Classical Mythology

IMAGES AND INSIGHTS

Classical Mythology

IMAGES AND INSIGHTS

Fifth Edition

Stephen L. Harris
Gloria Platzner
California State University, Sacramento

McGraw-Hill
Higher Education

Boston   Burr Ridge, IL   Dubuque, IA   New York   San Francisco   St. Louis
Bangkok   Bogotá   Caracas   Kuala Lumpur   Lisbon   London   Madrid   Mexico City
Milan   Montreal   New Delhi   Santiago   Seoul   Singapore   Sydney   Taipei   Toronto

The *McGraw·Hill* Companies

Mc Graw Hill McGraw-Hill
Higher Education

Published by McGraw-Hill, an imprint of The McGraw-Hill Companies, Inc., 1221 Avenue of the
Americas, New York, NY 10020. Copyright © 2008. All rights reserved. No part of this publication
may be reproduced or distributed in any form or by any means, or stored in a database or retrieval
system, without the prior written consent of The McGraw-Hill Companies, Inc., including, but
not limited to, in any network or other electronic storage or transmission, or broadcast for distance
learning.

This book is printed on acid-free paper.

2 3 4 5 6 7 8 9 0 DOC/DOC 0 9 8

ISBN: 978-0-07-353567-8
MHID: 0-07-353567-2

Editor in Chief: *Emily Barrosse*
Publisher: *Lisa Moore*
Sponsoring Editor: *Mark Georgiev*
Marketing Manager: *Pamela S. Cooper*
Editorial Assistant: *Marley Magaziner*
Production Editor: *Carey Eisner*
Manuscript Editor: *Jennifer Bertman*
Design Manager: *Cassandra Chu*
Text Designer: *Glenda King*
Cover Designer: *Adrian Morgan*
Art Editor: *Emma Ghiselli*
Photo Editor: *Alexandra Ambrose*
Photo Researcher: *Judy Mason*
Production Supervisor: *Dennis Fitzgerald*
Composition: *9pt Garamond by Newgen*
Printing: *45# New Era Matte, R. R. Donnelley & Sons*
Cover: © *Stapleton Collection/Corbis*

Credits: The credits section for this book begins on page C-1 and is considered an extension of the
copyright page.

Library of Congress Cataloging-in-Publication Data
Harris, Stephen L., 1937–
    Classical mythology : images and insights / Stephen L. Harris, Gloria Platzner. — 5th ed.
        p.   cm.
    Includes bibliographical references and index.
    ISBN-13: 978-0-07-353567-8
    ISBN-10: 0-07-353567-2
    1. Mythology, Classical.   I. Platzner, Gloria.   II. Title.
    BL723.H37   2008
    292.1'3—dc22

                                                                                    2007017317

The Internet addresses listed in the text were accurate at the time of publication. The inclusion of a
Web site does not indicate an endorsement by the authors or McGraw-Hill, and McGraw-Hill does
not guarantee the accuracy of the information presented at these sites.

www.mhhe.com

Preface to the Fifth Edition

Designed for undergraduate students, this book introduces readers to the exciting world of classical myth via the same approach taken by the Greeks and Romans themselves—primary works of art and literature. Beginning with the narrative poems of Hesiod and Homer, *Classical Mythology: Images and Insights* surveys the myths in generally chronological order, including the complete texts of six Greek plays and parts of two others, as well as several Homeric hymns. (For copyright reasons, the first scenes of Aeschylus's *Libation-Bearers* are omitted.) The primary readings are illuminated throughout by more than two hundred relevant examples of Greco-Roman painting, architecture, and sculpture. While reading Aeschylus's *Oresteia,* today's students can also study how Athenian vase painters, contemporaries of the playwright, responded to the drama's harrowing scenes of murder and revenge (Chapter 15). The adventures of Odysseus (Ulysses) similarly inspired artistic interpretations of the hero's struggles against gods and monsters (Chapter 13).

The opening chapters, further revised for the fifth edition, explore the nature and function of Greek myth. Emphasizing the relationship of myth to art, religion, history, politics, and society, the first chapter connects specific literary genres in which previously oral traditions were preserved (such as epic, lyric, and tragedy) to specific periods of Greek historical development and to the social and religious institutions they produced. In addition to offering some tentative definitions of myth, legend, saga, and folklore, this chapter also examines the particular qualities that distinguish Greek myth, including its humanism, patriarchal assumptions, political uses, and family orientation. The second chapter reviews a wide spectrum of theories that attempt to explain Greek myth, ranging from ancient commentaries to the diverse speculations of contemporary scholarship.

Each literary text in the collection, from Hesiod's *Theogony* and *Works and Days* to Virgil's *Aeneid* and Ovid's *Metamorphoses,* is prefaced with an essay that places the work in its historical and social context, inviting students to see the evolving interplay of myth and Greco-Roman society. The concept of the epic hero, such as Achilles or Odysseus, is thus viewed in its archaic setting, whereas the later heroes and heroines of tragedy—Oedipus, Antigone, Medea, and Pentheus—are examined in the context of the Athenian democracy.

New Features

Besides revising and expanding critical discussions of myth throughout the text, the authors have significantly updated coverage on several topics, ranging from new theories about humans being neurologically programmed to create mythic narratives to new archaeological discoveries about the geographical location of Odysseus's homeland, Ithaca. Chapter 1 now features a particularly useful box, "Tools for Studying Greek and Roman Myth," which provides an annotated list of indispensable references, authoritative works that cover the entire content of a classical myth and/or place it in its cultural and historical context. Keeping current with contemporary anthropological thought, Chapter 5, "The Divine Woman in Greek Mythology," has been carefully updated, showing more cogently how the widespread worship of a prehistoric goddess influenced later Greek concepts of feminine divinity. Discussions of several goddess figures in "The Olympian Family of Zeus" have accordingly been rewritten to accommodate new information (Chapter 6).

The authors have also revised coverage of the Homeric epics. In addition to a new box on the possible site of Ithaca, the *Odyssey* chapter now includes a detailed description and exploration of the thematic significance of Odysseus's visit to the perilous realm of Hades, as well as reflections on the series of recognition scenes that occur when the hero, disguised as a beggar, returns to his beleaguered home after an absence of twenty years. Discussion of the *Oresteia* has also been somewhat modified to include variant theories about the trilogy's interpretation. Additional text from the *Aeneid* has been added, including Virgil's description of the crucial duel between Turnus and Pallas (Book 10) and the famous depiction of Aeneas's shield (Book 8).

To emphasize the continuing impact that ancient myth exerts on contemporary thought, a new poem and a recent cartoon have been added to our final chapter, "The Persistence of Myth." To aid students in pursuing their study of myths, including material for research papers, the lists of references for each chapter have been thoroughly updated, incorporating many important new works of scholarship. The short lists of "Recommended Readings" from the previous edition have been integrated into the "Selected Bibliography" at the back of the book.

As in previous editions, the myths are presented in roughly the order in which they found (extant) written expression, allowing readers to perceive the ways in which Greek authors reinterpreted their traditions over time. Along with presenting the epic poems of Homer (mid-eighth century B.C.) and Hesiod (early seventh century B.C.), this text surveys several major gods to whom the "Homeric Hymns" were devoted: Demeter, Hermes, Apollo, and Dionysus. Myths dramatized in Athenian tragedy are also examined, showing how the playwrights transformed their inherited traditions to address the issues of Athens' democratic society of the fifth century B.C. Composed at a much later date (the late first century B.C. and early first century A.D.) the myths that Virgil and Ovid adapted to the sophisticated literary tastes and political realities of imperial Rome reveal a view of myth strikingly different from that of classical Greece (Chapters 18–20). The final chapter, reviewing mythology's enduring legacy, demonstrates the continuing vitality of myth in European and American thought (Chapter 21).

Pedagogical Features

Like its predecessors, the fifth edition of *Classical Mythology* offers numerous pedagogical devices to aid students who are undertaking their first systematic study of Greco-Roman myth. Each chapter begins with a "Key Topics/Themes" section that clearly summarizes the main points discussed. All major names and concepts appear in **boldface**, are given a pronunciation guide, and are concisely defined in an extensive glossary at the back of the book. (Although individual translators employ a variety of transliterations of Greek and Latin names, we generally use the standard anglicized spelling provided by the *Oxford Companion to Classical Literature*.) "Questions for Discussion and Review" appear at the end of each chapter. In addition, numerous boxes offer helpful information on a particular god, heroine, mythic concept, or other relevant subject, providing a stimulating counterpoint to the main text. Many of the charts, graphs, and illustrations also have captions featuring mini-essays on a wide variety of pertinent topics. An extensive chapter-by-chapter bibliography listing major scholarly publications is included at the end of the book. Finally, the book includes a detailed index, making it easy for readers to look up individual names, terms, and topics. The authors have attempted to make the new edition as reader-friendly as possible and hope that these features will enhance students' enjoyment of ancient myths and their enduring relevance to our common humanity.

For instructors using the fifth edition, a password-protected Web site at www .mhhe.com/harrismyth5 has an Instructor's Manual, test bank, multiple-choice quizzes, a glossary, flashcards, and more.

Classical Mythology: Images and Insights remains the only one-volume introduction to Greek and Roman myth that combines many complete works, and generous excerpts from others, with critical discussions of the myths' thematic content and historical background. A compendium of primary sources and critical analysis, it consistently directs readers to the dynamic way in which Greek and Roman writers revised their mythic heritage, reinterpreting ancient tradition to explore its meaning for new generations.

Acknowledgments

The authors are grateful to colleagues who reviewed earlier editions of *Classical Mythology* and offered helpful suggestions to make the fifth edition more effective. We particularly wish to thank:

Ken Burchenal, The University of Texas at San Antonio
Tony Hammer, Harper College
Andrea Mason, Washington State University
David Schenker, University of Missouri
Judith Sebesta, University of South Dakota

We would also like to thank our colleague Jeffrey Brodd at California State University, Sacramento, for his many valuable recommendations.

The authors also gratefully acknowledge the professional guidance provided by our previous sponsoring editors, Ken King and Jon-David Hague, who holds a doctorate in Classics from Boston University, and Mark Georgiev, our current sponsoring editor. We also thank Beth Ebenstein and Marley Magaziner who prepared the manuscript for production; Carey Eisner, our production editor; and Jennifer Bertman, for copyediting the manuscript.

Contents

PART THREE   Tragic Heroes and Heroines   541

CHAPTER **14**   **The Theater of Dionysus: Myth and the
Tragic Vision   543**

CHAPTER **15**   **The House of Atreus: Aeschylus's *Oresteia*   557**

PART FOUR   The World of Roman Myth   873

PART ONE

∽◦∞◦∽

The Nature and Function of Myth

Introduction to Greek Myth

KEY TOPICS/THEMES

An integral component of ancient Greek religious, political, and social culture, Greek myth originated with anonymous storytellers who created tales about gods and heroes that were transmitted orally for many generations before being crystallized in written form. The oldest surviving myths, from the Archaic period, are preserved in the epic poems of Homer and Hesiod (mid-eighth to early seventh centuries B.C.), who portray the gods as resembling idealized human beings in appearance, psychology, and behavior. Paralleling human social organization, the Homeric deities constitute a multigenerational family, headed by Zeus, king of the Olympian gods. The Athenian dramas of the Classical period (fifth century B.C.), a second major source of myth, similarly emphasize the distinctive qualities of anthropomorphism, humanism, competitiveness, and individuality. A fluid synthesis of ancient Near Eastern and Indo-European Bronze Age elements that evolved into disparate traditions during the Mycenean, Archaic, and Classical periods of Greek history, Greek myths were further modified by Roman authors, who typically adapted them for political and didactic purposes.

Almost twenty-five hundred years ago, the people of Athens built a new marble temple to honor **Athene** [uh-THEE-nuh], the goddess of wisdom after whom their city was named. Dedicated to Athene Parthenos (the virgin), the **Parthenon** (Figure 1-1) was designed to house a colossal statue of Athene by the sculptor Phidias. Phidias also decorated the temple's two pediments, triangular gables under its peaked roof, with sculptures representing key scenes from Athene's myth.

The east pediment, over the Parthenon's main entrance, depicted one of the crucial moments in Greek myth—the birth of Athene from **Zeus**, king of the gods. A

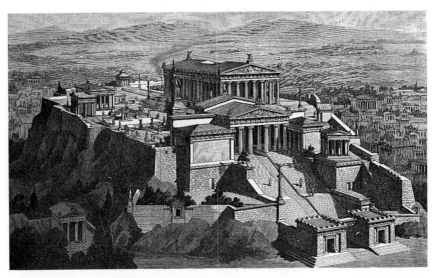

FIGURE 1-1   A Drawing of the Parthenon and Associated Structures on the Acropolis. The conviction that the goddess Athene presided over and defended their city inspired the Athenians of the mid-fifth century B.C. to create an extraordinary work of classical architecture, the temple dedicated to Athene Parthenos (the Virgin).

modern reconstruction of this scene shows an enthroned Zeus contemplating the daughter who has just sprung, clutching a warrior's spear and shield, from his head (Figure 1-2). Pictured behind Athene is an unlikely midwife, the god of fire and metalcraft, **Hephaestus** [he-FES-tuhs], who recoils from the ax blow he has boldly delivered to split Zeus's skull, providing a birth canal for the goddess. Seated to Zeus's right is his wife and sister, **Hera** [HEE-ra], who keenly observes her husband's latest display of power—his usurpation of the female's reproductive functions.

Although Athene is born from the male rather than the female parent, myth provides her with a mother of sorts, the goddess **Metis,** an embodiment of cunning intelligence who was Zeus's first wife. When Metis was already pregnant with Athene, Zeus, fearing fulfillment of the prophecy that she would eventually bear a son greater than his father, swallowed her. Assimilating Metis's intelligence into his own nature, Zeus then produced from his own body a child manifesting divine wisdom, a powerful daughter who supports her father's rule. Athene is not only Zeus's wise counselor, she is also the goddess of victory in war, the divine being who triumphs through clever strategy and ingenious planning (Figure 1-3).

Despite his position as king of the gods, Zeus's anxiety about being replaced by a younger, stronger rival is well founded, for at the time of Athene's birth Zeus only recently had overthrown an older generation of gods, the giant **Titans,** who had been led by Zeus's father, **Cronus.** (See Chapter 3 for Hesiod's account of the older deities who preceded Zeus as rulers of the universe.)

Myth also credits Zeus with giving birth to a second child, his son **Dionysus** [dye-oh-NYE-suhs], god of wine, intoxication, and emotional freedom (Figure 1-4). In contrast to Athene, who is literally Zeus's brainchild, a rational force for civilized

FIGURE 1-2   The Birth of Athene. In this modern reconstruction of the Parthenon's east pediment, the central figures of Zeus and Athene confront each other immediately after Athene, bearing a warrior's spear and shield, has burst from her father's head. Zeus's entire Olympian family has gathered to witness the prodigy, including his disapproving wife Hera, who sits holding a royal scepter, indicating her position as queen of heaven. Partly visible behind Athene's shield is the figure of Hephaestus, god of fire and the forge, who has just split Zeus's skull with his ax and now appears torn between his satisfaction at having struck Zeus and his fear of Zeus's reprisal. The scene is rife with family resentments: Hera is outraged by her husband's preemption of her maternal function. According to Hesiod, she, without male aid, gave birth to Hephaestus, who is entirely her son and who typically takes his mother's part in her endless quarrels with Zeus. To the viewer's right is the seated figure of Zeus's powerful brother Poseidon, god of sea and earthquakes. At the extreme right, Apollo, god of light and prophecy, appears with his lyre, a musical instrument symbolizing his patronage of music, harmony, and the creative intellect. *(Acropolis Museum, Athens)*

FIGURE 1-3   A Drawing of the Madrid Puteal. This circular bas-relief, thought to depict the scene of Athene's birth that Phidias created for the Parthenon's east pediment, shows Hephaestus recoiling behind Zeus's throne and Athene being crowned by the winged figure of Nike (Victory). As defender of the polis (city-state), Athene is also goddess of military victory through intelligent planning and strategy. Note that Zeus and Athene meet each other's gaze at the same eye level. The king of the universe is entranced by the daughter he has just produced—a brilliant image of the divine consciousness. For the Athenians, Zeus's unique relationship to Athene enhanced their prestige: the chief god's firstborn child was also their special protector and patron. *(Archaeological Museum, Madrid)*

FIGURE 1-4 The Birth of Dionysus. The painting on this crater (large wine vessel) shows the infant Dionysus, god of wine and intoxication, emerging from Zeus's thigh and surrounded by figures representing participants in the ecstatic Dionysian cult. Myth's insistence that both Athene's cool rationality and Dionysus's passionate sensuality derive from the same father-god conveys the Greek belief that both disciplined intellect and unrestrained emotion are part of the natural order and therefore equally divine. (*Museo Archeologico Nazionale, Taranto*)

order, Dionysus represents the nonrational forces of both physical nature and human emotion. Derived not from Zeus's head but from his thigh, he is a god who combines joyous sensuality with amoral aggression (see Chapters 8 and 17). As a son of Zeus, Dionysus is half-brother not only to Athene but also to Zeus's other divine offspring, including **Apollo,** who, like Athene, exemplifies the abstract intellect. A god of light, health, prophecy, and the creative arts, Apollo also presents a striking contrast to the emotional extremes of Dionysus (see Chapters 7 and 8).

These two images of Athene and Dionysus reveal much about Greek myth's presentation of the gods' complex, often contradictory, natures. That a single deity can produce, by himself, two such different offspring—a virgin goddess of formidable austerity and self-discipline and a wine god whose passions can reduce society to anarchy—suggests myth's power to integrate polar opposites. Among its many functions, myth confronts and defines tensions such as those between Athene's cerebral control and Dionysus's wild abandon, recognizing that these seemingly irreconcilable opposites express the contrarieties and conflicts inherent in human life. Both deities are necessary aspects of a cosmic whole encompassed in the Greek concept of the divine.

Greek Religion and the Nature of the Divine

The Parthenon sculptures depicting Athene's miraculous entrance into the world offer a good introduction to some distinctive characteristics of Greek myth, including its relationship to ancient Greek religion. For the Greeks, religion was very different from most modern conceptions of it. The Greeks had no sacred texts, such as the Judeo-Christian Bible or Islamic Qur'an (Koran), that purported to reveal ultimate truth, nor was it expressed in creeds or doctrines that officially articulated essential beliefs about the gods. Instead of utilizing a professional clergy or a dominant class of hereditary priests—in most cases, ordinary individuals performed the necessary rites and sacrifices—the Greeks acted out their sense of the *numinous,* the perceived experience of divine or sacred forces present in the world, by honoring *ta hiera,* "holy things." Operating without a supernatural revelation of the divine will, such as the Torah (Divine Instruction) that Israel's God disclosed to Moses at Mount Sinai, the Greeks communed with numinous entities through ritual and other time-honored practices. They learned of "holy things" through witnessing or participating in customary rites at home and at public festivals, as well as through hearing stories about the gods—myths that were also vividly rendered in the paintings, sculpture, architecture, and poetry that were part of their daily environment.

Phidias's representation of Athene's birth captures a climactic moment in the history of the **cosmos,** the Greek term denoting a stable, harmonious world order. The goddess's sudden appearance, leaping fully armed from Zeus's head, is a sacred event, a prodigy to which all the major gods are pictured as witnesses (Figure 1-5).

FIGURE 1-5   A Drawing of Phidias's Athene Parthenos. The Parthenon was built to house a cult statue of Athene that the sculptor Phidias created in ivory and gold. Approximately thirty-seven feet high, Phidias's rendition of Zeus's most formidable child, an embodiment of intellect and martial prowess, dominates the temple's lavish marble interior.

For the Greeks, it is an event of universal significance, causing heaven and earth to tremble in awe:

> Great Olympus itself [the mountain home of the gods] started to reel,
> Dazed by the might of the gray-eyed newcomer, and earth all around
> Cried out in fear, while the sea heaved, throwing up
> Purple billows and spewing forth sudden foam.
> The brilliant son of Hyperion [Helios, driver of the sun's chariot] halted his swift-footed
> horses,
> Forgetful of time. . . .
>
> —*Homeric Hymn to Athene,* trans. Thelma Sargent

Athene's arrival temporarily suspends the normal operations of nature—the earth shouts aloud, the sea roars in agitation, and the sun pauses in its orbit, struck with wonder at what the gods have brought forth.

In Phidias's artistic re-creation of this divine mystery, several distinctive aspects of Greek religion stand out. The gods are not one, but many; they have human shape and form; and they—as brothers, sisters, wives, children, or mistresses of Zeus—constitute a family. Whereas modern Judaism, Christianity, and Islam are characterized by **monotheism,** belief in one God, ancient religions (excepting that of Israel) embraced **polytheism,** belief in a multiplicity of gods. The monotheistic God is typically conceived as eternal (without beginning or ending), omnipotent (all-powerful), omniscient (all-knowing), and omnipresent (existing everywhere). By contrast, Zeus and his fellow Olympians, named for their dwelling place atop **Mount Olympus,** the highest peak in Thessaly, were viewed as immortal, but not eternal. As the myth of Athene's birth demonstrates, they did not always exist. Because Olympian rule has a beginning in time, it may also come to an end, an eventuality that on occasion causes Zeus some worry.

In some myths, the gods are also restricted by limited knowledge: at least early in his reign, Zeus cannot perceive other gods' thoughts, nor can he always see clearly into the future (see Zeus's conflict with Prometheus in Chapter 4). Although poets describe them as "deathless," the gods can be wounded and suffer pain, bleeding a clear liquid called **ichor** [IH-kohr]. Despite their superhuman strength, some gods can be defeated and even permanently imprisoned, as are the Titans, whom Zeus confines in the Underworld. They can also be misled or deceived, as when Hera beguiles Zeus or when Hephaestus tricks Hera (see Chapter 6).

Social and Political Functions of Myth

Although myth is closely related to Greek religion, it also served social and political functions, as exemplified in the tradition explaining how the city of Athens took its name from the goddess Athene. The mythic event in which the city's early inhabitants became the Athenians, identified as the special people of Athene, was the subject of the Parthenon's west pediment. At this end of the temple, Phidias carved sculptures depicting a momentous contest between Athene and her uncle **Poseidon** [poh-SYE-duhn], god of the sea and earthquakes, for the city's allegiance. In this competition for divine patronage, Athene offered the gift of a domestic olive tree, the fruit and oil of which eventually became the city's chief exports and source of economic prosperity, whereas Poseidon, somewhat cluelessly, produced only a salt-water spring. When the citizens' vote went to Athene, an angry Poseidon retaliated by flooding the city.

Besides granting Athens a unique relationship to the firstborn child of Greece's chief god, this tradition also explains why Athens, even after it became the world's first democracy, denied suffrage to its women. According to a late version of the myth recounted by the Christian theologian Augustine (fifth century A.D.), Athene triumphed over Poseidon by a single vote, that of a woman (Augustine, *City of God,* Book 18, Chapter 9, citing the Roman writer Varro [c. 116–27 B.C.] as his source). While retaining Athene as their divine patron, the male Athenians attempted to assuage Poseidon's wrath by punishing the women, depriving them of their right to vote, to pass on their names to their own children, or even to be called Athenians. Inherently paradoxical, this myth, establishing the foundation or justification for a restrictive political policy, credits women for making Athens the favorite city of a powerful goddess but at the same time blames them for a male god's violent behavior and strips them of their former participation in the democratic process.

A second myth linking Zeus's immortal daughter to Athenian origins is even more paradoxical. According to this tradition, Athene can remain perpetually virginal yet, in a sense, become the mother of one of the city's earliest rulers and hence a divine ancestor of the Athenian people. As austere and emotionally remote as she is wise and beautiful, Athene is nonetheless—on one recorded occasion only—the unwilling object of sexual desire—oddly enough, that of the lame god whose ax-blow brought her into the world. While visiting Hephaestus's forge to order new weapons, Athene unexpectedly finds herself fending off the god's passionate advances. During the struggle, Hephaestus ejaculates on Athene's thigh. Perhaps because Hephaestus's attempted rape is both clumsy and unsuccessful, Athene behaves with remarkable coolness: she neither recriminates nor plots revenge. Instead, she calmly takes a wool cloth, wipes the semen from her thigh, and tosses the moist rag aside.

Because a god's seed always bears fruit, when the enseminated wool falls on Mother Earth, a child, Erichthonius, is born. Accepting responsibility for the baby, Athene places Erichthonius in a basket and entrusts his care to the daughters of Cecrops, the mythical first king of Athens. Ignoring Athene's instructions, the young women look into the basket and are driven insane by the sight: either Erichthonius has the lower body of a serpent, a characteristic of earth's offspring, or he is guarded by frightening snakes. Athene then takes Erichthonius to her sacred precincts atop the **Acropolis** (the steep hill upon which the Parthenon and other public buildings stood), where he grows up to become Athens' king. Under Athene's guidance, Erichthonius is said to have invented the first four-horse chariot and founded the **Panathenaea** [pan-ath-e-NEE-uh], the annual festival held in the goddess's honor. Other myths ascribe these accomplishments to **Erechtheus** [e-REK-thee-uhs], another prehistoric ruler who is variously identified as the son or grandson of Erichthonius. The Erechtheum, a smalls temple famous for its porch roof supported by statues of young maidens, was built to accommodate Poseidon's salty spring, Athene's original olive tree, and the oldest wooden statue of the goddess. It still stands near the Parthenon.

Athene's contributions to the Athenian **polis** (city-state) include the establishment of a legal system to try cases of homicide, the inauguration of which is dramatized in Aeschylus's play the *Eumenides* (see Chapter 15). In inaugurating the rule of law to replace earlier chaotic practices of personal vengeance, Athene unequivocally champions the cause of civic order and harmony. In casting her vote to break a deadlocked jury in favor of a young man accused (rightfully) of murdering his mother, Athene announces that she, born without a mother, inevitably takes the male side in any controversy between the sexes, a position that helps to reinforce the Athenian social hierarchy in which women are subordinate to men. Aeschylus's drama, which raises crucial political and social issues embodied in a male–female conflict, is but one example of the many ways in which Greek myth explores the polarities of existence in terms of gender conflict. For the Greeks, some of their deepest concerns about human nature and society are expressed in myths that present male and female figures locked in constant struggle (see the myths of Agamemnon and Clytemnestra in Chapter 15 and of Jason and Medea in Chapter 17).

Although myth intimately associates Athene with her beloved Athens, which she defends against foreign invaders such as the all-female army of **Amazons** and other representatives of barbarism, she was also worshiped throughout Greece. We encounter the goddess in almost every tale of heroic myth, whatever the hero's native city, including the stories of **Heracles** (Hercules), **Jason, Perseus,** and **Theseus,** another early king of Athens (see Chapter 10). An important force in the *Iliad,* Homer's epic of the Greek war against Troy, she is also the central deity in the *Odyssey,* in which she largely engineers the long-delayed homecoming of the wandering hero **Odysseus** (Ulysses) (see Chapter 13).

Anthropomorphism

In both art and literature, the Greek gods resemble supremely privileged human beings, only incomparably stronger, more beautiful, and more powerful, blessedly immune to sickness, old age, or death. When not engaged in manipulating human beings for their own purposes, the Olympians frequently gather at heavenly banquets, where they dine on **ambrosia** and drink **nectar,** food that sustains their perpetual youthfulness.

Because they resemble humans not only physically but also psychologically, the gods betray character flaws typical of ordinary mortals, engaging in conspiracies and competitions for power and prestige, as well as sexual escapades of every description. Unlike the Judeo-Christian God, they do not jealously demand to be worshiped exclusively; they do, however, punish and even destroy mortals who deny them their due recognition, honor, and sacrifice. They typically favor individuals who, like Odysseus, properly acknowledge their importance by regularly offering prayers and animal sacrifices.

A Greek temple, such as the Parthenon, was literally the house of the god whose image it sheltered, a holy place where a supernatural power could reside among humans. In contrast to modern churches, synagogues, or mosques, the temple was not intended to hold a congregation. Greek worshipers assembled outside their sanctuaries to perform animal and other sacrifices on altars. The temple's interior was reserved for the divine presence and for the treasures that commonly were stored there, offerings from the devout. Some of the Greek world's largest and most elaborate shrines, such as the temple of Artemis at Ephesus—one of the Seven Wonders of the ancient world—impressed some viewers as a visible replica of the gods' celestial abode. As Philo of Byzantium (c. 200 B.C.) remarked, Artemis's sanctuary brought "the heavenly world of immortality . . . [down to] the earth."

The Divine Family

Just as the Greeks visualized the gods in their own idealized image and built earthly homes for them, so they ascribed to them the basic unit of their own social structure —the family. In Greek myth, all the gods are related, descended from the original divine couple **Gaea** (the earth) and **Uranus** (the sky). (See Hesiod's *Theogony* in Chapter 3 for a genealogy of the Olympian family.) A grandson of Gaea and Uranus, Zeus heads a divine **patriarchy,** a social organization marked by the supremacy of the father in a clan or family and a sociopolitical arrangement in which male leadership and values dominate. Wielding the thunderbolt to enforce his will, Zeus brooks no challenge to his supreme authority; he presides over the gods' councils and demands strict obedience from his sometimes fractious Olympian family. Although Zeus firmly maintains control of the universe, both material and spiritual, he shares its administration with other family members, assigning each of his siblings and divine children some function or sphere of activity.

The emotional ties, tensions, hostilities, and rivalries inherent in intergenerational human families, with older and younger generations often in conflict, characterize Zeus's Olympian household. Zeus's untamed sexual appetite, which drives him to beget children by mothers both human and divine, and Hera's consequent jealous rages add to the family's psychological stress. (See Chapters 3 and 6 for a discussion of some myths relating to the principal members of the Olympian family of Zeus.)

Although the Greeks honored their gods as potent forces that could either help or destroy them, they also found much to laugh at in their myths' projection of human foibles and family squabbles onto the divine realm. In the hands of some Greek poets, Zeus's adulteries, Hera's devious schemes, and Hephaestus's physical clumsiness were irresistible sources of humor. At the same time, Greek myth recognizes the enormous gulf between divinity and humanity—and humanity's inferior place in the cosmos. The gods typically assume human shape, but it is only the *appearance* of a mortal form: at will, Zeus can transform himself into a bolt of lightning, a raging bull, or a cosmic serpent. For all their anthropomorphism, the Greeks realized that their gods belonged to the *Other,* a dimension of reality profoundly different from the material realm to which humans are bound. Mysterious and unpredictable, the gods represent forces beyond human ability to control or comprehend. Greek deities may command themselves to appear in human likeness—and Greek artists delighted in so picturing them—but they belong to an unknowable mode of existence intrinsically different from that of humanity.

Tools for Studying Greek and Roman Myth*

The following reference works provide indispensable information about the content and nature of classical myth.

Apollodorus. *The Library of Greek Mythology*. Rev. ed. Trans. Robin Hard. (Oxford World Classics). New York: Oxford UP, 1999. A primary source for Greek myth.

Buxton, Richard. *The Complete World of Greek Mythology*. London: Thames and Hudson, 2004. A well-illustrated survey of major themes in Greek myth.

Carpenter, T. H. *Art and Myth in Ancient Greece*. London: Thames, 1991. Combines visual and textual illustrations of important myths.

Gantz, Timothy. *Early Greek Myth: A Guide to Literary and Artistic Sources*. Baltimore: Johns Hopkins UP, 1993. The only one-volume compendium of Greek myth, giving the ancient textual or artistic source for each myth.

Grimal, Pierre. *The Dictionary of Classical Mythology*. Trans. A. R. Maxwell-Hyslop. Oxford: Basil Blackwell, 1986. A comprehensive resource for all major figures in Greco-Roman myth.

Hornblower, Simon, and Antony Spawforth, eds. *The Oxford Classical Dictionary*, 3rd ed., rev. New York: Oxford UP, 2003. Includes entries on important historical and literary topics, such as "Athene," "Homer," "Tragedy," and "Troy."

Howatson, M. C., ed. *The Oxford Companion to Classical Literature*. 2nd ed. New York: Oxford UP, 1989. (Paperback, 2006). An invaluable reference to both historical writers and mythological characters.

The Literary Quality of Greek Myth and Its Association with Communal Observances

Although a component of virtually every world religion, myth—which typically conveys traditions about supernatural powers, cosmic origins, and the divine–human relationship—is notoriously hard to define. The word **myth**, taken from the Greek *mythos* (or *muthos*), literally means "utterance," or "something one says"—a traditional story commonly set in the remote past and involving the actions of divine beings and/or human heroes. As in other cultures, Greek myth was originally an *oral* phenomenon, created by anonymous storytellers and transmitted by word of mouth. During the long process of oral transmission, myth is highly fluid, open to the individual speaker's changes at every retelling. Even after myths were committed to writing, Greek poets felt free to create new versions of old stories, introducing new characters and events into traditional tales. Athenian playwrights were particularly inventive in reinterpreting and revising myth to heighten the onstage drama, as when Euripides has Medea kill her own children (see Chapter 17), an ac-

The following titles place myth in its social, historical, and/or religious context.

Burkert, Walter. *Greek Religion.* Trans. John Raffan. 1985. Reprint, Cambridge: Harvard UP, 2006. A detailed, scholarly study of the character and evolution of ancient Greek religious practices.

Buxton, Richard. *Imaginary Greece: The Contexts of Mythology.* 1994, Reprint, New York: Cambridge UP, 2002. Examines the sociohistorical background of Greek myth.

Edmunds, Lowell, ed. *Approaches to Greek Myth.* 1990. Reprint, Baltimore: Johns Hopkins UP, 2007. Includes helpful essays on "Myth and History" and "Indo-European and Greek Mythology."

Graf, Fritz. *Greek Mythology: An Introduction.* Trans. Thomas Marier. 1993. Reprint, Baltimore: Johns Hopkins UP, 1996. An excellent review of current scholarship on myth.

Price, Simon. *Religions of the Ancient Greeks.* 1999. Reprint, New York: Cambridge UP, 2004. A lucid exposition of Greek religion in the context of Greek social and political life.

Shapiro, H. A. *Myth into Art: Poet and Painter in Classical Greece.* New York: Routledge, 1994. Surveys vase paintings of scenes from epic, lyric, and dramatic poetry.

*For a list of recommended readings for each topic or literary work discussed, see the Selected Bibliography at the end of this book, organized by chapter.

tion absent from older versions of Medea's story. As a result, most myths survive in at least several different, even contradictory, versions.

In ancient Greece, these differences were reinforced by the region's rugged terrain and the geographical isolation of the polis. Because many Greek settlements were separated by steep mountain ranges or inhospitable coastlines, each polis tended to develop its own variation of popular myths, commonly attaching them to tales about the gods who favored their particular city, as Athene championed Athens, or about local heroes whose exploits enhanced the polis's reputation. Leading families of a given polis typically compiled genealogies linking members to famous leaders of the mythic past, thus boosting their local prestige while perpetuating the ancestral hero's story. Citizens could point out to visitors where heroes such as Heracles (Hercules), Orestes, or Oedipus had slain monsters, had died, or were buried. Whereas some tales remained of purely local interest, many others, spread abroad by sailors, traveling merchants, and itinerant poets, eventually became part of the national tradition. Stories of gods serving similar functions and heroes performing similar feats commonly merged, as when the myth about Heracles gradually incorporated the stories of innumerable strongmen. Only by slow degrees were Heracles' labors fixed at twelve—a popular number in Greek mythology, as well as in the Judeo-Christian Bible—and only over long spans of time were the identities, attributes, and number of the twelve Olympians also agreed on. The form in which Greek myth comes to us is thus the end result of a long evolutionary process.

Myths are categorized as *traditional* tales because they are passed on from one generation to the next as part of a particular people's cultural legacy. They are preserved and transmitted over time because they are seen as meaningful to the society that transmits them, helping to express a community's distinctive worldview—its values and its goals. Although no universally accepted definition of myth exists, Walter Burkert provides a useful generalization: a myth is "a traditional tale with secondary, partial reference to something of collective importance" (see Burkert in the Selected Bibliography).

In the Greek city-state, myth's "collective importance"—its pervasive role in the communal life of the polis—was demonstrated by the prominence given it at public festivals. Greek festivals were religious celebrations in which the community expressed its beliefs about the gods through both observance of religious rites and recitations by poets of time-honored stories about the Olympians and their relationship with humanity. Among its many religious holidays, Athens held two annual festivals—the Panathenaea, honoring Athene, and the City Dionysia, honoring Dionysus—that featured public performances of myths—events at which Athenians assembled to celebrate a common mythological heritage. The stories about gods and heroes performed at these two festivals were eventually written down, preserving our two principal sources of Greek myth—the epic poems of Homer and the tragic dramas of Aeschylus, Sophocles, and Euripides. Because these writers took their people's traditional tales about gods and heroes as their primary subject matter, Greek myth is preserved chiefly in works of highly sophisticated literature. Individual mythic scenes are preserved in Greek sculpture and vase painting, an important part of myth's legacy, but only in literary form do complete stories survive.

The Panathenaea

At the Panathenaea, held every July to celebrate Athene's birth, professional reciters of poetry, the **rhapsodes**, declaimed Homer's long narratives about the Trojan War (the *Iliad*) and a war hero's arduous quest to return home (the *Odyssey*). Although the Homeric epics were composed and transmitted orally for an extended period (perhaps attaining something like their present form about 750 B.C.), they were committed to writing no later than the sixth century B.C. (See Chapter 12 for a discussion of scholarly theories about Homeric authorship and the oral formulation of the epics.) The *Iliad* and the *Odyssey*, which many critics regard as the foundation literature of Western civilization, exerted a wide and enduring influence throughout Greece. The Homeric epics were panhellenic—belonging to all **Hellas** (the Greeks' name for their country) and an indispensable part of the national heritage. To an incalculable extent, they defined Greek concepts of both divinity and human heroism. According to Herodotus, a Greek historian (c. 450 B.C.), it was Homer and Hesiod (c. 675 B.C.), who definitively fixed popular ideas about the gods' individual personalities, physical appearance, and functions (*Histories,* Book 2,

Scholars do not agree on the precise definitions of *myth, legend, folklore,* and *saga,* or on the precise distinctions between them. Some scholars argue that attempts to differentiate between myth and other categories of traditional tales are misleading and that all traditional Greek narratives should be classed as myths. Others use *folklore* as the more comprehensive term, viewing it as encompassing the totality of traditionally derived and orally transmitted literature. Many critics, however, believe that it is possible—and helpful—to suggest more precise definitions, that the different terms represent closely related but separate categories. Given the lack of consensus, proposed definitions must be regarded as tentative, mere starting points for a study of traditional material and inevitably subject to debate and revision.

Most current definitions of *myth* (Greek, *mythos*) are extremely general. Walter Burkert proposed that it is a "traditional tale," a story passed on from generation to generation, that, as a secondary component, had a "collective importance" to the life of the community that preserved and transmitted it. Whereas myths typically originate orally during a preliterate period, Greek myth is primarily literary, surviving in written works of great artistry, such as the epics of Homer and the tragedies of Sophocles. Some Greek tales are often characterized as "divine myths," stories dealing with creation, the birth of the gods, and the relationship between divinity and humanity. Other myths focus on the deeds of mortal heroes and heroines, presenting human models of courage to be imitated or examples of wrongdoing to be avoided. Both types commonly function to express social values, norms of behavior, and/or the consequences of deviating from them. (For a discussion of different methods scholars use to interpret myth, see Chapter 2.)

The term **legend** is variously defined, with some critics using it to denote stories about humans, such as Jason's quest for the Golden Fleece, and others restricting its use to denote traditional tales that have some basis, however tenuous, in historical events. If the Mycenaean Greeks did lay siege to Troy, stories about the war may be legendary rather than strictly fictional. Collections of narratives about a particular enterprise, city, or family, such as the many interconnected tales about Troy, Thebes, or Argos and their ruling dynasties, are called *sagas*. A term originally used to describe Scandinavian tales dating from the twelfth through the fifteenth centuries A.D., *saga* typically refers to long, detailed narratives involving both gods and heroes that blend historical and fictional elements. Whereas legends and sagas commonly recount the exploits of a military *aristocracy* (a Greek term referring to government by the "best people"), **folktales** relate the activities of more humble persons. In contrast to myths, which feature major gods of sky and earth and which place heroes at a particular time or location, such as the Greek assault on Troy, folktales deal with lesser figures of popular imagination, such as witches, elves, giants, and fairies. **Folklore**, as the word implies, concerns the experiences of common folk in a vague, undefined era—fairy tales usually begin with "Once upon a time" or "In a kingdom far away"—and ordinarily does not include myth's characteristic preoccupation with the human spirit struggling against the limitations of its own mortality. Some literary works based on myth, such as the *Odyssey,* also contain elements of folklore—giant cannibals, sorceresses, magic spells, and assorted half-human monsters—as do tales of dragon-slaying heroes like Perseus.

Section 55). Even while allowing for Herodotus's rhetorical exaggeration, the Homeric epics indisputably provided the Greeks with their most persuasive models of heroic behavior and the interaction of gods and mortals. In the education of Greek boys, Homer's epics constituted the chief textbook.

Myths about the Homeric deities belonged to all the many city-states of Greece, but they could also be adapted to serve the interests of a particular polis. In adorning the Parthenon, Phidias combined portraits of the Homeric gods with scenes from his own city's unique festival, the Panathenaea, emphasizing Athene's special connection with Athens. Every fourth year, at the Great Panathenaea, celebrations were especially elaborate: besides extended recitations of the *Iliad* and the *Odyssey,* there were horse races, athletic games, and musical contests. The festivities climaxed in a solemn procession of Athens' leading citizens, as well as allies and visiting dignitaries, across the agora (marketplace) and up the high hill of the Acropolis, on which Athene's temple stood. Phidias made this ritual procession the subject of the Parthenon frieze, a long band of bas-relief sculptures running horizontally along the top of the walls inside the temple's exterior colonnade (Figure 1-6).

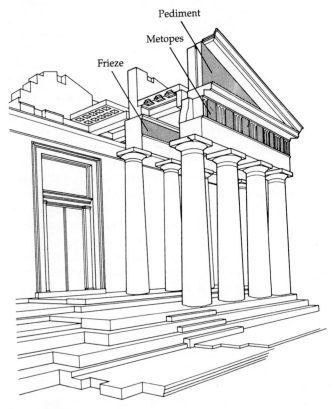

FIGURE 1-6   The Location of the Sculptures on the Parthenon. This cross section of Athene's temple shows the positions of the pediment sculptures, the frieze featuring scenes from the Panathenaea procession, and the metopes (architectural panels decorated with bas-reliefs).

FIGURE 1-7   Young Women Carrying the Peplos. In this scene based on the Panathenaea procession, aristocratic Athenian women carry the peplos, a sacred garment—lavishly embroidered with pictorial episodes from the goddess's myth—to clothe Athene's oldest cult statue on the Acropolis. *(British Museum, London)*

The east frieze depicts a panorama of Athene's chief worshipers, including those especially honored in carrying out one of the main purposes of the procession—a group of young Athenian women carrying the peplos, an intricately embroidered robe to be placed on the goddess's ancient statue in the Erechtheum (Figure 1-7). Like the Parthenon itself, the peplos was decorated with mythic motifs featuring Athene's triumphs—in this case, her defeat of the giants who had dared to attack Olympus (see Chapter 3). Other architectural sculptures of the Parthenon represent similar victories of civilization over savagery: a band of Lapiths, mountain tribesmen in Thessaly, overcome centaurs, male figures whose bestial nature is indicated by their horselike anatomy from the waist down (Figure 1-8). In another scene, heroes battle Amazons, female warriors who invaded prehistoric Attica, the territory governed by Athens, further emphasizing Athene's role in protecting civilized values.

In contrast to scenes depicting violent conflict on earth, the east frieze of the Parthenon presents the gods—invisible participants in the Panathenaea—as utterly calm and relaxed. Having demonstrated their ability to vanquish all opposition, the Olympians exhibit the serenity born of supreme confidence. The seated Apollo leans casually toward his uncle Poseidon, the tempestuous sea god, now in a calm mood, to exchange a private word; his twin sister, Artemis, patron of wildlife and the hunt, modestly adjusts the body-clinging folds of her diaphanous gown (Figure 1-9). In another Olympian group, even fierce **Ares** [AR-eez], god of war and bloodshed, exhibits total repose. His hands grasp the knee of a crossed leg while he shares a conversation with his aunt **Demeter** [de-MEE-ter], goddess of earth's fertility, and his two half-brothers, Hermes and Dionysus (Figure 1-10). Although probably already somewhat drunk (Dionysus's hand originally may have held a beaker of wine), the god of unbridled freedom—whose frenzy can elicit either joy or terror—is mellow.

FIGURE 1-8   A Centaur and a Lapith in Hand-to-Hand Combat. In this Parthenon metope, agents representing barbarism (the half-animal centaur) and civilization (the unarmed human warrior) battle for dominance. As defender of the civilized values of the polis, Athene champions the forces of rational order against savagery. (*British Museum, London*)

FIGURE 1-9   Olympian Gods, East Frieze of the Parthenon. A visible symbol of Athens' triumph over barbarian invaders (the Persians, who invaded Greece in 490 and 480–479 B.C.), the Parthenon (constructed c. 447–438 B.C.) embodies principles of cosmic order, a mythic theme reinforced by picturing the highest gods as present in Athene's sanctuary. Apollo, god of rational order, turns toward his uncle Poseidon, lord of the sea. Apollo's twin sister, Artemis, patron of women, wildlife, and the hunt, is at the right. (*Acropolis Museum, Athens*)

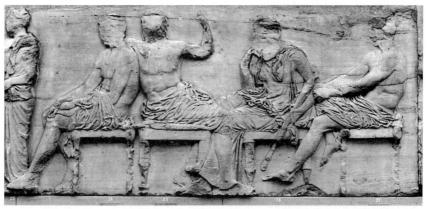

(a)

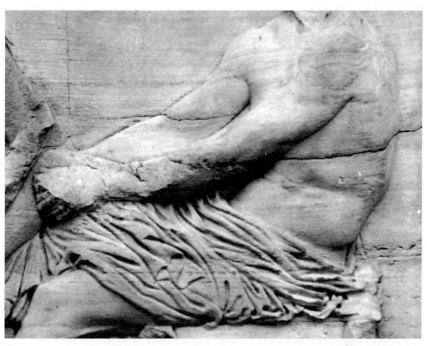

(b)

FIGURE 1-10   A Gathering of the Olympian Family, East Frieze of the Parthenon. (a) Although their faces have been obliterated, this seated quartet of gods still exhibits a divine grace and repose. With his arm raised, the wine god Dionysus leans confidentially against his half-brother Hermes (left), god of merchants, travelers, tricksters, gamblers, and thieves. Zeus's sister Demeter, great goddess of earth's fertility, turns an interested gaze on the tipsy Dionysus. Ares, god of violent aggression and bloodshed, appears on the right. (b) In this close-up of Ares, the god of war manifests an uncharacteristic serenity; his relaxed presence at the Panathenaea marks a time of peace. *(British Museum, London)*

Dionysus's right arm embraces the shoulders of **Hermes** [HER-meez], the ever-mobile trickster, god of travelers, thieves, and businessmen—and Zeus's trusted messenger.

Looking much as Homer describes them, the Olympian gods are assembled to observe the Panathenaean games, savor the fragrance of burnt-animal sacrifices, and offer favored humans the comfort of their presence and protection. Like all the Parthenon sculptures and friezes, Phidias's representation of Homeric divinities illustrates the close bond between myth and Greek society. The rituals of the Panathenaea, as well as the art and architecture of the Parthenon, serve multiple religious, social, and political purposes. Athene's preeminence among the gods and her unique link to Athens are consciously exploited to affirm the Athenians' identity as a divinely favored people and to validate both their distinctive customs and their right militarily to dominate less powerful Greek city-states.

The City Dionysia

The narrative poems of Homer and Hesiod, our oldest extant source of Greek myth, were composed during the **Archaic period** of Greek history (c. 800–480 B.C.). Some historians bracket the Archaic period by two epochal events: the founding of the Olympic Games in 776 B.C. and Greece's successful conclusion of the Persian Wars in 479 B.C. (see Chapter 14). The tragedies produced at the City Dionysia, the second major source of Greek myth, date from the **Classical period,** the epoch of phenomenal creativity that extends from 479 B.C., when the Greeks drove Persia's invading armies from their shores, to 323 B.C., the year in which Alexander the Great died. The period following Alexander's death is known as the **Hellenistic,** an era characterized by the widespread dissemination of classic Hellenic cultures throughout the region of the eastern Mediterranean and the Near East.

Established as an important Athenian festival in the sixth century B.C., the annual **City Dionysia** (also called the Great Dionysia) was dedicated to Dionysus and featured the production of ritual dramas emphasizing the suffering of a mythic figure, such as Oedipus or his daughter Antigone. Like the epic poets Homer and Hesiod, the Athenian dramatists who composed scripts for the wine god's celebration took myth as their primary subject, freely revising traditional stories for theatrical effect and adapting mythic themes to suit the sophisticated audiences of classical Athens. Along with the older epic poetry, the surviving plays by Aeschylus, Sophocles, and Euripides (fifth century B.C.) form our chief extant body of Greek mythology (see Chapters 14–17).

Other Literary Sources

In addition to our two main sources of Greek myth—archaic narrative poetry, such as Homer's *Iliad* and Hesiod's *Theogony,* and classical dramas by Athenian playwrights—Greek authors employed other literary genres in which myth is the chief topic. Writing in imitation of Homer, several (generally) anonymous poets later composed a series of hymns praising the twelve Olympians. Known collectively as the *Homeric Hymns,* they preserve important myths about the mother goddess Demeter, her daughter Persephone, the volatile Dionysus, the cunning Hermes, and the luminescent Apollo (see Chapters 5–8). These hymns, which vary considerably in length, were recited at festivals as prologues to the performance of the longer epics. Some Greek lyric poets, such as Stesichorus (sixth century B.C.), who wrote a narrative version of the *Oresteia,* and Pindar (c. 518–446 B.C.), who included numerous allusions to myth in his odes praising victorious athletes, regularly incorporated myths into their work.

Of Greek epic poetry after Homer, only a few long narratives, such as the *Voyage of the Argo (Argonautica)* by Apollonius of Rhodes (c. 295–215 B.C.), survive intact, preserving the story of Jason's quest for the Golden Fleece (see Chapter 17). Interestingly, the most comprehensive collection of Greek myths is not a literary composition by a major poet, but a prosaic textbook misnamed the *Library of Apollodorus.* Although this compendium of traditional tales is attributed to Apollodorus of Athens (c. 140 B.C.), scholars believe that it was actually compiled by an unknown hand two or three centuries later. The *Library* may have been intended as a sourcebook to aid Greek schoolchildren in learning the ancient myths, which, by the time of its publication, were already losing their former familiarity. Despite its lack of artistic flair, the *Library* is exceptionally valuable: arranging the myths in a generally chronological order, it begins with a creation story that largely parallels Hesiod's *Theogony* and narrates a wide range of heroic adventures, including those of such diverse figures as Bellerophon, Perseus, and Heracles. (See the discussion of heroes and heroines in Chapters 10 and 11.) The *Library* closes with the fall of Troy, traditionally regarded as the final great event in Greece's mythic past. In this epilogue to the Homeric poems, the writer adds fascinating details about the aftermath of the Trojan War, recounting the death of Odysseus. To the Greeks, the children of the warriors who had fought at Troy, such as Odysseus's son Telemachus and Agamemnon's son Orestes, constituted the last generation of heroes, with their lives the final chapter in Greece's mythic past. After the last heroes died, the world changed forever; never again did Zeus father human sons and daughters, leaving humankind to cope without divinely begotten leaders.

Although the *Library* was probably written in the late first or early second century A.D., approximately thirteen hundred years after the traditional date of the Greek assault on Troy, this compendium is believed to contain versions of some myths that are much older than the time of their written composition. Unlike the poets, who were interested in reshaping the myths for their own artistic purposes, the *Library*'s unknown author was chiefly interested in preserving them unchanged for posterity.

Pausanias, who wrote a *Guide to Greece* late in the second century A.D., was similarly concerned with recording ancient traditions. Devoting fourteen years to traveling throughout Greece, Pausanias describes what he saw and heard about the history, religious practices, and mythology of such important city-states as Athens, Thebes, and Sparta, as well as sacred institutions such as Apollo's Oracle at Delphi (see Chapter 7). His detailed report provides insight into the varying beliefs, rites, and customs prevailing in different parts of late classical Greece.

At a slightly earlier date, the Greek historian and biographer **Plutarch** (c. A.D. 46–120), best known for his *Parallel Lives* of eminent Greek and Roman leaders, recorded a number of local myths, particularly those of his native province of Boeotia and nearby Delphi, where he served as a priest of Apollo. Plutarch explores some popular beliefs not usually addressed by the great poets in his "On the Cessation of Oracles," which contains a discussion of demons (*daimones*), invisible beings intermediate between gods and men.

Distinctive Qualities of Greek Literary Myth

Poets writing in the three major literary categories in which Greek myth survives —epic narratives, lyric poetry, and tragic drama—imbue the myths with several distinctive qualities. Besides promoting such traits as anthropomorphism and consistently emphasizing family dynamics, Greek authors transmit a mythology that is characterized by humanism, individualism, competitiveness, and a modified pessimism based on their keen awareness of human mortality.

Humanism

In contrast to many other mythologies of antiquity, the majority of Greek myths ultimately focus on human heroes, a fact the Greeks themselves noted. Divine beings are important in most heroic tales, but their presence is typically intermittent and their influence indirect. Gods may operate invisibly behind the scenes, but it is the heroes' own struggles and suffering that occupy the foreground. Greek myth consistently expresses an anthropocentric (human-centered) cosmos. A worldview that places human consciousness squarely at the center of the universe, **humanism** asserts the intrinsic worth, dignity, and creative potential of each individual. "Man is the measure of all things," asserted fifth-century B.C. philosopher Protagoras, and it is human perception—guided by logic and moral principle—that defines the nature of reality. The human element is so fundamental to the Greek perspective that Hesiod's *Theogony* contains no reference to man's creation, perhaps because the poet could not conceive of a world without men—though he easily imagines one without women.

Although Hesiod does not include an account of human origins in the *Theogony,* he does allude to a tradition that gods and humans have a "common descent"—all derive ultimately from Gaea (Mother Earth). In addition to claiming a shared ancestry for gods and men, Pindar even asserts the divine–human affinity: in intellect and physical skill, men can perform deeds worthy of gods!

> Single is the race, single
> Of men and gods;
> From a single Mother [Gaea] we both draw breath.
> But a difference in power in everything keeps us apart;
> For one is nothing, but the brazen sky
> Stays a fixed habitation for ever.
> Yet we can in greatness of mind
> Or of body be like the immortals.

> —"Nemean VI," *The Odes of Pindar,* trans. C. M. Bowra

The poets' insistence that, through creative thought and heroic action, men can compete with gods, coupled with a grim awareness that even the greatest human accomplishments are eventually nullified by death, produces an almost painful tension in Greek myth. Greek humanism, particularly during the Classical period, exalted human achievements, but at the same time maintained a realistic view of human frailty. Although humanity's potential seems almost unlimited, and heroic ambition inspires men to strive with gods, both Homer and the tragic poets unanimously agree that humans betray a lamentable tendency to overreach and make fatal errors in judgment. Greek poets thus advocate a prudent self-discipline and reverence for the gods, reminding their audiences that implacable forces—fate and the sometimes unfathomable divine will—circumscribe human existence. As the example of Oedipus demonstrates, no human, no matter how lofty his status, can avoid fulfilling what the gods have decreed (see Chapter 16).

Individualism and Competitiveness

While recognizing the paradoxical tension between human assertiveness and human vulnerability, both Archaic and Classical myth emphasize a distinctively Greek focus on competitiveness and individual achievement. The Homeric heroes strive to surpass their peers and attain the foremost place—as judged by an admiring public—as the bravest, strongest, most skilled, and most eloquent. The Homeric warrior, such as Achilles or Ajax, prefers single, hand-to-hand combat with individual opponents of equal social rank to a mass assault on the enemy in which he might be lost in the crowd. Only in solo confrontations with another aristocratic fighter can he effectively demonstrate his superiority.

The career of Achilles, the *Iliad*'s leading character, illustrates both the glory and the enormous cost of unrestrained **individualism**: Achilles recognizes no equals and adamantly refuses to cooperate with his fellow Greek soldiers after Agamemnon unwisely appropriates his captive slave girl. By seizing Achilles' concubine, a living trophy of the hero's valor in battle, Agamemnon calls into question Achilles' status and reputation, subjecting him to public shame. When Hector, Troy's chief defender, slays Achilles' beloved comrade Patroclus, Achilles insists on avenging his friend, even though he knows that killing Hector will hasten his own death. The epic hero, represented by Achilles, unhesitatingly sacrifices everything, including life itself, to vindicate his honor and thereby earn undying fame (see Chapter 12).

Writers of tragedy similarly concentrate on single heroes caught up in circumstances that almost invariably bring about their destruction. Whereas the epic hero is typically a man of physical action who proves his worth by demonstrating indomitable courage and fighting skill, the tragic hero, such as Oedipus, explores the meaning of pain and defeat, plumbing depths of thought and feeling typically beyond those that epic warriors express.

Greek society routinely institutionalized the principle of individual competition: at virtually every public festival, poets, dancers, athletes, and musicians competed for prizes that were communal affirmations of their personal worth. Greece's most celebrated contests were held at the Olympic Games, which perpetuated the heroic ideal of a single competitor triumphing over all rivals. Awarding only a first prize, the Olympic judges acknowledged no second- or third-best entrants in such sports as foot racing, wrestling, boxing, discus throwing, and chariot racing. The winning athlete and the mythic hero, such as Achilles, Odysseus, Oedipus, or Antigone, share a common destiny: they stand alone, willing to risk all to accomplish feats that will elevate them over lesser mortals. As the myths never tire of saying, this obsessive quest for godlike preeminence is a noble goal, but it inevitably exacts a crushing toll.

In the universe postulated by Greek myth, humans are permanently barred from the divine enjoyment of everlasting life, a condition that threatens to rob individual lives of real meaning (compare Chapters 9 and 10). According to Homer, even the greatest heroes are condemned to spend eternity in the darkness of the Underworld, where significant action is no longer possible. Given the view that death ends all that makes life valuable, a belief well illustrated in the Homeric account of Odysseus's journey to the realm of the dead (*Odyssey,* Book 11), the high-risk environment in which the hero labors makes his efforts to excel all the more remarkable. Seeking his destiny on the battlefield or in other dangerous ventures, the hero finds himself in the paradoxical situation of pursuing immortality into the jaws of death. Dealing with themes of warfare, rage, murder, family strife, sexual aggression, and other acts of violence, many Greek myths are uncompromising in their insistence on the inevitability of human suffering and ultimate loss. Despite their repeated portrayals of noble heroes defeating evil adversaries, not many contain happy endings.

The world of Greek myth thus reflects the tensions, perplexities, and disappointments of Greek society. The gods possess everything that the Greek male desires or admires—eternal youth, good looks, honor, reputation, power, and the uninhibited assertion of individual selfhood. For all their superiority to mortals, however, the gods are driven by the same kinds of competitive ambition and jealous regard for their prerogatives that ruin the mental peace of human leaders. Worshiping divine beings who were largely projections of their own idealized (and fallible) selves, the Greeks created myths in which the gods are almost as fascinated by human activities as their mortal subjects are intrigued by the gods.

Myth and History

For the ancient Greeks, not only was myth a component of religion and a regulator of social norms, but it also took the role of prehistory, providing traditions about their supposed ancestors in the distant past. In the Greek view, the mythic past was indistinguishable from the historical past and included everything from the world's beginnings to the aftermath of the Trojan War. Having few historical facts about this ancient era, Greek storytellers typically regarded it as an almost magical era, qualitatively different from their own mundane time. It was an epoch in which gods communed freely and openly with humans, inviting mortals to their feasts and sometimes directly aiding heroes in their endeavors. Gods also took human lovers: mating with mortal women, Zeus sired many of the greatest heroes and heroines, including Perseus, Heracles, and Helen. The incomparable strength and beauty of the children thus produced was proof of their divine parentage. Even goddesses occasionally deigned to bestow their love on young men: Thetis, a beautiful sea nymph, bore Achilles to the mortal Peleus; and lovely Aphrodite seduced the Trojan shepherd-prince Anchises to produce Aeneas, who attained enormous prominence in later Roman myth (see the *Aeneid* in Chapter 19).

After the sons of heroes who had fought at Troy died, however, the mythic era came to an end, and the divine–human relationship changed forever. Zeus and the other Olympians no longer took mortal lovers, thereby precluding a new generation of heroes who could kill lions with their bare hands or descend to the Underworld and return unscathed. The Olympians withdrew permanently to Mount Olympus, thereafter communicating with humanity only through dreams, visions, or oracles delivered at prophetic shrines such as Delphi. Most commonly, the gods remained silent or sent highly ambiguous "signs" of their intentions, in the form of the flight of birds, the rustling of leaves in a sacred oak, or the appearance of the entrails of a sacrificial animal. (See Chapter 7 for a discussion of the Delphic Oracle.)

In contrast to the Greeks' view of myth as prehistory, modern scholars hotly debate whether myth has any connection with historical fact. Whereas some scholars believe that myth is entirely fiction, albeit fiction that conveys important truths about the nature of human experience, others think that some mythic events, such as the **Trojan War,** have a basis in actual events. During the nineteenth century, when most scholars insisted that the Trojan War was entirely fictional, the amateur German archaeologist Heinrich Schliemann (1822–1890) excavated the traditional site of **Troy,** near the modern village of Hissarlik in northwestern Turkey. He discovered that the site contained the ruins of a series of Bronze Age settlements, each built atop the rubble of its predecessor. Schliemann concluded that the ruin labeled Troy VII-A was the citadel Homer described in the *Iliad.* Some later archaeologists argued that Troy VII-A was too puny to fit the Homeric description; however, recent surveys of the site indicate that a slightly earlier city, Troy VI, was much larger and more impressively fortified than Schliemann's Troy VII-A. Troy VI, with its massive walls, was destroyed and burned about 1270 B.C., whereas Troy VII-A fell about 1190 B.C., when Mycenaean civilization was already in decline (Figure 1-11).

Having "found" Troy, Schliemann next excavated the site of **Mycenae** [mye-SEE-nee], a late Bronze Age city that Agamemnon, leader of the Greek forces against Troy, was said to have ruled. (See the map in Figure 1-17.) Schliemann discovered that Homer was correct in describing Mycenae as "rich in gold," for its royal tombs contained superbly crafted metalwork, including gold drinking vessels and gold death masks that had been placed over the faces of deceased kings. Referring to a particularly striking mask, Schliemann incorrectly claimed to have "looked upon the face of Agamemnon" (Figure 1-12), although the object in question subsequently was dated to a period considerably before the Trojan War. Recent studies accuse Schliemann of both careless error and outright deception in some of his claims, but his work stimulated other archaeological investigations of prehistoric Greece that have enabled us to understand some of the major developments in Greek history. If future discoveries produce evidence that prehistoric Greeks did indeed capture Troy, the famous war may prove to be legendary rather than purely mythic. (Recall that the term *legend* is commonly used to denote a tradition that has some core of historicity, no matter how embellished by later poetic interpretation.)

(All dates approximate and B.C.)

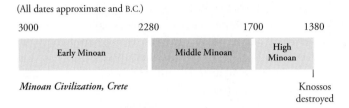

Minoan Civilization, Crete

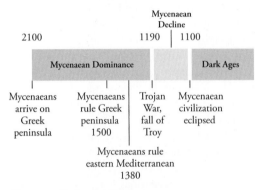

Mycenaean Civilization, Peloponnesus

FIGURE 1-11   Historical Time Lines. Although many Greek myths may have originated during the Mycenaean era (c. 1600–1100 B.C.), they were not written down until the Archaic period, after the Homeric epics were composed. The last great events of Greek myth concern the war against Troy and the homecomings of heroes such as Agamemnon, king of Mycenae, and Odysseus, king of Ithaca (c. 1190 B.C.). During the twelfth century B.C., the Mycenaean urban centers were destroyed, plunging Greece into the Dark Ages.

The Major Periods of Greek History

Greek culture of the historical period, including its mythology, is a synthesis of many older influences, including that of the ancient Near Eastern civilizations of Mesopotamia. (See Chapter 3 for a discussion of Near Eastern parallels to Hesiod's myth of world origins.) Archaeological evidence from Greece and the Aegean Islands indicates that an identifiably Greek culture did not begin to emerge until after the arrival of Indo-Europeans about 2100 B.C. **Indo-European** is a linguistic term designating an interrelated group of languages, including Greek, Latin, French, and English, that are spoken in Europe and parts of western Asia. Scholars believe that these linguistically related languages are descended from a proto-Indo-European tongue that may have originated in central Asia and, beginning in the fourth millennium B.C., spread to western Asia and then to Europe.

FIGURE 1-12   Mycenaean Death Mask. When the pioneering archaeologist Heinrich Schliemann excavated the circular shaft graves at Mycenae,
he found royal entombments that had miraculously escaped the plundering of ancient grave robbers. Although Schliemann thought that he had
"looked upon the face of Agamemnon" when he discovered this remarkable
gold mask, he had actually found a funerary artifact belonging to a period
of the Bronze Age that predates the traditional time of the Trojan War.
(National Museum, Athens)

Minoan Civilization

Long before the Indo-Europeans arrived in Greece, a people of unknown origins
had already created a highly sophisticated culture centered on the island of Crete
(see Figure 1-17). Characterized by huge palace complexes decorated with colorful
wall paintings, Cretan society developed during the early and middle Bronze Ages
(c. 3000–1600 B.C.). When Sir Arthur Evans (1851–1941), a British archaeologist,
excavated Cretan sites during the early twentieth century, he named the rediscovered culture the **Minoan** [Mih-NOH-an], after **Minos** [MYE-nohs], a mythical
king said to have reigned at Knossos, the largest of Crete's palaces. Evans, who
partly restored some of Knossos's grand courtyards, broad stairways, painted colonnades, and brilliant frescoes (Figure 1-13), found that the Minoans had achieved a
remarkable level of both artistic and technological development. Besides brighten-
ing their rooms with light wells and exquisite paintings, they equipped Knossos
with indoor plumbing and flush toilets, a combination of domestic elegance and

FIGURE 1-13   Minoan Figures [Priestesses?] from Knossos. The beauty and elegance characterizing aristocratic life at the Minoan royal palaces are evident in this fresco from Knossos. A vast multistory structure extending over many acres, the Knossos palace was excavated by Sir Arthur Evans in the early twentieth century. *(Archaeological Museum, Heraklion, Crete)*

convenience not matched again until the age of imperial Rome. The fact that Minoan palaces were not fortified also suggests that this luxury-loving people controlled the surrounding seas and did not fear enemy invasion.

For many centuries, Minoan culture dominated the Aegean, including settlements on Thera (modern Santorini), a volcanic island about sixty miles north of Crete. About 1628 B.C., the Thera volcano produced one of the region's largest eruptions since the Ice Age ended approximately ten thousand years earlier. The eruption buried a coastal town, named for the nearby modern village of Akrotiri, that has now been partly excavated. Like the Minoan palaces on Crete, this Bronze Age seaport boasted paved streets, an elaborate water supply and sewage system, indoor plumbing, and superb frescoes, including paintings of an urban waterfront and a naval fleet. Some historians believe that Plato's famous tale of **Atlantis,** an advanced civilization thought to have disappeared suddenly during a great natural disaster, may be based on dim memories of the catastrophic eruption of Thera. In the 1960s, some archaeologists theorized that the Thera disaster, which probably triggered giant tsunamis, may have sunk the Minoan fleet and destroyed many low-lying coastal settlements, paving the way for mainland invaders to seize control of Crete. Because the destruction of the Minoan palaces occurred almost two centuries after the great eruption, however, historians have concluded that Thera was not responsible for the demise of Minoan civilization. At present, only the equivalent of three city blocks of ancient Akrotiri have been uncovered from their thick shroud of volcanic ash; many more artifacts that will illuminate this pre-Greek culture probably still await discovery.

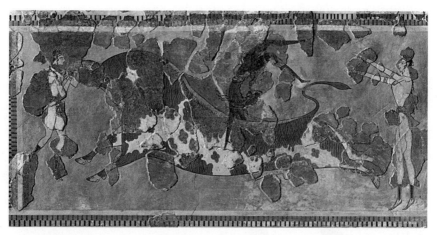

FIGURE 1-14 The Minoan "Bull Dance." This fresco from the Minoan palace at Knossos shows a young woman and a young man participating in an apparently death-defying ritual involving a Cretan bull. Such rites may have given rise to the myth of the flesh-devouring Minotaur, half-man and half-bull. Bull horns carved in stone formed a dominant architectural motif at Knossos, suggesting that for the Minoans the bull represented a divine force. In Greek myth, Poseidon, god of the sea (which the Minoans ruled), is represented by a bull. Poseidon also caused earthquakes, which sporadically devastated Crete and other parts of the Aegean. *(Archaeological Museum, Heraklion, Crete)*

Both the Minoan and other Aegean Island cultures appear to have worshiped the feminine principle of divinity. Although no written texts dating from Minoan times have yet been deciphered, an abundance of female figurines and other cult objects associated with the earth, fertility, and regeneration indicate that the "Divine Woman" was central to Minoan and other Aegean religions (see Chapter 5). The bull, a symbol of divine strength, also featured prominently in Minoan art (Figure 1-14).

Mycenaean Civilization

When Indo-Europeans arrived in Greece near the end of the third millennium B.C., they brought with them not only horses and an aggressive warrior mentality but also the worship of a male sky god. Zeus, head of the Greek **pantheon** (roster of officially recognized deities), is a direct descendant of the Indo-European concept of masculine divinity (Figure 1-15; see the discussion of Zeus in Chapter 6).

Borrowing heavily from the earlier Minoan culture, Indo-Europeans speaking an early form of Greek established a series of fortified cities on the Greek mainland, including Mycenae, after which archaeologists have named the Mycenaean civilization (c. 1650–1150 B.C.). Whereas the Minoans had constructed enormous palaces without fortifications, the Mycenaeans surrounded their hilltop settlements with massive defensive walls (Figure 1-16). They also appear to have worshiped a number of gods later included in the Greek pantheon. Mycenaean texts, a form of writing known as Linear B, reveal several familiar names, including Zeus and Hera (who

FIGURE 1-15   Bronze Statue of Zeus [or Poseidon]. This larger-
than-life bronze (c. 460 B.C.) probably represents the king of the
gods about to hurl a lightning bolt at some offending mortal. An
awesome embodiment of nature's power revealed in electrical
storms, Zeus is a sky god who also represents the Greek conviction that the universe is based on principles of justice and cosmic
harmony. When human crimes upset the world's moral balance,
Zeus punishes the guilty to restore the natural order, a view
expressed in Homer's *Odyssey* and other works of Greek myth.
(National Museum, Athens)

are linked), Poseidon, Artemis, Athene, Hermes, and Ares. Even Dionysus is mentioned, although some myths suggest that he was an import from Asia, a late arrival
on the Greek scene (see Chapter 8). Some Linear B passages feature dedications
to "all the gods," indicating a substantial number of recognized deities during the
Mycenaean era, perhaps forerunners of the Olympian family.

In his *Mycenaean Origin of Greek Mythology,* Martin P. Nilsson argued that
Greek myth assumed its distinctive qualities during the Mycenaean period. Noting
that many of the Homeric and other mythical heroes are associated with specific
Mycenaean cities—Agamemnon and Orestes with Mycenae, Heracles with Tiryns,
Nestor with Pylos, Oedipus with Thebes—Nilsson concluded that Homer, Hesiod,
and other early poets drew on oral traditions from the Mycenaean era in creating
their later versions of the myths. Unfortunately, archaeology has revealed only that
the Mycenaeans honored some of the same gods worshiped later in Greek history.

FIGURE 1-16 The Lion Gate at Mycenae. Unlike the Minoan palace complexes, Mycenaean cities were heavily fortified against attack. Originally, the carved lions—nine feet high—atop the huge stone slabs composing the city's main entryway probably had heads of bronze. After the collapse of Mycenaean civilization (c. 1150 B.C.), later generations referred to such massive defensive walls as *cyclopean,* believing that only a race of giants, the Cyclopes, could have built them.

Not a single Mycenaean story about gods or heroes has survived; we may infer from Minoan and Mycenaean frescoes and vase paintings that many of the scenes depicted have a religious/mythical significance, but we do not know what myths, if any, they may represent.

Scholars believe that Greek myth evolved gradually over time, perhaps largely from Bronze Age religious practices and other rituals. But it is not until the Archaic period, when the Homeric epics were composed, that we can be sure of the nature or content of any given myth. The earliest surviving representations of identifiable mythic scenes in art, such as Odysseus's blinding of the Cyclops, are roughly co-eval with the creation of the Homeric epics (eighth century B.C.). Whatever specific influence Mycenaean lore may have exerted on Greek literary myth must remain conjectural.

The Iron Age (Dark Ages)

As the Minoan civilization crumbled in the mid-fifteenth century B.C., perhaps as a result of Mycenaean assaults, so the great Mycenaean citadels fell about three hundred years later. Historians disagree about the causes of the Mycenaean collapse (c. 1200–1100 B.C.), but it may have resulted from multiple factors, including

Major Periods of Ancient Greek History

APPROXIMATE DATE B.C.	HISTORICAL EPOCH
c. 3000	Beginnings of Minoan culture on Crete
c. 2200–1450	Middle Minoan palace culture on Crete
c. 2100	Probable arrival of Indo-Europeans in Greece
1600–1200	Development of Mycenaean palace culture in Greece, initially dependent on Cretan models
1450	Mycenaeans take over Minoan Knossos on Crete

Between 1250 and 1150 B.C., there was a breakdown of settled conditions in the eastern Mediterranean and Asia Minor.

c. 1190	Destruction of Troy VII-A, the probable event that inspired traditions of the Trojan War and that may represent the last major enterprise of the Mycenaean Greeks
1200–1125	Widespread destruction of Mycenaean sites in Greece; Mycenae falls c. 1150 B.C.
1100–1000	Infiltration of Dorian Greeks (in myth, the return of the sons of Heracles); beginning of DARK AGES
1050–950	Migration of mainland Greeks to Aegean Islands and coast of Asia Minor; iron tools in use after 1050; period of crude geometric pottery
	ARCHAIC PERIOD
750–675	Age of Homer (c. 750 B.C.) and Hesiod (c. 675 B.C.); production of epic poems

new techniques in Iron Age warfare, ecological disaster, or even uprisings in which the ruling aristocracy was overthrown. Whatever factors produced the downfall of Mycenaean culture, it was followed by a long period—traditionally known as the **Dark Ages** (c. 1100–800 B.C.)—during which most of Greece suffered a severe decline in population, widespread economic impoverishment, and a corresponding deterioration of the material culture. With the disappearance of urban centers, the art of writing (Linear B) was also lost. The crude pottery surviving from this period contrasts strikingly with the richly decorated Minoan and Mycenaean artwork. Perhaps because much of Greece was gradually occupied by a people speaking a Dorian dialect, refugees from the older Mycenaean centers migrated from the mainland eastward across the Aegean Sea to settle along the coast of Ionia, in what is now western Turkey.

APPROXIMATE DATE B.C.	HISTORICAL EPOCH
	ARCHAIC PERIOD (*continued*)
600	Renaissance in Ionia (Asia Minor); birth of primitive science and philosophy in Miletus
546	Pisistratus establishes tyranny at Athens
534	First tragedy competition held at Athens
510	Expulsion of Hippias from Athens; establishment of world's first democracy
490–479	PERSIAN WARS: Marathon (490), Salamis (480), Plataea and Mycale (479)
	CLASSICAL PERIOD ("Golden Age" of Pericles at Athens)
431–404	Peloponnesian Wars between Athens and Sparta
406	Deaths of Euripides and Sophocles
338	Philip II of Macedonia conquers Athens and Thebes; end of Greek independence
336–323	Conquests of Alexander the Great, son of Philip II
	HELLENISTIC PERIOD
323	Successors of Alexander rule eastern Mediterranean world and Near East
146	Rome conquers Greece: Corinth is destroyed and Macedonia becomes a Roman province

The Archaic and Classical Periods

As the prosperity and material culture of these Ionian settlements gradually improved—largely through sea trade and interaction with the commercial centers of Asia Minor—a new and distinctively Greek civilization began to emerge at Ionian cities such as Miletus, Smyrna, and Halicarnassus. During the Archaic period (c. 800–480 B.C.), Greece was reborn as a network of hundreds of city-states scattered from Ionia in the eastern Aegean to Sicily and southern Italy in the west (Figure 1-17). Important symbols of the Greek renaissance were the founding of the panhellenic Olympic Games (traditionally in 776 B.C.) and the production of the Homeric epics. A possession of all the Greek peoples, Homer's *Iliad* and *Odyssey* crystallized ancient oral traditions that helped give the politically fragmented

FIGURE 1-17   Map of the Greek World. Minoan Crete, island home of the first European civilization, influenced the development of the mainland Mycenaean culture, the earliest proto-Greek culture. Note the locations of Mycenae, Sparta, and Troy, cities that figure prominently in Greek myth.

Greeks their collective identity. Some scholars even argue that the revival of writing in the mid-eighth century B.C.—with an alphabet borrowed from the Phoenicians—was achieved in order to transcribe the Homeric poems.

Following Greek victories during Persia's two invasions of Greece (490 and 480–479 B.C.), **Athens** formed a confederacy of Greek states, the Delian League, and assumed political leadership of Greece. During the half-century after the **Persian Wars,** Athens celebrated its ascendancy in an outburst of creative activity in works of art, architecture, history, philosophy, and drama. Even after it was militarily defeated by Sparta (with Persian aid) at the end of the **Peloponnesian Wars** (431–404 B.C.), Athens continued to be, as the Athenian leader Pericles had once stated, a "school for all Hellas," producing sculpture, painting, and literature that established standards of excellence for later generations. Because Greek myth is preserved in works of literature—epics, lyric poetry, and dramas—that stand as models of artistic achievement, it is known as *classical,* both the fountainhead and the inspiration of the West's subsequent creative impulses.

Differences Between Greek and Roman Mythology

Although classical mythology is essentially Greek myth, the Romans also contributed extensively to the field. Ovid, a leading Roman poet during the reign of Augustus (27 B.C.–A.D. 14), created the single most important collection of Greco-Roman tales—the *Metamorphoses.* Ovid's stories about gods and heroes changing their physical forms, undergoing a metamorphosis, were designed to reflect a late development in the Greek mythic tradition, one that influenced the literary tastes of a sophisticated Roman audience familiar with the Hellenistic poets and scholars of Alexandria, Egypt, the second largest city in the Roman Empire and a center of literary and artistic creativity. Although most of Ovid's tales were drawn from ancient Greek sources, he retold them in a witty and entertaining manner, a cosmopolitan touch pleasing to his Roman contemporaries. The *Metamorphoses,* for example, begins in the mythic realm, with stories of creation, gods, and heroes, but ultimately ties the ancient myths to specific events in Roman history, ending with the death and posthumous deification of Julius Caesar, which occurred only a year before the poet's birth. Taking a more solemnly didactic approach to revising Greek myth, the Roman poet Virgil (70–19 B.C.) celebrated distinctively Roman social, ethical, and political values, particularly the hero's self-discipline and self-sacrifice in serving gods and state. In his *Aeneid,* an epic of Rome's origins, Virgil adapted the tradition of Aphrodite's affair with the Trojan prince Anchises, which led to the birth of the hero Aeneas (see Chapter 6), to connect the glories of the Trojan conflict with the later founding of Rome by Aeneas's descendants, the twins Romulus and Remus (see Chapter 19). Because Roman poets such as Ovid and Virgil produced their adaptations of Greek myth not only at a much later time than the Greeks but also for different aesthetic and political purposes, as well as for a different audience, Roman mythology is discussed in a separate section (see Chapters 18–20).

In this text, we explore the major literary works embodying Greek and Roman myths in generally chronological order, beginning with Hesiod's narrative of creation and the birth of the gods (see Chapters 3 and 4). After surveying the prehistoric

Goddess figure, and poetic hymns to various Olympian gods, including Demeter, Hermes, Apollo, and Dionysus (see Chapters 5–9), we examine the defining nature and adventures of representative heroes and heroines (see Chapters 10 and 11). Extended excerpts from Homer's *Iliad* and *Odyssey,* epics narrating the Trojan War and the long-delayed homecoming of its most resourceful hero, illustrate both the heroic figure in action and a variety of heroes' relationships with the gods (see Chapters 12 and 13).

In contrast to the epics of Hesiod and Homer, which were probably composed orally in the eighth and early seventh centuries B.C. and which encompass Archaic traditions shared by all Greeks, the second main source of Greek myth, the tragic dramas of Aeschylus, Sophocles, and Euripides, were written specifically for an Athenian audience in the fifth century B.C. Commonly expressing the interests and concerns of democratic Athens, such plays as the *Agamemnon, Eumenides, Antigone, Medea,* and *Bacchae* (all given with the complete text) also highlight the roles of women and issues of gender conflict that Greek writers often used to express their sense of life's challenges and mysterious contrarieties.

Readers wishing to explore the different ways in which Greek and Roman mythographers handled similar topics and themes may find it instructive to compare Hesiod's account of creation and humanity's decline from a primal Golden Age (see Chapters 3 and 4) with Ovid's later, more urbane version of the tradition in the *Metamorphoses* (see Chapter 20), keeping in mind that Ovid wrote approximately seven hundred and fifty years after Hesiod and inhabited an entirely different cultural and intellectual environment. Similarly, the contrast between Homer's pessimistic description of the subterranean realm of the dead (the *Odyssey,* Book 11; see Chapter 13) and Virgil's far more philosophically informed portrayal of the Underworld in the *Aeneid* (Book 6; see Chapter 19) also illustrates the striking evolution of mythic ideas over the course of centuries (see also the discussion of Hades' kingdom in Chapter 9).

. . . .

Questions for Discussion and Review

1. According to Greek myth, what is unusual about the births of Athene (goddess of wisdom) and Dionysus (god of wine and emotional freedom)? Why do you suppose many ancient traditions tell of events that are literally impossible? Can you see any symbolic meaning in having Zeus, king of the gods, personally give birth to two such different divine children?

2. Suggest some possible definitions for the term *mythos.* What role does oral storytelling play in the origin and development of myth? Why do Greek myths survive in so many different versions?

3. Discuss the literary character of much Greek myth. What are the major written sources of classical myth?

4. Define the Minoan, Mycenaean, Archaic, Classical, and Hellenistic periods of Greek history. From which two periods do most of our literary sources of Greek myth derive?

5. Discuss the distinctive qualities of Greek mythology, including its literary character and emphasis on competitive action. Define the concepts of *humanism, anthropomorphism,* and *individualism* as they relate to Greek myth.

Works Cited

Sargent, Thelma, trans. *Homeric Hymn to Athene.* New York: Norton, 1973.

(For a list of recommended readings, see the Selected Bibliography at the back of this book.)

CHAPTER

2

Ways of Interpreting Myth

KEY TOPICS/THEMES

Although most Greeks apparently regarded their myths as plausible accounts of their remote past, some Greek thinkers were skeptical, criticizing the Homeric portrayal of the gods as unethical and attempting to rationalize the miraculous elements in myth. By contrast, modern scholars try to define the precise nature and purpose of myth, advancing various theories to explain its origin and functions. Some theorists argue that myths are largely prescientific responses to the external world of nature or social institutions. Externalist theories suggest that myths were designed to provide imaginative causes for natural phenomena, such as the cycle of day and night or the recurrence of the seasons; to give meaning to commonly observed rituals, such as religious sacrifices or initiation rites; or retroactively to justify social practices or institutions whose actual origins had been forgotten. Internalist theories propose that myth is a spontaneous product of the human mind, operating to express typically unconscious fears or desires, to chart the difficulties of psychological maturation, or to mediate the contrarieties of existence.

Ancient Ways of Viewing Myth

Archaic Views

Most ancient Greeks seem to have accepted their myths uncritically, as venerable traditions that preserved generally reliable accounts of the world's origins, the nature of divinity, and the distant past. Besides substituting for history and theology in the popular Greek imagination, myth offered examples of heroic action that promoted standards of courage and leadership for the ruling classes. After about 600 B.C., however, the rise of philosophy, with its use of reason and observation to interpret the world without dependence on inherited beliefs, produced thinkers who could be acutely critical of Homer's portrayal of the gods. Xenophanes, a writer who lived about two hundred years after Homer in the town of Colophon in Ionia (now western Turkey), was among the first to attack the Homeric gods as ethically deficient—guilty of theft, adultery, vindictiveness, and other acts that would shame most humans. Aware that a society's gods mirror the virtues and defects of the people who worship them, Xenophanes called attention to the Greeks' tendency to fashion gods in their own image:

1
Man made his gods, and furnished them
with his own body, voice and garments.

2
If a horse or lion or a slow ox
had agile hands for paint and sculpture,
the horse would make his god a horse,
the ox would sculpt an ox.

3
Our gods have flat noses and black skins
say the Ethiopians. The Thracians say
our gods have red hair and hazel eyes.

　　—*Greek Lyric Poetry*, trans. Willis Barnstone, p. 131

While rejecting myth's anthropomorphic gods as naive and morally objectionable, Xenophanes proposed that there exists a single, unknowable deity who informs and governs the universe by thought alone:

There is one God—supreme among gods and men—
who is like mortals in neither body nor mind.

　　—*Greek Lyric Poetry*, trans. Willis Barnstone

Although Xenophanes is sometimes regarded as the earliest Greek monotheist, some scholars believe that he was instead formulating a notion of cosmic unity and harmony that encompassed all divinity.

Another Archaic poet, Theagenes (c. 525 B.C.), agreed that a literal reading of Homeric myth was ethically unacceptable, but he suggested a method of interpretation by which the Greeks could retain their mythic heritage and also make it morally respectable. Theagenes, who lived in southern Italy, was allegedly the first to view the *Iliad* and *Odyssey* as allegories—narratives that are not to be read at face value, but that function metaphorically. In an **allegory,** all characters, places, and actions are symbolic of something else. According to Theagenes, who incorporated ideas from early Greek science into his allegorical reading of Homer, the gods fighting against one another in the Trojan War represent not real deities but natural phenomena. Thus, when Apollo or Helios battles Poseidon or Troy's river god Scamander, the conflict actually signifies celestial fire opposing its cosmic opposite, water. Similarly, Artemis represents the moon, and Hera the air. In Theagenes' view, the gods can also symbolize human qualities or dispositions: Aphrodite is desire; Ares, insanity; and Athene, intelligence.

Classical Views

The philosopher Anaxagoras ([an-ax-AG-o-ras] c. 500–428 B.C.) also avoided taking a literal view of myths that, at first blush, seem to present the gods behaving badly. In the Homeric tradition, Hermes steals Apollo's cattle; Zeus rapes the virgin Io; Ares seduces Hephaestus's wife, Aphrodite; and Hera persecutes her husband's innocent (although typically illegitimate) children. The list of divine misdemeanors seems endless. Adopting Theagenes' allegorical approach to resolve the ethical dilemma, Anaxagoras contended that the Homeric epics were really intended to expose the evil results of wrongdoing and thereby to teach virtue.

Myth's use of miraculous or otherwise "incredible" events also caused problems for many Greek intellectuals, who typically attempted to rationalize mythic "impossibilities." With few exceptions, most classical authors exploited the tools of philosophical reasoning only to explain away unrealistic aspects of old traditions. They did not question the existence of their gods, but merely the way the poets presented them. In his play the *Bacchae*, Euripides has the prophet Tiresias correct a popular misconception about Dionysus's birth from the thigh of Zeus. The mistaken view that Zeus literally carried Dionysus in his body after saving the embryo from a fire consuming the child's mother, Semele, results from the careless confusion of similar words. Zeus did not stitch the unborn child into his thigh (Greek, *meron*); instead, Tiresias says, he rescued the infant from Hera's jealous wrath by hiding him away and making, out of bright air, a replica of Dionysus's body, and then giving this false image to Hera as a hostage (*homeron*; Figure 2-1). Euripides' ingenious wordplay thus purges the myth of its irrational content while retaining the supernatural aspect of the story, a typical mode of classical interpretation.

FIGURE 2-1   The Birth of Dionysus from the Thigh of Zeus. In this bas-relief, the newborn Dionysus emerges from his father's lap and reaches out to Hermes, who prepares to wrap the infant in swaddling clothes. Whereas a few educated Greeks, such as the playwright Euripides and the philosopher Plato, tried to rationalize myth to make it seem more plausible, none seem to have questioned its fundamental relation to supposedly historical events in the distant past. Viewing myth as a purely imaginary creation—perhaps invented to express insights into physical nature, social institutions, or human psychology —is a modern, post-Enlightenment development. *(Vatican Museums, Rome)*

Some classical philosophers, notably the Athenian **Socrates** (c. 469–399 B.C.) and his disciple **Plato** (427–347 B.C.), were particularly offended by the poor moral example the Olympians set, objecting to such tales as Uranus's castration by his son Cronus, the father of Zeus, or Zeus's countless adulteries. Insisting that the gods must be viewed as entirely good and free of human passion, Plato banned Homeric myth from his ideal republic. Despite his aversion to poetic fictions, however, Plato himself freely revised selected myths to illustrate his teachings about an invisible spirit realm to which the soul returns after death (see Chapter 9).

A Hellenistic Theory

About two generations after Plato, Euhemerus of Messene proposed a revolutionary theory about the origin of the Greek gods. In his fictional travel story *Sacred Scripture* (*Hiera anagraphē,* c. 300 B.C.), Euhemerus described an imaginary island, Panchaia, in the Indian Ocean, that he claimed to have visited. According to this account, the islanders had erected a golden column inscribed with lists of prehistoric human kings, including such rulers as Uranus, Cronus, and Zeus! According to Euhemerus's startling interpretation, this column provided written evidence that the Homeric gods were originally mortal, ancient leaders who had been posthumously elevated to divine status. Known as Euhemerism, this view holds that Greek concepts about the gods derive from the postmortem deification of otherwise forgotten mortals. Euhemerism had a strong impact on the Hellenistic world, where successors to Alexander the Great were claiming divine honors, a practice that some Roman emperors later adopted.

Some Modern Interpretations of Myth

Despite Euhemerus's shocking assertion, however, or an occasional philosopher's rejection of its more brutal aspects, myth generally maintained its hold on Greco-Roman society until the Roman government's legitimization of Christianity as the official state religion in the fourth century A.D. Denounced by the Christian Church as being opposed to the true faith, classical religion and mythology were largely devalued in Western culture during the Middle Ages. Medieval scholars produced numerous handbooks or other compilations that summarized Greco-Roman myths, but these volumes were mostly devoted to reinterpreting myth as allegory, commonly as symbols of "higher truths" compatible with Christian doctrine. Ovid's tales were particularly subject to scholarly moralizing, as were traditions of the Trojan War. Although medieval theologians commonly identified Greek deities with demons, the rebirth of classical learning during the European Renaissance reintroduced myth to the world of art, literature, and scholarship. The development of modern scientific methodology during the Enlightenment (eighteenth century A.D.), with its emphasis on reason, objectivity, classification, and analysis, eventually inspired a renewed scholarly interest in myth. During the past two centuries, scholars have applied techniques from a variety of academic disciplines—including anthropology, cultural history, psychology, sociology, and religious studies—in studying myth and interpreting its significance.

Mythology has two general meanings. It can be defined as a set or system of myths, such as the vast collection of Greek and Roman tales known as classical mythology. It also refers to a methodological analysis of myths, particularly their form, purpose, and function. In trying to isolate some theme or principle that all myths have in common, scholars have produced many theories that claim to provide *the* correct key for understanding the precise nature of myth. Although no one theory or definition of myth has yet won universal acceptance, scholarly attempts to break myths down into their component parts and identify some unifying element behind their almost infinite variety have greatly increased our knowledge of what myths are and are not. Most scholarly theories fit into one of two broad categories: those that assume an external basis, such as a reaction to physical nature, for the creation of myth; and those that see mythmaking as spontaneous and internal, an instinctive expression of the human mind.

Externalist Theories: Myth as a Product of the Environment

The "externalists" typically view myth as a prescientific attempt to explain natural phenomena or to provide justifications for social, religious, or political customs or institutions. These theories generally view myth as a quasi-rational response to the physical or social environment.

Nature Myths   One of the first modern efforts to fashion a comprehensive theory of myth was, in fact, anticipated by Theagenes' argument that mythic characters and actions actually represent natural processes. The **nature myth** theory holds that myth is essentially a reaction to the awe-inspiring power of physical nature, particularly those phenomena that directly affect human life: the continuing cycles of day and night, sunshine and darkness, summer and winter, heat and cold, fair weather and foul, rainfall and drought, plant life and death.

Even casual readers will immediately recognize that many Greek tales personify (give human traits to) solar, atmospheric, meteorological, or other natural processes. Zeus, who gathers storm clouds, detonates thunder, and hurls lightning bolts, is, in some respects, a **personification** of meteorological forces. From another perspective, Zeus is also the divine being who is *revealed* through these natural phenomena. His brother Poseidon is lord of the sea and earthquakes, a volatile manifestation of natural energy that makes both sea and land violently roll and pitch, with potentially disastrous consequences for mortals.

Some of the older gods, whom the Greeks believed preceded the Olympians in time, are directly identified with astronomical objects or functions. The Titan **Hyperion** [hye-PEER-ee-uhn] (or his son **Helios** [HEE-lee-ohs]) is the sun, and **Selene** [se-LEE-nee] is the moon that typically rises as the sun sets—a cycle depicted at the two corners of the Parthenon's east pediment to frame the central scene of Athene's birth (see Figures 3-1 and 3-2). **Eos** [EE-ohs], whom Homer calls "rosy-fingered" and whom the Romans named **Aurora** [ah-ROR-uh], personifies the dawn. A few myths about Apollo, who in later traditions assumes Hyperion's duties as the sun god, illustrate solar movement, signified by Apollo's fiery chariot journeying daily across the sky.

Scholars advocating the nature myth theory—such as the nineteenth-century philologist F. Max Müller (1823–1900), whose work helped popularize the concept

—rigorously applied their view to the entire range of myth. If a particular myth's relation to natural phenomena was not immediately obvious, it was interpreted allegorically to make it fit the theory. According to Müller and others of his school, the Greeks used mythic figures and events to symbolize the tensions, oppositions, and seasonal changes in nature, such as the anxiety-producing alternation of flood and aridity that so profoundly affected the activities of sowing, growing, and harvesting on which the human community depended to survive.

Interpreting all myths as ingeniously disguised representations of natural phenomena, the nature myth theory fails to account for the full content of most myths. Zeus is undeniably a weather god, but he is also the champion of justice, hospitality, and legitimate kingship; defining him only as a personification of atmospheric turbulence explains none of his higher ethical functions. Artemis is commonly identified with the moon, but that does not explain her role as patron of childbirth and guardian of wildlife. Nor does regarding Dionysus, god of the vine, as merely an embodiment of the vegetative life cycle adequately explain his role as liberator of the human psyche.

Myth and Ritual   A more persistent and influential theory associates myth exclusively with **ritual,** a religious or quasi-religious ceremony in which a prescribed series of actions—accompanied by the repetition of traditional phrases—are scrupulously observed. At the annual festival of Dionysus in Athens, a parade featured representations of the god's mythic birth and death, as well as traditional songs and dances out of which Athenian tragedy is said to have developed. According to the ritualist view, promoted by several leading scholars at Cambridge University during the late nineteenth and early twentieth centuries, myths are the byproduct of such ritual enactments as those performed at Dionysian celebrations. They are stories invented to explain ceremonies whose real origins have long been forgotten. In his multivolume compendium of European myth, *The Golden Bough* (1890–1915), the English anthropologist Sir James Frazer (1854–1941) offered numerous examples from European folk rituals to illustrate the close bond between myth and ancient rites, particularly those that evoked plant, animal, and human fertility. Among others, Robert Graves (1895–1985), an English poet, novelist, and critic, maintained that myths derive from mimes, dances, and other performances given at public festivals. The Cambridge school, which included such distinguished critics as Jane Harrison and Gilbert Murray, argued that even supposedly sophisticated Greek myths were based on primitive, irrational customs. Stories of Heracles' labors and his later ascension to heaven were alleged to derive from oral recitations made at his purported tomb.

In some cases, such as the tale of Demeter and Persephone, there is a close correlation between ritual and myth. At Eleusis, a town about twelve miles northwest of Athens, celebrants reenacted the ancient story of Demeter's search for her young daughter, Persephone, who, unknown to her grieving mother, had been abducted by Hades and imprisoned in the Underworld. Overcome with sorrow and anger, Demeter expressed her displeasure by afflicting the earth with sterility, so that the grain that sustains all human and animal life could not grow, and the world faced starvation. The ritual she later taught the people of Eleusis to observe in her honor mirrored the course of her suffering: in addition to holding a torch-lit procession and consuming a special barley drink, public actions that recapitulated Demeter's nocturnal quest and the beverage she had created to refresh herself, devotees participated in secret rites they were forbidden to divulge. Persons who took part in Demeter's Great Mysteries, ceremonies of initiation into the goddess's worship, relived the goddess's movement from despair to joy when, by Zeus's order, her daughter was restored to her. (Demeter's myth and the Eleusinian Mysteries are discussed in detail in Chapter 5.)

A similar instance illustrating ritual's connection with myth occurs in a tale about the women of **Lemnos**, a volcanic island in the north Aegean. It was said that Aphrodite afflicted Lemnos's women with an offensive smell, so that their husbands rejected them. In retaliation, the wives murdered their husbands, leaving only women on the island. The situation changed unexpectedly when Jason, with his crew of heroes, the Argonauts, suddenly arrived on Lemnos to end the widows' celibacy. Welcoming the Argonauts as lovers, the women soon bore children who repopulated the island amid general rejoicing. The Lemnians' annual ritual mirrored the myth almost precisely: each year all fires were extinguished for nine days and family life ceased, with women eating garlic and separating themselves from the men, who apparently kept out of sight. After nine days, new fire was brought from Apollo's sacred island of Delos, and the hearth fires were rekindled; the inhabitants then held a festival expressing jubilation at the sexual reunion of husband and wife.

In both the Demeter–Persephone myth and that of the women of Lemnos, the action progresses from scenes of loss and deprivation to a climactic restoration (although Persephone's return is only partial; see the *Homeric Hymn to Demeter* in Chapter 5). Both myth and ritual reflect a consciousness of danger, the ever-present threat to civilized life posed by a possible loss of the food supply or of what fire represents, the ability to transform raw meat into cooked food and to create tools and weapons—the source of a uniquely human culture. The transition from grief to joy in both the Eleusinian and the Lemnian rites offers reassurance that potential disasters, including the sundering of basic family ties—the bonds linking mother and child or husband and wife—can be averted and communal life sustained.

The Charter Theory   The charter theory developed from direct observations of a preliterate people in the active process of making myth serve practical or social purposes. Stranded on the Trobriand Islands near New Guinea during the First World War, the Polish anthropologist Bronislaw Malinowski (1884–1942) noted that the Trobrianders used myth to validate existing communal institutions, beliefs, and practices. These "charter" **myths** are narratives that supply the rationale for some ritual or custom; they serve to justify the practice of a particular initiation rite or other ceremony and to promote its regular repetition, presumably to help maintain stability and communal order.

A few Greek myths seem to function as charters, justifying some debatable social or religious observance. In his poem of origins, the *Theogony*, Hesiod provides a foundation story to support the Greeks' habit of offering their gods only the least desirable parts of sacrificial animals. Like the biblical Hebrews and other ancient peoples, the Greeks shared communal meals with their divine protectors, eating cooked meat and burning the residue, which wafted its way to heaven as a column of smoke. According to Hesiod, when the newly empowered Olympian gods met with primitive men (women had not yet been created) at Mekone to "negotiate" humanity's obligation to offer animal sacrifices, the cunning Titan Prometheus slew a sacrificial ox, dividing its carcass into two unequal portions. Concealing the meat and hide beneath the ox's unappetizing stomach, he tricked Zeus, king of the gods, into accepting as the gods' share a pile of inedible bones covered with fat. Hesiod's story operates as a charter, a validation of the ancient practice of offering the gods only the least desirable parts of a sacrificial animal, the bones and fat, while human participants ate the tastier portions. Although Hesiod's Zeus severely punishes the human race on whose behalf Prometheus has acted, this subversive myth confirms, in typically Greek fashion, humanity's right to enjoy even that which the gods might wish to claim. While explaining the "how" or "what" of ritual sacrifice, applying the charter theory to this myth fails to account for the important "why"— the distinctive favoring of human welfare over divine prerogative.

Myth and Etiology   The etiological method sees myths as attempts to explain the cause or origin of things. From the Greek word for "cause" (*aition*), **etiology** encompasses two schools of thought. The first regards myth as primitive science, the product of naive minds trying to give plausible reasons for the present structure and operation of the natural world. Hesiod, for example, devotes part of his *Theogony* to narrating the origins of earth, sky, air, day, night, ocean, mountains, and other aspects of physical nature.

A more comprehensive etiological approach emphasizes the broadly explanatory purpose of myth. More than being mere prescientific attempts to account for the natural or social environment, myths can also give theological or metaphysical interpretations of the human condition. Hesiod's *Theogony* and *Works and Days* explain why humanity's possession of fire, which Zeus had wished to retain as an exclusively divine prerogative, led to a tragic alienation between men and gods. Hesiod links the forbidden fire motif to the creation of the first woman, Pandora, whom the gods mold from clay as a "lovely evil" to plague mankind. As Hesiod's poetry demonstrates, etiological myths can be richly diverse, ranging from narratives of cosmic evolution and divine–human conflict to the human male's highly ambivalent attitude toward women.

Although numerous myths serve an etiological purpose, many heroic tales ordinarily classified as myth have little to do with etiology. Most of Heracles' labors, Jason's quest for the Golden Fleece, Medea's vengeance on her faithless husband, Oedipus's tragic fall, and Theseus's slaying of the Minotaur are not concerned with explaining world origins or social institutions.

Internalist Theories: Myth as a Product of the Mind

Whereas the nature, ritual, charter, and etiological theorists view myths essentially as interpretations of the external world, a second major school of thought sees them as spontaneous expressions of the human mind. A study of the human psyche (the Greek word meaning "soul," or "center of consciousness"), **psychology** proposes an intimate link between myth and several mental processes.

Freudian Theory and Myth   Sigmund Freud (1856–1939) emphasized the importance of the unconscious in determining human behavior and beliefs. He also formulated psychoanalysis, a method of therapeutic analysis based on the theory that abnormal mental states result from the repression of emotions that the conscious mind rejects but that persist in the unconscious. In such works as *The Interpretation of Dreams*, Freud argued that dreams, which typically resemble myths in their imagery and narrative form, offer important clues to the human psyche. Dreams typically combine elements from everyday life—familiar objects, routines, and persons—with fantastic actions in which the dreamer can fly like Icarus (see Color Plates 12 and 13), descend into Hades' realm like Orpheus (see Figure 9-8), or battle dragons like Apollo or Perseus (see Chapters 7 and 10). Whether soaring above mountaintops or struggling with grotesque monsters, dreamers and mythic heroes inhabit a strangely fluid environment in which ordinary life expands to encompass extraordinary characters and actions that transcend the limits of nature. Although Freud at first viewed dreams as basically wish fulfillment, in later studies such as *Beyond the Pleasure Principle*, he recognized that they could also express the dreamer's most profound anxieties.

In analyzing numerous dreams, Freud discovered a common discrepancy between a dream's literal or manifest content and its latent meaning. According to Freudian theory, dreamers typically disguise antisocial or forbidden longings as seemingly harmless images; for example, a son may transfer feelings of extreme hostility toward his father to some apparently unrelated symbol, such as an attacking predator. In this process of transference, when the dreamer slays the wild beast, he releases hostile impulses toward what he perceives as a threatening figure—without actually having to acknowledge his socially unacceptable feelings toward his parent.

Like dreams, myths permit the individual to violate taboos with impunity: parental or other authority figures commonly appear as one secretly *feels* them to be. Thus, antagonism toward the mother transforms her into the man-devouring Sphinx or the snake-haired Gorgon Medusa, whose gaze emasculates men and turns them to stone. Oedipus can defeat the Sphinx (an image of the treacherous mother) by answering her riddle and then go on to commit incest with (and so destroy) the mother who had once abandoned him to be devoured by wild animals (see Chapter 16). By beheading Medusa, Perseus can kill what he hates in maternal power, psychologically freeing himself to rescue Andromeda, the future mother of his children.

Freud's most celebrated application of his psychoanalytical theories to myth relates to the story of Oedipus, a king of Thebes who unwittingly kills his father and marries his mother. According to Freud's theory of infantile sexuality, the male child passionately desires exclusive possession of his mother, whom he regards as the source of all nurturing pleasure. To claim the mother entirely, he must eliminate his male parent, whom he instinctively recognizes as his chief rival for his mother's affection. On growing older and discovering that both his incestuous feelings toward his mother and his hostility toward his father are prohibited, the boy experiences sexual guilt, which commonly takes the form of a fear of castration—punishment for the loss of male power that he had wished to inflict on his father.

In Sophocles' *Oedipus the King*, the hero literally acts out the Oedipal drive, and his doom graphically illustrates the high price society exacts for this transgression. Oedipus's wife, Jocasta (when not yet aware that she is also his mother), explicitly connects a son's incestuous desire with dream fulfillment but dismisses the accompanying feelings of anxiety. By contrast, when he learns the truth about his identity, Oedipus accepts responsibility for his acts: he figuratively castrates himself by gouging out his eyes, the organs of desire, and, through his self-inflicted mutilation, reaffirms the sanctity of the social norm. In sacrificing himself, Oedipus restores communal order, thereby redeeming the city of Thebes (see Chapter 16).

Because Greek plays typically dramatize conflicts between members of a single family, Freudian insights into the domestic psychodrama may offer helpful starting points in understanding many tragic myths. Some of Freud's disciples have noted that the myth of Electra, heroine of three separate Greek tragedies, is psychologically analogous to that of Oedipus. Idolizing the memory of her dead father, Agamemnon, Electra jealously plots to murder her mother, Clytemnestra (see Chapter 15).

In *The Glory of Hera,* Philip Slater applies some Freudian principles to illustrate the connection between actual Greek family life and the harrowing battles between family members in Greek myth. Slater points out that Greek boys were raised in an exclusively female environment during their early years and then abruptly transferred to an all-male society of school, gymnasium, and military camp, where they were inculcated with patriarchal values. It seems credible that Greek mothers entertained decidedly mixed feelings about their sons, taking pride in their achievements yet simultaneously resenting their enjoyment of opportunities denied to women. That youths who had first been acculturated by their mothers subsequently acquired a socially approved masculine contempt for all things feminine must have created considerable bitterness for Greek women.

Although the theory is highly controversial, some feminist critics propose that the anxiety about female hostility contained in some Greek myths has its roots in the distant past (see Chapter 5). In Homer's *Odyssey,* Agamemnon rails at his wife's treachery, a theme extensively developed in Aeschylus's *Oresteia* (see Chapter 15). Outstanding even in myth's portrait gallery of cruel and dangerous mothers, the Aeschylean Clytemnestra is not only a conniving adulteress but an unnatural mother, abusing her helpless daughter and lusting to kill her son Orestes. Aeschylus also identifies this monster-mother with the Furies, creatures addicted to torture and castration of males. In Euripides' play the *Hippolytus,* Phaedra develops an incestuous passion for her stepson and, when rejected, successfully contrives to destroy him. Two of Euripides' mothers, Agave in the *Bacchae* and the title heroine in the *Medea,* actually murder their sons, the former ripping her son's body to pieces (see Chapter 17).

Jung's Archetypal Myths   Although Freudian analysis yields important clues to the excessive behavior of a few mythic characters, some modern critics find the work of one of Freud's leading protégés (and later rival), the Swiss analytical psychologist Carl Jung (1875–1961), even more instructive. After studying thousands of myths from cultures all over the globe, Jung was struck by their similarity to dreams in which the same prominent figures kept appearing. It did not matter whether the myth—or dreamer—was Italian, Japanese, African, American, or Indonesian; figures such as the great mother, stern paternal judge, threatening stranger, clever trickster, or benign guide were consistently present. One would expect that basic human emotions such as fear, desire, and greed would dominate both dreams and myths, but Jung also found that certain situations and actions—journeys, encounters with frightening monsters, struggles with unidentified assailants—were universal. Jung identified these recurring mythic characters, situations, and events as archetypes.

An **archetype** is the primal form or original pattern of which all other things of the same kind are representatives or copies. In Western cultures, for example, paintings of Mary holding the infant Jesus convey an archetypal image of the mother figure, an ideal model of maternal tenderness. The Christian Madonna and child, in turn, are a relatively recent manifestation of images found throughout the ancient world, from Egyptian art that depicts Isis nursing a newborn Horus to Greek murals that show a tearful Demeter searching for her lost daughter, Persephone. A fundamental aspect of human existence, the imprint of a maternal image undoubtedly characterized the human psyche even in prehistory.

The Greek gods and/or heroes commonly represent archetypal characteristics or personalities, serving as paradigms for a whole class or category of human types: Zeus, the powerful father whose least frown may evoke terror; Prometheus, the heroic rebel who defies unjust authority; Hera, the strong wife who upholds the institution of matrimony that perpetuates her own subordination; Artemis, the female free spirit who roams wild, disdaining social restraints; Hermes, the epitome of swift mobility who delights in deceiving lesser intellects; Athene, the master planner and strategist who outwits the opposition; and Aphrodite, patron of love and desire who revels in the passions she arouses (see Chapters 4 and 6).

Because the same basic facts shape all human consciousness, major life events are also archetypal, including birth, sexual maturation, struggles with parents or other authority figures, fraternal rivalry, mating, competition for power, and sickness and death. Myth, therefore, typically involves archetypal actions suggesting transitions from one stage of being to another: the gods' struggle to overthrow parental control and assert their individual egos on a cosmic scale (see Chapter 3), or heroes' battles against evil monsters or their arduous journeys of discovery into strange and dangerous territory, commonly including a journey to the Underworld (see Chapters 10 and 13).

The myth of Icarus combines a form of Freudian wish fulfillment with an archetypal situation in which the human desire to experience near-absolute freedom overpowers even the instinct toward self-preservation (Figure 2-2). **Icarus** [IK-uh-ruhs] is the son of an Athenian craftsman, **Daedalus** [DEE-duh-luhs], prototype of the artist and inventor, who designs the labyrinth beneath the Knossos palace in which King Minos houses the flesh-eating Minotaur. When Minos refuses to permit the invaluable Daedalus to leave Crete, Daedalus makes wings of feathers and wax so that he and Icarus can escape from Minoan captivity. Aware of the perils of humans unnaturally behaving like birds, Daedalus warns his son not to fly too low lest his wings become waterlogged or too high lest the sun's heat melt the wax holding his feathers together. Suddenly given dizzying freedom from earthly constraints, Icarus soars heavenward, crossing the boundary between mortal and immortal spheres. Flying too close to the sun, Icarus can only watch in horror as his artificial wings disintegrate, plunging him to his death in the Aegean Sea. When granted the opportunity to break barriers that ordinarily separate humanity from the gods, Icarus, an image of human nature, cannot resist exploring the unknown

FIGURE 2-2   Daedalus and Icarus. In this bas-relief, Daedalus, prototype of the artist-inventor, makes wings of feathers and wax for his son Icarus. Ignoring his father's warning not to fly too high, Icarus rashly approaches too near to the sun, causing the wax holding his wings together to melt and precipitating his fatal fall into the sea. A cautionary tale about humans foolishly trespassing into the gods' realm, the Icarus myth is also an example of human wish fulfillment in which an adventuresome youth soars through the heavens like Zeus's eagle—and of the inevitable consequences when religious or societal laws are broken. *(Villa Albani, Rome)*

and forbidden. In Jungian terms, Icarus's failed quest to achieve fulfillment in an alien environment may stem from his inability to assimilate his father's cautionary wisdom. An archetype of the "wise old man," Daedalus is his son's animus, an internal guide whose advice, when rejected, leads to failure and death (see Color Plates 12 and 13).

Archetypal figures, events, and situations seem to pervade the consciousness of every ethnic group, whether belonging to a literate technological society or to a preliterate hunting-and-gathering community (Figure 2-3). For Jung, these archetypes spring from the collective unconscious, a term he used to denote the mental images, cognitive processes, patterns of symbols, innate memories, and intrinsic assumptions that all members of a given culture—or the entire human race—hold in common. According to Jungian theory, the collective unconscious spawns virtually all creative activity, including dreams, religious visions, and mythologies. Living in the twenty-first century, we can still relate intimately to myths of birth, testing, conflict, death, and rebirth that originated thousands of years ago because our unconscious minds have inherited these mythic archetypes from our distant ancestors.

FIGURE 2-3 A Female Archetype: Aphrodite. A personification of erotic desire and sensual pleasure, Aphrodite, as shown in this statue from Cyrene, North Africa (first century B.C.), was said to have been born from the sea, whose murky, unfathomable depths hide forms of life that are commonly so grotesque as to seem unimaginable. Hesiod's tradition of her sea origin (see Chapter 3) hints at the love goddess's connection with the human psyche's amoral unconscious and instinctual appetites. The Homeric tradition in which she is the daughter of Zeus and Dione (a Titan goddess), however, serves to place Aphrodite's rampant sexuality within the framework of cosmic order: as Zeus's child, Aphrodite (and the human sexuality she represents) must be subject to religious and social restraints. *(National Museum of Terme, Rome)*

Jung further postulated that the human unconscious also houses archetypal images of both the male and female principles. The **anima,** an internal expression of archetypal feminine wisdom and creativity, inhabits the minds of men and women. Correspondingly, the **animus,** which embodies essential masculine qualities, is present in both male and female psyches. Because the anima and animus are also partly determined by feelings derived from individuals' direct experiences with other men or women, these indwelling images can include negative perceptions of masculinity or femininity. A distorted anima can produce an internalized view of woman as dangerous or destructive (a Medusa or Fury). Similarly, a woman may perceive the male primarily as a potential rapist or tyrant, the way Zeus's brother Hades appears to Persephone when he abducts the young woman and imprisons her in the Underworld (see Chapter 5). In the healthy psyche, however, anima and animus achieve a harmonious relationship with each other, as they do in the reunion of Odysseus and his wife, Penelope (see Chapter 13).

In addition, the mind contains a sinister force that Jung called the **shadow,** a composite of unacknowledged negative elements—unconscious fear, hatred, envy, unsatisfied desire—within the human personality. As we shall discover, numerous myths about the Greco-Roman gods and heroes present a Jungian tension between a character's conscious intentions and an unacknowledged shadow self—repressed or undervalued aspects of the personality—that commonly functions counterproductively or self-destructively. Despite his victory over the Titans, Zeus is internally subverted by lust and a tyrannical egocentrism, as is Heracles by deadly outbursts of uncontrolled rage. Both god and hero ultimately triumph, but only after overcoming or assimilating some morally ambiguous aspect of their own natures.

Many contemporary interpreters of myth have been influenced by Freud or Jung, including Joseph Campbell, who has written numerous books applying Jungian insights to world myths. In such works as *The Masks of God* and *The Hero with a Thousand Faces,* Campbell explores the archetypal hero's adventures, particularly his tests of courage, honor, and self-knowledge. The hero's rite of passage typically features a cyclical process; a necessary separation from his original environment; a journey in which he encounters frightening, even supernatural, forces; an initiation into hitherto unknown regions, roles, or relationships; and an eventual return to his point of departure. These rites of passage represent the hero's stages of psychological development and maturation: by meeting challenges and surmounting obstacles, such heroes as Odysseus, Perseus, and Heracles fulfill their innate potential and grow into true selfhood, a process Jung called individuation.

Other important writers analyzing myth in psychological terms include Ernst Cassirer, Mircea Eliade, and Victor Turner. Cassirer argues that myth is no less than the mind's spontaneous creation of an emotionally satisfying cosmos, which it imposes on the external world. Myths satisfy because, like religion, they project symbolic meaning on the natural and human environment, imparting a significance otherwise absent in objective reality. In *Myth and Reality* and *The Sacred and the Profane,* Eliade, a philosopher and historian of religion, presents world myths as sacred tales emanating from a singularly creative era of prehistory.

Whereas Eliade emphasizes myth's relationship to a vanished epoch of unique holiness, Turner argues that myths serve a combined psychological and social purpose in the present, promoting liminal, or threshold, experiences. Whereas the charter approach sees myths associated with rituals operating primarily to justify or validate the ritual itself, Turner sees myth and ritual linked by their psychological function, helping to ease people through life's difficult transitions. Thus, stories involving certain rituals help individuals cope with various crises or changes in social position, including rites of passage for boys initiated into warrior status, for girls into marriageable womanhood, and for adults into roles of community leadership.

Structuralism and Myth Most psychological theorists regard myths as a natural expression of the psyche—one that functions therapeutically to purge unacceptable desire, provide creative energy, reconcile individuals to their environment, and attribute moral order and meaning to the universe. **Structuralism** further refines this concept, viewing myth as a reflection of the mind's binary organization. Structuralists, such as the Belgian anthropologist Claude Lévi-Strauss (1908–), observe that humans tend to see the world as a reflection of their own physical and cerebral structure. Equipped with two eyes, legs, arms, and hands and—most important—a brain divided into two hemispheres, humans automatically project a binary significance onto experience, typically dividing everything into polar opposites: right/left, light/dark, pleasure/pain, beautiful/ugly, good/evil, cooked/raw, civilized/savage. In Lévi-Strauss's view, myth deals with the perception and reconciliation of these opposites, which may be rendered as conflicts between natural order and human lawlessness, instinctual desire and social prohibition, or the divine will and human ambition. The many tensions inherent in the human predicament, such as the dichotomy between individual need and communal obligation, are the inspiration for myths created to resolve or mitigate these contradictory forces.

Jean-Pierre Vernant and Pierre Vidal-Naquet, contemporary French classical scholars who employ a modified structuralism in their studies of Greek myth, offer some intriguing reinterpretations. In *Myth and Tragedy in Ancient Greece,* Vernant and Vidal-Naquet emphasize the contradictions and confusions of reality that characterize the Greek tragic drama. Vernant's *Myth and Society in Ancient Greece* focuses on the alien quality of Greek culture, with its primeval traditions of ceremonial hunting, blood sacrifice, slavery, ritualized warfare, and religious ecstasy. Avoiding a literalist application of Lévi-Strauss's binary model, Vernant provides an insightful critique of structuralism that emphasizes the ambiguous, complex, and mercurial nature of myth.

Helpful as it can be in highlighting the oppositions and conflicts inherent in many myths, some scholars question structuralism's overly tidy binary approach, pointing out that not all myths present a quantitative division of opposites or even a formal linear development. In the story of Odysseus and Penelope, for instance, the two partners evince a complementary rather than conflicted relationship.

Narratology Some aspects of structuralism were anticipated in the work of the Russian folklorist Vladimir Propp. In his seminal *Morphology of the Folktale* (1928), Propp identified seven "spheres of action" and thirty-one "functions" that he believed were intrinsic to traditional tales. In analyzing a narrative's sequence of events, Propp emphasized that the action follows a distinctive pattern, giving traditional stories a recognizably similar structure. A term coined in 1969, **narratology** is the theory of narrative and narrative structure and the way in which they affect our perception. In her *Narratology,* Mieke Bal offers a theoretical system by which narrative texts, and their component parts, function to achieve a particular effect. Examining the role of the narrator, the narrative agent who tells a story, Bal emphasizes the concept of focalization, the point of view from which a story is written or told, as well as narrative events, the sequential changes in narrative action. Many Greek myths, for example, exhibit a coherent narrative pattern controlling the order of events. Heroic tales conform to a predictable order: born from the union of a divine being and a mortal, the hero typically combines godlike ambition with human vulnerability; he leaves home on a quest in which he confronts and defeats supernatural adversaries, passes difficult or perilous tests of courage and intelligence, and narrowly escapes death. His tasks may involve retrieving treasure from a guardian dragon and/or rescuing an endangered princess; his rewards commonly include winning the princess in marriage, gaining riches, and/or receiving a crown. Thus, Odysseus sails from Ithaca to Troy where he proves his mettle as a warrior; embarks on a long voyage home beset by ogres and lethal temptresses, all of which obstacles he overcomes; battles rivals successfully to demonstrate his right to claim the princess (in this case his wife, Penelope); and reclaims his property and kingship. Rarely is this sequence reversed: ordinarily, the hero does not first win a bride, find a treasure, and mount a throne, and only afterward wrestle a hydra, kill a Medusa, or descend to the Underworld.

Although the mythic narrative commonly observes the sequence of quest, challenge, struggle, victory, and reward, the order is far from universal. The tragic hero, in particular, may face his greatest threats and obstacles *after* he has attained matrimony, kingship, and fame. By cleverly and courageously solving the riddle of the Sphinx, Oedipus acquires a royal wife, crown, and reputation, only to lose it all in a fatal quest for his true identity (see Chapter 16). The "last acts" in the careers of such heroes as Agamemnon, Jason, and Heracles manifest this postreward reversal, which characteristically involves making a fatally flawed decision concerning their marital relationships.

Because myth takes the form of narrative—the sequential arrangement of action and its consequences over time—it expresses a linear and irrevocable movement in its characters' lives, a progression in which time's arrow flies in only one direction—toward death. As the ultimate shaping influence on the contours of even the greatest heroic endeavors, Greek myth's unrelenting emphasis on human mortality—the chief factor that distinguishes heroes from gods—gives most heroic tales a final, "vertical" twist. The graph of a hero's life typically features an upward progression as he climbs fame's pinnacle by performing immortal deeds, but it takes an abrupt downward turn near his career's end. In contrast to much folklore, Greek myth never concludes with a pronouncement that the tale's principal couple "lived happily ever after." Eschewing such optimism, Greek myth routinely recounts the manner and circumstances of the hero's death. Besides describing in detail the slaughter of military leaders who perish at Troy or in other wars, the narratives, with extraordinary consistency, encompass the demise of those who survive conflicts as well. From Heracles to Jason, and from Agamemnon to Odysseus (in post-Homeric lore), virtually no hero exits his myth alive; in most stories, the descent to Hades' realm is made explicit. As if to assure us of this universal morbidity, many tales include a visit to the Underworld, where the shades of dead heroes are interviewed, providing unimpeachable evidence that all personal narratives end at a state in which no further action is possible. (In rare cases, a mortal son of Zeus, such as Heracles, undergoes posthumous deification and joins the gods in heaven, thus transcending the linear confines of his story by entering a supranatural dimension; see Chapter 10.)

Feminist Approaches to Myth

Rather than constituting a "school" of mythography or sharing a single approach to interpreting myth, feminist scholars have collectively, and from an interdisciplinary perspective, focused on reemphasizing components of myth previously neglected or recovering knowledge of some aspects of mythmaking cultures previously unavailable. Feminist scholars have contributed especially to our understanding of the goddess figures and the rituals related to their worship, as well as their relationship to the male gods, and have explored the complexities of the gender system that myths inevitably touch on, both legitimizing and necessitating such studies.

Scholars such as Marija Gimbutas, who assembled and interpreted vast numbers of artifacts, have argued for extensive goddess worship throughout Europe prior to the advent of sky gods in the region. More recently, archaeologists have discovered goddess shrines carved into the mountainsides of Crete, thus overturning previous assumptions that the inhabitants of ancient Crete (whose society was one of the major sources of Greek culture) were a relatively "secular" people.

Similar shrines elsewhere, such as at Catal Huyuk in Anatolia (western Turkey), and ancient aboriginal shrines in Australia were found to share symbols resembling those described by Gimbutas, including circles or lozenges with a dot in the center, painted on the walls in red ochre. Explaining the recurrent themes found at these and other sites, mythographer Elinor Gadon and others explain what our consideration of the widespread worship of creator goddesses contributes to our understanding of the roles of Greek goddesses such as Gaea and Demeter (see Chapter 5). Other feminist scholars, such as Lucy Goodison and Christine Morris, examining the goddess artifacts in their archaeological context, find no evidence for a universally worshiped "Mother Goddess" figure. They argue instead for a variety of possible interpretations—which, however, in the absence of evidence, cannot be stipulated.

Still other feminist scholars have explored the social and psychological insights manifested in the goddess myths. Carol Gilligan, for example, uses contemporary psychological approaches to elucidate the stages of a woman's life as depicted in the story of Demeter and Persephone (see Chapter 5) and then applies that myth to the lives of modern women. Froma Zeitlin studies what the myths reveal about the role of the female as "other," both threatening and reinforcing the "norm" of male hegemony in Greek society.

Neurological Explorations of Myth

The newest approach to myths is not cultural but biological. For example, Klaus Manhart describes experiments conducted by Eugene D'Aquili and Andrew Newberg which revealed that when individuals (the subjects in the study were Catholic nuns and Buddhist monks) are in a state of intense prayer or meditation, the neurons in a section of the brain's parietal lobe (responsible for spatial orientation and awareness of one's body) stop firing. Another relevant factor is described by neurologist V. S. Ramachandran, who explains that not only do people who suffer temporal lobe seizures often have intense religious experiences, but stimulation of the temporal lobes in healthy subjects can also induce such experiences even if the subjects had no previous religious inclinations or beliefs.

In addition to the brain's potential for generating such responses, other studies demonstrate that our brains naturally tend to impose order and sense on our experience, and to attribute cause-effect relationships to perceptions from immediate to the cosmic, an attribute D'Aquili termed the "cognitive imperative." We have, it seems, a biologically conditioned need to construct stories to explain the nature of our world and our place in it. The fact that myths worldwide share preoccupations with the mysteries of creation, life and death, and the nature of the cosmos, these theorists argue, is biologically driven.

Our capacity to experience transcendence and our tendency to organize such perceptions into explicatory narratives, then, are rooted in brain structures, apparently unique to the human species, from which mythmaking, possibly like language itself, is what cognitive scientists call an "emergent phenomenon." We are, it seems, wired for myth! But while neurologists and cognitive scientists may help explain the generation of what we might call the "mythic imperative," they cannot, at least as of yet, address either the vast terrain encompassed by myths (which are, of course, not limited to cosmic issues) or the complexities that myths entail.

Lenses of Mythology

The large number of competing scholarly theories about the nature of myth suggests its diversity, elusiveness, and continuing power to elicit a broad range of human responses. Disparate theories abound because different scholars, influenced by their own cultural assumptions, commonly view myth through but one of the many different lenses by which the mythic eye perceives reality. As Wendy Doniger points out in her study of myth, theology, and politics, *The Implied Spider,* myth provides at least two lenses through which we see our universe: the microscope, which focuses on the details, the individual experience, the specific social, cultural, and/or political world with which myth engages; and the telescope, which offers a panorama of the "big picture," the universal images or experiences, the cosmic sweep—as well as innumerable intermediate angles of vision.

By offering a connection between these ocular possibilities, myth allows us to see the small world of individual experience through the lens of larger, universal reality and to experience the otherwise unimaginable cosmic vision through the concrete details of a particular narrative. To use Doniger's analogy, the advantage of employing an inclusive approach in viewing myth is that it permits us to examine myths simultaneously from both microscopic and telescopic perspectives, or to set the aperture of our lens at any point between.

The Autonomy of Myth

Although scholars continue to develop and refine theories that seek to provide the elusive key to understanding mythology, Greek myth has a vitality and inner logic that confounds attempts to make it conform to any given theory. Some modern efforts to reduce its diversities to fit a single monolithic interpretation recall the tale of **Procrustes,** a notorious thief and extortionist who kidnaped travelers and tied them to an iron bed. If a victim was too tall and his legs extended over the foot of the bed, they were chopped off; if the victim was too short, he was forcibly stretched out to fit the iron frame. To avoid any such Procrustean excess, this book tries not to force every myth discussed into one theoretical mold. The authors believe that several different methods provide valid approaches to particular myths, including some etiological, ritual, Freudian, Jungian, and structuralist techniques.

Myth Theory and the Birth of Athene

A single myth, such as the birth of Athene, yields a variety of meanings when different theories of myth are applied to the story. Athene's leaping forth, fully armed, from Zeus's head may violate our sense of reality, but it makes good sense from both externalist and internalist perspectives. Viewed as a nature myth, Athene's origin largely reflects the recognition that human thought takes place in the brain. The assertion that Zeus produced Athene from his own being represents a powerful statement about the intrinsic value of wisdom and its close relationship to divinity. In its etiological function, the myth describes a shift from feminine notions of divinity to patriarchal concerns: thought and cunning, formerly independent in an autonomous female, Metis, are now embodied in Zeus's daughter, subordinated to male rule. Athene's perpetual virginity means that her father will always be the decisive force in her life and that his influence will never be challenged by an ambitious son-in-law. Operating as a charter, the myth validates both patriarchy and the institution of marriage in which the husband has total control of his wife, even to the point of taking over her identity. Phidias's use of Athene's birth in the Parthenon sculptures also functions as a specific political statement, visually proclaiming Athens' unique connection with the highest gods (see Figure 1-2). As Athene is Zeus's first and favorite offspring, so the city she protects enjoys a special relationship with the king of heaven. The dreamlike image of pure thought issuing from the mind of the supreme deity and taking visible shape as Athens' supernatural patron explicitly validates Athenian social institutions.

In terms of Jungian psychology, Athene's birth from a male represents the archetypal union of the animus and the anima. As an example of psychoanalysis, it expresses the male fear of the castrating female: Zeus swallows Metis to prevent her from dominating him or producing a rival to his masculine power. In a Freudian sense, Zeus reenacts an Oedipal fear of competition with the father, imitating Cronus's method of preventing future rivalry by imprisoning all potential threats within his own body and then transforming feminine intelligence into a daughter under his control (see Chapter 3).

In some cases, the myths are presented theory-free, with an emphasis on the historical circumstances of their development. In most cases, discussion focuses on the *content* of the myth, a product of the human imagination.

· ·

Questions for Discussion and Review

1. How did Archaic and Classical Greeks interpret their myths? How does Euhemerism differ from the allegorical method? What was the ancient Greek belief about

Zeus's assimilation of Metis also illustrates the god's progression from a merely successful warrior, the fighter who defeated the Titans, to a mature ruler who understands the value of taking pragmatic Metis as his internal voice and wise-counseling Athene as his trusted confidante. By this act, a symbolic rite of passage, Zeus moves to a higher stage of development, a liminal experience that marks his strategic advance beyond the mere brute force that characterized his Titan predecessors. Finally, viewed from a binary or structuralist position, the myth expresses the benefit to humanity of reconciling its natural, instinctual, physical component (the young, undeveloped Zeus, who wins his throne largely through the destructiveness of his thunderbolts) with its higher potential centered in the rational intellect (Metis). The creative union of the body–mind dichotomy produces Athene, in whose person both strength (the military skill to defend civilized values) and intelligence (the ability to rule wisely) are harmonized.

Whereas some myths, such as the tale of Athene's birth, lend themselves to a broad spectrum of theoretical analyses, others seem to invite a distinctive mode of interpretation. Aeschylus's presentation of Orestes' dilemma dramatizes a conflict and final resolution of opposites, suggesting a structuralist approach —while still allowing for other approaches, such as a Freudian analysis of Orestes' tangled family relationships. In the Orestes plays, Aeschylus's characters seem to act out a dialectic between the id (amoral instinct), the ego (individual will), and the superego (divine law) (see the box in Chapter 15). By contrast, the *Odyssey*'s hero appears to undergo a process of individuation in which he learns and matures through contact with and the assimilation of archetypal principles of feminine wisdom, inviting a Jungian interpretation. At the same time, Homer's narrative may represent the hero's adventures as a complex series of initiations or rites of passage (see Chapter 13). Several elements in Hesiod's creation story, such as the origin of earth's topographical features, have an etiological component, explaining the process by which the world evolved into its present configuration.

myth's relation to history? In what ways could a city-state, such as Athens, employ myth to bolster its prestige or political authority?

2. Some nineteenth-century scholars regarded mythmaking as a quasi-scientific attempt to interpret the natural world and/or the human social environment. Describe the nature, ritual, charter, and etiological theories about the origin or purpose of myth.

3. Some scholars believe that mythmaking is an innate—and spontaneous—function of the human mind. Explain some psychologically based theories of myth, particularly the claims that Freud and Jung made about the operations of the human psyche. Define the terms *collective unconscious, anima, animus, archetype, shadow,* and *individuation.*

4. If humans tend to automatically perceive the world in terms of tensions between opposites, how can myth function to mediate these assumed contrarieties? Describe the structuralist position. According to some neurologists, how does the human brain seem to be "hard-wired" to create myth?

Works Cited

Barnstone, Willis, trans. *Greek Lyric Poetry*. Rev. ed. New York: Bantam Books, 1967.

PART TWO

~~~

Epic Myths and
the Heroic Quest

In the Beginning: Hesiod's Creation Story

KEY TOPICS/THEMES

In ancient Greek thought, the universe was a cosmos—a harmonious world order that evolved from Chaos, the primal Chasm or Abyss. Chaos and Gaea (Gaia; the earth) are the sources of all that exists, including seas, mountains, monsters, and gods. Celebrating the rise of Zeus to cosmic rulership, Hesiod's Theogony *traces the gods' descent from Gaea and her son, Uranus (the sky), who mate to produce the Titans, a race of giant deities led by Cronus. On Gaea's advice, Cronus emasculates his father, Uranus, separating sky from earth, and seizes control of the cosmos. Cronus, in turn, is overthrown by his youngest son, Zeus, who defeats the Titans in battle, imprisons them in Tartarus, and establishes his Olympian sovereignty.*

Some Greek scientists such as Aristarchus of Samos (c. 320 B.C.) correctly postulated that the earth is a globe, suspended in space, that orbits around the sun. Long before classical astronomers produced theories based on mathematical calculations, however, Greek poets such as Hesiod (c. 675 B.C.) promoted a mythic conception of the universe, based partly on ancient Near Eastern models and partly on commonsensical observations of their physical environment. The world structure reflected in Hesiod's *Theogony*, the Greeks' oldest and most influential creation account, is that which a careful observer might infer after taking a look around. When viewed from a hilltop affording a 360-degree panorama of the surrounding terrain, the earth's surface appears to extend an equal distance in all directions, forming a generally circular boundary. From this perspective, the sky resembles a huge bowl or dome that, from its highest point overhead, seems to curve evenly downward to the distant horizon.

FIGURE 3-1   Detail, East Pediment of the Parthenon. The Olympians assembled to witness Athene's miraculous birth were framed by personifications of the sun and moon. In this modern reconstruction, in the extreme left corner of the pediment appear the heads of celestial horses drawing the chariot of the rising sun (Helios). The reclining figure of Dionysus, awakening from sleep, faces Helios's fiery steeds. The Parthenon sculptures thus portray the gods inhabiting an invisible region above the solar and lunar orbits, reflecting their superior power and status. *(Acropolis Museum, Athens)*

FIGURE 3-2   Detail, East Pediment of the Parthenon. The moon (Selene) is shown descending below the horizon in the extreme right corner of the pediment. In this version of Athene's birth, the sculptor follows Homer and not Hesiod in portraying Aphrodite (the reclining figure immediately left of Selene) as the daughter of Dione, a Titan goddess not usually included among the Olympian family. Inhabiting the uppermost level of the three-story universe, the Olympians live high above the astronomical phenomena of physical nature. *(Acropolis Museum, Athens)*

The sun, rising in the East, appears to trace an arc across the sky before sinking into darkness in the West, typically to be followed by the moon's ascent. In addition, the viewer may assume that Olympus, dwelling place of the gods, lies somewhere above heaven's vault. This picture, in fact, is precisely the structure used to frame the scene of Athene's birth on the Parthenon's east pediment. In the extreme lower-left corner, horses pulling Helios's chariot rear their heads, heralding the sunrise (Figure 3-1); in the extreme right-hand corner, Selene pilots the moon's descending car (Figure 3-2). The family of gods gathered on Olympus presumably stands above the solar and lunar orbits.

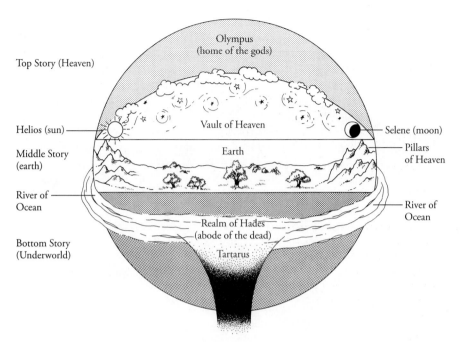

FIGURE 3-3 The Three-Story Universe. Following ancient traditions from the Near East, Greek mythographers conceived of the earth as a massive disk surrounded by a watery waste, the circular River of Ocean. The physical heavens arched overhead like an inverted bowl, the edges of which were supported by mountainous pillars—or held up by Atlas, the mightiest Titan. The Olympian gods lived somewhere above the clouds. Beneath the earth lay the eternally dark kingdom of Hades, a vast subterranean cavern housing the dead. Tartarus, a deep pit beneath Hades' main level, served as a prison for fallen Titans and the souls of notorious sinners.

Greek myth thus postulates a vertically structured three-story universe (Figure 3-3). The top level, infinitely beyond human reach, is an invisible heaven inhabited exclusively by gods untouched by human woes. The Olympian gods' carefree existence contrasts sharply with the harshness of life in the middle story—earth —where **Fate** assigns mortals an unequal mixture of joy and pain that inevitably ends in death. Conceived as a relatively flat disk, except where high mountains like Olympus seem to support the sky, the earth's circular surface is surrounded by **Ocean.** Rather than an open sea like the Atlantic, Ocean is an immeasurable river coiled around the central landmass. Far beneath earth is a cosmic basement, the kingdom of **Hades** [HAY-deez], Zeus's brother who rules over the Underworld. A dank subterranean cavern, Hades' realm permanently houses all the dead, who, according to Homer, exist only as disembodied shades flitting aimlessly in eternal darkness. Pitiless Hades allows no one, except for a few heroes, to escape from his gloomy dominion, effectively banishing all hope from the afterlife (see Chapter 9).

Lying beneath Hades' realm is **Tartarus,** a kind of cosmic subbasement, in which the Titans are confined. In Hesiod, Tartarus is a geographical space, a fathomless abyss, and an elemental entity with whom Gaea mates to produce the monster Typhoeus (see following section).

Egyptian Myths of Creation

Although Hesiod describes the cosmos as originating from Chaos, a primordial abyss or chasm, some later Greek thinkers, such as Thales of Miletus (c. 600 B.C.), speculated that water was the primal substance out of which the universe evolved, a view also found in Mesopotamian, Egyptian, and Hebrew traditions. Ancient cosmogonies (stories about the birth or origin of the cosmos) typically represented the major elements composing the world—earth, sky, atmosphere—as gods, a means by which thinkers in a prescientific age could denote the superhuman forces that fashioned and sustained the universe. Thus, the Babylonian epic poem *Enuma Elish* depicts the precreation waste of limitless water as the deities Apsu (sweet or potable water) and Tiamat (saltwater). Similarly, the Egyptian creation account associated with Heliopolis (meaning "City of the Sun") postulates a primordial expanse of water, called Nu, that had to be divided during the process of forming the world. According to the Heliopolis account, the sun god Atum arose out of Nu, standing on a solitary mound, a prototype of the inhabitable earth, surrounded by a vast watery chaos.

Atum, who in his divine being encompassed the totality of everything that exists, became the source of all other gods, the first two of whom he spewed forth in his semen. Producing Shu and Tefnut (thought to signify air and moisture, respectively), Atum initiated the proliferation of divine life that included Geb (the male principle, earth) and Nut (the female principle, sky). His progeny also included the gods who symbolized the divinely ordained structure of Egyptian society: Osiris, lord of the Underworld; his consort and sister Isis, symbolizing the royal throne; Seth, Osiris's destructive brother, a personification of chaos; Nephthys, sister of Isis and wife of Seth; and Horus, son of Osiris and Isis, who embodied the power of Osiris on earth, represented by Egypt's reigning pharaoh.

Although Atum, the supreme creator god who embodies the life-giving energy of the sun, presides over an ordered, harmonious system (the cosmos), the Egyptians apparently feared an eventual return of the original watery chaos. In

Hesiod's *Theogony* and Ancient Near Eastern Myth

The three-tier cosmos—heaven, earth, and Underworld—envisioned in Hesiod's *Theogony* encompasses both a **cosmogony** (cosmos + *gonos* [birth]), an account of the universe's physical origin and organization, and a **cosmology,** a metaphysical statement about the universe's nature and purpose. As its title implies, the *Theogony* (Birth of the Gods) is primarily a religious work, a vision of the gods' origins, progeny, and genealogy. Above all, Hesiod's purpose is to show how Zeus attained his position as ruler of the universe, thereby bringing stability and order to the cosmos.

In reading the *Theogony,* it is important to remember that Hesiod's version of primal events was only one among many that circulated in ancient Greece. Although only fragments of other creation traditions survive, their existence indicates

Egyptian cosmology (a philosophical view of the universe's nature and purpose), even after creation the primal waters continued to surround the world, separated from it by the vault of sky (Nut) and confined to subterranean regions by the overlying earth (Geb). The Egyptian notion of waters gathered above the atmosphere and below the earth is essentially that presented in Genesis 1, where Elohim (God) "divided the waters above the vault [sky, or firmament] from the waters under the vault" (Gen. 1:6–7). When God brings the flood, he simply releases the primal waters stored above the vault by activating the "sluices of heaven" (openings in the sky's broad dome) and causing "the springs of the great deep" (water-filled abyss beneath the earth) to break through to the surface (Gen. 7:11–12). (See also Exodus 20:4, which refers to "the waters beneath the earth," the underground remnant of primeval sea on which the dry land is precariously balanced.) Interestingly, the Egyptians had no tradition of a global deluge, perhaps because they received very little rain and anticipated the annual inundations of the Nile as a natural blessing that ensured the fertilization of their fields.

Another Egyptian account, devised by the priests of Ptah at Memphis during the thirteenth century B.C., offers a prototype of creation by divine thought and speech, a concept found not only in Genesis 1 but also in the New Testament Gospel of John. Ptah, after whom the nation of Egypt (the "Temple of Ptah") is named, was promoted by the Memphis priests as superior to all other deities, including Atum, the sun. According to a late version of the myth, inscribed on stone by order of Pharaoh Shabaka about 700 B.C., Ptah gave birth to all things, including the gods, by his "heart" and "tongue." Because many ancient languages, including biblical Hebrew, which has few abstract terms, used the word for "heart" to designate "mind" or "consciousness," Ptah created the universe by thinking it into existence, fashioning it by the power of his word. When Ptah conceived an idea of something, he then pronounced its name (identity), causing it to be—a process that God also follows in Genesis 1.

that no single account was generally accepted as fully authoritative. Hesiod's narrative, however, is the one most widely quoted by later authors, and, as indicated in Chapter 1, it forms the basis for the creation story in the *Library of Apollodorus*.

Etiological myths—narrating the cause or source of the world as we experience it today—are common all over the globe. Virtually every known culture, from Africa to Asia to Mesoamerica, has produced stories explaining the origins of heaven, earth, and human life. Like the *Theogony,* most creation accounts are largely religious, crediting divine beings with fashioning the cosmos, but they typically also have social and political functions. In Hesiod's case, the triumph of Zeus over his divine predecessors and his defeat of chaotic monsters are but the prelude to the establishment of the sociopolitical system that prevailed in the poet's own day. Although Hesiod begins his epic with the etiology of the gods, he concludes it with genealogies of heroes descended from the gods' couplings with mortal women. This section provides not only a transition from the realm of the divine to that of the human but also a validation of the aristocratic families who justified their rule of the Greek city-states by claiming divine descent. The *Theogony*'s final lines (not included in the excerpts that follow) originally formed a connection to a now-lost section of the poem called the *Catalogue of Women,* which recounted the births of heroes who reputedly became the ancestors of then-reigning dynasties. Thus, in addition to being a theological work, Hesiod's creation epic served as a charter supporting military and political leaders of the Archaic period—an elite class that likely formed the most influential part of his audience.

The cosmos Hesiod describes is essentially a *Greek* world: its long evolution from the primordial Chaos (chasm) inevitably culminates in the births of familiar Greek gods and heroes who uphold distinctively Greek social practices and institutions. In portraying this characteristically Greek universe, however, Hesiod not only incorporated a variety of Greek traditions but also borrowed and transformed seminal traditions inherited from the pre-Greek cultures of the ancient Near East, particularly Egypt and Mesopotamia.

The closest parallels to Hesiod's poem are found in the creation stories of Mesopotamia, where a people known as the Sumerians developed the first large urban centers almost three millennia before Hesiod's time. Known to the Greeks as "the land between the [Tigris and Euphrates] rivers," Mesopotamia is a flat, swampy region at the head of the Persian Gulf in what is now southern Iraq (Figure 3-4). Shortly after 3500 B.C., the Sumerians founded the earliest cities, such as Ur, the native city of the biblical patriarch Abraham, and Uruk, home to Gilgamesh, the first hero of Western myth (see the box on Gilgamesh in Chapter 10). A remarkably innovative group, the Sumerians produced a series of inventions ranging from the wheel, to the first law codes, to the art of writing. Some Sumerian literary texts and those of the Akkadians (Old Babylonians), a Semitic people who invaded Mesopotamia about 2000 B.C., contain the oldest surviving narratives about the origin of the gods, the creation of the universe, and a prehistoric flood that allegedly drowned most of earth's population. One version of Mesopotamian myth about the world's beginnings, transformed by Israelite monotheism, appears in the biblical book of Genesis; another form of Sumero-Akkadian lore, reshaped by Greek storytellers, appears in Hesiod, whose poetry integrates both Indo-European and Near Eastern motifs.

Besides inheriting the concept of a vertically ordered cosmos, Hesiod also reflects a Mesopotamian belief in a divine pantheon in which most of the gods were associated with either the sky and weather or the Underworld and fertility. In addition, Hesiod follows a tradition in the ***Enuma Elish,*** a Babylonian creation account, in which the chief sky god came to power only after battling and defeating older generations of gods. In the *Enuma Elish* (c. 1300 B.C.), the Babylonian deity **Marduk** earns his cosmic supremacy after overthrowing Tiamat, a personification of the sterile salt sea who is also the primordial dragon of precreation chaos. After slaying Tiamat, Marduk cuts her body in two, using one half to mold the earth and the other to form the vault of heaven; he then creates humanity from the blood of Tiamat's vanquished consort, Kingu. Similarly, in Hesiod's *Theogony,* Zeus—whom the Greeks identified with Marduk—battles the monster Typhoeus, like Tiamat a

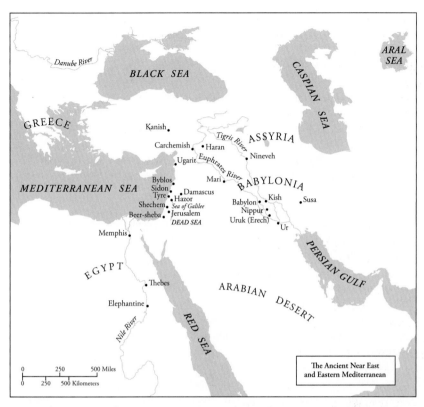

FIGURE 3-4   Map of the Ancient Near East. The Fertile Crescent, which extends from Mesopotamia at the head of the Persian Gulf northwestward through Syria and then southwestward through Canaan into Egypt, was the location of the world's oldest urban civilizations. Hesiod incorporates many traditions from ancient Mesopotamia into his account of the world's origins in the *Theogony*.

reptilian embodiment of chaotic violence. Only after eliminating such threats to cosmic order can Marduk and Zeus begin their successful reigns (Figure 3-17).

In both the Mesopotamian and Hesiodic traditions, violent conflict characterizes the creative process: sky and earth, once conjoined, are wrenched apart; the gods are fatally divided by intergenerational rivalry; the present harmonious universe is made possible only by the victory of a young sky god over older deities who threaten to destroy their own children. Both Marduk and Zeus assume the right to govern the world through their superior strength and martial skill, and both gods are able to retain power by advancing shrewd policies. After conquering their opponents, they wisely assign spheres of influence to other gods, establishing an orderly administration based on cooperation and the judicious delegation of authority.

Besides parallels to the *Enuma Elish,* the *Theogony* contains motifs from other ancient Near Eastern sources, such as the Hurrian-Hittite *Kingship in Heaven* and *Song of Ullikummi.* The account in which the usurping god Kumarbi bites off and

Mythical Attempts to Scale the Heavens

In the ancient world, temples or other shrines were typically viewed as sacred places where a divinity was perceived as present, where unseen spiritual forces intersected with material reality. In Mesopotamian cities, the most distinctive sacred structure was the **ziggurat** [ZIG-oo-rat], a massive, multitiered edifice of glazed brick, crowned by a small chapel at the top, that was believed to house the individual deity, such as Marduk, to whom the building was dedicated. With broad staircases connecting its several levels, the ziggurat was, like the spire of a Christian cathedral, a visible symbol, linking humans on earth with invisible powers inhabiting the sky (Figure 3-5).

Both biblical and Greek traditions echo aspects of the ziggurat's mythic function. In the Tower of Babel story in Genesis, ambitious humans impiously erect a tower high enough to reach heaven, only to have God throw it down. In the Greek version of this myth, the giants Ephialtes and Otus try to invade the divine realm by piling one huge mountain on top of another—Pelion on Ossa and Ossa on Olympus—until Zeus destroys them. In another Genesis narrative, the patriarch Jacob dreams of a colossal "ladder" or ramp by which supernatural figures ascend to or descend from heaven. Historians believe that Jacob's dream more accurately reflects the ziggurat's purpose: rather than a means for humans to trespass into the gods' territory, the ziggurat served as an artificial mountain on which divine beings could visit earth and human beings could rise partway to meet them. A holy place at which earth and heaven, mortals and gods, could commune with each other, the ziggurat filled a role resembling that of the Greek holy mountain of Parnassus, a sanctuary where Apollo reveals the gods' will to human questioners (see Chapter 7). The ziggurat, whose foundations lie beneath the earth's surface and whose pyramidal shape points toward heaven, is also a paradigm of the vertically structured universe. Although the Greeks did not erect comparable towers, their temples also enclosed sacred space in which a god was invisibly housed. For many Greeks, the gods' ultimate home was Mount Olympus; like the ziggurat, Olympus served as an earthly pedestal to which divine beings could descend.

swallows Anu's genitals anticipates the castration of Uranus, a crucial event in Hesiod's poem. In both the Greek and Near Eastern versions, as the vanquished god, Anu or Uranus, flees to the heavens, his severed genitals produce new divinities. Hesiod and his fellow Greeks probably absorbed these Near Eastern myths piecemeal, picking up narrative fragments from sailors, merchants, and other travelers who plied the trade routes between Mesopotamia and the eastern Mediterranean. The Phoenicians, a seafaring people from whom the Greeks borrowed the alphabet, were perhaps the chief mediators in transmitting the Near East's cultural legacy to Greece.

FIGURE 3-5 A Drawing of a Ziggurat. The Sumerians built the world's first skyscrapers, towers of sunbaked bricks known as ziggurats. In this artist's reconstruction of the ancient ziggurat at Ur, the chapel to Nanna, god of the moon, crowns the structure. These artificial mountains served as conduits connecting the human and divine realms, their ceremonial staircases providing the means by which gods descended to earth and mortals ascended to commune with them. Like the ziggurat, Greek temples enclosed sacred space visited by gods, present yet invisible, to accept human worship. *(British Museum, London)*

The Poet and His Inspiration

Intergenerational conflict among the gods is one of Hesiod's main themes, but he also wishes to show that conflict permeates every level of the cosmos, especially family and economic life on earth. Introducing an autobiographical subtheme, Hesiod states that his father, unable to prosper as a sea trader in Ionia, migrated west to Boeotia on the Greek mainland (Figure 3-6), where Hesiod was born to a life of poverty and hard work. Hesiod's poetry bristles with complaints about the slights and injustices he and other small landholders had to endure. According to Hesiod,

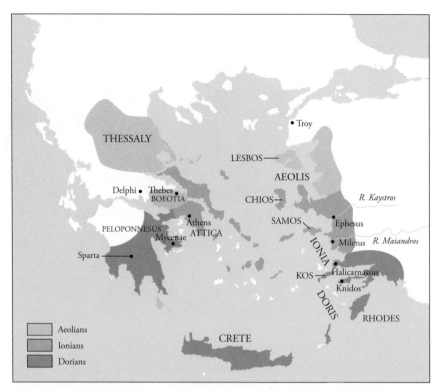

FIGURE 3-6   Map of Greece and the Aegean. Hesiod's father hailed from Ionia, the strip of Greek settlements along the west coast of Asia Minor (modern Turkey). Active in trade with older cultures in Egypt, Mesopotamia, and Phoenicia, the Ionian Greeks probably assimilated many ancient Near Eastern myths into local traditions. Hesiod, a native of rural Boeotia, reshaped some of these older tales in his account of the gods' origins, the *Theogony.*

his difficulties were compounded by the dishonesty and greed of his brother Perses, whom he accuses of bribing corrupt magistrates to award him an unfairly large portion of their father's modest estate. Much of Hesiod's second major poem, *Works and Days,* is aimed at correcting Perses' misbehavior, which allegedly stripped the poet of his rightful heritage and means of livelihood. (For a discussion of Hesiod's second poem, with its account of humanity's decline from an original Golden Age, see Chapter 4.)

The Muses

The most intriguing of Hesiod's allusions to his personal experience is that describing the origin of his poetic inspiration, which he claimed derived from an encounter on Mount Helicon with the **Muses** (Figure 3-7), the nine daughters of Zeus and **Mnemosyne** [nee-MAHS-ih-nee], a personification of memory. Hailed as the

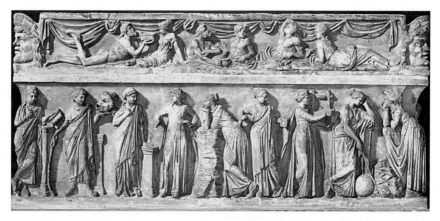

FIGURE 3-7 The Nine Muses. Each of the nine daughters of Zeus and Mnemosyne (memory) eventually became associated with a particular field of creativity, but Hesiod emphasizes only Calliope (Kalliope), inspirer of epic poetry. (The manual crafts, such as metallurgy, were under the direction of Hephaestus; Athene was the patron of weavers, spinners, and potters.) This bas-relief was discovered near Ostia, Italy. *(Capitoline Museum, Rome)*

source of artistic and intellectual creativity, the Muses become Hesiod's unseen companions, a spiritual link to Zeus and the divine authority that validates his poem. In typically blunt style, Hesiod has the Muses contrast the ignorance of his backwater environment with their divine omniscience:

> "Hillbillies and bellies, poor excuses for shepherds:
> We know how to tell many believable lies,
> But also, when we want to, how to speak the plain truth."
> So spoke the daughters of great Zeus, mincing their words.
> And they gave me a staff, a branch of good sappy laurel,
> Plucking it off, spectacular. And they breathed into me
> A voice divine, so I might celebrate past and future.
> And they told me to hymn the generation of the eternal gods,
> But always to sing of themselves, the Muses, first and last.

Hesiod receives the laurel branch, sacred to Apollo, patron of the Muses, to authenticate his revelation of the gods' origins. (We presume that the Muses are prepared to "speak the plain truth" in this case.) Although little more than a thousand lines long, one-fifteenth the length of the *Iliad*, Hesiod's *Theogony* is an enormously ambitious effort: an attempt to trace the history of the universe from its inception to the poet's own day. Honoring the goddesses' request, Hesiod begins each major segment of the poem with an invocation of the Muse, asking Mnemosyne's daughters to inspire him with creative success. Note that it is the Muses in their Olympian guise (lines 561–63) who inspire the poet to sing of the highest gods, transforming his song into a hymn exalting Zeus.

The Nine Daughters of Zeus and Mnemosyne

The source of all poetic, artistic, and intellectual inspiration, the Muses embody the Greek conviction that music—the most sublime expression of cosmic harmony—is a primary and integral part of the universe. Although Hesiod names the nine daughters of Zeus and Mnemosyne, it was only later that each Muse acquired a particular creative function. Their distinctive spheres of activity are:

1. Calliope—epic poetry
2. Clio—history
3. Polyhymnia—mime
4. Melpomone—tragedy
5. Thalia—comedy
6. Erato—lyric choral poetry
7. Euterpe—the flute
8. Terpsichore—light verse and dance
9. Urania—astronomy

The Origins of the Gods

Readers familiar with the biblical story of creation may find Hesiod's version of how all things began somewhat alien. Unlike the Genesis account, which describes a single deity fashioning heaven and earth out of a primordial watery chaos by the power of his word alone, the *Theogony* presents a polytheistic world spontaneously evolving from primal emptiness to a universe teeming with life.

Hesiod's starting point is **Chaos**, literally the yawning Chasm, Abyss, or "gaping Void" that early on somehow came into being—it did not necessarily exist throughout eternity. Hesiod's understanding of Chaos contrasts with that of Ovid in his *Metamorphoses*, where it is defined as anarchic dark matter that preceded the formation of the cosmos (see Chapter 20). For Hesiod, **Gaea** [JEE-uh] (Gaia), who is both the earth and the primordial mother, is also a primal entity. Gaea springs independently into existence, along with **Tartarus** [TAHR-tahr-uhs], the subterranean abyss that will later house monsters and fallen gods, and **Eros** [AIR-ohs], the driving force of procreative love. Although Chaos and Gaea, as well as some male deities, occasionally give birth without a mate, Eros's presence ensures that life will multiply chiefly through sexual reproduction. Like later Greek scientists and philosophers, Hesiod was keenly interested in organizing and classifying material, in this poem delineating the genealogies and familial relationships of three generations of gods.

Hesiod devotes considerable space to recounting the origins of almost innumerable deities who, in surviving myths, play relatively small roles, such as the children of Nyx (Night) or Nereus, a primeval water god. These long genealogical catalogues do not obscure his main purpose, however, which is to trace the divine succession that culminates in Zeus, whose reign is the ultimate goal of cosmic evolution.

The Rise of Zeus

Zeus is the grandson of the primal couple Gaea and her firstborn son, **Uranus** [OOR-a-nuhs] (Ouranos), a personification of the "starry sky," whom she produced

Two Different Accounts of Creation in Genesis

Greek myth's tolerance of diverse, even contradictory, traditions about what happened in the remote past was characteristic of most cultures in the ancient world. Like Hesiod and his counterparts in other ancient societies, biblical editors and compilers accepted differing versions of prehistoric events as equally venerable and worth preserving. In the opening chapters of Genesis, the first book of the Judeo-Christian Bible, editors combined two previously independent stories about the universe's beginnings. Scholars ascribe the first account (Gen. 1:1–2:4) to a priestly author writing in Mesopotamia during the sixth century B.C., when many upper-class Israelites were held captive in Babylon. This priestly narrative, which calls God *Elohim,* a generic term for "divine being," opens with a precreation chaos of undifferentiated waters similar to that in the Babylonian creation story, the *Enuma Elish.* Unlike the Babylonian tale, which features violent conflict between different generations of gods, however, the biblical narrative reshapes older myths of a primordial watery chaos to fit a monotheistic concept. In Genesis 1, a single deity—Elohim—transforms chaos into cosmos by his word alone, creating the world by a six-step process of separation, division, and differentiation.

In the priestly account, humans—both male and female—are fashioned at the same time and both in "the image of God." Following the formation of dry land, plants, and animals, humanity's appearance in the divine image is the climax of creation. In its second tale of origins (Gen. 2:5–25), it is not Elohim but **Yahweh** (the personal name of the biblical God) who creates, and he does so in an entirely different environment and in a different order. Instead of beginning with a watery chaos as the priestly author does in Genesis 1, the Yahwist writer (so called because he or she consistently identifies God as Yahweh) sets creation in an arid desert that has to be irrigated. Instead of making humanity's appearance the final event, the Yahwist states that, after Adam (whose name means "humankind") is formed from dust, the animals are fashioned and brought to Adam to name. Only when Yahweh discovers that no animal provides a suitable mate for his human creature does the Deity decide to create a woman. (For a comparison of Pandora, Adam, Eve, and humanity's alienation from its creator, see the box in Chapter 4.)

GENESIS*
THE ORIGIN OF THE WORLD AND OF MANKIND

The First Account of the Creation (Genesis 1:1–2:4)

1 In the beginning God created the heavens and the earth. Now the earth was a formless void, there was darkness over the deep, and God's spirit hovered over the water.

The Second Account of the Creation: Paradise (Genesis 2:5–25)

At the time when Yahweh God made the earth and heaven there was as yet no wild bush on the earth nor had any wild plant yet sprung up, for Yahweh God had not sent rain on the earth nor was there any

*From *The Jerusalem Bible.* Garden City, NY: Doubleday; London: Darton, Longman & Todd, 1966.

(continued)

Two Different Accounts of Creation in Genesis (*continued*)

God said, "Let there be light," and there was light. God saw that light was good, and God divided light from darkness. God called light "day," and darkness he called "night." Evening came and morning came: the first day.

God said, "Let there be a vault in the waters to divide the waters in two." And so it was. God made the vault, and it divided the waters above the vault from the waters under the vault. God called the vault "heaven." Evening came and morning came: the second day.

God said, "Let the waters under heaven come together into a single mass, and let dry land appear." And so it was. God called the dry land "earth" and the mass of waters "seas," and God saw that it was good.

God said, "Let the earth produce vegetation: seed-bearing plants, and fruit trees bearing fruit with their seed inside, on the earth." And so it was. The earth produced vegetation: plants bearing seed in their several kinds, and trees bearing fruit with their seed inside in their several kinds. God saw that it was good. Evening came and morning came: the third day.

God said, "Let there be lights in the vault of heaven to divide day from night, and let them indicate festivals, days and years. Let them be lights in the vault of heaven to shine on the earth." And so it was. God made the two great lights: the greater light to govern the day, the smaller light to govern the night, and the stars. God set them in the vault of heaven to shine on the earth, to govern the day and the night and to divide light from darkness. God saw that it was good. Evening came and morning came: the fourth day.

God said, "Let the waters teem with living creatures, and let birds fly above the earth within the vault of heaven." And so it was. God created great sea-serpents and every kind of living creature with which the waters teem, and every kind of winged creature. God saw that it

man to till the soil. However, a flood was rising from the earth and watering all the surface of the soil. Yahweh God fashioned man of dust from the soil. Then he breathed into his nostrils a breath of life, and thus man became a living being.

Yahweh God planted a garden in Eden which is in the east, and there he put the man he had fashioned. Yahweh God caused to spring up from the soil every kind of tree, enticing to look at and good to eat, with the tree of life and the tree of the knowledge of good and evil in the middle of the garden. A river flowed from Eden to water the garden, and from there it divided to make four streams. The first is named the Pishon, and this encircles the whole land of Havilah where there is gold. The gold of this land is pure, bdellium and onyx stone are found there. The second river is named the Gihon, and this encircles the whole land of Cush. The third river is named the Tigris, and this flows to the east of Ashur. The fourth river is the Euphrates. Yahweh God took the man and settled him in the garden of Eden to cultivate and take care of it. Then Yahweh God gave the man this admonition, "You may eat indeed of all the trees in the garden. Nevertheless of the tree of the knowledge of good and evil you are not to eat, for on the day you eat of it you shall most surely die."

Yahweh God said, "It is not good that the man should be alone. I will make him a helpmate." So from the soil Yahweh God fashioned all the wild beasts and all the birds of heaven. These he brought to the man to see what he would call them; each one was to bear the name the man would give it. The man gave names to all the cattle, all the birds of heaven and all the wild beasts. But no helpmate suitable for man was found for him. So Yahweh God made the man fall into a deep sleep. And while he slept, he took one of his ribs and enclosed it in flesh. Yahweh

was good. God blessed them, saying, "Be fruitful, multiply, and fill the waters of the seas; and let the birds multiply upon the earth." Evening came and morning came: the fifth day.

God said, "Let the earth produce every kind of living creature: cattle, reptiles, and every kind of wild beast." And so it was. God made every kind of wild beast, every kind of cattle, and every kind of land reptile. God saw that it was good.

God said, "Let us make man in our own image, in the likeness of ourselves, and let them be masters of the fish of the sea, the birds of heaven, the cattle, all the wild beasts and all the reptiles that crawl upon the earth."

God created man in the image of
 himself,
in the image of God he created him,
male and female he created them.

God blessed them, saying to them, "Be fruitful, multiply, fill the earth and conquer it. Be masters of the fish of the sea, the birds of heaven and all living animals on the earth." God said, "See, I give you all the seed-bearing plants that are upon the whole earth, and all the trees with seed-bearing fruit; this shall be your food. To all wild beasts, all birds of heaven and all living reptiles on the earth I give all the foliage of plants for food." And so it was. God saw all he had made, and indeed it was very good. Evening came and morning came: the sixth day.

2 Thus heaven and earth were completed with all their array. On the seventh day God completed the work he had been doing. He rested on the seventh day after all the work he had been doing. God blessed the seventh day and made it holy, because on that day he had rested after all his work of creating.

Such were the origins of heavens and earth when they were created.

God built the rib he had taken from the man into a woman and brought her to the man. The man exclaimed:

"This at last is bone from my bones,
 and flesh from my flesh!
This is to be called woman,
 for this was taken from man."

This is why a man leaves his father and mother and joins himself to his wife, and they become one body.

Now both of them were naked, the man and his wife, but they felt no shame in front of each other.

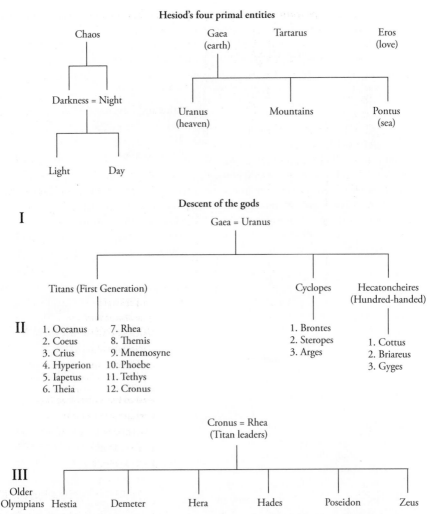

Hesiod's four primal entities

FIGURE 3-8   Genealogy of the Gods. According to Hesiod, all things that exist, including both gods and geographic features like mountains, rivers, and seas, owe their being to
the four primordial entities—Chaos, Gaea, Tartarus, and Eros. There is a direct line of
divine descent from the first parents, Gaea and Uranus, to the second generation of gods,
the Titans, to the third (reigning) generation of deities—the Olympians, headed by Zeus.

without a father (Figure 3-8). The incestuous union of Gaea and Uranus results in
the race of **Titans,** gigantic beings led by **Cronus** [KROH-nuhs] (Kronos), who
mates with his sister **Rhea** [REE-uh] to produce Zeus and his older siblings, the
future Olympians.

The Castration of Uranus and the Birth of Aphrodite

Of the scores of births catalogued in the *Theogony,* two—those of Aphrodite and
Athene—most strikingly represent the contradictory themes that Hesiod weaves

into his account. **Aphrodite** [af-roh-DYE-tee], the embodiment of love, beauty, and sexual desire, is the result of a grotesquely violent act—the castration of Uranus by his Titan son Cronus. Gaea, who deeply resents Uranus for his refusal to allow her the relief of giving birth to the many children painfully confined in her subterranean womb, initiates the events leading to her husband's dethronement and Aphrodite's miraculous appearance. Following his mother's instructions and using the adamantine sickle she fashioned for the purpose, Cronus, the "arch-deceiver," ambushes his parents during copulation and severs his father's genitals, which he throws into the sea.

This act, which permanently separates earth and sky, has a strangely paradoxical effect: drops of phallic blood touching the earth generate both giants and the Furies (Erinyes), dreaded female spirits who punish criminals guilty of slaying their kin. The sea foam that collects around Uranus's severed phallus is transformed into "golden" Aphrodite, the most beguilingly feminine of all goddesses, yet born without a female parent (Figure 3-9 and Color Plate 1). In the *Theogony,* Aphrodite's origin clearly testifies to her function as patron of masculine sexual pleasure. Ultimately, however, Aphrodite derives from two ancient Mesopotamian divinities—the Sumerian Inanna and the Babylonian Ishtar, powerful goddesses of love and war, and expressions of natural fertility, human sexual attraction, and violent aggression. (Homer more conventionally makes her the daughter of Zeus and Dione, daughter of Gaea and Uranus.)

FIGURE 3-9　Aphrodite Rising from the Sea. In Hesiod's version of her origin, the love goddess has no mother and is born from the sea foam surrounding the severed genitals of Uranus, the primal sky god. She rises from a watery element as if to demonstrate that a conscious awareness of human sexuality as a divine force is born from the universal unconscious. *(National Museum of Terme, Rome)*

The Origins of Sexual Attraction: Aristophanes' Speech in Plato's *Symposium*

Although Hesiod's *Theogony* does not include an account of humanity's creation, it emphasizes the crucial role of Eros (Love), the divine power that expresses itself through human sexual desire. In Hesiod's view, Eros is the procreative force responsible for populating the universe, generating both gods and heroes. About three and a half centuries after Hesiod's day, the Athenian philosopher Plato (427–347 B.C.) made Eros the subject of one of his most important dialogues, the *Symposium* (Figure 3-10). The fictional re-creation of a drinking party attended by some of Athens' most famous citizens, including Socrates, Agathon, Alcibiades, and the comic playwright Aristophanes, the *Symposium* contains numerous references to different myths about Eros's origin and purpose. Aristophanes, a fictive character whom Plato bases on the historical author of erotic comedies, offers an etiological myth to explain both the universality of sexual attraction and the reason for its diverse manifestations.

In the beginning, Aristophanes states, there were not merely two sexes—male and female—but three, the third being androgynous, composed of both male and female characteristics. The male sex derived from the sun, the female from the earth, and the androgynous from the moon, which the ancients believed to partake of both sun and earth. Originally, humans were twice the person they are now: round in shape, each had two heads, facing in opposite directions, as well as two sets of arms and legs. These double creatures could go either forward or backward without turning around. They could also use their eight limbs to turn cartwheels, rolling along at high speeds wherever they wished to go.

FIGURE 3-10   A Greek Symposium. An all-male drinking party, the symposium provided educated Greeks with a time-honored forum for discussing ideas, such as the nature of Love (Eros) that Plato makes the subject of his *Symposium,* in which the comic playwright Aristophanes proposes a creation myth that explains the origin and purpose of both heterosexual and homosexual love. *(British Museum, London)*

Strong and confident—their circular form indicating their completeness— these primordial humans were also intensely ambitious. Like the giants Ephialtes and Otus, sons of Poseidon who attempted to invade the heavens, early humans dared to challenge the gods with a direct attack. Zeus, who did not want to obliterate them with thunderbolts as he had the giants, decided instead to weaken humanity by splitting each person in two. As soon as Zeus bisected an individual, Apollo turned the creature's head around to face the side that had been cut, drawing skin over it "like a pouch with drawstrings" and tying the skin together in a knot on the abdomen, thus giving humans a navel.

With their ambition punished and their power diminished, humans ceased rivaling the gods and began to devote their energies to seeking the half of their original self that had been lost. The androgynes, who had resembled the biblical Adam before the female Eve was separated from his body, sought their other half in members of the opposite sex, forming heterosexual combinations. Those who had been all male naturally endeavored to reunite with members of the same sex, while formerly all-female beings longed to restore their basic nature by coupling with other women.

Human sexual attraction, Aristophanes declares, is inspired by a profound need to recapture the wholeness of personality that existed before Zeus bifurcated us (Figure 3-11). The playwright then conjures up the spirit of Hephaestus, the ingenious god of metalcraft, who offers to fuse together those lovers who desire total union with their beloved, melding the artificially divided two into one. By thus uniting humanity's fragmented nature, Eros enables lovers to regain the lost paradise of spiritual and physical completeness.

FIGURE 3-11   Scene from a Typical Symposium. A youth plays the diaulos (a kind of double oboe) for an older man who seems to forget the wine cup in his hand as he listens raptly. According to Aristophanes' story, Love (Eros) is the force that drives all people to seek out and commingle with the person who represents the part of their original nature that was lost when Zeus bifurcated primal humans. *(Louvre, Paris)*

FIGURE 3-12 *Aphrodite Crouching.* Pictured as if drying her hair after a bath (or after her emergence from earth's primordial sea), Aphrodite embodies a graceful charm that captivates even the gods. Judged the most beautiful of divinities, she and her companion (or son) Eros (god of love) inspire and manipulate every being in the universe, from Zeus to ordinary mortals. *(Rhodes Museum)*

Aphrodite rising from the sea, accompanied by the figures of Eros and Desire—and the vengeful Furies rising from blood-clotted earth—reveals the paradoxical aspects of Uranus's mutilation. Cronus's action leads the world another step closer to Zeus's inevitable reign, of which the love goddess will be a radiant ornament (Figure 3-12); however, it is also a savage betrayal of a kinsman that brings the spirits of hatred and revenge into being. Resulting from an act that combines sexual passion and violence, Aphrodite's birth expresses a characteristic Greek ambivalence about sexual love: although promising beauty and joy, it can also inspire acts of brutal aggression. Aphrodite's appearance prior to the birth of Zeus or any other Olympians also suggests the love goddess's primacy, both in time and in universal significance.

Consistent with his treacherous brutality, Cronus attempts to avoid Uranus's fate by devouring his own children, all of Zeus's older brothers and sisters (Figure 3-13), thereby imitating his father's life-denying policy and ensuring that any offspring who might escape his cannibalism—as Zeus does—will repeat his rebellion. With the exception of Prometheus, whose name means "forethought," the male Titans are not known for their intelligence.

The Separation of Earth and Sky

Cronus's overthrow of Uranus embodies several basic mythological themes. In many world traditions, an early stage of creation is the enforced separation of earth

FIGURE 3-13 Cronus Devouring One of His Children. Goya's famous painting (c. 1819–1823) of Cronus's cannibalistic attempt to prevent a son from replacing him as universal sovereign emphasizes the savagery of Zeus's Titan predecessors. In Hesiod's view of an evolving universe, Zeus's success in overthrowing Cronus represents the triumph of civilized justice over primitive brutality. *(Prado Museum, Madrid)*

and sky, a division necessary to achieve an inhabitable cosmos. In Egyptian tradition, which reverses the sexes of the two primal entities, the goddess Nut (the sky) is separated from her brother Geb (the earth) because their original embrace was so tight that their divine children had no room in which to be born. Accordingly, their father, Shu, god of the air, parted the incestuous couple, elevating Nut so that she arched her body far above Geb, thereby allowing the gods Isis, Osiris, Nephthys, and Seth to emerge into the atmosphere. Another Egyptian theme appearing in Hesiod's account is that of parent devouring child: it was said that, not only did Nut swallow the sun every night, but each morning she ate her own offspring, the stars, which, of course, were reborn every evening after sunset.

Rather than serving as a model or justification for sons in primitive societies to seize power from their aged fathers, the Uranus–Cronus conflict echoes a convention of ancient cosmogony. The creative process demands that sky be removed from earth in order for life to develop. As in the Egyptian tale, Hesiod's account makes it clear that new gods cannot appear until their divine parents are permanently riven. Representing the dark night sky, studded with brilliant stars, Uranus remains in the distant background—to be consulted occasionally, as when Rhea asks for his and Gaea's help. But heaven's extreme remoteness means that the sky plays little role in subsequent events, an impotence symbolized by Uranus's emasculation.

The tale of a primal deity whose body, like that of Uranus, suffers mutilation and then is used as building material to form part of the physical universe is common to mythology around the world. In the *Enuma Elish,* Marduk bifurcates Tiamat's corpse to construct earth and sky. In Scandinavian myth, the Norse creator gods slay Ymir, a huge frost giant, and make the earth from his body, the oceans from his blood, and the dome of heaven from his skull. Chinese myth offers a parallel account: a primordial deity, Pangu, exhausts himself performing the essential function of holding up the sky so that it will not fall and crush the earth, in effect sacrificing his life so that the cosmos can exist. In death, Pangu offers his body as the substance out of which the visible world is created.

The theme of primordial sacrifice, often taking the form of **sparagmos** [spuh-RAHG-mohs]—the ritual tearing apart of a sacrificial victim, divine or human— plays a significant role in Greek myth, not only in Hesiod's *Theogony* but also in narratives about Dionysus and mortal heroes (see Chapter 17). These, and many analogous creation stories from around the world, imply that the universe did not come into being without pain and loss, including the sacrificial suffering of divine beings. A god who, like Uranus, withdraws from the earthly scene or disappears altogether after his creative function is completed is called a *deus otiosus*. This shadowy figure, who can be defined as a god "at leisure" or "out of work," is familiar in the mythology of Africa, Mesoamerica, and ancient Canaan.

Some feminist scholars see in the myths of Uranus's mutilation a remnant of ancient matriarchal rites in which the primal goddess's consort was ritually killed (and perhaps eaten) to ensure fertility of flock and field, as well as that of the human community. Etiologically, the episode suggests the mysterious psychological affinity between love and hate, explains the enforced division of masculine and feminine principles in the cosmos, and offers a reason the "starry sky" (Uranus) is so remote from and seemingly irrelevant to human affairs. The myth is also a classic illustration of the Freudian domestic psychodrama, a father–son rivalry in which the mother sides with her ambitious male child to subvert the dominance of a tyrannical husband and father.

The Birth of Athene

After Zeus, again with Mother Gaea's help, has succeeded in conquering the Titans and imprisoning most of them in Tartarus, he sets about populating the universe in his own image. Although Zeus sires a prodigious number of divine beings and mortal heroes, Hesiod's designation of him as "father of gods and men" does not refer to his literal paternity. Zeus is "father" in his role as ruler of the divine patriarchy, protector and defender of the cosmic order.

The first of Zeus's seven successive wives is **Metis** [MEE-tis], a personification of the Greek word meaning "thought" or "cunning," a concept about which the Greeks had mixed feelings, particularly when it involved female astuteness. When Gaea and Uranus warn Zeus that he, too, may have a son strong enough to depose him, Zeus reacts in a way that echoes Cronus's cannibalism but significantly differs from it: he swallows Metis, already pregnant with their child. Whereas Cronus could ingest but not absorb his children, Zeus successfully incorporates Metis into himself, controlling female cunning by internalizing it as part of his character. By assimilating Metis, Zeus is able personally to give birth to his first child, **Athene,** a potent manifestation of her father's creative intelligence (Figure 3-14; see also Figures 1-2 and 1-3; see Chapter 2 for a discussion of theoretical interpretations of this myth).

FIGURE 3-14   The Birth of Athene. This crude but vigorous vase painting effectively illustrates Hesiod's tradition of Athene's birth from the head of Zeus (compare a much later version in Figure 1-2). Athene emerges from Zeus's skull thrusting a shield before her as Hephaestus gazes in amazement at the result of his ax-blow. *(British Museum, London)*

Goddess of Victory   The fact that Athene is born wearing a soldier's armor and accompanied by the figure of **Nike** (Victory) (see Figure 1-3) suggests that Zeus will use his intellect to defend his newly acquired power. Athene is not only the epitome of wisdom, but also the goddess of victory in war, the ingenious strategist who outmaneuvers all opponents. As defender of the Greek polis, she teaches the rational arts of logical argument and persuasion, replacing civil strife with disciplined cooperation (see Chapter 15).

Zeus will need to co-opt all of Athene's qualities because, as the Prometheus myth makes clear, only the acquisition of wisdom—and all the divine attributes that go with it—can protect him from falling as ignominiously as his predecessors. Although he will never again face enemies as formidable as those he defeats early in his reign, Zeus contains in his own patriarchal character the seeds of his potential undoing (see the discussion of Prometheus in Chapter 4). Even in his own household, Zeus encounters sporadic opposition, particularly from his sister-wife **Hera**, a goddess of marriage and domesticity, who may have been worshiped independently before the imposition of patriarchal religion reduced her to the status of Zeus's consort (Figure 3-15).

Hera and Hephaestus

Hera's rivalry with her husband, whose policies she regularly sabotages, appears at the outset of their relationship and pervades virtually all of the myths about her. Hesiod asserts that, as soon as Hera sees Zeus giving birth to Athene, she counters, without any male assistance, by producing a son who is entirely hers, **Hephaestus.**

FIGURE 3-15   The Marriage of Zeus and Hera. In this bas-relief (fifth century B.C.), Hera unveils herself to her new husband. The posture of the divine couple suggests the ambiguity of their relationship: while extending his arm as if to control his wife's movements, Zeus is also mesmerized by Hera's beauty. Although myth affirms the pair's sexual compatibility, their union is marred by his obsessive infidelities and her unforgiving jealousy. *(Archeological Museum, Palermo)*

(Because myth typically operates without regard for chronological sequence, the Parthenon sculptures of Athene's birth can show Hephaestus as already present on Olympus.) Just as Athene, Zeus's favorite child, consistently supports her father, so Hephaestus is his mother's devoted son, repeatedly taking Hera's side in his parents' many quarrels. In some versions of the myth, Hephaestus, the only imperfect Olympian, is born lame; in others, he becomes a cripple after Zeus hurls him down to earth for conspiring with Hera once too often. Although the myths of Olympian familial strife partly replay the deadly mother–son–father triangle of Gaea, Cronus, and Uranus, Zeus's superior wisdom and improved technological resources—his arsenal of thunderbolts—allow him to master the competitive dynamics of family life and thus maintain his throne. (For a variant tradition about Hephaestus's relationship to his mother, see the description of Hera in Chapter 6.)

FIGURE 3-16   Zeus Battling Typhoeus (Typhon). In this vase painting, after defeating the Titans, Zeus faces an even greater challenge to his sovereignty, the reptilian monster Typhoeus, child of Gaea and Tartarus. Typhoeus, shown here with only one head, is a Greek version of the Mesopotamian dragon of chaos and represents Gaea's final attempt to circumvent undisputed male rule of the universe. Originally, this serpent may have been a guardian of a prehistoric earth goddess, which later myth reinterpreted as a threat to Zeus's patriarchal regime. In this close-up of Typhoeus, the monster's lower torso ends in serpentine coils, and his scaly wings extend to blot out the sun. Although in Hesiod's account Zeus defeats him with overpowering thunderbolts, other myths indicate that Zeus almost suffers defeat from the dragon's attack. *(Antikensammlungen, Munich)*

Gaea and Typhoeus

Although Hesiod passionately supports a patriarchal society, in heaven as on earth, he seldom underestimates the crucial role of the feminine principle in cosmic history. Gaea, instrumental in every change in divine leadership, ultimately confirms Zeus's right to rule, but not before she has subjected him to a supreme test. Having contrived Uranus's downfall and tricked Cronus into vomiting up his children so that they can assist in Zeus's campaign against the Titans, she now presents Zeus with his most formidable opponent, the monster **Typhoeus** [tye-FEE-uhs], a Greek version of the ancient Near Eastern dragon of chaos (Figure 3-16). Gaea's "last-born child," Typhoeus, in some traditions called **Typhon,** is deliberately created by his mother's mating with Tartarus, here presented as a primal entity rather than an abyss below Hades' domain. With his hundred reptilian heads, fiery breath, and fierce, predatory shrieks, Typhoeus, who aspires to rule both gods and men, represents a frightening alternative to Zeus's benevolent despotism.

Some commentators note that Typhoeus, whom Hesiod depicts as an incarnation of cosmic evil, may be a distorted picture of the guardian serpent that was once associated with the worship of a prehistoric goddess, before she was dethroned

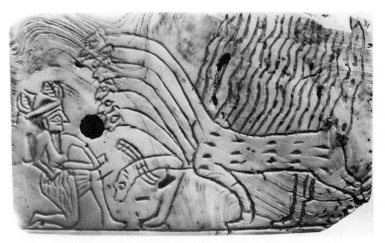

FIGURE 3-17   Mesopotamian God Battling a Seven-Headed Dragon. From the Sumerian early dynastic period (c. 2800–2600 B.C.), this plaque shows the Sumerian god Ninurta, a divine warrior and son of Enlil, the storm god, defeating the primal monster of chaos. In Hesiod's *Theogony,* Zeus assumes Ninurta's role as cosmic savior by overthrowing Typhoeus, the Greek version of the chaotic dragon. Biblical writers also adapted this ancient Near Eastern conflict myth to express their vision of the cosmic struggle between divine forces of Good and Evil (Ps. 74:12–17; Job 3:8; 26:13; 41:1–34; Isa. 27:1). The mythical dragon again rears his seven heads in the Christian Book of Revelation, where, identified with Satan and the devil, he is cast from heaven by the archangel Michael (Rev. 12:3, 9; 13:1; 17:3).

by male sky gods (Figure 3-17) (see Chapter 5). Other scholars suggest that the conflagration that ravages earth during Zeus's war with Typhoeus represents not only a patriarchal assault on Gaea but also a faint memory of some distant geological catastrophe, such as the devastating prehistoric eruptions of Mount Etna or Thera (Santorini).

Hesiod portrays Zeus defeating Typhoeus by merely summoning the full might with which he previously vanquished the Titans, but later traditions emphasize the great difficulty Zeus had in subduing this embodiment of universal disorder. According to Apollodorus, the cunning monster severs the tendons of Zeus's hands and feet and hides them, rendering the god impotent (a variation of Uranus's emasculation) until Zeus's clever son Hermes restores them to his father. In an elaboration from the fifth century A.D., Typhoeus steals Zeus's thunder and lightning, as well as his tendons, making the outcome of this battle between good and evil even more uncertain.

Although Gaea's last strategy to prevent Zeus's complete triumph fails, her ambivalent attitude toward the king of the gods lives on in Hera. According to some versions of the tale, Hera herself gives birth to Zeus's would-be nemesis Typhoeus (see Chapter 7, *Hymn to Pythian Apollo*), source of the violently destructive winds that sink ships and ravage crops. One tradition, preserved in Aeschylus's *Prometheus Bound,* states that Zeus finally defeated Typhoeus by burying him beneath Mount

Greek and Anglicized Spellings of Characters' Names in the *Theogony*

Because different translators adopt differing transliterations of Greek names, the names of characters in Greek myth and literature are spelled in a variety of ways. Whereas this text uses an Anglicized spelling, the version of Hesiod's *Theogony* included here adopts a spelling approximating the pronunciation of the original Greek. The following list provides a brief sampling of both forms of the names. (For a more complete list of variant spellings of gods' names, see Chapter 6; a similar list of characters' names in the *Iliad* appears in Chapter 12.)

Atropos (Atropus)   Okeanos (Oceanus)

Carberus (Cerberus)   Olympos (Olympus)

Gaia (Gaea)   Ouranos (Uranus)

Helikon (Helicon)   Phoibus Apollon (Phoebus Apollo)

Hephaistos (Hephaestus)   Pontos (Pontus)

Herakles (Heracles, Hercules)   Rheia (Rhea)

Klotho (Clotho)   Tartaros (Tartarus)

Kronos (Cronus)   Typhoios (Typhoeus)

Moirai (Moirae, the Fates)

Etna, Europe's largest and most active volcano. This etiological myth explains Etna's fiery outbursts as manifestations of Typhoeus's convulsive struggles to escape from his underground prison.

Hesiod's Worldview

In creating an orderly account that synthesizes ancient Near Eastern and native Greek traditions about the Greek gods' complex ancestry, functions, and kinships (a synthesis he probably inherited from earlier Greek poets), Hesiod portrays a universe that is inherently contradictory. The primal Chasm (Chaos) is the unlikely source of an exuberant proliferation of life that culminates in Zeus's joyous begetting of both mortal heroes and deathless gods, figures who will dominate the mythic environment. Each stage of cosmic development, however, is marked by acts of appalling violence—mutilation, cannibalism, treachery, war—illustrations of strife's power to trigger conflict on both the divine and human levels. Yet, even while celebrating the chief Olympian's ultimate triumph as the "bringer of good," Hesiod is deeply pessimistic about the human scene. He envisions a deteriorating world in which Zeus's reign inaugurates a progressive social and moral decline that imposes poverty and suffering on most of his human subjects (see Chapter 4).

THEOGONY*

Hesiod

INVOCATION TO THE MUSES

Begin our singing with the Helikonian Muses,   1
Who possess Mount Helikon, high and holy,
And near its violet-stained spring on petalsoft feet
Dance circling the altar of almighty Kronion,

And having bathed their silken skin in Permessos
Or in Horse Spring or the sacred creek Olmeios,
They begin their choral dance on Helikon's summit
So lovely it pangs, and with power in their steps
Ascend veiled and misted in palpable air
Treading the night, and in a voice beyond beauty   10
They chant:

   Zeus Aegisholder and his lady Hera
   Of Argos, in gold sandals striding,
   And the Aegisholder's girl, owl-eyed Athene,
   And Phoibos Apollo and arrowy Artemis,
   Poseidon earth-holder, earthquaking god,
   Modest Themis and Aphrodite, eyelashes curling,
   And Hebe goldcrowned and lovely Dione,
   Leto and Iapetos and Kronos, his mind bent,
   Eos and Helios and glowing Selene,   20
   Gaia, Okeanos, and the black one, Night,

And the whole eerie brood of the eternal Immortals.

And they once taught Hesiod the art of singing verse,
While he pastured his lambs on holy Helikon's slopes.
And this was the very first thing they told me,
The Olympian Muses, daughters of Zeus Aegisholder:

"Hillbillies and bellies, poor excuses for shepherds:
We know how to tell many believable lies,
But also, when we want to, how to speak the plain truth."
So spoke the daughters of great Zeus, mincing their words.   30
And they gave me a staff, a branch of good sappy laurel,
Plucking it off, spectacular. And they breathed into me
A voice divine, so I might celebrate past and future.
And they told me to hymn the generation of the eternal gods,
But always to sing of themselves, the Muses, first and last.

---

*Translation by Stanley Lombardo.

But why all this about oak tree or stone?

Start from the Muses: when they sing for Zeus Father
They thrill the great mind deep in Olympos,
Telling what is, what will be, and what has been,
Blending their voices, and weariless the sound   40
Flows sweet from their lips and spreads like lilies,
And Zeus' thundering halls shine with laughter,
And Olympos' snowy peaks and the halls of the gods
Echo the strains as their immortal chanting
Honors first the primordial generation of gods
Whom in the beginning Earth and Sky bore,
And the divine benefactors born from them;
And, second, Zeus, the Father of gods and men,
Mightiest of the gods and strongest by far;
And then the race of humans and of powerful Giants.   50
And Zeus' mind in Olympos is thrilled by the song
Of the Olympian Muses, the Storm King's daughters.

They were born on Pieria after our Father Kronion
Mingled with Memory, who rules Eleutherae's hills.
She bore them to be a forgetting of troubles,
A pause in sorrow. For nine nights wise Zeus
Mingled with her in love, ascending her sacred bed
In isolation from the other Immortals.
But when the time drew near, and the seasons turned,
And the moons had waned, and the many days were done,   60
She bore nine daughters, all of one mind, with song
In their breasts, with hearts that never failed,
Near the topmost peak of snowcapped Olympos.

There are their polished dancing grounds, their fine halls,
And the Graces and Desire have their houses close by,
And all is in bloom. And they move in the dance, intoning
The careful ways of the gods, celebrating the customs
Of all the Immortals in a voice enchanting and sweet.
Then they process to Olympos, a glory of pure
Sound and dance, and the black earth shrieks with delight   70
As they sing, and the drum of their footfalls rises like love
As they go to their father. He is king in the sky,
He holds the vajra thunder and flashing lightning.
He defeated his father Kronos by force, and He ordained
Laws for the gods and assigned them their rights.

Thus sing the Muses who have their homes on Olympos,

  The nine daughters born of great Zeus,

  Klio, Euterpe, Thalia, Melpomene,
  Terpsichore, Erato, Polyhymnia, Ourania,

  And Kalliope, the most important of all,   80

For she keeps the company of reverend kings.
When the daughters of great Zeus will honor a lord
Whose lineage is divine, and look upon his birth,
They distill a sweet dew upon his tongue,
And from his mouth words flow like honey. The people
All look to him as he arbitrates settlements
With judgments straight. He speaks out in sure tones
And soon puts an end even to bitter disputes.
A sound-minded ruler, when someone is wronged,
Sets things to rights in the public assembly,   90
Conciliating both sides with ease.
He comes to the meeting place propitiated as a god,
Treated with respect, preeminent in the crowd.
Such is the Muses' sacred gift to men.
For though it is singers and lyre players
That come from the Muses and far-shooting Apollo
And kings come from Zeus, happy is the man
Whom the Muses love. Sweet flows the voice from his mouth.
For if anyone is grieved, if his heart is sore
With fresh sorrow, if he is troubled, and a singer   100
Who serves the Muses chants the deeds of past men
Or the blessed gods who have their homes on Olympos,
He soon forgets his heartache, and of all his cares
He remembers none: the goddesses' gifts turn them aside.

Farewell Zeus's daughters, and bestow song that beguiles.
Make known the eerie brood of the eternal Immortals
Who were born of Earth and starry Sky,
And of dusky Night, and whom the salt Sea bore.
Tell how first the gods and earth came into being
And the rivers and the sea, endless and surging,   110
And the stars shining and the wide sky above;
How they divided wealth and allotted honors,
And first possessed deep-ridged Olympos.

Tell me these things, Olympian Muses,
From the beginning, and tell which of them came first.

THE FIRST GODS

In the beginning there was only Chaos, the Abyss,
But then Gaia, the Earth, came into being,
Her broad bosom the ever-firm foundation of all,
And Tartaros, dim in the underground depths,
And Eros, loveliest of all the Immortals, who   120
Makes their bodies (and men's bodies) go limp,
Mastering their minds and subduing their wills.

From the Abyss were born Erebos and dark Night.
And Night, pregnant after sweet intercourse
With Erebos, gave birth to Aether and Day.

Earth's first child was Ouranos, starry Heaven,
Just her size, a perfect fit on all sides.
And a firm foundation for the blessed gods.
And she bore the Mountains in long ranges, haunted
By the Nymphs who live in the deep mountain dells.   130
Then she gave birth to the barren, raging Sea
Without any sexual love. But later she slept with
Ouranos and bore Ocean with its deep currents,
And also: Koios, Krios, Hyperion, Iapetos,
        Theia, Rheia, Themis, Mnemosyne,
        Gold-crowned Phoibe and lovely Tethys.

THE CASTRATION OF OURANOS

After them she bore a most terrible child,
Kronos, her youngest, an arch-deceiver,
And this boy hated his lecherous father.

She bore the Cyclopes too, with hearts of stone,   140
Brontes, Steropes and ponderous Arges,
Who gave Zeus thunder and made the thunderbolt.
In every other respect they were just like gods,
But a lone eye lay in their foreheads' middle.
They were nicknamed Cyclopes because they had
A single goggle eye in their foreheads' middle.
Strong as the dickens, and they knew their craft.

And three other sons were born to Gaia and Ouranos,
Strong, hulking creatures that beggar description,
Kottos, Briareos, and Gyges, outrageous children.   150
A hundred hands stuck out of their shoulders,
Grotesque, and fifty heads grew on each stumpy neck.
These monsters exuded irresistible strength.
They were Gaia's most dreaded offspring,
And from the start their father feared and loathed them.
Ouranos used to stuff all of his children
Back into a hollow of Earth soon as they were born,
Keeping them from the light, an awful thing to do,
But Heaven did it, and was very pleased with himself.
Vast Earth groaned under the pressure inside,   160
And then she came up with a plan, a really wicked trick.
She created a new mineral, grey flint, and formed
A huge sickle from it and showed it to her dear boys.
And she rallied them with this bitter speech:

"Listen to me, children, and we might yet get even
With your criminal father for what he has done to us.
After all, he started this whole ugly business."

They were tongue-tied with fear when they heard this.
But Kronos, whose mind worked in strange ways,
Got his pluck up and found the words to answer her: 170

"I think I might be able to bring it off, Mother.
I can't stand Father; he doesn't even deserve the name.
And after all, he started this whole ugly business."

This response warmed the heart of vast Earth.
She hid young Kronos in an ambush and placed in his hands
The jagged sickle. Then she went over the whole plan with him.
And now on came great Ouranos, bringing Night with him.
And, longing for love, he settled himself all over Earth.
From his dark hiding-place, the son reached out
With his left hand, while with his right he swung   180
The fiendishly long and jagged sickle, pruning the genitals
Of his own father with one swoop and tossing them
Behind him, where they fell to no small effect.
Earth soaked up all the bloody drops that spurted out,
And as the seasons went by she gave birth to the Furies
And to great Giants gleaming in full armor, spears in hand,
And to the Meliai, as ash-tree nymphs are generally called.

THE BIRTH OF APHRODITE

The genitalia themselves, freshly cut with flint, were thrown
Clear of the mainland into the restless, white-capped sea,
Where they floated a long time. A white foam from the god-flesh   190
Collected around them, and in that foam a maiden developed
And grew. Her first approach to land was near holy Kythera,
And from there she floated on to the island of Kypros.
There she came ashore, an awesome, beautiful divinity.
Tender grass sprouted up under her slender feet.
                                            Aphrodite
Is her name in speech human and divine, since it was in foam
She was nourished. But she is also called Kythereia since
She reached Kythera, and Kyprogenes because she was born
On the surf-line of Kypros, and Philommedes because she loves
The organs of sex, from which she made her epiphany.   200
Eros became her companion, and ravishing Desire waited on her
At her birth and when she made her debut among the Immortals.
From that moment on, among both gods and humans,
She has fulfilled the honored function that includes
Virginal sweet-talk, lovers' smiles and deceits
And all of the gentle pleasures of sex.

But great Ouranos used to call the sons he begot
Titans, a reproachful nickname, because he thought
They had over-reached themselves and done a monstrous deed
For which vengeance later would surely be exacted.   210

OTHER EARLY GODS

And Night bore hateful Doom and black Fate
And Death, and Sleep and the brood of Dreams.
And sleeping with no one, the ebony goddess Night
Gave birth to Blame and agonizing Grief,
And to the Hesperides who guard the golden apples
And the fruit-bearing trees beyond glorious Ocean.
And she generated the Destinies and the merciless,
Avenging Fates, Clotho, Lachesis, and Atropos,
Who give mortals at birth good and evil to have,
And prosecute transgressions of mortals and gods.   220
These goddesses never let up their dread anger
Until the sinner has paid a severe penalty.
And deadly Night bore Nemesis too, more misery
For mortals; and after her, Deception and Friendship
And ruinous Old Age, and hard-hearted Eris.
And hateful Eris bore agonizing Toil,
Forgetfulness, Famine, and tearful Pains,
Battles and Fights, Murders and Manslaughters,
Quarrels, Lying Words and Words Disputatious,
Lawlessness and Recklessness, who share one nature,   230
And Oath, who most troubles men upon Earth
When anyone willfully swears a false oath.

And Pontos, the Sea, begot his eldest, Nereus,
True and no liar. And they call him Old Man
Because he is unerring and mild, remembèrs
What is right, and his mind is gentle and just.

. . . .

THE BIRTH OF THE OLYMPIANS

Later, Kronos forced himself upon Rheia,
And she gave birth to a splendid brood:

   Hestia and Demeter and gold-sandalled Hera,
   Strong, pitiless Hades, the underworld lord,
   The booming Earth-shaker, Poseidon, and finally   240
   Zeus, a wise god, our Father in heaven
   Under whose thunder the wide world trembles.

And Kronos swallowed them all down as soon as each
Issued from Rheia's holy womb onto her knees,
With the intent that only he among the proud Ouranians
Should hold the title of King among the Immortals.

For he had learned from Earth and starry Heaven
That it was fated for him, powerful though he was,
To be overthrown by his child, through the scheming of Zeus.
Well, Kronos wasn't blind. He kept a sharp watch   250
And swallowed his children.
                                    Rheia's grief was unbearable.
When she was about to give birth to Zeus our Father
She petitioned her parents, Earth and starry Heaven,
To put together some plan so that the birth of her child
Might go unnoticed, and she would make devious Kronos
Pay the Avengers of her father and children.
They listened to their daughter and were moved by her words,
And the two of them told her all that was fated
For Kronos the King and his stout-hearted son.   260
They sent her to Lyktos, to the rich land of Crete,
When she was ready to bear the youngest of her sons,
Mighty Zeus. Vast Earth received him when he was born
To be nursed and brought up in the wide land of Crete.
She came first to Lyktos, travelling quickly by night,
And took the baby in her hands and hid him in a cave,
An eerie hollow in the woods of dark Mount Aigaion.
Then she wrapped up a great stone in swaddling clothes
And gave it to Kronos, Ouranos' son, the great lord and king
Of the earlier gods. He took it in his hands and rammed it   270
Down into his belly, the poor fool! He had no idea
That a stone had been substituted for his son, who,
Unscathed and content as a babe, would soon wrest
His honors from him by main force and rule the Immortals.
It wasn't long before the young lord was flexing
His glorious muscles. The seasons followed each other,
And great devious Kronos, gulled by Earth's
Clever suggestions, vomited up his offspring,
[Overcome by the wiles and power of his son]
The stone first, which he'd swallowed last.   280
Zeus took the stone and set it in the ground at Pytho
Under Parnassos' hollows, a sign and wonder for men to come.
And he freed his uncles, other sons of Ouranos
Whom their father in a fit of idiocy had bound.
They remembered his charity and in gratitude
Gave him thunder and the flashing thunderbolt
And lightning, which enormous Earth had hidden before.
Trusting in these he rules mortals and Immortals.

PROMETHEUS

Then Iapetos led away a daughter of Ocean,
Klymene, pretty ankles, and went to bed with her.   290
And she bore him a child, Atlas, stout heart,

And begat ultraglorious Menoitios, and Prometheus,
Complex, his mind a shimmer, and witless Epimetheus,
Who was trouble from the start for enterprising men,
First to accept from Zeus the fabricated woman,
The Maiden. Outrageous Menoitios broadbrowed Zeus
Blasted into Erebos with a sulphurous thunderbolt
On account of his foolishness and excessive violence.
Atlas, crimped hard, holds up the wide sky
At earth's limits, in front of the shrill-voiced Hesperides,   300
Standing with indefatigable head and hands,
For this is the part wise Zeus assigned him.
And he bound Prometheus with ineluctable fetters,
Painful bonds, and drove a shaft through his middle,
And set a long-winged eagle on him that kept gnawing
His undying liver, but whatever the long-winged bird
Ate the whole day through, would all grow back by night.
That bird the mighty son of pretty-ankled Alkmene,
Herakles, killed, drove off the evil affliction
From Iapetos' son and freed him from his misery—   310
Not without the will of Zeus, high lord of Olympos,
So that the glory of Theban-born Herakles
Might be greater than before on the plentiful earth.
He valued that and honored his celebrated son.
And he ceased from the anger that he had before
Because Prometheus matched wits with mighty Kronion.

That happened when the gods and mortal men were negotiating
At Mekone. Prometheus cheerfully butchered a great ox
And served it up, trying to befuddle Zeus' wits.
For Zeus he set out flesh and innards rich with fat   320
Laid out on the oxhide and covered with its paunch.
But for the others he set out the animal's white bones
Artfully dressed out and covered with shining fat.
And then the Father of gods and men said to him:

"Son of Iapetos, my celebrated lord,
How unevenly you have divided the portions."
Thus Zeus, sneering, with imperishable wisdom.
And Prometheus, whose mind was devious,
Smiled softly and remembered his trickery:

"Zeus most glorious, greatest of the everlasting gods,   330
Choose whichever of these your heart desires."

This was Prometheus' trick. But Zeus, eternally wise,
Recognized the fraud and began to rumble in his heart
Trouble for mortals, and it would be fulfilled.
With both his hands he picked up the gleaming fat.

Anger seethed in his lungs and bile rose to his heart
When he saw the ox's white bones artfully tricked out.
And that is why the tribes of men on earth
Burn white bones to the immortals upon smoking altars.
But cloudherding Zeus was terribly put out, and said: 340

"Iapetos' boy, if you're not the smartest of them all.
So you still haven't forgotten your tricks, have you?"
Thus Zeus, angry, whose wisdom never wears out.
From then on he always remembered this trick
And wouldn't give the power of weariless fire
To the ashwood mortals who live on the earth.
But that fine son of Iapetos outwitted him
And stole the far-seen gleam of weariless fire
In a hollow fennel stalk, and so bit deeply the heart
Of Zeus, the high lord of thunder, who was angry   350
When he saw the distant gleam of fire among men,
And straight off he gave them trouble to pay for the fire.

PANDORA

The famous Lame God plastered up some clay
To look like a shy virgin, just like Zeus wanted,
And Athena, the Owl-Eyed Goddess,
Got her all dressed up in silvery clothes
And with her hands draped a veil from her head,
An intricate thing, wonderful to look at.
And Pallas Athena circled her head
With a wreath of luscious springtime flowers   360
And crowned her with a golden tiara
That the famous Lame God had made himself,
Shaped it by hand to please father Zeus,
Intricately designed and a wonder to look at.
Sea monsters and other fabulous beasts
Crowded the surface, and it sighed with beauty,
And you could almost hear the animals' voices.
He made this lovely evil to balance the good,
Then led her off to the other gods and men
Gorgeous in the finery of the owl-eyed daughter   370
Sired in power. And they were stunned,
Immortal gods and mortal men, when they saw
The sheer deception, irresistible to men.
From her is the race of female women,
The deadly race and population of women,
A great infestation among mortal men,
At home with Wealth but not with Poverty.
It's the same as with bees in their overhung hives
Feeding the drones, evil conspirators.

The bees work every day until the sun goes down, 380
Busy all day long making pale honeycombs,
While the drones stay inside, in the hollow hives,
Stuffing their stomachs with the work of others.
That's just how Zeus, the high lord of thunder,
Made women as a curse for mortal men,
Evil conspirators. And he added another evil
To offset the good. Whoever escapes marriage
And women's harm, comes to deadly old age
Without any son to support him. He has no lack
While he lives, but when he dies distant relatives 390
Divide up his estate. Then again, whoever marries
As fated, and gets a good wife, compatible,
Has a life that is balanced between evil and good,
A constant struggle. But if he marries the abusive kind,
He lives with pain in his heart all down the line,
Pain in spirit and mind, incurable evil.
There's no way to get around the mind of Zeus.
Not even Prometheus, that fine son of Iapetos
Escaped his heavy anger. He knows many things,
But he is caught in the crimp of ineluctable bonds. 400

THE TITANOMACHY

When their father Ouranus first grew angry
With Obriareus, and with his brothers,
Kottos and Gyges, he clamped down on them hard.
Indignant because of their arrogant maleness,
Their looks and bulk, he made them live underground.
So there they lived in subterranean pain,
Settled at the outermost limits of earth,
Suffering long and hard, grief in their hearts.
But the Son of Kronos, and the other Immortals
Born of Rheia and Kronos, took Earth's advice 410
And led them up back into the light, for she
Told them the whole story of how with their help
They would win glorious honor and victory.

For a long time they fought, hearts bitter with toil,
Going against each other in the shock of battle,
The Titans and the gods who were born from Kronos.
The proud Titans fought from towering Othrys,
And from Olympos the gods, the givers of good
Born of rich-haired Rheia after lying with Kronos.
They battled each other with pain in their hearts 420
Continuously for ten full years, never a truce,
No respite from the hostilities on either side,
The war's outcome balanced between them.

Then Zeus gave those three all that they needed
Of ambrosia and nectar, food the gods themselves eat,
And the fighting spirit grew in their breasts
When they fed on the sweet ambrosia and nectar.
Then the father of gods and men addressed them:

"Hear me, glorious children of Earth and Heaven,
While I speak my mind. For a long time now   430
The Titans and those of us born from Kronos
Have been fighting daily for victory and dominance.
Show the Titans your strength, the invincible might
Of your hands, oppose them in this grisly conflict
Remembering our kindness. After suffering so much
You have come back to the light from your cruel dungeon,
Returned by my will from the moldering gloom."

Thus Zeus, and the blameless Kottos replied:

"Divine One, what a thing to say. We already realize
That your thoughts are supreme, your mind surpassing,   440
That you saved the Immortals from war's cold light.
We have come from under the moldering gloom
By your counsel, free at last from bonds none too gentle,
O Lord, Son of Kronos, and from suffering unlooked for.
Our minds are bent therefore, and our wills fixed
On preserving your power through the horror of war.
We will fight the Titans in the crush of battle."

He spoke, and the gods who are givers of good
Heard him and cheered, and their hearts yearned for war
Even more than before. They joined grim battle again   450
That very day, all of them, male and female alike,
The Titans and the gods who were born from Kronos,
And the three Zeus sent from the underworld to light,
Dread and strong, and arrogant with might.
A hundred hands stuck out of their shoulders,
Grotesque, and fifty heads grew on each stumpy neck.
They stood against the Titans on the line of battle
Holding chunks of cliffs in their rugged hands.
Opposite them, the Titans tightened their ranks
Expectantly. Then both sides' hands flashed with power,   460
And the unfathomable sea shrieked eerily,
The earth crashed and rumbled, the vast sky groaned
And quavered, and massive Olympos shook from its roots
Under the Immortals' onslaught. A deep tremor of feet
Reached misty Tartaros, and a high whistling noise
Of insuppressible tumult and heavy missiles
That groaned and whined in flight. And the sound

Of each side shouting rose to starry heaven,
As they collided with a magnificent battle cry.

And now Zeus no longer held back his strength.   470
His lungs seethed with anger and he revealed
All his power. He charged from the sky, hurtling
Down from Olympos in a flurry of lightning,
Hurling thunderbolts one after another, right on target,
From his massive hand, a whirlwind of holy flame.
And the earth that bears life roared as it burned,
And the endless forests crackled in fire,
The continents melted and the Ocean streams boiled,
And the barren sea. The blast of heat enveloped
The chthonian Titans, and the flame reached   480
The bright stratosphere, and the incandescent rays
Of the thunderbolts and lightning flashes
Blinded their eyes, mighty as they were,
Heat so terrible it engulfed deep Chaos.
                                        The sight of it all
And its sound to the ears was just as if broad Heaven
Had fallen on Earth: the noise of it crashing
And of Earth being crushed would be like the noise
That arose from the strife of the clashing gods.
Winds hissed through the earth, starting off tremors   490
And swept dust and thunder and flashing bolts of lightning,
The weapons of Zeus, along with the shouting and din,
Into both sides. Reverberation from the terrible strife
Hung in the air, and sheer Power shone through it.

And the battle turned. Before they had fought
Shoulder to shoulder in the crush of battle,
But then Kottos, Briareos, and Gyges rallied,
Hungry for war, in the front lines of combat,
Firing three hundred stones one after the other
From their massive hands, and the stones they shot   500
Overshadowed the Titans, and they sent them under
The wide-pathed earth and bound them with cruel bonds—
Having beaten them down despite their daring—
As far under earth as the sky is above,
For it is that far from earth down to misty Tartaros.

TARTAROS

A bronze anvil falling down from the sky
Would fall nine days and nights and on the tenth hit earth.
It is just as far from earth down to misty Tartaros.
A bronze anvil falling down from earth
Would fall nine days and nights and on the tenth hit Tartaros   510

There is a bronze wall beaten round it, and Night
In a triple row flows round its neck, while above it grow
The roots of earth and the unharvested sea.

There the Titans are concealed in the misty gloom
By the will of Zeus who gathers the clouds,
In a moldering place, the vast earth's limits.
There is no way out for them. Poseidon set doors
Of bronze in a wall that surrounds it.
There Gyges and Kottos and stouthearted Briareos
Have their homes, the trusted guards of the Storm King, Zeus.   520

There dark Earth and misty Tartaros
And the barren Sea and the starry Sky
All have their sources and limits in a row,
Grim and dank, which even the gods abhor.
The gaping hole is immense. A man could not reach bottom
In a year's time—if he ever got through the gates—
But wind after fell wind would blow him about.
It is terrible even for the immortal gods,
Eerie and monstrous. And the house of black Night
Stands forbidding and shrouded in dark blue clouds.   530

In front the son of Iapetos supports the wide sky
With his head and indefatigable hands, standing
Immobile, where Night and Day greet each other
As they pass over the great threshhold of bronze.
One goes down inside while the other goes out,
And the house never holds both inside together,
But one of them is always outside the house
And traverses the earth while the other remains
Inside the house until her journey's hour has come.
One holds for earthlings the far-seeing light;   540
The other holds Death's brother, Sleep, in her arms:
Night the destroyer, shrouded in fog and mist.
There the children of black Night have their house,
Sleep and Death, awesome gods. Never does Helios
Glowing in his rays look upon these two
When he ascends the sky or from the sky descends.
One roams the earth and the wide back of the sea,
A quiet spirit, and is gentle to humans;
The other's heart is iron, unfeeling bronze,
And when he catches a man he holds on to him.   550
He is hateful even to the immortal gods.

In front of that stand the echoing halls
Of mighty Hades and dread Persephone,
Underworld gods, and a frightful, pitiless

Hound stands guard, and he has a mean trick:
When someone comes in he fawns upon him
Wagging his tail and dropping his ears,
But he will not allow anyone to leave—
He runs down and eats anyone he catches
Leaving Persephone's and Hades' gates.   560

And there dwells a goddess loathed by the Immortals,
Awesome Styx, eldest daughter of back-flowing Ocean.
She lives in a glorious house apart from the gods,
Roofed in towering stone, surrounded on all sides
With silver columns that reach up to the sky.
Seldom does Iris, Thaumas' swift-footed daughter,
Come bearing a message over the sea's wide back.
Whenever discord and strife arise among the gods,
Or any who have homes on Olympos should lie,
Zeus sends Iris to bring the gods' great oath   570
Back from afar in a golden pitcher, the celebrated water
That trickles down cold from precipitous stone.
Far underneath the wide-pathed earth it flows
From the holy river through midnight black,
A branch of Ocean, allotted a tenth of its waters.
Nine parts circle earth and the sea's broad back
In silvery currents returning to Ocean's brine.
But one part flows from stone, woe to the gods.
If ever a god who lives on snowcapped Olympos
Pours a libation of this and breaks his oath,   580
He lies a full year without any breath,
Not a taste of ambrosia, not a sip of nectar
Comes to his lips, but he lies breathless and speechless
On a blanketed bed, an evil coma upon him.
But when the long year brings this disease to its end,
Another more difficult trial is in store,
Nine years of exile from the everlasting gods,
No converse in council or at their feasts
For nine full years. In the tenth year finally
He rejoins the Immortals in their homes on Olympos.   590
Upon this the gods swear, the primordial, imperishable
Water of Styx, and it issues from a forbidding place.

There dark Earth and misty Tartaros
And the barren Sea and the starry Sky
All have their sources and limits in a row,
Grim and dank, which even the gods abhor.
There are shining gates and a bronze threshhold,
Deeply rooted and firmly fixed, a natural
Outgrowth. Beyond and far from all the gods

The Titans dwell, past the gloom of Chaos.   600
But the famous helpers of thunderous Zeus
Inhabit houses on Ocean's deep fundaments,
Kottos and Gyges. And Briareos for his bravery
Deep-booming Poseidon made his son-in-law,
And gave him Kymopoleia in marriage.

TYPHOIOS

When Zeus had driven the Titans from heaven,
                              Earth,
Pregnant by Tartaros thanks to golden Aphrodite,
Delivered her last-born child, Typhoios,
A god whose hands were like engines of war,   610
Whose feet never gave out, from whose shoulders grew
The hundred heads of a frightful dragon
Flickering dusky tongues, and the hollow eyesockets
In the eerie heads sent out fiery rays,
And each head burned with flame as it glared.
And there were voices in each of these frightful heads,
A phantasmagoria of unspeakable sound,
Sometimes sounds that the gods understood, sometimes
The sound of a spirited bull, bellowing and snorting,
Or the uninhibited, shameless roar of a lion,   620
Or just like puppies yapping, an uncanny noise,
Or a whistle hissing through long ridges and hills.
And that day would have been beyond hope of help,
And Typhoios would have ruled over Immortals and men,
Had the father of both not been quick to notice.
He thundered hard, and the Earth all around
Rumbled horribly, and wide Heaven above,
The Sea, the Ocean, and underground Tartaros.
Great Olympos trembled under the deathless feet
Of the Lord as he rose, and Gaia groaned.   630
The heat generated by these two beings—
Scorching winds from Zeus' lightning bolts
And the monster's fire—enveloped the violet sea.
Earth, sea, and sky were a seething mass,
And long tidal waves from the immortals' impact
Pounded the beaches, and a quaking arose that would not stop.
Hades, lord of the dead below, trembled,
And the Titans under Tartaros huddled around Kronos,
At the unquenchable clamor and fearsome strife.
When Zeus' temper had peaked he seized his weapons,   640
Searing bolts of thunder and lightning,
And as he leaped from Olympos, struck. He burned
All the eerie heads of the frightful monster,
And when he had beaten it down he whipped it until

It reeled off maimed, and vast Earth groaned.
And a firestorm from the thunderstricken lord
Spread through the dark rugged glens of the mountain,
And a blast of hot vapor melted the earth like tin
When smiths use bellows to heat it in crucibles,
Or like iron, the hardest substance there is,   650
When it is softened by fire in mountain glens
And melts in bright earth under Hephaistos' hands.
So the earth melted in the incandescent flame.
And in anger Zeus hurled him into Tartaros' pit.

And from Typhoios come the damp monsoons,
But not Notos, Boreas, or silverwhite Zephyros.
These winds are godsent blessings to men,
But the others blow fitfully over the water,
Evil gusts falling on the sea's misty face,
A great curse for mortals, raging this way and that,   660
Scattering ships and destroying sailors—no defense
Against those winds when men meet them at sea.
And others blow over endless, flowering earth
Ruining beautiful farmlands of sod-born humans,
Filling them with dust and howling rubble.

ZEUS IN POWER

So the blessed gods had done a hard piece of work,
Settled by force the question of rights with the Titans.
Then at Gaia's suggestion they pressed broad-browed Zeus,
The Olympian, to be their king and rule the Immortals.
And so Zeus dealt out their privileges and rights.   670

Now king of the gods, Zeus made Metis his first wife,
Wiser than any other god, or any mortal man.
But when she was about to deliver the owl-eyed goddess
Athena, Zeus tricked her, gulled her with crafty words,
And stuffed her in his stomach, taking the advice
Of Earth and starry Heaven. They told him to do this
So that no one but Zeus would hold the title of King
Among the eternal gods, for it was predestined
That very wise children would be born from Metis,
First the grey-eyed girl, Tritogeneia,   680
Equal to her father in strength and wisdom,
But then a son with an arrogant heart
Who would one day be king of gods and men.
But Zeus stuffed the goddess into his stomach first
So she would devise with him good and evil both.

Next he married gleaming Themis, who bore the Seasons,
And Eunomia, Dike, and blooming Eirene,

Who attend to mortal men's works for them,
And the Moirai, whom wise Zeus gave honor supreme:
Klotho, Lakhesis, and Atropos, who assign   690
To mortal men the good and evil they have.

And Ocean's beautiful daughter Eurynome
Bore to him the three rose-cheeked Graces,
Aglaia, Euphrosyne, and lovely Thalia.
The light from their eyes melts limbs with desire,
One beautiful glance from under their brows.

And he came to the bed of bountiful Demeter,
Who bore white-armed Persephone, stolen by Hades
From her mother's side. But wise Zeus gave her away.

And he made love to Mnemosyne with beautiful hair,   700
From whom nine Muses with golden diadems were born,
And their delight is in festivals and the pleasures of song,

And Leto bore Apollo and arrowy Artemis,
The loveliest brood of all the Ouranians
After mingling in love with Zeus Aegisholder.

Last of all Zeus made Hera his blossoming wife,
And she gave birth to Hebe, Eileithyia, and Ares,
After mingling in love with the lord of gods and men.

From his own head he gave birth to owl-eyed Athena,
The awesome, battle-rousing, army-leading, untiring   710
Lady, whose pleasure is fighting and the metallic din of war.
And Hera, furious at her husband, bore a child
Without making love, glorious Hephaistos,
The finest artisan of all the Ouranians.

From Amphitrite and the booming Earthshaker
Mighty Triton was born, who with his dear mother
And kingly father lives in a golden palace
In the depths of the sea, an awesome divinity.

And Aphrodite bore to shield-piercing Ares
Phobos and Deimos, awesome gods who rout   720
Massed ranks of soldiers with pillaging Ares
In icy war. And she bore Harmonia also,
Whom high-spirited Kadmos made his wife.

The Atlantid Maia climbed into Zeus' sacred bed
And bore glorious Hermes, the Immortals' herald.

And Kadmos' daughter Semele bore to Zeus
A splendid son after they mingled in love,

Laughing Dionysos, a mortal woman
Giving birth to a god. But they are both divine now.

And Alkmene gave birth to the might of Herakles   730
After mingling in love with cloud-herding Zeus.

And Hephaistos the glorious Lame God married
Blossoming Aglaia, youngest of the Graces.

Gold-haired Dionysos made blond Ariadne,
Minos' daughter, his blossoming wife,
And Kronion made her deathless and ageless.

And Herakles, Alkmene's mighty son,
Finished with all his agonizing labors,
Made Hebe his bride on snowy Olympos,
Daughter of Zeus and gold-sandalled Hera.   740
Happy at last, his great work done, he lives
Agelessly and at ease among the Immortals.

. . . .

Questions for Discussion and Review

1. Describe the structure of the mythic cosmos. Define *cosmogony and cosmology.*

2. At what point in cosmic history does Hesiod begin his account of world origins?
    Define the primordial entities of Chaos, Gaea, Eros, and Tartarus. What is Hesiod's
    major purpose in composing the *Theogony?* Why do you suppose he makes Zeus a
    third-generation god? What are the implications of a universe ruled by a god who is
    neither its creator nor eternal?

3. What role do the Muses play in the poetry of myth?

4. Discuss the unusual births of Aphrodite and Athene. What are the paradoxes in-
    volved in the love goddess's birth from an act of sexual mutilation and violence?
    How is Zeus able to give birth to Athene, and why does she issue from her father's
    head? Which theories of myth are useful in interpreting these births?

5. Discuss Zeus's battles with the Titans and with Typhoeus. What role does Gaea play
    in each change of divine administration? Why does she side with sons who over-
    throw their fathers? Why does she create Zeus's most formidable opponent?

6. Why does myth attribute at least seven principal wives to Zeus? What significance
    do you give to the fact that most of his early children are personifications of abstract
    qualities? Why does Zeus feel compelled to mate with so many females, both divine
    and human? In what sense is he "father of gods and men"? Why does he wait until
    after he has defeated all his enemies before embarking on his amorous exploits?

4

Alienation of the Human and Divine: Prometheus, Fire, and Pandora

KEY TOPICS/THEMES

In the Theogony, *Hesiod traced the world's evolution from its origins to the triumph of Zeus and the divine begetting of a race of mortal heroes; in his* Works and Days, *he tells of humanity's decline from a prehistoric Age of Gold to the present Age of Iron, a downward spiral introduced by the presence of Pandora, the first woman. Created by the gods to punish mankind for Prometheus's theft of fire, Pandora, ancestress of the "race of women," allegedly subverts the masculine values of order, independence, and dominion. Although Hesiod portrays Prometheus as a mere trickster, rightly imprisoned and tormented by Zeus's ravenous eagle, later Greek poets radically reinterpreted the fallen Titan's moral significance, transforming him into a champion of human liberty courageously opposed to Zeus's tyrannical regime.*

The dual themes of dynamic change and unending conflict that pervade Hesiod's creation account also dominate his view of human history. In his second major poem, the *Works and Days,* which describes humanity's steady decline from an original Golden Age, Hesiod praises Zeus for imposing lawful order on a previously chaotic universe but laments the undeniable fact that people are now much worse off than they were under Cronus's rule. Deterioration in human society, Hesiod says, is a consequence of Zeus's personal quarrel with **Prometheus** [proh-MEE-thee-uhs], the supremely cunning Titan who maneuvered Zeus into accepting the inferior part of animal sacrifices (see Chapter 2).

Humanity's Alienation from the Gods: Prometheus and Fire

According to Hesiod, Zeus's hostility toward early mankind (woman had not yet been created) springs from two acts by Prometheus that anger Zeus while significantly benefiting mortals. First, Prometheus tricks Zeus into reserving all the edible portions of animal sacrifices for human consumption, thereby enriching the human diet at the gods' expense. The clever Titan then steals fire from heaven to give mortals the ability to cook their food, forge tools and weapons, and otherwise establish a dominion over nature that distinguishes humanity from all other creatures. Prometheus's forbidden gift to humankind is a celestial flame that ignites the spark of civilization and further narrows the gap between gods and men.

Furious at Prometheus's subversion of his authority, the newly enthroned King of Heaven chains Prometheus to a mountain crag, where at dawn an eagle, Zeus's "winged hound," arrives to rip open the Titan's body and feast on his liver (Figure 4-1). Because he is immortal, Prometheus's entrails grow back after each assault, only to be devoured again when the eagle returns.

FIGURE 4-1   The Eagle of Zeus. Portrayed as both majestic and cruel, the eagle was not only "king of the air" but also a merciless predator that swept down on helpless prey, tearing it to pieces with razor-sharp talons. In the Prometheus myth, the eagle is Zeus's "winged hound," symbolizing both the god's mastery of the atmosphere and his cruelty to the Titan who attempted to deceive him, as illustrated on this archaic cup. *(Louvre, Paris)*

The Trickster

Prevalent throughout global myth—from the wily Coyote of Native American lore to the devious Loki in Norse myth—the trickster figure is typically cunning, quick-witted, and mischievous, a character who delights in his ability to outsmart others, demonstrating an ethical ambivalence that can work for either good or evil. In Greek myth, the trickster, whether human or divine, is usually a male character who falls into one of two broad categories: he is commonly either a culture hero whose deviant actions ultimately serve to benefit humankind or a subverter of cosmic order whose chicanery results in disaster.

According to Hesiod, the trickster mentality played a crucial role in shaping the cosmos and human society. From Uranus, the primal sky god, to his son Cronus, the Titan "arch-deceiver," to Zeus, the shrewdest god of all, the successive rulers of the universe employ deception and subterfuge to achieve their ends. Fearing that his offspring would grow up to replace him, Uranus began the "ugly business" of divine manipulation by clumsily attempting to subvert Gaea's reproductive powers, stuffing Mother Earth's newborn children back inside her body.

Despite his efforts to thwart nature, however, Uranus is soon outfoxed by his even more duplicitous son Cronus, who conspires with his mother Gaea to ambush and castrate his father, rendering "starry sky" permanently impotent. Although Cronus succeeds in overthrowing Uranus, he does not learn from his predecessor's mistakes; he repeats his father's fatal error by swallowing his own children, hoping to prevent them from supplanting him. But the Titan deceiver is soon outwitted by Gaea and her granddaughter Rhea, who dupe Cronus into gulping down a stone instead of his last-born son, Zeus. Forced to regurgitate the offspring he had proved unable to assimilate, Cronus is himself defeated and imprisoned by Zeus and his allies the Hecatoncheires, hundred-handed giants whom Zeus freed from Tartarus, where Uranus had confined them. Following his victory over the Titans, Zeus performs a variation of Cronus's cannibalism by ingesting Metis, the personification of female cunning, but with a significant difference: he is able to integrate Metis's intelligence into his own being, thus ensuring that he will have greater wisdom than his forebears and be able to perpetuate his reign. As Hesiod observes, no one can outmaneuver Zeus.

Hesiod's Prometheus, however, tries to do just that, ostensibly tricking Zeus into accepting an inferior sacrifice and then stealing heavenly fire to light the altars and hearths of mortals. (Hesiod insists that Zeus was not deceived, though other mythographers argue that he was.) Although Hesiod depicts Prometheus as a gratuitous troublemaker who has no more lofty ambition than to embarrass Zeus, Aeschylus attributes a more profound motivation to the Titan's theft of fire—an altruistic desire to benefit humanity. In *Prometheus Bound,* Aeschylus emphasizes that Prometheus (whose name means "Forethought") disobeys Zeus primarily because the Titan's philanthropy (love for humanity) prompts him to interfere with Zeus's plan to replace the human race with another species. In Aeschylus's vision, Prometheus acts to save humanity not only from extinction but also from crippling ignorance, teaching humankind all the arts of civilization and thereby guaranteeing its survival. In transforming Hesiod's Prometheus from a mere trickster to a heroic rebel who champions cosmic justice, Aeschylus adds a new dimension to the ancient tradition of divine subterfuge. Aeschylus's two other plays about Prometheus, now lost, dramatized the eventual reconciliation between the Olympian and the Titan, illustrating a cosmic evolution in which Zeus's irresistible power and Prometheus's ethical compassion are at last united in a single heavenly administration. For Aeschylus, Prometheus's ingenuity and foreknowledge—his ability to foresee consequences—are crucial to both humanity's preservation and the continuation of Zeus's reign—only Prometheus knows the means by which Zeus can escape suffering the same fate as his predecessors. In time, he voluntarily confides his secret to Zeus—that if the Olympian gives in to his passion for the sea nymph Thetis, the couple will have a son greater than his father. Disciplining his lust, Zeus orders Thetis to marry the mortal Peleus; their only child is the superhuman fighter Achilles, greater than any other hero of the Trojan War.

Although Prometheus undergoes extreme suffering for having offended Zeus, he avoids the fate of his fellow Titans: permanent imprisonment in Tartarus. Unlike Cronus or any of the other male Titans, he ultimately ascends to Olympus to act as Zeus's trusted counselor, a trickster whose endurance and wisdom have redemptive value for both gods and mortals.

Considering Zeus's extreme displeasure with Prometheus, it may seem surprising that he willingly embraces another celestial trickster—Hermes—who also delights in deceiving other gods, even lying to Zeus himself (see the *Homeric Hymn to Hermes* in Chapter 6). Despite his affinity with thieves and confidence men, Hermes is very much a part of the Olympian system: he is Zeus's acknowledged son—and wise enough to refrain from challenging his father's authority, acting instead as his valued messenger and herald. A crosser of boundaries and great distances, Hermes also takes on a task for which few other Olympians have a taste: he guides the souls of the newly dead to the Underworld. As inventive as he is duplicitous, Hermes is credited with making the first lyre, thereby introducing music of unprecedented beauty to the heavenly realm. His moral ambiguity notwithstanding, Hermes, who links the divine, human, and postmortem worlds and who understands the mysteries of dreams and death, is indispensable to Zeus's reign. (See Chapter 6 for a discussion of his character and major myths.)

It is perhaps inevitable that myth's most notorious human trickster, Autolycus, is a son of Hermes. The maternal grandfather of Odysseus (through his daughter Anticleia), Autolycus earned an unenviable reputation for thievery and false dealing, stealing his neighbors' cattle and, by rendering them invisible, avoiding detection. Although he excelled in cunning, Autolycus on one occasion was outsmarted by the even more unscrupulous Sisyphus, the mythical founder of Corinth. When Sisyphus came looking for his cattle, which Autolycus had stolen, he was able to reclaim them because he had previously put a distinctive marking

(continued)

The Trickster *(continued)*

on their hooves. In some variants, Sisyphus was said to have avenged himself on Autolycus by seducing his daughter Anticleia on the eve of her wedding to Laertes, thus becoming the biological father of Odysseus. For his attempts to outwit the immortals, even Death (Thanatos) itself, Sisyphus was condemned to push a boulder uphill for all eternity, putting an end to all his intrigues (see Chapter 9 for a description of the sins of Sisyphus). Whereas Sisyphus offends the gods with his trickery, Odysseus—the most resourceful and quick-witted of all Greek heroes—consistently honors them, reserving his skill in deceit for human opponents.

In the *Iliad*, Odysseus's ruse of the Trojan Horse brings victory to the Greek forces, after ten years of open warfare between the Greeks and Trojans had resulted only in a stalemate (see Chapter 12).

In the *Odyssey*, Odysseus demonstrates a phenomenal capacity for thinking himself out of tight situations, extricating himself and his men from imprisonment in the cave of the cannibalistic Cyclops and staging a surprise attack on the suitors of his wife, Penelope, scoring a triumph even though he is outnumbered almost a hundred to one. He is, in fact, so successful a deceiver that Athene, renowned among the gods for her clever schemes, confesses that if she were a mortal she would choose to be Odysseus, a human counterpart of her own divine craftiness (*Odyssey*, Book 13; see Chapter 13). Like Hermes, who also violates many conventions, Odysseus works his ploys within the Olympian order, taking care to respect Zeus's supremacy.

Greek myth, unlike that of many other cultures, depicts gods tricking other gods (as when Athene intervenes with Zeus to aid Odysseus while his enemy Poseidon is away in Ethiopia), or humans deceiving humans (as when Clytemnestra and Medea plot vengeance on their unsuspecting husbands), but rarely shows gods tricking humans. Rather than leading mortals into divinely engineered traps, gods commonly warn humans of the dangers of deviant behavior, as when Zeus dispatches Hermes to order Clytemnestra's illicit lover, Aegisthus, not to carry out his plot to murder Agamemnon (*Odyssey*, Book 1). Does this imply that Greek mythographers felt some degree of confidence in their anthropomorphic deities, a divine–human affinity that bred trust in divine rule?

The figure of Prometheus, whom Hesiod portrays as a mere trickster who deserves the punishment Zeus inflicts on him, has a far more complex role in Greek myth than Hesiod allows him. In other traditions, Prometheus was the divinity who created man, shaping him from clay and infusing him with life. Consistently concerned with human welfare, he is also the god who warns his mortal son **Deucalion** of Zeus's plan to annihilate humanity in a global flood, directing him to build a boat so that Deucalion and his wife, **Pyrrha,** can repopulate the world after the deluge recedes. (See the section "Prometheus and Deucalion's Flood" later in the chapter.)

The most complete treatment of Prometheus's character, suffering, and motive for giving humankind the means to survive Zeus's wrath and develop a technologically advanced culture appears in the tragedy ascribed to Aeschylus, *Prometheus Bound.* Whereas Hesiod recognizes neither altruism nor nobility of spirit in the Titan who defies Zeus to aid helpless mortals, Aeschylus explores the conflict between Zeus and Prometheus in terms of a crisis in the theological evolution of the universe (see following section).

In Hesiod's vision of human prehistory, Prometheus's interference with Zeus's plans brings only woe to humankind. In the beginning, before the Titan's rebellion, men "lived like gods," mingling freely with the Olympians at their earthly banquets. Such divine–human socializing was possible because "men and gods" enjoyed a close kinship; they shared a "common descent" from the original mother, Gaea. After Prometheus gives mankind fire, however, with all its cultural benefits, Zeus determines to counteract that gift by presenting men with his own irresistible bait that will effectively spoil the Promethean enlightenment. He orders the most inventive divine artisans—Hermes, Athene, and Hephaestus—to create the first woman, **Pandora** (Figure 4-2).

In giving etiological myth a religious interpretation that explains humanity's alienation from divinity, Hesiod emphasizes an interconnection among food, sacrifice, fire, cooking, and women. Man's final banquet with the gods signals the end of an era because the introduction of fire to cook raw meat severs human ties

FIGURE 4-2   Pandora as a Mannequin. In this vase painting, the newly fashioned Pandora receives gifts from the gods (including Athene, left), who have designed her to punish mortals for having received Prometheus's gift of fire. The presence of Ares with his spear and shield (right) hints that the appearance of woman on earth will elicit many a battle between the sexes. *(British Museum, London)*

to nature. The guilt incurred in killing a fellow creature, the sacrificial ox, is compounded by (unnaturally) cooking and eating it. By contrast, Zeus's eagle, which belongs to nature and is also a symbol of the god, eats raw flesh—Prometheus's liver. The myth's division of animal sacrifice into two disparate elements adds a further ambiguity: whereas the gods inhale only the intangible scent of burnt meat, men, as physical beings, must consume corruptible flesh to survive. Pandora, who arrives on the scene too late to dine with the gods but who, presumably, will preside over the civilized art of cooking, introduces yet another force dividing mortals from gods: the unresolved tension between male and female.

Humanity's Decline: Pandora and Eve

Despite significant differences, the two most influential forces in shaping the modern Western consciousness—the Greek and Judeo-Christian traditions—agree in regarding women as the catalyst of humanity's cataclysmic decline. In both the Greek and biblical worldviews, the cosmos is run by and for a male principle of divinity regarded as simultaneously the source of and the justification for a patriarchal society on earth. In the biblical and Hesiodic cosmologies alike, a previously all-male world order crumbles into chaos almost immediately after the first female is created.

Hesiod, whose personal distrust of women everywhere colors his account, wrote two significantly different versions of Pandora's creation. In the *Theogony,* in which Pandora is not named, Hesiod implies that only two gods, Hephaestus and Athene, were responsible for manufacturing this "sheer deception, irresistible to men." In the *Works and Days,* a whole array of divine beings contributes specific qualities to fashion a complex creature of tempting beauty who also functions, paradoxically, as Zeus's "evil" curse on mankind. Hephaestus molds Pandora of "earth and water," giving her the face of a goddess, and Athene imbues her with domestic skills. Then a procession of divinities, including Aphrodite, the Graces, the Seasons, and eloquent Persuasion, equip her with attributes ranging from sexual allure to luxurious tastes—"a great infestation among mortal men." Finally, Hermes endows Pandora with "a bitchy mind and a cheating heart." A trickster figure like Prometheus, Hermes is Zeus's instrument in giving men the feminine counterpart of the inferior animal sacrifice that Prometheus had led Zeus to accept at Mekone. Like the inedible bones and hide covered with an attractive pelt that Zeus selected as his part of the divine–human arrangement, Pandora is alluring on the outside but worthless within, an economic parasite who will subvert the benefits of Promethean fire. She is Zeus's trump card in outwitting even his trickiest opponents (see Color Plate 2).

In the *Works and Days,* Hesiod's picture of many deities lavishing diverse gifts on Pandora provides the context for his interpretation of her name, which he says means "all-gifted." Many scholars believe, however, that Hesiod either inherited or created a revised version of an older myth in which Pandora was originally an earth goddess called "Giver of All." Instead of portraying her as an active embodiment of divine generosity (see Chapter 5), Hesiod makes her the passive recipient of Olympian patriarchal largesse. Other versions of the Pandora myth indicate that the jar she brings with her contained not evils but blessings. In this tradition, Zeus gives her a jarful of good things as a wedding present for her marriage to **Epimetheus**

FIGURE 4-3   Epimetheus Accepting Pandora. In this vase painting, Zeus (far left) presides over his problematic gift to humanity—the first woman. Hermes, in a characteristic winged helmet, looks to Zeus for instructions as he persuades Epimetheus (second from the right) to accept Pandora, whose presence among men will partly cancel out the benefits of the fire brought by Prometheus. Pandora's rising from the earth suggests her origin as divinely shaped clay. The figure of Eros hovering over Pandora indicates Epimetheus's motive for ignoring his brother Prometheus's warning not to accept any gift from the Olympian gods. *(Ashmolean Museum, Oxford)*

[epih-MEE-thee-uhs], who is a brother of Prometheus and whose name means "after-thought" or "hindsight" (Figure 4-3). When she inevitably opens the jar, all the blessings fly out and return to heaven, which accounts for the present predominance of negative forces on earth. All these myths agree that Pandora, according to the divine purpose, catches Hope before it can escape, retaining the quality necessary to save humankind from despair. Hesiod's narrative implies that, except for hope, the contents of Pandora's jar were completely undesirable—disease, grief, hardship, and suffering, all the miseries that now afflict humankind. Even hope, as some critics suggest, may be an evil: it provides the illusion that life will improve, inducing people to bear the more transitory evils.

Pandora's arrival on earth thus ends the original Golden Age, shatters the link between humanity and divinity, and plunges human history into an irreversible downward spiral. As the feminine agent responsible for all of our subsequent misfortunes, Pandora serves the same mythic function as Eve in the Genesis story of Eden. According to Genesis 3, a serpent persuades Eve to eat forbidden fruit, a symbol of earth's fecundity. The fruit miraculously confers "knowledge of good and evil," a phrase denoting awareness of the entire spectrum of existence, a breadth of vision hitherto the exclusive property of divine beings. The prohibited fruit is the biblical counterpart to Promethean fire, the source of enlightenment that makes civilization possible and simultaneously severs humanity's primal bond with nature (Eden) (see the following box).

Biblical Parallels to the Pandora Myth: Adam, Eve, and the Loss of Paradise

Both the Greek and the biblical traditions blame the first woman for humanity's loss of its original paradise home. In Genesis 3, the author—whom scholars identify as the Yahwist because he or she consistently uses the personal name Yahweh to denote Israel's god—appropriates some of the same ancient Near Eastern traditions that the Greeks inherited. Like Hesiod, the Yahwist assumes that man existed in an ideal environment before God created womankind. The biblical author also echoes primordial traditions in associating Eve, the primal matriarch and "mother of all those who live" (Gen. 3:20) with distinctive symbols of the divine woman—a wise serpent, the Tree of Knowledge of Good and Evil (offering a cosmic perspective), and the Tree of Life. It is Eve, and not her absent husband, to whom the serpent points out the desirability of becoming "like God."

After Eve leads the way in humanity's assertion of selfhood—and the consequent alienation from an all-controlling Deity and a childlike unity with nature—Yahweh expels Adam and Eve from Eden, the garden he had created for them to "cultivate and take care of" (Gen. 2:16). (In Mesopotamian creation myths, the gods fashion humanity for a similar purpose, to maintain the gods' temples and parks.) Furious at humanity's attainment of divine knowledge, Yahweh states that, because the "man has become one of us [Yahweh and the other divine beings who make up the heavenly council], with his knowledge of good and evil, [h]e must not be allowed to [eat] . . . from the tree of life also . . . and live for ever" (Gen. 3:22). To prevent humanity from acquiring immortality, a jealously guarded divine prerogative, Yahweh orders "cherubs" (supernatural creatures who are part-animal and part-human) to bar the gates of Eden with a flaming sword. (To compare the two disparate creation accounts in Genesis, see the box in Chapter 3.)

THE FALL OF HUMANITY (GENESIS 3:1–24)*

3 The serpent was the most subtle of all the wild beasts that Yahweh God had made. It asked the woman, "Did God really say you were not to eat from any of the trees in the garden?" The woman answered the serpent, "We may eat the fruit of the trees in the garden. But of the fruit of the tree in the middle of the garden God said, 'You must not eat it, nor touch it, under pain of death.'" Then the serpent said to the woman, "No! You will not die! God knows in fact that on the day you eat it your eyes will be opened and you will be like God, knowing good and evil." The woman saw that the tree was good to eat and pleasing to the eye, and that it was desirable for the knowledge that it could give. So she took some of its fruit and ate it. She gave some also to her husband who was with her, and he ate it. Then the eyes of both of them were opened and they realized that they were naked. So they sewed fig leaves together to make themselves loincloths.

The man and his wife heard the sound of Yahweh God walking in the garden in the cool of the day, and they hid from Yahweh God among the trees of the garden.

*From *The Jerusalem Bible*. Garden City, NY: Doubleday; London: Darton, Longman & Todd, 1966.

But Yahweh God called to the man. "Where are you?" he asked. "I heard the sound of you in the garden," he replied. "I was afraid because I was naked, so I hid." "Who told you that you were naked?" he asked. "Have you been eating of the tree I forbade you to eat?" The man replied, "It was the woman you put with me; she gave me the fruit, and I ate it." Then Yahweh God asked the woman, "What is this you have done?" The woman replied, "The serpent tempted me and I ate."

Then Yahweh God said to the serpent, "Because you have done this,

"Be accursed beyond all cattle,
all wild beasts.
you shall crawl on your belly and eat dust
every day of your life.
I will make you enemies of each other:
you and the woman,
your offspring and her offspring.
It will crush your head
and you will strike its heel."

To the woman he said:

"I will multiply your pains in childbearing,
you shall give birth to your children in pain.
Your yearning shall be for your husband,
yet he will lord it over you."

To the man he said, "Because you listened to the voice of your wife and ate from the tree of which I had forbidden you to eat,

"Accursed be the soil because of you.
With suffering shall you get your food from it
every day of your life.
It shall yield you brambles and thistles,
and you shall eat wild plants.
With sweat on your brow
shall you eat your bread,
until you return to the soil,
as you were taken from it.
For dust you are
and to dust you shall return."

The man named his wife "Eve" because she was the mother of all those who live. Yahweh God made clothes out of skins for the man and his wife, and they put them on. Then Yahweh God said, "See, the man has become like one of us, with his knowledge of good and evil. He must not be allowed to stretch his hand out next and pick from the tree of life also, and eat some and live for ever." So Yahweh God expelled him from the garden of Eden, to till the soil from which he had been taken. He banished the man, and in front of the garden of Eden he posted the cherubs, and the flame of a flashing sword, to guard the way to the tree of life.

After Eve convinces her husband to sample the fruit, the couple suddenly realize that they are naked, that unlike animals they are unprotected and open to harm—the first painful cut from knowledge's two-edged sword. In rapid succession, Eve learns of her vulnerability to the pains of childbirth and to social domination by her male partner, **Adam,** whose name means "humankind." Forced into an awareness of their inevitable deaths, the pair are expelled from paradise, because Yahweh, the biblical Creator, does not want them to rival him further. Already possessed of divine knowledge, they might also eat of the Tree of Life and live forever, giving humanity the two qualities that distinguish mortals from gods—cosmic perspective and immortality. Greek myth also associates fruit from the Tree of Life with a guardian serpent and protective goddesses (see Figure 5-6).

The Bible and Greek myth similarly blame the introduction of women for breaking the divine–human connection that prevailed when man existed alone with his patriarchal deity. Hesiod, like the author of Genesis, insists that the price humanity pays for knowledge—a dangerous and divine commodity associated with the serpentine feminine principle—is loss of innocence, loss of peace, and loss of paradise, an environment in which no long-term threats to happiness are perceived. Like the post-Edenic world of Adam and Eve, what remains in Hesiod's experience is labor, pain, and awareness of death. Despite his suspicion of women, however, even Hesiod admits that the gods' female creation is, like the male of the species, "a mixture of good and bad"—in fact, a newly minted image of the contradictory system over which Zeus presides. Unlike the Genesis author, Hesiod does not charge the first woman with violating a divine prohibition. In contrast to Eve, Pandora receives no command not to touch a forbidden object or to open her jar. Indeed, Pandora's "jar" (or womb) must be opened for her to give birth to all subsequent humanity.

When Hesiod states that Hermes endows Pandora with "lies, coaxing words, and a thievish nature," he implicitly identifies her with Zeus's first wife, Metis, the embodiment of cunning. Whereas Zeus could claim Metis's mental acuity as his own by swallowing her, the human male cannot do the same with the female, whose ability to manipulate her mate remains a threat to his sense of masculine autonomy. In a Jungian interpretation, the Hesiodic male's unwillingness or inability to value or nurture the potentially empowering feminine principle within (the anima) condemns him to an unremitting battle of the sexes.

Humanity's Alienation from Nature as the Price of Civilization

In the myths of Pandora and Eve, it is the action of a woman that disrupts humanity's primal tie to nature. Some other traditions, however, take a more positive view of women's mythic role in helping the human psyche to distinguish itself from nature's mindlessness. In the Mesopotamian story of Gilgamesh and Enkidu, the civilizing of a savage male is used to show that human culture is necessarily—and tragically—based on alienation from natural instincts. Just as the Greek gods fashion Pandora to punish man for his godlike control of fire, so the Mesopotamian gods create Enkidu, a wild, hairy, human animal, to distract and rival Gilgamesh, a powerful king whose unfocused energies disrupt the state he rules (see the box in Chapter 10).

Like Adam before he tasted the fruit of knowledge, Enkidu identifies totally with nature, running naked with wild beasts and freeing them from traps laid by city dwellers. Only after a "holy one"—a priestess of the love goddess Ishtar—awakens his sexuality and teaches him the arts of civilization does Enkidu lose his affinity with the natural world. When animals, his former companions, flee from him because, thanks to the woman, he now carries the scent of humanity, Enkidu is forced to become a part of city life. He joins Gilgamesh in a heroic campaign against the destructive aspects of nature, such as the fire monster Humbaba and the "bull of heaven," a personification of drought and earthquake.

When Gilgamesh spurns Ishtar's offer of love in favor of bonding with Enkidu, whom he loves as a second self, the outraged goddess afflicts Enkidu with a terminal sickness. On his deathbed, Enkidu bitterly curses Ishtar's priestess, a temple prostitute, for having ensnared him in the net of civilization. Hearing Enkidu's dying words, the sun god Shamash wisely reminds him that his gains from acculturation—adventure, fame, and the love of Gilgamesh—far outweigh the loss of his original status as "natural man." Enkidu then pronounces a grateful blessing on the woman who initiated him into the larger possibilities of civilized awareness.

Hesiod's failure to perceive or articulate a comparable tribute to the feminine principle, though not shared by all Greek writers, characterizes much of his culture. Greek mythology, like the patriarchal society it reflects, is essentially a male mythology. A few Greek heroes, such as Perseus and Odysseus, learn to value and assimilate feminine wisdom (see Chapters 10 and 13), but female intelligence and assertiveness, the qualities of a Clytemnestra or Medea, are typically seen as threats to male security (see Chapters 15 and 17).

The Two Natures of Strife

In a cosmos organized on the principles of male competition and conflict, one in which the gods constantly battle or conspire against each other, it is not surprising that Hesiod regarded human wars and violence as inescapable. He saw the entire cosmos as permeated with manifestations of Strife (Eris), a personification of discord that takes two distinctive forms. Although both versions are daughters of Night, an offspring of Chaos, they are not equally bad. The first Strife triggers mindless aggression, driving men to slaughter each other; the second figure of Strife is milder, inspiring healthy competition and a striving after excellence that inspires people to produce their finest work, thus benefiting the entire community.

The Five Ages of Humanity

The Age of Gold

The *Works and Days* divides human history into five distinctive periods, all but one of which (the Age of Heroes) is symbolized by a metal more valuable than that which chronologically follows it. The initial Age of Gold, synonymous with the paradise that men inhabited before woman was created, flourished when Cronus ruled the world. Hesiod includes no account of man's creation, perhaps because he regarded the primal race as autochthonous (spontaneously born from the earth). According to a variant myth Apollodorus records, Prometheus was humanity's creator, fashioning man from earth and water. Even if Hesiod was familiar with this tradition, his disdain for Prometheus as a mere trickster who was justly punished for breaking Zeus's law would explain his omitting the story.

During this Age of Gold, aboriginal men live in peace and enjoy the same freedom from toil or anxiety as the gods. Like pure gold that never decays or rusts, humans live unblemished by old age or hardship until death takes them in the gentle guise of sleep. Even after their bodies perish, their indomitable spirits roam the earth, acting as invisible protectors and helpers of later generations.

The Age of Silver

Whereas Golden Age inhabitants are peaceful, all subsequent generations are perpetrators or victims of Strife's worst manifestation: bloody war. Represented by a less pure or costly metal, the Age of Silver demonstrates Hesiod's belief that each new historical epoch is inferior to the one before it and emphasizes a marked deterioration in the human condition. This second age is characterized by extreme opposites: people take a full hundred years to mature, but after leaving their "mother's side," they live only a short time, cut off by their "lack of wits." Although enjoying a century of preparation for life, as adults they behave like fools: they are the first race the Olympians directly create, but they refuse to acknowledge or worship their creators, which prompts Zeus to order their extinction. This failed experiment does not haunt earth's surface, as do specters of the Age of Gold, but is confined beneath the earth.

The Age of Bronze

Men of the third period are created by Zeus alone, reputedly from ash trees. Commonly used to make warriors' spears, ash wood is an appropriate source for Hesiod's Bronze Age soldiers, "who didn't eat any food at all"—they are incapable of peaceful activities like agriculture—and who mindlessly pursue violent conflict. Mirroring only one aspect of Zeus—his aggressive strength—the warriors achieve mutual extermination and posthumously sink even lower than their predecessors, into the dank pit of Hades.

The Age of Heroes

The next generation, a short-lived Age of Heroes, is an exception to Hesiod's narration of inexorable decline. Described as "juster and nobler" than the races that precede or succeed them, the mortals of this age are the great heroes who fight at Troy or Thebes. Most of these soldiers, whose deeds are celebrated in the Homeric epics, manage to kill each other off in their endless wars; but Zeus carries away some of the noblest to a remote paradise where they enjoy conditions that prevailed during the vanished Golden Age. This Edenic reward, reserved exclusively for Zeus's few favorites, corresponds to Homer's Elysium (or Isles of the Blest), to which the Olympian transports his son-in-law Menelaus (see Chapter 9).

Scholars believe that Hesiod's passage about Greek heroes—to which he assigns no characteristic metal and which interrupts the otherwise consistent historical decline—was inserted into an older tradition of four regressive ages that the Greeks borrowed from ancient Near Eastern sources. The biblical Book of Daniel offers a parallel tradition in which a huge statue, composed of four different metals, symbolizes four successive historical empires. The idol has a head of gold, chest and arms of silver, belly and thighs of bronze, legs of iron, and feet of mixed iron and clay. Daniel's vision of historical decline, echoing Hesiod's older image of historical epochs as increasingly degenerative, has helped to keep the myth of humanity's post-Edenic devolution alive in some Judeo-Christian circles.

The Age of Iron

The fifth and final epoch, that in which the poet and his audience lived, is the brutal Age of Iron. The least precious and most harsh metal, iron effectively symbolizes the hardness of heart that distinguishes the petty kings who economically exploit the class of impoverished small farmers and shepherds to which Hesiod belonged. The situation will only worsen, for Zeus already plans to wipe out the present generation as he had its forebears. Increasing signs of degeneracy will mark the end's approach: life will be so unbearable that even newborn infants will have gray hair. Natural affection among family members will disappear, and the normal social order will be reversed, with good men punished and evil rewarded. Qualities, such as Shame, that now hold wickedness in check, will flee in horror to Olympus, abandoning humanity to misery and grief.

Hesiod's view of history arbitrarily divided into five epochs of intensifying decline is essentially apocalyptic: he assumes not merely one end of the world—the doom rapidly overtaking the present system—but four earlier, divinely ordained mass extinctions. The gods thoroughly eradicate each successive race, allowing no survivors of one era to found the next and preventing any normal historical continuity. Human history, which flows inevitably toward the abyss, is thus a painful lesson teaching mortals that "there's just no way you can get around the mind of Zeus" (Figure 4-4).

Aeschylus's Transformation of the Prometheus Myth and Humanity's Salvation

Whereas Hesiod depicted Prometheus, the thief of heavenly fire, as a wily trickster whose attempts to outwit Zeus are appropriately punished, the Athenian dramatist Aeschylus (c. 525–456 B.C.) transformed Hesiod's crafty Titan into a heroic rebel who defies Zeus for largely altruistic reasons and who suffers willingly to benefit humanity. Although he borrows his subject from Hesiod, Aeschylus shows a radically different attitude toward both Zeus and Prometheus. Turning Hesiod's theology on its head, the playwright transforms the Titan into a champion of freedom and Zeus into a despot who rules without law, justice, or mercy.

In his *Prometheus Bound*, Aeschylus does not portray Zeus as the embodiment of cosmic justice whom Plato revered as "the god of gods, who rules according to law." Instead, the dramatist imagines Zeus as he may have been at the beginning of his reign—a force of raw power untempered by wisdom or compassion (Figure 4-5). Because this morally infantile Zeus is neither omnipotent (all-powerful)

FIGURE 4-4   Zeus Holding a (Vanished) Thunderbolt. Although the guarantor of universal justice, Zeus paradoxically rules over an imperfect human world typified by war and aggression. Hesiod views human history as an ever-downward spiral from an original Golden Age, which ended with two crucial events: the Promethean domestication of fire, source of all subsequent culture, and Zeus's introduction of women, the source of all men's domestic misery, into human society. *(Vatican Museums, Rome)*

FIGURE 4-5 Zeus and the Eagle. In his *Prometheus Bound,* Aeschylus portrays heaven's king as a despot and his imperial eagle, which he will send to devour the rebel Titan's liver, as a cruel agent of tyranny, as shown in this Roman statue of the Olympian king. Whereas Hesiod had depicted Prometheus as a wily trickster who deserved his punishment, Aeschylus transformed the myth by making Prometheus a savior of humankind, without whose gift of celestial fire, the symbol of all culture and technology, humanity could not have avoided the extinction that Zeus planned for it. *(Villa Albani, Rome)*

nor omniscient (all-knowing), he is vulnerable to fatal error. As Hyginus, an astronomer of the second century A.D., observed, "Zeus [when tricked by Prometheus] did not act with the brains of a god, nor did he foresee everything, as befits a god."

The Question of Authorship

Although most scholars attribute *Prometheus Bound* to the tragedian Aeschylus, some critics, such as Mark Griffith, question Aeschylean authorship of the play, ascribing it to another hand, perhaps that of Euphorion, a son of Aeschylus who was also a dramatist (see the Selected Bibliography at the end of the book). Certainly, *Prometheus Bound*'s highly critical portrait of Zeus differs sharply from Aeschylus's portrayal of a wise and just Zeus in the *Oresteia* (see Chapter 15). Because only six (or seven) of Aeschylus's ninety plays survive, however, it is impossible to be absolutely sure that the playwright did not, for dramatic effect, vary his picture of Zeus from play to play.

An Evolving Universe

In this text, we take the traditional view that *Prometheus Bound* is the first part of an Aeschylean trilogy, a series of three thematically related plays intended to be performed sequentially in a single day. The other two dramas, *Prometheus Unbound* and *Prometheus the Fire-Carrier,* exist only in fragments, primarily in citations from later writers. Enough references to the lost plays remain, however, to suggest that the conflict in *Prometheus Bound* represents the painful beginning of a complex evolutionary process in which Zeus—perhaps by developing qualities appropriate to divinity—eventually reconciles with the rebel Titan.

Although the means of their reconciliation is not specified, it appears that Aeschylus follows a tradition in which Zeus releases Prometheus from the mountain peak on which he has been impaled. According to Hesiod's version of the myth, Zeus permits his mortal son Heracles to kill the eagle that repeatedly shreds Prometheus's liver, chiefly to enhance Heracles' reputation. For Aeschylus, however, the god's change of heart is more significant: his evolving Zeus at last comes to value the Titan's superior wisdom and insight. By the end of the third play, we may assume that Zeus has not only liberated his former enemy but also sponsored his ascension to Olympus, where Prometheus is honored as the divine "fire-carrier." Making the wise Titan his heavenly companion, Zeus, in effect, restages his swallowing of Metis, assimilating the Promethean qualities that will equip him to rule wisely and thereby perpetuate his reign.

Prometheus and Humanity

In *Prometheus Bound,* however, Zeus's evolutionary growth has only begun: the godhead is divided, causing divine power (Zeus) to war against divine intelligence (Prometheus). The play opens with Zeus's henchmen, the unwilling Hephaestus and the allegorical figures of Might and Violence (the qualities by which Zeus then ruled), driving iron spikes through the Titan's flesh, immobilizing him on a barren crag. Silent during his mutilation, Prometheus later reveals that he stole fire not

FIGURE 4-6   The Creation of Man. In this densely figured scene carved on a Roman sarcophagus, Prometheus (seated, slightly left of center) acts like a divine potter, fashioning from clay the body of the first man, whose head he cradles on his lap. In a parallel to the birth of Athene (see Figure 1-2), the Olympians gather to observe humanity's creation. The gods' presence, crowding about the as-yet unconscious form, suggests that the new creature will be endowed with divine qualities that each deity represents. Although Aeschylus does not explicitly refer to this aspect of the Prometheus myth, he closely identifies the god with humanity, for whose cause Prometheus endures Zeus's wrath. *(National Museum, Naples)*

merely to defy Zeus but to rescue humanity from extinction. Zeus had planned to allow the human race to perish in ignorance and darkness, but Prometheus, feeling pity for helpless mortals, gave them fire and taught them the arts and skills of civilization, raising humanity from savagery to a consciousness of its potential.

Although Aeschylus—at least in this one surviving play—does not cite the tradition making Prometheus humanity's creator (Figure 4-6), he emphasizes the almost complete identification between the Titan and the race for whose benefit he suffers. As the nineteenth-century English romantic poet Percy Bysshe Shelley realized in his version of *Prometheus Unbound,* the suffering Titan is an image of the human mind, which, despite its physical bondage to oppressive rulers, remains free in thought to explore the vast universe and to contemplate its eventual liberation.

Complexities and Functions of the Prometheus Myth

Savior and Rebel

The tension between Zeus the despot and Zeus the future promulgator of justice is paralleled in the ambiguity of Prometheus's dual role as rebel and savior. From a human viewpoint, the Titan is a redeemer who endures unspeakable pain for the sake of mortals, whose continued existence he makes possible. From Zeus's perspective, however, he is a lawbreaker whose arrogance must be punished. As a savior figure who subverts divine authority, Prometheus reflects the Greeks' ambivalence toward individualism: although the intrinsic value of the individual was an indispensable component of Greek humanism, it was also recognized that extreme assertion of

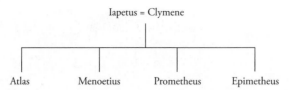

FIGURE 4-7   The Genealogy of Prometheus. According to Hesiod, Prometheus is the son of the Titans Iapetus and Clymene and the brother of Atlas—whom Zeus condemns to hold up the vault of the sky—and Epimetheus (Afterthought), a dimwit who accepts Pandora on behalf of mankind. Aeschylus, however, makes Prometheus (Forethought) a son of Themis, whom the playwright implicitly identifies with the earth goddess, Gaea, thus associating the rebel Titan with an aspect of earth's primal and prophetic powers. Although Prometheus had used his intelligence to help Zeus overthrow the Titans, in *Prometheus Bound* he must use it to maintain universal absolutes of justice and freedom, principles that Zeus's despotism threatens to obliterate.

individual rights can disrupt the public order. Individual rebels, even when championing a just cause, can collide destructively with legitimate authority, damaging both themselves and the state (see the discussion of Antigone's defiance of state law in Chapter 16). Some commentators suggest, in fact, that the play juxtaposes two equally plausible versions of the right: Zeus as established authority, to which appropriate deference must be paid, and Prometheus as the force of conscience and critical intelligence, which has an ethical obligation to oppose oppressive authority.

In Aeschylus's reinterpretation of the Prometheus myth, both Zeus and Prometheus can plausibly justify their respective positions, but it is the passage of slow time, with its potential for contemplative growth and ripened insight, that ultimately reconciles these polar opposites. After long eons, Zeus's political might and Prometheus's ethical right at last converge, bringing together king and rebel—uniting them in the Olympian council.

According to Hesiod, Prometheus is a second-generation Titan, the son of Iapetus and Clymene (Figure 4-7). Aeschylus, however, makes him the child of Themis, whom he implicitly identifies with Gaea, the Earth Mother, generator of gods and primeval source of justice. As a masculine counterpart to wise-counseling Gaea, Themis, and Athene, Prometheus attracts the loyalty of Ocean's daughters, who compose the chorus, a group of singers and dancers who comment on (and often judge) the characters and actions in a Greek play. In *Prometheus Bound,* the chorus is torn between sympathy for the hero's suffering and horror at the example of divine retribution he represents. When Prometheus refuses to submit to Zeus and thus end his pain, his obstinacy provokes the chorus to charge that he "misses the mark" of wise self-interest.

The word Aeschylus and other tragedians use to denote a character's tragic error is **hamartia**, a term drawn from archery that means "missing the mark." Although this is the same word translated as "sin" in English versions of the New Testament, it can apply to any quality or action, such as a mistake in judgment or even an excess of righteousness, that results in failure to hit the target of divine approval. In the chorus's pragmatic view, Prometheus's extreme ethical autonomy displays **hubris,** the blinding pride that typically afflicts the tragic hero (see Chapters 14 and 15).

FIGURE 4-8　Atlas and Prometheus. The brutality with which Zeus enforces his rule is vividly rendered in this archaic Spartan cup depicting two Titan brothers (c. 555 B.C.). The giant Atlas endures back-breaking pain, his shoulders bent against the weight of the heavenly vault he is condemned forever to support. Facing him while suffering even worse agony is Prometheus, whose flesh is being ripped by the beak and talons of Zeus's hungry eagle. Aeschylus's Prometheus can escape this repeated vivisection if he submits to Zeus's authority, an option he rejects because it means accepting his oppressor's right to enslave bodies and control minds. *(Vatican Museum, Rome)*

At the same time, Aeschylus makes it clear that Prometheus willingly bears excruciating pain because his is the last free mind in the universe, the sole remaining consciousness that can distinguish between absolutes of good and evil (Figure 4-8). To corrupt his awareness by conforming to Zeus's demands would be to extinguish the light that he had brought to earth. In this respect, Prometheus's intellectual honesty—a virtue—is the quality that occasions his suffering.

Io: A Victim of Zeus's Despotism

Two important scenes help convey Aeschylus's purpose in his startling reinterpretation of the Prometheus myth. The first introduces **Io**, a young woman driven almost insane by a stinging gadfly that Hera jealously sends to plague her. Unlike Prometheus, who has deliberately disobeyed Zeus, Io is merely an innocent victim of the despot's lust. Io's case illustrates the fate of vulnerable humanity when no restraints on a despot's whim exist. Her appearance near the middle of the play is particularly damning to the Olympian ruler: the bully who rapes her is too cowardly to protect Io from his wife's irrational fury. Both the King and Queen of Heaven are chillingly indifferent to the suffering they cause.

In the climactic episode, Hermes, portrayed as the swaggering emissary of a military junta, appears to announce the torments that Zeus will soon inflict on Prometheus. Ocean's daughters, who had earlier begged Prometheus to give up his resistance, now reject Hermes' advice to abandon the Titan. The chorus, which typically voices a mediating position between the tragic extremes of two battling opponents, unanimously decides to take Prometheus's side, even if it means sharing his punishment. Led by the chorus's example, the audience is confronted with a choice between seemingly irresistible power and helpless principle and is asked to opt for the latter.

The Secret: Only Prometheus Can Save Zeus

In Aeschylus's ironic vision, Prometheus's defiance of Zeus's injustice gives the Olympian an opportunity to save himself from the fate of his predecessors, Uranus and Cronus. Prometheus alone knows the cause of Zeus's future downfall—the Olympian's sexual hunger will drive him to beget (by the sea nymph Thetis) a son strong enough to displace him (see Chapter 12). In the lost plays, Prometheus voluntarily confides this secret to Zeus, rescuing the god from destruction by his own untamed impulses.

In turn, as Hermes prophesies, Prometheus will benefit from the redemptive act of a god willing to die for him. Although Aeschylus does not identify the deity who will sacrifice himself for Prometheus, Apollodorus states that this expiatory role is filled by the centaur Chiron (Figure 4-9). According to Apollodorus, when he is wounded by one of Heracles' poisoned arrows, Chiron suffers such exquisite agony that he is eager to die, and in perishing he somehow bestows his immortality on Prometheus. Because the Titan is already immortal, however, it is difficult to see how Chiron's vicarious sacrifice can benefit him. As Mark Griffith suggests, Hermes' prophecy may refer to either Chiron or Heracles, who not only frees Prometheus but also, as his final "labor," descends into the Underworld to fetch Cerberus (see Chapters 9 and 10).

Although Zeus finally accepts Prometheus among the Olympian immortals, one tradition states that, because he had sworn by the River Styx (a symbol of the gods' unbreakable oaths) that the Titan would never be released from his rock, Zeus forces Prometheus to wear a steel ring to which a fragment of the rock is attached. Prometheus is thus forever bound to a tangible reminder of Zeus's superior authority.

Scenes from *Prometheus Bound* are included after passages from the *Works and Days*.

Prometheus and Deucalion's Flood

Just as some traditions make Prometheus the divine potter who created humankind (in his image?), so others similarly portray him as humanity's savior when Zeus drowned the world in a flood. According to Aeschylus, Prometheus's theft of fire

FIGURE 4-9 Chiron. Wisest of the centaurs, Chiron instructs the young Achilles in playing the lyre. A son of Cronus and Philyra, daughter of Ocean, Chiron belongs to the generation of Zeus. He is famous for his kindness to humans, helping to bring up such heroes as Jason and Asclepius. According to Apollodorus, when Aeschylus states that Prometheus must suffer until another god is willing to die for him, he refers to Chiron, who was accidentally struck by one of Heracles' arrows, which inflicted an incurable wound. In unrelenting agony, Chiron gives his immortality to Prometheus (who in Apollodorus's version of the myth was apparently born mortal), thus providing a vicarious atonement for the Titan. Zeus then places Chiron in the sky as the constellation Centaurus. *(National Museum, Naples)*

originally was prompted by Zeus's early resolve to eliminate humanity and replace it with a new race. When the Titan's additional gifts to men—teaching the arts of civilization, such as architecture, writing, agriculture, and the domestication of animals—kept humanity from dying out through ignorance and poverty, Zeus then unleashed a global deluge to rid earth of its human population. Again, the quick-witted Titan subverted Zeus's intentions, warning his mortal son **Deucalion** and Deucalion's wife, **Pyrrha,** of Zeus's plan and instructing them to build a boat, thus ensuring humanity's survival. According to Apollodorus's *Library* and Ovid's *Metamorphoses* (see Chapter 20), after the floodwaters recede, an oracle from Themis, the wise mother of Prometheus, commands the pair to repopulate the world by casting the bones of their mother. Recognizing the earth, Gaea, as their maternal parent, Deucalion and Pyrrha obey the oracle by tossing fragments of earth's "bones" (rocks) over their shoulders. The stones that Deucalion throws become men, while those that Pyrrha throws become women—a tale reiterating the Hesiodic tradition that both gods and mortals are descendants of a common ancestor, the earth.

Like Hesiod's tale of succeeding generations of warring gods in the *Theogony,* the Greek myth of Deucalion's flood is a revised version of older Mesopotamian lore. Ancient Sumerian and Babylonian texts refer to a deluge in which the gods wiped out all of humanity except for one family, which survived by building an ark (rectangular wooden chest) to ride out the catastrophe. Detailed accounts of the disaster appear in the *Atrahasis Epic* and the *Epic of Gilgamesh,* which influenced not only the Greeks but also the authors of Genesis, who preserve the most famous version of this ancient Near Eastern story.

Perhaps one of the most significant parallels between the Gilgamesh flood narrative and that of Deucalion is the opposing roles played by two different gods, one of whom brings the disaster and the other of whom saves humanity by secretly warning a human favorite of the imminent danger. In the Gilgamesh epic, Enlil, the irritable god of storm, determines to exterminate humanity by flooding the earth. But Ea, the god of wisdom and a friend to humanity, warns a worthy individual, Utnapishtim (the Babylonian Noah), of the coming disaster. Following Ea's instructions to construct an ark and fill it with all kinds of animals, Utnapishtim and his wife survive the world's return to a watery chaos. When the flood is over and his ark is grounded on a mountaintop (the peak is Ararat in the biblical tale and Parnassus in the Greek), Utnapishtim sends out birds to find dry land; eventually, he leaves the ark to help repeople the earth. His most celebrated descendant is the hero Gilgamesh, a slayer of monsters and explorer of earth's remotest regions (see Chapter 10).

In Genesis, the three sons of Noah become the progenitors of all branches of the human race known to the early biblical writers, with Seth identified as the ancestor of the Semitic peoples, including Israel, and Japheth (Javen) the ultimate forebear of the Greeks. In the Greek adaptation of this Mesopotamian myth, Deucalion and Pyrrha (without throwing stones) produce Hellen, the eponymous ancestor (the person from whom a group reputedly takes its name) of the Greeks. In Hellen's honor, the historical Greeks called themselves **Hellenes** [HEL-lee-neez] and their country **Hellas** [HEL-luhs].

Traditions about humanity's decline from a lost Golden Age, evoked in Hesiod's *Works and Days,* as well as the stories of Prometheus's deeds and Deucalion's flood, provided the ancient Greeks with a mythic past that serves the purpose of history. In employing ancient tales to justify retroactively the values and practices of Hellenic society, including the tensions involved in gender inequality and other forms of social inequity, Hesiod and other storytellers leave many important questions unanswered. The tension between Hesiod's admiration for Zeus and his uncomfortable awareness that the god is largely responsible for humanity's miseries in the present Age of Iron goes unresolved. Three centuries after Hesiod's time, however, Aeschylus creatively reinterpreted the mythic conflict between Zeus, Prometheus, and the mortals whom Prometheus loved to explore further the issues of divine justice, individual freedom, and humanity's possible future in a fitfully evolving universe.

WORKS AND DAYS*

Hesiod

Muses of the sacred spring Pieria   1
Who give glory in song,
Come sing Zeus' praises, hymn your great Father
Through whom mortals are either
Renowned or unknown, famous or unfamed
As goes the will of great Zeus.
Easy for Him to build up the strong
And tear the strong down.
Easy for Him to diminish the mighty
And magnify the obscure.   10
Easy for Him to straighten the crooked
And wither the proud,

Zeus the Thunderer
Whose house is most high.

Bend hither your mind,
Hand down just judgments,
O Thou!

And as for me,
Well, brother Perses,
I'd like to state a few facts.   20

TWO KINDS OF STRIFE

It looks like there's not just one kind of Strife—
That's Eris—after all, but two on the Earth.
You'd praise one of them once you got to know her,
But the other's plain blameworthy. They've just got
Completely opposite temperaments.
One of them favors war and fighting. She's a mean cuss
And nobody likes her, but everybody honors her,
This ornery Eris. They have to: it's the gods' will.

The other was born first though. Ebony Night
Bore her, and Kronos' son who sits high in thin air   30
Set her in Earth's roots, and she's a lot better for humans.
Even shiftless folks she gets stirred up to work.
When a person's lazing about and sees his neighbor
Getting rich, because he hurries to plow and plant

---

*Translation by Stanley Lombardo.

And put his homestead in order, he tends to compete
With that neighbor in a race to get rich.

Strife like this does people good.

So potter feuds with potter
And carpenter with carpenter,
Beggar is jealous of beggar   40
And poet of poet.

Now, Perses, you lay these things up in your heart
And don't let the mischief-loving Eris keep you from work,
Spending all your time in the market eyeballing quarrels
And listening to lawsuits. A person hasn't any business
Wasting time at the market unless he's got a year's supply
Of food put by, grain from Demeter out of the ground.
When you've got plenty of that, you can start squabbling
Over other people's money.
                                 Not that you're going to get   50
Another chance with me. Let's settle this feud right now
With the best kind of judgment, a straight one from Zeus.
We had our inheritance all divided up, then you
Made off with most of it, playing up to those
Bribe-eating lords who love cases like this.
Damn fools. Don't know the half from the whole,
Or the real goodness in mallows and asphodel.

WHY LIFE IS HARD

You know, the gods never have let on
How humans might make a living. Else,
You might get enough done in one day   60
To keep you fixed for a year without working.
You might just hang your plowshare up in the smoke,
And all the fieldwork done by your oxen
And hard-working mules would soon run to ruin.
But Zeus got his spleen up, and went and hid
How to make a living, all because shifty Prometheus
Tricked him. That's why Zeus made life hard for humans.
He hid fire. But that fine son of Iapetos stole it
Right back out from under Zeus' nose, hiding
The flame in a fennel stalk. And thundering Zeus   70
Who rides herd on the clouds got angry and said:

"Iapetos' boy, if you're not the smartest of them all!
I bet you're glad you stole fire and outfoxed me.
But things will go hard for you and for humans after this.
I'm going to give them Evil in exchange for fire,
Their very own Evil to love and embrace."

That's what he said, the Father of gods and men,
And he laughed out loud. Then he called Hephaistos
And told him to hurry and knead some earth and water
And put a human voice in it, and some strength,   80
And to make the face like an immortal goddess' face
And the figure like a beautiful, desirable virgin's.
Then he told Athene to teach her embroidery & weaving,
And Aphrodite golden to spill grace on her head
And painful desire and knee-weakening anguish.
And he ordered the quicksilver messenger, Hermes,
To give her a bitchy mind and a cheating heart.
That's what he told them, and they listened to Lord Zeus,
Kronos' son. And right away famous old Gimpy
Plastered up some clay to look like a shy virgin   90
Just like Zeus wanted, and the Owl-Eyed Goddess
Got her all dressed up, and the Graces divine
And Lady Persuasion put some gold necklaces
On her skin, and the Seasons (with their long, fine hair)
Put on her head a crown of springtime flowers.
Pallas Athena put on the finishing touches,
And the quicksilver messenger put in her breast
Lies and wheedling words and a cheating heart,
Just like rumbling Zeus wanted. And the gods' own herald
Put a voice in her, and he named that woman   100
Pandora, because all the Olympians donated something,
And she was a real pain for human beings.

When this piece of irresistible bait was finished,
Zeus sent Hermes to take her to Epimetheus
As a present, and the speedy messenger-god did it.
Epimetheus didn't think on what Prometheus had told him,
Not to accept presents from Olympian Zeus but to send any
Right back, in case trouble should come of it to mortals.
No, Epimetheus took it, and after he had the trouble
Then he thought on it.   110
                          Because before that the human race
Had lived off the land without any trouble, no hard work,
No sickness or pain that the Fates give to men
(And when men are in misery they show their age quickly).
But the woman took the lid off the big jar with her hands
And scattered all the miseries that spell sorrow for men.
Only Hope was left there in the unbreakable container,
Stuck under the lip of the jar, and couldn't fly out:
The woman clamped the lid back on the jar first,
All by the plan of the Aegisholder, cloud-herding Zeus.   120
But ten thousand or so other horrors spread out among men,
The earth is full of evil things, and so's the sea.

Diseases wander around just as they please, by day and by night,
Soundlessly, since Zeus in his wisdom deprived them of voice.
There's just no way you can get around the mind of Zeus.

If you want, I can sum up another tale for you,
Neat as you please. The main point to remember
Is that gods and humans go back a long way together.

THE FIVE AGES

Golden was the first race of articulate folk
Created by the immortals who live on Olympos.   130
They actually lived when Kronos was king of the sky,
And they lived like gods, not a care in their hearts,
Nothing to do with hard work or grief,
And miserable old age didn't exist for them.
From fingers to toes they never grew old,
And the good times rolled. And when they died
It was like sleep just ravelled them up.
They had everything good. The land bore them fruit
All on its own, and plenty of it too. Cheerful folk,
They did their work peaceably and in prosperity,   140
With plenty of flocks, and they were dear to the gods.
And sure when Earth covered over that generation
They turned into holy spirits, powers above ground,
Invisible wardens for the whole human race.
They roam all over the land, shrouded in mist,
Tending to justice, repaying criminal acts
And dispensing wealth. This is their royal honor.

Later, the Olympians made a second generation,
Silver this time, not nearly so fine as the first,
Not at all like the gold in either body or mind.   150
A child would be reared at his mother's side
A hundred years, just a big baby, playing at home.
And when they finally did grow up and come of age
They didn't live very long, and in pain at that,
Because of their lack of wits. They just could not stop
Hurting each other and could not bring themselves
To serve the Immortals, nor sacrifice at their altars
The way men ought to, wherever and whenever. So Zeus,
Kronos' son, got angry and did away with them
Because they weren't giving the Blessed Gods their honors.   160
And when Earth had covered over that generation—
Blessed underground mortals is what they are called,
Second in status, but still they have their honor—
Father Zeus created a third generation
Of articulate folk, **Bronze** this time, not like

The silver at all, made them out of ash trees,
Kind of monstrous and heavy, and all they cared about
Was fighting and war. They didn't eat any food at all.
They had this kind of hard, untameable spirit.
Shapeless hulks. Terrifically strong. Grapplehook hands   170
Grew out of their shoulders on thick stumps of arms,
And they had bronze weapons, bronze houses,
And their tools were bronze. No black iron back then.
Finally they killed each other off with their own hands
And went down into the bone-chilling halls of Hades
And left no names behind. Astounding as they were,
Black Death took them anyway, and they left the sun's light.

So Earth buried that generation too,
And Zeus fashioned a fourth race
To live off the land, juster and nobler,   180
The divine race of **Heroes,** also called
Demigods, the race before the present one.
They all died fighting in the great wars,
Some at seven-gated Thebes, Kadmos' land,
In the struggle for Oidipous' cattle,
And some, crossing the water in ships,
Died at Troy, for the sake of beautiful Helen.
And when Death's veil had covered them over
Zeus granted them a life apart from other men,
Settling them at the ends of the Earth.   190
And there they live, free from all care,
In the Isles of the Blest, by Ocean's deep stream,
Blessed heroes for whom the life-giving Earth
Bears sweet fruit ripening three times a year.

[Far from the Immortals, and Kronos is their king,
For the Father of gods and men has released him
And he still has among them the honor he deserves.
Then the fifth generation: Broad-browed Zeus
Made still another race of articulate folk
To people the plentiful Earth.]   200
                                        I wish

I had nothing to do with this fifth generation,
Wish I had died before or been born after,
Because this is the **Iron Age.**
                        Not a day goes by
A man doesn't have some kind of trouble.
Nights too, just wearing him down. I mean
The gods send us terrible pain and vexation.
Still, there'll be some good mixed in with the evil,
And then Zeus will destroy this generation too,   210

Soon as they start being born grey around the temples.
Then fathers won't get along with their kids anymore,
Nor guests with hosts, nor partner with partner,
And brothers won't be friends, the way they used to be.
Nobody'll honor their parents when they get old
But they'll curse them and give them a hard time,
Godless rascals, and never think about paying them back
For all the trouble it was to raise them.
They'll start taking justice into their own hands,
Sacking each other's cities, no respect at all   220
For the man who keeps his oaths, the good man,
The just man. No, they'll keep all their praise
For the wrongdoer, the man who is violence incarnate,
And shame and justice will lie in their hands.
Some good-for-nothing will hurt a decent man
Slander him, and swear an oath on top of it.
Envy will be everybody's constant companion,
With her foul mouth and hateful face, relishing evil.
And then

>   up to Olympos from the wide-pathed Earth,   230
>   lovely apparitions wrapped in white veils,
>   off to join the Immortals, abandoning humans

There go **Shame** and **Nemesis.** And horrible suffering
Will be left for mortal men, and no defense against evil.

PROMETHEUS BOUND*
Aeschylus

[The reluctant Hephaestus, following Zeus's orders, has chained the rebel Titan to an isolated mountain crag, where the daughters of Ocean (forming the dramatic chorus) have come to sympathize with Prometheus in his agony. In the following speech, Prometheus—the most intelligent of the Titan generation—explains to the choral leader why he decided to help Zeus defeat the Titans, a debt that Zeus has repaid with unprecedented cruelty. Prometheus adds that he disobeyed the new cosmic ruler to protect humanity, whom Zeus intended to exterminate.]

Prometheus
Yes, [Zeus] is harsh, and a law to himself, I know it. And yet, crushed on this   1
    anvil, his heart shall be made malleable, till at last, when his age-long rage
    is at rest, we shall pledge our reconciliation.

Leader
Reveal it all. Explain from the beginning
What was the accusation on which Zeus
Seized you and inflicted this fearful ignominy.
If it is safe, let us hear the whole story.

Prometheus
To speak is painful. Silence is painful too.
I have no choice but misery either way.
When civil war flared up among the immortals,
Some plotting to throw Kronos out of heaven
And set Zeus up, while others were determined   10
That come what might Zeus shouldn't be their master,
The Titans, deaf to all my appeals for cunning
Trusted in a swift victory by force.
In vain I told them how my mother, Earth,
Whose vision had prefigured the world's future,
Had often warned me that skill in stratagem
Alone could win the upper hand in heaven.
They wouldn't hear of it, and so I decided
In concert with my mother to lend my aid
Where it was asked for, on the side of Zeus,   20
Who thus supported hurled old Kronos down
With all his great Titan confederates
Into the pitch-black dungeons of Tartarus.
These services the new emperor of heaven,

---

*Translation by George Thomson.

135

Infected like all tyrants with suspicion
Of his best friends, has rewarded as you see.
Now to your question of the charge against me.
Having usurped his father's throne, he invested
The Gods with dignities, ranks, offices,
And all the perquisites of authority,   30
But to humanity, whose wretchedness
Cried for relief, gave nothing. He intended
To leave mankind to perish. Only I
Had the courage to oppose him. I defied him.
I dared to save man from annihilation.
That was his pretext for the agony
That moves your sympathy and extorts my groans.
I pitied man more than myself, yet I
Am barred from pity, tortured mercilessly,
A monument to the perfidy of Zeus.   40

Leader
Iron has no feeling, there's no heart in stones.
All other natures cannot but dissolve
Like mine, Prometheus, to see what I see now.

Prometheus
Yes, I enjoy the pity of my friends.

Leader
Was that the whole of the evidence against you?

Prometheus
I saved man from remembering he's mortal.

Leader
What opiate could dull the thought of death?

Prometheus
Blind hope. In the human mind I settled hope.

Leader
Ah, what a great gift you have endowed him with!

Prometheus
And more than that, I provided him with fire.   50

Leader
What, is humanity now equipped with fire?

Prometheus
Yes, they use fire, and fire shall teach them arts.

Leader
Ah, this then is the accusation on which Zeus—

Prometheus
Yes, crushes me with interminable wrongs.

Leader
Is there no end set to your punishment?

Prometheus
No end, until *he* thinks it time to end it.

Leader
When will he? Oh what hope? Can you not see
You have sinned? Forgive me, to reproach you with it
Offends you and so pains me. Let us forget it
And seek somehow some means to your release.   60

Prometheus
Advice comes easily from one whose own
Feet are well out of the mire. All this I knew
From the beginning. I sinned deliberately.
I had to suffer for delivering mankind.
And yet I did not think the penalty
Would be so bitter as this solitude,
This creeping wastage in the barren hills.

. . . .

[In this next scene, Prometheus informs the chorus that he gave humanity much more than the gift of fire—he also taught humans the arts and technologies of civilization, enabling them to rise above the primal savagery to which Zeus had relegated them. From the development of logical reasoning to the invention of the alphabet, the gifts of Prometheus brought both mental enlightenment and increasing control over nature to humankind. He even gave them "blind hope," an attribute ordinarily associated with Pandora's jar, thereby imparting a conviction that humans will not only survive but eventually assume godlike mastery of their environment.

At a moment when the chorus, despairing over the Titan's prolonged suffering, is ready to urge him to end his pain by submitting to Zeus, the figure of Io appears. A young girl whom Zeus had brutally seduced and then abandoned to his wife's jealous vengeance—she is driven mad by the stings of a huge gadfly—Io begs Prometheus (whose name means "Forethought") to reveal her future. After foretelling her long wanderings throughout the earth, Prometheus predicts that a kinder Zeus will eventually come to her, in Egypt, with a "gentle touch," begetting a mortal hero and ending her afflictions.]

Prometheus
It is not pride or obstinacy that has prompted
My silence, but the bitter consciousness
Of what I have done to merit such maltreatment.   70
Who was it after all that first appointed
Their several powers for these new divinities?
You have heard that story and I will say no more,

But now listen to the sufferings of mankind,
In whom, once speechless, senseless, like an infant,
I have implanted the faculty of reason.
I speak of man not to reproach him, only
To proclaim the record of my services.
At first, with eyes to see, they saw in vain,
With ears to hear, heard nothing, groping through   80
Their lives in a dreamlike stupor, with no skill
In carpentry or brickmaking, like ants
Burrowing in holes, unpracticed in the signs
Of blossom, fruit, and frost, from hand to mouth
Struggling improvidently, until I
Charted the intricate orbits of the stars;
Invented number, that most exquisite
Instrument; formed the alphabet, the tool
Of history and chronicle of their progress;
Tamed the wild beasts to toil in pack and harness,   90
And yoked the prancing mounts of opulence,
Obedient to the rein, in chariots;
Constructed wheelless vehicles with linen
Wings to carry them over the trackless waters;
Yet, having bestowed all these discoveries
On man, I have none for myself to win
Deliverance from what I suffer for them.

Leader
It is a bitter irony that *you*
Should find yourself so helpless—a physician
Who taken sick despairs of his own skill.   100

Prometheus
There is more matter yet for you to admire
In the resource of my imagination,
And this above all—when sickness struck them down,
Having no herbal therapy to dispense
In salves and potions, their strength neglected ran
To waste in moping ignorance, till I
Compounded for them gentle medicines
To arm them in the war against disease.
And I set in order the forms of prophecy,
Interpreting the significance of dreams,   110
Voices, wayside meetings; trained them to observe
The flight of eagles, distinguishing the good
And evil auguries, describing for them
Their habits, matings, feuds, affinities;
Taught them to inspect the entrails, of what hue
And texture they must be for heaven's favor,
So leading them in to the difficult art

Of divination by burnt sacrifice.
And last, who else can boast to have unlocked
The earth's rich subterranean treasure-houses   120
Of iron, copper, bronze, silver and gold?
That is my record. You have it in a word:
Prometheus founded all the arts of man.

Leader
Temper your loyalty to mankind and take
Stock of your own condition. In this way
There is still hope that set at liberty
You shall return to greatness, the peer of Zeus.

Prometheus
No, that is not how all-determining Fate
Has shaped my destiny. Innumerable
Torments await me before I can be free.   130
Art is subservient to Necessity.

Leader
Who then is governor of Necessity?

Prometheus
The three Fates and the unforgetting Furies.

Leader
Is the sovereignty of Zeus second to these?

Prometheus
Yes, he cannot escape his destiny.

Leader
What *is* his destiny if not to reign forever?

Prometheus
No, that is a question which you must not ask me.

Leader
What can it be that you guard so jealously?

Prometheus
No, think of other things. The time to speak
Of that is still far distant. It must be hidden.   140
That is my secret, which if closely kept
Contains my sure hope of deliverance.

· · · · · · · · · · · · · ·

[Io's scene, not included here, follows. In the play's final scene, Zeus dispatches
Hermes, here portrayed as a swaggering flunky, to demand that Prometheus reveal
the secret cause of Zeus's prophesied fall from power. Only Prometheus knows that if
Zeus has a son by the sea nymph Thetis their union will produce a child greater than

his father, one strong enough to overthrow and replace Zeus, as the Olympian had dethroned Cronus. Much later, after the unchained Prometheus willingly saves Zeus from this fate by confiding Thetis's identity, the gods decide to marry her to a mortal, the young Peleus, so that her offspring will never rival Zeus. (See the discussion of Thetis and Peleus, the parents of mighty Achilles, in Chapter 12.) When Prometheus refuses to divulge the secret, a catastrophic storm and earthquake split the earth, hurling the Titan to his subterranean doom. After eons of torment underground, Prometheus will emerge again into daylight, only to be visited by Zeus's eagle, which will claw his body to shreds, feasting on his liver, which grows back only to be devoured again.

When Hermes warns the chorus of Prometheus's fate, the gentle nymphs, perhaps identifying with the plight of Io, a victim of male lust, openly defy Zeus by casting their lot with Prometheus, implicitly validating the Titan's position. Prometheus's final words call heaven and earth—all the natural world that preceded Zeus's reign—to witness the horror of divine injustice.]

[Zeus's messenger enters.]

Hermes
Prometheus, thief, inventor, intellectual,
Embittered protagonist of mortality,
You are hereby instructed to divulge
The secret which endangers the supreme power;
And pray spare me further interrogations
By giving plainly full particulars.
Zeus, you observe, is not intimidated.

Prometheus
What a solemn, stern, peremptory announcement,   150
Such as befits so highly-placed an official!
Upstarts parading in your citadel
As though it were impregnable! I have seen
Two tyrants tumble already from that throne,
And the third fall will be the most precipitate,
The most abject of all. Do you imagine
That these new gods can make me cringe? If so
You are much mistaken. Go back the way you came
And tell your master, there is no reply.

Hermes
Still unregenerate! Such gross impertinences   160
Have landed you already where you are.

Prometheus
I am not inclined, believe me, to exchange
My place for your obsequious errand-running.

Hermes
It is better no doubt to garrison this rock
Than serve as a trusted emissary of Zeus.

Prometheus

A petty tyrant's truculence! It is common.

Hermes

It almost seems you enjoy your punishment.

Prometheus

If only I may see my enemies,
With you among them, enjoy themselves as much!

Hermes

Do you hold me too responsible for all this?   170

Prometheus

I hate you all, the gods I served so well,
Who treat me so unjustly—hate you all!

Hermes

Yours is a desperate case, a mind diseased.

Prometheus

I hate my enemies, yes, incurably.

Hermes

You *would* have been insufferable if you'd prospered.

Prometheus

Oh, oh!

Hermes

Oh, oh! to Zeus that is a foreign language.

Prometheus

Time, as he grows old, will teach everything.

Hermes

He's been slow enough so far in teaching *you*.

Prometheus

Yes, or I wouldn't have spoken to an orderly.   180

Hermes

Do I understand then that you mean to flout him?

Prometheus

I will pay him what I owe him, and pay it all.

Hermes

I am not a child to be browbeaten like this.

Prometheus

You are indeed a child, a simpleton,
If you expect to get anything out of me.

Zeus can devise no instrument of torture
That will extract this revelation from me
Till he has freed me from these outrages.
So let him open fire with sulphurous flares,
Earthquakes, volcanoes, blizzards, hurricanes,   190
And make a tottering chaos of the world!
Nothing can force me to disclose the hand
Which shall put an end to his vile despotism.

Hermes
Pause to reflect, what can you gain by this?

Prometheus
All this was deeply meditated long ago.

Hermes
Can you not bring yourself, infatuate,
To learn the lesson of what you suffer now?

Prometheus
Implore the stones, admonish the wild waves,
But never imagine that his policies
Can make me bow and beg him like a woman   200
With outstretched, quivering, supplicating palms
To liberate me. That can never be.

Hermes
My words are wasted, all my remonstrances
Fall on deaf ears. You kick and plunge against
The checkrein like a colt just broken in.
Yet how precarious your self-confidence is!
Mere obstinate persistence, undirected
By sanity or expediency, leads nowhere.
Consider, if you disobey this order,
The storm that's brewing. First, he means to split   210
This icy crag from top to bottom, then
Inter your body deep in its embrace
For many centuries; and when at length
You see once more the light of day, to send you
His blood-red eagle, a daily visitor,
Punctual, unfailing, whose claws shall lacerate
Your flesh as it tears the day's meal from your liver
And this will go on indefinitely, until
Some god consents to take your place and go
Down to the dark of Tartarus and die.   220
That is the prospect, so make up your mind.
These are not empty menaces. Zeus is
Infallible. They will come true, every word.

So think it over carefully, and remember
To make your choice not obstinately but wisely.

Leader
Yes, we agree with Hermes. He is right.
He urges you to lay self-will aside
And follow the path of wisdom and discretion.
Being so wise, you must for shame comply.

Prometheus
I knew this message would come. Unashamed I defy him. I take back noth-   230
ing. And so let him now set his fireballs rolling! Let him scorch hill and
valley, blacken the sky, smoke out heaven, quench stars in the sea, and
then sweep me, plunged in the ironbound Tide of Necessity, down into
Tartarus—all this he can do but not kill me!

Hermes
He is mad, stark mad, you can see for yourselves. So now, stand clear! Having
offered your sympathy, hurry away! Stand clear from the volley of thunder!

Chorus
No, no, we refuse to desert him, we stay at his side to the end; for of all vile things
in the world the worst is a traitor.

Hermes
Very well, but remember that, caught in the whirlwind, you must not blame Zeus
for it, whimpering in the trap of your own sweet folly.

Prometheus
It is coming. The ground shakes. In the distance a rumble of thunder. Forked
lightning above, and the dust-clouds dance as the winds frolic madly, the crests
of the sea topple into the skies. It is on me, the full force of the fury of Zeus.
Mother Earth! O light of the world, moving in majesty in the heavenly spaces!
You see this injustice.

. . . .

Questions for Discussion and Review

1. Describe Prometheus's role in humanity's primal history. What does his gift of fire
   to mankind signify? Why does Zeus retaliate with the creation of Pandora? In what
   respects is the first woman a "lovely evil"? How does she resemble Eve in the Book
   of Genesis? Why do both Zeus and the biblical Yahweh try to prevent humans from
   acquiring forbidden knowledge?

2. Describe Hesiod's view of the two Strifes, and explain their role in the devolving
   history of humankind. Describe the four metallic ages and the Age of Heroes. Why
   does Hesiod regard human history as characterized by a downward spiral toward
   ultimate calamity?

3. Discuss the mythic themes of a lost Golden Age and primal fall from grace that appear in both Greek and biblical traditions. Does a Freudian or Jungian approach help explain this persistent myth?

4. What is Strife's (Eris's) function in Hesiod's concept of the world order?

5. How does the Athenian playwright Aeschylus, writing more than two centuries after Hesiod, change the character of Prometheus? At what ethical stage of his development do we find Zeus in this dramatic retelling of the myth? Why does Zeus operate primarily through the agencies of Might and Violence, allegorical figures who bind Prometheus to his rock?

6. Describe Io's thematic function in Aeschylus's version of the myth. In what way does her innocence of wrongdoing implicate Zeus? Why does the chorus, which usually represents a middle ground between two battling opponents, ultimately decide to take Prometheus's side, even though it means they must share in his punishment?

7. How does Aeschylus portray the Titan as both lawbreaker and savior who suffers for humanity? What qualities of the two opponents—Zeus and Prometheus—keep them in conflict? What changes in attitude and ethical maturity will eventually, after eons, allow them to reconcile so that divine power (Zeus) is again linked to divine wisdom and compassion (Prometheus)?

8. According to traditions not mentioned by either Hesiod or Aeschylus, Prometheus was both humankind's creator and its savior during Deucalion's flood. What new dimensions to his myth do these traditions add?

The Divine Woman in Greek Mythology

KEY TOPICS/THEMES

Creator goddesses in early Europe, some scholars claim, share with their nearly universal counterparts three functions: they are the source of the complete cycle that encompasses life, death, and rebirth—both literal and spiritual. Once the secrets of agriculture are mastered, such goddesses are associated with earth. As patriarchal systems overseen by male sky gods replace the older matriarchal ones, the functions of the Creator goddesses typically are parceled out among various goddesses who are subordinated to the male gods. Other scholars argue that there was no single Creator goddess, but rather, diverse figures subject to varying interpretations. Whatever conditions might have existed earlier, in extant Greek mythology, the primordial goddess is Gaea, whose functions under the Olympian system are most completely syncretized in the figure of Demeter. Her importance is emphatically revealed in the Eleusinian Mysteries performed in her honor.

The Great Goddess

Although discussions of classical myths have, throughout the ages, emphasized the male gods, modern feminist scholars, both male and female, have undertaken new explorations of the significance of the female deities. The extensive research of modern archaeologists has demonstrated that from the Paleolithic (Old Stone Age, 30,000–7000 B.C.) period through the Bronze Age (3500–1000 B.C.) in Europe, female images abound (Figure 5-1), while few images of warriors or heroes dating from before the Bronze Age have been found. Scholars such as Marija Gimbutas, who examined thousands of figures and other artifacts, along with cultural his-

FIGURE 5-1 Venus of Willendorf. Stone Age figures were typically depicted as pregnant and with enlarged breasts, illustrating the female's role as creator and sustainer of life. This small (4¾") limestone sculpture found in Austria (c. 30,000–25,000 B.C.) may represent a goddess, or may be a figure intended to assist, by sympathetic magic, in childbirth or fertility. *(Museum of Natural History, Austria)*

torians such as Anne Baring and Jules Cashford and others, who studied ancient shrines excavated at Catal Hüyük in Turkey, on Crete, and elsewhere, argue that, long before male gods were worshiped throughout the cultures of early Europe and the Mediterranean, worship of one or perhaps a variety of Creator goddesses prevailed. (The names of such deities are, of course, unknowable; hence, the term **Great Goddess** is sometimes used to distinguish these primordial figures from later goddesses who incorporated some of their functions.)

Some even postulate the existence of a peaceful matriarchal society in Old Europe, prior to its displacement by a weapons-loving, patriarchal one. There is no evidence, however, to suggest that worship of a female Creator goddess necessitated or corresponded with a matriarchal social organization. In fact, more recent excavations by Ian Hodder and others at Catal Hüyük, including analysis of bones and teeth of humans buried there (to look for signs of dietary differences that might indicate lifestyles differentiated by gender or social status) found evidence of a more complex society than terms like "matriarchy" or "patriarchy" can accurately describe.

As for the Great Goddess herself, as scholars such as Lucy Goodison, Christine Morris, and others have insisted, we cannot ascertain exactly what artifacts, removed from their physical or social context, actually meant to those who made or used them. Thus, to draw inferences from the objects themselves requires a leap beyond the limits of empirical evidence. Furthermore, scholars explain, not only is there a significant difference between a single Mother Goddess and a mother goddess as one among many deities, but images taken out of context are all too easily misinterpreted, based on the premises of the observer. (For example, Goodison and Morris point to a figurine from modern Tanzania of a pregnant female that could easily be misidentified as a goddess, but is actually used for initation rites for adolescent males.)

Although the controversy continues, the shrines, images, and artifacts remain, and surely had some important function. Furthermore, examples of Creator goddess figures occur in extant mythologies from all over the world: Gaea and Demeter in Greek myths, Ceres and Terra Mater in Roman myths, Inanna/Ishtar in Sumerian/Babylonian myths, Nerthus in Norse myths, as well as the Chinese goddess Nu Wa and the Hindu Devi in all her various incarnations, along with others too numerous to list. Naturally, the meanings and roles of such figures must have varied from one locale to another and changed over time as well. And though there was undoubtedly never a single widely dispersed divinity, these figures often shared many important characteristics.

The nearly universal distribution of Creator-goddess themes and images in extant mythologies reinforces the likelihood of earlier versions that did not survive. It remains plausible, then, that Creator goddesses were frequent attributes of the cultures of Old Europe. Moreover, given the fondness of ancient Greek culture for contradiction, for awareness rather than denial of tensions, as well as for the corollary emphasis on dialectic and debate in Greek philosophy and eventually in the political developments that evolved into the world's first democracy, it should not be surprising to find goddess religions and interest in female powers, whether or not they were ever actually dominant, subsisting right alongside the ostensibly predominant patriarchy that either came to prevail, or possibly had always done so.

But whether there was one Creator goddess or many different ones, or perhaps even none at all, we cannot help but note that the known goddesses of classical mythology that have come down to us manifest all of the characteristics that Gimbutas and others attribute to the nominal Great Goddess; thus, it is useful to consider her attributes as a conceptual model, if not as a literal figure. For convenience, this text will refer to the concept implied by such figures as the Creator goddess or the Great Goddess.

The Three Functions of the Great Goddess

The earliest European images typically depict female figures with enlarged breasts and abdomen; the woman or goddess is often shown as pregnant and sometimes in the act of giving birth, symbolizing her power to create and nourish (Figure 5-2). Representing a different perspective on the creation myths from that found in Hesiod's "official," clearly male-dominated narrative, such goddesses may have been perceived as powerful, creative beings who, by **parthenogenesis** (conception without sex), gave birth to the universe. In these early images, the Great Goddess was not associated with love or sex. Perhaps before humans understood the precise male role in procreation, the female ability to generate life from within herself seemed magi-

FIGURE 5-2   Artemis of Ephesus. Although she was a virgin goddess, Artemis, like most Greek goddesses, retained the association with childbirth and nurturing derived from the ancient Creator goddesses. In this alabaster and bronze sculpture (a Roman copy of a Greek original, c. 500 B.C.), her power to nourish is manifested in her multiple breasts. (Some scholars have suggested that the "breasts" are actually fruits or the testicles of sacrificed bulls.) The representations of many varieties of beasts and insects with which she is covered emphasize Artemis's power as a sustainer of animal as well as human life. *(National Museum, Naples)*

cal, a premise from which the idea of a Creator goddess might naturally emerge. Modern readers should surely understand this response: we know that some insects and lizards regularly procreate parthenogenetically, but when mammals like ourselves do it, it makes the headlines, as happened in 2004 when Japanese scientists manipulated the DNA of mouse egg cells so that the eggs developed into a fetal mouse, with no sperm involved. "Males not mandatory," read the headline. Completing the link between modern science and ancient myth, one such mouse, who has since had her own offspring by more conventional means, was named Kaguya, after a princess from a Japanese folk tale who was born from a bamboo stump. The motif of birth (or rebirth) from the trunk or stump of a tree occurs frequently in myths, as in the Egyptian tale of the goddess Isis, who resurrects her dead husband Osiris from the trunk of a tamarisk tree that had long since been cut down, or the Greek myth of Adonis, born from the tree-trunk womb into which his mother had been transformed (see Chapter 6).

Beyond the power of parthenogenesis, the Great Goddess is typically associated with three functions: she is the source of life, of death, and of transfiguration or rebirth. She is often described as having a triple nature as well, repeated in the patterns of heaven–earth–Underworld (the three-storied cosmos she encompasses), and of virginal maiden–nurturing mother–wise old woman (the three stages of a woman's life). Melding opposites within herself, such a deity thus encompasses both light and darkness, both upper and lower worlds, embracing the totality of the cycle of birth, death, and renewal in all its aspects—the terrifying along with the beneficent. Later, after humans came to recognize the life cycle of plants and learned to plant, grow, and harvest food, she was also identified as the grain goddess or earth goddess—responsible for the growth, death, and rebirth of vegetation—who now added these functions to the primal one of maintaining the eternal cycle of life, death, and regeneration.

Symbols of the Great Goddess

Although the guises in which the Great Goddess appears in myths throughout the world vary, certain key images remain constant—recurring symbols of an archetypal female principle shared by humans in all times and cultures.

Among the key symbols, perhaps the most prominent is the **serpent** (Figures 5-3, 5-4, and 5-5). Slithering underground as well as on the surface, the snake is privy to the mysteries of the Underworld, to the magic that transforms seeds into plants, and to the secrets of life, death, and rebirth. Because it sheds its skin each spring after a period of hibernation, the snake also symbolizes immortality, visually embodying the continuity of the eternal cycle. To emphasize that connection, the snake is sometimes depicted with its tail in its mouth. A related symbol is the tree (or its variants, the pillar or column or even a bamboo stump, like the princess in the Japanese fairy tale)—the Tree of Life, or the World Tree, with its roots in the Underworld and its branches in the heavens, often depicted with the serpent twined around its trunk (Figure 5-6).

The Great Goddess is also frequently associated with the moon, whose cycles of waxing and waning approximate the menstrual cycle, while the waxing of the moon

FIGURE 5-3   Atargatis, or Dea Syria. One of the many deities imported by the Romans as they enlarged their empire by conquest, this Syrian goddess is another variant of the Great Goddess. She is linked in this bronze sculpture with two of her most important symbols: the serpent and the tree. Both the serpent (which can penetrate the secrets of the Underworld and also renew itself by shedding its skin) and the tree (which bears fruit annually after a period of dormancy) symbolize the Goddess's power of rebirth or renewal, typically combined on this figure. The snake surrounds the goddess as it would the trunk of a tree so that her body, embraced by the serpent, figuratively becomes the Tree of Life. As in Figures 5-4 and 5-5, the serpent is depicted as a beautiful and benevolent creature. *(National Museum of Terme, Rome)*

from crescent to full suggests the swelling of the womb in pregnancy. Therefore, the worldwide connection of the moon with women's fertility is not surprising. Moreover, the moon then disappears from view for several nights, only to be "reborn" to begin the lunar cycle anew. This pattern is reflected in the many myths depicting a lunar goddess who mourns for a lover or child who dies or descends to the Underworld, or who descends herself and then returns to the upper world or arranges for the return/rebirth of the child or lover. The lunar cycle, recapitulating the cycle of life, death, and rebirth, creates a link between the physical and spiritual realms of existence. Some mythographers even speculate that the impulse of humans to engage in mythmaking is initially inspired by their imaginative response to the lunar cycle. Visible against the night sky, the moon also unites contradictory elements of light and darkness, unlike the sun, whose blinding light obliterates darkness.

Other symbols include various forms of a vessel (jar, vase, pot, oven, chest, chalice, grail), which depict the body of the Great Goddess and which often were decorated with breasts and abdomen. As a vessel, her body becomes the womb of creation, container of the waters of life. Thus, a descent to the Underworld becomes

FIGURE 5-4 A Snake Goddess from Knossos. The Minoans, whose civilization, centered on Crete, preceded and influenced the Greeks', also worshiped snake goddesses. In this unfortunately damaged figure, the goddess (or possibly her priestess), whose bared breasts reflect her nurturing function, is wearing a skirt with serpentine designs and holding aloft serpents, traditional symbols of the Goddess's mysteries—her knowledge of the secrets of life, death, and regeneration. *(Heraklion Museum, Knossos)*

FIGURE 5-5   A Ceremony in Honor of Lares. The Lares were male guardian spirits of the household, who had their counterparts in the guardian spirits of the state—Jupiter (the Roman Zeus), Juno (the Roman Hera), and, of course, Ceres (the Roman version of the grain goddess Demeter). In the top panel of this fresco from Pompeii, offerings are made to the Lares; in the bottom panel, as vegetation sprouts in abundance, the serpents appear to accept the offerings. *(National Museum, Naples)*

a return to the womb of the Great Goddess, the source of all life, a journey sometimes archetypally identified as a descent into the unconscious. As some scholars have noted, in many locations in Europe and Asia Minor, from Paleolithic-era cultures to civilizations as sophisticated as that of the Minoans on Crete, shrines to the Great Goddesses were located in caves.

Other common goddess symbols include birds (whose flight links earth and sky), sows (an image of fecundity), and cows (a source of nourishment and sustainer of life, whose horns recapitulate the shape of the crescent moon). For example, the Middle Eastern goddesses Astarte and Ishtar, and the Egyptian goddesses Isis, Hathor, and Nut are all represented as cow goddesses. In Greek mythology, the princess Europa, carried to Crete by Zeus in the form of a bull, may have been such a cow goddess, with the spread of her worship perhaps etiologically depicted in that story. In the earliest figures, the female forms probably depicting goddesses often are inscribed with lozenge shapes, frequently with a dot inside, perhaps representing the seed in the field.

FIGURE 5-6   Heracles in the Garden of the Hesperides. The Greek hero Heracles engages in several battles with serpents. To the male hero, unlike the goddesses (see Figures 5-3 through 5-5), the serpent is a threat, and he must either kill it (as Heracles does in some versions of this myth) or seduce its female guardians before he can acquire the Golden Apples of Immortality. It is notable that the hero—typically not satisfied with rebirth through his own offspring, through spiritual renewal in this life, or through the hope of resurrection in the hereafter—wants his immortality literally and is willing to risk the potentially fatal encounter with the serpent to obtain it. In this Athenian vase painting (fifth century B.C.), Heracles rests after his journey to the land of the setting sun, where the Greek version of the Tree of Life grows, guarded, of course, by a serpent. Heracles apparently has charmed the Hesperides (the nymphs who guard the Golden Apples that grow on that tree) into giving him one. *(British Museum, London)*

The Division of the Great Goddess's Functions

Eventually, some writers claim, the three aspects of the Great Goddess are divided into separate figures, each of which represents one aspect of her totality. In Greek mythology, some scholars speculate that this division may reflect, at least in part, the invasion of Europe by martial Indo-European cultures with their weapon-bearing male gods, whose symbols are linear and phallic—spears, swords, thunder-bolts, and other weapons; others, however, argue that there is no hard evidence for such an invasion. Some evidence suggests that the relationship between the Goddesses and the male deities may have been perceived as cooperative. For example, the Cretan cave shrines dedicated to the Goddess contain what most viewers interpret as representations of the horns of a bull god (although one archaeologist asserts that they are solar calendar symbols). Although we cannot reconstruct the precise process, we can note in Greek mythology, as in that of many other cultures, the presence of an original Creator goddess who does not retain her powers. Perhaps she was, as some suggest, divided, absorbed, and subordinated into forms not threatening to the more recently enthroned sky gods. Thus, her triple aspects as maiden–mother–old woman are redefined from the patriarchal perspective—in the three ways women could relate to men—as virgin–wife–mistress/whore and embodied in separate figures such as Athene, Hera, and Aphrodite. Or perhaps she was simply relegated to the background, as other local and/or imported goddesses became more prominent—although none was ever credited with the full range of powers attributed to the Creator goddess figures. The traditional Greek myths that have come down to us, tracing the generations from Gaea to Rhea to Hera, certainly reflect a narrowing of the goddesses' sphere of operations, although some essential functions, sometimes expressed in surprising contexts, are preserved.

However it evolved, the reign of patriarchy among the gods gives rise to a new archetype, the hero. In contrast to the feminine archetype, the masculine model of experience focused on the singular achievements of unique individuals, is linear, not cyclical, making death terrible and final. Thus the hero, whose primary role is to escape mortality and achieve personal transcendence, becomes necessary. From this new perspective, the feminine archetype is a threat that must be counteracted. The frequent association of the sun with male deities typically creates a system of dualism in which the universe becomes an arena of combat between opposing forces: the sky gods of sun and light are portrayed as "good," whereas the forces of darkness, including the Underworld functions of the Great Goddess, are seen as "evil." Thus, the snake becomes a dragon, with whom gods and heroes alike must do battle.

Gaea

In Greek myths, the original, parthenogenetic goddess is **Gaea**, one of the components of the primordial universe. She includes all levels of the cosmos within herself, mediating between the upper and lower worlds, between light and darkness, and between life and death. It is she who is the source of the physical universe, including the sky, personified as the god Uranus. Like most Creator goddesses, she is associated with the serpent image, such as Python, who guarded her sanctuary at Delphi.

As with many creation myths, the story of Gaea's creation describes a process of separation and differentiation. Stirred from stillness into motion, Gaea separates the male components out of herself and gives birth to the many forms of life that inhabit our world. Those varied life-forms must then struggle to preserve their uniqueness, in competition with all other life-forms. Life is the condition of **agon,** filled with struggle, tension, and unfulfilled desire. But that very tension produces a contradictory urge—the desire to return to the condition of undifferentiated wholeness. Borrowing the names of the Greek gods, Freud portrayed this contradictory state as tension between **Eros,** the life force, and **Thanatos**—after the Greek god of death—the return to the peace of the womb that is the death wish. In the Greek creation myth, it is Eros himself who ignites the desire that brings the universe as we know it into being, but it is also Eros whose universal amorous influence drives male and female gods toward reconnecting with their opposites.

The tension between these two opposing impulses—male and female—is reflected in worldwide myths in a variety of ways: as an expanding and contracting universe undergoing repeated cycles of creation and destruction; as gods or heroes who desire erotic reunion with the feminine force while pursuing ego-preserving or power-enhancing goals, often at the expense of the women and children in their lives; or as heroes who strive to attain the immortal condition of the male sky gods only to find that they must descend to the (feminine) Underworld in order to make the attempt. When Gaea creates the universe out of her wholeness, life happens, in all its glorious complexity, and with it the tensions between feminine and masculine, earth and sky, goddess and god, parent and child.

In the second stage of the Greek creation myth, as if acknowledging this tension, Gaea takes a step toward compromising with the masculine principle by acknowledging the male role in conception. According to Hesiod, she mates with Uranus and gives birth to offspring that include both deities (the Titans) and monsters (the Cyclopes and the hundred-handed giants) whom Uranus imprisons in the Underworld—the womb of the goddess—thus preventing the usurpation of his own powers by undoing hers, reversing the birth process.

Gaea and Her Consort

Though Uranus now nominally reigns as king of the gods, it is clearly Gaea who retains her functions as the source of life and death, conspiring with her children to overthrow Uranus by castrating him while he is making love to her—his desire for erotic reunion with the goddess undermining his impulses toward augmentation of his own powers. (In later myths and related rituals, the male god or consort, sometimes in the form of an animal, such as a horned bull, often must undergo **sparagmos,** a ritual in which he is dismembered—and commonly eaten raw—to ensure the renewal of life.) Gaea's bonds are clearly with her children, and her commitment is to the continuity of the cycle. By contrast, Uranus, whose interest is in the acquisition and maintenance of his personal power, sees his potentially violent children as threats and so imprisons them. Although from the masculine perspective this scene of primal violence might reflect the sons' Oedipal envy of their father, from the feminine point of view it perpetuates the power of the goddess, dispensing with the male after his biological function as provider of semen is fulfilled. The myth also reflects recurrent social phenomena. As has continued to occur in many modern cultures, including our own, Uranus fathers but does not "parent" his offspring, a situation that, in myth as in reality, is often accompanied by child abuse. The pattern of domination of the violent male by the goddess who bonds with her children is continued in the relationship of Rhea and Cronus, who, in turn, are overthrown by Zeus.

The Subordination of Gaea

Zeus's last battle, after his defeat of his father and the rest of the Titans, is with the dragon Typhoeus (see Chapter 3), a patriarchal revision of the World Serpent who

FIGURE 5-7   The Gorgon. As long as death is perceived as part of the ongoing cycle of life, death, and rebirth, the Great Goddess's serpent is portrayed as a beneficent creature. From the patriarchal perspective, however, death becomes the final blow to the hero's ego, and the Goddess's Underworld functions come to seem terrifying. The once-beautiful serpent is transformed into the hero's perpetual enemy, the dragon. The Goddess herself, in her death-related functions, is similarly transformed. The Greek Gorgons, three women with snakes for hair, were called Sthenno, Euryale, and Medusa (whose eyes turned men to stone). In this marble relief from the temple of Artemis at Corfu (sixth century B.C.), we see a Gorgon, whose bulging eyes, protruding tongue, and hair of snakes, along with her belt of entwined snakes, render her a truly hideous figure. *(Museum of Corfu)*

incorporates the feminine archetype now exclusively identified with the Goddess's **chthonic** [THOH-nik], or death-wielding aspect. Under Zeus's Olympian regime, the patriarchal gods are in firm control. Gaea largely fades from view, her triple functions most often syncretized with Demeter or divided into separate functions, each reinterpreted from the male perspective. The Great Goddess in her chthonic aspect is transformed by the patriarchal system into a hideous old hag, such as the **Gorgon** (Figure 5-7), or a witch, such as Hecate.

Hecate

In the *Theogony*, Hesiod attributes to **Hecate** [HEK-uh-tee] the powers of all the gods and considers her the deity most honored by Zeus. She has power associated with both earth and sea, and can offer as her gifts fertility of the soil, victory in contests or battle, and wealth through fishing, farming, and animal breeding. She is associated with Demeter, both because she helped Demeter in her search for her missing daughter Persephone and because of their shared fertility functions.

Because of her Underworld connection, Hecate is gradually stripped of her positive associations with wealth and plenty, and becomes identified exclusively with fearful associations. These include night, unlucky places such as crossroads, and the moon (a symbol shared with her younger associate Artemis, like whom she is sometimes said to be a daughter or granddaughter of Leto), as well as witchcraft and sorcery. Under patriarchal auspices, the dread goddess—perceived in youth as the beguiling but deadly femme fatale—in old age becomes a witch. Thus, in addition to her connection with the so often fatal-to-men Artemis, Hecate joins the ranks of the Gorgons, the Graiae, the Furies, and other loathsome and fearful inheritors of the death-giving function of the Great Goddess.

Earlier images of the Goddess include the spider as a weaver of the intricate web of life, which often took the shape of the sun disk (compare, for example, Grandmother Spider, the Cherokee Creator goddess who captures the sun and brings light to the world). But now such images are transformed into threats of entrapment— the web, the net, the noose—wielded by the beautiful-but-deadly spider woman who imprisons the free male, or by the terrifying old woman who freezes him in place by turning him to stone, rendering him impotent and symbolically repressing the unconscious forces the feminine archetype invokes. The other aspects of the Great Goddess (maid, mother) are reinvoked in forms clearly subordinate to Zeus: Athene, whose divine wisdom is reborn out of the mind of Zeus; Hera, whose protection of the institution of marriage supports the patriarchal social structure; and Aphrodite, in whom the creative cosmic energy of Eros is often reduced to the pursuit of sexual gratification. Despite the official subordination of the feminine, however, the fear of the castrating goddess remains.

The god of war himself, Ares, so glorious on the battlefield, is more easily humiliated in the bedroom, where he is outwitted by the love goddess's nonathletic husband, Hephaestus (see Chapter 6), and literally trapped in an invisible but binding web of sexual desires and jealousies. Similarly, human warrior-heroes such as Heracles and Jason, who model themselves on Ares, continue to be undone whenever they enter the world of the feminine (see Chapter 10).

Although reconciled under patriarchal rule with the reign of the male gods, the other Olympian goddesses, individually, retain some of Gaea's characteristics and symbols. Three of her aspects are embodied as virgin (Athene), wife (Hera), and lover (Aphrodite), while her chthonian aspects are manifested separately in goddesses such as Hecate and Artemis (see Chapter 6).

Demeter

Possibly the most complex of the goddess figures to survive the shift to patriarchy, **Demeter** [de-MEE-ter] embodies—albeit in somewhat domesticated form—all the functions of the Great Goddess except the capacity for parthenogenesis: Zeus is the father of **Persephone** [per-SEF-oh-nee], also known as **Kore** [KOHR-ee], or the Maiden (Figure 5-8). The story of Persephone—her abduction by Hades, her rape by and marriage to the Underworld god and her reunion with her mother—recapitulates Gaea's (as well as Rhea's) experiences directly. Demeter's child has been taken from her and thrust back into the Underworld by a male deity for his own nefarious purposes. Just as Uranus thrust Gaea's offspring back into the Underworld, or as Cronus swallowed Rhea's children, so Hades' realm opens up and swallows the maiden. Demeter thus has her fertility denied. Unlike Gaea, however, she cannot castrate or outwit either Hades or Zeus as her grandmother had done to Uranus, and her mother to Cronus. All she can do is withhold her services as grain goddess

FIGURE 5-8   Demeter and Persephone. In this stone relief from Eleusis (fifth century B.C.), Demeter is seated, holding her corn-tipped scepter and stalks of grain. She talks with her daughter Persephone (Kore, also known as the Maiden), who holds an agricultural implement. Not only their functions as grain goddesses but also the close mother–daughter bonds are implied in this bas-relief. *(Eleusis Museum)*

and negotiate a compromise with Zeus, king of the gods, under the auspices of his thoroughly patriarchal, if somewhat more rational, political regime.

This is a moment of extreme crisis: as happens in many myth systems, whether by fire or flood or drought or other means, humankind is at risk of being destroyed. However, unlike similar tales in some myth systems, the crisis is averted. Demeter has no choice but to accept Zeus's compromise, and with it, the patriarchal hierarchy she had attempted to resist. The seasons will henceforth proceed in their natural course, assuring both cosmic order and human survival. The annual coming of spring is the continuing sign of that promise.

According to one episode introduced into the story of Demeter's search for Persephone, Poseidon attempts to seduce his grieving sister. When Demeter tries to escape his unwelcome attentions by transforming herself into a mare, the sea god, in the form of a horse, nonetheless completes his rape, fathering a horse called Arion and a mysterious daughter named "the Mistress." The story connecting these two deities may reflect their early role in Bronze Age Arcadia in southern Greece, where they may have been important regional nature gods. At a major shrine in honor of Demeter, an image of the goddess with a horse's head was found, and a ritual celebrating the union of Demeter and Poseidon in the form of mare and stallion was probably performed in the region, suggesting that this story antedates the story of Persephone and the rituals at Eleusis.

In another fertility-related myth, Iasion, the son of Zeus and Electra, a daughter of the Titan Atlas, falls passionately in love with Demeter. One version of the myth suggests that she does not return his affection and that Iasion, in retaliation, tries to harm her, for which Zeus kills him with a thunderbolt. According to Hesiod's *Theogony,* Demeter reciprocates Iasion's love and lies with the hero in a thrice-plowed field, their union resulting in a son, Plutus. In this chthonic myth, Iasion is the male consort of a fertility goddess to whom Demeter gives seeds of wheat, making him an adjunct of her function as producer of grain. Greek art typically portrays their son **Plutus** [PLOO-tuhs], a personification of wealth, as a young man carrying a horn of plenty.

Demeter and Persephone

The most important myth about Demeter, the story of the abduction of her daughter, is a multifaceted tale that operates on several levels of meaning (Figure 5-9).

FIGURE 5-9   Demeter. An important aspect of the ancient Great Goddess, Demeter represents the fertility of earth's soil and hence the grain harvest on which the entire human community depends for survival. In this monumental statue, the seated goddess stares ahead unseeingly, blinded by grief for her daughter, Persephone, whom Zeus and Hades have secretly conspired to take from her. The myth of Demeter's agonized search for the abducted girl—hidden deep in Hades' underground realm —and Persephone's role in nature's annual cycle of death and regeneration represent one of the most important religious traditions of Greek civilization. *(British Museum, London)*

As a nature myth, the story of Persephone represents the seed, planted under the ground (the trip to the Underworld), watered by the rain (Zeus's intervention), and sprouting in the spring as grain, whose mature form is represented by Demeter. As an etiological myth, the story explains why we have seasons. As a charter myth, the story establishes the basis for several rituals, from the Eleusinian Mysteries and the Thesmophoria (festivals honoring Demeter) to the common practice by farmers' wives of setting an extra place at the table in honor of Demeter.

Rituals in Honor of Demeter

The two most important rituals in honor of Demeter reflect her two major functions: as source of the cycle of human life, death, and transfiguration, she inspires the Greater and Lesser Eleusinian Mysteries; as grain goddess, the protector of agricultural fertility, she is honored in the Thesmophoria.

The Eleusinian Mysteries   The **Eleusinian** [el-oo-SIN-ee-uhn] **Mysteries** were celebrated in the town of Eleusis (where Demeter rested in her wanderings in search of Persephone) and in the nearby city of Athens. Large numbers of men and women, led by officially approved priests, participated in the annual nine-day event each September and October. As in all mystery religions, participation in the emotionally intense ritual was restricted to initiates, who were forbidden to reveal the secret rites. As a result, little is known about the rites performed in the temple at Eleusis itself.

Such evidence as exists suggests that the Lesser Mysteries were celebrated earlier in the year in preparation for the Greater Mysteries. The rituals involved fasting, the wearing of costumes, and ritual purification in the sea, with the participants carrying sacrificial pigs. Processions—possibly symbolic of Persephone's trip to the Underworld or of Demeter's search for her daughter—took place along the Sacred Way between Athens and the temple of Demeter at Eleusis. During the procession, bawdy jokes and obscene gestures apparently were exchanged, enhancing the fertility component of the rituals. Within the temple, participants partook of a sacred drink of barley and water. Prayers were recited and sacred objects revealed. Some scholars believe that among the sacred objects revealed during the mystery was a single seed of grain. The rite may have included dramatic elements, possibly some form of enactment of a **hieros gamos** [HYE-rohs GAHM-ohs], or sacred marriage, presumably between Zeus and Demeter or Persephone, to produce a sacred child. The climax of the ritual was undoubtedly the final **epiphany** of the goddess, when her direct communion with or manifestation to the worshipers took place. Participating in the ritual, according to the *Homeric Hymn to Demeter,* enabled the soul to experience, in a direct and emotional way, the connection among death, life, and rebirth—to achieve spiritual renewal in the moment and to look forward confidently to "joy" after death, thus ensuring spiritual, and possibly literal, rebirth and immortality.

Demeter and Dionysus   The ritual itself may have gradually incorporated elements from the worship of Dionysus, a male counterpart of Demeter and Persephone. Indeed, Demeter's gift of bread, like Dionysus's wine, is a sacred symbol of transformation. Certainly, the dramatic elements—the procession and costumes, the ritualized jesting, and possibly the reenactment of some events in the myth —were analogous to the plays performed during the Dionysian festival (see Chapter 14). Dionysus shares with Demeter and Persephone not only some vaguely feminine attributes (the long, flowing garments and hair, for example) but also the reconciliation of polarities—the cyclical process of life, death, and rebirth and the terror and joy of the Bacchic ritual.

When Dionysus's mother, **Semele** [SEM-uh-lee], who made love to Zeus, was unable to sustain the epiphany of Zeus in his true form as lightning—the Divine Fire itself—she was burned to death in the flame. For a mere mortal, naked divinity—the godhead seen face-to-face—is destructive. In the mysteries of Demeter, as in those of Dionysus, the ritual provides a mediated form of ecstatic communion with the deity, perhaps less electrifying than Semele's direct confrontation, but more appropriate to the human worshiper, who can thus experience the love of the god and live to tell the tale.

The Thesmophoria

Unlike the Eleusinian Mysteries, which were open to initiates of both sexes, the **Thesmophoria** [thes-moh-FOHR-ee-uh], a sowing ritual, was practiced by women only (except for the actual killing of the sacrificial animals, which was performed by a man). This ritual involved placing the bodies of sacrificed pigs (symbols of the Great Goddess) into gullies filled with snakes, along with pinecones and cakes baked in phallic shapes. After three days, properly purified women were lowered into the pit, reenacting Persephone's descent to Hades, to retrieve the material, which was then mixed with the seeds for next year's crop to ensure plant, animal, and human fertility.

Psychological Components of the Demeter Myth

The Mediation of Contraries As described in the *Homeric Hymn to Demeter,* it is Zeus who arranges for the marriage of Persephone, negotiating the compromise between Hades and Demeter that will allow Persephone to remain for part of the year in the Underworld with her husband and for the other part back on earth with her mother. The myth thus mediates between the self-sufficient Great Goddess and the patriarchy, as well as between life and death. The Greeks referred to the souls of the dead, whose bodies were often buried in clay jars, as those who "rest in the womb of the Goddess." Clay pots with corn seeds were often kept near the hearth to ensure the renewal of life in the spring.

The myth also reconciles the Great Goddess with the patriarchy through the institution of marriage, itself a union of contraries. Presented as legalized rape, because it is ultimately justified by Zeus (see Color Plate 4), Persephone's marriage brings about her symbolic death and descent to the Underworld. But it also is the occasion for understanding women's mysteries and the cycle of existence. Unlike the heroes' descent to the Underworld, which was the climax of a literally death-defying quest for personal immortality (see Chapter 10), Persephone's descent results in marriage with Hades. Their marriage achieves a reconciliation of life and

FIGURE 5-10   Persephone and Hades. In this vase painting, the King and Queen of the Underworld are depicted in a pleasant domestic scene. Hades holds the cornucopia, or horn of plenty, suggesting the fertility aspects of these chthonian deities, as well as Persephone's adaptation to her adult role. *(British Museum, London)*

death, portrayed as part of a continuing cycle that includes her annual rebirth as she returns to the upper world to be reunited with Demeter (Figure 5-10).

The Feminine Archetype   As an embodiment of the feminine archetype, Demeter manifests the threefold nature of the Goddess as mother (creator), as grain goddess (source of sustenance), and as goddess of the mysteries (the link in the process of life, death, and renewal, and the source of spiritual rebirth or transformation). The Demeter myth also repeats the motif of the triple functions in the figures of the mother (Demeter), the maiden (Persephone), and the wise old woman (Hecate, who helps Demeter locate her missing daughter). Even the role of Persephone as Kore, the Maiden, is tripled: her virginity appears in the three aspects of the goddesses who accompany her to the fields—Athene, who personifies self-sufficient reason; Artemis, who shuns men; and Persephone herself, who is innocent because she is inexperienced.

Demeter and Female Values   Beyond sharing the functions and symbols of the archetypal female, the myth of Demeter explores feminine values. As contemporary psychologists have noted, the myth upholds a model of self-fulfillment at odds with the independent, autonomous path that the masculine archetype—the hero —personifies. The linear male archetype requires that the hero, a unique individual, separate himself from others—and from his father in particular—and go out to contend with powerful forces alone. In fact, the characteristic hostility between father and son in the archetypal male experience, as exemplified in the myths of Uranus and Cronus, requires the son to define himself by literally or symbolically killing or emasculating his father. By contrast, the female archetype exemplifies the importance of the continuity of the generations, especially the bond between mother and daughter, who must be reunited if life is to continue.

The hero, furthermore, achieves his quest by spurning his sexual attraction to women as a "temptation" that will weaken his drive toward immortality. The female, in contrast, experiences renewal by accepting her sexuality, which allows her to achieve the desired bond with her children. Thus, in giving birth, Demeter becomes, in effect, her daughter, while in growing up, Persephone becomes her mother. Like many women since who grew up and bore children of their own, only to discover that they shared unanticipated links with their mothers ("I'm turning into my own mother!" is a frequent observation), Persephone returns from the Underworld transformed into another version of Demeter, thus joining the endless pattern of such renewals. This ultimate identification of mother and daughter is reflected in the fact that they were referred to collectively as the Two Goddesses and that in many of the rituals their roles were interchangeable.

Agriculture and the Source of Civilization

The myth goes one step further and presents the female principle as the source of civilization itself via the invention of agriculture. Demeter, having agreed to renew her function as grain goddess, teaches her rites and mysteries to **Triptolemus** [trip-TOHL-e-muhs], whose name means "thrice-plowed field" (which may refer to a field ready for planting and/or to Demeter's having sex with him three times), and who is sometimes identified as the Holy Child of the Eleusinian rite (Figure 5-11). The reference to the "thrice-plowed field" may suggest a recapitulation or assimilation of the image of fertility in the story of Demeter's affair with Iasion. Some say that Demeter gives Triptolemus a plow and grain seed, instructing him to share the secrets of planting with the rest of the human race. What modern anthropologists call the agricultural revolution derives from this insight, allowing humans to settle into permanent locations while they plant seeds, tend their crops, and await the harvest. It is from these early villages that complex cultures, stable and enduring over time, will develop. And the development of agriculture, some people speculate, may have set the stage for our understanding of the human reproductive process, as well.

Demeter thus presents a rather different perspective on the source of civilization from the equivalent male myth, the story of Prometheus and the theft of fire (see Chapter 4). By giving fire—the divine spark—to men, Prometheus sets them free. Men are no longer dependent on Zeus's lightning and are now able to create both

FIGURE 5-11   Demeter, Triptolemus, and Persephone. In this
marble relief from Eleusis (fifth century B.C.), Demeter (holding
the scepter) and her daughter confide the secrets of agriculture to
Triptolemus and instruct him to spread the knowledge to the rest
of humankind. Humans are thus both blessed by the goddesses and
initiated into their mysteries. *(National Museum, Athens)*

civilization and the technology, including weapons, on which a more aggressive
model of civilization will be built. Prometheus's gift creates antagonism between
men and gods, reinforcing a model of hostility and separation, whereas the feminine myth emphasizes bonding and reconciliation—among the gods and between
gods and humans.

The connection between the two myths is, in fact, a direct one. According to
Hesiod, to punish humankind for Prometheus's "trickery" of Zeus on their behalf over the issue of the sacrifice, Zeus withholds from humanity the secret of the
grain—how to plant seeds. But Demeter's gift doesn't merely restore fertility to the
land; rather, Demeter teaches humans her own secret—how to grow crops—making them less dependent on her will and promoting a closer divine–human con-

nection. Whereas Prometheus gave humans Zeus's fire behind his back, against his will, Demeter's gift is freely offered, and presumably with Zeus's acquiescence.

The Demeter Myth and Female Psychology

Besides expressing the feminine archetype, the Demeter myth also explores the psychology of the individual female as she progresses through the life cycle from girlhood to old age, passing from virgin to lover to mother and, eventually, to the wisdom of age that is partly represented in the myth by Hecate, a lunar goddess whose capacity for vision is not obliterated by darkness. In the *Homeric Hymn to Demeter,* although she cannot literally see what has occurred, Hecate knows a rape when she hears one, and she acts, in defiance of Zeus, to help reunite mother and daughter. The last stage of the life cycle is also expressed by Demeter herself as, searching for her daughter, she travels disguised as an old woman.

The myth addresses the emotional experiences of both mother and daughter as they pass through the stages in the life of a woman. The mother must watch as her child is wrenched from her by the patriarchal institution of marriage and must struggle to restore the bond afterward, albeit under different auspices. For her part, the daughter must discard her former home and identity and subordinate herself to a male who now determines her functions, as well as the conditions under which she must live. But the change involves both gains and losses: the mother, relinquishing her protective bond to her child, gains a new friendship, on equal terms, with a now mature woman like herself; the daughter, losing the comforting protection of a parent, gains at least relative independence and new understanding of herself as an adult woman.

The innocent but ignorant Persephone, abducted by Hades, undergoes her first sexual experience: eating the pomegranate, a symbol of sexual knowledge like the fruit eaten by Eve in the Book of Genesis, Persephone thus passes on to another stage of feminine experience and cannot go back to the upper world or return to her previous condition of naive virginity. At some of her shrines, pomegranate amulets, symbols of fertility, were offered to Demeter. (Another interpretation identifies the pomegranate, with its red juice, as an emblem of the onset of menstruation, with the descent into the Underworld a reflection of a common taboo, practiced in many patriarchal societies, requiring the isolation of the female during the menstrual period.) The result for Persephone, as for Eve, is her first consciousness of herself as a woman and her initiation into the mysteries of the life cycle (see Color Plate 2). Like Eve, whose "apple" was originally a pomegranate, she has eaten from the Tree of Knowledge (Tree of Life) and is ready to emerge as an adult woman. No longer dependent entirely on either mother or husband, no longer exclusively either somebody's child or somebody's wife, she is ready to relate to both on her own terms. Persephone's new powers reflect her new state—once a naive girl, she has become Queen of the Underworld. Hades also is changed by her presence. Not only has the power of Eros been extended to his dread kingdom, thus embracing all three levels of the universe, but Hades himself has been transformed from sexual predator to spouse. Albeit under patriarchal auspices, the Underworld is thereby reclaimed, and the complete cycle encompassed by the Great Goddess is restored.

The *Homeric Hymn to Demeter*

Most of the "Homeric" hymns, a collection of poems by mostly unknown authors in honor of various deities in the Greek pantheon, were probably composed in the eighth to seventh centuries B.C. (A few may have been composed much later, in the Hellenistic period, between the fourth and second centuries B.C.) Varying in length from a few short lines to full-length narratives, these poems were presented at festivals as a prologue to recitations of longer poems or to musical performances and were traditionally attributed to Homer, a doubtful attribution already questioned by Hellenistic readers. The *Homeric Hymn to Demeter,* the longest of the poems, probably dates from the seventh century B.C. and is one of our major sources of information about the rituals performed at Eleusis.

Unusual for its time in that it highlights the female point of view, the *Homeric Hymn to Demeter* tells the story of the abduction of Persephone by Hades and describes Demeter's search for her and their eventual reunification. It also describes some of the mystery rites for Demeter celebrated at Eleusis, where Demeter is given refuge during her wanderings. Unlike other versions of the myth, the hymn does not mention Demeter's gift of agriculture to Triptolemus—the residents of Eleusis described in the poem seem already to engage in plowing—but stresses instead the goddess's promise of rebirth to her worshipers: the cult is presented as an alternative to the literal immortality that Demeter offers to **Demophon**, child of the king and queen of Eleusis. When his terrified mother interrupts the process of placing him in the Divine Fire, Demeter reveals her true identity to the queen and insists that a cult be started in her honor. In contrast to the goddess Thetis, who was unable to render her son Achilles fully immortal when she similarly placed him in the Divine Fire (see Chapter 10), thus leaving him a divided self, half-human and half-divine, Demeter offers Demophon, along with the rest of humanity, an alternative path to wholeness, the unity of body and spirit. Her gift is the promise of eternal bliss in the hereafter, through initiation in her Mysteries. The myth thus simultaneously charters the mystery and establishes its functions: a means of achieving communion with Demeter and of ensuring an alternative to the literal immortality that is too terrifying and too destructive a transformation for humans to undergo.

HOMERIC HYMN TO DEMETER*

Author unknown

Demeter I begin to sing[†]   1
the fair-tressed awesome goddess,
herself and her slim-ankled daughter whom Aidoneus[‡]
seized; Zeus, heavy-thundering and mighty-voiced, gave her,
without the consent of Demeter of the bright fruit and golden sword,
as she played with the deep-breasted daughters of Ocean,
plucking flowers in the lush meadow—roses, crocuses,
and lovely violets, irises and hyacinth and the narcissus,
which Earth grew as a snare for the flower-faced maiden
in order to gratify by Zeus's design the Host-to-Many,[‡]
a flower wondrous and bright, awesome for all to see,   10
for the immortals above and for mortals below.
From its root a hundredfold bloom sprang up and smelled
so sweet that the whole vast heaven above
and the whole earth laughed, and the salty swell of the sea.
The girl marveled and stretched out both hands at once
to take the lovely toy. The earth with its wide ways yawned
over the Nysian plain; the lord Host-to-Many rose up on her
with his immortal horses, the celebrated son of Kronos;
he snatched the unwilling maid into his golden chariot
and led her off lamenting. She screamed, with a shrill voice,   20
calling on her father, the son of Kronos highest and best.
Not one of the immortals or of humankind
heard her voice, nor the olives bright with fruit,
except the daughter of Persaios; tender of heart
she heard it from her cave, Hekate of the delicate veil.
And lord Helios, brilliant son of Hyperion, heard
the maid calling her father the son of Kronos. But he sat apart
from the gods, aloof in a temple ringing with prayers,
and received choice offerings from humankind.
Against her will Hades took her by the design of Zeus   30
with his immortal horses—her father's brother,
Commander- and Host-to-Many, the many-named son of Kronos.
So long as the goddess gazed on earth and starry heaven,
on the sea flowing strong and full of fish,

---

*Translation by Helene P. Foley.
†The following divine genealogy will assist the reader in following the text. Gaia (earth) and Ouranos (sky) are the parents of Rheia and Kronos, who are, in turn, parents of Zeus, Hades, and Demeter. Zeus and Hades are thus both sons of Kronos. Demeter and Zeus are the parents of Kore/Persephone.
‡Hades.

and on the beams of the sun, she still hoped
to see her dear mother and the race of immortal gods.
For so long hope charmed her strong mind despite her distress.
The mountain peaks and the depths of the sea echoed
in response to her divine voice, and her goddess mother heard.
Sharp grief seized her heart, and she tore the veil   40
on her ambrosial hair with her own hands.
She cast a dark cloak on her shoulders
and sped like a bird over dry land and sea,
searching. No one was willing to tell her the truth,
not one of the gods or mortals;
no bird of omen came to her as truthful messenger.
Then for nine days divine Deo* roamed over the earth,
holding torches ablaze in her hands;
in her grief she did not once taste ambrosia
or nectar sweet-to-drink, nor bathed her skin.   50
But when the tenth Dawn came shining on her,
Hekate met her, holding a torch in her hands,
to give her a message. She spoke as follows:
"Divine Demeter, giver of seasons and glorious gifts,
who of the immortals or mortal men
seized Persephone and grieved your heart?
For I heard a voice but did not see with my eyes
who he was. To you I tell at once the whole truth."
Thus Hekate spoke. The daughter of fair-tressed Rheia*
said not a word, but rushed off at her side   60
holding torches ablaze in her hands.
They came to Helios, observer of gods and mortals,
and stood before his horses. The most august goddess* spoke:
"Helios, respect me as a god does a goddess, if ever
with word or deed I pleased your heart and spirit.
The daughter I bore, a sweet offshoot noble in form—
I heard her voice throbbing through the barren air
as if she were suffering violence. But I did not see her with my eyes.
With your rays you look down through the bright air
on the whole of the earth and sea.   70
Tell me the truth about my child. Have you somewhere
seen who of gods or mortal men took her
by force from me against her will and went away?"
Thus she spoke and the son of Hyperion replied:
"Daughter of fair-tressed Rheia, mighty Demeter,
you will know the truth. For I greatly revere and pity you
grieving for your slim-ankled daughter. No other
of the gods was to blame but cloud-gathering Zeus,

*Demeter.

who gave her to Hades his brother to be called
his fertile wife. With his horses Hades   80
snatched her screaming into the misty gloom.
But, Goddess, give up for good your great lamentation.
You must not nurse in vain insatiable anger.
Among the gods Aidoneus is not an unsuitable bridegroom,
Commander-to-Many and Zeus's own brother of the same stock.
As for honor, he got his third at the world's first division
and dwells with those whose rule has fallen to his lot."
He spoke and called to his horses. At his rebuke
they bore the swift chariot lightly, like long-winged birds.
A more terrible and brutal grief seized the heart   90
of Demeter, angry now at the son of Kronos with his dark clouds.
Withdrawing from the assembly of the gods and high Olympus,
she went among the cities and fertile fields of men,
disguising her beauty for a long time. No one of men
nor deep-girt women recognized her when they looked,
until she came to the house of skillful Keleos,
the man then ruler of fragrant Eleusis.
There she sat near the road, grief in her heart,
where citizens drew water from the Maiden's Well
in the shade—an olive bush had grown overhead—   100
like a very old woman cut off from childbearing
and the gifts of garland-loving Aphrodite.
Such are the nurses to children of law-giving kings
and the keepers of stores in their echoing halls.
The daughters of Keleos, son of Eleusis, saw her
as they came to fetch water easy-to-draw and bring it
in bronze vessels to their dear father's halls.
Like four goddesses they were in the flower of youth,
Kallidikê, Kleisidikê, fair Demo, and Kallithoê,
who was the eldest of them all.   110
They did not know her—gods are hard for mortals to recognize.
Standing near her, they spoke winged words.
"Who are you, old woman, of those born long ago?
From where? Why have you left the city and do not
draw near its homes? Women are there in the shadowy halls,
of your age as well as others born younger,
who would care for you both in word and in deed."
They spoke, and the most august goddess replied:
"Dear children, whoever of womankind you are,
greetings. I will tell you my tale. For it is not wrong   120
to tell you the truth now you ask.
Doso's my name, which my honored mother gave me.
On the broad back of the sea I have come now from Crete,
by no wish of my own. By force and necessity pirate men
led me off against my desire. Then they

put into Thorikos in their swift ship, where
the women stepped all together onto the mainland,
and the men made a meal by the stern of the ship.
My heart did not crave a heartwarming dinner,
but racing in secret across the dark mainland   130
I escaped from my arrogant masters, lest
they should sell me, as yet unbought, for a price overseas.
Then wandering I came here and know not at all
what land this is and who lives here.
But may all the gods who dwell on Olympus
give you husbands to marry and children to bear,
such as parents wish for. Now pity me, maidens,
and tell me, dear children, with eager goodwill,
whose house I might come to, a man's
or a woman's, there to do for them gladly   140
such tasks as are done by an elderly woman.
I could nurse well a newborn child, embracing it
in my arms, or watch over a house. I could
spread out the master's bed in a recess
of the well-built chamber and teach women their work."
So spoke the goddess. To her replied at once Kallidikê,
a maiden unwed, in beauty the best of Keleos's daughters.
"Good mother, we mortals are forced, though it hurt us,
to bear the gifts of the gods; for they are far stronger.
To you I shall explain these things clearly and name   150
the men to whom great power and honor belong here,
who are first of the people and protect with their counsels
and straight judgments the high walls of the city.
There is Triptolemos subtle in mind and Dioklos,
Polyxenos and Eumolpos the blameless,
Dolichos and our own lordly father.
And all these have wives to manage their households.
Of these not one at first sight would scorn
your appearance and turn you away from their homes.
They will receive you, for you are indeed godlike.   160
But if you wish, wait here, until we come to the house
of our father and tell Metaneira our deep-girt mother
all these things straight through, in case she might bid
you come to our house and not search after others'.
For her only son is now nursed in our well-built hall,
a late-born child, much prayed for and cherished.
If you might raise him to the threshold of youth,
any woman who saw you would feel envy at once,
such rewards for his rearing our mother will give you."
Thus they spoke and she nodded her head. The girls   170
carried proudly bright jars filled with water and
swiftly they reached the great house of their father.

At once to their mother they told what they saw and heard.
She bade them go quickly to offer a boundless wage.
Just as hinds or heifers in the season of spring
bound through the meadow sated with fodder,
so they, lifting the folds of their shimmering robes,
darted down the hollow wagon-track, and their hair
danced on their shoulders like a crocus blossom.
They found the famed goddess near the road   180
just where they had left her. Then to the house
of their father they led her, She, grieved in her heart,
walked behind with veiled head. And her dark robe
swirled round the slender feet of the goddess.
They soon reached the house of god-cherished Keleos,
and went through the portico to the place where
their regal mother sat by the pillar of the close-fitted roof,
holding on her lap the child, her young offshoot. To her
they raced. But the goddess stepped on the threshold. Her head
reached the roof and she filled the doorway with divine light.   190
Reverence, awe, and pale fear seized Metaneira.
She gave up her chair and bade the goddess sit down.
But Demeter, bringer of seasons and giver of rich gifts,
did not wish to be seated on the shining seat.
She waited resistant, her lovely eyes cast down,
until knowing Iambe set out a well-built stool
for her and cast over it a silvery fleece.
Seated here, the goddess drew the veil before her face.
For a long time she sat voiceless with grief on the stool
and responded to no one with word or gesture.   200
Unsmiling, tasting neither food nor drink,
she sat wasting with desire for her deep-girt daughter,
until knowing Iambe jested with her and
mocking with many a joke moved the holy goddess
to smile and laugh and keep a gracious heart—
Iambe, who later pleased her moods as well.
Metaneira offered a cup filled with honey-sweet wine,
but Demeter refused it. It was not right, she said,
for her to drink red wine; then she bid them mix barley
and water with soft mint and give her to drink.   210
Metaneira made and gave the drink to the goddess as she bid.
Almighty Deo received it for the sake of the rite.
Well-girt Metaneira spoke first among them:
"Hail, lady, for I suppose your parents are not lowborn,
but noble. Your eyes are marked by modesty
and grace, even as those of justice-dealing kings.
We mortals are forced, though it may hurt us, to bear
the gifts of the gods. For the yoke lies on our necks.
But now you have come here, all that's mine will be yours.

Raise this child for me, whom the gods provided   220
late-born and unexpected, much-prayed for by me.
If you raise him and he comes to the threshold of youth,
any woman who saw you would feel envy at once,
such rewards for his rearing would I give you."
Rich-crowned Demeter addressed her in turn:
"Hail also to you, lady, may the gods give you blessings.
Gladly will I embrace the child as you bid me.
I will raise him, nor do I expect a spell or the Undercutter
to harm him through the negligence of his nurse.
For I know a charm more cutting than the Woodcutter;   230
I know a strong safeguard against a baneful bewitching."
So speaking, she took the child to her fragrant breast
with her divine hands. And his mother was glad at heart.
Thus the splendid son of skillful Keleos, Demophoön,
whom well-girt Metaneira bore, she nursed
in the great halls. And he grew like a divinity,
eating no food nor sucking [at a mother's breast];
[For daily well-crowned divine] Demeter anointed
him with ambrosia like one born from a god
and breathed sweetly on him, held close to her breast.   240
At night, she would bury him like a brand in the fire's might,
unknown to his own parents. And great was their wonder
as he grew miraculously fast; he was like the gods.
She would have made him ageless and immortal,
if well-girt Metaneira had not in her folly
kept watch at night from her fragrant chamber
and spied. But she shrieked and struck both thighs
in fear for her child, much misled in her mind,
and in her grief she spoke winged words.
"Demophoön, my child, the stranger buries you   250
deep in the fire, causing me woe and bitter cares."
Thus she spoke lamenting. The great goddess heard her.
In anger at her, bright-crowned Demeter snatched
from the flames with immortal hands the dear child
Metaneira had borne beyond hope in the halls and,
raging terribly at heart, cast him away from herself to the ground.
At the same time she addressed well-girt Metaneira:
"Mortals are ignorant and foolish, unable to foresee
destiny, the good and the bad coming on them.
You are incurably misled by your folly.   260
Let the god's oath, the implacable water of Styx, be witness,
I would have made your child immortal and ageless
forever; I would have given him unfailing honor.
But now he cannot escape death and the death spirits.
Yet unfailing honor will forever be his, because
he lay on my knees and slept in my arms.

In due time as the years come round for him,
the sons of Eleusis will continue year after year
to wage war and dread combat against each other.
For I am honored Demeter, the greatest   270
source of help and joy to mortals and immortals.
But now let all the people build me a great temple
with an altar beneath, under the sheer wall
of the city on the rising hill above Kallichoron.
I myself will lay down the rites so that hereafter
performing due rites you may propitiate my spirit."
Thus speaking, the goddess changed her size and appearance,
thrusting off old age. Beauty breathed about her and
from her sweet robes a delicious fragrance spread;
a light beamed far out from the goddess's immortal skin,   280
and her golden hair flowed over her shoulders.
The well-built house flooded with radiance like lightning.
She left the halls. At once Metaneira's knees buckled.
For a long time she remained voiceless, forgetting
to pick up her dear only son from the floor.
But his sisters heard his pitiful voice and
leapt from their well-spread beds. Then one took
the child in her arms and laid him to her breast.
Another lit the fire; a third rushed on delicate feet
to rouse her mother from her fragrant chamber.   290
Gathering about the gasping child, they bathed and
embraced him lovingly. Yet his heart was not comforted,
for lesser nurses and handmaids held him now.
All night they tried to appease the dread goddess,
shaking with fear. But when dawn appeared,
they explained to wide-ruling Keleos exactly
what the bright-crowned goddess Demeter commanded.
Then he called to assembly his innumerable people
and bid them build for fair-tressed Demeter
a rich temple and an altar on the rising hill.   300
Attentive to his speech, they obeyed at once and did
as he prescribed. It grew as the goddess decreed.
But once they finished and ceased their toil,
each went off home. Then golden-haired Demeter
remained sitting apart from all the immortals,
wasting with desire for her deep-girt daughter.
For mortals she ordained a terrible and brutal year
on the deeply fertile earth. The ground released
no seed, for bright-crowned Demeter kept it buried.
In vain the oxen dragged many curved plows down   310
the furrows. In vain much white barley fell on the earth.
She would have destroyed the whole mortal race
by cruel famine and stolen the glorious honor of gifts

and sacrifices from those having homes on Olympus,
if Zeus had not seen and pondered their plight in his heart.
First he roused golden-winged Iris to summon
fair-tressed Demeter, so lovely in form.
Zeus spoke and Iris obeying the dark-clouded
son of Kronos, raced swiftly between heaven and earth.
She came to the citadel of fragrant Eleusis   320
and found in her temple dark-robed Demeter.
Addressing her, she spoke winged words:
"Demeter, Zeus, the father, with his unfailing knowledge
bids you rejoin the tribes of immortal gods.
Go and let Zeus's word not remain unfulfilled."
Thus she implored, but Demeter's heart was unmoved.
Then the father sent in turn all the blessed immortals;
one by one they kept coming and pleading
and offered her many glorious gifts and whatever
honors she might choose among the immortal gods.   330
Yet not one could bend the mind and thought
of the raging goddess, who harshly spurned their pleas.
Never, she said, would she mount up to fragrant
Olympus nor release the seed from the earth,
until she saw with her eyes her own fair-faced child.
When Zeus, heavy-thundering and mighty-voiced,
heard this, he sent down the Slayer of Argos* to Erebos
with his golden staff to wheedle Hades with soft words
and lead back holy Persephone from the misty gloom
into the light to join the gods so that her mother   340
might see her with her eyes and desist from anger.
Hermes did not disobey. At once he left Olympus's height
and plunged swiftly into the depths of the earth.
He met lord Hades inside his dwelling,
reclining on a bed with his shy spouse, strongly reluctant
through desire for her mother. [Still she, Demeter,
was brooding on revenge for the deeds of the blessed gods.]
The strong Slayer of Argos stood near and spoke:
"Dark-haired Hades, ruler of the dead, Father Zeus   350
bids me lead noble Persephone up from Erebos
to join us, so that her mother might see her with her eyes
and cease from anger and dread wrath against the gods.
For she is devising a great scheme to destroy
the helpless race of mortals born on earth,
burying the seed beneath the ground and obliterating
divine honors. Her anger is terrible, nor does she go

*Hermes.

among the gods but sits aloof in her fragrant temple,
keeping to the rocky citadel of Eleusis."
Thus he spoke and Aidoneus, lord of the dead, smiled
with his brows, nor disobeyed king Zeus's commands. 360
At once he urged thoughtful Persephone:
"Go, Persephone, to the side of your dark-robed mother,
keeping the spirit and temper in your breast benign.
Do not be so sad and angry beyond the rest;
in no way among immortals will I be an unsuitable spouse,
myself a brother of father Zeus. And when you are there,
you will have power over all that lives and moves,
and you will possess the greatest honors among the gods.
There will be punishment forevermore for those wrongdoers
who fail to appease your power with sacrifices, 370
performing proper rites and making due offerings."
Thus he spoke and thoughtful Persephone rejoiced.
Eagerly she leapt up for joy. But he gave her to eat
a honey-sweet pomegranate seed, stealthily passing it
around her, lest she once more stay forever
by the side of revered Demeter of the dark robe.
Then Aidoneus commander-to-many yoked
his divine horses before the golden chariot.
She mounted the chariot and at her side the strong
Slayer of Argos took the reins and whip in his hands 380
and dashed from the halls. The horses flew eagerly;
swiftly they completed the long journey; not sea nor
river waters, not grassy glens nor mountain peaks
slowed the speed of the immortal horses,
slicing the deep air as they flew about these places.
He brought them to a halt where rich-crowned Demeter
waited before the fragrant temple. With one look she darted
like a maenad down a mountain shaded with woods.
On her side Persephone, [seeing] her mother's [radiant face],
[left chariot and horses,] and leapt down to run 390
[and fall on her neck in passionate embrace].
[While holding her dear child in her arms], her [heart
suddenly sensed a trick. Fearful, she] drew back
from [her embrace and at once inquired:]
"My child, tell me, you [did not taste] food [while below?]
Speak out [and hide nothing, so we both may know.]
[For if not], ascending [from miserable Hades],
you will dwell with me and your father, the
dark-clouded [son of Kronos], honored by all the gods.
But if [you tasted food], returning beneath [the earth,] 400
you will stay a third part of the seasons [each year],
but two parts with myself and the other immortals.

When the earth blooms in spring with all kinds
of sweet flowers, then from the misty dark you will
rise again, a great marvel to gods and mortal men.
By what guile did the mighty Host-to-Many deceive you?"
Then radiant Persephone replied to her in turn:
"I will tell you the whole truth exactly, Mother.
The Slayer of Argos came to bring fortunate news
from my father, the son of Kronos, and the other gods   410
and lead me from Erebos so that seeing me with your eyes
you would desist from your anger and dread wrath
at the gods. Then I leapt up for joy, but he stealthily
put in my mouth a food honey-sweet, a pomegranate seed,
and compelled me against my will and by force to taste it.
For the rest—how seizing me by the shrewd plan of my father,
Kronos's son, he carried me off into the earth's depths—
I shall tell and elaborate all that you ask.
We were all in the beautiful meadow—
Leukippê, Phaino, Elektra; and Ianthê;   420
Melitê, Iachê; Rhodeia; and Kallirhoê;
Melibosis; Tychê; and flower-faced Okyrhoê;
Khryseis; Ianeira; Akastê; Admetê;
Rhodopê; Plouto; and lovely Kalypso;
Styx; Ourania; and fair Galaxaura; Pallas,
rouser of battles; and Artemis, sender of arrows—
playing and picking lovely flowers with our hands,
soft crocus mixed with irises and hyacinth,
rosebuds and lilies, a marvel to see, and the
narcissus that wide earth bore like a crocus.   430
As I joyously plucked it, the ground gaped from beneath,
and the mighty lord, Host-to-Many, rose from it
and carried me off beneath the earth in his golden chariot
much against my will. And I cried out at the top of my voice.
I speak the whole truth, though I grieve to tell it."
Then all day long, their minds at one, they soothed
each other's heart and soul in many ways,
embracing fondly, and their spirits abandoned grief,
as they gave and received joy between them.
Hekate of the delicate veil drew near them   440
and often caressed the daughter of holy Demeter;
from that time this lady served her as chief attendant.
To them Zeus, heavy-thundering and mighty-voiced,
sent as mediator fair-tressed Rheia to summon
dark-robed Demeter to the tribes of gods; he promised
to give her what honors she might choose among the gods.
He agreed his daughter would spend one-third
of the revolving year in the misty dark and two-thirds

with her mother and the other immortals.
So he spoke and the goddess did not disobey his commands.   450
She darted swiftly down the peaks of Olympus
and arrived where the Rarian plain, once life-giving
udder of earth, now giving no life at all, stretched idle
and utterly leafless. For the white barley was hidden
by the designs of lovely-ankled Demeter. Yet as spring came on,
the fields would soon ripple with long ears of grain;
and the rich furrows would grow heavy on the ground
with grain to be tied with bands into sheaves.
There she first alighted from the barren air.
Mother and daughter were glad to see each other   460
and rejoiced at heart. Rheia of the delicate veil then said:
"Come, child, Zeus, heavy-thundering and mighty-voiced,
summons you to rejoin the tribes of the gods;
he has offered to give what honors you choose among them.
He agreed that his daughter would spend one-third
of the revolving year in the misty dark, and two-thirds
with her mother and the other immortals.
He guaranteed it would be so with a nod of his head.
So come, my child, obey me; do not rage overmuch
and forever at the dark-clouded son of Kronos.   470
Now make the grain grow fertile for humankind."
So Rheia spoke, and rich-crowned Demeter did not disobey.
At once she sent forth fruit from the fertile fields
and the whole wide earth burgeoned with leaves
and flowers. She went to the kings who administer law,
Triptolemos and Diokles, driver of horses, mighty
Eumolpos and Keleos, leader of the people, and revealed
the conduct of her rites and taught her Mysteries to all of them,
holy rites that are not to be transgressed, nor pried into,
nor divulged. For a great awe of the gods stops the voice.   480
Blessed is the mortal on earth who has seen these rites,
but the uninitiate who has no share in them never
has the same lot once dead in the dreary darkness.
When the great goddess had founded all her rites,
the goddesses left for Olympus and the assembly of the other gods.
There they dwell by Zeus delighting-in-thunder, inspiring
awe and reverence. Highly blessed is the mortal
on earth whom they graciously favor with love.
For soon they will send to the hearth of his great house
Ploutos, the god giving abundance to mortals.   490
But come, you goddesses, dwelling in the town of
fragrant Eleusis, and seagirt Paros, and rocky Antron,
revered Deo, mighty giver of seasons and glorious gifts,
you and your very fair daughter Persephone,

for my song grant gladly a living that warms the heart.
And I shall remember you and a new song as well.

. . . .

Questions for Discussion and Review

1. What are the three functions of the Great Goddess, and why are they important? Explain why and how her three functions are divided among the various Olympian goddesses.

2. One of the Great Goddess's primary symbols is the serpent. What aspects of the Goddess's power are symbolized by the serpent? Explain why the perception of the snake as depicted in myth changes from a beautiful and beneficent creature into a terrifying monster or dragon. How does that change reflect the transformation from matriarchal to patriarchal systems?

3. What roles and qualities do Demeter and Persephone share with Dionysus? How are they different? Discuss the similarities and differences in the rites celebrating these deities. How might the gender of each of these deities help explain the differences?

4. In the *Homeric Hymn to Demeter,* why does Demeter go to Eleusis? Why does she want to make the child Demophon immortal? How does the apparent inability of gods and humans to understand each other contribute to her failure? In what ways does the Eleusinian ritual she demands to compensate for the insult to her divinity assist her worshipers in communicating with the goddess?

5. What is the gift of Triptolemus to humankind? Explain the relevance of this myth to the development of agricultural communities. How does understanding the growth processes of plants aid humans in understanding their own lives? How might living in agricultural villages affect the lives of people who had previously lived as hunters of animals and gatherers of grain? What would that change contribute to the development of civilization?

Works Cited

Weiss, Rick. "Males not mandatory to these mice." *Washington Post.* Rpt. *Sacramento Bee,* April 22, 2004: A9.

The Olympian Family of Zeus: Sharing Rule of the Universe

KEY TOPICS/THEMES

Originally conceived as amoral forces—embodiments of natural processes and/or instinctual drives—the Greek gods eventually evolved into idealized images of humanity. Transformed by the poets to reflect Greek society's concept of aristocratic leadership, the Olympians typically enforce exacting standards of justice in earthly society while enjoying the option to behave capriciously when manipulating human lives.

According to Homer, after Zeus achieved mastery of the universe by vanquishing the Titans, he and his two brothers, Poseidon and Hades, cast lots to divide the world among themselves (*Iliad,* Book 15). In this apportionment of power, Zeus receives the sky, Poseidon the sea, and Hades the Underworld as their respective domains. The three divine rulers agree to share jurisdiction of the earth, assuming equal freedom to intervene in human affairs.

In the *Theogony,* however, with its emphasis on Zeus's supremacy, Hesiod states that, after Gaea advised the gods to invite Zeus to rule over them, Zeus himself decided which gods were to govern specific natural phenomena or facets of human activity, be it love or war. Leaving little in Zeus's administration to chance, Hesiod's account includes no casting of lots.

Whether achieved by a fated roll of the dice or through his personal shrewdness in assigning congenial spheres of influence to his brothers, sisters, and children, Zeus's reign—in direct contrast to that of his predecessors Uranus and Cronus—is characterized by lasting order and stability. Although he occasionally encounters

179

temporary opposition from members of his divine family, Zeus remains in power because he wisely gives each fellow Olympian the authority to govern independently his or her particular aspect of the cosmos and/or human society—whether it be Poseidon's control of the sea; Athene's patronage of the well-governed city-state; Apollo's jurisdiction over the creative arts, medicine, and prophecy; or Aphrodite's celebration of the ever-present erotic passion that drives both gods and humans.

In ascribing cosmic rule to a family of highly differentiated divine personalities, Greek myth not only projects typically Greek social hierarchies on heavenly Olympus but also helps to account for the contradictions and oppositions of the cosmos. Just as humans contend for power and influence in both the domestic sphere and the city-state, so the gods themselves, within the bounds of kin relationships, compete to attain their own goals, bringing a complex mixture of good and evil to human existence. In myth, the social-sexual dynamics of the Olympian family, as well as the volatile interaction of gods and mortals, reflects both Greek social realities and the endless vicissitudes of life itself.

A brilliant mosaic of nobility, splendor, and amoral passion, the Greek pantheon mirrors the values and contrarieties of the patriarchal society that fashioned it as a viable image of our essentially paradoxical universe. Although a few Greek thinkers, such as Plato, criticized the ethical flaws that myth ascribes to the gods (see Chapter 2), most classical writers delighted in exploring the psychological affinity that linked humans to divinity. Portraying a class of beings who achieve virtually every human wish, myth simultaneously emphasizes both the mysterious but painfully real gulf that forever separates humanity from the immortals and the glorious exploits of mortal heroes and heroines who exhibit a portion of the divine glory.

The Older Olympians

Although Homeric myth gives all of Zeus's siblings equal access to Mount Olympus, Hades, whose reign is largely confined to the dark nether regions, almost never appears there. Thus, despite being Zeus's brother, he is not usually counted among the twelve Olympians. When Dionysus, Zeus's son by the mortal princess Semele, is elevated to Olympus, the number of Olympians is kept at twelve by the demotion of Zeus's sister Hestia. (Membership in the Twelve varied slightly in different parts of Greece; see Figure 6-1 for a standard genealogy of the Olympians.)

Although the Greeks accepted the existence of many other deities of earth and sea, only the immediate family of Zeus lived on Olympus: every Olympian is a brother, sister, or child of Zeus. That Greek myth presents the major gods as constituting an extended family of parents, children, aunts and uncles—with its inevitable rivalries, conflicts, and sparring for power—is significant. Even at home on Olympus, Zeus is not free of domestic turmoil. As divine patriarch, he is forced to devote much of his time to settling disputes among quarreling brothers (see the *Hymn to Hermes*); adjudicating among some Olympians' rival agendas, such as Athene's and Poseidon's opposing intentions toward Odysseus (see Chapter 13); and, above all, dealing with Hera's persistent schemes to thwart his imperial will. On occasion, some of Zeus's nearest and dearest—including not only his wife and

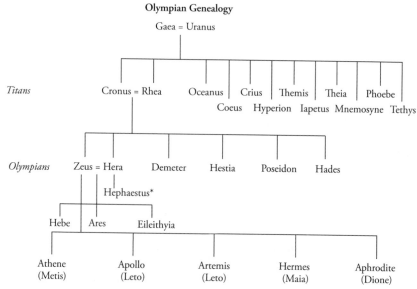

FIGURE 6-1   Genealogy of Zeus's Olympian Family. The Greek pantheon consists exclusively of close family members, all of whom are descendants of the original divine parents, Gaea and Uranus. The older Olympians—Zeus and his siblings—are offspring of the Titans Cronus and Rhea, while the younger are children of Zeus by various wives or, in the case of Hephaestus, of Hera. The names of Zeus's wives are enclosed in parentheses beneath the names of their divine offspring. (Hades, who lives in the Underworld, technically is not one of the Twelve.) *Although Hesiod has Hera produce Hephaestus parthenogenetically, Homer states that Zeus is his father.

his brother Poseidon but also his favorite daughter, Athene—conspire to challenge his authority.

In the *Iliad,* Achilles briefly refers to a plot hatched by Hera, Poseidon, and Athene to "bind" Zeus, a conspiracy aborted by the intervention of Achilles' mother, the sea nymph Thetis (*Iliad,* Book 1). After Thetis summons Briareus (also called Aegaeon), one of the hundred-armed giants who had helped Zeus defeat the Titans, the three divine conspirators hastily abandon their project. Homer gives no details about what the three gods hoped to achieve in binding Zeus. However, because the incident appears in the context of the Trojan War, the plotters may have intended to advance the Achaean (Greek) side, which all three supported. Athene's participation in the attempted coup is surprising, but this deviation from her customary role of dutiful daughter illustrates the fragility of the family bond, even on the heavenly level.

Despite intermittent disobedience or even treachery on the part of his closest relatives, Zeus generally reigns unopposed, successfully subordinating all other deities to his administration. Some gods who in early Greek history had enjoyed an existence independent of Zeus are, in the myths of the Archaic and Classical periods, brought under his jurisdiction. As Hesiod reports in the *Theogony,* some Olympians, such as Aphrodite, were once thought to have appeared long before Zeus was born. As generations of poets, including Homer, emphasized the supremacy of Zeus, however, these older gods were refashioned as Zeus's siblings or children, effectively placing them under his control. Such figures as Aphrodite, Poseidon, Artemis, and Hermes, who in prehistoric and Mycenaean times may have been Zeus's peers, were transformed during the Archaic and Classical periods into dependent family members supporting his patriarchy.

In the eighth and early seventh centuries B.C., respectively, Homer and Hesiod helped to establish the character and functions of the Olympians; during the later Archaic and Classical periods, Greek artists defined their physical appearance. The older generation of Zeus and his five siblings, the children of Cronus and Rhea, were depicted as physically mature, an unchanging perfection of early middle age. Although retaining the superb musculature of the athlete, Zeus and his brothers have the full beards and thick, flowing locks that proclaim their patriarchal status and their membership in the age group that typically governs society. Zeus's sisters —Hera, Demeter, and Hestia—are similarly portrayed as majestic, with the full figures of feminine maturity.

The following thumbnail character sketches briefly introduce the principal gods, surveying their essential qualities and functions and offering examples of their defining myths. The epic narratives, lyric hymns, and tragic dramas anthologized in this text show the gods operating in the fully realized literary context that the Greek poets created for them, maneuvering among themselves to achieve their individual objectives or influencing humans to carry out the divine will. Because the gods' characteristic motivations, behaviors, and passions are most effectively illustrated in these literary embodiments of myth, the discussion of each god provides references to specific works in which they appear. The gods' Latin names, which may be more familiar to many readers, are included in parentheses after the Greek name.

Zeus (Jupiter, Jove)

The closest that Greek religion came to conceptualizing a supreme being, **Zeus** is the awe-inspiring King of Heaven, the champion of justice, sworn oaths, lawful order, and hospitality, particularly the sacred obligations of the host–guest relationship (Figure 6-2). An Indo-European sky god, Zeus denotes the clear, luminous daylight sky; his name corresponds to that of a celestial deity from ancient India, *Dyaus pitar* (Greek, *Zeu pater*). In Roman myth, he is Jupiter (*Diespiter,* meaning "God [Zeus] the father"). The same root appears in the Latin *deus* ("god") and *dies* ("day") and the Greek *eudia* ("fair weather"), indicating Zeus's association with the bright light of day. In Homer's famous phrase, Zeus is also "the cloud-gatherer," the frightening power that generates storms, a function the Greeks also recognized in another of Zeus's epithets, *Ombrios* (bringer of rain). His most formidable weapon is the thunderbolt, blasts of lightning that he effectively employed to defeat the Titans. As a symbol of his masculine prowess, the lightning bolt represents both the scepter and spear by which he compels universal obedience and the divine phallus that brings rain (semen) to fertilize the earth.

The most ethically developed Olympian, Zeus represents the ultimate court of appeal to whose judgments both men and gods must submit. Unlike the Judeo-

FIGURE 6-2 Zeus Holding a Thunderbolt (or Poseidon Wielding His Trident). If this fifth-century B.C. bronze represents Zeus, the bearded patriarch is about to hurl a thunderbolt, the ultimate weapon by which he enforces his will. The epitome of masculine dignity, the King of Heaven has conquered all rivals, including his father, Cronus, and Gaea's chaotic serpent Typhoeus. His is the power that keeps the universe in moral equilibrium. *(National Museum, Athens)*

Christian or Islamic God, however, Zeus is neither omniscient nor all-powerful. His relation to Fate, the irresistible power of Necessity that directs the flow of history, is ambiguous. In many myths, Fate is a force superior to the gods; in the Homeric poems, Zeus almost always refrains from even contemplating a change in the heroes' individual destinies. For a fleeting moment, he is tempted to save from an early death his mortal son Sarpedon, an exceptionally brave and noble warrior who fought against the Greeks in the Trojan War. When confronted with Hera's scorn and the unpredictable consequences of interfering with destiny, however, Zeus reluctantly agrees not to intervene on Sarpedon's behalf. In some myths, it is difficult to determine whether Zeus accedes to the dictates of Fate because he does not wish

The Major Gods and Their Functions

GOD/ GODDESS	CHIEF ATTRIBUTES/FUNCTIONS/SHRINES
Zeus (Jupiter)	Son of Cronus and Rhea; conqueror of the Titans; king of the Olympian gods; brother and husband of Hera; guarantor of cosmic order and justice; patron of hospitality; regulator of weather, particularly thunder and lightning; protector of the free city-state; major cults on Crete and at Olympia where the Olympic Games were dedicated to him; Zeus's oracle at Dodona was reputedly the oldest in Greece. Symbols: the eagle, the thunderbolt, and (sometimes) a serpent.
Poseidon (Neptune)	Son of Cronus and Rhea; lord of the sea and earthquakes; husband of Amphitrite; major temples at the Isthmus of Corinth, where the Isthmian Games were held in his honor, and at Mount Mycale in Asia Minor. Symbols: the three-pronged trident or a giant bull.
Hades (Pluto, Dis)	Son of Cronus and Rhea; king of the Underworld; husband of Demeter's daughter Persephone. Symbol: a cap of invisibility.
Hera (Juno)	Daughter of Cronus and Rhea; sister and wife of Zeus; Queen of Heaven; patron of marriage and married women; principal sanctuaries near Argos and Mycenae and on Samos. Symbol: the peacock.
Demeter (Ceres)	Daughter of Cronus and Rhea; mother of Persephone by Zeus; patron of agriculture and source of the soil's fertility and grain harvest; founder, at Eleusis (near Athens), of the Eleusinian Mysteries, secret rites celebrating death and rebirth. Symbol: a sheaf of golden wheat.
Hestia (Vesta)	Daughter of Cronus and Rhea; virgin goddess of the hearth; as Vesta, her temple in the Roman forum housed a sacred flame symbolizing the city's eternity. Symbol: the household fire and hearth.
Athene (Minerva)	Daughter of Zeus (and Metis); virgin goddess of wisdom and victory in war; patron of weavers and potters; defender of the Greek polis and special protector of Athens; the Parthenon, her most famous sanctuary, stood atop the Athenian Acropolis, but she also had temples in Argos, Sparta, and many other Greek cities. Symbols: a warrior's helmet, spear, and shield; the aegis, a breastplate adorned with the Gorgon's head; and the owl.
Aphrodite (Venus)	Daughter of Zeus and Dione (Homer); according to Hesiod, she was born from seafoam surrounding the semen and severed genitals of Uranus; goddess of beauty, sexual love, and desire; wife of Hephaestus (Vulcan); lover of Ares (Mars); in Homer, the mother of Eros/Cupid. Symbol: the dove.

The Major Gods and Their Functions

GOD/ GODDESS	CHIEF ATTRIBUTES/FUNCTIONS/SHRINES
Hermes (Mercury)	Son of Zeus and Maia; messenger of Zeus; father of Pan, conductor of newly deceased souls to the Underworld; god of luck, sleep, dreams, magic, roads, and boundaries; patron of travelers, merchants, thieves, tricksters, athletes, and orators. Symbols: winged sandals, broad-brimmed traveler's hat, and the caduceus, a wand around which two serpents are entwined (also used by Asclepius, god of healing).
Apollo (Phoebus)	Son of Zeus and Leto; twin brother of Artemis; god of light, rationality, health, plague, prophecy, masculine beauty, music, and all the creative arts; patron of shepherds, the Muses, and the Delphic Oracle. His most sacred sites are found on Delos, his island birthplace, and at Delphi, where the Pythian Games were held in his honor. He later replaced Helios/Hyperion as the god who each day drove the sun's chariot across heaven. Symbol: bow and arrow, the lyre; later, the sun.
Artemis (Diana)	Daughter of Zeus and Leto; twin sister of Apollo; virgin goddess of wildlife and the hunt; patron of women and of childbirth; later identified, at Ephesus and elsewhere in Asia Minor, with Near Eastern fertility deities; she later assumed the functions of Selene, the moon. At Artemis's most famous festival, the Brauronia, young girls, pretending to be bears, underwent a rite of passage into maturity and qualification for marriage. The largest temple in the ancient world was dedicated to Artemis at Ephesus. Symbols: bow and arrow; later, the moon.
Hephaestus (Vulcan)	Son of Zeus and Hera or, according to Hesiod, son of Hera alone; husband of Aphrodite; god of fire, the forge, and metalcraft; builder of the gods' palace on Olympus. Major cults on Lemnos, the island to which he fell when hurled from heaven, and at Athens, where he was patron of many crafts. Symbol: hammer and anvil.
Ares (Mars)	Son of Zeus and Hera; god of violence, war, and frenzied aggression; lover of Aphrodite. Little honored in Greece, Ares was later identified with the Roman Mars, a more important Italian god of war and agriculture. Chief cult site: Rome. Symbol: the sword.
Dionysus (Bacchus)	Son of Zeus and the mortal virgin Semele, reborn from his father's thigh; god of wine, emotional freedom, and ecstasy; patron of wine festivals, such as the City Dionysia at Athens; inspirer of both tragedy and comedy, suffering and joy. Symbols: the grape vine, the actor's mask.

to upset the cosmic order or whether he cannot change the basic operation of a universe he did not create.

Hesiod complicates the relationship between Zeus and Fate by giving two contradictory accounts of Fate's origins. In one version, long before Zeus's birth, Night (Nyx) parthenogenetically delivers the **Moirae,** the three sisters who spin the threads and weave the patterns controlling mortal lives. In another, Zeus fathers the Moirae by Themis, whose name means "the right" or "established custom," thus implying that the god is both the source of and independent of Fate. Also by Themis, Zeus sires Lawfulness (Eunomia), Justice (Dike), and Peace (Eirene), indicating that he is the force that keeps the cosmos, including his household of fractious, egocentric deities, operating in relative harmony.

Because Zeus is a compendium of amoral nature, symbolized by the thunderbolt, and a projection of Greek patriarchal leadership, his character is correspondingly paradoxical. Warring against his imperial dignity as king, husband, father, and judge is Zeus's apparently uncontrollable sexual appetite, which compels him to pursue virtually every attractive person—mortal or immortal, male or female—within his considerable reach. In the *Theogony,* Hesiod validates this aspect of Zeus's character by highlighting the cosmic benefits of his divine hero's compulsive promiscuity. Zeus's extramarital affairs with goddesses, nymphs, and mortal women produce sons and daughters of extraordinary superiority. Who could object to liaisons that result in such gods as Apollo and Artemis or heroes such as Perseus and Heracles? In cataloguing Zeus's conquests and their offspring, Hesiod informs us that the chief Olympian's sexual adventures not only enrich the human gene pool with heroic stock but also populate the cosmos with beings who represent the highest values of civilization. Thus, Zeus begets such progeny as the Muses, who inspire all the creative arts, and other divine abstractions, including the Graces, personifications of beauty and charm, and the Seasons, guarantors of cosmic order. Without Zeus's virile generosity in siring these children, Hesiod implies, the universe would be no better than it was under the generally uncivilized Titans.

In modern astronomy, Zeus's amorous conquests have been commemorated in the sixteen moons circling our solar system's largest planet, which bears Zeus's Latin name, Jupiter. Taking their cue from classical mythology, astronomers named each of Jupiter's satellites after one of Zeus's lovers: these include **Europa,** a mortal woman whom he abducted in the form of a white bull; **Callisto,** a nymph who was part of Artemis's virgin retinue until Zeus seduced her and she was changed into a bear; **Io,** a mortal virgin whom Zeus brutally raped in the form of a bull (see Chapter 4); and **Ganymede,** a handsome Trojan youth whom Zeus desired and, in the guise of an eagle, seized and carried off to Olympus (Figure 6-3). The only one of Zeus's lovers permanently installed in heaven, Ganymede was made cupbearer of the gods, pouring out wine at Olympian banquets. If future astronomers discover additional moons orbiting Jupiter, they are unlikely to run out of lovers' names to bestow on them. Some ancient mythographers tallied no fewer than 115 different objects of Zeus's affections.

The god's lust, which is at once the instinctual "shadow" of Zeus's ostensibly rational persona and a projection of his will to control and dominate, at times produces a comic spectacle. Myth shows heaven's love-obsessed king sneaking about in disguise, abandoning his divine splendor to assume the form of a bull, swan,

The Major Classical Gods and Goddesses

ANGLICIZED NAME	TRANSLITERATED GREEK NAME	LATIN NAME
Zeus	Zeus	Jupiter, Jove
Poseidon	Poseidon	Neptune
Hades, Pluto	Hades, Plouton, Aidoneus	Pluto, Dis
Hera	Here	Juno
Hestia	Hestia	Vesta
Demeter	Demeter	Ceres
Athene (Athena)	Athene	Minerva
Aphrodite	Aphrodite	Venus
Hermes	Hermes	Mercury (Mercurius)
Phoebus Apollo	Phoibos Apollon	Phoebus Apollo
Artemis	Artemis	Diana
Hephaestus	Hephaistos	Vulcan (Vulcanus)
Ares	Ares	Mars
Dionysus, Bacchus, Bromius	Dionysos, Bakchos, Bromios	Liber
Pan	Pan	Faunus
Gaea	Gaia	Terra Mater
Uranus	Ouranos	Caelum
Cronus	Kronos	Saturn
Rhea, Cybele	Rheia, Kybele	Ops
Eros	Eros	Cupid (Cupido)
Eileithyia	Eileithyie	Lucina
Helios	Helios	Sol, Phoebus
Selene	Selene	Luna
Persephone, Cora	Persephone, Kore	Proserpina
Hebe	Hebe	Juventas

serpent, or eagle, images of the nonhuman power he represents—all in the (usually vain) hope of escaping his wife's ever-watchful eye. Although his desire can be cruelly exploitative, as it is with the unfortunate Io, many poets depict Zeus humorously, as henpecked by Hera at home and driven by an indefatigable libido abroad. Although the myths recounting Zeus's amorous adventures may serve to uphold a double standard that permits men greater sexual freedom than women, they also

FIGURE 6-3 Zeus and Ganymede. This terra-cotta statue depicts Zeus carrying off the Trojan boy Ganymede, whom the god will install on Olympus as his lover and cupbearer, the honored wine server at the gods' banquets. Shown striding forward in a rush to enjoy his prize, Zeus manifests the classical Greek attraction toward the physical beauty of young men. Although Hera objects passionately to her husband's liaisons with other goddesses, nymphs, and mortal women, she accepts Ganymede's presence in heaven, where the youth is identified with the zodiacal sign of Aquarius. *(Olympia Museum, Greece)*

remind us of the enormous variety and complexity of humanity's sexual nature. In Greek myth, Eros and Aphrodite overwhelm even the gods.

As divine patron of the Olympic Games (founded 776 B.C.), Zeus was honored by a large temple at Olympia, for which the Athenian sculptor Phidias (c. 438 B.C.) designed the ancient world's most famous representation of divinity. In creating this forty-foot-tall statue of Zeus, Phidias used the same method as for his earlier figure of Athene in the Parthenon—a technique known as chryselephantine, in which a wooden frame is overlaid with closely joined panels of ivory for the flesh and gold for the garments. Wishing to portray Zeus as Homer's majestic King of Heaven whose voice made all Olympus quake (*Iliad,* Book 1), Phidias depicted the enthroned god holding a winged figure of Victory (Nike) in his right hand and an enormous staff topped with a golden eagle in his left. At Zeus's feet was a large, shallow pool of olive oil that kept visitors from approaching the ornately bejeweled deity too closely. The pool reflected sunlight from the temple doorway onto Zeus's face (which otherwise would have been obscured by shadows in the windowless sanctuary) and may have provided moisture to keep Zeus's ivory skin from drying out.

Philo of Byzantium (c. 200 B.C.) expressed the sense of divinity commonly evoked by Phidias's masterpiece, which was early acknowledged as among the Seven Wonders of the ancient world: "Whereas we just wonder at the other six wonders, we kneel in front of this one in reverence because the execution of the skill is as incredible as the image of Zeus is holy." Although many classical writers echoed Philo's praise, the Roman geographer Strabo (c. 4 B.C.–A.D. 25) viewed the statue with an engineer's practicality, noting that if Phidias's Zeus were to stand up, his head would go through the temple's disproportionately low roof. Even more skeptical, the Roman satirist Lucian compared the hollow statue's hidden scaffolding—infested with rats and mice, he said—to the inferior reality lurking behind the grandiose images that kings and emperors present to the public.

As king of the gods, Zeus is the dominant figure in many myths, including Hesiod's account of Zeus as divine warrior whose military strength defeated and replaced older deities (see Chapters 3 and 4). Homer emphasizes Zeus's impressive dignity as the Olympian ruler who wisely arbitrates the competing claims of other Olympians, showing him presiding over the gods' heavenly councils (see the *Iliad*, Book 1, in Chapter 12, and the *Odyssey*, Book 1, in Chapter 13). By contrast, Zeus appears as an indulgent father to the mischievous infant Hermes, settling a dispute between two quarreling sons with benign good humor (see the *Homeric Hymn to Hermes* at the end of this chapter). Even when he does not visibly intervene in divine or human affairs, his is the controlling will that shapes the action of numerous heroic myths, including that of Agamemnon and his family in the *Oresteia* (see Chapter 15) and, as Jupiter, that of the hero Aeneas (see Chapter 19).

Hera (Juno)

The most powerful of the Olympian goddesses, **Hera** [HEE-ra] (Figure 6-4) is the only one to retain the creative power of parthenogenesis originally possessed by Gaea, albeit with somewhat diminished effectiveness: she produced by that method only the ungainly Hephaestus. Possibly descended from the Cretan snake goddess and also related to the Syrian Great Mother (see Figure 5-4), Hera is said to renew her virginity every spring as naturally as a serpent sheds its skin, an event celebrated annually in Argos, where she was the dominant deity long before her assimilation as the wife of Zeus, and where the cult of Hera paid widespread homage to her Bronze Age role in agriculture, adolescent initiations, and war. In the latter role, as defender of the citadel of Argos, Hera is associated with the Argive heroes, including Jason and the Argonauts and Agamemnon. She also made sure that Eurystheus, Heracles' nemesis (see Chapter 10), would be born before Zeus's human offspring, ensuring that the kingship would fall to a native Argive citizen. But her earliest and most important function was seasonal fertility. Evidence suggests that Hera was originally an earth goddess. In fact, the oldest ruins in the Peloponnese are

FIGURE 6-4 Hera. As the goddess of marriage and marital fidelity, Hera finds herself in an unending war against her brother-husband's promiscuity. Because her function is to uphold family values and punish those who violate them, she typically appears as an angry persecutor of Zeus's innumerable mistresses and their children. *(Vatican Museums, Rome)*

associated with Hera. Reinforcing her possible link to a Creator goddess is the title she bore in Sparta—"Hera Aphrodite." At her shrine at Samos, where offerings of pomegranates, a common fertility symbol, were made to her, she may have been worshiped as a tree goddess. Hera retains the primal goddess's features as patron of childbirth, a function doubled in her daughter **Eileithyia** [ye-lye-THYE-ya], also a childbirth goddess. Her portrayal as "cow-eyed" also connects her with divine fertility, and she is sometimes referred to as "cow-faced." A source of cosmic nourishment, her breasts give the milk that forms the Milky Way. The link to Gaea is similarly suggested in some variants in which it is Hera who is the parthenogenetic mother of the monster Typhoeus and who gives him to Python, guardian of the Delphic shrine, to raise (see Chapter 7).

Eventually represented as the wife of Zeus, Hera is interpreted under the patriarchy as the goddess of marriage. Thus, she is subject to a double standard of judging sexual behavior. She remains, as expected, sexually loyal to Zeus, while he constantly betrays her with other females, as well as males, both divine and human. According to some mythographers, his first extramarital affair was with Io, a priestess of Hera. Zeus turns Io into a heifer to protect her from the anger of Hera. (In some variants, it is Hera who turns Io into a cow to prevent her rape by Zeus, who then comes to Io in the form of a white bull.) (See the discussion of Io's role in Chapter 4.) When all ruses and other measures fail, a furious Hera sends a gadfly to torment the heifer; the gadfly pursues Io all the way to Egypt, where she is credited with spreading the worship of Demeter. Some versions even conflate Io with the Egyptian goddess Isis, who is often portrayed as the traditional "horned goddess." Although in this tale Hera and Io are rivals, some scholars see Io as a variant of Hera, who is also a cow goddess—a white cow married to Zeus in the form of a white bull.

Hera's power, manifest in her ability to metamorphose her rivals into animals, is also revealed in her ability to drive heroes like Heracles insane (see Chapter 10). Despite her power, she is portrayed under Zeus's regime as the stereotype of the nagging, jealous wife. The tension between Hera's assumption of some powers of the Creator goddess and her subordination under Zeus's rule is similar to the ambiguous status of another cow goddess, the Egyptian Nut (or Hathor, yet another Egyptian cow goddess, whose stories are often conflated with those of Nut). The sun god, Amon-Ra, in his form as a bull, descends into the womb of the goddess, sails all night through her belly, and is born again each morning as a golden calf, the bull calf of the sun, who then grows into a powerful bull, only to repeat the journey each night. The cow goddess who, in earlier myths, sacrificed the bull god to ensure renewal, is now depicted as his mother. The goddess is clearly essential to give birth (and rebirth) to the god. But the calf she bears each morning rules her world, and she is subordinated.

Hera has a similarly complex relationship with Zeus. As Zeus's wife, she reinforces marriage as a social institution, in effect chartering her own subordination. Indeed, Zeus's taking of many consorts, especially among the Titans and his Olympian sisters, effectively subordinates all the goddesses' powers to his own. After an early attempt at rebellion—a failed conspiracy, with Poseidon, to overthrow Zeus—Hera settles down into an uneasy but permanent relationship with her husband, reserving her anger for his many children by other females, divine and human. At the same time, her marriage transforms Zeus from an expendable source of conception (as were Uranus and Cronus) to a god of family love who, unlike his predecessors, maintains positive relationships with his children and whose reign is thus comparatively stable.

Despite her exalted status as Queen of Heaven, myth depicts Hera as leading a frustrating and generally unhappy existence, largely because her priorities collide head-on with the will of Zeus. Nor was Hera's childhood a secure and pleasant experience: along with Poseidon, Hades, Hestia, and Demeter, she was swallowed alive by her father, Cronus. Only when her mother, Rhea, beguiled Cronus into regurgitating his children did her life begin, and then she was sent to live with foster parents, Oceanus and Tethys, while Zeus battled Cronus and his Titan allies. Although Oceanus and Tethys were also Titans, as personifications, respectively, of the great river that surrounds the earth and the sea's inexhaustible fecundity, they were essential cosmic features and hence survived even as the other Titans fell. Grateful for their protection during her youth, Hera is said to have reconciled the couple after they had been divided by a bitter quarrel.

Unfortunately, Hera is less successful—and apparently much less diplomatic—in mediating differences in her own marriage to Zeus. Although she is the patron of weddings, wives, marriage, and family life, Hera rarely shares her husband's viewpoint and tries to subvert his plans whenever possible. In a famous incident from the *Iliad* (Books 14–15), Hera determines to manipulate events so that the Greeks will thoroughly trounce the Trojans, whom she hates (see Chapter 12). Accordingly, she borrows Aphrodite's erotically charmed girdle to seduce her husband and thereby distract his attention from the war. The couple make love atop lofty **Mount Ida,** which Zeus swathes in a thick cloud to ensure their privacy. When Zeus awakens from postcoital slumber, however, and realizes his wife's deception, he is furious, reminding Hera of the occasion on which he used his superior strength to suspend her from Olympus by her wrists, with huge anvils tied to her feet!

Hera also acts to spite Zeus when, in retaliation for his producing Athene without her aid, she—without *his* participation—conceives and, according to Hesiod, gives birth to Hephaestus, a defiant attempt to upstage Zeus's patriarchal self-sufficiency (although Homer names Zeus and Hera as Hephaestus's parents). In some versions of the myth, Hephaestus is born crippled, the only physically imperfect Olympian, and in disgust Hera throws the newborn out of heaven. Homer preserves two different versions of Hephaestus's fall. In one, after being thrown out by Hera, the lame god plunges into the sea where Thetis and her fellow sea nymphs rescue him (*Iliad,* Book 18). In the second, it is not Hera but Zeus—angry at Hephaestus's defense of his mother—who hurls him down from Olympus, to land on the volcanic island of Lemnos (*Iliad,* Book 1). In a sequel to the first version of this tale, Hephaestus avenges himself on his unaffectionate mother by designing and sending her a treacherous golden throne. Once seated on the throne, Hera is a prisoner: Hephaestus has contrived a golden chain that automatically wraps itself about the throne's occupant, holding her immobile. Only when Dionysus seeks him out, gets him drunk, and leads him back to Olympus does Hephaestus reluctantly consent to release his mother.

Despite her role as celestial wife, Hera is not a maternal figure, and Greek artists never depict her, as the Egyptians portrayed Isis, as a tender mother holding her child. In some accounts, the only child she and Zeus produce is Ares, the ill-tempered war god, who is a fitting symbol of his parents' contentious union. In others, the royal couple also produce Eileithyia, a goddess of childbirth, and **Hebe** [HEE-bee], a personification of blooming youth whom Zeus later replaces with Ganymede as the Olympians' cupbearer.

Interestingly, myth depicts none of the Olympian goddesses as prolific childbearers: Hestia, Athene, and Artemis remain virgins; and Demeter, for all her maternal devotion to Persephone, produces only two or three children. Even Aphrodite, the personification of sexuality and fertility, has few offspring. Although some myths make Eros (Cupid) her son by Ares, in Hesiod's *Theogony* Eros is a primal god who existed long before Aphrodite's birth.

While acknowledging that Homeric and other myths emphasize Hera's unattractive qualities, it is important to remember that her behavior may embody a reaction to the patriarchal usurpation of earlier goddesses' rights and privileges. Zeus's imperious refusal to be faithful to Olympus's highest goddess only emphasizes the male god's complete independence of the divine female. At the same time, Hera's cosmic importance is voiced in a myth about the newborn Heracles. In this tale,

Hermes finds Hera asleep and stealthily places the infant Heracles at the goddess's breast. When the baby begins to nurse, however, Hera awakens, thrusting Zeus's son aside before he can absorb the milk of immortality. But it is too late: a powerful jet of Hera's milk streams across the night sky, igniting thousands of brilliant stars. Visible every clear night, the Milky Way bears silent tribute to heaven's troubled queen, forming a display far more impressive than Jupiter's lonely, endlessly circling moons (see Color Plate 3).

Although Homer portrays her as a compelling presence at the gods' deliberations on Olympus, where she typically attempts (usually unsuccessfully) to persuade Zeus to conduct affairs according to her liking, myth accords Hera relatively few appearances on earth. A famous exception is her visit, disguised as a friendly old woman, to the Theban princess Semele, then pregnant with Dionysus. Although she deceives Semele into committing an act that destroys her, Hera fails to prevent the wine god's birth, and her subsequent attempts to harass and even kill the child are typical of her methods in dealing with her husband's illegitimate offspring (see Chapters 8 and 17). Hera's lack of sisterly feeling, even for innocent victims of Zeus's lust, and her unforgiving persecution of the noble Aeneas led Virgil, Rome's greatest poet, to ask, "Is vindictiveness an attribute of the celestial mind?"

Poseidon (Neptune)

Just as Zeus compels obedience with his thunderbolts, so **Poseidon** [poh-SYE-duhn] uses the trident, a huge three-pronged spear with which he generates monstrous sea waves to crush the ships of any who offend him (Figure 6-5). Like the restless element over which he rules, Poseidon is volatile, unpredictable, and quick to rage. Any sailor venturing into his realm must propitiate the god with acceptable sacrifices if he hopes to reach his destination safely. In the *Odyssey,* Poseidon represents the brutal power of nature against which the hero must pit his human intelligence in order to survive. Homer also suggests an important component of Poseidon's character through his son Polyphemus, an uncouth Cyclops who devours his guests and refuses to observe any code of civilized behavior (see Chapter 13).

Although master of the sea, Poseidon is also associated with land animals such as bulls and horses—images of masculine virility (Figure 6-6). When the earth rumbles and shakes, it is the effect of Poseidon, in the form of a colossal bull, bellowing and pawing the ground. As the invisible earthshaker, he was worshiped from Mycenaean times on as lord of earthquakes, a personification of seismic energy.

As an embodiment of natural violence and the begetter of monstrous offspring, Poseidon is a particularly dangerous god. If offended, he is merciless even to his worshipers; when the Phaeacians, once favorites of the sea's ruler, provide Odysseus with safe conduct back to Ithaca, he angrily turns their ship to stone and shatters their city's peace by convulsing the earth and elevating a mountain range to surround the city (*Odyssey,* Book 13). Not surprisingly, when humans first began to settle in cities, many were reluctant to choose Poseidon as their presiding deity. In fact, the list of gods who successfully competed against Poseidon to become the divine patrons of cities throughout Greece is impressive. In competition for Corinth, Poseidon lost to Helios (the Sun); for Aegina, to Zeus; for Troezen and Athens, to Athene; for Argos, to Hera; for Delphi, to Apollo; and for Naxos, to Dionysus.

FIGURE 6-5 Poseidon of Melos. This colossal marble statue of Poseidon, carved about 140 B.C. and found on the Greek island of Melos in 1877, portrays the strength and majesty of Zeus's brother. In his upraised right hand, Poseidon grasps a trident, the three-pronged instrument with which he stirs the sea to destructive fury during storms. Worshiped throughout Greece for his connection with shipping and navigation, he was patron of the Isthmian Games, held near his temple at the Isthmus of Corinth, perhaps because of Corinth's strategic location as a major seaport. Despite Poseidon's unpredictable rages, which wrecked ships and drowned sailors, his patronage was essential to the seafaring Greeks. *(National Archaeological Museum, Athens)*

Although widely recognized as a natural force that must be placated, Poseidon's surly temperament earned him a poor showing in mythic popularity contests.

Living along the rugged coastlines of Greece, the Aegean Islands, and Asia Minor (western Turkey), the Greeks were a seafaring people who naturally feared the Mediterranean storms that menaced their ships, a fact of life that made unavoidable a close relationship with Poseidon, lord of the dangerous element over which they traveled. Nonetheless, Poseidon has relatively few myths besides his unsuccessful contest with Athene for Athens' patronage (see Chapter 1) and, most important, his role as Odysseus's divine opponent in the *Odyssey* (see Chapter 13). In the *Iliad,* he took the side of the Greeks against Troy, reputedly because Laomedon, a Trojan king, had refused to pay him for his work on building Troy's defensive walls. In some traditions, Poseidon is the father of Theseus, slayer of the Minotaur and king of Athens (see Chapter 10).

Demeter (Ceres)

As goddess of the soil's fertility and its production of life-sustaining grain, **Demeter** [de-MEE-ter] is closely associated with agriculture, the Underworld, and the cycle

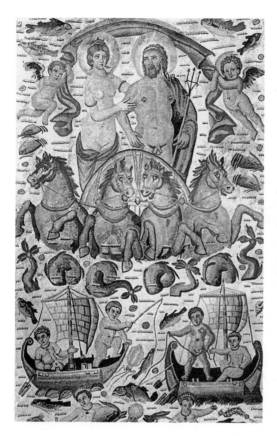

FIGURE 6-6   Poseidon and Amphitrite. In this mosaic from the Villa Stabiae (Pompeii) depicting Poseidon—with his wife, Amphitrite—driving a chariot triumphantly over the waves, the sea god is surrounded by symbols of his marine domain, including the ships of fishermen who depend on his goodwill to survive. Triton, the son of Poseidon and Amphitrite, had a human head and shoulders, but a fish tail from the waist down. Note the nimbi, or halos, encircling the couple's heads, a symbol of divinity later borrowed by Christian artists. *(Louvre, Paris)*

of life, death, and rebirth (see Chapter 5). Her principal myth—Hades' abduction of her daughter Persephone, the mother's earthwide search for her lost child, and the establishment of the Eleusinian Mysteries—is recounted in the *Homeric Hymn to Demeter*. In Euripides' tragedy the *Bacchae*, Demeter's gift of grain (the daily bread of life) is compared to Dionysus's gift of wine (the intoxicating beverage that eases life's pain) (see Chapter 17).

Hades (Pluto, Dis)

Even gloomier than the irascible Poseidon is **Hades** [HAY-deez], "Zeus of the Underworld," a chthonic figure who represents the darker, more sinister aspects of divinity, a polar opposite of Zeus's sunlit vitality. Although Hades is neither an evil being nor the cause of death, he is dreaded for his association with the hopeless dead, over whom he rules jointly with Persephone, his queen. Wearing a cap of invisibility, Hades may be present without being seen. For the ancient Greeks, the invisible god was virtually ubiquitous; one could not know when, figuratively, Hades' subterranean realm would suddenly open, drawing the living into a chasm of perpetual darkness.

Hades rarely appears in the upper world and figures prominently in only one major myth, the story of Persephone's abduction (see the *Homeric Hymn to Demeter* in Chapter 5). Also called **Pluto** [PLOO-toh] (*Plouton,* the "wealth giver") because gems and mineral riches are found under the earth, Hades has a grim and pitiless personality, his implacability reflecting the harsh natural law that condemns all living things to death. (Hades' subterranean kingdom, which played a major role in the Greek imagination, is described in Chapter 9; Odysseus's journey to the borders of Hades' realm is narrated in Chapter 13; and Aeneas's descent to the Underworld appears in Chapter 19).

Hestia (Vesta)

Zeus's unmarried sister **Hestia** [HES-tee-uh] is the only Olympian for whom no myths were created. An immortal virgin devoted exclusively to guarding the Olympian hearth and its life-sustaining fire, she represents the unmoving, fixed center of family life, both human and divine. A symbol of unchanging permanence, she never leaves her assigned place and so neither acts nor becomes involved in others' actions, a role that precludes her having any life story of her own. In Greek myth, her opposite is Hermes, who roams freely throughout the universe, an embodiment of divine restlessness and movement. Hestia's colorless passivity, though essential to her identification with the domestic hearth, ultimately resulted in her being demoted from the Olympian pantheon, to be replaced by the energetic Dionysus.

In Roman myth, Hestia was known as **Vesta** [VES-tuh] and figured more prominently in the civic cult as keeper of the sacred flame that symbolized Rome's essential life force. The Vestal Virgins, famous for remaining strictly celibate while performing their holy duties, were well-born women who tended Vesta's eternal flame in a temple near the Roman forum. Tradition decreed that any Vestal priestess who broke her oath of celibacy was to be buried alive. Released from their vows only at their fortieth birthday, the Vestals' peculiar circumstance gave birth to the adage that "life begins at forty."

The Younger Olympians

Zeus is the only Olympian deity whose children are major gods in their own right. Of the seven younger Olympians, only two are Hera's.

Athene (Minerva)

Like her half-brothers Hermes and Apollo, **Athene** [uh-THEE-nuh] is a complex deity whose many attributes and functions encompass contradictory elements. Although born without a mother, she takes a keen interest in women's activities, particularly the domestic arts of spinning and weaving. Late sixth-century B.C. artifacts reveal offerings to Athene that included loomweights, often in the shape of pomegranates (also offered to Hera and Demeter), reflecting her role as weaver of the web of life, death, and rebirth. Athene is also the patron of pottery making and carpentry (she directs the hero Jason in building his ship, the *Argo*). With Hephaestus, god of smiths and metalworkers, she shares the patronage of virtually all civilized, productive skills. Originally a Bronze Age goddess (her name appears in

Linear B tablets), she may have been, like Hera, descended from the Minoan snake goddess. Worshiped throughout the Greek world as the defender of cities, from both external attack and internal strife, she was particularly associated with Athens, where her statues, shrines, and marble temple dominated the Athenian skyline.

Her birth from Zeus's head, in which Athene appears fully armed with a warrior's spear, helmet, and shield, indicates her dual role as an embodiment of "male rationality" and a potent champion of patriarchal order. As she tells the audience in Aeschylus's play the *Eumenides,* she habitually takes the part of men—except for marrying one. Athene's perpetual virginity, like that of her half-sister Artemis, is a sign of her autonomy and independence; her foiling of Hephaestus's attempted rape reflects her resolve to maintain a life free of male domination, save that of her father (see Chapter 1). Although not a deity of war as such, Athene offers formidable opposition to any who threaten the Greek city-state (Figure 6-7). In crucial battles during the Persian invasion of Greece, she was said to have been invisibly present supporting the Greek side, inspiring Athenian soldiers to unprecedented acts of valor. Patron of civilized values, especially civic justice and order, Athene typically

FIGURE 6-7 The Mourning Athene. In this fifth-century B.C. bas-relief, a helmeted Athene leans on her spear while apparently reading an inscription listing the names of men who died defending her beloved Athens. Athenian myth consistently identified the goddess with their city's welfare. (*Acropolis Museum, Athens*)

FIGURE 6-8   Athene Holding a
Spear. In this statue, the warrior
goddess wears the aegis of Zeus—
a breastplate decorated with a fringe
of coiled snakes. A picture of Medusa,
whose gaze turned men to stone,
appears at the center of the aegis.
(*Archeological Museum, Naples*)

wins battles through forethought and strategy rather than physical violence, cleverly outmaneuvering enemies. (In a fight with Ares [Mars], god of war, however,
she uses the simple expedient of vanquishing her opponent by heaving a boulder on
him (*Iliad,* Book 21).

As a military figure, Athene customarily wears Zeus's special insignia, the **aegis**
[EE-jis], a goatskin shield or breastplate, decorated with a terrifying Gorgon's head
and a fringe of snakes, the latter an emblem of the older Cretan goddess (Figures 6-8
and 6-9). With the owl regarded as her sacred bird, she is commonly called "owl-
eyed" (*glaukopis*), an epithet that may be translated as "gray-eyed" or "bright-eyed,"
perhaps an index of her intelligence.

More than any other goddess, Athene befriends a whole series of heroes, including Perseus, Heracles, Jason, and Odysseus, who mirror her attributes of intelligence, resourcefulness, and determination to defend the civil order (see Chapters 10
and 13). In establishing the world's first law court at Athens, she promotes the art
of logical persuasion, rather than the application of brute strength or the seeking of
blood vengeance, to reconcile a city-state's opposing factions. Although a generous
guide to intelligent heroes, Athene can be pitiless to enemies: in the sole myth that
shows her exhibiting a humanlike vanity, competing with Hera and Aphrodite for

FIGURE 6-9 Athene Parthenos. This statue is a Roman copy of the original gold and ivory image of the goddess that the sculptor Phidias designed to place in the Parthenon, Athene's most famous temple (c. 438 B.C.). Now lost, Phidias's original work stood thirty-seven feet high, including the pedestal. In her role as warrior and defender of cities, Athene carries in her right hand an image of Victory, personification of success in battle, while her left hand grasps a massive shield. On her breastplate, she wears the Gorgon's head, symbol of the terrifying death-giving function of a chthonic goddess, while the serpent, symbol of divine mysteries, lies coiled behind her shield. *(National Museum, Athens)*

the honor of being judged the "most beautiful" goddess, she never forgives Paris, a callow Trojan prince who awards the coveted prize to the love goddess. In the *Iliad,* she vigorously supports the Greek attackers and relentlessly promotes Troy's destruction, determined to exterminate Paris's entire people for his slight of her austere charms. This animosity is in spite of the fact that the Trojans worship Athene as a major deity, honoring the **Palladium,** an ancient image of the goddess said to have descended from heaven (see Chapter 12). In the *Odyssey,* while lavishing help upon Odysseus, his wife Penelope, and their son Telemachus, she refuses to spare a single man from among Penelope's hundred unwanted suitors, urging the hero to slaughter them all (see Chapter 13).

Implacable toward those who offend her, Athene cruelly punishes Arachne, a young woman who foolishly challenges her to a contest of weaving skills, changing the impertinent mortal into a spider. In Sophocles' play *Ajax,* she excessively persecutes the title character, driving into madness a brave warrior whose major crime is his claim to deserve the golden armor of Achilles, which the goddess wishes to bestow upon her favorite, Odysseus.

Apollo

The sole Olympian whose name remains the same in Roman myth is **Apollo** (Apollon), the son of Zeus and Leto, daughter of the Titans Coeus and Phoebe. A god of multiple functions, he is primarily the giver of rational harmony—both mental and physical—and a seer of future events. As communicator of the gods' will to humanity, he establishes his main sanctuary at Delphi on **Mount Parnassus,** where his virgin priestess—known as the Pythia or Pythoness—issues cryptic pronouncements whose ambiguities are described as "oracular." The Delphic Oracle became the most respected and widely consulted institution of prophecy in the Greco-Roman world (see Chapter 7).

Often cited as the most typically Greek of all gods, Apollo is called **Phoebus**—the radiant, or shining, one, an embodiment of intellectual and spiritual enlightenment. In later myths, he assumes the duties of Hyperion (or Helios) and is identified with the sun. Apollo shares with his half-brother Hermes the patronage of rustic shepherds, flocks, and fields, but he is preeminently a symbol of sophisticated creativity, as indicated by his role as protector of the Muses. The **lyre** (a small stringed instrument used to accompany poets' songs) represents his artistic function.

Embodying a typically Greek paradox, Apollo is the great Archer King whose arrows can decimate whole armies or cities with plague, but he is also the bestower of the healing arts through his son **Asclepius** [as-CLEE-pee-uhs], the first physician. Apollo's characteristic use of the arrow as his chosen weapon well expresses the god's cool detachment. Unlike Ares or even Athene, he does not wield a sword at close quarters, but chooses instead to work his effects at a great distance (Figure 6-10).

A model of civilized self-discipline, Apollo is nonetheless capable of savage cruelty, as when he flays alive Marsyas, who claimed that he could play the flute more beautifully than the god. A satyr—an embodiment of carnality—Marsyas is Apollo's opposite, unthinking instinct untempered by the keen edge of intellect. (For a more complete discussion of Apollo's myths, including his typically unhappy love affairs, see Chapter 7.)

Artemis (Diana)

Artemis [AR-te-mis], Apollo's twin sister, was born first and immediately acted as midwife for the birth of her younger sibling. Although patron of midwifery and childbirth, a function she shares with Hera and Eileithyia, Artemis is a virgin who jealously guards her privacy.

Like her twin brother, Artemis embodies contradictory functions: she is both protector of wild animals and patron of the hunt. She also resembles Apollo in that

(a)

(b)

FIGURE 6-10   Apollo. This sculpture (c. 460 B.C.), from the west pediment of the temple of Zeus at Olympia, shows Apollo as upholder of civilized values, ending the battle between the Lapiths, a Greek tribe, and the savage centaurs who attacked them. (a) The sculptor's rendition of Apollo's serene and eternally youthful countenance expresses the Greek belief in the gods' freedom from distorting human emotion. Although the god appears here to intervene in a fierce battle, he remains unaffected by the surrounding turmoil. (b) Extending his arm to compel peace, Apollo restores order and harmony by his authoritative presence, a divine example to the warring states of Greece, which assembled near Zeus's Sanctuary every four years to stage the Olympian Games. *(Olympia Museum, Greece)*

FIGURE 6-11   Artemis and Apollo. In this vase painting, the twins Artemis and
Apollo aim their lethal arrows at the children of Niobe. A daughter of Tantalus who
has fourteen children (the number varies in different traditions), Niobe boasts that
she is superior to Leto, who has only two children. At Leto's request to avenge her
honor, Apollo and Artemis then slay all but two of Niobe's sons and daughters. Consumed with grief, Niobe dissolves in tears, becoming a rock from which a spring flows.
(Louvre, Paris)

she carries a quiver of arrows, with which she can inflict the pains of childbirth—or
even cause death. A famous vase painting shows Apollo and Artemis shooting down
the children of **Niobe,** who naively boasts that she is Leto's superior because she has
so many more sons and daughters (Figure 6-11).

A goddess of exceptional beauty, Artemis was also called "the dangerous one."
Associated with the mysterious nocturnal deity Hecate, it is she who manifests the
chthonic aspect of the feminine principle of divinity. Guardian of women's groups,
such as the Amazons, her symbol is the moon, which in its regular cycles of waxing
and waning, changing from a dark, invisible orb to a radiant beacon of the night
and back again, was an astronomical image of the female psyche.

FIGURE 6-12   Artemis and Actaeon. This vase painting depicts Artemis, goddess of the hunt, as she takes aim at Actaeon, for spying on her while bathing. As punishment, Artemis is about to turn Actaeon into a stag. As Actaeon kneels before her, we see his hounds already attacking the fallen hunter. *(James Fund and by special contributions. Courtesy, Museum of Fine Arts, Boston)*

Resembling Athene in her self-sufficiency and independence of men (who must nevertheless appeal to her as patron of the hunt), Artemis has powers that threaten male hegemony, and she is portrayed as terrifying, even deadly, to men who find themselves drawn to her physical allure. When the hunter Actaeon, a mortal cousin of Dionysus, observes the goddess bathing, thus violating the boundaries surrounding her divinity, she turns him into a stag, whereupon he is torn apart by his own hounds (Figure 6-12). Some writers suggest that Actaeon is a variant of the Horned God, a prehistoric deity, commonly seen as a consort of the goddess, who wore antlers as a symbol of his virility and who, in cultures that practiced such rituals, was mutilated and dismembered by women wearing dog masks. This ancient ritual in which a male sacrificial victim suffers vivisection—known as **sparagmos**—is also associated with myths involving Dionysus and the tragic drama that evolved from his worship (see Chapters 14 and 17).

As the "Lady of the Beasts" who spends much of her time in the fields and woods, Artemis is linked to the powers of instinct, nature, or unconscious drives often represented in animal form in dreams (Figure 6-13). She presides over women's mysteries and over the initiation of young girls into them (see Chapter 11 for a discussion of her festival, the Brauronia, in which girls took the role of bears). Preeminent in pursuing typically male tasks, such as the slaying of wild animals, Artemis, like Athene, wields men's weapons, upholding an image of freedom that human women must have envied. As skilled an archer as her twin brother Apollo, Artemis is the only goddess who, roaming the wilds far from Olympus, cannot effectively be subordinated to Zeus (Figure 6-14).

Artemis's most celebrated myth involves not a virgin companion of the goddess but a male worshiper, Hippolytus, son of **Theseus** [THEE-see-uhs], an early king of Athens. In Euripides' play the *Hippolytus,* the title hero, exclusively devoted to Artemis, chastity, and the hunt, denounces Aphrodite as no better than a prostitute, angering the love goddess, who then plots his destruction. Artemis, whom

FIGURE 6-13 Artemis. In this stone sculpture from Italy (c. 500 B.C.), Artemis is shown with a pair of lions. A deity of woods and fields, Artemis not only is a hunter but also has the capacity to tame and communicate with wild beasts, who flock to her. *(British Museum, London)*

FIGURE 6-14 Artemis of Gabii. Unlike Aphrodite, Artemis was traditionally shown clothed. In this copy of a sculpture from the fourth century B.C., Artemis, in her loose-fitting cloak and sandals, reaches to fasten or unfasten a pin on her right shoulder. Her lithe, graceful form, and delicate features convey her much-admired beauty, but her hair style—pulled back into a simple chignon—and her plain hunter's garb reflect her scorn of feminine fashion. *(Louvre, Paris)*

the celibate Hippolytus adores, does nothing to rescue him from a fellow goddess whom he has insulted.

In the Homeric epics, Artemis plays a relatively small role, supporting her brother Apollo's defense of the Trojans but appearing on the battlefield only once (*Iliad,* Book 21). As the Olympians side with either the Greeks or the Trojans, Artemis first berates her twin for refusing to tackle Poseidon and then is attacked by Hera, who knocks Artemis's bow and arrows to the ground with one hand while she repeatedly slaps the huntress's face with the other. Humiliated, Artemis flees for consolation to Zeus, who merely chuckles at the behavior of the women in his family.

Artemis's emotional detachment, and even cruelty, appears in numerous myths. When mortal women die suddenly or unexpectedly, Artemis commonly is seen as the cause. Not only does she gladly join her brother in killing the children of Niobe, but, according to some myths, she also demands the death of Agamemnon's daughter Iphigenia, although other accounts state that she prevented the human sacrifice by substituting a stag for the girl (see the box in Chapter 15).

Greek colonists of Asia Minor associated Artemis with older fertility goddesses of the Near East, depicting her as adorned either with fruitlike symbols of fecundity or with the testicles of bulls sacrificed at her altar (see Figure 5-2). The largest Greco-Roman temple, one of the Seven Wonders of the ancient world, was erected to Artemis at Ephesus. (For a discussion of Artemis's crucial role in Greek girls' rite of passage to adulthood, see Chapter 11.)

Hermes (Mercury)

Hermes [HER-meez], the son of Zeus and Maia, a daughter of the Titan Atlas, has even more attributes and spheres of influence than Apollo, but his primary function is to serve as Zeus's personal messenger, traveling swiftly over vast distances of land and sea to carry out his father's orders. As the Olympian counterpoint of Hestia's intractable fixity, Hermes represents mobility and the benefits that derive from it. The essence of physical movement, transitions, and communication, he is the patron of those who prosper through travel, trade, or theft. As the dispenser of good luck and prosperity, his image commonly appeared in the marketplace and on city gates and doorways—wherever barter or other business was conducted or journeys began or ended. Particularly in Athens, Hermes was depicted in the form of a quadrangular pillar crowned with the head of a bearded man and sporting an erect phallus (Figure 6-15). From about the sixth century B.C. on, these **ithyphallic** figures, the Hermae, served to guarantee the success of all kinds of undertakings, respectable and otherwise. In addition to delivering Zeus's orders throughout the cosmos and thereby supporting the divine order, Hermes was the patron of all who lived by movement and mental agility, including merchants, gamblers, highwaymen, and thieves.

Emphasizing his multiple functions and his extreme mobility, Greek vase painters typically portray Hermes wearing winged sandals and a broad-brimmed traveler's hat. He is also shown holding the **caduceus,** a wand entwined by two serpents and topped by a pair of wings, emblematic of his authority as Zeus's personal

FIGURE 6-15 Herm from Siphnos. In contrast to Praxiteles' elegant statue of Hermes (see Figure 6-16), this rustic Herm is a simple square column with a bearded head and an erect phallus carved in front. Similar Hermae were placed at street corners, gateways, and entrances to private houses and along country roads, where they elicited reverence from and offered divine protection to travelers. The erect phallus promised fertility and good luck to passersby. *(National Museum, Athens)*

messenger and herald. A symbol of the physician's healing art, the caduceus was a gift of Apollo and is also carried by Apollo's son Asclepius, the first physician. The most celebrated portrait of the god is the sculptor Praxiteles' statue of Hermes holding the infant Dionysus (see a copy in Figure 6-16), in which he resembles his half-brother Apollo, a lithe, clean-shaven athlete. As Homer describes him in the *Odyssey,*

> He'd taken on the likeness of a youth
> just come of age, blessed with a young man's grace.
>
> —*Odyssey,* Book 10, trans. Allen Mandelbaum

At one time, it was believed that Hermes evolved from an association with boundary markers—cairns or heaps of stone delimiting property lines. His name, however, appears in Linear B texts found on Crete and at such mainland sites as Pylos and Thebes, demonstrating that he was already an acknowledged deity in Mycenaean times.

In the *Homeric Hymn to Hermes,* an anonymous poet recounts Hermes' birth and early childhood, emphasizing the infant god's amazing ingenuity and equally

FIGURE 6-16 Hermes Holding the Infant Dionysus. Discovered in Olympia in 1877, this marble sculpture of Hermes was once thought to be an original work by Praxiteles (c. 350–340 B.C.), although many scholars now question this identification and regard the statue as a Hellenistic or Roman copy. In this portrayal of Zeus's divine messenger, the sculptor contrasts Hermes' sinuously muscular body with the almost tender expression on his face as he gazes at his half-brother, newly born from Zeus's thigh. Although Hermes commonly appears as a bearded, older male figure wearing a traveler's broad-brimmed hat and winged sandals, later Greek artists commonly present the god as a youthful athlete. (*Olympia Museum*)

astonishing amorality. According to this source (probably from the late sixth century B.C.), the newly born Hermes first lived with his mother, Maia, in a dank cave far from Olympus, an undesirable neighborhood that the ambitious baby soon resolves to quit. Gifted with singular precocity and phenomenal deceptiveness, Hermes devises a plan that will inevitably compel Zeus to notice him and effect a permanent change of residence from the rude cave to the celestial glories of Mount Olympus. Born in the morning, by midday Hermes has invented a new musical instrument—the seven-stringed lyre—which he fashions out of a tortoise shell; by evening he has stolen and hidden fifty head of Apollo's cattle, bringing the angry son of Leto to his cave in search of his lost property. When the devious Hermes denies knowledge of the theft, Apollo hauls the young rogue to Olympus, where Zeus, amused at the child's audacity—Hermes lies to Zeus himself—commands that the cattle be returned.

Exploiting Apollo's close identification with the Muses—and hence his passion for music—Hermes enraptures his older half-brother by playing the lyre, an instrument that produces more beautiful sounds than even the gods have previously heard. In exchange for permission to keep the stolen herd, Hermes gives Apollo the lyre, which thereafter becomes the god's chief symbol. Hermes also invents a reed pipe, the syrinx or panpipes, which Apollo similarly appropriates, trading the caduceus for it. The hymn concludes with Apollo not only pacified by Hermes' clever bargaining but henceforth also bound to him in a pact of eternal friendship. Only two days old, Hermes has succeeded in assuaging Apollo's wrath, learning from his erstwhile victim the art of divination, and convincing Zeus that his trickster son deserves to join the immortal company on Olympus.

Although the *Homeric Hymn to Hermes* touches on many of Hermes' attributes, it alludes only briefly to his important role as Psychopompos, the guide who escorts souls of the recently dead to their final rest in Hades' cheerless abode. Effortlessly transiting vast distances from heaven to earth to the Underworld, Hermes' itinerary connects all levels of the cosmos—from the throne of Zeus, where he hears the divine will, to the murky nether regions, where he delivers souls to **Charon,** the dread boatman who transports the dead across the River Styx (see Chapter 9).

Associated not only with unknown paths to Hades' mysterious realm but also with sleep, dreams, magic, and fortune-telling, Hermes was sometimes perceived as a conduit to mysticism and occult knowledge. By the fourth century A.D., when Greco-Roman society was crumbling, Hermes became identified with the Egyptian Thoth, a god of arcane wisdom, and was known as Hermes Trismegistus (Thrice-Greatest).

Except for the story of his infancy, Hermes is ordinarily featured as a subordinate figure in most extant myths, serving as Zeus's go-between. His diplomatic skills are featured in the *Iliad,* where he negotiates King Priam's recovery of his son's corpse from the fierce Achilles; in the *Odyssey,* he intervenes to give Odysseus a charm that will protect the hero from Circe's sorcery and, later, to persuade the possessive Calypso that she must release Odysseus from captivity on her remote island (see Chapter 13). His appearance as a blustering bully in *Prometheus Bound,* where he represents a tyrannical Zeus, seems out of character for this divine maker of mischief.

Unlike the other male Olympians, Hermes is not associated with killing or violence; his only murder is that of **Argus,** the hundred-eyed monster that Hera used to spy on Zeus, a deed that earns him the epithet "giant-slayer." Although generally well disposed toward humans, he remains—like the Norse god Loki—an incorrigible trickster, the bane of any unwary victim who crosses his path (see the box in Chapter 4). As his mother, Maia, correctly observed, he is destined to be a "great nuisance to mortal men and the undying gods!"

Hephaestus (Vulcan)

The tradition that **Hephaestus** [he-FES-tuhs] is entirely Hera's creation (although Homer makes Zeus the father) indicates the close bond between mother and son. Just as she is the upholder of domesticity, so Hephaestus is the house builder, the supremely gifted craftsman who single-handedly erects the gods' palatial dwelling on Olympus. God of fire and the forge, he manufactures Zeus's thunderbolts, fashions golden armor for Achilles, assists at Athene's birth, and creates the first woman, Pandora, from clay (see Chapter 4).

The marriage of the sooty, clumsy, lame god of the workshop to the lovely Aphrodite is a classic example of marital mismatching that inevitably leads to infidelity. Homer states that, when Hephaestus discovers his wife's adultery with Ares, he devises an invisible net to trap the guilty pair together in bed. Instead of offering sympathy to the wronged husband, Apollo and Hermes confess that they would be glad to exchange positions with Ares, provoking gales of "Olympian laughter." (See *The Loves of Ares and Aphrodite* at the end of the chapter.)

Despite Hephaestus's marginality as the only imperfect Olympian, his skills as blacksmith, valued by the many artisans in Greek society, were celebrated in cults throughout Greece. On Lemnos, where he landed when thrown down from Olympus, Hephaestus had a sanctuary at which rituals honoring the god were performed. In Athens, a popular cult linked him with Athene, the patron of weavers, spinners, and potters; between them, the two gods presided over virtually every manual art and craft. Every fifth year, a festival called the Hephaestia was held in honor of Athene and Hephaestus, which featured a torch race and elaborate sacrifices. The myth of Hephaestus's abortive attempt to rape Athene, which produced the earthborn Erichthonius, the supposed ancestor of the Athenians, suggests the centrality of this unlikely couple in Athenian life (see Chapter 1).

Because the northeastern Mediterranean is located in a geologically active region, with frequent earthquakes and volcanic eruptions, the fire god had a special prominence. Some myths indicate that Hephaestus built his smithy under Mount Etna in Sicily (the same volcano under which, according to other traditions, the monster Typhoeus was imprisoned). In Roman myth, Hephaestus was identified with the god Vulcan (Vulcanus), whose forge was said to be located under the Mediterranean island of Vulcano, from which the modern term *volcano* derives.

Aphrodite (Venus)

A personification of human sexual desire, **Aphrodite** [af-roh-DYE-tee] is the Greek counterpart to the ancient Near Eastern goddess of love and fertility known to the Sumerians as Inanna and to the Babylonians as Ishtar. The most important female deity in Mesopotamia, Inanna/Ishtar—the "Lady of Heaven"—appears prominently in the Gilgamesh epic, in which the hero refuses to mate with her because of her reputation for depriving her male lovers of their humanity, transforming them into snakes or moles before abandoning them altogether. A goddess of war as well as physical love, Ishtar made the battlefield her "playground," fighting invisibly alongside the kings she favored. Ishtar's violent and sinister qualities are mirrored in her sister Ereshkigal, ruler of the Mesopotamian Underworld.

Besides incorporating many traits of older Sumero-Babylonian goddesses, Aphrodite draws on characteristics of the Canaanite Astarte, the Egyptian Isis, and the Syrian Atargatis, including a connection to the sea, the primal "waters of life," and her unusual birth. Atargatis, for example, emerges from an egg that has fallen into the Euphrates River and is pushed to shore by fish; according to Hesiod, Aphrodite herself is born from the foam surrounding the severed genitals of Uranus, which

FIGURE 6-17   Aphrodite, Eros, and Pan. In this sculpture group (second century B.C.), a nude Aphrodite is surprised by Pan, the goat-shanked embodiment of physical lust. Although the goddess grips a sandal in her right hand with which to repel Pan's advances, she appears not altogether displeased by his attentions. The hovering figure of a smiling Eros seems to urge a rapprochement between the beauty and the beast. *(National Archaeological Museum, Athens)*

Cronus had flung into the sea (see Chapter 3). Floating to shore on a clamshell, Aphrodite rises from the sea in the last outpouring of the primeval gods' creative energies (see Color Plate 1). Accompanied by Eros (Love), the prime creative force of the universe and its life principle, Aphrodite precedes the Olympians in both time and cosmic importance, a powerful deity to whom all creation—human and divine—was subject (Figure 6-17).

From the patriarchal view, however, such a powerful force associated with a female probably aroused some anxiety, producing two conflicting perceptions of Aphrodite manifested even within Hesiod's *Theogony*. On the one hand, in the form of the male figure Eros (later portrayed as Aphrodite's son), love is the mysterious force that literally makes the world go round and to which the gods themselves succumb; on the other, Aphrodite is merely a flirtatious girl, a "laughter-loving" lightweight, a fitting companion to her lover, the athletic but not excessively bright Ares, god of war. As with her birth, her connection to the war god is perhaps a vestige of the dual role as patron of both love and war that Ishtar and other Near Eastern goddesses represented, and from which Aphrodite is descended. When Homer gives the alternative myth that she is the daughter of Zeus and Dione, a daughter of either Uranus and Gaea or the Titans Oceanus and Tethys, the poet more firmly subordinates her to the Olympian hierarchy.

In some traditions, Aphrodite bears Ares three children: Harmonia, a daughter who married Cadmus, founder of Thebes (see Chapter 17); and two sons whose names associate them with war, Phobos (Panic) and Deimos (Fear), who accompany their father into battle. Appropriately, modern astronomers have named the two small moons orbiting the red planet after Mars' two bellicose sons.

Perhaps reflecting her descent from ancient Near Eastern goddesses such as Inanna/Ishtar, who presided over ritual prostitution in Mesopotamian temples, Aphrodite is variously redefined as a wanton flirt who seduces men for the fun of it, as an adulterous mistress or lover, or as a whore. Consequently, she remains alluring, but her power is diminished: in a world in which marriage is sanctified, she has no legitimate social place. Aphrodite's own marriage to the lame and singularly unattractive, though highly intelligent Hephaestus is a failure: she betrays him with gods and mortals alike (see Color Plate 14). In striking contrast to human wives, Aphrodite enjoys a sexual freedom that, in ancient Greek society, only men possessed.

Aphrodite's liaisons with humans often have far-reaching, and even devastating, consequences. The *Homeric Hymn to Aphrodite,* which tells of her seduction of Anchises, the Trojan shepherd-prince, and the birth of their son Aeneas, illustrates Aphrodite's casual (almost masculine) approach to sex. After discovering that she and the Trojan youth are psychologically incompatible, Aphrodite blithely returns to Olympus, leaving Anchises to raise Aeneas by himself. The tradition that Anchises suffered premature aging after boasting of his affair with a goddess seems consistent with Gilgamesh's charge that Ishtar routinely drained her human lovers of their virility; sexual contact with a divinity invariably exacts a formidable toll. The myth of Aeneas's divine parentage later played an influential role in Roman culture, prompting the early emperors to claim descent from Aeneas, a mythic legacy that Virgil explores in the *Aeneid* (see Chapter 19).

Although her son Aeneas will eventually carry Troy's heritage with him from Asia Minor to Italy, where his descendants Romulus and Remus will found the city of Rome, it is Aphrodite's interference in Trojan affairs that brings about Troy's destruction. She promises the Trojan prince Paris the love of the world's most beautiful woman, Helen, the fulfillment of which sparks the conflagration of the Trojan War. That promise is made in exchange for the gift of a Golden Apple of Immortality from the Tree of Life belonging to Gaea, once again connecting Aphrodite to the primal goddess.

Whereas Paris and his entire people are destroyed for his acceptance of Aphrodite's promise of illicit love—for Helen was already married to the Greek Menelaus, king of Sparta (see Chapter 12)—another young man's refusal to accept Aphrodite's amorous gift results in his annihilation. Because Hippolytus, son of Theseus, king of Athens, spurns her and takes a vow of celibacy, she causes his stepmother, Phaedra, to become infatuated with him. When Hippolytus rejects Phaedra, she is both furious and heartbroken: she hangs herself, leaving behind a note for Theseus falsely accusing his son of attempted rape. The unfortunate Hippolytus, pursued by his enraged father, becomes entangled in the reins of his horses and is dragged to his death, fatally ensnared by the goddess he spurned.

Greco-Roman myth also offers several examples of the miserable fate awaiting persons who presume to live without experiencing the sexual love that Aphrodite represents. In Ovid's tale of Narcissus, the self-absorbed youth refuses love from both women and young men, an affront to the nature of the universe that dooms him (see Chapter 20).

Aphrodite's affair with **Adonis,** her most famous human lover, is also a source of grief for both. When the queen of Cyprus boasts that her daughter, Smyrna, is more beautiful than Aphrodite, the goddess exacts her revenge by causing Smyrna to seduce and be impregnated by her own father, whom she had gotten drunk. Realizing what has happened, the father tries to kill his daughter, whom Aphrodite turns into a myrrh tree to save her. When her father splits the tree open with his sword, the beautiful child Adonis emerges. Aphrodite then saves the child by concealing him in a chest, which she gives to Persephone to hide until he grows up. However, Persephone falls in love with the boy and refuses to relinquish him. Just as in the story of Demeter and Persephone, a compromise is worked out: Adonis will spend part of each year in the Underworld with Persephone and part in the upper world with Aphrodite. However, tricking Persephone, Aphrodite causes Adonis to remain with her in the upper world beyond his allotted time, thus arousing the jealousy of her divine lover, Ares. When Adonis is out hunting, Ares disguises himself as a boar and kills Adonis, whose blood penetrates the Underworld. To Jungian mythographers, Adonis personifies the archetype of the "eternal child," who seeks return to the womb. But in Greek myth, he doesn't stay there: transformed by the power of Aphrodite's love into the blood-red anemone (wind flower), Adonis emerges again as the flower each spring. Like his Near Eastern counterparts, Tammuz and Osiris, Adonis became the subject of a popular cult (see Color Plate 15).

Indeed, many details of the Aphrodite–Adonis tale underline the link between Aphrodite and her Near Eastern sources, allowing us a glimpse of the powers of the Creator goddesses that still are sustained beneath the surface of the charming but superficial nymph into which Aphrodite ostensibly was changed. But not even Zeus can entirely negate the power of Aphrodite, and the residue of the Creator goddesses keeps surfacing. Like the Babylonian myth of Ishtar and Tammuz, the tale of Aphrodite and Adonis incorporates the descent to the Underworld and the return to the upper world, in defiance of the Underworld goddess. Like the Egyptian myth of Isis and Osiris, it incorporates the entombing of the male in a tree, his subsequent release when the tree is split, and his rebirth. In all these tales, the transformational role of the ancient goddesses—givers of life, death, and rebirth—is brought about through the power of love that, dimmed but not obliterated, radiates still from the embrace of Aphrodite.

Whereas Aphrodite's power is evident in innumerable myths, including that of Jason's quest for the Golden Fleece, in which the goddess persuades Eros to make Medea fall in love with Jason, thus enabling her favorite to steal the fleece and sail his ship the *Argo* back to Greece (see Chapter 17), her most momentous appearance is as Aeneas's divine mother, advisor, and protector in the *Aeneid*. In revisiting the old myth of Aphrodite's affair with the Trojan Anchises and its unforeseen consequences to later history, the Roman poet Virgil portrays the goddess—now known by her Latin name Venus—as a far more dignified and majestic figure than she had been in many earlier traditions (Figure 6-18). In his epic, Virgil employs the same theme—of two different gods with conflicting intentions toward a long-

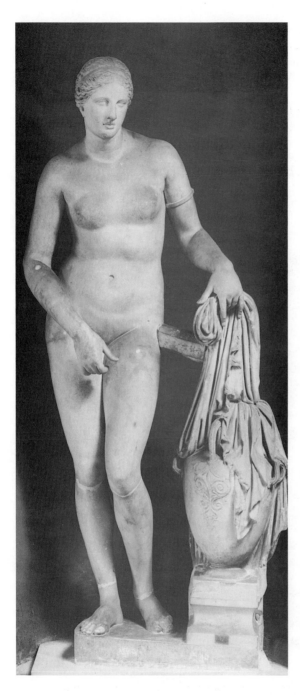

FIGURE 6-18 Aphrodite of Cnidos. Praxiteles' original sculpture of Aphrodite (c. 350–330 B.C.) was reportedly the first to depict the love goddess fully nude, establishing a tradition observed by most later artists. In this Roman copy, Aphrodite appears sensuous but detached, beautiful but not self-conscious. Her gaze turns inward in reflective repose, suggesting a combination of feminine beauty and mature self-awareness. *(Vatican Museum, Rome)*

suffering hero—that Homer had used in the *Odyssey,* with Venus (Aphrodite) taking Athene's role as the hero's champion, and Juno (Hera) the part of Poseidon, the hero's unforgiving enemy. Although Virgil's Venus behaves with impressive decorum to implement her long-term goal of bringing her son from Troy to Italy to become the forefather of the Roman people, she is still not above forcing a hapless mortal to forsake reason for love—in this case, ordering Eros (Cupid) to wound Dido, queen of Carthage, compelling her to fall in love with Aeneas, and thereby guaranteeing her help in rebuilding the hero's storm-wrecked fleet. Nor has Venus any compunction over Aeneas's abandonment of Dido when he abruptly leaves Carthage to fulfill his god-ordained destiny (see Chapter 19).

Eros (Cupid)

Either one of the oldest gods (Hesiod) or Aphrodite's son by Ares (Homer), **Eros** is a masculine aspect of the love goddess who projects arrows of fierce desire into the hearts of both gods and mortals (Figure 6-19). Although not one of the official twelve Olympians, he flits about Olympus as familiarly as he does on earth.

FIGURE 6-19 Aphrodite and Ares. Although married to Hephaestus, god of the forge, Aphrodite takes Ares as her favored lover. In this wall painting from Pompeii, the artist celebrates the union of the gods of love and war, illustrating the affinity between sexual desire and martial aggressiveness. Eros, the winged boy appearing on the upper left, is in some myths the son of Ares and Aphrodite, explaining the mixture of calculating detachment and passionate assertiveness in his character. He is shown placing an arrow in his bow, about to hurl the invisible dart of erotic obsession into the breast of some god or mortal. *(National Museum, Naples)*

Whereas the Greeks regarded Eros as an adolescent, the Romans pictured him as a chubby infant (Cupid) and identified his mother as Venus, a goddess of gardens and flowers. Eros may be related to the Hindu god Kama, who also shoots invisible arrows into the hearts of gods and humans to cause them to fall in love.

Ares (Mars)

Ares [AR-eez], the son of Zeus and Hera, is god of war in its most savage guise. A personification of combativeness and bloodthirsty frenzy, he represents the undisciplined aspects of masculine aggression, as well as a telling symbol of his parents' strife-torn marriage (Figure 6-20).

Although Ares exists only to fight and kill (or to commit adultery with Aphrodite), he is not the most effective Olympian warrior: when the gods descend to a Trojan battlefield, Athene has little trouble vanquishing the war god by hurling a

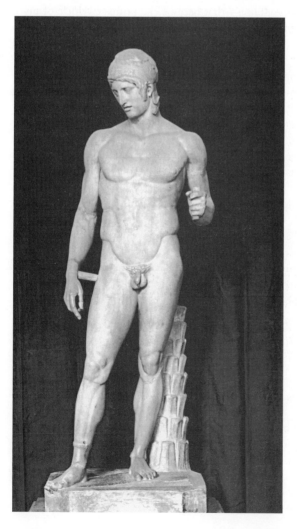

FIGURE 6-20   Ares. This Roman copy of a Greek original (c. 420–400 B.C.) depicts Ares in a moment of uncharacteristic repose; the god embodying humanity's irrational impulse to commit violence stands lost in contemplation. Although the Greeks were almost continuously at war, they rarely worshiped Ares, whom Zeus labeled "the most hated of the gods" for his hot temper and eagerness to overpower or kill. Later identified with a god of agriculture and war, Ares became the Roman Mars. *(Louvre, Paris)*

boulder at him (*Iliad*, Book 21). Earlier, she had inspired the Greek hero Diomedes to wound Ares, sending him yelping back to Olympus, where Zeus contemptuously labels him "the most hated of all the gods" (*Iliad*, Book 5). Athene's ability to achieve military victory through intelligence and planning, myth indicates, is clearly superior to Ares' mindless violence and cruelty.

Although the Greeks were almost continually at war, usually with fellow Greeks, they showed Ares scant respect. By contrast, the Romans, who associated Ares with Mars—their local god of agriculture and military conquest—regarded him as the divine father of Romulus, their city's founder, and patron of their far-flung empire (see *The Loves of Ares and Aphrodite*.)

Dionysus (Bacchus, Bromius, Liber)

The sole major deity in the Greek pantheon who is born human and must die to achieve immortality is **Dionysus**, god of wine, intoxication, and creative ecstasy (see Chapters 8 and 17 for his principal myths). Because his worship gave birth to an entirely new art form—the drama—that became the primary vehicle of myth during the fifth century B.C., this important aspect of the Dionysian cult is treated in a separate chapter. (See Chapter 14 for Dionysus's patronage of tragedy and comedy.)

When the latecomer Dionysus was added to the Olympian pantheon, the mythologically undeveloped Hestia was demoted to make room for him, thus keeping the traditional number of Olympians at twelve. Whereas the Olympians hold sway over the universe at large, a host of minor deities preside over geographically limited areas, specific activities, or particular landforms: lovely naiads (female nature spirits) inhabit springs, rivers, and lakes; dryads are the indwelling spirits of trees; and oreads live in mountainous terrain. **Pan**, who has a human torso and arms but the legs, ears, and horns of a goat, is a personification of all natural wild things (Figure 6-21). His name, derived from the root *pa*, means "guardian of flocks," designating his function as the god responsible for the fertility of shepherds and flocks. Like nature itself, Pan creates both beauty and terror: with the seven-reed syrinx (panpipe), he produces enchanting music; he also is the source of unreasoning fear (panic) that can unexpectedly freeze the human heart. With his horns, hairy shanks, cloven hooves, and lustful energy, Pan became in postclassical times a model for the physical shape of the Christian devil.

The Gods at Home: Adultery on Olympus

Whereas the majority of Greek myths focus on the earthly adventures of mortal heroes—the gods appearing only intermittently to influence the action—the Homeric epics feature several scenes depicting the gods alone in the privacy of their Olympian retreat. Early in both the *Iliad*, and the *Odyssey*, the gods hold heavenly councils at which they discuss such weighty matters as cosmic justice or the fate of outstanding heroes such as Achilles or Odysseus (*Iliad*, Book 1, and *Odyssey*, Book 1; see Chapters 12 and 13). In an episode dramatizing *The Loves of Ares and Aphrodite*, however, Homer offers a rare glimpse of the gods' behavior when they

FIGURE 6-21   Head of Pan. A god of wild nature, Pan combines the qualities of humans and beasts. He has the cloven hooves, horns, and hairy shanks of a goat, along with the head and torso of a human being, a visible image of the tension existing between the animal and the divine in the human psyche. In some myths, he is the son of Hermes, a god of goatherds, shepherds, gamblers, thieves, liars, traders, and other persons existing on the margins of civilized society. Although sometimes gentle, he can exhibit the cruel savagery of nature on the rampage, inspiring sudden terror in persons traveling through the woods or other isolated places. An embodiment of uninhibited male sexuality, Pan often shows up in the Dionysian retinue. *(J. Paul Getty Museum, Los Angeles)*

are not engaged in the serious business of administering the universe. This self-contained narrative from the *Odyssey*, presented as the song of a court minstrel named Demodocus, portrays the gods of love and war pursuing recreational sex, much as if they were aristocratic inhabitants of one of the ancient Minoan or Mycenaean palace complexes, where one noble might gain easy access to the wife of an absent peer (see Color Plate 11).

THE LOVES OF ARES AND APHRODITE*
Homer

[Demodocus's celebration of this adulterous affair—and the outraged Hephaestus's ingenious trap for his unfaithful wife and her ill-tempered lover—is remarkably light-hearted. When Hephaestus summons the other male deities (the goddesses stay away out of modesty) to witness the adulterers entangled in his invisible web (see Color Plate 14), the wronged husband receives no comfort or encouragement from his fellow gods. Apollo and Hermes only wish aloud that they could exchange places with Ares —a pleasure for which they would gladly bear public exposure and humiliation. After Poseidon orders their release from Hephaestus's trap, neither Aphrodite nor Ares is punished (although Ares is pledged to pay a fine for his misdeed); the lovers flee Olympus separately to nurse their wounded dignity in familiar earthly haunts.]

. . . .

Then Demodocus swept the strings of his lyre   1
And began his song. He sang of the passion
Between Ares and gold-crowned Aphrodite,
How they first made love in Hephaestus' house,
Sneaking around, and how the War God Ares
Showered her with gifts and shamed the bed
Of her husband, Hephaestus. But it wasn't long
Before Hephaestus found out. Helios told him
That he had seen them lying together in love.
When Hephaestus heard this heart-wrenching news   10
He went to his forge, brooding on his wrongs,
And set the great anvil up on its block
And hammered out a set of unbreakable bonds,
Bonds that couldn't loosen, bonds meant to stay put.
When he had wrought this snare, furious with Ares,
He went to his bedroom and spread the bonds
All around the bedposts, and hung many also
From the high roofbeams, as fine as cobwebs,
So fine not even the gods could see them.
When he had spread this cunning snare   20
All around the bed, he pretended to leave
On a trip to Lemnos, his favorite city.
Ares wasn't blind, and when he saw Hephaestus
On his way out, he headed for the house
Of the glorious smith, itching to make love
To the Cytherean goddess. She had been visiting

---

*From the *Odyssey*, Book 8. Translation by Stanley Lombardo.

Her father, Zeus, and was just sitting down
When Ares came in, took her hand, and said:
"Let's go to bed, my love, and lie down together.
Hephaestus has left town, off to Lemnos no doubt   30
To visit the barbarous Sintians."

This suggestion appealed to the goddess,
And they climbed into bed. They were settling in
When the chains Hephaestus had cunningly wrought
Fell all around them. They couldn't move an inch,
Couldn't lift a finger, and by the time it sank in
That there was no escape, there was Hephaestus,
Gimpy-legged and glorious, coming in the door.
He had turned back on his way to Lemnos
As soon as Helios, his spy, gave him the word.   40
He stood in the doorway, seething with anger,
And with an ear-splitting yell called to the gods:

"Father Zeus and all you blessed gods eternal,
Come see something that is as ridiculous
As it is unendurable, how Aphrodite,
Daughter of Zeus, scorns me for being lame
And loves that marauder Ares instead
Because he is handsome and well-knit, whereas I
Was born misshapen, which is no one's fault
But my parents', who should have never begotten me!   50
Come take a look at how these two
Have climbed into my bed to make love and lie
In each other's arms. It kills me to see it!
But I don't think they will want to lie like this
Much longer, no matter how loving they are.
No, they won't want to sleep together for long,
But they're staying put in my little snare
Until her father returns all of the gifts
I gave him to marry this bitch-faced girl,
His beautiful, yes, but faithless daughter."   60

Thus Hephaestus, and the gods gathered
At his bronze threshold.
                              Poseidon came,
The God of Earthquake, and Hermes the Guide,
And the Archer Apollo. The goddesses
All stayed home, out of modesty; but the gods
Stood in the doorway and laughed uncontrollably
When they saw Hephaestus' cunning and craft.
One of them would look at another and snigger:
"Crime doesn't pay."
                        "The slow catches the swift.

Slow as he is, old Gimpy caught Ares,   70
The fastest god on Olympus."
"Ares has to pay the fine for adultery."
That was the general drift of their jibes.
And then Apollo turned to Hermes and said:

"Tell me, Hermes, would you be willing
To be pinched in chains if it meant you could lie
Side by side with golden Aphrodite?"

And the quicksilver messenger shot back:

"I tell you what, Apollo. Tie me up
With three times as many unbreakable chains,   80
And get all the gods and goddesses, too,
To come here and look, if it means I can sleep
Side by side with golden Aphrodite."

The gods roared with laughter, except Poseidon
Who did not think it was funny. He kept
Pleading that Ares should be released,
And his words winged their way to Hephaestus:

"Let him go, and I will ensure he will pay you
Fair compensation before all the gods."

And the renowned god, lame in both legs: 90

"Do not ask me to do this, Poseidon.
Worthless is the surety assured for the worthless.
How could I ever hold you to your promise
If Ares slipped out of the bonds and the debt?"

Poseidon the Earthshaker did not back off:

"Hephaestus, if Ares gets free and disappears
Without paying the debt, I will pay it myself."

And the renowned god, lame in both legs:

"I cannot refuse you. It wouldn't be right."

And with that the strong smith undid the bonds,   100
And the two of them, free at last from their crimp,
Shot out of there, Ares to Thrace,
And Aphrodite, who loves laughter and smiles,
To Paphos on Cyprus, and her precinct there
With its smoking altar. There the Graces
Bathed her and rubbed her with the ambrosial oil
That glistens on the skin of the immortal gods.

And then they dressed her in beautiful clothes,
A wonder to see.

        This was the song
The renowned bard sang, and Odysseus   110
Was glad as he listened, as were the Phaeacians,
Men who are famed for their long-oared ships.

HOMERIC HYMN TO HERMES*
Author unknown

[Although Greek myth frequently celebrates Zeus's amorous adventures in seducing goddesses, nymphs, and mortal women, it rarely examines the aftermath of these divine dalliances from the perspective of the mother or her newborn child. The anonymous *Homeric Hymn to Hermes* is a rare exception, narrating the story of Maia, one of the seven daughters of the Titan Atlas, and her astoundingly precocious son, Hermes. (According to another myth, when pursued by Orion, Maia and her six sisters eventually were transformed into a famous astral constellation, the Pleiades.) Whereas Zeus's liaisons with human women produced mortal heroes, such as Heracles, that with the immortal Maia creates a full-fledged god, albeit one born in secret (his original home is an obscure cave on Mount Cyllene in Arcadia) and without public status (he has no official acknowledgment of his Olympian connections).

This thoroughly amoral poem delights in demonstrating that Hermes proved his right to recognition as Zeus's son—and an honored place among the gods of Olympus —through breath-taking boldness, lies, thievery, and deceit. If Homer presented the adultery of Ares and Aphrodite as a source of sophisticated humor, the hymn's author takes an even more cavalier approach to divine misbehavior. As noted in the discussion of Hermes' mutable character, the poet portrays this god of swift movement and boundary breaking as both preternaturally ingenious and totally unscrupulous, outwitting other gods and brazenly lying even to his father, the guarantor of cosmic truth and justice. Largely ignoring Hermes' more respectable functions, as Zeus's messenger and the guide of human souls to the Underworld, this tale highlights the Olympians' remarkable tolerance for deviant behavior among divine family members—provided it is done with the fearless audacity, impish charm, and effectiveness with which Hermes accomplishes his mischief. In sharp contrast to Hesiod's emphasis on Zeus's hostility toward Prometheus, the Olympian clan welcomes the trickster Hermes into their midst because he is one of them, an invaluable addition to their exclusive group of confirmed manipulators.]

Sing, Muse, of Hermes, the son of Zeus and Maia,   1
Guardian over Cyllene and sheep-rich Arcadia,
Luck-bringing messenger of the immortals, whom Maia,
Shy, lovely-haired nymph, brought forth of her union in love
With Zeus. Shunning the company of the blessed immortals,
She lived in a shadowy cave, where Zeus son of Cronos
Came often by night to lie with the lovely-haired nymph
In the deep silent hours when sweet sleep possessed white-armed
    Hera,
Escaping thereby the observance of undying gods and of men.

---

*Translation by Thelma Sargent.

But when the purpose of powerful Zeus was accomplished   10
And the tenth moon of Maia hung high in heaven,
She brought forth into the light, and his ruse was revealed.
The son she bore then was a versatile child, wily and wheedling,
A thief and a drover of cattle, a marshal of dreams,
By night a spy on watch at the gates, destined forthwith
To make manifest glorious deeds among the immortals.
Born in the morning, at midday he played on the lyre,
And at eventide stole the cows of far-shooting Apollo,
On the fourth day of the month—the day Maia bore him.
After he leapt from the immortal loins of his mother,   20
He tarried no longer to lie asleep in his holy cradle,
But rose up at once to go in search of the cows of Apollo.
He clambered over the sill of the high-vaulted cavern,
Where to his endless delight he discovered a tortoise—
Hermes it was who first made the tortoise a singer—
Coming upon it by chance at the gate of the courtyard
As, awkwardly mincing along on hesitant feet,
It browsed on the lush green grass in front of the dwelling.
Zeus' child, the luck-bringer, looked closely and laughed, and straightway
    spoke a word:
    "A most useful token for me already! Not I one to scorn it!   30
Hail, lovely creature, stamping the ground in the dance,
Comrade of the feast! Welcome indeed is your coming!
Where did you get that handsome bauble you wear, O tortoise,
You who live in the mountains—that patterned shell?
But let me carry you into the house. You will be useful
To me; I will show you no lack of honor, but first you must serve me.
Inside the house is better; out of doors there is danger.
Alive you will be a shield against baneful enchantment,
But if you should die, then would you sing with great beauty."
    So Hermes spoke and, picking the creature up with both hands,   40
Went back into the house with his lovely new plaything.
There with a knife of gray iron he cut off the legs
And bored out the life of the mountain-bred tortoise.
As a swift thought courses through the heart of a man
Who writhes under close-crowding troubles, or as sparks flash from his eyes,
So at the same moment did glorious Hermes merge plan and deed.
He fixed at measured intervals cut stalks of reed
Through the clean-scooped shell of the tortoise and spanning the back,
And, by a stroke of wisdom, stretched oxhide over the hollow.
He added two horns to the sides yoked by a crossbar,   50
From which he stretched taut seven strings made of sheepgut.
When it was finished, he lifted the lovely toy on his arm
And tried each string in turn with the plectrum, and under his hand
A strange new sound rang out, and the god, trying his skill,
Sang along in sweet random snatches, as at festivals

Boys in the springtime of youth maliciously carol—
Singing of Zeus son of Cronos and Maia, beautifully sandaled,
And of their former intimate love and communion,
Recounting the tale of his own famous birth and begetting.
He honored as well the handmaids of the nymph and her glorious halls   60
And the tripods throughout her household and caldrons galore.
    While yet Hermes sang, he yearned in his heart for new things.
He carried the hollow lyre to his holy wickerwork cradle
And there laid it down; then, craving the taste of flesh,
Forth from the sweet-scented chamber he sallied, and sprang to a lookout,
His mind turning over devices of deepest deception,
Deeds such as robbers arrange in the time of black night.
    Helios was driving his chariot and horses from earth
Downward toward Ocean when Hermes arrived all in haste
In Pieria's shadowy mountains, there where the heavenly cattle   70
Of the blessed immortal gods had their stables and, sheltered,
Placidly grazed the lovely meadows unmown and fragrant.
The son of Maia, far-sighted slayer of Argos,
Cut out from the sacred herd fifty loud-bellowing beasts,
And drove them by random ways through the sandy places,
Turning their hoofprints aside; then he chanced on the crafty conceit
Of reversing their hoofs, so that their forefeet came after,
Their hind feet before, and he himself walked behind them.
Then on the sandy shore of the sea he wove wicker sandals—
Marvelous things they were, unthought of, unheard of—   80
Intermingling tamarisk branches and myrtlelike boughs.
He tied up in a bundle an armful of new-sprouted wood,
Leaves and all, and bound as light sandals securely under his feet
The bundles of boughs he gathered, the glorious slayer of Argos,
Preparing thus for his journey home from Pieria
As one hard-pressed prepares for a wearisome road.
    But an old man tending his flowering vineyard saw him
As he hurried down to the plain through grassy Onchestos.
The son of glorious Maia spoke first and addressed him:
    "Old fellow, you who among your vines dig with bent shoulders,   90
Rich in wine will you be when all these vines bear
If you heed me and remember well in your heart,
Seeing, not to have seen, and, having heard, to be mute.
Be silent except when some harm has been done to your own."
    So much he said, then drove on with his herd of strong cattle.
On through countless shadowy mountains and rushing ravines
And flowery plains did glorious Hermes drive them,
Until divine night, his dark ally, had for the greater part
Covered her course, and dawn that calls man to work was fast breaking,
And shining Selene, daughter of royal lord Pallas,   100
Son fathered by Megamedes, had newly ascended her watchtower.
Down then to the river Alpheus Hermes, stout son of Zeus,

Drove the broad-fronted cattle of Phoebus Apollo.
Unwearied, at length they came to the high-vaulted byre
And the watering troughs before the magnificent meadow.
When Hermes had seen the loud-lowing cattle well sated with fodder,
He rounded them up and herded them into their stable,
Still munching on lotus and galingale sprinkled with dew.
Then the god gathered wood in abundance, and sought after
    the technique of fire.
Grasping a branch of bright laurel, he peeled off the bark with his knife,   110
Held close in the palm of his hand, and the hot blast burst forth.
Hermes thus first of all gave man fire and the kindling of fire.
Then he stacked thick in a pit dug in the ground
Dry, seasoned logs without stint, and the flame grew and brightened.
Sending far distant the blaze of hot-burning fire.
    While the power of glorious Hephaistos was feeding the flame,
Hermes, endowed with great strength, dragged out of the stable
To a spot near the fire two lowing, crumple-horned beasts,
And threw them, both panting, down on their backs on the ground,
And, rolling them over, forced back their heads and bored out their lives.   120
Deed he added to deed. He cut up the meat rich with fat,
And, piercing the morsels with wooden spits, roasted the flesh,
Along with the chine highly honored and the black blood
Confined in the entrails, and these he laid on the ground.
The hides he stretched on a steep slab of rough unhewn rock,
And so they remain even now, long ages since they were placed there—
Ages long past these events, and forever unchanging.
Next, joyous-hearted, Hermes hauled the rich meat
To a smooth, flat stone and divided it into twelve portions,
Sharing it out by lot, and conferring to each his due measure of honor.   130
Then, tempted, glorious Hermes yearned for a taste of the meat
Unreserved to the gods, for the pleasant odor of roasting
Distressed even him, an immortal, but his strong heart was steadfast;
No morsel slid down his holy throat however great was his yearning.
Instead, he carried inside the high-vaulted byre
The fat and a mound of roast flesh and, hoisting them quickly aloft,
There laid them up in remembrance of his youthful theft.
Then, gathering dry sticks together, he covered his traces,
Destroying all the feet and the thickly curled heads
Of the two slain beasts in the hot blaze of the fire.   140
    When all his work at last was completed, the god
Tossed his tamarisk sandals deep into the eddying Alpheus
And put out the embers and strewed over with sand the black ashes.
All through the night he labored, while the lovely light of Selene shone down,
Then at dawn scurried back to the shining peaks of Cyllene;
Nor did anyone either of blessed gods or of mortals
Encounter him on the long journey, or any dog bark.
Then luck-bringing Hermes, begotten by Zeus, turning sideways,

Made his way into the hall of his home through the keyhole
Like a breeze in autumn, or incorporeal mist.   150
He slipped straight through the cave to the rich inner chamber,
His silent feet making no sound as they might on the ground.
Climbing quickly back into his wickerwork cradle, glorious Hermes
Drew around him his swaddling wraps, enfolding his shoulders,
Seeming an infant newborn and helpless, and, as he lay,
Played with his hands at the coverings over his knees
While under his left arm he sheltered his lovely tortoise.
But the god eluded not the eye of the goddess his mother.
    "Where do you come sneaking home from, you rascal," she said,
    "at this time of night,
You of consummate wiles, clad in shamelessness? Very soon now,   160
I foresee, you will quickly be helplessly bound with strong bands
Close round the ribs by the hand of Leto's Apollo,
And carried bodily out the front door—not playing your tricks
Down in the glens and the hollows robbing betweentimes.
Back with you again where you came from! Your father begot you
To be a great nuisance to mortal men and the undying gods!"
    Hermes then answered her, craftily choosing his words:
"Mother mine, why do you welcome me with these threats and forebodings,
Like an innocent child who knows very little of evil,
A baby who shrinks with fright when his mother reproves him?   170
Me, I shall hit upon some clever scheme—what may be best—
And so provide food for you and for me for all time.
Not for us two, alone among the undying gods
Unfed by gifts and unprayed to, patiently here to abide as you bid.
Better to spend all our days among the immortals,
Rich and prosperous, owning productive acres of cornland,
Than to sit at home in a drafty cave. As to honor,
I too will enter into the rites Apollo enjoys.
But if my father withholds the gift, then indeed I will try—
And doubt not that I can—to become the prince among robbers.   180
And if the son of all-glorious Leto searches me out,
Something else even worse, I predict, will befall him,
For I will go and break into his great house at Pytho
And plunder it of its hoard of beautiful tripods and caldrons
And gold and flashing iron in abundance and many fine garments.
You shall see all of it, mother, if you desire."
    So with such words they spoke one to another, Hermes,
The son of Zeus of the aegis, and heavenly Maia.
Dawn, early-born, who brings light to mortals, was rising
Out of deep-flowing Ocean when Phoebus Apollo   190
Came, on his way, to Onchestos, the lovely green grove
Consecrate to Poseidon, loud-roaring Upholder of Earth.
There the son of all-glorious Leto found the old man

Grazing his beast by the path through, the hedge of his courtyard,
And Apollo, halting his strides, spoke first and addressed him:
    "Old man, you who gather the brambles of grassy Onchestos,
I come to this place from Pieria seeking my cattle,
All of the creatures cows all having long crumpled horns,
Part of my herd—the bull, blue-black, grazed alone,
Away from the others. And fierce-eyed dogs followed after the herd—   200
Four, like-minded as men. But the dogs and the bull
Were all left behind—a marvelous thing to have happened.
The cows strayed off at the time the sun was just setting,
Away from the soft, grassy meadow, away from the succulent pasture.
Tell me, old man born long ago, if by chance you have seen
Some man passing by on the road driving my cattle."
    The old man, replying, then spoke to him in these words:
"Dear friend, a difficult task to say all I have seen
With my eyes. For many wayfarers pass back and forth
On this road, some bent on evil, others on good.   210
Hard would it be to know all about every one.
But all day until sundown I was here in my vineyard
Digging about, tending my fruitful vines.
And I seemed, sir, to see—but I cannot certainly say—
A young child, some boy, who herded before him horned cattle,
An infant who carried a staff and roamed from one side to another,
But, oddly, he drove the cows backwards, their heads facing toward him."
    So spoke the old man, and Apollo, hearing his words,
The more quickly went on his way. Not long thereafter
He glimpsed a wide-winged bird of omen, and straightway he knew   220
That the culprit he sought was the child born of Zeus son of Cronos.
So, concealed by a purple cloud around his broad shoulders,
The son of Zeus, lord Apollo, rushed impetuously on
To most holy Pylos in search of his sway-gaited cattle.
Then he saw tracks, and Apollo, Far-Darter, cried out:
    "By my bow! What I see with my eyes is truly a wonder!
These tracks are surely the hoofprints of fine long-horned cattle,
But back they turn toward the asphodel meadow; these others—
Such prints are not those of man nor yet those of woman,
Nor of gray wolves, neither of bears, nor of lions,   230
Nor do I think they are those of a shaggy-necked centaur,
This creature that takes such enormous strides on swift feet.
Fearsome are these on this side of the path, more fearsome those on the other!"
    So saying, the son of Zeus, lord Apollo, sped on
And came to the forest-clad peak of Cyllene, to the shadowy cavern
Cut deep in the rock where Maia, the immortal nymph,
Had brought forth to light the child of Zeus son of Cronos.
A delicate fragrance hung over the hallowed mountain,
And flocks of long-shanked sheep grazed on the grass.

Far-shooting Apollo himself then stepped swiftly over   240
The threshold of stone and entered the cave dark with shadows.
    Now Hermes, the son of Zeus and of Maia, observing
The wrath of Apollo, Far-Darter, concerning his cattle,
Nestled deep into his sweet-smelling swaddling garments.
As wood ash envelops the glowing embers of tree trunks,
So Hermes buried himself when he saw the Far-Worker.
He made of himself a small bundle, drawing up arms
And legs toward his head, as though, fresh from his bath,
He was drifting into sweet slumber. In truth, wide awake
And watchful he lay, and held his lyre under his armpit.   250
But the son of Zeus and of Leto failed not to perceive
Both the beautiful nymph of the mountains and her dear son,
That little child, lying there wrapped in deceit.
Intently, Apollo looked round the cavernous dwelling,
Carefully peering into each dusky corner;
Then with a shiny key he unlocked three cupboards,
And found them full of nectar and lovely ambrosia.
Much gold and silver lay also within them, and many
Crimson and silvery robes of the nymph, such things
As are kept in the sacred homes of the blessed immortals.   260
When he had searched every nook of the cavernous dwelling,
The son of Leto turned and accosted glorious Hermes:
    "Boy, you who lie there in your wickerwork cradle,
Tell me at once what you have done with my cows,
Or we two shall fall out in a way neither seemly nor proper.
For I will take you and hurl you down into gloomy Tartaros,
Doomed to darkness, and helpless; nor shall your mother
Or father free and restore you to daylight, but under the earth
You shall wander forever, the leader among little people."
    Hermes then answered Apollo, craftily choosing his words: 270
"Son of Leto, what are all these harsh things that you say?
Have you come here seeking cows that graze in the meadows?
I have not seen them or heard of them, nor have I had
Word from another about them. I could disclose
Nothing about them, even to win a reward.
I am not a strong man, not like a rustler of cattle.
Not mine is this deed; I have quite other concerns.
Sleep do I care for more, and the milk of my mother,
To have swaddling clothes over my shoulders, and be given warm baths.
Let no one hear from what matter this quarrel arose,   280
For it would be a great wonder among the immortals
That a child newly born, a mere babe, should pass through the front door
Driving before him cows of the field. What nonsense you speak!
I was born yesterday. Soft are my feet and the ground beneath rough.
But, if you wish, I will swear a great oath by the head of my father:
Neither, I vow, am I myself guilty of what you accuse me,

Nor have I seen any other thief stealing your cows—
Whatever cows may be; I know them only by rumor."
    So Hermes spoke, his shrewd eyes sparkling and twinkling,
And he wiggled his eyebrows, glancing hither and yonder,   290
And absent-mindedly whistled, as if hearing an idle tale.
    Apollo who works from afar, softly laughing, replied:
"You little imp, you deceiver, wily of mind,
To hear you talk, I could well believe that last night
You broke into many a well-furnished house, and left more than
One poor wretch only the floor to sit on,
While you soundlessly went through the rooms, stripping them bare.
And many a shepherd dwelling alone in the fields
Will you harass in the mountain glens when you hunger for meat
And come upon herds of cattle and wool-bearing sheep.   300
But come, if you would not that this sleep now be your last,
Get down out of your cradle, companion of black night,
For now and hereafter this honor you hold among the immortals:
You shall for all time be known as the prince among robbers."
    So spoke Phoebus Apollo, and picked up the child
And carried him off. But the mighty slayer of Argos,
Musing as he was borne away in the arms of Apollo,
Sent forth an omen—a rude, importunate herald—
Exploding a belch from his belly, and followed that blast with a sneeze.
Apollo, hearing him, let Hermes fall from his arms to the ground   310
And, though longing to be on his way, sat down before him
And spoke a few words, gently gibing at Hermes:
    "Have no fear, little baby enveloped in swaddling clothes,
Son of Zeus and of Maia. I will yet find
My herd of strong cows, and by these very omens,
And you shall go before and show me the way."
    So he spoke, and Cyllenian Hermes quickly jumped to his feet,
And with both hands readjusted the swaddling wraps
Wound round his shoulders, pushing them up to his ears.
Then he turned and spoke a word to Apollo: 320
    "Where do you carry me, Far-Worker, hottest-tempered of all gods?
Is it because of your cows that you rave so and persecute me?
Oh, I would that the race of cows would perish, believe me!
I did not steal your cows or see any other who did—
Whatever cows may be; I know them only by rumor.
But dispense and receive right before Zeus son of Cronos."
    So over each separate term they disputed and wrangled,
Hermes the shepherd and Leto's beautiful son,
And each one held fast. But Apollo, with unerring voice
Not without ground did he clash with glorious Hermes   330
Over his cows, but the wily Cyllenian tried
With ruses and tricks and flattering words to deceive
The lord of the silver bow. Yet, finding the other

Fertile in tricks of his own, he of many devices,
Leading, rapidly trotted ahead through the sand,
And the son of Zeus and of Leto followed behind.
Soon they came to the heights of sweet-smelling Olympus,
The surpassingly beautiful children of Zeus son of Cronos,
And to their father, for there lay the scale of justice for both.
A convocation was being assembled on snow-capped Olympus,   340
And the undying gods gathered together just after gold-enthroned dawn.
   Hermes and lord Apollo, god of the silver bow,
Stood side by side seeking judgment before the knees of their father.
Then high-thundering Zeus spoke a word to his son shining in beauty:
   "Phoebus, where do you come from driving this winsome captive,
This child newly born, having the look of a herald?
Serious business, this, that you bring to the council of gods!"
   Lord Apollo who works from afar replied in return:
"Father, you will soon hear an incredible tale,
Though you taunt me and hold that I alone care for plunder.   350
I found a child—this very one—a burglar and thief,
In the hills of Cyllene after traveling far through the land.
Another such mocker have I never seen among gods,
Or men, for that matter, as many swindlers on earth as there are.
He stole my cows from their meadow and drove them away
In the dusk of evening along the shore of the loud-roaring sea,
Making directly for Pylos. The tracks behind him were double,
The tracks of a monster, tracks to give rise to wonder,
The spoor of an ingenious devil. As for the cows,
The black dust proclaimed that their footsteps led toward the asphodel
      meadow.   360
He himself wandered aside from the path, and—I cannot explain it—
Traversed the sandy places on neither his feet nor his hands.
By some other means he knew he pursued his journey—
Some magic—as if one might walk on slender young oak trees.
So long as he drove the cows through the sandy places,
The tracks they left in the dust were all very clear,
But when he had put behind him the long stretch of sand,
The hoofprints of cows and his own tracks faded away
And soon became indiscernible on the hard ground.
A man, a mortal, noticed him heading for Pylos   370
Driving before him the herd of broad-fronted cattle.
When he had quietly shut them in for the night,
He returned to his home, playing with fire here and there on the way,
Then silently as black night he crept into his cradle
Down in the darkness of the dim cave—not even
An eagle on watch would have spotted him with his sharp eyes.
The child, when I charged him, rubbed his eyes hard, inventing fresh schemes,
Then at once, careless of consequence, uttered a word:
'I have not seen them or heard of them, nor have I had

Word from another about them. I could disclose   380
Nothing about them, even to win a reward.'"
    When he had spoken, Phoebus Apollo sat down.
Hermes then, standing opposite, made his defense,
Pointing at Zeus son of Cronos, king of all gods.
    "Zeus, father, to you will I tell the absolute truth,
For I am unfailingly honest and do not know how to lie.
He came to our cave in search of his sway-gaited cows
Early this morning, just as the sun was new-rising.
None of the blessed gods had he brought along with him—
No observer or witness—but with great show of force   390
Demanded of me to make known what I had done with his cows,
And strongly threatened to hurl me down into broad Tartaros.
He bears the delicate bloom of joyful young manhood,
While I, a baby, was born yesterday—he too knows this.
I am not a strong man, not like a drover of cattle.
Believe me, for you profess to be my father too.
I did not drive his cows home—so may I prosper!—
Nor did I cross over the threshold. This that I speak is the truth.
Helios and the other gods I hold in high reverence,
You do I love, and I care too for him. You yourself know   400
That I am not guilty, but I will swear a great oath—
Not by these well-adorned porticoes of the immortals!
Sometime, somehow, strong as he is, I will pay Phoebus back
For his ruthless grilling. But you, father, come to the aid of the younger."
    So spoke Cyllenian Hermes, the slayer of Argos,
Rapidly blinking his eyes, his swaddling wraps,
Undiscarded, draped carelessly over his arm.
Zeus laughed aloud seeing his child wise in evil
Denying well and with cunning all knowledge concerning the cattle.
He bade them both then, with their minds in agreement, set out   410
And seek after the cows, with Hermes the guide leading the way
And pointing out to Apollo, without thought of mischief,
The place where he had concealed the herd of fine cattle.
And Zeus son of Cronos nodded, confirming his word.
Hermes, brilliant in splendor, obeyed, for the will
And purpose of Zeus, aegis-bearer, quickly prevailed.
    Then the two surpassingly beautiful children of Zeus
Hastened to sandy Pylos, and came to the ford of the Alpheus
And the fields and the high-vaulted byre where by night the cattle were
    sheltered.
Hermes then, going inside the stony cave of the byre,   420
Drove out into the light the herd of fine cattle.
But the son of Leto, glancing around, saw the hides
Stretched on a towering rock, and sharply addressed glorious Hermes:
    "How were you able, you devious-minded child,
To slaughter two cows, being so very newborn and helpless?

I myself shudder to think of the strength to be yours
Hereafter. There is no need for you to grow tall,
Little Cyllenian, son of heavenly Maia."
    So spoke Apollo, and twisted around in his hands
Tough willow shoots with which to fashion strong fetters,   430
Desiring to bind glorious Hermes. But bonds would not hold him,
And the willow withes fell off at a distance around him
And took root in the earth underfoot and began to grow
There on the spot, shooting up quickly and twining around
One another and all the cattle that graze in the meadows,
By the will of Hermes of dissembling mind, while Apollo
Looked on in amazement. Then the strong slayer of Argos
Covertly scanned the ground, his eyes sparkling with fire,
Seeking to find a hollow to hide in, but Hermes,
As he had designed, easily soothed the Far-Darter,   440
Son of most glorious Leto, obdurate though he was.
Taking his lyre upon his left arm, he tried out
Each string in turn with the plectrum, and under his hand
The lyre resounded uncannily. Phoebus Apollo
Laughed aloud with delight. The lovely sound
Of heavenly music went straight through his heart, and sweet longing
Possessed him as he listened, enraptured. As he played on,
Enticingly stroking his lyre, the young son of Maia,
Gaining assurance, sidled up to the left
Of Phoebus Apollo, and soon, still calling forth   450
Clear strains from the lyre, he burst into song—and lovely his voice—
Telling of how the immortal gods and black earth
First came to be, and how each was allotted his portion.
Mnemosyne, mother of Muses, first of the gods
He honored with song, for to her Maia's son was apportioned by lot.
Hermes, the son brilliant in splendor of Zeus,
Hymned the undying gods according to age,
And told the tale of how each one was born, relating
All things in order, to the sweet strains of the lyre on his arm.
The anguish of helpless desire laid hold on the heart of Apollo,   460
And he cried out to Hermes, addressing him with winged words:
    "Killer of cows, prankster, industrious child,
Comrade of the feast, your invention is worth fifty cows!
I think we shall very soon peacefully settle our quarrel.
Now come, tell me this, versatile son of Maia:
Has this wondrous object been yours since your birth, or did one
Of the immortal gods or someone of mortal mankind
Give you this royal gift and coach you in heavenly song?
So amazing is this new sound that I hear
That no man, I swear, can ever have heard it before,   470
Nor any of the immortals who have their homes on Olympus
Save you, you robber, son of Zeus and of Maia.

What art can this be? What music for hearts bent with sorrow?
What path of life? For here in truth are combined
Three pleasures to choose from—merriment, love, and sweet slumber.
I, though attendant upon the Olympian Muses,
Who take careful thought for the dance and the bright strains of song,
The swelling chant and the sweet shrilling of pipes,
Never before have I cared so much in my heart
For other displays of skill by festive young men.   480
Son of Zeus, I am astonished, so lovely your playing!
And now, since although indeed you are little you have such remarkable talent,
Sit down here, my friend, and heed the voice of your elders.
Now fame and glory will be yours among the immortals,
For both you yourself and your mother—I truly proclaim it.
I swear by this cornelwood shaft I will make you a leader
Renowned and blessed among the immortals and give you rich gifts,
And to the end of the world I will never deceive you."
    Hermes then answered him, craftily choosing his words:
"You question me closely, Far-Worker, but not out of envy   490
Would I deny you the means of learning my art.
This very day you shall know it. Toward you would I always be
Kindly in words and intending. But you in your heart, son of Zeus,
Well know all things, for you sit foremost among the immortals,
Both brave and strong, and Zeus wise in counsel loves you
And with all justice has granted you glorious favors.
From the divine voice of Zeus they say you have learned
The honors due to the gods, Far-Worker, and know
By oracular power all that Zeus has decreed.
I have heard too that you are exceedingly rich;   500
It is for you to choose to learn whatever delights you.
But since now your heart is set on playing the lyre,
Receive it from me, and sing and play and be happy,
And you, my friend, on me bestow future glory.
Sing well as you hold in your hands the clear-voiced companion,
For you are skilled in beautiful speech according to order.
Then, carefree, carry joy to the bounteous feast,
The lovely choral dance, and the brilliant carousal
By night and day. For whoever with wisdom and skill
Inquires of it, him will it teach, in a voice loud and clear,   510
All manner of things agreeable to the mind,
Being played lightly with delicate, intimate touches,
For it loathes painful toil. But he who, witless to start with, asks roughly,
Him will it answer with wavering notes and uncertain noises.
But it is for you to choose to learn whatever delights you.
Son radiant in splendor of Zeus, I will give you this lyre,
And I in turn, Far-worker, will graze down the pastures
Of mountain and horse-feeding plain with cattle that dwell in the meadows.
Then cows shall be covered by bulls and bring forth in abundance

Calves, both heifers and bull calves. So there is no reason for you,   520
Shrewd at a trade as you are, to fly into a rage."
    So speaking, he held out the lyre, and Phoebus Apollo received it,
And of his own will gave into the hand of Hermes
The shining scourge, and ordained him herder of cattle,
And the son of Maia, rejoicing received it. Then Apollo,
Lord who works from afar, Leto's illustrious son,
Took the lyre upon his left arm and tried out with the plectrum
Each string in turn, and under his deft touch the strains
Of unearthly music rang out, while the god sang along.
    Then together they turned the cows back toward the sacred meadow,   530
And themselves, the surpassingly beautiful children of Zeus,
Hastened once more to snowy Olympus, exultant
Over the lyre. Zeus wise in counsel was glad
And brought his sons together in friendship. Hermes,
From that moment when, having taught Apollo the art,
He gave the longed-for lyre as a token into his hands
And the Far-Darter took it upon his left arm and played—
Hermes from that time forever loved Leto's son,
And so even now. Then from his vast store of knowledge
Hermes devised a new art and, joining cut reeds,   540
Fashioned the syrinx, whose shrill sound is heard from afar.
    Then Apollo, the son of Leto, spoke words to Hermes:
"I am afraid, son of Maia, guide, wily of mind,
Lest you should steal from me the lyre and my bent bow together,
For from Zeus you hold the honor of bringing to men
Throughout the all-nourishing earth business of barter.
But if you dare swear to me the great oath of the gods,
Either by nodding your head or by the strong waters of Styx,
You would do all I could ask for to ease and win over my heart."
    The son of Maia then, nodding his head, solemnly vowed   550
Never to steal the Far-Darter's many possessions
And never to venture near his thickly built house, and Apollo,
Son of Leto, nodded in turn, vowing friendship and love
And swearing to hold dearer than Hermes no other
Among the immortals—neither god nor man born of Zeus.
And father Zeus sent out an eagle, confirming the oath.
Then Apollo furthermore swore: "You only, Hermes,
Among the immortal gods and all others besides
Will I adopt as a symbol of my heart's trust and esteem.
I will give you, moreover, a beautiful wand of blessing and riches,   560
Wrought of gold, triply entwined, to protect you, unharmed,
And bring to conclusion all contests of words and of deeds
Of the good that I claim to know from Zeus's divine voice.
But the art of prophecy, friend, god-cherished child,
About which you ask—it is not ordained that you learn it,

Or any other immortal; the mind of Zeus alone knows it.
I bound myself by a pledge, nodding, and swore a strong oath
That no one apart from me of the gods everlasting
Should ever share the wise-minded counsel of Zeus.
So do not press me, gold-wanded brother, to make clear his will   570
And reveal the decrees and intentions of far-seeing Zeus.
As for mankind, one man will I harm and another man benefit,
Greatly perplexing the tribes of unenviable men,
He who comes to my shrine, guided there by the cries
And flight of birds of sure omen, will reap a rich harvest
From my oracular voice, and I will not deceive him.
But he who, foolishly trusting in idly twittering birds,
Desires to inquire through my oracle into things beyond knowing
And to understand more than the gods everlasting—that man
I say travels the road without profit, though his gifts I would take.   580
    "And this too I will tell you, son of all-glorious Maia
And of Zeus, aegis-bearer, of gods the spirit of luck.
Certain holy ones are there, three of them, sisters and virgins,
Adorned with swift wings, on whose heads has been sprinkled white barley,
Who live in a dwelling under a ledge of Parnassos.
Teachers of prophecy are they apart from me—
That art I studied while yet a boy tending cattle,
And my father at that time cared not at all.
From their mountain home they flit from one place to another,
Feeding on honeycombs, and they bring all things to fulfillment.   590
When they are inspired by eating pale golden honey,
Graciously then are they willing to utter the truth,
But if deprived of the sweet food of the gods,
They speak false words and swarm in confusion around one another.
These, then, I give you. Inquire sincerely of them
And be content in your heart. If you should so teach some mortal,
Often, if he is lucky, will he hear your response.
Take these, son of Maia, and watch over crumple-horned cattle
That graze in the meadows, and horses and mules long-enduring."
    So spoke Apollo, and out of high heaven the father,   600
Zeus himself, brought to fulfillment the words of his son.
Zeus commanded besides that glorious Hermes rule over
All birds of omen and fiery-eyed lions and boars with white tusks,
And dogs and flocks, as many as broad earth feeds—
Over all beasts that move on the land—and moreover appointed
Hermes his son to serve as sole courier to Hades,
Who, though receiving no gifts, will himself give no unworthy prize.
    Thus lord Apollo showed love for the young son of Maia
With all these affectionate tokens, and Zeus son of Cronos
Besides showered favor upon him. Consorting with all gods and mortals,   610
Seldom he helps them, but everlastingly cozens

The tribes of mortal mankind throughout the dark night.
  And so farewell to you, son of Zeus and of Maia;
Yet I will remember you and another song too.

. . . .

Questions for Discussion and Review

1. According to Homer, how do Zeus and his brothers decide on their respective spheres of influence? How does Zeus share power with various members of his family?

2. Why do you think Greek myth uses the model of the human family to depict the gods? Discuss some of the family dynamics at work among the Olympians.

3. In what specific ways do the individual gods resemble humans? In what respects are they qualitatively different? Discuss myth's portrayal of the gods as it reveals a typically Greek anthropomorphism, humanism, individualism, and competitiveness, as well as an anthropocentric view of the universe.

4. In Homer's song about the affair between Ares and Aphrodite, does the fact of divine adultery threaten the stability of the Olympian family or social structure? Why or why not?

5. In the *Homeric Hymn to Hermes,* how do the young god's actions illustrate his unique qualities of inventiveness, roguery, and skillfulness in manipulating others to his own advantage? Why do you suppose the Greeks, who valued Zeus for upholding cosmic justice and the sacredness of the sworn oath, also accepted a lying and thieving god such as Hermes?

In Touch with the Gods: Apollo's Oracle at Delphi

KEY TOPICS/THEMES

Located on the slopes of Mount Parnassus, Apollo's shrine at Delphi was widely regarded as the spiritual center of the Greek world, a place where humans could consult the god to whom Zeus had given the art of prophecy. Apollo's word (oracle) was transmitted through his virgin priestess, the Pythia, named in honor of the Python, which Apollo slew when he established his Delphic rule. A sanctuary where myth and ritual combined to affirm humanity's communion with divine powers, Delphi linked the worlds of flesh and spirit.

Two of Zeus's sons—Apollo and Dionysus —embody strikingly different aspects of the human psyche: rational intellect and instinctual sensuality. Perhaps because these two forces, and the tension between them, are so crucial in human experience, the two young gods—more than any other of Zeus's male children—inspired myths and ceremonies that profoundly influenced Greek life. The worship of Dionysus, whose character and myth express life's dangerous mutability, gave birth to the Athenian tragic drama (see Chapter 14); the cult of Apollo created a practical institution that allowed humans to communicate, albeit imperfectly, with the gods (Figure 7-1).

The Shrine at Delphi: Communing with the Gods

Whereas the living could visit Olympus or Hades' abode only in their imagination, the Greeks believed that a few sacred places on earth also provided limited access to the invisible realm of divine beings. Communicating with the gods was, however, a

FIGURE 7-1 Apollo. Patron of the Muses and god of rationality, health, and prophecy, Apollo is also an eternal ephebe (a youth schooled in the strict discipline of mind
and body). An embodiment of the Greek ideal of proportion, strength, and masculine
beauty, Apollo presides over his mantic shrine at Delphi, where his priestess, the Pythia,
communicates the god's will to human questioners. Known as the Belvedere, this marble
statue is a Roman copy of a Greek bronze from the Hellenistic period, the era following Alexander's conquests and the assimilation of Greek culture throughout the eastern
Mediterranean world. (*Vatican Museums, Rome*)

procedure fraught with mystery and ambiguity, for Zeus had bestowed the patronage of clairvoyance and prophecy on Apollo, a deity known to distance himself from direct contact with mortals. Aloof and remote, Apollo transmitted Zeus's will through a series of mediators, commonly phrasing his responses in cryptic terms more comprehensible to other gods than to the human questioners.

The prophetic shrines, the gods' words spoken there, and the persons authorized to convey and interpret the typically obscure messages were all designated by the term **oracle.** One of the oldest oracles was that of Zeus at Dodona in Epirus, where the Olympian's utterances were said to issue from a sacred oak tree, perhaps via the sound of the wind rustling its leaves. A few foreign oracles, particularly that of Zeus Ammon at Siwa in the Libyan desert, which was consulted by Alexander the Great, also enjoyed a high reputation among the Greeks.

By far the most popular and influential oracle, however, was that of Apollo at **Delphi** [DEL-phee], to which thousands of Greeks flocked each year to seek enlightenment from their god. Originally called **Pytho** [PYE-thoh], Delphi occupied a spur of rugged Mount Parnassus thousands of feet above the adjacent Pleistos River valley (Figure 7-2). Delphi's site combined the beauty of wild nature with the sophistication of classical architecture; these sacred precincts encompassed a large theater, a stadium where the Pythian Games were held in the god's honor, and a magnificent columned temple where the Pythia (or Pythoness), Apollo's clairvoyant priestess, gave ethical advice and issued predictions about the future that many believed were divinely inspired (Figure 7-3).

FIGURE 7-2   Map Showing the Location of Delphi, Thebes, and Athens. Situated high on the wooded slopes of Mount Parnassus, Delphi's site combines the beauty of wild nature with the sophistication of classical architecture, including the ruins of Apollo's temple, an amphitheater, and a stadium where the Pythian Games were held in the god's honor.

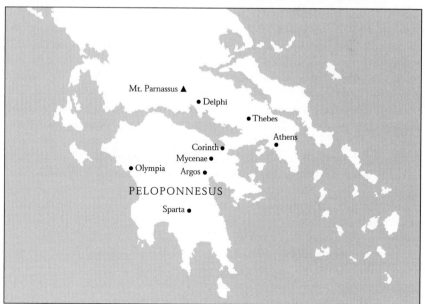

FIGURE 7-3   Reconstruction of Delphi's Magnificent Shrines. Depicted in this model are a colossal bronze statue of Apollo (right center), the god's chief temple (center), and a large amphitheater where thousands of people assembled to attend musical performances, poetic recitations, and dance exhibitions staged to honor the divine patron of artistic creativity.

Delphi's reputation, which reached its peak between the seventh and fifth centuries B.C., was so widespread that foreign kings, as well as Greek rulers, built numerous lavishly decorated shrines along its Sacred Way. These miniature temples, crammed with treasures, were erected in gratitude for (or in hope of eliciting) the god's wise counsel and diplomatic intervention in settling political disputes both at home and abroad. Although some complained that the Delphic priesthood favored Sparta and other conservative city-states, Apollo's oracles were generally peaceful in tone and calculated to promote a viable balance of political power and harmony among Greece's many warring factions. The facade of Apollo's temple was inscribed with maxims urging the Greeks to practice moderation: "Nothing in Excess" (*mēden agan*) and "Know Yourself" (*gnōthi sauton*)—an exhortation to remember one's human limitations and to avoid behaving as if one were a god (Figure 7-4).

Delphi's centrality in Greek religion was expressed in the belief that it stood at the exact center of earth's surface. Zeus, it was said, had released two equally swift eagles that flew in opposite directions around the globe; they met at Delphi, where an ancient carved stone, perhaps a meteor fragment, the omphalos (Figure 7-5), was kept in the temple and identified as the navel of the earth. The omphalos was also reputed to be the stone—the substitute body of Zeus—that Cronus had swallowed instead of his youngest son, the predestined ruler of the universe. Equating Apollo's sanctuary with the cosmic nucleus—Delphi literally means "womb"—the myth not only validated the priestly institution of prophecy but also exalted Apollo

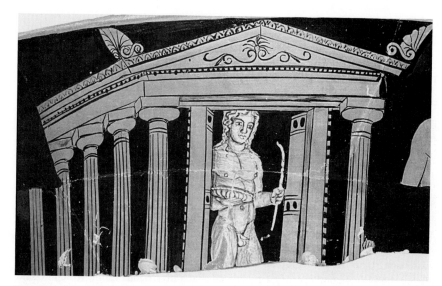

FIGURE 7-4 Temple of Apollo at Delphi. This detail of a vase painting shows the statue of the Archer King—characteristically holding the bow from which he propels his arrows of plague or healing (invisibly)—in his Doric temple at Delphi. The temple walls were inscribed with famous proverbs advocating self-knowledge and self-control. (*Allard Pierson Museum, Amsterdam*)

FIGURE 7-5 Delphic Omphalos. The social and spiritual centrality of Delphi was expressed in the myth that Apollo's sacred place of worship was literally the geographic center of the world: it is the place where Zeus's two eagles met when, departing from the same point, they flew at equal speeds around the globe. Delphi's connection with themes of birth and rebirth is suggested by its name, which means "womb," and the presence of the omphalos, a stone representing earth's navel. According to tradition, the original omphalos was the stone that Cronus swallowed instead of Zeus. Shown here is a carved replica of the "navel" stone. (*Delphi Museum*)

as the essential divinity whose far-ranging intelligence unites the realms of heaven and earth.

Prehistoric Delphi

Positioned at the foot of two soaring rocky cliffs, the Phedriads, Delphi was regarded as a holy site long before Apollo's arrival there. In addition to its spectacular mountainscape, the site was famous as a place where some persons experienced the invisible presence of divine beings willing to commune with mortals.

Archaeologists have only recently found evidence supporting an ancient tradition that, at the site of Apollo's temple, a cleft in the rocks formerly emitted strangely intoxicating fumes that may have been partly responsible for the trances and ecstatic utterances of the Oracle there. The Roman geographer Strabo (c. 64 B.C.–A.D. 25) stated that "the seat of the oracle is a cavern hollowed down in the depths . . . from which arises pneuma [spirit, breath, or vapor] that inspires a divine state of possession." The Greek biographer Plutarch, who served as Apollo's priest at Delphi during the early second century A.D., agreed that a mysterious vapor, which he said smelled as sweet as perfume, issued from a crevice at the sanctuary, adding that the fumes probably were triggered by the region's frequent earthquakes.

In the 1920s, French investigators concluded that there had never been any volcanic emissions in the Delphi area (assuming that only volcanic gases were likely to have caused the phenomena Strabo and Plutarch described), a verdict that effectively dismissed the tradition as pure fiction, and one that the academic community generally accepted for seventy years. In the late 1990s and early 2000s, however, Greek and American researchers found that Apollo's temple actually sat at the intersection of two active geologic faults (one previously unknown), deep fractures in the earth's crust that may have provided channels for subterranean vapors of nonvolcanic origin to reach the surface. Earth movements along the Delphi fault system repeatedly fractured the bitumen-permeated limestone underlying the area, heating the rock and permitting groundwater laden with hydrocarbons to percolate upward. Analysis of hydrocarbon gases in springs near the temple revealed the presence of methane and ethylene, the latter of which has a sweet odor and can induce a narcotic effect. Ethylene, researchers note, was once used as an anaesthetic; in small doses, it produces a floating sensation and feelings of euphoria, though in large quantities it can be fatal. (See the works by Broad; Jelle De Boer and colleagues; and Piccardi in the Selected Bibliography under Chapter 7.) As Plutarch observed in *On the Cessation of Oracles*, when the women acting as Apollo's Oracle inhaled the intoxicating vapors, they commonly went into a trance; afterward, some of them died.

In Aeschylus's play the *Eumenides,* the Pythia summarizes Delphi's prehistory, noting that Apollo's rule followed that held by several ancient goddesses. After Gaea, the primordial fount of wisdom, came her equally wise daughter **Themis** [THEE-mis] (Eternal Law), who was Zeus's second wife and one of the few Titans to remain influential under Olympian jurisdiction. An aspect of the Great Goddess, Themis taught her male successor the art of prophecy, a debt Apollo acknowledged by allowing Themis's priestesses to continue officiating at a small altar within

Delphi's precincts. Although we can not take the Pythia's speech as historical fact, Aeschylus does preserve a tradition that a succession of goddesses presided at Delphi long before Apollo established his cult there.

Apollo's Prehistory

Just as Delphi has a complex history of religious development, so does the figure of the god who eventually came to dominate it. Although Apollo does not appear in the Linear B texts under that name, the term *Paian or Paion* is listed among the gods at Knossos during the Mycenaean period. In Homer, this term is applied both to a god of healing and to Apollo in his dual role of healer and bringer of pestilence, an office featured prominently in Book 1 of the *Iliad* and in Sophocles' play *Oedipus Rex* (see Chapters 12 and 16, respectively). The same term, rendered in English as **paean,** is given to Apollo's cult hymn, named for its repeated cry *"ie, ie Paian,"* which was used as a refrain. According to tradition, the paean was introduced from Crete to Sparta early in the seventh century B.C. and was performed at Apollo's Spartan festivals.

Lacking evidence that Apollo was worshiped during the Bronze Age, most scholars believe that his cult became prominent only during the Dark Ages following the collapse of Mycenaean civilization in the twelfth century B.C. (see Chapter 1). By the Archaic period, when the oral traditions underlying the epics of Homer and Hesiod evolved, the concept of Apollo was already well developed. Both the *Iliad* and the *Odyssey* refer to his oracular shrine at Delphi and/or his sacred birthplace on the remote island of Delos. Although Apollo's origins remain uncertain (he was not originally a sun god), some scholars trace aspects of his cult to the Dorian word *apella,* or "assembly," an annual gathering of adult males at which initiated youths were admitted to the social group.

Apollo and Initiation

Apollo's connection with young men, their education, and their initiation into adult society is central to his religious significance. Consistently depicted in artworks as youthful, long-haired, handsome, and athletic, Apollo is the eternal **ephebe,** a term designating a class of youths, approximately eighteen to twenty years old, who underwent systematic educational and physical training in order to serve the polis as hoplites (heavily armed infantrymen). Apollo's association with the Muses—patrons of poetry, song, dance, and music—probably stems from his function as educator of young men, who studied the arts as part of their preparation for military service and other obligations of full citizenship. In time, Apollo also became the patron of philosophy, so involved in the promotion of rationality and logical thought that, according to one source, he became the father of Plato, the foremost thinker of classical Greece.

Presiding over the ephebes' rite of passage from boyhood to full citizenship and military responsibility, Apollo received the sacrifice of their long hair, which was cut short as part of a ritual symbolizing their transition to a new stage of life. Some scholars regard Achilles, a young warrior without wife or family, as a salient example of the ephebe, a novice soldier who fights far from home (at Troy) to win the respect of his peers.

Apollo and the Dragon: The Transition from Earth Goddess to Sky God

As if reflecting the historical transition from chthonic powers to Olympian sky gods (see Chapters 3 and 5), myths about the establishment of Apollo's worship at Delphi involve an epochal battle between female and male principles of divinity. According to the Homeric *Hymn to Pythian Apollo*, the single most important account of Apollo's mythic origins, the conflict originates in Hera's anger toward Zeus for having produced Athene by himself. As granddaughter of Gaea and as the Queen of Heaven, Hera inherits a primal goddess's prerogatives and is outraged when Zeus ignores her exclusive right to bear divine children. After her attempt to duplicate Zeus's reproductive autonomy results only in the malformed Hephaestus, Hera abandons her husband's bed and, without male help, conceives and bears **Typhon** (Typhoeus), the monstrous serpent whose strength rivals that of Zeus. She entrusts Typhon's upbringing to **Python** [PYE-thuhn], a female dragon who guards the ancient sanctuary of Gaea and Themis at Delphi. According to the Delphic hymn, the monster does not challenge Zeus directly, but is associated with Python, the serpent who will threaten Zeus's noblest son, Apollo. (Compare Hesiod's account in the *Theogony,* in which Gaea, not Hera, is the dragon's mother; see Chapter 3.)

Apollo's Birth

Birth stories about an infant predestined for unusual achievement, whether as a national leader or a future god—such as the biblical Moses or Jesus of Nazareth—typically involve grave dangers from which the child narrowly escapes. Hera tries to eliminate Apollo and Artemis by preventing their birth. After Zeus impregnates their mother, **Leto** [LEE-toh], daughter of the Titans Coeus and Phoebe, Hera so terrorizes the world that no land on earth will give Leto a safe place to deliver her children. When Leto at last finds refuge on a barren floating island, Ortygia (Island of Quails), Hera then refuses to allow Eileithyia, goddess of childbirth, to leave Olympus, causing Leto to remain in agonizing labor for nine days. Only after Athene persuades Hera to assuage her anger by giving her a gigantic gold and amber necklace does Hera permit Eileithyia to visit Ortygia and effect Leto's safe delivery. Apollo later transforms his birthplace into the island of Delos, permanently fixing it in the midst of the Cyclades, where it became an important religious center honoring Zeus's Olympian twins. Serving an etiological function, this tale accounts for Delos's name (meaning "brilliant"): it was here that the god of light first beheld the sun's bright rays.

Festivals and Ceremonies of Delphi

The Pythian Games

Whereas the first part of the *Hymn to Pythian Apollo* tells the story of Apollo's birth, the second part (composed earlier, in the seventh century B.C.) narrates the god's founding of his oracular shrine at Pytho (Delphi). After traversing Greece and settling at Delphi, Apollo faces an immediate challenge to his new cult. Python, reputedly a child of Gaea and mentor of Typhon (embodiment of Hera's bitter hatred of Zeus's patriarchy), ravages the countryside, slaughtering sheep and humans alike. Only three days old, Apollo achieves his first victory with the bow, shooting an arrow through Python and ridding the world of a destructive pest. In memory of this feat, Apollo's Delphic Oracle, a virgin prophetess empowered to speak in his name, is called the **Pythia** [PITH-ee-uh]. Further commemorating Python's defeat, Apollo establishes the Pythian Games (Figure 7-6), which were held every four years and which were second only to the Olympics in importance among Greece's

(a)   (b)

FIGURE 7-6 The Charioteer. (a) This Greek bronze of a charioteer standing in calm triumph at the moment of victory displays the classic ideals of simplicity, symmetry, and serenity—qualities of conscious restraint associated with Apollonian balance. Victors at the Pythian Games, held every four years at Delphi, were crowned with laurel wreaths cut from the valley of Tempe. This is one of the few statues to retain eyes of inlaid metal. (b) The Charioteer once stood in a bronze chariot pulled by four bronze horses. It owes its preservation to an earthquake that toppled it into a drain, burying it under an avalanche. *(Delphi Museum)*

athletic competitions. As befits a festival honoring the Muses' patron, the Pythian Games also emphasized performances in music, poetry, and dance.

The Stepterion: Guilt and Purification

Although Apollo must eradicate his older rival in order to establish his Delphic rites, he readily acknowledges moral responsibility for having slain Python, the serpent guardian of Gaea's ancient shrine. Voluntarily exiling himself from Olympus, Apollo withdraws to the valley of Tempe, where he works as a shepherd for King **Admetus.** Setting the example of a god who performs slave labor to purge himself of guilt, Apollo creates a paradigm of expiation for mortals who seek to purify themselves (Figure 7-7). After his purification, Apollo, crowned with laurel leaves,

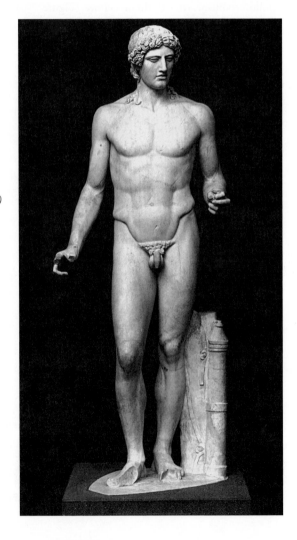

FIGURE 7-7   Apollo at Delphi. This Roman copy of the original (450 B.C.) Greek statue depicts the god as one of the athletes who competed in Delphi's Pythian Games. Embodying the principle of a healthy mind in a healthy body, Apollo presides over rites of purification that can remove guilt and restore offenders to participation in Greek society. *(Kassel Museum)*

returns to Delphi at midsummer and inaugurates the first Pythia, Herophile, who is inspired to foretell the Trojan War.

Because of Apollo's example, Delphi became a holy asylum where exiles could ritualistically rid themselves of moral pollution, as Orestes does when he is cleansed with sacrificial pig's blood, ceremonially, if not legally or ethically, absolving him from the crime of having murdered his mother. In general, Apollo's Delphic myth helped to promote a more humane moral order in which Greek society was encouraged to abandon its ancient demands for bloody retaliation by recognizing the superiority of justice tempered with mercy—an innovation that Aeschylus celebrates in his Oresteia (see Chapter 15).

In classical times, every eight years, the priests of Delphi reenacted Apollo's slaying of Python in a religious drama called the *Stepterion*. The rite took place on an ancient threshing floor (the *halos*), where a young boy representing the infant god was guided by priests to a hut in which the dragon lurked. After launching an arrow into the hut and supposedly killing the hidden serpent, the boy then pantomimed Apollo's flight to Tempe, where the god atoned for Python's death.

Consulting the Oracle

Persons wishing to ask questions of the Pythia followed a strictly regulated procedure: applicants first washed themselves in water from the nearby Castalia Spring; paid a fee, the size of which was determined by officiating priests; and sacrificed an animal, usually a sheep or goat that was "perfect," in the sense that it had no visible defects. Before the animal's throat was cut on Apollo's altar, priests doused it with cold spring water; if it shivered or trembled, the day was deemed propitious, and the god could be expected to offer a reply.

After washing in Castalia's waters, the Pythia, accompanied by priests similarly purified, entered the temple, where she burned an offering of laurel and barley flour in a sacred flame kept perpetually alight on Apollo's hearth. The priestess then descended into an underground chamber where she seated herself on a tripod—a high, three-legged stand that normally held a bowl or cauldron used in cooking (Figure 7-8). Perched on the tripod, she prepared to receive the god's spirit. After drinking water from the sacred spring and chewing bay or laurel leaves, the Pythia went into a trance during which she uttered phrases that were unintelligible to the questioner waiting in an adjoining room. A priest then wrote down her words, translating them into Greek verses, commonly using dactyl hexameters, the meter of epic poetry.

Typically couched in highly obscure terms, many of the Pythia's oracles have been preserved, chiefly in inscriptions and the histories of Herodotus. In a famous, but probably spurious, episode involving **Croesus**, [KREE-SUS], a king of Lydia (sixth century B.C.), regarded as the world's wealthiest ruler, Herodotus reports that the king disastrously failed to cope with oracular ambiguity. Threatened by the rapidly expanding empire of Persia under Cyrus the Great, Croesus determined to halt the expansion. Before taking action, however, he sought the Delphic Oracle's advice; he was told that if he crossed the Persian border a great nation would fall.

FIGURE 7-8   The Pythia, Sitting atop a Tripod in Her God's Delphic Sanctuary. Holding a laurel branch in one hand, Apollo's virgin priestess gazes intently at the contents of a bowl she holds in her other hand, perhaps reading there an answer to the question posed by the petitioner standing before her. At the height of its reputation, during the sixth and fifth centuries B.C., Delphi attracted pilgrims from throughout the eastern Mediterranean world. Sophocles' *Oedipus Rex* was written, in part, to demonstrate the inescapable truth of Apollo's oracles. *(Staatliche Museen, Berlin)*

Thinking that Persia's imperialist aspirations were doomed, Croesus boldly attacked Cyrus, only to have his own capital city, Sardis, captured by Persian troops and his kingdom incorporated into the Persian Empire. After narrowly escaping being burned alive—Herodotus states that Apollo sent a storm that quenched the flames—Croesus indignantly asked the Delphic priestess how she could have so misled him. The Pythia's reply was mild: if Croesus did not understand the first oracle, he should have made a second inquiry.

During the two Persian invasions of Greece (490 and 480–479 B.C.), the Delphic Oracle at first seemed to favor submitting to the hitherto undefeated Persian armies, perhaps to avoid the severe reprisals that the invaders would inflict after overcoming Greek resistance. When at last the Pythia reluctantly conceded that the Greeks should place their trust in "the wooden wall," Themistocles, Athens' resourceful leader, argued that Apollo advised relying on the Greeks' warships. After the combined Greek fleet managed to sink most of the Persian armada at the Battle of Salamis, causing the Persians to withdraw, it seemed clear that Themistocles—and Apollo's oracle—was right. The oracle's part in the Persian Wars offers an interesting example of a religious institution whose authority was based on myth exerting a significant influence on historical events.

Sophocles used one of the oldest myths, that of Oedipus and his doomed royal house of Thebes, to dramatize the infallibility of Apollo's Delphic pronouncements. Oedipus's career and those of his equally tragic children, Antigone, Eteocles, and Polyneices—hedged about by cryptic oracles—serve to confirm that the god speaks truly through his priestess and that no one can escape fulfilling Delphi's prophecies. (See Chapter 16, Sophocles' *Oedipus Rex*.)

Despite such unqualified support as Sophocles gave in his Oedipus plays, Delphi's prestige rapidly declined after the fifth century B.C. With the rise of Macedonian imperialism, under King Philip and his son Alexander, Greek city-states like Attica and Boeotia (the state bordering Delphi) were absorbed into a larger political system and lost much of their confidence in divine institutions, along with their autonomy. After Rome seized control of Greece in 146 B.C., Delphi became even more a religious curiosity or cultural artifact than a source of living faith. A few Roman emperors—such as Hadrian, with his friend Herodes Atticus—provided money to rebuild its stadium and restore its shrines, but even before new gods arrived from Palestine and declared Apollo's cult obsolete, the sanctuary had fallen into disuse and ruin (Figure 7-9). When Julian (A.D. 360–363), the only non-Christian emperor after Constantine, attempted to revive worship of the classical gods and sent an envoy to Delphi, it is said that an aged Pythia gave this response:

> Tell the king the fairwrought hall has fallen to the ground,
> no longer has Phoebus a hut, nor a prophetic laurel,
> nor a spring that speaks. The water of speech even is quenched.

Apollo's Loves

Apollo's primary form of communication with humanity was through his oracles, but the god also developed relationships with individual human lovers. Like his father, Zeus, he formed liaisons with members of both sexes, but unlike Zeus, he was typically unlucky in love. Although the model of manly beauty, Apollo frequently suffered the pangs of rejection; even when accepted, he commonly lost his beloved through betrayal or death. The story of his first unrequited passion, for **Daphne,** a beautiful mountain nymph, foreshadows his legacy of loss and sexual frustration. When Apollo pursues her, Daphne flees him like the plague, praying (in some traditions) to Zeus to preserve her virginity. In an instant, Daphne is changed into a bay or laurel tree, leaving her pursuer inconsolable. As a memorial

FIGURE 7-9 The Site of Delphi. Although Delphi's shrines now lie in ruins, the site retains, for many, an almost mystical attraction. Only the foundations and a few columns remain of Apollo's temple, but the pointed cypress is an evergreen reminder of one of the god's earliest loves, the youth Cyparissus.

of his unconsummated love, Apollo makes a crown of laurel leaves, an emblem that was later awarded to victors in the Pythian Games.

Apollo also loved a youth named **Cyparissus**, who, in turn, was devoted to a pet stag. When Cyparissus accidentally kills the stag, he resolves to die himself, grieving so intensely for his animal friend that he refuses Apollo's pleas to transfer his affection to the god. Drained by excessive weeping, he gradually loses his human form and is transformed into a cypress. Even today, a scattering of cypress trees punctuates the rocky slopes of Parnassus, standing as upright, evergreen reminders of Apollo's passion.

In the god's most celebrated affair, a stunningly handsome boy named **Hyacinthus** is the object of Apollo's desire. Although this time the god's affection is returned, the relationship still ends unhappily. While throwing the discus together, a favorite pastime of Greek lovers, Hyacinthus, perhaps accidentally, steps in the way of Apollo's hurtling discus, which strikes him fatally in the head. (One version of the myth states that **Zephyrus,** the West Wind, also loved Hyacinthus and, when spurned by the youth, jealously diverts the discus's trajectory, causing it to strike the young man.) His mind indelibly imprinted by the sight of blood streaming over

Hyacinthus's white skin, Apollo transforms the boy's corpse into a flower whose white petals are marked in red, mimicking the letters *AI,* signifying the Greeks' cry of sorrow.

Apollo's Son Asclepius: The Divine Gift of Healing

Although these myths of unfulfilled love provide etiologies of various plants or blossoms, symbols of the ephemerality of mortal youth and beauty, the story of Apollo and Coronis, equally unsatisfying to the god, serves a different purpose. Coronis, a princess of Thessaly, is already pregnant by Apollo when she leaves Zeus's most attractive son for a human lover. According to one tradition, the god is informed of Coronis's humiliating infidelity with a mere mortal by a gossipy crow. In Pindar's version of the tale, the all-seeing god does not need a bird of ill omen to bring the bad news; rather, he discerns the truth himself and sends his sister Artemis to kill Coronis for her treachery.

The unborn child is preserved, however, and given to **Chiron,** wisest of the centaurs, to raise. Created by the union of divinity and fallible humanity, and tutored by a creature half-human and half-horse, the child **Asclepius** becomes one of myth's most potent symbols of human endeavor. Inheriting from his father the art of healing, Asclepius is the first physician, using his divine legacy to combat disease and cure mortals of their afflictions (Figure 7-10). When Asclepius becomes so skilled at practicing medicine that he learns how to revive even the dead, Zeus, alarmed at this violation of nature, kills him with a thunderbolt. Outraged at his son's undeserved fate, Apollo promptly retaliates by killing the Cyclops who had forged Zeus's lightning. Regarding Apollo's act as rebellion, Zeus momentarily contemplates imprisoning the god of light in Tartarus's infernal darkness.

Closely associated with that of Apollo, the cult of Asclepius, whom tradition granted posthumous immortality, flourished throughout Greece. When pilgrims visited the rural shrine at Epidaurus, where Asclepius's most famous temple stood, they followed a peculiar ritual in which reptilian symbols of Gaea and other chthonic goddesses played a major part. (Both Apollo and Asclepian practitioners bore the **caduceus,** with its two serpents entwined about a staff, which some mythographers interpret as a phallic symbol and others as a representation of the Tree of Life, an image associated with the divine woman's powers of regeneration.) Patients seeking a cure slept overnight on the temple floor, typically experiencing incubation, the receiving of dreams in which the god prescribes the method of healing. Combining Apollonian reason with sympathetic magic (a ritual acting out of what one wants to take place), the Epidaurus physicians applied their skills to replicating on individual humans the ancient Delphic rite of cleansing and purification.

As the god of rationality, cerebral control, and moderation, Apollo is characteristically cool and emotionally detached, shooting his invisible arrows of plague from vast distances and communicating indirectly through obscure pronouncements. Through his son Asclepius, however, he gives humankind an invaluable gift, endowing physicians with the power to heal and restoring the balance between disease and health.

FIGURE 7-10   Asclepius and a Suppliant. Apollo punishes wrongdoing by inflicting plagues on entire communities that harbor the guilty, as he does in the *Iliad* and *Oedipus Rex,* but he also confers the benefits of medicine on humanity through his human son Asclepius, the first physician. Myth presents Asclepius as so potent a healer that he can restore even the dead to life. Zeus ends this disruption of natural processes—and assertion of human skill against the limits of mortality—by killing Asclepius, an act that outrages Apollo and brings him temporarily into conflict with the King of Heaven. In this votive plaque, Asclepius tends to the wounded arm of a suppliant. *(Archaeological Receipts Fund [TAP], Greece)*

HYMN TO THE PYTHIAN APOLLO*

Cynaethus (Kynaithos) of Chios

[One of the longest and oldest of the poems praising an Olympian god, the *Hymn to Apollo* is divided into two parts: the opening section narrates the god's birth on the Aegean island of Delos, and the second describes the young deity's search for a suitable place to establish his Oracle, an earthly abode where he can communicate Zeus's will to humanity. The first part (not included here) tells of Hera's jealous attempt to prevent Leto from giving birth to the divine twins, Apollo and Artemis, and of Leto's agonized wanderings around the eastern Mediterranean in search of asylum. Only tiny Delos, a poor and insignificant island, agrees to provide a birthplace, for which it is rewarded by becoming a major center of Apollo's cult.

Illustrating Apollo's universal worship in the Greek world, which will include sanctuaries on both Delos and the mainland, the poet then recounts the god's establishment of his oracular shrine at Delphi, then called Pytho after Python, the monstrous serpent that the god slays there. After ridding his sacred place of its predatory guardian, Apollo recruits a ship's crew of Cretan sailors to found his priesthood. The fact that a group from a distant location are selected as priests emphasizes the panhellenic nature of Apollo's prophetic institution, in effect removing it from the exclusive control of local peoples.

The hymn also contains two significant variations on generally accepted myths. In this poem, it is Hera (not Gaea, as in Hesiod) who, through the chthonic power of parthenogenesis, bears the chaotic dragon Typhon (Typhoeus), whom she gives to the equally repellant Python to raise. In addition, the poet does not mention the Pythia, Apollo's female prophet. Nor does he include the tradition that a series of female deities, such as Gaea or Themis, maintained a prophetic office at Delphi (Pytho) before Apollo's arrival. For the hymn's author, Apollo establishes a completely masculine (Olympian) institution on an empty site, previously uninhabited and free of goddess cults. The only previous female occupant is a monster whose death and putrefaction gave the place its ancient name.]—*Pytho* is a Greek verb meaning "I rot."

The glorious son of Leto   1
goes to steep Pytho,
playing his hollow lyre,
wearing divine and perfumed clothes.
And his lyre makes a lovely sound
with its gold pick.
And then, like a thought,
he goes to Olympos
from earth, to the house of Zeus

---

*Translation by Charles Boer.

253

where the other gods   10
are gathered.
And suddenly the gods
are only concerned with
the lyre and song,
and all together the Muses sing
the divine gifts of the gods,
each one answering the other
with a beautiful voice,
and the suffering of men,
what they have   20
from the immortal gods,
how they live,
mindless, helpless,
how they can't find
a cure for death
or a defense against age.

[While roaming Greece looking for a sacred place to locate his sanctuary, the young
Apollo first wishes to set up his shrine at an enchantingly cool spring that belonged
to Telphusa, its guardian nymph. Not wanting a powerful god at her favorite place,
Telphusa persuades Apollo to settle elsewhere. After arriving at Delphi, called Pytho
in this tradition, Apollo slays its guardian serpent, the "she-dragon" Python. He then
lays the foundations of his temple and recruits a band of sailors from Minoan Crete to
serve as his first Delphic priests.]

There lord Phoebus Apollo
decided to make his lovely temple,
and he said this:
"It's here that I'm inclined   30
to build a very beautiful temple,
an oracle for mankind,
where everybody will always bring
perfect sacrifices, whether they live
in the rich Peloponnesus
or in Europe, or in the islands
that are surrounded by waves,
because they will be looking for oracles.
And I will give out oracles
to all of them, accurate advice, too,   40
I'll give it to them
in my rich temple."

And when he had said this,
he started laying out the foundations,
which were wide and very long throughout.
And over these
the sons of Erginus, Trophonius

and Agamedes, who were loved
by the immortal gods,
laid out a stone base.   50
And the innumerable tribes of men
built the temple out of smooth stone,
to be the subject of song
for all time.
But near this place there was a spring
that was flowing beautifully,
and there the lord, the son of Zeus,
killed the big fat she-dragon,
with his mighty bow.
She was a wild monster   60
that worked plenty of evil
on the men of earth,
sometimes on the men themselves,
often on their sheep with their thin feet.
She meant bloody misery.
She once received from Hera,
who sits on a golden throne,
the dreaded, cruel Typhaon,
and raised him, a sorrow for mankind.
Hera had given him birth once   70
when she was mad at father Zeus,
when the son of Cronos himself
was giving birth to glorious Athena
in his head. The lady Hera
got angry then, and said this
to the gods who were assembled:
"Listen to me,
all you gods and goddesses,
how Zeus who gathers the clouds
has begun to dishonor me,   80
after he has made me
his dearly beloved wife.
Without me, he has given birth
to bright-eyed Athena,
who stands out from all the blessed gods.
But my own boy, Hephaestus,
the one I myself gave birth to,
was weak among all the gods,
and his foot was shrivelled,
why it was a disgrace to me,   90
a shame in heaven,
so I took him in my hands
and threw him out and he fell
into the deep sea.

The daughter of Nereus, Thetis,
with her silver feet,
took him and brought him up
with her sisters.
I wish she would have done us blessed gods
some other favor!   100
Well, you crafty devil,
what do you plan to do now?
How did you dare give birth,
alone, to bright-eyed Athena?
Wouldn't I have given birth for you?
At least I was called your wife
among the gods
who live in this big heaven.
Watch out now that I don't plan
some trouble for you later on: 110
yes in fact I will plan something,
that a son will be born to me
who will stand out among the immortal gods,
and it won't shame your sacred marriage
or mine. But I won't come to your bed,
I'll go far away from you
and stay with the immortal gods,"
She said all this
and went away from the gods,
her heart very angry. The lady Hera,   120
with her cow-eyes, then prayed,
and struck the ground
with the flat of her hand, and said:
"Listen to me now,
Earth and wide Heaven overhead,
and you Titan gods
who live under the earth
around big Tartarus,
from whom we get both men and gods.
Listen to me now,   130
all of you, and give me a child
separate from Zeus, and yet one
who isn't any weaker than him
in strength. In fact,
make him stronger than Zeus,
just as Zeus who sees so far
is stronger than Cronos."
She cried this out
and beat the ground
with her thick hand.   140
And then Earth,

who brings us life;
was moved. And when she saw it,
she was very happy.
And she expected a fulfillment.
From that point on,
for a full year,
she didn't go once
to the bed of wise Zeus.
She didn't even sit   150
in her elaborate chair,
as she used to do,
giving him good advice.
No, she stayed in her temples,
the lady Hera, with her cow-eyes,
where many people prayed,
and she enjoyed their sacrifices.
But when the months and days
were finished, and the seasons
came and went with the turning year,   160
she bore something
that didn't resemble the gods,
or humans, at all: she bore
the dreaded, the cruel, Typhaon,
a sorrow for mankind.
Immediately the lady Hera,
with her cow-eyes, took it
and gave it to her (the she-dragon),
bringing one wicked thing to another.
And she received it.   170
And it used to do
plenty of terrible things
to the famous tribes of mankind.

Whoever encountered the she-dragon,
it was doomsday for him,
until the lord Apollo,
who works from a distance,
shot a strong arrow at her.
And she lay there,
torn with terrible pain,   180
gasping deeply, and rolling around
on the ground.
She made an incredible, wonderful noise.
She turned over again and again,
constantly, in the wood.
And then life left her,
breathing up blood.

And Phoebus Apollo boasted:
"Rot right there now,
on the ground that feeds man.   190
You won't live anymore
to be a monstrous evil to humans
who eat the fruit of the earth
that feeds so many, and
who will bring perfect sacrifices here.
Typhoeus won't save you
from hard death,
nor the infamous Chimera,
but right here the black earth
and the bright sun will rot you."   200
Phoebus said this, gloating over her,
and darkness covered her eyes.
And the sacred power of the sun
rotted her out right there,
which is why the place is called Pytho (rot),
and why they give the lord
the name of Pythian, because it was right there
that the power of the piercing sun
rotted the monster out.
And then Phoebus Apollo   210
understood in his mind
how that beautifully flowing stream
had deceived him,
and he went for Telphusa, furious,
and he got there fast.
He stood very close to her
and said this:
"Telphusa, you weren't going to deceive my mind
and keep this lovely place
just for your beautifully flowing waters   220
to go on flowing.
My fame will also come from this place,
and not just yours alone."
Apollo, who works from a distance,
said this, and pushed over a mountain top
along with a rock-slide,
and covered over her streams.
And he made an altar in a shaded grove,
very near the beautifully flowing stream.
And everybody prays to the lord there   230
by calling him Telphusian,
because he disfigured the streams
of sacred Telphusa.
Then Phoebus Apollo thought over

in his heart who the priests should be
that he would bring in
to serve him in rocky Pytho.
And while he was thinking about it,
he spotted a fast ship on the wine-sea,
in which there were many men,   240
and good men, Cretans from Minoan Cnossos,
who make sacrifices to the lord
and announce the laws
of Phoebus Apollo with his gold sword,
whatever he says, answering
from his laurel tree in the valley of Parnassus.
They were sailing
in their black ship, for business
and profit, to sandy Pylos,
to the men of Pylos.   250
But it was Phoebus Apollo
who met them. He jumped into the sea,
like a dolphin, and onto their fast ship,
and he lay there,
a big, frightening monster.
And none of these men thought about it
in their hearts, enough to understand,
and they wanted to throw the dolphin off.
But he kept rocking the black ship
all over, and he rattled the black ship's beams.   260
So they sat back, scared and silent,
in their ship. And they didn't let go
the cables in their hollow black ship,
and they didn't let out the sail
of their dark-prowed ship, but
they kept sailing, as they had before
with the ship fastened with ox-rope.
And a fierce south wind
beat their fast ship from behind.
And first they passed by Malea,   270
and down the Laconian coast
until they came to that city
that is garlanded by the sea,
Taenarum, the land of the Sun,
who makes men happy.
Here the sheep of Lord Sun,
with their thick fleece,
are always eating,
and live in a joyful land.
Here the men wanted to land   280
their ship, and go ashore,

and think over the great wonder
and see with their eyes
if the monster would stay on the deck
of their hollow ship,
or whether it would jump back
into the salt sea that's so full of fish.
But their well-built ship
did not obey the rudders,
it kept on going   290
along the rich coast of Peloponnesus,
and lord Apollo, who works from a distance,
guided it easily with his breath.
It plied its way and came to Arena,
and to lovely Argyphia, and to Thryon,
the ford of the Alpheus, and to Aepy,
well situated, and to sandy Pylos,
to the men of Pylos. But it went on,
past Cruni and Chalcis,
past Dyme and marvellous Elis,   300
where the Epei are in power.
And while it was heading for Pherae,
rejoicing in the breeze of Zeus,
the steep mountain of Ithaca
appeared to them beneath the clouds,
and Dulichium and Same
and the woodland Zacynthus.
But when they had passed
the entire Peloponnesus, towards Crisa,
that enormous gulf appeared to them   310
which closes off the rich Peloponnesus.
A great west wind came up, clear,
by order of Zeus, blowing furiously
out of the sky, so that the ship
would cease, as soon as possible,
its journey over the salt sea.
And that's when they started sailing back
towards dawn and the sun.
The lord Apollo, son of Zeus,
led them. They reached Crisa,   320
which you see from a distance,
vine country, and harbor.
Their sea-going ship went aground here
on the sands.

Then the lord Apollo,
who works from a distance,
jumped from the ship,

like a star at mid-day.
Sparks flew off him all over,
and their light reached the sky.   330
He entered his shrine,
past the tripods,
which were very valuable,
and he made a fire,
revealing his arrows,
and the brightness filled all of Crisa.
And the wives and daughters
of the Crisans, beautifully dressed,
howled at this blast of Phoebus,
for he put great fear in each of them.   340
And then he leaped out,
like a thought, to speed to the ship again,
in the shape of a man
who is quick and strong,
an adolescent, his wide shoulders
covered with his hair.
He spoke to the men
and said winged words:
"Strangers, who are you?
Where do you come from,   350
sailing the waterways?
Was it for business
or do you wander recklessly
over the sea, like pirates
who roam around
risking their lives
as they do evil to strangers?
Why do you stand around like this,
grieving, why don't you go ashore,
why don't you put away the gear   360
of your black ship—which is the custom
among men who eat bread,
whenever they come from the sea
to land, in their black ships,
weary with work.
A desire for sweet food
usually seizes their minds right away."
He said this
and put courage in their breasts,
and the leader of the Cretans   370
answered him back and said:
"Stranger, even though you are not like
ordinary men, neither in your size or shape,
but like the immortal gods,

good health to you and hello,
and may the gods give you
good fortune.
Tell me honestly,
so that I may be sure,
what country is this?   380
what land? what people live here?
We were thinking of somewhere else
when we went sailing
over the great deep sea
to Pylos, from Crete,
which is where we boast our origin.
And now we've come on our ship here,
not at all willingly,
and we want to return,
we want another route, other paths.   390
One of the immortal gods
brought us here against our will."
Then Apollo, who works from a distance,
answered them:
"Strangers, you who once lived before this
around the very wooded Cnossos,
you will not be going back again
to the city you love,
or to your beautiful houses,
or to your dear wives. Instead,   400
you will take care of my rich temple
that is honored by many men.
I am the son of Zeus. I am Apollo.
I brought you here
over the great deep sea.
I intended no evil for you.
Instead, you will take care of my rich temple
that is so honored by all men.
You will get to know
the plans of the gods,   410
and by their will
you will forever be honored,
on and on through every single day.
But come on, do what I say right now.
First, lower the sails
and set the cables free,
and then pull the fast ship
up on land. Take out your stuff,
and everything in the balanced ship,
and make an altar on the beach of the sea.   420
Light a fire on it

and offer up white barley
and then stand around the altar
and pray. And since it was as a dolphin
that I first jumped on to your fast ship
in the misty sea, pray to me
as Delphinus. And the altar itself
will be called Delphinus,
as well as All-seeing, forever.
And then eat dinner   430
by your fast black ship
and pour an offering to the blessed gods
who live on Olympos.
And after you've satisfied your desire
for delicious food, come with me
and sing 'Io Paean,' 'Hail Healer,'
until you get to the place
where you will take care of my rich temple."

Apollo said this.
And the men heard him very well,   440
and they obeyed him.
First the men lowered the sail,
and set free the cables,
and lowered the mast with the forestays
on the mast-hold. And then the men
went up on the beach of the sea.
They dragged the fast ship
onto land out of the sea, up on the sand,
and they put big props under it.
And they made an altar   450
on the beach of the sea,
and lit a fire, and made an offering
of white barley, and they prayed,
standing around the altar,
as he told them to.
And then they had dinner
next to their fast black ship
and poured an offering to the blessed gods
who live on Olympos.
And when they had satisfied their desire   460
for food and drink, they started to go.
The lord Apollo, the son of Zeus,
led them, holding a lyre in his hands,
playing it beautifully,
walking high and nicely.
And the Cretans followed him, dancing,
to Pytho, and they sang "Io Paean"

just like the paean-singers of Crete,
and like those men in whose breasts
the divine Muse has put   470
beautifully sounding song.
Not tired at all in their feet,
they approached the ridge, and then,
right away, they reached Parnassus
and that lovely place where they were to live
honored by many men.
He led them, and showed them
his sacred shrine and his rich temple.
But their spirit was moved
in their dear breasts,   480
and the leader of the Cretans asked him:
"O lord, you brought us here
far from our loved ones
and our fatherland, because
it seemed good in your heart,
how are we to live now?
We have to ask you that.
This place isn't any good for vineyards
and it isn't very desirable for pasture,
to live here very well,   490
and to serve mankind."

And then Apollo, the son of Zeus,
smiled on them, and said:
"What foolish people you are,
what wretches, that in your hearts
you want trouble, and painful work,
and distress. Now I'm going to tell you something,
something pleasing, and put it in your heads:
Even if each one of you,
with a knife in your hand,   500
were to kill sheep constantly,
there would still remain
an endless supply, all in fact
that the famous tribes of mankind
bring here for me.
So guard my temple,
and welcome the tribes of mankind
who gather here, and tell them
most important of all,
what my will is.   510
And maintain justice in your hearts.
But if any of you is disobedient,
or careless, or contemptuous,

or if there are any idle words
or incidents or arrogance,
which is, after all, the custom
among human beings, then other men
will become your masters,
and they will subdue you with force
forever. Now everything has been said.   520
Guard it in your hearts."
And so, farewell,
son of Zeus and Leto.
But I will remember you
in other hymns.

. . . .

Questions for Discussion and Review

1. Apollo is commonly described as the quintessential Greek deity. What characteristics distinguish him from other Olympians?

2. Describe the prophetic institution at Delphi: its physical setting, mythic traditions (including the story of Apollo's unusual birth and Hera's wrath), and religious function in classical Greek society. Why is the Pythia always a woman? How is her prophetic office connected with female deities who reigned at Delphi before Apollo's arrival?

3. How are the themes of guilt and purification involved in Apollo's myth, as well as in later human rituals at Delphi?

4. Discuss Apollo's generally unsatisfying love affairs. Why does myth present the most physically and intellectually gifted young male Olympian as almost invariably suffering erotic rejection or loss? Is it because he is an ephebe, lacking the mature authority that ensures Zeus's success in love? Explain the reasons for your answer.

5. Connect the myth of Asclepius with that of his father.

CHAPTER

8

Dionysus: Rooted in Earth and Ecstasy

KEY TOPICS/THEMES

If Apollo represents the conscious mind subject to rational control, Diony-sus, the "twice-born" son of Zeus and Semele, embodies both the human unconscious and the instinctual life force that animates nature. As god of the vine and bestower of intoxication, he shatters conventional restraints and permits humans to act out extremes of emotion and behavior. Some later Greek poets and mystics linked Dionysus's cult to that of Orpheus, emphasizing the god's connections with the Underworld and spiritual regeneration.

Dionysus and Apollo: Contrasts and Connections

Greek tradition held that each year Apollo left his sanctuary at Delphi to live with the Hyperboreans, a mythical tribe inhabiting the extreme north, an unexpectedly idyllic region ruled by **Boreas** (North Wind). During Apollo's seasonal absence, **Dionysus** reigned in Delphi for the three winter months. A more radical change in divine patronage is difficult to imagine: Apollo, symbol of moderation and mental balance, is replaced by a nonrational power that liberates humans to explore emotional and behavioral extremes (Figure 8-1). In the absence of rational control, the unconscious, with all its amoral energy, can flourish.

Despite their fundamental differences, however, Apollo and Dionysus share some important qualities. As sons of Zeus by different mothers, the two half-broth-ers manifest their father's indomitable will to power, as well as his creative drive. Born under difficult, and even bizarre, circumstances, both gods spend their early youth recruiting new worshipers, establishing their respective cults, and winning general recognition of their divinity. Although Apollo is identified with disciplined

266

FIGURE 8-1 Dionysus Pictured as an Ephebe. The multiple, even paradoxical qualities
of Dionysus are clearly rendered in this bas-relief from Herculaneum, a Greco-Roman
city buried by an eruption of Mount Vesuvius in A.D. 79. Shown as a youthful athlete in
a moment of relaxation, the god extends his right hand to refill a firmly gripped wine cup
while he loosely holds the phallic thyrsus (a pinecone-tipped shaft) in his left hand. The
apparent serenity of the scene is undercut by the presence of a panther snarling beneath
Dionysus's chair. An unpredictable compendium of sensuous pleasure and latent savagery,
the god encompasses the opposing forces of beneficence and violence characteristic of both
human nature and the natural cycle of life and death. *(National Museum, Naples)*

intellect and Dionysus with spontaneous emotion, both are associated with the phenomenon of ecstasy (Greek, *ecstasis*), a term meaning "to stand outside oneself," to abandon rational control and surrender oneself to an overwhelming emotion. Overcome by his spirit, Apollo's priestess, the Pythia, falls into a trance and speaks in tongues, a religious behavior known as glossolalia. When possessed by Dionysus, his followers similarly change their normal conduct, breaking into wild dances and experiencing a rapturous sense of union with their god. Both gods represent the principle of *enthousiasmos,* a state of being inspired, filled with a divine presence that kindles fervor and zeal in the human soul.

This affinity between seeming opposites suggests an underlying unity between these two sons of Zeus. Apollo and Dionysus are, in fact, two equally important aspects of the human psyche, which, like the Delphic administration, alternates between conscious self-discipline and emotional self-abandonment. In strikingly different ways, both gods transcend the limits of the flesh to link humanity with divinity.

The two Greek gods most closely identified with artistic creativity, Apollo and Dionysus both inspire poetry, song, and dance. Their musical styles, however, are strongly opposed: Apollo's golden lyre, with its limpid melodies, evokes feelings of harmony and serenity. The timbrel (a small hand drum resembling a modern tambourine), which Dionysus invents, is beaten to furious, erratic rhythms that express the wine god's passionate, impulsive nature (Figure 8-2). While Apollo's worshipers sing the **paean,** an elegantly lyrical hymn of praise, Dionysus's followers perform the **dithyramb** [DITH-i-ram], an impassioned choral dance from which, according to Aristotle, the tragic drama evolved.

The Dionysian Myth

Historical Origins

Although some myths present Dionysus as a god foreign to Greek culture, his name appears in ancient Mycenaean inscriptions composed about 1250 B.C., indicating that his cult was indigenous to Greece. The persistent tradition that this wildly nonconforming deity was really a foreign import may represent many Greeks' collective denial that his socially disruptive qualities were really Greek. Dionysian antics seemed to violate cherished Greek ideals of reason and order. The god's name seems to include "Zeus" as its first element, but scholarly attempts to interpret Dionysus as meaning "son of Zeus" have not been widely accepted. Because the infant Dionysus was, for a time, raised by nymphs living on Mount Nysa (location unknown), some historians suggest that the name may mean "Zeus of Nysa."

Dionysus is commonly identified with other male fertility gods of the ancient Near East, including the Mesopotamian and Syrian Tammuz (Dumuzi), whose name means "proper son," the true offspring of divinity; the Near Eastern Adonis (a Semitic term meaning "lord," or "master"); and the Egyptian **Osiris,** who is dismembered by his jealous brother Set, reassembled by his devoted sister-wife Isis, and subsequently reborn as ruler of the Land of the Dead. All of these youthful figures have similar stories: they undergo a violent death—typically by being torn

FIGURE 8-2   Dionysus Riding on a Panther. In this mosaic from Delos, birthplace of
Apollo and Artemis, a sullen and heavy-eyed Dionysus carries a thyrsus and a timbrel
(a small, drumlike instrument beaten to hypnotic rhythms). Music, song, and dance were
important in the cults of both Apollo and Dionysus, but the wine god's followers typically
gave impassioned performances of a wild, ecstatic nature—a stark contrast to the limpid
melodies of Apollo's lyre. In this rendition, the panther is even larger than the god, an indi-
cation of the untamed and dangerous animal power inherent in Dionysian impulses. *(Ecole
Française d'Archéologie, Athens)*

asunder—descend into the Underworld, and are ultimately reborn as immortal
beings.

   Myths about Dionysus's entrance into Greece reflect the Greeks' deep ambivalence about this troubling god who provides freedom from everyday reality but
stimulates potentially antisocial conduct as well. The most common tradition presents him as both native born and the proselytizer of a strange foreign cult. In Euripides' play the *Bacchae* (the title refers to female devotees of **Bacchus** [BAH-kuhs],
another name for Dionysus), the god returns to Thebes, site of his initial birth,
from Asia Minor, where he has recruited a throng of enthusiastic female worshipers (Figure 8-3). Suspicious of its "un-Greek" excesses, the Theban king Pentheus
(Dionysus's own cousin) bans the new religion and imprisons the god (disguised as

FIGURE 8-3 Dancing Maenad. This cup painting shows a maenad, a nymph or woman possessed by Dionysus's spirit, carrying a thyrsus and the body of a small panther. Unlike the formal Olympian religion, the cult of Dionysus allowed the expression of extreme emotion. Caught up in the spirit of frenzied music and dance, the worshiper could experience ecstasy, a joyous feeling in which the celebrant temporarily escaped the limitations of the self and experienced a sense of union with the divine.

Confined to narrow roles in most Greek society, women could enjoy an orgiastic liberation at various Dionysian festivals. *(Museum Antiker Kleinkunst, Munich)*

a gentle youth), who then exacts a savage vengeance on the entire city (see Chapter 17, the *Bacchae*).

Dionysus's Double Birth

Just as she tried to prevent Leto from delivering Apollo and Artemis, so Hera does her best to keep Dionysus from being born. Determined to thwart Zeus's efforts to populate Olympus with children who are not her own offspring, Hera disguises herself as a harmless old lady and appears to **Semele** (a daughter of Cadmus, king of Thebes), whom Zeus has seduced. She convinces the naive princess that the mysterious lover who visits her under cover of darkness is actually an ogre. Following Hera's instructions, Semele makes her paramour—Zeus in human form—promise to grant whatever she asks: she then demands that her lover appear as he really is. Despite Zeus's attempts to dissuade her, Semele insists that he keep his vow, compelling Zeus to reveal his essential force, a blaze of lightning that incinerates the young woman. From her flaming corpse, Zeus snatches the embryo of Dionysus, which he places in his thigh until the child is fully formed. After several months, as if to spite Hera again (she never forgives Athene's motherless entrance into the world), from his own body Zeus gives birth to Dionysus, who is thus a god twice-born (Figure 8-4).

Unlike Athene, who springs from Zeus's brain, Dionysus issues from his father's thigh, a male fertility god who represents the life force energizing plants, animals, and humans. In the poet Dylan Thomas's phrase, he is "the force that through the

FIGURE 8-4   The Birth of Dionysus. Surrounded by figures associated with his ecstatic cult, the infant Dionysus emerges from his father's thigh. The second (and last) of Zeus's children to be born from their father's body, Dionysus represents the ever-changing natural world and the instinctual component of the human psyche, a counterbalance to Athene's conscious intellect. As their respective birth myths suggest, Athene and Dionysus demonstrate that reason and nonrationality spring from the same powerful source. *(Museo Archeologico Nazionale, Taranto)*

green fuse drives the flower." Dionysus's nature is varied and complex, but among other things he is god of the vine, a deity representing the growth, death, and rebirth of vegetation. A masculine counterpart of Persephone, whose presence stimulates the earth to produce grain and whose absence brings winter's sterility, Dionysus symbolizes the annual vegetative cycle. His chief gift to humanity is the fruit of the vine—wine that gladdens the hearts of all, from peasant laborers toiling in vineyards to carefree gods feasting on Olympus.

Like the paradoxical god himself, Dionysus's intoxicating gift is double-edged: wine can temporarily ease anxiety and heighten the capacity for pleasure, but its effects can also induce severe mental disorientation, followed by debilitating illness. As one of the world's first mood-altering beverages, wine triggers the rapid changes in personality and behavior that typify Dionysus's protean character (Figure 8-5).

FIGURE 8-5   Dionysus and
His Alter Ego. The only major
Olympian born from the union
of Zeus with a mortal woman,
Dionysus is also the only deity
who undergoes sparagmos (the
physical tearing asunder of a
young male) and rebirth, an
aspect of his myth that links
him with the mysteries of the
natural life cycle. In this vase
painting, a bearded Dionysus, draped in leopard skins,
contemplates the slim figure
of a youth holding the wine
god's identifying emblems: a
wine cup and a grapevine. In
beholding his youthful image,
a renewal of self symbolized
by the flourishing vine, the
mature Dionysus comprehends
both psychological and physical transformation, the strange
process by which nature re-
creates life. In the Orphic religion, Dionysus's descent to and
return from the Underworld
foreshadows the human soul's
quest for immortality. *(Museo
Archeologico Nazionale, Ferrara)*

As a god of fluids—wine, blood, sap, and semen—he undergoes sudden transformations of mood and physical shape, appearing one moment as a seductive adolescent offering a brimming chalice of wine and the next as a savage bull ready to
gore any offender. Greek vase painters, who decorated wine vats, mixing bowls, and
drinking cups with scenes from Dionysian myth, commonly showed the god as a
handsome youth lounging in a chariot bedecked with vine branches and ivy and
drawn by panthers or leopards—feline predators ready to tear flesh at the slightest
provocation.

Dionysus's Youth and Foreign Travels

Myths about Dionysus's early career are many and diverse. Although the following
summary draws on a variety of sources originating at different periods of Greek history, two main themes consistently dominate the disparate narratives: the god rep-

resents strange foreign customs, and he repeatedly confronts opponents hostile to him and his religion. His first enemy is his father's wife. Showing the same malice that motivated her persecution of Leto and Heracles, Hera pursues the infant Dionysus, punishing all who try to help Semele's son. After Hermes takes the child to Semele's sister, **Ino,** who disguises him as a girl, Hera falls on Dionysus's protectors, driving both Ino and her husband, King Athamas, mad (Figure 8-6). This time Zeus transports Dionysus far from Greece, changing his son into a young goat and hiding him on Mount Nysa, where nymphs tenderly care for the child.

Dionysus's discovery of wine, his chief contribution to humanity, also involves his initiation into the mysteries of love and death. The young god's first lover is Ampelus, a youth who is gored to death by an enraged bull. When he discovers Ampelus's bloodied corpse lying in the dust, Dionysus, who has never known sorrow before, weeps unashamedly. Watered by divine tears, Ampelus's body shoots forth a vine that bears ruddy fruit, its color reflecting the boy's rosy complexion. Just as Apollo's grief transformed Hyacinthus into a fragrant symbol of perishable beauty, so Dionysus recreates Ampelus as a plant whose grape clusters, properly fermented, induce in partakers the same intoxicating joy that his first love gave to the wine god. Demeter's bread and Athene's olive were necessary for existence, but Dionysus's beverage surpassed other divine gifts in liberating the human spirit.

The first person to whom Dionysus teaches the art of making wine is Icarius, an old gardener who hospitably receives the god when he appears as a human stranger. Obedient to the god's command, Icarius then travels around the countryside, supplying wine to the thirsty and instructing farmers in viniculture. When some shepherds overindulge and think that they have been poisoned, they murder Icarius, who is dressed in the skin of a goat he had earlier killed for eating his grapevines. According to one tradition, it was then that men first danced around a slain goat, a performance that allegedly developed into the choral "goat song" of tragedy (see Chapter 14).

Observing Dionysus's vulnerability after the death of Ampelus, Hera seizes the opportunity to afflict him with insanity, compelling him to wander crazily through Egypt, Syria, and Asia Minor. (The inexperienced young god's erratic behavior may also have resulted from an overfondness for his own inebriating invention.)

Eventually regaining his sanity, Dionysus continues to roam the earth, acquiring some attributes of foreign deities and punishing those who fail to honor him. When in Phrygia (a region in modern Turkey), Dionysus is initiated into the orgiastic rites of **Cybele** [SIB-e-lee], an eastern fertility goddess whom the Greeks commonly identified with Rhea, mother of the Olympians. Dionysus next travels to Thrace, where King Lycurgus foolishly attempts to imprison him. After afflicting the king with madness and rendering his entire land barren, Dionysus orders Lycurgus tied to four horses, which bolt in four different directions, ripping the king's body apart. According to another version of the story, after Dionysus drives the king to kill his son, Dryas, Lycurgus is eaten alive by wild horses.

In the most famous tale involving the god's rejection by a mortal unable to perceive his divinity, Dionysus, disguised as a vulnerable youth, returns to his native city, Thebes, where young king Pentheus denounces him and his female followers as foreign threats to the social order. After Pentheus imprisons the youth

FIGURE 8-6 Ino and the Infant Dionysus. When Hera attempts to destroy the newly born Dionysus, Zeus places his child in the care of Ino, a sister of Dionysus's mother, Semele. Hera punishes Ino and her husband, Athamas, by driving them mad, causing Ino to throw herself into the sea, where she is transformed into the nymph Leucothea. In this bucolic scene, Ino gives the child a drink from the Horn of Plenty while sheep graze peacefully and a satyr plays the syrinx (a multireed instrument invented by Pan or, in some accounts, by his father, Hermes). Even as a baby, Dionysus's presence causes a huge vine—inhabited by nesting birds, a serpent, and other symbols of the life force—to spring up and shelter him. *(Lateran Museum, Rome)*

FIGURE 8-7   Dionysus Transforming a Ship's Mast into a Vine. In the last myth ascribed
to Dionysus, the god, traveling disguised as a gentle youth, is kidnapped by pirates and
held for ransom. When the sailors fail to recognize his divinity, the god changes them
into dolphins and causes a massive vine, bearing huge clusters of grapes, to grow over
the abductors' ship. Dionysus's divinity is thus revealed in a natural phenomenon—the
vine sprouting miraculously in an unnatural environment. *(Museum Antiker Kleinkunst,
Munich)*

and threatens to kill him, Dionysus exacts a terrible revenge, his spirit possessing
Pentheus's mother, Agave, who, in a frenzy, tears her son to shreds. (For Euripides'
dramatization of the Dionysus–Pentheus conflict, see Chapter 17, the *Bacchae*.)

The *Hymn to Dionysus* relates one of the wine god's final adventures, his kidnapping by Tyrrhenian pirates and the miraculous growth of vines and ivy that
suddenly overwhelms the abductors' ship (Figure 8-7). For their offense, the sailors
are changed into dolphins (which explains why these sea mammals are friendly to
humans). The abrupt transformation of Dionysus from a submissive youth into a
ravening lion is typical of the god's terrifying changeability, a theme that Euripides
emphasizes in the *Bacchae* (see Chapter 17).

The Dionysian Retinue

While invading India, which he subdues partly by magic and partly by armed force, Dionysus attracts a host of rustic demigods to his train. His retinue includes throngs of **satyrs** [SAY-terz] and **silens** [sih-LEENZ], wild creatures combining the features of bearded men with aspects of horses, such as pointed ears and a tail. By the fourth century B.C., artists gave satyrs a more goatlike appearance, apparently modeling them on images of Pan—generally human above the waist but goat-shaped below. The animal most closely associated with Dionysus's revels, the goat is not only the god's preferred sacrificial offering but also the form in which Dionysus customarily appears to his followers.

Called fauns by the Romans, satyrs are famous for their sexual prowess, which artists typically emphasize by depicting them with oversized (and fully erect) penises. Symbols of unrestrained male libido, they are unabashedly lecherous, spending much of their time drinking wine and/or pursuing wood nymphs or other young men (Figures 8-8 and 8-9). Whereas satyrs are generally youthful, the similarly human–animal hybrids known as silens are usually pictured as old men whose bestial appearance and antic behavior belie their inner wisdom. By about the sixth century B.C., writers and artists amalgamated the concepts of satyrs and silens, using the terms interchangeably to denote virtually identical members of Dionysus's sacred band.

Possessed by the god's frenzied spirit, many women also join the retinue: these **bacchants** (also called **bacchae**) reveal their oneness with nature by dressing in tiger or fawn skins and bedecking themselves with vine leaves and ivy (Figure 8-10), **Maenads** [MEE-nadz], literally "mad women," were inspired with Dionysian mania to leave their cities and gather by night in rugged mountains, where, through ritual singing and dancing, they achieved religious ecstasy (Figure 8-11).

Dionysus's Marriage to Ariadne

At the end of the *Theogony*, Hesiod tells us that, in what became a dominant tradition, "gold-haired Dionysus" marries "blond **Ariadne**," daughter of Minos, king of Knossos on Crete, and that Zeus approves the union by making the human bride immortal. According to the standard version of the myth, Theseus, after Ariadne helps him slay the Minotaur, flees with her from Crete but then abandons her on the island of Dia (Naxos), where Dionysus subsequently appears and claims her as his wife. Homer, however, complicates the Dionysus–Ariadne relationship by stating that Artemis kills Ariadne on the island, apparently with the wine god's complicity (*Odyssey*, Book 11). The two stories are difficult to reconcile, for if Dionysus, perhaps jealous of Ariadne's liaison with Theseus (whom Homer implies has not yet slept with her), allows (requests?) Artemis, divine protector of virginity, to punish the young woman for unchastity, the widespread tradition of his eternal marriage to Ariadne seems puzzling. (Some interpreters suggest that Ariadne was already pledged to Dionysus at the time she fled Crete with Theseus, which would explain the god's displeasure.) Another variant states that Athene ordered Theseus to abandon Ariadne because Dionysus had previously claimed her, a version depicted on numerous vase paintings.

(a)

(b)

FIGURE 8-8 A Drunken Satyr.
(a) This marble study (known as the
Barberini Faun) of a reclining satyr
sleeping off his hangover suggests the
combination of sensuality and strength
characteristic of members of Dionysus's
retinue. Although many Greek vase
paintings depict satyrs as having the
form of a goat from the waist down, others show them as largely human except
for their overlarge heads and horse tails.
(b) The satyr's face, with its full lips,
heavy brows, and hornlike locks of hair,
also indicates his bestial traits. These
hybrid creatures, generally indifferent
to everything except the satisfaction of
their appetites, personify the human sex
drive uninhibited by civilized restraints.
(Hirmer Fotoarchiv, Munich)

FIGURE 8-9   Pan Pursuing
a Young Goatherd. In this vase
painting (c. 480 B.C.), a lustful
Pan (depicted with a goat's head,
beard, and horns) chases a young
man. A prominently ithyphallic
statue of Hermes (right) sets the
tone for this erotic scene. *(James
Fund and by special contributions.
Courtesy, Museum of Fine Arts,
Boston)*

FIGURE 8-10   Hephaestus, a Bacchante, and a Satyr. After reconciling with Hera—who
threw him out of heaven—Hephaestus returns to Olympus in a Dionysian procession.
Fortified by Dionysus's gift of intoxication and clutching a beaker of wine, Hephaestus
carefully looks down to avoid a misstep as he follows an ecstatic bacchante and a piping
satyr. *(Louvre, Paris)*

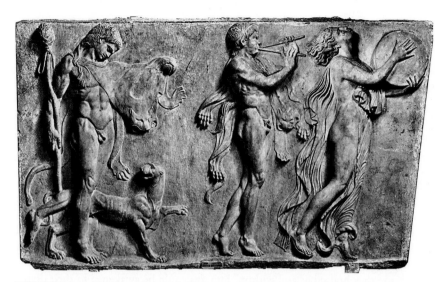

FIGURE 8-11 Dionysus, Pan, and a Maenad. In this bas-relief, a cavorting maenad beating a timbrel leads a musical procession typical of Dionysian celebrations. She is followed by the nature god Pan—wearing a panther skin and playing pipes—and an inebriated Dionysus, who walks carefully, gazing down with fond affinity at his ubiquitous panther. *(National Museum, Naples)*

At an Athenian festival held in February, the Anthesteria, the communal celebration of new wine included a ritual acting out of the sacred marriage (*hieros gamos*) between Dionysus and Ariadne. On the festival's second day, a figure representing the Athenian king (Theseus) surrendered his wife to Dionysus, whose presence was symbolized by a pillar crowned by a mask of the god. In an abrupt reversal of mood, the following day was devoted to sacrificing to the chthonian powers of the Underworld, thus ritually linking the opposing forces of love and death.

Dionysus Zagreus: A Dying and Rising God

Although Dionysus is the embodiment of nature's vital life force, myth also associates him with the mysteries of suffering, death, and rebirth. Because he exemplifies the unending cycle of birth, growth, and decay—the joy and terror that characterize the natural world—mythographers created a wide range of traditions connecting Dionysus with both creation and dissolution, giving his story a dimension that embraces both heaven and the Underworld and portraying him as a mediator of cosmic oppositions.

Beginning in the sixth century B.C., some Greek writers forged an association between the myth of Dionysus and that of Orpheus, the poet who had descended into the Underworld to bring back his deceased wife, Eurydice (see Chapter 9). An esoteric tradition known as **Orphism**, allegedly based on Orpheus's secret teachings, promoted a variation of the Dionysian myth that offered a different version of his double birth and that linked the wine god more closely with the regenerative powers of the Underworld. According to Orphic teaching, Dionysus is originally the son of Zeus and Persephone. Zeus plans to enthrone his divine son, who combines his celestial power with chthonic wisdom, as king of the universe. The ever-jealous Hera, however, induces the Titans to kill Dionysus by tearing him to pieces and devouring him. Acting for her father, Athene manages to save the child's heart, which she gives to Zeus, who swallows it (as he had Metis) and then impregnates Semele. The son of Zeus and Persephone, re-formed in Semele's womb, is reborn as **Dionysus Zagreus** [ZAG-re-uhs].

Zeus punishes the Titans by striking them with lightning, carbonizing the giant cannibals who dared to kill the son of god. Orphic religion taught that the human race sprang from the Titans' ashes, which accounted for humanity's dual nature: human beings were rebels against the gods, but they also contained elements of the divine, the flesh of Zeus's son that the Titans had consumed. Although imbued with evil impulses (the Titan heritage), humanity was also infused with a spark of divinity (Dionysus's body).

Because they housed a "god within," humans could be awakened to their divine potential. Through ritual purification and a communal meal of wine and flesh—Dionysus's symbolic blood and body—initiates could, in the next world, eventually share their god's eternal life. The material body (*sōma*), meanwhile, was simply the soul's prison (*sēma*); death was merely the freeing of the soul to attain its spiritual home, the realm of the gods (see Chapter 9, "The Transmigration of Souls").

Dionysus's Descent into Hades' Kingdom

An earthier account linking Dionysus with the afterlife involves his descent into Hades' realm to find Semele and install her on Mount Olympus. Dionysus, who does not know the way to the Underworld, searches for an entrance near Lake Lerna, a supposedly bottomless body of water. When he asks directions from a young man named Prosymnus (or Polymnus), the youth agrees to reveal the path if Dionysus will have sex with him on his return. After ascending from the nether regions, Dionysus finds that Prosymnus has died during his absence. Resolved to keep his promise, however, Dionysus fashions a stick into an appropriately phallic shape, plants it on Prosymnus's grave, and performs the desired sexual act.

Athens's annual festival honoring the god, the City Dionysia, featured an elaborate procession in which participants carried a statue of Dionysus and replicas of his sacred phallus (symbol of divine virility). The secret rituals through which worshipers were initiated into the Dionysian cult also included a climactic unveiling of an oversized model of the god's penis.

Erotic and fertility motifs in the Dionysian cult persisted well into Roman times. Wall paintings in the famous Villa of the Mysteries near Pompeii (buried by an eruption of Mount Vesuvius in A.D. 79) depict a variety of scenes from the Dionysian initiation ceremonies (Figure 8-12).

Providing a warmer emotional climate than that offered by the distant Olympians, the Dionysian Mysteries were extremely popular throughout Greece and Italy. Although Rome's senate banned the Bacchanalia in 186 B.C., the wine god's rites continued to be observed well into the Christian era.

(a)

(b)

(c)

FIGURE 8-12   Dionysian Initiation Ceremonies. These Roman wall paintings from the Villa of the Mysteries in Pompeii (c. 60–40 B.C.) depict a series of rituals performed during the initiation of candidates into the Dionysian Mysteries. (a) Confined largely to the home, many Greek and Roman women apparently found in Bacchic rites a means of emotional release. (b) A young novice, who has probably just undergone a ritual whipping, lays her head on the lap of an older woman who offers comfort. (c) Figures from the Dionysian retinue, one holding a theatrical mask associated with Bacchus, act out preparatory rituals of initiation into the wine god's cult. (d) A woman is about to uncover the god's sacred genitalia, a climactic element illustrating the mysterious integration of sex, ecstasy, suffering, and spiritual rebirth that Dionysus represents. *(Pompeii, Italy)*

(continued)

(d)

FIGURE 8-12   (*Continued*)

The religion ascribed to Orpheus mediated between the orgiastic passion of Dionysus and the austere control of Apollo, suggesting the essential unity of these ostensibly antithetical deities. Promoting a balance between emotion and intellect, as well as strict personal ethics and thoughtful preparation for the next life, Orphism anticipated many of the doctrines of Christianity. Not surprisingly, early Christian artists commonly used the figure of Orpheus—or even Dionysus—to depict their incarnation of the dying and rising god.

Dionysus of Thebes and Jesus of Nazareth

As many scholars have observed, some myths of Dionysus foreshadow beliefs and ceremonies associated with Jesus of Nazareth, providing a thematic continuity between these disparate figures who, in their deaths and rebirths to immortality, mediate between the divine and human realms. In the *Bacchae,* Euripides' dramatization of the ancient myth of Dionysus's return to Thebes, his birthplace, the wise prophet Tiresias underscores the theological significance of the wine god and his liberating beverage. As he tells Pentheus, the young king of Thebes, two powerful gods, Demeter and Dionysus, have given humanity two indispensable gifts: grain to sustain life and wine to make life bearable. Tiresias urges Pentheus to see the divinity present in these gifts:

> This new God whom you dismiss,
> no words of mine can attain
> the greatness of his coming power in Greece. Young man,
> two are the forces most precious to mankind.
> The first is Demeter, the Goddess.
> She is the Earth—or any name you wish to call her—

and she sustains humanity with solid food.
Next comes the son of the virgin, Dionysus,
bringing the counterpart to bread, wine
and the blessings of life's flowing juices.
His blood, the blood of the grape,
lightens the burden of our mortal misery.
When, after their daily toils, men drink their fill,
sleep comes to them, bringing release from all their troubles.
There is no other cure for sorrow. Though himself a God,
it is his blood we pour out
to offer thanks to the Gods. And through him,
we are blessed.

—EURIPIDES, *Bacchae,* trans. Michael Cacoyannis

Bread and/or wine, tangible emblems of divine care for mortals, played important roles in some Greco-Roman mystery religions, with food and beverage emblematic of earth's fecundity filling sacred dining tables at which initiates communed with their gods. Christian writers frame Jesus' public ministry with feasts involving bread and wine. In John's Gospel, Jesus' first miraculous act is to change water into wine at a Jewish wedding, a "sign" of his divinity that seems to mimic the wine-making magic of some Dionysian priests. In the Gospels of Mark, Matthew, and Luke (but not, strangely, John), Jesus hosts a final Passover dinner with his friends at which he announces that the bread he disburses is his "body" and the wine he passes around his "blood." The next day, Roman soldiers execute him, his wounding and crucifixion a form of sparagmos, the ritual sacrifice of God's beloved son.

The Gospels also state that partway through his career of miraculous healings and exorcisms, when large crowds flocked to him seeking cures for their afflictions, Jesus returned to his hometown of Nazareth—only to have his former neighbors publicly doubt his supernatural abilities and reject his authority. Mark tells the story most baldly:

> Then he [Jesus] left that place, and he comes to his hometown and his disciples follow him. When the sabbath day arrived, he started teaching in the synagogue; and many who heard him were astounded and said so: "Where's he getting this?" and "What's the source of all this wisdom?" and "Who gave him the right to perform such miracles? This is the Carpenter, isn't it? Isn't he Mary's son? And who are his brothers, if not James and Judas and Simon? And who are his sisters, if not our neighbors?" And they were resentful of him.
>
> Jesus used to tell them: "No prophet goes without respect, except on his home turf and among his relatives and at home!"
>
> He was unable to perform a single miracle there, except that he did cure a few by laying hands on them, though he was always shocked at their lack of trust. (Mark 6:1–6, *Scholar's Version*)

In describing the hero's return to the scene of his early life, Mark notes that he is received without "respect" or "trust." No one in Nazareth recognizes that "Mary's son" is a figure of divine origin: the reference to Jesus as his mother's child implies illegitimacy; in Israelite tradition a male is always identified by his father's name.

Scholars of world religion and mythology detect numerous parallels between the stories of heroes and gods from widely different cultures and periods. Tales of mortal heroes who ultimately become gods characterize the ancient traditions of Egypt, Mesopotamia, India, Greece, and Rome, as well as the native cultures of Mesoamerica and North America. In comparing the common elements found in the world's heroic myths, scholars discern a number of repeated motifs that form a distinctive pattern. Although Jesus is a historical figure and Dionysus a mythic being, their received life stories reveal components of an archetypal pattern, including the hero's birth to a divine parent; his narrow escape from attempts to kill him as an infant; his "missing" formative years; his sudden appearance as a young adult manifesting miraculous gifts; his struggle with evil forces; his return to his place of origin, commonly resulting in rejection; his betrayal, suffering, and death; and his elevation to divine status, followed by the establishment of a new cult honoring his name.

DIONYSUS	JESUS
Is son of Zeus, king of the Greek gods	Is Son of God (Mark 15:39)
Is son of Semele, a virgin princess of Thebes	Is son of Mary, a virgin of Nazareth (Luke 2)
Survives an attempt by Hera to kill him as an infant	Survives an attempt by King Herod to kill him as an infant (Matt. 2)
Performs miracles to inspire faith in his divinity	Performs healings and other miracles (Mark 1–2)
Battles supernatural evil in the form of Titans	Resists Satan; exorcizes demons (Mark 1–3; Matt. 4; Luke 4)
Returns to his birthplace, where he is denied and rejected by family and former neighbors	Returns to his hometown, where he is rejected and threatened with death (Mark 6; Luke 4)
Invents wine; promotes his gift to humanity throughout the world	Transforms water into wine (John 2); makes wine the sacred beverage in communion (Mark 14)
Suffers wounding and death at the hands of the Titans	Suffers wounding and crucifixion at the hands of the Romans (Mark 15; John 19)
Descends into the Underworld	Descends into the Underworld (1 Pet. 3:19; 4:6)
Rises to divine immortality, joining his father Zeus on Olympus	Resurrected to glory; reigns in heaven at God's right hand (Phil. 2; Acts 7:55–57)
Evangelizes the world, establishing his universal cult	Directs followers to evangelize the world (Matt. 28:19–20)
Punishes opponents who denied his divinity	Will return to pass judgment on non-believers (Matt. 24–25; Rev. 19–20)

Defining Jesus solely by his blood relationships—mother, brothers, and sisters—the Nazarenes make it impossible for him to demonstrate his divine powers. "Shocked at their lack of trust," the one who routinely works miracles abroad among strangers was "unable to perform a single miracle there." In Luke's version of the episode, the author introduces a telling incident absent in Mark's account: the people of Nazareth not only reject Jesus' claims to supernatural gifts but try to kill him.

> Everyone in the synagogue was filled with rage when they heard [Jesus speak]. They rose up, ran him out of town, and led him to the brow of the hill on which the town was built, intending to hurl him over it. But he slipped away through the throng and went on his way. (Luke 4:28–30, *Scholar's Version*)

Like the citizens of Thebes who refused to believe that the son of Zeus had been born among them and had now unexpectedly returned to offer spiritual liberation, the Nazarenes could not recognize Jesus as the Son of God who had come home to heal them. Unlike Dionysus, however, Jesus does not threaten to avenge his slighted divinity on the rejecting—and insulting—townspeople.

In interpreting the significance of Jesus's life to a Greco-Roman audience, New Testament authors employed numerous parallels to Dionysian myth. Like the son of Zeus and the mortal Semele, Jesus has a divine father and a human mother; as Dionysus is spirited away to hide from Hera's wrath, so the infant Jesus is taken to Egypt to escape King Herod's murderous rage; as Dionysus performs miracles to demonstrate his divine sonship, so does Jesus; as the evil Titans inflict sparagmos on Dionysus, so the benighted Romans crucify Jesus; as Dionysus descends into Hades' realm to rescue his mother, so Jesus descends into Tartarus to preach to "spirits in prison"; as Zeus raises the slain Dionysus to immortal life in heaven, so the biblical God resurrects the glorified Jesus to sit at his right hand.

The Book of Revelation draws another analogy linking Jesus with Dionysus. Whereas Luke's Gospel preserves a tradition in which Jesus consistently showed patience and forgiveness toward people who did not value him, the author of Revelation does not hesitate to transform the historical Jesus into a cosmic being determined to execute merciless judgment on his enemies. In Revelation's visions, the nonviolent prophet from Nazareth is portrayed as a traditionally mythic avenger, a divine warrior-king who returns to earth not as a sacrificial lamb but as a ferocious lion, ready to slaughter the multitudes who do not accept his divinity.

> And now I saw heaven open, and a white horse appear, its rider [Christ] was called Faithful and True; he is a judge with integrity, a warrior for justice. His eyes were flames of fire, and his head was crowned with many coronets; . . . his cloak was soaked in blood. . . . From his mouth there came a sharp sword to strike the pagans with; he is the one who will rule them with an iron scepter, and tread out the wine of Almighty God's fierce anger. . . . (Rev. 19:11–16, *New English Bible*)

The myth of a deity, "despised and rejected of men," who suddenly reappears to punish unbelievers who had failed to acknowledge his supernatural status, pervades global mythology. In tales about Dionysus and in theological speculations about Jesus, the archetypal pattern of the suffering hero, posthumously deified, is clearly manifest. If the *Bacchae*'s author were to visit contemporary Western society, he would probably not be surprised to find that some elements of the Bacchic tradition persist into the twenty-first century. Although significantly modified by Christian theology, in Revelation's mythic picture of Jesus' Second Coming, the story of Dionysus's catastrophic return to Thebes lives on in the Western imagination (see Chapter 17).

HYMN TO DIONYSUS*

Author Unknown

[In this brief hymn extolling Dionysus's ability to work wonders, the poet offers a variation on the god's reputation for severely punishing those who fail to recognize or honor his divinity. Whereas Dionysus decrees horrible and painful deaths for such opponents as Lycurgus and Pentheus (see Chapter 17), he merely deprives the pirates who try to kidnap him of their human form, transforming the men into dolphins (an etiological myth that explains why dolphins are generally well disposed to humans).

The poem vividly illustrates both Dionysus's power over nature and his mutability, his knack for changing shape and for making even a foreign element—the untilled sea—produce the fruit of the vine that normally grows only on land. When forced on board the pirate ship, the god causes a grapevine to spring up miraculously, entwining itself over the ship's masts, while floods of fragrant wine bubble forth from nowhere. Dionysus, who first appears as a vulnerable adolescent with long, dark hair (though the *Theogony* refers to him as "gold-haired"), then metamorphoses into a lion, revealing the fierce and dangerous nature previously hidden by his gentle guise. Only one member of the crew, the helmsman Hecator, is spared the wine god's wrath: he alone had the wit to recognize the presence of a god on board, urging the other sailors to free their mysterious captive and thus avoid the inevitable consequences of insulting a deity. Whereas his obtuse mates are condemned to an animal existence, Hecator not only receives divine favor and earthly riches but also is given a special revelation of Dionysus's identity and unique parentage.]

What I remember now   1
is Dionysus, son of
glorious Semele, how he appeared
by the sand of an empty sea,
how it was far out, on a promontory, how
he was like a young man,
an adolescent.

      His dark hair
was beautiful, it
blew all around him, and   10
over his shoulders, the strong
shoulders, he held a purple cloak.

      Suddenly,
pirates appeared, Tyrrhenians,
they came on the sea wine
sturdily in their ship

---

*Translation by Charles Boer.

and they came fast.
A wicked fate drove them on.

    They saw him,
they nodded to each other,   20
they leaped out
and grabbed him,
they pulled him
into their boat
jumping for joy!

They thought he was
the son of
one of
Zeus's favorite kings:
they wanted to tie him up   30
hard.

    The ropes wouldn't hold.
      Willow ropes,
they fell right off him, off
arms and legs.
    He smiled at them,
motionless,
in his dark eyes.

    The helmsman saw this,
he immediately cried out,   40
he screamed out to his men:
    "You fools!
    What powerful god is this
whom you've seized,
whom you've tied up?
Not even our ship,
sturdy as it is,
not even our ship
can carry him.
Either this is Zeus,   50
or it's Apollo, the silver-bow,
or else it's Poseidon!
He doesn't look like
a human person,
he's like the gods
who live on Olympus.
Come on!
Let's unload him, right now,
let's put him
on the dark land.   60

Don't tie his hands
or he'll be angry, he'll
draw terrible winds to us,
he'll bring us a big storm!"
    That's what he said.

The captain, however,
in a bitter voice,
roared back:
    "You fool,
    look at the wind!   70
    Grab the ropes,
    draw the sail.
    We men
    will take care of him.
        I think
    he'll make it to Egypt,
    or Cyprus,
    or to the Hyperboreans,
    or even further.
    In the end   80
    he'll tell
    who his friends are,
    and his relatives,
    and his possessions.
    A god sent him to us."
        He said this,
then he fixed the mast
and the sail of the ship.
And the wind began to blow
into the sail. And then   90
they stretched the rigging.
    Suddenly,
wonderful things
appeared to them.
        First of all,
wine broke out, babbling,
bubbling over their speedy black ship,
it was sweet, it was fragrant,
its odor was divine.
Every sailor who saw it   100
was terrified.
        Suddenly,
a vine sprang up,
on each side,
to the very top of the sail.
And grapes, all over,

clung to it.
And a dark ivy
coiled the mast,
it blossomed with flowers   110
and yielded
pleasing fruit.
      Suddenly,
all the oar-locks
became garlands.
When they saw this
they cried to the helmsman
then and there
to steer their ship
to land.   120
      But
the god became a lion,
an awful lion
high up on the ship,
and he roared at them
terribly.
      And then,
in their midst,
he put a bear,
a bear with a furry neck,   130
and it made gestures.
It threatened,
and the lion,
on the high deck,
scowled down.
      Everybody
fled to the stern,
they panicked, they ran
to the helmsman, because
the head of the helmsman was cool.   140
      But
the lion, suddenly,
leaped up, it seized
the captain!
They all wanted to escape
such a doom
when they saw it.
They all jumped ship
into the sea, they jumped
into the divine sea.   150
They became dolphins.
      As for the helmsman,
he was saved:

the god pitied him,
he made him very rich,
and told him this:
  "Courage, divine Hecator,
  I like you.
  I am Dionysus
  the ear-splitter.   160
  My mother,
  Cadmaean Semele,
  had me
  when she slept with Zeus."

    Farewell,
  son of Semele,
  who had such a beautiful face.
  Without you,
  the way to compose a sweet song
  is forgotten.   170

. . . .

Questions for Discussion and Review

1. Describe both the similarities and the differences between Apollo and Dionysus. In
   what areas do their attributes overlap? How do both gods inspire states of ecstasy or
   enthusiasm in their followers?

2. Summarize the story of Dionysus's double birth. Why does myth present this particular god as being twice-born, first from Semele's womb and then from the body
   of Zeus? How is this double birth thematically related to the Orphic myth that describes the death and rebirth of Dionysus (as Zagreus)?

3. Why do many myths present this god of wine, intoxication, and sensuality as "un-
   Greek"? Why does myth picture him traveling among foreign nations and afflicted
   with madness? What does his retinue of satyrs, panthers, maenads, and goats imply
   about Dionysus's connection with both nature and human psychology?

4. Specify the Orphic variations in Dionysus's myth. How is his ecstatic cult linked
   to that of Orpheus and Orphism? What do these two figures have in common with
   each other—or with Apollo?

Land of No Return: The Gloomy Kingdom of Hades

KEY TOPICS/THEMES

Hades and Persephone, King and Queen of the Underworld, rule over a gloomy realm inhabited by fearful monsters and shades of the dead. In the Homeric epics, the entrance to Hades' subterranean domain is located far to the north, beyond the River of Ocean that encircles the earth's central landmass. The Odyssey *portrays Hades' kingdom, eternally dark and cheerless, as the permanent prison of almost all dead souls; only a few of Zeus's favorites are sent to the Isles of the Blest (also called Elysium), an earthlike paradise. As Greek concepts of individual responsibility developed over time, however, many poets and philosophers argued that a person's behavior in this life determined one's fate after death. After the sixth century B.C., the old Homeric view of Hades' realm was typically modified to accommodate all righteous souls in Elysium, with the wicked atoning for their crimes in Tartarus. In his speculations about the soul's posthumous fate, Plato (c. 427–347 B.C.) employs Orphic teachings symbolically to create a vision of the afterlife based on ethical justice. Plato's interpretation of myths about the next world forms an indispensable link between the Homeric view of Hades (*Odyssey, Book 11) *and that pictured, seven centuries later, in Virgil's* Aeneid *(Book 6), which incorporates many Platonic ideas and themes.*

The Homeric View of the Afterlife

The Greeks expressed their desire for perpetual youth, beauty, and everlasting life in myths about the gods. By contrast, myths about their heroes revealed a painful awareness of the limits that death imposes on all human striving. The Greek hero's passion to seize every opportunity for fame and individual achievement springs largely from his certainty that every quality he values—strength, good looks, even divine favor—will inevitably be taken from him. The tension between life's unrealized possibilities and the prospect of oblivion in Hades' kingdom casts a chilling shadow across the mythic landscape.

Greek heroes' eagerness to court danger and risk their lives in fighting monsters or winning glory on the battlefield should be read in the light of Greek beliefs about the grim finality of Hades' domain. Although success in accomplishing great deeds could earn them undying fame, experiencing death before they had achieved their goals was to suffer permanent and total loss. As Homer repeatedly emphasizes, the souls of young warriors killed at Troy left this world bitterly lamenting the sacrifice of their youth and manhood. They would find no comfort or compensation in the dark world below.

Although Greek and Roman ideas about the afterlife changed over time, eventually incorporating diverse views of the next world, the Homeric epics provide the earliest—and most influential—vision of Hades' realm. In the *Odyssey*, Homer emphasizes the extreme dread with which his heroes regard the Underworld. When Circe, a wise enchantress, informs Odysseus that he must travel into Hades' realm —in effect, die before his time—the hero feels his heart shatter within him (*Odyssey*, Books 9 and 11). Far from being an escape from earthly woes into a higher realm of light and beauty, death signified only one thing: permanent imprisonment in a dark world utterly devoid of joy, purpose, or hope. In journeying to Hades' realm, Odysseus is forced to confront both the fact of his own mortality and the unspeakable bleakness of the soul's unsatisfying half-life in the netherworld. The ghost of Achilles, once the Greeks' most vital hero, hastens to assure Odysseus that he would rather be a poor man's living slave than king of all the dead.

Writing in the sixth century B.C., the lyric poet Anacreon contemplated his own fear of death with similar pessimism:

> for the lightless chasm of death is dreadful
> and the descent appalling: once cast down into [Hades], there is no return.
>
> —*Greek Lyric Poetry*, trans. Willis Barnstone, p. 127

The Homeric picture of Hades' dominion underscores both the finality of death and the impossibility of any satisfying contact between the living and the dead. Illustrating the unbridgeable gap between the two, Homer describes Odysseus reaching out to embrace the shade (disembodied spirit) of his mother, Anticleia, only to find that he can no more grasp her shadowy form than he can hold a puff of smoke. Death, personified as **Thanatos** [THAN-a-tohs], severs even the closest ties of kinship and affection.

While depriving the soul of substance, death simultaneously impairs memory, reason, and will. The throng of souls gathered near Odysseus are witless, gibbering specters until they are allowed to drink sacrificial blood, which temporarily restores their mental faculties and verbal abilities. Following Circe's instructions, Odysseus performs an elaborate chthonic ritual to summon the dead and briefly establish communication with them. The long trench he digs functions as both a symbolic grave and a boundary separating the realms of life and death, a frontier that neither the living nor the dead may cross. Into the trench Odysseus pours a mixed libation (ceremonial drink offering) representing the earth's bounty, such as honey, grain, and wine, as well as the blood of black rams, animals peculiarly sacred to Hades. The belief that blood is the essence of life was widespread in the ancient world. As the Book of Leviticus declares, "The life of the soul [living creature] is in the blood." Dead souls hunger for it.

The first soul whom Odysseus encounters is that of Elpenor, one of his men who had recently perished after falling off Circe's roof. Elpenor begs Odysseus to give him a proper burial, without which no soul can find peace (see Figure 13-8). So certain was the Greek conviction that funeral ceremonies were indispensable in securing posthumous rest that Oedipus's daughter Antigone risks her life to perform final rites for her brother Polyneices (see Chapter 16). This obligation to the dead also spurs Priam, king of Troy, to brave Achilles' wrath to retrieve the body of his slain son Hector (see Chapter 12).

Survival Through Descendants

Although the Homeric Hades offers a bleak picture of the soul's condition after death, it also includes a slightly more positive element—the belief that one may live on through one's descendants and that their accomplishments may somehow enhance one's own postmortem existence. After informing Odysseus that he would rather be alive as a pauper's slave than the most envied soul in Hades' kingdom, Achilles rejoices in Odysseus's news that Neoptolemus, Achilles' warrior son, has won universal admiration for his courage and skill in battle. Buoyed by this revelation of his progeny's fame, Achilles strides proudly away across the Plain of Asphodel (a dreary region dotted with funereal plants related to the iris family), the only soul in the Homeric netherworld to manifest any degree of joy.

The Location and Geography of Hades' Realm

In Homer's account, Odysseus reaches Hades by sailing northward across the River of Ocean, earth's far boundary where sky's vault touches the ground and the sun sinks into darkness. Odysseus's journey to the land of the dead, across a foggy, desolate waste, roughly parallels that of Gilgamesh to the faraway island retreat of the Sumerian king's immortal ancestor, Utnapishtim. The Homeric concept of the afterlife, in fact, strikingly resembles older Mesopotamian beliefs about the Underworld: the ghost of Enkidu informs his friend Gilgamesh that departed souls mourn forever in a mildew- and worm-infested dungeon.

The Hebrew Bible (Old Testament) paints a similarly grim picture: all the dead, both good and bad, are permanently housed in an underground region called Sheol, a Hebrew counterpart of the Homeric Hades. Reduced to impotent shadows or wraiths (called *repaim*), the dead languish in mindless inactivity. As if paraphrasing Achilles' pessimism, the author of Ecclesiastes argues that it is better to be a "live dog" than a "dead lion," "because in Sheol, for which you are bound, there is neither doing nor thinking, neither understanding nor wisdom" (Eccles. 9:5, 10).

Over the centuries, numerous poets contributed to myths about Hades, providing more details about its topography. Five great subterranean rivers were said to encompass or flow through the Underworld: the **Styx** (Abhorrent) is Hades' principal stream, personified by a river goddess, a daughter of Ocean, who sided with Zeus in his battle with the Titans. As a result, Zeus honored her by decreeing that an oath invoking the Styx was inviolable, even by the gods. The **Acheron** [AK-e-rahn] (Distress), like the Styx, is commonly represented as Hades' official boundary across which all souls pass on the way to their allotted places below.

Cocytus [koh-SYE-tuhs] (Lament), variously defined as a branch of the Acheron or Styx, and **Phlegethon** or Pyriphlegethon (Fire Flaming) are the two other rivers Greek myth placed in Hades. In Plato's "Myth of Er," a mystical vision of the afterlife that concludes his *Republic,* the philosopher adds a "river of unmindfulness" that runs through a plain named Lethe. Roman poets later made **Lethe** [LEE-thee] (Oblivion) the name of Hades' fifth river. Drinking Lethe's waters caused souls about to be reincarnated in new bodies to forget their past lives and sufferings (see Chapter 19, Virgil's *Aeneid*). The Christian poet Dante borrowed the four Greek rivers to intersect his *Inferno* and relocated Lethe atop the Mount of Purgatory so that purified souls could drink its waters to erase all memory of sin before ascending to heaven.

Elysium

In the *Odyssey,* Homer briefly refers to **Elysium** [e-LIZ-ih-uhm], garden islands of earthly delights located far to the west at the extreme edge of the world, an Eden to which Zeus sends a very few of his favorites. Homer cites Menelaus as one of the isles' future inhabitants, not because Agamemnon's brother is virtuous, but because he is married to Helen, the beautiful daughter whom Zeus, in the shape of a swan, had sired by Leda. This mythic paradise, which was later also known as the **Elysian Fields,** echoes the Mesopotamian myth of Dilmun, an Edenic island where some heroic souls could posthumously continue to enjoy life's sensual pleasures.

Residents of Hades' Domain

Hades, also called *Aidoneus,* the "invisible" or "unseen one," represents the universality of death's hold on humanity. His queen, Persephone, whom the *Homeric Hymn to Demeter* originally associates with flowers and other emblems of youthful beauty (see Chapter 5), comes to share her husband's pitilessness (Figure 9-1). Emphasizing death's utter finality, the couple permits no one (except a few heroes) to escape Hades' confines. The rare myths in which the two rulers allow a shade to return to earth, as when the poet Orpheus persuades them to release his beloved wife, Eurydice, only serve to highlight the bitter inevitability of loss (see Ovid's "Orpheus and Eurydice" in Chapter 20).

Besides reflecting the natural law condemning all that lives to perish, the Kingdom of Hades also encompasses childlike fears of monsters and other bogeymen that lurk in the dark. **Cerberus** [SER-ber-uhs], the hound of hell, is a three-headed (or fifty-headed) dog with a mane (or tail) of snakes who guards the Underworld's entrance. The **Furies** (Erinyes), generated from the blood of Uranus's castration, have their home here, as does, in later myth, **Eurynomos** [oo-RIH-noh-mohs], a demonic figure associated with death and decay. Even more images of

FIGURE 9-1   Hades and Persephone. This vase painting shows Hades and Persephone, King and Queen of the Underworld, in a pose typical of Greek domestic life, as if they were an ordinary couple. The implications of Hades extending a bowl toward his wife, in effect inviting her to partake, are paradoxical. Because Demeter's inexperienced daughter accepted hospitality—in the form of pomegranate seeds (the symbol of marriage)—from Hades, she was forced to remain in his gloomy kingdom for part of each year (see Chapter 5). Hades' bowl, however, is also a cornucopia (or Horn of Plenty), a symbol of riches—gold and gems—excavated from his subterranean realm. Although dreaded as lord of the dead, Hades was also honored as Pluto, god of wealth. *(British Museum, London)*

pain and terror appear in the nightmare abyss of Tartarus (discussed in the next section).

In contrast to Homer, who represented the dead as being admitted directly to the Plain of Asphodel, later mythographers emphasized the soul's symbolic crossing of Hades' watery frontier. **Charon** [KA-rohn], a hideous creature whose job is to ferry souls across the Styx or Acheron, demands a monetary fee for his services (Figure 9-2). (Because souls unable to pay were not allowed to cross over, the Greeks had a custom of burying the dead with coins in their hands or mouths.)

Less frightening in appearance, but equally intimidating to the newly dead, are the figures of **Minos**, a legendary ruler of Minoan Crete, and his brother **Rhadamanthus.** Renowned for their justice, after their deaths they are appointed judges in the netherworld. Plato adds a third judge, Aeacus, a son of Zeus famous for his piety. As originally conceived, these magistrates function primarily to assign souls their respective positions in Hades' domain or to arbitrate their futile quarrels. In later times, when writers began to distinguish between the respective fates of good and of evil persons, Minos and Rhadamanthus determined whether each soul would enjoy the bliss of Elysium or the agony of Tartarus.

Persephone: Queen of the Underworld

Whereas myth utilizes two male deities—Zeus and Hades—to symbolize the polar opposites of celestial light and netherworld darkness, in Persephone, Queen of the Underworld, myth combines in a single female figure the contrarieties of life and death, beauty and terror. In her annual cycle of birth, death, and rebirth, she illustrates the extreme contrasts of existence that perplexed the Greek imagination. When released from her husband's subterranean kingdom to return to earth's surface each spring, she brings a renewal of life, causing nature to emerge from winter's deathlike trance and explode in green leaf and varicolored blossom. Spring's flowers, in fact, were an integral element in Persephone's myth before Hades' chariot transported her from sunlit fields to realms of perpetual darkness (see Chapter 5). In tension with her positive image as the seasonal catalyst of earth's fertility and the burgeoning joy of her mother, Demeter, however, is Persephone's ongoing role as Hades' wife and co-regent, in which she assumes the sinister aspects of her dark and sterile environment. She becomes, in fact, a Greek amalgamation of two Near Eastern goddesses—Ishtar, divine patron of love, war, and fertility, and her sister Ereshkigal, goddess of the Sumero-Babylonian Underworld. Ereshkigal, guardian of all the dead, is the chthonic mirror image of her heavenly sister, who, paradoxically, inspires both sexual reproduction and martial slaughter. In attributing several of these disparate functions to one goddess, Greek myth insists on Persephone's encompassing of the polar opposites of life and death, affirming the ultimate unity of the life cycle.

In administering death's domain with her husband (by whom, significantly, she has no children), Persephone exercises considerable power, even micromanaging the movements of dead souls. When Odysseus approaches the netherworld's entrance, Persephone herself determines which shades he will be allowed to interview, and in which order (*Odyssey*, Book 11). She personally makes decisions about special concessions sometimes granted to individual souls, as when she permits the blind prophet Tiresias to retain his powers of reason even after death—in contrast to the majority, whom death robs of their wits. To signal the end of Odysseus's encounter with the spirits, Homer invokes Persephone's lethal traits, portraying the hero as terrified lest Hades' queen dispatch her most terrifying weapon, the Gorgon, whose gaze turns men to stone, inflicting the permanent rigidity (rigor mortis) of death.

Thanatos's (Death's) twin brother **Hypnos** (Sleep) also inhabits the Underworld. A fatherless child of Night, he is commonly depicted as a winged youth who pours soporific liquid from a horn or gently touches the weary with a leafy branch. Generally regarded as friendly toward humans, Hypnos appears in Greek funerary art as a kindly figure helping to carry the souls of the recently dead to the next world (Figure 9-3). His son **Morpheus,** the god of dreams, often visits sleepers in human shape, sometimes conveying messages from the dead.

FIGURE 9-2 Charon. As depicted in this vase painting, Charon is the mythical figure symbolizing the soul's transition from life to death. Described as hideous and frightening, he is the sole means of transporting the newly dead across the Styx or Acheron, subterranean rivers marking the boundaries of the Underworld. Reluctantly, he ferries a few bold heroes, such as Heracles and Aeneas, across waters separating the worlds of light and darkness. *(National Museum, Athens)*

Although not a resident of Hades, Hermes is associated with the Underworld because of his role as Psychopompos, the guide of souls to their final abode (Figure 9-4). An embodiment of fluid movement, Hermes easily crosses the boundaries separating the living and the dead. Escorting both newly deceased souls and a few living heroes on their visits to Hades' kingdom, Hermes became known as a repositor of occult secrets, a source of arcane knowledge about the afterlife.

Tartarus

In Hesiod's *Theogony*, **Tartarus** is both an elemental deity by whom Gaea conceives Typhoeus (Typhon) and an amorphous cosmic cellar in which the fallen Titans are chained in oppressive darkness. Described as lying as far beneath Hades as Olym-

FIGURE 9-3   A Warrior's Departing Soul. This vase painting (c. 510 B.C.) shows the three figures traditionally associated with the soul's transference from earthly life to the Underworld. The winged figures Thanatos (Death) and Hypnos (Sleep) carry the body of Sarpedon, a hero of the *Iliad*. Hermes, in his role of Psychopompos (Guide of Souls), appears in the center. *(Metropolitan Museum of Art, New York)*

pus is above the earth, Tartarus is an almost bottomless pit of anguish and despair, a divine torture chamber foreshadowing popular Christian notions of hell.

Notorious Sinners

During his visit to the Underworld, Odysseus witnesses the sufferings inflicted on three archetypal criminals—Tityus, Tantalus, and Sisyphus—all of whom post-Homeric tradition incarcerated in Tartarus. A giant son of Gaea, Tityus attempted to rape Leto, the mother of Apollo and Artemis. For this sacrilege, he is punished by being tied spread-eagled on the ground and having two vultures continually feed on his liver. His punishment, identical to that of Prometheus, is also an emasculation, a stripping of power and virility from one who impiously tried to compete with Zeus.

Odysseus also sees **Tantalus,** a son of Zeus who became king of Lydia, afflicted with intolerable hunger and thirst. Although standing in a pool of water, he is unable to slake his thirst because, every time he lowers his head to drink, the water level

(a)   (b)

FIGURE 9-4   Charon, Hermes, and the Soul of a Woman. In this vase painting, the artist depicts Hermes (Psychopompos), guide of the recently dead, conducting the soul of a
young woman (a) to Charon's boat (b). Because the ancient Greeks believed that Charon
demanded a fee for his services, corpses were commonly buried or cremated with a coin
in their mouths. Shades (disembodied spirits) without the necessary payment—or those
whose bodies had not been properly buried—were denied passage, preventing them from
finding peace in the netherworld. According to one tradition, when Charon refused to
transport someone, the person's ghost was condemned to wander disconsolately for a hundred years before it found rest. *(Staatliche Antikensammlungen, Munich)*

recedes. Similarly, when he reaches toward the fruit growing above his head, the
branches move just beyond his grasp. Experiencing insatiable desire that is eternally
unsatisfied, Tantalus lends his name to the English verb *tantalize* (which means "to
tease or frustrate by appearing to promise something that is never given").

Myth gives several different accounts of Tantalus's crime. In one version, Tantalus, living at the dawn of time, when humans dined with gods, abused Olympian
hospitality by stealing ambrosia and giving it to undeserving mortals. In another
account, Tantalus irresponsibly divulged secrets gleaned from divine table talk. In
the most common variant, Tantalus is said to have tested divine omniscience by
serving the gods the flesh of his son **Pelops** [PEE-lahps]. Only Demeter, distracted
by her grief for Persephone, ate part of Pelops's body (his shoulder), which Zeus
replaced with gleaming ivory when he restored the boy to life. In this version of the

FIGURE 9-5   Sisyphus in Tartarus. In Book 11 of the *Odyssey,* Homer describes the post-mortem torments of a few souls who have directly offended the gods. The reputed founder of Corinth, Sisyphus was notorious for his cunning, which included successfully plotting to outwit Death and live to a ripe old age. When he finally dies, however, the gods condemn him to push a huge boulder uphill, only to have it roll down again just before he reaches the summit. This exercise in obsessive futility illustrates the gods' harsh treatment of those who attempt to thwart natural law: human ingenuity can no more forestall death than a falling boulder can escape the force of gravity. *(Vatican Museums, Rome)*

myth, Tantalus, for his sin of cannibalism, must suffer from a ravenous appetite that is never satisfied, making him a prime example of the gods' retributive justice.

Odysseus also sees **Sisyphus** [SIS-ih-fuhs] (reputed founder of the city of Corinth), who is forced to roll a huge stone uphill, only to have it roll back down, so that he must endlessly repeat a painfully strenuous but meaningless act (Figure 9-5). Like Tityus and Tantalus, Sisyphus was a trickster who tried to dupe or outwit the gods. When Sisyphus was alive, he betrayed Zeus by revealing one of his seductions, provoking the Olympian to send Thanatos (Death) to haul him off to Hades. Sisyphus, however, succeeded in overpowering Thanatos, chaining him so that mortals ceased to die. After Ares released Thanatos, Sisyphus was dragged into the Underworld, but not before he instructed his wife not to bury his body but to leave it in the street. His powers of deception undiminished, Sisyphus next persuaded Hades and Persephone to permit him to return to earth to punish his negligent wife. As soon as he arrived above ground, Sisyphus refused to return, frustrating death by living to a ripe old age. The gods, of course, have the last laugh, ingeniously devising a torment that keeps him too busy to devise any further tricks.

A fourth notorious sinner, **Ixion,** dared to assault Hera, as if to take Zeus's place in heaven. For his arrogance, Ixion is bound to a fiery wheel, which rolls perpetually

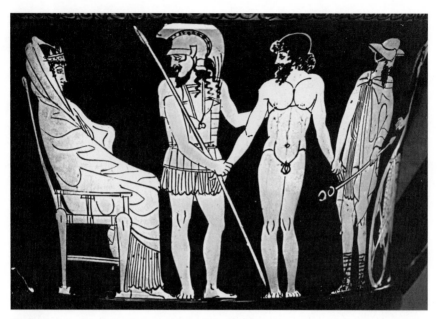

FIGURE 9-6   Hera Condemning Ixion. Like Sisyphus, Ixion was a trickster who presumed to acquire prerogatives reserved only for the gods. After Ixion tried to rape Hera —thereby taking Zeus's place—he was affixed to an iron wheel that whirled aimlessly through the dark abyss, an image of human impotence when pitted against divine power. *(British Museum, London)*

through the air (Figure 9-6). Whereas these four are prototypes of human error, in later myth, the ordinary inhabitant of Tartarus is a human soul, sent there to be purged of the qualities that spawned evil deeds or, in some extreme cases, to endure eternal punishment.

Descents into the Underworld

In Greco-Roman myth, only a tiny handful of the most esteemed heroes succeed in reaching—and returning alive from—the House of Hades. In virtually every case, tales of a descent into the netherworld (*katabasis*) form one episode in a chain of events involving the hero's learning to overcome fear and endure pain. Odysseus and Heracles are both famous for undergoing trials that severely test their courage and resourcefulness. Confronting the ultimate challenge—death's negation of all human achievement—not only places the hero's life in perspective but also enables him to experience symbolic annihilation and rebirth. Odysseus and Aeneas (a Trojan prince), in particular, emerge from Hades' realm with a renewed sense of purpose that allows them either to reclaim a patrimony (Odysseus) or to found a new homeland (Aeneas), thus successfully completing their predestined lifework.

A hero's worthiness to face death without being destroyed is typically linked to the presence of an Olympian protector: Athene supports Heracles and Odysseus, while Aphrodite (Venus) inspires her son Aeneas to negotiate the chthonic perils of Hades. Similarly, Love (Eros) is the force that motivates Orpheus, the first musician and poet, to rescue his dead wife, Eurydice, from Hades' prison. It is also a form of love that drives Dionysus, then still mortal, to retrieve his mother, Semele, from Hades (see Chapter 8).

The Descent of Heracles

Odysseus's last conversation in the Underworld is with Heracles, the strongest, bravest, and longest-suffering of all Greek heroes. Although hailing Odysseus as a fellow hero, Heracles pointedly reminds him that in life he (Heracles) had already accomplished a much more difficult descent. The last of Heracles' Twelve Labors requires him to kidnap Cerberus (Figure 9-7) and exhibit the hellhound to his cow-

FIGURE 9-7   Heracles Capturing Cerberus. As his final and most challenging labor, Heracles descends into the Underworld to subdue Cerberus, the savage three-headed hound that guards the entrance to Hades. By bringing Cerberus into the upper world, Heracles attains the extreme limits of heroism, braving the terrors of death and demonstrating that human courage and intelligence—when supported by the gods (Athene and Hermes act as his guides)—may accomplish the impossible. Heracles' successful quest, carried out with divine aid and approval, contrasts strongly with the prideful ambitions of Sisyphus, Ixion, and Tantalus. *(Louvre, Paris)*

ardly master, Eurystheus. Like Odysseus, before his journey Heracles sought the guidance of an earth-goddess figure and was initiated into the Mysteries of Demeter at Eleusis, where he was taught the means of safely traversing Death's kingdom (see Chapter 10).

Although most traditions state categorically that no Olympian ever sets foot in Hades, in the Heracles myth both Athene (Victorious Wisdom) and Hermes (Safe Travel) act as his guides. As Psychopompos (Guide of Souls), Hermes normally withdraws to Olympus immediately after depositing souls at Hades' portals. According to Apollodorus, however, on this occasion he remains at Heracles' side, reminding him that the monsters he encounters, such as the Gorgon Medusa, are shadows cast by his own fears. With divinely inspired courage, Heracles dares to face Hades himself, winning the implacable god's permission to take Cerberus—on the condition that he use none of his usual weapons.

Heracles not only performs unprecedented feats of strength, such as capturing Cerberus with his bare hands, but also exercises his equally notable sense of compassion in freeing several heroes from Hades' prison. Besides rescuing Theseus (see the next section), he releases Apollo's son, Asclepius, allowing the master physician's healing influence again to benefit humanity at such shrines as Epidaurus.

Although he escapes Hades with Cerberus in tow, Heracles must obey universal law in returning there after his death. As Homer observes, however, Heracles differs from all other Underworld inhabitants: his image remains below, but his real self, or soul, ascends to join his father and other gods on Mount Olympus. Homer does not pursue the implications of Heracles' dual nature, his paradoxical sharing of both human death and Olympian immortality. By placing Heracles' appearance last in Odysseus's Underworld experience, however, Homer indirectly anticipates subsequent philosophic speculations about humanity's duality—its division into perishable body and deathless spirit—views that shape Orphic and Platonic concepts of the virtuous soul's posthumous reward in Elysium.

The Descent of Theseus

Theseus, a legendary king of Athens who supposedly lived in Minoan times, is the rare example of a hero who dared to enter Hades' kingdom with unworthy motives—and with disastrous consequences. The Athenian hero, whose father was Poseidon, was the devoted friend of **Pirithous** [pye-RITH-oh-uhs], a mortal son of Zeus. Because they were both the offspring of gods, they decided that only daughters of Zeus would make acceptable wives. After abducting Helen from Sparta and finding that she was too young to marry, Theseus and Pirithous descended into Hades' realm for the purpose of kidnaping Persephone. While in the Underworld searching for its queen, the heroes accepted an invitation to dine with Hades, who lived up to his reputation as a host who makes all visitors permanently welcome. Seated at the banquet, they found that they were immobilized in their chairs, unable to rise. Not until Heracles arrived in the netherworld was Theseus released, and then he lost part of his buttocks when Heracles literally tore him from his seat, a crude surgery that reputedly accounted for the subsequent prevalence of slim hips among Athenian youths. Theseus's tragedy is that he returned to life without the person he loved best: the gods denied Pirithous permission to leave, imprisoning him forever in the chair of oblivion. Like Gilgamesh and Achilles, Theseus was deprived of his alter ego, condemned to exist without the beloved companion whose presence alone had given meaning to his adventure.

The Descent of Orpheus

The descent myth that has had the most enduring influence—commemorated for millennia in Western art, religion, and philosophy—is that of **Orpheus** [OR-fee-uhs], who entered Hades' realm to retrieve his adored wife, **Eurydice** [oo-RIH-dih-see], who had died of a poisonous snakebite. A mortal figure who combines elements of rational Apollo and ecstatic Dionysus, Orpheus is the archetypal creative artist, expressing powerful emotions in poetry of irresistible beauty. When Orpheus performs on his lyre, given him by Apollo, the entire world is captivated by his song: gods, mortals, wild animals, and even stones respond joyously (Figure 9-8). In the still darkness of death's lair, Orpheus's music charms Hades' fiercest monsters, including Cerberus and the Furies, who quietly let him pass. Singing of his love for Eurydice, Orpheus reduces Hades and Persephone to tears, winning their permission to reclaim his wife—provided he does not look at or speak to her until after they have emerged into the world of light.

Orpheus's fatal error is as inevitable as Adam's tasting of the forbidden fruit or Pandora's opening of the jar of woes. His loss of Eurydice is final (Figure 9-9), poignantly illustrating the Greeks' realistic assessment of such romantic notions as Love (Eros) having the power to overcome Death (Thanatos).

Although Orpheus is primarily identified with Apollo's lucidity and musicality, his story after losing Eurydice parallels events in Dionysus's myth, including a violent death by sparagmos and eventual deification. According to one tradition, after discovering how cruelly the universe fails to honor or protect married love, Orpheus renounces women and devotes himself to winning the young men of Thrace, who

FIGURE 9-8 Orpheus Charming Wild Beasts with His Singing. A personification of musical skill, Orpheus was the world's most effective, if not its first, poet. Accompanying his own singing on the lyre, he charmed the gods, reduced wild animals to peaceful contemplation (as shown in this Roman mosaic), and even persuaded Hades and Persephone to release his beloved Eurydice from the confines of death. Orpheus's ability to create beauty and to tame animal instincts, as well as his descent into the Underworld, made him the subject of a religious cult, Orphism, that initiated converts into the rites and purifications necessary to achieve happiness in the afterlife. (*National Museum, Palermo*)

FIGURE 9-9   Hermes, Eurydice, and Orpheus. This bas-relief captures the moment at which Orpheus, having won Hades' permission to bring his beloved wife, Eurydice, back to the living world, breaks the prohibition not to look back at her until they have reached earth's sunlit surface. Hermes immediately appears to reclaim the veiled Eurydice, whose right arm he grasps. The most creative of all musicians, whose art even the gods admire, fails to overcome the iron grip of death. Orpheus does, however, benefit others by the arcane knowledge he acquires of the afterlife, establishing a mystery cult whose rituals purify the soul and prepare it for a safe journey to Elysium. *(Louvre, Paris)*

flock to hear him play (see Figure 14-7). Furious at Orpheus's neglect, some Thracian women, followers of Dionysus, attack the poet, tearing him apart and scattering his body parts over the earth. Even when severed from his body and cast into the sea, however, the poet's head remains fully alive and—still singing—washes ashore on the island of Lesbos. While Apollo preserves the miraculously vital head from harm and Dionysus punishes his murderous followers by turning them into oak trees, the gods agree to validate Orpheus's incomparable musicianship by transforming his lyre into the constellation Lyra and granting his soul immortality in Elysium (see "The Death of Orpheus" in Chapter 20).

Because he had penetrated the mysteries of the Underworld and overcome its terrors, Orpheus was regarded as a source of esoteric knowledge about the afterlife. A whole body of poems and hymns, known as the Orphic literature, was (falsely) ascribed to him, including mythological texts about the world's origins and about Dionysus's rebirth after the Titans had dismembered and eaten him (see Chapter 8). Orphic poetry not only influenced Dionysian mystery cults but also promised initiates help after death, offering magic spells, secret passwords, and ritual practices that enabled newly deceased souls to find safe passage through Hades' dangerous realm. Persons initiated into these mysteries were sometimes buried with gold leaves inscribed with the formulae necessary to answer correctly when brought before an underworld tribunal over which Persephone, queen of the nether region, presided.

Most modern scholars believe that **Orphism** was less a formal religion than a highly diverse set of occult beliefs and practices based on Orphic literature. In Orphic teaching, humankind, formed from the ashes of Titans who had murdered and consumed the young Dionysus, bore a collective guilt for this primal crime, a contamination that had to be cleansed through ritual purification. Paralleling the doctrines of the philosopher Pythagoras (sixth century B.C.), Orphism fostered a belief in metempsychosis—the doctrine that the soul underwent a series of rebirths in new bodies, pursuing a quest for spiritual cleansing that would eventually permit its escape from the wheel of reincarnation. In this view, the netherworld became a place of ultimate regeneration.

Evolving Ideas About the Afterlife

For all its gloom, in the Homeric Underworld the human soul is too important to suffer extinction at death, maintaining a tenuous survival and retaining some individual identity. Hades is viewed as a Freudian or Jungian dreamlike state in which disembodied souls, like sleepers caught in a nightmare, experience a paralysis that renders them unable to control their actions or environment. Souls float helplessly amid flickering shadows, insubstantial as clouds that dissolve and re-form without purpose or volition. For Homer, death is being trapped in a murky dreamland where the rational will loses all ability to make choices or influence events.

Greek ideas about the afterlife, however, changed significantly over time. In Book 11 of Homer's *Odyssey,* except for some notorious sinners, all of the dead are housed indiscriminately in a dank cave, with no hope of seeing light again. By contrast, in Book 6 of Virgil's *Aeneid,* written approximately seven hundred years later, souls are assigned qualitatively different fates, with the virtuous enjoying a splendidly illuminated paradise and the wicked unspeakable torment. During the centuries between Homer and Virgil, Greek philosophers such as Pythagoras, Socrates, and Plato transformed beliefs about the spirit world, the nature of the human soul, and the ethical purpose of life.

The Transmigration of Souls

Perhaps the first Greek thinker to articulate a doctrine about the soul's transmigration—that at death it passes into another earthly body—was **Pythagoras** (sixth century B.C.), a philosopher who established a school or society in Croton in southern Italy. Pythagoras's contribution to Greek thought lies in two fields, mathematics and mysticism. In his scientific endeavors, he not only formulated the famous geometric theorem named after him (involving the hypotenuse of a right triangle) but also discovered that the ratio of musical intervals produced by a vibrating string on a musical instrument can be expressed numerically. From this discovery, Pythagoras extrapolated that the entire universe can be understood as a vast structure of numerical relationships.

In his speculations about the soul, which he apparently conceived as a combination of mind and life force, Pythagoras claimed to remember his previous incarnations. A legend in his own day, he was also said to hear the music of the spheres, the tones produced as the planets followed their orbits in heaven. Among the many subsequent thinkers inspired by Pythagoreanism was Empedocles (c. 492–432 B.C.), a poet and philosopher from Sicily. According to Empedocles, who allegedly recalled having been a shrub, a fish, and a girl in previous incarnations, the soul passes through many physical forms during the various aeons-long cycles into which cosmic history is divided.

The most complete discussions of the nature of the soul, its postmortem survival, and its rebirth in new bodies appear in the works of the Athenian philosopher **Plato** (427–347 B.C.; Figure 9-10). Profoundly influenced by Orphic tradition and the teachings of Pythagoras, Plato argued that the human soul is immortal, originating in heaven but descending to earth in a kind of fall from grace, where it is trapped in a physical body. In such dialogues as the *Phaedo* and the *Phaedrus,* he contends that the human being is a duality composed of an invisible, eternal soul and a perishable material body tied to the natural processes of change and death. Plato's most detailed vision of the soul's fate after death is contained in the "Myth of Er," a narrative that concludes the *Republic.*

An extended parable of eschatological justice, Plato's myth draws heavily on Orphic doctrines involving purification and regeneration. Er, who narrates the tale, is a soldier seemingly killed in battle who for ten days lies in a comatose state, during which his soul leaves his body and journeys to a spiritual realm where the recently dead gather for judgment. In Er's near-death experience, which strikingly resembles similar reports published in recent centuries, he witnesses the mysterious process of reincarnation in which souls choose their new lives on earth. After spending their allotted time, either in heaven or a place of torment, souls reassemble in the plain or meadow where fates are decided. Some persons who have experienced a thousand

FIGURE 9-10   Plato. One of the world's most influential thinkers, Plato used myths from the Orphic tradition to provide symbols for his vision of the soul's fate after death. Plato's "Myth of Er"—which includes an account of the soul's reincarnation in new bodies to continue a necessary process of learning and purification—provided a view of human destiny that Virgil adopted in the Aeneid. *(Granger Collection, New York)*

years of bliss in heaven choose unwisely because they have been virtuous merely from habit, not from philosophic conviction. Others, having painfully learned the value of righteousness from having endured a millennium of punishment for previous misdeeds, select a worthy new life. Mythic characters appear to illustrate some principles that determine individual choices: Orpheus, disgusted with human love, decides to become a swan; Odysseus, weary of laboring for distinction, chooses to return as an ordinary person. In Plato's universe, the gods, symbols of perfect virtue, are not responsible for human folly or wickedness or the suffering it brings: each soul freely adopts its own destiny.

Plato's contribution to myths about the netherworld forms an indispensable link connecting the Homeric view of Hades and the more sophisticated picture given in Virgil's *Aeneid* (see Chapter 19). Virgil (70–19 B.C.) follows Plato not only in assuming an essential polarity in human nature—the body–soul dichotomy—but also in portraying an afterlife in which souls are spiritually cleansed before returning to earth in new bodies. Combining mystical and ethical values, Virgil presents a complex Hades compartmentalized into contrasting regions such as Elysium and Tartarus, each representing a positive or negative aspect of the human psyche. For Pythagoras, Plato, and Virgil, the next world, no longer a land of no return, becomes a gateway to the soul's future growth and regeneration.

Christianity, which inherited many of its concepts from Greco-Roman tradition, also contributed to the mythic theme of descent into the Underworld. According to the New Testament, after his crucifixion Jesus of Nazareth descended into Tartarus, preaching to spirits imprisoned in its darkness (1 Pet. 3:19; 2 Pet. 2:4). From these brief passages, a belief developed that Jesus entered the netherworld on Good Friday to rescue the souls of righteous persons who had died before he ascended and opened the way to heaven. In medieval theology, this doctrine was known as the harrowing of hell.

For Homer's depiction of souls in Hades' kingdom, see Book 11 of the *Odyssey* (see Chapter 13); for a later, more developed vision of the afterlife, see Virgil's account of Aeneas's descent into the Underworld in Book 6 of the *Aeneid* (see Chapter 19).

. . . .

Questions for Discussion and Review

1. Why does the universal fact of death cast a sinister shadow over the efforts of Greek heroes to perform unparalleled actions and achieve undying fame?

2. Describe the Homeric picture of Hades' realm (see the *Odyssey,* Book 11). Where is the netherworld located, and what are its chief geographic features? Who or what dwells there?

3. Discuss the differences between Elysium and Tartarus and the posthumous state of their respective inhabitants.

4. For what reasons do certain Greek heroes descend into the Underworld? What rites of passage characterize their journeys into and from the land of Death?

5. Compare the Homeric Hades with the afterworld postulated by Virgil in the *Aeneid* (see Chapter 19). In what ways do ideas about Hades' realm evolve over time?

Works Cited

Barnstone, Willis, trans. *Greek Lyric Poetry.* Rev. ed. New York: Bantam, 1967.

Heroes of Myth: Man Divided Against Himself

KEY TOPICS/THEMES

The heroes of Greek myths—from Perseus and Heracles to Achilles and Odysseus—share certain characteristics or experiences: a divine parent or ancestor, physical strength, courage and skill, the performance of "impossible" feats, an encounter with chthonic powers (often an actual trip to the Underworld), and a quest for immortality. For the early heroes, that quest often ends in their achieving some form of divine status, whereas later heroes have to settle for a reputation that endures though they themselves cannot. Each hero, however, also has his own unique characteristics. Perseus, possibly the earliest of the heroes, is unusual in his positive relationships with women, both divine and human; other heroes, like Heracles, Theseus, and Jason, experience difficulties in their dealings with women. In all the heroes after Perseus, we see an inner division, men pulled in two directions: toward the fulfillment of their godlike capacity to excel, on the one hand, and toward the expression of their instinctive savagery or violence, on the other. In other figures, like Phaethon, the reckless flight of the hero toward immortality is used to teach a lesson on the dangers of excessive ambition.

The Heroic Pattern

The adventures of the Greek heroes, like those of heroes everywhere, typically follow a traditional pattern. The hero is often born in an unusual (or unnatural) fashion and, as an infant, faces terrible danger, which, of course, he survives. The hero often has two fathers—a divine, "real" one, and a human father figure, from whom he often faces threats. According to Freudian theorists, these threats represent a projection of the hero's own hostility toward his father, whom he perceives as a rival for his mother's affections. This fantasy of having a "good" divine father and a "bad" human one is, these theorists suggest, the hero's way of coping with the guilt at his unconscious desire to kill his biological father. The hero also often demonstrates prodigious powers, even in childhood. On reaching adulthood, he craves adventure and, seeking to test his own powers, embarks on a quest or series of quests: a journey of discovery during which he will learn about himself, his society, and his universe.

In the course of that quest, he is eventually isolated from his fellow humans and, all alone, must do battle with nightmarish creatures or monsters, usually including some in serpent or dragon form—all variants of the serpents of the ancient goddesses. The hero also does battle with barbarians who would destroy Greek civilization, such as Amazons, female warriors considered to be "savage" (see Chapter 11). Both Theseus and Heracles were depicted as battling the Amazons, and Theseus is said to have protected Athens from invasions by these monstrous women who threatened patriarchal powers. Ultimately, the hero must confront the divine or cosmic powers themselves. His journey often culminates in a trip to the Underworld, from which he returns, bringing a new awareness of himself, his limitations, and his relationship to the forces that govern the universe.

The hero's trip to the Underworld has been interpreted as a descent into the "womb" of the earth goddess, connecting the masculine ego of the hero with the feminine principle; others see the trip as a descent into the unconscious. Thus, rejoining the animus with the anima, the hero's psyche can be made whole. Additionally, by connecting with both upper and lower worlds, the hero participates in the cycle of life, death, and rebirth that the goddess religions once embraced. In the competitive, linear world of the sky gods, the hero, being merely mortal, is at a serious disadvantage: his quest to defy death, to achieve literal immortality, is doomed. But in descending to the Underworld, the hero recognizes the necessity of experiencing the whole cycle, however terrifying. Ascending once more to the upper world, he achieves spiritual rebirth. Unlike Dionysus, the "twice-born" god who descends into human incarnation in the womb of a human mother and is born again out of his divine parent, the human hero descends into the womb of the goddess and reclaims his spiritual life, which is his link to the divine world.

The Hero as Redeemer

The hero as a redemptive figure emerges in myths as humans enter the fallen world, the world of time, of decay and death. In Hesiod's account of the Ages of Man, the Age of Heroes follows immediately after the Bronze and Silver Ages, and the implicit function of the hero is to redeem humanity, a process begun by Prometheus's defiance of Zeus. Prometheus's gifts to humankind of sacrifice and fire serve to reconnect the fallen world of mortals to the world of the gods, at least symbolically. Sacrifice restores a form of mediated communication with the gods—the communion established by the symbolic sharing of a meal. Fire provides both the means for humans to cook their food (and thus to obliterate the obvious signs of their penchant for violence—that, like animals, humans kill to eat) and the means to create technology (to use fire to forge weapons, for example). The hero's function, too, is

The Heroic Pattern: Archetypal Events

Anthropologists, folklorists, and other scholars have surveyed traditions about the hero figure in representative cultures of the world and have compiled lists of characteristics that typify the hero's life. The following list is adapted from one published by the folklorist and mythographer Lord Raglan.

1. The hero's mother is a royal virgin, and
2. His father is a king.
3. The circumstances of his conception and birth are unusual, and
4. He is reputed to be the son of a god.
5. At birth, an attempt is made, often by his father or maternal grandfather, to kill him, but
6. He is spirited away, and
7. He is reared by foster parents in a distant land.
8. On reaching manhood, he returns or travels to his future kingdom.
9. He often journeys to the Underworld, or the shades of the dead may visit him.
10. After he triumphs over the king and/or a giant, dragon, or wild beast,
11. He marries a princess, often the daughter of his predecessor, and
12. He becomes king.
13. Eventually, he loses favor with the gods and/or his subjects, and
14. He meets a mysterious death.
15. His children do not succeed him.
16. His body is not buried, but
17. He has one or more holy sepulchers.

Other mythographers find different patterns. Joseph Campbell describes the heroic pattern as a "monomyth":

1. The hero is separated from his familiar surroundings and goes on a journey alone.
2. He undergoes a mysterious initiation, during which he grapples with supernatural powers and gains a new understanding of himself in relation to his community and the gods.
3. He returns to share the new vision with his fellows.

redemptive: by his half-divine nature, his glorious deeds, and his relentless pursuit of immortality, he uplifts humanity from its dismal condition and reminds it of its godlike potential.

Nevertheless, he remains half-human and must therefore die. For the hero, the final burden of his humanity is the necessity of confronting his own mortality. In the polarities of the hero's experiences, nature and culture, and the human and the divine, converge to produce a being who is contradictory in his very essence.

Protesting this condition, the ancient Sumerian hero **Gilgamesh** asks of the sun god, "If this quest is not to be achieved, why did you create in me the irresistible urge to attempt it?" The hero of Greek mythology, from Heracles to Achilles and Odysseus, is similarly trapped by his very nature into undertaking, and usually achieving, the impossible—paradoxically pursuing death in order to achieve immortality, a potentially tragic endeavor.

The Isolation of the Hero

At the same time, the more successful he is at reconnecting humanity, by example or imaginatively, with the divine realm, the more the hero constitutes, by his very nature, a potential threat or rival to the gods. It is no accident that heroes are typically objects of enmity of one deity or another.

The divided nature of the hero also creates a psychological dilemma. In his singular drive to burst through the tantalizingly transparent ceiling of mortality, the hero figure is isolated by his own uniqueness: no one understands his compulsion toward excess. Culminating the process of individuation begun at creation, the hero is the ultimate unique individual—and yet he craves human companionship and love. For the ancient Sumerian hero Gilgamesh, the gods provided a companion, Enkidu, to ease his loneliness. But even Enkidu, while sharing Gilgamesh's enormous courage and skill, fails to understand his friend's determination to do combat with Humbaba, the terrifying deity of the forest. For Gilgamesh, the mere fact of mortality is enough to fuel the compulsion to achieve something extraordinary—or to die trying.

The ultimate isolation of the hero figure is even more emphatically evident in his relationship with women. For such a hero, essentially a warrior, the female is at best a distraction and at worst a threat. The bonds of love, domestic contentment, and/or sexual indulgence are destructive to the heroic task. To succeed in his quest—to fulfill his godlike aspirations—the hero must eschew the banal comforts of ordinary life that would bind him to the earth to which his body will eventually be returned. Although there are exceptions, such as Odysseus (see Chapter 13), the hero must typically reject, tame, or even kill the women in his life, lest he be tamed (and thus psychologically destroyed) or killed by them. The enmity of Hera, goddess of marriage, toward Heracles likewise reflects this essential antagonism.

The Hero and Society

In his role as protector of society, the hero is also a divided being. Charged with defending civilization from rampaging beasts or monsters or human enemies who would destroy it and return humankind to the savage condition from which it has only barely emerged, the hero has unique gifts that allow him to protect society from threats to personal, economic, or cultural survival. In addition, by his exploits and travels, he adds to humanity's body of knowledge, both geographic and historical: Gilgamesh, for example, brings back knowledge of the world before the Flood, recovering the prehistory of Uruk and recording it for future generations.

The product, furthermore, of a newly urbanized society, the hero, whose "official" job is protecting his city, represents an emergent civilization's self-consciousness, both of its pride in its own glorious achievements (the *Epic of Gilgamesh* opens with extended praise for the awesome walls, temples, and gardens of Gilgamesh's city, Uruk) and of its incipient awareness that these gains, however amazing, are dependent on humans' willingness to commit themselves to maintaining that civilization. But humans are all too capable of backsliding into savagery and losing all they have gained. It is the hero who bears the burden of protecting society, often on behalf of (or in place of) the kings who organize the armies or appoint the tasks. Paradoxically, the hero's martial skills, his potential for violence, and his often impulsive nature put civilization at risk: when we first meet Gilgamesh, he's causing havoc in Uruk, raping the women and distracting the men from their work. Similarly, the heroes in Hesiod's Bronze Age are so violent that they destroy each other, and the men of the Age of Heroes, whose exploits are recounted in the myths, constitute a second attempt at redemption, while providing models for young men in Greek society to emulate.

The social role of mythic heroes also acquired a political dimension, as cities that were, or could claim to be, associated with specific heroes took advantage of those figures' reputations to glorify their own public images or to justify their political agendas. Thus, the myths of both Perseus and Heracles are associated with the Argolid region, which included the cities of Sparta and Thebes (where Heracles was born), both rivals to Athens. The myths of both heroes spread quickly throughout Greece, while the Attic city of Athens did everything possible to enhance the stories and cults of its own mythic past through the figure of Theseus.

The Hero as Centaur: Image of the Divided Self

Though required for his martial skill and willingness to serve in times of war or other threat, the hero often becomes, in times of peace, a danger to the civilization he is charged with protecting. Furthermore, by encouraging and rewarding his capacity for violence when it serves society's needs and then complaining about its inability to control him when he continues to act in the same fashion once the immediate threat is resolved, humanity creates conflicting sets of demands that result in an inner division in the hero's own nature. In that inner division, the hero, despite his frequent battles with the creatures, resembles the **centaur**—a literally divided creature.

Combining a human head and upper torso with a horse's rear end, the centaurs—beings with a capacity for intelligence, knowledge, and wisdom but possessing voracious appetites and aggressive instincts—embody the best and worst of human potentialities, brains and brawn inextricably joined.

Two stories about centaurs exemplify their inherent contradictions. In their usual manifestation, the centaurs embody animal nature, raw and unrestrained. They are said to eat uncooked food and are unable to control themselves when drinking wine: invited to the wedding of a Lapith princess, the centaurs characteristically get drunk and attempt to carry off and rape the Lapith women. A horrible battle follows in which King Pirithous and his guests, including Heracles and Theseus, finally drive the centaurs away.

Gilgamesh: The First Hero of World Myth

The oldest surviving account of a hero's adventures appears in the Sumero-Babylonian *Epic of Gilgamesh*. Tales about Gilgamesh, a legendary king of Uruk, one of Mesopotamia's first city-states, were composed in Sumeria as early as the second millennium B.C. The most complete version of his story, however, was compiled by the poet Sin-leqe-unnini in about the seventh century B.C. Although once widely distributed throughout the Near East (fragments have been found from Iraq to Israel), the epic was unknown to the modern world until the mid-nineteenth century. While excavating Nineveh, the ancient capital of Assyria, in the 1850s, archaeologists discovered a royal library consisting of thousands of baked clay tablets inscribed in cuneiform, the wedge-shaped writing that the Sumerians had invented about 3200 B.C. Although partly damaged, the Nineveh library's twelve tablets containing the Gilgamesh epic, supplemented by fragments from other sources, reveal a hero who strikingly anticipates major figures from later world mythology.

The Gilgamesh narrative has two distinct parts. In the first, the hero strongly bonds with a wild man, Enkidu, whom the gods created out of clay to be his life-partner. After the two friends demonstrate their courage and martial skill by slaying monsters such as the fiery Humbaba and the ferocious "bull of heaven," a manifestation of drought and earthquake, Gilgamesh makes a fatal decision: he rejects the sexual advances of Ishtar, the powerful goddess of love and war, and the divine patron of his city, Uruk. Ishtar, furious over the insult to her charms, persuades the heavenly council to punish Gilgamesh by afflicting Enkidu with a lethal disease. Gilgamesh, overwhelmed by grief and terrified by his first personal encounter with death, experiences a crisis that changes his life: he determines to find a way to escape human mortality.

In the epic's second part, Gilgamesh embarks on a long and dangerous quest to find the remote island home of his ancestor, Utnapishtim (the Babylonian Noah). Because Utnapishtim is the only man to have survived the global deluge and the only person to whom the gods have granted immortality, Gilgamesh hopes to acquire from him the secret of everlasting life.

In his desperate pursuit of life eternal, Gilgamesh endures intense suffering, finally arriving exhausted at Utnapishtim's faraway paradise. Scoffing at his descendant's unrealistic attempt to avoid death, Utnapishtim reminds Gilgamesh that his host's possession of immortality stems from unique, unrepeatable circumstances: being selected by Ea, a wise and compassionate god, to build an ark, stock it with pairs of all animals, and thus survive a cataclysm that annihilated all humanity. In pity at Gilgamesh's despair, Utnapishtim's wife persuades her husband to reveal that a plant capable of miraculously restoring youth grows at the bottom of the sea. After risking his life to retrieve the plant, Gilgamesh begins his journey back to Uruk, only to have the plant stolen from him and eaten by a snake. Ironically, the serpent is thus able to shed its skin, ostensibly renewing its life, whereas mortal humans forever lack the ability to rejuvenate.

During his search for Utnapishtim, Gilgamesh meets Siduri, a wise barmaid and minor goddess, who tells him that he will never find the everlasting life he seeks, for the gods reserve immortality exclusively for themselves. Instead of wearing himself out trying to achieve divinity, she says, he must accept the ordinary consolations of humanity's mortal state, enjoying each day as if it were a festival.

In important ways, Gilgamesh's story establishes the model or pattern for the subsequent heroes of Greek and Roman myth. In his inexhaustible struggle to win undying fame through displays of strength and valor, he resembles Achilles, the *Iliad*'s central character. Like Achilles, Gilgamesh also has a divine mother, the goddess Ninsun, from whom he presumably inherits his superhuman qualities and godlike aspiration. He also anticipates Achilles in identifying with a beloved friend, a second self, whose death precipitates the major turning point in his career. The second part of Gilgamesh's myth, a dangerous journey across the "waters of death" that includes traversing such diverse mythical sites as the realm of absolute darkness (Erebus) and the brightly jeweled "garden of the gods," foreshadows Odysseus's heroic quest in the *Odyssey*. As Odysseus provokes the hostility of Poseidon, which costs him all of his companions, so Gilgamesh elicits Ishtar's curse that robs him of Enkidu. Both men survive the divine wrath, but only after enduring great hardship and pain do they succeed in returning to their respective homes.

In its entirety, Gilgamesh's myth encompasses aspects typical of a Greek hero. These characteristic elements include the hero's divine parentage, royal status, personal courage, phenomenal strength, skill in waging war and/or vanquishing monsters, irresistible drive to surpass all rivals, conflict with a divine adversary, posthumous fame and/or deification, and confrontation with death, typically in the guise of a visit to the Underworld. (Besides braving the "valley of the shadow of death," Gilgamesh also beholds Enkidu's ghost, who reveals to him the gloomy nature of the afterlife.) In many cases, such as those of Gilgamesh and Odysseus, the hero's tale takes a circular form, with his travels among strange and perilous domains followed by a return to his place of origin. But the returning hero does not come back empty-handed: he brings with him invaluable knowledge of distant lands and peoples, as well as a fuller understanding of his role as a mortal human. Imparting otherwise inaccessible wisdom to others—Gilgamesh has his adventures inscribed in stone on Uruk's walls, and Odysseus conveys all he saw and did to his wife, Penelope—the hero enriches the community with his life-affirming experience.

By contrast, the leader of the centaurs, **Chiron** [KYE-rahn], is temperate and wise—indeed, a great teacher of both gods and men, instructing Asclepius, for example, in the art of medicine. Unlike the other centaurs, Chiron embodies all that culture and civilization have to offer. His reward is to be shot with a poisoned arrow by Heracles—in one of that hero's irrational (and ironically centaurlike) moments—as Chiron is attempting to stop the centaurs' rampage at the Lapith wedding. In agony but unable to die, Chiron generously offers to trade places with Prometheus, releasing the latter from the rock (see Chapter 4). Chiron, like Perseus, is finally transformed into a constellation, Centaurus, while the centaurlike Heracles will ultimately be elevated to divine status.

Indeed, whether or not they are metamorphosed into constellations, most of the heroes are deified in some fashion and become the object of hero cults. At their purported tombs, or at shrines dedicated to them, offerings are made and rituals performed. Thus, Heracles, transformed into a god, marries Hebe and enters directly into the pantheon of Olympian gods (Figure 10-1). In Euripides' *Heracleidae,* Heracles and Hebe intercede from the heavens and, in direct response to a prayer

FIGURE 10-1   The Marriage of Heracles and Hebe. In this vase painting (c. 350 B.C.), Heracles (with his club) stands next to the seated Hebe, whose attendants prepare her for the wedding. Eros hovers over the pair, while Desire stands on the knee of the seated Aphrodite on the right. *(Staatliche Museen, Berlin)*

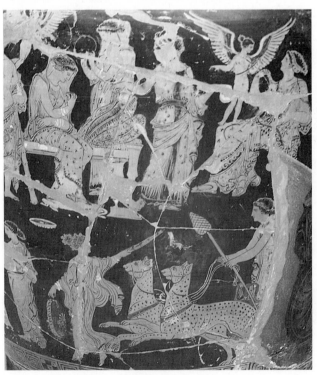

for help, miraculously cause Heracles' now elderly former assistant, Iolaus, to be young again for just one day, in order to take revenge on Eurystheus, who has been attempting to destroy Heracles' mother and his children. Theseus, too, is invoked after his death as a protector of Athens, and Odysseus, likewise, has cults established in his honor. Even Oedipus, once considered a source of such dire pollution that no city would allow him entry, undergoes apotheosis and ascends to the heavens in a cloud of glory at his death in the sacred grove of the Eumenides to remain a source of perpetual blessing to the people of Athens (see Chapter 16).

The Early Hero: Perseus

Perseus is one of the earliest of the Greek heroes. Although he shares some of the traits later seen in Heracles and has some similar adventures, Perseus is distinguished by some important differences. Whereas other heroes often have difficulties in their encounters with women, whether human or divine, Perseus performs all of his exploits either with the aid or on behalf of women, and he maintains mutually supportive relationships with them throughout his career. Perhaps because he is less estranged from the feminine powers, Perseus does not journey to the Underworld.

Perseus's Early Life

Perseus's mother, **Danae** [DA-na-ee], had been imprisoned in a bronze tower by her father, Acrisius, king of Argos. He wanted to sequester her from all men in order to protect his rulership by preventing the fulfillment of a prophecy that a son of Danae would kill him. But Zeus, who is attracted to her beauty, comes to her in a shower of golden rain, releasing the procreative power that Acrisius had attempted to restrain, a tale that recapitulates the relationships between Gaea and Uranus, and Rhea and Cronus. The child conceived by this miraculous intervention is, like most of the heroes who follow, half-divine. Although their response to later heroes is sometimes ambivalent, the gods seem to identify closely with Perseus. When Perseus is born, Acrisius sets his daughter and grandson adrift at sea in a chest, an archetypal symbol of both coffin and womb, connecting Perseus to the cycle of life, death, and rebirth that is the traditional province of the Great Goddess. From the very beginning of the myth of Perseus, the opposing powers of male and female, human and divine, are more closely reconciled than they will be in later hero myths.

Danae and the child are protected by Zeus, and, instead of drowning, they float safely to shore on the island of Seriphus, where they are taken in by the fisherman Dictys and where Perseus is raised. But further danger threatens, as the hero experiences the hostility of yet another father-substitute, Dictys's brother, King Polydectes, who desires Danae. When she refuses him, Perseus protects her, offering to bring Polydectes instead any gift of his choice. The shrewd king demands the head of **Medusa,** one of the three Gorgons, knowing that the attempt will be fatal, thus ridding himself of Perseus and giving himself free access to Danae. Perseus, of course, does not hesitate to volunteer for impossible missions, possessing, by virtue of his divine parentage, the courage and skill to succeed.

Perseus and the Gorgon

The gods, however, are concerned that, being half-human, Perseus lacks powers sufficient to the formidable task he faces. Athene therefore steps in to help, warning Perseus of the difficulties he will encounter and telling him to visit the sisters of the Gorgon, the **Graiae** [GRYE-eye]—old, gray hags from birth, with one eye and one tooth to share among them. Snatching the eye, Perseus forces them to reveal the location of the nymphs who possess magical weapons: a pouch, a pair of winged sandals (possibly Hermes') that will enable him to fly, and a cap of invisibility, which may have belonged to Hades. Hermes gives him a sickle of adamant, an unbreakable stone. Perseus also takes his polished bronze shield (in some versions, a mirror), possibly a gift from Athene.

The terrifying, deadly aspects of the Great Goddess are portrayed in the Graiae and the Gorgons, whose powers are tamed by the hero in a striking inversion of Gaea's plan for the castration of Uranus by a sickle; here, however, it is the power of the female that is nullified. (In fact, for Freudian psychologists, decapitation is an unconscious image of castration; thus, the fear of Medusa, whose head is seen as a symbol of the female genitalia, represents the male fear of castration.) However, even while destroying the terrifying chthonic powers of the female, Perseus does not reject feminine powers altogether: his weapons—a pouch, mirror (shield), pair of sandals, and cap—are more "feminine" and less aggressive than those of typical heroes (we cannot imagine Heracles or Achilles needing to be invisible to his enemies) and depend for their efficacy on magic, rather than on the considerable strength and intelligence of the hero himself. Even his sickle, an agricultural tool, is reminiscent not only of Gaea's arranged castration of Uranus but also of Demeter's gift of agriculture to humankind.

Furthermore, borrowing divine powers for the purposes of his quest, Perseus literally assumes, at least temporarily, powers like flight and invisibility that humans may dream of but that are reserved for the gods. He thus becomes, in effect, a demigod, foreshadowing his final stellar transformation and reconciling the human and the divine more completely than later heroes ever could.

Arriving at the Gorgons' cave, Perseus finds the petrified statues of men who had looked in the faces of the horrifying creatures. Waiting until the Gorgons are asleep, Perseus dons his cap of invisibility. But even though they cannot see him, he is still in danger: if he, too, looks into Medusa's face, he will be turned to stone. As clever as he is brave, Perseus enters the cave backward, looking into his shield (mirror) so he won't have to look directly into the terrible face. When he cuts off Medusa's head, a winged horse—**Pegasus**—springs from her neck (Figure 10-2). Placing the head in his pouch, Perseus flies off and escapes.

Medusa herself is a complex figure. Her golden wings and her hair of snakes are symbols inherited from the Great Goddess figures (the Egyptian goddess Isis, for example, was often depicted as a winged goddess), linking the upper and lower worlds in a single figure. Variously described as inhabiting a region near the limits of the ocean or the Garden of the Hesperides, she maintains her connection to the primal Goddess of the Tree (or the Waters) of Life. Like Artemis, Medusa is a guardian of the women's mysteries, of the secrets of the early goddesses whose chthonic aspects she has come to represent. Perseus's entrance into the Gorgon's

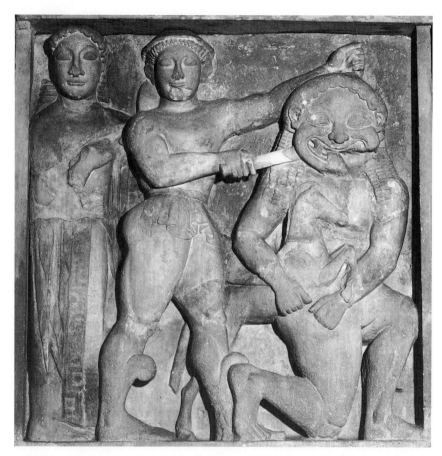

FIGURE 10-2   Perseus Slaying Medusa. This limestone relief from the temple at Selinus (550–540 B.C.) depicts Perseus cutting off the head of the Gorgon Medusa. Athene looks on as Pegasus, the winged horse, springs forth. Perseus will later give the head to Athene, thus effectively transferring this terrifying aspect of the Great Goddess's powers to the representative of the wisdom of Zeus. *(National Museum, Palermo)*

cave is thus a symbolic entrance into the Underworld, and, like his successors in the heroic tradition, he escapes alive. When Perseus avoids looking at Medusa directly, wisely viewing her reflected image rather than her face, he is astutely avoiding the fate of Actaeon and other males who spy on those mysteries.

Medusa's link to the upper world of the heavens, where the sky gods now rule, is also evident in her connection with the sacred horses who pull the chariot of the sun, an image common to many myth systems. According to one tradition, she makes love to (or is raped by) Poseidon, who comes to her in the form of a horse; in other versions of that story, she takes the form of either a mare or a woman from the waist up, with a mare's lower half. The products of this union are Chrysaor, a human warrior, and Pegasus, the winged horse, who will fly across the heavens pulling the chariot of Zeus that bears his thunderbolt—a variant of the sunchariot.

Medusa is thus closely connected to both the upper world and the Underworld, as were the primal goddesses themselves. As the mother of the sacred horse of the sky god, she asserts her powers as a creator figure whose realm includes the light and the darkness.

Perseus's Other Adventures

On the way home, Perseus comes to the Garden of the Hesperides (as Heracles will later) where Atlas, afraid that Perseus will steal the Golden Apples, offends the hero, who turns Atlas into a mountain of stone by using the Gorgon's head.

Taking the long way home (as will both Heracles and Theseus), Perseus stops in Ethiopia, where he sees Princess **Andromeda** chained to a rock, at the mercy of a sea monster. Her mother, Cassiopeia, it seems, boasted of being more beautiful than the sea nymphs, and an angry Poseidon, in response, sent the sea monster to punish the Ethiopians. Andromeda's father, King Cepheus, was told that only the sacrifice of his daughter would rid the kingdom of the monster.

Perseus offers to rescue Andromeda in exchange for her hand in marriage. Her parents, despite her previous betrothal to Phineus, agree, whereupon Perseus kills the monster (see Color Plate 7). He is then attacked by Phineus and his allies, but he wins the battle by removing the Gorgon's head from his sack (while he himself looks the other way) and turning his opponents to stone. Perseus and Andromeda have a son, Perses, who becomes king of Ethiopia (and was said to be the ancestor of the Persians).

Perseus's Return

Perseus's story, much of which is recounted in Apollodorus's *Library,* embodies the complete cycle of the heroic rite of passage—departure, testing, triumph, and return. Returning home at last with Andromeda, Perseus finds his mother still pursued by Polydectes. Perseus uses the Gorgon's head once again to turn Polydectes and his followers to stone. Perseus then returns his magical weapons to Hermes, who restores them to the nymphs. No longer a demigod, Perseus nevertheless brings with him a gift—the Gorgon's head—which he gives to Athene. The powers of the Great Goddess are now assimilated by Athene—who personifies the wisdom of Zeus—as she puts the Gorgon's head, with its power to bind men by turning them to stone (possibly an image of impotence), behind her masculine weapon of war, her shield.

We may be witnessing in Perseus the emergence of the hero figure as he is differentiated from the various aspects of the goddess figure at an early stage in the shift from a matriarchal to a patriarchal system. Unlike the later, more exclusively "masculine" heroes, whose power depends on separating themselves from women (except, of course, for Odysseus; see Chapter 13), Perseus derives his power directly from females, who give him magical weapons. His heroic acts are performed not in isolation, in pursuit of immortality or reputation, but in defense of women: to save his mother from rape or Andromeda from a sea monster. Finally, whereas the later heroes typically have difficulty settling down into peaceful, domestic lives, Perseus does exactly that, insisting on marrying Andromeda, bringing her back to his mother, and becoming the progenitor of a large and successful family.

Perseus as King

Following his return home, Perseus visits his grandfather, Acrisius, hoping to be reconciled. But at the funeral games for a friend, Perseus throws a discus that goes off course and hits his grandfather, killing him and fulfilling the prophecy that a son of Danae would kill Acrisius. Reluctant to assume his grandfather's throne at Argos after the accident, Perseus trades cities with his cousin Megapenthes, now king of Tiryns. Perseus had earlier petrified Megapenthes' father, Proetus, for attacking his own brother, Acrisius (Perseus's grandfather), and usurping his throne. Perseus thus becomes ruler of Tiryns and, eventually, Mycenae.

According to one tradition, Megapenthes eventually kills Perseus to avenge his father. But most versions describe Perseus as living a long and happy life with Andromeda, who bears him one daughter and five more sons, establishing a political dynasty that rules in Argos for several generations and whose descendants include both Heracles and Eurystheus, who will assign Heracles to his labors.

The Death of Perseus

One of the earliest functions of the Perseus myth may have been etiological: the myth explains the origin of several constellations. At their deaths, Athene transforms Perseus and Andromeda into constellations (as did Poseidon on the deaths of Cassiopeia and Cepheus). More importantly, the hero here fulfills, in the most literal way, the quest for immortality that underlies the heroic myth. Thus, without incurring the enmity of the gods, Perseus completes the cycle through his heavenly rebirth and acquires the fully divine status—the reunification of the divided self, half-human and half-divine—that later heroes will risk death to achieve.

But the reconciliation is not to last. Rarely afterward will male and female, human and god, coexist so harmoniously in a single being. The seeds of the new, more exclusively patriarchal hero figure have been planted. Out of the severed neck of Medusa springs the winged horse Pegasus, whose famous rider, **Bellerophon** [bel-LER-oh-fahn], will be a new kind of hero who accepts the magical bridle that enables him to mount the horse and kill the **Chimaera** (a fire-breathing monster—part lion, part goat, and part serpent). Bellerophon also fought the Amazons and performed other amazing feats. However, not content, as Perseus was, to return the magical weapons to the gods and settle down to enjoy his fame and the kingdom and bride he has won, Bellerophon mounts the divine steed once more, in an attempt to leap the barriers to the heavens themselves, thus provoking the gods' hostility—a hero, in other words, much like Heracles.

The Archetypal Hero: Heracles

It is **Heracles** [HER-a-kleez], about whom stories multiplied and spread throughout the Greek world, who sets the model for Greek mythological heroes—extraordinary men who often combine the courage and strength of the gods with the bestial instincts of centaurs. The son of Zeus and a mortal woman—**Alcmene**—Heracles inherits a divided nature, half-human and half-divine; Zeus was said to have extended the night for three days in order to conceive such a son. Yet the two halves never come together for Heracles as they did for Perseus. As befits the son of a god, Heracles is unnaturally brave, strong, and clever, possessed of the spark of the divine fire that always seems, somehow, excessive when embodied in merely human form. Of course, as a hero must, he uses those gifts to protect and preserve society and to enlarge human knowledge. Bound by his human inheritance, however, he is also capable of animal-like behavior, committing acts sometimes ridiculous, sometimes irrational, and sometimes extremely violent. It is thus no accident that few heroes are as closely associated with the centaur as is Heracles, the dual components of his nature as abruptly juxtaposed as they are in the mismatched halves of that bifurcated creature. A being divided against himself, Heracles embodies the quintessential heroic predicament: how to fulfill the demands of the godlike desire for knowledge and achievement that drive him while bound to a mortal body that can neither fly nor turn invisible and that will surely die.

The Life of Heracles

Like most heroes, Heracles is threatened even as an infant. Ever jealous of Zeus's infidelities, Hera hates Heracles from his birth. In fact, the hero's name, which means "Glory of Hera," may reflect the fact that every attempt by Hera to destroy Heracles instead merely enhances his heroic status. According to one myth, Zeus tries to subvert her antagonism by tricking Hera into nursing the infant while she sleeps. When she awakes and discovers the child, she angrily pulls him from her breast, spilling the milk that becomes the Milky Way. Furious, she tries to get rid of him, sending a serpent into his cradle and thereby reenacting his father's own battle with the serpent of the goddess, Typhoeus (Figure 10-3). The prodigious infant, of course, strangles the serpent. Even though Heracles continues to foil Hera's attempts to destroy him, however, he cannot foil his own nature.

His early exploits reveal the ambiguity of Heracles' heroism. Turning his prowess to beneficial use, he kills a marauding lion that had been devouring the flocks of King Thespius. He also sleeps with the king's fifty daughters on their father's invitation, either on fifty successive nights or all on one night, rivalling his own father's rampant sexual exploits. Extraordinary service, extraordinary appetites—these are, from the first, combined in Heracles.

One of the most popular of Greek heroes, Heracles has many stories told about his life, our sources for which include Apollodorus, Apollonius of Rhodes (the *Argonautica*), and Homer. These stories cover not just the famous Twelve Labors but a whole range of exploits that run the gamut from the serious to the comic and from the grotesque to the tragic. For instance, in his role as civic hero, Heracles helps many kings—leading armies, defeating enemies, and building and defending cities. He is also credited with founding the Olympic Games. He doesn't always play by the rules, though: in one account, he cuts off the noses and ears of an enemy's ambassadors and sends them back with the body parts hung around their necks. His innate brutality sometimes erupts in his private life as well. Married to **Megara** [ME-ga-ra] as a reward for his services to her father, Heracles settles down into domestic life. The couple has several children, and the hero appears to be happy. One night, however, in a fit of uncontrollable rage—perhaps sent by the still-angry Hera—he slays his wife and children, a tragic event dramatized in Euripides' play

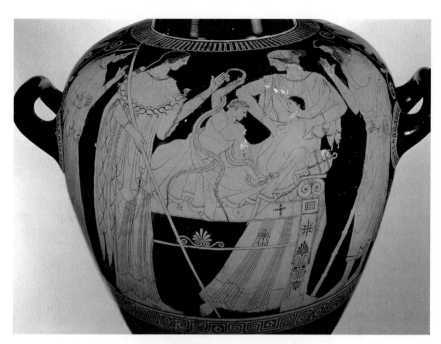

FIGURE 10-3   Baby Heracles Strangling Snakes. In this vase painting (c. 480 B.C.), the hero's prodigious skill is multiplied as he battles not one but two deadly serpents while his terrified half-brother tries to escape. *(Réunion des Musées Nationaux)*

Heracles. Perhaps the strength, drive, and energy that define his heroic identity could not brook a life of mere domestic contentment. A savior in times of threat or war, the hero becomes a menace in time of peace: trained to use his strength to kill and to glory in his violent victories, how does he control the violence or repress the glorying ego when he leaves the battlefield and returns to civilized life?

The Twelve Labors and Other Stories

As expiation for his crime of domestic violence, Heracles is forced to perform Twelve Labors (some versions mention only ten) for King Eurystheus, each one designed (probably at the instigation of Hera) to destroy him. Typical of the pattern of the heroic quest, Heracles' first labors are physical. Using his enormous strength and intelligence, Heracles kills the **Hydra**—a many-headed water snake whose heads would immediately regrow if cut off—by cleverly instructing a friend to use a torch to sear the neck of each head as the hero severs it. He also captures the Arcadian boar (also called the Erymanthian boar, after Mount Erymanthus, where he catches it) and the Cretan bull and tames the man-eating Thracian horses.

But even the very first of the labors reveals the savage core of the hero's heart. In killing the ravaging lion of Nemea, whose skin was impervious to human weapons, Heracles uses brute force by choking it to death with his bare hands (Figure 10-4). Required to bring back its skin as proof of the deed, Heracles demonstrates his

FIGURE 10-4   Heracles' First Labor: Battling with the Nemean Lion. An illustration of the hero's amazing strength, this vase painting shows the hero strangling with his bare hands the lion whose skin is impenetrable to human weapons. After cleverly skinning it with its own claws, he wears its pelt as a cloak, a symbol of the savage element of the hero's nature. *(University of Pennsylvania Museum, Philadelphia)*

cleverness by using its own claws to skin the lion. From this time forward, Heracles wears the lion skin as a cloak, as if he himself has become the marauding beast. Further manifesting his animal nature and suggesting his regression to a precivilized state, Heracles shapes his famous club at this point, substituting this primitive weapon for the more conventional and equally famous bow that had been his trademark (Figures 10-5 and 10-6).

Many stories depict Heracles' animal-like qualities, describing him as unusually hairy and prone to bouts of excessive drunkenness, often in the company of centaurs. During one such episode, he shoots the good centaur, Chiron, by mistake, his strong right arm going into action before his brain is engaged: like many heroes after him, Heracles' instinct is to shoot first and ask questions later. In other tales, he is depicted comically, the object of sometimes coarse jokes. On one such occasion, he captures two enemy soldiers and slings them from a pole over his shoulders. Faced with a close-up view of the hero's hairy rear end, the two soldiers begin to laugh. Finding their laughter momentarily amusing, Heracles actually releases them.

FIGURE 10-5   Heracles Shooting His Bow. This statue (c. 490–
475 B.C.) from the temple of Aphaia at Aegina portrays Heracles
in the act of shooting his famous bow and wearing the armor of a
conventional Greek warrior. The stable posture, calm expression,
and firmly outstretched arm suggest rationality, self-control, and
supreme self-confidence. *(Glyptothek, Munich)*

On the positive side, several of the labors present the hero in his civic function as preserver of society and civilized life—killing the Stymphalian birds who
were plaguing one town or cleaning out the Augean stables by diverting two rivers
through the barn. Another task involved bringing back the belt of the Amazon
queen Hippolyte: perhaps she yielded to him, or perhaps he killed her for it; either
way, he "tamed" a formidable female opponent.

In the most incredible series of labors, Heracles fulfills the hero's most significant
function—to extend the parameters of human experience, to embody the scope of
the human imagination stretched to its limits, and to retrieve powers and knowledge otherwise limited to the gods. Heracles undertakes, literally, to extend the
boundaries of the known world by traveling to the ends of the earth, to the unknown reaches of the North in pursuit of the Golden Hind (Figure 10-7) and to
the Garden of the **Hesperides** [hes-PER-ih-deez] in the mythical West to obtain
the goddess's Golden Apples of Immortality.

In all his quests, Heracles calls on his divine gifts to commit death-defying acts,
but, tainted by his human inheritance, he must finally confront the most formi-

FIGURE 10-6 Heracles with His Club. This Roman copy, known as the Hercules Farnese, of a statue by Lysippus (original from the late fourth century B.C.) shows Heracles, in contrast to the traditional hero of Figure 10-5, to be larger, hairier, and more muscular than the earlier version. The increased brawn, along with the grim expression, adds to the savage image conveyed by the huge, rather primitive-looking club with the lion skin, complete with claws, draped over it: in this image, the warrior-hero has been transformed into a brute. *(National Museum, Naples)*

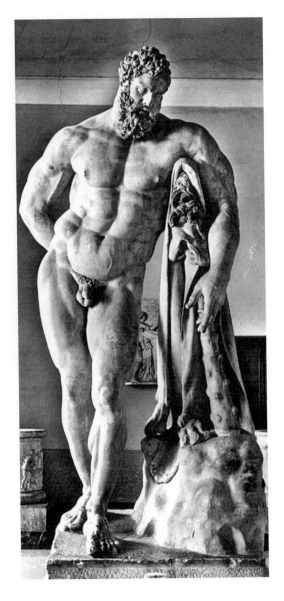

dable obstacle of all: his own death. Twice, Heracles voyages to the Underworld, undertaking the archetypal rite of passage that all heroes must fulfill in this most urgent of human quests—to find a loophole to escape the ultimate trap of mortality. On separate trips to the Underworld, Heracles brings back the cattle of the giant **Geryon** (who may be the herdsman of the dead) and **Cerberus**, the three-headed hound of Hades, shooting the King of the Underworld in the process. Having thus gone to the Land of the Dead and been reborn twice—having taken on Death (Hades) himself, and won—Heracles transcends the limits of the human condition, achieving literally what most heroes can achieve only in the form of an

FIGURE 10-7   Heracles' Third Labor: Pursuing the Cerynitian Hind. The two conflicting aspects of the hero illustrated in Figures 10-5 and 10-6 are captured in this vase painting: as the daring explorer, Heracles pursues the mythical Golden Hind into the unknown
North and brings back its golden antlers; as a creature of brute force, he wears the lion skin
and, relinquishing his weapons (here held for him by two goddesses, possibly Athene and
Artemis), he pulls off the antlers with his bare hands. *(British Museum, London)*

immortal reputation. Heracles, like most hero figures, thus mediates the most extreme of contradictions—not only those of nature and culture but those of life and
death as well.

The Death of Heracles

There are innumerable stories about Heracles apart from the labors, among them the
voyage with Jason and the Argonauts—another mythic anachronism, because Jason and the Argonauts do not appear until several generations after Heracles' death.
During that voyage, the tables are turned on Heracles. Like many Greek heroes, he
has an intimate, and even erotic, relationship with a young male friend, **Hylas,** who
disappears on shore, apparently abducted by a water nymph who falls in love with
him. (Freudian theorists see the water nymph—the pool maiden who lures men to
their deaths—as an expression of the fear of the female genitalia, much as decapitation of the Gorgon represents the male fear of castration.) Heracles' search for him
proves fruitless, and he is eventually forced to sail on without him.

FIGURE 10-8   Heracles and Nessus. In his last heroic exploit,
Heracles grabs Nessus by the hair and puts his foot on the creature's back, as the lying centaur offers one last gesture of supplication. This vase painting (c. 620 B.C.) is one of many illustrations of
Heracles' associations with the creatures whose physically divided
natures reflect his own inner divisions—part god, part brute. Nessus's role in the death of Heracles reflects the destructive potential
of the conflicting drives at work in the warrior-hero. *(National
Museum, Athens)*

The many sides of the hero are summed up in the story of Heracles' death. Having remarried, this time to **Deianeira** [dee-ya-NYE-ra], the sister of a friend, Heracles is still unable to rest contentedly at home. Eventually, weary of his erotic and
heroic escapades, Deianeira sets out in pursuit of Heracles, determined to bring him
home. Unable to cross a river in her path, she accepts a ride from a centaur, **Nessus,** who ferries her halfway across and then tries to rape her. Fortunately, Heracles
comes along just in time to shoot the centaur and rescue his wife (Figure 10-8). The
dying centaur offers Deianeira a way to ensure Heracles' commitment to her: he
tells her to collect Nessus's blood, now mixed with the poisonous blood of the Hydra on Heracles' arrows, and to smear it on his shirt. As dramatized in Sophocles'
Women of Trachis, when Heracles dons the shirt, the mixture eats through his flesh,
and, destroyed by Deianeira's attempt to domesticate him, Heracles dies in agony.

Heracles was said to have no grave. According to some versions of the myth,
his soul goes to the Underworld while only his reputation endures; other versions,
however, portray Heracles as raised up by the gods from his funeral pyre to dwell in
Olympus (Figure 10-9). There, he is reconciled to Hera and married to her daughter

FIGURE 10-9   The Apotheosis of Heracles. In this vase painting
(c. 410 B.C.), Heracles is raised from the funeral pyre and carried to the
heavens in Athene's chariot, leaving his clothing behind but taking his
club and lion skin with him. While satyrs look curiously at the place
where the missing corpse should have been, two women bring water to
put out the fire. *(Antikensammlungen, Munich)*

Hebe (whose name means "youth"), who may be a surrogate for the goddess herself,
fulfilling at last the quest for immortality that is central to the heroic endeavor.
As Hera's son-in-law, Heracles formally reconciled with the feminine powers, and
Hera and "the Glory" that is now truly hers are rejoined. Homer, combining both
versions in the *Odyssey* (Book 11), describes Heracles' human part remaining as a
shade in Hades while his divine self takes up residence with the gods. The hero remains divided in death as in life—as complex as human nature itself.

   With this final transfiguration, the ongoing conflict between the masculine hero
and the feminine principle is at last transcended. The hero can safely participate in
this *hieros gamos* (sacred marriage) between the hero and the goddess: because she is
no longer an obstacle to his pursuit of immortality, he is not compelled to abandon
her. Nor does he need to use violence or risk death to pursue the same goal. Thus,
the inherent contradictions in the hero's nature are at last resolved: in death, if not
in life, the beast and the god are reconciled.

Other Heroes: Theseus and Jason

Other heroes share many of the characteristics exemplified by the myths of Heracles: the divine parentage or ancestry; the amazing feats and pursuit of impossible
quests; the problems with the women in their lives; and, finally, despite their heroic

The Twelve Labors of Heracles

1. **Killing the Nemean lion,** whose hide was impervious to weapons. Heracles chokes the lion to death with his bare hands and uses its own claws to skin it. Thenceforth, he wears its pelt as a cloak. He also fashions his famous club at this time to substitute for his trademark bow.

2. **Killing the Hydra,** a many-headed water snake whose heads would immediately grow back when severed. To prevent the heads from regenerating, Heracles arranges for a friend to sear the necks with a torch as each head is severed. Heracles then applies its poisonous gall to his arrows. (Eurystheus refused to count this labor because Heracles had help.)

3. **Capturing the Golden Hind,** a golden-horned deer sacred to Artemis. To capture the deer, Heracles has to pursue it for a year. In some versions, he has to travel to the mythical North, the land of the Hyperboreans, to find it. (Note: the sequence of the third and fourth labors is sometimes reversed.)

4. **Capturing the Erymanthian boar,** which he has to pursue into territory occupied by the centaurs. While he is there, his host, the centaur Pholus, opens a barrel of wine, thereby attracting the other centaurs, who attack Heracles. Heracles drives them off, but in the process he accidentally wounds both his host and the good centaur, Chiron, with poisoned arrows.

5. **Cleaning the Augean stables,** for which Heracles demands a promise of payment from King Augeas. He accomplishes this unpleasant task by diverting the course of a river (or two) to wash through the barn. Because Augeas refuses to pay him, Heracles later returns with an army. (Eurystheus refused to count this labor, too, because Heracles demanded payment.)

6. **Removing the Stymphalian birds,** whose droppings were creating a public nuisance in an Arcadian town. (According to some versions, they also

achievements, their oddly nonheroic deaths. In addition, as the role of the hero and that of king or ruler converge, the lives of the heroes increasingly involve political problems.

Theseus

The hero **Theseus** follows (sometimes quite literally) in the footsteps of Heracles. His mother is Aethra, daughter of King Pittheus of Troezen; his father's identity is somewhat ambiguous, in that his mother slept with **Aegeus** [EE-jee-uhs] (king of Athens) and the sea god Poseidon on the same night. As a sign and test for the youngster, Aegeus leaves a sword and a pair of sandals under a heavy stone. Lifting the stone, the prodigious child Theseus asserts simultaneously his political and divine inheritance.

ate human flesh.) Heracles drives away these birds by using brass rattles to frighten them off and by shooting many of them as they fly away.

7. **Capturing the Cretan bull,** the bovine parent of the Minotaur. Bringing it back, Heracles releases it near Marathon. (Theseus has to recapture it later.)

8. **Capturing the Thracian horses,** property of King Diomedes. To tame the horses, which eat human flesh, Heracles feeds their owner to them. While the guest of King Admetus, Heracles rescues Admetus's wife, Alcestis, from death—actually wrestling with Death (Thanatos) in the process.

9. **Bringing back the girdle (belt) of Hippolyte,** the Amazon queen. Hippolyte gives the girdle to Heracles willingly, which angers Hera, who persuades the other Amazons that Heracles was actually kidnapping Hippolyte. When they attack Heracles' ship, he kills the queen, believing she has lied to him, and keeps the belt.

10. **Bringing back the cattle of Geryon,** the three-headed giant sometimes identified as the herdsman of the dead. On this trip, the hero sets up the Pillars of Heracles at the western entrance to the Mediterranean.

11. **Bringing back the Golden Apples of the Hesperides,** apples of immortality that grow on the Tree of Life in the garden in the mythical West, where the sun sets. According to some versions, the Titan Atlas retrieves the apples while Heracles holds up the sky in his place.

12. **Capturing Cerberus** (the three-headed, or fifty-headed, hound of Hades). In order to accomplish this task, Heracles is first initiated into the Eleusinian Mysteries to learn how to safely traverse the kingdom of Hades. In some versions, he shoots Hades himself, wounding him in the process.

Early Adventures   Rivaling Heracles in the number of tales told about him (variously recounted by Plutarch, Apollodorus, and others), Theseus is also similar to Heracles in the specific adventures he encounters (Figure 10-10). Setting out for Athens, the young Theseus rids the road of various threats to travelers: a robber who beats his victims with a bronze club (reminiscent of Heracles' club), which Theseus seizes; another who ties his victims to a pair of pine trees bent to the ground, which, when released, tear them in two; another who pushes his victims over a cliff to be devoured by a giant sea turtle; and another who wrestles all passersby to death. Like Heracles, Theseus kills a menacing wild boar. He also punishes Procrustes on the same iron bed used by the brigand to torture his victims.

Some of Theseus's adventures were actually identical to those of Heracles. Theseus, sent by his father (who was prompted, in turn, by his dangerous current wife, Medea) to catch the same Cretan bull once captured by Heracles, brings it back

FIGURE 10-10   The Deeds of Theseus. Surrounding the central illustration in which
Theseus kills the Minotaur, this vase painting depicts (clockwise from the top) the encounter with Corynetes, whose bronze club Theseus keeps after defeating this savage threat to
travelers; the defeat of Procrustes, on whose bed unwary travelers were either stretched or
cut off at the ankles if they did not fit; the battle with Sceiron, who robbed travelers after
pretending to wash their feet and then threw them off a cliff to be devoured by a giant
turtle; the capture of the Cretan bull, which Theseus brings back alive; the defeat of Sinis,
who killed travelers by tying them to one or two bent-over pine trees that he would then
release, either catapulting them to their deaths or tearing them in two; and the defeat of the
wild boar (or sow) whose father was Typhon. *(British Museum, London)*

successfully. The presence of this myth in the stories of both heroes suggests the
importance of destroying the power of the matriarchal goddesses on Crete, which,
long after Crete's disappearance as a political force, persisted as these deities were
absorbed into the Greek pantheon (see Chapter 11). And Heracles and Theseus,
several generations removed from each other, even share adventures. Theseus joins
Heracles on the voyage of the Argonauts and on his expedition against the Amazons. With Heracles, he is present at the Lapith wedding when the centaurs attack and helps drive them off. And, of course, Heracles rescues Theseus when he is
trapped in the Underworld (see Chapter 9).

The Labyrinth Theseus's most famous exploit is his adventure on Crete. By order of King Minos of Crete, the Athenians were forced to send a tribute of seven men and seven women every nine years to be devoured by the **Minotaur,** the hybrid offspring of Minos's wife, **Pasiphae** [pah-SIF-a-ee], and the Cretan bull. Hoping to free Athens from this threat, Theseus volunteers to go along as one of the seven men. Before Theseus departs, his father asks him to change his ship's black sail to a white one in the event of his successful return.

Attracted to the hero, Minos's daughter **Ariadne** [ar-ih-AD-nee] procures the help of **Daedalus** [DEE-duh-luhs], who informs Theseus how to kill the Minotaur and escape (via an unrolled ball of string) from the labyrinth where the Minotaur is kept (Figure 10-11). Theseus, of course, succeeds and returns to Athens but forgets to change sails. His father, seeing the ship approaching with black sails, believes his son has died and commits suicide by jumping off a cliff (or from the walls of Athens).

From a historical perspective, this myth may reflect a shift in the center of power in the Mediterranean from Crete to the mainland, thus ending the condition of the Greek coastal city-states as tributaries of the Cretan empire. Enormous Cretan palaces, such as the one at Knossos, with its endless rooms and corridors, could easily have given rise, as some historians have suggested, to legends of a "labyrinth" in its basement.

FIGURE 10-11 Theseus and the Minotaur. As shown in this vase painting, Theseus takes his sword to the Minotaur, here depicted with a human body but a bull's tail and head. As with Heracles and the centaurs, the multiple associations of hero with beasts (especially divided creatures like the Minotaur, half-man and half-bull) suggest the battle with the beast within: the savage drives normally repressed within the labyrinth of the unconscious that the life of the warrior-hero forces to the surface. *(British Museum, London)*

FIGURE 10-12   The Goddess of the Double Axe. In this wall painting from the palace of Minos (c. 1500 B.C.), the goddess (or her priestess) displays the labrys, or double-headed axe, to her worshipers. *(Knossos, Crete)*

Undoubtedly more significant are archaeologists' discoveries of shrines to the Minoan snake goddess built deep into the recesses of Cretan mountain caves, where bull horns and other images of the bull god, consort to the goddess, are also found. The entrances and underground passageways to these shrines themselves constitute a kind of labyrinth. The word *labrys,* furthermore, means "double-headed axe," and the labyrinth of the myth thus also suggests the palace at Knossos, where sculptures, wall paintings, and vases employ that symbol of the goddess, as well as the cave temples where she was worshiped (Figure 10-12) and where double-headed gold axes, presumably belonging to the goddess, have been found.

Some scholars note that Theseus appears to be a much later Athenian creation—the earliest visual representations appear in the seventh century B.C., and the earliest literary references date from the late sixth or early fifth century B.C.—which would deny in the Theseus myths reflections of any changes in Cretan or Mycenaean politics or religion. But the fact that Homer provides us with the first literary references to the Trojan War does not preclude some basis of historicity, preserved for centuries in oral tradition, in the myths of Troy. And references to Cretan politics or lifestyles or to the palace of Minos, long since buried (and excavated in our own time), should be no more surprising—or necessarily purely fantastic—than Homer's reference to citadels like Tiryns.

Questions of historicity aside, the archetypal components of the labrys, the central image of this myth, prevail. The double-headed axe, whose shape is recapitulated in the curved bull horns, is also associated with the butterfly, symbol of transformation. In the image of the labyrinth, then, life and death, sacrifice and renewal, converge on each other. From the mythic perspective, we can thus see in the story of Theseus's descent into the labyrinth the persistence of the Cretan snake goddess, herself the source of many of the Greek goddesses, part of whose worship was carried out in the Cretan bull dance painted on palace walls and numerous vases excavated at Knossos. Such ceremonies often involved the ritual mating of the goddess in her cow form with the bull god, who would then be sacrificed, perhaps in place of the king, to ensure the renewal of fertility. The intercourse between Queen

Pasiphae, in her cow costume, and the bull may be the narrative form of that ritual. Similarly, Theseus's entry into the center of the labyrinth, following the string that Ariadne offers (acting here in the role of priestess of the Goddess), suggests a retracing of the umbilical link to the womb where the mysteries of the Goddess are hidden, followed by rebirth into the upper world. And his killing of the bull and the subsequent destruction of the labyrinth may, some scholars suggest, reflect the shift from the ancient Cretan goddess religion to the patriarchal system that supplanted it in Greece.

Some scholars see the myths of Theseus, from his birth to his return to Athens, where he assumes his role as king, as a rite of passage that also charters Athenian initiation rites for ephebes (young men age eighteen to twenty during their period of military training). Theseus himself is credited with founding the Oschophoria, a ritual procession out of the city led by two boys dressed as girls. Leaving as immature boys who have not yet attained their adult male roles, and thus the equivalent of girls, they race back as men, proving their masculine skills as "swift-footed" athletes and warriors. The feast day of Theseus, the Thereia, a festival featuring competition in torch racing, javelin throwing, and other military exercises, likewise celebrated Theseus's mature role as warrior-king.

Theseus's Women   Women are involved in many of Theseus's adventures, as they are in those of Heracles, but none of the relationships ends happily. For example, Theseus sails from Crete with Ariadne but abandons her on the way home on the island of Naxos, where (according to variant myths) she is killed by Artemis, or marries the god Dionysus, or commits suicide, grieving for Theseus.

Theseus also seduces and/or defeats the Amazon queen Hippolyte (or her sister Antiope), whose forces then invade Athens but are, in turn, defeated. This relationship produces a son, **Hippolytus** [hip-PAHL-ih-tuhs], who comes to cause Theseus great distress. Having married **Phaedra** [FE-drah], the sister of Ariadne, Theseus leaves her with Hippolytus while he goes to Troezen. As dramatized in Euripides' play *Hippolytus,* Phaedra falls in love with the young man, but he refuses her advances, having taken a vow of celibacy in honor of the goddess Artemis. Furious at being rejected, Phaedra tells Theseus that Hippolytus raped her and then kills herself. Theseus calls on Poseidon to kill his son, and the god obligingly sends a bull from the sea to terrify Hippolytus's chariot horses, which bolt, overturning the chariot. Trapped in the reins, Hippolytus is dragged to his death. Artemis then informs Theseus that Hippolytus was innocent and that Aphrodite, angry at the boy's exclusive devotion to Artemis, is responsible for the catastrophe. In some oblique way, of course, Theseus's own unpredictable erotic urges are to blame. It was he, after all, who, driven by his lust, abandoned Ariadne for Phaedra and then, like Heracles, went off on other adventures, leaving Phaedra, in turn, alone.

The myths tell of many marriages of Theseus, but, like Heracles, he engages in no meaningful or lasting relationships. In yet another example of sexual misadventures, Theseus, along with his friend Pirithous, kidnaps the child Helen, in order to fulfill an ambition to marry a daughter of Zeus, something Heracles achieved only after death. The audacious pair then fix on a scheme to bring Persephone up from the Underworld for Pirithous. Both are bound by Hades to iron chairs for eternity, but only Pirithous remains in the nether realm. Theseus is rescued from the Underworld by Heracles, but his relationship with the feminine powers remains destructive. The hero can no more domesticate the divine than the human women in his life can domesticate the hero.

Political Problems   Theseus's kidnapping of Helen brings down the wrath of the Spartans, who attack Athens, rescue her in Theseus's absence, and establish a rival, Menestheus, on the throne. This is not the first time Theseus has to protect his rule against usurpers. Earlier, Medea had played on his father's rivalry with his uncle Pallas, brother to Aegeus, who, with his fifty sons, kept trying to take over rulership of Athens. When Medea persuades Aegeus to send Theseus to capture the Cretan bull, it is with the hope that he won't return, so that her own sons can succeed to the throne. This failing, she tries to poison Theseus, but Aegeus fortunately recognizes the sword his son wears and foils her plan. Pallas and his sons repeatedly rebel, and eventually Theseus kills them, but he has to go into exile to Troezen as a result. Despite the political threats, Theseus manages to unify Athens, form a central government, and forge alliances with surrounding towns, thus establishing his own dominions.

In fact, one scholar, Henry J. Walker, insists that the Athenians co-opted and expanded on the already popular Theseus myths in order to develop a specifically Athenian hero, the equivalent of Heracles, who was the pride of Sparta. Thus, Theseus is credited with unifying Attica and protecting Athens, its main city-state, from invasion. In 476 B.C., the Athenians are said to have been instructed by an oracle to find the body of Theseus and bring it to Athens, where his central cults and shrines were located. Theseus's deeds were celebrated in sculptures decorating the Athenian treasury at Delphi, as well as the Parthenon. He was even associated with Athenian democracy, although in the myths he rules Athens as a king, and Athenian politicians explicitly identified themselves with their hero. In one version (Euripides' *Suppliant Women*), Theseus is depicted as bequeathing his kingdom to the Athenian people, and was thus credited with inspiring the Athenian constitution.

The Death of Theseus   Theseus's death may also have resulted from political rivalries. Traveling to Scyrus to get allies to help him evict the usurper Menestheus, Theseus either falls or is pushed off a cliff, recapitulating the death of his own father. Like Heracles' death, however, Theseus's less-than-glorious demise is followed by a transfiguration to divine status. Honored by the Athenians—who believed that the spirit of Theseus watched over their city, aiding them in the war against the Persians and even appearing at the Battle of Marathon—Theseus was worshiped as a god.

Jason

The most equivocal of the heroes, **Jason** shares the heroic traits of Heracles and Theseus—the divine ancestry, the search for glory, the performing of impossible tasks—but in a somewhat diminished (if not ironic) and oddly eclectic form. Thus, although we have a single extended source for most of the details, it almost seems as if the myth of Jason were constructed from scraps of the myths of other heroes.

The son of Aeson of Iolcos, Jason is the grandson of Aeolus, who may be the wind god or a human with the same name. Aeson's brother, **Pelias** [PEE-lih-uhs], usurped the throne of Iolcos, so when Jason is born, his parents have him raised in secret by the centaur Chiron. Also reminiscent of Theseus's myth, a sandal is one of the signs Jason displays on his return. Pelias had been told by an oracle that a man descended from Aeson and wearing one sandal would kill him: on the trip to Iolcos, Jason loses one sandal while helping Hera, disguised as an old woman, cross a river. Thus, according to one account, when Jason returns to Iolcos lacking one sandal, Pelias recognizes him instantly and determines to get rid of him.

The Golden Fleece   To dispose of Jason, Pelias sends him to obtain the **Golden Fleece.** This is an impossible mission given that the fleece is located in the distant land of Colchis, ruled by King Aeetes, who has a reputation for treating visitors abominably. To gain glory, Jason, like Perseus and Theseus, accepts this challenge and sets about organizing an expedition—one of the most famous in Greek mythology—of **Argonauts** (sailors on the ship the *Argo,* commissioned for this purpose). All the heroes—whether of Jason's generation or not, including Heracles, Orpheus, and, in some versions, Theseus, share the quest (Figure 10-13). After a series

FIGURE 10-13   Attic Red Figure Crater from Orvieto. Except for the figures of Athene, wearing a warrior's helmet and carrying a spear (left), and Heracles, wearing a lion skin and holding a club (center), easily identifiable by their characteristic insignia or apparel, scholars disagree on the identities of the other figures. Although commonly described as a scene depicting the Argonauts who accompanied Jason on his quest for the Golden Fleece, the painting (c. 450 B.C.) may, in fact, represent Heracles' descent into the Underworld. If so, the two seated heroes are Theseus and his friend Pirithous, who had rashly invaded Hades' realm to abduct Persephone as a wife for Pirithous (see Chapter 9). *(Louvre, Paris)*

FIGURE 10-14   Jason Approaching the Golden Fleece. In this vase painting, Athene is shown overseeing Jason's approach to the Golden Fleece. Her presence underscores Jason's heroism here, in contrast to his later adventures, from which she is conspicuously absent. *(Metropolitan Museum of Art)*

of adventures in which they do battle with human rivals and monsters, propitiate the Phrygian mother goddess Cybele, and avoid, with Athene's help, being crushed by the Clashing Rocks, they arrive at Colchis.

Hera, meanwhile, has a vested interest in the quest: having been insulted by Pelias, who worships the other gods but scorns Hera, she wants Pelias dead and believes that no one but **Medea** [me-DEE-a] can accomplish that. Thus, she wants Jason to bring Medea back with him. Athene also supports the operation, and Aphrodite assists by causing Medea to fall in love with Jason on his arrival (Figure 10-14).

Just as Ariadne did with Theseus, Medea helps Jason obtain the Golden Fleece, but with a difference. Before Aeetes will give Jason the fleece, he orders the hero to perform another impossible feat: he must yoke a fire-breathing bull, plow a field, and sow it with dragon's teeth, left over, apparently, from the founding of Thebes by **Cadmus.** Just as in the Theban myth, Jason must kill the armed men who germinate from these teeth. Protected by a drug that Medea gives him, which he applies to himself and his weapons, Jason performs the task, only to find that Aeetes reneges on his promise and plans to attack the Argonauts.

Jason must therefore steal the fleece and escape in secret. But unlike Theseus, who killed the Minotaur, Jason doesn't actually fight the serpent or dragon guarding the tree on which the Golden Fleece is hung; rather, Medea, trusting Jason's promise to marry her, just as Ariadne had trusted Theseus's, casts a spell to put the creature to sleep so that Jason can safely remove the object of his quest. To prevent pursuit by Aeetes, Medea kills and dismembers the corpse of her younger brother, tossing the pieces in the sea so that her father will be obliged to stop and retrieve them in order to give his son a proper burial. Not even the savage Heracles, who cut off the ears and noses of his enemy's ambassadors, could match such gratuitous violence.

The Role of Hecate   As Perseus was aided by Athene, so Jason continues to be helped by Medea. But again, although both Athene and Hera continue to support the Argonauts' mission, the contrasts are significant: Perseus attacks the Gorgons, the terrifying aspect of the primordial Goddess, and delivers up their power to the Olympian goddess Athene; Jason, for his part, propitiates the chthonic powers, performing rituals in honor of **Hecate** [HEK-uh-tee] (some of whose powers Medea shares) both before and after his trials. It is the power of Hecate that allows him both to obtain the fleece and to escape afterward. And whereas heroes like Theseus and Heracles descend to the Underworld to subdue the power of Hades and defy mortality, Jason enters only the barbaric region of Colchis, portrayed in myth as a remote and savage place where witchcraft and sorcery flourish and where, rather than defy the chthonic powers, he succumbs to them.

From this point on, the acts that Jason allows Medea to perform on his behalf become even more appalling, while Jason himself behaves increasingly less like a hero and more like a self-serving coward who uses women as a means to gain his objectives. Ultimately, his quest for glory yields to a crass desire for wealth and status. Meanwhile, the Olympians who supported the Argonauts' voyage disappear. In the absence of the gods, the tension between the human and the divine that sustained, however tragically, the heroic endeavor likewise vanishes. The myths of Jason seem to fall into two distinct groups: the more conventional, heroic stories from his birth and early adventures through the capture of the Golden Fleece, and those depicting his return and the subsequent events, in which the heroic quest for victory over time—for the power of immortality—degenerates into a quest for power in merely human, and thus venial, terms.

Jason's Return   When Jason returns with the Golden Fleece, his uncle Pelias— who has in the meantime killed Jason's father and thereby prompted his mother's suicide—is still on the throne. Medea, however, trading on her reputation as a sorceress, convinces Pelias's daughters that their aging father will be rejuvenated if they kill him, dismember the corpse, and cook it. They perform Medea's prescribed ritual—but, of course, without the desired result.

Having succeeded to the throne of Iolcos by this somewhat questionable method, Jason forfeits the trust of the people, and he and Medea are forced to leave. Whereas other heroes typically have strong regional associations—Perseus and Heracles with Mycenae and Tiryns, for example, and Theseus with Athens—Jason, already abandoned by the gods, becomes a man without a country. Emigrating to Corinth, he and Medea set up residence and have two children. But Jason is not content and, as dramatized in Euripides' *Medea* (see Chapter 17), decides to fulfill his ambition for power by abandoning Medea and marrying the princess of Corinth, daughter of King Creon, an ironic inversion of the typical heroic achievement of status in spite of or even in defiance of marriage. He also demands custody of the two children, claiming that he can support them better as spouse of the princess than he can as Medea's common-law husband.

Medea   Refusing to yield, Medea poisons the princess and King Creon and (at least in Euripides' version) kills the children. She then escapes in a dragon-powered chariot to Athens, where she has been promised asylum by King Aegeus in return for her promise to cure his infertility. (The child thus conceived, when Aegeus stops off briefly in Troezen and makes love to Aethra as he is returning to Athens, turns out to be none other than Theseus, who, in the typically timeless world of intersecting myths, had already accompanied Jason on his voyage to Colchis.)

In her role as the source of fertility, as in her continuing connection with dragons—the dragon that guards the Golden Fleece and the winged dragon that pulls the chariot given to her as a gift by her grandfather, Helios—Medea carries out the creative and transformative functions of the primordial Goddess. But as was true of Medusa, with whom Medea shares a link with the serpents/dragons and the sunchariot, these powerful symbols are now reinterpreted, as was the role of Medea's divine counterpart, Hecate, in a more perverse and terrifying fashion as evidence of her witchcraft. Nevertheless, Medea drives the chariot of the sun, and unlike Phaethon, whose attempt to drive the vehicle ended in a fatal crash, she has no difficulty. The powers she commands are so awesome that it's no wonder Jason is no match for her. If the sky gods and the heroes who emulate them have succeeded in decapitating the ancient Goddess, driving her underground and transforming her into a witch or sorceress, then in figures like Medea the Goddess has her revenge.

The Death of Jason   Jason's death is the most inglorious of all of the heroes'. Bereft of friends and family as he sits, dejected, under the prow of his rotting ship, he is killed when a beam falls and hits him on the head. Jason is not elevated—as are Theseus, Perseus, and Heracles—to the status of divinity, nor is he made into the object of a cult. With Jason, in death as in the latter part of his life, the hero figure has reached a new low.

The Upper Limits of Human Ambition: Phaethon

The Greeks were fascinated by heroes in the excessive Heracleian mold—indeed, they admired no hero more than Achilles, who shares many of the earlier heroes' qualities. But a society that came to value the Apollonian way of self-knowledge and moderation could hardly maintain that such heroes were appropriate role models. If myths about Heracleian heroes emphasize the transcendent elements of the fractionalized hero—half-human, half-divine—other myths, providing an alternative perspective on the heroic impulse, reminded the Greeks of the necessary limits on human ambition. The myths of Icarus (see Chapter 2) and Phaethon, young men who defy those limits, reinforce the need for humans to be aware of their own limitations and to exercise self-control. But no one makes songs to the memories of those who walk the middle way: the Golden Mean is not the road that heroes travel.

When Clymene tells her son **Phaethon** [FEE-e-thahn] that he is actually the son of Helios, the sun god, the young man travels to the god's palace and requests proof of his divine paternity. Helios (or Apollo, in Ovid's later retelling in the *Metamorphoses*) promises to grant any wish that his son might make. Admiring the glorious chariot of the sun that his father drives, Phaethon asks to drive it himself for one day. Although he knows that the chariot is beyond the boy's powers, Helios is bound by his promise and reluctantly yields.

Phaethon is eager to test the power of the marvelous vehicle and starts off with great exuberance, but, as his father predicted, he loses control of the steeds. They veer off course: first, bolting up into the heavens, they leave a visual reminder of the havoc Phaethon causes, the great scar of the Milky Way; then, careening down, they set the earth on fire from the intense heat of the sun. To save the earth from destruction, Zeus is forced to kill Phaethon with a lightning bolt. Once again, overconfidence and the desire to take on tasks better suited to the gods prove deadly. Mortals need to be reminded: half-divine is simply not enough.

(Many other figures illustrate the heroic experiences in a variety of ways. For primary readings illustrating the myths of heroes, see Chapters 12 and 13, on the Homeric epics, and Chapters 15–17, on the Athenian tragedies.)

. . . .

Questions for Discussion and Review

1. In what ways is Perseus similar to Heracles and Theseus? In what ways is he different? Discuss the ways in which their semidivine natures influence their adventures, their relationships with women, and their political affairs, as well as their status after death.

2. For the heroes of Greek myths, the ultimate adventure is going to the Underworld and coming back alive. Why do Heracles and Theseus venture to the Underworld? How does the quest help them achieve the immortality they desire?

3. The standard pattern of the heroic rite of passage includes the hero's separation from his normal environment, his initiation to or encounter with supernatural forces, and his return bearing some new understanding to share with his community. Choose a significant example from the adventures of Perseus, Heracles, and Theseus, and explain how each follows this pattern. In each case, what new understanding does the hero achieve?

4. Does Jason also undergo a rite of passage? Explain what elements of Jason's adventures fit the archetypal pattern of separation and initiation. Does Jason also return with any new insight or understanding? Explain your position.

Heroines of Myth:
Women in Many Roles

KEY TOPICS/THEMES

The patterns of the heroines' stories differ from those of the heroes. The most common type of heroine is the "perfect" wife or mother of the hero, who serves him all her life and remains loyal even after his death. She may even, like Alcestis, offer to die for him. Other heroines, sometimes described as "helper maidens," aid heroes in completing their journeys or fulfilling their tasks. When such heroines, like Ariadne, switch roles and become lovers of the heroes, however, they often are abandoned. Rejecting the role of victim, some heroines try to be heroes on the masculine model, attempting to outdo the heroes at their own game, as Clytemnestra does. But such attempts to violate gender roles invariably either fail or are fatal to the heroine. Alternatively, still other heroines, like Iphigenia, embrace catastrophe from the outset, entering the Underworld as brides of Death. The smallest but most impressive group of heroines combine the best elements of the other types and succeed in attaining their goals and relating to their hero-husbands or lovers. In rare instances, they may even, like Psyche, achieve immortality.

The Heroine: Women's Mysteries in a Man's World

Heroine is a term that must be used with caution in describing women in Greek mythology. Certainly, in many myths, females play a central role, and in the literary works based on mythic themes, such as the plays of the great Greek dramatists, females are often the protagonists. But unlike their male counterparts, who embodied the ideal of the warrior that most young boys would aspire to emulate, women in the myths are rarely held up as models for young girls, and even more rarely for the same qualities of strength and courage that the male heroes displayed.

Nor do the heroines often go on quests or engage in combat with monsters or gods. Although a few, such as Andromeda, become constellations, they usually are granted that gift only when their husbands likewise achieve stellar status. Furthermore, the ultimate lure of ascension to divinity does not motivate heroines, as it does the heroes. There are no heroines who seek, as Gilgamesh does, to live forever, or even, like Heracles, Achilles, or Hector, to leave behind a name that will endure for eternity, repeating the pattern of the gods, who want to rule forever (and thus try to destroy their children). In fact, even when women are granted divine status and transformed into goddesses, their names are usually changed, so that the prospect of earning an "immortal name" has no meaning for them. Ino, for example, a sister of Semele who is driven mad and kills her children, is transformed into a sea goddess and renamed Leukothea. And although cults were established and offerings made to these figures, they were made under the new name or under that of the goddess with whom the heroine was associated. For the women, perhaps reflecting the cyclical pattern of the Creator goddess whose role is cosmic maintenance, eternal life happens, if they are fortunate, through the survival of their children. This is why the myths of Hecuba and Andromache, who lose all their children (as in Euripides' *Trojan Women*), are so tragic.

Women's Rituals

These differences reflect similar contrasts in the rites of passage for women. The archetypal male rite of passage involves the initiate's separation from the community, isolation while he grapples with supernatural forces, and victorious return to the community bearing new insights into himself and his relationship to society, the gods, and the cosmos. For the Greek heroes, it is the goddess Athene, embodying the wisdom of Zeus and the martial skill of the warrior, who supports them in their trials. The female rites of passage, in contrast, are collective rather than individual experiences. And it is the goddess Artemis who not only presides over the initiation of young girls but also is usually associated with the lives of the heroines thereafter.

The initiation ritual for girls was called the Brauronia, after the location of Artemis's shrine at Brauron, in Attica, where the ritual, performed by girls before they reached puberty, took place. The most important part of the ritual was the Arkteia, in which the girls ran as "bears," either nude or wearing short garments (Figure 11-1). It is instructive that a man becomes a full-fledged hero by killing a savage beast—whether lion, boar, or monster—while a girl becomes a woman by becoming one. Races are not unusual in women's initiations in many cultures. Bruce Lincoln, in his study of women's rituals, describes how Navajo girls, for example, undergo the "Kinaalda of Changing Woman," which also includes a race in which the initiands pursue the course of the sun and reenact creation—the emergence of life from successive underworlds onto the earth's surface. Participating in the initiation ritual, the girl is led to understand her relationship to the world of nature.

In the Brauronia, the connection to the natural world is emphasized through the act of playing the bear. Artemis, of course, as goddess of the beasts, is the bear

FIGURE 11-1　The Brauronia. This fragment of a vase painting (c. 440–430 B.C.) shows girls racing in the nude, while bear and deer, symbols of the goddess Artemis, are depicted in the lower section. *(Israel Museum, Jerusalem)*

goddess, and she often appears as a doe or a she-bear. But she is also goddess of the hunt and thus unites the pursuing huntress with the hunted animal—life with death—as did the primordial goddesses themselves. Not surprisingly, Artemis has links with all three levels of the cosmos: with the heavens, both as Olympian twin sister of Apollo and in her connection with the lunar cycle; with the earth as the lady of the beasts; and with the Underworld in her association with Hecate, her Underworld counterpart. Furthermore, as a virgin goddess who nevertheless is patron of childbirth, she prepares young girls for their roles as brides and future mothers. In fact, the clothes of women who died in childbirth (shot by the golden arrows of Artemis, as those who succumbed to disease were shot by the silver arrows of her twin, Apollo) were offered to Artemis at Brauron.

Running as a bear, each girl enters the sisterhood of Artemis and, leaving the cave of her childhood hibernation behind, becomes the bear goddess, as well as her eventual potential victim. For, unlike Artemis herself and her small band of followers who shun the society of men, the initiand cannot become a virgin goddess: for a female, marriage and subsequent motherhood were the only ways to enter adult society. The inevitable end of the chase is perhaps best revealed in the fate of **Callisto,** one of Artemis's followers. Attracted to her but unable to approach one who avoids male society, Zeus tricks Callisto by disguising himself as Artemis until it is too late for her to escape. Impregnated by the god, Callisto is forced to leave Artemis's band of followers. After the birth of her son, Callisto is turned into a bear—a clear insult to the bear goddess—by Hera, angered by her husband's infidelity and the means he used to carry it out, or perhaps by Artemis herself. Callisto wanders in the forest alone for years while her son Arcas grows up not knowing his mother. One day while out hunting, he encounters the she-bear and is prevented from unwittingly committing matricide only by the intervention of Zeus himself, who transforms Callisto into the Great Bear constellation. The tale of Callisto underlines the fate of a woman who refuses the conventional path. Callisto can never return to her human self—even enshrined in the heavens, she remains perpetually the Bear.

The girl racing as a she-bear in the Brauronia ritual celebrates the final moments of the freedom of childhood, before puberty transforms her into a woman, ready to accept her sexuality and enter the world where men—and gods—prevail. Prepared by her understanding of both the role she must relinquish and the one she must soon assume, the initiand is ready for the onset of puberty and the marriage that will follow: in the life of a woman, Artemis must become Persephone.

The Amazons

There were, of course, women in Greek mythology who refused this path, who manifested skills and insisted on freedoms associated with those of the warrior-heroes. The **Amazons,** a tribe of formidable female warriors who lived apart from men, engaged in combat with most of the male heroes: Bellerophon, Heracles, and Theseus, for example, all fought and defeated the Amazons (Figure 11-2), and Achilles is described as having done battle with the Amazon queen, Penthesilia (Figure 11-3), only realizing after having killed her and removed her armor that she was a woman (see Chapter 12). But whereas standing up to Achilles confirms the Trojan Hector

FIGURE 11-2 Heracles and the Amazons. In this vase painting (c. 560 B.C.), Heracles, in his lion skin, is attacking an Amazon named Andromache (not Hector's wife), as other soldiers fight other Amazon warriors. *(Courtesy Museum of Fine Arts, Boston)*

FIGURE 11-3   Achilles and Penthesilia. This vase painting (c. 530 B.C.) shows Achilles about to kill the Amazon queen Penthesilia. In this version, Penthesilia wears a leopard skin cloak, reminiscent of Heracles' lion skin. *(British Museum, London)*

as a true hero, being a worthy opponent to Achilles made Penthesilia—an Amazon! Then, as now, to be an "Amazon" was to be an aberration, a kind of monstrosity, like the dragon that the hero, defender of civilization, must destroy, thus putting these savage, upstart females back in their place. The skills displayed by female warriors in such myths never suggested the possibility that a normal woman could, given equivalent encouragement and training, wield weapons, serve in the military, or exhibit the courage or develop the physical skills of men. Indeed, Amazons seem to have existed in myths largely to be defeated by male heroes—unless they were abducted and made to conform to the standard social model. The Amazon queen Antiope (or Hippolyte), for example, was abducted by Theseus and bore him a son, Hippolytus.

Patterns of the Heroine Myths

In Greek mythology, as in Greek society, the male clearly is the norm. As many readers have noted, Hesiod speaks of the "damnable race of women," as if they are less than fully human—artificial creatures, attractive on the outside but serving to undermine the world of men. Thus, heroes abound while heroines are rather scarce. And when women in the myths are heroines, they are always portrayed in terms of their relationship to their fathers or sons, husbands or lovers—the real "heroes." In that capacity, those who properly fulfill those roles, as defined from the men's perspective, are held up as models of loyalty and obedience (such as Alcestis, or Helen in Euripides' *Helen*). Those who, for various reasons, refuse to do so are condemned as whores (such as Helen in the *Iliad* or Clytemnestra in Aeschylus's *Agamemnon*), witches (such as Medea), or monsters (such as Agave). But the rewards of wifely virtue and the consequences of rebellion end up the same: the women who are loyal and obedient to their hero-husbands often end up as widows, typically either enslaved or themselves soon dead as well; those who defy the established order often end up being killed or martyring themselves. And whereas deceased male heroes have songs and stories immortalizing their deeds, have cults established in their honor, and may even be deified, the women rarely enjoy such consolations.

The heroines in the myths, then, fall into several patterns, which sometimes overlap. First are the wives or mothers of heroes, whose bravery consists of remaining loyal even in the face of death (unless rescued by a male hero). Second are the helper-maidens, whose function is to assist the heroes in their quests (often to be unceremoniously dumped when their assistance is no longer needed). Next, the hero "impersonators" are strong, independent women who step outside the boundaries of traditional gender roles and, in conscious imitation of the heroes, defy kings or kill their enemies, only to be deemed traitors or murderers, and thus be exiled or killed. Then there are the brides of Death (Hades), who martyr themselves rather than compromise their integrity. Finally, there are the victorious heroines, exceptional women who somehow manage to retain their independence and to pursue their goals aggressively and yet remain within the context of gender-coded behavior. Typically, these women are not yet married or are married but long separated from their husbands. But the conditional, derivative nature of such "independence" is reflected in the fact that all of these exceptional women are fortunate in having fathers, suitors, or husbands who are unusual in their willingness to submit to the women's judgments. As Euripides' Medea notes, the rare woman who is lucky enough to have a good husband can find happiness; a woman not so lucky is condemned to a life of grief (see Chapter 17). But unlike Persephone, even if she finds marriage to be hell, she cannot return to her mother.

The Heroine as Mother or Wife

As might be expected, the role of the heroine in Greek mythology reflects the role of women in Greek society. Thus, the most frequently occurring role of the heroine is that of the mother or wife of the hero, with variants as daughter/sister or concubine/slave. As idealized in these roles as the male heroes are in theirs, the heroines are expected to be submissive, obedient, and loyal, no matter what—even willing to risk death to remain true to their husbands, just as their male counterparts are portrayed as willing to risk death to attain glory.

Mothers and Daughters of the Heroes

To be the mother of a hero, of course, a woman must first be the consort of a god. For the human mother of semidivine heroes, the experience of the divine *raptus* is the high point of their lives, and the consequences they suffer afterward are decidedly unpleasant. The most extreme example is **Semele,** impregnated by Zeus, who comes to her in human form. But when, goaded by Hera, she insists on making love to the god in his natural form (as lightning), she has a brief but electrifying experience and then, consumed by the fire of divine passion, goes up in smoke. Thus, Zeus has to rescue his son, who will become the incarnated god, Dionysus, and implant the fetus in his thigh (see Chapter 8). In some versions, Semele (renamed Thyone) is immortalized, but given that what she wanted was not immortal life but divine love, this could hardly have consoled her.

   Those women who experience the divine passion in mediated form may survive the encounter, but their lives are no happier for it. Danae, for example has her moment of bliss as she is inseminated by Zeus's golden rain (Figure 11-4), but although Zeus prevents Danae and the child Perseus from drowning, she is thereafter harassed by one man after another and must repeatedly be saved from potential rape by Perseus. In Euripides' *Heracleidae* (the children of Heracles), both Heracles' mother, Alcmene, and his children are endangered once the hero is no longer available to protect them, because Heracles' old nemesis Eurystheus, who imposed the labors on the hero, seeks their death. When Eurystheus leads his army to Athens, where Heracles' family has taken refuge, an oracle predicts that the only way to save the city from destruction is to sacrifice a virgin to Persephone. In the play, Macaria, Heracles' daughter, bravely volunteers to die, willing to sacrifice herself in order to save the city and her brothers. For this, she is praised as a truly heroic woman, a worthy daughter of her father. And although the rest of the family is eventually rescued through the divine intervention of the deified Heracles and Hebe, the message is clear: heroes are brave if they fight their enemies; heroines are brave if they sacrifice themselves. It is, in fact, typically women who are sacrificed in the myths. (In a rare exception, such as Euripides' *Iphigenia Among the Taurians,* in which male sacrifice is threatened, this gender reversal is proof that the scene occurs in

FIGURE 11-4   Danae and the Shower of Gold. In this vase painting (c. 410 B.C.), Danae reclines on her couch, readying herself to receive Zeus's shower of gold, which will engender the child Perseus. *(Louvre, Paris)*

a "savage" country, and not in "civilized" Greece, where Iphigenia herself was the designated sacrifice.)

Wives of the Heroes

The wives of the heroes fare no better. Hecuba, queen and wife of Priam, king of Troy, as well as mother of Hector, is taken into slavery when the city falls, as is Hector's wife, Andromache. In Euripides' *Trojan Women,* Andromache laments that, the more she embodied the wifely virtues, the more she made herself attractive to the Greeks as a slave. She describes how she worked at being the most virtuous wife possible—staying indoors, avoiding gossip, remaining quiet in her husband's presence. In Euripides' *Andromache,* she adds that, to please Hector, she joined him in admiring the women with whom he had affairs. She even went so far as to nurse Hector's illegitimate children, outdoing Hera, goddess of marriage, herself, who in a similar situation refused to nurse Heracles. The result of such absolute loyalty to a man who insists on seeking glory on the battlefield despite his awareness that his death will result in her enslavement (see Chapter 12), is that her son is killed and she becomes the slave of **Neoptolemus,** son of Achilles, who killed her husband. She then finds herself in the same situation—she and her child by Neoptolemus are threatened with death, and Neoptolemus himself is killed. Again, the reward for the sacrifices she makes as a dutiful wife (or slave) is loss and death and the opportunity to continue to sacrifice.

Heracles' wife, Megara, experiences an even more calamitous end to her role as hero's wife. Threatened by Lycus, who usurps Heracles' rulership while the hero is in the Underworld, Megara (as depicted in Euripides' *Heracles*) offers to die, along with her sons, to preserve her dignity. Her husband returns just in time to rescue his family, but almost immediately he goes mad and kills both Megara and their children. Once again, marriage to a hero proves deadly.

Alcestis: The Model Wife

The most extreme example, and the one held up as the ideal model of a loyal wife, is **Alcestis**. The eldest daughter of Pelias, king of Iolcus, Alcestis is admired both for her virtue and for her beauty. She has so many suitors for marriage that her father resorts to a contest for the bride of the kind that abounds in fairy tales: to win her hand, a suitor must harness two wild beasts to a chariot. Aided by Apollo, **Admetus** succeeds in harnessing a lion and a boar, and so wins his bride.

Admetus, ruler of Pherae, is a good man and an especially good host. When Apollo, forced to serve for a year as slave to a mortal as punishment for an offense to Zeus, is sent to serve Admetus, the latter refuses to take advantage of the god's position and treats him as an honored guest, thus endearing himself to the god. However, despite Admetus's piety and the mutual love that he and his new bride share, the marriage has a rather inauspicious beginning. It seems that Admetus, filled with gratitude to Apollo, forgot to honor Artemis, who prepares young girls for adulthood and marriage. Artemis expresses her anger by filling the bridal chamber with snakes. And although Admetus, when informed of his omission, makes the requisite sacrifices, the bride, in entering her marriage bed, has entered into the nightmare chasm of the Underworld, where the serpent goddess resides: in marriage, even to a virtuous and worthy man, every woman reenacts the experience of Persephone.

Alcestis bears two children, but her happiness is cut short when Admetus falls ill and dies. According to various versions of the myth, Apollo either persuades Artemis or tricks the Fates (by getting them drunk) and thereby obtains permission to release Admetus from the Underworld, if a substitute can be found. In a reversal of the usual mythological pattern wherein the goddess, descending to the Underworld, wins release by providing a substitute, usually her husband or consort (as in the Sumerian-Babylonian myths of Inanna/Ishtar and Dumuzi/Tammuz, or its many variants, from the Egyptian Isis and Osiris to Aphrodite and Adonis in the Greek tradition), in this case it is Alcestis who dutifully offers herself as the substitute for her husband when his elderly parents refuse to sacrifice themselves.

Alcestis willingly goes with Thanatos, god of death, to the Underworld, while her inconsolable husband mourns for her—although his love didn't stop him from accepting her offer. Alcestis thus becomes what she has, in fact, been from the moment of her entry into the marriage chamber—indeed, from the moment she entered that chariot ominously yoked to wild beasts—like Persephone herself, a bride of Death. (Reinforcing the connection to Persephone, some scholars claim that Alcestis was at one time, in early Greek culture, an Underworld goddess figure like Persephone at Pherae, with Admetus a version of Hades.)

Alcestis's reenacting of Persephone's experiences is completed when, in one version of the story, Persephone, sharing the admiration of the gods for Alcestis's extreme devotion to her husband's welfare, releases her, sending her back to her husband. In other versions, such as the one in Euripides' play *Alcestis,* it is Heracles, happening to arrive as a guest in Admetus's house just as the funeral procession begins, who defeats Thanatos in a wrestling match and gains the power to resurrect his host's dead wife. Thus, although both the hero Heracles and the heroine Alcestis, in their respective myths, enter the Underworld and return, only he does so on his own powers, fighting with Death (as he has done before); she depends on her male rescuer. And whereas Heracles, as a result of his Underworld journeys, undergoes a symbolic rebirth that will have its counterpart in his ascension to Olympus, Alcestis merely gets sent back to that same marriage chamber.

Admetus is overjoyed to have his wife back. However, he is far more apologetic, in Euripides' play, to Heracles for having, in his grief, neglected his duties as a host than he is to his wife for having accepted her offer in the first place. Alcestis's own feelings about being returned to an ostensibly loving husband who let her dwell in the Underworld in his place aren't addressed in the play. But she is held up forever after as a model wife—an example for all Greek wives to emulate.

The Heroine as Helper-Maiden

Electra

A variant of the heroine as wife or mother of the hero is the helper-maiden (who may or may not be the hero's spouse, lover, or sister), whose role is to assist the hero in fulfilling his quest. **Electra,** for example, is credited with assisting her brother, Orestes, in avenging the murder of their father, Agamemnon (see Chapter 15). In Aeschylus's *Libation Bearers* and Sophocles' *Electra,* she is portrayed as encouraging her brother and assisting him in gaining access to the palace and the intended victims, their mother, Clytemnestra, and her lover, Aegisthus. When Orestes, driven mad and pursued by the Furies, is required by Apollo to go into exile to expiate Clytemnestra's murder, Electra, whose role is clearly secondary, even insignificant, is left behind (see Chapter 15). In Euripides' version, the roles are almost reversed: portrayed as hating her mother, Electra deceives Clytemnestra by pretending to be pregnant, in order to entrap her, and actually stabs Clytemnestra herself. Perhaps because she shares the role of "hero" here, and is not simply Orestes' assistant, her reward is to be married to his friend Pylades.

Medea

Most helper-maidens end up in decidedly less pleasant circumstances. And they seem to multiply the risk if, having served as helper-maiden to the hero, they opt to become his wife or lover as well. Medea, for example, helps the Argonaut, Jason, obtain the Golden Fleece from the dragon that guards it, on the condition that he take her with him from the remote land of Colchis to Greece as his wife. She

FIGURE 11-5   Dionysus and Ariadne. Greek image from Falerii
Veteres. In this painting, Ariadne is represented as one of Dionysus's
maenads. *(Museo Nazionale de Villa Giulia, Roma, Italy)*

continues to assist him to overcome the obstacles he encounters (for an extended
discussion of Medea, see Chapter 17), but none of that prevents Jason from abandoning her for a younger, wealthier, and better-connected woman.

Ariadne

Ariadne, daughter of King Minos of Crete, has a similar experience as helper-
maiden. Having fallen in love with Theseus, Ariadne helps him by giving him
instructions on how to kill the Minotaur and escape the labyrinth; like Medea, she
does so on the condition that he take her with him afterward. Although Theseus,
like Jason, succeeds thanks to her assistance, he does not reward her as promised.
Having escaped with Ariadne and her younger sister, Phaedra, on board his ship,
he abandons Ariadne on the island of Naxos and marries Phaedra instead. In some
versions of the myth, Ariadne commits suicide or dies of grief; in others (such as in
Hesiod's *Theogony*), she marries the god Dionysus (or his priest) (Figure 11-5). But
though Hesiod describes her as being made immortal, as would be appropriate to
the wife of a god, another version describes her as being killed by Artemis, perhaps
for failing to preserve her chastity, or perhaps for violating a previous betrothal to
Dionysus by making love to Theseus. Dionysus, in yet another version, turns her
into a constellation, the Corona Borealis, when she dies, after the golden crown he
gave her at their wedding.

Even given the apparent contradictions of the variants of the myth, one fact remains constant—despite all Ariadne has done for him, out of love, Theseus leaves her. Athene, helper of heroes, is the model for the helper-maidens. But for Athene, self-contained virgin goddess and personification of divine wisdom, crossing the line between helping heroes and loving them is never an issue. For the human women, the attraction of half-divine, or at least divinely inspired, men represents a temptation that few can resist, and Aphrodite supplants Athene. (In fact, some scholars claim that Ariadne was originally a Cretan goddess who was worshiped in many places, such as Cyprus, as Aphrodite/Ariadne.) Similarly, in Euripides' *Medea,* Jason claims that Medea assisted him, not of her own accord, but under the spell of Aphrodite. And although, in various versions of the Ariadne myth, the motive for Artemis's involvement is unclear, in mythic terms it is entirely appropriate. Unable, like Callisto, to remain forever in Artemis's band, a young woman must leave the remote country or protected island where she grows up and, falling under the spell of Aphrodite, as Aphrodite herself fell in love with Adonis, entrust herself to a man who will lead her either to happiness or to grief. In the case of the helper-maidens, it is all too often the latter.

The Heroine as Hero-Impersonator

Yet another type of heroine is the one who, not content with either being confined to the woods of her childhood with Artemis or being the victim of a hero-husband or lover, chooses instead an independent life. However, because there are no socially acceptable avenues for achieving independence for heroines who demand freedom from the restrictions of gender barriers but who do not choose to opt out of "normal" society and live in isolation from men, as the Amazons do, the only available models are the male heroes. These heroines seek to outdo the heroes at their own game. In a male-dominated world, however, such enterprises are doomed, and the heroines who choose to rebel against traditional gender restrictions are bound, sooner or later, either to yield to the inevitable and conform to social expectations or to self-destruct.

Atalanta

Undoubtedly the most attractive, as well as the most successful, of such heroines is **Atalanta**. Atalanta combines the exceptional physical and martial prowess of the Amazons with the hunting skills of the followers of Artemis. In fact, in some versions, she is exposed to die at birth because her father wanted only sons but is nursed by she-bears and becomes a virgin huntress in the mode of Artemis's followers. (Some scholars claim that there may actually have been two Atalantas who share the same skills and whose stories are conflated in the myths.) But unlike either the members of Artemis's band or the Amazons, Atalanta does not eschew the company of men. Instead, she challenges them, joining the heroes in their games and adventures. For example, in some versions, such as Apollodorus's, she sails with the Argonauts and participates in the famous Calydonian boar hunt, in which the best Greek warriors kill a vicious boar sent by Artemis to destroy Calydon because

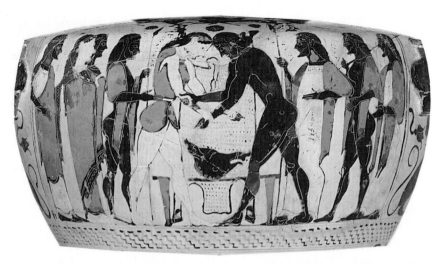

FIGURE 11-6 Atalanta and Peleus. In this vase painting (c. 530 B.C.), Atalanta wrestles with Peleus for the boar's hide at the funeral games for Pelias. Although Peleus is one of the greatest heroes of his time, Atalanta wins the match. *(Antikensammlungen, Munich)*

its king, Oineus, forgot to sacrifice to her. Atalanta gets in the first shot, and Meleager, who finishes off the beast, gives her the hide. But his uncles, insulted that a woman is granted such an honor over themselves, go to war over it. (Several years ago, when a woman first successfully dove off an extremely high cliff in Mexico into shallow water beneath, an annual challenge that previously only men had attempted, a retired diver who had accomplished the same death-defying feat in his youth was quoted in American newspapers as saying, "If a woman can do it, what's the point?" It is this same attitude that Atalanta confronts in Meleager's uncles.) Atalanta also participates in the funeral games for Pelias (father of Alcestis and uncle of Jason), during which she wrestles with the hero Peleus (father of Achilles) for the prize of a boar's hide (or head), winning the match (Figure 11-6).

Atalanta seeks out challenges, and the men she contends with, unlike Meleager's uncles, often find her intriguing and attractive, so she has many suitors. But Atalanta does not want to marry, for marriage would mean an end to her freedom. To forestall that dreaded fate, Atalanta, in the best-known tale of her exploits, sets up a rather unusual bride contest: she will race against each of her suitors; if he wins, she will marry him, but if he loses, he will forfeit his life. In some versions, she makes the challenge even more insulting to the men: she will grant them a head start and will even run carrying weapons, thus handicapping herself still further; but if she overtakes the runner before he reaches the finish line, she will kill him herself on the spot. In other versions, the identity of the suitors varies—usually it is Hippomenes or Melanion—but the outcome remains the same. Hippomenes has three golden apples given to him by Aphrodite, and he carries these in the race. As he runs, he drops each of the apples in turn, and when Atalanta slows to pick them up, he wins the race—and a bride.

Many young girls in our own time were raised on this story, presented (on records, tapes, and television) as a tale of "liberation"—of a strong woman free to set her own terms and conditions and to define her life as she chooses. But in ancient Greece, Atalanta and her peers enjoyed no such freedom. The choice (marriage or death) that she imposes on her suitors also applies to herself, and the she-bear who runs a race as a type of Artemis, in a version of the Brauronia, must succumb to Aphrodite and marry in the end.

According to one tradition, Aphrodite, angry that Hippomenes forgot to thank her for the apples, sends such an overwhelming fit of desire to the pair that they make love right on the spot—in a temple to Zeus—and are turned into lions for that sacrilege. Thus, like Callisto, Atalanta the huntress becomes the hunted. But in another version, she has a child (by Meleager or Melanion) and becomes, after all, the mother she never intended to be. Either way, the possibility for a grown woman to preserve her independence without being exiled from society or killed outright is nil.

Agave

Other rebellious heroines resort to more extreme measures in seeking the freedom and equality that society denies them. Of all the "rebel" heroines, **Agave** [a-GAY-vee] is the most extreme example of a woman who violates gender-role expectations to her own destruction. Driven mad by the god Dionysus (see Chapter 17), Agave, who has explicitly rejected the confinement of traditional female roles, tries to be Artemis and Heracles at once. After killing her son, Pentheus, who has spied on the mysteries of the god's rites, Agave can only briefly sustain the illusion that the head of her son, which she brings back from the mountains, is indeed that of the "lion" she boasts of having killed with her bare hands—making her even braver, she declares, than men, who must use weapons. Ironically, in this grotesque parody of Heracles' famous labor, she becomes more like that hero than she intended. After killing the Nemean lion, Heracles wore its skin and chose a club, rather than his bow, as his weapon, a fitting metamorphosis for a man who had already become a savage, killing his wife and children in a fit of madness also sent by a deity. In her "heroic" act of defiance, Agave destroys all the real possibilities open to her as a woman: neither a virgin huntress nor, any longer, a mother, she has no options left but madness and exile.

Clytemnestra

Clytemnestra [Klye-tem-NES-tra], Agamemnon's wife, is another "rebel" heroine who consciously defies gender boundaries. In Aeschylus's play *Agamemnon,* she is portrayed as living, while her husband has been absent for a decade prosecuting the war at Troy, the life of an independent, and even "professional," woman, ruling the city of Argos in his place (see Chapter 15). Her daughter Iphigenia having been sacrificed by Agamemnon, Clytemnestra has no interest in being a mother to her other children: she has long since sent her son, Orestes, to live abroad, and she ignores her now-grown daughter, Electra. In fact, the role of mother seems not to have had much appeal for her. In Aeschylus's play, the nurse comments that it was she, rather than Clytemnestra, who cared for Orestes as a baby.

For ten years, Clytemnestra has ruled competently, albeit perhaps more firmly than the citizens would like. She has also taken a lover, Agamemnon's cousin Aegisthus, with whom she lives openly. And she has organized an efficient intelligence service—a network of spies and messengers to inform her about her husband's return. Not expecting decisive leadership from a woman, the old men of the city repeatedly describe her as behaving "like a man." And, indeed, she does behave like a man—like any hero on the battlefield of Troy. When Agamemnon finally returns home, an enraged Clytemnestra stabs him with a sword, along with his slave and concubine Cassandra. When the murders are accomplished, she boasts of her deed, gloating over the fallen warrior just as Achilles and his peers did on the battlefield, proclaiming, "This is my work, and I claim it." But behavior that is glorious for a man on the battlefield is monstrous for a woman in the palace. Although her action is no illusion, Clytemnestra can no more get away with being an Achilles than Agave can be a Heracles. When the battle of the sexes turns literal, she loses even if she wins. Of course, her son, Orestes, will have to avenge his father's murder by killing her. And unlike the story of Zeus's intervention in Callisto's experience, no god steps in to prevent that matricide. On the contrary, Apollo himself ordains it, while Clytemnestra, like the loathsome Furies who emerge from the Underworld to take up her cause after her death, is deemed savage and barbaric. This is in contrast to "civilized" Apollo and Athene who, in Aeschylus's *Eumenides,* assert that the survival of Athenian democracy depends on keeping the "unnatural" female powers in their rightful, thoroughly subordinated place. Clearly, when women step out of line, mayhem ensues.

When heroes like Achilles or Hector face death, they are consoled by the fact that, if they go down fighting, their names will be glorified and their deeds celebrated forever. By contrast, neither Clytemnestra nor Agave is reconciled to her fate. In Aeschylus's *Eumenides,* Clytemnestra's ghost is still arguing her case—futilely, of course—against Apollo and Athene, while Agave remains so alienated and enraged at Dionysus that, even in exile, she tries with equal futility to ambush the god himself.

The Heroine as Bride of Death

Although at marriage every young maiden (Kore) enters the chamber of snakes, gateway to the Underworld, and becomes Persephone, for another group of heroines, entry into the Underworld represents an alternative to marriage. Such heroines as Cassandra, Iphigenia, and Antigone (see Chapter 16 for an extended discussion) become brides of Thanatos (Death) rather than of living husbands, either human or divine. (Girls who died before they could be married were likewise called "brides of Hades.")

Cassandra

The Trojan princess **Cassandra,** a priestess of Apollo, has the misfortune to attract the erotic attentions of that god. When Cassandra rebuffs his advances, he gives her the gift of prophetic vision, hoping to win her over, but she does not yield, holding him off instead with vague promises of future satisfaction. As Apollo's prophet, Cassandra becomes the oracle, the medium through which the divine communicates with the human. But the price Apollo demands is that she accept the divine *raptus*. To be the consort of a god carries risks, as the fate of Semele shows. Indeed, Cassandra is doomed whether she accepts or rejects the divine consummation. Determined to preserve her chastity, she denies the god and, as punishment, is driven mad, so that no one believes her prophecies. Thus, though she accurately foretells the doom of Troy, her predictions are dismissed as lunatic ravings.

In her enforced inability to share her vision or be believed or taken seriously, Cassandra is in the same position as every Greek woman. Andromache, for example, in the *Iliad*, gives her husband, Hector, sound strategic advice and also accurately predicts her own fate and that of their child if Hector ignores her advice and consequently dies in battle. But she is dismissed and sent back to her weaving, her admittedly sound but "womanly" voice not heeded.

Having relinquished her power as an oracle and refused the *hieros gamos* (sacred marriage) with Apollo, Cassandra is left to the world of mortal men, where her attempt to preserve her chastity is in any case futile. When her prophecies prove true and Troy falls, she is raped by Aias on the altar of Athene, an ironic commentary on her attempt to be, as oracle, a variant of the virgin goddess of divine wisdom. Cassandra is brought to Greece as Agamemnon's slave (according to some versions, along with the two sons she bore him), where she is slain by Clytemnestra.

In Aeschylus's play, Cassandra laments her tragic predicament: having refused to be the bride of Apollo, she must instead become the bride of Death. Although her death is literally unavoidable, her final act is one she consciously chooses, wresting out of the hands of fate the only kind of freedom still possible: she rejects her role as prophet of the god whose visions have enslaved her. Entering the palace to confront the death she knows awaits her, Cassandra demonstrates the same heroic acceptance of fate and determination to go forward that heroes manifest when facing death on the battlefield.

Iphigenia

Iphigenia [if-ih-jeh-NYE-a], daughter of Agamemnon and Clytemnestra, finds herself likewise trapped and also chooses death, both for patriotic reasons and as a literal substitute for marriage. When Agamemnon decides to sacrifice her to the goddess Artemis, in order, he believes, for the Greek armada assembled at Aulis to be permitted to sail for Troy, he sends for her, under the pretense that he is going to marry her to Achilles. When she arrives, according to Euripides' *Iphigenia at Aulis,* expecting to be married to the greatest living hero, she discovers her father's true intention. Her mother, Clytemnestra, is appalled and prevails on Achilles, who knew nothing of the arrangements, to prevent the tragedy. Iphigenia herself, however, accepts her death, a willing sacrifice. Arguing that one man is worth more than ten thousand women, Iphigenia offers her body to Artemis, for "Hellas." The taking of Troy, she declares, will be her marriage and her children. Achilles, in turn, praises her for her nobility. Wearing garlands and sprinkled with holy water, she goes to the altar of death that should have been the altar of marriage, singing the praises of Artemis.

In some versions of the myth, the sacrifice is carried out, but in Euripides' play, a deer is miraculously substituted for the girl, who is spirited away by Artemis. (Some scholars see the deer, like the bear into which Callisto is transformed, as linked with local cults in honor of Artemis, Lady of the Beasts.) In Euripides' *Iphigenia Among the Taurians,* we next find her as a priestess of Artemis, isolated in a savage land and presiding over gruesome, bloody rites of human sacrifice. It is a place of death, a kind of Underworld, where all strange men are slain as offerings to the goddess, a gender-inverted corollary of the usual order—women, not men, are sacrificed—and of Iphigenia's own experience at Aulis. When her brother, Orestes, and his friend Pylades arrive there, Iphigenia's prior situation is reversed—now her brother is the intended victim of the goddess, and his sister the rescuer. However, even though she manages to save the pair and succeeds in sailing off with them to Greece, clearly there will be no marriage for her.

Iphigenia complains of her life without husband or children and without the usual feminine occupations such as weaving, symbol of the connected web of life; she regrets that, as priestess of Artemis, she is denied the opportunity to make offerings to Hera, goddess of marriage. Recollecting the horror of Aulis, she insists that her father married her to Hades rather than to Achilles. She has been the bride of Death and guardian of the gateway to the Underworld but has, in fact, been denied the consummation even of that "marriage."

At the end of Euripides' play, Athene appears and decrees that Iphigenia will return to Greece and establish a temple to Artemis at Brauron. According to the play, Athene then "charters" the Brauronia. She declares that a priest will put a knife to a man's throat and draw blood, a symbolic sacrifice in compensation for Iphigenia's life. In a reversal of Alcestis's story, the "sacrificed" men are substitutes for Iphigenia in the Underworld, allowing her to be restored to life.

Iphigenia herself will become the Keeper of the Keys of the feminine mysteries, guardian of the rituals at Brauron at which young girls are initiated. But whereas the girls, after running as she-bears in Artemis's ritual, go on to follow the path of Persephone—they reach puberty, marry, and, like Demeter, have children—Iphigenia herself will have no such life. She will die and be buried, Athene says, at Brauron. And the garments of women who die in childbirth (in other words, who are sacrificed to Artemis, goddess of childbirth) will be consecrated as offerings to Iphigenia, stand-in for the virgin goddess, albeit under different names: according to Hesiod, she is renamed Artemis Einodia, later identified with Hecate. In effect frozen in time, a grown woman fixated at the stage before puberty, Iphigenia is condemned to remain perpetually unfulfilled.

The Victorious Heroines

Among all these women who suffer either because of or despite their strengths, one small group of heroines stands out. These are the lucky few who manage to retain their independence and yet remain within the context of gender-coded behavior as proper helper-maidens, as wives or daughters to the heroes, or as consorts to the gods.

Nausicaa

Daughter of King Alcinuous and Queen Arete of Scheria, the princess **Nausicaa** [na-SIK-ay-a] meets the hero Odysseus, in Homer's epic, after his last adventure in the supernatural world (see Chapter 13). Crossing the sea from Calypso's island on a raft and nearly drowning, Odysseus at last drags himself ashore and falls asleep. When he awakens, Nausicaa and her handmaidens are playing ball on the beach while waiting for their laundry to dry. When Odysseus—naked, hair matted, and covered with brine—crawls out from under a bush and approaches them, the young women scream and flee. Only Nausicaa stands her ground. When he greets her, he compares her to Artemis, thus reassuring her that he both admires her beauty and respects her virginity (Figure 11-7). Offering him a cloak and inviting him to the palace, Nausicaa as helper-maiden sets in motion the event that represents the culmination of Odysseus's journey, his return to Ithaca, for her father will eventually arrange for the hero's safe transportation home.

Despite her youth and unmarried state, Nausicaa is neither shy nor naive. She demonstrates her sophistication when she insists that Odysseus go to the palace

FIGURE 11-7 Odysseus and Nausicaa. In this vase painting (c. 440 B.C.), the women doing laundry keep their distance or run away; only Nausicaa turns to face the hero. Here, Athene looks on approvingly. *(Antikensammlungen, Munich)*

separately, apart from herself and her maids, to prevent the townspeople from gossiping about the disreputable-looking man the princess picked up on the beach. Clearly, this courageous, intelligent, and witty young woman finds Odysseus attractive, as he finds her. But unlike other helper-maidens, she assists him simply because he is a human being in need, and "wanderers and beggars come from Zeus," as she says, without attaching herself to him as a condition. She does not initiate an erotic relationship with him, nor he with her. Attractive as she is, Odysseus is by this time in his travels beyond any temptation—he wants only to return to his wife, Penelope. As a result, Odysseus and Nausicaa are free to engage in subtle flirtation and to give and receive help with no disastrous consequences to either party. When the king generously offers Odysseus a ship full of treasure and free passage home if he wants to leave, and half his kingdom and his daughter if he wants to stay, Odysseus chooses to go, wishing Nausicaa "wedded bliss"—with someone else. Of course, in a patriarchal society, her father still has the right to give her to any man of his choice. But perhaps King Alcinuous has noticed his daughter's affinity for their heroic visitor and will respect such preferences in a future choice of son-in-law as well. And because Nausicaa has remained self-possessed and emotionally detached and, unlike Ariadne, has not thrown herself at the first hero who comes ashore on the island of her childhood, she can accept Odysseus's parting blessing in the generous spirit in which it was given. She will undoubtedly, one imagines, choose her own mate wisely when she is ready.

Penelope

Combining the roles of helper-maiden with those of the ideal wife and mother, Odysseus's wife **Penelope,** as described in Homer's *Odyssey,* is far more than a model of patience and loyalty, the traits for which she is usually (and properly) acclaimed. Of course, as devoted wife of the hero and mother to their son Telemachus, Penelope manifests those ideal qualities far beyond what social convention requires. Her husband has been gone for twenty years: ten years fighting the war at Troy and, in effect, "missing in action" for the following ten years. Unlike Alcmene or Megara, though, Penelope is not a helpless victim waiting to be rescued. Legally permitted to remarry after such an interval, she persists in her determination to wait, hoping that her husband will somehow make it home. But her determination reflects not a sense of duty or piety, but rather her genuine love for Odysseus, just as his determination to return to her motivates his own increasingly desperate journey (see Chapter 13).

Surrounded by one hundred rowdy "suitors" who have taken over her home and attempted to assassinate her son, Penelope has for a year postponed acting on their demand that she "choose" one of them by pretending to weave a shroud of death for her elderly father-in-law, as her last duty to Odysseus's family, but secretly unraveling most of her work each night. As a weaver, she is aligned with the life-maintaining goddess, weaver of the web of life: she daily weaves to keep her hope—and her marriage—alive and nightly unweaves the shroud, as if to keep death at bay that much longer. Appropriately, it is Athene, goddess of weaving, who inspires Penelope to devise the trick of unweaving the shroud. But Athene is also protector of heroes and goddess of the defensive war that saves the home. On both grounds, she clearly has an interest in reuniting Odysseus's family. That Penelope's divine patron is not Artemis but Athene, who combines masculine and feminine principles, aligns the heroine with the wisdom of Zeus in its feminine manifestation, effectively combining animus and anima.

It is precisely this combination that enables Penelope not only to outwit the suitors, and thus make Odysseus's return possible, but also to function as his helper-maiden when at last he does return, disguised as a beggar, to Ithaca. Although it may be that she recognizes him right away, she does not reveal his identity, for to do so would probably mean his death at the suitors' hands. As if to emphasize that awareness, and the incredible self-restraint required of her, Homer shows instead the old nurse, Eurycleia, as she recognizes Odysseus and swears to keep his identity secret—unless, perhaps, she tells Penelope. If Penelope has indeed recognized him, from this point on, Odysseus's survival depends on his wife's behavior. Thus, she is, in effect, in control—and, significantly, Odysseus accepts his subordination. If, however, she has not yet recognized him, his victory is still dependent on her next moves.

Penelope as helper-maiden assists the hero by courageously arranging a mock "bride contest" among the suitors: the famous "test of the bow." She takes a real risk here—the bow in the wrong hands could mean disaster, so she must trust Odysseus implicitly just as he does her. Knowing that no one but Odysseus could either string the hero's marvelous weapon or use it with his near-miraculous precision, and trusting that his skills after all this time are still functional, she manages to remove the weapon from the storeroom so that Odysseus can get his hands on it. With his wife's assistance, the hero is now armed for the inevitable battle. Without ever needing to communicate directly, this equally heroic pair instinctively act as a team.

Once all the suitors have been killed, Penelope reserves a final test for Odysseus himself. Unlike Atalanta, however, Penelope uses the test to strengthen, rather than to avoid, her marriage, Ostensibly an identity check, the test determines whether Odysseus is still the loving husband who sailed off to war twenty years ago and whether, therefore, he deserves to have her back. Thus, she challenges Odysseus to reveal the secret sign of their marriage bed, the culminating point of both of their journeys.

Unlike Alcestis's marriage chamber, the bedroom of Odysseus and Penelope is no chamber of snakes. Perhaps because, unlike most of her peers, Penelope was neither abducted nor given away to a stranger—her marriage to Odysseus was a love match from the start—there is no aura of the Underworld here. On the contrary, it is the Tree of Life that grows in their bedroom. In Homer's epic, Odysseus describes how he constructed the bed, carving the first bedpost from a live olive tree still rooted in the earth, making the others to match, and then weaving a bed of oxhide thongs between them. In a complete reversal of standard construction techniques, Odysseus built the bed first, and then constructed the room around the bed and the rest of his home around the bedroom, making the marriage chamber the center of his very existence.

And not only did he build the bed with his own hands (a rather unusual action for a king, even of a small island), he wove the oxhide thongs himself as well. Thus, just as Penelope has heroically held off one hundred suitors by herself during his absence, Odysseus has been a weaver. And, like his wife, he has, without violating gender roles, combined animus and anima to create a marriage that is enduring, mutually sustaining, and capable of surviving change and growth. When they are eventually reunited, Homer, in an epic simile, compares her achievements at home to those of a shipwrecked sailor, pursued by Poseidon, who survives to crawl up at last on the beach, a literal description of Odysseus's own adventures, thus equating Penelope's heroism with her husband's. It is not surprising, then, that Odysseus's attitude toward domestic life reverses that of conventional heroes like Heracles or Hector, or that he has literally turned down the unattainable gift they died for—immortality—in order to have what they could have had all along but rejected or destroyed—a happy marriage.

Psyche

Of all the Greek heroines, perhaps the most remarkable is **Psyche.** The myth of Eros and Psyche is sometimes interpreted as an allegory of the relationship between the soul (Psyche, whose name means both "soul" and "butterfly," ancient symbol of the Goddess as source of spiritual transformation) and the divine (the god Eros), in which marriage represents the mystical union of the soul with the deity. The tale also weaves together strands from all the patterns of the mythic heroine's experience. As Heracles is the archetypal hero, Psyche is the archetypal heroine.

Possessing unearthly beauty, Psyche is taken to be a goddess, a second Aphrodite, and is worshiped accordingly, arousing the fury of Aphrodite herself, presented in Apuleius's tale (the earliest narrative source for this story) as the Creator goddess. Psyche is distressed by this misidentification, because, as a result, she has no suitors while her older sisters, of merely ordinary attractiveness, are already married. Aphrodite is enraged that a mere mortal girl should receive the prayers and offerings that are due to the goddess. She sends her son Eros (called by his Latin name, Cupid, in Apuleius's version) to cause Psyche to fall in love with the vilest man possible. But Eros falls in love with her himself and craves her for his own bride.

When an oracle tells Psyche's father that she must be married to a monstrous dragon, she is led, in a procession that is both marriage rite and funeral, to a high mountain crag and abandoned to be the bride of Death. Alone and about to plunge into a chasm from which, like Persephone, she can never emerge in the same state, Psyche is "every bride."

Then, as in a fairy tale (such as "Beauty and the Beast"), Psyche awakens to find herself in a magnificent palace, where she is waited on by invisible servants. Every night her husband, whom she does not know to be the god Eros, comes to her in the dark, and she is forbidden to look on him, on pain of losing him forever. Thus, Psyche, like Persephone, has become the queen of a luxurious netherworld kingdom. But unlike Persephone, she is a mortal, not a goddess, and like Semele, she cannot look on the face of her divine consort directly. Like Semele, too, she conceives a divine child who, Eros tells her, will be a god if she makes no attempt to see her husband but a mortal if she should ever see him. Psyche's predicament is thus one that almost every Greek woman experiences at marriage: she is separated from her family and made to live in what is a hell for her, despite its attractive furnish-

Color Plate 1　Sandro Botticelli, *Birth of Venus*, c. 1480. Botticelli's graceful and modest Venus (the Roman name for Aphrodite) floats serenely on her shell, gently propelled by the Zephyrs, embodiments of the west wind, whose breezes waft her toward the shore, and attended by one of the Hours (holding a robe to cloak the goddess as soon as she arrives) who presides over her birth. The painting may have been inspired by written accounts of a lost work from ancient Greece, the Aphrodite Anadyomene (Aphrodite Rising from the Sea) by Apelles, an artist at the court of Alexander the Great. Apelles's picture, in turn, ultimately derives from Hesiod's description of the love goddesses's origin in the *Theogony* (see Chapter 3). (*Uffizi, Florence.*)

Color Plate 2   Jean Cousin the Elder, *Eva Prima Pandora*, 1538. Cousin's painting explicitly identifies the biblical first woman, Eve, whose eating of forbidden fruit causes humanity's Fall from grace, with "the first Pandora," the primal human female whom the Greek gods created to plague mankind and bring the paradisal Golden Age to an end. With one hand on her jar (containing both blessings and woes), and the other on a skull (grim symbol of human mortality), she contemplates the paradox of her creation: all life's gifts (and potential evils) that belong to the material world reside in her jar; their release will introduce the bewildering mixture of pain and pleasure, strife and death, that Hesiod says have characterized human existence ever since woman's initial appearance on earth (see Chapter 6). (*Louvre, Paris.*)

Color Plate 3   Jacopo Tintoretto, *The Origin of the Milky Way.* The Venetian painter Tintoretto (1518–1594) here captures a crucial moment in Greek myth, one involving both the perennial power struggle between Zeus (Jupiter) and Hera (Juno) and a cosmic phenomenon, the birth of a new galaxy. Set in Hera's celestial boudoir, this scene depicts the startled Queen of Heaven leaping from her bed just as Zeus's messenger Hermes (Mercury) (top right) places the infant Heracles (Hercules) at the sleeping goddess's breast, causing her milk to jet skyward, igniting a fountain of sparkling stars (see Chapter 5). Hera's angry rejection of Zeus's illegitimate child, born to a human mother, Alcmene, thwarts her husband's attempt to render Heracles immortal by absorbing divine nourishment from his wife and condemns the hero to a life of hardship and pain (see Chapter 10). Hera's sacred bird, the watchful peacock, occupies the lower right corner, while Zeus is symbolically present in the form of his eagle with a thunderbolt in its claws. (*National Gallery, London.*)

Color Plate 4   Thomas Hart Benton, *Persephone,* 1938. In this updating of the ancient myth of Persephone's abduction by Hades, an American painter depicts Demeter's virgin daughter as an innocently voluptuous (and vulnerable) figure in a rural midwestern setting, unconsciously inciting the lust of the Underworld's ruler, here shown as a lecherous voyeur about to intrude on the young woman's serenity. The transformation of an as-yet unawakened maiden associated with nature's gentle flowering into Hades's wife and grim queen of the netherworld is about to begin. (*The Nelson-Atkins Museum of Art, Kansas City, Missouri. Purchase acquired through the Yellow Freight Foundation Art Acquisition Fund and the generosity of Mrs. Herbert O. Peet, Richard J. Stern, the Doris Jones Stein Foundation, the Jacob L. and Ella C. Loose Foundation, Mr. and Mrs. Richard M. Levin, and Mr. and Mrs. Marvin Rich. © 2000 T. H. Benton and R. P. Benton Testamentary Trusts/Licensed by VAGA, New York, NY.*)

Color Plate 5 Jean-Auguste-Dominique Ingres, *Jupiter and Thetis,* 1811. Ingres's neo-classical painting employs the heroic themes characteristic of the Roman revival popular during the Napoleanic era in France. A rather stern and upright Jupiter stares straight ahead, maintaining his composure, though seemingly annoyed by Thetis's request that he assist Achilles in that hero's defiance of Agamemnon. Jupiter's determination to see his ultimate commitment to order prevail is suggested by the god's angry-looking eagle at the right, balanced by the figure of Juno (Hera) at the left. Jupiter's foot, extended slightly over the base of the throne, rests over a bas-relief depicting the battle of gods and giants, as if, having once established order, he must now put his foot down and do so again. The pyramidal form of the composition, with its apex at Jupiter's head, reinforces the painting's insistence on Jupiter as the enforcer of cosmic order. (*Musée Granet, Palais de Malte, Aix-en-Provence, France.*)

Color Plate 6   Peter Paul Rubens, *The Judgment of Paris,* c. 1633–1635. Unlike his earlier version of the same subject, in which Rubens placed the victorious Venus at the center, this painting shows a young Paris gazing admiringly at Venus (the middle of the three goddesses), who returns his look as he extends the apple. But while Minerva (Athene) on the left and Juno (Hera) on the right look on in apparent detachment, their bodies curve away from the enraptured shepherd. In typical Baroque counterpoint to this seemingly calm scene complete with grazing sheep, it is Juno who, despite losing the contest, occupies the physical center of the canvas. Juno's peacock makes menacing gestures at Paris's sleeping dog, while the curve of the peacock's tail begins a visual sweep upward through the light clouds between the trees where we find Allecto, the Fury, watching the action below in anticipation of the disastrous consequences of Paris's choice. That motif is echoed in the war helmet temporarily laid aside by Minerva, along with her shield, which bears the contorted face of the Gorgon Medusa. (*National Gallery, London.*)

Color Plate 7   Perseus Frees Andromeda. In this wall painting from the House of the
Dioscuri in Pompeii, the hero Perseus, son of Zeus and the mortal Danae, releases
Andromeda, a princess of Ethiopia, from the rock where she had been chained as a sacri-
fice to a ravenous sea monster (lower right). In his hand, Perseus carries the head of the
Gorgon Medusa that he uses to petrify his opponents and a scimitar given him by the god
Hermes, who has also loaned the hero his winged footwear. According to variants of this
myth, Perseus was also temporarily given a cap of invisibility by Hades, a mirror by
Athene (so that he could avoid looking directly at Medusa and thereby escape being
turned to stone), and a special bag by the nymphs in which to keep the severed head.
Favored by the gods, the hero thus temporarily acquired divine attributes while battling
against injustice or other evils. (*Museo Archeologico Nazionale, Naples.*)

Color Plate 8   Andromache Pouring a Stirrup-Cup for Hector on the Eve of His Fatal Battle with Achilles, c. 475 B.C. In their last quiet moment together, Hector and Andromache reveal, with their downcast looks, their contemplation of Hector's impending death that Andromache has already predicted. As if in confirmation of that fate, the vase painter has positioned the couple with Hector's weapons occupying the space between them, his spear-handle dividing them symbolically in the composition as they were about to be literally divided. (*Henry Lillie Pierce Fund, 1898. Courtesy Museum of Fine Arts, Boston. Reproduced with permission. Courtesy of the Museum of Fine Arts, Boston.*)

ings; she has no meaningful relationship with her husband, apart from sex; and she has to deal with a hostile mother-in-law!

Psyche accepts the arrangement, but her jealous sisters tell her that she is married to a monster and convince her not only to look on him (as Hera tricked Semele) but to kill him. With heroic courage, Psyche uncovers a lantern and, like every hero confronting a dragon, is about to cut Eros's head off when she sees the sleeping god. Awed at the divine presence, she touches the tip of his arrow, pricks her finger, and thus falls passionately in love with him. At that moment, pricking her own finger and falling in love with the god she clearly sees, she experiences mature love, independently given, rather than accepted blindly as the condition of her marriage, as would be the case for any girl married off to a stranger in the usual way. Psyche, by contrast, has become the aggressor, not the victim. In fact, Apuleius says that she "becomes a man" at that moment. And Eros is wounded, not just in his shoulder by a drop of oil from her lantern, but in his self-serving premise that it is necessary to keep his bride in the dark. Thus far, he has used her to satisfy his own desires, and although he has kept her housed and fed in luxury, the couple have no relationship at all: "love" as an erotic fantasy or a housekeeping arrangement is not enough.

Awakened by the pain of the oil burning his shoulder, Eros leaves, flying up into the heavens, with Psyche clinging to him, until she drops back to earth. Like Pandora, she has seen the divine secret and suffers a fall. But whereas heroes like Actaeon suffered death for seeing the beauty of Artemis too directly, Eros is a gentler god, and Psyche does not die.

Unsuccessful in a suicide attempt, Psyche goes searching for her husband, who is at his mother's house, suffering from his wound. Still angry, Aphrodite now imposes a series of labors on Psyche, the only heroine to go on a quest like those of the male heroes. Like Odysseus, the goal of whose labors is a return to Penelope, Psyche's labors will bring about her reunion with Eros. But where the heroes are helped by gods (or helper-maidens), Psyche is assisted by nature.

Her first task is to sort an immense heap of various grains, which she does with the help of the ants—another folk and fairy tale motif. Her second task is reminiscent of Jason's—to bring back some of the golden fleece of wild sheep who attack humans, driven into a frenzy by the heat of the sun. Instructed by a reed on the river bank, Psyche waits until the sheep are asleep to gather the wool that clings to the twigs in the grove.

Psyche's third and fourth tasks are akin to those of Heracles himself. Ordered to bring back water from the high mountain stream that is the source of the rivers of the Underworld, an inaccessible height guarded by fierce dragons, she is assisted by the eagle of Zeus himself, who honors Eros by helping his bride, in memory of his having brought Ganymede to Zeus. For her last labor, Psyche must venture into the Underworld and bring back in a casket a small portion of Persephone's beauty to present to Aphrodite. Psyche understands that she is being sent to her death. Mounting a tower to try again to commit suicide, she hears the tower itself instruct her on how to enter the Underworld, taking two coins (for Charon, the ferryman) and two barley cakes (for Cerberus, the hound of Hades). To succeed, she will need to resist the temptation to open the casket that Persephone gives her. Once again, the Pandora theme enters the story as curiosity overwhelms Psyche. On returning to the upper world, she opens the casket and falls into a deathlike sleep.

Here, again, myth and fairy tale converge as Psyche becomes a "sleeping beauty"; as in the fairy tale, meaningful life is suspended until her marriage. Having recovered, meanwhile, Eros locates his bride and awakens her with a prick of one of his arrows. He puts sleep back into the casket, in effect burying the adolescent girl, who experiences rebirth as a mature woman. Psyche has emerged from the cocoon of unconsciousness and become the butterfly. Like Eros, she now has her own wings. When Psyche awakens, it is to accept her mature role as wife. With animus and anima now joined, the relationship of Eros and Psyche resembles that of Odysseus and Penelope, except that Eros is divine and Psyche is mortal. To make the couple more compatible, Zeus gives Psyche a drink of the nectar of the gods and immortalizes her, and the marriage is formalized at last. Psyche and Eros, like Heracles and Hebe, will be married for all eternity. But unlike Heracles, Psyche has achieved transfiguration through love, not war, and the divine child who is born to Psyche is called Pleasure. As a heroine myth, the story of Psyche contains all the possibilities, but as for Psyche herself, there are none like her. (For primary readings illustrating the myths of heroines, see Chapters 12 and 13, on the Homeric epics, and Chapters 15–17, Athenian tragedies.)

. . . .

Questions for Discussion and Review

1. Using Theseus or Heracles as an example, explain how the heroic version of the trip to the Underworld is similar to that of Persephone, who undergoes a rite of passage of her own. Explain the similarities and differences between the separation, initiation, and return of the male, as modeled in the myths of the heroes, and that of the female, as exemplified by the myth of Persephone's abduction and eventual return.

2. What components do the myths of heroines share with the hero myths? What are some significant differences?

3. Using Heracles and Alcestis as examples, compare and contrast the Underworld associations of the male and female heroic patterns.

4. Heroines sometimes rebel against the limitations imposed on women by trying to be "heroes" in their own right. How successful are they? Explain how the behavior of either Atalanta or Clytemnestra is modeled on that of the male heroes.

5. Some heroines are remarkable in bringing together "masculine" and "feminine" qualities to become successful women with satisfying lives and relationships with their spouses. Using Penelope and Psyche as examples, explain what traits and experiences these heroines share.

12

Heroes at War: The Troy Saga

KEY TOPICS/THEMES

At the wedding of Peleus and Thetis, the uninvited goddess of discord, Eris, tosses a golden apple. When three goddesses fight over it, Zeus throws it off Mount Olympus. It is found by Paris, prince of Troy, who gives it to the goddess Aphrodite in return for her promise of the love of the most beautiful woman in the world. That woman is Helen, wife of Menelaus, king of Sparta. When she runs off to Troy with Paris, the Greeks and Trojans go to war. The myth of the Trojan War may recall a historical military encounter. According to the myth, after a ten-year siege, Troy is conquered by Odysseus's trick of the Trojan Horse. In the Iliad, *Homer tells of a quarrel between the general Agamemnon and the hero Achilles in the Greek camp in the ninth year of the war.*

The Decision of Paris

The story of the **judgment** (or decision) **of Paris** is seminal to the study of Greek mythology, not only because it is the seed from which so many myths arise, but also because it is a paradigm of the complex world in which those myths reside. The story involves a minor sea goddess, **Thetis,** and a mortal man, **Peleus,** who are about to wed. Zeus, it seems, has heard a prophecy, perhaps revealed by Prometheus in exchange for his freedom, that a child of his, possibly by Thetis, will one day usurp his throne. To prevent such a threat, Zeus marries off Thetis, to whom he is sexually attracted, to a human prince, guaranteeing that any child of hers will be half-human, and so no threat to his divinity. Or perhaps Zeus is simply punishing her, as one variant account suggests, for refusing, out of loyalty to Hera, who raised her, to yield to his sexual advances; or perhaps, according to yet another variant, he is rewarding Peleus for his uncommon valor.

Zeus invites to the wedding all the gods and goddesses except one—**Eris,** the goddess of strife, or discord. Naturally, she arrives uninvited and tosses at the assembled guests a golden apple bearing the inscription "For the fairest."

Three goddesses—Hera, Athene, and Aphrodite—quarrel over the apple. Determined to preserve harmony, Zeus throws the apple down off Mount Olympus. It lands in a field outside Troy, where **Paris,** son of King Priam of Troy, is tending sheep. Picking up the apple, Paris is startled by the sudden appearance of the three goddesses, each of whom asks for it, offering him a gift in exchange (see Color Plate 6). One scholar, Joan O'Brien, argues that the three proffered gifts represented the triple functions of Mycenean Hera, who may herself have presented Paris with the choices, thus provoking the ensuing war and ensuring Troy's destruction. According to most versions, though, all three goddesses are involved. Hera, queen of the gods, offers power over all of Asia Minor, but Paris will one day inherit his father's kingdom, so he turns her down. Athene offers wisdom, but, like many young men, Paris is sure that he already possesses all the wisdom he needs. Aphrodite offers the love of the most beautiful woman in the world, and, to a young man whose only company is a flock of sheep, she clearly wins the prize (Figure 12-1). The goddesses, one exultant and the other two enraged, disappear—perhaps it was a dream. Paris goes back to his sheep.

FIGURE 12-1   The Judgment of Paris. This Roman bas-relief from the Casali Altar shows Paris (seated, right) negotiating with the three goddesses—Athene (left), Hera (center), and Aphrodite (right, shown partially disrobed)—while Hermes holds the golden apple that he has delivered to the Trojan prince. *(Vatican Museums, Rome)*

Shortly thereafter, King **Priam** calls for his son, now old enough to assume some political responsibilities, and sends him on his first diplomatic mission—to the home of **Menelaus** [men-e-LAY-uhs], king of Sparta. Or perhaps, prompted by Aphrodite, he chooses on his own to go. Menelaus's wife, **Helen**, is the most beautiful woman in the world because of her half-divine parentage. She is the daughter of a mortal woman, **Leda**, and Zeus, who appeared to Leda (who would not betray her husband, Tyndareus, with another man) in the form of a great white swan. In another variant, Paris already knows of Helen's beauty and goes to Sparta intending to kidnap her.

While Paris is a guest in Menelaus's home, Menelaus leaves for a brief trip of his own. Left alone with Helen, Paris seduces her. Or perhaps he abducts her, as well as stealing some of Menelaus's treasure, and returns to Troy. When, despite official protests, Paris refuses to return Helen, Priam feels honor-bound to defend his son, though it means war with Menelaus. The latter, however, has many powerful allies: when **Tyndareus**, Helen's supposed father, was ready to marry her off, he summoned all the heroes—the princes of noble families—as potential suitors. Before announcing his choice, Tyndareus made them all swear to support Helen's husband should he ever call on their aid. Thus begins the **Trojan War**—ten years of death and chaos, consequences of a bad choice.

The Historicity of Troy

One of the most important sets of myths in the corpus of Greek mythology, the saga of Troy may also have at least one of its roots in history. The ancient Greeks certainly thought so: Herodotus, for example, discusses Troy early in his *Histories*, treating that war as the source of the continuing animosity between Greeks and "Asians"—specifically, the Persians. Although anachronisms (such as references to post–Bronze Age technology, especially iron, and to later rituals and burial customs) demonstrate that the *Iliad* was composed several centuries after the events described, modern scholars have reason to believe that the *Iliad* has at least some loose basis in actual historical events.

Situated at the entrance to the Hellespont, the narrow sea link between the Mediterranean and the Black Sea, Troy occupied a highly strategic location. Modern excavations have revealed a wealthy city of long standing, with some of its affluence possibly the result of exacting taxes from merchant ships traveling this critical seagoing trade route between East and West. And archaeological evidence attests that, somewhere around 1250 B.C., Troy VII-A was looted and burned by unidentified aggressors, possibly after a long siege.

Even if those unknown aggressors were Greek, the exact nature of the conflict that may have occurred between the Trojans and the Mycenaean city-states is likewise unknown. Various theories include a feud over a dynastic marriage (Herodotus remarks that only the Greeks would be stupid enough to go to such lengths to fight to retrieve a woman); the pressure of migrations and/or invasions by the **Dorians,** another Greek-speaking people entering the region at the time; a population explosion in mainland Greece that was unsupportable by the local economy; and a wave of migrations and/or raids prompted by that same struggling economy.

Until recently, excavations at Troy had uncovered a series of cities destroyed and rebuilt on the site, all of them far too small to have withstood a protracted siege such as the myths and Homer's epic describe. But more recent excavations have revealed a much larger outer wall, and thus a city far more extensive than previously believed to exist (see Chapter 1). Furthermore, although scholars had previously suggested that Troy was not near enough to the coast either to pose a serious threat to ships passing through the Hellespont or to fit the description of the field of war as Homer describes it (with the Greeks encamped on the beach and the battlefield between them and the city gates), very recent geological studies have revealed that the current landscape is significantly different from what it was in the Bronze Age, when the coastline was indeed much closer to the city than is now the case. Recent archaeological discoveries at Pylos, including studies of animal bones, also confirm the surprising accuracy of some of the poem's details, such as the descriptions of the sacrifices of bulls. Thus, although we have no definitive knowledge of the actual nature of the historical link between Troy and Mycenaean Greece, we have every reason to accept some basis of historicity in the legends.

The Implications of the Story

One of the most popular bodies of material in Greek mythology, the stories that make up the saga of Troy have been retold in numerous variations by many writers. Among the most important narrative sources for the pre- and post-*Iliad* materials are Apollodorus's *Library,* Ovid's *Metamorphoses,* and various works by unknown writers, often fragments, collectively referred to as the "Epic Cycle" (among them the *Cypria* and the *Little Iliad*), as well as Hyginus's *Fabulae.* Examples of the many dramatic sources include plays by Aeschylus (the *Oresteia*), Euripides (*Iphigenia at Aulis, Iphigenia Among the Taurians, Orestes,* and *Trojan Women*), and Sophocles (*Aias,* and *Philoctetes*). The alternative versions of parts of the story of the judgment of Paris and the endless sequels—including the sacrifice of Agamemnon's daughter Iphigenia, the destruction of Troy, the death of Achilles, the murder of Agamemnon and Orestes' revenge, and the wanderings of Odysseus, as well as many other tales—reflect the multiform and open-ended nature of Greek myths. Such a complex network of overlapping but often contradictory tales inevitably prompts us to ask where the saga of Troy truly begins: is it with Paris's judgment, with Zeus's rape of Leda (as the modern Irish poet W. B. Yeats asserts—see Chapter 21) or with the genesis of a universe that, as Hesiod describes it in the *Theogony,* emerged out of chaos at its inception? The beginning and end of the story of the decision of Paris are obscured in the mysteries of the creation and destruction of the universe itself.

The Timelessness of Myth

The myths occur in a timeless world, or at least they refuse to submit to the rules of human chronology and logic. Consider, for example, **Achilles** [a-KIL-leez], the child born of the marriage of Peleus and Thetis. Goddesses, like human females, apparently carry their offspring for nine months. Presumably, then, Achilles is born within a year of the marriage. If, meanwhile, Paris's embassy to Menelaus begins several months after the incident of the apple and lasts for a year, and even if it takes, as the myths attest, a year for the Greeks to assemble their troops and another for the armada to set sail for Troy, then Achilles would have been two years old when the war began and twelve when it ended. According to some variants, Helen and Paris spent a ten-year honeymoon on Crete before returning to Troy, but even that interval would have made Achilles twelve years old at the start of the war—still too young for the experiences attributed to him. Before the war starts, Achilles is already the Greeks' most renowned hero, and his friend Patroclus may have been one of the suitors for Helen's hand before her marriage to Menelaus. Stretching the time frame still further, before the war is over, Achilles' son, Neoptolemus, is old enough to join the battle and become a hero in his own right. No reasonable computation can make sense of these numbers in terms of human time. We may ask questions about the chronology, but the myth, in its own timeless realm, refuses to address them.

Conflict in Society and the Cosmos

On a social level, Zeus, god of family love and of guest–host relationships, sanctifies values that preserve the sacred institution of marriage, harmony within families, and civilized modes of social and political exchange that maintain order. This larger cosmic perspective is reflected in political terms in the emerging concept of the Greeks as a nation, witnessed in the *Iliad*, as scholars have noted, in the collective names by which the Greeks refer to themselves: Hellenes, Danaans, Argives, **Achaeans.** Paris, making off with Menelaus's wife while a guest in the Spartan king's home, violates these god-ordained relationships. But personal and familial loyalty are also important under the older kinship system, in which the clan is the source of security, values, and justice. When Priam, believing that honor and family love oblige him to stand behind his son despite his poor judgment, refuses to abide by the prevailing social norms, opting instead to show loyalty to the clan, the two systems clash. In a world already in transition, the crisis forces these two systems into open conflict, releasing the aggressions that all such social systems usually manage to keep in check. The veneer of civilized life is stripped away, and the world is plunged into war.

It is not just social structures that can change. The cosmos itself in which the myth occurs is dynamic: although Zeus's regime appears stable, there are recurrent hints, however obscure, that it will not be eternal. Change is inherent in the nature of things, and not even the immortal gods rule forever. The powers under control of the gods in this cosmos, furthermore, are limited. Zeus is in command, but not control, of the universe. He cannot by fiat decree discord nonexistent: evil exists, and Zeus, like the rest of us, must cope with it. The disharmony in the human world, moreover, is both a consequence and a reflection of the disharmony in a cosmos at war with itself. The Trojan War, like the war between the Titans and the Olympians, reflects an ambiguous and contradictory universe in which, as Hesiod pointed out, a mixture of good and evil is the best one can hope for.

The Human and the Divine

The myth of the decision of Paris also depicts, in terms characteristic of Greek myth, the conjunction of the human and the divine. So closely connected are the two—the gods so like humans, the humans so godlike—that marriage is possible between them. But such marriages are fraught with difficulties: although they remain amicable, Peleus and Thetis soon separate—they may love each other, but they fail to understand each other. Post-Homeric versions of the tale describe how Thetis, attempting to erase the father's human taint from her child, dips Achilles in the divine fire (or water), holding him by the heel. For all her efforts, though, she cannot erase his paternal inheritance: "Achilles' heel" signifies not a personal weakness but the human, and therefore necessarily mortal, condition itself. Meanwhile, Peleus, terrified that Thetis's efforts will destroy his son, attempts unsuccessfully to stop her. They are clearly incompatible and must carry on their lives on separate planes.

The gods, furthermore, lack the power either to control human nature or to compel human fate: Thetis can neither make Achilles immortal nor prevent him from going to Troy. Thus, within the limits of mortality, humans have the freedom to act: just as Paris freely chooses to give the apple to Aphrodite, so Achilles freely chooses to go to Troy, and both must accept responsibility for their fates. Indeed, Paris, dangling an apple over the heads of three goddesses, already has, in a way perhaps even he does not understand, more power than Hera can offer him.

The myth of the decision of Paris suggests a universe of infinite, though ambiguous, options; it offers humans the freedom to choose, but no guarantees or clear-cut guides. Paris chooses love, sacrificing power and wisdom: Could he have chosen better? Would raw power, unguided by wisdom or love, have been preferable? What about an abstract wisdom, untempered by love and lacking the power to act? In opting for love, Paris defines himself, as do Achilles and Hector when they choose to fight (and die) for glory. Each lives the life and death he has chosen. For all its trappings of prophecies and oracles, Greek myth depicts in the story of the decision of Paris a world of human freedom and moral responsibility, in which every option is fraught with awe and terror, and every life contains the possibilities at once for transcendence and for tragedy.

The Trojan Cycle Continues: Events Preceding the *Iliad*

The Gathering of the Troops

When Menelaus calls up his allies, the most powerful Greek princes and their troops, led by Menelaus's brother, **Agamemnon**, begin gathering at the port of Aulis. Only two, **Odysseus** [oh-DIS-ee-uhs] and Achilles, fail to appear.

Odysseus is married to Helen's cousin Penelope, who has recently given birth to their son, Telemachus. Devoted to his family, Odysseus is reluctant to leave them when the call to arms comes. When Agamemnon's ambassadors arrive, Odysseus pretends to be insane, but when they test him by placing the baby in front of the plow he is driving, Odysseus immediately acts to save his son, thus revealing the pretense. Once committed to the war effort, however, Odysseus becomes the most loyal officer and the prime strategist and morale builder of the Greek troops.

Odysseus's first assignment is to locate and recruit the missing Achilles. In a desperate attempt to protect her son from the prophecy that he will perish if he participates in the Trojan War, Thetis insists that he hide on the island of Scyros, disguised as a girl. Disguising himself, in turn, as a merchant, Odysseus travels to Scyros and displays before the local women an assortment of beautiful garments and one suit of armor. While the women examine the dresses, Achilles' attention is immediately drawn to the armor. Thus found out, Achilles comes willingly. Achilles' hiding as a girl, indistinguishable from the women, to emerge in armor as "swift-footed Achilles," recapitulates the Oschophoria, the initiation ritual for ephebes (see Chapter 10) about to become adult warriors.

The Events at Aulis

With the armada assembled at Aulis, the goddess Artemis, perhaps angered by Agamemnon's boast that his skill at hunting exceeded hers, causes the winds to die down, thus preventing the ships from embarking for Troy. When he appeals to the gods for some clue as to how to proceed, Agamemnon is informed by the prophet **Calchas** that he must sacrifice his daughter Iphigenia (see Chapters 11 and 15). Only then do the ships set sail. The war on Troy, intended to save a family, begins by destroying one, and the effort is tainted from the start.

The Outbreak of War

While the Greeks have been mustering their troops and preparing for the invasion, the Trojans have been gathering allies of their own. When the Greeks, after seizing some outlying cities, land on the beaches at Troy, they find a city whose walls are impregnable and whose many allies prevent the Greeks from creating a total blockade. The river Scamander also runs through the city, providing an abundant water supply. A well-fortified city whose lifelines of food and water are secure can wait out even the longest siege, and so the Trojans are in no immediate danger. If they choose to remain inside the walls, they are safe; if they elect to come out and fight, they have a safe retreat nearby. The Greeks, meanwhile, in a temporary encampment far from home, are at a strategic and psychological disadvantage.

For nine years, the Greek troops remain camped on the beaches. Battles are fought, men are killed, prisoners are taken and held or ransomed, but the war itself remains stalemated, with the Trojans unable to drive the Greeks from their shores and the Greeks unable to breach the walls and take the city. The level of frustration is high on both sides. It is at this point that Homer picks up the story in his epic poem the *Iliad*.

The Homeric Epics

The Question of Authorship

The *Iliad* and the *Odyssey* are traditionally attributed to **Homer,** a poet about whom we know virtually nothing beyond the speculation that he may have lived on an island off the coast of Asia Minor between 800 and 700 B.C. Legends depicting

Homer as blind may have been extrapolated from his portrayal of the blind bard, Demodocus, in the *Odyssey*. However, because Homer also describes a sighted bard in the same epic, we must infer the possibility of embellishment by Homer's admirers, placing him in the tradition of the blind prophet of the myths, Tiresias, who, undistracted by surface appearances, sees moral truths, just as the poet must.

Both poems exhibit what scholars agree are signs of oral composition: fixed epithets and adjectives ("wily Odysseus," "swift-footed Achilles"), set speeches made by one character and repeated verbatim by another, and genealogies of characters, weapons, and even animals. Both poems also share qualities of style and, to a lesser extent, structure. Thus, some scholars believe that one poet composed both works. The poems' perspectives, however—on the characteristics of the gods, the role of women, the value of the heroic life, and the nature of the universe itself—differ radically. Did a single poet change his mind about many important issues? We have clear evidence from more recent times of poets who have done just that. Were these poems perhaps composed by one poet and later modified by different hands who wrote them down? Or were they composed by different poets and possibly later recorded by the same editor? We have, to date, no verifiable answers to these questions. Although the multiple-authorship theory is the most common one among modern scholars, for ease of reference, this text will henceforth cite Homer as the author of both texts.

The Literary Transformations: Myth into Epic

Both poems make extensive use of inherited mythic materials. But neither is merely a retelling of traditional stories. Literary devices such as the use of dialogue and of an omniscient narrator (the all-knowing author who can reveal what his characters, human or divine, are thinking and can comment on the tale directly) allow the poet to impose his own perspective on the myths.

Furthermore, the author has shaped the received material into a specific literary form, the epic. Choosing to compose in the epic genre (or literary type) itself constitutes an interpretation of the myths. The epic entails what were undoubtedly, by Homer's time, already formal conventions: the proem (the opening passages establishing the author's central concerns), the semidivinity of the hero, and the hero's descent into the Underworld. The choice of the epic form—traditionally, for the Greeks, the highest of the genres—also establishes the author's conviction of the seriousness and grandeur of his subject. A long narrative poem celebrating the achievements of a culture and the deeds of the hero who protects it, the epic is itself an expression of pride in one's civilization.

Epics transform their mythic sources in other ways as well. In contrast to the timeless world of myth, the epic is rooted in human time. In the *Iliad*, for example, the poet keeps reminding his audience of the passage of time: time taken for the cremation of corpses; time remembered in the genealogies; time compared (as the aged Nestor does, recalling the days of his youth, when heroes were *really* spectacular). In the *Odyssey*, time is even more prominent: ten years for the war, followed by ten years of wandering; the growth of Telemachus; the aging of Penelope and Odysseus. Even his dog, Argos, a pup when Odysseus left, reminds us, as he wags his tail one last time in joy at Odysseus's return before expiring, of the inexorable drive toward death that lends such urgency to human experience.

Besides using (and, indeed, expanding) the possibilities of the epic form, Homer also selected and transformed the available mythic material to reflect his own thematic perspectives. Thus, whereas the traditional myth presents a narrative that is itself simple but open-ended, the literary work presents a more complicated but closed narrative with a defined beginning, middle, and end.

Homer also uses epic similes (extended comparisons) to ground his works in the soil of real human experience, despite the presence of the gods and the quasi-supernatural adventures of the heroes. He thereby allows us to imagine the more remote actions in terms of the more familiar. Thus, although we have surely never seen a monster like Scylla reach down, pluck a man off a ship, and devour him, we have probably seen a man fishing from a rock who casts his line and plucks a fish from the water, a more common experience to which Homer, in a simile in the *Odyssey,* compares the more fantastic one. Similarly, although we are not half-divine and may not understand what it feels like to possess the heroes' superhuman powers, we can surely understand how using a tool extends the power of the human hand; thus, Paris, in a simile, compares Hector's prowess to a sharpened ax-edge that extends the powers of the hero.

Other literary devices, some of which Homer probably invented (the cliff-hanger and the interrupted flashback), also help shape the material. Consider, for example, the startling juxtaposition in the great chase scene in the *Iliad.* Achilles chases Hector three times around the walls of Troy before he finally catches and kills his rival (see Color Plate 9). But in the midst of the scene, Homer interrupts the chase for an extended description of how, on that spot in the days before the war, women used to do the laundry. What better way to remind the audience of the values that, in their preoccupation with personal glory and impending death, both heroes have forgotten: both sides in the war ostensibly are fighting for the right to carry on their prosaic domestic lives, the right to keep their families and their daily rituals intact, the right to do the laundry in peace.

The *Iliad*

Omitting all mention of the Promethean prophecy (that a child of Thetis's by Zeus would, if conceived, grow up to usurp his father's throne), of the decision of Paris and the divine quarrel that precedes the war, and of the failed attempt of Thetis to immortalize her son, Homer centers the *Iliad* squarely in the human world. Unlike the *Odyssey,* which opens on Mount Olympus with the gods in council, the *Iliad* begins in the Greek encampment. The gods do not appear until the priest Chryses, offended at Agamemnon's refusal to ransom his daughter, calls on Apollo to intervene. Nor does the poet choose to chronicle the war itself: neither the sacrifice of Iphigenia, nor the death of Achilles, nor the sack of Troy is ever mentioned. Beginning instead with a single event in the ninth year of the stalemated war, Homer chooses to focus entirely on the quarrel between Achilles and Agamemnon and its consequences in order to explore some central questions that must be raised in a society in which kings are warriors and warriors are heroes. What does it mean to be a hero? How valid is the code of honor by which the hero lives? What are the hero's potentials and limitations? How far can the hero go in pursuing his goals without either offending the gods or alienating himself from the human community? How does the hero commit violent acts to defend his civilization without undermining the values he is fighting for? And, finally, how can the hero create a meaningful life for himself in the face of certain death?

The Hero's Nature

The heroes we meet in the *Iliad* are, like Heracles, divided souls. Gifted with enormous energy and the drive to use it, they take an aggressive stance toward life, whether in the characteristic "shoot first, ask questions later" attitude or in the irresistible impulse always to "go forward," to attack their problems or their enemies head-on. Hector can no more sit contentedly inside the walls of Troy and simply outwait the Greeks—however logical a strategy that might be—than Achilles can remain sulking in his tent or hiding safely at home. Each can fulfill his gifts, his inner nature, only by being what he is. Just as Paris is a born lover whose gifts are the blessing of Aphrodite, so Achilles and Hector are, by nature, warriors. But to fulfill their needs as godlike warriors, they must violate their social needs as human beings.

The Hero's Two Fates   Achilles is presented with not one but two fates: to die gloriously at Troy or to live anonymously at home. The choices confronting him, however, are at best ambiguous. For individuals like Achilles and Hector, to choose inaction is to suffer the death of the soul that occurs when one's identity is shattered; but to choose action is to choose to die, sooner or later, in battle. Doomed whether he goes or stays, such an individual is confronted by the same tragic paradox that beset Heracles: to escape the mortality that is the inevitable lot of humanity, the hero strives to immortalize his name by pursuing glory. But in order to choose death with honor, he must, of course, choose death. Propelled by the enormous heroic energy that consumes as it inspires them, both Hector and Achilles arrive at the same moment of recognition and make the same decision: "Let it come." For the epic hero, as for the hero of the later tragedies, the readiness is all.

The Hero's Reputation

The *Iliad* describes a world in which the glory of a hero is not merely the consequence of divine gifts. Rather, his reputation must be publicly confirmed. Unique by virtue of his skills, the hero nevertheless must depend on the community to confer heroic status, signified through rank, rewards, prizes, songs, and stories. It is all too easy, then, to confuse the outward signs of heroism with the intrinsic merit and the amazing deeds of the true hero. Both Agamemnon and Achilles confuse the rank of general and the status of hero with the outward signs of respect from their troops or peers. Forgetting that a general needs his troops, Agamemnon neglects his responsibilities to his men, dwells on his own need for "prizes" sufficient for his rank, and suffers by losing men and battles (Figure 12-2). Forgetting that even heroes need the bonds of human society, Achilles, humiliated by having his "prize"

FIGURE 12-2   Agamemnon Leading Briseis Away from Achilles' Tent. In this vase painting (c. 480–470 B.C.), Agamemnon cruelly grabs Briseis by the wrist, dragging her from Achilles' tent. *(Louvre, Paris)*

FIGURE 12-3   The Armor of Achilles. In this vase painting (c. 460 B.C.), Thetis embraces her son, who is still grieving for the death of Patroclus. Athene is present, on the left, to lend her support to the re-arming of the despondent hero. His new shield is held by two Nereids, one of whom, herself saddened by the spectacle of Achilles' grief, covers her own face. *(British Museum, London)*

publicly removed, withdraws from the field and suffers by losing his beloved friend **Patroclus** [pa-TROH-kluhs] (Figure 12-3).

Achilles and Hector   Enraged by grief, Achilles forgets his human limitations and imagines that he can stand up to a raging river god, commit atrocities against the dead, and ignore the need to eat. Only when he is at last reconciled with Priam, whose son, **Hector**, Achilles has killed and whose corpse he refuses to release

FIGURE 12-4   Priam Pleading with Achilles for the Body of Hector. In this vase painting, the bearded Priam, leaning on his staff, appeals to Achilles, shown here reclining under his famous helmet and shield, for the return of his son Hector's corpse, here stretched under Achilles' chair. Rejecting the gifts offered by Priam's followers, Achilles turns his face from the old man. *(Kunsthistorisches Museum, Vienna)*

(Figure 12-4), does he belatedly recognize that the demands of the belly signify communion with the gods (as men pray and sacrifice some of each meal), the limits of the merely human body, and the bonds that unite humans into a community (as men feast together). Only then does Achilles emerge from the shell of egocentricity and begin to say *we* instead of *I*.

Hector exhibits similar confusion. Determined to protect his family and honor, he confuses honor with blind loyalty and fights in what he knows is an unworthy cause. He, too, knows that the inevitable consequence will be the destruction of the very city for which he sacrifices himself.

Diomedes   Among these exalted but tragic heroes, one figure emerges as a more moderate alternative—**Diomedes** [dye-oh-MEE-deez] "of the loud war cry." Formidable in battle, willing and able to take on and defeat even the gods themselves, he nevertheless knows when to stop. He is able to accept limits, whether required by the rules of courtesy (he will not, for example, fight **Glaucus**, the Trojan descendant of a guest-friend of Diomedes' own grandfather) or by direct orders from the gods (urged on by Athene, Diomedes wounds both Aphrodite and Ares, but when Apollo tells him not to attack any more gods, he obeys). Although he possesses the courage and the skills of the hero, he is not driven to meet experience head-on in defiance of the consequences. He is, furthermore, as persuasive in the assembly as he is effective on the battlefield. No Greek songs or epics celebrate Diomedes. Nevertheless, he possesses the kind of balance that the Greeks later came to admire.

Greek and Anglicized Spellings of Characters' Names in the *Iliad*

Because different translators adopt differing English transliterations of Greek names, the names of characters in Greek literature are spelled in a variety of ways. Whereas this text uses an Anglicized spelling, the translation of the *Iliad* included here adopts a spelling approximating the pronunciation of the original Greek. The following list provides a sampling of both versions of the names. (For a similar list of variant spellings of gods' names, see Chapter 6.)

Aias (Ajax)	Hektor (Hector)
Aineias (Aeneas)	Kalkhas (Calchas)
Akhaians (Achaeans)	Khryseis (Chryseis)
Akhilleus (Achilles)	Klytaimnestra (Clytemnestra)
Glaukos (Glaucus)	Menelaos (Menelaus)
Hekabe (Hecuba)	Patroklos (Patroclus)

(Much later, by the fifth century B.C., the qualities exhibited by Diomedes—the equal development of mind and body, the rational way of self-knowledge and self-control—would become the ideals of classical Greek culture.)

Odysseus   The most gifted speaker among the Greeks, Odysseus is able to use his characteristic diplomacy and common sense to his advantage—for example, persuading the Greeks not to retreat to their ships, stepping into the gap when Agamemnon's leadership momentarily falters, and preserving discipline and morale. However, even though we get to see him in action as a great soldier (rescuing the corpse of Patroclus, for example, along with his usual companion, Ajax), his most noteworthy activities are his intelligence operations, such as sneaking into Troy in disguise or wreaking havoc at night in the Trojan encampment. His use of disguises and deceptions, of course, eventually helps the Greeks to win (via the strategem of the **Trojan Horse,** a clever ruse that Homer does not include in the *Iliad*). Indeed, the Greeks valued his services, but heroes do not sneak about in disguise or under cover of darkness. Behaving as if the aim is to win the war and get home instead of to display one's heroic prowess in a game, Odysseus is a somewhat ambiguous hero (see Chapter 13).

The Gods

If the human world is confused, the realm of the Olympians is equally disordered. Divided among themselves, the gods nag, quarrel, lie, deceive, and, of course, take sides—Hera, Poseidon, and Athene favor the Greeks, while Apollo, Artemis, and Aphrodite favor the Trojans. Ares, the two-faced god of war, simply enjoys the sport and, while usually pro-Trojan, on some occasions fights on both sides. Zeus himself, although temporarily yielding to Thetis's request to support Achilles in his

The Gods' Alignment in the Trojan War		
PRO-GREEK	NEUTRAL	PRO-TROJAN
Hera	Zeus	Apollo
Athene		Aphrodite
Poseidon		Artemis
Hephaestus		Ares

quarrel with Agamemnon (see Color Plate 5), is relatively neutral, having worshipers and favorite heroes on both sides and even a son, Sarpedon, among the Trojans. He would prefer a peaceful compromise, or at least an agreement by the other gods not to intervene. But he is unable to arrange the former or to prevent the latter.

The Gods' Intervention in Human Affairs The gods intervene in human affairs in a variety of ways. They affect the action indirectly by encouraging the men to commit acts of courage, by sending dreams that inspire fear or affect morale, and by producing clouds of darkness to cover retreats or to interrupt battles. More directly, they intervene by assuming human disguises and entering the battlefield, where they block the path of arrows or actually fight, both as aggressors (as when Apollo knocks the wind out of Patroclus, setting him up to be killed) and as targets (as when both Ares and Aphrodite are wounded by Diomedes). Unlike the human combatants, however, the gods bleed **ichor** [IH-kohr] instead of blood and cannot really be hurt—being immortal, they need only to retreat to Olympus, where a balm applied by Hephaestus instantly cures all wounds. The gods of the *Iliad* may appear superficially human in their behavior, but the crucial distinction remains: gods simply do not die. For the gods, then, the war is like a game in which they cheer on their favorite teams and players and occasionally spill over onto the playing field. Ultimately, the fate of individual humans is of little real consequence to them.

The Powers and Limitations of the Gods The gods of the *Iliad* are not omnipotent: they preside over but do not absolutely control the universe. Zeus, for example, "father of gods and men," is unable to force the Olympians to comply with his wishes. And although he may rattle their wine cups with his thunderbolts or threaten to dangle recalcitrant deities from a chain off Mount Olympus, he is, in fact, apparently unwilling or unable to do so—nor could he without abrogating his role as a god who (unlike his father and grandfather) rules by persuasion, not violence.

Nor can the gods control human behavior. Despite his own preference for a negotiated solution, Zeus cannot force the warring parties to make peace or compel Achilles to return to Priam Hector's body, which he drags for eleven days past the tomb of Patroclus to avenge his friend's death at Hector's hands (Figure 12-5). The gods do, however, reinforce the values of courtesy and the guest–host relationship

FIGURE 12-5   Achilles Dragging the Body of Hector past the Tomb of Patroclus. In this image (early fifth century B.C.), Achilles is shown dragging Hector's corpse, which he has lashed to his chariot, past Patroclus's tomb to avenge the death of his dear friend. In attempting to mutilate the body, Achilles violates the gods' requirement that the dead be respected and given proper burial. *(Metropolitan Museum of Art, New York)*

applicable to humans and gods alike. Thus Zeus, who owes a debt of gratitude to Thetis, obliges her by assenting to her request that he help Achilles. And Apollo, who was a guest-friend at the wedding of Peleus and Thetis, cannot now violate that bond by stealing Hector's corpse from their son Achilles. On similar grounds, it is clear to all, even to the Trojans themselves, that the Trojans must eventually lose the war for having violated the sanctity of the bonds between guest and host, as well as the sacred institution of marriage. At the moment when Paris, a guest in Menelaus's home, seduced and absconded with his wife and treasure, he doomed the city of Troy.

For the humans, the acknowledgment of obligations to the gods includes piety, especially the expression of their gratitude to the gods. Apollo, for instance, brings down the plague in the Greek camp in answer to the prayers of the pious Trojan priest Chryses. This divine–human connection is also made through rituals, especially various forms of sacrifice and communion, from pouring off some wine to share with the gods at each meal to sacrificing an entire animal; such rituals are symbolic expressions of the human dependence on the gods for their physical and spiritual well-being. But although the gods react firmly to punish violations of these universal values, they do not necessarily reward piety in corresponding fashion: Hector, admired by the gods, especially Apollo, as a pious man, is nevertheless abandoned to his fate when he confronts Achilles. Not even Apollo can enable Hector to defeat a better fighter than himself. The gods may regret the death of Hector, but they do not prevent it. Unlike the morally neat and essentially comic world of the *Odyssey,* in which the good are eventually rewarded and the wicked struck by lightning bolts, thereby ensuring happy endings, the *Iliad* depicts a more unpredictable and thus potentially tragic world.

Human Destiny

It is not the gods, furthermore, who dictate human destiny. Rather, humans determine their own fate, the inevitable consequences of their own freely chosen acts.

The essential freedom of individuals is signified in the *Iliad* by three recurring motifs: the dual destinies, the image of the scales, and the two urns.

The dual destinies of humans are best symbolized by the alternative fates of Achilles, who is destined to live a long but unremarkable life *if* he chooses to stay at home or a short but glorious life *if* he chooses to fight at Troy. Thus, his fate is not predetermined but conditional: when he makes his choice, the consequences follow. And that choice, to be meaningful, must transcend external coercion of any kind, whether divine or human, and derive instead from a sense of his own integrity. His truly heroic nature is fulfilled not merely by the use of his special gifts but, more importantly, by his acceptance of moral responsibility for his own fate.

On the gods' part, the sense of alternative destinies—of a universe of freedom and possibilities—is reflected in the image of the scales in which Zeus weighs the fate of humans. Each time, Zeus suspends the scales by the midpoint and reads what they reveal. Although on one level the image concretizes the act of divine judgment, it also suggests that Zeus does not determine which pan rises up or which sinks down, any more than holding up a thermometer determines the temperature of the air.

The implications of a world in which humans are free to choose among complex possibilities are perhaps most concretely stated by Achilles himself, when he describes the two urns from which Zeus doles out gifts. Like Pandora's jar, the urns contain both blessings and curses, pleasures and pains, good news and bad news. Unfortunate individuals, Achilles explains, experience nothing but suffering; fortunate individuals experience great joy along with the suffering. He cites his father, Peleus, as an example: heroic, wealthy, married to a goddess, and father to a son he can be proud of, Peleus is blessed beyond the hopes of most men. But he will also have to confront his son's early death and to grow old and die alone. Only the gods live happily forever; mixed blessings are the best humans can hope for.

The Heroic Code

Homer's portrayal of the code by which the heroes live is equally ambivalent. On the positive side, we are compelled to admire the hero's strength, courage, and skill; his intensity and drive; and his willingness to risk all. On the negative side, we watch in dismay as his excessive strength and zeal lead to uncontrolled violence and as his need to fight undermines his good sense and moral values. On the positive side, we admire the hero's dedication; his loyalty to friends, family, and society; and his commitment to keep promises. Achilles fights in a cause not his own, for a promise he made, and the depth of his friendship with Patroclus is a model of devotion. On the negative side, we witness emotional and behavioral excesses as heroic commitments turn into misdirected loyalty, such as Priam's in defending his son, right or wrong, or Hector's in fighting for what he admits is a bad cause, or Achilles' in stubbornly persisting in his attempts to mutilate Hector's corpse. Dragging the body around his camp, tied to the axle of his chariot, Achilles violates the "prime directive" of the Greek world—respect for the dead—thus prompting outrage even among the gods who have favored him (except for Hera, who continues to support him).

Even more chilling, perhaps, is Achilles' stated wish to eat Hector's body raw, a fantasy that involves not only cannibalism, but reversion to the animal state, reversing the gift of Prometheus that shifted the balance of human existence from nature to culture. Joan O'Brien argues that Achilles' rage here reflects that of Hera, who likewise threatened to devour raw both Priam and Troy itself. There may be some correlation implied, but as we know from all-too-frequent modern instances of excessive savagery on the part of otherwise honorable soldiers, it is war itself that can finally break the tenuous bonds of civilization and set loose the beast within.

The heroic code calls for high ideals—respect among equals, courtesy toward others, and adherence to the rules, on the field and off. But it also encourages a corollary contempt for inferiors. Modern readers, who no longer live in a society strictly divided along class lines, can't help but notice how Odysseus, for example, trying to keep the demoralized troops from departing, speaks respectfully to his fellow officers but insults the common soldiers.

The Heroic Combat   Similarly, we share the hero's pride as he glories in victory, and we are dismayed as that pride gives way to vain egotism, to gloating over the fallen. And we are always reminded that victory for one hero necessitates death for another. The ideal model of heroic combat is the single combat between two heroes who respect each other's reputation, skill, and family; who fight face-to-face according to the rules of warfare; whose encounter, like a game, is monitored by a referee; who keep the armor but respect the corpse if they win; and who part as friends if they battle to a draw.

The point of such combat (for example, the match between Hector and Ajax) is not to defeat an enemy but to enhance one's heroic reputation. To the gods, war is a game. When war is presented as a challenge match between two heroic contenders with a taste for extreme sports, humans, too, can easily idealize warfare as a glorious game, an opportunity for the heroes to exhibit their godlike skills. But, as many readers have noted, it is a zero-sum game in which there are ultimately no winners. And the illusion of the game is all too easily shattered, giving way to savagery, as when Achilles captures and beheads twelve anonymous Trojans to avenge Patroclus's death.

Worse, in the heat of battle, the game, with its dream of glory, turns into a nightmare, and we are forced to watch in extreme close-up as brains spatter or guts spill out onto the ground. The climactic encounter between Achilles and Hector takes place on a quasi-surreal plane where there are no rules, no umpires, and no escape. The gods may, at their discretion, turn their attention from the war to their dinner, as Hephaestus suggests. Meanwhile, Hector, chased by the relentless Achilles around and around the walls of Troy, is trapped in a nightmare from which he will never awaken.

The Role of Women

If the heroes are trapped in a nightmare, it is at least one of their own choosing. Modern readers will recognize that the real victims in the masculine world of the epics are the women. Legally the property of their husbands or fathers, women are treated as loot—the booty of war—or given as prizes in athletic games. (In fact, their value was equated to that of draft animals; Achilles, for example, offers as a prize one woman good at crafts, valued at four oxen.) Several centuries later, the playwright Euripides will follow up the stories of the women in such plays as

Trojan Women and *Hecuba;* but no one in the Homeric epics asks how a **Chryseis** or a **Briseis** feels about being captured and forced to service the sexual needs of Agamemnon or Achilles.

But even those women who are not literally slaves are trapped, whether they remain within the body of the family or free themselves from its confines. Helen, for example, the cause of it all, leaves her husband and family to follow her lover, only to find herself surrounded by hostile Trojans, her only refuge a lover who is reluctant to fight for her and for whom she has come to feel contempt. Nor do we find any instances of Menelaus's expressing any love for Helen. His highly ornamental property has been taken, and his pride offended; it is not Helen herself that Menelaus wants, for all her beauty. And Agamemnon openly expresses contempt for his own wife, Clytemnestra. With the singular exception of Odysseus, the Greek heroes, for all that they are fighting to restore family love, express little love for their own wives. The family bonds they feel are exclusively patriarchal, the ties between fathers and sons.

In contrast to Helen, both Hector's mother, **Hecuba** [HEK-oo-ba], and his wife, **Andromache** [an-DROM-a-kee], remain entirely devoted to their families. Indeed, the household of Hector, Andromache, and the child, Astyanax, is presented as a model family—husband and wife utterly devoted to each other and openly affectionate with the child, their love so embracing that it even encompasses the horses, whom they name and pamper as family pets. It is ironic that we see the Greeks, ostensibly the pro-family side in this war, living in a military camp, having abandoned their own families to fight for the reunion of Menelaus's, while the Trojans, responsible for the breakup of Menelaus's family, are portrayed as ideal models of family love. Despite the mutual love of Hector and Andromache, she is nevertheless trapped in a society in which her needs and perceptions are not taken as seriously as those of the warriors (see Color Plate 8).

The traditional female role in the heroic myths is, of course, that of the temptress who tries to distract the hero from his quest, enticing him to indulge himself in the rewards and comforts of everyday life—food, sex, children, wealth. The Babylonian goddess of love and war, Ishtar, tempts Gilgamesh by attempting to seduce him, offering herself (as Calypso will later do to Odysseus) as his bride. He spurns her offer, pointing out that she has turned her previous lovers into animals (as Circe will do to Odysseus's crew—see Chapter 13). For the hero, to yield to such temptations is to cut himself off from expressing those heroic qualities that lift him out of the mundane world and allow him to fulfill his godlike potential. In the *Iliad,* it is Aphrodite, the goddess of love, who plays that role (along with her human counterpart, Helen), although her function as a war goddess, clear in the "judgment of Paris" myth, is attenuated in the epic, in which golden apples play no part and she is portrayed as an incompetent warrior. Nevertheless, her spirit prevails in Paris, who is more at home in the bedroom than on the battlefield, and even Achilles himself withdraws from battle in a quarrel over a woman.

Similarly, the Sumerian-Babylonian wine goddess Siduri tempts Gilgamesh with prosaic creature comforts, attempting to persuade him to abort his journey to the Underworld. The *Iliad*'s counterpart to Siduri is Andromache herself, who also tempts Hector with the comforts of domestic life. Andromache thus has a dual role in the epic. From the conventional heroic perspective, as temptress, she attempts to dissuade Hector from going into battle, an offer he, of course, dismisses, sending her back to her "woman's" pursuits—child care and weaving. From another perspective, as a manifestation of the wise goddess, she counsels commitment to the family and to achieving continuity through one's children.

Not compelled by nature or training into fitting the heroic mold, Andromache is free to see the truth that no one else in the epic, apart from the narrator, will acknowledge: Hector's compulsion to fight is strategically unnecessary and, worse, destructive to the very family that he is fighting to save. She tells him as much—the price of his glory is her enslavement: she and the child will be taken as slaves by the Greeks. Stay inside the walls, she advises, or at least don't go beyond the nearby fig tree, which could thus literally be a "Tree of Life," reminding us of the archetypal symbol of the feminine principle.

Compelled both by their nature and by social conditioning, Hector and Achilles cannot acknowledge the feminine aspect of their own natures, their anima. Hector recognizes the validity of Andromache's argument but, being a hero, cannot act on it: he *must* go forward. Achilles, too, rejects the protective urging of his mother and ends up bringing about the death of his best friend, Patroclus, who, wearing his armor and assuming Achilles' identity, becomes an alter ego whose death prefigures Achilles' own. This exclusively masculine heroic code is destructive to families, destructive to peace, and destructive to civilization itself, which requires the stability of affection and commitment and the peace in which to nurture the relationships of domestic life. But the social code of the Bronze Age, as depicted in the *Iliad,* reinforced traditional heroic attitudes. To stay at home was associated with the feminine principle: grown men fought; women, children, and old men stayed at home. Paris, who prefers making love to making war, is accused by Hector of skulking at home "like a woman."

Holding up the heroic code for us to view from a variety of often conflicting perspectives, the *Iliad* asks questions but does not offer answers. This is in keeping with the artist's role, as described by the bard Demodocus, to see the truth, in all its complexity, and to tell it. By showing us Andromache's perspective and reminding us of it in the brief glimpse of domestic life when he pauses to reflect on doing the laundry in the midst of the chase scene, Homer comments ironically on the limits of the heroic model. The hero so narrowly defined cannot achieve wholeness. Such partial consciousness is self-destructive, not just to the body but to the personality as well. And it is the women who are given the last word, as they lament the death of Hector.

But for all these brief glimpses of the role of women, Homer's focus in the *Iliad* remains largely, if somewhat ambivalently, on the hero. Achilles is, after all, the most revered of all the Greek heroes, and the *Iliad* celebrates his glory even as it questions the value of the war by which he achieved it. The feminine principle will have to lie in wait until, in the *Odyssey,* a new kind of hero emerges to effect the reconciliation of opposites, the integration of the divided self. Achilles' phallic instrument of destruction, his Pelian ash, was presumably once a tree, the symbol of the feminine principle. In the *Odyssey,* Odysseus is said to have carved the olive tree (symbol of Athene) not into a spear but into a marriage bed, leaving it still rooted in the earth, the primordial mother—the phallus and the Tree of Life rejoined.

The Conclusion of the *Iliad*

The epic ends with the funeral of Hector—a celebration of the life of a heroic individual, a ritual that affirms, even in the face of death, the value of life. Although the saga of Troy is carried on in the myths through the eventual death of Achilles and the defeat of the Trojans, in the epic, the renewed commitment of Achilles and the death of Hector make the fate of both Achilles and Troy inevitable. Rather than describing them, however, Homer chooses for his climactic point the moment of reconciliation—of the hero and his society, of honor and integrity, of life and death.

The Rite of Passage   In many myths, the hero's rite of passage is literal—he is separated from his community, goes on a journey, often to the Underworld, and returns with new knowledge, as did Gilgamesh, Heracles, Odysseus, and Aeneas. Perhaps more like the heroes of the later tragedies, Achilles' journey has been to the hell within. Retreating to his tent, he isolates himself physically, but his more important isolation is psychological. Like Gilgamesh, he loses his best friend. Abandoning society, Gilgamesh dons animal skins and travels to the Underworld. Similarly, while Achilles does not literally travel to the Underworld, in his rage he behaves like an animal, while the Underworld comes to him, literally, in the form of Patroclus's shade (his ghost or spirit) and the corpses he heaps up—in perverse tribute to his friend—in his camp, which quickly takes on an atmosphere of the realm of Death. It also comes to him psychologically as he undergoes the experiences of separation and alienation, descends into the depths of grief and murderous rage, and does battle with the gods themselves. Returning with new insight into the ambiguous nature of human experience and the limits of mortality, he is at last reconciled with the community of his fellow humans. The ego-driven hero with the hair-trigger temper of the opening chapters, obsessed with honor defined externally as public reputation, has yielded, albeit after great loss, to a more mature, more compassionate, more self-controlled Achilles who will be a hero because his own integrity, and not merely his public image, requires it. Later playwrights and philosophers, from Aeschylus to Socrates, would argue that humans "must suffer to be wise." If that is the case, then Achilles has earned—and paid for—his wisdom.

The Trojan Cycle Completed

Although the *Iliad* ends with the funeral of Hector, the myths continue the story to the end of the war and beyond. One of the many related stories tells of Penthesilea, the Amazon queen who disguises herself in a man's armor and fights with incredible skill until she is killed by Achilles himself (see Chapter 11).

The Death of Achilles

Achilles himself is eventually killed at the gates of Troy by an arrow in the heel, shot, according to some versions, by Paris, who was hiding behind the city walls. Other versions credit Apollo with the fatal shot or describe Apollo as guiding Paris's hand.

Achilles' corpse and armor are rescued by Odysseus and **Ajax**; Achilles' ashes are buried in a golden urn together with the ashes of Patroclus, and a huge mound is erected as a memorial, but the rescuers can't agree on which of them is to receive the armor. They present their cases in speeches before the assembly, and Odysseus, always a masterful speaker, is awarded the honor. Ajax, furious at being thus humiliated, goes mad. In a fit of insanity much like Heracles', he attacks the Greek leaders in their sleep, only to have Athene redirect his rage toward the horses and cattle. When he returns to his senses and realizes what he has done, he commits suicide.

Still the war goes on. The Greeks are told of prophecies that several tasks must be accomplished before they can defeat Troy. For example, they must bring Neoptolemus, Achilles' son, to join the battle: he does so and becomes a hero in his own right. They must bring the **Palladium**, a statue of Athene, from the city of Troy; Odysseus, once again operating as the Greeks' major intelligence agent, sneaks into Troy disguised as a beggar to accomplish the theft. Furthermore, the Greeks must bring the bow of Heracles from the island of Lemnos, where they had abandoned Philoctetes (the owner of the bow) because of a snakebite he'd suffered, which caused an agonizing wound that smelled so foul the troops could not bear to be near him.

The Trojan Horse

When all the assigned tasks are accomplished but the walls of Troy are still not breached, it is Odysseus who devises the trick that ends the war. He designs a hollow wooden horse in which he hides with a group of Greek officers. The prophetess **Cassandra** tries to warn the Trojans, but no one understands her warnings. A priest, **Laocoon** [lay-AHK-oh-ahn], also tries to warn them, but he is prevented from doing so by Poseidon, who sends a sea serpent to strangle him and his sons.

A soldier named **Sinon** is assigned to deliver the horse to the Trojans as a peace offering from the Greek armies, which pretend to be departing. Sinon claims to have been abandoned as a deserter and to be seeking asylum. The Trojans open the gates and bring the hollow horse inside the city, where they begin a great victory celebration. When the Trojans are at last asleep, Odysseus and his men emerge from the horse and open the gates for the Greek forces, which have silently assembled just outside. Once inside the city, they defeat the Trojans. The men (all but Aeneas and his household) are killed, the women and children taken prisoner, and the city looted and burned. After ten years of battling for honor and glory, after all those deaths, the city of Troy falls to a clever trick. The games, the heroic battles, the sacrifices—all have proved futile; intelligence, not prowess, is the weapon that brings victory.

The Return of the Achaeans

The battle won, the Greeks divide up the loot and sail for home. But their ten-year struggle has already set in motion consequences far beyond the military victory. The myths that spin off from the war detailing the returns of Agamemnon (see Chapter 15) and Odysseus (see Chapter 13) relate the problems of a postwar world struggling to return to normalcy or to create a new kind of order.

ILIAD*

Homer

BOOK 1

Anger be now your song, immortal one,   1
Akhilleus' anger, doomed and ruinous,
that caused the Akhaians loss on bitter loss
and crowded brave souls into the undergloom,
leaving so many dead men—carrion
for dogs and birds; and the will of Zeus was done:
Begin it when the two men first contending
broke with one another—
                              the Lord Marshal
Agamémnon, Atreus' son, and Prince Akhilleus.

Among the gods, who brought this quarrel on?   10
The son of Zeus by Lêto. Agamémnon
angered him, so he made a burning wind
of plague rise in the army: rank and file
sickened and died for the ill their chief had done
in despising a man of prayer.
This priest, Khrysês, had come down to the ships
with gifts, no end of ransom for his daughter;
on a golden staff he carried the god's white bands
and sued for grace from the men of all Akhaia,
the two Atreidai most of all:
                              "O captains   20
Meneláos and Agamémnon, and you other
Akhaians under arms!
The gods who hold Olympos, may they grant you
plunder of Priam's town and a fair wind home,
but let me have my daughter back for ransom
as you revere Apollo, son of Zeus!"

Then all the soldiers murmured their assent:

"Behave well to the priest. And take the ransom!"

But Agamémnon would not. It went against his desire,
and brutally he ordered the man away: 30
"Let me not find you here by the long ships
loitering this time or returning later,

---

*Translation by Robert Fitzgerald.

old man; if I do,
the staff and ribbons of the god will fail you.
Give up the girl? I swear she will grow old
at home in Argos, far from her own country,
working my loom and visiting my bed.
Leave me in peace and go, while you can, in safety."

So harsh he was, the old man feared and obeyed him,
in silence trailing away   40
by the shore of the tumbling clamorous whispering sea,
and he prayed and prayed again, as he withdrew,
to the god whom silken-braided Lêto bore:

"O hear me, master of the silver bow,
protector of Ténedos and the holy towns,
Apollo, Sminthian, if to your liking
ever in any grove I roofed a shrine
or burnt thighbones in fat upon your altar—
bullock or goat flesh—let my wish come true:
your arrows on the Danáäns for my tears!"   50

Now when he heard this prayer, Phoibos Apollo
walked with storm in his heart from Olympos' crest,
quiver and bow at his back, and the bundled arrows
clanged on the sky behind as he rocked in his anger,
descending like night itself. Apart from the ships
he halted and let fly, and the bowstring slammed
as the silver bow sprang, rolling in thunder away.
Pack animals were his target first, and dogs,
but soldiers, too, soon felt transfixing pain
from his hard shots, and pyres burned night and day.   60
Nine days the arrows of the god came down
broadside upon the army. On the tenth,
Akhilleus called all ranks to assembly. Hêra,
whose arms are white as ivory, moved him to it,
as she took pity on Danáäns dying.
All being mustered, all in place and quiet,
Akhilleus, fast in battle as a lion,
rose and said:
              "Agamémnon, now, I take it,
the siege is broken, we are going to sail,
and even so may not leave death behind: 70
if war spares anyone, disease will take him . . .
We might, though, ask some priest or some diviner,
even some fellow good at dreams—for dreams
come down from Zeus as well—
why all this anger of the god Apollo?

Has he some quarrel with us for a failure
in vows or hekatombs? Would mutton burned
or smoking goat flesh make him lift the plague?"
Putting the question, down he sat. And Kalkhas,
Kalkhas Thestórides, came forward, wisest   80
by far of all who scanned the flight of birds.
He knew what was, what had been, what would be,
Kalkhas, who brought Akhaia's ships to Ilion
by the diviner's gift Apollo gave him.
Now for their benefit he said:
                              "Akhilleus,
dear to Zeus, it is on me you call
to tell you why the Archer God is angry.
Well, I can tell you. Are you listening? Swear
by heaven that you will back me and defend me,
because I fear my answer will enrage   90
a man with power in Argos, one whose word
Akhaian troops obey.
                      A great man in his rage is formidable
for underlings: though he may keep it down,
he cherishes the burning in his belly
until a reckoning day. Think well
if you will save me."

Said Akhilleus:
              "Courage,
Tell what you know, what you have light to know.
I swear by Apollo, the lord god to whom
you pray when you uncover truth,   100
never while I draw breath, while I have eyes to see,
shall any man upon this beachhead dare
lay hands on you—not one of all the army,
not Agamémnon, if it is he you mean,
though he is first in rank of all Akhaians."

The diviner then took heart and said:
                              "No failure
in hekatombs or vows is held against us.
It is the man of prayer whom Agamémnon
treated with contempt: he kept his daughter,
spurned his gifts: for that man's sake the Archer   110
visited grief upon us and will again.
Relieve the Danáäns of this plague he will not
until the girl who turns the eyes of men
shall be restored to her own father—freely,
with no demand for ransom—and until
we offer up a hekatomb at Khrysê.
Then only can we claim him and persuade him."

He finished and sat down. The son of Atreus,
ruler of the great plain, Agamémnon,
rose, furious. Round his heart resentment   120
welled, and his eyes shone out like licking fire.
Then, with a long and boding look at Kalkhas,
he growled at him:
                    "You visionary of hell,
never have I had fair play in your forecasts.
Calamity is all you care about, or see,
no happy portents; and you bring to pass
nothing agreeable. Here you stand again
before the army, giving it out as oracle
the Archer made them suffer because of me,
because I would not take the gifts   130
and let the girl Khrysêis go; I'd have her
mine, at home. Yes, if you like, I rate her
higher than Klytaimnestra, my own wife!
She loses nothing by comparison
in beauty or womanhood, in mind or skill.

For all of that, I am willing now to yield her
if it is best; I want the army saved
and not destroyed. You must prepare, however,
a prize of honor for me, and at once,
that I may not be left without my portion—   140
I, of all Argives. It is not fitting so.
While every man of you looks on, my girl
goes elsewhere."

Prince Akhilleus answered him:

"Lord Marshal, most insatiate of men,
how can the army make you a new gift?
Where is our store of booty? Can you see it?
Everything plundered from the towns has been
distributed; should troops turn all that in?
Just let the girl go, in the god's name, now;   150
we'll make it up to you, twice over, three
times over, on that day Zeus gives us leave
to plunder Troy behind her rings of stone."

Agamémnon answered:
                    "Not that way
will I be gulled, brave as you are, Akhilleus.
Take me in, would you? Try to get around me?
What do you really ask? That you may keep
your own winnings, I am to give up mine
and sit here wanting her? Oh, no:
the army will award a prize to me   160

and make sure that it measures up, or if
they do not, I will take a girl myself,
your own, or Aías', or Odysseus' prize!
Take her, yes, to keep. The man I visit
may choke with rage; well, let him.
But this, I say, we can decide on later.

Look to it now, we launch on the great sea
a well-found ship, and get her manned with oarsmen,
load her with sacrificial beasts and put aboard
Khrysêis in her loveliness. My deputy,   170
Aías, Idómeneus, or Prince Odysseus,
or you, Akhilleus, fearsome as you are,
will make the hekatomb and quiet the Archer."

Akhilleus frowned and looked at him, then said:

"You thick-skinned, shameless, greedy fool!
Can any Akhaian care for you, or obey you,
after this on marches or in battle?
As for myself, when I came here to fight,
I had no quarrel with Troy or Trojan spearmen:
they never stole my cattle or my horses,   180
never in the black farmland of Phthía
ravaged my crops. How many miles there are
of shadowy mountains, foaming seas, between!
No, no, we joined for you, you insolent boor,
to please you, fighting for your brother's sake
and yours, to get revenge upon the Trojans.
You overlook this, dogface, or don't care,
and now in the end you threaten to take my girl,
a prize I sweated for, and soldiers gave me!

Never have I had plunder like your own   190
from any Trojan stronghold battered down
by the Akhaians. I have seen more action
hand to hand in those assaults than you have,
but when the time for sharing comes, the greater
share is always yours. Worn out with battle
I carry off some trifle to my ships.
Well, this time I make sail for home.
Better to take now to my ships. Why linger,
cheated of winnings, to make wealth for you?"

To this the high commander made reply: 200

"Desért, if that's the way the wind blows. Will I
beg you to stay on my account? I will not.
Others will honor me, and Zeus who views
the wide world most of all.

                    No officer
is hateful to my sight as you are, none
given like you to faction, as to battle—
rugged you are, I grant, by some god's favor.
Sail, then, in your ships, and lord it over
your own battalion of Myrmidons. I do not
give a curse for you, or for your anger.   210
But here is warning for you:
                    Khrysêis
being required of me by Phoibos Apollo,
she will be sent back in a ship of mine,
manned by my people. That done, I myself
will call for Brisêis at your hut, and take her,
flower of young girls that she is, your prize,
to show you here and now who is the stronger
and make the next man sick at heart—if any
think of claiming equal place with me."

A pain like grief weighed on the son of Pêleus,   220
and in his shaggy chest this way and that
the passion of his heart ran: should he draw
longsword from hip, stand off the rest, and kill
in single combat the great son of Atreus,
or hold his rage in check and give it time?
And as this tumult swayed him, as he slid
the big blade slowly from the sheath, Athêna
came to him from the sky. The white-armed goddess,
Hêra, sent her, being fond of both,
concerned for both men. And Athêna, stepping   230
up behind him, visible to no one
except Akhilleus, gripped his red-gold hair.

Startled, he made a half turn, and he knew her
upon the instant for Athêna: terribly
her grey eyes blazed at him. And speaking softly
but rapidly aside to her he said:

"What now, O daughter of the god of heaven
who bears the stormcloud, why are you here? To see
the wolfishness of Agamémnon?
Well, I give you my word: this time, and soon,   240
he pays for his behavior with his blood."

The grey-eyed goddess Athêna said to him:

"It was to check this killing rage I came
from heaven, if you will listen. Hêra sent me,
being fond of both of you, concerned for both.
Enough: break off this combat, stay your hand

upon the sword hilt. Let him have a lashing
with words, instead: tell him how things will be.
Here is my promise, and it will be kept:
winnings three times as rich, in due season,   250
you shall have in requital for his arrogance.
But hold your hand. Obey."
                          The great runner,
Akhilleus, answered
                    "Nothing for it, goddess,
but when you two immortals speak, a man
complies, though his heart burst. Just as well.
Honor the gods' will, they may honor ours."
On this he stayed his massive hand
upon the silver pommel, and the blade
of his great weapon slid back in the scabbard.
The man had done her bidding. Off to Olympos,   260
gaining the air, she went to join the rest,
the powers of heaven in the home of Zeus.

But now the son of Pêleus turned on Agamémnon
and lashed out at him, letting his anger ride
in execration:

              "Sack of wine,
you with your cur's eyes and your antelope heart!
You've never had the kidney to buckle on
armor among the troops, or make a sortie
with picked men—oh, no; that way death might lie.
Safer, by god, in the middle of the army—   270
is it not?—to commandeer the prize
of any man who stands up to you! Leech!
Commander of trash! If not, I swear,
you never could abuse one soldier more!

But here is what I say: my oath upon it
by this great staff: look: leaf or shoot
it cannot sprout again, once lopped away
from the log it left behind in the timbered hills;
it cannot flower, peeled of bark and leaves;
instead, Akhaian officers in council   280
take it in hand by turns, when they observe
by the will of Zeus due order in debate:
let this be what I swear by then: I swear
a day will come when every Akhaian soldier
will groan to have Akhilleus back. That day
you shall no more prevail on me than this
dry wood shall flourish—driven though you are,
and though a thousand men perish before

the killer, Hektor. You will eat your heart out,
raging with remorse for this dishonor   290
done by you to the bravest of Akhaians."
He hurled the staff, studded with golden nails,
before him on the ground. Then down he sat,
and fury filled Agamémnon, looking across at him.
But for the sake of both men Nestor arose,
the Pylians' orator, eloquent and clear;
argument sweeter than honey rolled from his tongue.
By now he had outlived two generations
of mortal men, his own and the one after,
in Pylos land, and still ruled in the third.   300
In kind reproof he said:

     "A black day, this.
Bitter distress comes this way to Akhaia.
How happy Priam and Priam's sons would be,
and all the Trojans—wild with joy—if they
got wind of all these fighting words between you,
foremost in council as you are, foremost
in battle. Give me your attention. Both
are younger men than I, and in my time
men who were even greater have I known
and none of them disdained me. Men like those   310
I have not seen again, nor shall: Peiríthoös,
the Lord Marshal Dryas, Kaineus, Exádios,
Polyphêmos, Theseus—Aigeus' son,
a man like the immortal gods. I speak
of champions among men of earth, who fought
with champions, with wild things of the mountains,
great centaurs whom they broke and overpowered.
Among these men I say I had my place
when I sailed out of Pylos, my far country,
because they called for me. I fought   320
for my own hand among them. Not one man
alive now upon earth could stand against them.
And I repeat: they listened to my reasoning,
took my advice. Well, then, you take it too.
It is far better so.
     Lord Agamémnon,
do not deprive him of the girl, renounce her.
The army had allotted her to him.
Akhilleus, for your part, do not defy
your King and Captain. No one vies in honor
with him who holds authority from Zeus.   330
You have more prowess, for a goddess bore you;
his power over men surpasses yours.

But, Agamémnon, let your anger cool.
I beg you to relent, knowing Akhilleus
a sea wall for Akhaians in the black waves of war."
Lord Agamémnon answered:
                              "All you say
is fairly said, sir, but this man's ambition,
remember, is to lead, to lord it over
everyone, hold power over everyone,
give orders to the rest of us! Well, one   340
will never take his orders! If the gods
who live forever made a spearman of him,
have they put insults on his lips as well?"

Akhilleus interrupted:
                        "What a poltroon,
how lily-livered I should be called, if I
knuckled under to all you do or say!
Give your commands to someone else, not me!
And one more thing I have to tell you; think it
over: this time, for the girl, I will not
wrangle in arms with you or anyone,   350
though I am robbed of what was given me;
but as for any other thing I have
alongside my black ship, you shall not take it
against my will. Try it. Hear this, everyone:
that instant your hot blood blackens my spear!"

They quarreled in this way, face to face, and then
broke off the assembly by the ships. Akhilleus
made his way to his squadron and his quarters,
Patróklos by his side, with his companions.

Agamémnon proceeded to launch a ship,   360
assigned her twenty oarsmen, loaded beasts
for sacrifice to the god, then set aboard
Khryséis in her loveliness. The versatile
Odysseus took the deck, and, all oars manned,
they pulled out on the drenching ways of sea.
The troops meanwhile were ordered to police camp
and did so, throwing refuse in the water;
then to Apollo by the barren surf
they carried out full-tally hekatombs,
and the savor curled in crooked smoke toward heaven.   370

That was the day's work in the army.
                                      Agamémnon
had kept his threat in mind, and now he acted,
calling Eurybatês and Talthýbios,
his aides and criers:

"Go along," he said,
"both of you, to the quarters of Akhilleus
and take his charming Brisêis by the hand
to bring to me. And if he balks at giving her
I shall be there myself with men-at-arms
in force to take her—all the more gall for him."
So, ominously, he sent them on their way,   380
and they who had no stomach for it went
along the waste sea shingle toward the ships
and shelters of the Myrmidons. Not far
from his black ship and hut they found the prince
in the open, seated. And seeing these two come
was cheerless to Akhilleus. Shamefast, pale
with fear of him, they stood without a word;
but he knew what they felt and called out:

                                          "Peace to you,
criers and couriers of Zeus and men!
Come forward. Not one thing have I against you: 390
Agamémnon is the man who sent you
for Brisêis. Here then, my lord Patróklos,
bring out the girl and give her to these men.
And let them both bear witness before the gods
who live in bliss, as before men who die,
including this harsh king, if ever hereafter
a need for me arises to keep the rest
from black defeat and ruin.

                              Lost in folly,
the man cannot think back or think ahead
how to come through a battle by the ships."   400
Patróklos did the bidding of his friend,
led from the hut Brisêis in her beauty
and gave her to them. Back along the ships
they took their way, and the girl went, loath to go.

Leaving his friends in haste, Akhilleus wept,
and sat apart by the grey wave, scanning the endless sea.
Often he spread his hands in prayer to his mother:

"As my life came from you, though it is brief,
honor at least from Zeus who storms in heaven
I call my due. He gives me precious little.   410
See how the lord of the great plains, Agamémnon,
humiliated me! He has my prize,
by his own whim, for himself."

                              Eyes wet with tears,
he spoke, and her ladyship his mother heard him
in green deeps where she lolled near her old father.
Gliding she rose and broke like mist from the inshore

grey sea face, to sit down softly before him,
her son in tears; and fondling him she said:
"Child, why do you weep? What grief is this?
Out with it, tell me, both of us should know."   420
Akhilleus, fast in battle as a lion,
groaned and said:
           "Why tell you what you know?
We sailed out raiding, and we took by storm
that ancient town of Eëtíôn called Thêbê,
plundered the place, brought slaves and spoils away.
At the division, later,
they chose a young girl, Khrysêis, for the king.
Then Khrysês, priest of the Archer God, Apollo,
came to the beachhead we Akhaians hold,
bringing no end of ransom for his daughter;   430
he had the god's white bands on a golden staff
and sued for grace from the army of Akhaia,
mostly the two Atreidai, corps commanders.
All of our soldiers murmured in assent:
'Behave well to the priest. And take the ransom!'
But Agamémnon would not. It went against his desire,
and brutally he ordered the man away.
So the old man withdrew in grief and anger.
Apollo cared for him: he heard his prayer
and let black bolts of plague fly on the Argives.   440

One by one our men came down with it
and died hard as the god's shots raked the army
broadside. But our priest divined the cause
and told us what the god meant by plague.

I said, 'Appease the god!' but Agamémnon
could not contain his rage; he threatened me,
and what he threatened is now done—
one girl the Akhaians are embarking now
for Khrysê beach with gifts for Lord Apollo;
the other, just now, from my hut—the criers   450
came and took her, Briseus' girl, my prize,
given by the army.
           If you can, stand by me:
go to Olympos, pray to Zeus, if ever
by word or deed you served him—
and so you did, I often heard you tell it
in Father's house: that time when you alone
of all the gods shielded the son of Krónos
from peril and disgrace—when other gods,
Pallas Athêna, Hêra, and Poseidon,
wished him in irons, wished to keep him bound,   460

you had the will to free him of that bondage,
and called up to Olympos in all haste
Aigaion, whom the gods call Briareus,
the giant with a hundred arms, more powerful
than the sea-god, his father. Down he sat
by the son of Krónos, glorying in that place.
For fear of him the blissful gods forbore
to manacle Zeus.
        Remind him of these things,
cling to his knees and tell him your good pleasure
if he will take the Trojan side   470
and roll the Akhaians back to the water's edge,
back on the ships with slaughter! All the troops
may savor what their king has won for them,
and he may know his madness, what he lost
when he dishonored me, peerless among Akhaians."

Her eyes filled, and a tear fell as she answered:

"Alas, my child, why did I rear you, doomed
the day I bore you? Ah, could you only be
serene upon this beachhead through the siege,
your life runs out so soon.   480
Oh early death! Oh broken heart! No destiny
so cruel! And I bore you to this evil!

But what you wish I will propose
To Zeus, lord of the lightning, going up
myself into the snow-glare of Olympos
with hope for his consent.
        Be quiet now
beside the long ships, keep your anger bright
against the army, quit the war.
        Last night
Zeus made a journey to the shore of Ocean
to feast among the Sunburned, and the gods   490
accompanied him. In twelve days he will come
back to Olympos. Then I shall be there
to cross his bronze doorsill and take his knees.
I trust I'll move him."

        Thetis left her son
still burning for the softly belted girl
whom they had wrested from him.

        Meanwhile Odysseus
with his shipload of offerings came to Khrysê.
Entering the deep harbor there
they furled the sails and stowed them, and unbent

forestays to ease the mast down quickly aft 500
into its rest; then rowed her to a mooring.
Bow-stones were dropped, and they tied up astern,
and all stepped out into the wash and ebb,
then disembarked their cattle for the Archer,
and Khrysêis, from the deepsea ship. Odysseus,
the great tactician, led her to the altar,
putting her in her father's hands, and said:

"Khrysês, as Agamémnon's emissary
I bring your child to you, and for Apollo
a hekatomb in the Danáäns' name. 510
We trust in this way to appease your lord,
who sent down pain and sorrow on the Argives."

So he delivered her, and the priest received her,
the child so dear to him, in joy. Then hastening
to give the god his hekatomb, they led
bullocks to crowd around the compact altar,
rinsed their hands and delved in barley baskets,
as open-armed to heaven Khrysês prayed:

"Oh hear me, master of the silver bow,
protector of Ténedos and the holy towns, 520
if while I prayed you listened once before
and honored me, and punished the Akhaians,
now let my wish come true again. But turn
your plague away this time from the Danáäns."

And this petition, too, Apollo heard.
When prayers were said and grains of barley strewn,
they held the bullocks for the knife, and flayed them,
cutting out joints and wrapping these in fat,
two layers, folded, with raw strips of flesh,
for the old man to burn on cloven faggots, 530
wetting it all with wine.
       Around him stood
young men with five-tined forks in hand, and when
the vitals had been tasted, joints consumed,
they sliced the chines and quarters for the spits,
roasted them evenly and drew them off.
Their meal being now prepared and all work done,
they feasted to their hearts' content and made
desire for meat and drink recede again,
then young men filled their winebowls to the brim,
ladling drops for the god in every cup. 540
Propitiatory songs rose clear and strong
until day's end, to praise the god, Apollo,

as One Who Keeps the Plague Afar; and listening
the god took joy.

                      After the sun went down
and darkness came, at last Odysseus' men
lay down to rest under the stern hawsers.

When Dawn spread out her finger tips of rose
they put to sea for the main camp of Akhaians,
and the Archer God sent them a following wind.
Stepping the mast they shook their canvas out,   550
and wind caught, bellying the sail. A foaming
dark blue wave sang backward from the bow
as the running ship made way against the sea,
until they came offshore of the encampment.
Here they put in and hauled the black ship high,
far up the sand, braced her with shoring timbers,
and then disbanded, each to his own hut.

Meanwhile unstirring and with smoldering heart,
the godlike athlete, son of Pêleus, Prince
Akhilleus waited by his racing ships.   560
He would not enter the assembly
of emulous men, nor ever go to war,
but felt his valor staling in his breast
with idleness, and missed the cries of battle.

Now when in fact twelve days had passed, the gods
who live forever turned back to Olympos,
with Zeus in power supreme among them.

                             Thetis
had kept in mind her mission for her son,
and rising like a dawn mist from the sea
into a cloud she soared aloft in heaven   570
to high Olympos. Zeus with massive brows
she found apart, on the chief crest enthroned,
and slipping down before him, her left hand
placed on his knees and her right hand held up
to cup his chin, she made her plea to him:

"O Father Zeus, if ever amid immortals
by word or deed I served you, grant my wish
and see to my son's honor! Doom for him
of all men comes on quickest.

                       Now Lord Marshal
Agamémnon has been highhanded with him,   580
has commandeered and holds his prize of war.
But you can make him pay for this, profound
mind of Olympos!

Lend the Trojans power,
until the Akhaians recompense my son
and heap new honor upon him!"
                          When she finished,
the gatherer of cloud said never a word
but sat unmoving for a long time, silent.
Thetis clung to his knees, then spoke again:

"Give your infallible word, and bow your head,
or else reject me. Can you be afraid   590
to let me see how low in your esteem
I am of all the gods?"
                          Greatly perturbed,
Lord Zeus who masses cloud said:
                          "Here is trouble.
You drive me into open war with Hêra
sooner or later:
she will be at me, scolding all day long.
Even as matters stand she never rests
from badgering me before the gods: I take
the Trojan side in battle, so she says.

Go home before you are seen. But you can trust me   600
to put my mind on this; I shall arrange it.
Here let me bow my head, then be content
to see me bound by that most solemn act
before the gods. My word is not revocable
nor ineffectual, once I nod upon it."

He bent his ponderous black brows down, and locks
ambrosial of his immortal head
swung over them, as all Olympos trembled.
After this pact they parted: misty Thetis
from glittering Olympos leapt away   610
into the deep sea; Zeus to his hall retired.
There all the gods rose from their seats in deference
before their father; not one dared
face him unmoved, but all stood up before him,
and thus he took his throne.
                          But Hêra knew
he had new interests; she had seen
the goddess Thetis, silvery-footed daughter
of the Old One of the sea, conferring with him,
and, nagging, she inquired of Zeus Kroníon:

"Who is it this time, schemer? Who has your ear?   620
How fond you are of secret plans, of taking
decisions privately! You could not bring yourself,

could you, to favor me with any word
of your new plot?"
                    The father of gods and men
said in reply:
                    "Hêra, all my provisions
you must not itch to know.
You'll find them rigorous, consort though you are.
In all appropriate matters no one else,
no god or man, shall be advised before you.
But when I choose to think alone,   630
don't harry me about it with your questions."
The Lady Hêra answered, with wide eyes:

"Majesty, what a thing to say. I have not
'harried' you before with questions, surely;
you are quite free to tell what you will tell.
This time I dreadfully fear—I have a feeling—
Thetis, the silvery-footed daughter
of the Old One of the sea, led you astray.
Just now at daybreak, anyway, she came
to sit with you and take your knees; my guess is   640
you bowed your head for her in solemn pact
that you will see to the honor of Akhilleus—
that is, to Akhaian carnage near the ships."

Now Zeus the gatherer of cloud said:
                                        "Marvelous,
you and your guesses; you are near it, too.
But there is not one thing that you can do about it,
only estrange yourself still more from me—
all the more gall for you. If what you say
is true, you may be sure it pleases me.
And now you just sit down, be still, obey me,   650
or else not all the gods upon Olympos
can help in the least when I approach your chair
to lay my inexorable hands upon you."
At this the wide-eyed Lady Hêra feared him,
and sat quite still, and bent her will to his.
Up through the hall of Zeus now all the lords
of heaven were sullen and looked askance. Hêphaistos,
master artificer, broke the silence,
doing a kindness to the snowy-armed
lady, his mother Hêra.

                    He began: 660
"Ah, what a miserable day, if you two
raise your voices over mortal creatures!

More than enough already! Must you bring
your noisy bickering among the gods?
What pleasure can we take in a fine dinner
when baser matters gain the upper hand?
To Mother my advice is—what she knows—
better make up to Father, or he'll start
his thundering and shake our feast to bits.
You know how he can shock us if he cares to—   670
out of our seats with lightning bolts!
Supreme power is his. Oh, soothe him, please,
take a soft tone, get back in his good graces.
Then he'll be benign to us again."
He lurched up as he spoke, and held a winecup
out to her, a double-handed one,
and said:

Hephaestus → "Dear Mother, patience, hold your tongue,
no matter how upset you are. I would not
see you battered, dearest.
                    It would hurt me,
and yet I could not help you, not a bit.   680
The Olympian is difficult to oppose.
One other time I took your part he caught me
around one foot and flung me
into the sky from our tremendous terrace.
I soared all day! Just as the sun dropped down
I dropped down, too, on Lemnos—nearly dead.
The island people nursed a fallen god."

He made her smile—and the goddess, white-armed Hêra,
smiling took the winecup from his hand.
Then, dipping from the winebowl, round he went   690
from left to right, serving the other gods
nectar of sweet delight.
                    And quenchless laughter
broke out among the blissful gods
to see Hêphaistos wheezing down the hall.
So all day long until the sun went down
they spent in feasting, and the measured feast
matched well their hearts' desire.
So did the flawless harp held by Apollo
and heavenly songs in choiring antiphon
that all the Muses sang.
                    And when the shining   700
sun of day sank in the west, they turned
homeward each one to rest, each to that home
the bandy-legged wondrous artisan
Hêphaistos fashioned for them with his craft.

The lord of storm and lightning, Zeus, retired
and shut his eyes where sweet sleep ever came to him,
and at his side lay Hêra, Goddess of the Golden Chair.

BOOK 2

[Zeus sends a false dream to Agamemnon to persuade him to take the field. Pretending that they are going to give up and return home, Agamemnon first tests the resolve of the troops, who run for the ships. Odysseus has to persuade them to return to the assembly, appealing to the courage of the officers and threatening the rank and file. Thersites, an ugly and cowardly but impudent member of the troops, challenges Agamemnon verbally in the assembly, but Odysseus threatens him and then beats him into submission. Offering a ritual sacrifice, Agamemnon prays to Zeus for victory. Zeus accepts the sacrifice but, carrying out his promise to Thetis to support Achilles in his quarrel, does not grant Agamemnon's request. The array of commanders and their respective troops on both the Greek and Trojan sides is described.]

BOOK 3

[Paris (also known as Alexandros), hanging back from battle, contrasts his gifts as a lover with Hector's as a hero. Paris is persuaded to enter the battle and proposes a single combat between himself and Menelaus. Aphrodite rescues him from this combat, setting him down in his own room and sending him back to Helen, who is now regretful of the life she has chosen and contemptuous of her lover.]

BOOK 4

[The gods in council discuss the war. Zeus expresses his esteem for both sides. He wants peace, but Athene and Hera want to punish the Trojans, while Aphrodite wants to save them. Despite Zeus's desire for compromise, the gods continue to get involved in the battles. Ares urges the Trojans on; Athene encourages the Greeks.]

BOOK 5

[Athene encourages the Greek warrior Diomedes, even urging him to fight the goddess Aphrodite:]

. . . .

As this man fled, Eurýpylos leapt after him
with drawn sword, on the run, and struck his shoulder,
cutting away one heavy arm: in blood
the arm dropped, and death surging on his eyes
took him, hard destiny.
                         So toiled the Akhaians
in that rough charge. But as for Diomêdês,
you could not tell if he were with Akhaians
or Trojans, for he coursed along the plain
most like an April torrent fed by snow,
a river in flood that sweeps away his bank;   10
no piled-up dyke will hold him, no revetment
shielding the bloom of orchard land, this river

suddenly at crest when heaven pours down
the rain of Zeus; many a yeoman's field
of beautiful grain is ravaged: even so
before Diomêdês were the crowded ranks
of Trojans broken, many as they were,
and none could hold him.

                      Now when Pándaros
looked over at him, saw him sweep the field,
he bent his bow of horn at Diomêdês   20
and shot him as he charged, hitting his cuirass
in the right shoulder joint. The winging arrow
stuck, undeflected, spattering blood on bronze.
Pándaros gave a great shout:

                      "Close up, Trojans!
Come on, charioteers! The Akhaian champion
is hit, hit hard; I swear my arrowshot
will bring him down soon—if indeed it was
Apollo who cheered me on my way from Lykia!"

Triumphantly he shouted; but his arrow
failed to bring Diomêdês down. Retiring   30
upon his chariot and team, he stood
and said to Sthénelos, the son of Kapanéus:

"Quick, Sthénelos, old friend, jump down
and pull this jabbing arrow from my shoulder!"

Sthénelos vaulted down and, pressed against him,
drew the slim arrow shaft clear of his wound
with spurts of blood that stained his knitted shirt.
And now at last Diomêdês of the warcry
prayed aloud:

                  "Oh hear me, daughter of Zeus
who bears the stormcloud, tireless one, Athêna!   40
If ever you stood near my father and helped him
in a hot fight, befriend me now as well.
Let me destroy that man, bring me in range of him,
who hit me by surprise, and glories in it.
He swears I shall be blind to sunlight soon."

So ran his prayer, and Pallas Athêna heard him.
Nimbleness in the legs, sure feet and hands
she gave him, standing near him, saying swiftly:

"Courage, Diomêdês. Press the fight
against the Trojans. Fury like your father's   50
I've put into your heart: his never quailed—
Tydeus, master shieldsman, master of horses.

I've cleared away the mist that blurred your eyes
a moment ago, so you may see before you
clearly, and distinguish god from man.
If any god should put you to the test
upon this field, be sure you are not the man
to dare immortal gods in combat—none,
that is, except the goddess Aphrodítê.
If ever she should join the fight, then wound her   60
with your keen bronze."
                              At this, grey-eyed Athêna
left him, and once more he made his way
into the line. If he had burned before
to fight with Trojans, now indeed blood-lust
three times as furious took hold of him.
Think of a lion that some shepherd wounds
but lightly as he leaps into a fold:
the man who roused his might cannot repel him
but dives into his shelter, while his flocks,
abandoned, are all driven wild; in heaps   70
huddled they are to lie, torn carcasses,
before the escaping lion at one bound
surmounts the palisade. So lion-like,
Diomêdês plunged on Trojans.

. . . .

[Diomedes then fights the Trojan Aeneas, Aphrodite's son. The goddess attempts to
rescue him, but she is wounded in the hand by Diomedes. Apollo steps in to carry
out the rescue, and Diomedes even tries to take him on. Back on Olympus, where
Aphrodite has retreated to have her wound healed, Dione relates other instances when
humans have injured gods. Ares then enters the fray, and Athene urges Diomedes to
attack him, too. With Athene's help, Diomedes wounds the god of war himself and
drives him from the field.]

BOOK 6

[The battle continues. Diomedes encounters Glaucus, a Trojan. When they discover
that their grandfathers were guest-friends, they exchange armor in token of continued
friendship and go on to fight other members of the opposing armies instead. Returning from the field, Hector talks with his wife, Andromache:]

. . . .

"Up to the great square tower of Ilion   1
she took her way, because she heard our men
were spent in battle by Akhaian power.
In haste, like a madwoman, to the wall
she went, and Nurse went too, carrying the child."

At this word Hektor whirled and left his hall,
taking the same path he had come by,
along byways, walled lanes, all through the town

until he reached the Skaian Gates, whereby
before long he would issue on the field.   10
There his warmhearted lady
came to meet him, running: Andrómakhê,
whose father, Eëtíôn, once had ruled
the land under Mount Plakos, dark with forest,
at Thêbê under Plakos—lord and king
of the Kilikians. Hektor was her lord now,
head to foot in bronze; and now she joined him.
Behind her came her maid, who held the child
against her breast, a rosy baby still,
Hektoridês, the world's delight, as fresh   20
as a pure shining star. Skamándrios
his father named him; other men would say
Astýanax, "Lord of the Lower Town,"
as Hektor singlehanded guarded Troy.
How brilliantly the warrior smiled, in silence,
his eyes upon the child! Andrómakhê
rested against him, shook away a tear,
and pressed his hand in both her own, to say:

"Oh, my wild one, your bravery will be
your own undoing! No pity for our child,   30
poor little one, or me in my sad lot—
soon to be deprived of you! soon, soon
Akhaians as one man will set upon you
and cut you down! Better for me, without you,
to take cold earth for mantle. No more comfort,
no other warmth, after you meet your doom,
but heartbreak only. Father is dead, and Mother.
My father great Akhilleus killed when he
besieged and plundered Thêbê, our high town,
citadel of Kilikians. He killed him,   40
but, reverent at last in this, did not
despoil him. Body, gear, and weapons forged
so handsomely, he burned, and heaped a barrow
over the ashes. Elms were planted round
by mountain-nymphs of him who bears the stormcloud.
Then seven brothers that I had at home
in one day entered Death's dark place. Akhilleus,
prince and powerful runner, killed all seven
amid their shambling cattle and silvery sheep.
Mother, who had been queen of wooded Plakos,   50
he brought with other winnings home, and freed her,
taking no end of ransom. Artemis
the Huntress shot her in her father's house.
Father and mother—I have none but you,
nor brother, Hektor; lover none but you!

Be merciful! Stay here upon the tower!
Do not bereave your child and widow me!
Draw up your troops by the wild figtree; that way
the city lies most open, men most easily
could swarm the wall where it is low: 60
three times, at least, their best men tried it there
in company of the two called Aías, with
Idómeneus, the Atreidai, Diomêdês—
whether someone who had it from oracles
had told them, or their own hearts urged them on."

Great Hektor in his shimmering helmet answered:

"Lady, these many things beset my mind
no less than yours. But I should die of shame
before our Trojan men and noblewomen
if like a coward I avoided battle,   70
nor am I moved to. Long ago I learned
how to be brave, how to go forward always
and to contend for honor, Father's and mine.
Honor—for in my heart and soul I know
a day will come when ancient Ilion falls,
when Priam and the folk of Priam perish.
Not by the Trojans' anguish on that day
am I so overborne in mind—the pain
of Hékabê herself, or Priam king,
or of my brothers, many and valorous,   80
who will have fallen in dust before our enemies—
as by your own grief, when some armed Akhaian
takes you in tears, your free life stripped away.
Before another woman's loom in Argos
it may be you will pass, or at Messêis
or Hypereiê fountain, carrying water,
against your will—iron constraint upon you.
And seeing you in tears, a man may say:
'There is the wife of Hektor, who fought best
of Trojan horsemen when they fought at Troy.'   90
So he may say—and you will ache again
for one man who could keep you out of bondage.
Let me be hidden dark down in my grave
before I hear your cry or know you captive!"

As he said this, Hektor held out his arms
to take his baby. But the child squirmed round
on the nurse's bosom and began to wail,
terrified by his father's great war helm—
the flashing bronze, the crest with horsehair plume
tossed like a living thing at every nod.   100
His father began laughing, and his mother

laughed as well. Then from his handsome head
Hektor lifted off his helm and bent
to place it, bright with sunlight, on the ground.
When he had kissed his child and swung him high
to dandle him, he said this prayer:

                          "O Zeus
and all immortals, may this child, my son,
become like me a prince among the Trojans.
Let him be strong and brave and rule in power
at Ilion; then someday men will say   110
'This fellow is far better than his father!'
seeing him home from war, and in his arms
the bloodstained gear of some tall warrior slain—
making his mother proud."

                    After this prayer,
into his dear wife's arms he gave his baby,
whom on her fragrant breast
she held and cherished, laughing through her tears.
Hektor pitied her now. Caressing her,
he said:

            "Unquiet soul, do not be too distressed
by thoughts of me. You know no man dispatches me   120
into the undergloom against my fate;
no mortal, either, can escape his fate,
coward or brave man, once he comes to be.
Go home, attend to your own handiwork
at loom and spindle, and command the maids
to busy themselves, too. As for the war,
that is for men, all who were born at Ilion,
to put their minds on—most of all for me."

He stooped now to recover his plumed helm
as she, his dear wife, drew away, her head   130
turned and her eyes upon him, brimming tears.
She made her way in haste then to the ordered
house of Hektor and rejoined her maids,
moving them all to weep at sight of her.
In Hektor's home they mourned him, living still
but not, they feared, again to leave the war
or be delivered from Akhaian fury.

Paris in the meantime had not lingered:
after he buckled his bright war-gear on
he ran through Troy, sure-footed with long strides.   140
Think how a stallion fed on clover and barley,
mettlesome, thundering in a stall, may snap
his picket rope and canter down a field

to bathe as he would daily in the river—
glorying in freedom! Head held high
with mane over his shoulders flying,
his dazzling work of finely jointed knees
takes him around the pasture haunts of horses.
That was the way the son of Priam, Paris,
ran from the height of Pergamos, his gear   150
ablaze like the great sun,
and laughed aloud. He sprinted on, and quickly
met his brother, who was slow to leave
the place where he had discoursed with his lady.
Aléxandros was first to speak:
                        "Dear fellow,"
he said, "have I delayed you, kept you waiting?
Have I not come at the right time, as you asked?"

And Hektor in his shimmering helm replied:

"My strange brother! No man with justice in him
would underrate your handiwork in battle;   160
you have a powerful arm. But you give way
too easily, and lose interest, lose your will.
My heart aches in me when I hear our men,
who have such toil of battle on your account,
talk of you with contempt. Well, come along.
Someday we'll make amends for that, if ever
we drive the Akhaians from the land of Troy—
if ever Zeus permit us, in our hall,
to set before the gods of heaven, undying
and ever young, our winebowl of deliverance."   170

BOOK 7

[Hector challenges the Greeks to single combat. Ajax is selected by lot from the volunteers:]

. . . .
"we have no fear of any. No man here   1
will drive me from the field against my will,
not by main force, not by a ruse. I hope
I was not born and bred on Sálamis
to be a dunce in battle."

                    At this the soldiers
prayed to Zeus. You might have heard one say,
his eyes on heaven:

                    "Father Zeus, from Ida
looking out for us all: greatest, most glorious:
let Aías win the honor of victory!

Or if you care for Hektor and are inclined   10
to favor him, then let both men be even
in staying power and honor!"
                              So they prayed,
while Aías made his brazen helmet snug,
fitted his shield and sword strap. He stepped out
as formidable as gigantic Arês,
wading into the ranks of men, when Zeus
drives them to battle in bloodletting fury.
Huge as that, the bastion of Akhaians
loomed and grinned, his face a cruel mask,
his legs moving in great strides. He shook   20
his long spear doubled by its pointing shadow,
and the Argives exulted. Now the Trojans
felt a painful trembling in the knees,
and even Hektor's heart thumped in his chest—
but there could be no turning back; he could not
slip again into his throng of troops;
he was the challenger. Aías came nearer,
carrying like a tower his body shield
of seven oxhides sheathed in bronze—a work
done for him by the leather-master Tykhios   30
in Hylê: Tykhios made the glittering shield
with seven skins of oxhide and an eighth
of plated bronze. Holding this bulk before him,
Aías Telamônios came on
toward Hektor and stood before him. Now he spoke,
threatening him:

               "Before long, man to man,
Hektor, you'll realize that we Danääns,
have our champions, too—I mean besides
the lionhearted breaker of men, Akhilleus.
He lies now by the beaked seagoing ships   40
in anger at Lord Marshal Agamémnon.
But here are those among us who can face you—
plenty of us. Fight then, if you will!"

To this, great Hektor in his shimmering helmet
answered:

               "Son of the ancient line of Télamôn,
Aías, lordly over fighting men,
when you try me you try no callow boy
or woman innocent of war. I know
and know well how to fight and how to kill,
how to take blows upon the right or left   50
shifting my guard of tough oxhide in battle,

how to charge in a din of chariots,
or hand to hand with sword or pike to use
timing and footwork in the dance of war.
Seeing the man you are, I would not trick you
but let you have it with a straight shot,
if luck is with me."

                    Rifling his spear,
he hurled it and hit Aías' wondrous shield
square on the outer and eighth plate of bronze.
The spearhead punched its way through this and through   60
six layers, but the seventh oxhide stopped it.
Now in his turn great Aías made his cast
and hit the round shield braced on Hektor's arm.
Piercing the bright shield, the whetted spearhead
cut its way into his figured cuirass,
ripping his shirt along his flank; but he
had twisted and escaped the night of death.
Now both men disengaged their spears and fell
on one another like man-eating lions
or wild boars—no tame household creatures. Hektor's   70
lancehead scored the tower shield—but failed
to pierce it, as the point was bent aside.
Then Aías, plunging forward, rammed his spear
into the round shield, and the point went through
to nick his furious adversary, making
a cut that welled dark blood below his ear.
But Hektor did not slacken, even so.
He drew away and in one powerful hand
picked from the plain a boulder lying there,
black, rough and huge, and threw it   80
hitting Aías' gigantic sevenfold shield
square on the boss with a great clang of bronze.
Then Aías lifted up a huger stone
and whirled, and put immeasurable force
behind it when he let it fly—as though
he flung a millstone—crushing Hektor's shield.
The impact caught his knees, so that he tumbled
backward behind the bashed-in shield. At once
Apollo pulled him to his feet again,
and now with drawn swords toe to toe   90
they would have doubled strokes on one another,
had not those messengers of Zeus and men,
the heralds, intervened—one from the Trojans,
one from the Akhaian side—for both
Idaíos and Talthýbios kept their heads.
They held their staves out, parting the contenders,
and that experienced man, Idaíos, said:

"Enough, lads. No more fighting. The Lord Zeus,
assembler of bright cloud, cares for you both.
Both are great spearmen, and we all know it.   100
But now already night is coming on,
and we do well to heed the fall of night."

Said Aías Telamônios in reply:

"Idaífos; call on Hektor to say as much.
He was the one who dared our champions
to duel with him. Let him take the lead.
Whatever he likes, I am at his disposition."

Hektor in his shimmering helmet answered:

"Aías, a powerful great frame you had
as a gift from god, and a clear head; of all   110
Akhaians you are toughest with a spear.
And this being shown, let us break off our duel,
our bloodletting, for today. We'll meet again
another time—and fight until the unseen
power decides between these hosts of ours,
awarding one or the other victory.
But now already night is coming on,
and we do well to heed the fall of night.
This way you'll give them festive pleasure there
beside the ships, above all to your friends,   120
companions at your table. As for me,
as I go through Priam's town tonight
my presence will give joy to Trojan men
and to our women, as in their trailing gowns
they throng the place of god with prayers for me.
Let us make one another memorable gifts,
and afterward they'll say, among Akhaians
and Trojans: 'These two fought and gave no quarter
in close combat, yet they parted friends.'"

This he said, and lifting off his broadsword,   130
silver-hilted, in its sheath, upon
the well-cut baldric, made a gift of it,
and Aías gave his loin-guard, sewn in purple.
Each then turned away. One went to join
the Akhaian troops; the other joined his Trojans,
and all were full of joy to see him come
alive, unhurt, delivered from the fury
of Aías whose great hands no man withstood.
Almost despairing of him still, they led him
into the town.   140

.   .   .   .   .

[The Greeks and Trojans agree to a one-day truce to bury their dead.]

BOOK 8

Dawn in her saffron robe came spreading light   1
on all the world, and Zeus who plays in thunder
gathered the gods on peaked Olympos' height,
then said to that assembly:

            "Listen to me,
immortals, every one,
and let me make my mood and purpose clear.
Let no one, god or goddess, contravene
my present edict; all assent to it
that I may get this business done, and quickly.
If I catch sight of anyone slipping away   10
with a mind to assist the Danáäns or the Trojans,
he comes back blasted without ceremony,
or else he will be flung out of Olympos
into the murk of Tartaros that lies
deep down in underworld. Iron the gates are,
brazen the doorslab, and the depth from hell
as great as heaven's utmost height from earth.
You may learn then how far my power
puts all gods to shame.
             Or prove it this way:
out of the zenith hang a golden line   20
and put your weight on it, all gods and goddesses.
You will not budge me earthward out of heaven,
cannot budge the all-highest, mighty Zeus,
no matter how you try.
            But let my hand
once close to pull that cable—up you come,
and with you earth itself comes, and the sea.
By one end tied around Olympos' top
I could let all the world swing in mid-heaven!
That is how far I overwhelm you all,
both gods and men."

            They were all awed and silent,   30
he put it with such power. After a pause,
the grey-eyed goddess Athêna said:

            "O Zeus,
highest and mightiest, father of us all,
we are well aware of your omnipotence,
but all the same we mourn the Akhaian spearmen
if they are now to meet hard fate and die.
As you command, we shall indeed
abstain from battle—merely, now and again,
dropping a word of counsel to the Argives,
that all may not be lost through your displeasure."   40

The driver of cloud smiled and replied:

"Take heart,
dear child, third born of heaven. I do not speak
my full intent. With you, I would be gentle."

Up to his car he backed his bronze-shod team
of aerial runners, long manes blowing gold.
He adorned himself in panoply of gold,
then mounted, taking up his golden whip,
and lashed his horses onward. At full stretch
midway between the earth and starry heaven
they ran toward Ida, sparkling with cool streams,   50
mother of wild things, and the peak of Gárgaron
where are his holy plot and fragrant altar.
There Zeus, father of gods and men, reined in
and freed his team, diffusing cloud about them,
while glorying upon the crest he sat
to view the far-off scene below—Akhaian
ships and Trojan city.
                              At that hour
Akhaian fighting men with flowing hair
took a meal by their huts and armed themselves.
The Trojans, too, on their side, in the city,   60
mustered under arms—though fewer, still
resolved by dire need to fight the battle
for wives' and children's sake.
                              Now all the gates
were flung wide and the Trojan army sortied,
charioteers and foot, in a rising roar.

When the two masses met on the battle line
they ground their shields together, crossing spears,
with might of men in armor. Round shield-bosses
rang on each other in the clashing din,
and groans mingled with shouts of triumph rose   70
from those who died and those who killed: the field
ran rivulets of blood. While the fair day
waxed in heat through all the morning hours
missiles from both sank home and men went down,
until when Hêlios bestrode mid-heaven
the Father cleared his golden scales. Therein
two destinies of death's long pain he set
for Trojan horsemen and Akhaian soldiers
and held the scales up by the midpoint. Slowly
one pan sank with death's day for Akhaians.   80

          . . . .

BOOK 9

[Fearing for the safety of their ships, the Greeks hold a feast and, in the assembly that follows, agree to petition Achilles to return to battle. Admitting an error of judgment, Agamemnon itemizes a list of munificent gifts he will give to Achilles if the hero will return. The one remaining condition is that Achilles must bow to Agamemnon. Odysseus, Ajax, and Phoenix—Achilles' old tutor—are appointed as ambassadors to Achilles, who makes a feast of his own to welcome them:]

.   .   .   .

And Prince Akhilleus led them in. He seated them   1
on easy chairs with purple coverlets,
and to Patróklos who stood near he said:

"Put out an ampler winebowl, use more wine
for stronger drink, and place a cup for each.
Here are my dearest friends beneath my roof."

Patróklos did as his companion bade him.
Meanwhile the host set down a carving block
within the fire's rays; a chine of mutton
and a fat chine of goat he placed upon it,   10
as well as savory pork chine. Automédôn
steadied the meat for him, Akhilleus carved,
then sliced it well and forked it on the spits.
Meanwhile Patróklos, like a god in firelight,
made the hearth blaze up. When the leaping flame
had ebbed and died away, he raked the coals
and in the glow extended spits of meat,
lifting these at times from the firestones
to season with pure salt. When all was done
and the roast meat apportioned into platters,   20
loaves of bread were passed round by Patróklos
in fine baskets. Akhilleus served the meat.
He took his place then opposite Odysseus,
back to the other wall, and told
Patróklos to make offering to the gods.
This he did with meat tossed in the fire,
then each man's hand went out upon the meal.
When they had put their hunger and thirst away,
Aías nodded silently to Phoinix,
but Prince Odysseus caught the nod. He filled   30
a cup of wine and lifted it to Akhilleus,
saying:
            "Health, Akhilleus. We've no lack
of generous feasts this evening—in the lodge
of Agamémnon first, and now with you,
good fare and plentiful each time.
It is not feasting that concerns us now,

however, but a ruinous defeat.
Before our very eyes we see it coming
and are afraid. By a blade's turn, our good ships
are saved or lost, unless you arm your valor.   40
Trojans and allies are encamped tonight
in pride before our ramparts, at our sterns,
and through their army burn a thousand fires.
These men are sure they cannot now be stopped
but will get through to our good ships. Lord Zeus
flashes and thunders for them on the right,
and Hektor in his ecstasy of power
is mad for battle, confident in Zeus,
deferring to neither men nor gods. Pure frenzy
fills him, and he prays for the bright dawn   50
when he will shear our stern-post beaks away
and fire all our ships, while in the shipways
amid that holocaust he carries death
among our men, driven out by smoke. All this
I gravely fear; I fear the gods will make
good his threatenings, and our fate will be
to die here, far from the pastureland of Argos.
Rouse yourself; if even at this hour
you'll pitch in for the Akhaians and deliver them
from Trojan havoc. In the years to come   60
this day will be remembered pain for you
if you do not. No remedy, no remedy
will come to hand, once the great ill is done.
While there is time, think how to keep this evil
day from the Danáäns!
             My dear lad,
how rightly in your case your father, Pêleus,
put it in his farewell, sending you out
from Phthía to take ship with Agamémnon!
'Now as to fighting power, child,' he said,
'if Hêra and Athêna wish, they'll give it.   70
Control your passion, though, and your proud heart,
for gentle courtesy is a better thing.
Break off insidious quarrels, and young and old,
the Argives will respect you for it more.'
That was your old father's admonition:
you have forgotten. Still, even now, abandon
heart-wounding anger. If you will relent,
Agamémnon will match this change of heart
with gifts. Now listen and let me list for you
what just now in his quarters he proposed: 80
seven new tripods, and ten bars of gold,
then twenty shining caldrons, and twelve horses,

thoroughbreds, that by their wind and legs
have won him prizes: any man who owned
what these have brought him would not lack resources,
could not be pinched for precious gold—so many
prizes have these horses carried home.
Then he will give you seven women, deft
in household handicraft: women of Lesbos
chosen when you yourself took Lesbos town,   90
as they outshone all womankind in beauty.
These he will give you, and one more, whom he
took away from you then: Briseus' daughter,
concerning whom he adds a solemn oath
never to have gone to bed or coupled with her,
as custom is, my lord, with men and women.
These are all yours at once. If the immortals
grant us the pillaging of Priam's town,
you may come forward when the spoils are shared
and load your ship with bars of gold and bronze.   100
Then you may choose among the Trojan women
twenty that are most lovely, after Helen.
And then, if we reach Argos of Akhaia,
flowing with good things of the earth, you'll be
his own adopted son, dear as Orestês,
born long ago and reared in bounteous peace.
He has three daughters now at home, Khrysóthemis,
Laódikê, and Iphiánassa.
You may take whom you will to be your bride
and pay no gift when you conduct her home   110
to your ancestral hall. He'll add a dowry
such as no man has given to his daughter.
Seven flourishing strongholds he'll give to you:
Kardamylê and Enopê and Hirê
in the wild grassland; holy Phêrai too,
and the deep meadowland of Ántheia,
Aipeia and the vineyard slope of Pêdasos,
all lying near the sea in the far west
of sandy Pylos. In these lands are men
who own great flocks and herds; now as your liegemen,   120
they will pay tithes and sumptuous honor to you,
prospering as they carry out your plans.
These are the gifts he will arrange if you
desist from anger.
            Even if you abhor
the son of Atreus all the more bitterly,
with all his gifts, take pity on the rest,
all the old army, worn to rags in battle.
These will honor you as gods are honored!

And ah, for these, what glory you may win!
Think: Hektor is your man this time: being crazed   130
with ruinous pride, believing there's no fighter
equal to him among those that our ships
brought here by sea, he'll put himself in range!"

Akhilleus the great runner answered him:

"Son of Laërtês and the gods of old,
Odysseus, master soldier and mariner,
I owe you a straight answer, as to how
I see this thing, and how it is to end.
No need to sit with me like mourning doves
making your gentle noise by turns. I hate   140
as I hate Hell's own gate that man who hides
one thought within him while he speaks another.
What I shall say is what I see and think.
Give in to Agamémnon? I think not,
neither to him nor to the rest. I had
small thanks for fighting, fighting without truce
against hard enemies here. The portion's equal
whether a man hangs back or fights his best;
the same respect, or lack of it, is given
brave man and coward. One who's active dies   150
like the do-nothing. What least thing have I
to show for it, for harsh days undergone
and my life gambled, all these years of war?
A bird will give her fledglings every scrap
she comes by, and go hungry, foraging.
That is the case with me.
Many a sleepless night I've spent afield
and many a day in bloodshed, hand to hand
in battle for the wives of other men.
In sea raids I plundered a dozen towns,   160
eleven in expeditions overland
through Trojan country, and the treasure taken
out of them all, great heaps of handsome things,
I carried back each time to Agamémnon,
He sat tight on the beachhead, and shared out
a little treasure; most of it he kept.
He gave prizes of war to his officers;
the rest have theirs, not I; from me alone
of all Akhaians, he pre-empted her.
He holds my bride, dear to my heart. Aye, let him   170
sleep with her and enjoy her!

                    Why must Argives
fight the Trojans? Why did he raise an army
and lead it here? For Helen, was it not?

Are the Atreidai of all mortal men
the only ones who love their wives? I think not.
Every sane decent fellow loves his own
and cares for her, as in my heart I loved
Brisêis, though I won her by the spear.
Now, as he took my prize out of my hands,
tricked and defrauded me, he need not tempt me;   180
I know him, and he cannot change my mind.
Let him take thought, Odysseus, with you
and others how the ships may be defended
against incendiary attack. By god,
he has achieved imposing work without me,
a rampart piled up overnight, a ditch
running beyond it, broad and deep,
with stakes implanted in it! All no use!
He cannot hold against the killer's charge.
As long as I was in the battle, Hektor   190
never cared for a fight far from the walls;
his limit was the oak tree by the gate.
When I was alone one day he waited there,
but barely got away when I went after him.
Now it is I who do not care to fight.
Tomorrow at dawn when I have made offering
to Zeus and all the gods, and hauled my ships
for loading in the shallows, if you like
and if it interests you, look out and see
my ships on Hellê's waters in the offing,   200
oarsmen in line making the sea-foam scud!
And if the great Earthshaker gives a breeze,
the third day out I'll make it home to Phthía.
Rich possessions are there I left behind
when I was mad enough to come here; now
I take home gold and ruddy bronze, and women
belted luxuriously, and hoary iron,
all that came to me here. As for my prize,
he who gave her took her outrageously back.
Well, you can tell him all this to his face,   210
and let the other Akhaians burn
if he in his thick hide of shamelessness
picks out another man to cheat. He would not
look me in the eye, dog that he is!
I will not share one word of counsel with him,
nor will I act with him; he robbed me blind,
broke faith with me: he gets no second chance
to play me for a fool. Once is enough.
To hell with him, Zeus took his brains away!
His gifts I abominate, and I would give   220
not one dry shuck for him. I would not change,

not if he multiplied his gifts by ten,
by twenty times what he has now, and more,
no matter where they came from: if he gave
what enters through Orkhómenos' town gate
or Thebes of Egypt, where the treasures lie—
that city where through each of a hundred gates
two hundred men drive out in chariots.
Not if his gifts outnumbered the sea sands
or all the dust grains in the world could Agamémnon   230
ever appease me—not till he pays me back
full measure, pain for pain, dishonor for dishonor.
The daughter of Agamémnon, son of Atreus,
I will not take in marriage. Let her be
as beautiful as pale-gold Aphrodítê,
skilled as Athêna of the sea-grey eyes,
I will not have her, at any price. No, let him
find someone else, an eligible Akhaian,
kinglier than I.

        Now if the gods
preserve me and I make it home, my father   240
Pêleus will select a bride for me.
In Hellas and in Phthía there are many
daughters of strong men who defend the towns.
I'll take the one I wish to be my wife.
There in my manhood I have longed, indeed,
to marry someone of congenial mind
and take my ease, enjoying the great estate
my father had acquired.

        Now I think
no riches can compare with being alive,
not even those they say this well-built Ilion   250
stored up in peace before the Akhaians came.
Neither could all the Archer's shrine contains
at rocky Pytho, in the crypt of stone.
A man may come by cattle and sheep in raids;
tripods he buys, and tawny-headed horses;
but his life's breath cannot be hunted back
or be recaptured once it pass his lips.
My mother, Thetis of the silvery feet,
tells me of two possible destinies
carrying me toward death: two ways: 260
if on the one hand I remain to fight
around Troy town, I lose all hope of home
but gain unfading glory; on the other,
if I sail back to my own land my glory
fails—but a long life lies ahead for me.
To all the rest of you I say: 'Sail home:

you will not now see Ilion's last hour,'
for Zeus who views the wide world held his sheltering
hand over that city, and her troops
have taken heart.

            Return, then, emissaries,   270
deliver my answer to the Akhaian peers—
it is the senior officer's privilege—
and let them plan some other way, and better,
to save their ships and save the Akhaian army.
This one cannot be put into effect—
their scheme this evening—while my anger holds.
Phoinix may stay and lodge the night with us,
then take ship and sail homeward at my side
tomorrow, if he wills. I'll not constrain him."

After Akhilleus finished, all were silent,   280
awed, for he spoke with power.
Then the old master-charioteer, Lord Phoinix,
answered at last, and let his tears come shining,
fearing for the Akhaian ships:

                "Akhilleus,
if it is true you set your heart on home
and will not stir a finger to save the ships
from being engulfed by fire—all for this rage
that has swept over you—how, child, could I
be sundered from you, left behind alone?
For your sake the old master-charioteer,   290
Pêleus, made provision that I should come,
that day he gave you godspeed out of Phthía
to go with Agamémnon. Still a boy,
you knew nothing of war that levels men
to the same testing, nothing of assembly
where men become illustrious. That is why
he sent me, to instruct you in these matters,
to be a man of eloquence and action.
After all that, dear child, I should not wish
to be left here apart from you—not even   300
if god himself should undertake to smooth
my wrinkled age and make me fresh and young,
as when for the first time I left the land
of lovely women, Hellas. I went north
to avoid a feud with Father, Amyntor
Orménidês. His anger against me rose
over a fair-haired slave girl whom he fancied,
without respect for his own wife, my mother.
Mother embraced my knees and begged that I
make love to this girl, so that afterward   310

she might be cold to the aging man. I did it.
My father guessed the truth at once, and cursed me,
praying the ghostly Furies that no son
of mine should ever rest upon his knees:
a curse fulfilled by the immortals—Lord
Zeus of undergloom and cold Perséphonê.
I planned to put a sword in him, and would have,
had not some god unstrung my rage, reminding me
of country gossip and the frowns of men;
I shrank from being called a parricide   320
among the Akhaians. But from that time on
I felt no tie with home, no love for lingering
under the rooftree of a raging father.
Our household and our neighbors, it is true,
urged me to stay. They made a handsome feast
of shambling cattle butchered, and fat sheep;
young porkers by the litter, crisp with fat,
were singed and spitted in Hêphaistos' fire,
rivers of wine drunk from the old man's store.
Nine times they spent the night and slept beside me,   330
taking the watch by turns, leaving a fire
to flicker under the entrance colonnade,
and one more in the court outside my room.
But when the tenth night came, starless and black,
I cracked the tight bolt on my chamber door,
pushed out, and scaled the courtyard wall, unseen
by household men on watch or women slaves.
Then I escaped from that place, made my way
through Hellas where the dancing floors are wide,
until I came to Phthía's fertile plain,   340
mother of flocks, and Pêleus the king.
He gave me welcome, treated me with love,
as a father would an only son, his heir
to rich possessions. And he made me rich,
appointing me great numbers of retainers
on the frontier of Phthía, where I lived
as lord of Dolopês. Now, it was I
who formed your manhood, handsome as a god's,
Akhilleus: I who loved you from the heart;
for never in another's company   350
would you attend a feast or dine in hall—
never, unless I took you on my knees
and cut your meat, and held your cup of wine.
Many a time you wet my shirt, hiccuping
wine-bubbles in distress, when you were small.
Patient and laborious as a nurse
I had to be for you, bearing in mind

that never would the gods bring into being
any son of mine. Godlike Akhilleus,
you were the manchild that I made my own   360
to save me someday, so I thought, from misery.
Quell your anger, Akhilleus! You must not
be pitiless! The gods themselves relent,
and are they not still greater in bravery,
in honor and in strength? Burnt offerings,
courteous prayer, libation, smoke of sacrifice,
with all of these, men can placate the gods
when someone oversteps and errs. The truth is,
prayers are daughters of almighty Zeus—
one may imagine them lame, wrinkled things   370
with eyes cast down, that toil to follow after
passionate Folly. Folly is strong and swift,
outrunning all the prayers, and everywhere
arriving first to injure mortal men;
still they come healing after. If a man
reveres the daughters of Zeus when they come near,
he is rewarded, and his prayers are heard;
but if he spurns them and dismisses them,
they make their way to Zeus again and ask
that Folly dog that man till suffering   380
has taken arrogance out of him.
                          Relent,
be courteous to the daughters of Zeus, you too,
as courtesy sways others, and the best.
If Agamémnon had no gifts for you,
named none to follow, but inveighed against you
still in fury, then I could never say,
'Discard your anger and defend the Argives—'
never, no matter how they craved your help.
But this is not so: he will give many things
at once; he promised others; he has sent   390
his noblest men to intercede with you,
the flower of the army, and your friends,
dearest among the Argives. Will you turn
their words, their coming, into humiliation?"

. . . .

[Achilles having rejected their offer, the Greeks decide to continue without him.]

BOOK 10

[Odysseus and Diomedes carry out a night raid. After capturing and interrogating a Trojan soldier, they kill him and use the intelligence thus obtained to slay thirteen Trojans and steal their horses.]

BOOK 11

[The Greeks continue the battle with incredible valor. Agamemnon charges into the enemy ranks, slaughtering Trojans as he goes. Then Agamemnon, Diomedes, and Odysseus are wounded. Achilles, intensely curious about the fate of his fellow soldiers, sends his beloved friend Patroclus for news. Nestor persuades Patroclus to don his friend's armor and enter the battle disguised as Achilles. Patroclus agrees and returns to tell Achilles of the plan.]

BOOK 12

[The Trojans plan to attack the ships, led by Sarpedon (a son of Zeus) and Hector. They almost succeed, and the Greeks are beaten back around the ships. Zeus sends a portent—an eagle carrying a blood-red snake, which strikes its captor; when the eagle lets go in pain, the snake falls among the Trojan troops. A Trojan officer, Poulydamas, interprets the omen as a warning to the Trojans to retreat from the Greek ships, but Hector refuses.]

BOOK 13

[While Zeus turns his attention elsewhere, Poseidon rallies the Greeks, inspiring them to fight off the Trojan attack. The gods, at cross purposes, continue to intervene on both sides.]

BOOK 14

[The recently wounded Greek heroes return to battle. Hera adorns herself with scents and fine clothes, and deceives Aphrodite into loaning her the enchanted girdle of desire. Hera uses it to entice Zeus to make love to her, in order to distract him from the war. Afterward, Zeus falls asleep. Meanwhile, Hector is wounded.]

BOOK 15

[Zeus discovers that he has been tricked and that meanwhile Poseidon has been intervening to help the Greeks. Zeus insists that the Greeks must continue to lose until the Trojans actually reach the ships so that Achilles will send Patroclus into the battle. He predicts the death of his own son, Sarpedon, at Patroclus's hands, the death of Patroclus and the consequent return of Achilles to battle, and the death of Hector. Then, Zeus promises, he will turn the tide of war to favor the Greeks.]

BOOK 16

[The Trojans set fire to the ships. Seeing the flames, Achilles tells Patroclus that the time has come to go into combat to protect the Greeks from total destruction. Patroclus arms for battle but does not have the strength to wield Achilles' spear, the famous Pelian ash. He leads the Myrmidons, Achilles' troops, into battle, wearing his friend's highly visible armor. Seeing the famous helmet, the Trojans are terrified. Patroclus encounters Sarpedon, and Zeus is divided between his desire to protect his son and his need to allow Patroclus to kill him to protect the Greeks. Reminding him that death is the fate of all men, Hera persuades him to allow Sarpedon's death. Then Patroclus encounters Hector:]

. . . .

                                      And fierce   1
Patróklos hurled himself upon the Trojans,
in onslaughts fast as Arês, three times, wild
yells in his throat. Each time he killed nine men.
But on the fourth demonic foray, then
the end of life loomed up for you, Patróklos.
Into the combat dangerous Phoibos came
against him, but Patróklos could not see
the god, enwrapped in cloud as he came near.
He stood behind and struck with open hand   10
the man's back and broad shoulders, and the eyes
of the fighting man were dizzied by the blow.
Then Phoibos sent the captain's helmet rolling
under the horses' hooves, making the ridge
ring out, and dirtying all the horsehair plume
with blood and dust. Never in time before
had this plumed helmet been befouled with dust,
the helmet that had kept a hero's brow
unmarred, shielding Akhilleus' head. Now Zeus
bestowed it upon Hektor, let him wear it,   20
though his destruction waited. For Patróklos
felt his great spearshaft shattered in his hands,
long, tough, well-shod, and seasoned though it was;
his shield and strap fell to the ground; the Lord
Apollo, son of Zeus, broke off his cuirass.
Shock ran through him, and his good legs failed,
so that he stood agape. Then from behind
at close quarters, between the shoulder blades,
a Dardan fighter speared him: Pánthoös' son,
Euphórbos, the best Trojan of his age   30
at handling spears, in horsemanship and running:
he had brought twenty chariot fighters down
since entering combat in his chariot,
already skilled in the craft of war. This man
was first to wound you with a spear, Patróklos,
but did not bring you down. Instead, he ran back
into the mêlée, pulling from the flesh
his ashen spear, and would not face his enemy,
even disarmed, in battle. Then Patróklos,
disabled by the god's blow and the spear wound   40
moved back to save himself amid his men.
But Hektor, seeing that his brave adversary
tried to retire, hurt by the spear wound, charged
straight at him through the ranks and lunged for him
low in the flank, driving the spearhead through.
He crashed, and all Akhaian troops turned pale.
Think how a lion in his pride brings down

a tireless boar; magnificently they fight
on a mountain crest for a small gushing spring—
both in desire to drink—and by sheer power   50
the lion conquers the great panting boar:
that was the way the son of Priam, Hektor,
closed with Patróklos, son of Menoitios,
killer of many, and took his life away.
Then glorying above him he addressed him:

"Easy to guess, Patróklos, how you swore
to ravage Troy, to take the sweet daylight
of liberty from our women, and to drag them
off in ships to your own land—you fool!
Between you and those women there is Hektor's   60
war-team, thundering out to fight! My spear
has pride of place among the Trojan warriors,
keeping their evil hour at bay.
The kites will feed on you, here on this field.
Poor devil, what has that great prince, Akhilleus,
done for you? He must have told you often
as you were leaving and he stayed behind,
'Never come back to me, to the deepsea ships,
Patróklos, till you cut to rags
the bloody tunic on the chest of Hektor!'   70
That must have been the way he talked, and won
your mind to mindlessness."

.   .   .   .

[Reminding Hector that his own death is imminent—at Prince Achilles' hands—
Patroclus dies.]

BOOK 17

[Hector strips Patroclus's corpse of Achilles' armor and wears it. Zeus comments on
the inevitability of Hector's death. Ajax rescues the corpse.]

BOOK 18

[Achilles mourns for Patroclus and acknowledges his responsibility for his friend's
death. Vowing revenge, he determines to reenter the battle, ready to face his own
death in order to destroy Hector. He vows not to bury Patroclus until he brings back
the mutilated corpse of Hector and cuts the throats of twelve Trojans in tribute to
his friend. But now he has no war gear. Thetis appeals to Hephaestus to forge a new
shield for Achilles. Hephaestus decorates the shield with scenes from two cities in
which disputes occur, one solving the dispute by formal debate, the other by war. He
also provides a cuirass (breastplate), helmet, and greaves (shin armor):]

.   .   .   .

                                   "On this account   1
I am here to beg you: if you will, provide
for my doomed son a shield and crested helm,

good legging-greaves, fitted with ankle clasps,
a cuirass, too. His own armor was lost
when his great friend went down before the Trojans.
Now my son lies prone on the hard ground in grief."

The illustrious lame god replied:

                    "Take heart.
No trouble about the arms. I only wish
that I could hide him from the power of death   10
in his black hour—wish I were sure of that
as of the splendid gear he'll get, a wonder
to any one of the many men there are!"

He left her there, returning to his bellows,
training them on the fire, crying, "To work!"
In crucibles the twenty bellows breathed
every degree of fiery air: to serve him
a great blast when he labored might and main,
or a faint puff, according to his wish
and what the work demanded.
                    Durable   20
fine bronze and tin he threw into the blaze
with silver and with honorable gold,
then mounted a big anvil in his block
and in his right hand took a powerful hammer,
managing with his tongs in his left hand,

His first job was a shield, a broad one, thick,
well-fashioned everywhere. A shining rim
he gave it, triple-ply, and hung from this
a silver shoulder strap. Five welded layers
composed the body of the shield. The maker   30
used all his art adorning this expanse.
He pictured on it earth, heaven, and sea,
unwearied sun, moon waxing, all the stars
that heaven bears for garland: Plëïadês,
Hyadês, Oríôn in his might,
the Great Bear, too, that some have called the Wain,
pivoting there, attentive to Oríôn,
and unbathed ever in the Ocean stream.

He pictured, then, two cities, noble scenes:
weddings in one, and wedding feasts, and brides   40
led out through town by torchlight from their chambers
amid chorales, amid the young men turning
round and round in dances: flutes and harps
among them, keeping up a tune, and women
coming outdoors to stare as they went by.
A crowd, then, in a market place, and there

two men at odds over satisfaction owed
for a murder done: one claimed that all was paid,
and publicly declared it; his opponent
turned the reparation down, and both   50
demanded a verdict from an arbiter,
as people clamored in support of each,
and criers restrained the crowd. The town elders
sat in a ring, on chairs of polished stone,
the staves of clarion criers in their hands,
with which they sprang up, each to speak in turn,
and in the middle were two golden measures
to be awarded him whose argument
would be the most straightforward.
                      Wartime then;   60
around the other city were emplaced
two columns of besiegers, bright in arms,
as yet divided on which plan they liked:
whether to sack the town, or treat for half
of all the treasure stored in the citadel.
The townsmen would not bow either: secretly
they armed to break the siege-line. Women and children
stationed on the walls kept watch, with men
whom age disabled. All the rest filed out,
as Arês led the way, and Pallas Athêna,   70
figured in gold, with golden trappings, both
magnificent in arms, as the gods are,
in high relief, while men were small beside them.
When these had come to a likely place for ambush,
A river with a watering place for flocks,
they here disposed themselves, compact in bronze.
Two lookouts at a distance from the troops
took their posts, awaiting sight of sheep
and shambling cattle. Both now came in view,
trailed by two herdsmen playing pipes, no hidden
danger in their minds. The ambush party   80
took them by surprise in a sudden rush;
swiftly they cut off herds and beautiful flocks
of silvery grey sheep, then killed the herdsmen.
When the besiegers from their parleying ground
heard sounds of cattle in stampede, they mounted
behind mettlesome teams, following the sound,
and came up quickly. Battle lines were drawn,
and on the riverbanks the fight began
as each side rifled javelins at the other.
Here then Strife and Uproar joined the fray,   90
and ghastly Fate, that kept a man with wounds
alive, and one unwounded, and another
dragged by the heels through battle-din in death.

This figure wore a mantle dyed with blood,
and all the figures clashed and fought
like living men, and pulled their dead away.

Upon the shield, soft terrain, freshly plowed,
he pictured: a broad field, and many plowmen
here and there upon it. Some were turning
ox teams at the plowland's edge, and there   100
as one arrived and turned, a man came forward
putting a cup of sweet wine in his hands.
They made their turns-around, then up the furrows
drove again, eager to reach the deep field's
limit; and the earth looked black behind them,
as though turned up by plows. But it was gold,
all gold—a wonder of the artist's craft.

He put there, too, a king's field. Harvest hands
were swinging whetted scythes to mow the grain,
and stalks were falling along the swath   110
while binders girded others up in sheaves
with bands of straw—three binders, and behind them
children came as gleaners, proffering
their eager armfuls. And amid them all
the king stood quietly with staff in hand,
happy at heart, upon a new-mown swath.
To one side, under an oak tree his attendants
worked at a harvest banquet. They had killed
a great ox, and were dressing it; their wives
made supper for the hands, with barley strewn.   120

A vineyard then he pictured, weighted down
with grapes: this all in gold; and yet the clusters
hung dark purple, while the spreading vines
were propped on silver vine-poles. Blue enamel
he made the enclosing ditch, and tin the fence,
and one path only led into the vineyard
on which the loaded vintagers took their way
at vintage time. Lighthearted boys and girls
were harvesting the grapes in woven baskets,
while on a resonant harp a boy among them   130
played a tune of longing, singing low
with delicate voice a summer dirge. The others,
breaking out in song for the joy of it,
kept time together as they skipped along.

The artisan made next a herd of longhorns,
fashioned in gold and tin: away they shambled,
lowing, from byre to pasture by a stream
that sang in ripples, and by reeds a-sway.

Four cowherds all of gold were plodding after
with nine lithe dogs beside them.
On the assault,   140
in two tremendous bounds, a pair of lions
caught in the van a bellowing bull, and off
they dragged him, followed by the dogs and men.
Rending the belly of the bull, the two
gulped down his blood and guts, even as the herdsmen
tried to set on their hunting dogs, but failed:
trading bites with lions for those dogs,
who halted close up, barking, then ran back.

And on the shield the great bowlegged god
designed a pasture in a lovely valley,   150
wide, with silvery sheep, and huts and sheds
and sheepfolds there.
A dancing floor as well
he fashioned, like that one in royal Knossos
Daidalos made for the Princess Ariadnê.
Here young men and the most desired young girls
were dancing, linked, touching each other's wrists,
the girls in linen, in soft gowns, the men
in well-knit khitons given a gloss with oil;
the girls wore garlands, and the men had daggers
golden-hilted, hung on silver lanyards.   160
Trained and adept, they circled there with ease
the way a potter sitting at his wheel
will give it a practice twirl between his palms
to see it run; or else, again, in lines
as though in ranks, they moved on one another:
magical dancing! All around, a crowd
stood spellbound as two tumblers led the beat
with spins and handsprings through the company.

Then, running round the shield-rim, triple-ply,
he pictured all the might of the Ocean stream.   170

Besides the densely plated shield, he made
a cuirass, brighter far than fire light,
a massive helmet, measured for his temples,
handsomely figured, with a crest of gold;
then greaves of pliant tin.

Now when the crippled god
had done his work, he picked up all the arms
and laid them down before Akhilleus' mother,
and swift as a hawk from snowy Olympos' height
she bore the brilliant gear made by Hêphaistos.

. . . .

BOOK 19

[Thetis brings the new armor to Achilles and promises to preserve Patroclus's corpse from decay until Achilles has fulfilled his promise. Achilles then returns to the assembly. Agamemnon and Achilles mutually apologize for their respective folly and rage, although Agamemnon blames Zeus for "stealing his wits" and repeats his offer of gifts. Odysseus reminds the impatient Achilles that the men need to eat before fighting:]

. . . .

Akhilleus answered: "Excellency,   1
Lord Marshal Agamémnon, make the gifts
if you are keen to—gifts are due; or keep them.
It is for you to say. Let us recover
joy of battle soon, that's all!
No need to dither here and lose our time,
our great work still undone. When each man sees
Akhilleus in a charge, crumpling the ranks
of Trojans with his bronze-shod spear, let each
remember that is the way to fight his man!"   10
Replied Odysseus, the shrewd field commander:

"Brave as you are, and like a god in looks,
Akhilleus, do not send Akhaian soldiers
into the fight unfed! Today's mêlée
will not be brief, when rank meets rank, and heaven
breathes fighting spirit into both contenders.
No, tell all troops who are near the ships to take
roast meat and wine, for heart and staying power.
No soldier can fight hand to hand, in hunger,
all day long until the sun goes down!   20
Though in his heart he yearns for war, his legs
go slack before he knows it: thirst and famine
search him out, and his knees fail as he moves.
But that man stayed with victualing and wine
can fight his enemies all day: his heart
is bold and happy in his chest, his legs
hold out until both sides break off the battle!
Come, then, dismiss the ranks to make their breakfast.
Let the Lord Marshal Agamémnon
bring his gifts to the assembly ground   30
where all may see them; may your heart be warmed.
Then let him swear to you, before the Argives,
never to have made love to her, my lord,
as men and women by their nature do.
So may your heart be peaceable toward him!
And let him sate your hunger with rich fare
in his own shelter, that you may lack nothing
due you in justice. Afterward, Agamémnon,

you'll be more just to others, too. There is
no fault in a king's wish to conciliate
a man with whom he has been quick to anger!"   40

And the Lord Marshal Agamémnon answered:

"Glad I am to hear you, son of Laërtês,
finding the right word at the right time
for all these matters. And the oath you speak of
I'll take willingly, with all my heart,
and will not, before heaven, be forsworn.
Now let Akhilleus wait here, though the wargod
tug his arm; and all the rest of you
wait here assembled till the gifts have come   50
down from our quarters, and our peace is made.
For you, Odysseus, here is my command:
choose the finest young peers of all Akhaia
to fetch out of my ship those gifts we pledged
Akhilleus yesterday; and bring the women.
Let Talthýbios prepare for sacrifice,
in the army's name, a boar to Zeus and Hêlios."
Replied Akhilleus:

        "Excellency, Lord Marshal,
another time were better for these ceremonies,
some interval in the war, and when I feel   60
less passion in me. Look, those men lie dead
whom Hektor killed when Zeus allowed him glory,
and yet you two propose a meal! By god,
I'd send our soldiers into action now
unfed and hungry, Have a feast, I'd say,
at sundown, when our shame has been avenged!
Before that, for my part, I will not swallow
food or drink—my dear friend being dead,
lying before my eyes, bled white by spear-cuts,
feet turned to his hut's door, his friends in mourning   70
around him. Your concerns are none of mine.
Slaughter and blood are what I crave, and groans
of anguished men!"

        But the shrewd field commander
Odysseus answered:

        "Akhilleus, flower and pride
of the Akhaians, you are more powerful
than I am—and a better spearman, too—
only in sizing matters up I'd say
I'm just as far beyond you, being older,
knowing more of the world. So bear with me.
Men quickly reach satiety with battle   80
in which the reaping bronze will bring to earth

big harvests, but a scanty yield, when Zeus,
war's overseer for mankind, tips the scales.
How can a fasting belly mourn our dead?
So many die, so often, every day,
when would soldiers come to an end of fasting?
No, we must dispose of him who dies
and keep hard hearts, and weep that day alone.
And those whom the foul war has left unhurt
will do well to remember food and drink,   90
so that we may again close with our enemies,
our dangerous enemies, and be tough soldiers,
hardened in mail of bronze. Let no one, now,
be held back waiting for another summons:
here is your summons! Woe to the man who lingers
beside the Argive ships! No, all together,
let us take up the fight against the Trojans!"

He took as escort sons of illustrious Nestor:
Phyleus' son Mégês, Thoas, and Meríonês,
and the son of Kreion, Lykomêdês, and   100
Melánippos, to Agamémnon's quarters.
No sooner was the work assigned than done:
they brought the seven tripods Agamémnon
promised Akhilleus, and the twenty caldrons
shining, and the horses, a full dozen;
then they conducted seven women, skilled
in housecraft, with Brisêis in her beauty.
Odysseus weighed ten bars of purest gold
and turned back, followed by his young Akhaians,
bearing the gifts to place in mid-assembly.   110

. . . .

[Refusing to eat, Achilles reluctantly agrees to allow the others to do so. Achilles, meanwhile, yokes his team. Xanthus, one of his magical horses, speaks, his voice given him by Hera to prophesy Achilles' death. Achilles already knows this but is committed to satisfying his rage against Hector, whatever the cost to himself.]

BOOKS 20 AND 21

[The armies gather again. Now Zeus gives the gods permission to get engaged in the battle. Poseidon removes Aeneas from danger, saving him for Troy's future destiny. Achilles moves through the Trojan army like a forest fire, killing Trojans and trampling them in the blood and dust. In contrast to his earlier practices, he refuses to take or ransom prisoners, instead tossing body after body into the river. He tells one victim that, however heroic, he himself will die:]

. . . .

"A morning comes or evening or high noon   1
when someone takes my life away in war,
a spear-cast, or an arrow from a bowstring."

At this the young man's knees failed, and his heart;
he lost his grip upon the spear
and sank down, opening his arms. Akhilleus
drew his sword and thrust between his neck
and collarbone, so the two-edged blade went in
up to the hilt. Now face down on the ground
he lay stretched out, as dark blood flowed from him,   10
soaking the earth. Akhilleus picked him up
by one foot, wheeled, and slung him in the river
to be swept off downstream. Then he exulted:

"Nose down there with fishes. In cold blood
they'll kiss your wound and nip your blood away.
Your mother cannot put you on your bed
to mourn you, but Skamánder whirling down
will bear you to the sea's broad lap,
where any fish that jumps, breaking a wave,
may dart under the dark wind-shivered water   20
to nibble white fat of Lykáôn. Trojans,
perish in this rout until you reach,
and I behind you slaughtering reach, the town!
The god-begotten river swiftly flowing
will not save you. Many a bull you've offered,
many a trim-hooved horse thrown in alive
to Xánthos' whirlpools. All the same, you'll die
in blood until I have avenged Patróklos,
paid you back for the death-wounds of Akhaians   30
cut down near the deep-sea-going ships
far from my eyes."

                        On hearing this, the river
darkened to the heart with rage. He cast
about for ways to halt prodigious Akhilleus'
feats of war and keep death from the Trojans.
Meanwhile the son of Pêleus took his spear
and bounded straight for Asteropaíos,
burning to kill this son of Pêlegôn,
whom the broad river Áxios had fathered
on Periboia, eldest of the daughters
of Akessámenos. Whirling, deep-running   40
river that he was, Áxios loved her.
And now Akhilleus made for Asteropaíos,
who came up from the stream-bed to confront him,
holding two spears. And Xánthos, in his anger
over all the young men dead, cut down
by Akhilleus pitilessly in the stream,
gave heart to this contender. As they drew near,
the great runner and prince was first to speak:

"Who are you, soldier? Where do you come from,
daring to challenge me? Grief comes to all   50
whose sons meet my anger."

                                          Pêlegôn's
brave son replied:
                                          "Heroic son of Pêleus,
why do you ask my birth? I am a native
of rich farmland, Paiônia; Paiônês
are the spearmen I command. Today the eleventh
dawn came up since I arrived at Ilion.
My line began, if you must know, with, Áxios,
mover of beautiful water over land,
who fathered the great spearman, Pêlegôn,
and Pêlegôn is said to have fathered me.   60
But now again to battle, Lord Akhilleus."

That was his prideful answer. Then Akhilleus
lifted his Pêlian ash. His enemy,
being ambidextrous, cast both spears at once
and failed. With one he hit Akhilleus' shield
but could not pierce it, for the gold plate held,
the god's gift; with his other spear he grazed
the hero's right forearm. Dark blood ran out,
but, craving manflesh still, the spear passed on
and fixed itself in earth. In turn, Akhilleus,
putting his heart into the cast to bring down   70
Asteropaíos, rifled his ashwood spear.
He missed him, hitting the high bank of the river,
where the long shaft punched in to half its length.
The son of Pêleus, drawing sword from hip,
lunged forward on his enemy, who could not
with his big fist work the spear loose: three times
he tried to wrench it from the arching bank,
three times relaxed his grip, then put his weight
into a fourth attempt to break the shaft,   80
and bent it; but Akhilleus closed
and killed him with a sword stroke. Near the navel
he slashed his belly; all his bowels dropped out
uncoiling to the ground. He gasped, and darkness
veiled his eyes. Upon his chest Akhilleus
mounted, and then bent to strip his armor,
gloating:

                                    "This way you'll rest. It is rough work
to match yourself with children of Lord Zeus,
river's offspring though you are. You claimed
descent from a broad river; well, I claim   90

descent from Zeus almighty. My begetter,
lord over many Myrmidons, was Pêleus,
the son of Aíakos, a son of Zeus.
Zeus being stronger than the seaward rivers,
so are his offspring than a river's get!
Here's a big river for you, flowing by,
if he had power to help you. There's no fighting
Zeus the son of Krónos. Akhelôïos
cannot rival him; neither can the might
of the deep Ocean stream—from whom all rivers   100
take their waters, and all branching seas,
all springs and deep-sunk wells. And yet he too
is terrified by the lightning flash of Zeus
and thunder, when it crashes out of heaven."

With this he pulled from the bank's overhang
his bronze-shod spear, and, having torn the life
out of the body, left it there, to lie
in sand, where the dark water lapped at it.
Then eels and fish attended to the body,
picking and nibbling kidney fat away.   110
As for Akhilleus, he ran onward, chasing
spearmen of Paiônia in their rout
along the eddying river: these had seen
their hero vanquished by the hand and blade
and power of Akhilleus. Now he slew
Thersílokhos, Mydôn, and Astýpylos,
Mnêsos, Thrásios, Ainios, Ophelestês,
and would have killed far more, had not the river,
cold with rage, in likeness of a man,
assumed a voice and spoken from a whirlpool: 120

"O Akhilleus, you are first in power
of all men, first in waywardness as well,
as gods forever take your side. If Zeus
has given you all Trojans to destroy,
destroy them elsewhere, do your execution
out on the plain! Now my blue watercourses
back up, filled with dead; I cannot spend
my current in the salt immortal sea,
being dammed with corpses. Yet you go on killing
wantonly. Let be, marshal of soldiers."   130

Akhilleus the great runner answered:

                              "Aye,
Skamánder, child of Zeus, as you require,
the thing shall be. But as for killing Trojans,
arrogant enemies, I take no rest

until I back them on the town and try out
Hektor, whether he gets the best of me
or I of him."

      At this he hurled himself
upon the Trojans like a wild god. The deep
and swirling river then addressed Apollo:
"All wrong, bow of silver, child of Zeus!   140
You have not worked the will of Zeus. How often
he made you free to take the Trojan side!
You could defend them until sunset comes,
till evening darkens grainland."

        "As he spoke,
the great spearman Akhilleus in a flash
leapt into midstream from the arching bank.
But he, the river, surged upon the man
with all his currents in a roaring flood,
and swept up many of the dead, who jostled
in him, killed by Akhilleus. He ejected   150
these to landward, bellowing like a bull,
but living men he kept in his blue streams
to hide them in deep places, in backwaters.
Then round Akhilleus with an ominous roar
a wave mounted. It fell against his shield
and staggered him, so that he lost his footing.
Throwing his arms around a leafy elm
he clung to it; it gave way, roots and all,
and tore the bank away, and dipped its branches
in the clear currents, damming up the river   160
when all had fallen in. The man broke free
of swirling water, turned into the plain
and ran like wind, in fear. But the great god
would not be shaken off: with his dark crest
he reared behind to put the Prince Akhilleus
out of action and protect the Trojans.
Akhilleus led him by a spear-throw, running
as fast as the black eagle, called the hunter,
strongest and swiftest of all birds: like him
he flashed ahead, and on his ribs the bronze   170
rang out with a fierce clang. At a wide angle
he fled, and the river with tremendous din
flowed on behind. Remember how a farmer
opens a ditch from a dark reservoir
to water plants or garden: with his mattock
he clears away the clods that dam the stream,
and as the water runs ahead, smooth pebbles
roll before it. With a purling sound

it snakes along the channel, going downhill,
outrunning him who leads it: so the wave   180
sent by the river overtook Akhilleus
momently, in spite of his great speed,
as gods are stronger than men are. Each time
the great battlefield runner, Prince Akhilleus,
turned to make a stand—to learn if all
the immortal gods who own the sweep of heaven
chased him—every time, the rain-fed river's
crest buffeted his back, and cursing
he leapt high in the air. Across his knees
the pressure of swift water tired him,   190
and sand was washed away under his feet.
Lifting his eyes to heaven, Akhilleus cried:

"Father Zeus, to think that in my travail
not one god would save me from the river—
only that! Then I could take the worst!
None of the gods of heaven is so to blame
as my own mother, who beguiled me, lying,
saying my end would come beneath Troy's wall
from flashing arrows of Apollo. Ah,
I wish Hektor had killed me; he's their best.   200
Then one brave man would have brought down another.
No, I was fated to ignoble death,
whelmed in a river, like a swineherd's boy
caught by a winter torrent as he crosses."

Now as he spoke, Poseidon and Athêna,
taking human form, moved near and stood,
and took his hands to tell him what would calm him.
Poseidon was the speaker:

                              "Son of Pêleus,
do not be shaken overmuch or fearful,
seeing what gods we are, your two allies,   210
by favor of Zeus—myself and Pallas Athêna.
The river is not destined to pull you down.
He will fall back, and you will soon perceive it.
Meanwhile here's good counsel, if you'll take it.
Do not allow your hands to rest from war—
from war that treats all men without distinction—
till you have rolled the Trojan army back
to Ilion, every man of them who runs,
and shut them in the wall. Then when you've taken
Hektor's life, retire upon the ships.   220
We give you glory; it is yours to win."

        .   .   .   .

[When even Achilles' skill and rage prove inadequate before the rushing flood of the river god Scamander, the gods rush in to rescue Achilles.]

BOOK 22

[At last, Achilles and Hector meet on the battlefield:]

. . . .

The old man wrenched at his grey hair and pulled out   1
hanks of it in both his hands, but moved
Lord Hektor not at all. The young man's mother
wailed from the tower across, above the portal,
streaming tears, and loosening her robe
with one hand, held her breast out in the other,
saying:

     "Hektor, my child, be moved by this,
and pity me, if ever I unbound
a quieting breast for you. Think of these things,
dear child; defend yourself against the killer   10
this side of the wall, not hand to hand.
He has no pity. If he brings you down,
I shall no longer be allowed to mourn you
laid out on your bed, dear branch in flower,
born of me! And neither will your lady,
so endowed with gifts. Far from us both,
dogs will devour you by the Argive ships."

With tears and cries the two implored their son,
and made their prayers again, but could not shake him.
Hektor stood firm, as huge Akhilleus neared.   20
The way a serpent, fed on poisonous herbs,
coiled at his lair upon a mountainside,
with all his length of hate awaits a man
and eyes him evilly: so Hektor, grim
and narrow-eyed, refused to yield. He leaned
his brilliant shield against a spur of wall
and in his brave heart bitterly reflected:

"Here I am badly caught. If I take cover,
slipping inside the gate and wall, the first
to accuse me for it will be Poulýdamas,   30
he who told me I should lead the Trojans
back to the city on that cursed night
Akhilleus joined the battle. No, I would not,
would not, wiser though it would have been.
Now troops have perished for my foolish pride,
I am ashamed to face townsmen and women.
Someone inferior to me may say:

'He kept his pride and lost his men, this Hektor!'
So it will go. Better, when that time comes,
that I appear as he who killed Akhilleus   40
man to man, or else that I went down
fighting him to the end before the city.
Suppose, though, that I lay my shield and helm
aside, and prop my spear against the wall,
and go to meet the noble Prince Akhilleus,
promising Helen, promising with her
all treasures that Aléxandros brought home
by ship to Troy—the first cause of our quarrel—
that he may give these things to the Atreidai?
Then I might add, apart from these, a portion   50
of all the secret wealth the city owns.
Yes, later I might take our counselors' oath
to hide no stores, but share and share alike
to halve all wealth our lovely city holds,
all that is here within the walls. Ah, no,
why even put the question to myself?
I must not go before him and receive
no quarter, no respect! Aye, then and there
he'll kill me, unprotected as I am,
my gear laid by, defenseless as a woman.   60
No chance, now, for charms from oak or stone
in parley with him—charms a girl and boy
might use when they enchant each other talking!
Better we duel, now at once, and see
to whom the Olympian awards the glory."
These were his shifts of mood. Now close at hand
Akhilleus like the implacable god of war
came on with blowing crest, hefting the dreaded
beam of Pélian ash on his right shoulder.
Bronze light played around him, like the glare   70
of a great fire or the great sun rising,
and Hektor, as he watched, began to tremble.
Then he could hold his ground no more. He ran,
leaving the gate behind him, with Akhilleus
hard on his heels, sure of his own speed.
When that most lightning-like of birds, a hawk
bred on a mountain, swoops upon a dove,
the quarry dips in terror, but the hunter,
screaming, dips behind and gains upon it,
passionate for prey. Just so, Akhilleus   80
murderously cleft the air, as Hektor
ran with flashing knees along the wall.
They passed the lookout point, the wild figtree
with wind in all its leaves, then veered away

along the curving wagon road, and came
to where the double fountains well, the source
of eddying Skamánder. One hot spring
flows out, and from the water fumes arise
as though from fire burning; but the other
even in summer gushes chill as hail   90
or snow or crystal ice frozen on water.
Near these fountains are wide washing pools
of smooth-laid stone, where Trojan wives and daughters
laundered their smooth linen in the days
of peace before the Akhaians came. Past these
the two men ran, pursuer and pursued,
and he who fled was noble, he behind
a greater man by far. They ran full speed,
and not for bull's hide or a ritual beast
or any prize that men compete for: no,   100
but for the life of Hektor, tamer of horses.
Just as when chariot-teams around a course
go wheeling swiftly, for the prize is great,
a tripod or a woman, in the games
held for a dead man, so three times these two
at full speed made their course round Priam's town,
as all the gods looked on. And now the father
of gods and men turned to the rest and said:

"How sad that this beloved man is hunted
around the wall before my eyes! My heart   110
is touched for Hektor; he has burned thigh flesh
of oxen for me often, high on Ida,
at other times on the high point of Troy.
Now Prince Akhilleus with devouring stride
is pressing him around the town of Priam.
Come, gods, put your minds on it, consider
whether we may deliver him from death
or see him, noble as he is, brought down
by Pêleus' son, Akhilleus."

            Grey-eyed Athêna
said to him:

            "Father of the blinding bolt,   120
the dark stormcloud, what words are these? The man
is mortal, and his doom fixed, long ago.
Would you release him from his painful death?
Then do so, but not all of us will praise you."

Zeus who gathers cloud replied:

            "Take heart,
my dear and honored child. I am not bent

on my suggestion, and I would indulge you.
Act as your thought inclines, refrain no longer."

So he encouraged her in her desire,
and down she swept from ridges of Olympos.   130
Great Akhilleus, hard on Hektor's heels,
kept after him, the way a hound will harry
a deer's fawn he has startled from its bed
to chase through gorge and open glade, and when
the quarry goes to earth under a bush
he holds the scent and quarters till he finds it;
so with Hektor: he could not shake off
the great runner, Akhilleus. Every time
he tried to sprint hard for the Dardan gates
under the towers, hoping men would help him,   140
sending missiles down, Akhilleus loomed
to cut him off and turn him toward the plain,
as he himself ran always near the city.
As in a dream a man chasing another
cannot catch him, nor can he in flight
escape from his pursuer, so Akhilleus
could not by swiftness overtake him,
nor could Hektor pull away. How could he
run so long from death, had not Apollo
for the last time, the very last, come near   150
to give him stamina and speed?
                             Akhilleus
shook his head at the rest of the Akhaians,
allowing none to shoot or cast at Hektor—
none to forestall him, and to win the honor.
But when, for the fourth time, they reached the springs,
the Father poised his golden scales.
                             He placed
two shapes of death, death prone and cold, upon them,
one of Akhilleus, one of the horseman, Hektor,
and held the midpoint, pulling upward. Down
sank Hektor's fatal day, the pan went down   160
toward undergloom, and Phoibos Apollo left him.
Then came Athêna, grey-eyed, to the son
of Pêleus, falling in with him, and near him,
saying swiftly:

          "Now at last I think
the two of us, Akhilleus loved by Zeus,
shall bring Akhaians triumph at the ships
by killing Hektor—unappeased
though he was ever in his thirst for war.
There is no way he may escape us now,

not though Apollo, lord of distances,   170
should suffer all indignity for him
before his father Zeus who bears the stormcloud,
rolling back and forth and begging for him.
Now you can halt and take your breath, while I
persuade him into combat face to face."

These were Athêna's orders. He complied,
relieved, and leaning hard upon the spearshaft
armed with its head of bronze. She left him there
and overtook Lord Hektor—but she seemed
Dêíphobos in form and resonant voice,   180
appearing at his shoulder, saying swiftly:

"Ai! Dear brother, how he runs, Akhilleus,
harrying you around the town of Priam!
Come, we'll stand and take him on."

                              "To this,
great Hektor in his shimmering helm replied:

"Dêíphobos, you were the closest to me
in the old days, of all my brothers, sons
of Hékabê and Priam. Now I can say
I honor you still more
because you dared this foray for my sake,   190
seeing me run. The rest stay under cover."

Again the grey-eyed goddess Athêna spoke:

"Dear brother, how your father and gentle mother
begged and begged me to remain! So did
the soldiers round me, all undone by fear.
But in my heart I ached for you.
Now let us fight him, and fight hard.
No holding back. We'll see if this Akhilleus
conquers both, to take our armor seaward,
or if he can be brought down by your spear."   200

This way, by guile, Athêna led him on.
And when at last the two men faced each other,
Hektor was the first to speak. He said:

"I will no longer fear you as before,
son of Pêleus, though I ran from you
round Priam's town three times and could not face you.
Now my soul would have me stand and fight,
whether I kill you or am killed. So come,
we'll summon gods here as our witnesses,
none higher, arbiters of a pact: I swear   210

that, terrible as you are,
I'll not insult your corpse should Zeus allow me
victory in the end, your life as prize.
Once I have your gear, I'll give your body
back to Akhaians. Grant me, too, this grace."

But swift Akhilleus frowned at him and said:

"Hektor, I'll have no talk of pacts with you,
forever unforgiven as you are.
As between men and lions there are none,
no concord between wolves and sheep, but all   220
hold one another hateful through and through,
so there can be no courtesy between us,
no sworn truce, till one of us is down
and glutting with his blood the wargod Arês.
Summon up what skills you have. By god,
you'd better be a spearman and a fighter!
Now there is no way out. Pallas Athêna
will have the upper hand of you. The weapon
belongs to me. You'll pay the reckoning
in full for all the pain my men have borne,   230
who met death by your spear."

                                   He twirled and cast
his shaft with its long shadow. Splendid Hektor,
keeping his eyes upon the point, eluded it
by ducking at the instant of the cast,
so shaft and bronze shank passed him overhead
and punched into the earth. But unperceived
by Hektor, Pallas Athêna plucked it out
and gave it back to Akhilleus. Hektor said:

"A clean miss. Godlike as you are,
you have not yet known doom for me from Zeus.   240
You thought you had, by heaven. Then you turned
into a word-thrower, hoping to make me lose
my fighting heart and head in fear of you.
You cannot plant your spear between my shoulders
while I am running. If you have the gift,
just put it through my chest as I come forward.
Now it's for you to dodge my own. Would god
you'd give the whole shaft lodging in your body!
War for the Trojans would be eased
if you were blotted out, bane that you are."   250

With this he twirled his long spearshaft and cast it,
hitting his enemy mid-shield, but off

and away the spear rebounded. Furious
that he had lost it, made his throw for nothing,
Hektor stood bemused. He had no other.
Then he gave a great shout to Dêíphobos
to ask for a long spear. But there was no one
near him, not a soul. Now in his heart
the Trojan realized the truth and said:

"This is the end. The gods are calling deathward.   260
I had thought
a good soldier, Dêíphobos, was with me,
He is inside the walls. Athêna tricked me.
Death is near, and black, not at a distance,
not to be evaded. Long ago
this hour must have been to Zeus's liking
and to the liking of his archer son.
They have been well disposed before, but now
the appointed time's upon me. Still, I would not
die without delivering a stroke,   270
or die ingloriously, but in some action
memorable to men in days to come."

With this he drew the whetted blade that hung
upon his left flank, ponderous and long,
collecting all his might the way an eagle
narrows himself to dive through shady cloud
and strike a lamb or cowering hare: so Hektor
lanced ahead and swung his whetted blade.
Akhilleus with wild fury in his heart
pulled in upon his chest his beautiful shield—   280
his helmet with four burnished metal ridges
nodding above it, and the golden crest
Hêphaistos locked there tossing in the wind.
Conspicuous as the evening star that comes,
amid the first in heaven, at fall of night,
and stands most lovely in the west, so shone
in sunlight the fine-pointed spear
Akhilleus poised in his right hand, with deadly
aim at Hektor, at the skin where most
it lay exposed. But nearly all was covered   290
by the bronze gear he took from slain Patróklos,
showing only, where his collarbones
divided neck and shoulders, the bare throat
where the destruction of a life is quickest.
Here, then, as the Trojan charged, Akhilleus
drove his point straight through the tender neck,
but did not cut the windpipe, leaving Hektor

able to speak and to respond. He fell
aside into the dust. And Prince Akhilleus
now exulted:

        "Hektor, had you thought   300
that you could kill Patróklos and be safe?
Nothing to dread from me; I was not there.
All childishness. Though distant then, Patróklos'
comrade in arms was greater far than he—
and it is I who had been left behind
that day beside the deepsea ships who now
have made your knees give way. The dogs and kites
will rip your body. His will lie in honor
when the Akhaians give him funeral."

Hektor, barely whispering, replied: 310

"I beg you by your soul and by your parents,
do not let the dogs feed on me
in your encampment by the ships. Accept
the bronze and gold my father will provide
as gifts, my father and her ladyship
my mother. Let them have my body back,
so that our men and women may accord me
decency of fire when I am dead."

Akhilleus the great runner scowled and said:

"Beg me no beggary by soul or parents,   320
whining dog! Would god my passion drove me
to slaughter you and eat you raw, you've caused
such agony to me! No man exists
who could defend you from the carrion pack—
not if they spread for me ten times your ransom,
twenty times, and promise more as well;
aye, not if Priam, son of Dárdanos,
tells them to buy you for your weight in gold!
You'll have no bed of death, nor will you be
laid out and mourned by her who gave you birth.   330
Dogs and birds will have you, every scrap."

Then at the point of death Lord Hektor said:

"I see you now for what you are. No chance
to win you over. Iron in your breast
your heart is. Think a bit, though: this may be
a thing the gods in anger hold against you
on that day when Paris and Apollo
destroy you at the Gates, great as you are."

Even as he spoke, the end came, and death hid him;
spirit from body fluttered to undergloom,   340
bewailing fate that made him leave his youth
and manhood in the world. And as he died
Akhilleus spoke again. He said:

"Die, make an end. I shall accept my own
whenever Zeus and the other gods desire."

At this he pulled his spearhead from the body,
laying it aside, and stripped
the bloodstained shield and cuirass from his shoulders.
Other Akhaians hastened round to see
Hektor's fine body and his comely face,   350
and no one came who did not stab the body.
Glancing at one another they would say:

"Now Hektor has turned vulnerable, softer
than when he put the torches to the ships!"

And he who said this would inflict a wound.
When the great master of pursuit, Akhilleus,
had the body stripped, he stood among them,
saying swiftly:

                    "Friends, my lords and captains
of Argives, now that the gods at last have let me
bring to earth this man who wrought   360
havoc among us—more than all the rest—
come, we'll offer battle around the city,
to learn the intentions of the Trojans now.
Will they give up their strongpoint at this loss?
Can they fight on, though Hektor's dead?"

· · · · · · · · · · · · · ·

[Achilles lashes Hector's corpse through the feet to his chariot and drags the body,
attempting to defile it. Horrified, Hector's parents and wife express their grief.]

BOOKS 23 AND 24

[The shade of Patroclus appeals to Achilles to ask for quick burial so his soul can find
rest in the Underworld. For eleven days Achilles mourns, each day dragging Hector's
body around the burial mound of Patroclus. But Apollo protects the corpse from
disfigurement. Achilles holds funeral games in honor of Patroclus. By the twelfth day,
many of the gods want to steal Hector's body. Apollo argues that Achilles' behavior is
savage and inhuman:]

· · · · · · · · · · · · · · ·

                                        He yoked   1
his team, with Hektor

tied behind, to drag him out, three times
around Patróklos' tomb. By day he rested
in his own hut, abandoning Hektor's body
to lie full-length in dust—though Lord Apollo,
pitying the man, even in death,
kept his flesh free of disfigurement.
He wrapped him in his great shield's flap of gold
to save him from laceration. But Akhilleus
in rage visited indignity on Hektor   10
day after day, and, looking on,
the blessed gods were moved. Day after day
they urged the Wayfinder to steal the body—
a thought agreeable to all but Hêra,
Poseidon, and the grey-eyed one, Athêna.
These opposed it, and held out, since Ilion
and Priam and his people had incurred
their hatred first, the day Aléxandros
made his mad choice and piqued two goddesses,
visitors in his sheepfold: he praised   20
a third, who offered ruinous lust.
Now when Dawn grew bright for the twelfth day,
Phoibos Apollo spoke among the gods:
"How heartless and how malevolent you are!
Did Hektor never make burnt offering
of bulls' thighbones to you, and unflawed goats?
Even in death you would not stir to save him
for his dear wife to see, and for his mother,
his child, his father, Priam, and his men:
they'd burn the corpse at once and give him burial.   30
Murderous Akhilleus has your willing help—
a man who shows no decency, implacable,
barbarous in his ways as a wild lion
whose power and intrepid heart
sway him to raid the flocks of men for meat.
The man has lost all mercy;
he has no shame—that gift that hinders mortals
but helps them, too. A sane one may endure
an even dearer loss: a blood brother,
a son; and yet, by heaven, having grieved   40
and passed through mourning, he will let it go.
The Fates have given patient hearts to men.
Not this one: first he took Prince Hektor's life
and now he drags the body, lashed to his car,
around the barrow of his friend, performing
something neither nobler in report
nor better in itself. Let him take care,

or, brave as he is, we gods will turn against him,
seeing him outrage the insensate earth!"

Hêra whose arms are white as ivory   50
grew angry at Apollo. She retorted:

"Lord of the silver bow, your words would be
acceptable if one had a mind to honor
Hektor and Akhilleus equally.
But Hektor suckled at a woman's breast,
Akhilleus is the first-born of a goddess—
one I nursed myself. I reared her, gave her
to Pêleus, a strong man whom the gods loved.
All of you were present at their wedding—
you too—friend of the base, forever slippery!—   60
came with your harp and dined there!"

                              Zeus the stormking
answered her:

                    "Hêra, don't lose your temper
altogether. Clearly the same high honor
cannot be due both men. And yet Lord Hektor,
of all the mortal men in Ilion,
was dearest to the gods, or was to me.
He never failed in the right gift; my altar
never lacked a feast
of wine poured out and smoke of sacrifice—
the share assigned as ours. We shall renounce   70
the theft of Hektor's body; there is no way;
there would be no eluding Akhilleus' eye,
as night and day his mother comes to him.
Will one of you now call her to my presence?
I have a solemn message to impart:
Akhilleus is to take fine gifts from Priam,
and in return give back Prince Hektor's body."

At this, Iris who runs on the rainy wind
with word from Zeus departed. Midway between
Samos and rocky Imbros, down she plunged   80
into the dark grey sea, and the brimming tide
roared over her as she sank into the depth—
as rapidly as a leaden sinker, fixed
on a lure of wild bull's horn, that glimmers down
with a fatal hook among the ravening fish.
Soon Iris came on Thetis in a cave,
surrounded by a company of Nereids
lolling there, while she bewailed the fate

of her magnificent son, now soon to perish
on Troy's rich earth, far from his fatherland.   90
Halting before her, Iris said:

                    "Come, Thetis,
Zeus of eternal forethought summons you."

Silvery-footed Thetis answered:

                    "Why?
Why does the great one call me to him now,
when I am shy of mingling with immortals,
being so heavyhearted? But I'll go.
Whatever he may say will have its weight."
That loveliest of goddesses now put on
a veil so black no garment could be blacker,
and swam where windswift Iris led. Before them   100
on either hand the ground swell fell away.
They rose to a beach, then soared into the sky
and found the viewer of the wide world, Zeus,
with all the blissful gods who live forever
around him seated. Athêna yielded place,
and Thetis sat down by her father, Zeus,
while Hêra handed her a cup of gold
and spoke a comforting word. When she had drunk,
Thetis held out the cup again to Hêra.
The father of gods and men began:

                    "You've come   110
to Olympos, Thetis, though your mind is troubled
and insatiable pain preys on your heart.
I know, I too. But let me, even so,
explain why I have called you here. Nine days
of quarreling we've had among the gods
concerning Hektor's body and Akhilleus.
They wish the Wayfinder to make off with it.
I, however, accord Akhilleus honor
as I now tell you—in respect for you
whose love I hope to keep hereafter. Go, now,   120
down to the army, tell this to your son:
the gods are sullen toward him, and I, too,
more than the rest, am angered at his madness,
holding the body by the beaked ships
and not releasing it. In fear of me
let him relent and give back Hektor's body!
At the same time I'll send Iris to Priam,
directing him to go down to the beachhead
and ransom his dear son. He must bring gifts
to melt Akhilleus' rage."

Thetis obeyed,
leaving Olympos' ridge and flashing down
to her son's hut. She found him groaning there,
inconsolable, while men-at-arms
went to and fro, making their breakfast ready—
having just put to the knife a fleecy sheep.
His gentle mother sat down at his side,
caressed him, and said tenderly:

"My child,
will you forever feed on your own heart
in grief and pain, and take no thought of sleep
or sustenance? It would be comforting
to make love with a woman. No long time
will you live on for me: Death even now
stands near you, appointed and all-powerful.
But be alert and listen: I am a messenger
from Zeus, who tells me the gods are sullen toward you
and he himself most angered at your madness,
holding the body by the beaked ships
and not releasing it. Give Hektor back.
Take ransom for the body."

"Said Akhilleus:
"Let it be so. Let someone bring the ransom
and take the dead away, if the Olympian
commands this in his wisdom."

"So, that morning,
in camp, amid the ships, mother and son
conversed together, and their talk was long.
Lord Zeus meanwhile sent Iris to Ilion.

"Off with you, lightfoot, leave Olympos, take
my message to the majesty of Priam
at Ilion. He is to journey down
and ransom his dear son upon the beachhead.
He shall take gifts to melt Akhilleus' rage,
and let him go alone, no soldier with him,
only some crier, some old man, to drive
his wagon team and guide the nimble wagon,
and afterward to carry home the body
of him that Prince Akhilleus overcame.
Let him not think of death, or suffer dread,
as I'll provide him with a wondrous guide,
the Wayfinder, to bring him across the lines
into the very presence of Akhilleus.
And he, when he sees Priam within his hut,
will neither take his life nor let another

130

140

150

160

170

enemy come near. He is no madman,
no blind brute, nor one to flout the gods,
but dutiful toward men who beg his mercy."

. . . .

[Inspired by Zeus, Priam goes alone through enemy lines to appeal to Achilles to
return Hector's corpse for burial:]

                              "Noble sons
I fathered here, but scarce one man is left me.
Fifty I had when the Akhaians came,
nineteen out of a single belly, others
born of attendant women. Most are gone.
Raging Arês cut their knees from under them.   180
And he who stood alone among them all,
their champion, and Troy's, ten days ago
you killed him, fighting for his land, my prince,
Hektor.
         It is for him that I have come
among these ships, to beg him back from you,
and I bring ransom without stint.
                              Akhilleus,
be reverent toward the great gods. And take
pity on me, remember your own father.
Think me more pitiful by far, since I
have brought myself to do what no man else   190
has done before—to lift to my lips the hand
of one who killed my son."

                    Now in Akhilleus
the evocation of his father stirred
new longing, and an ache of grief. He lifted
the old man's hand and gently put him by.
Then both were overborne as they remembered:
the old king huddled at Akhilleus' feet
wept, and wept for Hektor, killer of men,
while great Akhilleus wept for his own father
as for Patróklos once again; and sobbing   200
filled the room.
                    But when Akhilleus' heart
had known the luxury of tears, and pain
within his breast and bones had passed away,
he stood then, raised the old king up, in pity
for his grey head and greybeard cheek, and spoke
in a warm rush of words:

                    "Ah, sad and old!
Trouble and pain you've borne, and bear, aplenty.

Only a great will could have brought you here
among the Akhaian ships, and here alone
before the eyes of one who stripped your sons,   210
your many sons, in battle. Iron must be
the heart within you. Come, then, and sit down.
We'll probe our wounds no more but let them rest,
though grief lies heavy on us. Tears heal nothing,
drying so stiff and cold. This is the way
the gods ordained the destiny of men,
to bear such burdens in our lives, while they
feel no affliction. At the door of Zeus
are those two urns of good and evil gifts
that he may choose for us; and one for whom   220
the lightning's joyous king dips in both urns
will have by turns bad luck and good. But one
to whom he sends all evil—that man goes
contemptible by the will of Zeus; ravenous
hunger drives him over the wondrous earth,
unresting, without honor from gods or men.
Mixed fortune came to Pêleus. Shining gifts
at the gods' hands he had from birth: felicity,
wealth overflowing, rule of the Myrmidons,
a bride immortal at his mortal side.   230
But then Zeus gave afflictions too—no family
of powerful sons grew up for him at home,
but one child, of all seasons and of none.
Can I stand by him in his age? Far from my country
I sit at Troy to grieve you and your children.
You, too, sir, in time past were fortunate,
we hear men say. From Makar's isle of Lesbos
northward, and south of Phrygia and the Straits,
no one had wealth like yours, or sons like yours.
Then gods out of the sky sent you this bitterness: 240
the years of siege, the battles and the losses.
Endure it, then. And do not mourn forever
for your dead son. There is no remedy.
You will not make him stand again. Rather
await some new misfortune to be suffered."

The old king in his majesty replied:

"Never give me a chair, my lord, while Hektor
lies in your camp uncared for. Yield him to me
now. Allow me sight of him. Accept
the many gifts I bring. May they reward you,   250
and may you see your home again.
You spared my life at once and let me live."

Akhilleus, the great runner, frowned and eyed him
under his brows:

        "Do not vex me, sir," he said.
"I have intended, in my own good time,
to yield up Hektor to you. She who bore me,
the daughter of the Ancient of the sea,
has come with word to me from Zeus. I know
in your case, too—though you say nothing, Priam—
that some god guided you to the shipways here.   260
No strong man in his best days could make entry
into this camp. How could he pass the guard,
or force our gateway?
        Therefore, *let me be.*
Sting my sore heart again, and even here,
under my own roof, suppliant though you are,
I may not spare you, sir, but trample on
the express command of Zeus!"

        When he heard this,
the old man feared him and obeyed with silence.
Now like a lion at one bound Akhilleus
left the room. Close at his back the officers   270
Automédôn and Álkimos went out—
comrades in arms whom he esteemed the most
after the dead Patróklos. They unharnessed
mules and horses, led the old king's crier
to a low bench and sat him down.
Then from the polished wagon
they took the piled-up price of Hektor's body.
One khiton and two capes they left aside
as dress and shrouding for the homeward journey.
Then, calling to the women slaves, Akhilleus   280
ordered the body bathed and rubbed with oil—
but lifted, too, and placed apart, where Priam
could not see his son—for seeing Hektor
he might in his great pain give way to rage,
and fury then might rise up in Akhilleus
to slay the old king, flouting Zeus's word.
So after bathing and anointing Hektor
they drew the shirt and beautiful shrounding over him.
Then with his own hands lifting him, Akhilleus
laid him upon a couch, and with his two   290
companions aiding, placed him in the wagon.
Now a bitter groan burst from Akhilleus,
who stood and prayed to his own dead friend:

        "Patróklos,
do not be angry with me, if somehow

even in the world of Death you learn of this—
that I released Prince Hektor to his father.
The gifts he gave were not unworthy. Aye,
and you shall have your share, this time as well."

The Prince Akhilleus turned back to his quarters.
He took again the splendid chair that stood   300
against the farther wall, then looked at Priam
and made his declaration:
                              "As you wished, sir,
the body of your son is now set free.
He lies in state. At the first sight of Dawn
you shall take charge of him yourself and see him.
Now let us think of supper. We are told
that even Niobê in her extremity
took thought for bread—though all her brood had perished,
her six young girls and six tall sons. Apollo,
making his silver longbow whip and sing,   310
shot the lads down, and Artemis with raining
arrows killed the daughters—all this after
Niobê had compared herself with Lêto,
the smooth-cheeked goddess.
                              She has borne two children,
Niobê said, How many have I borne!
But soon these two destroyed the twelve.

                                          Besides,
nine days the dead lay stark, no one could bury them,
for Zeus had turned all folk of theirs to stone.
The gods made graves for them on the tenth day,
and then at last, being weak and spent with weeping,   320
Niobê thought of food. Among the rocks
of Sipylos' lonely mountainside, where nymphs
who race Akhelôïos river go to rest,
she, too, long turned to stone, somewhere broods on
the gall immortal gods gave her to drink.

Like her we'll think of supper, noble sir.
Weep for your son again when you have borne him
back to Troy; there he'll be mourned indeed."

In one swift movement now Akhilleus caught
and slaughtered a white lamb. His officers   330
flayed it, skillful in their butchering
to dress the flesh; they cut bits for the skewers,
roasted, and drew them off, done to a turn.
Automédôn dealt loaves into the baskets
on the great board; Akhilleus served the meat.
Then all their hands went out upon the supper.

When thirst and appetite were turned away,
Priam, the heir of Dárdanos, gazed long
in wonder at Akhilleus' form and scale—
so like the gods in aspect. And Akhilleus   340
in his turn gazed in wonder upon Priam,
royal in visage as in speech. Both men
in contemplation found rest for their eyes,
till the old hero, Priam, broke the silence:
"Make a bed ready for me, son of Thetis,
and let us know the luxury of sleep.
From that hour when my son died at your hands
till now, my eyelids have not closed in slumber
over my eyes, but groaning where I sat
I tasted pain and grief a thousandfold,   350
or lay down rolling in my courtyard mire.
Here for the first time I have swallowed bread
and made myself drink wine.
                        Before, I could not."

Akhilleus ordered men and servingwomen
to make a bed outside, in the covered forecourt,
with purple rugs piled up and sheets outspread
and coverings of all fleece laid on top.
The girls went out with torches in their hands
and soon deftly made up a double bed.
Then Akhilleus, defiant of Agamémnon,   360
told his guest:

            "Dear venerable sir,
you'll sleep outside tonight, in case an Akhaian
officer turns up, one of those men
who are forever taking counsel with me—
as well they may. If one should see you here
as the dark night runs on, he would report it
to the Lord Marshal Agamémnon. Then
return of the body would only be delayed.
Now tell me this, and give me a straight answer:
How many days do you require   370
for the funeral of Prince Hektor?—I should know
how long to wait, and hold the Akhaian army."

Old Priam in his majesty replied:

"If you would have me carry out the burial,
Akhilleus, here is the way to do me grace.
As we are penned in the town, but must bring wood
from the distant hills, the Trojans are afraid.
We should have mourning for nine days in hall,
then on the tenth conduct his funeral
and feast the troops and commons;   380

on the eleventh we should make his tomb,
and on the twelfth give battle, if we must."

Akhilleus said:

> "As you command, old Priam,
> the thing is done. I shall suspend the war
> for those eleven days that you require."

He took the old man's right hand by the wrist
and held it, to allay his fear.

. . . .

[Achilles allows Priam eleven days for Hector's funeral rites, suspending the war until the twelfth day. Aided by Hermes, Priam escapes with the body earlier than the time Achilles had appointed. Helen mourns for him, as her protector among the Trojans who revile her. The funeral rites over and the death mound completed, the Trojans hold a feast in honor of Hector, tamer of horses.]

. . . .

Questions for Discussion and Review

1. Zeus tries to disinvite Eris, the spirit of strife, or discord, from the wedding of Peleus and Thetis, just as he arranged Thetis's marriage to forestall the birth of a child of hers who might usurp his throne. When Zeus overthrew the Titans, he restored peace and harmony to the universe. Why, then, can he not exclude Eris, even by divine decree?

2. When Zeus tosses the golden apple off Mount Olympus, in a last-ditch attempt to preserve harmony, not even the gods foresee the consequences: ten years of war among gods and humans alike. What does this failure of foresight tell us about the limitations on the powers of the gods and the nature of the universe they inhabit?

3. Compare the Greeks' and Trojans' attitudes toward the family, using specific examples from the *Iliad.*

4. Throughout the *Iliad,* scenes of feasting abound, often associated with ceremonial occasions. Why is feasting so important in the *Iliad?* What kinds of bonds are formed or confirmed through feasting?

5. Diomedes and Patroclus are both great fighters—Diomedes even takes on several gods in battle and wins—but neither is considered as extraordinary as Achilles. What makes Achilles different?

6. How are Achilles and Hector alike? How are they different? What qualities does each share with the archetypal hero Heracles?

7. How do the gods in the *Iliad* feel about the humans? How seriously do they take human affairs? Why do they get involved at all? Give specific examples to support your answer.

8. At the end of the *Iliad,* Troy still stands, its walls intact. Explain why you think the city survives so long, despite Achilles' efforts.

CHAPTER

13

A Different Kind of Hero: The Quest of Odysseus

KEY TOPICS/THEMES

The resourceful hero of Homer's Odyssey *differs significantly from the brash young warriors who besiege Troy. Whereas Achilles, Ajax, and their peers strive to win undying fame by displaying physical strength, courage, and fighting skill, Odysseus cultivates the qualities of intelligence and ingenuity that will ensure his survival in a strange and unpredictable world. In a series of encounters with powerful women and goddesses, such as Circe, Calypso, and Athene, he further develops his native cunning and hones the mental skills that at last enable him to defeat his wife's hundred unwanted suitors and reunite with Penelope, his feminine counterpart, thus bringing this strand of the Troy saga to a peaceful conclusion.*

Differences Between the *Iliad* and the *Odyssey*

A popular Greek tradition accounts for differences between the *Iliad* and the *Odyssey* by assuming that the war poem was written in Homer's youth while the generally peaceful world depicted in the story of Odysseus's homecoming was a product of the poet's old age. Noting the unusually large cast of female characters who play key roles in the *Odyssey*—from the goddess Athene to Odysseus's aged nurse, Eurycleia—some modern critics suggest that the author was a woman. A few add that she even left a self-portrait in the figure of **Nausicaa** [nah-SIK-ay-a], a remarkably competent princess who acts as the hero's patron at the court of her parents, King **Alcinous** [al-SIN-oh-uhs] and Queen **Arete** [a-REE-tee].

Whoever the poet(s)—the same person who wrote the *Iliad* or an entire school of nameless geniuses—the *Odyssey* is a worthy sequel to the "Song of Ilium." It contains an enormous mass of traditional material about the hero's wanderings from

460

Troy to Ithaca, which the poet shapes into a smoothly flowing narrative that builds inexorably toward the climax of Odysseus's long-delayed reunion with his beloved wife, Penelope.

The differences between the two epics are instructive. In the *Iliad,* the action is concentrated along the narrow beaches where the Greek army is bivouacked or within the besieged city of Troy. In the *Odyssey,* the world opens up to encompass the entire Mediterranean basin, with the restless hero roaming from Asia Minor to Africa to Europe, encountering previously unknown peoples and strange customs. Odysseus even leaves the material realm behind, journeying to the murky kingdom of the dead. With the possible exceptions of Virgil's *Aeneid* or Dante's *Divine Comedy,* no work of literature offers a more comprehensive tour of earth, heaven, and netherworld or a more dazzling parade of the gods, monsters, sorcerers, warriors, ghosts, heroes, and villains that inhabit mythology's three-tier universe.

Homer's Structuring of the *Odyssey*

The *Iliad* immediately introduces its two leading opponents, Achilles and Agamemnon, and pursues the consequences of their quarrel in generally chronological order straight through to the end of the poem. The *Odyssey's* structure is more complex: the hero who gives the epic its name and who imprints the narrative with his distinctive personality does not appear until Book 5. Homer devotes the first four books to describing the effects in **Ithaca** of Odysseus's nineteen-year absence and the quest that his son **Telemachus** [tee-LEM-a-kuhs] undertakes in search of his lost father.

Apart from flashbacks recounting the hero's earlier adventures, the action covers about six weeks: the time it takes Odysseus to leave Calypso's island (where he has spent seven years as the goddess's love slave), suffer a near-fatal shipwreck, wash ashore at the Phaeacians' hospitable kingdom, be transported to Ithaca, and plot and execute his revenge on the hundred suitors who compete to replace him as king of Ithaca by marrying his wife, **Penelope** (Figure 13-1). Although Zeus points out in Book 1 the cause of Poseidon's hostility, which delays Odysseus's homecoming by ten years, we do not learn exactly how or why the hero blinded the sea god's son **Polyphemus** until almost the middle of the epic.

To the *Odyssey's* central section (Books 8–12), in which the ingenious hero narrates his own story, Homer relegates the poem's most fantastic elements. Singing for his supper at the court of King Alcinous, Odysseus regales his audience with tales of man-eating giants, amorous nymphs, and messages from the recently dead, including Achilles and Agamemnon. From Book 13 to the poem's conclusion, Odysseus is back in the familiar world of Ithacan politics, struggling to find a way to defeat the suitors and resume his mundane duties as husband, father, and king. In these later scenes of pragmatic conflict, the supernatural is represented only by the Olympians, rational administrators of the daylight world.

Demodocus: The Blind Singer

Some ancient commentators believed that, in his portrayal of **Demodocus** [de-MAH-dah-kuhs], the blind poet whose songs delight the Phaeacian court (Book 8),

Has the Location of Homeric Ithaca Been Found?

Homer's fabled epics continue to fascinate a large public, including many archaeologists determined to prove that such characters as Agamemnon, Achilles, Hector, and Odysseus were real historical figures. In his excavations at the sites of Troy and Mycenae during the nineteenth century, Heinrich Schliemann showed that these Late Bronze Age cities truly existed and that the Homeric tales of war and adventure may have had some basis in historical events. Mycenean invaders, the prototypes of Homer's Achaean warriors, may actually have laid siege to a trade-rich city in Asia Minor (Ilion or Troy) about 1190 B.E.

Following Schliemann's example, some twenty-first-century archaeologists and classicists continue to seek confirmation that at least some epic figures, including Odysseus, were real people. Although the Ionian island of Ithaca, located off the west coast of mainland Greece, has long been identified as the same Ithaca that Homer says was Odysseus's home, some prominent archaeologists dispute that claim. In a new book co-authored by an archaeologist, a classical scholar, and a geologist, the authors insist that a peninsula called Paliki on the nearby island of Kefalonia is really the site of Odysseus's palace, where he famously slew his wife's one hundred suitors. According to this theory, the geography of Kefalonia matches the *Odyssey*'s description of Ithaca much more closely than the largely barren island now bearing that name. (See Bittlestone, Diggle, and Underhill in the Selected Bibliography for Chapter 13.) In the epic, a large mountain, the "tree-clad Mount Neriton," dominated Odysseus's island and could be seen for miles out at sea. Kefalonia's Mount Aenos (a modern name) is the highest peak in the Ionian islands and fits the Homeric description. In addition, the *Odyssey*'s allusion to the Cave of the Nymphs, said to be less than two days walk from the town of Ithaca, is matched by a cave containing impressive stalactites and ponds of water. Whereas modern Ithaca lacks a sufficient water supply, Kefalonia has several streams, as well as a small lake. Unlike Ithaca, the coastline of Paliki also boasts a navigable bay and several other topographical features corresponding to those Homer mentions.

Because the Homeric epics portray such psychologically vivid characters, many readers—both amateur and professional—seem persuaded that the epic heroes are modeled on once-living persons rather than being based solely on the imaginative creativity of ancient Greek poets. The temptation to interpret some archaeological finds as evidence for the historicity of particular Homeric figures is strong. When researchers found a gold brooch similar to that belonging to Homer's Odysseus (*Odyssey,* Book 19) in a Bronze Age tomb on Kefalonia, it was argued that the hero's final resting place had been discovered. Verification that Kefalonia—or one of the many other sites that researchers have suggested—is the Homeric Ithaca will have to await extensive archaeological excavations. It may be that researchers eventually will unearth artifacts showing that one site rather than another better conforms to the Homeric conception of Odysseus's island kingdom, or even that the character of Odysseus may have been derived from that of a historic Mycenaean leader. In the meantime, scholars caution us that the Homeric poems are creative fiction and their enduring value does not depend on their historicity.

(a)

(b)

FIGURE 13-1   Odysseus Slaying the Suitors. Caught unaware by the sudden revelation of Odysseus's identity (a), the drunken suitors (b) cower before a deadly hail of arrows flying from the hero's longbow. Although a few of the young nobles courting Penelope are far less reprehensible than Antinous, the most arrogant of the suitors, Fate marks them all for sudden death because of their communal guilt in violating hospitality and seeking to take the place of their legitimate king. *(Staatliche Museen, Berlin)*

Homer created an idealized self-portrait. Although the tradition that Homer was blind may derive from Demodocus's sightlessness, few modern critics view Homer's description of the Phaeacian bard as autobiographical. Demodocus's plight, in fact, represents the conventional paradox afflicting mortal recipients of divine favor: a person whom the gods single out for special attention typically receives a bitter-sweet, two-edged gift. The Muse who lavishes "matchless love" on Demodocus and inspires his incomparable poetry also robs him of his eyes. The *Odyssey*'s author, however, certainly presents Demodocus as a supreme artist who deserves all the honor and respect that King Alcinous and his courtiers bestow on him. Odysseus remarks that Demodocus's poetic skills are so great that either Apollo or the Muse herself must have taught the poet his art.

Homer's description of Demodocus's creative role offers an important glimpse into the creative process by which Greek minstrels fashioned epics. In the first of three poems Demodocus recites, accompanied on his harp, he celebrates "heroes" whom his songs have already made famous "throughout the world." The bard's function is indispensable if a hero's "glory" is to last: the accomplishments of an Achilles will live on only when a great poet recounts them in memorable verse. In his second poem, Demodocus moves from heroes to gods, singing of the adulterous love of Ares and Aphrodite, a theme that evokes Paris's illicit affair with Helen, the cause of the Trojan War. (See Chapter 6 for the text of Demodocus's song of Ares and Aphrodite.) His third poem, recounting Odysseus's infamous ruse of the wooden horse, serves multiple purposes: besides refocusing narrative attention on Odysseus and crediting him for the long-delayed Greek victory, it skillfully advances Homer's plot. Until Demodocus sings of the Trojan Horse, Odysseus is an anonymous stranger at the Phaeacian court; his tearful response to the minstrel's art motivates him to reveal his identity as the hero whose peerless ingenuity Demodocus has just praised. When Alcinous recognizes his guest as the instrument of Troy's fall, he provides Odysseus with a Phaeacian ship that transports the hero back to Ithaca.

A Different Kind of Hero

Whereas numerous aristocratic warriors contend for our interest in the *Iliad,* a single personality dominates the *Odyssey.* All other characters, from the doting Athene to the cannibalistic Laestrygonians, are defined exclusively by their relationship to Odysseus. Odysseus has the courage, fighting skills, and leadership abilities that characterize the epic hero, but he is defined primarily in terms of the extraordinary intelligence that equips him to cope with unexpected and dangerous situations away from the battlefield. He also differs from his colleagues at Troy in his emphasis on solving problems through cunning and strategy rather than brute force. His most famous ruse, the Trojan Horse (which Demodocus describes in Book 8), results in the capture of Troy when direct attacks and military brawn fail.

Greek myth customarily explains the hero's superiority by making him the descendant of a god. Although Odysseus, unlike Achilles, has two mortal parents, **Laertes** [lay-ER-teez] and **Anticleia** [an-tih-KLEE-a], non-Homeric tradition assigns him a divine ancestor in **Autolycus** [ah-TUHL-ih-kuhs], his maternal grandfather. Reputedly a son of Hermes, Autolycus embodies some of his father's less de-

The Sequence of Events in the Homeward Voyage of Odysseus

After Odysseus's ruse of the wooden horse results in Troy's fall (c. 1190 B.C.), Odysseus and his men set sail for Ithaca. Along the way, he endures various trials.

1. Odysseus raids Ismarus, city of the Cicones in southern Thrace, where some of his men are killed.

2. A storm drives Odysseus's small fleet southward, away from Ithaca.

3. Odysseus stops briefly in the land of the Lotus-Eaters.

4. On the island of the Cyclopes, Polyphemus eats six of his men and brings Poseidon's curse on Odysseus.

5. After staying a month with Aeolus, Odysseus sails within sight of Ithaca, but his suspicious men open Aeolus's bag of winds, creating a gale that drives them back to the wind god's island.

6. The Laestrygonians destroy all of Odysseus's fleet except for his own ship.

7. Odysseus spends a year as Circe's lover. The wise enchantress directs his journey to the Underworld.

8. Forewarned by Circe, Odysseus hears the Sirens' songs and passes between Scylla and Charybdis.

9. Marooned on the island of Helios, Odysseus's crew eat the sun god's sacred cattle, for which Zeus sinks his ship and drowns his crewmen.

10. His ship lost, Odysseus is swept alone back through the narrow straits of Scylla and Charybdis. He is eventually cast ashore on Calypso's island, where he is detained for seven years.

11. After Hermes carries Zeus's order to Calypso, Odysseus is allowed to build a raft and sail toward home, until Poseidon destroys his craft, leaving him to drown.

12. Odysseus comes ashore on the island of Scheria, the kingdom of the Phaeacians ruled by King Alcinous and Queen Arete, whose sailors transport the hero back to Ithaca.

sirable attributes, including a penchant for thievery and deception, qualities some later writers, such as Sophocles, also ascribe to Odysseus. As Homer portrays him, however, Odysseus is entirely human, making his refusal when the nymph **Calypso** offers him immortality all the more significant (Book 5).

Brains Versus Brawn   Distinguished by brains rather than an exceptional physique, Odysseus lacks Achilles' commanding height and good looks (Figure 13-2). He has the physical strength to string a huge bow that other men cannot even bend (Book 21), and he competes successfully with younger athletes at Alcinous's court, but this middle-aged hero must rely on Athene to apply a divine cosmetic

FIGURE 13-2 The Head of Odysseus. The central character of Homer's *Odyssey* differs qualitatively from the *Iliad*'s impetuous heroes. Distinguished by brains rather than brawn, the middle-aged Odysseus is a human counterpart of his divine patron Athene, using forethought and ingenuity to overcome the obstacles confronting him on his long journey back to Ithaca. In this portrait of the experience-weary Odysseus, the sculptor suggests both the physical strain caused by the hero's labors and his resolve to take on new challenges. (*Archaeological Museum, Sperlonga*)

that makes him appear taller and handsomer whenever he needs to make a good impression. When circumstances dictate, Athene also changes Odysseus's appearance for the worse, withering his skin to make his disguise as an aged beggar more convincing. These physical transformations, repeated throughout the epic, suggest Odysseus's chameleon-like traits, his uncanny ability to take on a variety of roles, from commander and king to pauper and suppliant.

Differences between Achilles and Odysseus run more than skin deep. Whereas Achilles represents the aristocratic warrior, an archetypal ephebe whose chief attributes are strength, martial skill, and courage, Odysseus manifests the less spectacular quality of seasoned prudence. The ability to exercise foresight, discretion, and rational self-control, prudence is the trait that most commonly (but not always) distinguishes Odysseus's behavior. Whereas Achilles' brawn and bloodlust well suit his military career, Odysseus's quick-witted caution proves crucial in negotiating the obstacles, temptations, and dangers that the gods strew, like so many land mines, along his path through the postwar world.

The *Iliad*'s warrior-heroes, obsessively competing for personal glory, condemn themselves to early deaths. Sacrificing their future is a necessary price for the posthumous fame that poets, singing of their prowess in war, eventually bestow on them. The shrewd, aging hero of the *Odyssey,* however, is not predestined to share the tragic end of Achilles and his comrades. In the epic's opening scene, set on Mount Olympus, Zeus promises Athene that her beloved Odysseus will safely reach

Ithaca. Even Poseidon, who persecutes Odysseus for his mutilation of Polyphemus, cannot resist the collective will of the other Olympians.

Zeus's first words sound a theme of heavenly justice that shapes the *Odyssey's* moral universe. Mortals, he says, blame the gods for their troubles, but in reality people bring suffering on themselves, far exceeding the lot—the mixture of good and evil apportioned to each person—that Necessity decrees. Zeus then cites the example of **Aegisthus** [ee-JIS-thuhs], who had ignored Hermes' warning not to seduce **Clytemnestra** [klye-tem-NES-tra] or murder her husband, Agamemnon. As a result, Aegisthus is slain by **Orestes** [ah-RES-teez], the son of Agamemnon and Clytemnestra, who boldly avenges his father's death, an act of filial devotion that the gods heartily approve.

Zeus's remarks introduce three important issues: first, if the suitors succeed in their plot to kill Odysseus, Telemachus will be called on to reenact Orestes' vengeance; second, like Aegisthus, Odysseus will cause many of his own problems; and finally, the Olympians govern the world according to a principle of retributive justice that rewards persons honoring divine law and punishes the disobedient. Cosmic balance is maintained by ensuring that every crime is paid for by an appropriate punishment. The gods also distinguish among degrees of guilt: Odysseus's men, who deliberately break a divine prohibition, forfeit their lives, whereas Odysseus, who also suffers for his mistakes, avoids directly offending Zeus and survives (Figure 13-3).

FIGURE 13-3 The Head of Zeus. In the *Odyssey,* Zeus enforces the principles of cosmic justice, punishing such lawbreakers as the suitors and assuring Athene that her protégé Odysseus will safely regain his rightful place at Ithaca. Odysseus's marked reverence for the gods and his resourcefulness and persistence ensure that, in spite of considerable pain and suffering, he will survive and reach his goal. Unlike the tragic vision of the *Iliad,* in which death claims even the best and bravest, the *Odyssey* presents a relatively optimistic worldview, albeit one shadowed by the prospect of a grim afterlife in Hades' realm (see Book 11). *(Vatican Museums, Rome)*

FIGURE 13-4 The Blinding of Polyphemus. In the *Odyssey's* opening pages, Zeus warns that humans bring greater sorrows on themselves than Necessity decrees, a truth illustrated by the hero's behavior with the Cyclops Polyphemus. Forgetting that a military leader must always plan ahead for possible retreat, Odysseus guides his men into a fatal trap, the cannibal Cyclops's cave. Although he devises a means of blinding Polyphemus and escaping with the men the giant has not yet eaten, Odysseus compounds his errors by

boasting of his cleverness to the Cyclops and revealing his hitherto concealed identity, a burst of hubris (excessive pride) that brings the curse of Poseidon on him. Because of this uncharacteristic rashness, Odysseus suffers a ten-year delay in his homecoming, as well as the loss of his men. *(Eleusis Museum)*

Odysseus's Error with Polyphemus   Zeus does not mention Odysseus's partial responsibility for his delayed homecoming, but the hero later confesses that at least once he violated his own standards of prudence, with disastrous results. In his encounter with the Cyclops Polyphemus, Odysseus goes beyond offending mere mortals by incurring the wrath of Poseidon, lord of the sea over which he and his men must travel. Odysseus imprudently enters Polyphemus's cave, where the cannibalistic giant blocks the cave entrance with a huge stone and greedily devours several of his men. After getting the monster drunk and blinding him (Figure 13-4), Odysseus devises a way to escape the cave by tying his companions and himself to the undersides of Polyphemus's rams (Figure 13-5). Proud to have blinded Polyphemus and escaped alive, Odysseus temporarily acts as if he has lost his wits: boasting of his cleverness, he abandons the protective alias he has used, announcing to the infuriated Cyclops that, far from being "Noman," he has a famous identity, and he proceeds to divulge both his name and his address. The Cyclops's prayer to his father, Poseidon, is immediately granted: Odysseus will suffer an agonizing ten-year delay in reaching home, the loss of all his men, and the certainty of great trouble on arriving in Ithaca.

The Polyphemus episode throws a long shadow over Odysseus's career, eventually necessitating his journey to Hades to consult the blind prophet **Tiresias** [tih-REE-sih-as] about the future consequences of his recklessness (Book 11). Alerted to the self-destructive aspects of his nature—the impulsive pride that subverts his rational control—Odysseus henceforth behaves with redoubled prudence. By cautiously anchoring his vessel a safe distance off an unfamiliar shore, he escapes the

FIGURE 13-5   Escape from Polyphemus's Cave. Tying himself to the underside of a large ram, Odysseus escapes from the Cyclops's lair. Odysseus's device to save himself and his men is successful, but its effect is immediately undercut by his impulsively revealing his identity—including his name and address—to Polyphemus. *(Anonymous gift in memory of L. D. Caskey. Courtesy, Museum of Fine Arts, Boston)*

fate of his men when the Laestrygonians destroy their eleven ships (Figure 13-6). He also learns to accept being the "Noman" that he had merely pretended to be in the Cyclops's cave. When shipwrecked naked on the Phaeacians' island, Odysseus is a stranger without name, country, rank, possessions, identity—or even clothing. Although he later boasts of his adventures at the Phaeacian court, he is careful to keep his true identity a secret until it is safe to disclose his name. On Athene's advice, he even reenters his own palace as a social nonentity, wearing the rags of a foreign beggar.

Athene: Wise Guide and Mentor

Odysseus's exceptionally intimate relationship with his divine patron is virtually unique in Greek myth. When the two, both in disguise, meet on the beach near Ithaca, each delights in the other's efforts to deceive (Book 13). The phenomenon of a mortal successfully matching wits with the goddess of wisdom elicits Athene's unstinted praise. Describing herself and Odysseus as possessing "the two shrewdest minds in the universe," Athene tells her favorite that he is "far and away the best man on earth for plotting strategies," while she is similarly "famed among gods for [her] clever schemes." The affinity between Athene and Odysseus surpasses their shared attribute of mental agility, for man and goddess both set intellect to work, manipulating others to further their own private agendas (Figure 13-7). As

FIGURE 13-6   Odysseus in the Land of the Laestrygonians. In this episode with the cannibalistic Laestrygonians, Odysseus demonstrates that he has learned from his earlier encounter with Polyphemus. Whereas Odysseus thoughtlessly had led his men into the Cyclops's cave without bothering to learn anything of his putative host's disposition, he now approaches the unknown with caution. By anchoring his ship a safe distance offshore, Odysseus and his crew escape the fate of the rest of his fleet, who imprudently moor their vessels along the beach and are destroyed when the giant Laestrygonians smash their ships with huge boulders. This painting, in which some of the figures are identified with their names in Greek, is part of a colorful frieze decorating the house of a wealthy Roman on the Esquiline Hill in Rome (c. 50–40 B.C.). *(Biblioteca Apostolica Vaticana, Rome)*

Athene maneuvers Zeus into circumventing Poseidon's vendetta, so Odysseus artfully exploits the suitors' drunken overconfidence to arrange his revenge. As giver of victory, Athene helps Odysseus plan his strategy—the reconquest of Ithaca—but, goddesslike, she does not actively intervene during his hand-to-hand battle with the suitors until he has already demonstrated both the will and the ability to win.

In her final appearance, Athene again materializes as Mentor, an old Ithacan friend of Odysseus, ordering the families of the slain suitors to cease their vendetta against Ithaca's king. With her last words, she demands that Odysseus also control his anger, the emotion that generates the blood lust of war. As it did throughout the poem, Athene's presence—the unexpected effulgence of rational thought—points the way out of difficulty, restores order among Ithaca's warring factions, and guides mortals toward a fulfillment of the divine will.

Odysseus and Images of the Feminine

Circe   Almost every stage of Odysseus's voyage is marked by an encounter with a woman or a goddess, each of whom typically first challenges and then assists the

FIGURE 13-7   Athene in
Profile. Although slightly cor-
roded, this bronze sculpture
of Athene vividly conveys the
goddess's bright-eyed intelligence. A personification of
the human ability to achieve
victory through effective
forethought, Athene advances
the careers of several heroes
who are characterized by their
capacity to learn through
experience, including Perseus, Heracles, and Odysseus.
In preparing for Odysseus's
ultimate return to Ithaca and
resumption of his kingship,
Athene cleverly manipulates
almost every character in the
Odyssey, from the Olympian
Zeus to an Ithacan swineherd.
(National Museum, Athens)

hero. After escaping the Laestrygonians, Odysseus's next adventure takes place on
the island of **Circe** [SIR-see], an enchantress who turns men into swine. Like the
demigoddess Calypso, who will later hold Odysseus in thrall for seven long years,
Circe is a powerful female who threatens the hero's masculine identity because she
plies the art of reducing human males to their animal natures. Exercising total
control over their respective domains, she and Calypso represent isolated cultural
pockets in which the feminine principle still holds sway—matriarchal islands in a
vast patriarchal sea.

Significantly, the only two occasions on which the grand patriarch Zeus sends
his male emissary (Hermes) to aid Odysseus are when the hero's masculine autonomy is jeopardized by a captivating female. Hermes rushes to Odysseus's side the
moment he sets foot in Circe's dangerous terrain, giving him a mythical herb, the
moly plant, to counteract the effect of her magic, thus protecting him from a loss of
manhood.

As a wise manifestation of the ancient Goddess, Circe soon becomes Odysseus's
host, lover, and guide. Once Odysseus has demonstrated his ability to resist her manipulation and claimed the right to assert his own maleness (threatening her with
his phallic sword), Circe freely accepts him as her equal partner. Functioning as an
aspect of his anima (Penelope is its full expression), Circe imparts the secret knowledge of such chthonic goddesses as Gaea, Demeter, and Persephone. Circe reveals
as well the hidden path to the Underworld (Figure 13-8), instructing Odysseus in
the sacred rituals necessary to consult the dead and enabling him to complete the
rite of passage in which he undergoes symbolic death and rebirth (Books 10–12).

FIGURE 13-8   Odysseus in Hades' Kingdom, Although Circe at first appears as a threat to Odysseus's manhood, she becomes his partner and guide, wisely preparing him to avoid the dangers and pitfalls he must encounter on subsequent wanderings. A mistress of occult knowledge, she instructs Odysseus on the correct path to the Underworld and the proper rituals for safely inquiring of the dead. In this vase painting, the shade of Elpenor (left) hails his former captain (center), asking that his yet unburied corpse be interred and a monument be erected to his memory. That Odysseus enjoys divine protection in his risky journey to Hades' realm is indicated by the presence of Hermes (right), who escorts the recently dead to their final rest. *(William Amory Gardner Fund. Courtesy Museum of Fine Arts, Boston)*

Journey to the House of Hades   Explicitly following Circe's directions, Odysseus and his men sail their ship through darkness and thick fog to the "stream of Ocean," the mighty river encircling the earth's central landmass. Reaching the entrance to Hades' subterranean realm, Odysseus disembarks on Ocean's desolate shore to dig a square pit into which he pours offerings of grain, milk, wine, and other products of earth's fertility. The key ingredient in this chthonic ritual, however, is the dark blood of sacrificial sheep that gushes into the pit, providing the vital liquid that will temporarily animate ghosts of the dead who soon crowd eagerly around the pooled blood.

In Greek myth's most extensive portrayal of the afterlife, Homer not only describes the pitiable condition of the dead but also dramatizes how Odysseus personally is affected by his direct experience of human mortality. (For a discussion of evolving Greek concepts about the afterlife, see Chapter 9.) The resourceful hero, world-famous for repeatedly using his wits to escape death, must now face death's inexorable reality. Each ghost whom Odysseus encounters serves to illustrate the limits of his heroic striving and at the same time to define his sense of self-identity, demonstrating what he is and what he is not. First to speak is the shade of newly dead **Elpenor,** one of Odysseus's less capable men who had managed to kill himself by getting drunk and falling off the roof of Circe's house (Figure 13-8). Elpenor, whose corpse still lies where he fell, claims the right that all military commanders owe their fallen men, a decent burial and a memorial to save his name from oblivion, an obligation that Odysseus promises to fulfill.

Far more important to Odysseus is the next ghost, that of his mother, Anticleia, who has recently died in Ithaca mourning for her long-absent son. Although Odysseus longs to speak with her, he prevents her from drinking the sacrificial blood until after he has accomplished Circe's purpose in sending him to Hades' gates—consulting with the famed Theban prophet Tiresias. Displaying an Apollonian self-discipline that places fulfillment of his heroic quest above even filial love, Odysseus reveals an emotional hardness consistent with his character throughout the *Odyssey*. After his almost Dionysian impulsiveness with Polyphemus, he never again allows spontaneous emotion—even a hero's pride—to override his rational self-interest, a reclaiming of his country, crown, and wife. Adopting iron self-control when he returns to Ithaca, Odysseus, unlike Achilles or the other heroes at Troy, will deny his real identity, temporarily abandoning his royal status and claims to public honor by disguising himself as a homeless beggar subject to insult and mistreatment. In Hades' house, he learns to cultivate an Apollonian detachment that will help ensure his future survival.

From Tiresias's prophecy about the dangers still awaiting him, Odysseus learns that he must steel himself to endure bitter enmity of the gods, a prolonged delay in his homecoming, and, if his men harm the cattle of Helios, the loss of all his companions. Once home, without ships or men, he will find no immediate welcome, only the obstacle of eliminating Penelope's one hundred predatory suitors. Even after he succeeds in killing the suitors, he will not be free to enjoy his patrimony, for he must then go on another long journey—so far inland that people there will not know what a ship's oar is—to reconcile with Poseidon, the god who blocks his progress toward home. Only after hearing Tiresias's dire warnings, does Odysseus allow his mother to taste the sheep blood and recognize her son. Anticleia's shade offers the good news that Penelope remains loyal to her truant husband, but when Odysseus tries to embrace her, he finds that she is as insubstantial as smoke or mist. By permanently depriving the soul of physical form, death renders any natural expression of affection impossible.

In meeting the ghosts of his fallen comrades from Troy, Odysseus further defines himself in relation to the illustrious dead. When Agamemnon's shade obsessively agonizes over his wife Clytemnestra's treachery—she and her lover Aegisthus had given the Greek commander in chief an ignominious death upon his return home—he presents a tragic alternative to Odysseus's own situation. Only Penelope's fidelity protects her husband from Agamemnon's fate, and their son Telemachus from being obligated to imitate Agamemnon's son Orestes by committing matricide (see the *Oresteia,* Chapter 15). The encounter with Achilles, greatest of all the Greek warriors, not only highlights the vast difference between Odysseus and the *Iliad*'s superhero, it also calls into question the older epic's cult of heroism. Achilles responds to Odysseus's flattering praise by telling him bluntly that he would rather be the slave of "some poor dirt farmer" than king of all the dead. Having achieved his heroic goal of winning ultimate glory—already being celebrated by Achaean poets at that time—Achilles now realizes that posthumous fame is little consolation for the grim fact of death. As a living visitor to Hades' abode who will soon return to the sunlit world, Odysseus has the incomparable advantage. As if partially to bridge the chasm between them, however, Odysseus is able to brighten Achilles' gloom with the news that his son Neoptolemus has won honor as a brave fighter, a report that momentarily brings joy to Achilles' heart.

By contrast, Odysseus's sighting of the ghost of **Ajax**, second only to Achilles as the Greeks' finest warrior, brings no pleasure to either of the former comrades. Still deeply offended that the Greeks—under Athene's guidance—had awarded the slain Achilles' golden armor to the wily Odysseus instead of to him, Ajax refuses to speak or otherwise acknowledge Odysseus's presence. Apparently stung by Ajax's snub—and perhaps aware that the armor indeed had been given to the less worthy competitor—Odysseus tries in vain to win any sign that Ajax forgives or exonerates him. He must live with the consciousness that he had wronged a more deserving man and profited unfairly from Athene's favoritism.

His mood darkened after confronting troubling moral failures, Odysseus next witnesses the torments of men who had grievously offended the gods. Although he does not descend into the Underworld and remains standing at Hades' portal, Odysseus nonetheless beholds Minos, a human son of Zeus, judging the dead, and the giant hunter Orion brandishing his huge bronze club as if to threaten the mortal intruder. Plunged next into visions of Tartarus, Odysseus observes the punishments of notorious sinners: Tithos, who had raped Leto, Apollo's mother, endures eternal pain as vultures feast on his liver; Tantalus, suffering constant hunger and thirst, has food and water kept just beyond his reach; and Sisyphus, the trickster who had tried to outwit death, is condemned to push a heavy boulder uphill only to have it tumble down again, forcing endless repetition of his futile labor.

Last of all, Odysseus beholds the image of Heracles, an archetypal hero who had gained undying glory long before the Trojan War and whose deeds included a descent into Hades' realm to capture **Cerberus,** the hound of hell, and bring the monstrous watchdog back to earth's surface. Heracles had not only preceded Odysseus to the netherworld and back, he had also far surpassed him when Zeus elevated his formerly mortal son to immortality on Olympus. Thus, the Ithacan wanderer finds that the shade with whom he converses is only a phantom: the real Heracles now dwells in heaven with the gods, an apotheosis that will not be extended to Odysseus. With Heracles' departure, Odysseus's courage also deserts him. Terror-stricken at death's power to destroy all that the living value—he fears that the Gorgon will suddenly appear to turn him to flint, reducing the hero to a mere tombstone—Odysseus flees back to his ship.

Dangerous Aspects of the Feminine   Having bravely separated from the living world and personally experienced humanity's ultimate destiny in Hades' dark abode, Odysseus—now initiated into the chthonic mysteries—returns to Circe and confides his encounter with death's realm. He will repeat this story again, to his Phaeacian hosts, and finally to Penelope. But first he must face other manifestations of chthonic peril. Circe instructs Odysseus how to minimize his losses from two particularly deadly aspects of the feminine—**Scylla** [SIL-la] (Figure 13-9) and **Charybdis** [ka-RIB-dis], the man-devouring monsters he must encounter before

FIGURE 13-9 Scylla. According to tradition, Scylla was once
human but was changed into a cannibalistic monster by a rival in
love. Described as having six heads, each with a triple row of teeth,
and a circle of vicious dogs encompassing her waist, she lived in
a cave above a narrow strait (traditionally the Straits of Messina
between Sicily and Italy), opposite the whirlpool of Charybdis.
As portrayed in this Roman bronze bowl, Scylla reaches out to
grasp and devour one of Odysseus's men while her dogs maul other
victims. Circe warns Odysseus that he must sacrifice a few of his
men to Scylla in order to avoid having his entire crew drowned in
Charybdis. Thanks to Circe's wise advice, Odysseus survives both
encounters with these two destructive manifestations of feminine
dominance. *(British Museum, London)*

his initiation into life and kingship is complete. Perceiving Odysseus's omnivo-
rous curiosity and need for risk taking, Circe further instructs him on how to hear
the **Sirens'** irresistible song without falling victim to their fatal attraction (Figure 13-10). Although a threat to men dominated by their bestial appetites (such
as Odysseus's intellectually undeveloped companions), Circe exemplifies the Great
Goddess's beneficence to those worthy of her help.

In the final test that qualitatively distinguishes Odysseus from his remaining men,
the hero wisely heeds Circe's warning to refrain from eating the sacred cattle of Helios. The men, becalmed for weeks on an inhospitable island, give in to their physical
appetites, slaughtering and feasting on the sun god's property, an impious act that
Zeus punishes by later incinerating their ship with his thunderbolt. Only Odysseus,
wise enough to sacrifice his immediate well-being in order to win the gods' approval,

Post-Homeric Traditions About Odysseus and His Family

The *Odyssey* ends with Athene insisting that Odysseus make peace with the dead suitors' families, although Tiresias's earlier prophecy about the hero's eventual reconciliation with his divine enemy, Poseidon, hints at Odysseus's future adventures (not covered in the Homeric epic). A later narrative poem, the *Telegonia* (ascribed to Eugammon of Cyrene and known only from brief summaries), states that, after sacrificing to Hades, Persephone, and Tiresias (denizens of the Underworld to which Odysseus's bloody revenge had consigned the suitors), Odysseus leaves Ithaca and travels to Thesprotia, where he makes his obligatory peace offering to Poseidon. While among the Thesprotians (people of mythic King Thesprotus), Odysseus becomes the lover of Callidice, queen of the region, who gives birth to their son, Polypoetes. When Callidice dies, Odysseus turns the kingdom over to the young Polypoetes and returns home to Ithaca, where he finds that Penelope has borne him a second son, Poliporthes.

In the meantime, Odysseus's son by Circe, Telegonus (not mentioned in Homer but noted in Hesiod's *Theogony*), has gone in search of his father (reenacting Telemachus's quest in the *Odyssey*). After landing in Ithaca and raiding its cattle, Telegonus is beset by Ithacan herdsmen, who are aided by their king, Odysseus. Unaware of his father's identity, Telegonus kills Odysseus with a spear tipped with the poisonous tail of a stingray, only to be overcome with remorse when he learns whom he has slain. (Tiresias's prophecy that Odysseus will not die at sea is thus given an ironic twist: the hero is killed on land by the venom of a sea creature.) Telegonus then flees to Circe's island, taking Odysseus's body, Penelope, and his half-brother, Telemachus, with him. After Circe makes them immortal, Telegonus marries Penelope and Telemachus marries Circe. In one variant of the tradition, Circe restores Odysseus to life and, after dispatching Penelope and Odysseus's two sons to the Isles of the Blest (Elysium; see Chapter 9), Circe at last marries the hero herself.

Other post-Homeric variations of the myth focus on Penelope's fate. Apollodorus cites a tradition in which Penelope is seduced by Antinous, her most aggressive suitor, for which Odysseus sends her back to her father, Icarius, where she becomes Hermes' mistress and gives birth to the rustic god Pan. Some later poets claim that Pan, a figure of unbridled lust, was the result of an orgy in which Penelope coupled with *all* of her hundred suitors—a gratuitous slander against Homer's portrait of human fidelity.

In still another version, after slaying the suitors, Odysseus receives an oracle directing him to Epirus, where he makes love to Euippe, the daughter of his host,

survives Zeus's wrath. He is then made to endure, on Calypso's isle, **Ogygia** [oh-JIJ-ih-a], the most extended test of his patience, purpose, and manhood.

Calypso In contrast to Circe, who coolly relinquishes her lover as soon as he asks to leave, Calypso represents a different threat to Odysseus's psyche—the demands of untrammeled female sexuality. Although it may seem that Odysseus has found

Tryimmas (a contrast to his restrained behavior with King Alcinous's daughter Nausicaa). When the son of this union, Euryalus, grows up, his mother sends him to Ithaca with sealed proofs of his parentage. Odysseus is not at home when Euryalus arrives. Penelope, recognizing in him the illegitimate child of a rival, later jealously persuades her husband that the youth is a threat to his life. Reverting to his earlier imprudent conduct, Odysseus impulsively kills the stranger, thus becoming guilty of his son's murder.

Some Athenian dramatists were extremely critical of Odysseus's ethical character. In his tragedy *Philoctetes,* Sophocles portrays Odysseus as an amoral example of middle-aged expediency. After receiving an oracle that only possession of Heracles' famous bow can ensure the Greeks' victory at Troy, Odysseus does not hesitate to manipulate Achilles' naive son, Neoptolemus, into inadvertently deceiving the wounded Philoctetes, whom the Greeks had previously abandoned on the island of Lemnos, persuading him to relinquish Heracles' bow.

As this cursory sampling of post-Homeric myth indicates, Greek and Roman writers delighted in spinning endless new tales about Odysseus and his diverse escapades. A quintessentially human paradox of intelligence and passion, foresight and recklessness, Odysseus continued to fascinate the European imagination long after the fall of Rome. For Dante, the supreme poet of medieval Roman Catholicism, Odysseus (Ulysses) symbolizes the pride of intellect that drives men to violate God-ordained boundaries. In Dante's *Inferno* (Canto 26; see the reading in Chapter 21), the poet imagines Odysseus's last journey into realms never before explored by mortals, an impious ambition that Christendom's God punishes in hell. By contrast, in a poem written in 1842, the English poet Alfred, Lord Tennyson, depicts the aged Greek hero as embodying a modern spirit of scientific heroism, his insatiable thirst to experience new life representing the finest of human aspiration (see the reading in Chapter 21).

Homer's successors, ancient and modern, present an enormous range of possible fates for Odysseus after his return to Ithaca. As Hesiod's evolving cosmos is a seedbed of almost unlimited potential, so Odysseus's multifaceted character presents endless opportunities for further development. Inhabiting a timeless dimension limited only by the human imagination, he confronts an open-ended universe, simultaneously journeying through parallel worlds and creating a legion of selves acting out their individual destinies. In his infinite variety—transcending time and culture—Odysseus illustrates the boundless exuberance of the mythical hero.

paradise with a goddess who drags him to her bed every night for seven years, we must remember that the hero is no longer a young man of unlimited virility. Besides the potentially castrating effects of Calypso's dominance, Odysseus—imprisoned on an island literally in the middle of nowhere—is deprived of the normal challenges and opportunities that society affords. A Greek hero cannot fulfill his destiny in total isolation from other human beings.

FIGURE 13-10   Odysseus and the Sirens. Understanding Odysseus's insatiable desire to undergo extremes of experience, wise Circe instructs him how to hear the Sirens' (creatures half-woman, half-bird) lethal song without being destroyed. As shown in this vase painting (early fifth century B.C.), his men row obliviously, their ears stopped with beeswax, while Odysseus listens to the Sirens' irresistible call, struggling against the bonds that prevent him from impulsively giving in to their fatal attraction. Stunned by her failure to lure a man to his death, one Siren self-destructs, plunging into the sea (right center). *(British Museum, London)*

Calypso's outrage when Hermes brings Zeus's command—given at Athene's urging—to release Odysseus reflects a female deity's deep resentment at the Olympian autocracy. Some critics view Calypso's offer to make Odysseus immortal as the echo of a prehistoric rite in which the Goddess's male consort was sacrificed, his shed blood fertilizing the ground and enhancing Gaea's fecundity. As in the Heracles myth, a hero's immortality is attained only after death and transfiguration, a posthumous deification that Odysseus rejects.

Odysseus's refusal to disavow the burden of mortality also marks a radical departure from the hero's traditional quest for divine status. Rather than deny his mortal humanity, he embraces it, spurred partly by his loyalty to Penelope, who, unlike Calypso, will grow old and die. After his prolonged contact with the wisdom of figures like Circe, Odysseus chooses to remain fixed in the earthly life cycle that includes aging and death, the wise acceptance of natural law expressed by the Great Goddess (see Chapter 5).

In his close rapport with goddesses and his employment of their gifts, Odysseus is reminiscent of earlier heroes, such as Perseus and Heracles. Like Heracles, another of Athene's select favorites, Odysseus is associated with a bow that only he can utilize and with a perilous journey into Hades' kingdom, a parallel that Homer underscores in the climax of Book 11. Combining many traits of Perseus and Heracles, Odysseus exceeds them in the intense solitariness of his quest: no other Greek hero is more completely alone, deals with more terrifying supernatural forces, develops a higher degree of self-reliance, or returns to his place of origin with greater insight than Odysseus. In negotiating the dangerous and complex rites of passage, few heroes can match Odysseus's versatility or success.

Recognitions When the Phaeacian ship deposits Odysseus on Ithaca's shores, displeasing Poseidon, who vindictively changes the ship and its crew into a rock, Odysseus is at last brought face-to-face with his divine protector, Athene. It is the first of several scenes in which loyal friends or family members recognize the hero, but it is a strange one: both Odysseus and Athene disguise their true identities and both spin tall tales about their false characters. Although each party is aware of who the other is, the two tricksters compete in weaving plausible stories to deceive the other. Overjoyed at this mortal's audacity in attempting to outwit a goddess, Athene pays him a compliment greater than any other mythic deity gives a human: if she were mortal, she would be Odysseus! She then transforms her favorite beyond recognition, prematurely aging him and giving him the appearance of a decrepit beggar.

Reduced to a social nonentity, Odysseus must now feel his way cautiously into Ithacan society, discovering who remains loyal to the absent king and contriving a way to ambush the suitors. Playing a beggar's role, Odysseus endures humiliating insults from the more arrogant suitors, but a faithful goatherd, Eumaeus, offers him hospitality, the mark of a man Zeus approves. Although he secretly reveals his identity to Telemachus and engages in intimate conversations with Penelope while still in disguise, he prudently refrains from suggesting his identity to any other member of his household. Poignantly, the first to recognize his returned master is Odysseus's old hunting dog, Argus, who immediately dies at the shock. When the aged nurse, Eurycleia, while washing the stranger's feet, recognizes him by a scar on his thigh, Odysseus ruthlessly grasps her by the throat and threatens to kill the old woman if she does not keep quiet. In Odysseus's mind, the Apollonian self-control he had cultivated during the visit to Hades' kingdom is essential to his success: nothing, not even the affection of Eurycleia, who had been a surrogate mother to him, must be allowed to interfere with his plan to take the suitors by surprise. Odysseus's almost repellent emotional coldness is most apparent in the painfully long delay of his self-revelation to Penelope.

Penelope During Odysseus's visit to the Underworld (Book 11), the ghost of Agamemnon, obsessed by Clytemnestra's betrayal, warns him never to trust even the best of wives. Although Odysseus ignores Agamemnon's spectral advice and confides fully in Penelope after their reunion, the implied parallel between the two kings' potential fate is cited repeatedly. The key difference in this equation is Penelope's distinctive character, which makes her far more than a conventional model of the submissive and patient wife. As intelligent, perceptive, and resourceful as her husband, she shares Odysseus's prudence and inventiveness, demonstrated by her delaying tactics with the suitors: her feigned promise to marry as soon as she finishes weaving a burial shroud for Laertes (Figure 13-11)—which she covertly unravels at night—keeps the suitors at bay for years. Penelope's ability to test men's mettle ranges from the deadly trial of skill she sets up for the suitors to a final ruse

FIGURE 13-11 Telemachus and Penelope. This vase painting shows the faithful Penelope sitting mournfully at her loom, pining for the husband she has not seen for almost twenty years. Homer portrays Penelope as Odysseus's equal in prudence and cunning, for she devises a scheme of keeping her one hundred unwanted suitors waiting for years while she weaves a burial shroud for Laertes, her father-in-law, unraveling at night what she creates by day. Telemachus, who reaches young manhood on the eve of his father's long-delayed return, sets out on an arduous journey to gather news of Odysseus's whereabouts. Most of the *Odyssey*'s first four books are devoted to an account of Telemachus's travels to Pylos and Sparta, where he hears characters from the *Iliad*—old King Nestor, Menelaus, and Helen—sing Odysseus's praises. *(Museo Archeologico, Chiusi, Italy)*

about the immovability of her marriage bed. Her use of this image—a place of sexual union secretly fashioned from the trunk of an olive tree, Athene's unique gift to the Greeks—suggests Penelope's association with peaceful fecundity, a benevolent expression of the same qualities that Circe and Calypso represent, but without the attendant danger.

As weaver, keeper of nuptial secrets, and guardian of an olive trunk symbolizing the Tree of Life, Penelope implicitly functions as a priestess of feminine divinity. Her characteristic task of weaving also links Penelope to the feminine aspects of

Athene, who is patron of women's handicrafts and protector of the home. Despite her ostensible powerlessness when pressured by the suitors, Penelope is also in control of her destiny. Although Penelope's endurance matches that of her peripatetic husband, the excessive duration of Odysseus's absence stretches the marriage bond to its utmost limit. At the moment of Odysseus's return, she appears to have exhausted her capacity for waiting and seems ready to make an active choice for her future life.

In a Jungian interpretation, Penelope—a feminine counterpart of the "godlike Odysseus"—embodies her husband's anima, an appropriately human expression of Circe's chthonic wisdom. The couple's long-delayed reunion signifies a rejoining of the heroic animus and anima, a commingling that marks the completion of their respective natures and the fulfillment of their mutual quest. In one of myth's great ironies, during the night in which this archetypal pair renew their conjugal bond,

FIGURE 13-12   The Warrior Athene. Authoritatively grasping her shield and spear, Athene prepares to do battle. As defender of the city-state and goddess of victory in war, Athene intervenes on Odysseus's behalf not only to defeat the suitors but also to cut short a potential civil conflict and restore peace to Ithaca. The *Odyssey* concludes with Athene's decisive action, pacifying the vengeful relatives of the slain suitors and curtly ordering Odysseus to give up his anger. Unlike Ares, who glories in the vicious frenzy of mass slaughter, Athene employs her military skills primarily to impose the benefits of peace. *(Munich Museum)*

Odysseus confides to his wife that he must leave her again. The hero's fate necessitates another extended journey into unknown lands, this time to seek a reconciliation with his divine enemy, Poseidon.

Homer concludes the *Odyssey* by placing his hero's reunion with Penelope in the larger context of Ithacan politics. At the beginning of Book 24, it looks as if Odysseus will have to shed more of his people's blood, for the suitors' male relatives are honor-bound to avenge the young men's deaths. Zeus and Athene, however, intervene to end the feud and reestablish civic order, a climactic reconciliation of warring opposites in which Athene, again disguised as Mentor, has the final word, bringing the long Troy saga to a peaceful close (Figure 13-12).

ODYSSEY*

Homer

BOOK 1

Speak, Memory—
              Of the cunning hero,   1
The wanderer, blown off course time and again
After he plundered Troy's sacred heights.
                         Speak
Of all the cities he saw, the minds he grasped,
The suffering deep in his heart at sea
As he struggled to survive and bring his men home
But could not save them, hard as he tried—
The fools—destroyed by their own recklessness
When they ate the oxen of Hyperion the Sun,
And that god snuffed out their day of return.   10

                Of these things,
Speak, Immortal One,
And tell the tale once more in our time.

By now, all the others who had fought at Troy—
At least those who had survived the war and the sea—
Were safely back home. Only Odysseus
Still longed to return to his home and his wife.
The nymph Calypso, a powerful goddess—
And beautiful—was clinging to him
In her caverns and yearned to possess him.
The seasons rolled by, and the year came   20
In which the gods spun the thread

For Odysseus to return home to Ithaca,
Though not even there did his troubles end,
Even with his dear ones around him.
All the gods pitied him, except Poseidon,
Who stormed against the godlike hero
Until he finally reached his own native land.

But Poseidon was away now, among the Ethiopians,
Those burnished people at the ends of the earth—
Some near the sunset, some near the sunrise—   30
To receive a grand sacrifice of rams and bulls.
There he sat, enjoying the feast.

---

*Translation by Stanley Lombardo.

                    The other gods
Were assembled in the halls of Olympian Zeus,
And the Father of Gods and Men was speaking.
He couldn't stop thinking about Aegisthus,
Whom Agamemnon's son, Orestes, had killed:

"Mortals! They are always blaming the gods
For their troubles, when their own witlessness
Causes them more than they were destined for!
Take Aegisthus now. He marries Agamemnon's   40
Lawful wife and murders the man on his return
Knowing it meant disaster—because we did warn him,
Sent our messenger, quicksilver Hermes,
To tell him not to kill the man and marry his wife,
Or Agamemnon's son, Orestes, would pay him back
When he came of age and wanted his inheritance.
Hermes told him all that, but his good advice
Meant nothing to Aegisthus. Now he's paid in full."

Athena glared at him with her owl-grey eyes:

"Yes, O our Father who art most high—   50
That man got the death he richly deserved,
And so perish all who would do the same.
But it's Odysseus I'm worried about,
That discerning, ill-fated man. He's suffered
So long, separated from his dear ones,
On an island that lies in the center of the sea,
A wooded isle that is home to a goddess,
The daughter of Atlas, whose dread mind knows
All the depths of the sea and who supports
The tall pillars that keep earth and heaven apart.   60
His daughter detains the poor man in his grief,
Sweet-talking him constantly, trying to charm him
Into forgetting Ithaca. But Odysseus,
Longing to see even the smoke curling up
From his land, simply wants to die. And yet you
Never think of him, Olympian. Didn't Odysseus
Please you with sacrifices beside the Greek ships
At Troy? Why is Odysseus so odious, Zeus?"

Zeus in his thunderhead had an answer for her:

"Quite a little speech you've let slip through your teeth,   70
Daughter. How could I forget godlike Odysseus?
No other mortal has a mind like his, or offers
Sacrifice like him to the deathless gods in heaven.
But Poseidon is stiff and cold with anger
Because Odysseus blinded his son, the Cyclops

Polyphemus, the strongest of all the Cyclopes,
Nearly a god. The nymph Thoösa bore him,
Daughter of Phorcys, lord of the barren brine,
After mating with Poseidon in a scalloped sea-cave.
The Earthshaker has been after Odysseus   80
Ever since, not killing him, but keeping him away
From his native land. But come now,
Let's all put our heads together and find a way
To bring Odysseus home. Poseidon will have to
Put aside his anger. He can't hold out alone
Against the will of all the immortals."

And Athena, the owl-eyed goddess, replied:

"Father Zeus, whose power is supreme,
If the blessed gods really do want
Odysseus to return to his home,   90
We should send Hermes, our quicksilver herald,
To the island of Ogygia without delay
To tell that nymph of our firm resolve
That long-suffering Odysseus gets to go home.
I myself will go to Ithaca
To put some spirit into his son—
Have him call an assembly of the long-haired Greeks
And rebuke the whole lot of his mother's suitors.
They have been butchering his flocks and herds.
I'll escort him to Sparta and the sands of Pylos   100
So he can make inquiries about his father's return
And win for himself a name among men."

Athena spoke, and she bound on her feet
The beautiful sandals, golden, immortal,
That carry her over landscape and seascape
On a puff of wind. And she took the spear,
Bronze-tipped and massive, that the Daughter uses
To level battalions of heroes in her wrath.
She shot down from the peaks of Olympus
To Ithaca, where she stood on the threshold   110
Of Odysseus' outer porch. Holding her spear,
She looked like Mentes, the Taphian captain,
And her eyes rested on the arrogant suitors.

They were playing dice in the courtyard,
Enjoying themselves, seated on the hides of oxen
They themselves had slaughtered. They were attended
By heralds and servants, some of whom were busy
Blending water and wine in large mixing bowls,
Others wiping down the tables with sponges
And dishing out enormous servings of meat.   120

Telemachus spotted her first.
He was sitting with the suitors, nursing
His heart's sorrow, picturing in his mind
His noble father, imagining he had returned
And scattered the suitors, and that he himself,
Telemachus, was respected at last.
Such were his reveries as he sat with the suitors.
And then he saw Athena.

He went straight to the porch,
Indignant that a guest had been made to wait so long.
Going up to her he grasped her right hand in his   130
And took her spear, and his words had wings:

"Greetings, stranger. You are welcome here.
After you've had dinner, you can tell us what you need."

Telemachus spoke, and Pallas Athena
Followed him into the high-roofed hall.
When they were inside he placed her spear
In a polished rack beside a great column
Where the spears of Odysseus stood in a row.
Then he covered a beautifully wrought chair
With a linen cloth and had her sit on it   140
With a stool under her feet. He drew up
An intricately painted bench for himself
And arranged their seats apart from the suitors
So that his guest would not lose his appetite
In their noisy and uncouth company—
And so he could inquire about his absent father.
A maid poured water from a silver pitcher
Into a golden basin for them to wash their hands
And then set up a polished table nearby.
Another serving woman, grave and dignified,   150
Set out bread and generous helpings
From the other dishes she had. A carver set down
Cuts of meat by the platter and golden cups.
Then a herald came by and poured them wine.

Now the suitors swaggered in. They sat down
In rows on benches and chairs. Heralds
Poured water over their hands, maidservants
Brought around bread in baskets, and young men
Filled mixing bowls to the brim with wine.
The suitors helped themselves to all this plenty,   160
And when they had their fill of food and drink,
They turned their attention to the other delights,
Dancing and song, that round out a feast.
A herald handed a beautiful zither

To Phemius, who sang for the suitors,
Though against his will. Sweeping the strings
He struck up a song. And Telemachus,
Putting his head close to Pallas Athena's
So the others wouldn't hear, said this to her:

"Please don't take offense if I speak my mind.   170
It's easy for them to enjoy the harper's song,
Since they are eating another man's stores
Without paying anything—the stores of a man
Whose white bones lie rotting in the rain
On some distant shore, or still churn in the waves.
If they ever saw him make landing on Ithaca
They would pray for more foot speed
Instead of more gold or fancy clothes.
But he's met a bad end, and it's no comfort to us
When some traveler tells us he's on his way home.   180
The day has long passed when he's coming home.
But tell me this, and tell me the truth:
Who are you, and where do you come from?
Who are your parents? What kind of ship
Brought you here? How did your sailors
Guide you to Ithaca, and how large is your crew?
I don't imagine you came here on foot.
And tell me this, too. I'd like to know,
Is this your first visit here, or are you
An old friend of my father's, one of the many   190
Who have come to our house over the years?"

Athena's seagrey eyes glinted as she said:

"I'll tell you nothing but the unvarnished truth.
I am Mentes, son of Anchialus, and proud of it.
I am also captain of the seafaring Taphians.
I just pulled in with my ship and my crew,
Sailing the deep purple to foreign ports.
We're on our way to Cyprus with a cargo of iron
To trade for copper. My ship is standing
Offshore of wild country away from the city,   200
In Rheithron harbor under Naion's woods.
You and I have ties of hospitality,
Just as our fathers did, from a long way back.
Go and ask old Laertes. They say he never
Comes to town any more, lives out in the country,
A hard life with just an old woman to help him.
She gets him his food and drink when he comes in
From the fields, all worn out from trudging across
The ridge of his vineyard plot.

I have come
Because they say your father has returned, 210
But now I see the gods have knocked him off course.
He's not dead, though, not godlike Odysseus,
No way in the world. No, he's alive all right.
It's the sea keeps him back, detained on some island
In the middle of the sea, held captive by savages.
And now I will prophesy for you, as the gods
Put it in my heart and as I think it will be,
Though I am no soothsayer or reader of birds.
Odysseus will not be gone much longer
From his native land, not even if iron chains 220
Hold him. He knows every trick there is
And will think of some way to come home.
But now tell me this, and I want the truth:
Tall as you are, are you Odysseus' son?
You bear a striking resemblance to him,
Especially in the head and those beautiful eyes.
We used to spend quite a bit of time together
Before he sailed for Troy with the Argive fleet.
Since then, we haven't seen each other at all."

Telemachus took a deep breath and said: 230

"You want the truth, and I will give it to you.
My mother says that Odysseus is my father.
I don't know this myself. No one witnesses
His own begetting. If I had my way, I'd be the son
Of a man fortunate enough to grow old at home.
But it's the man with the most dismal fate of all
They say I was born from—since you want to know."

Athena's seagrey eyes glinted as she said:

"Well, the gods have made sure your family's name
Will go on, since Penelope has borne a son like you. 240
But there is one other thing I want you to tell me.
What kind of a party is this? What's the occasion?
Some kind of banquet? A wedding feast?
It's no neighborly potluck, that's for sure,
The way this rowdy crowd is carrying on
All through the house. Any decent man
Would be outraged if he saw this behavior."

Telemachus breathed in the salt air and said:

"Since you ask me these questions as my guest—
This, no doubt, was once a perfect house, 250
Wealthy and fine, when its master was still home.

But the gods frowned and changed all that
When they whisked him off the face of the earth.
I wouldn't grieve for him so much if he were dead,
Gone down with his comrades in the town of Troy,
Or died in his friends' arms after winding up the war.
The entire Greek army would have buried him then,
And great honor would have passed on to his son.
But now the whirlwinds have snatched him away
Without a trace. He's vanished, gone, and left me   260
Pain and sorrow. And he's not the only cause
I have to grieve. The gods have given me other trials.
All of the nobles who rule the islands—
Doulichium, Samî, wooded Zacynthus—
And all those with power on rocky Ithaca
Are courting my mother and ruining our house.
She refuses to make a marriage she hates
But can't stop it either. They are eating us
Out of house and home, and will kill me someday."

And Pallas Athena, with a flash of anger: 270

"Damn them! You really do need Odysseus back.
Just let him lay his hands on these mangy dogs!
If only he would come through that door now
With a helmet and shield and a pair of spears,
Just as he was when I saw him first,
Drinking and enjoying himself in our house
On his way back from Ephyre. Odysseus
Had sailed there to ask Mermerus' son, Ilus,
For some deadly poison for his arrowheads.
Ilus, out of fear of the gods' anger,   280
Would not give him any, but my father
Gave him some, because he loved him dearly.
That's the Odysseus I want the suitors to meet.
They wouldn't live long enough to get married!
But it's on the knees of the gods now
Whether he comes home and pays them back
Right here in his halls, or doesn't.
                                So it's up to you
To find a way to drive them out of your house.
Now pay attention and listen to what I'm saying.
Tomorrow you call an assembly and make a speech   290
To these heroes, with the gods as witnesses.
The suitors you order to scatter, each to his own.
Your mother—if in her heart she wants to marry—
Goes back to her powerful father's house.
Her kinfolk and he can arrange the marriage,
And the large dowry that should go with his daughter.

And my advice for you, if you will take it,
Is to launch your best ship, with twenty oarsmen,
And go make inquiries about your long-absent father.
Someone may tell you something, or you may hear   300
A rumor from Zeus, which is how news travels best.
Sail to Pylos first and ask godly Nestor,
Then go over to Sparta and red-haired Menelaus.
He was the last home of all the bronzeclad Greeks.
If you hear your father's alive and on his way home,
You can grit your teeth and hold out one more year.
If you hear he's dead, among the living no more,
Then come home yourself to your ancestral land,
Build him a barrow and celebrate the funeral
Your father deserves. Then marry off your mother.   310
After you've done all that, think up some way
To kill the suitors in your house either openly
Or by setting a trap. You've got to stop
Acting like a child. You've outgrown that now.
Haven't you heard how Orestes won glory
Throughout the world when he killed Aegisthus,
The shrewd traitor who murdered his father?
You have to be aggressive, strong—look at how big
And well-built you are—so you will leave a good name.
Well, I'm off to my ship and my men,   320
Who are no doubt wondering what's taking me so long.
You've got a job to do. Remember what I said."

And Telemachus, in his clear-headed way:

"My dear guest, you speak to me as kindly
As a father to his son. I will not forget your words.
I know you're anxious to leave, but please stay
So you can bathe and relax before returning
To your ship, taking with you a costly gift,
Something quite fine, a keepsake from me,
The sort of thing a host gives to his guest."   330

And Athena, her eyes grey as saltwater:

"No, I really do want to get on with my journey.
Whatever gift you feel moved to make,
Give it to me on my way back home,
Yes, something quite fine. It will get you as good."

With these words the Grey-eyed One was gone,
Flown up and away like a seabird. And as she went
She put courage in Telemachus' heart
And made him think of his father even more than before.

Telemachus' mind soared. He knew it had been a god,   340
And like a god himself he rejoined the suitors.

  .   .   .   .

BOOKS 2–4

[Aware that Telemachus has now matured sufficiently to pose a threat to their plans,
the suitors conspire to get rid of him. Prompted by Athene, Telemachus leaves Ithaca
to search for news of his father, traveling first to the court of old King Nestor at Pylos
and then, accompanied by Nestor's son Pisistratus, visiting Sparta and hearing his
father's praises sung by Menelaus and Helen. With Athene's help, Telemachus escapes
the suitors' ambush and returns unharmed to Ithaca.]

BOOK 5

[While Telemachus gathers testimony about his father's heroic reputation, Odysseus
remains trapped on Calypso's remote island, Ogygia, where for seven years he has
nightly made love to the amorous nymph and spent his empty days weeping for home.
Dispatched at Athene's request, Hermes appears to order Calypso to free her reluctant
lover:]

Dawn reluctantly   1
Left Tithonus in her rose-shadowed bed,
Then shook the morning into flakes of fire.

Light flooded the halls of Olympus
Where Zeus, high Lord of Thunder,
Sat with the other gods, listening to Athena
Reel off the tale of Odysseus' woes.
It galled her that he was still in Calypso's cave:

"Zeus, my father—and all you blessed immortals—
Kings might as well no longer be gentle and kind   10
Or understand the correct order of things.
They mights as well be tryannical butchers
For all that any of Odysseus' people
Remember him, a godly king as kind as a father.
No, he's still languishing on that island, detained
Against his will by that nymph Calypso,
No way in the world for him to get back to his land.
His ships are all lost, he has no crew left
To row him across the sea's crawling back.
And now the islanders are plotting to kill his son   20
As he heads back home. He went for news of his father
To sandy Pylos and white-bricked Sparta."

Storm Cloud Zeus had an answer for her:

"Quite a little speech you've let slip through your teeth,
Daughter. But wasn't this exactly your plan

So that Odysseus would make them pay for it later?
You know how to get Telemachus
Back to Ithaca and out of harm's way
With his mother's suitors sailing in a step behind."

Zeus turned then to his son Hermes and said: 30

"Hermes, you've been our messenger before.
Go tell that ringleted nymph it is my will
To let that patient man Odysseus go home.
Not with an escort, mind you, human or divine,
But on a rickety raft—tribulation at sea—
Until on the twentieth day he comes to Schería
In the land of the Phaeacians, our distant relatives,
Who will treat Odysseus as if he were a god
And take him on a ship to his own native land
With gifts of bronze and clothing and gold,   40
More than he ever would have taken back from Troy
Had he come home safely with his share of the loot.
That's how he's destined to see his dear ones again
And return to his high-gabled Ithacan home."

Thus Zeus, and the quicksilver messenger
Laced on his feet the beautiful sandals,
Golden, immortal, that carry him over
Landscape and seascape on a puff of wind.
And he picked up the wand he uses to charm
Mortal eyes to sleep and make sleepers awake.   50

Holding this wand the tough quicksilver god
Took off, bounded onto Pieria
And dove through the ether down to the sea,

   Skimming the waves like a cormorant,
   The bird that patrols the saltwater billows
   Hunting for fish, seaspume on its plumage,

Hermes flying low and planing the whitecaps.

When he finally arrived at the distant island
He stepped from the violet-tinctured sea
On to dry land and proceeded to the cavern   60
Where Calypso lived. She was at home.
A fire blazed on the hearth, and the smell
Of split cedar and arbor vitae burning
Spread like incense across the whole island.
She was seated inside, singing in a lovely voice
As she wove at her loom with a golden shuttle.
Around her cave the woodland was in bloom,
Alder and poplar and fragrant cypress.

Long-winged birds nested in the leaves,
Horned owls and larks and slender-throated shorebirds   70
That screech like crows over the bright saltwater.
Tendrils of ivy curled around the cave's mouth,
The glossy green vine clustered with berries.
Four separate springs flowed with clear water, criss-
Crossing channels as they meandered through meadows
Lush with parsley and blossoming violets.
It was enough to make even a visiting god
Enraptured at the sight. Quicksilver Hermes
Took it all in, then turned and entered
The vast cave.
        Calypso knew him at sight.   80
The immortals have ways of recognizing each other,
Even those whose homes are in outlying districts.
But Hermes didn't find the great hero inside.
Odysseus was sitting on the shore,
As ever those days, honing his heart's sorrow,
Staring out to sea with hollow, salt-rimmed eyes.

Calypso, sleek and haloed, questioned Hermes
Politely, as she seated him on a lacquered chair:

"My dear Hermes, to what do I owe
The honor of this unexpected visit? Tell me   90
What you want, and I'll oblige you if I can."

The goddess spoke, and then set a table
With ambrosia and mixed a bowl of rosy nectar.
The quicksilver messenger ate and drank his fill,
Then settled back from dinner with heart content
And made the speech she was waiting for:

"You ask me, goddess to god, why I have come.
Well, I'll tell you exactly why. Remember, you asked.
Zeus ordered me to come here; I didn't want to.
Who would want to cross this endless stretch   100
Of deserted sea? Not a single city in sight
Where you can get a decent sacrifice from men.
But you know how it is: Zeus has the aegis,
And none of us gods can oppose his will.
He says you have here the most woebegone hero
Of the whole lot who fought around Priam's city
For nine years, sacked it in the tenth, and started home.
But on the way back they offended Athena,
And she swamped them with hurricane winds and waves.
His entire crew was wiped out, and he   110
Drifted along until he was washed up here.
Anyway, Zeus wants you to send him back home. Now.

The man's not fated to rot here far from his friends.
It's his destiny to see his dear ones again
And return to his high-gabled Ithacan home."
He finished, and the nymph's aura stiffened.
Words flew from her mouth like screaming hawks:

"You gods are the most jealous bastards in the universe—
Persecuting any goddess who ever openly takes
A mortal lover to her bed and sleeps with him.   120
When Dawn caressed Orion with her rosy fingers,
You celestial layabouts gave her nothing but trouble
Until Artemis finally shot him on Ortygia—
Gold-throned, holy, gentle-shafted assault goddess!
When Demeter followed her heart and unbound
Her hair for Iasion and made love to him
In a late-summer field, Zeus was there taking notes
And executed the man with a cobalt lightning blast.
And now you gods are after me for having a man.
Well, I was the one who saved his life, unprying him   130
From the spar he came floating here on, sole survivor
Of the wreck Zeus made of his streamlined ship,
Slivering it with lightning on the wine-dark sea.
I loved him, I took care of him, I even told him
I'd make him immortal and ageless all of his days.
But you said it, Hermes: Zeus has the aegis
And none of us gods can oppose his will.
So all right, he can go, if it's an order from above,
Off on the sterile sea. How I don't know.
I don't have any oared ships or crewmen   140
To row him across the sea's broad back.
But I'll help him. I'll do everything I can
To get him back safely to his own native land."

The quicksilver messenger had one last thing to say:

"Well send him off now and watch out for Zeus' temper.
Cross him and he'll really be rough on you later."

With that the tough quicksilver god made his exit.

Calypso composed herself and went to Odysseus,
Zeus' message still ringing in her ears.
She found him sitting where the breakers rolled in.   150
His eyes were perpetually wet with tears now,
His life draining away in homesickness.
The nymph had long since ceased to please.
He still slept with her at night in her cavern,
An unwilling lover mated to her eager embrace.
Days he spent sitting on the rocks by the breakers,

Staring out to sea with hollow, salt-rimmed eyes.
She stood close to him and started to speak:
"You poor man. You can stop grieving now
And pining away. I'm sending you home.   160
Look, here's a bronze axe. Cut some long timbers
And make yourself a raft fitted with topdecks,
Something that will get you across the sea's misty spaces.
I'll stock it with fresh water, food and red wine—
Hearty provisions that will stave off hunger—and
I'll clothe you well and send you a following wind
To bring you home safely to your own native land,
If such is the will of the gods of high heaven,
Whose minds and powers are stronger than mine."

Odysseus' eyes shone with weariness. He stiffened,   170
And shot back at her words fletched like arrows:

"I don't know what kind of send-off you have in mind,
Goddess, telling me to cross all that open sea on a raft,
Painful, hard sailing. Some well-rigged vessels
Never make it across with a stiff wind from Zeus.
You're not going to catch me setting foot on any raft
Unless you agree to swear a solemn oath
That you're not planning some new trouble for me."

Calypso's smile was like a shower of light.
She touched him gently, and teased him a little: 180

"Blasphemous, that's what you are—but nobody's fool!
How do you manage to say things like that?
All right. I swear by Earth and Heaven above
And the subterranean water of Styx—the greatest
Oath and the most awesome a god can swear—
That I'm not planning more trouble for you, Odysseus.
I'll put my mind to work for you as hard as I would
For myself, if ever I were in such a fix.
My heart is in the right place, Odysseus,
Nor is it a cold lump of iron in my breast."   190

With that the haloed goddess walked briskly away
And the man followed in the deity's footsteps.
The two forms, human and divine, came to the cave
And he sat down in the chair which moments before
Hermes had vacated, and the nymph set out for him
Food and drink such as mortal men eat.
She took a seat opposite godlike Odysseus
And her maids served her ambrosia and nectar.
They helped themselves to as much as they wanted,
And when they had their fill of food and drink   200

Calypso spoke, an immortal radiance upon her:
"Son of Laertes in the line of Zeus, my wily Odysseus,
Do you really want to go home to your beloved country
Right away? Now? Well, you still have my blessings.
But if you had any idea of all the pain
You're destined to suffer before getting home,
You'd stay here with me, deathless—
Think of it, Odysseus!—no matter how much
You missed your wife and wanted to see her again.
You spend all your daylight hours yearning for her.   210
I don't mind saying she's not my equal
In beauty, no matter how you measure it.
Mortal beauty cannot compare with immortal."

Odysseus, always thinking, answered her this way:

"Goddess and mistress, don't be angry with me.
I know very well that Penelope,
For all her virtues, would pale beside you.
She's only human, and you are a goddess,
Eternally young. Still, I want to go back.
My heart aches for the day I return to my home.   220
If some god hits me hard as I sail the deep purple,
I'll weather it like the sea-bitten veteran I am.
God knows I've suffered and had my share of sorrows
In war and at sea. I can take more if I have to."

The sun set on his words, and the shadows darkened.
They went to a room deep in the cave, where they made
Sweet love and lay side by side through the night.

. . . .

BOOKS 6–8

[After building a raft and leaving Calypso, Odysseus sails the open sea for seventeen days, at last coming in sight of the island of Scheria, land of the Phaeacians. When Poseidon, returning from Ethiopia, observes his enemy approaching land, the angry god raises a storm that destroys Odysseus's raft. Washed ashore after nearly drowning, Odysseus is befriended by Nausicaa, daughter of the Phaeacian king Alcinous and his wife Arete, who takes him to her parents' court. Moved by the bard Demodocus's singing of the Trojan Horse episode (a brilliant example of the hero's successful cunning), Odysseus reveals his identity and tells the Phaeacians of his fantastic adventures from the time he left Troy until his final shipwreck.]

BOOK 9

[Odysseus narrates his narrow escape when he and his men were trapped in the cave of Polyphemus, the cannibalistic Cyclops. He describes his ruse of getting the one-eyed giant drunk:]

.   .   .   .

"At evening he [Polyphemus, the Cyclops] came, herding his fleecy sheep.   1
He drove them straight into the cave, drove in
All his flocks in fact. Maybe he had some
Foreboding, or maybe some god told him to.
Then he lifted the doorstone and set it in place,
And sat down to milk the goats and bleating ewes,
All in good order, and setting the sucklings
Beneath their mothers. His chores done,
Again he seized two of my men and made his meal.
Then I went up to the Cyclops and spoke to him,   10
Holding an ivy-wood bowl filled with dark wine.

'Cyclops, have some wine, now that you have eaten
Your human flesh, so you can see what kind of drink
Was in our ship's hold. I was bringing it to you
As an offering, hoping you would pity me
And help me get home. But you are a raving
Maniac! How do you expect any other man
Ever to visit you after acting like this?'

He took the bowl and drank it off, relishing
Every last, sweet drop. And he asked me for more: 20

'Be a pal and give me another drink. And tell me
Your name, so I can give you a gift you'll like.
Wine grapes grow in the Cyclopes' land, too.
Rain from the sky makes them grow from the earth.
But this—this is straight ambrosia and nectar.'

So I gave him some more of the ruby-red wine.
Three times the fool drained the bowl dry,
And when the wine had begun to work on his mind,
I spoke these sweet words to him:

                              'Cyclops,
You ask me my name, my glorious name,   30
And I will tell it to you. Remember now,
To give me the gift just as you promised.
Noman is my name. They call me Noman—
My mother, my father, and all my friends, too.'

He answered me from his pitiless heart:

'Noman I will eat last after his friends.
Friends first, him last. That's my gift to you.'

He listed as he spoke and then fell flat on his back,
His thick neck bent sideways. He was sound asleep,

Belching out wine and bits of human flesh   40
In his drunken stupor. I swung into action,
Thrusting the stake deep in the embers,
Heating it up, and all the while talking to my men
To keep up their morale. When the olivewood stake
Was about to catch fire, green though it was,
And was really glowing, I took it out
And brought it right up to him. My men
Stood around me, and some god inspired us.
My men lifted up the olivewood stake
And drove the sharp point right into his eye,   50
While I, putting my weight behind it, spun it around
The way a man bores a ship's beam with a drill,
Leaning down on it while other men beneath him
Keep it spinning and spinning with a leather strap.
That's how we twirled the fiery-pointed stake
In the Cyclops' eye. The blood formed a whirlpool
Around its searing tip. His lids and brow
Were all singed by the heat from the burning eyeball
And its roots crackled in the fire and hissed
Like an axe-head or adze a smith dips into water   60
When he wants to temper the iron—that's how his eye
Sizzled and hissed around the olivewood stake.
He screamed, and the rock walls rang with his voice.
We shrank back in terror while he wrenched
The blood-grimed stake from his eye and flung it
Away from him, blundering about and shouting
To the other Cyclopes, who lived around him
In caverns among the windswept crags.
They heard his cry and gathered from all sides
Around his cave and asked him what ailed him: 70

'Polyphemus, why are you hollering so much
And keeping us up the whole blessed night?
Is some man stealing your flocks from you,
Or killing you, maybe, by some kind of trick?'

And Polyphemus shouted out to them:

'Noman is killing me by some kind of trick!'

They sent their words winging back to him:

'If no man is hurting you, then your sickness
Comes from Zeus and can't be helped.
You should pray to your father, Lord Poseidon.'   80

They left then, and I laughed in my heart
At how my phony name had fooled them so well.

Cyclops meanwhile was groaning in agony.
Groping around, he removed the doorstone
And sat in the entrance with his hands spread out
To catch anyone who went out with the sheep—
As if I could be so stupid. I thought it over,
Trying to come up with the best plan I could
To get us all out from the jaws of death.
I wove all sorts of wiles, as a man will   90
When his life is on the line. My best idea
Had to do with the sheep that were there, big,
Thick-fleeced beauties with wool dark as violets.
Working silently, I bound them together
With willow branches the Cyclops slept on.
I bound them in threes. Each middle sheep
Carried a man underneath, protected by
The two on either side: three sheep to a man.
As for me, there was a ram, the best in the flock.
I grabbed his back and curled up beneath   100
His shaggy belly. There I lay, hands twined
Into the marvelous wool, hanging on for dear life.
And so, muffling our groans, we waited for dawn.

When the first streaks of red appeared in the sky,
The rams started to bolt toward the pasture.
The unmilked females were bleating in the pens,
Their udders bursting. Their master,
Worn out with pain, felt along the backs
Of all of the sheep as they walked by, the fool,
Unaware of the men under their fleecy chests.   110
The great ram headed for the entrance last,
Heavy with wool—and with me thinking hard.
Running his hands over the ram, Polyphemus said:

'My poor ram, why are you leaving the cave
Last of all? You've never lagged behind before.
You were always the first to reach the soft grass
With your big steps, first to reach the river,
First to want to go back to the yard
At evening. Now you're last of all. Are you sad
About your master's eye? A bad man blinded me,   120
Him and his nasty friends, getting me drunk,
Noman—but he's not out of trouble yet!
If only you understood and could talk,
You could tell me where he's hiding. I would
Smash him to bits and spatter his brains
All over the cave. Then I would find some relief
From the pain this no-good Noman has caused me.'

He spoke, and sent the ram off through the door.
When we had gone a little way from the cave,
I first untangled myself from the ram   130
And then untied my men. Then, moving quickly,
We drove those fat, long-shanked sheep
Down to the ship, keeping an eye on our rear.
We were a welcome sight to the rest of the crew,
But when they started to mourn the men we had lost
I forbade it with an upward nod of my head,
Signaling each man like that and ordering them
To get those fleecy sheep aboard instead,
On the double, and get the ship out to sea.
Before you knew it they were on their benches   140
Beating the sea to white froth with their oars.
When we were offshore but still within earshot,
I called out to the Cyclops, just to rub it in:

'So, Cyclops, it turns out it wasn't a coward
Whose men you murdered and ate in your cave,
You savage! But you got yours in the end,
Didn't you? You had the gall to eat the guests
In your own house, and Zeus made you pay for it.'

He was even angrier when he heard this.
Breaking off the peak of a huge crag   150
He threw it toward our ship, and it carried
To just in front of our dark prow. The sea
Billowed up where the rock came down,
And the backwash pushed us to the mainland again,
Like a flood tide setting us down at the shore.
I grabbed a long pole and shoved us off,
Nodding to the crew to fall on the oars
And get us out of there. They leaned into it,
And when we were twice as far out to sea as before
I called to the Cyclops again, with my men   160
Hanging all over me and begging me not to:

'Don't do it, man! The rock that hit the water
Pushed us in and we thought we were done for.
If he hears any sound from us, he'll heave
Half a cliff at us and crush the ship and our skulls
With one throw. You know he has the range.'

They tried, but didn't persuade my hero's heart—
I was really angry—and I called back to him:

'Cyclops, if anyone, any mortal man,
Asks you how you got your eye put out,   170

Tell him that Odysseus the marauder did it,
Son of Laertes, whose home is on Ithaca.'

He groaned, and had this to say in response:

'Oh no! Now it's coming to me, the old prophecy.
There was a seer here once, a tall handsome man,
Telemos Eurymides. He prophesied well
All his life to the Cyclopes. He told me
That all this would happen some day,
That I would lose my sight at Odysseus' hands.
I always expected a great hero   180
Would come here, strong as can be.
Now this puny, little, good-for-nothing runt
Has put my eye out—because he got me drunk.
But come here, Odysseus, so I can give you a gift,
And ask Poseidon to help you on your way.
I'm his son, you know. He claims he's my father.
He will heal me, if he wants. But none
Of the other gods will, and no mortal man will.'

He had his say and then prayed to Poseidon,
Stretching his arms out to starry heaven: 190

'Hear me, Poseidon, blue-maned Earth-Holder,
If you are the father you claim to be.
Grant that Odysseus, son of Laertes,
May never reach his home on Ithaca.
But if he is fated to see his family again,
And return to his home and own native land,
May he come late, having lost all companions,
In another's ship, and find trouble at home.'

He prayed, and the blue-maned sea-god heard him.
Then he broke off an even larger chunk of rock,   200
Pivoted, and threw it with incredible force.
It came down just behind our dark-hulled ship,
Barely missing the end of the rudder. The sea
Billowed up where the rock hit the water,
And the wave pushed us forward all the way
To the island where our other ships waited
Clustered on the shore, ringed by our comrades
Sitting on the sand, anxious for our return.
We beached the ship and unloaded the Cyclops' sheep,
Which I divided up as fairly as I could   210
Among all hands. The veterans gave me the great ram,
And I sacrificed it on the shore of the sea
To Zeus in the dark clouds, who rules over all.

I burnt the thigh pieces, but the god did not accept
My sacrifice, brooding over how to destroy
All my benched ships and my trusty crews.

So all the long day until the sun went down
We sat feasting on meat and drinking sweet wine.
When the sun set and darkness came on
We lay down and slept on the shore of the sea.   220
Early in the morning, when the sky was streaked red,
I roused my men and ordered the crews
To get on deck and cast off. They took their places
And were soon whitening the sea with their oars.

We sailed on in shock, glad to get away alive
But grieving for the comrades we had lost."

BOOK 10

**[In telling his story to the Phaeacians, Odysseus makes clear that he—unlike his
men—had learned from the Cyclops episode. Thus, he explains, when his small fleet
approached the unknown land of the Laestrygonians to gather needed supplies,
Odysseus took the precaution of anchoring his ship a safe distance from shore. Before learning anything about the local inhabitants' treatment of strangers, however,
Odysseus's crewmen unwisely moored their ships along the Laestrygonian shore:]**

. . . .
"The harbor we came to is a glorious place,   1
Surrounded by sheer cliffs. Headlands
Just out on either side to form a narrow mouth,
And there all the others steered in their ships
And moored them close together in the bay.
No wave, large or small, ever rocks a boat
In that silvery calm. I alone moored my black ship
Outside the harbor, tying her up
On the rocks that lie on the border of the land.
Then I climbed to a rugged lookout point   10
And surveyed the scene. There was no sign
Of plowed fields, only smoke rising up from the land.

I sent out a team—two picked men and a herald—
To reconnoiter and find out who lived there.
They went ashore and followed a smooth road
Used by wagons to bring wood from the mountains
Down to the city. In front of the city
They met a girl drawing water. Her father
Was named Antiphates, and she had come down
To the flowing spring Artacia,   20
From which they carried water to the town.
When my men came up to her and asked her

Who the people there were and who was their king,
She showed them her father's high-roofed house.
They entered the house and found his wife inside,
A woman, to their horror, as huge as a mountain top.
At once she called her husband, Antiphates,
Who meant business when he came. He seized
One of my men and made him into dinner.
The other two got out of there and back to the ships,   30
But Antiphates had raised a cry throughout the city,
And when they heard it, the Laestrygonians
Came up on all sides, thousands of them,
Not like men but like the Sons of the Earth,
The Giants. They pelted us from the cliffs
With rocks too large for a man to lift.
The sounds that came from the ships were sickening,
Sounds of men dying and boats being crushed.
The Laestrygonians speared the bodies like fish,
And carried them back for their ghastly meal.   40
While this was happening I drew my sword
And cut the cables of my dark-prowed ship,
Barking out orders for the crew to start rowing
And get us out of there. They rowed for their lives,
Ripping the sea, and my ship sped joyfully
Out and away from the beetling rocks,
But all of the others were destroyed as they lay.

We sailed on in shock, glad to get out alive
But grieving for the comrades we'd lost.
And we came to Aeaea, the island that is home   50
To Circe, a dread goddess with richly coiled hair
And a human voice. She is the sister
Of dark-hearted Aeetes, and they are both sprung
From Helios and Perse, daughter of Ocean.
Some god guided us into a harbor
And we put in to shore without a sound.
We disembarked and lay there for two days and nights,
Eating our hearts out with weariness and grief.
But when Dawn combed her hair in the third day's light,
I took my sword and spear and went up   60
From the ship to open ground, hoping to see
Plowed fields, and to hear human voices.
So I climbed to a rugged lookout point
And surveyed the scene. What I saw was smoke
Rising up from Circe's house. It curled up high
Through the thick brush and woods, and I wondered
Whether I should go and have a closer look.
I decided it was better to go back to the ship

And give my crew their meal, and then
Send out a party to reconnoiter.   70
I was on my way back and close to the ship
When some god took pity on me,
Walking there alone, and sent a great antlered stag
Right into my path. He was on his way
Down to the river from his pasture in the woods,
Thirsty and hot from the sun beating down,
And as he came out I got him right on the spine
In the middle of his back. The bronze spear bored
All the way through, and he fell in the dust
With a groan, and his spirit flew away.   80
Planting my foot on him, I drew the bronze spear
Out of the wound and laid it down on the ground.
Then I pulled up a bunch of willow shoots
And twisted them together to make a rope
About a fathom long. I used this to tie
The stag's feet together so I could carry him
Across my back, leaning on my spear
As I went back to the ship. There was no way
An animal that large could be held on one shoulder.
I flung him down by the ship and roused my men,   90
Going up to each in turn and saying to them:

'We're not going down to Hades, my friends,
Before our time. As long as there is still
Food and drink in our ship, at least
We don't have to starve to death.'

When they heard this, they drew their cloaks
From their faces, and marveled at the size
Of the stag lying on the barren seashore.
When they had seen enough, they washed their hands
And prepared a glorious feast. So all day long   100
Until the sun went down we sat there feasting
On all that meat, washing it down with wine.
When the sun set and darkness came on,
We lay down to sleep on the shore of the sea."

[Odysseus continues his narration: because of the Laestrygonians' savage assault, the fleet that Odysseus commanded after leaving Troy is reduced to a single ship, which puts ashore on Circe's enchanted island. A powerful sorceress, Circe changes a group of Odysseus's unwary men into swine. Forewarned by Hermes, Zeus's Olympian messenger, Odysseus first threatens Circe with his sword, forcing her to return his men to human shape. He then becomes her lover, benefiting greatly from Circe's extensive knowledge and wise advice:]

"When Dawn brushed the eastern sky with rose,
I called my men together and spoke to them:

'Listen to me, men. It's been hard going.
We don't know east from west right now,
But we have to see if we have any good ideas left.
We may not. I climbed up to a lookout point.   110
We're on an island, ringed by the endless sea.
The land lies low, and I was able to see
Smoke rising up through the brushy woods.'

This was too much for them. They remembered
What Antiphates, the Laestrygonian, had done,
And how the Cyclops had eaten their comrades.
They wailed and cried, but it did them no good.
I counted off the crew into two companies
And appointed a leader for each. Eurylochus
Headed up one group and I took the other,   120
And then we shook lots in a bronze helmet.
Out jumped the lot of Eurylochus, brave heart,
And so off he went, with twenty-two men,
All in tears, leaving us behind in no better mood.

They went through the woods and found Circe's house
In an upland clearing. It was built of polished stone
And surrounded by mountain lions and wolves,
Creatures Circe had drugged and bewitched.
These beasts did not attack my men, but stood
On their hind legs and wagged their long tails,   130
Like dogs fawning on their master who always brings
Treats for them when he comes home from a feast.
So these clawed beasts were fawning around my men,
Who were terrified all the same by the huge animals.
While they stood like this in the gateway
They could hear Circe inside, singing in a lovely voice
As she moved about weaving a great tapestry,
The unfading handiwork of an immortal goddess,
Finely woven, shimmering with grace and light.
Polites, a natural leader, and of all the crew   140
The one I loved and trusted most, spoke up then:

'Someone inside is weaving a great web,
And singing so beautifully the floor thrums with the sound.
Whether it's a goddess or a woman, let's call her out now.'

And so they called to her, and she came out
And flung open the bright doors and invited them in.
They all filed in naively behind her,
Except Eurylochus, who suspected a trap.
When she had led them in and seated them
She brewed up a potion of Pramnian wine   150
With cheese, barley, and pale honey stirred in,

And she laced this potion with insidious drugs
That would make them forget their own native land.
When they had eaten and drunk, she struck them
With her wand and herded them into the sties outside.
Grunting, their bodies covered with bristles,
They looked just like pigs, but their minds were intact.
Once in the pens, they squealed with dismay,
And Circe threw them acorns and berries—
The usual fare for wallowing swine.   160

Eurylochus at once came back to the ship
To tell us of our comrades' unseemly fate,
But, hard as he tried, he could not speak a word.
The man was in shock. His eyes welled with tears,
And his mind was filled with images of horror.
Finally, under our impatient questioning,
He told us how his men had been undone;

'We went through the woods, as you told us to,
Glorious Odysseus, and found a beautiful house
In an upland clearing, built of polished stone.   170
Someone inside was working a great loom
And singing in a high, clear voice, some goddess
Or a woman, and they called out to her,
And she came out and opened the bright doors
And invited them in, and they naively
Filed in behind her. But I stayed outside,
Suspecting a trap. And they all disappeared,
Not one came back. I sat and watched
For a long, long time, and not one came back.'

He spoke, and I threw my silver-studded sword   180
Around my shoulders, slung on my bow,
And ordered Eurylochus to retrace his steps
And lead me back there. But he grabbed me by the knees
And pleaded with me, wailing miserably:

'Don't force me to go back there. Leave me here,
Because I know that you will never come back yourself
Or bring back the others. Let's just get out of here
With those that are left. We might still make it.'

Those were his words, and I answered him:

'All right, Eurylochus, you stay here by the ship.   190
Get yourself something to eat and drink.
I'm going, though. We're in a really tight spot.'

And so I went up from the ship and the sea
Into the sacred woods. I was closing in

On Circe's house, with all its bewitchment,
When I was met by Hermes. He had a golden wand
And looked like a young man, a hint of a moustache
Above his lip—youth at its most charming.
He clasped my hand and said to me:

'Where are you off to now, unlucky man,   200
Alone, and in rough, uncharted terrain?
Those men of yours are up in Circe's house,
Penned like pigs into crowded little sties.
And you've come to free them? I don't think so.
You'll never return; you'll have to stay there, too.
Oh well, I will keep you out of harm's way.
Take this herb with you when you go to Circe,
And it will protect you from her deadly tricks.
She'll mix a potion and spike it with drugs,
But she won't be able to cast her spell   210
Because you'll have a charm that works just as well—
The one I'll give you—and you'll be forewarned.
When Circe strikes you with her magic wand,
Draw your sharp sword from beside your thigh
And rush at her with murder in your eye.
She'll be afraid and invite you to bed.
Don't turn her down—that's how you'll get
Your comrades freed and yourself well loved.
But first make her swear by the gods above
She will not unsex you when you are nude,   220
Or drain you of your manly fortitude.'

So saying, Hermes gave me the herb,
Pulling it out of the ground, and showed it to me.
It was black at the root, with a milk-white flower.
Moly, the gods call it, hard for mortal men to dig up,
But the gods can do anything. Hermes rose
Through the wooded island and up to Olympus,
And I went on to Circe's house, brooding darkly
On many things. I stood at the gates
Of the beautiful goddess' house and gave a shout.   230
She heard me call and came out at once,
Opening the bright doors and inviting me in.
I followed her inside, my heart pounding.
She seated me on a beautiful chair
Of finely wrought silver, and prepared me a drink
In a golden cup, and with evil in her heart
She laced it with drugs. She gave me the cup
And I drank it off, but it did not bewitch me.
So she struck me with her wand and said:
'Off to the sty, with the rest of your friends.'   240

At this, I drew the sharp sword that hung by my thigh
And lunged at Circe as if I meant to kill her.
The goddess shrieked and, running beneath my blade,
Grabbed my knees and said to me wailing:

'Who are you, and where do you come from?
What is your city and who are your parents?
I am amazed that you drank this potion
And are not bewitched. No other man
Has ever resisted this drug once it's past his lips.
But you have a mind that cannot be beguiled.   250
You must be Odysseus, the man of many wiles,
Who Quicksilver Hermes always said would come here
In his swift black ship on his way home from Troy.
Well then, sheath your sword and let's
Climb into my bed and tangle in love there,
So we may come to trust each other.'

She spoke, and I answered her:

'Circe, how can you ask me to be gentle to you
After you turned my men into swine?
And now you have me here and want to trick me   260
Into going to bed with you, so that you can
Unman me when I am naked. No, Goddess,
I'm not getting into any bed with you
Unless you agree first to swear a solemn oath
That you're not planning some new trouble for me.'

Those were my words, and she swore an oath at once
Not to do me any harm, and when she finished
I climbed into Circe's beautiful bed.

Meanwhile, her serving women were busy,
Four maidens who did all the housework,   270
Spirit women born of the springs and groves
And of the sacred rivers that flow to the sea.
One of them brought rugs with a purple sheen
And strewed them over chairs lined with fresh linen.
Another drew silver tables up to the chairs
And set golden baskets upon them. The third
Mixed honey-hearted wine in a silver bowl
And set out golden cups. The fourth
Filled a cauldron with water and lit a great fire
Beneath it, and when the water was boiling   280
In the glowing bronze, she set me in a tub
And bathed me, mixing in water from the cauldron
Until it was just how I liked it, and pouring it over
My head and shoulders until she washed from my limbs

The weariness that had consumed my soul.
When she had bathed me and rubbed me
With rich olive oil, and had thrown about me
A beautiful cloak and tunic, she led me to the hall
And had me sit on a silver-studded chair,
Richly wrought and with a matching footstool. 290
A maid poured water from a silver pitcher
Over a golden basin for me to wash my hands
And then set up a polished table nearby.
And the housekeeper, grave and dignified,
Set out bread and generous helpings
From all the dishes she had. She told me to eat,
But nothing appealed. I sat there with other thoughts
Occupying my mind, and my mood was dark.
When Circe noticed I was just sitting there,
Depressed, and not reaching out for food, 300
She came up to me and spoke winged words:

'Why are you just sitting there, Odysseus,
Eating your heart out and not touching your food?
Are you afraid of some other trick? You need not be.
I have already sworn I will do you no harm.'

So she spoke, and I answered her:

'Circe, how could anyone bring himself—
Any decent man—to taste food and drink
Before seeing his comrades free?
If you really want me to eat and drink, 310
Set my men free and let me see them.'

So I spoke, and Circe went outside
Holding her wand and opened the sty
And drove them out. They looked like swine
Nine or ten years old. They stood there before her
And she went through them and smeared each one
With another drug. The bristles they had grown
After Circe had given them the poisonous drug
All fell away, and they became men again,
Younger than before, taller and far handsomer. 320
They knew me, and they clung to my hands,
And the house rang with their passionate sobbing.
The goddess herself was moved to pity.

Then she came to my side and said:

'Son of Laertes in the line of Zeus,
My wily Odysseus, go to your ship now
Down by the sea and haul it ashore.

Then stow all the tackle and gear in caves
And come back here with the rest of your crew.'

So she spoke, and persuaded my heart.   330
I went to the shore and found my crew there
Wailing and crying beside our sailing ship.
When they saw me they were like farmyard calves
Around a herd of cows returning to the yard.
The calves bolt from their pens and run friskily
Around their mothers, lowing and mooing.
That's how my men thronged around me
When they saw me coming. It was as if
They had come home to their rugged Ithaca,
And wailing miserably they said so to me: 340

'With you back, Zeus-born, it is just as if
We had returned to our native Ithaca.
But tell us what happened to the rest of the crew.'

So they spoke, and I answered them gently:

'First let's haul our ship onto dry land
And then stow all the tackle and gear in caves.
Then I want all of you to come along with me
So you can see your shipmates in Circe's house,
Eating and drinking all they could ever want.'

They heard what I said and quickly agreed.   350
Eurylochus, though, tried to hold them back,
Speaking to them these winged words:

'Why do you want to do this to yourselves,
Go down to Circe's house? She will turn all of you
Into pigs, wolves, lions, and make you guard her house.
Remember what the Cyclops did when our shipmates
Went into his lair? It was this reckless Odysseus
Who led them there. It was his fault they died.'

When Eurylochus said that, I considered
Drawing my long sword from where it hung   360
By my thigh and lopping off his head,
Close kinsman though he was by marriage.
But my crew talked me out of it, saying things like:

'By your leave, let's station this man here
To guard the ship. As for the rest of us,
Lead us on to the sacred house of Circe.'

And so the whole crew went up from the sea,
And Eurylochus did not stay behind with the ship

But went with us, in mortal fear of my temper.
Meanwhile, back in Circe's house, the goddess 370
Had my men bathed, rubbed down with oil,
And clothed in tunics and fleecy cloaks.
We found them feasting well in her halls.
When they recognized each other, they wept openly
And their cries echoed throughout Circe's house.
Then the shining goddess stood near me and said:

'Lament no more. I myself know
All that you have suffered on the teeming sea
And the losses on land at your enemies' hands.
Now you must eat, drink wine, and restore the spirit 380
You had when you left your own native land,
Your rugged Ithaca. You are skin and bones now
And hollow inside. All you can think of
Is your hard wandering, no joy in your heart,
For you have, indeed, suffered many woes.'

She spoke, and I took her words to heart.
So we sat there day after day for a year,
Feasting on abundant meat and sweet wine.
But when a year had passed, and the seasons turned,
And the moons waned and the long days were done, 390
My trusty crew called me out and said:

'Good god, man, at long last remember your home,
If it is heaven's will for you to be saved
And return to your house and your own native land.'
They spoke, and I saw what they meant.
So all that long day until the sun went down
We sat feasting on meat and sweet red wine.
When the sun set and darkness came on,
My men lay down to sleep in the shadowy hall,
But I went up to Circe's beautiful bed 400
And touching her knees I beseeched the goddess:

'Circe, fulfill now the promise you made
To send me home. I am eager to be gone
And so are my men, who are wearing me out
Sitting around whining and complaining
Whenever you happen not to be present.'

So I spoke, and the shining goddess answered:

'Son of Laertes in the line of Zeus,
My wily Odysseus—you need not stay
Here in my house any longer than you wish. 410
But there is another journey you must make first—

To the house of Hades and dread Persephone,
To consult the ghost of Theban Tiresias,
The blind prophet, whose mind is still strong.
To him alone Persephone has granted
Intelligence even after his death.
The rest of the dead are flitting shadows.'

This broke my spirit. I sat on the bed
And wept. I had no will to live, nor did I care
If I ever saw the sunlight again.   420
But when I had my fill of weeping and writhing,
I looked at the goddess and said:

'And who will guide me on this journey, Circe?
No man has ever sailed his black ship to Hades.'

And the goddess, shining, answered at once:

'Son of Laertes in the line of Zeus,
My wily Odysseus—do not worry about
A pilot to guide your ship. Just set up the mast,
Spread the white sail, and sit yourself down.
The North Wind's breath will bear her onwards.   430
But when your ship crosses the stream of Ocean
You will see a shelving shore and Persephone's groves,
Tall poplars and willows that drop their fruit.
Beach your ship there by Ocean's deep eddies,
And go yourself to the dank house of Hades.
There into Acheron flow Pyriphlegethon
And Cocytus, a branch of the water of Styx.
And there is a rock where the two roaring rivers
Flow into one. At that spot, hero, gather yourself
And do as I say.
                    Dig an ell-square pit,   440
And around it pour libation to all the dead,
First with milk and honey, then with sweet wine,
And a third time with water. Then sprinkle barley
And pray to the looming, feeble death-heads,
Vowing sacrifice on Ithaca, a barren heifer,
The herd's finest, and rich gifts on the altar,
And to Tiresias alone a great black ram.
After these supplications to the spirits,
Slaughter a ram and a black ewe, turning their heads
Toward Erebus, yourself turning backward   450
And leaning toward the streams of the river.
Then many ghosts of the dead will come forth.
Call to your men to flay the slaughtered sheep
And burn them as a sacrifice to the gods below,

To mighty Hades and dread Persephone.
You yourself draw your sharp sword and sit there,
Keeping the feeble death-heads from the blood
Until you have questioned Tiresias.
Then, and quickly, the great seer will come.
He will tell you the route and how long it will take   460
For you to reach home over the teeming deep.'

Dawn rose in gold as she finished speaking.
Circe gave me a cloak and tunic to wear
And the nymph slipped on a long silver robe
Shimmering in the light, cinched it at the waist
With a golden belt and put a veil on her head.
I went through the halls and roused my men,
Going up to each with words soft and sweet:

'Time to get up! No more sleeping late.
We're on our way. Lady Circe has told me all.'   470

So I spoke, and persuaded their heroes' hearts.
But not even from Circe's house could I lead my men
Unscathed. One of the crew, Elpenor, the youngest,
Not much of a warrior nor all that smart,
Had gone off to sleep apart from his shipmates,
Seeking the cool air on Circe's roof
Because he was heavy with wine.
He heard the noise of his shipmates moving around
And sprang up suddenly, forgetting to go
To the long ladder that led down from the roof.   480
He fell headfirst, his neck snapped at the spine,
And his soul went down to the house of Hades.

As my men were heading out I spoke to them:

'You think, no doubt, that you are going home,
But Circe has plotted another course for us,
To the house of Hades and dread Persephone,
To consult the ghost of Theban Tiresias.'

This broke their hearts. They sat down
Right where they were and wept and tore their hair,
But no good came of their lamentation.   490

While we were on our way to our swift ship
On the shore of the sea, weeping and crying,
Circe had gone ahead and tethered a ram and a black ewe
By our tarred ship. She had passed us by
Without our ever noticing. Who could see
A god on the move against the god's will?"

BOOK 11

"When we reached our black ship   1
We hauled her onto the bright saltwater,
Set up the mast and sail, loaded on
The sheep, and boarded her ourselves,
Heartsick and weeping openly by now.
The dark prow cut through the waves
And a following wind bellied the canvas,
A good sailing breeze sent by Circe,
The dread goddess with a human voice.
We lashed everything down and sat tight,   10
Leaving the ship to the wind and helmsman.
All day long she surged on with taut sail;
Then the sun set, and the sea grew dark.

The ship took us to the deep, outermost Ocean
And the land of the Cimmerians, a people
Shrouded in mist. The sun never shines there,
Never climbs the starry sky to beam down at them,
Nor bathes them in the glow of its last golden rays;
Their wretched sky is always racked with night's gloom.
We beached our ship there, unloaded the sheep,   20
And went along the stream of Ocean
Until we came to the place spoken of by Circe.

There Perimedes and Eurylochus held the victims
While I dug an ell-square pit with my sword,
And poured libation to all the dead,
First with milk and honey, then with sweet wine,
And a third time with water. Then I sprinkled
White barley and prayed to the looming dead,
Vowing sacrifice on Ithaca—a barren heifer,
The herd's finest, and rich gifts on the altar,   30
And to Tiresias alone a great black ram.
After these supplications to the spirits,
I cut the sheeps' throats over the pit,
And the dark blood pooled there.
                            Then out of Erebus
The souls of the dead gathered, the ghosts
Of brides and youths and worn-out old men
And soft young girls with hearts new to sorrow,
And many men wounded with bronze spears,
Killed in battle, bearing blood-stained arms.
They drifted up to the pit from all sides   40
With an eerie cry, and pale fear seized me.
I called to my men to flay the slaughtered sheep
And burn them as a sacrifice to the gods,

To mighty Hades and dread Persephone.
Myself, I drew my sharp sword and sat,
Keeping the feeble death-heads from the blood
Until I had questioned Tiresias.
First to come was the ghost of Elpenor,
Whose body still lay in Circe's hall,
Unmourned, unburied, since we'd been hard pressed.   50
I wept when I saw him, and with pity in my heart
Spoke to him these feathered words:

'Elpenor, how did you get to the undergloom
Before me, on foot, outstripping our black ship?'

I spoke, and he moaned in answer:

'Bad luck and too much wine undid me.
I fell asleep on Circe's roof. Coming down
I missed my step on the long ladder
And fell headfirst. My neck snapped
At the spine and my ghost went down to Hades.   60
Now I beg you—by those we left behind,
By your wife and the father who reared you,
And by Telemachus, your only son,
Whom you left alone in your halls—
When you put the gloom of Hades behind you
And beach your ship on the Isle of Aeaea,
As I know you will, remember me, my lord.
Do not leave me unburied, unmourned,
When you sail for home, or I might become
A cause of the gods' anger against you.   70
Burn me with my armor, such as I have,
Heap me a barrow on the grey sea's shore,
In memory of a man whose luck ran out.
Do this for me, and fix in the mound the oar
I rowed with my shipmates while I was alive.'

Thus Elpenor, and I answered him:

'Pitiful spirit, I will do this for you.'

Such were the sad words we exchanged
Sitting by the pit, I on one side holding my sword
Over the blood, my comrade's ghost on the other.   80

Then came the ghost of my dead mother,
Anticleia, daughter of the hero Autolycus.
She was alive when I left for sacred Ilion.
I wept when I saw her, and pitied her,

But even in my grief I would not allow her
To come near the blood until I had questioned Tiresias.

And then he came, the ghost of Theban Tiresias,
Bearing a golden staff. He knew me and said:
'Odysseus, son of Laertes, master of wiles,
Why have you come, leaving the sunlight   90
To see the dead and this joyless place?
Move off from the pit and take away your sword,
So I may drink the blood and speak truth to you.'

I drew back and slid my silver-studded sword
Into its sheath. After he had drunk the dark blood
The flawless seer rose and said to me:

'You seek a homecoming sweet as honey,
Shining Odysseus, but a god will make it bitter,
For I do not think you will elude the Earthshaker,
Who has laid up wrath in his heart against you,   100
Furious because you blinded his son. Still,
You just might get home, though not without pain,
You and your men, if you curb your own spirit,
And theirs, too, when you beach your ship
On Thrinacia. You will be marooned on that island
In the violet sea, and find there the cattle
Of Helios the Sun, and his sheep, too, grazing.
Leave these unharmed, keep your mind on your homecoming,
And you may still reach Ithaca, though not without pain.
But if you harm them, I foretell doom for you,   110
Your ship, and your crew. And even if you
Yourself escape, you will come home late
And badly, having lost all companions
And in another's ship. And you shall find
Trouble in your house, arrogant men
Devouring your wealth and courting your wife.
Yet vengeance will be yours, and when you have slain
The suitors in your hall, by ruse or by sword,
Then you must go off again, carrying a broad-bladed oar,
Until you come to men who know nothing of the sea,   120
Who eat their food unsalted, and have never seen
Red-prowed ships or oars that wing them along.
And I will tell you a sure sign that you have found them,
One you cannot miss. When you meet another traveler
Who thinks you are carrying a winnowing fan,
Then you must fix your oar in the earth
And offer sacrifice to Lord Poseidon,
A ram, a bull, and a boar in its prime.
Then return to your home and offer

Perfect sacrifice to the immortal gods   130
Who hold high heaven, to each in turn.
And death will come to you off the sea,
A death so gentle, and carry you off
When you are worn out in sleek old age,
Your people prosperous all around you.
All this will come true for you as I have told.'

Thus Tiresias. And I answered him:

'All that, Tiresias, is as the gods have spun it.
But tell me this: I see here the ghost
Of my dead mother, sitting in silence   140
Beside the blood, and she cannot bring herself
To look her son in the eye or speak to him.
How can she recognize me for who I am?'

And Tiresias, the Theban prophet:

'This is easy to tell you. Whoever of the dead
You let come to the blood will speak truly to you.
Whoever you deny will go back again.'

With that, the ghost of Lord Tiresias
Went back into Hades, his soothsaying done.
But I stayed where I was until my mother   150
Came up and drank the dark blood. At once
She knew me, and her words reached me on wings:

'My child, how did you come to the undergloom
While you are still alive? It is hard for the living
To reach these shores. There are many rivers to cross,
Great bodies of water, nightmarish streams,
And Ocean itself, which cannot be crossed on foot
But only in a well-built ship. Are you still wandering
On your way back from Troy, a long time at sea
With your ship and your men? Have you not yet come   160
To Ithaca, or seen your wife in your halls?'

So she spoke, and I answered her:

'Mother, I came here because I had to,
To consult the ghost of the prophet Tiresias.
I have not yet come to the coast of Achaea
Or set foot on my own land. I have had nothing
But hard travels from the day I set sail
With Lord Agamemnon to go to Ilion,
Famed for its horses, to fight the Trojans.
But tell me truly, how did you die?   170
Was it a long illness, or did Artemis

Shoot you suddenly with her gentle arrows?
And tell me about my father and my son,
Whom I left behind. Does the honor I had
Still remain with them, or has it passed
To some other man, and do they all say
I will never return? And what about my wife?
What has she decided, what does she think?
Is she still with my son, keeping things safe?
Or has someone already married her,   180
Whoever is now the best of the Achaeans?'

So I spoke, and my mother answered at once:

'Oh, yes indeed, she remains in your halls,
Her heart enduring the bitter days and nights.
But the honor that was yours has not passed
To any man. Telemachus holds your lands
Unchallenged, and shares in the feasts
To which all men invite him as the island's lawgiver.
Your father, though, stays out in the fields
And does not come to the city. He has no bed   190
Piled with bright rugs and soft coverlets
But sleeps in the house where the slaves sleep,
In the ashes by the fire, and wears poor clothes.
In summer and autumn his vineyard's slope
Is strewn with beds of leaves on the ground,
Where he lies in his sorrow, nursing his grief,
Longing for your return. His old age is hard.
I died from the same grief. The keen-eyed goddess
Did not shoot me at home with her gentle shafts,
Nor did any long illness waste my body away.   200
No, it was longing for you, my glorious Odysseus,
For your gentle heart and your gentle ways,
That robbed me of my honey-sweet life.'

So she spoke, and my heart yearned
To embrace the ghost of my dead mother.
Three times I rushed forward to hug her,
And three times she drifted out of my arms
Like a shadow or a dream. The pain
That pierced my heart grew ever sharper,
And my words rose to my mother on wings: 210

'Mother, why do you slip away when I try
To embrace you? Even though we are in Hades,
Why can't we throw our arms around each other
And console ourselves with chill lamentation?
Are you a phantom sent by Persephone
To make me groan even more in my grief?'

And my mother answered me at once:

'O my child, most ill-fated of men,
It is not that Persephone is deceiving you.
This is the way it is with mortals.   220
When we die, the sinews no longer hold
Flesh and bones together. The fire destroys these
As soon as the spirit leaves the white bones,
And the ghost flutters off and is gone like a dream.
Hurry now to the light, and remember these things,
So that later you may tell them all to your wife.'

That was the drift of our talk."

. . . .

[*The shade of Agamemnon appears:*]
"When holy Persephone had scattered
The women's ghosts, there came the ghost
Of Agamemnon, son of Atreus,   230
Distraught with grief. Around him were gathered
Those who died with him in Aegisthus' house.
He knew me as soon as he drank the dark blood.
He cried out shrilly, tears welling in his eyes,
And he stretched out his hands, trying to touch me,
But he no longer had anything left of the strength
He had in the old days in those muscled limbs.
I wept when I saw him, and with pity in my heart
I spoke to him these winged words:

'Son of Atreus, king of men, most glorious   240
Agamemnon—what death laid you low?
Did Poseidon sink your fleet at sea,
After hitting you hard with hurricane winds?
Or were you killed by enemy forces on land,
As you raided their cattle and flocks of sheep
Or fought to capture their city and women?'

And Agamemnon answered at once:

'Son of Laertes in the line of Zeus,
My crafty Odysseus—No,
Poseidon did not sink my fleet at sea   250
After hitting us hard with hurricane winds,
Nor was I killed by enemy forces on land.
Aegisthus was the cause of my death.
He killed me with the help of my cursed wife
After inviting me to a feast in his house,
Slaughtered me like a bull at a manger.
So I died a most pitiable death,
And all around me my men were killed

Relentlessly, like white-tusked swine
For a wedding banquet or dinner party   260
In the house of a rich and powerful man.
You have seen many men cut down, both
In single combat and in the crush of battle,
But your heart would have grieved
As never before at the sight of us lying
Around the wine-bowl and the laden tables
In that great hall. The floor steamed with blood.
But the most piteous cry I ever heard
Came from Cassandra, Priam's daughter.
She had her arms around me down on the floor   270
When Clytemnestra ran her through from behind.
I lifted my hands and beat the ground
As I lay dying with a sword in my chest,
But that bitch, my wife, turned her back on me
And would not shut my eyes or close my lips
As I was going down to Death. Nothing
Is more grim or more shameless than a woman
Who sets her mind on such an unspeakable act
As killing her own husband. I was sure
I would be welcomed home by my children   280
And all my household, but she, with her mind set
On stark horror, has shamed not only herself
But all women to come, even the rare good one.'

Thus Agamemnon, and I responded:

'Ah, how broad-browed Zeus has persecuted
The house of Atreus from the beginning,
Through the will of women. Many of us died
For Helen's sake, and Clytemnestra
Set a snare for you while you were far away.'

And Agamemnon answered me at once: 290

'So don't go easy on your own wife either,
Or tell her everything you know.
Tell her some things, but keep some hidden.
But your wife will not bring about your death,
Odysseus. Icarius' daughter,
Your wise Penelope, is far too prudent.
She was newly wed when we went to war.
We left her with a baby boy still at the breast,
Who must by now be counted as a man,
And prosperous. His father will see him   300
When he comes, and he will embrace his father,
As is only right. But my wife did not let me
Even fill my eyes with the sight of my son.

She killed me before I could do even that,
But let me tell you something, Odysseus:
Beach your ship secretly when you come home.
Women just can't be trusted any more.
And one more thing. Tell me truthfully
If you've heard anything about my son
And where he is living, perhaps in Orchomenus,   310
Or in sandy Pylos, or with Menelaus in Sparta.
For Orestes has not yet perished from the earth.'

So he spoke, and I answered him:

'Son of Atreus, why ask me this?
I have no idea whether he is alive or dead,
And it is not good to speak words empty as wind.'

Such were the sad words we had for each other
As we stood there weeping, heavy with grief.

Then came the ghost of Achilles, son of Peleus,
And those of Patroclus and peerless Antilochus   320
And Ajax, who surpassed all the Danaans,
Except Achilles, in looks and build.
Aeacus' incomparable grandson, Achilles, knew me,
And when he spoke his words had wings:

'Son of Laertes in the line of Zeus,
Odysseus, you hard rover, not even you
Can ever top this, this bold foray
Into Hades, home of the witless dead
And the dim phantoms of men outworn.'

So he spoke, and I answered him: 330

'Achilles, by far the mightiest of the Achaeans,
I have come here to consult Tiresias,
To see if he has any advice for me
On how I might get back to rugged Ithaca.
I've had nothing but trouble; and have not yet set foot
On my native land. But no man, Achilles,
Has ever been as blessed as you, or ever will be.
While you were alive the army honored you
Like a god, and now that you are here
You rule the dead with might. You should not   340
Lament your death at all, Achilles.'

I spoke, and he answered me at once:

'Don't try to sell me on death, Odysseus.
I'd rather be a hired hand back up on earth,
Slaving away for some poor dirt farmer,

Than lord it over all these withered dead.
But tell me about that boy of mine.
Did he come to the war and take his place
As one of the best? Or did he stay away?
And what about Peleus? What have you heard?   350
Is he still respected among the Myrmidons,
Or do they dishonor him in Phthia and Hellas,
Crippled by old age in hand and foot?
And I'm not there for him up in the sunlight
With the strength I had in wide Troy once
When I killed Ilion's best and saved the army.
Just let me come with that kind of strength
To my father's house, even for an hour,
And wrap my hands around his enemies' throats.
They would learn what it means to face my temper.'   360

Thus Achilles, and I answered him:

'I have heard nothing of flawless Peleus,
But as for your son, Neoptolemus,
I'll tell you all I know, just as you ask.
I brought him over from Scyros myself,
In a fine vessel, to join the Greek army
At Troy, and every time we held council there,
He was always the first to speak, and his words
Were never off the mark. Godlike Nestor and I
Alone surpassed him. And every time we fought   370
On Troy's plain, he never held back in the ranks
But charged ahead to the front, yielding
To no one, and he killed many in combat.
I could not begin to name them all,
All the men he killed when he fought for us,
But what a hero he dismantled in Telephus' son,
Eurypylus, dispatching him and a crowd
Of his Ceteian compatriots. Eurypylus
Came to Troy because Priam bribed his mother.
After Memnon, I've never seen a handsomer man.   380
And then, too, when all our best climbed
Into the wooden horse Epeius made,
And I was in command and controlled the trapdoor,
All the other Danaan leaders and counselors
Were wiping away tears from their eyes
And their legs shook beneath them, but I never saw
Neoptolemus blanch or wipe away a tear.
No, he just sat there handling his sword hilt
And heavy bronze spear, and all he wanted
Was to get out of there and give the Trojans hell.   390
And after we had sacked Priam's steep city,

He boarded his ship with his share of the loot
And more for valor. And not a scratch on him.
He never took a hit from a spear or sword
In close combat, where wounds are common.
When Ares rages anyone can be hit.'

So I spoke, and the ghost of swift-footed Achilles
Went off with huge strides through the fields of asphodel,
Filled with joy at his son's preeminence.

The other ghosts crowded around in sorrow,   400
And each asked about those who were dear to him.
Only the ghost of Telamonian Ajax
Stood apart, still furious with me
Because I had defeated him in the contest at Troy
To decide who would get Achilles' armor.
His goddess mother had put it up as a prize,
And the judges were the sons of the Trojans
And Pallas Athena. I wish I had never won.
That contest buried Ajax, that brave heart,
The best of the Danaans in looks and deeds,   410
After the incomparable son of Peleus.
I tried to win him over with words like these:

'Ajax, son of flawless Telamon,
Are you to be angry with me even in death
Over that accursed armor? The gods
Must have meant it to be the ruin of the Greeks.
We lost a tower of strength to that armor.
We mourn your loss as we mourn the loss
Of Achilles himself. Zeus alone
Is to blame. He persecuted the Greeks   420
Terribly, and he brought you to your doom.
No, come back, Lord Ajax, and listen!
Control your wrath and rein in your proud spirit.'

I spoke, but he said nothing. He went his way
To Erebus, to join the other souls of the dead.
He might yet have spoken to me there, or I
Might yet have spoken to him, but my heart
Yearned to see the other ghosts of the dead.

There I saw Minos, Zeus' glorious son,
Scepter in hand, judging the dead   430
As he sat in the wide-gated house of Hades;
And the dead sat, too, and asked him for judgments.

And then Orion loomed up before me,
Driving over the fields of asphodel

The beasts he had slain in the lonely hills,
In his hands a bronze club, forever unbroken.

And I saw Tityos, a son of glorious Earth,
Lying on the ground, stretched over nine acres,
And two vultures sat on either side of him
And tore at his liver, plunging their beaks   440
Deep into his guts, and he could not beat them off.
For Tityos had raped Leto, a consort of Zeus,
As she went to Pytho through lovely Panopeus.

And I saw Tantalus there in his agony,
Standing in a pool with water up to his chin.
He was mad with thirst, but unable to drink,
For every time the old man bent over
The water would drain away and vanish,
Dried up by some god, and only black mud
Would be left at his feet. Above him dangled   450
Treetop fruits, pears and pomegranates,
Shiny apples, sweet figs, and luscious olives.
But whenever Tantalus reached up for them,
The wind tossed them high to the shadowy clouds.

And I saw Sisyphus there in his agony,
Pushing a monstrous stone with his hands.
Digging in hard, he would manage to shove it
To the crest of a hill, but just as he was about
To heave it over the top, the shameless stone
Would teeter back and bound down to the plain.   460
Then he would strain every muscle to push it back up,
Sweat pouring from his limbs and dusty head.

And then mighty Heracles loomed up before me—
His phantom that is, for Heracles himself
Feasts with the gods and has as his wife
Beautiful Hebe, daughter of great Zeus
And gold-sandaled Hera. As he moved
A clamor arose from the dead around him,
As if they were birds flying off in terror.
He looked like midnight itself. He held his bow   470
With an arrow on the string, and he glared around him
As if he were always about to shoot. His belt,
A baldric of gold crossing his chest,
Was stark horror, a phantasmagoria
Of Bears, and wild Boars, and green-eyed Lions,
Of Battles, and Bloodshed, Murder and Mayhem.
May this be its maker's only masterpiece,
And may there never again be another like it.

Heracles recognized me at once,
And his words beat down on me like dark wings: 480

'Son of Laertes in the line of Zeus,
Crafty Odysseus—poor man, do you too
Drag out a wretched destiny
Such as I once bore under the rays of the sun?
I was a son of Zeus and grandson of Cronus,
But I had immeasurable suffering,
Enslaved to a man who was far less than I
And who laid upon me difficult labors.
Once he even sent me here, to fetch
The Hound of Hell, for he could devise   490
No harder task for me than this. That hound
I carried out of the house of Hades,
With Hermes and grey-eyed Athena as guides.'

And Heracles went back into the house of Hades.
But I stayed where I was, in case any more
Of the heroes of yesteryear might yet come forth.
And I would have seen some of them—
Heroes I longed to meet, Theseus and Peirithous,
Glorious sons of the gods—but before I could,
The nations of the dead came thronging up   500
With an eerie cry, and I turned pale with fear
That Persephone would send from Hades' depths
The pale head of that monster, the Gorgon.

I went to the ship at once and called to my men
To get aboard and untie the stern cables.
They boarded quickly and sat at their benches.
The current bore the ship down the River Ocean.
We rowed at first, and then caught a good tailwind."

BOOK 12

[Odysseus continues relating his adventures. He tells the Phaeacians of his encounter
with the enchanting Sirens, strange creatures whose irresistible song lures mariners
to their destruction. Following Circe's directions, Odysseus stops the ears of his men
with wax so that they cannot hear the Sirens' beautiful but deadly music and has himself lashed to the ship's mast, allowing him to listen but preventing him from throwing himself overboard. Next he confronts two equally lethal female monsters: Scylla,
a six-headed giant cannibal, and Charybdis, a ship-crushing whirlpool. Forced to
navigate his fragile bark through the narrow strait separating these two aspects of
the devouring feminine principle, Odysseus explains that he heeded Circe's advice to
lose a few of his men to Scylla rather than the entire crew to Charybdis. In this section, Odysseus also tells how the last of his fellow sailors were killed—for having disobeyed the divine command not to eat the sacred cattle of Helios, god of the sun:]

. . . .

"I spoke, they obeyed. But I didn't mention   1
Scylla. There was nothing we could do about that,
And I didn't want the crew to freeze up,
Stop rowing, and huddle together in the hold.
Then I forgot Circe's stern warning
Not to arm myself no matter what happened.
I strapped on my bronze, grabbed two long spears
And went to the foredeck, where I thought
Scylla would first show herself from the cliff.
But I couldn't see her anywhere, and my eyes   10
Grew weary scanning the misty rock face.

We sailed on up the narrow channel, wailing,
Scylla on one side, Charybdis on the other
Sucking down saltwater. When she belched it up
She seethed and bubbled like a boiling cauldron
And the spray would reach the tops of the cliffs.
When she sucked it down you could see her
Churning within, and the rock bellowed
And roared, and you could see the sea floor
Black with sand. My men were pale with fear.   20
While we looked at her, staring death in the eyes,
Scylla seized six of my men from our ship,
The six strongest hands aboard. Turning my eyes
To the deck and my crew, I saw above me
Their hands and feet as they were raised aloft.
They cried down to me, calling me by name
That one last time in their agony.
                              You know
How a fisherman on a jutting rock
Casts his bait with his long pole. The horned hook
Sinks into the sea, and when he catches a fish   30
He pulls it writhing and squirming out of the water.
Writhing like that my men were drawn up the cliff.
And Scylla devoured them at her door, as they shrieked
And stretched their hands down to me
In their awful struggle. Of all the things
That I have borne while I scoured the seas,
I have seen nothing more pitiable.

When we had fled Charybdis, the rocks,
And Scylla, we came to the perfect island
Of Hyperion the Sun, where his herds ranged   40
And his flocks browsed. While our black ship
Was still out at sea I could hear the bleating
Of the sheep and the lowing of the cattle
As they were being penned, and I remembered

The words of the blind seer, Theban Tiresias,
And of Circe, who gave me strict warnings
To shun the island of the warmth-giving Sun.
And so I spoke to my crew with heavy heart:

'Hear my words, men, for all your pain.
So I can tell you Tiresias' prophecies
And Circe's, too, who gave me strict warnings
To shun the island of the warmth-giving Sun,
For there she said was our gravest peril.
No, row our black ship clear of this island.'

This broke their spirits, and at once
Eurylochus answered me spitefully:

'You're a hard man, Odysseus, stronger
Than other men, and you never wear out,
A real iron-man, who won't allow his crew,
Dead tired from rowing and lack of sleep,
To set foot on shore, where we might make
A meal we could enjoy. No, you just order us
To wander on through the swift darkness
Over the misty deep, and be driven away
From the island. It is at night that winds rise
That wreck ships. How could we survive
If we were hit by a South Wind or a West,
Which sink ships no matter what the great gods want?
No, let's give in to black night now
And make our supper. We'll stay by the ship,
Board her in the morning, and put out to sea.'

Thus Eurylochus, and the others agreed.
I knew then that some god had it in for us,
And my words had wings:

                    'Eurylochus,
It's all of you against me alone. All right,
But swear me a great oath, every last man:
If we find any cattle or sheep on this island,
No man will kill a single cow or sheep
In his recklessness, but will be content
To eat the food immortal Circe gave us.'

They swore they would do just as I said,
And when they had finished the words of the oath,
We moored our ship in a hollow harbor
Near a sweet-water spring. The crew disembarked
And skillfully prepared their supper.
When they had their fill of food and drink,

50

60

70

80

They fell to weeping, remembering how Scylla
Had snatched their shipmates and devoured them.
Sweet sleep came upon them as they wept.
Past midnight, when the stars had wheeled around,   90
Zeus gathered the clouds and roused a great wind
Against us, an ungodly tempest that shrouded
Land and sea and blotted out the night sky.
At the first blush of Dawn we hauled our ship up
And made her fast in a cave where you could see
The nymphs' beautiful seats and dancing places.
Then I called my men together and spoke to them:

'Friends, there is food and drink in the ship.
Let's play it safe and keep our hands
Off those cattle, which belong to Helios,   100
A dread god who hears and sees all.'

So I spoke, and their proud hearts consented.

Then for a full month the South Wind blew,
And no other wind but the East and the South.
As long as my men had grain and red wine
They didn't touch the cattle—life was still worth living.
But when all the rations from the ship were gone,
They had to roam around in search of game—
Hunting for birds and whatever they could catch
With fishing hooks. Hunger gnawed at their bellies.   110

I went off by myself up the island
To pray to the gods to show me the way.
When I had put some distance between myself
And the crew, and found a spot
Sheltered from the wind, I washed my hands
And prayed to the gods, but all they did
Was close my eyelids in sleep.

                     Meanwhile,
Eurylochus was giving bad advice to the crew:

'Listen to me, shipmates, despite your distress.
All forms of death are hateful, but to die   120
Of hunger is the most wretched way to go.
What are we waiting for? Let's drive off
The prime beef in that herd and offer sacrifice
To the gods of broad heaven. If we ever
Return to Ithaca, we will build a rich temple
To Hyperion the Sun, and deposit there
Many fine treasures. If he becomes angry
Over his cattle and gets the other gods' consent
To destroy our ship, well, I would rather

Gulp down saltwater and die once and for all
Than waste away slowly on a desert island.'

Thus Eurylochus, and the others agreed.
In no time they had driven off the best
Of Helios' cattle, pretty, spiral-horned cows
That were grazing close to our dark-prowed ship.
They surrounded these cows and offered prayers
To the gods, plucking off tender leaves
From a high-crowned oak in lieu of white barley,
Of which there was none aboard our benched ship.
They said their prayers, cut the cows' throats,
Flayed the animals and carved out the thigh joints,
Wrapped these in a double layer of fat
And laid all the raw bits upon them.
They had no wine to pour over the sacrifice
And so used water as they roasted the entrails.
When the thighs were burned and the innards tasted,
They carved up the rest and skewered it on spits.

That's when I awoke, bolting upright.
I started down to the shore, and as I got near the ship
The aroma of sizzling fat drifted up to me.
I groaned and cried out to the undying gods:

'Father Zeus, and you other immortals,
You lulled me to sleep—and to my ruin—
While my men committed this monstrous crime!'

Lampetiê rushed in her long robes to Helios
And told him that we had killed his cattle.
Furious, the Sun God addressed the immortals:

'Father Zeus, and you other gods eternal,
Punish Odysseus' companions, who have insolently
Killed the cattle I took delight in seeing
Whenever I ascended the starry heaven
And whenever turned back from heaven to earth.
If they don't pay just atonement for the cows
I will sink into Hades and shine on the dead.'

And Zeus, who masses the clouds, said:

'Helios, you go on shining among the gods
And for mortal men on the grain-giving earth.
I will soon strike their ship with sterling lightning
And shatter it to bits on the wine-purple sea.'

All this I heard from rich-haired Calypso,
Who said she heard it from Hermes the Guide.
When I reached the ship I chewed out my men,

Giving each one an earful. But there was nothing
We could do. The cattle were already dead.
Then the gods showed some portents
Directed at my men. The hides crawled,
And the meat, both roasted and raw,
Mooed on the spits, like cattle lowing.

Each day for six days my men slaughtered oxen
From Helios' herd and gorged on the meat.   180
But when Zeus brought the seventh day,
The wind tailed off from gale force.
We boarded ship at once and put out to sea
As soon as we had rigged the mast and sail.

When we left the island behind, there was
No other land in sight, only sea and sky.
Then Zeus put a black cloud over our ship
And the sea grew dark beneath it. She ran on
A little while, and then the howling West Wind
Blew in with hurricane force. It snapped   190
Both forestays, and the mast fell backward
Into the bilge with all of its tackle.
On its way down the mast struck the helmsman
And crushed his skull. He fell from the stern
Like a diver, and his proud soul left his bones.
In the same instant, Zeus thundered
And struck the ship with a lightning bolt.
She shivered from stem to stern and was filled
With sulfurous smoke. My men went overboard,
Bobbing in the waves like sea crows   200
Around the black ship, their day of return
Snuffed out by the Sun God.
I kept pacing the deck until the sea surge
Tore the sides from the keel. The waves
Drove the bare keel on and snapped the mast
From its socket; the leather backstay
Was still attached, and I used this to lash
The keel to the mast. Perched on these timbers
I was swept along by deathly winds.

Then the West Wind died down,   210
And, to my horror, the South Wind rose.
All that way, back to the whirlpool,
I was swept along the whole night through
And at dawn reached Scylla's cliff
And dread Charybdis. She was sucking down
Seawater, and I leapt up
To the tall fig tree, grabbed hold of it

And hung on like a bat. I could not
Plant my feet or get myself set on the tree
Because its roots spread far below   220
And its branches were high overhead,
Long, thick limbs that shaded Charybdis.
I just grit my teeth and hung on
Until she spat out the mast and keel again.
It seemed like forever. Finally,
About the hour a man who has spent the day
Judging quarrels that young men bring to him
Rises from the marketplace and goes to dinner,
My ship's timbers surfaced again from Charybdis.
I let go with my hands and feet   230
And hit the water hard beyond the spars.
Once aboard, I rowed away with my hands.
As for Scylla, Zeus never let her see me,
Or I would have been wiped out completely.

I floated on for nine days. On the tenth night
The gods brought me to Ogygia
And to Calypso, the dread, beautiful goddess,
Who loved me and took care of me.
But I have told that tale only yesterday,
Here in your hall, to yourself and your wife,   240
And I wouldn't bore you by telling it again."

BOOKS 13-23

[After the Phaeacians transport him safely home to Ithaca, Odysseus, with Athene's
help, disguises himself as a wandering beggar. Having revealed his identity only to
Telemachus and his faithful swineherd Eumaeus, Odysseus covertly plots his revenge
on the suitors. Athene inspires Penelope to propose that she will marry the man who
can string her lost husband's great bow and shoot an arrow through twelve ax heads,
a feat that only the most worthy hero can accomplish. After stringing the bow, Odysseus and his few supporters exact vengeance on the suitors, slaughtering every one in
the great hall. Wondering at this unexpected turn of events, Penelope is called to meet
her husband for the first time in twenty years. From Book 23:]

. . . .

And Penelope, ever cautious: 1

"Dear nurse, don't gloat over them [the dead suitors] yet.
You know how welcome the sight of him
Would be to us all, and especially to me
And the son he and I bore. But this story
Can't be true, not the way you tell it.
One of the immortals must have killed the suitors,
Angry at their arrogance and evil deeds.
They respected no man, good or bad,

So their blind folly has killed them. But Odysseus   10
Is lost, lost to us here, and gone forever."

And Eurycleia, the faithful nurse:

"Child, how can you say this? Your husband
Is here at his own fireside, and yet you are sure
He will never come home! Always on guard!
But here's something else, clear proof:
The scar he got from the tusk of that boar.
I noticed it when I was washing his feet
And wanted to tell you, but he shrewdly clamped
His hand on my mouth and wouldn't let me speak.   20
Just come with me, and I will stake my life on it.
If I am lying you can torture me to death."

Still wary, Penelope replied:

"Dear nurse, it is hard for you to comprehend
The ways of the eternal gods, wise as you are.
Still, let us go to my son, so that I may see
The suitors dead and the man who killed them."

And Penelope descended the stairs, her heart
In turmoil. Should she hold back and question
Her husband? Or should she go up to him,   30
Embrace him, and kiss his hands and head?
She entered the hall, crossing the stone threshold,
And sat opposite Odysseus, in the firelight
Beside the farther wall. He sat by a column,
Looking down, waiting to see if his incomparable wife
Would say anything to him when she saw him.
She sat a long time in silence, wondering.
She would look at his face and see her husband,
But then fail to know him in his dirty rags.
Telemachus couldn't take it any more: 40

"Mother, how can you be so hard,
Holding back like that? Why don't you sit
Next to father and talk to him, ask him things?
No other woman would have the heart
To stand off from her husband who has come back
After twenty hard years to his country and home.
But your heart is always colder than stone."

And Penelope, cautious as ever:

"My child, I am lost in wonder
And unable to speak or ask a question   50
Or look him in the eyes. If he really is

Odysseus come home, the two of us
Will be sure of each other, very sure.
There are secrets between us no one else knows."

Odysseus, who had borne much, smiled,
And his words flew to his son on wings:

"Telemachus, let your mother test me
In our hall. She will soon see more clearly.
Now, because I am dirty and wearing rags,
She is not ready to acknowledge who I am.   60
But you and I have to devise a plan.
When someone kills just one man,
Even a man who has few to avenge him,
He goes into exile, leaving country and kin.
Well, we have killed a city of young men,
The flower of Ithaca. Think about that."

And Telemachus, in his clear-headed way:

"You should think about it, Father. They say
No man alive can match you for cunning.
We'll follow you for all we are worth,   70
And I don't think we'll fail for lack of courage."

And Odysseus, the master strategist:

"Well, this is what I think we should do.
First, bathe yourselves and put on clean tunics
And tell the women to choose their clothes well.
Then have the singer pick up his lyre
And lead everyone in a lively dance tune,
Loud and clear. Anyone who hears the sound,
A passerby or neighbor, will think it's a wedding,
And so word of the suitors' killing won't spread   80
Down through the town before we can reach
Our woodland farm. Once there we'll see
What kind of luck the Olympian gives us."

They did as he said. The men bathed
And put on tunics, and the women dressed up.
The godlike singer, sweeping his hollow lyre,
Put a song in their hearts and made their feet move,
And the great hall resounded under the tread
Of men and silken-waisted women dancing.
And people outside would hear it and say: 90

"Well, someone has finally married the queen,
Fickle woman. Couldn't bear to keep the house

For her true husband until he came back."
But they had no idea how things actually stood.

Odysseus, meanwhile, was being bathed
By the housekeeper, Eurynome. She
Rubbed him with olive oil and threw about him
A beautiful cloak and tunic. And Athena
Shed beauty upon him, and made him look
Taller and more muscled, and made his hair   100
Tumble down his head like hyacinth flowers.

> Imagine a craftsman overlaying silver
> With pure gold. He has learned his art
> From Pallas Athena and Lord Hephaestus,
> And creates works of breathtaking beauty.

So Athena herself made his head and shoulders
Shimmer with grace. He came from the bath
Like a god, and sat down on the chair again
Opposite his wife, and spoke to her and said:

"You're a mysterious woman.
                    The gods   110
Have given to you, more than to any
Other woman, an unyielding heart.
No other woman would be able to endure
Standing off from her husband, come back
After twenty hard years to his country and home.
Nurse, make up a bed for me so I can lie down
Alone, since her heart is a cold lump of iron."

And Penelope, cautious and wary:

"You're a mysterious man.
                    I am not being proud
Or scornful, nor am I bewildered—not at all.   120
I know very well what you looked like
When you left Ithaca on your long-oared ship.
Nurse, bring the bed out from the master bedroom,
The bedstead he made himself, and spread it for him
With fleeces and blankets and silky coverlets."

She was testing her husband.
                    Odysseus
Could bear no more, and he cried out to his wife:

"By God, woman, now you've cut deep.
Who moved my bed? It would be hard
For anyone, no matter how skilled, to move it.   130
A god could come down and move it easily,

But not a man alive, however young and strong,
Could ever pry it up. There's something telling
About how that bed's built, and no one else
Built it but me.
          There was an olive tree
Growing on the site, long-leaved and full,
Its trunk thick as a post. I built my bedroom
Around that tree, and when I had finished
The masonry walls and done the roofing
And set in the jointed, close-fitting doors,   140
I lopped off all of the olive's branches,
Trimmed the trunk from the root on up,
And rounded it and trued it with an adze until
I had myself a bedpost. I bored it with an auger,
And starting from this I framed up the whole bed,
Inlaying it with gold and silver and ivory
And stretching across it oxhide thongs dyed purple.
So there's our secret. But I do not know, woman,
Whether my bed is still firmly in place, or if
Some other man has cut through the olive's trunk."   150

At this, Penelope finally let go.
Odysseus had shown he knew their old secret.
In tears, she ran straight to him, threw her arms
Around him, kissed his face, and said:

"Don't be angry with me, Odysseus. You,
Of all men, know how the world goes.
It is the gods who gave us sorrow, the gods
Who begrudged us a life together, enjoying
Our youth and arriving side by side
To the threshold of old age. Don't hold it against me   160
That when I first saw you I didn't welcome you
As I do now. My heart has been cold with fear
That an imposter would come and deceive me.
There are many who scheme for ill-gotten gains.
Not even Helen, daughter of Zeus,
Would have slept with a foreigner had she known
The Greeks would go to war to bring her back home.
It was a god who drove her to that dreadful act,
Or she never would have thought of doing what she did,
The horror that brought suffering to us as well.   170
But now, since you have confirmed the secret
Of our marriage bed, which no one has ever seen—
Only you and I and a single servant, Actor's daughter,
Whom my father gave me before I ever came here
And who kept the doors of our bridal chamber—
You have persuaded even my stubborn heart."

This brought tears from deep within him,
And as he wept he clung to his beloved wife.

> Land is a welcome sight to men swimming
> For their lives, after Poseidon has smashed their ship   180
> In heavy seas. Only a few of them escape
> And make it to shore. They come out
> Of the grey water crusted with brine, glad
> To be alive and set foot on dry land.

So welcome a sight was her husband to her.
She would not loosen her white arms from his neck,
And rose-fingered Dawn would have risen
On their weeping, had not Athena stepped in
And held back the long night at the end of its course
And stopped gold-stitched Dawn at Ocean's shores   190
From yoking the horses that bring light to men,
Lampus and Phaethon, the colts of Dawn.

Then Odysseus said to his wife:

"We have not yet come to the end of our trials.
There is still a long, hard task for me to complete,
As the spirit of Tiresias foretold to me
On the day I went down to the house of Hades
To ask him about my companions' return
And my own. But come to bed now,
And we'll close our eyes in the pleasure of sleep."   200

And Penelope calmly answered him:

"Your bed is ready for you whenever
You want it, now that the gods have brought you
Home to your family and native land.
But since you've brought it up, tell me
About this trial. I'll learn about it soon enough,
And it won't be any worse to hear it now."

And Odysseus, his mind teeming:

"You are a mystery to me. Why do you insist
I tell you now? Well, here's the whole story.   210
It's not a tale you will enjoy, and I have no joy
In telling it.
          Tiresias told me that I must go
To city after city carrying a broad-bladed oar,
Until I come to men who know nothing of the sea,
Who eat their food unsalted, and have never seen
Red-prowed ships or the oars that wing them along.
And he told me that I would know I had found them

When I met another traveler who thought
The oar I was carrying was a winnowing fan.
Then I must fix my oar in the earth   220
And offer sacrifice to Lord Poseidon,
A ram, a bull, and a boar in its prime.
Then at last I am to come home and offer
Grand sacrifice to the immortal gods
Who hold high heaven, to each in turn.
And death shall come to me from the sea,
As gentle as this touch, and take me off
When I am worn out in sleek old age,
With my people prosperous around me.
All this Tiresias said would come true."   230

Then Penelope, watching him, answered:

"If the gods are going to grant you a happy old age,
There is hope your troubles will someday be over."

While they spoke to one another,
Eurynome and the nurse made the bed
By torchlight, spreading it with soft coverlets.
Then the old nurse went to her room to lie down,
And Eurynome, who kept the bedroom,
Led the couple to their bed, lighting the way.
When she had led them in, she withdrew,   240
And they went with joy to their bed
And to their rituals of old.

              Telemachus and his men
Stopped dancing, stopped the women's dance,
And lay down to sleep in the shadowy halls.

After Odysseus and Penelope
Had made sweet love, they took turns
Telling stories to each other. She told him
All that she had to endure as the fair lady
In the palace, looking upon the loathsome throng
Of suitors, who used her as an excuse   250
To kill many cattle, whole flocks of sheep,
And to empty the cellar of much of its wine.
Odysseus told her of all the suffering
He had brought upon others, and of all the pain
He endured himself. She loved listening to him
And did not fall asleep until he had told the whole tale.

He began with how he overcame the Cicones
And then came to the land of the Lotus-Eaters,
And all that the Cyclops did, and how he

Paid him back for eating his comrades. 260
Then how he came to Aeolus,
Who welcomed him and sent him on his way,
But since it was not his destiny to return home then,
The stormwinds grabbed him and swept him off
Groaning deeply over the teeming saltwater.
Then how he came to the Laestrygonians,
Who destroyed his ships and all their crews,
Leaving him with only one black-tarred hull.
Then all of Circe's tricks and wiles,
And how he sailed to the dank house of Hades 270
To consult the spirit of Theban Tiresias
And saw his old comrades there
And his aged mother who nursed him as a child.
Then how he heard the Sirens' eternal song,
And came to the Clashing Rocks,
And dread Charybdis and Scylla,
Whom no man had ever escaped before.
Then how his crew killed the cattle of the Sun,
And how Zeus, the high lord of thunder,
Slivered his ship with lightning, and all his men 280
Went down, and he alone survived.
And he told her how he came to Ogygia,
The island of the nymph Calypso,
Who kept him there in her scalloped caves,
Yearning for him to be her husband,
And how she took care of him, and promised
To make him immortal and ageless all his days
But did not persuade the heart in his breast.
Then how he crawled out of the sea in Phaeacia,
And how the Phaeacians honored him like a god 290
And sent him on a ship to his own native land
With gifts of bronze and clothing and gold.

He told the story all the way through,
And then sleep, which slackens our bodies,
Fell upon him and released him from care.

The Grey-eyed One knew what to do next.
When she felt that Odysseus was satisfied
With sleep and with lying next to his wife,
She roused the slumbering, golden Dawn,
Who climbed from Ocean with light for the world. 300
Odysseus got up from his rose-shadowed bed
And turned to Penelope with these instructions:

"My wife, we've had our fill of trials now,
You here, weeping over all the troubles
My absence caused, and I, bound by Zeus

To suffer far from the home I yearned for.
Now that we have both come to the bed
We have long desired, you must take charge
Of all that is mine in the house, while I
See to replenishing the flocks and herds   310
The insolent suitors have depleted.
I'll get some back on raids, some as tribute,
Until the pens are full again. But now,
I want you to know I am going to our farm
To see my father, who has suffered terribly
On my account. You don't need me to tell you
That when the sun rises the news will spread
That I have killed the suitors in our hall. So,
Go upstairs with your women and sit quietly.
Don't look outside or speak to anyone."   320

Odysseus spoke and put on his beautiful armor.
He woke Telemachus, and the cowherd
And swineherd, and had them arm also.
They strapped on their bronze, opened the doors
And went out, Odysseus leading the way.
It was light by now, but Athena hid them
In darkness, and spirited them out of the city.

. . . .

[Odysseus is successfully reunited with Penelope and resumes his role as husband, father, and master of his household, but he has yet to reestablish his role as king. Ancient laws of blood vengeance demand that relatives of the slain suitors uphold their families' honor by killing the young men's slayer. In Book 24, Odysseus, his aged father Laertes, his son Telemachus, and a few loyal retainers prepare to fight the suitors' angry kinsmen, threatening to plunge Ithaca into anarchy. At this point, Athene intervenes with Zeus, who promises to make the suitors' relatives forget their grievances and conclude a pact to accept Odysseus as their permanent king. (Zeus also directs a lightning bolt at the feuding Ithacans to emphasize his intention.) Commanding Odysseus to renounce his anger, Athene (still in Mentor's form) restores peace and civic order to Ithacan society.]

. . . .

Questions for Discussion and Review

1. Discuss the ways in which Odysseus both resembles and differs from other heroes of myth, particularly Achilles and Heracles. What personal qualities enable him to overcome the obstacles or survive the dangers that beset him on his long journey home from Troy?

2. Describe the ethical principles operating in the universe of the *Odyssey*. What are the ethical connections between the actions of individual human beings and their subsequent experiences? How do Zeus and the other Olympians regard wrongdoing?

In view of this cosmic ethos, how does Odysseus contribute to his own suffering? Be sure to consider the Polyphemus episode.

3. Discuss Athene's dominant role in the *Odyssey*. Why does she so intensely favor Odysseus, Penelope, and their family?

4. Women and goddesses play extremely important parts in Odysseus's education. Specify what the hero learns from Athene, Circe, Calypso, Nausicaa, the Sirens, and Penelope. Explain how Freudian or Jungian motifs may be operating in Odysseus's relationship with women, including his mother, aged nurse, and wife.

5. In Book 11, Homer suggests a link between Heracles and Odysseus. What qualities and experiences do the two heroes share? Why is Odysseus so solitary a figure, and why does he undergo so much of his testing and learning completely alone? At the end of the epic, how does Homer place Odysseus back in the context of human society?

PART THREE

Tragic Heroes
and Heroines

The Theater of Dionysus: Myth and the Tragic Vision

KEY TOPICS/THEMES

Athens' annual festival honoring Dionysus, the City Dionysia, gave birth to a new art form—theatrical productions of both tragedy and comedy, the two modes reflecting the paradoxical qualities of the wine god. Whereas tragedy emphasizes Dionysus's frightening mutability—nature's irresistible law of change that sparks unexpected reversals in human fortune— comedy celebrates the beneficent life force he embodies. The great Athenian playwrights reworked ancient myths illustrating Dionysian motifs of suffering, sacrifice, rebirth, and reintegration.

Greek myth makes its primary impact today in two major literary forms: the narrative poetry of Homer (c. 750 B.C.) and Hesiod (c. 675 B.C.), and the dramatic poetry of Athenian playwrights who wrote almost three hundred years later. The nearly three centuries separating Homeric epic from the oldest surviving Greek play, the *Persians* of Aeschylus (c. 472 B.C.), witnessed enormous changes in Greek society. In 508 B.C., Athens instituted the world's first democratic constitution, only to have this nascent democracy threatened by two successive Persian military invasions—successfully repelled at the crucial battles of Marathon (490 B.C.) and Salamis (480 B.C.)—in both of which Aeschylus, dramatist and citizen-soldier, participated (Figure 14-1). Some of these social and political developments, including the establishment of a jury system, are reflected in the Athenian drama's creative transformation of mythological themes to fit a newly democratic society. Indeed, in many respects, the dramatic festival, with its official, highly politicized opening ceremonies, represents the city's pride in its own accomplishments.

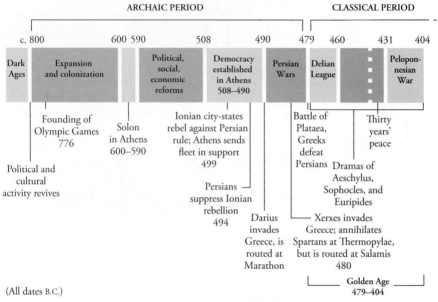

FIGURE 14-1　Developments in Greek History from the End of the Dark Ages to the Peloponnesian War (c. 800–404 B.C.). As this time line indicates, Greece went through a rapid period of development in the centuries immediately following the Dark Ages. Increased trade and exchange of ideas with older civilizations of the Near East brought both economic and intellectual growth as Greek city-states evolved an art and way of life that eventually gave birth to the cultural flowering of the fifth century B.C. The leading city-states, Athens and Sparta, united to repel two major invasions from Persia (the Persian Wars, 490 and 480–479 B.C.), after which victories Athens, by then the world's first democracy, pursued a policy of cultural and military imperialism. Threatened by Athenian expansion, Sparta engaged Athens in a series of devastating conflicts (the Peloponnesian War, 431–404 B.C.), which resulted in Athens' collapse and Sparta's exhaustion. Except for the comedies of Aristophanes and one comedy by Menander, all surviving Greek plays were written between the end of the Persian Wars and the deaths of Sophocles and Euripides, just two years before Athens' surrender to Sparta in 404 B.C.

　　In the hands of the greatest Athenian playwrights—Aeschylus, Sophocles, and Euripides—the ancient traditions were creatively reworked and applied to the social and political issues confronted by Athens' newly democratic institutions. Many of the surviving tragedies show how myth was used to highlight problems facing a democracy, particularly the crucial interaction of powerful leaders with the citizenry. In play after play, mythical heroes and heroines act out conflicts that divide the community and threaten its political stability; in many cases, the dramas emphasize the disastrous consequences to the state when rulers unilaterally refuse to heed popular opinion or effect a workable compromise between opposing points of view. The heroine of Sophocles' *Antigone,* for example, openly disobeys a law that she considers both unjust and contrary to custom and family duty. Creon, Antigone's uncle and ruler of Thebes, is equally inflexible, insisting that he alone has the right to make and enforce the city's laws. As the chorus observes, both Creon and Antigone express valid principles—he about the necessity of submitting to lawful order and she about a higher obligation toward blood kin—but their refusal to compromise not only destroys both but also plunges the state into chaos (see Chapter 16).

The difficulties involved when two unyielding opponents are both right—at least from their individual perspectives—generate dramatic conflict in most of the plays anthologized in this book. Even Zeus, whom the author of *Prometheus Bound* depicts as arbitrary and unjust at the beginning of his reign, manifests the perils of rigidity that result from administrative inexperience. New to power, he presumes to rule the universe without compassion or wisdom, qualities that, paradoxically, he must acquire from Prometheus if his government is to survive (see Chapter 4). Euripides' *Bacchae* presents a similarly arbitrary ruler, a young king who denies the value of Dionysian freedom and rejects all advice, including the wise counsel of Tiresias, Apollo's prophet. At the climax of his *Oresteia,* three plays about the ruling house of Mycenae, Aeschylus dramatizes the establishment in Athens of a basic democratic institution, a court of law empowered to settle disputes and to punish or pardon offenders. So important is this development in the evolution of civilization that the playwright shows Olympians descending from heaven to legitimize the legal system, with Athene representing the will of Zeus as she achieves a compromise between the ancient practice of blood vengeance and the emergent system of democratic justice.

The City Dionysia and the Birth of Drama

Whereas the gods and heroes of Homer and Hesiod belonged to all Greece, helping to define the Greek people's collective identity, it was principally in Athens that ancient myths were recast in an entirely new art form—dramatic performances in the theater of Dionysus. Although both tragedy and comedy began in rituals honoring Dionysus, details about their origins and development are unknown. In his *Poetics,* Aristotle (384–322 B.C.) briefly remarks that tragedy "originated with the authors of the dithyramb" and "advanced by slow degrees" until "it found its natural form, and there it stopped." The **dithyramb,** an ecstatic choral song celebrating the wine god's prowess, was an integral part of an important Athenian festival dedicated to Dionysus's worship, the **City** (or **Great**) **Dionysia,** reputedly established by the Athenian leader **Pisistratus** about 534 B.C. Some historians, however, believe that the City Dionysia was established, or thoroughly reorganized, only at the end of the sixth century B.C.

Although the City Dionysia regularly featured a dithyrambic contest among Athens' ten tribes, each of which had a chorus of fifty men and another of fifty boys dancing and singing a Dionysian hymn, only one example of the dithyramb has survived—the opening choral ode of Euripides' *Bacchae* (see Chapter 17). Held annually in early March, the City Dionysia began with a noisy procession of citizens carrying emblems of the god's cult, including grotesque masks (representing his diverse manifestations), sacred phalluses, and an effigy of the mutilated and dismembered Dionysus, a practice that Herodotus traces to similar Egyptian processions in honor of Osiris, god of death and rebirth (see Chapter 8). Celebrating the making of new wine (Figure 14-2), many participants generously sampled Dionysus's liquid gift, happily exploring the potentialities of intoxication. Raucous merrymaking

FIGURE 14-2   Dionysus and Satyrs Making Wine. The bearded god of wine joins satyrs (depicted here as men with pointed ears and horse tails) in a vintage revel. According to Aristotle, tragedy evolved from the dithyramb, a wild, ecstatic dance associated with such Dionysian festivals. A highly mutable deity symbolizing the ever-changing forces of physical and human nature, Dionysus is the patron of drama, both the painful reversals of tragedy and the joyous resolution of conflicts in comedy. *(Antiken Museum, Basle)*

combined with solemn ritual as celebrants offered sacrifices to the volatile deity who embodied life's irregular cycles of joy, grief, death, and rebirth. A priest of Dionysus presided over the entire five-day affair, occupying a prominent seat of honor in the front row of the theater.

When Pisistratus or his successors established a competition among playwrights as the major event of the City Dionysia, the procedure required that each contestant submit a set of three tragedies and a **satyr play,** a wild farce exploiting the comic potential of overtly sexual elements in Dionysian tradition. Each of the three dramatic categories—tragedy, satyr play, and comedy—staged at the City Dionysia represented a distinct aspect of Dionysus's complex nature. A jury selected by lot awarded first, second, and third places to three different sets of dramas and their accompanying satyr plays, which were publicly presented on three successive days beginning at dawn.

According to a perhaps dubious tradition, the initial winner of the tragic competition was **Thespis,** who reportedly created the first role for an actor by culling a single performer from the traditional Dionysian chorus of singers and dancers. For the first time, an actor stood in opposition to the choral leader, engaging in dialogue that could lead to true dramatic conflict, the essence of effective theater.

Tragedy

The new art form that Thespis allegedly introduced, and which Aeschylus later brought to artistic maturity, is called **tragedy,** a term combining the Greek words

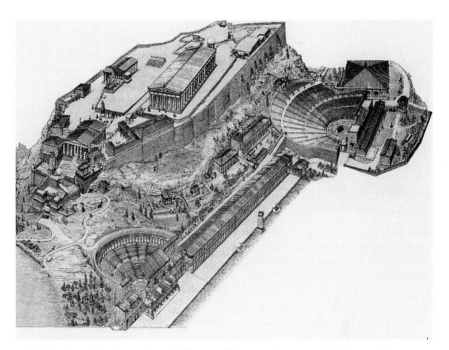

FIGURE 14-3   The Acropolis and Theater of Dionysus (upper right). The transformation of ancient Greek myth into dramatic presentations began in Athens during the late sixth century B.C. as part of a citywide festival honoring Dionysus. At that time, the Athenian tyrant Pisistratus reportedly established a contest among playwrights, whose tragedies were staged in an open-air amphitheater on the slopes of the Acropolis. The original theater of Dionysus, where the plays of Aeschylus, Sophocles, and Euripides had their premieres, was extensively reconstructed in the fourth century B.C. The scene pictured here shows the Acropolis area, including the much later theater of Herodes Atticus (lower left), as it appeared toward the end of the second century A.D. *(Reconstruction by Al N. Oikonomides)*

tragos (he-goat) and *oide* (song). The "goat song" may derive its rustic name from the loincloths of goatskin worn by the all-male chorus. (Women were not permitted to appear onstage, and all roles, including prominent females such as Aphrodite, Clytemnestra, and Helen of Troy, were filled by men wearing masks, wigs, and long robes.) According to another theory, "goat song" refers to the attendees' shouts and chants when a goat was sacrificed on Dionysus's altar to inaugurate the festival. Whatever the origin of its name, tragedy (*tragoidia*) rapidly became the dominant force for reinterpreting the significance of old myths for the Athenian public. Crowds of 15,000 or more packed the theater of Dionysus—a semicircular amphitheater cut into the south flank of the Acropolis (Figure 14-3)—to witness the latest adaptations of myth in new works of dramatic art. (Today, the theater at Epidaurus [Figure 14-4] stands as the best-preserved theater in Greece and is still used for the performance of classical tragedy.)

After witnessing his premiere tragedy, Thespis's first audience is said to have asked in disgust, "What has this to do with Dionysus?" Although Dionysus's shrine, altar, and priest were featured prominently in the theater, Thespis—like

FIGURE 14-4   The Theater at Epidaurus. The best-preserved theater in Greece, the great amphitheater at Epidaurus is still used for performances of classical tragedy and modern opera. Although drama was an Athenian invention, the art form quickly became popular and spread throughout the Greek world, resulting in the building of theaters like this one in Greece, Sicily, Italy, and Ionia. Many Greek theaters had such good acoustics that well-trained actors could project their speeches with near-perfect clarity even to the back rows. *(Ancient Art and Art Collection)*

most of the playwrights who followed him—did not confine himself to staging episodes from Dionysian myth. Tragedy was firmly committed to the spirit of the wine god, with his tragic suffering, death, rebirth, and ascension to heaven, but from the beginning, Greek dramatists freely used myths about other gods and heroes as their primary subject matter. Only one surviving tragedy, Euripides' *Bacchae* (c. 406 B.C.), features Dionysus as a leading character, although he appears in some comedies, such as Aristophanes' *Frogs* (405 B.C.). The two plays offer startlingly different portraits of the wine god: Euripides presents Dionysus as an irresistible natural force that destroys all who oppose it, whereas Aristophanes shows the deity as a (relatively) good-natured drunk interested in restoring theatrical productions to the high standards they had prior to the deaths of Sophocles and Euripides in 406 B.C.

Reversal of Roles and Rules   Although Dionysus did not regularly appear as a dramatic character, his paradoxical nature permeates all the plays. As a god of release who brings together life and death, violence and peace, freedom and control, male and female, his spirit presides over the plays that explore all these contradictions, depicting characters whose excesses violate norms and boundaries of all kinds. This kind of "letting go," of the release of conventional social norms and restrictions, is characteristic of the "Feast of Fools," of which the City Dionysia (like the modern New Orleans festival Mardi Gras) is an example. Such celebrations typically include heavy alcohol consumption, elaborate costumes, social- and gender-role reversal, and, often, ritual mockery of established rules and rulers, all in the interests of reestablishing normal order when the feast is over.

Dionysus's blurring of conventional gender roles is evident in his characteristically feminine garb and androgynous nature, as well as in the significant role of women in his myth and traditional rituals. This "gender-bending" is especially highlighted in the dramas by the fact that male actors wearing female costumes played all the female parts, often refracting the gender roles in an even more complex way when those "female" characters, like Clytemnestra in the *Agamemnon* or Agave in the *Bacchae,* adopt behavioral models, such as the hunter or warrior, that are overtly "masculine," albeit with horrendous results. Thus, although eventually reaffirming the supremacy and normalcy of the male perspective as necessary for preserving rational order, the plays explore both the limits of socially confirmed gender roles and the "feminine" components of masculine identity.

The settings of the plays also contribute to the exploration of gender roles. Unlike the epics and other heroic narratives, in which the open road, sea, or battlefield dominate, the plays all take place within the confines of the city—the container of the domestic space, the sphere of feminine values. As many readers (most notably, Froma Zeitlin) have noted, the plays negotiate the boundary between inside (the woman's sphere) and outside (the man's space), private and public, as the characters move through the doorways between these realms. In exploring the murky domestic relationships of public figures, a topic of fascination then as now, the plays breach the barriers between these gender-divided spaces in both directions, usually with catastrophic consequences.

Tragedy as the Athenians knew it differed qualitatively from the scholarly process of scanning a play's printed text that most readers experience today. Besides being a religious celebration that explored mysteries of life and death, dramatic presentations were communal events in which heightened emotions and sometimes shocking new insights were shared by thousands of people. The bare bones of a tragedy's script, which is all that remains to us, cannot convey the visual and auditory spectacle of the majestic ritual—accompanied by music and dance—in which Oedipus's self-deceptions were inexorably peeled away or Medea's scheme to murder her own children moved, without a hint of divine interference, toward its unspeakable fulfillment.

Catharsis   Uniting words and music to engage both intellect and emotion, Greek tragedy strives for an immediate and powerful impact on its audience. Aristotle defined tragedy in terms of the emotional response it elicited: by arousing strong feelings of pity and fear in spectators, tragedy is able to relieve or purge these emotions, achieving **catharsis.** Thus, tragedy's ultimate effect is to produce not depression, but exhilaration, a conscious lightening of emotive burdens.

The Satyr Play

Whereas Athenian tragedy underscored the terrifying unpredictability of change that can suddenly transform the lives of city-states and their leaders, the satyr play (which followed a series of three tragedies) provided a welcome alternative to confrontations of pain. Like tragedy, satyric drama used mythical plots and characters, but it did not take them seriously. The chorus, invariably composed of Dionysus's lewdly energetic half-human satyrs (Figure 14-5), wore horses' tails and ears and sported huge artificial penises, emblems of the god's sensuality and procreativity.

FIGURE 14-5   A Maenad and a Satyr. Heads thrown back in rapture, these wildly dancing figures display the effects of ecstasy—literally the standing outside of oneself, the
escape from individual self-awareness to experience a sense of unity with their god. Liberating people from the constraints of reason and custom, Dionysian possession permitted
extremes of feeling and behavior, a freedom to express instinctual drives and appetites,
appropriately represented by the satyr, who combines bestial and human traits. The animal
component of the uninhibited psyche is also implied by the snake coiled around the maenad's left arm and by the panther accompanying the horse-tailed satyr. Innocent of civilized taboos, the satyr unself-consciously pursues the fulfillment of emotional and sexual
impulses, a characteristic acknowledged and honored in the satyr plays presented after the
tragic dramas. *(Metropolitan Museum of Art, New York)*

The satyrs' humorous antics and obscene jokes provoked audience laughter, a counterbalance to tragedy's evocation of pity and fear.

Most satyr plays have been lost. Only Euripides' *Cyclops,* a burlesque of Odysseus's
encounter with the Cyclops Polyphemus (from the *Odyssey*), survives intact. Parts of
Aeschylus's *Drawers of Nets* and Sophocles' *Trackers* also exist in fragmental form.

Comedy

Athens added productions of comedy to the City Dionysia in 486 B.C. and established a separate comic festival, the Lenaea, about 440 B.C. Aristotle states that

FIGURE 14-6   Maenads Dancing. The Athenian painter Macron created this scene of joyous abandon in the early fifth century B.C. Women dressed as maenads and carrying thyrsi dance in honor of Dionysus. One woman holds aloft an animal, possibly intended for sacrifice. The juxtaposition of joy and sacrifice in these spirit-possessed worshipers is echoed in the Dionysian drama, which pits the high aspirations of heroes against the inevitable changes in human fortunes. *(State Museum, Berlin)*

comedy developed from the behavior of choral leaders who carried replicas of Dionysus's phallus in the Dionysian processions. As bands of revelers sang and danced (Figure 14-6), their leaders exchanged ribald banter with onlookers, spontaneously creating the forerunner of comic dialogue. The Greek word for comedy, *komoidia,* means "komos-singing" and is derived from the word *komos,* meaning "parade of revelers." Exploiting the humor inherent in humanity's (and the gods') diverse sexual activity, comedy offers a positive counterpoint to tragedy's solemn worldview. Like the satyr play, comedy promotes reconciliation of conflict and a reintegration of the disparate elements composing the Dionysian life force.

The Tragic Vision

The dramatic festival in honor of Dionysus took place in a society that saw itself as an embodiment of the spirit of Apollo, by now associated with moderation, self-control, and enlightenment through the pursuit of knowledge. The democratic constitution established in Athens in 508 B.C. was itself a model of Apollonian rationalism, with its system of checks and balances, its principle of the rule of the majority of citizens, and its use of debating and voting as instruments of problem solving. The ancient Apollonian way, which encouraged awareness of one's human limitations and place in the social and universal order, was precisely appropriate for a democratic society.

An essentially conservative people, however, despite the remarkable political changes they had instituted, the citizens of Athens and its sister city-states in Greece retained the old mythic heroes, even while rethinking their relationship to life in an urban, democratic state. Democracy requires a well-informed citizenry capable of self-restraint and willing, in principle and practice, to compromise, to abide by the will of the majority. There was clearly a gap between the old heroes, who always "go forward" and refuse to compromise, and the ideal citizens of the new city-state. The perfect expression of a feudal society in which the warrior is king, the old-style "hero" no longer fits comfortably into a world in which all citizens were "equal" by law.

Further, for the exceptional, "heroic" individual, Apollo's demands for self-knowledge and moderation in all things are inherently contradictory: what the tragic protagonist knows—when he or she truly acquires self-knowledge—is precisely the capacity for extremes of feeling and behavior that define the hero's extraordinary nature. The path to self-knowledge that Dionysus provides differs markedly from that of Apollo, a "binder" god who asks that we be reasonable and obey the rules. Dionysus, in contrast, is a god of spontaneous release and, as such, is much more in keeping with the heroic spirit.

The Dionysian drive toward self-exploration through freedom, through exuberance, through a breaking down of the barriers of inhibition and prohibition, reveals the full range of one's potentialities, however irrational and even terrifying those might be. Thus, the tragedies that open each Dionysian festival plunge one into the realm of the chaotic forces within the human mind, beyond the reach of the outer world of reason and moral imperatives. There, one must explore urges—including incest, matricide or patricide, and infanticide—that violate the most basic taboos of civilized life. By bursting beyond such absolute and universal limits, however, the tragic protagonist provokes awesome and terrifying cosmic reactions. Thus, tragedy makes possible—even demands—an awareness of one's connection to the incomprehensible, and seemingly irrational, mysteries of the universe. As the English poet William Blake wrote, "The road of excess leads to the palace of wisdom." Between these two divergent paths—of Dionysian freedom and Apollonian restraint, of instinct and taboo, of nature and civilization, of internal psychological needs and external social responsibilities—lies the uncharted territory that the **protagonist** (main character) of Greek tragedy must traverse.

Myth into Drama

Drama is an ideal vehicle for raising questions or exploring possibilities. In drama, there is no narrative voice, as there is in fiction (or epic), that tells us how to respond to the story—assuring us, for example, despite occasional appearances to the contrary, that Odysseus is a "wise and pious man" who therefore deserved to be rewarded by the gods. In drama, each character speaks and acts in ways that reflect only his or her personal motives or viewpoints. By setting various characters in motion and allowing them to state their conflicting views, the dramatist presents several different perspectives on any action for the audience to contemplate.

Greek dramatists were not expected to create original plots for their tragedies. Rather, the tragedies were all based on inherited myths. But in transforming myths into dramatic form, the tragedies combined the intrinsic potentialities of the original myths with the heroic aspirations of the epic traditions, as well as with the spirit of the rituals of Dionysus during which they were performed. Further, authors often took advantage of the multiple perspectives of the dramatic medium to question accepted views, to probe conventional responses, and to explore new approaches to experience.

The Tragic Hero

Like the heroes of the epics from whom the tragic protagonists are probably at least in part descended, the tragic protagonists are noble, both in lineage and in character. But perhaps because the tragedies were all performed live before an urban audience, they updated the mythic materials and expressed the heroes' qualities in slightly more realistic, or at least accessible, ways. Thus, instead of tracing their descent from the gods, the heroes are often members of leading families; and instead of performing incredible feats of physical prowess and courage in battle, they exhibit unusual moral courage and integrity. The myths that the writers of tragedy selected to dramatize, too, are often about domestic problems that involve violence: marital quarrels, sibling rivalry, incest, or the murder of a wife, husband, parent, or child. And whereas epic heroes may descend to Hades, the hell to which the tragic heroes descend often lies within the tormented recesses of their own minds, where the Jungian shadow, the unconscious capacity for evil, lurks.

Like the epic heroes, the tragic heroes possess extraordinary qualities. And like their epic predecessors, it is often their unique gifts that both get them into terrible predicaments and allow them to rise above those same predicaments. Thus, it is Oedipus's determination and skill at solving riddles that are the sources of his greatness; it is that very same determination and skill that bring about the confrontation with the truth that proves his own undoing. Similarly, in Sophocles' earliest play about the family of Oedipus, it is Antigone's moral commitment—her respect for the dead—that brings about both her courageous defiance and her martyrdom.

Trapped between conflicting demands, both external and internal, and possessing natures whose best qualities, under duress, often prove self-destructive, the tragic heroes are doomed to suffer. And because they are important people, their suffering ripples outward, encompassing others. The role of the tragic hero, however (perhaps like that of the scapegoat in the Dionysian ritual who took on the sins of the community and was sacrificed in order to relieve the worshipers of the burden of sin), is to take the communal suffering on him- or herself. The epic hero Achilles, by his extraordinary martial prowess, becomes the Greeks' point man, the major target of Trojan soldiers. So Oedipus takes the people's sorrows on himself, sending to the oracle to deal with their needs; so Orestes assumes the burden Apollo thrusts on him, of avenging the injustice of Agamemnon's murder; so Oedipus's daughter Antigone single-handedly takes on the duty of preserving moral law in her community. Only by plumbing the depths of pain can the tragic protagonist explore the limits of human knowledge.

Like the mythic heroes, the tragic protagonists expand the parameters of human experience. But where heroes like Heracles pushed back geographic and physical boundaries, the tragic protagonists push back psychic boundaries, breaking through the comfortable barriers of habit, convention, and illusion. "Man must suffer to be

FIGURE 14-7   Orpheus Playing His Lyre. A mythic figure who experiences the loss, spiritual growth, and acquisition of insight through sufferings that characterize the tragic hero, Orpheus also has the tragic protagonist's ability to articulate a poetic response to the griefs he experiences. Music—in the form of instrumental playing, choral song, and dance—was an integral part of the tragic performance, as it was to Orpheus as a symbol of the creative artist. This vase painting shows Orpheus singing for the young men of Thrace, perhaps only moments before frenzied maenads are to tear him to shreds—a sparagmos he shares not only with Dionysus but also with tragic figures such as Pentheus. *(Staatliche Museen, Berlin)*

wise," says the chorus in Aeschylus's *Agamemnon;* alternatively, as Sophocles' Tiresias (in *Oedipus Rex*) puts it, "To be wise is to suffer." The mythic and epic heroes embark on physical quests and learn through painful experience—such as losing one's best friend in battle or watching one's fellows be devoured by monsters—or through direct confrontation with the ultimate suffering (death) via descent to the Underworld. Tragedy typically turns these heroic quests inward: the tragic heroes suffer an inner torment of their own, a kind of psychological sparagmos, and the depth of their anguish is the measure of their heroism (Figure 14-7).

"Suffering is the sole origin of consciousness," wrote the Russian novelist Dostoyevsky, a statement that aptly describes the tragic protagonist. Conversely, the inability to suffer, or to perceive or experience horror, characterizes the morally blind. For example, in Aeschylus's *Agamemnon,* even when directly presented with the truth, the chorus refuses to see it and only reiterates, like a verbal talisman, "May good prevail in the end." At the opposite end of the scale, too much suffering produces unconsciousness and, ultimately, death (permanent unconsciousness). Consciousness and the awareness of pain are the conditions of a morally responsible existence. Unwilling to face the horror of her life, Oedipus's wife, Jocasta, commits suicide. Unable to confront the tragic burden of suffering, both the chorus and Jocasta are dramatic foils for (contrasts to) the tragic hero: to live on the unbearable pinnacle of agony without the merciful unconsciousness of death is Oedipus's tragic fate. Similarly, the chorus of Trojan slave women in the *Libation-Bearers* may cheer when Orestes kills Clytemnestra: they aren't the ones who have to confront the Furies and are, in fact, blind to their presence. While the chorus celebrates victory, it is Orestes who suffers torment.

The Tragic Universe

Such tragedies tend to depict the universe in a very particular and characteristic way. The universe is governed by divine beings whose presence, actual or implied, lends significance to the actions of the human beings whose lives the gods affect; however, the universe is anthropocentric (human centered). The gods affect human lives, but their responses to human actions are utterly unpredictable. Communication between humans and gods is not as easy as it was in the myths and epics, when the gods spoke with humans directly. In the world of the tragedies, direct, unmediated communication with the gods does occur (as in Euripides' *Bacchae*), but more rarely. Apollo and Athene do not stroll casually along the streets of downtown Athens chatting with the heroes, as they did at Troy or Ithaca. Such communication is more usually indirect—through rituals, prayers, prophecies, and oracles—and thus subject to misinterpretation. The gods speak in riddles, and humans struggle to understand, often with devastating results. But the heroes' nature is such that they will insist on trying, on blindly confronting the invisible limits of the cosmic order head-on, using whatever tools—reason, moral integrity, courage, persistence—are at their disposal.

The Tragic Mystery The tragic universe, furthermore, is not morally tidy—justice does not always prevail, nor can humans count on the gods to reward virtue and punish evil. The gods' actions are often incomprehensible, and the more the heroes try to penetrate the mystery, the more they suffer. Just as the epic heroes' efforts to achieve literal immortality are doomed, so the efforts of the tragic heroes to find clarity, to assert the rational need for a moral universe, invariably fail. Even for the most gifted, well-intentioned heroes, there is no certainty. Things unaccountably change: **peripeteia** [pair-ih-pe-TEE-uh] (reversal), as Aristotle pointed out, defines the tragic experience. In the world of the tragedies, questions like "Why do bad things happen to good people?" have no clear-cut answers beyond a recognition of the mystery at the heart of the universe. The gods are mysterious to humans; they exist and often make impossible demands on us, but we cannot clearly ascertain or comprehend what they really want of us.

Moral Freedom Although humans cannot hope to understand the gods, they can at least understand the consequences of their own actions. Thus, in the ambiguous, often paradoxical world of the tragedies, the protagonist typically accepts responsibility for his or her fate, regardless of what the gods may or may not have done to bring it about. Fated or not, we must act as if we are free. In so doing, in rejecting the role of victim and defining ourselves as free moral agents, we wrench human existence out of the hands of the gods and reclaim it as our own. Through intense struggle and sacrifice, the tragic protagonist achieves a kind of moral transcendence that is both ennobling in itself and reassuring of the value of the struggle.

Often culminating in a sudden burst of insight beyond the limits of ordinary sense experience, the tragic hero's experience corresponds loosely with the epiphany and consequent communion of the Dionysian ritual. As scholars have noted, the original ritual was also cathartic. The irrational drives were called up and released, allowing the worshiper to continue to function within the confines of ordinary, civilized life. So, too, in tragedy, order is restored in the world of the play: plagues and civil disruptions end, and Furies are given socially useful tasks. This restoration comes, of course, at the price of enormous sacrifice. We cannot return, exactly, to our previous condition: we have looked into the abyss and will not readily forget its vastness looming beneath our feet. But for the struggle to continue, the community must survive. Thus, tragedy prepares the way for what follows: the release of tension in the satyr play, and the confirmation and reintegration in the comedy that concludes the dramatic festival. Only in the experience of the entire dramatic cycle can Apollo and Dionysus at last be reconciled. (For the primary works illustrating Athenian tragedy, see Chapters 15–17.)

· ·

Questions for Discussion and Review

1. Describe Dionysus's relation to the origin of Greek tragedy. Why do you suppose this particular god, with his passion and unpredictability, became the inspirer of Athenian drama, including tragedies, satyr plays, and comedies? Given that most surviving Greek plays do not feature the wine god as a major character, why are his nature and spirit relevant to the tragic vision?

2. Discuss the similarities and differences between tragic and epic heroes. What heroic qualities do they share? In what different ways does each accept enormous challenges, descend to the Underworld, and return bearing new insights? Using examples from your readings, explain in what sense each appears to achieve success or failure.

3. Epic heroes are trapped in a paradoxical situation—to pursue immortality, they must risk death. In what sense are tragic heroes similarly caught in a paradox?

4. Peripeteia (reversal) describes the plot of a tragedy: the protagonist begins in an enviable condition, often possessing wealth, power, and prestige, and ends in an unenviable condition, suffering torment or even death. But the concept of reversal also applies to the tragic vision itself. Explain how this reversal of fortune helps bring about the protagonist's understanding of the inevitability of change, the limits of human knowledge, or the nature of the gods.

The House of Atreus:
Aeschylus's *Oresteia*

KEY TOPICS/THEMES

In three sequential plays, Aeschylus dramatizes the tragic effects of Clytem-nestra's murder of Agamemnon, king of Argos, and the ordeal of their son, Orestes, who is forced to avenge his father's death by killing his own mother. In the final play, which pits chthonic forces (the Furies) against the Olympian sky gods, Athene intervenes in Orestes' plight to mediate between the ancient principles of blood vengeance and new laws of civic order.

Aeschylus's Drama of Crime and Redemption

The only surviving Greek trilogy, Aeschylus's *Oresteia* was first produced in 458 B.C., two years before the playwright's death. A sweeping reinterpretation of Homeric myth, the three plays examine the causes and consequences of Agamemnon's murder by his wife, **Clytemnestra,** and the unbearable dilemma facing their son, Orestes, who is compelled to kill his own mother to avenge his father's death. Although Aeschylus inherited his characters and dramatic situation from Homer, he turned this domestic tragedy of adultery and matricide into a cosmic event: Orestes, after whom the trilogy is named, affords the gods an opportunity to redefine the nature of justice and establish a new concept of divinity that transforms both religion and Greek society.

According to one influential interpretation, the playwright's major theme is the force of evolutionary change, in both the human and divine spheres, that ultimately unites contrarieties and mediates a bipolar view of existence. Incorporating a dominant motif of the Prometheus trilogy, Aeschylus explores the implications of the Greek belief that gods are not eternal and unchanging but, like humans, are born, grow, and attain ethical maturity only with the slow passing of time. Time eventually heals the breach between Zeus and Prometheus, ultimately merging the Titan's superior intelligence with Zeus's Olympian administration. In the *Oresteia,* Aeschylus shows the influence on human society of Zeus's moral evolution, a process that reaches its climax in the *Eumenides* when the hostile spirits of blood vengeance (the **Erinyes** [e-RIN-ih-eez], or **Furies**) are transformed into benign protectors and sources of blessing for Athene's people. By the *Eumenides'* conclusion, we realize that Agamemnon's murder and his son's revenge are primarily an opportunity for a divinely guided legal and moral revolution: acts of personal barbarism (the vendetta) are replaced by courts of law that recognize and enforce the civilized values of clemency.

Aeschylus and the Athenian Democracy

For Aeschylus, the ancient myth of Agamemnon's doomed house—its crimes, punishments, and ultimate regeneration—serves as a powerful statement about the Athenian democracy. In dramatizing this tale of murder and retribution, Aeschylus focuses on the story's outcome: the gods' ability to redeem the effects of sin and guilt through the institution of democratic procedures, particularly courts of law in which juries composed of free citizens, each with a single vote, evaluate difficult questions of justice. Working together as a cooperative body of equals, the Athenian jurors share power in wrestling with issues of life and death—all under the benign direction of Athene, who emphasizes that no one person, not even so exalted a personage as an Olympian goddess, has the right to make unilateral decisions.

> This is too grave a case for mortal minds,
> Nor is it right that I [Athene] should judge an act
> Of blood shed with such bitter consequences.

Only the community acting as a whole, encompassing both its divine and human components, can resolve the ethical complexities that Orestes' crime presents to the polis. In the end, Athene pointedly credits "Zeus of the assembly" (the democracy's governing body) for having won the day, ushering her people to a higher stage of civilization.

An Overview

In his *Poetics,* the earliest extant discussion of Greek epic and tragedy, Aristotle (384–322 B.C.) described the well-made drama as having a single major action, without distracting subplots. He added that the time covered in the play's events should be confined to "one revolution of the sun," a twenty-four-hour period, so that the temporal duration of events on stage generally corresponded to the audience's sense of real time. Critics in the Renaissance and Enlightenment subsequently interpreted Aristotle's descriptive comments as formal prescriptions for the "three unities" of time, place, and action, imposing formal restrictions that supposedly intensify a drama's tragic effect.

Conceived on a grand scale perhaps never surpassed in world theater, the *Oresteia*—written more than a century before Aristotle's *Poetics*—boldly ignores any confines of time or place. Aeschylus gave his trilogy an epic scope, covering events

FIGURE 15-1   Map of the Northeastern Peloponnesus. The area of Greece south of the Gulf of Corinth is called the Peloponnesus, named after Pelops, son of Tantalus. During the Mycenaean period (c. 1600–1100 B.C.), this area was dominated by heavily fortified cities such as Mycenae, Sparta, Tiryns, and Pylos, all of which figure prominently in Greek mythology. Although Mycenae is traditionally the site of Agamemnon's capital, in his version of the myth Aeschylus transferred it to Argos, the setting of his *Agamemnon* and *Libation-Bearers.*

that span at least a decade and setting the action all over Greece (Figure 15-1). The first play, the *Agamemnon,* opens in Argos, a Peloponnesian city south of Mycenae, shortly before Agamemnon's return home from Troy. The second play, the *Choephoroe (Libation-Bearers),* takes place several years later, after Orestes has grown to young manhood and returned from exile. In the third play, the *Eumenides,* the scene shifts from the Peloponnesian peninsula to Delphi, where Orestes, pursued by the Furies, seeks purification. For the final act, after another year has passed, Aeschylus transfers the action to Athens, where Orestes is tried before a specially convened tribunal on the **Areopagus** (Hill of Ares), a rocky spur of the Acropolis.

The original issues of blood vengeance and filial duty that dominate in Argos become in Athens matters of civic law and religious ethics. To signal the extreme importance that Zeus attaches to Orestes' case, divine beings miraculously appear to participate in the court proceedings: the Furies act as prosecutor, Apollo as chief witness for the defense, and Athene as judge. The *Oresteia* reaches its climax not in

Orestes' acquittal and absolution but in Athene's transformation of the Furies (Erinyes) into the Kindly Ones (Eumenides), thus fulfilling Zeus's plan.

As a coda to the tragic action, Aeschylus created a satyr play based on an episode in the *Odyssey:* Menelaus's comic encounter with **Proteus,** a sea god who has the Dionysian ability to change into any form he desires. The play has been lost, but it probably involved a farcical version of the Homeric account, with Proteus metamorphosing himself successively into a lion, serpent, panther, boar, body of water, and tree. If Aeschylus followed Homer's account, we may suppose that the play featured this sequence of incidents: after a satiric **agon** (the contest or struggle featured in tragedy), Menelaus at last forces Proteus to use his prophetic gifts to foretell the Greek leader's successful return—with the now repentant Helen—to Sparta. Offering a pleasurable contrast to Agamemnon's bloody homecoming, Menelaus's adventure concludes the Dionysian tragic cycle by sexually reuniting the couple whose marital problems helped precipitate the Trojan War. In another of the many versions of Helen's reunion with Menelaus, the wronged husband seems ready to take vengeance on his faithless wife, despite Helen's all-but-irresistible allure (Figure 15-2).

Important Elements and Themes

The Choruses   The *Oresteia*'s three very different choruses are integral parts of Aeschylus's design. The *Agamemnon* chorus is composed of Argive citizens who, even ten years before the play opens, were too old to fight at Troy and are now reduced to the status of passive onlookers. Feebly protesting Clytemnestra's take-charge attitude, they fail to perceive her homicidal intent, even when **Cassandra,** a clairvoyant Trojan princess, explicitly describes her visions of Agamemnon's imminent death. Although physically impotent and unequal to the challenge of the queen's conspiracy, the chorus is a rich repository of traditional wisdom and religious insight. The first choral ode sounds two of Aeschylus's principal themes: that wisdom is won only through suffering and that the integrity of Zeus, the supreme god, ensures that universal moral order will ultimately prevail.

Both the second and third parts of the *Oresteia* are named after their respective choruses. The *Libation-Bearers* are captive women whom Clytemnestra orders to carry ritual drink offerings (libations) to the tomb of Agamemnon, whose ghost now troubles his widow's dreams. The enslaved women embody a typically Aeschylean paradox: although they have lost husbands, families, and homeland through Agamemnon's conquests, they are united in honoring their slain captor and hating his arrogant queen. Their cry of triumph over the regicides' dead bodies echoes Clytemnestra's joyous shout in the *Agamemnon* when she first learns of her husband's approach and anticipates the glad cries accompanying the Eumenides' ritual procession that concludes the trilogy.

In the third play, the *Eumenides,* the chorus consists of Furies (Erinyes), savage spirits of vengeance whom Athene will eventually domesticate as the **Eumenides** (oo-MEN-ih-deez), or "Kindly Ones." They first appear at the end of the *Libation-Bearers* when, as Gorgonlike horrors, they rush on stage to seize Orestes, determined to destroy the matricide in both body and soul. In Aeschylus's vision of the

FIGURE 15-2   Menelaus and Helen. In this vase painting, Menelaus, who has reclaimed Helen after the fall of Troy, threatens her with his sword. Although the *Odyssey* portrayed Helen respectfully, restoring her to Sparta with queenly rank and privileges, other Greek myths reported that Menelaus executed the woman who had betrayed him for Paris (whereas still others insisted that only a phantom Helen had eloped to Troy). Clytemnestra, who is married to Menelaus's brother, resembles her sister, Helen, in being an equally unfaithful wife, but far more deadly. *(British Museum, London)*

gods' evolution, the Furies represent ancient chthonic (earth-oriented) powers who oppose the new ouranic (sky god) deities of Olympus. According to Hesiod, they were generated from drops of blood falling on Gaea from Uranus's severed genitals and are thus both earthborn and the product of castration, a primordial crime against the father. Despite their differences in appearance and function, they are half-sisters of Aphrodite, who was also created from Uranus's mutilation, and thus aspects of the divine feminine. Commensurate with their origin, the Furies punish crimes against blood kin, especially of children against their parents. Aeschylus makes them daughters of Night (Nyx), sister of Erebus (Infernal Darkness), perhaps because this ancestry emphasizes their natural opposition to Apollo, the luminous eye of heaven.

The Curse on the House of Atreus   To illustrate his view that the gods are determined to end wanton bloodshed and expunge even the deepest guilt, Aeschylus examines one of the most spectacularly dysfunctional families in all of Greek

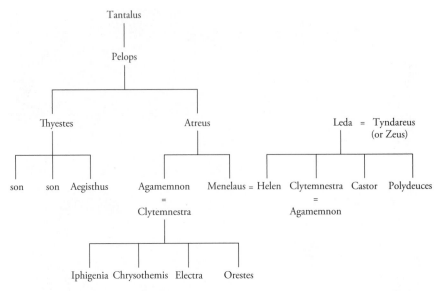

FIGURE 15-3   Genealogy of the House of Atreus. As this genealogical chart indicates, Agamemnon and his family are descended from a long line of royal criminals, including perpetrators of murder, adultery, incest, and cannibalism. In the *Oresteia,* Aeschylus takes on the issue of whether such deeply ingrained guilt—inherited but also compounded anew in each succeeding generation—can be cleansed or its cycle of violent crime and equally heinous vengeance be brought to a peaceful end.

myth. The royal house (dynasty) of **Atreus** [AY-tre-uhs] (Figure 15-3), father of Agamemnon and Menelaus, inherits a proclivity toward evil from a distant ancestor, Tantalus, the man who murdered and cooked his own son, serving Pelops's dismembered body to the gods presumably to test their omniscience (see Chapter 9). Although the Tantalus myth may function primarily to warn against human sacrifice—the Olympians summarily reject Tantalus's offering and condemn him to Tartarus—it anticipates the equally vile crime of Atreus himself. Atreus and his brother **Thyestes** engage in a bitter feud after the latter commits adultery with Atreus's wife, Aerope. Pretending a reconciliation, Atreus invites Thyestes to a banquet, where his unsuspecting brother dines on the flesh of his sons.

Although Aeschylus does not use it, one version of the Atreus myth emphasizes the incestuous origin of Thyestes' son Aegisthus, who avenges the wrongs done to his side of the family. After an oracle decrees that only a son conceived in incest could effect the desired revenge, Thyestes impregnates his daughter, Pelopia, who gives birth to Aegisthus. In this tradition, Aegisthus grows up to kill his uncle Atreus, become Clytemnestra's lover, and murder Agamemnon.

The Sacrifice of Iphigenia   Before leaving Argos for Troy, Agamemnon, acting on a priest's oracle, supposedly from Artemis, compounds the family sins by sacrificing his daughter, **Iphigenia** [if-ih-je-NYE-a], Clytemnestra's favorite child (Figure 15-4). In the *Agamemnon,* the chorus states that Argos's king slaughtered

FIGURE 15-4 The Sacrifie of Iphigenia. For Iphigenia's mother, Agamemnon's sin in sacrifiing their daughter is unforgivable. Clytemnestra sees herself as fully justified in avenging her child by killing the murderer, who is also her husband and king, an act that perpetuates the curse on the House of Atreus. In this Roman wall painting (c. A.D. 63–79) of Iphigenia at Aulis, the port from which the Greek fleet under Agamemnon's command departed for Troy, a veiled figure hides her face in grief while in the sky above, Artemis rides a stag to rescue the girl, a version of the myth absent in Aeschylus's trilogy but dramatized by Euripides (see the box on pp. 643–644). *(National Museum, Naples)*

his virgin daughter because he felt obligated to do so, "coerced" by priest and army to expedite the voyage to Troy. Other poets, however, assigned Agamemnon different motives, with some ascribing Iphigenia's murder to her father's ambition. When the unruly Greek army, assembled at the seaport of Aulis, threatens to disperse because the gods withhold fair sailing winds, threatening to rob Agamemnon of his main chance at glory, he exchanges his child for the opportunity to sack Troy. In his *Iphigenia at Aulis,* Euripides examines the pressures that Agamemnon's soldiers, eager to seize Troy's gold, impose on their commander, making him the pawn of their collective greed and blood lust.

Cassandra's Prophecy   When Troy falls, Agamemnon adds to his guilt by desecrating the city's holy shrines and massacring even those who seek asylum in the gods' sanctuaries. In his treatment of the myth, Aeschylus implies Agamemnon's impiety by showing the conqueror bringing home Cassandra, a virgin priestess of Apollo, whom he has violated and enslaved as his concubine. A daughter of Priam and Hecuba, Cassandra bears a heavy burden: she is a prophet who foresees the future with frightening accuracy, but no one ever believes her. This intensely frustrating predicament results from Cassandra's wish to protect her virginity, a symbol of her integrity and commitment to her prophetic office, even from the god who endowed her with clairvoyance. When Apollo attempted to seduce her, Cassandra rebuffed him: the Delphic god could not retract his gift, but he cursed her with an undeserved inability to make others understand her visions (Figure 15-5).

Near the end of the *Agamemnon,* as she obeys Clytemnestra's order to enter the royal palace, where the queen will butcher her, Cassandra strips off the emblems of Apollo's service, throwing down her prophet's veil and staff. Betrayed by her god, exploited by Agamemnon, and slaughtered by his wife, Cassandra is a victim of brutality both human and divine. Even the chorus, which is generally sympathetic to her plight, seems willfully blind to her warnings of impending disaster. In death, as in life, she is utterly alone, trapped in her solitary, unwanted vision.

The *Agamemnon*

With its long choral songs and stately pace, the *Agamemnon* moves slowly but inexorably toward a powerful confrontation between Greece's victorious commander in chief and the wife who has ruled Argos in his absence. While Agamemnon remains outside the palace in his war chariot, with a procession of soldiers, captives, and booty in his train, Clytemnestra occupies the high ground of the ceremonial steps that she will force her husband to ascend in a way that offends the gods and marks his doom. The agon (struggle) between husband and wife is no contest: Clytemnestra, superior in intelligence and will, knows how to bend Agamemnon to her purpose, goading his vanity until he accepts her dare to walk up the steps she has covered with priceless carpets. Persuading Agamemnon publicly to commit hubris—a prideful act that elicits divine retribution—she manipulates him into taking on himself an honor reserved only for gods: a conquering hero, he treads the crimson runner, a blood-red path leading to the palace interior.

Delighted that Agamemnon has escaped the dangers of war so that she can have the pleasure of killing him herself, Clytemnestra impales her husband on Aegisthus's sword, transforming his bath into a bloody sea (Figure 15-6). Carrying her gore-stained weapon as she emerges from the palace, Clytemnestra takes full credit for the regicide, for she sees herself as heaven's instrument of justice, the executioner of her daughter's killer. Acting alone, Clytemnestra struck her husband, humiliating him with her "woman's hand." Aegisthus, who later snarls loudly at the disapproving chorus, is little more than the queen's lapdog.

Grieving for Iphigenia as Demeter had for Persephone, Clytemnestra seems to champion women's rights, taking vengeance against a male ruler who sacrificed his daughter to further his political ambitions. Clytemnestra, however, does not mani-

FIGURE 15-5   Apollo and Cassandra [or a Muse]. If this vase painting depicts Apollo
offering himself to Cassandra, a princess of Troy and the god's virgin priestess, it evokes
the source of Cassandra's conflicted role in the *Agamemnon*. According to one tradition,
Cassandra at first consents to the god's wish to sleep with her but later refuses to make love,
attempting to retain both her religious office and her independence. Although he cannot
rescind his prophetic gift, the rejected Apollo takes away Cassandra's credibility so that no
one will ever believe her predictions. Tormented by her knowledge of the future and her
powerlessness to make others accept her vision, Cassandra appears in the *Agamemnon* as a
demented clairvoyant, possessed by a god's spirit but unable to warn others or save herself.
(Henry Lillie Pierce Fund. Courtesy, Museum of Fine Arts, Boston)

fest feminine solidarity as such, but only so far as there exists a blood tie between
females, particularly mother and a favored daughter. Even in this human bond,
however, Clytemnestra is deficient. While she fixates on Iphigenia and her fate,
Clytemnestra shows little affection for her younger daughter, **Electra**, of whom she
would be glad to dispose. She also has no compunction about hacking Cassandra to

FIGURE 15-6   The Death of Agamemnon. In Aeschylus's play, Clytemnestra boasts that she killed Agamemnon with her own hands. In this vase painting (c. 470 B.C), however, the artist follows the Homeric tradition, showing Aegisthus (with sword, at left) as the murderer of Agamemnon (center), who is caught in a netlike garment. Clytemnestra rushes in (far left), while another female figure (to the right of Agamemnon), probably the couple's daughter Electra, throws up her hands in horror. At the extreme right, another woman, perhaps Cassandra, attempts to flee. *(William Francis Warden Fund. Courtesy, Museum of Fine Arts, Boston)*

death with an ax (Figure 15-7), although the Trojan woman is clearly an unwilling victim of male dominance. Like Hera, Clytemnestra regards her husband's mistresses not as members of an exploited sisterhood but solely as affronts to her pride, rivals she can exterminate without a qualm.

The only character who appears in all three parts of the *Oresteia*—as a murderess in the *Agamemnon,* a murder victim in the *Libation-Bearers,* and a ghost demanding revenge in the *Eumenides*—Clytemnestra is a magnificent figure whose fate raises profoundly disturbing questions about the relative value of male and female lives in Greek society. Even stronger than Medea, the only other mythic woman whose outrage against male perfidy approaches her own level of passionate hatred, Clytemnestra never wavers in her resolution or breaks down under duress. For many men in Aeschylus's audience, Clytemnestra must have epitomized the problem posed by an extraordinary female: how to deal with a woman whose wit, energy, initiative, and drive exceed that of most men. As Orestes observes after slaying his mother, such a woman cannot be trusted. Aeschylus struggles with this issue, not altogether satisfactorily to some modern critics, throughout the *Oresteia*.

FIGURE 15-7 Clytemnestra About to Kill Cassandra. Although she loathes her husband, Clytemnestra is furious when Agamemnon brings home as his concubine Cassandra, the daughter of Priam and Hecuba. At the moment depicted in this red-figured cup, Cassandra meets the fate she had earlier foreseen but been helpless to avoid. As the victim of a powerful king's lust and his wife's savage jealousy, Cassandra resembles the mythic objects of Zeus's unwanted affection, such as Io or Leda. *(National Museum, Ferrara)*

The *Libation-Bearers*

Orestes, weeping alone at his father's neglected tomb, opens the *Libation-Bearers* with a brief prologue invoking Hermes, guide of the dead. Disguised as a traveling peddler because he knows that his mother would kill him in a minute to ensure her own safety, Orestes prepares to face the contradictory divine forces that push him to the brink of insanity. If he fails to obey Apollo's order to honor his father by slaying his mother, Phoebus will curse him. If he commits this most unnatural of crimes, the Furies will not only kill him but claim his soul as well.

Clytemnestra's dream that she takes a poisonous snake to her breast reflects both her unacknowledged guilt and the impending arrival of Orestes, whom she nursed but briefly before sending into exile. As Apollo's human servant, a furtive agent sent

FIGURE 15-8   Orestes About to Kill Aegisthus. As Orestes draws back his sword to plunge it into the man who usurped his father's throne, Clytemnestra rushes in, raising an ax to defend her lover. Despite presenting her justifications for killing Iphigenia's murderer in the *Agamemnon,* in the *Libation-Bearers* Aeschylus reduces sympathy for Clytemnestra by showing her readiness to slaughter her own son to protect her position. This vase painting may have been produced about the time of the *Oresteia's* first performance (458 B.C.). Whereas Greek artists commonly depicted scenes of violence, Greek dramatists always had such acts occur offstage, typically to be described later by an eyewitness or a messenger. *(William Francis Warden Fund. Courtesy, Museum of Fine Arts, Boston)*

to cleanse his homeland of evil, Orestes does not hesitate to kill Aegisthus (Figure 15-8) but almost fails to complete the act that fulfills his duty to Agamemnon. At the crucial moment when Orestes seems unable to strike Clytemnestra, his companion, **Pylades** [PYE-la-deez]—who dogs his friend's footsteps throughout the play but speaks only on this occasion—repeats Apollo's command: the gods give Orestes no freedom to choose. Obediently, he kills his mother (Figure 15-9) and is immediately besieged by fiends.

FIGURE 15-9   Orestes Killing Aegisthus. Although Orestes' hand
is occupied driving his sword through Aegisthus, his eyes are already
fixed on his next victim, his mother. Clytemnestra's attempted flight
(left) will soon be cut short by her son's avenging blade. *(Kunsthistorisches Museum, Vienna)*

Aeschylus emphasizes that no one except Orestes can see the Furies. The chorus,
to whom they are invisible, is baffled by Orestes' anguish, a suggestion that, in this
scene, Aeschylus presents the Furies as hallucinatory, psychological projections of
the mother slayer's overpowering guilt. (In the *Eumenides,* these figures are visible
not only to Orestes and the gods but to Apollo's human priestess and, presumably,
to Orestes' jurors as well.)

The *Eumenides*

Apollo's priestess, the Pythia, delivers the *Eumenides'* prologue, a review of Delphi's
mythic history emphasizing the sanctuary's religious evolution: she reminds us that,

FIGURE 15-10   Orestes Clinging to the Omphalos at Delphi. In this dramatic painting of a scene from the *Eumenides,* Apollo extends his right arm to banish the Furies from his sanctuary as his suppliant Orestes clutches the sacred "navel" stone, imploring the god to protect him. As the divine administrator of purification rites, Apollo cleanses Orestes of ritual guilt for having killed his mother, Clytemnestra; but only Athene's court of justice can legally absolve him of the crime and permanently deliver him from the vengeful Furies. Although she does not appear in the *Oresteia,* the figure at the right, holding a bow and accompanied by a hunting dog, may be Artemis, who shares her brother's loathing for the Furies. *(National Museum, Naples)*

before Apollo founded his oracle, a succession of earth goddesses presided there, including Themis and Phoebe, the "shining one," a daughter of Gaea and Uranus. The change from a chthonic to an ouranic cult foreshadows the play's climactic reversal: in the public arena of Orestes' trial, where gods of earth and sky contend for supremacy, the Olympians will gain universal control.

In the trial scene, binary tensions building throughout the trilogy gather in sharp focus: male is pitted against female, innovation against tradition, intellect against emotion, the rule of law against individual excess, and civilization against barbarism. Presenting the world as divided between two polar opposites, Aeschylus's impassioned characters identify its most savage components with the female principle, associating the Furies with cruelty, darkness, death, and slaughter, whereas Apollo, the quintessential male figure, is seen as allied with clemency, purity, light, health, rationality, and moderation (Figure 15-10).

The characters' assault against the negative shadow of a primal female divinity reaches a peak when, in a burst of misogyny, Apollo claims that the mother is not a real parent but merely the "nurse" or incubator of the seed that the father deposits in her. Phoebus cites Athene as the casebook example of a father's ability to produce children without female aid, a mythic allusion that serves primarily to endorse the

FIGURE 15-11   Athene. Extending her hand as if in appeal, this bronze Athene could well represent the goddess in her role at Orestes' trial before the Areopagus. Acting as mediator between Apollonian concern for masculine authority and the Furies, passion to avenge matricide, Athene uses the rhetorical arts of persuasion to tame chthonic energy and bring it into the service of her city-state. Fulfilling the will of Zeus, the sky gods succeed in establishing a new concept of civil justice, but the primitive fear of punishment for wrong-doing remains an integral part of the Greek experience. Accepting Athene's invitation to inhabit an underground grotto beneath the sunlit Acropolis, the Eumenides (Kindly Ones) remain a potent, unseen force—ancient promoters of the vendetta ironically transformed into inhibitors of future violence. *(National Museum, Athens)*

Athenian patriarchy: in terms of legal and social practice, only the male has genuine parental status.

Apollo's reference to Athene's motherless birth also functions symbolically to associate her, as rational consciousness and civilization, with the male principle. By contrast, the Furies—unconscious instinct and savage nature—are seen as Athene's polar opposite, a devouring feminine appetite for blood.

Although Athene does not explicitly endorse Apollo's argument, she unequivocally sides with male authority. Declaring that she cannot support the cause of a woman who kills her husband, Athene casts the deciding vote for Orestes' acquittal (Figure 15-11). (The jurors had reached a deadlock on the defendant's guilt; a vote evenly divided was equivalent to a not-guilty verdict.) Many critics have traditionally assumed that Apollo and Athene prefer mercy to strict justice and are concerned with establishing the legal principle of extenuating circumstances (in Orestes' case, the Oracle's command) in exonerating a defendant. Aeschylus's text, however, mentions neither compassion nor legal rationales.

FIGURE 15-12   Orestes and Electra. Athens' three greatest playwrights—Aeschylus, Sophocles, and Euripides—all dramatized the myth in which Electra and Orestes conspire to murder their mother. In both Aeschylus's *Libation-Bearers* and Sophocles' *Electra,* the two matricides are depicted as noble instruments of the gods' will, a heroic conception expressed in this monumental sculpture of Agamemnon's avengers. By contrast, Euripides' *Electra* portrays Orestes as a weakling dominated by his neurotic sister, a deranged creature driven by her thwarted desire for her dead father and sexual jealousy of her mother. *(National Museum, Naples)*

Orestes' victory (Figure 15-12) is necessary for Aeschylus to move on to his primary interest—Athene's use of persuasion to change the hostile Furies into a force for human good. Behaving as a divine exemplar of democratic principles, at the climax of the trial scene Athene employs rational argument to reconcile opposing factions. Like many leaders of the Athenian democracy, Athene must mediate between time-honored traditions beloved by many and political innovations that will radically change life in the polis. Alluding only briefly to her power to coerce—she has access to Zeus's thunderbolts—Athene prefers to offer civic honors and other benefits to the Furies, gradually making them realize the advantages of democratic compromise. Realizing that enemies can be changed into supporters only if they *willingly* agree to abandon their old allegiances, Athene persists in enumerating the benefits that will accrue to the Furies if they cooperate. By cultivating in the Furies a new awareness of their true self-interest, a recognition that turns bitter foes into helpful friends, Athene demonstrates the inestimable value of persuasive speech in the democratic process.

In the Prometheus trilogy, Aeschylus portrayed divine power split between the punishing strength of Zeus and the pain-racked compassion of Prometheus, a division that gradually evolved into the reconciliation and union of a previously bifurcated godhead. In the *Oresteia,* Aeschylus also presents two opposing aspects of divinity—the Furies and the Olympians—merging into a harmonious whole. For Aeschylus, there is no question of banishing the Furies or imprisoning them in Tartarus, as Zeus had done with the deposed Titans. (As they correctly observe, they function as single-minded detectives and executioners, in effect doing Zeus's dirty work for him.) Instead, Aeschylus uses a metaphor of the democratic process—the rhetorical art of persuasion by which political opponents can rationally settle their differences—to achieve a workable union between the divine anger that penalizes evil and the divine goodwill that heals and redeems.

Apollo, who leaves the stage immediately after the jury's verdict, cannot mediate the issues because, as god of beauty and purification, he has no common ground with the Furies, whom he sees only as filthy hags bespattered with gore from tortures and executions. Athene functions as mediator because she, like the daughters of Night, is also a female deity (although born of a male) and possesses both chthonic perception (from Metis) and ouranic wisdom (from Zeus). Her success in changing potential destroyers of the state into benign guardians fulfills the will of Zeus and unites Dionysian energy with Apollonian intelligence.

Transformed into the Eumenides, these night terrors act as a stabilizing influence in human society, inspiring a useful fear that prohibits wrong-doing—a repressive function that Athene explicitly approves—and simultaneously conferring the chthonic blessing of fertility. The Eumenides' torch-lit installation in a subterranean grotto beneath the Acropolis is an appropriate analogue to their Dionysian presence in the human unconscious, where their instinctual energy complements Apollo's rational intellect.

A few years after the *Oresteia*'s premiere, Athene's new temple, the Parthenon, was built atop the Acropolis, a gleaming symbol of the polis's collective awareness. Standing above the Eumenides' underground chapel and beneath heaven's light, Athene's marble shrine visibly linked the dim, mysterious world of primal earth with the bright sky of Zeus.

Conflict and Opposition in the Myth of the House of Atreus

Before Aeschylus transformed the stories of Agamemnon and Orestes to illustrate the conflict between matriarchal and patriarchal forces in Greek society, the myth of the House of Atreus featured a more traditional competition for power between male figures. Mythic events that took place before the action of Aeschylus's *Agamemnon* typically emphasize father–son and brother–brother conflict, usually involving murder and revenge. Agamemnon's ancestor, Tantalus, kills his son, Pelops, and attempts to feed his flesh to the Olympian gods—an act that condemns him to eternal torment in Tartarus. Tantalus's descendants, Atreus and Thyestes, engage in a fraternal rivalry that culminates in Atreus's murder of Thyestes' sons and the cannibalistic banquet in which Thyestes unwittingly devours his children's flesh.

In the Homeric version of the subsequent conflict between the son of Atreus (Agamemnon) and the son of Thyestes (Aegisthus), it is Aegisthus, presumably acting alone, who kills Agamemnon. In Aeschylus's tragedy, however, it is Clytemnestra who boasts that her husband is slain by her own hand, thereby setting the stage for an intense struggle involving the respective rights and authority of a strong woman pitted against a less effectual man (who is also a head of state). Aeschylus's dramatization of the struggle reaches a climax in the trial scene of the *Eumenides,* in which virtually all the principal characters in the *Oresteia* are depicted as polar opposites. Aeschylus's resolution of the battle between old and new, male and female, anarchy and order utilizes the powerful image of Athene, who shares qualities with both sides of the conflict and successfully mediates between them. Aeschylus's dramatic use of ancient myth to illustrate the reconciliation of opposing forces in Greek society (and the human psyche) lends itself to, among other approaches, a structuralist interpretation of the drama.

I

Traditions and Qualities Associated with the Feminine Principle:

Clytemnestra—powerful female who avenges wrongs

Iphigenia—innocent girl sacrificed to male ambition

The Furies—Night's daughters, spirits of blood vengeance, identified with darkness, violence, torture, bloodshed, castration, punishment, instinct, hatred, fear, irrationality, anarchy, inflexible justice, and age-old tradition

II

Traditions and Qualities Associated with the Masculine Principle:

Agamemnon—rightful king and father, treacherously murdered

Orestes—compelled by divine command to avenge his father

Apollo—immortal son of Zeus, identified with light, peace, spiritual insight, mental and physical health, masculine autonomy, ethical purification, moderation, restraint, rationality, stability, clemency, and divine innovation

III

Athene—immortal daughter of Zeus who was born without a mother, identified with rationality, wisdom, courage, defense of civic order, military victory, creative skill, virginity, emotional self-sufficiency, intellectual freedom, ethical commitment, democracy, legal justice, and the art of persuasion.

In the final scene of the *Eumenides,* Athene acts as a mediator who reconciles the opposing claims of chthonic tradition and ouranic innovation. By the end of his three-part drama, Aeschylus has clearly demonstrated his conviction that the ancient Mycenaean legacy has evolved into a new concept of social justice that finds completion and fulfillment in the Athenian court of law. For Aeschylus and his audience, Athens—with its democracy guided by the Zeus-born embodiment of divine wisdom—is the culmination and ultimate achievement of Greek historical development.

AGAMEMNON*

Aeschylus

CHARACTERS

WATCHMAN

CHORUS [OF OLD MEN, *citizens of Argos*]

CLYTEMNESTRA [*queen of Argos*]

HERALD [*messenger of Agamemnon*]

AGAMEMNON [*king of Argos, commander of Achaean forces at Troy*]

CASSANDRA [*daughter of Priam and Hecuba*]

AEGISTHUS [*son of Thyestes, lover of Clytemnestra*]

CAPTAIN OF THE GUARD

The scene is the entrance to the palace of the Atreidae. Before the doors stand shrines of the gods. [A WATCHMAN *is posted on the roof.]*

Watchman

I've prayed God to release me from sentry duty   1
All through this long year's vigil, like a dog
Couched on the roof of Atreus, where I study
Night after night the pageantry of this vast
Concourse of stars, and moving among them like
Noblemen the constellations that bring
Summer and winter as they rise and fall.
And I am still watching for the beacon signal
All set to flash over the sea the radiant
News of the fall of Troy. So confident   10
Is a woman's spirit, whose purpose is a man's.
Every night, as I turn in to my stony bed,
Quilted with dew, not visited by dreams,
Not mine—no sleep, fear stands at my pillow
Keeping tired eyes from closing once too often;
And whenever I start to sing or hum a tune,
Mixing from music an antidote to sleep,
It always turns to mourning for the royal house,
Which is not in such good shape as it used to be
But now at last may the good news in a flash
Scatter the darkness and deliver us!   20

Translation of the Agamemnon, Libation-Bearers, *and* Eumenides *by George Thomson.*

[The beacon flashes.]
O light of joy, whose gleam turns night to day,
O radiant signal for innumerable
Dances of victory! Ho there! I call the queen,
Agamemnon's wife, to raise with all the women
Alleluias of thanksgiving through the palace
Saluting the good news, if it is true
That Troy has fallen, as this blaze portends;
Yes, and I'll dance an overture myself.
My master's dice have fallen out well, and I   30
Shall score three sixes for this nightwatching.
[A pause.]
Well, come what will, may it soon be mine to grasp
In this right hand my master's, home again!
[Another pause.]
The rest is secret. A heavy ox has trodden
Across my tongue. These walls would have tales to tell
If they had mouths. I speak only to those
Who are in the know, to others—I know nothing.
[The WATCHMAN *goes into the palace. Women's cries are heard. Enter* CHORUS OF
OLD MEN.*]*

Chorus

It is ten years since those armed prosecutors of Justice, Menelaus and Agamemnon, twin-sceptred in God-given sovranty, embarked in the thousand ships
crying war, like eagles with long wings beating the air over a robbed mountain
nest, wheeling and screaming for their lost children. Yet above them some god,
maybe Apollo or Zeus, overhears the sky-dweller's cry and sends after the robber a Fury.
*[*CLYTEMNESTRA *comes out of the palace and unseen by the elders places offerings before
the shrines.]*
Just so the two kings were sent by the greater king, Zeus, for the sake of a
promiscuous woman to fight Paris, Greek and Trojan locked fast together in
the dusty betrothals of battle. And however it stands with them now, the end is
unalterable; no flesh, no wine can appease God's fixed indignation.

As for us, with all the able-bodied men enlisted and gone, we are left here   40
leaning our strength on a staff; for, just as in infancy, when the marrow is still
unformed, the War-god is not at his post, so it is in extreme old age, as the
leaves fall fast, we walk on three feet, like dreams in the daylight.
[They see CLYTEMNESTRA.*]*
O Queen, what news? what message sets light to the altars? All over the
town the shrines are ablaze with unguents drawn from the royal stores and
the flames shoot up into the night sky. Speak, let us hear all that may be made
public, so healing the anxieties that have gathered thick in our hearts; let the
gleam of good news scatter them.
*[*CLYTEMNESTRA *goes out to tend the other altars of the city.]*
Strength have I still to recall that sign which greeted the two kings

Taking the road, for the prowess of song is not yet spent.
I sing of two kings united in sovranty, leading
Armies to battle, who saw two eagles
Beside the palace
Wheel into sight, one black, and the other was white-tailed,
Tearing a hare with her unborn litter.
Ailinon cry, but let good conquer!

Shrewdly the priest took note and compared each eagle with each king,   50
Then spoke out and prefigured the future in these words:
"In time the Greek arms shall demolish the fortress of Priam;
Only let no jealous God, as they fasten
On Troy the slave's yoke,
Strike them in anger; for Artemis loathes the rapacious
Beagles of Zeus that have slaughtered the frail hare,
Ailinon cry, but let good conquer!
O Goddess, gentle to the tender whelp of fierce lions
As to all young life of the wild,
So now fulfil what is good in the omen and mend what is faulty.   60
And I appeal unto the Lord Apollo,
Let not the north wind hold the fleet storm-bound,
Driving them on to repay that feast with another,
Inborn builder of strife, feud that fears no man, it is still there,
Treachery keeping the house, it remembers, revenges, a child's death!"*
Such, as the kings left home, was the seer's revelation.
Ailinon cry, but let good conquer!

Zeus, whoe'er he be, if so it best
Please his ear to be addressed,
So shall he be named by me.   70
All things have I measured, yet
None have found save him alone,
Zeus, if a man from a heart heavy-laden
Seek to cast his cares aside.

Long since lived a ruler of the world,
Puffed with martial pride, of whom
None shall tell, his day is done;
Also, he who followed him
Met his master and is gone.

Zeus the victorious, gladly acclaim him;   80
Perfect wisdom shall be yours;
Zeus, who laid it down that man
Must in sorrow learn and through
Pain to wisdom find his way.

---

*Iphigenia

When deep slumber falls, remembered wrongs
Chafe the bruised heart with fresh pangs, and no
Welcome wisdom meets within.
Harsh the grace dispensed by powers immortal,
Pilots of the human soul.
Even so the elder prince,   90
Marshal of the thousand ships,
Rather than distrust a priest,
Torn with doubt to see his men
Harbor-locked, hunger-pinched, hard-oppressed,
Strained beyond endurance, still
Watching, waiting, where the never-tiring
Tides of Aulis ebb and flow:

And still the storm blew from mountains far north,
With moorings windswept and hungry crews pent
In rotting hulks,   100
With tackling all torn and seeping timbers,
Till Time's slow-paced, enforced inaction
Had all but stripped bare the bloom of Greek manhood.
And then was found but one
Cure to allay the tempest—never a blast so bitter—
Shrieked in a loud voice by the priest, "Artemis!" striking the Atreidae with
    dismay, each with his staff smiting the ground and weeping.

And then the king spoke, the elder, saying:
"The choice is hard—hard to disobey him,
And harder still
To kill my own child, my palace jewel,   110
With unclean hands before the altar
Myself, her own father, spill a maid's pure blood.
I have no choice but wrong.
How shall I fail my thousand ships and betray my comrades?
So shall the storm cease, and the men eager for war clamor for that virginal
    blood righteously! So pray for a happy outcome!"

And when he bowed down beneath the harness
Of cruel coercion, his spirit veering
With sudden sacrilegious change,
He gave his whole mind to evil counsel.
For man is made bold with base-contriving   120
Impetuous madness, first cause of much grief.
And so then he slew his own child
For a war to win a woman
And to speed the storm-bound fleet from the shore to battle.

She cried aloud "Father!", yet they heard not;
A girl in first flower, yet they cared not,

The lords who gave the word for war.
Her father prayed, then he bade his vassals
To seize her where swathed in folds of saffron
She lay, and lift her up like a yearling   130
With bold heart above the altar,
And her lovely lips to bridle
That they might not cry out, cursing the House of Atreus,
With gags, her voice sealed with brute force and crushed.
And then she let fall her cloak
And cast at each face a glance that dumbly craved compassion;
And like a picture she would but could not greet
Her father's guests, who at home
Had often sat when the meal was over,
The cups replenished, with all hearts enraptured   140
To hear her sing grace with clear unsullied voice for her loving father.

The end was unseen and unspeakable.
The task of priestcraft was done.
For Justice first chastens, then she presses home her lesson.
The morrow must come, its grief will soon be here,
So let us not weep today.
It shall be made known as clear as daybreak.
And so may all this at last end in good news,
For which the queen prays, the next of kin and stay of the land of Argos.
[CLYTEMNESTRA *appears at the door of the palace.*]
Our humble salutations to the queen!   150
Hers is our homage, while our master's throne
Stands empty. We are still longing to hear
The meaning of your sacrifice. Is it good news?

Clytemnestra
Good news! With good news may the morning rise
Out of the night—good news beyond all hope!
My news is this: The Greeks have taken Troy.

Chorus
What? No, it cannot be true! I cannot grasp it.

Clytemnestra
The Greeks hold Troy—is not that plain enough?

Chorus
Joy steals upon me and fills my eyes with tears.

Clytemnestra
Indeed, your looks betray your loyalty.   160

Chorus
What is the proof? Have you any evidence?

Clytemnestra
Of course I have, or else the Gods have cheated me.

Chorus
You have given ear to some beguiling dream.

Clytemnestra
I would not come screaming fancies out of my sleep.

Chorus
Rumors have wings—on these your heart has fed.

Clytemnestra
You mock my intelligence as though I were a girl.

Chorus
When was it? How long is it since the city fell?

Clytemnestra
In the night that gave birth to this dawning day.

Chorus
What messenger could bring the news so fast?

Clytemnestra
The God of Fire, who from Ida sent forth light   170
And beacon by beacon passed the flame to me.
From the peak of Ida first to the cliff of Hermes
On Lemnos, and from there a third great lamp
Was flashed to Athos, the pinnacle of Zeus;
Up, up it soared, luring the dancing fish
"To break surface in rapture at the light;
A golden courier, like the sun, it sped
Post-haste its message to Macistus, thence
Across Euripus, till the flaming sign
Was marked by the watchers on Messapium,   180
And thence with strength renewed from piles of heath
Like moonrise over the valley of Asopus,
Relayed in glory to Cithaeron's heights,
And still flashed on, not slow the sentinels,
Leaping across the lake from peak to peak,
It passed the word to burn and burn, and flung
A comet to the promontory that stands
Over the Gulf of Saron, there it swooped
Down to the Spider's Crag above the city,
Then found its mark on the roof of this house of Atreus,   190
That beacon fathered by Ida's far-off fires.
Such were the stages of our torch relay,
And the last to run is the first to reach the goal.

That is my evidence, the testimony which
My lord has signaled to me out of Troy.

Chorus
Lady, there will be time later to thank the Gods.
Now I ask only to listen: speak on and on.

Clytemnestra
Today the Greeks have occupied Troy.
I seem to hear there a very strange street-music.
Pour oil and vinegar into one cup, you will see   200
They do not make friends. So there two tunes are heard.
Slaves now, the Trojans, brothers and aged fathers,
Prostrate, sing for their dearest the last dirge.
The others, tired out and famished after the night's looting,
Grab what meal chance provides, lodgers now
In Trojan houses, sheltered from the night frosts,
From the damp dews delivered, free to sleep
Off guard, off duty, a blissful night's repose.
Therefore, provided that they show due respect
To the altars of the plundered town and are not   210
Tempted to lay coarse hands on sanctities,
Remembering that the last lap—the voyage home—
Lies still ahead of them, then, if they should return
Guiltless before God, the curses of the bereaved
Might be placated—barring accidents.
That is my announcement—a message from my master.
May all end well, and may I reap the fruit of it!

Chorus
Lady, you have spoken with a wise man's judgment.
Now it is time to address the gods once more
After this happy outcome of our cares.   220

Thanks be to Zeus and to gracious Night, housekeeper of heaven's embroidery,
who has cast over the towers of Troy a net so fine as to leave no escape for old
or young, all caught in the snare! All praise to Zeus, who with a shaft from his
outstretched bow has at last brought down the transgressor!

"By Zeus struck down!" The truth is all clear
With each step plainly marked. He said, Be
It so, and so it was. A man denied once
That heaven pays heed to those who trample
Beneath the feet holy sanctities. He lied wickedly;
For God's wrath soon or late destroys all sinners filled
With pride, puffed up with vain presumption,
And great men's houses stocked with silver
And gold beyond measure. Far best to live   230

Free of want, without grief, rich in the gift of wisdom.
Glutted with gold, the sinner kicks
Justice out of his sight, yet
She sees him and remembers.

As sweet temptation lures him onwards
With childlike smile into the death-trap,
He cannot help himself. His curse is lit up
Against the darkness, a bright baleful light.
And just as false bronze in battle hammered turns black and shows
Its true worth, so the sinner time-tired stands condemned.   240
His hopes take wing, and still he gives chase, with foul crimes branding all his
    people.
He cries to deaf heaven, none hear his prayers.
Justice drags him down to hell as he calls for succor.
Such was the sinner Paris, who
Rendered thanks to a gracious
Host by stealing a woman.

She left behind her the ports all astir
With throngs of men under arms filing onto shipboard;
She took to Troy in lieu of dowry death.
A light foot passed through the gates and fled,   250
And then a cry of lamentation rose.
The seers, the king's prophets, muttered darkly:
"Bewail the king's house that now is desolate,
Bewail the bed marked with print of love that fled!"
Behold, in silence, without praise, without reproach,
They sit upon the ground and weep.
Beyond the wave lies their love;
Here a ghost seems to rule the palace!
Shapely the grace of statues,
Yet they can bring no comfort,   260
Eyeless, lifeless and loveless.

Delusive dream shapes that float through the night
Beguile him, bringing delight sweet but unsubstantial;
For, while the eye beholds the heart's desire,
The arms clasp empty air, and then
The fleeting vision fades and glides away
On silent wing down the paths of slumber.
The royal hearth is chilled with sorrows such as these,
And more; in each house from end to end of Greece
That sent its dearest to wage war in foreign lands   270
The stout heart is called to steel itself
In mute endurance against
Blows that strike deep into the heart's core:

Those that they sent from home they
Knew, but now they receive back
Only a heap of ashes.

The God of War holds the twin scales of strife,
Heartless gold-changer trafficking in men,
Consigning homeward from Troy a jar of dust fire-refined,
Making up the weight with grief,   280
Shapely vessels laden each
With the ashes of their kin.
They mourn and praise them saying, "He
Was practiced well in sword and spear,
And he, who fell so gallantly—
All to avenge another man's wife":
It is muttered in a whisper
And resentment spreads against each of the royal warlords.
They lie sleeping, perpetual
Owners each of a small   290
Holding far from their homeland.

The sullen rumors that pass mouth to mouth
Bring the same danger as a people's curse,
And brooding hearts wait to hear of what the night holds from sight.
Watchful are the Gods of all
Hands with slaughter stained. The black
Furies wait, and when a man
Has grown by luck, not justice, great,
With sudden turn of circumstance
He wastes away to nothing, dragged   300
Down to be food in hell for demons.
For the heights of fame are perilous.
With a jealous bolt the Lord Zeus in a flash shall blast them.
Best to pray for a tranquil
Span of life and to be
Neither victor nor vanquished.

—The news has set the whole town aflame.
Can it be true? Perhaps it is a trick.
—Only a child would let such fiery words
Kindle his hopes, then fade and flicker out.   310
—It is just like a woman
To accept good news without the evidence.
—An old wives' tale, winged with a woman's wishes,
Spreads like wildfire, then sinks and is forgotten.

We shall soon know what the beacon signifies,
Whether it is true or whether this joyful daybreak
Is only a dream sent to deceive us all.

Here comes a messenger breathless from the shore,
Wearing a garland and covered in a cloud
Of dust, which shows that he has news to tell,   320
And not in soaring rhetoric of smoke and flame,
But either he brings cause for yet greater joy,
Or else,—no, let us abjure the alternative.
Glad shone the light, as gladly breaks the day!
[Enter HERALD.*]*

Herald
O joy! Argos, I greet you, my fatherland!
Joy brings me home after ten years of war.
Many the shattered hopes, but this has held.
Now I can say that when I die my bones
Will lie at rest here in my native soil.
I greet you joyfully, I greet the Sun,   330
Zeus the All-Highest, and the Pythian King,
Bending no more against us his fatal shafts,
As he did beside Scamander—that was enough,
And now defend us, Savior Apollo; all
The Gods I greet, among them Hermes, too,
Patron of messengers, and the spirits of our dead,
Who sent their sons forth, may they now prepare
A joyful welcome for those whom war has spared.
Joy to the palace and to these images
Whose faces catch the sun, now, as of old,   340
With radiant smiles greet your sovran lord,
Agamemnon, who brings a lamp to lighten you
And all here present, after having leveled
Troy with the mattock of just-dealing Zeus,
Great son of Atreus, master and monarch, blest
Above all living men. The brigand Paris
Has lost his booty and brought down the house of Priam.

Chorus
Joy to you, Herald, welcome home again!

Herald
Let me die, having lived to see this day!

Chorus
Your yearning for your country has worn you out.   350

Herald
So much that tears spring to the eyes for joy.

Chorus
Well, those you longed for longed equally for you.

Herald
Ah yes, our loved ones longed for our safe return.

Chorus
We have had many anxieties here at home.

Herald
What do you mean? Has there been disaffection?

Chorus
Never mind now. Say nothing and cure all.

Herald
Is it possible there was trouble in our absence?

Chorus
Now, as you said yourself, it would be a joy to die.

Herald
Yes, all has ended well. Our expedition
Has been successfully concluded, even though in part   360
The issue may be found wanting. Only the Gods
Prosper in everything. If I should tell you all
That we endured on shipboard in the night watches,
Our lodging the bare benches, and even worse
Ashore beneath the walls of Troy, the rains
From heaven and the dews that seeped
Out of the soil into lice-infested blankets;
If I should tell of those winters, when the birds
Dropped dead and Ida heaped on us her snows;
Those summers, when unruffled by wind or wave   370
The sea slept breathless under the glare of noon—
But why recall that now? It is all past,
Yes, for the dead past never to stir again.
Ah, they are all gone. Why count our losses? Why
Should we vex the living with grievance for the dead?
Goodbye to all that for us who have come back!
Victory has turned the scale, and so before
This rising sun let the good news be proclaimed
And carried all over the world on wings of fame:
"These spoils were brought by the conquerors of Troy   380
And dedicated to the Gods of Greece."
And praise to our country and to Zeus the giver
And thanks be given. That is all my news.
[CLYTEMNESTRA *appears at the palace door.*]

Chorus
Thank God that I have lived to see this day!
This news concerns all, and most of all the queen.

Clytemnestra
I raised my alleluia hours ago,
When the first messenger lit up the night,
And people mocked me saying, "Has a beacon
Persuaded you that the Greeks have captured Troy?
Truly a woman's hopes are lighter than air."   390
But I still sacrificed, and at a hundred
Shrines throughout the town the women chanted
Their endless alleluias on and on,
Singing to sleep the sacramental flames,
And now what confirmation do I need from you?
I wait to hear all from my lord, for whom
A welcome is long ready. What day is so sweet
In a woman's life as when she opens the door
To her beloved, safe home from war? Go and tell him
That he will find, guarding his property,   400
A wife as loyal as he left her, one
Who in all these years has kept his treasuries sealed,
Unkind only to enemies, and knows no more
Of other men's company than of tempering steel.
[Exit.]

Herald
Such a protestation, even though entirely true,
Is it not unseemly on a lady's lips?

Chorus
Such is her message, as you understand,
Full of fine phrases plain to those who know.
But tell us now, what news have you of the king's
Co-regent, Menelaus? Is he too home again?   410

Herald
Lies cannot last, even though sweet to hear.

Chorus
Can you not make your news both sweet and true?

Herald
He and his ships have vanished. They are missing.

Chorus
What, was it a storm that struck the fleet at sea?

Herald
You have told a long disaster in a word.

Chorus
Has no one news whether he is alive or dead?

Herald
Only the Sun, from whom the whole earth draws life.

Chorus
Tell us about the storm. How did it fall?

Herald
A day of national rejoicing must not be marred
By any jarring tongue. A messenger who comes   420
With black looks bringing the long prayed-against
Report of total rout, which both afflicts
The state in general and in every household leaves
The inmates prostrate under the scourge of war—
With such a load upon his lips he may fitly
Sing anthems to the Furies down in hell;
But when he greets a prospering people with
News of the war's victorious end—how then
Shall I mix foul with fair and find words to tell you
Of the blow that struck us out of that angry heaven?   430
     Water and Fire, those age-old enemies,
Made common cause against the homebound fleet.
Darkness had fallen, and a northerly gale
Blew up and in a blinding thunderstorm
Our ships were tossed and buffeted hull against hull
In a wild stampede and herded out of sight;
Then, at daybreak, we saw the Aegean in blossom
With a waving crop of corpses and scattered timbers.
Our ship came through, saved by some spirit, it seems,
Who took the helm and piloted her, until   440
She slipped under the cliffs into a cove.
There, safe at last, incredulous of our luck,
We brooded all day, stunned by the night's disaster.
And so, if any of the others have survived,
They must be speaking of us as dead and gone.
May all yet end well! Though it is most to be expected
That Menelaus is in some great distress,
Yet, should some shaft of sunlight spy him out
Somewhere among the living, rescued by Zeus,
Lest the whole house should perish, there is hope   450
That he may yet come home. There you have the truth.

Chorus
Tell us who invented that
Name so deadly accurate?
Was it one who presaging
Things to come divined a word
Deftly tuned to destiny?
Helen—hell indeed she carried

To men, to ships, to a proud city, stealing
From the silk veils of her chamber, sailing seaward
With the Zephyr's breath behind her;   460
And they set forth in a thousand ships to hunt her
On the path that leaves no imprint,
Bringers of endless bloodshed.

So, as Fate decreed, in Troy,
Turning into keeners kin,
Furies, instruments of God's
Wrath, at last demanded full
Payment for the stolen wife;
And the wedding song that rang out
To greet the bride from beyond the broad Aegean   470
Was in time turned into howls of imprecation
From the countless women wailing
For the loved ones they had lost in war for her sake,
And they curse the day they gave that
Welcome to war and bloodshed.

An old story is told of an oxherd who reared at his hearth a lion-cub, a pet for
    his children,
Pampered fondly by young and old with dainty morsels begged at each meal
    from his master's table.

But Time showed him up in his true nature after his kind—a beast savaging
    sheep and oxen,
Mad for the taste of blood, and only then they knew what they had long
    nursed was a curse from heaven.

And so it seemed then there came to rest in Troy   480
A sweet-smiling calm, a clear sky, seductive,
A rare pearl set in gold and silver,
Shaft of love from a glancing eye.
She is seen now as an agent
Of death sent from Zeus, a Fury
Demanding a bloody bride-price.
[Enter CLYTEMNESTRA.*]*
From ancient times people have believed that when
A man's wealth has come to full growth it breeds
And brings forth tares and tears in plenty.
No, I say, it is only wicked deeds   490
That increase, fruitful in evil.
The house built on justice always
Is blest with a happy offspring.

And yet the pride bred of wealth often burgeons anew
In evil times, a cloud of deep night,
Spectre of ancient crimes that still

Walks within the palace walls,
True to the dam that bore it.

But where is Justice? She lights up the smoke-darkened hut.
From mansions built by hands polluted   500
Turning to greet the pure in heart,
Proof against false praise, she guides
All to its consummation.

[*Enter* AGAMEMNON *in a chariot followed by another chariot carrying* CASSANDRA
and spoils of war.]

Agamemnon, conqueror, joy to our king! How shall my greeting neither fall
short nor shoot too high? Some men feign rejoicing or sorrow with hearts untouched; but those who can read man's nature in the book of the eyes will not
be deceived by dissembled fidelity. I declare that, when you left these shores
ten years ago to recover with thousands of lives one woman, who eloped of her
own free will, I deemed your judgment misguided; but now in all sincerity I
salute you with joy. Toil happily ended brings pleasure at last, and in time you
shall learn to distinguish the just from the unjust steward.

Agamemnon
First, it is just that I should pay my respects
To the land of Argos and her presiding Gods,
My partners in this homecoming as also
In the just penalty which I have inflicted on
The city of Troy. When the supreme court of heaven
Adjudicated on our cause, they cast   510
Their votes unanimously against her, though not
Immediately, and so on the other side
Hope hovered hesitantly before it vanished.
The fires of pillage are still burning there
Like sacrificial offerings. Her ashes
Redolent with riches breathe their last and die.
For all this it is our duty to render thanks
To the celestial powers, with whose assistance
We have exacted payment and struck down
A city for one woman, forcing our entry   520
Within the Wooden Horse, which at the setting
Of the Pleiads like a hungry lion leapt
Out and slaked its thirst in royal blood.
As to your sentiments, I take due note
And find that they accord with mine. Too few
Rejoice at a friend's good fortune. I have known
Many dissemblers swearing false allegiance.
One only, though he joined me against his will,
Once in the harness, proved himself a staunch
Support, Odysseus, be he now alive or dead.   530
All public questions and such as concern the Gods

I shall discuss in council and take steps
To make this triumph lasting; and if here or there
Some malady comes to light, appropriate
Remedies will be applied to set it right.
Meanwhile, returning to my royal palace,
My first duty is to salute the Gods
Who led me overseas and home again.
Victory attends me; may she remain with me!

Clytemnestra
Citizens of Argos, councillors and elders,   540
I shall declare without shame in your presence
My feelings for my husband. Diffidence
Dies in us all with time. I shall speak of what
I suffered here, while he was away at the war,
Sitting at home, with no man's company,
Waiting for news, listening to one
Messenger after another, each bringing worse
Disasters. If all his rumored wounds were real,
His body was in shreds, shot through and through.
If he had died—the predominant report—   550
He was a second Geryon, an outstretched giant
With three corpses and one death for each,
While I, distraught, with a knot pressing my throat,
Was rescued forcibly, to endure still more.
    And that is why our child is not present here,
As he should be, pledge of our marriage vows,
Orestes. Let me reassure you. He lives
Safe with an old friend, Strophius, who warned me
Of various dangers—your life at stake in Troy
And here a restive populace, which might perhaps   560
Be urged to kick a man when he is down.
    As for myself, the fountains of my tears
Have long ago run dry. My eyes are sore
After so many nights watching the lamp
That burnt at my bedside always for you.
If I should sleep, a gnat's faint whine would shatter
The dreams that were my only company.
    But now, all pain endured, all sorrow past,
I salute this man as the watchdog of the fold,
The stay that saves the ship, the sturdy oak   570
That holds the roof up, the longed-for only child,
The shore despaired-of sighted far out at sea.
God keep us from all harm! And now, dearest,
Dismount, but not on the bare ground! Servants,
Spread out beneath those feet that have trampled Troy
A road of royal purple, which shall lead him

By the hand of Justice into a home unhoped-for,
And there, when he has entered, our vigilant care
Shall dispose of everything as the Gods have ordained.

Agamemnon
Lady, royal consort and guardian of our home,   580
I thank you for your words of welcome, extended
To fit my lengthy absence; but due praise
Should rather come from others; and besides,
I would not have effeminate graces unman me
With barbarous salaams and beneath my feet
Purple embroideries designed for sacred use.
Honor me as a mortal, not as a god.
Heaven's greatest gift is wisdom. Count him blest
Who has brought a long life to a happy end.
I shall do as I have said, with a clear conscience.   590

Clytemnestra
Yet tell me frankly, according to your judgment.

Agamemnon
My judgment stands. Make no mistake about that.

Clytemnestra
Would you not in time of danger have vowed such an act?

Agamemnon
Yes, if the priests had recommended it.

Clytemnestra
And what would Priam have done, if he had won?

Agamemnon
Oh, he would have trod the purple without a doubt.

Clytemnestra
Then you have nothing to fear from wagging tongues.

Agamemnon
Popular censure is a potent force.

Clytemnestra
Men must risk envy in order to be admired.

Agamemnon
A contentious spirit is unseemly in a woman.   600

Clytemnestra
Well may the victor yield a victory.

Agamemnon
Do you set so much store by your victory?

Clytemnestra
Be tempted, freely vanquished, victor still!

Agamemnon
Well, if you will have it, let someone unlace
These shoes, and, as I tread the purple, may
No far-off god cast at me an envious glance
At the prodigal desecration of all this wealth!
Meanwhile, extend your welcome to this stranger.
Power tempered with gentleness wins God's favor.
No one is glad to be enslaved, and she   610
Is a princess presented to me by the army,
The choicest flower culled from a host of captives.
And now, constrained to obey you, setting foot
On the sacred purple, I pass into my home.

Clytemnestra
The sea is still there, nothing can dry it up,
Renewing out of its infinite abundance
Unfailing streams of purple and blood-red dyes.
So too this house, the Gods be praised, my lord,
Has riches inexhaustible. There is no counting
The robes *I* would have vowed to trample on,   620
Had some oracle so instructed, if by such means
I could have made good the loss of one dear soul.
So now your entry to your hearth and home
Is like a warm spell in the long winter's cold,
Or when Zeus from the virgin grape at last
Draws wine, coolness descends upon the house
(For then from the living root the new leaves raise
A welcome shelter against the burning Dog-Star)
As man made perfect moves about his home.
[Exit AGAMEMNON.*]*
Zeus, perfecter of all things, fulfil my prayers   630
And fulfil also your own purposes!
[Exit.]

Chorus
What is this delirious dread,
Ominous, oracular,
Droning through my brain with unrelenting
Beat, irrepressible prophet of evil?
Why can I not cast it out
Planting good courage firm
On my spirit's empty throne?
In time the day came
When the Greeks with anchors plunged   640
Moored the sloops of war, and troops
Thronged the sandy beach of Troy.

So today my eyes have seen
Safe at last the men come home.
Still I hear the strain of stringless music,
Dirge of the Furies, a choir uninvited
Chanting in my heart of hearts.
Mortal souls stirred by God
In tune with fate divine the shape
Of things to come; yet   650
Grant that these forebodings prove
False and bring my fears to naught.

If a man's health be advanced over the due mean,
It will trespass soon upon sickness, who stands
Next neighbor, between them a thin wall.
So does the vessel of life
Launched with a favoring breeze
Suddenly founder on reefs of destruction.
Caution seated at the helm
Casts a portion of the freight   660
Overboard with measured throw;
So the ship may ride the storm.
Furrows enriched each season with showers from heaven
Banish hunger from the door.
But if the red blood of a man spatters the ground, dripping and deadly, then who
Has the magical power to recall it?
Even the healer who knew
Spells to awaken the dead,
Zeus put an end to his necromancy.
Portions are there preordained,   670
Each supreme within its own
Province fixed eternally.
That is why my spirit groans
Brooding in fear, and no longer it hopes to unravel
Mazes of a fevered mind.
[Enter CLYTEMNESTRA]

Clytemnestra
You, too, Cassandra, come inside! The merciful
Zeus gives you the privilege to take part
In our domestic sacrifice and stand
Before his altar among the other slaves there.
Put by your pride and step down. Even Heracles   680
Submitted once to slavery, and be consoled
In serving a house whose wealth has been inherited
Over so many generations. The harshest masters
Are those who have snatched their harvest out of hand.
You shall receive here what custom prescribes.

Chorus
She is speaking to you. Caught in the net, surrender.

Clytemnestra
If she knows Greek and not some barbarous language,
My mystic words shall fill the soul within her.

Chorus
You have no choice. Step down and do her will.

Clytemnestra
There is no time to waste. The victims are   690
All ready for the knife to render thanks
For this unhoped-for joy. If you wish to take part,
Make haste, but, if you lack the sense to understand,—
[To the CHORUS.*]*
Speak to her with your hands and drag her down.

Chorus
She is like a wild animal just trapped.

Clytemnestra
She is mad, the foolish girl. Her city captured,
Brought here a slave, she will be broken in.
I'll waste no words on her to demean myself.
[Exit.]

Cassandra
Oh! oh! Apollo!

Chorus
What blasphemy, to wail in Apollo's name!   700

Cassandra
Oh! oh! Apollo!

Chorus
Again she cries in grief to the god of joy!

Cassandra
Apollo, my destroyer! a second time!

Chorus
Ah, she foresees what is in store for her.
She is now a slave, and yet God's gift remains.

Cassandra
Apollo, my destroyer! What house is this?

Chorus
Do you not know where you have come, poor girl?
Then let us tell you. This is the House of Atreus.

Cassandra

Yes, for its very walls smell of iniquity,
A charnel house that drips with children's blood.   710

Chorus

How keen her scent to seize upon the trail!

Cassandra

Listen to them as they bewail the foul
Repast of roast meat for a father's mouth!

Chorus

Enough! Reveal no more! We know it all.

Cassandra

What is it plotted next? Horror unspeakable,
A hard cross for kinsfolk.
The hoped-for savior is far away.

Chorus

What does she say? This must be something new.

Cassandra

Can it be so—to bathe one who is travel-tired,
And then smiling stretch out   720
A hand followed by a stealthy hand!

Chorus

She speaks in riddles, and I cannot read them.

Cassandra

What do I see? A net!
Yes, it is she, his mate and murderess!
Cry alleluia, cry, angels of hell, rejoice,
Fat with blood, dance and sing!

Chorus

What is the Fury you have called upon?
Helpless the heart faints with the sinking sun.
Closer still draws the stroke.

Cassandra

Ah, let the bull beware!   730
It is a robe she wraps him in, and strikes!
Into the bath he slumps heavily, drowned in blood.
Such her skilled handicraft.

Chorus

It is not hard to read her meaning now.
Why does the prophet's voice never have good to tell,
Only cry woes to come?

Cassandra
Oh, pitiful destiny! Having lamented his,
Now I lament my own passion to fill the bowl.
Where have you brought me? Must I with him die?

Chorus
You sing your own dirge, like the red-brown bird   740
That pours out her grief-stricken soul,
Itys, Itys! she cries, the sad nightingale.

Cassandra
It is not so; for she, having become a bird,
Forgot her tears and sings her happy lot,
While I must face the stroke of two-edged steel.

Chorus
From whence does this cascade of harsh discords
Issue, and where will it at last be calmed?
Calamity you cry—O where must it end?

Cassandra
O wedding day, Paris accurst of all!
Scamander, whose clear waters I grew beside!   750
Now I must walk weeping by Acheron.

Chorus
Even a child could understand.
The heart breaks, as these pitiful cries
Shatter the listening soul.

Cassandra
O fall of Troy, city of Troy destroyed!
The king's rich gifts little availed her so
That she might not have been what she is now.

Chorus
What evil spirit has possessed
Your soul, strumming such music upon your lips
As on a harp in hell?   760

Cassandra
Listen! My prophecy shall glance no longer
As through a veil like a bride newly-wed,
But bursting towards the sunrise shall engulf
The whole world in calamities far greater
Than these. No more riddles, I shall instruct,
While you shall verify each step, as I
Nose out from the beginning this bloody trail.
Upon this roof—do you see them?—stands a choir—
It has been there for generations—a gallery

Of unmelodious minstrels, a merry troop   770
Of wassailers drunk with human blood, reeling
And retching in horror at a brother's outraged bed.
Well, have I missed? Am I not well-read in
Your royal family's catalogue of crime?

Chorus
You come from a far country and recite
Our ancient annals as though you had been present.

Cassandra
The Lord Apollo bestowed this gift on me.

Chorus
Was it because he had fallen in love with you?

Cassandra
I was ashamed to speak of this till now.

Chorus
Ah yes, adversity is less fastidious.   780

Cassandra
Oh, but he wrestled strenuously for my love.

Chorus
Did you come, then, to the act of getting child?

Cassandra
At first I consented, and then I cheated him.

Chorus
Already filled with his gift of prophecy?

Cassandra
Yes, I forewarned my people of their destiny.

Chorus
Did your divine lover show no displeasure?

Cassandra
Yes, the price I paid was that no one listened to me.

Chorus
Your prophecies seem credible enough to us.

Cassandra
Oh!
Again the travail of the prophetic trance   790
Runs riot in my soul. Do you not see them
There, on the roof, those apparitions—children
Murdered by their own kin, in their hands

The innards of which their father ate—oh
What a pitiable load they carry! For that crime
Revenge is plotted by the fainthearted lion,
The stay-at-home, stretched in my master's bed
(Being his slave, I must needs call him so),
Lying in wait for Troy's great conqueror.
Little he knows what that foul bitch with ears   800
Laid back and rolling tongue intends for him
With a vicious snap, her husband's murderess.
What abominable monster shall I call her—
A two-faced amphisbaene or Scylla that skulks
Among the rocks to waylay mariners,
Infernal sea-squib locked in internecine
Strife—did you not hear her alleluias
Of false rejoicing at his safe return?
Believe me or not, what must be will be, and then   810
You will pity me and say, She spoke the truth.

Chorus
The feast of Thyestes I recognized, and shuddered,
But for the rest my wits are still astray.

Cassandra
Your eyes shall see the death of Agamemnon.

Chorus
No, hush those ill-omened lips, unhappy girl!

Cassandra
There is no Apollo present, and so no cure.

Chorus
None, if you speak the truth; yet God forbid!

Cassandra
Pray God forbid, while they close in for the kill!

Chorus
What man is there who would plot so foul a crime?

Cassandra
Ah, you have altogether misunderstood.

Chorus
But how will he do it? That escapes me still.   820

Cassandra
And yet I can speak Greek only too well.

Chorus
So does Apollo, but his oracles are obscure.

Cassandra

Ah, how it burns me up! Apollo! Now
That lioness on two feet pours in the cup
My wages too, and while she whets the blade
For him promises to repay my passage money
In my own blood. Why wear these mockeries,
This staff and wreath, if I must die, then you
Shall perish first and be damned. Now we are quits!
Apollo himself has stripped me, looking upon me   830
A public laughingstock, who has endured
The name of witch, waif, beggar, castaway,
So now the god who gave me second sight
Takes back his gift and dismisses his servant,
Ready for the slaughter at a dead man's grave.
Yet we shall be avenged. Now far away,
The exile shall return, called by his father's
Unburied corpse to come and kill his mother.
Why weep at all this? Have I not seen Troy fall,
And those who conquered her are thus discharged.   840
I name this door the gate of Hades: now
I will go and knock, I will take heart to die.
I only pray that the blow may be mortal,
Closing these eyes in sleep without a struggle,
While my life blood ebbs quietly away.

Chorus

O woman, in whose wisdom is so much grief,
How, if you know the end, can you approach it
So gently, like an ox that goes to the slaughter?

Cassandra

What help would it be if I should put it off?

Chorus

Yet, while there is life there's hope—so people say.   850

Cassandra

For me no hope, no help. My hour has come.

Chorus

You face your end with a courageous heart.

Cassandra

Yes, so they console those whom life has crossed.

Chorus

Is there no comfort in an honorable death?

Cassandra

O Priam, father, and all your noble sons!
[She approaches the door, then draws back.]

Chorus
What is it? Why do you turn back, sick at heart?

Cassandra
Inside there is a stench of dripping blood.

Chorus
It is only the blood of their fireside sacrifice.

Cassandra
It is the sort of vapor that issues from a tomb.
I will go now and finish my lament   860
Inside the house. Enough of life! O friends!
I am not scared. I beg of you only this:
When the day comes for them to die, a man
For a man, woman for woman, remember me!

Chorus
Poor soul condemned to death, I pity you.

Cassandra
Yet one word more, my own dirge for myself.
I pray the Sun, on whom I now look my last,
That he may grant to my master's avengers
A fair price for the slave-girl slain at his side.
O sad mortality! when fortune smiles,   870
A painted image; and when trouble comes,
One touch of a wet sponge wipes it away.
[Exit.]

Chorus
And her case is even more pitiable than his.
Human prosperity never rests but always craves more, till blown up with pride
it totters and falls. From the opulent mansions pointed at by all passersby none
warns it away, none cries, "Let no more riches enter!" To him was granted the
capture of Troy, and he has entered his home as a god, but now, if the blood of
the past is on him, if he must pay with his own death for the crimes of bygone
generations, then who is assured of a life without sorrow?

Agamemnon
Oh me!

Chorus
Did you hear?

Agamemnon
Oh me, again!

Chorus
It is the King. Let us take counsel!
　1　I say, raise a hue and cry!
　2　Break in at once!   880

3 Yes, we must act.
4 *They* spurn delay.
5 They plot a tyranny.
6 Must we live their slaves?
7 Better to die.
8 Old men, what can we do?
9 We cannot raise the dead.
10 His death is not yet proved.
11 We are only guessing.
12 Let us break in and learn the truth!   890

[The doors are thrown open, and CLYTEMNESTRA *is seen standing over the bodies of* AGAMEMNON *and* CASSANDRA, *which are laid out on a purple robe.]*

Clytemnestra
All that I said before to bide my time
Without any shame I shall now unsay. How else
Could I have plotted against an enemy
So near and seeming dear and strung the snare
So high that he could not jump it? Now the feud
On which I have pondered all these years has been
Fought out to its conclusion. Here I stand
Over my work, and it was so contrived
As to leave no loophole. With this vast dragnet
I enveloped him in purple folds, then struck   900
Twice, and with two groans he stretched his legs,
Then on his outspread body I struck a third blow,
A drink for Zeus the Deliverer of the dead.
There he lay gasping out his soul and drenched me
In these deathly dew-drops, at which I cried
In sheer delight like newly-budding corn
That tastes the first spring showers. And so,
Venerable elders, you see how the matter stands.
Rejoice, if you are so minded. I glory in it.
With bitter tears he filled the household bowl;   910
Now he has drained it to the dregs and gone.

Chorus
How can you speak so of your murdered king?

Clytemnestra
You treat me like an empty-headed woman.
Again, undaunted, to such as understand
I say—commend or censure, as you please—
It makes no difference—here is Agamemnon,
My husband, dead, the work of this right hand,
Which acted justly. There you have the truth.

Chorus
Woman, what evil brew have you devoured to take

On you a crime that cries out for a public curse?   920
Yours was the fatal blow, banishment shall be yours,
Hissed and hated of all men.

Clytemnestra
Your sentence now for me is banishment,
But what did you do then to contravene
His purpose, when, to exorcise the storms,
As though picking a ewe-lamb from his flocks,
Whose wealth of snowy fleeces never fails
To increase and multiply, he killed his own
Child, born to me in pain, my best-beloved?
Why did you not drive *him* from hearth and home?   930
I bid you cast at me such menaces
As make for mastery in equal combat
With one prepared to meet them, and if, please God,
The issue goes against you, suffering
Shall school those grey hairs in humility.

Chorus
You are possessed by some spirit of sin that stares
Our of your bloodshot eyes matching your bloody hands.
Dishonored and deserted of your kin, for this
Stroke you too shall be struck down.

Clytemnestra
Listen! By Justice, who avenged my child,   940
By the Fury to whom I vowed this sacrament,
No thought of fear shall enter through this door
So long as the hearth within is kindled by
Aegisthus, faithful to me now as always.
Low lies the man who insulted his wedded wife,
The darling of the Chryseids at Troy,
And stretched beside him this visionary seer,
Whom he fondled on shipboard, both now rewarded,
He as you see, and she swanlike has sung
Her dying ditty, his tasty side dish, for me   950
A rare spice to add relish to my joy.

Chorus
Oh, for the gift of death
To bring the long sleep that knows no waking,
Now that my lord and loyal protector
Breathes his last. For woman's sake
Long he fought overseas,
Now at home falls beneath a woman's hand.
    Helen, the folly-beguiled, having ravaged the city of Troy,
    She has set on the curse of Atreus
    A crown of blood beyond ablution.   960

Clytemnestra

Do not pray for death nor turn your anger against one woman as the slayer of
   thousands!

Chorus

Demon of blood and tears
Inbred in two women single-hearted!
Perched on the roof he stands and preens his
Sable wings, a carrion-crow.
Loud he croaks, looking down
Upon the feast spread before him here below.

Clytemnestra

Ah now you speak truth, naming the thrice-fed demon, who, glutted with
   blood, craves more, still young in his hunger.

Chorus

When will the feast be done?
Alas, it is the will of Zeus,   970
Who caused and brought it all to pass.
Nothing is here but was decreed in heaven.

Clytemnestra

It was not my doing, nor am I Agamemnon's wife, but a ghost in woman's
   guise, the shade of the banqueter whom Atreus fed.

Chorus

How is the guilt not yours?
And yet the crimes of old may well
Have had a hand, and so it drives
On, the trail of internecine murder.

Clytemnestra

What of *him?* Was the guilt not his, when he killed the child that I bore him?
   And so by the sword he has fallen.

Chorus

Alas, the mind strays. The house is falling.
A storm of blood lays the walls in ruins.   980
Another mortal stroke for Justice' hand
Will soon be sharpened.
   Oh me, who shall bury him, who sing the dirge?
   Who shall intone at the tomb of a blessed spirit
   A tribute pure in heart and truthful?

Clytemnestra

No, I'll bury him, but without mourners. By the waters of Acheron Iphigenia
   is waiting for him with a kiss.

Chorus

The charge is answered with countercharges.

The sinner must suffer: such is God's will.
The ancient curse is bringing down the house
In self-destruction. 990

Clytemnestra
That is the truth, and I would be content that the spirit of vengeance should
    rest, having absolved the house from its madness.
[Enter AEGISTHUS *with a bodyguard.]*

Aegisthus
Now I have proof that there are Gods in heaven,
As I gaze on this purple mesh in which
My enemy lies, son of a treacherous father.
His father, Atreus, monarch of this realm,
Was challenged in his sovran rights by mine,
Thyestes, his own brother, and banished him
From hearth and home. Later he returned
A suppliant and found sanctuary, indeed
A welcome; for his brother entertained him 1000
To a feast of his own children's flesh, of which
My father unsuspecting took and ate.
Then, when he knew what he had done, he fell
Back spewing out the slaughtered flesh and, kicking
The table to the floor, with a loud cry
He cursed the House of Pelops. That is the crime
For which the son lies here. And fitly too
The plot was spun by me; for as a child
I was banished with my father, until Justice
Summoned me home. Now let me die, for never 1010
Shall I live to see another sight so sweet.

Chorus
Aegisthus, if it was you who planned this murder,
Then be assured, the people will stone you for it.

Aegisthus
Such talk from the lower benches! Even in dotage
Prison can teach a salutary lesson.
Better submit, or else you shall smart for it.

Chorus
You woman, who stayed at home and wallowed in
His bed, you plotted our great commander's death!

Aegisthus
Orpheus led all in rapture after him.
Your senseless bark will be snuffed out in prison. 1020

Chorus
You say the plot was yours, yet lacked the courage
To raise a hand but left it to a woman!

Aegisthus
As his old enemy, I was suspect.
Temptation was the woman's part. But now
I'll try my hand at monarchy, and all
Who disobey me shall be put in irons
And starved of food and light till they submit.

Chorus
Oh, if Orestes yet beholds the sun,
May he come home and execute them both!

Aegisthus
Ho, my guards, come forward, you have work to do.   1030

Captain of the Guard
Stand by, draw your swords!

Chorus
We are not afraid to die.

Aegisthus
Die! We'll take you at your word.

Clytemnestra
Peace, my lord, and let no further wrong be done.
Captain, sheathe your swords. And you, old men,
Go home quietly. What has been, it had to be.
Scars enough we bear, now let us rest.

Aegisthus
Must I stand and listen to their threats?

Chorus
Men of Argos never cringed before a rogue.

Aegisthus
I shall overtake you yet—the day is near.   1040

Chorus
Not if Orestes should come home again.

Aegisthus
Vain hope, the only food of castaways.

Chorus
Gloat and grow fat, blacken justice while you dare!

Aegisthus
All this foolish talk will cost you dear.

Chorus

Flaunt your gaudy plumes and strut beside your hen!

Clytemnestra

Pay no heed to idle clamor. You and I,
Masters of the house, shall now direct it well.

LIBATION-BEARERS

Aeschylus

CHARACTERS

ORESTES *[son of Agamemnon and Clytemnestra]*

CHORUS *[captive slave women who carry libations (religious drink offerings) to Agamemnon's tomb]*

SERVANT

CLYTEMNESTRA *[Orestes' mother and queen of Argos]*

ELECTRA *[daughter of Agamemnon and Clytemnestra who aids her brother in his revenge]*

NURSE

AEGISTHUS *[Clytemnestra's lover and co-ruler of Argos]*

PYLADES *[Orestes' friend]*

[The *Libation-Bearers* opens several years after Agamemnon's murder when Orestes, disguised as a foreign peddler and accompanied by his friend Pylades, secretly returns to Argos. After revealing his identity to his sister Electra, who is also eager to avenge their father's death, Orestes arranges to lure Aegisthus and Clytemnestra into the palace, where—obeying Apollo's command—he will kill them. In the following scene, midway through the play, Orestes explains his intentions to the chorus of captive women, whose personal hatred of Clytemnestra causes them to support the royal siblings' plan to butcher their mother. Orestes tells the eager chorus exactly how he will lure Clytemnestra (the *"she"* to whom he refers in line 1) and Aegisthus to their deaths:]

. . . .

Orestes

It is soon told. First, *she* must go inside   1
To see that our enterprise is well concealed,
So that the couple whose cunning killed a king
Be caught by cunning, as Apollo has commanded.
Then I, with my true friend here, Pylades,
Disguised as travelers, shall approach the door
Speaking the Phocian dialect, and if no
Doorkeeper opens to us, since it is a house
Bewitched with sin, we will wait till the passersby
Take stock and say, "Where is Aegisthus? Why   10
Does he close his doors against these strangers?"—then,
Stepping across the threshold, if I find
That scoundrel seated on my father's throne,
Or if he should come to greet me, lifting up
To mine those eyes that shall soon be cast down,

608

Before he can ask, "Where is the stranger from?"
My steel shall strike, and so a Fury never
Starved shall drain a third great draught of blood.
And so to *you* I say, keep a close watch
[To ELECTRA.*]*
Inside the house, and to *you* I commend   20
[To the CHORUS.*]*
Silence in season and timeliness in speech.
The rest is for my comrade's eyes alone
To guide me in this ordeal of the sword.

Chorus
Fearful beasts bringing much
Harm to man breed on earth;
Monsters huge hid from sight lurk beneath
Smiling seas; and baleful lights sweeping through the vaulted skies
Swing suspended over all
Creatures that fly and that walk on the ground; and remember
How they rage, the stormy blasts.   30

Yet the deeds dared by man's
Forward spirit who shall tell?
Woman too, whose perverse loves contrive
Crimes of blood provoking bloodstained revenges, sin for sin.
Once a woman's lawless lust
Gains the supremacy, swiftly it brings to destruction
Wedded ties in beast and man.

Those who cannot grasp the truth, let them
Take thought touching that
Flash of torchlit treachery,   40
Which the black heart of Althaea plotted,
By whose hand the firebrand was burnt which
Dated back to the day her child
Cried as he issued from her
Womb, and measured his span of life
On to the death appointed.

No less wicked too was Scylla, whose
False heart foe-beguiled
Dared the death of dearest kin,
All for one necklace rare, wrought of fine gold,   50
A gift brought from Crete; hence in secret,
While in slumber her Nisus lay,
Ah, she shore his immortal
Locks—a pitiless heart was hers!
Hermes led him to darkness.

And since I call back to mind the wicked crimes
Of old . . . —To no purpose! *This* unhallowed, vile

Union, which the world abhors,
A wife's deceit framed against a warrior—
Have you no harsh words to censure that?   60
I praise the hearth where no fires of passion burn,
A meek heart such as graces woman.
—Of all the crimes told in tales the Lemnian
Is chief, a sin cried throughout the world with such
Horror that, if men relate
Some monstrous outrage, they call it Lemnian.
Abhorred of man, scorned of God,
Their seed is cast out for evermore;
For none respect what the Gods abominate.
Is *this* not well and justly spoken?   70

A sword of piercing steel is poised
To strike well home, which unerring Justice
Shall thrust to cleave the hearts of all
Those who trample underfoot
The sanctities
Of Zeus, to ungodly deeds inclining.

The tree of Justice shall not fall,
And Fate's strong hand forges steel to arm her.
There comes to wipe away with fresh
Blood the blood of old a son,   80
Obeying some
Inscrutable Fury's deadly purpose.
[Enter ORESTES, *and* PYLADES. *They go up to the door.]*

Orestes
Ho there! Ho! I call a third time: ho!
Let Aegisthus grant us hospitality!
[A SERVANT *comes to the door.]*

Servant
All right, I hear you. Where is the stranger from?

Orestes
Announce me to your masters. I bring them news.
Go quickly, for Night's chariot draws on
The hour for travelers to seek repose.
Let someone in authority come out,
A woman, or more properly a man;   90
For we can speak more freely man to man.
*[*CLYTEMNESTRA *comes to the door, attended by* ELECTRA.]*

Clytemnestra
Strangers, declare your wishes. Here you shall have
A welcome such as the house is noted for—
Warm baths and beds to ease the travel-tired

And the presence of an honest company;
But if you have in mind some graver matter,
That is man's business, and to men we shall impart it.

Orestes
I am a stranger from Phocis, and I have come
To Argos on an errand of my own;
But as I shod my feet to take the road,   100
A man came up to me whom I did not know—
Strophius the Phocian was his name, he said,—
"Stranger," he said to me, "if you are bound
For Argos, please inform the parents of
Orestes that their son is dead, and bring
An answer back, whether they wish to fetch
His body or leave it here duly lamented
And laid to rest an exile even in death."
That was the message. Whether I now address
One in authority and near to him   110
I do not know, but his parents should be told.

Electra
Oh, it is all over, all pitilessly destroyed!
O irresistible curse of our ancestors
So widely ranging! Even that which seemed
Safely disposed beyond the reach of harm
Has been brought down by an arrow from afar,
Leaving me desolate, stripped of all I loved.
And now Orestes—he who wisely resolved
To keep his foot outside the miry clay,
Now that one hope that might at last have purged   120
The house of wickedness, do not mark it as present.

Orestes
I could have wished, visiting such a house
On which God smiles, that happier news had made
Me known to you; for nothing brings such delight
As the gentle intercourse of host and stranger.
But I would have deemed it wrong not to fulfil
My solemn promise to those I love so dearly.

Clytemnestra
You shall be entertained as you deserve.
You are welcome notwithstanding; for, if you
Had not brought the news, others would have come.   130
Now it is time for you to be attended.
[*To* ELECTRA.]
Escort them in and wait upon their needs.
Do this, I tell you, as you shall answer for it.

Meanwhile I shall inform the master of
The house and shall consult all our friends
What should be done concerning this event.
[CLYTEMNESTRA, ELECTRA, ORESTES, *and* PYLADES *go into the palace.*]

Chorus
How soon shall our voices be lifted in praise of Orestes? O Earth, O Tomb,
   now is the time to strengthen his hand; let Hermes arise out of the darkness
   to look down on the contest!
[*The* NURSE *comes out of the palace.*]
It seems the stranger is already making mischief.
Here is Orestes' old nurse, bathed in tears.
What is it, Cilissa? What brings you to the gates? 140

Nurse
My mistress has commanded me to bring
Aegisthus to the strangers instantly,
That he may hear their message man from man.
Before the servants she affects a sorrowful
Demeanor, yet with a lurking smile
At news that makes her happy, and he too
Will now be overjoyed. What years of grief
Are locked up in this breast, which I have borne
Within these walls—old, mixed-up memories—
And now Orestes, who was entrusted to me 150
Out of his mother's arms—my dearest care—
And what a troublesome child he was!
For sure, like a dumb animal, a senseless babe
Must needs have a nurse's wits to nourish it.
A child in swaddling clothes cannot declare
His wants, that he would eat or drink or make
Water, nor will his belly wait upon
Attendance. Nurses must have second sight,
And even so they may be deceived, and then
Must wash the linen white—such was my task 160
Tending Orestes, his father's son and heir;
And now he is dead, they tell me, and I must take
The news to him whose wickedness infects
The house, and watch how it warms his heart.

Chorus
With what equipment did she bid him come?

Nurse
Equipment? How? I do not understand you.

Chorus
Attended by his retinue, or alone?

Nurse
He is told to bring his royal bodyguard.

Chorus
Then, as you hate him, not a word about that!
Tell him to come alone, and come at once,   170
Come and fear nothing and feed his happy heart.

Nurse
Can it be that you see some good in the report?

Chorus
Who knows but Zeus may yet turn an ill wind?

Nurse
How, if our last hope, Orestes, is gone?

Chorus
A good prophet would not read it so.

Nurse
Have you reason to doubt that the news is true?

Chorus
Go, take your message and do as you are told.
The Gods will care for what is their concern.

Nurse
I will go. God grant that all is for the best!

Chorus
Hear us, O Father Zeus, hear our prayer!   180
Grant that those win the day who would see
Lawlessness at last dethroned!
Nothing we ask but what is just: O Zeus, defend us!
   Let the champion who has gone in
   Be upheld now in the fray. Zeus, who has made him
   Great, shall take at will a twofold recompense and threefold.

Think of that lordly sire whose untried
Colt is now yoked and all set to run!
Lay a steady, guiding hand
Upon the rein until the breathless race is over!   190

Grant that he may grasp the great
Prize the Gods have kept for him
Here—his ancient heritage.
So with vengeance fresh redeem
The full debt of those ancestral crimes.
   Let us rejoice and set a crown on the palace!

O let it soon be revealed
Gleaming and friendly and free
Out of the veil of encircling darkness!
Hermes too shall lend a hand,   200
Named the keen and cunning one.
Much at will he can reveal.
Night he draws before the eyes
With voice veiled that none may understand.

Thus, with all done at last,
Music set to breezes fair,
Women's shrill songs of joy
Shall be heard, "All is well!"
Bringing peace to those we love.
And with stout heart, as she cries "Child!"   210
Let him cry "Father!" and kill her!

May his heart turn to stone,
Hard as Perseus', merciless!
Make the end bloody, wipe
Clean the old stain, that this
House may win deliverance!
[Enter AEGISTHUS.*]*

Aegisthus
I come in answer to the summons.
Strangers, they say, have brought unwelcome news,
Orestes' death, another wound to open
Old sores in this sad house. How shall I judge   220
Whether it is true or women's idle rumor?

Chorus
We have heard it, but go inside and ask
The strangers. Make enquiry on the spot.

Aegisthus
I want to see that messenger and ask
If he was present at the death. They shall
Not hoodwink me. My wits are wide awake.
*[*AEGISTHUS *enters the palace.]*

Chorus
Zeus, what shall I say? The moment has come, with the fate of the house on a
knife's edge. Is it to fall, or shall the son be restored to the wealth of his fathers?
That is the issue, and he faces alone two monsters—may he prove master!
[A cry is heard within.]
He is at work. Better stand clear awhile, in case
It goes against him. The issue has been decided.
[The SERVANT *comes to the door.]*

Servant

Oh, oh! My master has been murdered!   230
Oh me! A third cry for the dead! Help!
Unbolt the women's chambers! And yet even
A strong hand is too weak to help the dead.
Ho!
They must be deaf or sleeping. All my cries
Are wasted. Where is Clytemnestra? What
Is she doing? Now, it seems, her own
Head must bend beneath the axe of Justice.
[CLYTEMNESTRA *comes to the door.*]

Clytemnestra

What is it? What is the meaning of that shout?

Servant

It means the living are being killed by the dead.   240

Clytemnestra

Ah me, a riddle! yet I can read its meaning.
Quick, let me have a man-axe, then we shall see
Who wins, who loses. It has come to this.
[ORESTES *and* PYLADES *come out of the palace.*]

Orestes

I have been looking for you. He is all right.

Clytemnestra

Aegisthus, dearest love! Oh, he is dead!

Orestes

You love him? Well, then you shall share his grave,
Faithful in everything even to death.

Clytemnestra

O stay, my son! Dear child, have pity on
This bosom where in slumber long ago
Your toothless gums drew in the milk of life!   250

Orestes

Pylades, what shall I do? Shall I spare my mother?

Pylades

What then hereafter of the oracles
And solemn declarations of Apollo?
Better that men should hate you than the Gods.

Orestes

Your counsel shall prevail. Come with me. I
Shall kill you by his side. Since you preferred
Him to my father while he lived, die with him!

Clytemnestra
I brought you up—let me grow old with you!

Orestes
What, live with you, my father's murderess!

Clytemnestra
Fate had a hand, my son, in your father's end. 260

Orestes
Yes, the same fate which now decrees your own.

Clytemnestra
Have you no dread of a mother's curse, my child?

Orestes
Your child no more, because you cast me out.

Clytemnestra
No, not cast out—I sent you away to friends.

Orestes
Son of a royal father, foully sold!

Clytemnestra
What then was the payment that I took for you?

Orestes
For very shame I cannot answer that.

Clytemnestra
No, no! Remember too *his* faithlessness!

Orestes
Do not reproach him. It was for you he toiled abroad.

Clytemnestra
It is hard for a woman parted from her man. 270

Orestes
What but his labor keeps her safe at home?

Clytemnestra
So then, my son, you mean to kill your mother?

Orestes
It is not I, it is you who kill yourself.

Clytemnestra
Beware of the hell-hounds of a mother's curse!

Orestes
And how, if I spare you, escape from his?

Clytemnestra
My pleas are fruitless—warm tears at a cold tomb.

Orestes
My father's destiny has determined yours.

Clytemnestra
Ah me, I gave birth to a snake and not a son.

Orestes
That panic-stricken nightmare was prophetic.
Wrong shall be done to you for the wrong you did.   280
[They go into the palace.]

Chorus
I mourn for them both, and yet, since the tale
Of bloodshed is now crowned in brave Orestes,
I choose to have it so, that this great house
May rise again and not perish utterly.

Upon the sons of Priam Justice in time did bring
Heavy and harsh judgment;
To Agamemnon too and to his house it came,
A double lion, double strife.
On to the goal he held his course heaven-sped,
Following well the Lord Apollo's command.   290
   Cry Alleluia, lift up in the house a song,
   Deliverance from evil and the waste of wealth,
   From rough, thorny ways.

Yes, he has come, the God who with a sly assault
Ambushes evildoers;
Deftly his hand was guided in the battle by
The child of Zeus the truly-named,
Whom it is right that mortals call Righteousness.
Deadly the blast she breathes on those that shed blood.
Just as Apollo cried out of his holy shrine,   300
So does his word advance never at fault against
The ingrown disease which in the house is lodged;
For God's will is always stronger than sin.
   On us the light has shone! Now let the fallen house
   Out of the shadows rise; for it was long enough
   The chains of evil held it down.

It shall be purified in the appointed time,
When he has cleansed the hearth of the defiling sin,
And all those who wept shall have their sorrow turned
To joy, greeting man's salvation from wrong.   310
[The doors are opened and torches lit within, revealing the bodies of AEGISTHUS *and* CLY-
TEMNESTRA *laid out in purple robes on a couch, with* ORESTES *standing over them.]*

Orestes
See here our country's double tyranny!
How stately were they sitting on their thrones,
Both pledged to slay my father and so doomed
To die themselves together—they kept their word.
See here the snare which they contrived to enmesh
My father's hands and feet—what shall I call it?
A pit for wild beasts, or a winding-sheet,
Or a cloak spread by some highwayman to catch
The passing traveler? Come, spread it out,
This skilful masterpiece, that he who is   320
Father of all creation and looks down
On the whole world, the Sun, having observed
My mother's wicked handiwork, may stand
My witness at the judgment which is to come
And certify that I put her to death
Justly—as for Aegisthus, he has paid
The penalty prescribed for adulterers;
But she, who plotted this horror for her own
Husband, to whom she bore within her womb
Children, a load of love which now has turned   330
To hate, as they have shown by their sharp fangs—
What do you think of her? If she had been
A scorpion or sea-snake, her very touch
Would rot the unbitten hand. Rather than share
House with such a monster, may the Gods
Destroy me and my children and children's children!

Chorus
With a fearful death she has paid for her foul deed, reaping the crop which she
   sowed with her own hand.

Orestes
The deed was hers, was it not? I have a witness,
This robe, that here she plunged Aegisthus' sword:
See how bloodstains have joined with time and worn   340
The dye out of the pattern! I am now present,
Now only, to praise and lament my father,
Greeting this web that wove his death and weeping
For all that has been done and suffered here,
For the whole race, and for my own fate too,
Bearing the stains of this grim victory.

Chorus
All men have been born to sorrow, which is present for some today and is
   stored up for others.

Orestes
So then, to tell you plainly—I do not know
How it will end—my wits are out of hand
Like horses that with victory in sight   350
Shy and dash wildly off the course—so I feel
Here at the heart a throbbing—but while I have
My senses, I declare that I killed my mother
In a just cause, because she killed my father
And that I was driven to do it in obedience
To the oracle of Apollo, who proclaimed
That, if I did it, I should be cleared of guilt,
And that, if not—I will not name the penalty,
Something beyond imagination; and so,
Garlanded with these sprigs of supplication,   360
I make my way to his prophetic shrine
And the glorious light of his undying fire,
A suppliant stained with blood; for he commanded me
To seek no hearth but his; and meanwhile I
Call on my fellow-countrymen to give
In time to come their evidencc, how all this
Was brought about, an outcast, leaving to
Their safekeeping, in life and death, my name.

Chorus
You must not bend your lips to such ill-omened
Talk after delivering your country and   370
With one swift stroke lopping two dragons' heads.

Orestes
Look! Do you see those women, like Gorgons,
All clothed in black, their heads and arms entwined
With writhing snakes! How can I escape?

Chorus
What imaginings are these, O father's dearest
Son? Stay and fear nothing. You have won.

Orestes
Imaginings! They are real enough to me.
Can you not see them? Hounds of a mother's curse!

Chorus
It is the blood still dripping from your hands
That confuses your wits, but it will pass.   380

Orestes
O Lord Apollo! See how thick they come,
And from their eyes are oozing gouts of blood!

Chorus

You shall be purified! Apollo's touch
Shall save you and from all troubles set you free.

Orestes

You cannot see them, and yet how plain they are!
They are coming to hunt me down. Away, away!
[Exit.]

Chorus

Good luck, and may God guide you to the end!
This is the third storm to have struck the house: first, the slaughter of children;
next, the fall of the great king who had conquered Troy; and now—is it final
destruction or deliverance at last? When shall the curse be laid to rest?

EUMENIDES

Aeschylus

CHARACTERS

PRIESTESS *[the prophetic oracle of Apollo at Delphi]*

APOLLO *[god of healing, disease, and prophecy who purifies Orestes at Delphi]*

ORESTES *[the matricide who seeks exoneration at history's first murder trial in Athens]*

GHOST OF CLYTEMNESTRA *[the spirit of Orestes' murdered mother]*

CHORUS *[the Furies, whom Athene (Athena) transforms into the Eumenides (Kindly Ones)]*

ATHENE (ATHENA) *[goddess of wisdom and protector of the city-state]*

JUDGES

ESCORT OF WOMEN *[Athenian women who escort the Eumenides to their new shrine in Athens]*

[Before the temple of Apollo at Delphi. Enter the PRIESTESS.]

Priestess

First among all the gods to whom this prayer   1
Shall be addressed is the first of prophets, Earth;
And next her daughter, Themis, who received
The oracular shrine from her; third, another
Daughter, Phoebe, who having settled here
Bestowed it as a birthday gift, together
With her own name, on Phoebus; whereupon,
Leaving his native isle of Delos and landing
In Attica, he made his way from there
Attended by the sons of Hephaestus, who tamed   10
The wilderness and built a road for him;
And here Zeus, having inspired him with his art,
Set him, the fourth of prophets, on this throne,
His own son and interpreter, Apollo.
Together with these deities I pay
Homage to Athena and to the nymphs that dwell
In the Corycian caves on the rugged slopes
Of Parnassus, where Dionysus led
His troop of frenzied Bacchants to catch and kill
King Pentheus like a mountain-hare; and so,   20
After calling on Poseidon and the springs
Of Pleistus, watering this valley, and last
On Zeus the All-Highest, who makes all things perfect,

621

I take my seat on the oracular throne,
Ready to be consulted. Let all Greeks
Approach by lot according to the custom
And I shall prophesy to them as God dictates.
[She enters the temple, utters a loud cry, and returns.]
O horror, horror! I have been driven back
Strengthless, speechless, a terror-struck old woman,
By such a sight as was never seen before.   30
Entering the shrine I saw at the navel-stone
In the posture of a suppliant a man
Who held an olive-branch and an unsheathed sword
In hands dripping with blood; and all round him,
Lying fast asleep, a gruesome company
Of women—yet not women—Gorgons rather;
And yet not Gorgons; them I saw once in a picture
Of the feast of Phineus: these are different.
They have no wings, and are all black, and snore,
And drops ooze from their eyes, and the rags they wear   40
Unutterably filthy. What country could
Have given such creatures birth, I cannot tell.
Apollo is the master of this house,
So let him look to it, healer, interpreter,
Himself of other houses purifier.
[The inside of the temple is revealed, as described, with APOLLO *and* HERMES *standing beside* ORESTES.]*

Apollo
I will keep faith, at all times vigilant,
Whether at your side of far away, and never
Mild to your enemies, whom you now see
Subdued by sleep, these unloved virgins, these
Children hoary with age, whose company   50
Is shunned by God and man and beast, being born
For evil, just as the abyss from which they come
Is evil, the bottomless pit of Tartarus.
Yet you must fly before them, hotly pursued,
Past island cities and over distant seas,
Enduring all without faltering, until
You find sanctuary in Athena's citadel,
And there, embracing her primeval image, you
Shall stand trial, and after healing words
From me, who commanded you to kill your mother,   60
You shall be set free and win your salvation.

Orestes
O Lord Apollo, you have both wisdom and power,
And, since you have them, use them on my behalf!

Apollo
Remember, endure and have no fear! And you,

[handwritten margin note:] —Appollo promosises to protect orestes from the Furries

Hermes, go with him, guide him, guard his steps,
An outcast from mankind, yet blest of Zeus.
[Exeunt HERMES *and* ORESTES. *Enter the ghost of* CLYTEMNESTRA.*]*

Clytemnestra
Oho! asleep! What good are you to me asleep?
While I, deserted and humiliated,
Wander, a homeless ghost. I warn you that
Among the other spirits of the dead   70
(The taunt of murder does not lose its sting
In the dark world below) I am the accused
And not the accuser, with none to defend me,
Brutally slain by matricidal hands.
Look on these scars, and remember all
The wineless offerings which I laid upon
The hearth for you at many a solemn midnight—
All now forgotten, all trampled underfoot!
And *he* is gone! Light as a fawn he skipped
Out of your snare and now he laughs at you.   80
Oh hear me! I am pleading for my soul!
O goddesses of the underworld, awake!
I, Clytemnestra, call you now in dreams!

Chorus
Mu!

Clytemnestra
Ah, you may mew, but he is fled and gone.
He has protectors who are no friends of mine.

Chorus
Mu!

Clytemnestra
Still so drowsy, still so pitiless?
Orestes has escaped, the matricide!

Chorus
Oh, no!   90

Clytemnestra
Still muttering and mumbling in your sleep!
Arise, do evil! Is not that your task?

Chorus
Oh, oh!

Clytemnestra
How sleep and weariness have made common cause
To disenvenom the foul dragon's rage!

Chorus
Oh, oh! where is the scent? Let us mark it down!

Clytemnestra
Yes, you may bay like an unerring hound,
But still you are giving chase only in your dreams.
What are you doing? Rise, slothful slugabeds,
Stung by the scourge of my rebukes, arise   100
And blow about his head your bloody breath,
Consume his flesh in bellifuls of fire!
Come on, renew the chase and hunt him down!
[Exit.]

Chorus
We have been put to shame! What has befallen us?
The game has leapt out of the snare and gone.
In slumber laid low, we let slip the prey.

Aha, son of Zeus! pilferer, pillager!
A God, to steal away the matricide!
A youth to flout powers fixed long ago!

In dream I felt beneath the heart a swift   110
Charioteer's sharp lash.
Under the ribs, under the flank
It rankles yet, red and sore,
Like the public scourger's blow.

This is the doing of the younger gods.
Dripping with death, red drops
Cover the heel, cover the head.
Behold the earth's navel-stone
Thick with heavy stains of blood!

His own prophetic cell he has himself defiled,   120
Honoring mortal claims, reckless of laws divine,
And dealing death to Fates born of old.
He injures us and yet *him* he shall never free,
Not in the depths of hell, never shall he have rest
But suffer lasting torment below.

Apollo
Out, out! Be off, and clear this holy place
Of your foul presence, or else from my golden bow
Shall spring a snake of silver and bite so deep
That from your swollen bellies you shall spew
The blood which you have sucked! Your place is where   130
Heads drop beneath the axe, eyes are gouged out,
Throats slit, and men are stoned, limbs lopped, and boys
Gelded, and a last whimper heard from spines
Spiked writhing in the dust. Such celebrations,
Which fill heaven with loathing, are your delight.

Off with you, I say, and go unshepherded,
A herd shunned with universal horror!

Chorus
O Lord Apollo, hear us in our turn!
You are not an abettor in this business.
You are the culprit. On you lies the whole guilt.   140

Apollo
Explain yourselves. How do you make that out?

Chorus
It was at your command that he killed his mother.

Apollo
I commanded him to take vengeance for his father.

Chorus
So promising the acceptance of fresh blood.

Apollo
I promised to absolve him from it here.

Chorus
Why do you insult the band that drove him here?

Apollo
This mansion is not fit for your company.

Chorus
But this is the task that has been appointed to us.

Apollo
What is this privilege that you are so proud of?

Chorus
To drive all matricides from hearth and home.   150

Apollo
And what of a woman who has killed her husband?

Chorus
That is not manslaughter within the kin.

Apollo
So then you set at naught the marriage-bond
Sealed by Zeus and Hera, and yet what tie
Is stronger, joined by Fate and watched over
By Justice, than the joy which Aphrodite
Has given to man and woman? If you let those
Who violate that covenant go unpunished,
You have no right to persecute Orestes.

Why anger here, and there passivity?   160
On this in time Athena shall pass judgment.

Chorus
We shall give chase and never let him go.

Apollo
Pursue him then, and make trouble for yourselves.

Chorus
No words of yours can circumscribe our powers.

Apollo
I would not have your powers even as a gift.

Chorus
Then take your proud stand by the throne of Zeus.
Meanwhile a mother's blood is beckoning to us,
And we must go and follow up the trail.

Apollo
And I will still safeguard the suppliant.
A wrong unheard-of in heaven and on earth   170
Would be his protest, if I should break faith.

[A year passes. Before a shrine of Athena at Athens. Enter ORESTES.*]*

Orestes
O Queen Athena, I have come here in obedience
To the Lord Apollo. Grant me sanctuary,
An outcast, yet with hands no longer sullied, for
The edge of my pollution has been worn
Off on countless paths over land and sea;
And now, in accordance with his word, present
Before your image, I entreat you to
Receive me here and pass the final judgment.

Chorus
Step where our dumb informer leads the way;   180
For as the hounds pursue a wounded fawn,
So do we dog the trail of human blood.
How far we have traveled over land and sea,
Faint and footsore but never to be shaken off!
He must be somewhere here, for I smell blood.

—Beware, I say, beware!
Look on all sides for fear he find some escape!
—Ah, here he is, desperate,
Clasping that image awaiting trial.
—It cannot be! The mother's blood   190
That he has spilt is irrecoverable.

—Ravenous lips shall feed upon his living flesh
And on his blood—a lush pasturage.
—And others shall he see in hell, who wronged
Parents, guests or gods;
For Hades is a stern inquisitor of souls,
Recording all things till the hour of judgment.

Orestes
Taught by long suffering, I have learnt at what
Times it is right to keep silence and when
To break it, and in this matter a wise   200
Instructor has charged me to speak. The stain
Of matricide has been washed out in the flow
Of swine's blood by Apollo. I could tell
Of many who have given me lodging and no
Harm has befallen them from my company;
And now with lips made pure I call upon
Athena to protect me and so join
Our peoples as allies for all time to come.
Wherever she may be, on Libyan shores
Or by the stream of Trito, where she came   210
To birth, or like a captain keeping watch
On the heights of Phlegra against some enemy,
O may she come—far off, she can still hear me—
And from my sufferings deliver me!

Chorus
Neither Apollo nor Athena can
Save your soul from perdition, a feast for fiends.
Have you no answer? Do you spurn us so,
Fattened for us, our consecrated host?

Let us dance and declare in tune with this grim music the laws which it is ours
to enforce on the life of man. It is only those that have blood on their hands
who need fear us at all, but from them without fail we exact retribution.

Mother Night, your children cry! Hear, black Night!   220
It is ours to deal by day and dark night judgment.
The young god Apollo has rescued the matricide!
  Over the blood that has been shed
  Maddening dance, melody desperate, deathly,
  Chant to bind the soul in hell,
  Spell that parches flesh to dust.

This the Fates who move the whole world through
Have assigned to us, a task for all future ages,
To keep watch on all hands that drip red with kindred blood.
  Over the blood that has been shed   230
  Maddening dance, melody desperate, deathly,

Chant to bind the soul in hell,
Spell that parches flesh to dust.

Such are the powers appointed us from the beginning,
None of the Gods of Olympus to eat with us, while we
Take no part in the wearing of white—no,
Other pleasures are our choice—
   Wrecking the house, hunting the man,
   Hard on his heels ever we run,
   And though his feet be swift we waste and wear him out.   240

Hence it is thanks to our zealous endeavor that from such
Offices Zeus and the Gods are exempted, and yet he
Shuns us because we are covered in blood, not
Fit to share his majesty.
   Wrecking the house, hunting the man,
   Hard on his heels ever we run,
   And though his feet be swift we waste and wear him out.

— Furies

Glories of men, how bright in the day is their splendor,
Yet shall they fade in the darkness of hell,
Faced with our grisly attire and dancing   250
Feet attuned to sombre melodies.
   Nimble the feet leap in the air,
   Skip and descend down to the ground,
   Fugitive step suddenly tripped up in fatal confusion.

Caught without knowing he stumbles, his wickedness blinds him,
Such is the cloud of pollution that hangs
Over him and on his house, remembered
Many generations after him.
   Nimble the feet leap in the air,
   Skip and descend down to the ground,   260
   Fugitive step suddenly tripped up in fatal confusion.

Our task is such. With long memories
We keep constant watch on human sin.
What others spurn is what we prize,
Our heaven their hell, a region of trackless waste,
Both for the quick and dead, for blind and seeing too.

What wonder then that men bow in dread
At these commandments assigned to us
By Fate—our ancient privilege?
We are not without our own honors and dignities,   270
Though we reside in hell's unfathomable gloom.
[*Enter* ATHENA.]

Athena

I heard a distant cry, as I was standing
Beside Scamander to take possession of

The lands which the Achaean princes have
Bestowed on my people in perpetuity;
And thence I have made my way across the sea
In wingless flight; and now, as I regard
Before my shrine this very strange company,
I cannot but ask, in wonder, not in fear,
Who you may be. I address you all in common,   280
This stranger here who is seated at my image,
And you, who are not human in appearance
Nor yet divine; but rather than speak ill
Without just cause let me receive your answer.

Chorus
Daughter of Zeus, your question is soon answered.
We are the dismal daughters of dark Night,
Called Curses in the palaces of hell.

Athena
I know your names then and your parentage.

Chorus
And now let us inform you of our powers.

Athena
Yes, let me know what office you perform.   290

Chorus
We drive the matricide from hearth and home.

Athena
Where? In what place does his persecution end?

Chorus
A place where joy is something quite unknown.

Athena
Is that your hue and cry against this man?

Chorus
Yes, because he dared to kill his mother.

Athena
Was he driven to it perhaps against his will?

Chorus
What force could drive a man to matricide?

Athena
It is clear there are two parties to this case.

Chorus
We challenged him to an ordeal by oath.

Athena

You seem to seek only the semblance of justice.   300

Chorus

How so? Explain, since you are so rich in wisdom.

Athena

Do not use oaths to make the wrong prevail.

Chorus

Then try the case yourself and give your judgment.

Athena

Will you entrust the verdict to my charge?

Chorus

Yes, a worthy daughter of a worthy father.

Athena

Stranger, what is your answer? Tell us first
Your fatherland and family and what
Misfortune overtook you, and then answer
The charge against you. If you have taken your stand
Here as a suppliant with full confidence   310
In the justice of your cause, now is the time
To render on each count a clear reply.

Orestes

O Queen Athena, first let me remove one doubt.
I am not a suppliant seeking purification.
I was already cleansed before I took
This image in my arms, and I can give
Evidence of this. The manslayer is required
To keep silent until he has been anointed
With sacrificial blood. That has been done,
And I have traveled far over land and sea   320
To wear off the pollution. So, having set
Your mind at rest, let me tell you who I am.
I come from Argos, and my father's name—
For asking me that I thank you—was Agamemnon,
The great commander, with whom not long ago
You wiped out Troy. He died an evil death,
Murdered on his return by my blackhearted
Mother, who netted him in a bath of blood.
And therefore I, restored from banishment,
In retribution for my father's death,   330
I killed my mother; and yet not I alone—
Apollo too must answer for it, having

Warned me what anguish would afflict me if
I should fail to take vengeance on the guilty.
Whether it was just or not, do you decide.

Athena
This is too grave a case for mortal minds,
Nor is it right that I should judge an act
Of blood shed with such bitter consequences,
Especially since you have come to me
As one already purified, who has done no wrong   340
Against this city. But your opponents here
Are not so gentle, and, if their plea
Should be rejected, the poison dripping from
Their angry bosoms will devastate my country.
The issue is such that, whether I let them stay
Or turn them out, it is fraught with injury.
But be it so. Since it has come to this,
I will appoint judges for homicide,
A court set up in perpetuity.
Do you prepare your proofs and witnesses,   350
Then I, having selected from my people
The best, will come to pass a final judgment.
[Exit.]

Chorus
Now the world shall see the downfall of old commandments made
Long ago, if the accurst matricide should win his case.
Many a bitter blow awaits parents from their own children in the times to come.

We who had the task to watch over human life shall now
Cease to act, giving free rein to deeds of violence.
Crime shall spread from house to house like a plague, and whole cities shall be
      desolate.

Then let no man stricken cry
Out in imprecation, "Oh   360
Furies!" Thus shall fathers groan,
Thus shall mothers weep in vain,
Since the house of righteousness
Lies in ruins, overthrown.

Times there are when fear is good,
Keeping watch within the soul.
Needful too are penalties.
Who of those that have not nursed
Wholesome dread within them can
Show respect to righteousness?   370
Choose a life despot-free, yet restrained by rule of law.

God has appointed the mean as the master in all things.
Wickedness breeds pride, but from wisdom is brought forth
Happiness prayed for by all men.

So, we say, men must bow down before the shrine of Right.
Those who defy it shall fail; for the ancient commandments
Stand—to respect parents and honor the stranger.
Only the righteous shall prosper.
The man who does what is right by choice, not constraint,
Shall prosper always; the seed of just men shall never perish.   380
Not so the captain who ships a load of ill-gotten gains.
Caught in the gathering storm his proud sail shall be torn from the masthead.

He cries to deaf ears, no longer able to ride
The gale, and meanwhile his guardian spirit is close beside him
And scoffs to see him despair of ever again making port,
Dashed on the reefs of Justice, unlooked-on and unlamented.

[Enter ATHENA *with the* JUDGES, *followed by citizens of Athens.]*

Athena
Herald, give orders to hold the people back,
Then sound the trumpet and proclaim silence,
For while this new tribunal is being enrolled,
It is right that all should ponder on its laws,   390
Both the litigants here whose case is to be judged,
And my whole people for all generations.
[Enter APOLLO.]

Chorus
Apollo, what is there here that concerns you?
We say you have no authority in this matter.

Apollo
I come both as a witness, the accused
Having been a suppliant at my sanctuary
And purified of homicide at my hands,
And also to be tried with him, for I too
Must answer for the murder of his mother.
Open the case, and judge as you know how.   400

Apollo to Athena

Athena
The case is open. You shall be first to speak.
[To the CHORUS.]
The prosecutors shall take precedence
And first inform us truthfully of the facts.

Chorus
Many in number, we shall be brief in speech.
We beg you to answer our questions one by one.
First, is it true that you killed your mother?

Orestes
I killed her. That is true, and not denied.

Chorus
So then the first of the three rounds is ours.

Orestes
You should not boast that you have thrown me yet.

Chorus
Next, since you killed her, you must tell us how. 410

Orestes
Yes, with a drawn sword leveled at the throat.

Chorus
Who was it who impelled or moved you to it?

Orestes
The oracle of this God who is my witness.

Chorus
The God of prophecy ordered matricide?

Orestes
Yes, and I have not repented it to this day.

Chorus
You *will* repent it, when you have been condemned.

Orestes
My father shall defend me from the grave.

Chorus
Having killed your mother, you may well trust the dead!

Orestes
She was polluted by a double crime.

Chorus
How so? Explain your meaning to the judges. 420

Orestes
She killed her husband and she killed my father.

Chorus
She died without bloodguilt, and you still live.

Orestes
Why did you not hunt her when she was alive?

Chorus
She was not bound by blood to the man she killed.

Orestes
And am I then bound by blood to my mother?

Chorus
Abandoned wretch, how did she nourish you
Within the womb? Do you repudiate
The nearest and dearest tie of motherhood?

Orestes
Apollo, give your evidence. I confess
That I did this deed as I have said.   430
Pronounce your judgment: was it justly done?

Apollo
Athena's appointed judges, I say to you,
Justly, and I, as prophet, cannot lie.
Never from my prophetic shrine have I
Said anything of city, man or woman
But what my father Zeus has commanded me.
This plea of mine must override all others,
Since it accords with our great father's will.

Chorus
Your argument is, then, that Zeus commanded you
To charge Orestes with this criminal act   440
Regardless of the bond between son and mother?

Apollo
It is not the same, to murder a great king,
A woman too to do it, and not in open
Fight like some brave Amazon, but in such
Manner as I shall now inform this court.
On his return from battle, bringing home
A balance for the greater part of good,
She welcomed him with fine words and then, while
He bathed, pavilioned him in a purple robe
And struck him down and killed him—a man and king   450
Whom the whole world had honored. Such was the crime
For which she paid. Let the judges take note.

Chorus
According to your argument Zeus gives
Precedence to the father; yet Zeus it was
Who cast into prison his own father Kronos.
Judges, take note, and ask him to explain.

Apollo
Abominable monsters, loathed by gods
And men, do you not understand that chains
Can be unfastened and prison doors unlocked?

But once the dust has drunk a dead man's blood,   460
He can never rise again—for that no remedy
Has been appointed by our almighty Father,
Although all else he can overturn at will
Without so much effort as a single breath.

Chorus
See what your plea for the defendant means.
Is this not what he did—to spill his mother's
Blood on the ground? And shall he then be allowed
To live on in his father's house? What public
Altar can he approach and where find fellowship?

Apollo
The mother is not a parent, only the nurse   470
Of the seed which the true parent, the father,
Commits to her as to a stranger to
Keep it with God's help safe from harm. And I
Have proof of this. There can be a father
Without a mother. We have a witness here,
This daughter of Olympian Zeus, who sprang
Armed from her father's head, a goddess whom
No goddess could have brought to birth. Therefore,
Out of goodwill to your country and your people
I sent this suppliant to seek refuge with you,   480
That you, Athena, may find in him and his
A faithful ally for all time to come.

Athena
Enough has now been spoken. Are you agreed
That I call on the judges to record
Their votes justly according to their conscience?

Apollo
Our quiver is empty, every arrow spent.
We wait to hear the issue of the trial.

Athena
And has my ruling your approval too?

Chorus
Sirs, you have heard the case, and now declare
Judgment according to your solemn oath.   490

Athena
Citizens of Athens, hear my declaration
At this first trial in the history of man.
This great tribunal shall remain in power
Meeting in solemn session on this hill,
Where long ago the Amazons encamped

When they made war on Theseus, and sacrificed
To Ares—hence its name. Here reverence
For law and inbred fear among my people
Shall hold their hands from evil night and day,
Only let them not tamper with the laws,   500
But keep the fountain pure and sweet to drink.
I warn you not to banish from your lives
All terror but to seek the mean between
Autocracy and anarchy; and in this way
You shall possess in ages yet unborn
An impregnable fortress of liberty
Such as no people has throughout the world.
With these words I establish this tribunal
Grave, quick to anger, incorruptible,
And always vigilant over those that sleep.   510
Let the judges now rise and cast their votes.

Chorus
We charge you to remember that we have
Great power to harm, and vote accordingly.

Apollo
I charge you to respect the oracles
Sanctioned by Zeus and see that they are fulfilled.

Chorus
By interfering in what is not your office
You have desecrated your prophetic shrine.

Apollo
Then was my Father also at fault when he
Absolved Ixion, the first murderer?

Chorus
Keep up your chatter, but, if our cause should fail,   520
We shall lay on this people a heavy hand.

Apollo
Yes, you will lose your case, and then you may
Spit out your poison, but it will do no harm.

Chorus
Insolent youth mocks venerable age.
We await the verdict, ready to let loose
Against this city our destructive rage.

Athena
The final judgment rests with me, and I
Announce that my vote shall be given to Orestes.
No mother gave me birth, and in all things

Save marriage I commend with all my heart   530
The masculine, my father's child indeed.
Therefore I cannot hold in higher esteem
A woman killed because she killed her husband.
If the votes are equal, Orestes wins.
Let the appointed officers proceed
To empty the urns and count the votes.

Orestes
O bright Apollo, how shall the judgment go?

Chorus
O black mother Night, are you watching this?

Orestes
My hour has come—the halter or the light.

Chorus
And ours—to exercise our powers or perish.   540

Apollo
Sirs, I adjure you to count carefully.
If judgment errs, great harm will come of it,
Whereas one vote may raise a fallen house.

Athena
He stands acquitted on the charge of bloodshed,
The human votes being equally divided.

Orestes
Lady Athena, my deliverer,
I was an outcast from my country, now
I can go home again and live once more
In my parental heritage, thanks to you
And to Apollo and to the third, the Savior,   550
Who governs the whole world. Before I go
I give my word to you and to your people
For all posterity that no commander
Shall lead an Argive army in war against
This city. If any should violate this pledge,
Out of the graves which shall then cover us
We would arise with adverse omens to
Obstruct and turn them back. If, however,
They keep this covenant and stand by your side,
They shall always have our blessing. And so farewell!   560
May you and your people always prevail
Against the assaults of all your enemies!
[Exit.]

Chorus
Oho, you junior gods, since you have trod under foot

The laws of old and robbed us of our powers,
We shall afflict this country
With damp contagion, bleak and barren, withering up the soil,
Mildew on bud and birth abortive. Venomous pestilence
Shall sweep your cornlands with infectious death.
To weep?—No! To work? Yes! To work ill and lay low the people!
So will the maids of Night mourn for their stolen honors.   570

Athena
Let me persuade you to forget your grief!
You are not defeated. The issue of the trial
Has been determined by an equal vote.
It was Zeus himself who plainly testified
That Orestes must not suffer for what he did.
I beg you, therefore, do not harm my country,
Blasting her crops with drops of rank decay
And biting cankers in the early buds.
Rather accept my offer to stay and live
In a cavern on this hill and there receive   580
The adoration of my citizens.

Chorus
Oho, you junior gods, etc.

Athena
No, *not* dishonored, and therefore spare my people!
I too confide in Zeus—why speak of that?—
And I alone of all the Olympian gods
Know of the keys which guard the treasury
Of heaven's thunder. But there is no need of that.
Let my persuasion serve to calm your rage.
Reside with me and share my majesty;
And when from these wide acres you enjoy   590
Year after year the harvest offerings
From couples newly-wed praying for children,
Then you will thank me for my intercession.

Chorus
How can you treat us so?
Here to dwell, ever debased, defiled!
Hear our passion, hear, black Night!
For the powers once ours, sealed long, long ago
Have by the junior gods been all snatched away.

Athena
You are my elders, and therefore I indulge
Your passion. And yet, though not so wise as you,   600
To me too Zeus has granted understanding.
If you refuse me and depart, believe me,

This country will yet prove your heart's desire,
For as the centuries pass so there will flow
Such glory to my people as will assure
To all divinities worshipped here by men
And women gathered on festive holidays
More honors than could be yours in any other
City throughout the world. And so, I beg you,
Keep from my citizens the vicious spur 610
Of internecine strife, which pricks the breast
Of manhood flown with passion as with wine!
Abroad let battle rage for every heart
That is fired with love of glory—that shall be theirs
In plenty. So this is my offer to you—
To give honor and receive it and to share
My glory in this country loved by heaven.

Chorus
How can you, etc.

Athena
I will not weary in my benedictions,
Lest it should ever be said that you, so ancient 620
In your divinity, were driven away
By me and by my mortal citizens.
No, if Persuasion's holy majesty,
The sweet enchantment of these lips divine,
Has power to move you, please, reside with me.
But, if you still refuse, then, since we have made
This offer to you, it would be wrong to lay
Your hands upon us in such bitter rage.
Again, I tell you, it is in your power to own
This land attended with the highest honors. 630

Chorus
Lady Athena, what do you offer us?

Athena
A dwelling free of sorrow. Pray accept.

Chorus
Say we accept, what privileges shall we have?

Athena
No family shall prosper without your grace.

Chorus
Will you ensure us this prerogative?

Athena
I will, and bless all those that worship you.

Chorus
And pledge that assurance for all time to come?

Athena
I need not promise what I will not perform.

Chorus
Your charms are working, and our rage subsides.

Athena
Here make your dwelling, where you shall win friends.   640

Chorus
What song then shall we chant in salutation?

Athena
A song of faultless victory—from land and sea,
From skies above let gentle breezes blow
And breathing sunshine float from shore to shore;
Let crops and cattle increase and multiply
And children grow in health and happiness,
And let the righteous prosper; for I, as one
Who tends flowers in a garden, cherish fondly
The seed that bears no sorrow. That is your part,
While I in many a battle shall strive until   650
This city stands victorious against all
Its enemies and renowned throughout the world.

Chorus
We accept; we agree to dwell with you
Here in Athens, which by grace of Zeus
Stands a fortress for the gods,
Jeweled crown of Hellas. So
With you now we join in prayer
That smiling suns and fruitful soils unite to yield
Lifelong joy, fortune fair,
Light and darkness reconciled.   660

Athena
For the good of my people I have given homes in the city to these deities,
whose power is so great and so slowly appeased; and, whenever a man falls foul
of them, apprehended to answer for the sins of his fathers, he shall be brought
to judgment before them, and the dust shall stifle his proud boast.

Chorus
Free from blight may the early blossom deck
Budding trees, and may no parching drought
Spread across the waving fields.
Rather Pan in season grant
From the flocks and herds a full

Return from year to year, and from the rich
Store which these gods vouchsafe
May the Earth repay them well!

Athena

Guardians of my city, listen to the blessings they bring, and remember that their power is great in heaven and hell, and on earth too they bring to some glad music and to some lives darkened with weeping. 670

Chorus

Free from sudden death that cuts
Short the prime of manhood, blest
In your daughters too, to whom
Be granted husband and home, and may the dread Fates
Keep them safe, present in every household,
Praised and magnified in every place!

Athena

Fair blessings indeed from powers that so lately were averted in anger, and I thank Zeus and the spirit of persuasion that at last there is no strife left between us, except that they vie with me in blessing my people.

Chorus

Peace to all, free from that
Root of evil, civil strife!
May they live in unity, 680
And never more may the blood of kin be let flow!
Rather may all of them bonded together
Feel and act as one in love and hate!

Athena

From these dread shapes, so quick to learn a new music, I foresee great good for my people, who, if only they repay their favors with the reverence due, shall surely establish the reign of justice in a city that will shine as a light for all mankind.

[*Enter* ESCORT OF WOMEN, *carrying crimson robes and torches.*]

Chorus

Joy to you all in your justly appointed riches,
Joy to all the people blest
With the Virgin's love, who stands
Next beside her Father's throne!
Wisdom man has learnt at last.
Under her protection this 690
Land enjoys the grace of Zeus.

Athena

Joy to you also, and now let me lead you in torchlight to your new dwelling place! Let solemn oblations speed you in joy to your home beneath the earth, and there imprison all harm while still letting flow your blessings!

Chorus
Joy to you, joy, yet again we pronounce our blessing.
Joy to all the citizens,
Gods and mortals both alike.
While you hold this land and pay
Homage to our residence,
You shall have no cause to blame
Chance and change in human life.

Athena
I thank you for your gracious salutations,   700
And now you shall be escorted in the light
Of torches to your subterranean dwelling,
Attended by the sacristans of my temple
Together with this company of girls
And married women and others bowed with years.
Women, let them put on these robes of crimson,
And let these blazing torches light the way,
That the goodwill of our new co-residents
Be shown in the manly prowess of your sons!
[The CHORUS *put on the crimson robes and a procession is formed led by young men in armor, with the* CHORUS *and the* ESCORT *following, and behind them the citizens of Athens. The rest is sung as the procession moves away.]*

Chorus of the Escort
Pass on your way, O powers majestic,   710
Daughters of darkness in happy procession!
People of Athens, hush, speak fair!

Pass to the caverns of earth immemorial
There to be worshipped in honor and glory!
People of Athens, hush, speak fair!

Gracious and kindly of heart to our people,
Come with us, holy ones, hither in gladness,
Follow the lamps that illumine the way!
O sing at the end alleluia!

Peace to you, peace of a happy community,   720
People of Athens! Zeus who beholds all
Watches, himself with the Fates reconciled.
O sing at the end alleluia!

Orestes and Iphigenia

In the *Eumenides,* Orestes disappears immediately after the jury returns its verdict exonerating him, for Aeschylus is less interested in the young man's individual fate than he is in promoting Zeus's supremacy. Other poets, however, wrote extensively of Orestes' subsequent adventures, in several cases adapting the myths in a way that settles old scores involving Agamemnon and the Trojan War.

In Euripides' play *Iphigenia in Tauris,* when Orestes asks Apollo how to rid himself of the madness that (in spite of the Furies' domestication) still plagues him, the god directs him to Tauris (in modern Turkey), where he is to find and retrieve an ancient statue of Artemis. When Orestes and Pylades (Figure 15-13) arrive in Tauris, they are immediately imprisoned, for it is the local custom to sacrifice all strangers to their goddess. Brought before the high priestess of Artemis (Figure 15-14), the two captives discover that she is none other than Orestes' sister Iphigenia, whom the goddess had spirited away at the moment the priest at Aulis was about to cut her throat. Reunited, the two siblings carry off Artemis's statue and, with Pylades, attempt to escape by ship. As Thoas, king of the region,

FIGURE 15-13   Orestes and Pylades. Orestes' constant companion, Pylades is the son of Strophius, king of Phocis, and his wife, Anaxibia, sister of Agamemnon. Because he speaks only once in the *Oresteia,* his single line—to remember Apollo's command—has compelling force. After accompanying Orestes on his wanderings, Pylades eventually marries his friend's sister Electra. This marble group expresses the quality of heroic friendship that characterizes their myth. *(Louvre, Paris)*

(continued)

Orestes and Iphigenia (*continued*)

FIGURE 15-14 Artemis. Just as her brother Apollo plays a major role in promoting Orestes' filial duty in avenging his male parent, so Artemis figures prominently in the life of Agamemnon's virgin daughter, Iphigenia. Abhorring human sacrifice, Artemis (in one version of the story) intervenes at the moment Iphigenia is about to be killed, spiriting the girl away and leaving a deer in her place. In Euripides' *Iphigenia in Tauris,* the goddess installs Iphigenia as her priestess among a barbarian tribe (the Tauri), where custom demands that all strangers be sacrificed. Artemis manipulates events so that Iphigenia, Orestes, and Pylades escape to their homeland. This Roman work, known as *Diana of Versailles* (possibly copied from a Greek original), shows the goddess in her paradoxical function as both protector of  wild creatures, such as the deer she shields with her left hand, and patron of the hunt, represented by the arrows she draws from a quiver with her right hand. *(Louvre, Paris)*

is about to capture them, Athene suddenly appears to effect their safe return to Greece, where they build a temple to Artemis in Attica.

Other episodes in the Orestes myth deal with his marriage and return to Argos. When Orestes was still an infant, Agamemnon had engaged his son to Hermione, daughter of Helen and Menelaus, but, at Troy, Menelaus broke his word and married the girl instead to Neoptolemus (Pyrrhus), the only son of Achilles. After returning from Tauris, the adult Orestes visits Hermione at Sparta while Neoptolemus is at Delphi consulting the Oracle. Reenacting the elopement of Helen and Paris, Orestes abducts Hermione, taking her to Delphi, where, on her advice, he arranges Neoptolemus's death by provoking a riot in which his rival is killed. In the fates of their respective sons, the old argument between Achilles and Agamemnon dramatized in the *Iliad*'s opening scenes is at last settled to the latter's dynastic advantage.

In the final part of his mythic cycle, Orestes eventually succeeds to the throne of both Argos and Sparta, uniting the kingdoms of Agamemnon and Menelaus. When a plague devastates Sparta, the Oracle states that the epidemic will abate only when the cities of Asia Minor destroyed in the Trojan War are rebuilt. Orestes accordingly founds new colonies on the sites of the ruined cities, restoring the shrines of their respective gods and ameliorating the divine displeasure that had cursed the Greeks for their violations of holy places during the war. The murderous violence that had afflicted the House of Atreus for generations ends with Orestes: myth grants the son of Agamemnon and Clytemnestra a reign of seventy years and a peaceful death at age ninety.

. . . .

Questions for Discussion and Review

1. Compare Aeschylus's treatment of the Agamemnon–Clytemnestra conflict with Homer's account in the *Odyssey* (Books 1 and 11). What new themes or elements does Aeschylus add to the story?

2. What inspires Clytemnestra's monumental hatred of her husband? How does Aeschylus present her side of the issue? Why does Aegisthus also seek revenge on Agamemnon?

3. Define Orestes' dilemma in the *Libation-Bearers*. Do you think that Aeschylus's original audience would agree that Orestes made the right choice in obeying Apollo's command? Why does the chorus side with Orestes and Electra, and why are its members unable to see the Furies when they appear to Orestes?

4. The myth of the House of Atreus emphasizes family violence and dysfunctional relationships. How do you think Freud's theory of the domestic psychodrama applies to the power struggles in the *Agamemnon* and *Libation-Bearers*? Describe the elements of love and hate in the relations between Agamemnon, Clytemnestra, Iphigenia, Electra, and Orestes.

5. In the *Eumenides*, Aeschylus presents ideas and traditions in fierce opposition. How would you use the structuralist theory of interpreting myth when analyzing Athene's reconciliation of Greek religious and social divisions embodied in the Furies and Apollo? What mediating function does Athene serve in assimilating the Furies into the new Olympian order? Do the characters give the traditional feminine principle sufficient credit? Explain.

The Tragic House of Laius: Sophocles' Oedipus Cycle

KEY TOPICS/THEMES

One of the most popular playwrights of his age, Sophocles was a prolific writer whose plays (seven of which survive) encompass a wide variety of tragic experiences. His three plays on the myth of Oedipus have stimulated debate among critics from Aristotle's time to the present. Oedipus Rex *(which means "Oedipus the King," the Latin title of the play called* Oedipus Tyrannus*) presents the hero in pursuit of the riddle of his identity. Oedipus, who thought he had long since escaped the fate decreed by the oracle, discovers that he has indeed killed his father and married his mother. The play is a complex study of the human psyche, with its innermost secrets bared and its conflicting philosophical and metaphysical dimensions explored.* Oedipus at Colonus *continues the story as Oedipus, at the end of his long exile, comes to the seat of the Eumenides and fulfills the "awful destiny" as prophesied. Finally,* Antigone *dramatizes the tragic story of Oedipus's older daughter, who chooses to die rather than leave her traitorous brother Polyneices' body unburied.*

The World of Sophocles

Born in approximately 496 B.C., Sophocles lived for ninety years through a remarkable century in the history of ancient Greece. The development of democracy; the rise of Athens to a position of political and cultural preeminence; the achievements of Greek artists, architects, writers, philosophers, and mathematicians—all contributed to the sense of pride and the spirit of optimism that prevailed throughout what is commonly called the "classical age" of Greece.

The Athenian constitution had established what its citizens believed to be rational mechanisms for governing society, for preventing special-interest groups or individuals from gaining too much power, and for procuring justice, as Aeschylus's celebration of the jury system in the *Eumenides* attests. But even such careful planning could not prevent abuses within the system or external conflicts. The Peloponnesian War between Sparta and Athens and their respective allies, which erupted in 431 B.C., shattered many illusions, as rival political and economic factions took advantage of the war-generated anxiety and confusion to promote their own positions and power. Just as the myths describe people turning to their heroes to protect them in times of crisis, so the Athenians turned to their generals, who sometimes served them well (as did **Pericles** [PER-ik-leez]) and sometimes betrayed them (as did the highly popular Alcibiades, who, rejected by a more conservative faction, sold out to the Spartans).

But even before these unnerving events, the rapid pace of cultural changes led people to reexamine their traditional perspectives on human experience and the relationship of humans to the gods. For example, the emergence of a new group of philosophers called "Sophists" argued, in contrast to the more traditional, idealistic philosophers like Socrates and Plato, that absolute truth is unknowable, and that skill at rhetoric—the art of persuasion, now sprung loose from its traditional ties to the pursuit of truth—was in any case more relevant to citizens of a democracy, thus anticipating modern political practices. (The Sophists also offended traditionalists by charging tuition for teaching these skills to students.) In order to develop the techniques of political manipulation, the Sophists had to explore the motivations of human behavior. Thus, they are credited with initiating the systematic study of human psychology as a science. In addition, they contributed to the development of modern approaches to both science and criminal justice by encouraging skepticism regarding preconceived ideas and beliefs, and insisting on evidence as the basis for conclusions.

Already undermined by such changes, people's confidence in a rationally ordered world was beginning to falter. In the work of playwrights like Sophocles, we can see those doubts beginning to emerge, a slightly dissonant voice in tense counterpoint to the upbeat public music of conventional attitudes and beliefs. It is at just such a transitional moment—when trust in the centrality of human experience, expressed in the assertion of the Sophist philosopher Protagoras that "man is the measure of all things," perseveres alongside a growing distrust in the commitment of the gods to act accordingly—that tragedy of the kind we witness in the Oedipus plays becomes especially relevant.

Sophocles: The Citizen and Writer

Sophocles himself actively participated in the life, both political and artistic, of his time, serving in various elected offices and writing more than 125 plays, often in competition with his older contemporary Aeschylus and younger contemporary Euripides. A highly successful playwright, he won first prize in the dramatic competition twenty times, and after his death a hero cult was founded in his name.

Of Sophocles' many plays, only seven have survived, among them the three dramas on the family of **Oedipus** [E-dih-puhs]. Unlike Aeschylus's Oresteian trilogy,

Sophocles' three plays were not written as a set and presented simultaneously—forty years separated the first (*Antigone*) from the last (*Oedipus at Colonus*). Nor were they written in chronological order: *Antigone,* the first of the three to be written, is the last in the narrative sequence, picking up the story of **Antigone's** [an-TIG-oh-nee] defiance of her uncle, **Creon** [KREE-on], and her subsequent martyrdom. Her story is set in the aftermath of the civil war between Oedipus's sons, **Eteocles** [e-TEE-oh-kleez] and **Polyneices** [pol-ih-NYE-seez], that followed the death of Oedipus, which is depicted in Sophocles' last play, *Oedipus at Colonus.* And not only do the plot details, characterizations, and ideas and attitudes differ among the three, but the approach to tragedy as a mode of defining human experience changes from one play to the next.

Oedipus Rex

Perhaps no classical Greek play has stimulated as much critical discussion and debate, beginning with the philosopher Aristotle, as has Sophocles' *Oedipus Rex.* The exact date of *Oedipus Rex* is uncertain, but most scholars place it between 429 and 425 B.C. Shortly before, in 430 B.C., plague had broken out in Athens, perhaps a result of overcrowding and stress on the sanitation systems when refugees, seeking safety during the Peloponnesian War, crowded into the city. The Athenian audience would have recognized the description of the plague in Thebes in the opening scene of the play as immediately relevant to their own contemporary experience.

Psychological Dimensions

The psychoanalyst Sigmund Freud argued that *Oedipus Rex* is relevant—to all audiences—for another reason as well. Every male child, Freud believed, unconsciously desires to kill his father and to marry his mother, psychologically predetermined to do so simply because he is a human male. The Greek gods, of course, committed with impunity such acts as castrating a father or marrying a sister. Indeed, as many scholars have noted, Oedipus's situation re-creates that of Cronus and Zeus, who castrate or make war on (that is, symbolically kill) their fathers and marry their sisters, who, in turn, take over the role of their respective mothers. For humans, however, these universally forbidden impulses must be neither openly expressed nor even consciously acknowledged, and the resulting tension may give rise to a form of neurosis that Freud named, after Sophocles' protagonist, the "Oedipus complex" (see Chapter 2).

From the Jungian perspective as well, the male child must free himself from the clutches of the "Terrible Mother" who would entrap him, in order to establish his masculine identity. To do so, he must also abandon her protection, which, though it presents a safe harbor from the dangers of the world, nevertheless confines him in an infantile, and thus "feminized," state. Jocasta's desperate attempts to keep Oedipus from confronting the painful truth in some respects (albeit from different motives) recapitulate Thetis's attempt to prevent Achilles from going to Troy by forcing him to hide, disguised as a woman, on the island of Naxos. To become full-fledged men, both heroes must sever the maternal bonds—Achilles to join the company of heroes, and Oedipus, who thus far on his journey has gone from one mother in Corinth to another in Thebes, to deny Jocasta and thus become, at last, himself.

Theories such as Freud's or Jung's notwithstanding, Sophocles and his audience clearly had a keen interest in human psychology. Indeed, many Greek tragedies are concerned with the violation of universal taboos against matricide, patricide, and incest. In *Oedipus Rex,* we find such impulses addressed directly and the sources of such behavior explored. For example, **Jocasta** [joh-KAS-ta], Oedipus's wife, seems to believe that appalling urges (such as those described by Freud) are common and that (also like Freud) they are revealed in dreams. Speaking of the desire to marry one's mother, she tells Oedipus, "Many a man has dreamt as much." Even more remarkable is her insistence, several millennia before Freud, on the necessity of the mechanism that Freud would later call *repression:* "Such things must be forgotten," she insists, "if life is to be endured." But whereas Jocasta dismissed these impulses as insignificant, Freud saw them as determinants of the human personality. Further, he compared Oedipus's detective work—tracking down the secrets of his identity—to the psychoanalytic process of ferreting out and confronting the contents of the unconscious.

In *Oedipus Rex,* two forms of the failure of knowledge—the people's indifference to the identity of their king's murderer and Oedipus's ignorance of his own identity—produce illness, whether pathology (the plague) or what in other circumstances might appear to be psychosis (Oedipus's acting out of the primal taboos). In both cases, Oedipus's discovery of the truth has a cathartic effect. The plague presumably is over, and Oedipus has completed his excruciating voyage of self-discovery and achieved at last a state of wholeness not possible while the truth about himself lay hidden.

Apollo and Fate

In both cases, it is Apollo who calls attention through his oracle to the conditions that prevail: he reveals to Oedipus the initial prophecy regarding his parents and, later, the Thebans' failure to find and punish the killer of their king. It is also Apollo, as the source of the oracle's pronouncements, who is behind the original statements about what is usually called the *fate* of King **Laius** [LAY-uhs] and of Oedipus himself.

One of the important issues the play raises is whether Apollo, in articulating the "fate" of Oedipus, is decreeing what will happen to Oedipus no matter what actions he takes and what choices he makes, or whether, as god of prophecy, Apollo is simply foreseeing what actually happens to Oedipus as a result of his own free choices. That is, to what degree do the gods choose Oedipus's destiny for him? To what degree is he in control of his own life? In modern terms, we might ask the same question in another way: Does nature or nurture—that is, genetic makeup or training and experience—determine an individual's behavior? Sophocles provides several clues that occur at the precise juncture of these two possible explanations of the events in Oedipus's life, so that, no matter how we phrase the question, the answer remains tantalizingly ambiguous. Modern readers might also note that the oracle becomes a "self-fulfilling" prophecy: the mere fact of its revelation prompts Oedipus to leave his home and family in Corinth. Going out on the road to seek his fortune elsewhere, he will eventually encounter the man who turns out to be his biological father, thus setting in motion the whole chain of catastrophic events. As a prophetic god, to what degree is Apollo "responsible" for the consequences of the oracle's utterances?

In the play, the first and most obvious signal that Apollo interferes with events in the lives of humans is the plague that has been visited on Thebes and its inhabitants. Punished by Apollo, god of health (and therefore of illness), for their negligence in the serious matter of regicide (the murder of a king), the people of Thebes are suffering grievously. The oracle's message, which would have been taken as seriously by the members of the Athenian audience as it was by the characters in the play, is that the plague will continue until the murderer is apprehended and exiled. And although the play does not explicitly refer to the lifting of the plague, that expectation is presumably fulfilled when Oedipus agrees to exile himself as Apollo demands.

Other components of the play also seem to support the claim that fate controls human experience—the remarkable series of coincidences, for example. The more Oedipus tries to escape the path laid out for him by the oracle, the more he is trapped into fulfilling it. Thus, the man he kills at the crossroads turns out to be his father; the city that rewards him for solving the riddle of the **Sphinx** turns out to be his birthplace; and the woman to whom he is married turns out to be his mother.

Tiresias   Another figure whose presence seems to validate the oracle's authority is **Tiresias** [tih-REE-sih-as], prophet of Apollo. According to the myths, Tiresias was blinded by Hera (or possibly Athene) for witnessing the goddess bathing—a view of the gods too intimate for mere mortals. He was also punished (for killing the female of a pair of copulating snakes he encountered) by being made to spend one year as a woman, after which he retained both male and female sexual characteristics. In another variant, when asked which gender enjoyed sex more, Tiresias angered Hera by replying that the woman had more pleasure. She punished him by blinding him. According to these myths, Zeus compensated Tiresias for his physical blindness by giving him the gift of inner sight, or prophetic vision. Blind to distracting surface appearances, Tiresias is gifted as well with the wholeness of perspective that comes from a wider range of human experience than is available to mortals restricted to a single gender: as an androgynous human, at once male and female, he represents the psyche in which animus and anima are balanced. In the earlier epics, as well as in the tragedies, Tiresias had long since become a symbol of wisdom and insight into the will of the gods. Nevertheless, the clear perception and open revelation of that will is fraught with danger to humans. The gods speak in riddles while themselves remaining obscure and mysterious to us. Seeing a deity too close up, too clearly, in "natural," undisguised or unmediated form, brought death to the Theban princess Semele, who made love to Zeus, and to her nephew Actaeon, who observed the naked Artemis. Similarly, piercing the veil that hides the nature of the deities from human perception, and having the temerity to reveal what he saw, resulted in the blinding of Tiresias, who saw more of (or farther into) Hera than is permitted.

The blinding of Oedipus, who likewise tries to rip the veil off the divine mysteries, is also, from the gods' perspective, appropriate, if not inevitable. When Tiresias tells Oedipus, "To be wise is to suffer," he knows whereof he speaks. Dismissing

Tiresias's warning, Oedipus, ever the rationalist, persists in his demand for clarity of vision, for a logical explanation of the mysteries of the gods. However, to turn the light of human reason on the divine mysteries is to render oneself unable to see them. Thus, blinding himself to the mysteries of Dionysus, another Theban, Pentheus, was mutilated (see Chapter 17); Oedipus's self-blinding is a variant on the sparagmos theme.

Civic Responsibility   For all the ways in which fate is operative in the world of drama, Sophocles strictly circumscribes its sphere of operations. For example, the myths about Oedipus's family include references to a "curse" on the House of Labdacus, his grandfather. Such curses were presumed to be passed on from one generation to the next, until they were expiated to the gods' satisfaction. Sophocles, however, never even alludes to such a possibility, apparently excluding inherited pollution as a relevant factor in Oedipus's life.

Further, within the context of the play itself, Apollo is not initially concerned with Oedipus's violations of the primal taboos against patricide and incest. When the play opens, the prophecy has long since been fulfilled. Nevertheless, Oedipus has lived in Thebes for years, an honored leader, beloved husband, and loving parent. The sin that has angered Apollo was committed not by Oedipus but by the people of Thebes. Thus, some readers see the play as essentially political and equate Oedipus's fall with the potential failure of Athens itself. The city, after all, had been jarred by the war and the plague from its pride and confidence in its rationally ordered system, and tempted by leaders who would behave like a "tyrannos" of earlier times, developments that threatened the survival of Athenian democracy and put Athens at risk of becoming another Thebes.

Long regarded as being rooted in violence since its legendary founder, **Cadmus,** sowed dragon's teeth to create the city's first inhabitants, a race of armed men (see Chapter 17), **Thebes** had a reputation—much like that of Italy as depicted in the plays of the European Renaissance—as a place where evil reigned, where any form of corruption was possible. Thebes was, further, an enemy to Athens, having taken the side of the Persians during the Persian Wars and even fighting the Athenians during the Peloponnesian War. The Athenian audience would undoubtedly have been gratified to watch as, in Sophocles' portrayal, the Thebans, absorbed in their own affairs, engaged in a merely token investigation of the murder of their king while the perpetrator went unpunished. It is thus the people of Thebes—not Oedipus—who are punished by the plague. This is the message that Creon bears when he returns from the oracle: Justice and civic health must be restored. Nor does Apollo speak of blinding as the desired sanction for regicide; exile (the typical sentence imposed by Athens on offenders) is the punishment Apollo requires. Oedipus's self-blinding is done by his own choice.

Oedipus's Character

Sophocles not only sets limits to the scope of fate in the play but also provides for alternative explanations of the events surrounding Oedipus's life. Although fate may provide one explanation for Oedipus's leaving Corinth to go out on the road, where he will encounter his father, Laius, Oedipus's character provides another.

FIGURE 16-1 The Abandoned Oedipus
Being Rescued. The vase painter depicts the
shepherd bringing the infant Oedipus to the
childless royal couple in Corinth. The child
clings to his rescuer, whose evident compassion contrasts markedly with the cruelty of
Oedipus's biological parents. *(Cabinet des
Modailles, Paris)*

Laius thought he could control his destiny by taking preventive action. Thus, to
prevent fulfillment of his predicted murder by his own son, he had the child's ankles pierced and bound (hence the name *Oedipus,* meaning "swollen foot") and
abandoned the child on a mountainside to die rather than accept responsibility for
murdering his own son. How could he predict that the child would be rescued by a
sympathetic shepherd and delivered to Corinth, to be adopted by the childless royal
couple (Figure 16-1)? Oedipus similarly chose to leave Corinth, believing that he
could prevent the oracle's fulfillment and evade the inevitable guilt. Both acts—intended to preempt the will of the gods and to avoid or change destiny—ironically
help to bring it about. Thus, the son's experience recapitulates the father's. Both are
bound up in the set of innate human responses long attested to in even the most
ancient of Greek myths of the creation and the generations of the gods—responses
that produce rivalry and potential violence between fathers and sons and that express themselves in the typical "heroic," ego-driven obsession with permanence,
with the linear extension of the self through time.

Father and son likewise make similar behavioral choices. Fate may or may not
play a role in the extraordinary circumstances that place father and son at the crossroads at the same critical moment. But the more important question is, how do
individuals respond to the circumstances in which they find themselves? In the case
of Laius and Oedipus, pride and anger surely determine what happens when their

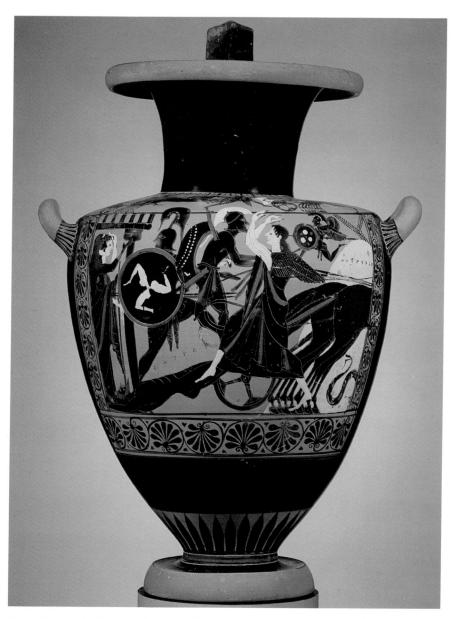

Color Plate 9 Achilles with the Body of Hector, c. 560 B.C. The painting on this Athenian water jar illustrates a dramatic scene from Book 24 of the *Iliad.* Wearing a plumed helmet and carrying a shield with a triskele, a figure composed of three legs joined together, Achilles mounts his chariot, to which he has tied the body of Hector. Achilles looks back at Hecuba and Priam, who lament this public degradation of their son's corpse. Achilles's driver stands in the chariot, holding the horses's reins as Iris, a winged figure personifying the rainbow, arrives from Olympus. Repelled by Achilles's shameful mistreatment of the fallen Trojan hero, the Olympian gods have determined that Achilles must return Hector's body to his parents for honorable burial. (*William Francis Warden Fund. Courtesy Museum of Fine Arts, Boston. Reproduced with permission. Courtesy of the Museum of Fine Arts, Boston.*)

Color Plate 10   Nicolas Poussin, *Bacchanalian Revel before a Term of Pan.* Whereas Apollo personifies the value of rational clarity, harmonious balance, and self-discipline, his half-brother Dionysus (also called Bacchus) represents the joyful release from care found in spontaneous emotion and unrestrained self-expression (see Chapters 8 and 17). In this work of the seventeenth-century French painter Nicolas Poussin, the artist presents a surprisingly light-hearted version of the wild, ecstatic dance inspired by Dionysian possession. The garlanded statue of Pan, half-bestial god of untamed nature and instinctive sensuality, gleefully presides over the revelry, its rigid immobility contrasting with the supple and energetic movement of the human figures. In Poussin's benign vision of earthy merriment, even the potential menace of a satyr threatening to assault a young woman is belied by her smiling lack of concern about his intensions (bottom right), while a companion holding a gold vase raised to clobber the offending satyr is in turn gently restrained by the arm of a nymph standing behind her. (*National Gallery, London*).

Color Plate 11   Sandro Botticelli, *Venus and Mars*, 1485. In this Renaissance painting, fauns play with Mars's helmet and spear while the war god, exhausted after his amorous exertions, sleeps. Venus herself, calm and composed, looks on, clearly the controlling figure here, despite Mars's weapons. (*National Gallery, London.*)

Color Plate 12 Pieter Breughel, the Elder, *The Fall of Icarus*, 1555–1556. The "heroic" figure of Icarus, emblem of the aspirations of Renaissance humanism, is here shifted off to an insignificant corner. The legs of the boy, barely visible in the lower right-hand corner of the painting, hardly create a splash, while the farmer goes on plowing, the ship goes on sailing, and the shepherd doesn't even look up: Icarus is nobody special. (*Musées Royaux des Beaux-Arts, Brussels.*)

Color Plate 13   Marc Chagall, *The Fall of Icarus,* 1975. In contrast to Breughel's version of this subject (see Color Plate 12), Icarus is the central figure in Chagall's painting. With upraised wings aflame, the figure of Icarus, the largest in the painting, suggests a fallen angel who hurtles, not toward water, but toward a landscape already ablaze. The sun, depicted with menacing geometric rays, seems already darkened, as if its light as well as its heat have been transferred, via Icarus's rebellion, to the crowds of people who watch, already caught up in the tragedy about to take place. (*Private collection, St. Paul de Vence, France.*)

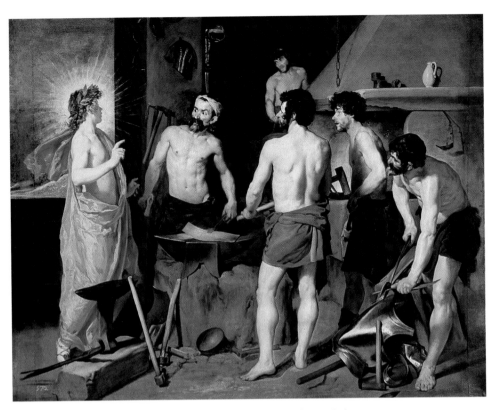

Color Plate 14   Diego Velázquez, *The Forge of Vulcan,* 1630. Velázquez's dramatic painting is based on the bard Demodocus's song about the illicit love affair between Aphrodite (Venus) and Ares (Mars) (*Odyssey,* Book 8). The Spanish painter depicts the precise moment at which the sun god, Helios, whose celestial perspective enables him to see everything, informs Hephaestus (Vulcan) that his wife and her paramour are then engaged in an act of adultery, bringing the god's labor to a sudden stop. The slight frame and fair skin of Helios (left), whose garlanded head radiates a solar brilliance, contrasts markedly with the darker complexions and sinuous musculature of Hephaestus and his four assistants. Although momentarily rendered immobile by the unwelcome news, the ingenious god of metalcraft soon devises a way to trap and expose the guilty lovers to public shame (see Chapter 6). (*Museo del Prado, Madrid.*)

Color Plate 15   Titian, *Venus and Adonis,* 1562. Titian shows Venus's lover, Adonis, about to leave for the hunt during which he will be killed. Characteristically, the stability of the typical Renaissance composition of geometric forms (compare figures 21-15 and 21-16) is hinted at but shattered in this painting. The legs of Venus's contorted body point out of the frame of the painting, while Adonis's spear points at another angle, and the hunting dogs strain their leashes in the opposite direction altogether, all beneath a swirling vortex of cloud formations. (*National Gallery, London.*)

Color Plate 16   Salvador Dali, *The Metamorphosis of Narcissus,* 1936–1937. Turning to classical myths just as Picasso did to express the complexities of the modern world (see Figure 21-5), Dali took as his subject the story of Narcissus, who fell in love with his own reflection in a pond and was turned into the flower that bears his name. In this painting, Dali comments on the self-destructive potential, the essentially narcissistic nature, of psychoanalysis. (Expressing his usual wit, he brought this painting to show Freud when he met the "father of psychoanalysis"!) The figure on the left stares inward at itself, its face a blank to the external world. To the right, the figure of the hand (the psychoanalyst?) that holds an egg—simultaneously the head and embryo of the self—recapitulates the figure on the left. Immobilized in stone, the egg burst forth in flower, reborn in the act of self-analysis. But it does so alone, apart from the dance of humanity that has receded to the background. The "crack" in the egg/head on the left reveals the result: the flower, too, will soon be petrified—reduced to an image, the life, like the color, has gone out of it. (*Tate Gallery, London.*)

paths intersect. What but pride in his status as king could prompt Laius to order passersby out of his way? What but pride in his own worth could prompt Oedipus to refuse the request? And what but uncontrollable anger could drive Oedipus to commit an act of "road rage," killing an old man for what he perceives to be an insult?

Oedipus may be in control of his rational decisions, but when angered, all restraints disappear, and he lashes out at whatever targets present themselves—the old heroic impulse that prompts heroes to attack first and worry about consequences later, as did Achilles and Hector. Thus, describing his encounter with Laius, Oedipus says, "Him I struck, for I was angry." Compelled by similar emotional responses, he lashes out at Creon, who is trying to help him, and at Tiresias, whom he himself has summoned, irrationally accusing both of crimes and conspiracies. Perhaps what Oedipus inherited from his father are not curses but the genetic predisposition toward personality traits. His frustration results in extreme anger combined with a dissociative response—primal instinct split off from the normal, rational responses of the brain. Denying the oracle, Oedipus experiences Dionysian freedom and excess, untempered by Apollonian restraint. And while Oedipus's behavior does not directly cause his ultimate suffering, it certainly potentiates the train of events that will end in tragedy.

The Importance of Riddles

Further, no oracle speaks of Oedipus's analytical intelligence—his extraordinary skill at solving riddles—nor does the oracle mention his courage in being willing even to confront the Sphinx, who had killed all previous challengers. In his relentless pursuit of evidence and unraveling of clues, Oedipus, drama's first detective hero, displays skills that the Sophists would have admired. Had Oedipus been less intelligent or courageous, his marriage with the now-widowed Jocasta—his reward for saving Thebes from the ravenous creature—could not have taken place. It is one of the play's many riddles that his virtues themselves become sources of his unhappiness.

As many readers note, riddles are central to the play in many ways. Behind the riddles in which Tiresias speaks and the riddle of Oedipus's identity, the unraveling of which forms the plot, lies the riddle of the Sphinx (Figure 16-2): "What walks on four legs in the morning, two legs in the afternoon, and three legs in the evening?" The answer, as Oedipus knew, to his own undoing, is "man," or, as we would now state it, humans, who crawl on all fours in infancy, walk upright throughout most of their lives, and lean on a cane in old age. Oedipus was satisfied that he knew the answer. But although he could solve the riddle by providing the correct word, as in some kind of diabolical quiz show, and thus escape the fatal penalty, he failed to understand its significance.

The riddle implies, first, that humans are all fated, at least in the sense that they are all destined to lose control even over their own bodies as they age and eventually to die: independence is a brief, transitory interval between the respective inadequacies of infancy and old age. The human will is free only in relative terms. During the crisis in Thebes, Oedipus believes that he is totally in charge: "I, Oedipus, whose name is known from afar." In the opening scene of the play, Oedipus

FIGURE 16-2   Oedipus Being Questioned by the Sphinx. As depicted in this vase painting, the Sphinx (part woman, part lion, part eagle) poses the riddle to Oedipus, who sits, looking her right in the eye, with his chin resting on his hand and his legs casually crossed. His air of bemused self-assurance suggests that he is patiently, if somewhat patronizingly, waiting for her to finish the question so that he can state aloud the answer he has already deduced. *(Vatican Museums, Rome)*

comes out himself to greet the suppliants and, before the opening lines are spoken, has already taken appropriate action. He has no inkling at this stage that the illusion of control is about to be shattered or that the general human condition applies to him.

Another major implication of the riddle is that humans are by nature a riddle—a mystery even to themselves. Is it possible for humans to truly know themselves, as Apollo commands? Oedipus may be able to follow the clues and fill in the blank surface data of his identity—his birthplace and the name of his parents—but there are depths to his own psyche that he doesn't even begin to suspect until the very last. Even Jocasta, who doesn't want to know, recognizes the horror before Oedipus does—that an admired and respected individual, an upright citizen and community leader, conceals beneath his conscious self a shadow self that is capable of the most appalling crimes. The monster that the hero must confront is now the libidinous beast within. He is no more in control of his psyche than he will be of his body in old age.

The Male and Female Principles

The Sphinx, a winged creature with the head of a woman and the body of a lion, combines the ancient symbols of the Great Goddess, with her birds and beasts. Like all heroes, Oedipus must defeat her to fulfill his role. One modern poet, Muriel Rukeyser, suggests, in her witty revision of the myth, that Oedipus misses the point of the riddle, and thus fails to recognize his mother, because he is blind to the riddle's feminine component: saying "man," he excludes women. The word *man* includes women, Rukeyser's Oedipus argues. "That's what you think," replies the Sphinx. Although Rukeyser is commenting on Oedipus's sexist language, the poem also touches on his larger failure, in the myth itself, to acknowledge the feminine principle.

In his conventional masculine-heroic identification of his integrity with the need to pursue his quest for his identity to its bitter end, regardless of the consequences, Oedipus is determined to "go forward always," like Hector or any other hero. And, as for the epic heroes, who can die young if they pursue glory in war or face psychic self-annihilation if they withdraw, "going forward" is the only choice consistent with Oedipus's sense of integrity. To "go forward" is to precipitate inevitable catastrophe; to choose otherwise would be to self-destruct, to give the deathblow to his very identity. Further, like all those other heroes who follow in the footsteps of Heracles, Oedipus, who had already separated himself from the family he had in Corinth, destroys the one he acquired in Thebes: his wife/mother is dead, and no normal future for his daughters is now possible. It is no mere coincidence that, like the Sphinx who was also destroyed by Oedipus, Jocasta realized the truth long before Oedipus but was destroyed when he "solved" the riddle and answered the question. Like many other women in Greek mythology, from Megara and Andromache to Clytemnestra and Agave, Jocasta finds that the heroic approach to experience, whether assumed by their husbands or, in a reversal of roles, by the women themselves, is destructive to women both in literal terms and in the only two roles they are allowed: marriage and motherhood.

Unlike Heracles' quests, though, Oedipus's quest is an internal one. From the archetypal perspective, the descent into the unconscious is the descent into the womb of the mother, the exploration of the female principle that thereby makes possible the recovery of the anima. The very quest that destroys Oedipus's actual mother allows him to find the mother within himself. It is only when Oedipus, having discovered the truth, accepts the mystery of his fate and of the gods' role in bringing it about, and so resigns himself to his condition of metaphysical blindness, that he is reconciled with the feminine principle, as was Tiresias before him. It is only now that Oedipus can speak of his love for his children and his pity for the suffering they will have to endure. It is thus appropriate that, as the myths attest, when Oedipus goes out on the road again, this time in exile, it will be one of his daughters, and not one of his sons, who will guide him on his final journey.

The Metaphysical Dimensions of the Oedipus Myth

Perhaps the most important implication of Oedipus's response to the Sphinx's riddle is that Oedipus—the supreme riddler—believes that all questions have answers and that humans can ascertain those answers by applying their wits and their logic. But adherence to the way of Apollo—god of intellect, logic, and riddles—to the exclusion of Dionysus and his mysteries is as unsatisfactory, and as destructive, as is the reverse. That some questions have no answers, that some mysteries are insoluble, and that the cosmos of the gods may be as far beyond the reach of human reason as the human psyche is beneath it never occurs to him. Why do terrible things happen to good people who are trying to do the right thing? Why do the gods call down such fates on individuals even before they are born? Humans who have suffered have always asked, "Why me?" and "Why now?" Destiny or choice? **Peripeteia**—reversal—happens, whether or not we can explain it. The play poses a riddle that seems to have no definitive answer.

Once awakened from his illusion that life has a clear purpose and that he is in rational control, Oedipus comes finally to accept the mystery—that the gods are not obliged to explain themselves to humans and that mere human logic is insufficient to explain their intentions or even to know whether they have any. Logic presupposes observable facts and relationships and thus can hardly be an adequate guide in a world in which the blind see but the sighted do not. Oedipus, in his blindness, literalizes the condition of all tragic heroes—of all humanity—groping blindly in a world they must inhabit but cannot comprehend.

Oedipus's Triumph

Recognizing that Apollo is in some indecipherable way behind the events in his life, Sophocles' Oedipus nevertheless freely asserts his own integrity and insists on taking responsibility for his acts. His father, Laius, had exposed his son to the elements instead of simply killing him, presumably to avoid being held responsible for the child's death: when he died, it would be the gods' doing. For Oedipus, blaming the gods would represent another attempt to escape. Instead, Oedipus insists, whatever Apollo might or might not have contributed to the circumstances in his life, "I did it." Paradoxically, his newfound awareness of the truth about his limits, of his essential ignorance, of the fact that he cannot ever know to what extent Apollo is responsible for his life's course, liberates him.

From the first, Oedipus accepts his role as scapegoat—just as in the ancient ritual—taking the people's sins on himself and ultimately redeeming them through his sacrifice and suffering. The plague lifts, and order is restored in Thebes. At the same time, he redeems himself, asserting his freedom even while accepting the burdens that fate has heaped on him. Not only does he impose pain on himself, in his self-blinding, an act far more intense than anything Apollo required, but he also reaches a kind of moral transcendence. To Oedipus's infinite credit, when all the pieces begin falling into place as a result of his logical investigation, he confronts the truth squarely. No longer attempting to avoid the inevitable, Oedipus now insists (as heroes must), "Let it come." In a moment of blinding insight, he recognizes the horror within. At that moment, in one of the play's many ironies, Apollo and Dionysus—control and excess, fate and freedom—converge on each other.

By putting his eyes out, an ironic reversal of his previous failure to see, Oedipus confronts the reality that only the gods have seen and that is more than mortal eyes can bear. Like Tiresias, Oedipus acquires true vision, his unflinching awareness of the truth in all its complexity. He may stop the flow of sensory data, but he cannot shut off his mind. What is dredged up from the depths of his psyche cannot again be repressed. The sighted Oedipus had been blind; the blinded Oedipus becomes, like Tiresias, a seer.

In an act of supreme moral courage, when death would be the easy way out, Oedipus chooses to live with the curse of awareness, with the knowledge that is pain. As Tiresias had said, "To be wise is to suffer." Following the archetypal path of mythic heroes, Oedipus experiences total alienation from his community, descends to the depth of his own inner hell, and returns. Hero and victim, subject and object of his own quest, the maimed king is transformed by his experience. Only now—when the terrible burden has been lifted and his fate is fulfilled—is Oedipus at last truly free.

Oedipus at Colonus

It is this redeemed Oedipus, now walking on three legs, as the riddle predicted, whom Sophocles, in his final play (produced posthumously, in 401 B.C.), sets on the road to Colonus, a village on the outskirts of Athens where the playwright himself had been born. Tradition asserted that Oedipus was buried there and that a shrine devoted to Oedipus, Theseus, and other ancient heroes was located on the spot. In the nearly twenty-five years between the creation of *Oedipus Rex* and *Oedipus at Colonus,* Sophocles reconsidered the myth, changing his mind about Oedipus himself, as well as about some specific details in the play. For example, in *Oedipus Rex,* Oedipus was ready to go into exile immediately, though it is not clear that he actually did so; in *Oedipus at Colonus,* his exile had apparently been delayed, and his daughter Antigone, a child in the earlier play, has reached adulthood and guided her blind father on his journey.

Meanwhile, Oedipus's sons, Eteocles and Polyneices, have taken over the government of Thebes from Creon, who had been ruling as regent. But the brothers quarreled, and Polyneices, now married to the daughter of the king of Argos, is leading an army against Thebes. Further complicating the situation, the oracle has revealed that victory and prosperity will be assured for whichever city earns Oedipus's goodwill while he lives and secures the right to retain his bones when he dies. Thus, Oedipus's sons—who shunned their father as a defiler of civilized society during his exile and are now about to do battle with each other—want the old man back as a guarantor of their rival claims to power over Thebes.

Contemporary Relevance

The threat of war, particularly the war Oedipus predicts between Thebes and Athens, would have been immediately relevant to the Athenian audience—in fact, Thebes and Athens, on opposite sides in the Peloponnesian War, had recently fought a minor battle. Some Athenians credited their victory in that encounter to the presence of the shrine and the blessing that Oedipus had bestowed on the city. Colonus had already been burned by the Spartans in 406 B.C. and was in ruins. The Athenians would, of course, also have responded enthusiastically to the play's praise of Athens as a city of justice and law.

Similarities and Differences Between the Two Oedipus Plays

Oedipus Rex and *Oedipus at Colonus* share a thread of common contemporary references. Other components of the earlier play are also retained in *Oedipus at Colonus.* For example, Oedipus still is tainted by his sins, so that the inhabitants of Colonus are at first terrified of allowing him to stay. Even though several cities compete for the right to keep his remains nearby, within their jurisdiction, none wants Oedipus, alive or dead, to enter its precincts. Only the Eumenides, or Furies (tactfully called the "Kindly Ones"), who are themselves shunned by humans and gods alike, allow him to enter their sacred grove unharmed.

In his unremitting anger, the Oedipus of the last play is also portrayed as being like the earlier character. This time, his anger is largely directed against his son Polyneices, who, like his father, refuses to back down and will pursue his intended war against Thebes despite pleas from his sister and warnings from his father.

Sophocles' final portrayal of Oedipus, however, while continuing that of *Oedipus Rex* in some respects, is also very different in others. In fact, in many ways, the later play inverts the earlier. In *Oedipus Rex* the hero insisted on his moral responsibility for his acts whereas, in *Oedipus at Colonus,* he insists on his essential innocence, blaming the gods for the sinful acts he unwittingly committed and arguing that his self-blinding was an overreaction in the heat of the moment. And whereas earlier his greatness lay in his determination to wrench his destiny from the hands of fate and to shunt the gods aside, now he relishes the role of victim: here, "suffering, not doing," is his strength.

Oedipus's innocence is underscored first by the approval of that favorite mythic hero Theseus and further by the thunder—the sign from Zeus—that reverberates through the play. And whereas, in the earlier play, Oedipus wrongly attacked the innocent Tiresias and Creon, in this play, Creon is depicted, as he is in Sophocles' earlier *Antigone,* as self-serving and tyrannical, manipulating Oedipus for his own political purposes and abusing Oedipus's daughters.

In contrast to his insistence in the earlier play on self-sufficiency, Oedipus now admits his dependency and confesses his loneliness. Whereas before he couldn't wait to see what fate would bring, he has now learned patience. Similarly, out of his earlier alienation, isolated in his exile and blindness, he perceives the extent of his love for his daughters, for the bonds of the human world from which he has been long estranged, at just that moment when he is about to leave the human world for good.

The Reconciliation of Opposites

Oedipus at Colonus does not merely invert the conditions of the earlier play, however; in this play, opposites are reconciled in a series of paradoxes. Thus, Oedipus is here a victim who has been patient through terrible suffering. But he is no saint;

rather, he has become himself an avenger, a "Fury"—cursing his son directly (in contrast to the passive curse transferred from Laius to Oedipus in the earlier play). The victim of fate has also become its active agent. In the earlier play, too, Oedipus was the sighted man who was blind. Now, the blinded Oedipus sees: having come guided by Antigone, he finds his own way to the "holy mystery" of his end. And, having once repudiated their interference in his life, he now achieves reconciliation with the gods through the acceptance of their will.

The Dread Goddesses

While king of Thebes, the heroic Oedipus rejected the feminine principle, defying the various avatars of the Great Goddess, who is privy to the secrets of life and death; the Sphinx, who knew the secret of the riddle, "What is man?"; and Jocasta, who knew from the very first the secrets of the human psyche and who was presented in the earlier play in the usual heroic mode—the temptress whose attempts to get the hero to abort his quest had to be spurned. Now, just as Oedipus rejects his sons, he embraces the feminine principle, abandoning the light of the intellect for the chthonic darkness of the "dread goddesses": Oedipus, who has broken all taboos, commits one final violation in entering the sacred grove of the Eumenides. Instead of destroying him, however, they accept him, as if, having committed all forbidden acts, Oedipus has now transcended all taboos: nothing is now forbidden to him.

Death and Transfiguration

The final paradox of the play, of course, is the apotheosis of Oedipus, as he experiences death and possibly even transfiguration, the "holy mystery," which only Theseus is permitted to witness. Having descended to the depths, Oedipus is at last not only freed but deified as well. The cursed one is now himself a dispenser of curses and blessings—the former to his son, the latter to Athens as the play's conclusion depicts the chartering of the hero's cult. Like the Furies, he has become one of the Kindly Ones.

Antigone

The earliest of Sophocles' plays on the family of Oedipus, *Antigone* (c. 442–441 B.C.) follows the tragic story of the House of Laius after Oedipus's death. The civil war between Oedipus's sons over rulership of Thebes is over. Both brothers are dead, but Eteocles, who defended Thebes, is buried with honor, while the corpse of Polyneices, who attacked Thebes, is left unburied at the orders of Creon, who now assumes rulership.

Creon argues that the security of the state demands that traitors be punished. Offended at this act of utter impiety (proper burial of the dead being required by the gods if the soul is to find eternal rest), Antigone argues that the gods are a higher authority than the state and, courageously defying Creon's orders, she attempts to bury her brother's body herself.

Ostensibly a debate, Sophocles' *Antigone* has been variously interpreted as focused on the conflicting demands of the state and the individual, or of the political order (Creon's claim that to honor a traitor is to invite anarchy) and religious principles (Antigone's claim that to refuse to bury a corpse constitutes blasphemy), or even of family-based chthonic religion centered on the cult of the dead and the public, ouranic religion of the city. The play does, in fact, include several formal debates on such issues. Seen exclusively as a topical drama, the play seems to lack the explicitly "mythological" components of the two later plays of Sophocles' Oedipus cycle—*Oedipus Rex,* with its Apollonian oracles and riddles, and *Oedipus at Colonus,* with its Furies and the final apotheosis of the hero. It is, rather, in the rite of passage of the heroine herself that we may perceive the subtle mythical dimensions of Antigone's story.

The Tyranny of Creon

Composed at the height of the Athenian experiment in democracy, *Antigone,* not surprisingly, is concerned with political issues and is, in fact, the most overtly political of Sophocles' surviving plays. When the play opens, Creon has just assumed the kingship by default; Eteocles and Polyneices, Oedipus's sons, have died in the civil war that ended so recently that Polyneices' body still lies intact, just outside the city walls.

Precariously installed on the throne, Creon is understandably apprehensive about his ability to maintain civic order in a city that has just emerged from chaos. No sooner does he issue his first edict, meant to shore up his rulership by invoking the patriotism of the citizens, than it is violated, and as it turns out, by a member of his own family—his niece, Antigone, who is also engaged to his son **Haemon.** Antigone at first secretly gives the body a ritual or symbolic burial, covering it with a token coating of dust, but when her work is undone on Creon's orders, she is caught repeating the act. When Antigone then insists on defying Creon publicly, he is on the spot, aware that he is being "tested."

The debate begins rationally enough. But Creon keeps ratcheting up the terms of the argument as his anger incrementally increases. When Creon first hears about the "burial," he lashes out, blaming "anarchists" and imagining bribery and corruption everywhere. And from the first, something clearly is amiss in his methods of governance: his own sentry is afraid to do his duty and swears he will not return to Creon's presence. The chorus supports Creon to his face, but Haemon describes "whispers" of negative public opinion, voiced only out of the hearing of Creon, who terrifies the citizens. If Oedipus was the model ruler, taking the people's suffering on himself, Creon is the reverse.

In a democracy such as Athens', of course, there may be a conflict between two "right" positions. But it isn't long before Creon has reduced the alternatives in government to anarchy or tyranny—he must be obeyed "in all things, great and small, just and unjust," an argument that reaches its logical conclusion in Creon's most extreme assertion that "the State is the King." "Only," replies Haemon, "if the State is a desert" (or, perhaps, the surely sympathetic Athenian audience might have added, if the state is Sparta, where dictatorship reigned). In the swiftness with which Creon moves from reasoned debate to tyrannical abuse, Sophocles vividly dramatizes the necessity of a democratic leader's listening to both sides of an issue and to the "voice of the Demos." By obstinately standing alone, Creon reveals the folly of equating the leader's will with the welfare of the polis. In his rage, Creon threatens to execute Ismene, Antigone's younger sister, too, but Haemon's warnings about public opinion have apparently sunk in, and he quickly backs down.

The Prophecies of Tiresias

However, Creon refuses to yield on the punishment of Antigone, and even the arrival of Tiresias, who denounces him and predicts catastrophe, fails to persuade Creon to change his course. In fact, he accuses Tiresias, just as Oedipus had, of accepting bribes and fronting for conspirators. However, by bringing in Tiresias, as he would in *Oedipus Rex,* Sophocles has, in effect, called in the heavy artillery: the dichotomy was false all along. The gods, Tiresias tells Creon, are offended at the denial of burial rites, and Creon was simply wrong to make it an issue in the first place. Reminded by the ever-fearful chorus that Tiresias always speaks the truth, Creon relents—but too late to prevent the deaths of Antigone, of Haemon, or of Creon's wife, Eurydice, who commits suicide on hearing of her son's death.

To his credit, Creon belatedly acknowledges his guilt. But unlike the realization of Oedipus, there is no sense of transcendence in Creon's admission and subsequent fate. He behaved stupidly, and others paid the price. Helped into the palace by members of the chorus, Creon has forfeited the authority he wrongly set out to enhance while setting in motion a chain of personal tragedies. In fact, some readers see Creon, rather than Antigone, as the real protagonist of the play. But while he certainly receives the greatest amount of attention in the play, he has nothing of the "hero" about him. Fearful of losing his authority, fearful of public opinion and of his niece's potential power to sway that against him, fearful of Tiresias's prophecies and finally of the gods themselves, Creon is an ordinary man trapped in an extraordinary position. The utmost demands are made on his compassion, insight, and leadership, and he demonstrates that he is capable of none of those qualities. In effect, Sophocles uses Creon as an example of what a leader should *not* do.

Antigone's Roles

When we encounter Antigone in the opening lines of the play, she has already made the fatal decision to defy Creon's orders and risk death by carrying out the burial rite, symbolically sprinkling some dirt and wine over the corpse of her brother. A loyal sister, Antigone is first presented as a variant of the traditional heroine as loyal wife or mother. Initially, carrying out the ritual on her brother's behalf is the extent of her intention. She plans to have her younger sister, Ismene, help her. But as she encounters resistance first from Ismene and then from Creon, she grows more defiant and, in the process, increasingly assumes the masculine hero's stance.

Antigone as Hero-Impersonator   Ismene first raises the gender issue, protesting that she and her sister are "just weak women" who "cannot fight with men." In response, like any of the male heroes whose women want to keep them inside the protective walls of the home or city, Antigone rejects Ismene's advice, dismissing her beloved younger sister lest she find her "hateful."

From this point on, Antigone increasingly isolates herself—from her sister, with whom she refuses to share the blame, or credit, for her act; from the chorus, whose potential sympathy she undermines through her defiance; from her fiancé, to whom she never even asks to speak; and finally, from the world of the living altogether. The ultimate hero's quest—the journey to the Underworld—is one that must be made unaccompanied. Thus, we are not surprised to find Antigone declaring that to risk death in pursuit of what Ismene calls "impossible things" is preferable to the "worst of deaths—death without honor." Moving beyond the simple, pious motive with which she began—burial of the body—Antigone has added another—the quest for personal honor—thus aligning herself with the traditional heroic model.

Ismene, however, is right: conventionally, "weak women" do not fight civic authority, do not stand up to a king with an army and the apparent weight of public opinion, as expressed by the chorus, behind him. Antigone has entered uncharted territory—a woman "impersonating" a male hero. We can see the transformation in progress as she carries out her mission. The first time she buries the body, she does so in secret, at night; the second time, she does so in broad daylight. And when she is hauled before the king, she is outspoken, even calling him a "fool" in public, as bold in her verbal assault as Achilles was in confronting Agamemnon—perhaps more so, since she has no sword to back up her fighting words.

Her integrity, courage, and aggressiveness stand out even more in contrast to the chorus, well-to-do older men of Thebes who, afraid to speak up to Creon, only whisper behind his back until Tiresias validates Antigone's position. Then they literally change their tune. Even Haemon is initially deferential, claiming to value his father's "wisdom" more than any marriage. Only gradually, after failing to persuade his father to be reasonable, and using the grounds of public opinion to cover for his own, does Haemon come to Antigone's defense. The chorus's comment, which they intend as a criticism, reveals to us the awesome extent of Antigone's heroic achievement: Antigone, they declare, has "passed beyond all human daring."

Creon, who is certainly blind to his own political folly, responds instantly to Antigone's bursting of the shackles of gender. "Pride? In a slave?" he asks, although Antigone is referred to by the sentry as "Princess Antigone," a social role Creon must have honored when he allowed his own son Haemon to be betrothed to her. If she is a "slave," it is to the social conventions that confine females to the status of "weak women" and destroy them when they prove otherwise. Creon goes on to accuse Antigone not only of "double insolence" in breaking the law and boasting of having done so but, worse, of breaking that social code: "Who is the man here, she or I, if this crime goes unpunished?" If Creon lashes out at Antigone and refuses to yield despite the pleas of Haemon, the pressure of public opinion, and the warnings of Tiresias, the mouthpiece of the gods, it is because it is more than "law" and civic authority that Creon is defending: it is his masculine identity.

Antigone as Bride of Death   Heroines who opt for the masculine heroic model traditionally do not fare well. Those who, like Clytemnestra or Agave, commit crimes in liberating themselves from oppressive gender roles are suitably punished by the gods or their human agents. Those like Atalanta, whose only "crime" is the defiance of social convention itself, find themselves undone by the goddess the chorus refers to as "merciless Aphrodite." Antigone, however, commits no crimes in the eyes of the gods, nor does she stoop to pick up any golden apples that the love goddess might have planted in her path. Rather, like Iphigenia and other heroines from Alcestis to Psyche, she becomes a bride of Death. But unlike those heroines, who take on that role as victims because they must, Sophocles' Antigone chooses that role consciously, almost too eagerly, from the earliest stages of her development as a heroine. "It is the dead, not the living," she tells Ismene, "who make the longest demands." And when she is condemned by Creon, she refuses to allow Ismene to "lessen" her death "by sharing it." The distinction between them, Antigone insists, is that Ismene is "alive" but "I belong to Death."

It is not just that she accepts Death as a sacrifice in the name of piety, as Iphigenia does in the name of patriotism. It is, rather, that she reaches out and embraces Death. She does so, furthermore, as a substitute for marriage. Once again, the contrast to Iphigenia is revealing. Lured to the sacrificial altar on the pretense that she will be married to Achilles, Iphigenia finds that she will be "married" to Death instead. But though she accepts the necessity of her sacrifice, she did not choose that fate for herself. Antigone, in contrast, intentionally elects to be the bride of Death.

Creon, too, has substituted death for love not only literally, for Antigone, but for himself as well. Ordering the death of his own son's intended bride, Creon dismisses the concept that love represents anything more than sex: "There are places enough for him to push his plow." Just as government, for Creon, is a kingdom of one, fitting only for a desert, so marriage is a self-serving arrangement. Creon has shut himself off from any meaningful human relationships. During his debate with Haemon, Creon asks, "If I permit my own family to rebel, how shall I earn the world's obedience?" To defend his kingship, he has shut himself off from his family, and he ends up with neither. His loss of his family is the inevitable consequence of that hardening of the heart.

The chorus asks Creon, "Do you really intend to steal this girl from your son?" as if sexual jealousy were the mainspring of his action. "No," replies Creon, "Death will do that for me." Even the erotic envy he denies would have been, in some way, more human, more alive. As if to remind us of the contrast, the only deities the chorus refers to in the play are Aphrodite, Eros, and Dionysus, god of joy and passion, to whom they sing a hymn. But neither Antigone nor Creon hears the music of the wine god. Creon's vulgar substitution of Death for sex has its counterpart in Antigone's substitution, albeit nobler in purpose, of Death for love. Both impulses are life-denying: Eros is supplanted by Thanatos. It is not Creon, but Death, who is rival to Haemon in courtship of Antigone. And she emphatically chooses Death over Haemon.

Antigone "Stoned to Death"   Summoned by Death to the Underworld where, she says, there is "no bridesong," Antigone compares herself to Niobe, who was turned to stone because she could not stop weeping over the loss of her children. Antigone says she feels the "loneliness of her death in mine." Yet, unlike Niobe, Antigone has chosen isolation. She has rejected Ismene and, though she laments being denied the prospect of marriage, she makes no mention of Haemon, as if she has already passed not only "far beyond all human daring" but far beyond all human love as well, and has "come at last to a place of stone" that is both her tomb and the marriage bed on which Haemon will join her in death.

Creon had originally decreed that whoever dared to bury Polyneices would be stoned to death; instead, as if internalizing that decree, Antigone has turned her heart to stone, shutting off all feeling. Of course, her family betrayed her: the consequences of her parents' incestuous marriage and her brothers' self-destructive warfare left her bereft of any family apart from her sister. Ismene's refusal to help with the burial seems to have severed Antigone's last family bond. For all her insistence that she was acting out of love for her brother, she seems to have been more in love with death. In burying Polyneices, she was also burying the last vestige of her capacity to love. Enclosed in a stony prison of self where no further betrayal or loss is possible, she has ironically become a counterpart to Creon, and the stone vault in which she is entombed becomes a fitting emblem for her psychological state. Entering the cave that will be her tomb, a "vaulted bride-bed in eternal rock," she becomes, like Persephone, a bride of Hades, hanging herself there with her bridal veil. Unlike the goddess, though, Antigone will not be able to return to the world of the living.

Every hero, of course, enters the Underworld, and Antigone has thus far followed the heroic path. For the male hero, however, the journey to the Underworld is a turning point, to be followed, in the usual structure of the heroic quest, by the hero's return, his rebirth into the world of the living, bearing new knowledge and the possibility of transcendence in the hereafter. Even Oedipus, the pollution of whose incestuous marriage Antigone sees as causing the destruction of her own, undergoes apotheosis and becomes the object of a hero cult.

For a woman, however, the journey to the Underworld is usually a one-way trip. Having elected to pursue the heroic course instead of letting go of the dead and accepting marriage to Haemon, Antigone has chosen to martyr herself, a choice confirmed by the swiftness with which she ends her own life, preempting Creon's reversal and decision to release her, which come moments too late to prevent her death or those of Haemon and Eurydice to follow.

Haemon as Nexus

It is Haemon who provides the nexus between the major strands of Sophocles' drama—the political and the personal, the masculine and the feminine. The long debate during which Haemon tries, patiently and rationally, to persuade his father to bury Polyneices and free Antigone stands in stark counterpoint to the later scene in which, entering the cave, Creon finds Haemon embracing Antigone's corpse, bewailing his lost love. Now the language of debate, a suitable vehicle for political discourse but an inadequate one for powerful emotions, gives way to silence. Haemon speaks "not a word": love and hatred speak more profoundly through the language of the body. Having embraced Antigone, Haemon attempts to stab his father and, missing, turns the sword on himself. Both Haemon and Antigone began with a rational determination to act according to the demands of political wisdom or piety. Both end their lives in irrational and tragically unnecessary acts of suicide. Standing on the brink of the abyss, of a world beyond the reach of reason, Antigone leaps, and Haemon follows.

Haemon is highly unusual among Greek heroes: dying for love had not become the romantic tradition that Sophocles' play foreshadows—the *liebestod* (love-and-death) theme—and that would later elevate the deaths of heroes, from Shakespeare's Romeo to Goethe's Werther or Wagner's Tristan, to the level of the sublime. It is, after all, the task of the mythological hero to rescue the maiden from death, not to join her there—to release the terrified girl chained to a rock or entombed, as Perseus rescued Andromeda and Heracles freed Hesione (a Trojan princess likewise chained to a rock). Heracles even released Alcestis from the Underworld itself. Compared to the traditional Greek mythological hero, who must reject the erotic or domestic temptation that would deflect him from his quest, Haemon has behaved in a way normally associated with women. Alcestis may be willing to die, and Medea to kill, for love. Jason scorns Medea, though, for being so concerned about love in the first place, a response he contemptuously attributes to the influence of Aphrodite. In Sophocles' play, it is Antigone-as-hero who implicitly denies Aphrodite, and Haemon who is under the goddess's spell. Creon had condemned Antigone for appropriating the male role. As Antigone increasingly adopts the heroic male attitudes, her fiancé, rejecting his father's mode, increasingly appropriates the traditionally feminine response. For Haemon, love achieves what the sword failed to accomplish. Thus, Haemon opens a new path to transcendence for the hero, mediating the opposition of Eros and Thanatos and, like Antigone, finding fulfillment in the joining of love and death.

Antigone and *Romeo and Juliet*

Over two thousand years later, an English playwright would create a highly similar double death scene in another drama of young lovers tragically caught up in a world of violence and political rivalry, itself influenced by Greco-Roman mythology—the tragic tale of the young lovers, Pyramus and Thisbe, recounted by the Roman poet Ovid in his *Metamorphoses*. But the tragedy of Haemon and Antigone only superficially resembles that of Shakespeare's *Romeo and Juliet,* and the difference is instructive. Shakespeare's lovers mutually commit themselves to love, and they die in the attempt to make their marriage possible. But while Romeo, like Haemon, kills himself on entering the tomb and finding his beloved dead, Haemon and Antigone are no "star-crossed lovers." Whereas Romeo begins by defying his father and hers in order to share his love with Juliet, Haemon begins by declaring that obedience to his father means more to him than marriage. Then, as the grip of "merciless Aphrodite" grows increasingly powerful, and as he becomes increasingly enraged with his father and determined first to defend Antigone and then to die with her if he cannot live with her, the trajectory of her path moves in the opposite direction, away from love, away from the affirmation of life.

Juliet's death is an accident of timing, not, at least initially, a choice. She enters the tomb where she will die expecting the fairy-tale ending, to be awakened with a kiss. Antigone, in contrast, has no wish to be awakened and strangles herself with the bridal veil she would have worn to wed Haemon. When Haemon embraces her in death, she has not merely died before him, as Juliet did Romeo; she has long since abandoned the world of the living and left him far behind.

OEDIPUS REX*

Sophocles

CHARACTERS

OEDIPUS, *king of Thebes*

A PRIEST

CREON, *brother-in-law of Oedipus*

CHORUS *of Theban elders*

TEIRESIAS, *a prophet*

JOCASTA, *sister of Creon, wife of Oedipus*

MESSENGER

SERVANT *of Laius, father of Oedipus*

SECOND MESSENGER

(silent) ANTIGONE *and* ISMENE, *daughters of Oedipus*

SCENE

Before the palace of OEDIPUS *at Thebes. In front of the large central doors, an altar; and an altar near each of the two side doors. On the altar steps are seated suppliants —old men, youths, and young boys—dressed in white tunics and cloaks, their hair bound with white fillets. They have laid on the altars olive branches wreathed with wool-fillets.*

The old PRIEST OF ZEUS *stands alone facing the central doors of the palace. The doors open, and* OEDIPUS, *followed by two attendants who stand at either door, enters and looks about.*

Oedipus

O children, last born stock of ancient Cadmus,   1
What petitions are these you bring to me
With garlands on your suppliant olive branches?
The whole city teems with incense fumes,
Teems with prayers for healing and with groans.
Thinking it best, children, to hear all this
Not from some messenger, I came myself,
The world renowned and glorious Oedipus.
But tell me, aged priest, since you are fit
To speak before these men, how stand you here,   10
In fear or want? Tell me, as I desire

---

*Translation by Albert S. Cook.

To do my all; hard hearted I would be
To feel no sympathy for such a prayer.

Priest
O Oedipus, ruler of my land, you see
How old we are who stand in supplication
Before your altars here, some not yet strong
For lengthy flight, some heavy with age,
Priests, as I of Zeus, and choice young men.
The rest of the tribe sits with wreathed branches,
In market places, at Pallas' two temples,
And at prophetic embers by the river.   20
The city, as you see, now shakes too greatly
And cannot raise her head out of the depths
Above the gory swell. She wastes in blight,
Blight on earth's fruitful blooms and grazing flocks,
And on the barren birth pangs of the women.
The fever god has fallen on the city,
And drives it, a most hated pestilence
Through whom the home of Cadmus is made empty.
Black Hades is enriched with wails and groans.
Not that we think you equal to the gods   30
These boys and I sit suppliant at your hearth,
But judging you first of men in the trials of life,
And in the human intercourse with spirits:—
You are the one who came to Cadmus' city
And freed us from the tribute which we paid
To the harsh-singing Sphinx. And that you did
Knowing nothing else, unschooled by us.
But people say and think it was some god
That helped you to set our life upright.   40
Now Oedipus, most powerful of all,
We all are turned here toward you, we beseech you,
Find us some strength, whether from one of the gods
You hear an omen, or know one from a man.
For the experienced I see will best
Make good plans grow from evil circumstance.
Come, best of mortal men, raise up the state.
Come, prove your fame, since now this land of ours
Calls you savior for your previous zeal.
O never let our memory of your reign   50
Be that we first stood straight and later fell,
But to security raise up this state.
With favoring omen once you gave us luck;
Be now as good again; for if henceforth
You rule as now, you will be this country's king,
Better it is to rule men than a desert,

Since nothing is either ship or fortress tower
Bare of men who together dwell within.

Oedipus
O piteous children, I am not ignorant
Of what you come desiring. Well I know 60
You are all sick, and in your sickness none
There is among you as sick as I,
For your pain comes to one man alone,
To him and to none other, but my soul
Groans for the state, for myself, and for you.
You do not wake a man who is sunk in sleep;
Know that already I have shed many tears,
And travelled many wandering roads of thought.
Well have I sought, and found one remedy;
And this I did: the son of Menoeceus, 70
Creon, my brother-in-law, I sent away
Unto Apollo's Pythian halls to find
What I might do or say to save the state.
The days are measured out that he is gone;
It troubles me how he fares. Longer than usual
He has been away, more than the fitting time.
But when he comes, then evil I shall be,
If all the god reveals I fail to do.

Priest
You speak at the right time. These men just now
Signal to me that Creon is approaching. 80

Oedipus
O Lord Apollo, grant that he may come
In saving fortune shining as in eye.

Priest
Glad news he brings, it seems, or else his head
Would not be crowned with leafy, berried bay.

Oedipus
We will soon know. He is close enough to hear.—
Prince, my kinsman, son of Menoeceus,
What oracle do you bring us from the god?

Creon
A good one. For I say that even burdens
If they chance to turn out right, will all be well.

Oedipus
Yet what is the oracle? Your present word 90
Makes me neither bold nor apprehensive.

Creon
If you wish to hear in front of this crowd
I am ready to speak, or we can go within.

Oedipus
Speak forth to all. The sorrow that I bear
Is greater for these men than for my life.

Creon
May I tell you what I heard from the god?
Lord Phoebus clearly bids us to drive out,
And not to leave uncured within this country,
A pollution we have nourished in our land.

Oedipus
With what purgation? What kind of misfortune?   100

Creon
Banish the man, or quit slaughter with slaughter
In cleansing, since this blood rains on the state.

Oedipus
Who is this man whose fate the god reveals?

Creon
Laius, my lord, was formerly the guide
Of this our land before you steered this city.

Oedipus
I know him by hearsay, but I never saw him.

Creon
Since he was slain, the god now plainly bids us
To punish his murderers, whoever they may be.

Oedipus
Where are they on the earth? How shall we find
This indiscernible track of ancient guilt?   110

Creon
In this land, said Apollo. What is sought
Can be apprehended; the unobserved escapes.

Oedipus
Did Laius fall at home on this bloody end?
Or in the fields, or in some foreign land?

Creon
As a pilgrim, the god said, he left his tribe
And once away from home, returned no more.

Oedipus
Was there no messenger, no fellow wayfarer
Who saw, from whom an inquirer might get aid?

Creon
They are all dead, save one, who fled in fear
And he knows only one thing sure to tell.   120

Oedipus
What is that? We may learn many facts from one
If we might take for hope a short beginning.

Creon
Robbers, Apollo said, met there and killed him
Not by the strength of one, but many hands.

Oedipus
How did the robber unless something from here
Was at work with silver, reach this point of daring?

Creon
These facts are all conjecture. Laius dead,
There rose in evils no avenger for him.

Oedipus
But when the king had fallen slain, what trouble
Prevented you from finding all this out?   130

Creon
The subtle-singing Sphinx made us let go
What was unclear to search at our own feet.

Oedipus
Well then, I will make this clear afresh
From the start. Phoebus was right, you were right
To take this present interest in the dead.
Justly it is you see me as your ally
Avenging alike this country and the god.
Not for the sake of some distant friends,
But for myself I will disperse this filth.
Whoever it was who killed that man   140
With the same hand may wish to do vengeance on me.
And so assisting Laius I aid myself.
But hurry quickly, children, stand up now
From the altar steps, raising these suppliant boughs.
Let someone gather Cadmus' people here
To learn that I will do all, whether at last
With Phoebus' help we are shown saved or fallen.

Priest
Come, children, let us stand. We came here

First for the sake of what this man proclaims.
Phoebus it was who sent these prophecies 150
And he will come to save us from the plague.

Chorus

Strophe A

O sweet-tongued voice of Zeus, in what spirit do you come
From Pytho rich in gold
To glorious Thebes? I am torn on the rack, dread shakes my fearful mind,
Apollo of Delos, hail!
As I stand in awe of you, what need, either new
Do you bring to the full for me, or old in the turning times of the year?
Tell me, O child of golden Hope, undying Voice!

Antistrophe A

First on you do I call, daughter of Zeus, undying Athene
And your sister who guards our land, 160
Artemis, seated upon the throne renowned of our circled Place,
And Phoebus who darts afar;
Shine forth to me, thrice warder-off of death;
If ever in time before when ruin rushed upon the state,
The flame of sorrow you drove beyond our bounds, come also now.

Strophe B

O woe! Unnumbered that I bear
The sorrows are! My whole host is sick, nor is there a sword of thought
To ward off pain. The growing fruits
Of glorious earth wax not, nor women
Withstand in childbirth shrieking pangs. 170
Life on life you may see, which, like the well-winged bird,
Faster than stubborn fire, speed
To the strand of the evening god.

Antistrophe B

Unnumbered of the city die.
Unpitied babies bearing death lie unmoaned on the ground.
Grey-haired mothers and young wives
From all sides at the altar's edge
Lift up a wail beseeching, for their mournful woes.
The prayer for healing shines blent with a grieving cry;
Wherefore, O golden daughter of Zeus, 180
Send us your succour with its beaming face.

Strophe C

Grant that fiery Ares, who now with no brazen shield
Flames round me in shouting attack
May turn his back in running flight from our land,
May be borne with fair wind

To Amphitrite's great chamber
Or to the hostile port
Of the Thracian surge.
For even if night leaves any ill undone
It is brought to pass and comes to be in the day.   190
O Zeus who bear the fire
And rule the lightning's might,
Strike him beneath your thunderbolt with death!

Antistrophe C

O lord Apollo, would that you might come and scatter forth
Untamed darts from your twirling golden bow;
Bring succour from the plague; may the flashing
Beams come of Artemis,
With which she glances through the Lycian hills.
Also on him I call whose hair is held in gold,
Who gives a name to this land,   200
Bacchus of winy face, whom maidens hail!
Draw near with your flaming Maenad band
And the aid of your gladsome torch
Against the plague, dishonoured among the gods.

Oedipus
You pray; if for what you pray you would be willing
To hear and take my words, to nurse the plague,
You may get succour and relief from evils.
A stranger to this tale I now speak forth,
A stranger to the deed, for not alone
Could I have tracked it far without some clue,   210
But now that I am enrolled a citizen
Latest among the citizens of Thebes
To all you sons of Cadmus I proclaim
Whoever of you knows at what man's hand
Laius, the son of Labdacus, met his death,
I order him to tell me all, and even
If he fears, to clear the charge and he will suffer
No injury, but leave the land unharmed.
If someone knows the murderer to be an alien
From foreign soil, let him not be silent;   220
I will give him a reward, my thanks besides.
But if you stay in silence and from fear
For self or friend thrust aside my command,
Hear now from me what I shall do for this;
I charge that none who dwell within this land
Whereof I hold the power and the throne
Give this man shelter whoever he may be,
Or speak to him, or share with him in prayer
Or sacrifice, or serve him lustral rites,

But drive him, all, out of your homes, for he   230
Is this pollution on us, as Apollo
Revealed to me just now in oracle.
I am therefore the ally of the god
And of the murdered man. And now I pray
That the murderer, whether he hides alone
Or with his partners, may, evil coward,
Wear out in luckless ills his wretched life.
I further pray, that, if at my own hearth
He dwells known to me in my own home,
I may suffer myself the curse I just now uttered.   240
And you I charge to bring all this to pass
For me, and for the god, and for our land
Which now lies fruitless, godless, and corrupt.
Even if Phoebus had not urged this affair,
Not rightly did you let it go unpurged
When one both noble and a king was murdered!
You should have sought it out. Since now I reign
Holding the power which he had held before me,
Having the selfsame wife and marriage bed—
And if his seed had not met barren fortune   250
We should be linked by offspring from one mother:
But as it was, fate leapt upon his head.
Therefore in this, as if for my own father
I fight for him, and shall attempt all
Searching to seize the hand which shed that blood,
For Labdacus' son, before him Polydorus,
And ancient Cadmus, and Agenor of old.
And those who fail to do this, I pray the gods
May give them neither harvest from their earth
Nor children from their wives, but may they be   260
Destroyed by a fate like this one, or a worse.
You other Thebans, who cherish these commands,
May Justice, the ally of a righteous cause,
And all the gods be always on your side.

Chorus
By the oath you laid on me, my king, I speak.
I killed not Laius, nor can show who killed him.
Phoebus it was who sent this question to us,
And he should answer who has done the deed.

Oedipus
Your words are just, but to compel the gods
In what they do not wish, no man can do.   270

Chorus
I would tell what seems to me our second course.

Oedipus
If there is a third, fail not to tell it too.

Chorus
Lord Teiresias I know, who sees this best
Like lord Apollo; in surveying this,
One might, my lord, find out from him most clearly.

Oedipus
Even this I did not neglect; I have done it already.
At Creon's word I twice sent messengers.
It is a wonder he has been gone so long.

Chorus
And also there are rumors, faint and old.

Oedipus
What are they? I must search out every tale.   280

Chorus
They say there were some travellers who killed him.

Oedipus
So I have heard, but no one sees a witness.

Chorus
If his mind knows a particle of fear
He will not long withstand such curse as yours.

Oedipus
He fears no speech who fears not such a deed.

Chorus
But here is the man who will convict the guilty.
Here are these men leading the divine prophet
In whom alone of men the truth is born.

Oedipus
O you who ponder all, Teiresias,
Both what is taught and what cannot be spoken,   290
What is of heaven and what trod on the earth,
Even if you are blind, you know what plague
Clings to the state, and, master, you alone
We find as her protector and her saviour.
Apollo, if the messengers have not told you,
Answered our question, that release would come
From this disease only if we make sure
Of Laius' slayers and slay them in return
Or drive them out as exiles from the land.
But you now, grudge us neither voice of birds   300
Nor any way you have of prophecy.
Save yourself and the state; save me as well.

Save everything polluted by the dead.
We are in your hands; it is the noblest task
To help a man with all your means and powers.

Teiresias
Alas! Alas! How terrible to be wise,
Where it does the seer no good. Too well I know
And have forgot this, or would not have come here.

Oedipus
What is this? How fainthearted you have come!

Teiresias
Let me go home; it is best for you to bear   310
Your burden, and I mine, if you will heed me.

Oedipus
You speak what is lawless, and hateful to the state
Which raised you, when you deprive her of your answer.

Teiresias
And I see that your speech does not proceed
In season; I shall not undergo the same.

Oedipus
Don't by the gods turn back when you are wise,
When all we suppliants lie prostrate before you.

Teiresias
And all unwise; I never shall reveal
My evils, so that I may not tell yours.

Oedipus
What do you say? You know, but will not speak?   320
Would you betray us and destroy the state?

Teiresias
I will not hurt you or me. Why in vain
Do you probe this? You will not find out from me.

Oedipus
Worst of evil men, you would enrage
A stone itself. Will you never speak,
But stay so untouched and so inconclusive?

Teiresias
You blame my anger and do not see that
With which you live in common, but upbraid me.

Oedipus
Who would not be enraged to hear these words
By which you now dishonor this our city?   330

Teiresias
Of itself this will come, though I hide it in silence.

Oedipus
Then you should tell me what it is will come.

Teiresias
I shall speak no more. If further you desire,
Rage on in wildest anger of your soul.

Oedipus
I shall omit nothing I understand
I am so angry. Know that you seem to me
Creator of the deed and worker too
In all short of the slaughter; if you were not blind,
I would say this crime was your work alone.

Teiresias
Really? Abide yourself by the decree   340
You just proclaimed, I tell you! From this day
Henceforth address neither these men nor me.
You are the godless defiler of this land.

Oedipus
You push so bold and taunting in your speech;
And how do you think to get away with this?

Teiresias
I have got away. I nurse my strength in truth.

Oedipus
Who taught you this? Not from your art you got it.

Teiresias
From you. You had me speak against my will.

Oedipus
What word? Say again, so I may better learn.

Teiresias
Didn't you get it before? Or do you bait me?   350

Oedipus
I don't remember it. Speak forth again.

Teiresias
You are the slayer whom you seek, I say.

Oedipus
Not twice you speak such bitter words unpunished.

Teiresias
Shall I speak more to make you angrier still?

Oedipus
Do what you will, your words will be in vain.

Teiresias
I say you have forgot that you are joined
With those most dear to you in deepest shame
And do not see where you are in sin.

Oedipus
Do you think you will always say such things in joy?

Teiresias
Surely, if strength abides in what is true.   360

Oedipus
It does, for all but you, this not for you
Because your ears and mind and eyes are blind.

Teiresias
Wretched you are to make such taunts, for soon
All men will cast the selfsame taunts on you.

Oedipus
You live in entire night, could do no harm
To me or any man who sees the day.

Teiresias
Not at my hands will it be your fate to fall.
Apollo suffices, whose concern it is to do this.

Oedipus
Are these devices yours, or are they Creon's?

Teiresias
Creon is not your trouble; you are yourself.   370

Oedipus
O riches, empire, skill surpassing skill
In all the numerous rivalries of life,
How great a grudge there is stored up against you
If for this kingship, which the city gave,
Their gift, not my request, into my hands—
For this, the trusted Creon, my friend from the start
Desires to creep by stealth and cast me out
Taking a seer like this, a weaver of wiles,
A crooked swindler who has got his eyes
On gain alone, but in his art is blind.   380
Come, tell us, in what clearly are you a prophet?
How is it, when the weave-songed bitch was here
You uttered no salvation for these people?
Surely the riddle then could not be solved

By some chance comer; it needed prophecy.
You did not clarify that with birds
Or knowledge from a god; but when I came,
The ignorant Oedipus, I silenced her,
Not taught by birds, but winning by my wits,
Whom you are now attempting to depose,   390
Thinking to minister near Creon's throne.
I think that to your woe you and that plotter
Will purge the land, and if you were not old
Punishment would teach you what you plot.

Chorus
It seems to us, O Oedipus our king,
Both this man's words and yours were said in anger.
Such is not our need, but to find out
How best we shall discharge Apollo's orders.

Teiresias
Even if you are king, the right to answer
Should be free to all; of that I too am king.   400
I live not as your slave, but as Apollo's.
And not with Creon's wards shall I be counted.
I say, since you have taunted even my blindness,
You have eyes, but see not where in evil you are
Nor where you dwell, nor whom you are living with.
Do you know from whom you spring? And you forget
You are an enemy to your own kin
Both those beneath and those above the earth.
Your mother's and father's curse, with double goad
And dreaded foot shall drive you from this land.   410
You who now see straight shall then be blind,
And there shall be no harbour for your cry
With which all Mount Cithaeron soon shall ring,
When you have learned the wedding where you sailed
At home, into no port, by voyage fair.
A throng of other ills you do not know
Shall equal you to yourself and to your children.
Throw mud on this, on Creon, on my voice—
Yet there shall never be a mortal man
Eradicated more wretchedly than you.   420

Oedipus
Shall these unbearable words be heard from him?
Go to perdition! Hurry! Off, away,
Turn back again and from this house depart.

Teiresias
If you had not called me, I should not have come.

Oedipus
I did not know that you would speak such folly
Or I would not soon have brought you to my house.

Teiresias
And such a fool I am, as it seems to you.
But to the parents who bore you I seem wise.

Oedipus
What parents? Wait! What mortals gave me birth?

Teiresias
This day shall be your birth and your destruction.   430

Oedipus
All things you say in riddles and unclear.

Teiresias
Are you not he who best can search this out?

Oedipus
Mock, if you wish, the skill that made me great.

Teiresias
This is the very fortune that destroyed you.

Oedipus
Well, if I saved the city, I do not care.

Teiresias
I am going now. You, boy, be my guide.

Oedipus
Yes, let him guide you. Here you are in the way.
When you are gone you will give no more trouble.

Teiresias
I go when I have said what I came to say
Without fear of your frown; you cannot destroy me.   440
I say, the very man whom you long seek
With threats and announcements about Laius' murder—
This man is here. He seems an alien stranger,
But soon he shall be revealed of Theban birth,
Nor at this circumstance shall he be pleased.
He shall be blind who sees, shall be a beggar
Who now is rich, shall make his way abroad
Feeling the ground before him with a staff.
He shall be revealed at once as brother
And father to his own children, husband and son   450
To his mother, his father's kin and murderer.

Go in and ponder that. If I am wrong
Say then that I know nothing of prophecy.

Chorus

Strophe A

Who is the man the Delphic rock said with oracular voice
Unspeakable crimes performed with his gory hands?
It is time for him now to speed
His foot in flight, more strong
Than horses swift as the storm.
For girt in arms upon him springs
With fire and lightning, Zeus' son   460
And behind him, terrible,
Come the unerring Fates.

Antistrophe A

From snowy Parnassus just now the word flashed clear
To track the obscure man by every way,
For he wanders under the wild
Forest, and into caves
And cliff rocks, like a bull,
Reft on his way, with care on care
Trying to shun the prophecy
Come from the earth's mid-navel,   470
But about him flutters the ever living doom.

Strophe B

Terrible, terrible things the wise bird-augur stirs.
I neither approve nor deny, at a loss for what to say,
I flutter in hopes and fears, see neither here nor ahead;
For what strife has lain
On Labdacus' sons or Polybus' that I have found ever before
Or now, whereby I may run for the sons of Labdacus
Is sure proof against Oedipus' public fame
As avenger for dark death?

Antistrophe B

Zeus and Apollo surely understand and know   480
The affairs of mortal men, but that a mortal seer
Knows more than I, there is no proof. Though a man
May surpass a man in knowledge,
Never shall I agree, till I see the word true, when men blame Oedipus,
For there came upon him once clear the winged maiden
And wise he was seen, by sure test sweet for the state.
So never shall my mind judge him evil guilt.

Creon

Men of our city, I have heard dread words
That Oedipus our king accuses me.

I am here indignant. If in the present troubles 490
He thinks that he has suffered at my hands
One word or deed tending to injury
I do not crave the long-spanned age of life
To bear this rumor, for it is no simple wrong
The damage of this accusation brings me;
It brings the greatest, if I am called a traitor
To you and my friends, a traitor to the state.

Chorus
Come now, for this reproach perhaps was forced
By anger, rather than considered thought.

Creon
And was the idea voiced that my advice 500
Persuaded the prophet to give false accounts?

Chorus
Such was said. I know not to what intent.

Creon
Was this accusation laid against me
From straightforward eyes and straightforward mind?

Chorus
I do not know. I see not what my masters do;
But here he is now, coming from the house.

Oedipus
How dare you come here? Do you own a face
So bold that you can come before my house
When you are clearly the murderer of this man
And manifestly pirate of my throne? 510
Come, say before the gods, did you see in me
A coward or a fool, that you plotted this?
Or did you think I would not see your wiles
Creeping upon me, or knowing, would not ward off?
Surely your machination is absurd
Without a crowd of friends to hunt a throne
Which is captured only by wealth and many men.

Creon
Do you know what you do? Hear answer to your charges
On the other side. Judge only what you know.

Oedipus
Your speech is clever, but I learn it ill 520
Since I have found you harsh and grievous toward me.

Creon
This very matter hear me first explain.

Oedipus
Tell me not this one thing: you are not false.

Creon
If you think stubbornness a good possession
Apart from judgment, you do not think right.

Oedipus
If you think you can do a kinsman evil
Without the penalty, you have no sense.

Creon
I agree with you. What you have said is just.
Tell me what you say you have suffered from me.

Oedipus
Did you, or did you not, advise my need   530
Was summoning that prophet person here?

Creon
And still is. I hold still the same opinion.

Oedipus
How long a time now has it been since Laius—

Creon
Performed what deed? I do not understand.

Oedipus
—Disappeared to his ruin at deadly hands.

Creon
Far in the past the count of years would run.

Oedipus
Was this same seer at that time practising?

Creon
As wise as now, and equally respected.

Oedipus
At that time did he ever mention me?

Creon
Never when I stood near enough to hear.   540

Oedipus
But did you not make inquiry of the murder?

Creon
We did, of course, and got no information.

Oedipus
How is it that this seer did not utter this then?

Creon
When I don't know, as now, I would keep still.

Oedipus
This much you know full well, and so should speak:—

Creon
What is that? If I know, I will not refuse.

Oedipus
This: If he had not first conferred with you
He never would have said that I killed Laius.

Creon
If he says this, you know yourself, I think;
I learn as much from you as you from me.   550

Oedipus
Learn then: I never shall be found a slayer.

Creon
What then, are you the husband of my sister?

Oedipus
What you have asked is plain beyond denial.

Creon
Do you rule this land with her in equal sway?

Oedipus
All she desires she obtains from me.

Creon
Am I with you two not an equal third?

Oedipus
In just that do you prove a treacherous friend.

Creon
No, if, like me, you reason with yourself.
Consider this fact first: would any man
Choose, do you think, to have his rule in fear   560
Rather than doze unharmed with the same power?
For my part I have never been desirous
Of being king instead of acting king.
Nor any other man has, wise and prudent.
For now I obtain all from you without fear.
If I were king, I would do much unwilling.
How then could kingship sweeter be for me
Than rule and power devoid of any pain?
I am not yet so much deceived to want

Goods besides those I profitably enjoy.   570
Now I am hailed and gladdened by all men.
Now those who want from you speak out to me,
Since all their chances' outcome dwells therein.
How then would I relinquish what I have
To get those gains? My mind runs not so bad.
I am prudent yet, no lover of such plots,
Nor would I ever endure others' treason.
And first as proof of this go on to Pytho;
See if I told you truly the oracle.
Next proof: see if I plotted with the seer;   580
If you find so at all, put me to death
With my vote for my guilt as well as yours.
Do not convict me just on unclear conjecture.
It is not right to think capriciously
The good are bad, nor that the bad are good.
It is the same to cast out a noble friend,
I say, as one's own life, which best he loves.
The facts, though, you will safely know in time,
Since time alone can show the just man just,
But you can know a criminal in one day.   590

Chorus
A cautious man would say he has spoken well.
O king, the quick to think are never sure.

Oedipus
When the plotter, swift, approaches me in stealth
I too in counterplot must be as swift.
If I wait in repose, the plotter's ends
Are brought to pass and mine will then have erred.

Creon
What do you want then? To cast me from the land?

Oedipus
Least of all that. My wish is you should die,
Not flee to exemplify what envy is.

Creon
Do you say this? Will you neither trust nor yield?   600

Oedipus
[No, for I think that you deserve no trust.]

Creon
You seem not wise to me.

Oedipus
                    I am for me.

Creon
You should be for me too.

Oedipus

No, you are evil.

Creon
Yes, if you understand nothing.

Oedipus

Yet I must rule.

Creon
Not when you rule badly.

Oedipus

O city, city!

Creon
It is my city too, not yours alone.

Chorus
Stop, princes. I see Jocasta coming
Out of the house at the right time for you.
With her you must settle the dispute at hand.

Jocasta
O wretched men, what unconsidered feud   610
Of tongues have you aroused? Are you not ashamed,
The state so sick, to stir up private ills?
Are you not going home? And you as well?
Will you turn a small pain into a great?

Creon
My blood sister, Oedipus your husband
Claims he will judge against me two dread ills:
Thrust me from the fatherland or take and kill me.

Oedipus
I will, my wife; I caught him in the act
Doing evil to my person with evil skill.

Creon
Now may I not rejoice but die accursed   620
If ever I did any of what you accuse me.

Jocasta
O, by the gods, believe him, Oedipus.
First, in reverence for his oath to the gods,
Next, for my sake and theirs who stand before you.

Chorus
Hear my entreaty, lord. Consider and consent.

Oedipus
What wish should I then grant?

Chorus
Respect the man, no fool before, who now in oath is strong.

Oedipus
You know what you desire?

Chorus
                  I know.

Oedipus
                         Say what you mean.

Chorus
Your friend who has sworn do not dishonour
By casting guilt for dark report.   630

Oedipus
Know well that when you ask this grant from me,
You ask my death or exile from the land.

Chorus
No, by the god foremost among the gods,
The Sun, may I perish by the utmost doom
Godless and friendless, if I have this in mind.
But ah, the withering earth wears down
My wretched soul, if to these ills
Of old are added ills from both of you.

Oedipus
Then let him go, though surely I must die
Or be thrust dishonoured from this land by force.   640
Your grievous voice I pity, not that man's;
Wherever he may be, he will be hated.

Creon
Sullen you are to yield, as you are heavy
When you exceed in wrath. Natures like these
Are justly sorest for themselves to bear.

Oedipus
Will you not go and leave me?

Creon
                    I am on my way.
You know me not, but these men see me just.

Chorus
O queen, why do you delay to bring this man indoors?

Jocasta
I want to learn what happened here.

Chorus
Unknown suspicion rose from talk, and the unjust devours.   650

Jocasta
In both of them?

Chorus
                    Just so.

Jocasta
                              What was the talk?

Chorus
Enough, enough! When the land is pained
It seems to me at this point we should stop.

Oedipus
Do you see where you have come? Though your intent
Is good, you slacken off and blunt my heart.

Chorus
O lord, I have said not once alone,
Know that I clearly would be mad
And wandering in mind, to turn away
You who steered along the right,
When she was torn with trouble, our beloved state.   660
O may you now become in health her guide.

Jocasta
By the gods, lord, tell me on what account
You have set yourself in so great an anger.

Oedipus
I shall tell you, wife; I respect you more than these men.
Because of Creon, since he has plotted against me.

Jocasta
Say clearly, if you can; how started the quarrel?

Oedipus
He says that I stand as the murderer of Laius.

Jocasta
He knows himself, or learned from someone else?

Oedipus
No, but he sent a rascal prophet here.
He keeps his own mouth clean in what concerns him. 670

Jocasta
Now free yourself of what you said, and listen.
Learn from me, no mortal man exists
Who knows prophetic art for your affairs,
And I shall briefly show you proof of this:
An oracle came once to Laius. I do not say
From Phoebus himself, but from his ministers
That his fate would be at his son's hand to die—
A child, who would be born from him and me.
And yet, as the rumor says, they were strangers,
Robbers who killed him where three highways meet. 680
But three days had not passed from the child's birth
When Laius pierced and tied together his ankles,
And cast him by others' hands on a pathless mountain.
Therein Apollo did not bring to pass
That the child murder his father, nor for Laius
The dread he feared, to die at his son's hand.
Such did prophetic oracles determine.
Pay no attention to them. For the god
Will easily make clear the need he seeks.

Oedipus
What wandering of soul, what stirring of mind 690
Holds me, my wife, in what I have just heard!

Jocasta
What care has turned you back that you say this?

Oedipus
I thought I heard you mention this, that Laius
Was slaughtered at the place where three highways meet.

Jocasta
That was the talk. The rumour has not ceased.

Oedipus
Where is this place where such a sorrow was?

Jocasta
The country's name is Phocis. A split road
Leads to one place from Delphi and Daulia.

Oedipus
And how much time has passed since these events?

Jocasta
The news was heralded in the city scarcely 700
A little while before you came to rule.

Oedipus
O Zeus, what have you planned to do to me?

Jocasta
What passion is this in you, Oedipus?

Oedipus
Don't ask me that yet. Tell me about Laius.
What did he look like? How old was he when murdered?

Jocasta
A tall man, with his hair just brushed with white.
His shape and form differed not far from yours.

Oedipus
Alas! Alas! I think unwittingly
I have just laid dread curses on my head.

Jocasta
What are you saying? I shrink to behold you, lord.   710

Oedipus
I am terribly afraid the seer can see.
That will be clearer if you say one thing more.

Jocasta
Though I shrink, if I know what you ask, I will answer.

Oedipus
Did he set forth with few attendants then,
Or many soldiers, since he was a king?

Jocasta
They were five altogether among them.
One was a herald. One chariot bore Laius.

Oedipus
Alas! All this is clear now. Tell me, my wife,
Who was the man who told these stories to you?

Jocasta
One servant, who alone escaped, returned.   720

Oedipus
Is he by chance now present in our house?

Jocasta
Not now. Right from the time when he returned
To see you ruling and Laius dead,
Touching my hand in suppliance, he implored me
To send him to fields and to pastures of sheep
That he might be farthest from the sight of this city.

So I sent him away, since he was worthy
For a slave, to bear a greater grant than this.

Oedipus
How then could he return to us with speed?

Jocasta
It can be done. But why would you order this?   730

Oedipus
O lady, I fear I have said too much.
On this account I now desire to see him.

Jocasta
Then he shall come. But I myself deserve
To learn what it is that troubles you, my lord.

Oedipus
And you shall not be prevented, since my fears
Have come to such a point. For who is closer
That I may speak to in this fate than you?
Polybus of Corinth was my father,
My mother, Dorian Merope. I was held there
Chief citizen of all, till such a fate   740
Befell me—as it is, worthy of wonder,
But surely not deserving my excitement.
A man at a banquet overdrunk with wine
Said in drink I was a false son to my father.
The weight I held that day I scarcely bore,
But on the next day I went home and asked
My father and mother of it. In bitter anger
They took the reproach from him who had let it fly.
I was pleased at their actions; nevertheless
The rumour always rankled; and spread abroad.   750
In secret from mother and father I set out
Toward Delphi. Phoebus sent me away ungraced
In what I came for, but other wretched things
Terrible and grievous, he revealed in answer;
That I must wed my mother and produce
An unendurable race for men to see,
That I should kill the father who begot me.
When I heard this response, Corinth I fled
Henceforth to measure her land by stars alone.
I went where I should never see the disgrace   760
Of my evil oracles be brought to pass,
And on my journey to that place I came
At which you say this king had met his death.
My wife, I shall speak the truth to you. My way

Led to a place close by the triple road.
There a herald met me, and a man
Seated on colt-drawn chariot, as you said.
There both the guide and the old man himself
Thrust me with driving force out of the path.
And I in anger struck the one who pushed me,   770
The driver. Then the old man, when he saw me,
Watched when I passed, and from his chariot
Struck me full on the head with double goad.
I paid him back and more. From this very hand
A swift blow of my staff rolled him right out
Of the middle of his seat onto his back.
I killed them all. But if relationship
Existed between this stranger and Laius,
What man now is wretcheder than I?
What man is cursed by a more evil fate?   780
No stranger or citizen could now receive me
Within his home, or even speak to me,
But thrust me out; and no one but myself
Brought down these curses on my head.
The bed of the slain man I now defile
With hands that killed him. Am I evil by birth?
Am I not utterly vile if I must flee
And cannot see my family in my flight
Nor tread my homeland soil, or else be joined
In marriage to my mother, kill my father,   790
Polybus, who sired me and brought me up?
Would not a man judge right to say of me
That this was sent on me by some cruel spirit?
O never, holy reverence of the gods,
May I behold that day, but may I go
Away from mortal men, before I see
Such a stain of circumstance come to me.

Chorus
My lord, for us these facts are full of dread.
Until you hear the witness, stay in hope.

Oedipus
And just so much is all I have of hope,   800
Only to wait until the shepherd comes.

Jocasta
What, then, do you desire to hear him speak?

Oedipus
I will tell you, if his story is found to be
The same as yours, I would escape the sorrow.

Jocasta

What unusual word did you hear from me?

Oedipus

You said he said that they were highway robbers
Who murdered him. Now, if he still says
The selfsame number, I could not have killed him,
Since one man does not equal many men.
But if he speaks of a single lonely traveller,   810
The scale of guilt now clearly falls to me.

Jocasta

However, know the word was set forth thus
And it is not in him now to take it back;
This tale the city heard, not I alone.
But if he diverges from his previous story,
Even then, my lord, he could not show Laius' murder
To have been fulfilled properly. Apollo
Said he would die at the hands of my own son.
Surely that wretched child could not have killed him,
But he himself met death some time before.   820
Therefore, in any prophecy henceforth
I would not look to this side or to that.

Oedipus

Your thoughts ring true, but still let someone go
To summon the peasant. Do not neglect this.

Jocasta

I shall send without delay. But let us enter.
I would do nothing that did not please you.

Chorus

Strophe A

May fate come on me as I bear
Holy pureness in all word and deed,
For which the lofty striding laws were set down,
Born through the heavenly air   830
Whereof the Olympian sky alone the father was;
No mortal spawn of mankind gave them birth,
Nor may oblivion ever lull them down;
Mighty in them the god is, and he does not age.

Antistrophe A

Pride breeds the tyrant.
Pride, once overfilled with many things in vain,
Neither in season nor fit for man,
Scaling the sheerest height

Hurls to a dire fate
Where no foothold is found.   840
I pray the god may never stop the rivalry
That works well for the state.
The god as my protector I shall never cease to hold.

Strophe B

But if a man goes forth haughty in word or deed
With no fear of the Right
Nor pious to the spirits' shrines,
May evil doom seize him
For his ill-fated pride,
If he does not fairly win his gain
Or works unholy deeds,   850
Or, in bold folly lays on the sacred profane hands.
For when such acts occur, what man may boast
Ever to ward off from his life darts of the gods?
If practices like these are in respect,
Why then must I dance the sacred dance?

Antistrophe B

Never again in worship shall I go
To Delphi, holy navel of the earth,
Nor to the temple at Abae,
Nor to Olympia,
If these prophecies do not become   860
Examples for all men.
O Zeus, our king, if so you are rightly called,
Ruler of all things, may they not escape
You and your forever deathless power.
Men now hold light the fading oracles
Told about Laius long ago
And nowhere is Apollo clearly honored;
Things divine are going down to ruin.

Jocasta

Lords of this land, the thought has come to me
To visit the spirits' shrines, bearing in hand   870
These suppliant boughs and offerings of incense.
For Oedipus raises his soul too high
With all distresses; nor, as a sane man should,
Does he confirm the new by things of old,
But stands at the speaker's will if he speaks terrors.
And so, because my advice can do no more,
To you, Lycian Apollo—for you are nearest—
A suppliant, I have come here with these prayers,
That you may find some pure deliverance for us:

We all now shrink to see him struck in fear,   880
That man who is the pilot of our ship.

Messenger
Strangers, could I learn from one of you
Where is the house of Oedipus the king?
Or best, if you know, say where he is himself.

Chorus
This is his house, stranger; he dwells inside;
This woman is the mother of his children.

Messenger
May she be always blessed among the blest,
Since she is the fruitful wife of Oedipus.

Jocasta
So may you, stranger, also be. You deserve
As much for your graceful greeting. But tell me   890
What you have come to search for or to show.

Messenger
Good news for your house and your husband, lady.

Jocasta
What is it then? And from whom have you come?

Messenger
From Corinth. And the message I will tell
Will surely gladden you—and vex you, perhaps.

Jocasta
What is it? What is this double force it holds?

Messenger
The men who dwell in the Isthmian country
Have spoken to establish him their king.

Jocasta
What is that? Is not old Polybus still ruling?

Messenger
Not he. For death now holds him in the tomb.   900

Jocasta
What do you say, old man? Is Polybus dead?

Messenger
If I speak not the truth, I am ready to die.

Jocasta
O handmaid, go right away and tell your master

The news. Where are you, prophecies of the gods?
For this man Oedipus has trembled long,
And shunned him lest he kill him. Now the man
Is killed by fate and not by Oedipus.

Oedipus
O Jocasta, my most beloved wife,
Why have you sent for me within the house?

Jocasta
Listen to this man, and while you hear him, think   910
To what have come Apollo's holy prophecies.

Oedipus
Who is this man? Why would he speak to me?

Jocasta
From Corinth he has come, to announce that your father
Polybus no longer lives, but is dead.

Oedipus
What do you say, stranger? Tell me this yourself.

Messenger
If I must first announce my message clearly,
Know surely that the man is dead and gone.

Oedipus
Did he die by treachery or chance disease?

Messenger
A slight scale tilt can lull the old to rest.

Oedipus
The poor man, it seems, died by disease.   920

Messenger
And by the full measure of lengthy time.

Oedipus
Alas, alas! Why then do any seek
Pytho's prophetic art, my wife, or hear
The shrieking birds on high, by whose report
I was to slay my father? Now he lies
Dead beneath the earth, and here am I
Who have not touched the blade. Unless in longing
For me he died, and in this sense was killed by me.
Polybus has packed away these oracles
In his rest in Hades. They are now worth nothing.   930

Jocasta
Did I not tell you that some time ago?

Oedipus
You did, but I was led astray by fear.

Jocasta
Henceforth put nothing of this on your heart.

Oedipus
Why must I not still shrink from my mother's bed?

Jocasta
What should man fear, whose life is ruled by fate,
For whom there is clear foreknowledge of nothing?
It is best to live by chance, however you can.
Be not afraid of marriage with your mother;
Already many mortals in their dreams
Have shared their mother's bed. But he who counts   940
This dream as nothing, easiest bears his life.

Oedipus
All that you say would be indeed propitious,
If my mother were not alive. But since she is,
I still must shrink, however well you speak.

Jocasta
And yet your father's tomb is a great eye.*

Oedipus
A great eye indeed. But I fear her who lives.

Messenger
Who is this woman that you are afraid of?

Oedipus
Merope, old man, with whom Polybus lived.

Messenger
What is it in her that moves you to fear?

Oedipus
A dread oracle, stranger, sent by the god.   950

Messenger
Can it be told, or must no other know?

Oedipus
It surely can. Apollo told me once
That I must join in intercourse with my mother
And shed with my own hands my father's blood.

---

*That is, a bright comfort.

Because of this, long since I have kept far
Away from Corinth—and happily—but yet
It would be most sweet to see my parents' faces.

Messenger
Was this your fear in shunning your own city?

Oedipus
I wished, too, old man, not to slay my father.

Messenger
Why then have I not freed you from this fear,   960
Since I have come with friendly mind, my lord?

Oedipus
Yes, and take thanks from me, which you deserve.

Messenger
And this is just the thing for which I came,
That when you got back home I might fare well.

Oedipus
Never shall I go where my parents are.

Messenger
My son, you clearly know not what you do.

Oedipus
How is that, old man? By the gods, let me know.

Messenger
If for these tales you shrink from going home.

Oedipus
I tremble lest what Phoebus said comes true.

Messenger
Lest you incur pollution from your parents?   970

Oedipus
That is the thing, old man, that always haunts me.

Messenger
Well, do you know that surely you fear nothing?

Oedipus
How so? If I am the son of those who bore me.

Messenger
Since Polybus was no relation to you.

Oedipus
What do you say? Was Polybus not my father?

Messenger
No more than this man here but just so much.

Oedipus
How does he who begot me equal nothing?

Messenger
That man was not your father, any more than I am.

Oedipus
Well then, why was it he called me his son?

Messenger
Long ago he got you as a gift from me.   980

Oedipus
Though from another's hand, yet so much he loved me!

Messenger
His previous childlessness led him to that.

Oedipus
Had you bought or found me when you gave me to him?

Messenger
I found you in Cithaeron's folds and glens.

Oedipus
Why were you travelling in those regions?

Messenger
I guarded there a flock of mountain sheep.

Oedipus
Were you a shepherd, wandering for pay?

Messenger
Yes, and your saviour too, child, at that time.

Oedipus
What pain gripped me, that you took me in your arms?

Messenger
The ankles of your feet will tell you that.   990

Oedipus
Alas, why do you mention that old trouble?

Messenger
I freed you when your ankles were pierced together.

Oedipus
A terrible shame from my swaddling clothes I got.

Messenger
Your very name you got from this misfortune.

Oedipus
By the gods, did my mother or father do it? Speak.

Messenger
I know not. He who gave you knows better than I.

Oedipus
You didn't find me, but took me from another?

Messenger
That's right. Another shepherd gave you to me.

Oedipus
Who was he? Can you tell me who he was?

Messenger
Surely. He belonged to the household of Laius.   1000

Oedipus
The man who ruled this land once long ago?

Messenger
Just so. He was a herd in that man's service.

Oedipus
Is this man still alive, so I could see him?

Messenger
You dwellers in this country should know best.

Oedipus
Is there any one of you who stand before me
Who knows the shepherd of whom this man speaks?
If you have seen him in the fields or here,
Speak forth; the time has come to find this out.

Chorus
I think the man you seek is no one else
Than the shepherd you were so eager to see before.   1010
Jocasta here might best inform us that.

Oedipus
My wife, do you know the man we just ordered
To come here? Is it of him that this man speaks?

Jocasta
Why ask of whom he spoke? Think nothing of it.
Brood not in vain on what has just been said.

Oedipus

It could not be that when I have got such clues,
I should not shed clear light upon my birth.

Jocasta

Don't, by the gods, investigate this more
If you care for your own life. I am sick enough.

Oedipus

Take courage. Even if I am found a slave   1020
For three generations, your birth will not be base.

Jocasta

Still, I beseech you, hear me. Don't do this.

Oedipus

I will hear of nothing but finding out the truth.

Jocasta

I know full well and tell you what is best.

Oedipus

Well, then, this best, for some time now, has given me pain.

Jocasta

O ill-fated man, may you never know who you are.

Oedipus

Will someone bring the shepherd to me here?
And let this lady rejoice in her opulent birth.

Jocasta

Alas, alas, hapless man. I have this alone
To tell you, and nothing else forevermore.   1030

Chorus

O Oedipus, where has the woman gone
In the rush of her wild grief? I am afraid
Evil will break forth out of this silence.

Oedipus

Let whatever will break forth. I plan to see
The seed of my descent, however small.
My wife, perhaps, because a noblewoman
Looks down with shame upon my lowly birth.
I would not be dishonoured to call myself
The son of Fortune, giver of the good.
She is my mother. The years, her other children,   1040
Have marked me sometimes small and sometimes great.
Such was I born! I shall prove no other man,
Nor shall I cease to search out my descent.

Chorus

Strophe

If I am prophet and can know in mind,
Cithaeron, by tomorrow's full moon
You shall not fail, by mount Olympus,
To find that Oedipus, as a native of your land,
Shall honour you for nurse and mother.
And to you we dance in choral song because you bring
Fair gifts to him our king.   1050
Hail, Phoebus, may all this please you.

Antistrophe

Who, child, who bore you in the lengthy span of years?
One close to Pan who roams the mountain woods,
One of Apollo's bedfellows?
For all wild pastures in mountain glens to him are dear.
Was Hermes your father, who Cyllene sways,
Or did Bacchus, dwelling on the mountain peaks,
Take you a foundling from some nymph
Of those by springs of Helicon, with whom he sports the most?

Oedipus

If I may guess, although I never met him,   1060
I think, elders, I see that shepherd coming
Whom we have long sought, as in the measure
Of lengthy age he accords with him we wait for.
Besides, the men who lead him I recognize
As servants of my house. You may perhaps
Know better than I if you have seen him before.

Chorus

Be assured, I know him as a shepherd
As trusted as any other in Laius' service.

Oedipus

Stranger from Corinth, I will ask you first,
Is this the man you said?

Messenger

                         You are looking at him.   1070

Oedipus

You there, old man, look here and answer me
What I shall ask you. Were you ever with Laius?

Servant

I was a slave, not bought but reared at home.

Oedipus

What work concerned you? What was your way of life?

Servant
Most of my life I spent among the flocks.

Oedipus
In what place most of all was your usual pasture?

Servant
Sometimes Cithaeron, or the ground nearby.

Oedipus
Do you know this man before you here at all?

Servant
Doing what? And of what man do you speak?

Oedipus
The one before you. Have you ever had congress with him?   1080

Servant
Not to say so at once from memory.

Messenger
That is no wonder, master, but I shall remind him,
Clearly, who knows me not; yet well I know
That he knew once the region of Cithaeron.
He with a double flock and I with one
Dwelt there in company for three whole years
During the six months' time from spring to fall.
When winter came, I drove into my fold
My flock, and he drove his to Laius' pens.
Do I speak right, or did it not happen so?   1090

Servant
You speak the truth, though it was long ago.

Messenger
Come now, do you recall you gave me then
A child for me to rear as my own son?

Servant
What is that? Why do you ask me this?

Messenger
This is the man, my friend, who then was young.

Servant
Go to destruction! Will you not be quiet?

Oedipus
Come, scold him not, old man. These words of yours
Deserve a scolding more than this man's do.

Servant
In what, most noble master, do I wrong?

Oedipus
Not to tell of the child he asks about.   1100

Servant
He speaks in ignorance, he toils in vain.

Oedipus
If you will not speak freely, you will under torture.

Servant
Don't, by the gods, outrage an old man like me.

Oedipus
Will someone quickly twist back this fellow's arms?

Servant
Alas, what for? What do you want to know?

Oedipus
Did you give this man the child of whom he asks?

Servant
I did. Would I had perished on that day!

Oedipus
You will come to that unless you tell the truth.

Servant
I come to far greater ruin if I speak.

Oedipus
This man, it seems, is trying to delay.   1110

Servant
Not I. I said before I gave it to him.

Oedipus
Where did you get it? At home or from someone else?

Servant
It was not mine. I got him from a man.

Oedipus
Which of these citizens? Where did he live?

Servant
O master, by the gods, ask me no more.

Oedipus
You are done for if I ask you this again.

Servant
Well then, he was born of the house of Laius.

Oedipus
One of his slaves, or born of his own race?

Servant
Alas, to speak I am on the brink of horror.

Oedipus
And I to hear. But still it must be heard. 1120

Servant
Well, then, they say it was his child. Your wife
Who dwells within could best say how this stands.

Oedipus
Was it she who gave him to you?

Servant
Yes, my lord.

Oedipus
For what intent?

Servant
So I could put it away.

Oedipus
When she bore him, the wretch.

Servant
She feared bad oracles.

Oedipus
What were they?

Servant
They said he should kill his father.

Oedipus
Why did you give him up to this old man?

Servant
I pitied him, master, and thought he would take him away
To another land, the one from which he came.
But he saved him for greatest woe. If you are he 1130
Whom this man speaks of, you were born curst by fate.

Oedipus
Alas, alas! All things are now come true.
O light, for the last time now I look upon you;
I am shown to be born from those I ought not to have been.

I married the woman I should not have married,
I killed the man whom I should not have killed.

Chorus

Strophe A

Alas, generations of mortal men!
How equal to nothing do I number you in life!
Who, O who, is the man
Who bears more of bliss   1140
Than just the seeming so,
And then, like a waning sun, to fall away?
When I know your example,
Your guiding spirit, yours, wretched Oedipus.
I call no mortal blest.

Antistrophe A

He is the one, O Zeus,
Who peerless shot his bow and won well-fated bliss,
Who destroyed the hook-clawed maiden,
The oracle-singing Sphinx,
And stood a tower for our land from death;   1150
For this you are called our king,
Oedipus, are highest-honoured here,
And over great Thebes hold sway.

Strophe B

And now who is more wretched for men to hear,
Who so lives in wild plagues, who dwells in pains,
In utter change of life?
Alas for glorious Oedipus!
The selfsame port of rest
Was gained by bridegroom father and his son,
How, O how did your father's furrows ever bear you, suffering man?   1160
How have they endured silence for so long?

Antistrophe B

You are found out, unwilling, by all seeing Time.
It judges your unmarried marriage where for long
Begetter and begot have been the same.
Alas, child of Laius,
Would I had never seen you.
As one who pours from his mouth a dirge I wail,
To speak the truth, through you I breathed new life,
And now through you I lulled my eye to sleep.

Second Messenger

O men most honoured always of this land   1170
What deeds you shall hear, what shall you behold!

What grief shall stir you up, if by your kinship
You are still concerned for the house of Labdacus!
I think neither Danube nor any other river
Could wash this palace clean, so many ills
Lie hidden there which now will come to light.
They were done by will, not fate; and sorrows hurt
The most when we ourselves appear to choose them.

Chorus
What we heard before causes no little sorrow.
What can you say which adds to that a burden?   1180

Second Messenger
This is the fastest way to tell the tale;
Hear it: Jocasta, your divine queen, is dead.

Chorus
O sorrowful woman! From what cause did she die?

Second Messenger
By her own hand. The most painful of the action
Occurred away, not for your eyes to see.
But still, so far as I have memory
You shall learn the sufferings of that wretched woman:
How she passed on through the door enraged
And rushed straight forward to her nuptial bed,
Clutching her hair's ends with both her hands.   1190
Once inside the doors she shut herself in
And called on Laius, who has long been dead,
Having remembrance of their seed of old
By which he died himself and left her a mother
To bear an evil brood to his own son.
She moaned the bed on which by double curse
She bore husband to husband, children to child.
How thereafter she perished I do not know,
For Oedipus burst in on her with a shriek,
And because of him we could not see her woe.   1200
We looked on him alone as he rushed around.
Pacing about, he asked us to give him a sword,
Asked where he might find the wife no wife,
A mother whose plowfield bore him and his children.
Some spirit was guiding him in his frenzy,
For none of the men who are close at hand did so.
With a horrible shout, as if led on by someone,
He leapt on the double doors, from their sockets
Broke hollow bolts aside, and dashed within.
There we beheld his wife hung by her neck   1210
From twisted cords, swinging to and fro.
When he saw her, wretched man, he terribly groaned

And slackened the hanging noose. When the poor woman
Lay on the ground, what happened was dread to see.
He tore the golden brooch pins from her clothes,
And raised them up, and struck his own eyeballs,
Shouting such words as these "No more shall you
Behold the evils I have suffered and done.
Be dark from now on, since you saw before
What you should not, and knew not what you should."   1220
Moaning such cries, not once but many times
He raised and struck his eyes. The bloody pupils
Bedewed his beard. The gore oozed not in drops,
But poured in a black shower, a hail of blood.
From both of them these woes have broken out,
Not for just one, but man and wife together.
The bliss of old that formerly prevailed
Was indeed, but now upon this day
Lamentation, madness, death, and shame—
No evil that can be named is not at hand.   1230

Chorus
Is the wretched man in any rest now from pain?

Second Messenger
He shouts for someone to open up the doors
And show to all Cadmeans his father's slayer,
His mother's—I should not speak the unholy word.
He says he will hurl himself from the land, no more
To dwell cursed in the house by his own curse.
Yet he needs strength and someone who will guide him.
His sickness is too great to bear. He will show it to you
For the fastenings of the doors are opening up,
And such a spectacle you will soon behold   1240
As would make even one who abhors it take pity.

Chorus
O terrible suffering for men to see,
Most terrible of all that I
Have ever come upon. O wretched man,
What madness overcame you, what springing daimon
Greater than the greatest for men
Has caused your evil-daimoned fate?
Alas, alas, grievous one,
But I cannot bear to behold you, though I desire
To ask you much, much to find out,   1250
Much to see,
You make me shudder so!

Oedipus
Alas, alas, I am grieved!

Where on earth, so wretched, shall I go?
Where does my voice fly through the air,
O Fate, where have you bounded?

Chorus
To dreadful end, not to be heard or seen.

Strophe A

Oedipus
O cloud of dark
That shrouds me off, has come to pass, unspeakable,
Invincible, that blows no favoring blast.   1260
Woe,
O woe again, the goad that pierces me,
Of the sting of evil now, and memory of before.

Chorus
No wonder it is that among so many pains
You should both mourn and bear a double evil.

Antistrophe A

Oedipus
Ah, friend,
You are my steadfast servant still,
You still remain to care for me, blind.
Alas! Alas!
You are not hid from me; I know you clearly,   1270
And though in darkness, still I hear your voice.

Chorus
O dreadful doer, how did you so endure
To quench your eyes? What daimon drove you on?

Strophe B

Oedipus
Apollo it was, Apollo, friends
Who brought to pass these evil, evil woes of mine.
The hand of no one struck my eyes but wretched me.
For why should I see,
When nothing sweet there is to see with sight?

Chorus
This is just as you say.

Oedipus
What more is there for me to see,   1280
My friends, what to love,
What joy to hear a greeting?
Lead me at once away from here,

Lead me away, friends, wretched as I am,
Accursed, and hated most
Of mortals to the gods.

Chorus
Wretched alike in mind and in your fortune,
How I wish that I had never known you.

Antistrophe B

Oedipus
May he perish, whoever freed me
From fierce bonds on my feet, 1290
Snatched me from death and saved me, doing me no joy.
For if then I had died, I should not be
So great a grief to friends and to myself.

Chorus
This also is my wish.

Oedipus
I would not have come to murder my father,
Nor have been called among men
The bridegroom of her from whom I was born.
But as it is I am godless, child of unholiness,
Wretched sire in common with my father.
And if there is any evil older than evil left, 1300
It is the lot of Oedipus.

Chorus
I know not how I could give you good advice,
For you would be better dead than living blind.

Oedipus
That how things are was not done for the best—
Teach me not this, or give me more advice.
If I had sight, I know not with what eyes
I could ever face my father among the dead,
Or my wretched mother. What I have done to them
Is too great for a noose to expiate.
Do you think the sight of my children would be a joy 1310
For me to see, born as they were to me?
No, never for these eyes of mine to see.
Nor the city, nor the tower, nor the sacred
Statues of gods; of these I deprive myself,
Noblest among the Thebans, born and bred,
Now suffering everything. I tell you all
To exile me as impious, shown by the gods
Untouchable and of the race of Laius.
When I uncovered such a stain on me,

Could I look with steady eyes upon the people? 1320
No, No! And if there were a way to block
The spring of hearing, I would not forbear
To lock up wholly this my wretched body.
I should be blind and deaf.—For it is sweet
When thought can dwell outside our evils.
Alas, Cithaeron, why did you shelter me?
Why did you not take and kill me at once, so I
Might never reveal to men whence I was born?
O Polybus, O Corinth, O my father's halls,
Ancient in fable, what an outer fairness, 1330
A festering of evils, you raised in me.
For now I am evil found, and born of evil.
O the three paths! Alas the hidden glen,
The grove of oak, the narrow triple roads
That drank from my own hands my father's blood.
Do you remember any of the deeds
I did before you then on my way here
And what I after did? O wedlock, wedlock!
You gave me birth, and then spawned in return
Issue from the selfsame seed; you revealed 1340
Father, brother, children, in blood relation,
The bride both wife and mother, and whatever
Actions are done most shameful among men.
But it is wrong to speak what is not good to do.
By the gods, hide me at once outside our land,
Or murder me, or hurl me in the sea
Where you shall never look on me again.
Come, venture to lay your hands on this wretched man.
Do it. Be not afraid. No mortal man
There is, except myself, to bear my evils. 1350

Chorus
Here is Creon, just in time for what you ask
To work and to advise, for he alone
Is left in place of you to guard the land.

Oedipus
Alas, what word, then, shall I tell this man?
What righteous ground of trust is clear in me,
As in the past in all I have done him evil?

Creon
Oedipus, I have not come to laugh at you,
Nor to reproach you for your former wrongs.
[To the attendants]
If you defer no longer to mortal offspring,
Respect at least the all-nourishing flame 1360

Of Apollo, lord of the sun. Fear to display
So great a pestilence, which neither earth
Nor holy rain nor light will well receive.
But you, conduct him to the house at once.
It is most pious for the kin alone
To hear and to behold the family sins.

Oedipus
By the gods, since you have plucked me from my fear,
Most noble, facing this most vile man,
Hear me one word—I will speak for you, not me.

Creon
What desire do you so persist to get?   1370

Oedipus
As soon as you can, hurl me from this land
To where no mortal man will ever greet me.

Creon
I would do all this, be sure. But I want first
To find out from the god what must be done.

Oedipus
His oracle, at least, is wholly clear;
Leave me to ruin, an impious parricide.

Creon
Thus spake the oracle. Still, as we stand
It is better to find out sure what we should do.

Oedipus
Will you inquire about so wretched a man?

Creon
Yes. You will surely put trust in the god.   1380

Oedipus
I order you and beg you, give the woman
Now in the house such burial as you yourself
Would want. Do last rites justly for your kin.
But may this city never be condemned—
My father's realm—because I live within.
Let me live in the mountains where Cithaeron
Yonder has fame of me, which father and mother
When they were alive established as my tomb.
There I may die by those who sought to kill me.
And yet this much I know, neither a sickness   1390
Nor anything else can kill me. I would not
Be saved from death, except for some dread evil.

Well, let my fate go wherever it may.
As for my sons, Creon, assume no trouble;
They are men and will have no difficulty
Of living wherever they may be.
O my poor grievous daughters, who never knew
Their dinner table set apart from me,
But always shared in everything I touched—
Take care of them for me, and first of all   1400
Allow me to touch them and bemoan our ills.
Grant it, lord,
Grant it, noble. If with my hand I touch them
I would think I had them just as when I could see.
[CREON's *attendants bring in* ANTIGONE *and* ISMENE.]
What's that?
By the gods, can it be I hear my dear ones weeping?
And have you taken pity on me, Creon?
Have you had my darling children sent to me?
Do I speak right?

Creon
You do. For it was I who brought them here,   1410
Knowing this present joy your joy of old.

Oedipus
May you fare well. For their coming may the spirit
That watches over you be better than mine.
My children, where are you? Come to me, come
Into your brother's hands, that brought about
Your father's eyes, once bright, to see like this.
Your father, children, who, seeing and knowing nothing,
Became a father whence he was got himself.
I weep also for you—I cannot see you—
To think of the bitter life in days to come   1420
Which you will have to lead among mankind.
What citizens' gatherings will you approach?
What festivals attend, where you will not cry
When you go home, instead of gay rejoicing?
And when you arrive at marriageable age,
What man, my daughters, will there be to chance you,
Incurring such reproaches on his head,
Disgraceful to my children and to yours?
What evil will be absent, when your father
Killed his own father, sowed seed in her who bore him,   1430
From whom he was born himself, and equally
Has fathered you whence he himself was born.
Such will be the reproaches. Who then will wed you?
My children, there is no one for you. Clearly
You must decay in barrenness, unwed.

Son of Menoeceus—since you are alone
Left as a father to them, for we who produced them
Are both in ruin—see that you never let
These girls wander as beggars without husbands,
Let them not fall into such woes as mine.   1440
But pity them, seeing how young they are
To be bereft of all except your aid.
Grant this, my noble friend, with a touch of your hand.
My children, if your minds were now mature,
I would give you much advice. But, pray this for me,
To live as the time allows, to find a life
Better than that your siring father had.

Creon
You have wept enough here, come, and go inside the house.

Oedipus
I must obey, though nothing sweet.

Creon
                              All things are good in their time.

Oedipus
Do you know in what way I go?

Creon
                              Tell me, I'll know when I hear.   1450

Oedipus
Send me outside the land.

Creon
                              You ask what the god will do.

Oedipus
But to the gods I am hated.

Creon
                              Still, it will soon be done.

Oedipus
Then you agree?

Creon
                              What I think not I would not say in vain.

Oedipus
Now lead me away.

Creon
                              Come then, but let the children go.

Oedipus
Do not take them from me.

Creon
Wish not to govern all,
For what you ruled will not follow you through life.

Chorus
Dwellers in native Thebes, behold this Oedipus
Who solved the famous riddle, was your mightiest man.
What citizen on his lot did not with envy gaze?   1460
See to how great a surge of dread fate he has come!
So I would say a mortal man, while he is watching
To see the final day, can have no happiness
Till he pass the bound of life, nor be relieved of pain.

ANTIGONE*

Sophocles

CHARACTERS

ANTIGONE

ISMENE

EURYDICE

CREON

HAEMON

TEIRESIAS

A SENTRY

A MESSENGER

CHORUS

SCENE

Before the palace of CREON, *King of Thebes. A central double door, and two lateral doors. A platform extends the length of the façade, and from this platform three steps lead down into the "orchestra," or chorus-ground.*

TIME

Dawn of the day after the repulse of the Argive army from the assault on Thebes.

PROLOGUE

*[*ANTIGONE *and* ISMENE *enter from the central door of the palace.]*

Antigone
Ismenê, dear sister,   1
You would think that we had already suffered enough
For the curse on Oedipus:
I cannot imagine any grief
That you and I have not gone through. And now—
Have they told you of the new decree of our King Creon?

Ismene
I have heard nothing: I know
That two sisters lost two brothers, a double death
In a single hour; and I know that the Argive army
Fled in the night; but beyond this, nothing.   10

---

*Translation by Dudley Fitts and Robert Fitzgerald.

715

Antigone

I thought so. And that is why I wanted you
To come out here with me. There is something we must do.

Ismene

Why do you speak so strangely?

Antigone

Listen, Ismenê:
Creon buried our brother Eteoclês
With military honors, gave him a soldier's funeral,
And it was right that he should; but Polyneicês,
Who fought as bravely and died as miserably—
They say that Creon has sworn
No one shall bury him, no one mourn for him,   20
But his body must lie in the fields, a sweet treasure
For carrion birds to find as they search for food.
That is what they say, and our good Creon is coming here
to announce it publicly; and the penalty—
Stoning to death in the public square!
                                   There it is,
And now you can prove what you are:
A true sister, or a traitor to your family.

Ismene

Antigonê, you are mad! What could I possibly do?

Antigone

You must decide whether you will help me or not.

Ismene

I do not understand you. Help you in what?   30

Antigone

Ismenê, I am going to bury him. Will you come?

Ismene

Bury him! You have just said the new law forbids it.

Antigone

He is my brother. And he is your brother, too.

Ismene

But think of the danger! Think what Creon will do!

Antigone

Creon is not strong enough to stand in my way.

Ismene

Ah sister!
Oedipus died, everyone hating him

For what his own search brought to light, his eyes
Ripped out by his own hand; and Iocastê died,
His mother and wife at once: she twisted the cords   40
That strangled her life; and our two brothers died,
Each killed by the other's sword. And we are left:
But oh, Antigonê,
Think how much more terrible than these
Our own death would be if we should go against Creon
And do what he has forbidden! We are only women,
We cannot fight with men, Antigonê!
The law is strong, we must give in to the law
In this thing, and in worse. I beg the Dead
To forgive me, but I am helpless: I must yield   50
To those in authority. And I think it is dangerous business
To be always meddling.

Antigone

                          If that is what you think,
I should not want you, even if you asked to come.
You have made your choice, you can be what you want to be.
But I will bury him; and if I must die,
I say that this crime is holy: I shall lie down
With him in death, and I shall be as dear
To him as he to me
                          It is the dead,
Not the living, who make the longest demands:
We die for ever . . .
                          You may do as you like,   60
Since apparently the laws of the gods mean nothing to you.

Ismene

They mean a great deal to me; but I have no strength
To break laws that were made for the public good.

Antigone

That must be your excuse, I suppose. But as for me,
I will bury the brother I love

Ismene

                          Antigonê,
I am so afraid for you!

Antigone

                          You need not be:
You have yourself to consider, after all.

Ismene

But no one must hear of this, you must tell no one!
I will keep it a secret, I promise!

Antigone

Oh tell it! Tell everyone!
Think how they'll hate you when it all comes out   70
If they learn that you knew about it all the time!

Ismene
So fiery! You should be cold with fear.

Antigone
Perhaps. But I am doing only what I must.

Ismene
But can you do it? I say that you cannot.

Antigone
Very well: when my strength gives out, I shall do no more.

Ismene
Impossible things should not be tried at all.

Antigone
Go away, Ismenê:
I shall be hating you soon, and the dead will too,
For your words are hateful. Leave me my foolish plan:
I am not afraid of the danger; if it means death,   80
It will not be the worst of deaths—death without honor.

Ismene
Go then, if you feel that you must.
You are unwise,
But a loyal friend indeed to those who love you.
[Exit into the Palace. ANTIGONE *goes off, L. Enter the* CHORUS.*]*

PARODOS

Strophe 1

Chorus
Now the long blade of the sun, lying
Level east to west, touches with glory
Thebes of the Seven Gates. Open, unlidded
Eye of golden day! O marching light
Across the eddy and rush of Dircê's stream,
Striking the white shields of the enemy   90
Thrown headlong backward from the blaze of morning!

Choragos
Polyneicês their commander
Roused them with windy phrases,
He the wild eagle screaming
Insults above our land,
His wings their shields of snow,
His crest their marshalled helms.

Antistrophe 1

Chorus

Against our seven gates in a yawning ring
The famished spears came onward in the night;
But before his jaws were sated with our blood,   100
Or pinefire took the garland of our towers,
He was thrown back; and as he turned, great Thebes—
No tender victim for his noisy power—
Rose like a dragon behind him, shouting war.

Choragos

For God hates utterly
The bray of bragging tongues;
And when he beheld their smiling,
Their swagger of golden helms,
The frown of his thunder blasted
Their first man from our walls.   110

Strophe 2

Chorus

We heard his shout of triumph high in the air
Turn to a scream; far out in a flaming arc
He fell with his windy torch, and the earth struck him.
And others storming in fury no less than his
Found shock of death in the dusty joy of battle.

Choragos

Seven captains at seven gates
Yielded their clanging arms to the god
That bends the battle-line and breaks it.
These two only, brothers in blood,
Face to face in matchless rage,   120
Mirroring each the other's death,
Clashed in long combat.

Antistrophe 2

Chorus

But now in the beautiful morning of victory
Let Thebes of the many chariots sing for joy!
With hearts for dancing we'll take leave of war:
Our temples shall be sweet with hymns of praise,
And the long night shall echo with our chorus.

SCENE 1

Choragos

But now at last our new King is coming:
Creon of Thebes, Menoikeus' son.
In this auspicious dawn of his reign   130

What are the new complexities
That shifting Fate has woven for him?
What is his counsel? Why has he summoned
The old men to hear him?
[Enter CREON *from the Palace, C. He addresses the* CHORUS *from the top step.]*

Creon
Gentlemen: I have the honor to inform you that our Ship of State, which recent storms have threatened to destroy, has come safely to harbor at last, guided by the merciful wisdom of Heaven. I have summoned you here this morning because I know that I can depend upon you: your devotion to King Laïos was absolute; you never hesitated in your duty to our late ruler Oedipus; and when Oedipus died, your loyalty was transferred to his children. Unfortunately, as you know, his two sons, the princes Eteoclês and Polyneicês, have killed each other in battle; and I, as the next in blood, have succeeded to the full power of the throne.

I am aware, of course, that no Ruler can expect complete loyalty from his subjects until he has been tested in office. Nevertheless, I say to you at the very outset that I have nothing but contempt for the kind of Governor who is afraid, for whatever reason, to follow the course that he knows is best for the State; and as for the man who sets private friendship above the public welfare,—I have no use for him, either. I call God to witness that if I saw my country headed for ruin, I should not be afraid to speak out plainly; and I need hardly remind you that I would never have any dealings with an enemy of the people. No one values friendship more highly than I; but we must remember that friends made at the risk of wrecking our Ship are not real friends at all.

These are my principles, at any rate, and that is why I have made the following decision concerning the sons of Oedipus: Eteoclês, who died as a man should die, fighting for his country, is to be buried with full military honors, with all the ceremony that is usual when the greatest heroes die; but his brother Polyneicês, who broke his exile to come back with fire and sword against his native city and the shrines of his fathers' gods, whose one idea was to spill the blood of his blood and sell his own people into slavery—Polyneicês, I say, is to have no burial: no man is to touch him or say the least prayer for him; he shall lie on the plain, unburied; and the birds and the scavenging dogs can do with him whatever they like.

This is my command, and you can see the wisdom behind it. As long as I am King, no traitor is going to be honored with the loyal man. But whoever shows by word and deed that he is on the side of the State,—he shall have my respect while he is living, and my reverence when he is dead.

Choragos
If that is your will, Creon son of Menoikeus,
You have the right to enforce it: we are yours. 140

Creon
That is my will. Take care that you do your part.

Choragos
We are old men: let the younger ones carry it out.

Creon
I do not mean that: the sentries have been appointed.

Choragos
Then what is it that you would have us do?

Creon
You will give no support to whoever breaks this law.

Choragos
Only a crazy man is in love with death!

Creon
And death it is; yet money talks, and the wisest
Have sometimes been known to count a few coins too many.
[Enter SENTRY *from L.]*

Sentry
I'll not say that I'm out of breath from running, King, because every time I stopped to think about what I have to tell you, I felt like going back. And all the time a voice kept saying, "You fool, don't you know you're walking straight into trouble?"; and then another voice: "Yes, but if you let somebody else get the news to Creon first, it will be even worse than that for you!" But good sense won out, at least I hope it was good sense, and here I am with a story that makes no sense at all; but I'll tell it anyhow, because, as they say, what's going to happen's going to happen, and—

Creon
Come to the point. What have you to say?   150

Sentry
I did not do it. I did not see who did it. You must not punish me for what someone else has done.

Creon
A comprehensive defense! More effective, perhaps,
If I knew its purpose. Come: what is it?

Sentry
A dreadful thing . . . I don't know how to put it—

Creon
Out with it!

Sentry
          Well, then;
The dead man—
          Polyneicês—

[Pause. The SENTRY *is overcome, fumbles for words.* CREON *waits impassively.]*
out there—

someone,—

New dust on the slimy flesh!
[Pause. No sign from CREON.*]*
Someone has given it burial that way, and
Gone . . .
[Long pause. CREON *finally speaks with deadly control:]*

Creon
And the man who dared do this?

Sentry

I swear I   160
Do not know! You must believe me!

Listen:
The ground was dry, not a sign of digging, no,
Not a wheeltrack in the dust, no trace of anyone.
It was when they relieved us this morning: and one of them,
The corporal, pointed to it.

There it was,
The strangest—

Look:
The body, just mounded over with light dust: you see?
Not buried really, but as if they'd covered it
Just enough for the ghost's peace. And no sign
Of dogs or any wild animal that had been there.   170

And then what a scene there was! Every man of us
Accusing the other: we all proved the other man did it,
We all had proof that we could not have done it.
We were ready to take hot iron in our hands,
Walk through fire, swear by all the gods.
It was not I!
I do not know who it was, but it was not I!
*[*CREON's *rage has been mounting steadily, but the* SENTRY *is too intent upon his story*
to notice it.]
And then, when this came to nothing, someone said
A thing that silenced us and made us stare
Down at the ground: you had to be told the news,   180
And one of us had to do it! We threw the dice,
And the bad luck fell to me. So here I am,
No happier to be here than you are to have me:
Nobody likes the man who brings bad news.

Choragos
I have been wondering, King; can it be that the gods have done this?

Creon *[Furiously:]*
Stop!
Must you doddering wrecks
Go out of your heads entirely? "The gods!"
Intolerable!
The gods favor this corpse? Why? How had he served them?   190
Tried to loot their temples, burn their images,
Yes, and the whole State, and its laws with it!
Is it your senile opinion that the gods love to honor bad men?
A pious thought!—
                    No, from the very beginning
There have been those who have whispered together,
Stiff-necked anarchists, putting their heads together,
Scheming against me in alleys. These are the men,
And they have bribed my own guard to do this thing.
[Sententiously:]
Money!
There's nothing in the world so demoralizing as money.   200
Down go your cities,
Homes gone, men gone, honest hearts corrupted,
Crookedness of all kinds, and all for money!
[To SENTRY:]
                         But you—!
I swear by God and by the throne of God,
The man who has done this thing shall pay for it!
Find that man, bring him here to me, or your death
Will be the least of your problems: I'll string you up
Alive, and there will be certain ways to make you
Discover your employer before you die;
And the process may teach you a lesson you seem to have missed: 210
The dearest profit is sometimes all too dear:
That depends on the source. Do you understand me?
A fortune won is often misfortune.

Sentry
King, may I speak?

Creon
                    Your very voice distresses me.

Sentry
Are you sure that it is my voice, and not your conscience?

Creon
By God, he wants to analyze me now!

Sentry
It is not what I say, but what has been done, that hurts you.

Creon

You talk too much.

Sentry

Maybe; but I've done nothing.

Creon

Sold your soul for some silver: that's all you've done.

Sentry

How dreadful it is when the right judge judges wrong!   220

Creon

Your figures of speech
May entertain you now; but unless you bring me the man,
You will get little profit from them in the end.
[Exit CREON *into the Palace.]*

Sentry

"Bring me the man"—!
I'd like nothing better than bringing him the man!
But bring him or not, you have seen the last of me here.
At any rate, I am safe!
[Exit SENTRY.*]*

ODE I

Chorus

Strophe 1

Numberless are the world's wonders, but none
More wonderful than man; the stormgray sea
Yields to his prows, the huge crests bear him high;   230
Earth, holy and inexhaustible, is graven
With shining furrows where his plows have gone
Year after year, the timeless labor of stallions.

Antistrophe 1

The lightboned birds and beasts that cling to cover,
The lithe fish lighting their reaches of dim water,
All are taken, tamed in the net of his mind;
The lion on the hill, the wild horse windy-maned,
Resign to him; and his blunt yoke has broken
The sultry shoulders of the mountain bull.

Strophe 2

Words also, and thought as rapid as air,   240
He fashions to his good use; statecraft is his,
And his the skill that deflects the arrows of snow,
The spears of winter rain: from every wind

He has made himself secure—from all but one:
In the late wind of death he cannot stand.

Antistrophe 2

O clear intelligence, force beyond all measure!
O fate of man, working both good and evil!
When the laws are kept, how proudly his city stands!
When the laws are broken, what of his city then?
Never may the anarchic man find rest at my hearth,   250
Never be it said that my thoughts are his thoughts.

SCENE II

[Re-enter SENTRY *leading* ANTIGONE.*]*

Choragos
What does this mean? Surely this captive woman
Is the Princess, Antigonê. Why should she be taken?

Sentry
Here is the one who did it! We caught her
In the very act of burying him.—Where is Creon?

Choragos
Just coming from the house
[Enter CREON, *C.]*

Creon
                             What has happened?
Why have you come back so soon?

Sentry *[Expansively:]*
                             O King,
A man should never be too sure of anything:
I would have sworn
That you'd not see me here again: your anger   260
Frightened me so, and the things you threatened me with;
But how could I tell then
That I'd be able to solve the case so soon?

No dice-throwing this time: I was only too glad to come!
Here is this woman. She is the guilty one:
We found her trying to bury him.
Take her, then; question her; judge her as you will.
I am through with the whole thing now, and glad of it.

Creon
But this is Antigonê! Why have you brought her here?

Sentry

She was burying him, I tell you!

Creon *[Severely:]*

                                Is this the truth?   270

Sentry

I saw her with my own eyes. Can I say more?

Creon

The details: come, tell me quickly!

Sentry

                          It was like this:
After those terrible threats of yours, King,
We went back and brushed the dust away from the body.
The flesh was soft by now, and stinking.
So we sat on a hill to windward and kept guard.
No napping this time! We kept each other awake.
But nothing happened until the white round sun
Whirled in the center of the round sky over us:
Then, suddenly,   280
A storm of dust roared up from the earth, and the sky
Went out, the plain vanished with all its trees
In the stinging dark. We closed our eyes and endured it
The whirlwind lasted a long time, but it passed;
And then we looked, and there was Antigonê!

I have seen
A mother bird come back to a stripped nest, heard
Her crying bitterly a broken note or two
For the young ones stolen. Just so, when this girl
Found the bare corpse, and all her love's work wasted,   290
She wept, and cried on heaven to damn the hands
That had done this thing.
                        And then she brought more dust
And sprinkled wine three times for her brother's ghost.

We ran and took her at once. She was not afraid,
Not even when we charged her with what she had done.
She denied nothing.
                     And this was a comfort to me,
And some uneasiness: for it is a good thing
To escape from death, but it is no great pleasure
To bring death to a friend.
                        Yet I always say
There is nothing so comfortable as your own safe skin!   300

Creon *[Slowly, dangerously:]*

And you, Antigonê,
You with your head hanging,—do you confess this thing?

Antigone
I do. I deny nothing.

Creon [*To* SENTRY:]
                    You may go.
[*Exit* SENTRY. *To* ANTIGONE:]
Tell me, tell me briefly:
Had you heard my proclamation touching this matter?

Antigone
It was public. Could I help hearing it?

Creon
And yet you dared defy the law.

Antigone
                    I dared.
It was not God's proclamation. That final Justice
That rules the world below makes no such laws.

Your edict, King, was strong,   310
But all your strength is weakness itself against
The immortal unrecorded laws of God.
They are not merely now: they were, and shall be,
Operative for ever, beyond man utterly.

I knew I must die, even without your decree:
I am only mortal. And if I must die
Now, before it is my time to die,
Surely this is no hardship: can anyone
Living, as I live, with evil all about me,
Think Death less than a friend? This death of mine   320
Is of no importance; but if I had left my brother
Lying in death unburied, I should have suffered.
Now I do not.
                    You smile at me. Ah, Creon,
Think me a fool, if you like; but it may well be
That a fool convicts me of folly.

Choragos
Like father, like daughter: both headstrong, deaf to reason!
She has never learned to yield.

Creon
                    She has much to learn.
The inflexible heart breaks first, the toughest iron
Cracks first, and the wildest horses bend their necks
At the pull of the smallest curb.
Pride? In a slave?   330
This girl is guilty of a double insolence,
Breaking the given laws and boasting of it.

Who is the man here,
She or I, if this crime goes unpunished?
Sister's child, or more than sister's child,
Or closer yet in blood—she and her sister
Win bitter death for this!
[To SERVANTS:]
                              Go, some of you,
Arrest Ismenê. I accuse her equally.
Bring her: you will find her sniffling in the house there.

Her mind's a traitor: crimes kept in the dark   340
Cry for light, and the guardian brain shudders;
But how much worse than this
Is brazen boasting of barefaced anarchy!

Antigone
Creon, what more do you want than my death?

Creon
                                        Nothing.
That gives me everything.

Antigone
                    Then I beg you: kill me.
This talking is a great weariness: your words
Are distasteful to me, and I am sure that mine
Seem so to you. And yet they should not seem so:
I should have praise and honor for what I have done.
All these men here would praise me   350
Were their lips not frozen shut with fear of you.
[Bitterly:]
Ah the good fortune of kings
Licensed to say and do whatever they please!

Creon
You are alone here in that opinion.

Antigone
No, they are with me. But they keep their tongues in leash.

Creon
Maybe. But you are guilty, and they are not.

Antigone
There is no guilt in reverence for the dead.

Creon
But Eteoclês—was he not your brother too?

Antigone
My brother too.

Creon
    And you insult his memory?

Antigone *[Softly:]*
The dead man would not say that I insult it.   360

Creon
He would: for you honor a traitor as much as him.

Antigone
His own brother, traitor or not, and equal in blood.

Creon
He made war on his country. Eteoclês defended it.

Antigone
Nevertheless, there are honors due all the dead.

Creon
But not the same for the wicked as for the just.

Antigone
Ah Creon, Creon,
Which of us can say what the gods hold wicked?

Creon
An enemy is an enemy, even dead.

Antigone
It is my nature to join in love, not hate.

Creon *[Finally losing patience:]*
Go join them, then; if you must have your love,   370
Find it in hell!

Choragos
But see, Ismenê comes:
[Enter ISMENE, *guarded.]*
Those tears are sisterly, the cloud
That shadows her eyes rains down gentle sorrow.

Creon
You too, Ismenê,
Snake in my ordered house, sucking my blood
Stealthily—and all the time I never knew
That these two sisters were aiming at my throne!
              Ismenê,
Do you confess your share in this crime, or deny it?
Answer me.   380

Ismene
Yes, if she will let me say so. I am guilty.

Antigone *[Coldly:]*
No, Ismenê. You have no right to say so.
You would not help me, and I will not have you help me.

Ismene
But now I know what you meant; and I am here
To join you, to take my share of punishment.

Antigone
The dead man and the gods who rule the dead
Know whose act this was. Words are not friends.

Ismene
Do you refuse me, Antigonê? I want to die with you:
I too have a duty that I must discharge to the dead.

Antigone
You shall not lessen my death by sharing it.   390

Ismene
What do I care for life when you are dead?

Antigone
Ask Creon. You're always hanging on his opinions.

Ismene
You are laughing at me. Why, Antigonê?

Antigone
It's a joyless laughter, Ismenê.

Ismene
                        But can I do nothing?

Antigone
Yes. Save yourself. I shall not envy you.
There are those who will praise you; I shall have honor, too.

Ismene
But we are equally guilty!

Antigone
                    No more, Ismenê.
You are alive, but I belong to Death.

Creon *[To the* CHORUS:*]*
Gentlemen, I beg you to observe these girls:
One has just now lost her mind; the other,   400
It seems, has never had a mind at all.

Ismene
Grief teaches the steadiest minds to waver, King.

Creon
Yours certainly did, when you assumed guilt with the guilty!

Ismene
But how could I go on living without her?

Creon
                                        You are.
She is already dead.

Ismene
                    But your own son's bride!

Creon
There are places enough for him to push his plow.
I want no wicked women for my sons!

Ismene
O dearest Haemon, how your father wrongs you!

Creon
I've had enough of your childish talk of marriage!

Choragos
Do you really intend to steal this girl from your son?   410

Creon
No; Death will do that for me

Choragos
                    Then she must die?

Creon [*Ironically:*]
You dazzle me.
                —But enough of this talk!
[*To* GUARDS:]
You, there, take them away and guard them well:
For they are but women, and even brave men run
When they see Death coming.
[*Exeunt* ISMENE, ANTIGONE, *and* GUARDS.]

ODE II

Chorus

Strophe 1

Fortunate is the man who has never tasted God's vengeance!
Where once the anger of heaven has struck, that house is shaken
For ever: damnation rises behind each child
Like a wave cresting out of the black northeast,
When the long darkness under sea roars up   420
And bursts drumming death upon the windwhipped sand.

Antistrophe 1

I have seen this gathering sorrow from time long past
Loom upon Oedipus' children: generation from generation
Takes the compulsive rage of the enemy god.
So lately this last flower of Oedipus' line
Drank the sunlight! but now a passionate word
And a handful of dust have closed up all its beauty.

Strophe 2

   What mortal arrogance
   Transcends the wrath of Zeus?
Sleep cannot lull him, nor the effortless long months   430
Of the timeless gods: but he is young for ever,
And his house is the shining day of high Olympos.
   All that is and shall be,
   And all the past, is his.
No pride on earth is free of the curse of heaven.

Antistrophe 2

   The straying dreams of men
   May bring them ghosts of joy:
But as they drowse, the waking embers burn them;
Or they walk with fixed eyes, as blind men walk.
But the ancient wisdom speaks for our own time: 440
   Fate works most for woe
   With Folly's fairest show.
Man's little pleasure is the spring of sorrow.

SCENE III

Choragos

But here is Haemon, King, the last of all your sons.
Is it grief for Antigonê that brings him here,
And bitterness at being robbed of his bride?
[*Enter* HAEMON.]

Creon

We shall soon see, and no need of diviners.
                          —Son,
You have heard my final judgment on that girl:
Have you come here hating me, or have you come
With deference and with love, whatever I do.   450

Haemon

I am your son, father. You are my guide.
You make things clear for me, and I obey you.
No marriage means more to me than your continuing wisdom.

Creon

Good. That is the way to behave: subordinate

Everything else, my son, to your father's will.
This is what a man prays for, that he may get
Sons attentive and dutiful in his house,
Each one hating his father's enemies,
Honoring his father's friends. But if his sons
Fail him, if they turn out unprofitably,   460
What has he fathered but trouble for himself
And amusement for the malicious?
                                        So you are right
Not to lose your head over this woman.
Your pleasure with her would soon grow cold, Haemon,
And then you'd have a hellcat in bed and elsewhere.
Let her find her husband in Hell!
Of all the people in this city, only she
Has had contempt for my law and broken it.

Do you want me to show myself weak before the people?
Or to break my sworn word? No, and I will not.   470
The woman dies.

I suppose she'll plead "family ties." Well, let her.
If I permit my own family to rebel,
How shall I earn the world's obedience?
Show me the man who keeps his house in hand,
He's fit for public authority.
                                        I'll have no dealings
With law-breakers, critics of the government:
Whoever is chosen to govern should be obeyed—
Must be obeyed, in all things, great and small,
Just and unjust! O Haemon,   480
The man who knows how to obey, and that man only,
Knows how to give commands when the time comes.
You can depend on him, no matter how fast
The spears come: he's a good soldier, he'll stick it out.
Anarchy, anarchy! Show me a greater evil!
This is why cities tumble and the great houses rain down,
This is what scatters armies!

No, no: good lives are made so by discipline.
We keep the laws then, and the lawmakers,
And no woman shall seduce us. If we must lose,   490
Let's lose to a man, at least! Is a woman stronger than we?

Choragos
Unless time has rusted my wits,
What you say, King, is said with point and dignity.

Haemon *[Boyishly earnest:]*
Father:
Reason is God's crowning gift to man, and you are right

To warn me against losing mine. I cannot say—
I hope that I shall never want to say!—that you
Have reasoned badly. Yet there are other men
Who can reason, too; and their opinions might be helpful.
You are not in a position to know everything   500
That people say or do, or what they feel:
Your temper terrifies them—everyone
Will tell you only what you like to hear.
But I, at any rate, can listen; and I have heard them
Muttering and whispering in the dark about this girl.
They say no woman has ever, so unreasonably,
Died so shameful a death for a generous act:
"She covered her brother's body. Is this indecent?
She kept him from dogs and vultures. Is this a crime?
Death?—She should have all the honor that we can give her!"   510

This is the way they talk out there in the city.

You must believe me:
Nothing is closer to me than your happiness.
What could be closer? Must not any son
Value his father's fortune as his father does his?
I beg you, do not be unchangeable:
Do not believe that you alone can be right.
The man who thinks that,
The man who maintains that only he has the power
To reason correctly, the gift to speak, the soul—   520
A man like that, when you know him, turns out empty.

It is not reason never to yield to reason!

In flood time you can see how some trees bend,
And because they bend, even their twigs are safe,
While stubborn trees are torn up, roots and all.
And the same thing happens in sailing:
Make your sheet fast, never slacken,—and over you go,
Head over heels and under: and there's your voyage.
Forget you are angry! Let yourself be moved!
I know I am young; but please let me say this: 530
The ideal condition
Would be, I admit, that men should be right by instinct;
But since we are all too likely to go astray,
The reasonable thing is to learn from those who can teach.

Choragos
You will do well to listen to him, King,
If what he says is sensible. And you, Haemon,
Must listen to your father.—Both speak well.

Creon
You consider it right for a man of my years and experience
To go to school to a boy?

Haemon
                  It is not right
If I am wrong. But if I am young, and right,   540
What does my age matter?

Creon
You think it right to stand up for an anarchist?

Haemon
Not at all. I pay no respect to criminals.

Creon
Then she is not a criminal?

Haemon
The City would deny it, to a man.

Creon
And the City proposes to teach me how to rule?

Haemon
Ah. Who is it that's talking like a boy now?

Creon
My voice is the one voice giving orders in this City!

Haemon
It is no City if it takes orders from one voice.

Creon
The State is the King!

Haemon
                 Yes, if the State is a desert.   550
[Pause.]

Creon
This boy, it seems, has sold out to a woman.

Haemon
If you are a woman: my concern is only for you.

Creon
So? Your "concern"! In a public brawl with your father!

Haemon
How about you, in a public brawl with justice?

Creon
With justice, when all that I do is within my rights?

Haemon
You have no right to trample on God's right.

Creon *[Completely out of control:]*
Fool, adolescent fool! Taken in by a woman!

Haemon
You'll never see me taken in by anything vile.

Creon
Every word you say is for her!

Haemon *[Quietly, darkly:]*
                     And for you.
And for me. And for the gods under the earth.   560

Creon
You'll never marry her while she lives.

Haemon
Then she must die.—But her death will cause another.

Creon
Another?
Have you lost your senses? Is this an open threat?

Haemon
There is no threat in speaking to emptiness.

Creon
I swear you'll regret this superior tone of yours!
You are the empty one!

Haemon
                 If you were not my father,
I'd say you were perverse.

Creon
You girlstruck fool, don't play at words with me!

Haemon
I am sorry. You prefer silence.

Creon
                Now, by God—!   570
I swear, by all the gods in heaven above us,
You'll watch it, I swear you shall!
[To the SERVANTS:*]*
                Bring her out!

Bring the woman out! Let her die before his eyes!
Here, this instant, with her bridegroom beside her!

Haemon
Not here, no; she will not die here, King.
And you will never see my face again.
Go on raving as long as you've a friend to endure you.
[*Exit* HAEMON.]

Choragos
Gone, gone.
Creon, a young man in a rage is dangerous!

Creon
Let him do, or dream to do, more than a man can.   580
He shall not save these girls from death.

Choragos
                                                        These girls?
You have sentenced them both?

Creon
                                        No, you are right.
I will not kill the one whose hands are clean.

Choragos
But Antigonê?

Creon [*Somberly:*]
                        I will carry her far away
Out there in the wilderness, and lock her
Living in a vault of stone. She shall have food,
As the custom is, to absolve the State of her death.
And there let her pray to the gods of hell:
They are her only gods:
Perhaps they will show her an escape from death,   590
Or she may learn,
                        though late,
That piety shown the dead is pity in vain.
[*Exit* CREON.]

ODE III
Chorus
Strophe

Love, unconquerable
Waster of rich men, keeper
Of warm lights and all-night vigil
In the soft face of a girl:
Sea-wanderer, forest-visitor!

Even the pure Immortals cannot escape you,
And mortal man, in his one day's dusk,
Trembles before your glory.   600

Antistrophe

Surely you swerve upon ruin
The just man's consenting heart,
As here you have made bright anger
Strike between father and son—
And none has conquered but Love!
A girl's glance working the will of heaven:
Pleasure to her alone who mocks us,
Merciless Aphroditê.

SCENE IV

Choragos   [*As* ANTIGONE *enters guarded:*]
But I can no longer stand in awe of this,
Nor, seeing what I see, keep back my tears.   610
Here is Antigonê, passing to that chamber
Where all find sleep at last.

Strophe 1

Antigone

Look upon me, friends, and pity me
Turning back at the night's edge to say
Good-by to the sun that shines for me no longer;
Now sleepy Death
Summons me down to Acheron, that cold shore:
There is no bridesong there, nor any music.

Choragos

Yet not unpraised, not without a kind of honor,
You walk at last into the underworld;   620
Untouched by sickness, broken by no sword.
What woman has ever found your way to death?

Antigone

Antistrophe 1

How often I have heard the story of Niobê,
Tantalos' wretched daughter, how the stone
Clung fast about her, ivy-close: and they say
The rain falls endlessly
And sifting soft snow; her tears are never done.
I feel the loneliness of her death in mine.

Chorus

But she was born of heaven, and you
Are woman, woman-born. If her death is yours,   630

A mortal woman's, is this not for you
Glory in our world and in the world beyond?

Strophe 2

Antigone
You laugh at me. Ah, friends, friends
Can you not wait until I am dead? O Thebes,
O men many-charioted, in love with Fortune,
Dear springs of Dircê, sacred Theban grove,
Be witness for me, denied all pity,
Unjustly judged! and think a word of love
For her whose path turns
Under dark earth, where there are no more tears.   640

Chorus
You have passed beyond human daring and come at last
Into a place of stone where Justice sits
I cannot tell
What shape of your father's guilt appears in this.

Antistrophe 2

Antigone
You have touched it at last; that bridal bed
Unspeakable, horror of son and mother mingling:
Their crime, infection of all our family!
O Oedipus, father and brother!
Your marriage strikes from the grave to murder mine.
I have been a stranger here in my own land: 650
All my life
The blasphemy of my birth has followed me.

Chorus
Reverence is a virtue, but strength
Lives in established law: that must prevail.
You have made your choice,
Your death is the doing of your conscious hand.

Epode

Antigone
Then let me go, since all your words are bitter,
And the very light of the sun is cold to me.
Lead me to my vigil, where I must have
Neither love nor lamentation; no song, but silence.   660
[CREON interrupts impatiently.]

Creon
If dirges and planned lamentations could put off death,
Men would be singing for ever.
[To the SERVANTS:*]*
                              Take her, go!

You know your orders: take her to the vault
And leave her alone there. And if she lives or dies,
That's her affair, not ours: our hands are clean.

Antigone
O tomb, vaulted bride-bed in eternal rock,
Soon I shall be with my own again
Where Persephonê welcomes the thin ghosts underground:
And I shall see my father again, and you, mother,
And dearest Polyneicês—

                    dearest indeed   670
To me, since it was my hand
That washed him clean and poured the ritual wine:
And my reward is death before my time!

And yet, as men's hearts know, I have done no wrong.
I have not sinned before God. Or if I have,
I shall know the truth in death. But if the guilt
Lies upon Creon who judged me, then, I pray,
May his punishment equal my own.

Choragos
                    O passionate heart,
Unyielding, tormented still by the same winds!

Creon
Her guards shall have good cause to regret their delaying.   680

Antigone
Ah! That voice is like the voice of death!

Creon
I can give you no reason to think you are mistaken.

Antigone
Thebes, and you my fathers' gods,
And rulers of Thebes, you see me now, the last
Unhappy daughter of a line of kings,
Your kings, led away to death. You will remember
What things I suffer, and at what men's hands,
Because I would not transgress the laws of heaven.
[To the GUARDS, *simply:]*
Come: let us wait no longer.
[Exit ANTIGONE, *L., guarded.]*

ODE IV
Chorus
Strophe 1

All Danaê's beauty was locked away   690
In a brazen cell where the sunlight could not come:

A small room, still as any grave, enclosed her.
Yet she was a princess too,
And Zeus in a rain of gold poured love upon her.
O child, child,
No power in wealth or war
Or tough sea-blackened ships
Can prevail against untiring Destiny!

Antistrophe 1

And Dryas' son also, that furious king,
Bore the god's prisoning anger for his pride: 700
Sealed up by Dionysos in deaf stone,
His madness died among echoes.
So at the last he learned what dreadful power
His tongue had mocked:
For he had profaned the revels,
And fired the wrath of the nine
Implacable Sisters that love the sound of the flute.

Strophe 2

And old men tell a half-remembered tale
Of horror done where a dark ledge splits the sea
And a double surf beats on the gray shores: 710
How a king's new woman, sick
With hatred for the queen he had imprisoned,
Ripped out his two sons' eyes with her bloody hands
While grinning Arês watched the shuttle plunge
Four times: four blind wounds crying for revenge,

Antistrophe 2

Crying, tears and blood mingled.—Piteously born,
Those sons whose mother was of heavenly birth!
Her father was the god of the North Wind
And she was cradled by gales,
She raced with young colts on the glittering hills   720
And walked untrammeled in the open light:
But in her marriage deathless Fate found means
To build a tomb like yours for all her joy.

SCENE V

[Enter blind TEIRESIAS, *led by a boy. The opening speeches of* TEIRESIAS *should be in singsong contrast to the realistic lines of* CREON.*]*

Teiresias
This is the way the blind man comes, Princes, Princes,
Lock-step, two heads lit by the eyes of one.

Creon
What new thing have you to tell us, old Teiresias?

Teiresias
I have much to tell you: listen to the prophet, Creon.

Creon
I am not aware that I have ever failed to listen.

Teiresias
Then you have done wisely, King, and ruled well.

Creon
I admit my debt to you. But what have you to say?   730

Teiresias
This, Creon: you stand once more on the edge of fate.

Creon
What do you mean? Your words are a kind of dread.

Teiresias
Listen, Creon:
I was sitting in my chair of augury, at the place
Where the birds gather about me. They were all a-chatter,
As is their habit, when suddenly I heard
A strange note in their jangling, a scream, a
whirring fury; I knew that they were fighting,
Tearing each other, dying
In a whirlwind of wings clashing. And I was afraid.   740
I began the rites of burnt-offering at the altar,
But Hephaistos failed me: instead of bright flame,
There was only the sputtering slime of the fat thigh-flesh
Melting: the entrails dissolved in gray smoke,
The bare bone burst from the welter. And no blaze!

This was a sign from heaven. My boy described it,
Seeing for me as I see for others.

I tell you, Creon, you yourself have brought
This new calamity upon us. Our hearths and altars
Are stained with the corruption of dogs and carrion birds   750
That glut themselves on the corpse of Oedipus' son.
The gods are deaf when we pray to them, their fire
Recoils from our offering, their birds of omen
Have no cry of comfort, for they are gorged
With the thick blood of the dead.
                              O my son,
These are no trifles! Think: all men make mistakes,
But a good man yields when he knows his course is wrong,
And repairs the evil. The only crime is pride.

Give in to the dead man, then: do not fight with a corpse—
What glory is it to kill a man who is dead?   760

Think, I beg you:
It is for your own good that I speak as I do.
You should be able to yield for your own good.

Creon
It seems that prophets have made me their especial province.
All my life long
I have been a kind of butt for the dull arrows
Of doddering fortune-tellers!
                              No, Teiresias:
If your birds—if the great eagles of God himself
Should carry him stinking bit by bit to heaven,
I would not yield. I am not afraid of pollution: 770
No man can defile the gods.
                              Do what you will,
Go into business, make money, speculate
In India gold or that synthetic gold from Sardis,
Get rich otherwise than by my consent to bury him.
Teiresias, it is a sorry thing when a wise man
Sells his wisdom, lets out his words for hire!

Teiresias
Ah Creon! Is there no man left in the world—

Creon
To do what?—Come, let's have the aphorism!

Teiresias
No man who knows that wisdom outweighs any wealth?

Creon
As surely as bribes are baser than any baseness.   780

Teiresias
You are sick, Creon! You are deathly sick!

Creon
As you say: it is not my place to challenge a prophet.

Teiresias
Yet you have said my prophecy is for sale.

Creon
The generation of prophets has always loved gold.

Teiresias
The generation of kings has always loved brass.

Creon
You forget yourself! You are speaking to your King.

Teiresias
I know it. You are a king because of me.

Creon

You have a certain skill; but you have sold out.

Teiresias

King, you will drive me to words that—

Creon

                                Say them, say them!

Only remember: I will not pay you for them.   790

Teiresias

No, you will find them too costly.

Creon

                         No doubt. Speak:

Whatever you say, you will not change my will.

Teiresias

Then take this, and take it to heart!
The time is not far off when you shall pay back
Corpse for corpse, flesh of your own flesh.
You have thrust the child of this world into living night,
You have kept from the gods below the child that is theirs:
The one in a grave before her death, the other,
Dead, denied the grave. This is your crime:
And the Furies and the dark gods of Hell   800
Are swift with terrible punishment for you.

Do you want to buy me now, Creon?
                               Not many days,
And your house will be full of men and women weeping,
And curses will be hurled at you from far
Cities grieving for sons unburied, left to rot
Before the walls of Thebes.

These are my arrows, Creon: they are all for you.
[*To* BOY:]
But come, child: lead me home.
Let him waste his fine anger upon younger men.
Maybe he will learn at last   810
To control a wiser tongue in a better head.
[*Exit* TEIRESIAS.]

Choragos

The old man has gone, King, but his words
Remain to plague us. I am old, too,
But I cannot remember that he was ever false.

Creon

That is true. . . . It troubles me.

Oh it is hard to give in! but it is worse
To risk everything for stubborn pride.

Choragos
Creon: take my advice.

Creon
                    What shall I do?

Choragos
Go quickly: free Antigonê from her vault
And build a tomb for the body of Polyneicês.   820

Creon
You would have me do this?

Choragos
                        Creon, yes!
And it must be done at once: God moves
Swiftly to cancel the folly of stubborn men.

Creon
It is hard to deny the heart! But I
Will do it: I will not fight with destiny.

Choragos
You must go yourself, you cannot leave it to others.

Creon
I will go
        —Bring axes, servants:
Come with me to the tomb. I buried her, I
Will set her free.
                Oh quickly!
My mind misgives—   830
The laws of the gods are mighty, and a man must serve them
To the last day of his life!
[Exit CREON.*]*

PÆAN
Strophe 1
Choragos
God of many names

Chorus
                O Iacchos
                        son
of Kadmeian Sémelê
                O born of the Thunder!

Guardian of the West

Regent

of Eleusis' plain

O Prince of maenad Thebes

and the Dragon Field by rippling Ismenos:

Antistrophe 1

Choragos

God of many names

Chorus

the flame of torches

flares on our hills

the nymphs of Iacchos

dance at the spring of Castalia: 840

from the vine-close mountain

come ah come in ivy:

Evohé evohé! sings through the streets of Thebes

Strophe 2

Choragos

God of many names

Chorus

Iacchos of Thebes

heavenly Child

of Sémelê bride of the Thunderer!

The shadow of plague is upon us:

come

with clement feet

oh come from Parnasos

down the long slopes

across the lamenting water

Antistrophe 2

Choragos

Iô Fire! Chorister of the throbbing stars!
O purest among the voices of the night!
Thou son of God, blaze for us! 850

Chorus

Come with choric rapture of circling Maenads
Who cry *Iô Iacche!*

God of many names!

EXODOS

[Enter MESSENGER, *L.]*

Messenger
Men of the line of Kadmos, you who live
Near Amphion's citadel:
                              I cannot say
Of any condition of human life "This is fixed,
This is clearly good, or bad." Fate raises up
And Fate casts down the happy and unhappy alike:
No man can foretell his Fate.
                              Take the case of Creon:
Creon was happy once, as I count happiness:
Victorious in battle, sole governor of the land,   860
Fortunate father of children nobly born.
And now it has all gone from him! Who can say
That a man is still alive when his life's joy fails?
He is a walking dead man. Grant him rich,
Let him live like a king in his great house:
If his pleasure is gone, I would not give
So much as the shadow of smoke for all he owns.

Choragos
Your words hint at sorrow: what is your news for us?

Messenger
They are dead. The living are guilty of their death.

Choragos
Who is guilty? Who is dead? Speak!

Messenger
                              Haemon.   870
Haemon is dead; and the hand that killed him
Is his own hand.

Choragos
                    His father's? or his own?

Messenger
His own, driven mad by the murder his father had done.

Choragos
Teiresias, Teiresias, how clearly you saw it all!

Messenger
This is my news: you must draw what conclusions you can from it.

Choragos
But look: Eurydicê, our Queen:
Has she overheard us?
[Enter EURYDICE from the Palace, C.]

Eurydice

I have heard something, friends:
As I was unlocking the gate of Pallas' shrine,
For I needed her help today, I heard a voice   880
Telling of some new sorrow. And I fainted
There at the temple with all my maidens about me.
But speak again: whatever it is, I can bear it:
Grief and I are no strangers.

Messenger

                              Dearest Lady,
I will tell you plainly all that I have seen.
I shall not try to comfort you: what is the use,
Since comfort could lie only in what is not true?
The truth is always best.

                    I went with Creon
To the outer plain where Polyneicês was lying,
No friend to pity him, his body shredded by dogs.   890
We made our prayers in that place to Hecatê
And Pluto, that they would be merciful. And we bathed
The corpse with holy water, and we brought
Fresh-broken branches to burn what was left of it,
And upon the urn we heaped up a towering barrow
Of the earth of his own land.

                              When we were done, we ran
To the vault where Antigonê lay on her couch of stone.
One of the servants had gone ahead,
And while he was yet far off he heard a voice
Grieving within the chamber, and he came back   900
And told Creon. And as the King went closer,
The air was full of wailing, the words lost,
And he begged us to make all haste. "Am I a prophet?"
He said, weeping, "And must I walk this road,
The saddest of all that I have gone before?
My son's voice calls me on. Oh quickly, quickly!
Look through the crevice there, and tell me
If it is Haemon, or some deception of the gods!"

We obeyed; and in the cavern's farthest corner
We saw her lying: 910
She had made a noose of her fine linen veil
And hanged herself. Haemon lay beside her.
His arms about her waist, lamenting her,
His love lost under ground, crying out
That his father had stolen her away from him.

When Creon saw him the tears rushed to his eyes
And he called to him: "What have you done, child? Speak to me.

What are you thinking that makes your eyes so strange?
O my son, my son, I come to you on my knees!"
But Haemon spat in his face. He said not a word,   920
Staring—
       And suddenly drew his sword
And lunged. Creon shrank back, the blade missed; and the boy,
Desperate against himself, drove it half its length
Into his own side, and fell. And as he died
He gathered Antigonê close in his arms again,
Choking, his blood bright red on her white cheek.
And now he lies dead with the dead, and she is his
At last, his bride in the houses of the dead.
[Exit EURYDICE *into the Palace.]*

Choragos
She has left us without a word. What can this mean?

Messenger
It troubles me, too; yet she knows what is best,   930
Her grief is too great for public lamentation,
And doubtless she has gone to her chamber to weep
For her dead son, leading her maidens in his dirge.

Choragos
It may be so: but I fear this deep silence.
[Pause.]

Messenger
I will see what she is doing. I will go in.
[Exit MESSENGER *into the Palace. Enter* CREON *with attendants, bearing* HAEMON's
body.]*

Choragos
But here is the King himself: oh look at him,
Bearing his own damnation in his arms.

Creon
Nothing you say can touch me any more.
My own blind heart has brought me
From darkness to final darkness. Here you see   940
The father murdering, the murdered son—
And all my civic wisdom!

Haemon my son, so young, so young to die,
I was the fool, not you; and you died for me.

Choragos
That is the truth; but you were late in learning it.

Creon
This truth is hard to bear. Surely a god
Has crushed me beneath the hugest weight of heaven,
And driven me headlong a barbaric way
To trample out the thing I held most dear.

The pains that men will take to come to pain! 950
[Enter MESSENGER *from the Palace.*]

Messenger
The burden you carry in your hands is heavy,
But it is not all: you will find more in your house.

Creon
What burden worse than this shall I find there?

Messenger
The Queen is dead.

Creon
O port of death, deaf world,
Is there no pity for me? And you, Angel of evil,
I was dead, and your words are death again.
Is it true, boy? Can it be true?
Is my wife dead? Has death bred death?

Messenger
You can see for yourself. 960
[*The doors are opened, and the body of* EURYDICE *is disclosed within.*]

Creon
Oh pity!
All true, all true, and more than I can bear!
O my wife, my son!

Messenger
She stood before the altar, and her heart
Welcomed the knife her own hand guided,
And a great cry burst from her lips for Megareus dead,
And for Haemon dead, her sons; and her last breath
Was a curse for their father, the murderer of her sons.
And she fell, and the dark flowed in through her closing eyes.

Creon
O God, I am sick with fear. 970
Are there no swords here? Has no one a blow for me?

Messenger
Her curse is upon you for the deaths of both.

Creon

It is right that it should be. I alone am guilty.
I know it, and I saw it. Lead me in,
Quickly, friends.
I have neither life nor substance. Lead me in.

Choragos

You are right, if there can be right in so much wrong.
The briefest way is best in a world of sorrow.

Creon

Let it come,
Let death come quickly, and be kind to me.   980
I would not ever see the sun again.

Choragos

All that will come when it will; but we, meanwhile,
Have much to do. Leave the future to itself.

Creon

All my heart was in that prayer!

Choragos

Then do not pray any more: the sky is deaf.

Creon

Lead me away. I have been rash and foolish.
I have killed my son and my wife.
I look for comfort; my comfort lies here dead.
Whatever my hands have touched has come to nothing.
Fate has brought all my pride to a thought of dust.   990
[As CREON is being led into the house, the CHORAGOS advances and speaks directly to
the audience.]

Choragos

There is no happiness where there is no wisdom;
No wisdom but in submission to the gods.
Big words are always punished,
And proud men in old age learn to be wise.

· ·

Questions for Discussion and Review

1. In what ways does Sophocles' portrayal of the chorus reflect the Athenians' attitude toward Thebes? Why are the Theban citizens punished with the plague? Why would Sophocles' Athenian audience consider Thebes to be a city whose citizens were corrupt?

2. Does the chorus's last speech in *Oedipus Rex* adequately explain what has happened to Oedipus? Why or why not? When they state the "lesson" of Oedipus's story, do they understand his insights into the human psyche or the nature of the gods?

3. What is the riddle of the Sphinx? What answer does Oedipus give? How is it possible for Oedipus to give the "right" answer without fully understanding what it means? Discuss the aspects of the riddle that Oedipus fails to understand. How does that failure of understanding reflect Oedipus's self-image?

4. Jocasta knows the truth about Oedipus before he himself completes his investigation, and she wants him to stop asking questions so that they can continue their lives as before. What does her attitude reveal about her? Contrast her response to Oedipus's.

5. *Antigone* includes several extended arguments on the rights of the individual versus the laws of the state and on the gods' laws versus human laws. Discuss the arguments that Antigone, Haemon, and Creon make on either side of these debates. How does Sophocles tell us who is right?

6. Explain how both Antigone and Haemon cross traditional gender boundaries. What factors motivate each to do so? In what ways does that violation of social conventions enlarge their spheres of action or enhance their awareness? In what ways does it contribute to their tragedies?

7. *Antigone* is named for its heroine, but some critics consider Creon to be the play's protagonist. Explain which character you consider to be the true protagonist, and defend your choice.

Works Cited

Rukeyser, Muriel. "Myth." *A Muriel Rukeyser Reader*. Ed. Jan Heller Levi. New York: Norton, 1994.

CHAPTER

17

A Different Perspective on Tragedy: Euripides' *Medea* and the *Bacchae*

KEY TOPICS/THEMES

More than any other Athenian playwright whose works have survived, Euripides transforms myths about gods and heroes, reinterpreting them in ways his Athenian audiences found puzzling and even offensive. In the Medea (c. 431 B.C.), he addresses the plight of a strong, intelligent, and articulate woman trapped in a society in which women were supposed to be none of those things. (Having few rights, they endured various forms of oppression and exploitation.) Medea's common-law husband, Jason, famed leader of the Argonauts, had won the Golden Fleece only with the aid of Medea. In this play, he has not only abandoned Medea, a foreigner and a sorceress, for a new Greek bride, the attractive princess of Corinth, but also demands custody of his and Medea's two young sons. Euripides uses Medea's savage response to her predicament (she kills both her children to prevent Jason from taking them) as a source of commentary on the condition of women in Athens and on the conventions of tragedy itself.

In the Bacchae, *written twenty-five years later, Euripides dramatizes the ancient myth recounting Dionysus's return to his home city of Thebes and the terrible vengeance that the god exacts on all who fail to honor his divinity. Like the* Medea, *the* Bacchae *features a homicidal mother, Agave, who—crazed by Dionysian possession—tears her son Pentheus, king of Thebes, to shreds. In both tragedies, female characters' extremes of emotion plunge the city-state into chaos and ruin. Like Medea, Agave resents the oppressive conditions imposed on women and responds violently. Euripides uses her actions to comment on both the social conventions*

753

*governing gender and the emotional and spiritual components of the hu-
man psyche.*

Euripides

A younger contemporary of Aeschylus and Sophocles, Euripides (c. 485–406 B.C.) was considered somewhat unconventional, both personally and intellectually. A loner who had his own private library, Euripides took little part in the public affairs that dominated the lives of most of his fellow Athenians.

Euripides wrote eighty-eight plays, of which eighteen survive. His fellow play-wrights (especially Sophocles) were interested in his work, and he achieved enor-mous popularity after his death, when revivals began to be performed. Neverthe-less, he won only four first prizes at the City Dionysia in his lifetime. His rather complex plays may have seemed too strange, too repulsive, or possibly even too decadent for his generally conservative audience. In his last year, he left Athens altogether and went to Macedonia.

The Woman's Perspective

It is easy to see why Euripides' *Medea* (431 B.C.) might have startled an audience ac-customed to plays like those of Aeschylus or Sophocles. The play stresses the female perspective, which was not in itself unusual, but Euripides provides a sympathetic portrayal both of one woman's plight in particular and of all women in general. Like the typical helper-maiden, **Medea** has done everything for **Jason**, giving up, in exchange for his false promise to marry her, her home, her family ties, and her reputation. She even saved his life by helping him obtain the Golden Fleece. In fact, Jason's success in that endeavor depended almost entirely on Medea. According to the various myths describing the Argonauts' expedition (not, of course, included in Euripides' play), Medea gave Jason the magical means to yoke the fire-breathing bulls and plow the field, to slay the armed men who sprang from the sowed dragon's teeth, and to put to sleep the dragon that guarded the Golden Fleece. Jason had, in other words, more help from Medea than any other hero had in completing his appointed tasks. Among traditional heroes, only Perseus is given magical aids, and none of those either render his opponents harmless to him or relieve him of the need to figure out on his own how to make effective use of the divinely given equipment. Once Jason has obtained the Golden Fleece, Medea also enables the Argonauts to escape the wrath of her father, Aeëtes. After they arrive in Iolcus, she continues to help him by conspiring in the killing of his uncle, **Pelias,** who had usurped the throne of Aeson (Jason's father) and would have killed Jason. Similar to Ariadne's abandonment by Theseus, Medea's reward is to have Jason desert her in Corinth for a younger, richer, and prettier (if not very bright) woman, who happens to be the daughter of the king.

Medea had the misfortune to fall in love with a hero who turned out to be, after all, merely a man—and not a very admirable one at that. Early in the play, Jason denies Medea's part in helping him get the Golden Fleece, insisting that it was Cypris (Aphrodite), not Medea, who saved him. Other versions of the myth assert that Aphrodite, at the request of Hera and Athene, sends Eros to cause Medea to fall in love with Jason, knowing that he will be unable to fulfill his quest without her intervention. But loving Jason does not automatically entail her betrayal of her father in order to help him. Indeed, the myths portray her as struggling with the conflicting demands of love for the hero and loyalty to her family. In Euripides' play, however, no one but Jason puts forth such an excuse, and he clearly has a vested interest in now denying her any credit or gratitude for her services to him as helper-maiden. Her unofficial "marriage" in ruins, the only meaningful role Medea has left is that of mother. But Jason, demanding custody of the children, seeks to deprive her of that, too. Utterly isolated in the unfamiliar city to which he has brought her, she speaks convincingly both of the woman's role—trapped whether she marries or not—and of society's negative attitude toward strong, intelligent, and articulate women.

The Heroic Medea

Medea, however, has other resources. Her role as helper-maiden having come to its typical conclusion, Medea takes on the role of hero herself. Indeed, she has all the strengths more typically associated with male tragic protagonists in the heroic mold: the intensity, the refusal to compromise, the sense of total commitment, and the ability to perform heroic acts. The leader of the chorus of townswomen implies that all mothers are heroic: Medea, she says, has, like the Argonauts, passed between the "grey Clashing Rocks" that guard the sea route to Colchis, which she also associates with the dangers of childbirth. Apart from Euripides' play, the mythic tradition accentuates the heroic side of Medea even further by portraying her, like many male heroes, as a founder of cities. According to Herodotus, for example, after leaving Corinth, Medea goes to Athens, whence she likewise must flee for attempting to poison King Aegeus's son, Theseus (see Chapter 11). She then settles in Iran, where she becomes the eponymous ancestor of an entire nation: the inhabitants, previously called "Arians," changed their name to "Medes," after Medea. Other versions portray her as marrying Achilles after her death and living with her heroic male counterpart in the Elysian Fields.

Words Versus Action

Medea believes that, like all heroes, she has the gods on her side—not just **Hecate**, her personal deity, but also **Themis**, Lady of Vows, and Zeus, protector of oaths, whose lightning is identified with Medea's fury. For the Greeks, oaths were not simply casually uttered words—they were sacred. Breaking a vow was a major violation that even the gods themselves would hesitate to commit. Yet Jason is a breaker of oaths—specifically, the vows he made to Medea when he needed her help. Hence his fate, which Medea foresees, is fully deserved. Some readers thus argue that Medea is acting as an agent of Zeus, carrying out divine retribution against Jason. But it is not Jason who dies—it is the princess, whose only crime is to have been superficial, and the children, whose offenses consist merely of being Jason's sons. To her credit, Medea does not resort to such extreme acts readily.

By the time we meet Medea, she has already exhausted all other avenues, but even now, despite her rage, she is still engaged in last-ditch attempts to use rhetoric, not violence. In fact, many speeches in the play are about rhetoric—about the use of words and the logic of arguments. But words mean nothing to a breaker of vows; once the link between rhetoric and truth is broken, words become mere babble. Jason never listens to Medea's arguments. And while he accuses her of being verbally aggressive (women should presumably be quiet!), she accuses him, quite properly, of using empty words. In language as in life, Jason confuses style with substance, just as he opts for the style of a successful life (a "good" home, adequate income) while ignoring the foundation of familial bonds on which a good home must rest.

Jason's actions have not matched his words; Medea's will. She, too, has made a vow—to Queen Hecate. And she openly does what she says: she announces her intentions, carries out the murders, and, just as Clytemnestra had done, acknowledges the deeds afterward.

Once determined to act, Medea announces, "From now on all words are superfluous." It is from this point in the play that she speaks Jason's language—the language of clichés and lies, weapons in the war between the sexes. Only then does she engage in a bit of playacting, miming the stereotypical "feminine" role—a weak creature given to crying instead of acting—in order to beguile Jason into unwittingly cooperating with her scheme to send the children with gifts to the princess! Naturally, unable to accept the truth about Medea or his dependence on her, he immediately accepts this lie.

Tragedy and the Irrational

Like most tragic protagonists, Medea is also a passionate woman, as extreme in her love as she is in her hatred. We watch what happens when the irrational forces that tragedy always confronts (here depicted as almost elemental forces, "like a rock, or a wave of the sea") drive Medea to act out uncontrollable impulses that end up hurting those she loves: killing her brother, landing Jason in exile, and, finally, like Agave, murdering her own children. But like Agave, Medea is a woman, for whom all such actions are deemed inexcusable. The gods, and the male heroes like Heracles who follow their divine models, may get away with destroying their children, but no expiatory rituals release women from that sin.

Medea and Corinthian Ritual

Medea does allude, in the last scene of Euripides' play, to a ritual she will establish to expiate "this impious murder," but she seems to be referring to chartering a ritual by which the Corinthians will expiate their own guilt, rather than one by which Medea will do so herself. The ambiguity of that reference may be rooted in actual

Corinthian rituals related to Medea, as well as in the complex and varied myths about her, not all of which portray her as killing her own children. Hesiod, for example, makes no mention of killing children. And according to Pindar, Zeus falls in love with Medea in Corinth, but she rejects his advances. Hera rewards Medea by promising to make her children immortal if Medea will bring them to her temple. In an oddly symmetrical inversion of the story of Medea's false promise to rejuvenate the father of the Iolcan princesses, Medea delivers her children to Hera's temple. However, the children die there, and Medea has to flee Corinth, despite the fact that the children's death is not her fault. According to some scholars, one function of this myth may have been to charter a Corinthian ritual that involved seven boys and seven girls annually being sent to serve in the temple of Hera, as well as the Corinthians' practice of offering sacrifices to Medea's children during an important festival.

In some versions of the myth, many Corinthian children die when Medea leaves Corinth, and the cult of Medea's children is instituted, on the gods' instructions, to halt these deaths. In fact, some scholars suggest that Medea may originally have been a Corinthian goddess of childbirth and nursing mothers, equivalent to Hera, whose cult displaces hers. Similarly, although he does not connect her either to Hera or to the city of Corinth, Hesiod describes Medea as a goddess, granddaughter of Helios, the sun god, and a goddess named Perseis, whose children are Circe and Medea's father, Aeëtes. Medea's mother, according to Hesiod, is Idyia, a sea goddess. But childbirth goddesses like Hera and Artemis could turn on the women in labor who appealed to them, slaying the mother or child or both, just as Apollo could be god of both health and disease. Medea, as patron of childbirth, could likewise share that ambiguous potential—another possible source of her role as "unnatural" mother.

Another View of Medea

The varying traditions in the Medea myths give rise to a complex figure who incorporates contradictory roles: Greek and foreigner, helper-maiden and murderer, mother/wife and child-killer, normal woman and witch, mortal and goddess. Euripides makes no mention of any ritual other than Medea's single reference at the end of the play. And his Medea certainly kills her own children. Indeed, some scholars suggest that Euripides may have introduced the infanticide as a typically melodramatic, theatrical device. But the playwright does take advantage of the varied and contradictory mythic resources to offer his audience a highly complex, multifaceted heroine.

One of the most important characteristics of drama is its capacity to hold up multiple points of view for the audience's inspection. In this play, as in many others, Euripides enhances that multiplicity of perspectives. No sooner do we begin to accept one perspective, than he shifts the angle slightly and a different perspective emerges. Thus, no sooner do we begin to sympathize with Medea's predicament and to see her as a strong, tragic heroine, than we find ourselves confronting another side of Medea. For example, portraying herself as victim, she does not mention that she eloped with Jason willingly; further, although marriage is in some ways always

FIGURE 17-1   Medea and Aegeus. Medea is shown, in this medallion from an Attic cup, appealing to the elderly figure of Aegeus, king of Athens, promising to make him fertile in exchange for his assurance of safe refuge for her in his city (see Chapter 11). He accepts her offer, thus enabling Medea to proceed with her planned murders. *(Vatican Museums, Rome)*

a betrayal of the woman's family, she alienated her father in more than the usual way—she killed her younger brother Apsyrtus and scattered the pieces of his corpse over the waves to stop her father's pursuit of Jason and the fleeing Argonauts. Nor does she mention her role as a practitioner of the magical arts of the chthonic goddess, Hecate, whom she reveres above all deities. Although Medea may not literally be a witch, she clearly has a sophisticated knowledge of poisons, as well as of fertility potions, and can command the services of dragons.

Other playwrights had, of course, written plays with strong female protagonists—even protagonists who, like Medea, committed crimes (Clytemnestra, for example). But those women eventually paid for their crimes, whereas Medea avoids punishment. In fact, she escapes to Athens, where King Aegeus gives her refuge (Figure 17-1) (a fact that Euripides stresses, taking a jab at the Athenian audience, whose attitudes toward women were much like Jason's, and perhaps warning them of the dangers of their views). Further, heroines like Clytemnestra performed their murders according to convention, decorously offstage, describing the result but not dwelling on the techniques; Medea's poisoning of the princess, in contrast, is described in all its gory detail.

A Proletarian Perspective

Before we can decide whether Medea is a hero or a monster, Euripides shifts the viewpoint yet again, revealing still another unusual perspective. Unlike the essentially aristocratic focus on the noble protagonists in other tragedies of the time, in Euripides' plays, the voice of the common people often represents the most legitimate or compelling vision. In the *Medea,* the most sensible voices are those of the tutor, the nurse, and the chorus of Medea's neighbors—ordinary women of Corinth who sympathize with her predicament as a woman (indeed, what woman could fail to identify with such statements as "I had rather fight three battles than bear one child"?) and who share her hatred of Jason. In fact, they become co-conspirators who, knowing of Medea's plans, neither intervene nor report the danger. But even they, who are willing to go so far as to make themselves accessories to murder, draw the line at attacking the children. They are capable of moral distinctions: Jason deserves punishment; the children do not. Medea is capable only of rage that lashes out whenever she is angered: "May it be an enemy and not a friend she hurts," says the nurse, implying that either is possible. Once again, such unfocused rage is entirely within the heroic tradition, as when Aias, angered over his failure to win Achilles' armor, tries to kill the Greek soldiers in their sleep; when intercepted by Athene, he vents his rage on the horses and cattle instead.

In explicit statements as well, the nurse comments on the perversity of a self-indulgent upper class that, like the warrior-heroes who represent its highest aspirations, is not answerable to its neighbors. "Great people," she observes, tend to be excessive, vindictive, and violent tempered, and when they fall, their ruin is that much more complete. "What is moderate is best," she concludes. On the surface, her advocacy of moderation may seem to resemble that of the chorus in Sophocles' *Oedipus Rex,* where it applied to not asking too many questions or to not insisting on pursuing ideas to their logical conclusions. For Sophocles' chorus, adhering to "what is moderate" is a way of avoiding trouble, of keeping a low profile, suitable to people who lack the courage of heroes. In Euripides' play, the women of the chorus are much more independent and aggressive. And the moderation that the nurse recommends applies not to knowledge but to behavior; what she advocates is not cowardice or passivity but self-control.

The Tragic Hero Revisited

Medea and Jason, of course, are "great people": Medea is the daughter of the king of Colchis, and Jason is the rightful heir to the kingdom of Iolcos and the hero of the Argonauts. The fact that they are without the status that derives from owning property, a situation referred to frequently in the play, is a reminder of the connection between power and territory. Having no place where they belong, these "important people" still behave as if power is theirs; but it isn't. The fact is, they are both dispossessed—Jason by political usurpation, Medea by marriage and exile. And we see them in action not through the idealized medium of myth—of epic quests and extraordinary feats of courage and skill—but back at home, close up. If we see "heroes" here, we see them as they really are, stripped of their public masks; and instead of a domestic quarrel presented as high tragedy (as in Aeschylus's *Agamemnon*), we have domestic drama presented on its own terms.

In the fate of these "displaced" persons, we confront the displacement of an entire class structure: the feudal society in which the warrior-hero and the landed aristocrat were interchangeable has long since become, except in the still-revered ancient myths, an anachronism. Agamemnon and Clytemnestra argued about pride and its relationship to human morality and the gods, while Oedipus and Jocasta discussed fate and free will. But Jason and Medea argue about where the money is coming from, whose fault the divorce is, who started the quarrels, and who gets custody of the kids. When Medea kills their two sons rather than allow Jason to take possession of them, we are on all-too-familiar territory (Figure 17-2). We see the headlines all the time: "Mother of Two, Distraught over Divorce and Loss of Custody Battle, Poisons Ex-Husband's New Flame, Kills Children." Seen close up, heroes suddenly look more like ordinary people.

Of the two, it is clearly Medea who comes closest to the conventional tragic protagonist of Greek drama. It is she who suffers; she who feels guilt for the death of the children (even as she plans their death); she who is carried away by an irre-

FIGURE 17-2   Medea
Killing Her Children.
This vase painting (c. 350–
320 B.C.) dramatizes
Medea's monstrous vio-
lence, as she wields a sword
to stab her son to death.
(Louvre, Paris)

sistible tide of passionate hatred, as she had earlier been by the irrational power of passionate love; she who has the courage to acknowledge her deeds; and she who, in typical heroic fashion, much like Oedipus, refuses to compromise.

Jason

The great Jason, who not only acquired his reputation but, indeed, survived only with Medea's help, will not acknowledge his complicity in the crimes she committed on his behalf and so is revealed as a lying coward, using women for his own gain—first Medea and now the princess. He "consoles" Medea with the comment that, after all, she's better off now because she lives in Greece instead of among "barbarians" (another of Euripides' sarcastic references to the Athenians' snobbery). And, although Medea's role as "foreigner" is increasingly emphasized throughout the play, it is clear, in context, that Jason is making yet another excuse for his own self-serving behavior. Jason's pitiful argument reaches a low point of logic when he asserts that it would be better if men could have children on their own and women did not exist!

The predicted death of Jason is the final nontragic point in what has been a mockery of the heroic life. He will die not on the battlefield nor in pursuit of some great revelation; rather, he will be struck on the head by a rotten beam as he sleeps under the prow of his ship—a fittingly ignominious death.

Euripides' Indictment of Tragic Violence

In traditional tragedies, like those of Aeschylus and Sophocles, important people commit appalling deeds: they go mad; they kill their husbands, mothers, or children; they commit incest. And because they do so, ostensibly, in pursuit of justice or freedom or integrity, their passions—and their violence—are portrayed nobly. "This is my deed, and I claim it," boasts Clytemnestra of her murder of Agamemnon, reenacting the heroic stand that the heroes of the *Iliad* made over the corpses of their foes. And Orestes, in Aeschylus's *Oresteia,* kills his mother with far less hesitation than Medea shows in killing her children. But whereas Aeschylus brings in Pylades to utter his one line, telling Orestes, in effect, "Do it," and thus justifying Orestes' act, Euripides has the chorus express their revulsion for Medea's murder of her children, which reinforces our own horror at her deed. Thus, whereas Aeschylus presents Orestes as a noble individual trapped, through no fault of his own, in an unfortunate predicament, Euripides forces us to confront the brutality of the act.

Further, in Aeschylus's plays, we do not get to see the vomiting of blood, the spilling of guts on the floor, or the writhing of the corpse. And perhaps because we are not forced to watch the violent acts, it is easier for us to go along with the illusion that such deeds can somehow be ennobling. Euripides, however, stops us short. Forbidden to literally enact violence on the stage, he gets around the restriction by describing the details of the princess's death, forcing us to see, however much we might sympathize with Medea in her predicament, how truly revolting and immoral such behavior is. If Jason the Argonaut has become Jason the hypocritical coward, so Medea the wronged woman has become Medea the psychotic housewife who enjoys hearing about her horrorific deeds. Violence, far from being ennobling or transforming, far from precipitating some kind of tragic insight into oneself, as was the case with heroes like Oedipus, produces only the sadistic relishing of the deeds.

Heroes are special, convinced that because of their divine ancestry and their unique drives and accomplishments, they are not bound by the same limits as other people. It is perfectly logical to assume, as both Jason and Medea do in this play, that somehow their needs reflect the gods' will and that they are free to enact their desires, however extreme. If these people are what heroes are like and these deeds are what heroes do, then perhaps we would do better to reserve our admiration for the tutors, the nurses, the village girls, and the peasants, who are the only rational or moral characters in many of Euripides' plays.

The Tragic Universe Parodied

Tragedies typically take place in an unpredictable universe in which the gods do not inevitably return good for good and evil for evil. Thus, the suffering of the tragic protagonist is usually disproportionate to whatever sins he might have committed or mistakes he might have made. Euripides turns this universe on its head and explores its underside: if the good can suffer, so the wicked can prosper. At the end of Euripides' version of *Electra,* for example, Orestes' acquittal is guaranteed in advance even though he stabbed Aegisthus in the back. Further, Electra, who in this version slays her mother with her own hand, gets to marry Orestes' friend Pylades and, presumably, live happily ever after, while the self-sacrificing peasant who aided and protected her is bought off with a few coins.

The Athenian audience was fond of parody, although it was usually associated with comedy. In fact, Euripides was himself parodied in Aristophanes' comedies the *Frogs* and *Thesmophoriazusae.* To incorporate parody in a tragedy, however, was more unusual. One scene in Euripides' *Electra* makes clear the playwright's intentional parody of his fellow tragic dramatists—in this case, the recognition scene in Aeschylus's the *Libation-Bearers* (see Chapter 15). In Euripides' play, Electra asks whether a man would still wear the same size shirt he wore as a boy; whether the color of his hair, surely shared by many, is of any use as an identifying clue; and whether a man's footprint is likely to be the same size as his sister's. Poking fun at the absurdities of Aeschylus's version of the story, Euripides reveals the parodic (and more realistic) elements of his own.

The *Medea,* too, though it does not mock any specific play, seems to ask us to reconsider the traditional tragic vision rooted in the glorious heroic values of the ancient myths: their characters, actions, and social, sexual, and moral premises. The "excessive" quality that seemed decadent to some of Euripides' more conservative contemporaries may, in fact, be the instrument of a radical revisionist taking a new look at an old story.

The Play's Conclusion

And so it is with Medea. We last see her on the roof of her home, about to fly off with the bodies of her children in a chariot drawn by dragons (Figure 17.3). Her

FIGURE 17-3 Medea and the Dragons. In this vase painting (c. 400 B.C.), Medea drives the sun-chariot of her grandfather, Helios, drawn by a pair of dragons, across the sky. Beneath, Jason (on the left) and the nurse and tutor (on the right, mourning over the corpses of the children) look on. The symbols here associated with Medea connect her with the primordial Creator goddess whose powers encompass heaven, earth, and netherworld. Beyond the circle of the sun's rays that contain the dragons, ancient symbols of the goddess, are winged Furies, dreaded avengers who surround and support Medea. Placing Medea in the center of the sun-disk, in control of the powers of light and darkness, this vase painting attributes to Medea extraordinary cosmic powers. *(Cleveland Museum of Art)*

"punishment" is to escape to Athens, where she will be supported and protected by the king. In the play's final speech—one that was apparently so compelling to Euripides that he used it again at the end of the *Bacchae*—the chorus comments on the unpredictable nature (the unreliability) of the gods: what we counted on is not what actually happened; the gods are not answerable to us, nor do they run the universe according to our needs or expectations.

In the *Odyssey,* when Odysseus prepares to fight the suitors, Zeus gives a sign, a crack of thunder, as a warning to the suitors and as a reminder that his will is being carried out. In the last scene of the *Medea,* Jason calls, as he has before, on the gods, asking for a sign, but fruitlessly: Medea gloats that no god will respond to him, an oath-breaker. But neither do the gods provide Medea with such symbolic sanctions. Jason lives, and he will die in a humiliating way, the very sort of unheroic death that Achilles and Odysseus most feared—the prosaic death of a failure, not a hero. (And why is he sleeping under the prow of his ship? No longer having any women to exploit, is he now homeless?) Nor will even that fate occur just yet. Who is to say whether his fate represents the delayed action of angry gods or a random accident?

The same ambiguity surrounds Medea's fate. Is her escape an act of divine intervention? The chariot and dragons, she explains, were a gift from Helios, her grandfather, as, indeed, Hesiod had attested. Is this vehicle, like Odysseus's bow or Achilles' shield, one of the special attributes of heroes, or did the chariot appear at that moment, a special dispensation to reward her behavior? Either way, Medea has powers beyond those of ordinary mortals. She drives the chariot of the Sun and commands its dragons. Nor does Medea, unlike Phaethon, find that task beyond her power. She has, as well, the power of life (she gave the old king, Aegeus, the gift of fertility), of death, and possibly even of rebirth, a skill alluded to when, according to some versions of the myth, she instructs the daughters of Jason's wicked uncle Pelias to kill their father. She tells them to place the dismembered pieces of his corpse into a cauldron that supposedly will bring about his regeneration—a mockery of ancient sparagmos rituals. To demonstrate the procedure, Medea had killed, cooked, and resurrected a ram in the same cauldron. In fact, Medea's powers recall those of the primal goddess herself. No wonder, in this thoroughly patriarchal society, that she is depicted as a witch!

Further, the deity Medea has appealed to most frequently is Hecate, the dread triple goddess (sometimes depicted as having three heads) of the Underworld. (Medea invokes Zeus only in his role as oath-keeper, not as guardian of moral values such as family love—how could she, who kills her own children?) And neither Helios nor Hecate, as some scholars have pointed out, had local cults in Athens and so would have come across as exotic "foreign" gods to the Athenian audience, as strange (and "barbaric") as Medea herself must have seemed.

Perhaps, when Medea taunted Jason with the notion that he thinks the "old gods" no longer prevail, she meant not "traditional" gods but an older generation of gods—more elemental, more primitive, from the Athenian view. If such bizarre and unfamiliar gods indeed now have the upper hand, and heroes like Jason, beloved in ancient myth, are denigrated, then truly, as the chorus remarks, "the world's great order is reversed." Not only has a woman, conventionally thought to be too helpless to plot and carry out such deeds, assumed the active, heroic role in this drama, but the usual gods, despite the expectations of both Jason and Medea, seem to have "ceased to rule" as enforcers of moral law. If that is so, then what is to stop Medea, strong, clever, and daring, from escaping divine as well as human retribution?

If strange, even chthonic, gods like Hecate are truly supporting Medea (as would be appropriate for a woman driven by the nonrational passions of love and hate), then it is the law of vengeance they enforce, along with the implacable inviolability of oaths. We are thrust back into an amoral universe such as the one the Furies tried, unsuccessfully, to maintain in Aeschylus's *Oresteia*. There, they were displaced, for the moment, by a new world order based on compassion and justice. In the *Medea,* we seem to be back in a world in which powerful and natural, but nonrational, forces prevail and human concepts like family love and justice are easily abrogated. And although Medea seems to recapitulate the powers of the primordial Goddess, she has clearly perverted them, under the pressure of an oppressive social structure, to unnatural uses. Once again, we have a tragedy in which the feminine powers are invoked, giving voice to new perspectives, but those same powers, first repressed and then explosively released, are ultimately revealed to be irrational and dangerous in the extreme.

At the end of the play, Medea takes off for Athens, a telling prompt to the Athenian audience to contemplate possible consequences when the proper order, especially the hierarchy of genders, is undermined. Ostensibly devoted to freedom and equality, Athens nevertheless oppressed its women just as Jason did. The city was, further, presently involved in what would end up being a mutually destructive war with the militaristic, old-style heroes of Sparta. Perhaps presenting the audience with the spectacle of a world gone mad, given over to irrational passions, in which order and justice could no longer be counted on (if they ever could), was not as unrealistic as the play's fantastic details, taken out of context, might suggest. Perhaps in these circumstances, a dramatic vision of a world turned upside down was entirely appropriate.

The *Bacchae*: Euripides' Tragic Vision

The only surviving tragedy that features Dionysus in a leading role is not only one of the last Greek dramas written but also one of the most perplexing. Composed about 406 B.C., shortly before Euripides' death, the *Bacchae* dramatizes the myth of Dionysus's return to Thebes, his birthplace, where the god exacts a horrific revenge on his native city for its citizens' failure to honor his divinity. Whereas in the *Medea*, the playwright examined the seamy underside of "heroic" tragedy, in this play, Euripides takes the Athenian theater back to its Dionysian roots, the wine god's ecstatic cult, and explores the implications of its passionate, potentially destructive nature. To many modern readers, the *Bacchae* is genuinely disturbing, in part because neither of its leading characters—Dionysus or **Pentheus** [PEN-thee-uhs], king of Thebes—seems particularly sympathetic. The wine god appears violent and merciless, while Pentheus is revealed as a hollow figure, his stubborn opposition to Dionysian religion a product of his fatal inability to confront Dionysian elements in himself. In exposing Pentheus's personal flaws, particularly the young ruler's refusal to take sage advice or compromise his overly rigid position, Euripides also highlights the old myth's relevance to democratic society. Like the unbending Creon in Sophocles' *Antigone*, Pentheus fails as a political leader because he values only his own viewpoint, foolishly ignoring representatives of the larger community. As the prophet Tiresias warns Pentheus, "The powerful man who matches insolence with glibness is worse than a fool. He is a public danger!"

The *Bacchae* is named for its chorus, a group of foreign women passionately devoted to Dionysus, also known as **Bacchus**. These bacchants, who have followed their god from Asia Minor to Greece, worship Dionysus voluntarily and gratefully, reveling in the emotional freedom and sense of joyous unity with nature that he imparts (Figure 17-4). Their opening song, in which the Asian bacchants dance

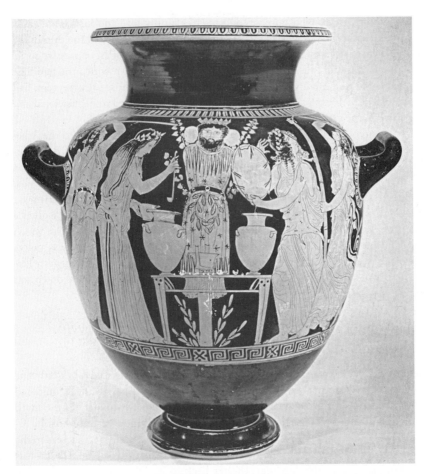

FIGURE 17-4   Dionysus and Bacchants. Surrounded by dancing maenads, two
women place ivy garlands on an effigy of Dionysus. Euripides' tragedy is named after
its chorus—Asian bacchants who voluntarily worship their god. By contrast, Theban
women are compelled against their will to honor Bromius (another name for Dionysus)
(National Archaeological Museum, Naples)

wildly, praising Dionysus's holy and irresistible gifts, is the only extant example
of a dithyramb, the ancient choral ode associated with Dionysus's prehistoric rituals (Figure 17-5). By contrast, a group of Theban women, who do not appear on
stage until near the drama's conclusion, perform the god's rites unwillingly, under
divine compulsion. Driven into madness by the god's disorienting power, the Theban bacchants, led by Pentheus's mother, **Agave** [a-GAY-vee], have abandoned their
homes, husbands, and children and fled to the nearby hills of Cithaeron, where
they reportedly nurse the young of wild animals and drink the milk and wine that
miraculously spout from the earth. The proliferation of miracles and natural signs,
including an earthquake that shakes Thebes to its foundations, unmistakably denotes a divine presence at work. These unpredictable suspensions of natural law,
however, serve only to stiffen Pentheus's resistance—and confirm his doom.

FIGURE 17-5   A Dancing Maenad. As a young satyr pipes, a bare-breasted maenad
dances, clad only in a scanty leopard skin. Pentheus assumes that any woman allowed the
freedom to express her inner feelings during Dionysian orgies will totally abandon her
civilized roles, indulging in sexual excess. *(British Museum, London)*

Pentheus

In the *Bacchae,* Euripides goes far beyond reinterpreting a cautionary myth that
highlights the perils of mortals' failure to recognize or properly revere a god in
their midst. Besides illustrating the folly of human insensitivity to divine visita-
tions, the playwright also explores the tragic character flaws causing the Theban
leader's spiritual blindness. Ironically, the trait that prompts Pentheus's stubborn
opposition to Dionysian freedom is his lack of Apollonian self-knowledge, a defect
that leads him to succumb to **hubris** [HYOO-bris], or excessive pride. Unable to
understand himself, including the Dionysian aspects of his own nature, he also
violates Apollo's edict against excess, foolishly pitting his human will against divine
force. Contemptuously rejecting the claim that Zeus had fathered the child his aunt
Semele had mysteriously borne, Pentheus compounds his blasphemy by imprisoning Dionysus and condemning him to death. In failing to "know [him]self"—and
thereby the limits of human reason—Pentheus also fails to exercise Apollonian self-
restraint, guaranteeing a tragic fate.

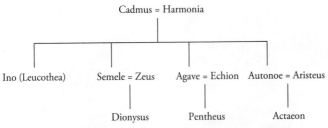

FIGURE 17-6   The Four Daughters of Cadmus. Three of the four
daughters of Cadmus and Harmonia bore sons—all first cousins
—who suffered sparagmos: Dionysus, son of Semele and Zeus, was
dismembered by the Titans; Actaeon, son of Autonoe and Aristeus,
was ripped to pieces by his hunting dogs; Pentheus, son of Agave and
Echion, was torn limb from limb by a band of spirit-possessed women
that included his mother. Ino also suffered a tragic fate: driven mad by
Hera for sheltering the young Dionysus, she threw herself into the sea
and was transformed into the sea nymph Leucothea, the "white goddess," a personification of sea spray.

Although Euripides emphasizes Pentheus's unacknowledged psychological affinity with Dionysus, the Athenian audience would also have been aware of Pentheus's blood kinship (Figure 17-6). The inflexible Theban king and the god of
intoxication are first cousins. Pentheus is the son of Agave, sister of Semele, and
Echion, one of the Spartoi—men generated from the teeth of a dragon that Pentheus's grandfather **Cadmus** slew before founding the city of Thebes. According to
this etiological myth, Cadmus, son of the Phoenician king Agenor, was dispatched
to search for his sister Europa after she had been abducted by Zeus. When consulting the Oracle at Delphi, he was told to found a city where a cow lay down. This
led Cadmus to the site of Thebes, where he killed its guardian dragon (Figure 17-7)
and sowed the dragon's teeth, from which a throng of young warriors sprang up.
Most of the dragon-born soldiers immediately killed each other in hand-to-hand
combat, but five, including Echion, were still living when Cadmus founded Thebes.
Although the *Bacchae* repeatedly mentions that Cadmus passed the city's rulership
on to his young grandson Pentheus, tradition offers no clue to Echion's disappearance from the scene.

Born to the aunt of a god and a man derived from the primordial goddess's
serpent, Pentheus should be expected to recognize his cousin's divinity, making his
adamant refusal to do so all the more puzzling. As Euripides makes clear, however,
Pentheus's relentless hostility to the young stranger, garlanded in ivy and bearing
a thyrsus, who suddenly shows up to wreak havoc in Thebes, springs from a deep
anxiety about his own sexual identity: the young king sees in the seductive youth
too much of what he fears in himself (Figure 17-8). Euripides' Dionysus appears
wearing the mask of a slight, rather effeminate young man, whose long golden curls
and suspicious preference for women's company Pentheus mocks. But the Euripidean Pentheus also wears a mask, posing ostentatiously as a tough soldier who
bravely guards his city against the kind of foreign defilement that the stranger tries
to introduce. A stalwart defender of Greek masculinity, Pentheus condemns Dio-

FIGURE 17-7 Cadmus and the Serpent. Athenian playwrights seemed to delight in dramatizing the tragic errors promulgated by the rulers of Thebes, which was one of Athens' most bitter enemies at the time Euripides wrote the *Bacchae* (c. 406 B.C.). In Euripides' play, the aged Cadmus, Thebes' mythical founder, suffers both exile and loss of his humanity, condemned by Dionysus to be changed into a serpent. Cadmus's transformation is an ironic reversal of his earlier heroic act of killing the serpent (dragon) that once guarded the site of Thebes. Following Athene's advice, Cadmus sowed the dragon's teeth, out of which sprang a band of armed warriors, the Spartoi, who fought one another until only five were left. One of the survivors, Echion, married Cadmus's daughter Agave and became the father of Pentheus. In this bowl, Cadmus advances with drawn sword toward the rearing serpent. *(Louvre, Paris)*

nysus's worshiper as his moral opposite: soft, undisciplined, vain, and ineffectual. In fact, however, Dionysus and Pentheus share important qualities, including sensuality, socially prohibited desires, and a will to power, but whereas these attributes are a source of strength to the god, they trigger his mortal opponent's disgrace and destruction.

Pentheus's Transformation

In the play's major reversal (peripeteia), the two leading characters' respective masks are stripped away, revealing that each is the opposite of what he had previously appeared. At the outset, Pentheus—king, soldier, and law enforcer—ostensibly has the power to humiliate and kill the stranger whose effeminacy so outrages him, making Dionysus's supposed priest a legal sacrifice to his masculine authority. Midway through the play, however, Dionysus takes charge of the action, manipulating Pentheus into unmasking his feminine component, the androgynous traits he found so disturbing in the stranger.

Every man in Euripides' audience must have cringed when the actor portraying a Greek military leader reappeared on stage outfitted in a woman's wig, gown, and flowing veil. But it is just such a moment that allows for a temporary enlargement of Pentheus's vision—briefly, he "sees double," acquiring another stance from which to achieve insight. In that moment, his action self-reflexively recapitulates the nature of the dramatic festival itself, wherein actors in gender-reversed costumes play women's roles, illuminating the relationship between male and female, transcending boundaries on stage as they are transcended in the androgynous god

FIGURE 17-8   A Rest-
ing Satyr. Satyrs, images of
uninhibited male sexuality, are
traditional companions of Dionysus. This Roman copy of a
Greek original (c. 350–330 B.C.)
combines strength and sensuality, expressing the sexual mag-
netism that so terrifies Pentheus
when he is confronted with
Dionysus disguised as a girlish
youth. *(Vatican Museums, Rome)*

of wine himself. In costume, in an assumed identity very different from our own, we can "let go" of the constraints and inhibitions that preclude self-knowledge by disguising ourselves even from ourselves: theater, like wine, can be liberating, and Dionysus's connection with both is not accidental. Unlike the audience, however, Pentheus is incapable of sustaining the moment of vision, and it quickly degener- ates into parody. The feminine self that Pentheus displays is not the wise anima of a mature human being but the caricature of a simpering, preening female, coyly adjusting her Bacchic regalia and flirting with the stranger. At this point, Pentheus and Dionysus have changed places: the god has assumed total control, and the king who tried to execute him is his future sacrificial victim.

Dionysus condemns Pentheus to die, not as a brave man fighting for his city but as a transvestite voyeur torn to pieces by women on whom he had come to spy (Figure 17-9). Refusing to recognize that Dionysus embodies the instinctual passion inherent in every human psyche—and is therefore a divine power that only fools ignore—Pentheus suffers the supreme penalty for failing to know himself.

FIGURE 17-9   The Death of Pentheus. Refusing to accept the religious validity of Dionysian irrationality, Pentheus becomes its victim. Exhibiting irresistible strength when possessed by the god's spirit, maenads—including Pentheus's mother, Agave—prepare to dismember the young king, whom Dionysus makes them perceive as a dangerous lion. This Pompeiian fresco vividly illustrates the hallucinatory quality of religious frenzy and its potential for fanatical violence. *(National Archaeological Museum, Naples)*

FIGURE 17-10   The Death of Actaeon. The young hunter Actaeon, son of Cadmus's daughter Autonoe—and therefore also a cousin of Pentheus—is torn to pieces by his fifty hunting dogs on the hills of Cithaeron outside Thebes. According to one account, he accidentally observes the nude Artemis bathing, for which intrusion the goddess incites his hounds against him. Actaeon's sparagmos foreshadows that of Pentheus. *(James Fund and by Special Contributions. Courtesy, Museum of Fine Arts, Boston)*

Denying Bacchus the proper sacrifice owed the god, he himself becomes the ritual sacrifice, his dismemberment reenacting Dionysus's own sparagmos by the Titans (see Chapter 8). Like his cousin **Actaeon** [ak-TEE-ahn], who offended Artemis and was consequently torn to pieces by his hunting dogs (Figure 17-10), Pentheus learns too late the absolute necessity of respecting the gods' prerogatives.

As Pentheus replays the scene of Dionysian suffering, the god changes his physical shape to reflect the bestial energies previously concealed when he appeared as a languid adolescent. Manifesting his divine–animal unity, Dionysus is simultaneously a horned bull, a lion, and a luminous deity. The ethical contradictions intrinsic to nature—its beauty, power, and cruelty—are sublimely combined in this frighteningly natural god (Figure 17-11).

Agave

Pentheus's nagging fear of what may result if human nature is liberated from its socially imposed restraints is abundantly justified in the manner of his death—at the hands of his own mother, Agave. Divine possession removes traditional inhibitions, allowing Agave to realize her potential in purely masculine terms, reversing the socially prescribed dichotomy between male and female. As racer, hunter, fighter, and executioner, she proves the equal of any Theban soldier. But the cost of her lib-

FIGURE 17-11   Celebrating the Death of Pentheus. In this scene, a satyr pipes to the enthroned Dionysus, as triumphant maenads brandish the severed limbs of Pentheus. *(Courtesy Dr. E. Borowski, Toronto)*

eration is tragically high, paradoxically stripping Agave of her freedom of rational choice.

Although the *Bacchae* may present Agave primarily as an object lesson in the folly of resisting divine power, her plight suggests other possibilities as well. In throwing off societal prohibitions, she reveals a startling kinship with Artemis, the goddess who eschews traditionally feminine duties, such as motherhood and weaving, to pursue savage beasts in the wilderness. Like Artemis, Agave not only revels in the freedom to hunt game and use weapons but also enacts the goddess's prerogative to inflict sparagmos on any male who dares to invade her sacred privacy. As Artemis incites the mutilation and death of Actaeon, so Agave dismembers the man who spies on women's mysteries (Figure 17-12). That her victim turns out to be her own son dramatizes the tragic alternatives available to women in a patriarchal society: the inner destruction of the psyche resulting from being oppressed and lacking opportunity to achieve real fulfillment in the world of action, or the outer destruction resulting from murdering husbands or children.

As a goddess and childless (although associated with childbirth), Artemis escapes the dilemma that entangles such human figures as Agave, Medea, and Clytemnestra. As a mortal woman and a mother, however, Agave is trapped, with no avenue of escape. The episode underscores the divided nature of gender roles, which, once again, have been violated in order to reinforce the boundaries. Such reversals, led by a festive "Lord of Misrule" (a role here taken by Dionysus himself), should lead the costumed, often gender-reversed, revelers to a new harmony, as happens in Shakespeare's *Twelfth Night,* a comic example of a Feast of Fools wherein a male actor portrays a woman who, in turn, plays the part of a man. But unlike the donning of costumes by Pentheus or by the actor playing Agave's part in the Dionysian Feast of Fools, Agave as a hero-impersonator doesn't enact a role. Rather, she acts out her resentment of oppression, revealing not only the difference between a tragedy enacted on stage and one actually performed but also the contrast between male and female "heroes." Asking her father to hang her "trophy," the head of the "lion" she believes she has killed, on his wall, Agave unconsciously mocks the "heroic" ego and the socially approved glorification of men as hunters and killers. Once again, we find Euripides offering a radical perspective on conventional attitudes. At the same time, however, as in every Feast of Fools, traditional norms and authorities are mocked only to have them subsequently restored. Agave has gone too far, from the one extreme, of "rational" denial, to the other, of "irrational" delusion. The tragic nature of her predicament is evident when Agave, believing that she has killed a lion with her bare hands, compares herself to Heracles—an ironic comparison that highlights the differences between their situations. Heracles, too, incurred blood guilt when, in a fit of madness, he slew his wife and children. In sharp contrast to Agave, however, Heracles was given a way to expiate his crime: he was sent on a series of quests that allow him to fulfill his heroic nature. Agave, who has staged a similarly deadly rebellion against domesticity, is permitted no redemptive action, but instead is condemned to permanent exile. Once again, as in the *Medea,* the association of women with irrational excess, with a lack of control of their passions, is blatantly emphasized.

Euripides creates one of the most powerful **anagnorisis** (recognition) scenes in all drama when he shows Agave, carrying Pentheus's severed head, in a struggle against a return to ordinary reality. Her desperate attempts to remain under Dionysus's spell, to avoid confronting the results of her terrible experiment with total freedom, produce one of the most excruciating scenes of madness ever devised for the theater. Her response reveals a startling schizophrenic state. She speaks of being "split in two": half of her identity (which she describes in the third person as "she") has been destroyed; the remaining half ("me") is numb, her life now an endless nothingness.

Having been forced to experience Dionysian ecstasy and coerced into releasing a killer instinct that she loathes, Agave is in a unique position to assess the value of Bacchanalian frenzy (as depicted in Figures 17-5 and 17-9). With returning sanity, she realizes that the god has violated the integrity of her personality, blinded her moral vision, robbed her of choice, and exploited her hitherto unexpected potential for aggression and impulsive violence. Agave's rationalism, which made her unable to believe that Semele's child was Zeus-begotten, resembles that of Jocasta, the unhappy wife of Oedipus, who is similarly punished for doubting that the gods personally influence human affairs (see Chapter 16). At the end of the play, Agave makes the only gesture of freedom still available to her: she rejects Dionysus and all he stands for. She resolves to go as far from "cursed Cithaeron" as possible, to a place where the thyrsus and Dionysian revels are unknown. Guilty of shedding a kinsman's blood, Agave is not allowed to join Pentheus in death: polluted and exiled, she must wander the earth to ponder and suffer the consequences of having discovered her affinity with nature's animal savagery.

Agave's decisive rejection of divine possession has echoes in other myths. According to one story, the bereaved mother's scorn for Dionysus was so strong that, in exile from Thebes, she climbed a tree and lay in wait to attack him with a weapon. As the gods' human pawn, Agave resembles Cassandra, a Trojan princess who was also Apollo's prophet. Both women find that union with a god, despite its emotional gratification, is a poisonous gift that deprives them of personal autonomy and mental peace. Just as Apollo stripped Cassandra of her credibility when she repulsed his advances, so Dionysus arbitrarily deprives Agave of the civilized bonds that might keep her from acting on the incipient violence in her soul. Driven to madness by the machinations of their divine patrons, Agave and Cassandra illustrate the paradox of religious commitment: while offering unparalleled rapture and insight, the gods punish mercilessly those who give less than complete submission. Agave's mental independence and skepticism about Semele's conception, and Cassandra's wish to keep her body inviolate, even from Apollo, spark the wrath of the gods, who demand unconditional surrender. The opposing tenets of religious devotion and Greek humanism are not easily reconciled—except in the Asian maenads, who claim to have found grace and peace in Dionysian possession.

Tiresias

In contrast to Agave and Pentheus, Apollo's prophet Tiresias does not hesitate to accept the wine god as Zeus's legitimate son. Although aged and blind, Tiresias decks himself out in the Bacchic regalia, advising Pentheus not to resist the divine will. The only character in the play whom Dionysus does not punish, Tiresias successfully balances the unavoidable contrarieties of control and freedom.

Although Euripides does not refer to it, his audience probably would have been familiar with another myth involving Tiresias's uncanny ability to assimilate polar opposites. Having been changed from man to woman and back again, Tiresias can appreciate Dionysian mutability and androgyny (see Chapter 16). Appearing in virtually every myth associated with Thebes' ill-fated royal house, Tiresias typically offers advice that all rulers, from Cadmus and Pentheus to Oedipus and Creon, unwisely reject. He retains his prophetic powers even after death, continuing to foretell the future in Hades (see *Odyssey,* Book 11, in Chapter 13).

Tiresias's accommodation of both Apollo and Dionysus, masculine control and androgynous surrender, parallels Delphi's historic accommodation of two radically different aspects of godhood. By making room for Dionysus—his temple also stood on the flanks of Mount Parnassus—the Delphic compromise between the conflicting demands of mental lucidity and sensuous abandon helped to contain (and control) incipiently dangerous human tendencies. Acknowledging its inevitability, Delphi—and democratic Athens—honored the principle of nonrationality by creating institutions to give it limited expression, restricting Dionysian revels to annually scheduled festivals.

Cadmus: Expediency No Substitute for Passion

Although Cadmus, the aged dragon slayer, also appears to honor the new god, his reverence is only lip service. Cadmus's advice urging Pentheus to accept Dionysus insults the god in its shallow expediency: Pentheus should at least pretend he believes that Zeus was Semele's lover, for such a rumor enhances the status of Thebes' royal house. Disdaining such lukewarm acquiescence, Dionysus condemns Cadmus to exile and eventual transformation into a serpent, reducing the former king in old age to the status of the reptile he had slain in his prime.

Dionysus's Pitiless Judgment

Like Zeus in Aeschylus's *Prometheus Bound,* the triumphant Dionysus is incapable of pity, oblivious to Agave's pain or Cadmus's despair. In Euripides' final scene, compassion for human suffering is no more part of the divine character than it is of nature, which sheds no tears for victims of earthquake, cyclone, or flood.

An aspect of nature that transcends moral judgment, Dionysus is as implacable as Hades or Persephone. In Euripides' mythic vision, sympathy for others and concern for their anguish are strictly human responses to tragic loss: Agave and Cadmus can express pity for each other's suffering, but the god—impervious to everything but the brute fact of his power—cannot connect with mortals foolish enough to reject his divine reality.

The *Bacchae* and the Festival of Dionysus

The ostensibly logical Pentheus, like his mother, Agave, and their fellow Thebans, refuse to believe that Semele was miraculously impregnated by Zeus and that her child, Dionysus, survived the conflagration and is now a god appearing in human form. Such a claim, after all, defies logic and the evidence of the senses: the "Stranger" who is walking about the streets of the city is visibly human. Euripides' play has already addressed the way in which Apollo's requirement of self-knowledge can be achieved by letting go of the self through acting (or watching others act). The play also calls dramatic attention to another essential relationship between Apollo, god of reason and moderation, and Dionysus, god of passion and excess, a relationship especially important in a culture whose self-concept was defined by the Apollonian model. After all, Dionysus is a god whose very being requires a response beyond the reaches of the intellect. And for those who cannot negate reason but who set it aside when appropriate, human redemption through a "marriage" with the divine is possible, just as was offered by Demeter in the Eleusinian Mysteries, when a *hieros gamos,* a sacred marriage, may have been performed for worshipers who, like the actors in the theater, came to Eleusis dressed in costumes.

The physical marriage of human and god in Greek mythology rarely succeeds: Thetis and Peleus prove incompatible, and Semele goes up in smoke. And although the vulgar-minded Pentheus is capable of imagining only sexual orgies where none occurred, the divine *raptus,* the spiritual union of the soul with the god, retains an erotically charged component. Unlike the worship of Apollo, a more distant god who typically communicated with humans through the intermediaries of prophet or oracle, the religion of Dionysus, despite having been "tamed" and urbanized in Athens into the form of a theatrical festival, remains a mystery religion, whose initiates experience, in a direct, personal, and highly emotional way, the epiphany—the miraculous appearance of the god—among them. And because the god is incarnated in human form, the humans who love him are not consumed in the divine fire. Agave's calling down divine wrath upon herself is one obviously undesirable way to relate to a divinity such as Dionysus; the other is the "Holy Joy" of which the maenads sing. Athens saw itself, if perhaps somewhat smugly, as the epitome of rational accomplishment in such areas as the arts, science, mathematics, philosophy, and politics. But no logical deduction or mathematical theorem can supply "proof" of the existence of a god. Centered on the spiritual core of the Dionysian festival, Euripides' play provides a reminder that belief in any deity, whether the god of reason or the god of wine and passion, requires a leap of faith. This is not, however, a passage into madness or savagery, but a letting go, a leap that transcends rationality and accesses the capacity for spiritual experience that distinguishes the human species, elevating humanity, however briefly, to the realm of divinity and thereby fulfilling the very purpose of the Festival of Dionysus.

MEDEA*

Euripides

CHARACTERS

NURSE *to Medea*

TUTOR *to Medea's children*

CHILDREN, *the two sons of Medea and Jason*

CHORUS *of Corinthian women*

MEDEA

CREON, *king of Corinth*

JASON

AEGEUS, *king of Athens*

MESSENGER

Soldiers, servants, and attendants

[The action takes place before the house of MEDEA *in Corinth.* MEDEA'S *old* NURSE *is standing at the door.]*

Nurse

If only Argo's hull had never flown	1
Between the Clashing Rocks to Colchis' shore,	
And if the pine in Pelion's woods had never	
Been chopped down, to put oars into the hands	
Of heroes who went out in Pelias' name	
To fetch the Golden Fleece! My mistress then,	
Medea, would never have fallen in love with Jason	
And sailed with him to the walls of Iolkos' land,	
Or persuaded the daughters of Pelias to kill	
Their father; would not be living here	10
In Corinth, with her husband and her children,	
Giving pleasure to the country she has chosen for her exile.	
Everything she did was for Jason's sake,	
And that's the best way of avoiding risks,	
For a wife to have no quarrel with her husband.	
But love's turned sour, there's hatred everywhere.	
Jason deserts my mistress and his children	
And seeks a royal alliance, marrying	
The daughter of Creon, ruler of this land,	

---

*Translation by Peter D. Arnott.

While poor Medea is left wretched and dishonored   20
To cry "You promised," and remind him of the hand
He pledged in faith, and calls on heaven to see
What she has done for him—and her reward.
She lies without eating, her body abandoned to grief,
Weeping herself thinner with each day that passed
Since first she knew her husband was unfaithful,
Never lifting her head or raising her eyes
From the ground, as deaf as rock or water
To anyone who gives her good advice.
Except, at times, she lifts her snow-white neck   30
And mourns to herself for the loss of her dear father
And the home and country she betrayed to come
Away with a man who now cares nothing for her.
Poor lady, she has come to learn the hard way
What it means to have no country to go back to.
She hates her children, takes no joy in seeing them;
I'm afraid she has something dreadful in her mind.
She's a dangerous woman; he who picks a fight
With her won't come off victor easily.
Here come her children, leaving their games behind;   40
They don't know anything about their mother's
Sorrows; youth is no friend to grief.
[Enter MEDEA's *two small sons, with their* TUTOR.*]*

Tutor
My mistress' time-worn piece of household property,
What are you doing standing here alone
Before the gates, soliloquizing on misfortune?
However could Medea do without you?

Nurse
Old fellow, guardian of Jason's children,
Good servants take it as a personal sorrow
When trouble and misfortune touch their masters.
And I was moved to such a pitch of misery   50
I longed to come outside, to tell
Heaven and earth about Medea's troubles.

Tutor
Poor lady, has she not stopped weeping yet?

Nurse
O blessed ignorance! Not halfway, hardly started.

Tutor
The fool—if I may speak so of my mistress;
She knows nothing of her more recent troubles.

Nurse
What is it, old man? Don't keep it to yourself!

Tutor
Nothing. I'm sorry that I said so much.

Nurse
By your beard, don't keep it from your fellow-servant.
I'll swear to keep it secret if I must.   60

Tutor
I heard somebody saying, and pretended not to listen,
When I was at the place where the old men sit
Playing draughts around the holy fountain of Peirene,
That Creon, this country's ruler, was about
To send Medea with her children into exile
Away from Corinth. Whether this tale is true
I cannot say; I hope it may not be so.

Nurse
Will Jason be content to see his sons
So treated, even though he's quarrelled with their mother?

Tutor
When loyalties conflict, the old one loses.   70
He has no love for any in this house.

Nurse
Why then, we are ruined, if we must add new sorrow
Before we have got rid of the old one.

Tutor
This is no time to tell Medea
What has happened; be quiet, keep it to yourself.

Nurse
My children, do you see what your father's like?
I hope he—no, he is my master still,
Even though he's proved a traitor to his loved ones.

Tutor
Who isn't? Have you only just now realized
That no man puts his neighbor before himself?   80
Some have good reason, most are out for profit,
Just as he neglects his sons for his new wife's sake.

Nurse
Go indoors, my children, everything will be all right.
You keep them to themselves as much as possible,
Don't bring them near their mother when she's angry.

I saw that wild bull look come in her eyes
As if she meant them harm. I know too well
She'll keep her anger warm till someone's hurt.
May it be enemies, and not her friends!
*[*MEDEA's *voice is heard from inside the house.]*

Medea
Oh,   90
I am wretched and oppressed with troubles.
I wish I were dead, I wish I were dead.

Nurse
What did I tell you, dear children? Your mother
Is stirring her heart and her anger with it.
Get along indoors as quickly as possible,
Don't go within sight of her, don't come near her,
Beware of her temper, the wild beast lurking
In that desperate mind of hers.
Come now, hurry along indoors;
It's clear that her smoldering anger will burst   100
Into flames as her passion increases.
Her spirit's too big for her, uncontrollable;
What will she do when provoked?

Medea
Oh,
I have suffered things, I have suffered things
Worth a world of weeping. Unhappy sons,
May you die with your father, the whole house perish!

Nurse
Oh dear, oh dear, what a state I am in!
What have your children to do with their father's
Wickedness, why hate them?
Oh, my darling children,   110
I'm terrified something will happen to you.
It's bad when a queen is angry; she rarely submits,
Gets her own way in most things, and changes
Her mood without warning.
[Exeunt CHILDREN *and* TUTOR.*]*
It's better if you've been used to a life
Without any ups or downs; I'd rather
Grow old in peace than be a great lady.
Moderation's a word that's good to hear
And the greatest blessing that men could have.
Excess can never bring profit; when heaven's   120
Angry, the great ones are hit the hardest.
[Enter the CHORUS *of Corinthian women.]*

Chorus

I heard the voice, I heard the cry
Of Colchis' unhappy daughter.
It is ringing still; tell us, old woman.
I was inside at my door, and heard her crying.
I cannot be happy when the home is troubled,
When the home is one I love.

Nurse

Home! There is no home, that's past and gone.
Jason is wrapped up in his new wife,
And my mistress sits pining away in her room   130
And her friends can say nothing to comfort her.

Medea

I wish
That lightning from heaven would split my head open!
What have I to live for now?
Why can I not leave this hateful life
And find repose in death?

Chorus

Zeus, heaven and earth, do you hear
How the wretched wife is weeping?
Why do you pray for that hateful sleep?
Fool, would you wish your death sooner?   140
This is no way to pray. If your husband
Honors another wife, it has happened
To others, don't take it to heart.
Zeus will see justice done; don't wear
Yourself out with lamenting your husband.

Medea

Goddess of justice, Queen Artemis,
You see how I suffer, who bound
My husband, curse him, with oaths?
I pray I may see him perish
And his wife, and all the house   150
Who have dared unprovoked to wrong me.
My father, my country, how shamefully
I left you, and killed my own brother.

Nurse

Do you hear what she says, how she cries
To Themis in prayer, and to Zeus
Whom we honor as keeper of oaths?
One thing is certain, my mistress
Won't let go her anger for nothing.

Chorus

If she would only come out here to see us,
If she would only hear what we have to say,   160
To see if her bitterness would melt
And her anger disappear.
I hope I shall always be ready
To stand by my friends. Go inside, old woman,
And fetch her out of the house; and hurry,
Before she can harm the household;
That's the way her grief is going.

Nurse

I'll do it, but I'm afraid
I shan't be able to move her.
Still, it's a labor of love.   170
She's angry, and glares at her servants
Like a lioness guarding her cubs
When anyone comes with a message.
You wouldn't be wrong to consider
The old poets not clever but fools
Who wrote music for dinners and banquets,
Pleasant tunes for men who were happy,
But nobody ever discovered
How to use all this music and singing
To lessen a man's load of trouble   180
That brought death and misfortune and ruin.
It would certainly be an advantage
To use music for healing! Why waste it
On dinners? There's pleasure enough
In a banquet, who wants any more?
[Exit.]

Chorus

I heard the voice heavy with grief
Bitterly mourning the faithless
Husband who married and left her,
Blaming her wrongs on the gods,
The justice of Zeus, the sworn oath   190
That started her difficult crossing
Through the gates of the salt foggy sea
To the opposite shores of Greece.
[Enter MEDEA.*]*

Medea

Women of Corinth, I have come outside
To avoid your disapproval. I know there are many
Conceited people; some keep themselves to themselves,
Others show it in public, while others still, who take

Things quietly, will find themselves called idlers.
The eyes are no good judges, when a man
Dislikes another at sight before she knows   200
His character, when there is nothing against him.
A foreigner especially should conform.
I'd even blame a native for presuming
To annoy his fellow citizens through lack of manners.
For me, this unexpected blow that fell
Has shattered me; it is the end, I only want to die.
The man to whom I gave my all, as well he knows,
Has turned out utterly false—my husband.
Of all things living that possess a mind
We women are the most unfortunate.   210
To start with, we must put ourselves to vast expense
To buy ourselves a husband, take a master for
Our bodies—a worse evil than the other:
And everything depends on this, whether we take a good man
Or a bad one; divorce is not respectable
For women, we may not deny our husbands.
Coming to new manners and a new way of life,
A woman needs second sight to know how best
To manage her bedfellow; no-one taught her at home.
And if we work hard at it, and our husband   220
Lives with us without struggling against the yoke
We are to be envied; if not, death comes at last.
When a man is bored with the company in his household
He can go out to find his consolation.
We women have only one soul-mate to look to.
They tell us we can spend our lives at home
In safety, while they go out to fight the wars.
How illogical! I'd rather stand three times
In the battlefield than bear one child.
But we have different stories, you and I;   230
You have a city, and a father's home,
And friendly company, a life you can enjoy.
I have no home, no country; I am despised
By my husband, something brought back from abroad;
I have no mother, no brother, no family
Where I can find a refuge from my troubles.
So this is the favor I will ask of you:
If the means offer, or I can find some way
To pay my husband back for the wrong he has done me,
Keep my secret. At other times a woman is timid,   240
Afraid to defend herself, frightened at the sight
Of weapons; but when her marriage is in danger
There is no mind bloodthirstier than hers.

Chorus

I will; for you have every right to punish him.
I do not wonder that you are distressed.
But I can see Creon, ruler of this land,
Approaching with some new decision to tell us.
[Enter CREON.*]*

Creon

You with the scowling face, who hate your husband,
Medea, I command you leave this land
An exile, taking your two children with you   250
Without delay. I come to execute
My own decree, and shall not go back home
Till I have seen you past our boundaries.

Medea

Alas, my ruin is complete;
My enemies pursue full-sailed, and I
Can find no friendly harbor from calamity.
But though I am persecuted I will ask one thing:
For what reason, Creon, do you banish me?

Creon

I am afraid of you. Why veil my words?
Afraid you will do my child some dreadful harm.   260
And many things contribute to my fear:
You are clever, and accomplished in black arts,
And angry that your husband has deserted you.
I hear you threaten—so I am informed—
To act against the bridegroom and the bride
And the father too. I had rather be safe than sorry.
Better be hated, woman, by you now,
Than soften and repent my weakness later.

Medea

This has happened before. It is not the first time, Creon,
I have been the victim of my reputation.   270
No sensible man should ever have his sons
Brought up more clever than the average.
Apart from being told they waste their time
They earn the spite and envy of their neighbors.
You'll be called good-for-nothing, not intelligent,
For holding unconventional ideas;
And if the know-alls find your reputation
Exceeding theirs, the state will turn against you.
And I am one of those to whom it happened.
I am clever, so some people envy me,   280

Some call me idle, some the opposite,
While others hate me; but they exaggerate.
You fear me? Do you think you will be hurt?
I am in no state—do not be nervous, Creon—
To commit an offence against the authorities.
How have you wronged me? You bestowed your daughter
On the man your heart desired. It is my husband
That I hate.
But I suppose you know what you are doing.
I do not grudge you any of your good fortune.   290
Let the marriage stand, and prosper; but permit me
To stay here. Though I am the injured party
I shall not raise my voice against my betters.

Creon
Your words are smooth enough, but I fear your heart
Is already plotting mischief, and by so much less
I trust you than I did before.
A fiery temper, in woman as in man,
Is easier to guard against than silent cunning.
So get you gone without more argument.
You may be sure that no arts you can use   300
Will keep you here, now you have turned against us.

Medea
No, by your knees, and by your child the bride!

Creon
Go, it is useless, you cannot persuade me.

Medea
Will you turn me away and not listen to my prayers?

Creon
My family comes first in my affections.

Medea
My country, how strongly I recall you now.

Creon
I love my country too, after my children.

Medea
Oh, what a bitter curse is love to men.

Creon
Well, that depends on circumstances, I suppose.

Medea
O Zeus, remember who began these sorrows.   310

Creon
Get out, you fool, and trouble me no further.

Medea
I have my troubles; trouble me no further.

Creon
Soon my men will drive you out by force.

Medea
No! Spare me that, at least. I beg you, Creon—

Creon
You seem determined, woman, to be difficult.

Medea
No. I will go. It was not that I wanted.

Creon
Then why resist? Why do you not leave the country?

Medea
Permit me to remain here this one day,
To make my mind up where I am to go,
And where to keep my children, since their father   320
Prefers to leave his sons without protection.
You are a father; you have sons yourself,
And therefore should be well disposed to mine.
I do not care for myself if I am banished
But I am wretched if they are in trouble.

Creon
I never had the heart to play the tyrant.
My conscience has always been my disadvantage.
Woman, I know that I am making a mistake,
But your request is granted. But I warn you,
If the light of heaven falls on you tomorrow   330
Here with your sons inside our boundaries
You die. This is my final word.
And now, if stay you must, remain one day,
Too little time to do the harm I dread.
[Exit.]

Chorus
How troubled you are, unfortunate lady!
Where will you turn? What home, what country
Will give you protection?
Medea, god has plunged you in a sea of troubles
And there is no land in sight.

Medea

Beaten on every side; who can deny it?   340
But not in this, so do not think I am.
There are still trials for this new-married pair
And no small sorrow for their families.
You think I would have fawned upon this man
Unless I were working for my own advantage?
I would not have touched him, not have spoken to him.
But he has gone so far in foolishness
That when he could have foiled my plans
By sending me to exile, he allowed me stay
One day, in which I shall make corpses of   350
Three of my enemies—father, girl, my husband.
And I have many ways to work their deaths
And do not know where first to try my hand—
Whether to set their wedding house on fire,
Or creep indoors to where their bedroom is
And thrust a sharpened sword into their hearts.
One thing prevents me; if I should be caught
Entering the house and plotting against it
I shall die the laughing-stock of my enemies.
No. It is best to go direct, the way in which I am   360
Most skilled, and poison both of them.
Ah then,
Suppose them dead; what city will receive me?
What host will offer me home and security
In some safe country, and protect my life?
No-one. Then I shall wait a little while,
And if some tower of safety should appear,
By stealth and cunning I shall murder them.
But if misfortune should drive me out helpless,
I shall take the sword, even though it means my death,   370
And kill them.
No, by the Queen of Night whom above all
I honor and have chosen as my partner,
Dark Hecate dwelling in the corners of my hearth,
No man shall wound my heart and still live happy.
I will make them curse the day they married,
Curse this alliance and my banishment.
Then come, Medea, call on all the skill
You have in plotting and contriving;
On to the crime! This is the test of courage.   380
Look to your wrongs! You must not let yourself
Be mocked by Jason's Sisyphean wedding,
You, a royal child, descended from the Sun.
You have the skill; moreover you were born

A woman; and women are incapable of good,
But have no equal in contriving harm.

Chorus
The sacred rivers flow back to their sources,
The appointed order of things is reversed.
It is men whose minds are deceitful, who take
The names of their gods in vain,   390
And women the future will honor in story
As leaders of upright lives.
Glory is ours! And the slanderous tongues
That attacked womankind shall be stilled.

You Muses of past generations, inspire
No more the refrain that woman is fickle.
We were not given the wit by Phoebus
Apollo, the master of songs,
To strike from the lyre its heavenly music.
If it were so, I should sing   400
In answer to men; for history tells
As much of men's lives as of ours.

In passion you sailed from the land
Of your fathers, and saw the twin rocks
Of the sea fall open before you.
Now you live among strangers, exchange
Your couch for a husbandless bed;
Without rights and distressed you are driven
An exile out of the land.

The spell of the oath has been broken; no longer   410
Has Greece any shame, it has flown to the winds.
Poor lady, your father's home
Will offer you shelter no more
In time of distress; your marriage
Is lost to a queen who descends
On your house as a second bride.
[Enter JASON.*]*

Jason
I have noticed many times, this not the first,
How willfulness runs on to self-destruction.
You could have kept this country as your home
By obeying the decisions of your betters,   420
But futile protests send you into exile.
They do not worry me. You can go on
Forever saying Jason is a scoundrel;
But when it comes to slandering your rulers,

Count yourself lucky you were only banished.
I wanted you to stay—tried all the time
To pacify the anger of the king;
But you persevered in folly, and continually
Spoke ill of him, and so you must be banished.
However, I shall not desert my friends   430
In spite of their behavior, but am here to see
That you and your children do not go out penniless
Or in need of anything; for banishment
Brings many hardships. Hate me though you may,
I could never bring myself to bear you malice.

Medea
Oh, devil! Devil! This is the worst abuse
My tongue can find for your lack of manliness.
You come to me, my mortal enemy,
Hateful to heaven and to all mankind?
This is not venturesome, this is not courage,   440
To look friends in the face whom you have wronged,
But the most detestable of human weaknesses,
Yes, shamelessness! But I am glad you came,
For I can ease my overburdened heart
Abusing you, and you will smart to hear.
I shall begin my tale at the beginning.
I saved your life, as every single Greek
Who sailed with you on board the Argo knows,
When you were sent to tame the bulls that breathed fire,
And yoke them, and sow death in the field.   450
The dragon that encircled with his coils
The Golden Fleece and watched it without sleeping
I killed for you, and lit your path to safety.
For you I left my father and my home
And sailed to Iolkos and Mount Pelion
With you, and showed more eagerness than sense.
I brought on Pelias the worst of ends,
Death at his children's hands, and ruined his house.
All this I suffered for your worthless sake,
To be abandoned for another woman,   460
Though I had borne you children! Were I barren
You might have some excuse to marry again.
I have no faith in your promises; I cannot tell
If you believe in the old gods still, or think
There is some newer standard of morality—
You have broken your oath to me, you must know that.
Oh, this my right hand, that you wrung so often!
These knees, at which you fell; how am I deceived
In a false lover, cheated of my hopes.

But come, I will open my heart to you as to a friend— 470
Though what fair treatment could I hope from you?
Yet will I; you will feel more shame to answer.
Where should I turn now? To my father's home?
The country I betrayed to come with you?
Or Pelias' wretched daughters? They would give
A gracious welcome to their father's murderess.
For that is how it is. I have estranged myself
From friends at home, and those I should not hurt
I have made mortal enemies for your sake.
In recompense, how happy have you made me 480
Among Greek women, what a paragon
Of rectitude I married, to my sorrow,
When I am exiled, cast out of the land
Without a friend. My sons are all I have.
A fine reproach for this new-married man
When his sons and she who saved him wander beggars.
O Zeus, why have you given men clear marks
To help them tell true gold from counterfeit,
While nature sets no stamp upon men's bodies
To help us tell the true man from the false! 490

Chorus
Tempers run high, and cannot soon be soothed,
When those who have once loved begin to quarrel.

Jason
I must show myself no mean speaker, so it seems,
But like the sea-wise steersman of a ship
Close-haul my canvas, lady, and run before
The storm of your verbosity. Since you
Have raised this monument to your own kindness,
I hold that Cypris was the guardian of my voyages,
No other god or man. You are quick-witted, true,
But it would be ungenerous to explain 500
You were compelled by Love's unerring shafts to save me.
However, I shall not go too deeply into that;
Where you did help me, you did not do badly.
But you have profited by my escape
More than you lost by it. Let me explain:
To start with, instead of living among savages
You live in Greece and come to learn our laws
And how to live by justice, not brute force.
Besides, all Greece has learned how clever you are.
You're famous! If you still lived at the ends 510
Of the earth, nobody would have heard of you.
If only my good fortune made me famous,

I would not ask for riches, nor the power
To sing a sweeter song than Orpheus did.
So much for what you have to say about
My labors; you began the argument.
For your reproaches on my royal marriage,
I'll show you first of all how clever I was,
Second, how prudent, and third, that I am my sons'
And your best friend. Please do not interrupt me.   520
When, with this irretrievable misfortune
Behind me, I came here from Iolkos' land,
What better piece of luck could I have found
Than this, an exile marry a princess?
Not that you bored me—the sore point with you—
Or that I was infatuated with a new wife
Or anxious for a larger family;
I'm satisfied with those I already have.
No! My main reason was that we should live well,
Not have to count our pennies. I'm aware   530
How all friends turn against you when you're poor.
I wanted to bring my children up as sons of mine
Should be, and give my sons by you some brothers.
If I could join our families and make them one,
I'd count myself a happy man. You need no sons,
But it profits me to add to those I have. Is this
So reprehensible? It's only jealousy
That makes you think so. But things have come to such a pass
That women think marriage is the only thing that matters.
When once your sole possession is endangered,   540
Whatever's good and right for you to do
You fight it. There ought to be some other way
For men to get their sons, there ought to be
No women; then a man could live his life in peace.

Chorus
Jason, you have made a pretty speech,
But I will be bold, and say what I think:
It was criminal to desert your wife.

Medea
The world and I have very different views.
The bad man who is clever with his tongue
In my opinion asks for double punishment.   550
He prides himself on his power to talk his way
Out of everything, nothing frightens him. But he
Is not so clever as he thinks. So do not make
Fine speeches, or think to play the innocent
With me. One word will throw you. If you were honest

You should have told me of your wedding plans,
Not kept them secret from the ones that loved you.

Jason
Much good you would have done my wedding plans, I must say,
If I'd told you of them, when even now
You can't disguise the anger in your heart.   560

Medea
It was not that. You thought it might cause talk
To have a foreign wife when you grew older.

Jason
I tell you it was not for the woman's sake
I made the royal alliance that I did,
But as I said before, to offer you
Protection, and beget young kings to be
My sons' new brothers, towers of strength to us.

Medea
Give me no happiness involving pain
Or joy that will not leave the mind in peace.

Jason
You should know better; pray for something else,   570
Never to judge good fortune to be bad
Or count yourself hard done by when all's well.

Medea
Go on, insult me! You have a place to go
While I am an exile from the land and friendless.

Jason
You brought it on yourself, blame no-one else.

Medea
How? Did I marry and abandon you?

Jason
Calling down blasphemous curses on the king.

Medea
Yes, you will find me a curse to your house too.

Jason
I refuse to discuss this matter any further.
But if you want my money, to assist   580
You and your children when you are gone,
Speak out; I am ready to be open-handed,
And give you introductions to my friends

Who will assist you. It is foolish to refuse;
Let your anger rest, and you will profit by it.

Medea
I want no truck with any friends of yours
Or anything from you, so do not offer it.
A bad man's gifts bring no-one any good.

Jason
Very well! But I call on heaven to witness
I have done everything possible for you and your sons.   590
Your stubbornness rejects your friends; you don't know
When you are well off. So much the worse for you.
[Exit.]

Medea
Yes, go; you are too eager for your new bride
To stay any longer outside her house.
Go and be married! God will echo me,
This marriage may be such you will disown it.

Chorus
Love unrestrained can bring
No worth or honor with it,
But coming in small measure
There is no power more gracious.   600
Never let fly at me
Great Queen, the unerring shafts
Of your golden arrows, tipped
In the poison of desire.

Let moderation be
My guide, the gods' best gift.
Dread Aphrodite, never
Send strife and argument
To attack my heart and make
Me long for other loves,   610
But learn to honor marriage
And let love lie in peace.

Oh, let me never lose you,
My country and my home,
Or learn the thorny ways
Of poverty, the worst
Of life's calamities.
No! Let me rather die
And see life's brief day done.
This is the greatest sorrow,   620
The loss of fatherland.

I know; I do not learn
The tale from the lips of others.
No home or friend to share
The depths of your distress.
Dishonored be the man
Who honors not his friends
And locks his heart away;
No friend shall he be of mine.
[Enter AEGEUS.*]*

Aegeus
Give you joy, Medea; this is the best way   630
Men know to start a conversation with their friends.

Medea
And joy to you, wise Aegeus, son of Pandion.
Where are you from? What brings you to our country?

Aegeus
From Apollo's ancient oracle at Delphi.

Medea
What took you there, to earth's prophetic center?

Aegeus
To inquire how children might be born to me.

Medea
What, are you still without a son at your age?

Aegeus
Yes, by some whim of providence I have no heir.

Medea
Are you married? Or have you never had a wife?

Aegeus
I am no stranger to the marriage bond.   640

Medea
And what did Phoebus have to say about it?

Aegeus
Words too wise for a man to understand.

Medea
Then may I know the oracle's reply?

Aegeus
Most certainly, for cleverness is what we need.

Medea
Then tell me, if you may, what Phoebus said.

Aegeus
Not to loosen the wineskin's hanging foot—

Medea
Until you had arrived somewhere, or done something?

Aegeus
Until I reached my ancestral hearth again.

Medea
And what directs your journey through this country?

Aegeus
There is a man called Pittheus, King of Troezen—   650

Medea
Old Pelops' son, with a great reputation for piety.

Aegeus
I want to tell him what the oracle has said.

Medea
He is a wise man, skillful in such matters.

Aegeus
And the oldest of my military allies.

Medea
I hope you are lucky, and achieve your heart's desire.
[She breaks down, and turns away her head.]

Aegeus
Why do you turn away, and look so pale?

Medea
Aegeus, my husband is the worst of men.

Aegeus
What's this you say? Tell me about your troubles.

Medea
Jason, unprovoked, has done me wrong.

Aegeus
What has he done to you? Tell me more clearly.   660

Medea
Put another woman over his household in my place.

Aegeus
He would not dare to treat you so despicably!

Medea
Too truly; and I, the old love, am dishonored.

Aegeus
Was it for love of her, or hate of you?

Medea
Much love he has; the man was born unfaithful.

Aegeus
Take no notice, if he's as worthless as you say.

Medea
He was in love with marrying a king's daughter.

Aegeus
Who gives her to him? Tell me the whole story.

Medea
Creon, the ruler of this land of Corinth.

Aegeus
You have good reason for your grief, my lady.   670

Medea
It is the end; and I am banished too.

Aegeus
On whose orders? This is a new wrong you speak of.

Medea
It is Creon who sends me into exile from the land.

Aegeus
And Jason lets him? This is unforgivable.

Medea
He says not, but he has resigned himself.
[She falls at his feet.]
But I beseech you, by the beard I clasp,
And throw myself a suppliant at your knees,
Have pity, have pity on my misery,
And do not see me thrown out destitute.
Let me come to your country and live at your hearthside;   680
So may your great desire come to fruition
And give you children, and allow you to die happy.
You do not know what good fortune you have found.

I can put a stop to your childlessness, and give
You issue, with the potions that I know.

Aegeus

I am anxious for many reasons, lady,
To grant your request; first, my religious scruples,
And then your promise that I should have sons,
For in this there is nothing else that I can do.
But this is how I stand. If you can reach my country   690
I'll endeavor to protect you as in duty bound.
But one thing I must make clear from the start:
I am not willing to take you from this country.
If you can make your own way to my home
I will keep you safe and give you up to no-one,
But you must make your own escape from Corinth.
I would not give offence, even to strangers.

Medea

So let it be, then. If you swear an oath
To do this, I have nothing more to ask.

Aegeus

Do you not trust me? What is it puts you off?   700

Medea

I trust you; but the house of Pelias is against me,
And Creon. Oath-bound, you could never yield
Me to them when they came to take me away.
A promise unsupported by an oath
Would allow you to befriend them, and obey
Their summons when it came. My cause is weak,
While they have power and money on their side.

Aegeus

You show great thought for the future in what you say.
But, if you wish it, I shall not refuse.
My own position will be unassailable   710
If I have an excuse to offer your enemies,
And you will run less risk. Come, name your gods.

Medea

Swear by the plain of Earth, and by the Sun,
My father's father; add the whole family of gods.

Aegeus

That I will do or not do what? Say on.

Medea

Never to drive me from the land yourself

Or willingly yield me to my enemies
When they come for me, as long as you do live.

Aegeus
I swear by Earth, by the holy light of sun,
By all the gods, to do as you have said.   720

Medea
Enough. What penalty if you break your oath?

Aegeus
What comes to men who take their gods in vain.

Medea
Now go your way in peace. All will be well.
I shall come to your country as soon as I have done
What I intend to do, and won my heart's desire.

Chorus
Now Hermes, God of Travelers,
Give you safe conduct home,
And may the desire that you cherish
So eagerly be fulfilled.
You have shown, Aegeus,   730
What a good man you are.
[*Exit* AEGEUS.]

Medea
O Zeus, Zeus' daughter Justice, light of Sun,
Now shall we have a glorious triumph, friends,
Upon our enemies; our feet are on the path.
Now is there hope my enemies will pay
The penalty. This man has shown himself,
Where we were weakest, a haven for my plans.
In him my ship may find safe anchorage;
To Athena's fortress city shall I go!
And now I will reveal you all my plans.   740
Hear what I have to say; it will not please you.
One of my servants I shall send to Jason
And ask him to come here before my face.
And when he comes, I shall say soft words to him,
That I agree with him, and all is well;
That the royal match he abandons me to make
Is for my advantage, and a good idea.
I shall entreat him that my sons should stay—
Not to allow my sons to be insulted
In a strange country by my enemies,   750
But to kill the daughter of the king with cunning.
I shall send them both with presents in their hands,

A fine-spun robe, a golden diadem.
If she accepts the gifts and puts them on
She will die in agony and all who touch her,
With such deadly poison shall I anoint my gifts.
Now I must leave this story, and lament
The dreadful thing that then remains for me to do.
I will kill my sons; no man shall take them from me.
And when the house of Jason lies in ruins,   760
I shall fly this land, setting my darlings' death
Behind me, most unspeakable of crimes.
The scorn of enemies is unendurable.
But let it go; for what have I to live for?
I have no home, no country, no escape from misery.
I made my mistake the day I left behind
My father's home, seduced by speeches from
A Greek who heaven knows will pay for them.
The sons I bore him he will never see
Alive after this day, nor father more   770
On his new-married bride, condemned to die
In agony from my poisons as she deserves.
No-one shall call me timorous or weak
Or stay-at-home, but quite the opposite,
A menace to my enemies and help to friends;
Those are the people that the world remembers.

Chorus
Since you have taken me into your confidence,
I should like to help you, but must still uphold
The laws of men. I say you cannot do this.

Medea
There is nothing else I can do. But you have excuse   780
For speaking so, you have not known my sufferings.

Chorus
But will you have the heart to kill your children?

Medea
Yes; it is the way I can most hurt my husband.

Chorus
But you will be the most unhappy of women.

Medea
So be it; there can be no compromise.
[Calling the NURSE.*]*
You; go at once and fetch Jason here.
We have no secrets from each other, you and I.
And breathe no word to anyone of my plans,

As you love your mistress, as you are a woman.
[Exit NURSE.*]*

Chorus
Happy of old were the sons of Erechtheus,   790
Sprung from the blessed gods, and dwelling
In Athens' holy and untroubled land.
Their food is glorious wisdom; they walk
With springing step in the crystal air.
Here, so they say, golden Harmony first
Saw the light, the child of the Muses nine.

And here too, they say, Aphrodite drank
Of Cephisus' fair-flowing stream, and breathed
Sweet breezes over the land, with garlands
Of scented roses entwined in her hair,   800
And gave Love a seat on the throne of Wisdom
To work all manner of arts together.

How then will this city of sacred waters,
This guide and protector of friends, take you,
Your children's slayer, whose touch will pollute
All others you meet? Think again of the deaths
Of your children, the blood you intend to shed.
By your knees, by every entreaty we beg you
Not to become your children's murderess.

Where will you find the boldness of mind,   810
The courage of hand and heart, to kill them?
How will you strike without weeping, how
Be constant to stain your hands in their blood
When your children kneel weeping before you?
[Enter JASON.*]*

Jason
I come at your request; although you hate me,
This favor you shall have. So let me hear
What new demand you have to make of me.

Medea
Jason, I ask you to forgive the words
I spoke just now. The memory of our
Past love should help you bear my evil temper.   820
Now I have taken myself to task and found
I was to blame. "Fool, why am I so mad?
Why should I quarrel with those who want to help me,
And why antagonize the men in power
And my husband, who works only for my advantage
In making this royal marriage, and begetting

New brothers for my sons? Why not lay down
My anger, why resent what the gods provide?
Are not the children mine, and am I not
An exile from the land, without a friend?"   830
Such were my thoughts, and then I realized
What foolishness my futile anger was.
Now I agree with you, and think you provident
In gaining us this connection, and myself a fool.
I should have been your go-between and shared
Your plans, stood by your marriage-bed,
And had the joy of tending your new bride.
But we are what we are; I will not say bad,
But women. But you should not take bad example
And answer my stupidity with yours.   840
Now I submit, agree that I was wrong
Before, but come to saner judgment now.
My children, here, my children, leave the house,
Come out to greet your father, and with me
Bid him goodbye; be reconciled to friends
And let your anger rest beside your mother's.
[The CHILDREN *appear from the house, and go to* JASON.*]*
We are at peace; there is no anger now.
Come, take his hand.
[aside]   Oh, the pity of it;
There is something still unseen, but my mind knows it.
Children, will you live long to stretch out   850
Your loving arms, as now? Oh pity, pity;
How near I am to tears, how full of fear.
[aloud]
At last I have stopped the quarrel with their father
And brought tears of forgiveness to their eyes.

Chorus
And my eyes too are wet with running tears.
I pray we have no troubles worse than these.

Jason
I approve this mood, and do not blame the other.
It is natural for a woman to show resentment
When her husband smuggles in a second marriage.
But now your mind has turned to better things   860
And learned—at last—which policy must win.
Done like a sensible woman!
[To the CHILDREN.*]*
Your father hasn't forgotten you, my boys.
God willing, you'll be well provided for.
I'll see you here in Corinth at the top
Beside your brothers. Just grow up; your father

Will see to the rest, and any god that fancies you.
I want to see you, when you've grown young men,
Stout fellows, head and shoulders above my enemies.
Medea, what are these tears upon your cheeks?   870
Why do you turn your face away from me?
Why aren't you happy at the things I say?

Medea
It is nothing. I was thinking of my children.

Jason
Don't worry. I shall see them well set up.

Medea
I shall try to be brave, not mistrust what you say;
But we women are the weaker sex, born weepers.

Jason
Why so unhappy, lady, for these children?

Medea
I am their mother. When you prayed that they might live,
Compassion came, and said, "Will it be so?"
For what you came here to discuss with me,   880
Part has been said, the rest remains to say.
Since the king thinks good to send me from the land,
I too think it is good, and I acknowledge it,
Not to embarrass you or the authorities
By staying. I am not welcome in this house.
Yes, I will leave this country, go to exile;
But that your hand alone may rear my sons,
I pray you, beg the king to let them stay.

Jason
I doubt I will succeed, but I must try.

Medea
Then you must tell your new wife, the princess,   890
To beg her father to remit their banishment.

Jason
I'll do it. Yes, I think I can persuade her.

Medea
You will, if she is a woman like the rest of us.
And I shall lend my shoulder to this labor,
And send her gifts more beautiful by far
Than any man has ever seen, I know—
A fine-spun robe, a golden diadem.
My sons shall take them. One of my servants,

Go bring the robes as quickly as you can.
She will be not once blessed but a thousand times,   900
Having you, the best of men, to be her husband,
And owning ornaments which once the Sun,
My father's father gave to his descendants.
[A servant brings the presents from the house.]
Here, take this dowry, children, put it in the hands
Of the happy royal bride. She will not think lightly of it.

Jason
What are you doing? Why deprive yourself?
Do you think the royal house lacks robes?
Do you think we have no gold? Keep them,
Don't give them away. If my wife respects me at all,
She will prefer my wish to presents, I can tell you.   910

Medea
Not so; they say that gifts can move the gods.
A piece of gold is worth a thousand speeches.
Her luck is in, god give her more of it.
A queen, so young. I'd willingly give my life
To save my sons from banishment, not only gold.
Go to the halls of wealth, my sons, beseech
The new wife of your father and my queen,
And beg her not to send you into exile.
Give her the presents—this is most important—
Into her own hands.   920
Now hurry; bring your mother back good news
That you have accomplished what she sets her heart on.
[Exeunt CHILDREN *and* JASON.*]*

Chorus
There is no hope now for the children's lives,
No hope any longer; they go to their deaths,
And the bride, poor bride, will accept the gift
Of the crown worked of gold,
And with her own hands make death an adornment
To set in her yellow hair.

The unearthly splendor and grace of the robe
And the crown worked of gold will persuade her to wear them.   930
She will soon be attired to marry the dead.
Into such a snare is she fallen,
Into such deadly fate, poor girl, and will never
Escape from the curse upon her.

And you, unhappy man, bitter bridegroom,
Who make an alliance with kings,

Unknowing you send your sons to their deaths
And bring on your bride the worst of ends.
How are you deceived in your hopes of the future.

And next to theirs we mourn your sorrows,   940
Unhappy mother of sons,
Who, to repay your husband for leaving
Your bed, and going to live with another
Woman, will kill your children.
[Enter the TUTOR, *leading the two* CHILDREN.*]*

Tutor
Mistress! Your children are reprieved from exile!
The royal bride was pleased to take into her hands
Your gifts, and with your sons is peace.
Why does good fortune leave you so confused?
Why do you turn your face the other way?
Why aren't you happy at the things I say?   950

Medea
Alas.

Tutor
        Your words and mine are out of tune.

Medea
Alas again.

Tutor
                Is there some meaning to my words
I do not know? Am I wrong to think them good?

Medea
You have said what you have said; I do not blame you.

Tutor
Why do you drop your eyes, begin to weep?

Medea
Because there is necessity, old man. The gods
And my pernicious schemings brought these things to pass.

Tutor
Be brave: your children will bring you home again.

Medea
I shall send others home before they do.

Tutor
You are not the only mother to lose her children.   960
Mankind must bear misfortune patiently.

Medea

And so shall I. But go inside the house
And see about my children's daily needs.
[Exit TUTOR.*]*
My sons, my sons, you have a city now
And home, where when we've said our sad goodbye
You will stay for ever, parted from your mother.
I go in exile to another land
Before I have had the joy of seeing you happy,
Before I have made your marriage beds, and seen
Your brides, and carried torches at your weddings.   970
My willfulness has brought its own reward.
For nothing did I toil to bring you up,
For nothing did I labor, and endure
The pangs I suffered in your hour of birth.
Once I had in you, oh, once, such splendid hopes,
To have you by my side as I grew old
And when I died, your loving arms around me,
What all men long for. This sweet dream is now
Destroyed. When you and I have parted
My life will be forlorn and desolate.   980
Your loving eyes will never look upon
Your mother again, you go to another life.
My sons, my sons, why do you look at me?
Why smile at me the last smile I shall see?
Oh, oh, what shall I do? Women, my heart
Is faltering when I look at their bright eyes.
I cannot do it; I renounce the plans
I made before, my children shall go with me.
Why should I use their sufferings to hurt
Their father, and so doubly hurt myself?   990
Not I, not I; I renounce my plans.
And yet—what is happening to me? Shall I let
My enemies go scot-free and earn their scorn?
Be bold, Medea. Why, what a coward am I
That can allow my mind talk of relenting.
Go in, my children. He who may not be
Present at my sacrifice without sin,
On his own head be it; my hand is firm.
[She turns to follow the CHILDREN *into the house, and then pauses.]*
Do not do this, my heart, do not do this!
Spare them, unhappy heart, let my sons go.   1000
They will live with you in exile and make you glad.
No, by the fiends that dwell in Hell below,
It shall never come to this, that I allow
My sons to be insulted by my enemies.
[A noise of shouting is heard off-stage.]

So; it is finished; there is no escape.
The crown is on her head, the royal bride
Is dying in her robes, this I know well.
And I must tread my own unhappy road;
Far worse the road on which I send my sons.
I want to speak to them. Here, children, give   1010
Your mother your hand, let mother hold your hand.
Oh dearest hand, oh lips I hold most dear,
Dear face, and dear bright eyes, may you be happy—
But in another place; your father leaves
You nothing here. Oh, sweet embrace,
The feel of your skin, the scent of your sweet breath;
Go away! Go away! I have no strength
To look on you, my sorrows overwhelm me.
Women, I know what evil I am to do,
But anger has proved stronger than our reason   1020
And from anger all our greatest ills arise.
[The CHILDREN *go into the house.]*

Chorus
I have often allowed my mind
To speculate, enter into arguments
Lying outside a woman's province.
But there is a Muse in women too
To help us to wisdom; not in all,
But look far enough, and you may find a few
On whom the Muse has smiled.

And I say that those men and women
Who do not know what it means to have children   1030
Are blessed above parents in this world.
A child can bring joy, or bitter pain;
What can the childless know of these?
And those whose fortune it is to be barren
Are spared a world of worry.
But we see that those who tend
The delicate plant of youth in their houses
Have care at their side every hour of the day;
How they will bring their children up,
How they will leave them the means to live,   1040
Will they grow up to be good or bad?
There is no way of knowing.

Then the unkindest blow:
Suppose young bodies grow sturdy and strong
To make parents proud; then if Fate decides,
Down goes Death to the house of Hades,
Taking the children's bodies with him.

How should it profit a man, if heaven
Adds this, the bitterest grief, to his sorrows
Only for loving his children?   1050

Medea
Friends, I have awaited my fortune this long while,
Anxious to see which way events would turn.
And now I can see one of Jason's servants
Approaching; he is running, out of breath,
Sure sign of some new horror to report.
[Enter a MESSENGER.*]*

Messenger
You who have outraged all laws, and done
This dreadful crime; run, run away, Medea!
Take ship or chariot, and do not scorn their aid!

Medea
What have I done, that I should run away?

Messenger
The royal bride is dead, and with her   1060
Her father Creon; it was your poisons killed them.

Medea
You tell a glorious tale. From this time on
I'll number you among my friends and benefactors.

Messenger
Are you in your right mind? Have you gone insane,
To work the ruin of the royal house
And laugh, and not be afraid of what I tell you?

Medea
There is a great deal I could say
To answer you. Do not be hasty, friend,
But tell me how they died. My pleasure will
Be doubled, if their deaths were horrible.   1070

Messenger
When the two children, your sons, came with their father
And presented themselves at the house where the bride lived,
We servants, who sympathized with your misfortunes,
Were glad, and rumor soon buzzed about the house
That you had patched up the old quarrel with your husband.
Some kissed their hands, and some
Their golden heads; and I was so delighted
I followed the children to the women's quarters.
Our mistress—her we honor in your place—
Only had eyes for Jason, and didn't see   1080

The children, when they came in at first.
And then she turned her pretty head the other way,
Angry they should have been let in. But Jason
Tried to pacify her anger and resentment
And said, "You must not be at odds with friends.
Stop sulking, turn your head this way again;
You must believe your husband's friends are yours.
Accept their gifts, and supplicate your father
To reprieve the boys from exile, for my sake."
When she saw the finery, she couldn't hold out longer,   1090
But did everything he asked. Before the children
And their father had gone far outside the house
She took the pretty robe and put it on,
And set the golden crown around her curls,
Arranging them before a shining mirror
And smiling at her ghostly image there.
Then she stood up, and left the throne, and trod
Her white feet delicately round the room,
Delighted with the gifts, and every now and then
She made a leg and studied the effect.   1100
And then there was a sight that scared us all:
Her color goes, she stumbles sideways, back
Towards the throne, and hardly stops herself
From falling on the floor.
Then some old waiting maid, who must have thought
The fit was sent by Pan, or by some god,
Began to pray; and then she saw her mouth
All white with running froth, the eyeballs starting from
Their sockets, and her body pale and bloodless; and then
She screamed so loud the screaming drowned the prayer.   1110
Someone went straight away to fetch
Her father, someone to her new husband,
To tell them what was happening to the bride,
And the house rang everywhere with noise of running feet.
Already, in the time a practised runner
Could run a hundred yards, the princess
Recovered from her speechless, sightless swoon
And screamed in anguish. It was terrible;
From two directions the pain attacked her.
The golden circlet twining round her hair   1120
Poured forth a strange stream of devouring fire,
And the fine-spun robe, the gift your children gave her,
Had teeth to tear the poor girl's pretty skin.
She left the throne and fled burning through the room,
Shaking her head this way and that,
Trying to dislodge the crown, but it was fixed
Immovably, and when she shook her hair

The flames burnt twice as fiercely.
Then, overcome with pain, she fell to the ground.
Only her father would have recognized her.   1130
Her eyes had lost their settled look, her face
Its natural expression, and the blood
Dripped from her head to mingle with the fire.
The flesh dropped from her bones like pine-tears, torn
By the unseen power of the devouring poison,
We saw, and shuddered; no-one dared
To touch the corpse, we had her fate for warning.
But her old father, who knew nothing of what had happened,
Came running in, and flung himself on the body,
Began to weep, and flung his arms around her,   1140
And kissed her, crying "Oh, unhappy child,
What god has killed you so inhumanly?
Who takes you from me, from the grave of my
Old age? If I could die with you, my child!"
And then he stopped his tears and lamentations
And tried to raise his old body up again,
But clung fast to the robe, as ivy clings
To laurel branches. Then there was a ghastly struggle,
He trying to raise himself from off his knees,
She holding him down; and when he pushed her off   1150
He tore the aged flesh from off his bones.
And then he fought no more; the poor old man
Gave up the ghost, the struggle was too much for him.
The bodies of the princess and her father
Lie side by side, a monument to grief.
Your part in this affair is none of my business.
You will find your own escape from punishment.
Life is a shadow; I have thought so often,
And I am not afraid to say that those
Who seem wise among men, and accomplished talkers,   1160
Must pay the heaviest penalty of all.
No man is happy. He might grow more prosperous
Than other men, if fortune comes his way,
But happy he can never be.
[Exit.]

Chorus
This is the day of heaven's visitation
On Jason, and he has deserved it richly.
But we have only tears for your misfortune,
Poor child of Creon, who must go to Hades
Because of Jason's wedding.

Medea
Women, my task is fixed: as quickly as possible   1170
To kill my children and to fly this land,

And not by hesitation leave my sons
To die by other hands more merciless.
Whatever happens, they must die; and since they must,
I, who first gave them life, shall give them death.
Come, steel yourself, my heart; why do you hesitate
To do this dreadful thing which must be done?
Come, my unhappy hand, take up the sword
And go to where life's misery begins.
Do not turn coward; think not of your children,   1180
How much you loved them, how you bore them; no,
For this one day forget you are a mother;
Tomorrow you may weep. But though you kill them, yet
You love them still; and my poor heart is broken.
[She goes into the house.]

Chorus
Earth and all-seeing light of the Sun,
Look down, look down on a woman destroyed
Before she raises her murderous hand
Against her babes. From a golden age
Was she born, and we fear divine blood
Will be shed by mortals. Restrain her, great light   1190
Of heaven, hold her back, drag her forth from the house,
This accursed murderess driven by furies.
Did you toil for your sons in vain, did you labor
For nothing to bring your darlings to birth
When you left behind you the angry straits
Where ships are crushed in the grim grey rocks?
Why has their weight of anger fallen
Upon your heart, this lust for the kill?
The death of kindred is mortals' curse
And heaven sends sorrows meet for the murderers,   1200
Calamities falling upon the house.
[The CHILDREN *are heard screaming inside the house.]*
Do you hear them? Do you hear the children crying?
Oh wretched woman, woman possessed.

First child
What shall I do? How avoid my mother's hand?

Second child
I cannot tell, dear brother; we are dying.

Chorus
Shall we enter the house? We ought to stop
The murder of the children.

First child
Help us in heaven's name, in our necessity.

Second child
The sword is near, and death is closing round us.

Chorus
Woman, you must have a heart of stone   1210
Or iron, that can kill with your own hand
The fruit of your own womb.

One woman, one woman only
I have heard of before this time
Who laid hands on her darling children—
The heaven-demented Ino
Whom Hera made mad, and drove abroad.
And because of her children's dying
The wretched mother drowned,
Leaping from cliff to water   1220
To join her two sons in death.
What worse could the world still hold?
Oh, women, how many sorrows begin
In your bed; what a count of ills
You have brought to mankind already.
[Enter JASON.*]*

Jason
You women, standing close beside the house,
Is she indoors, Medea, that has done
This dreadful crime, or has she taken flight?
She needs must hide herself beneath the earth
Or raise herself on wings to heaven's height   1230
To escape the vengeance of the royal house.
How can she think, when she has killed the king,
That she can escape out of this house unharmed?
It is not her I am thinking of, but my sons;
I leave her to the people she has wronged,
But I am here to save my children's lives
For fear my kinsmen may intend some harm to me
In vengeance for the mother's bloody murder.

Chorus
Jason, you do not know the full extent
Of your sorrows, or you would not have spoken so.   1240

Jason
What is it? Does she want to kill me too?

Chorus
Your sons are dead; it was their mother killed them.

Jason
What do you say? You have destroyed me, woman.

Chorus
You have no children now; remember them.

Jason
Where did she kill them? In the house or outside?

Chorus
Unbar the door and you will see their bodies.

Jason
What are you waiting for, men? Unbar the doors,
Break them down, so that I may see this double blow,
My dead sons, and she whose blood will pay for theirs.
[MEDEA *appears above the roof of the house in a fiery chariot drawn by snakes, clasping
the bodies of her* CHILDREN.]

Medea
Why hammer on the doors, and try to unbar them,   1250
Seeking the bodies and their murderess?
No need of that. If you want anything from me,
Say what you wish; your hand will never touch me,
So strong the chariot my father's father,
The Sun, gave me to keep away my enemies.

Jason
Abomination! Woman more than any other
Hateful to heaven and to all mankind.
You dared, their mother, thrust the sword
Into their bodies, rob me of my sons,
And show yourself before the world when you   1260
Had done this foul and most abominable of murders?
You death must pay for this. Oh, now I know
What I did not see before, it was a fatal curse
To bring you from your foreign land to Greece,
Traitor to your father and the land that reared you.
The gods have turned your fury on my head.
You killed your own brother there at your hearthside
Before you set foot on our good ship's deck,
And that was your beginning; married to
The man you see before you, mother of his sons,   1270
Because I left you, you have killed your children.
There is no woman throughout Greece would dare
Do such a thing, and these I overlooked
To marry you, my ruin and my curse.
No woman, but a lioness, more fierce by nature
Than Tyrrhenian Scylla. I could go on abusing you
Forever, and not touch you; such hardness were you born with.
Go, foul woman, children's murderess;
My part to stay and weep for my misfortunes.

No new-wed bride with whom to share my joy,   1280
No children whom I fathered and brought up
To live with me; I have no children.

Medea
There is a great deal that I could have said
To answer you, if heaven did not know
How we have dealt with each other, you and I.
Did you think you could desert my marriage bed,
Make me your laughingstock, and still live happy?
Neither your queen nor Creon your new father
Could banish me from Corinth with impunity.
So call me lioness if you will, call me   1290
A Scylla haunting the Tyrrhenian rocks,
I tore your heart for you, and you deserved it.

Jason
You too have paid; you hurt yourself as much.

Medea
I do, but gain by it, so do not laugh.

Jason
Oh children, what a mother you have found.

Medea
Oh children, dying from your father's malady.

Jason
It was not my hand that killed them; do not say that.

Medea
No, your defiance, and your second marriage.

Jason
You make my marriage an excuse for murder?

Medea
You think it is a little thing for women?   1300

Jason
For decent women. You think bad of everything.

Medea
Your sons are dead, and this will tear your heart.

Jason
My sons live still as curses on your head.

Medea
The gods know who began this misery.

Jason
They know then your abominable mind.

Medea
You are detestable; I hate your bitter tongue.

Jason
I yours. We have an easy remedy, to part.

Medea
How then? What shall I do? I too am eager.

Jason
Give me my sons to bury and to mourn.

Medea
No! I shall bury them with my own hands,   1310
Taking them to the Mountain-Mother's shrine
To ensure their tomb will keep its dignity
Untouched by enemies. I will inaugurate
A solemn rite and festival in this land
Of Sisyphus, for future time to expiate
This impious murder; then I go to Erechtheus' land
To live with Aegeus, son of Pandion.
And you will meet the base death you deserve,
Crushed by a relic of your ship, the Argo,
Now you have wept the end of this new wedding.   1320

Jason
May Erinys and bloody Justice
Avenge the death of my children.

Medea
What god, what power, will listen to you,
False swearer, betrayer of friends?

Jason
Foul woman, children's murderess.

Medea
Go home, and bury your dead.

Jason
I go, with two sons to mourn for.

Medea
You will not miss them yet; wait till you are older.

Jason
My darling children.

Medea

Not yours but mine.

Jason

And yet you killed them.

Medea

To give you pain.

Jason

Oh, how I long to kiss   1330
The soft lips of my children.

Medea

You would fondle and talk to them now,
Then you rejected them.

Jason

In heaven's name let me feel
The soft touch of my children's bodies.

Medea

No, you are wasting your breath.
[Exit.]

Jason

Zeus, do you hear how she mocks me,
How she tortures me, this accursed
Lioness, slayer of children?
But with what little power is left me   1340
I call upon heaven to see
My sufferings, and summon the gods
To witness how she prevents me
From giving my children burial.
I wish I had never begot them
To see them destroyed by you.

Chorus

Many things are wrought by Zeus in Olympus
And heaven works much beyond human imagining.
The looked-for result will fail to materialize
While heaven finds ways to achieve the unexpected.   1350
So it has happened in this our story.

BACCHAE*

Euripides

CHARACTERS

DIONYSUS, *also called Bromius and Bacchus*

CHORUS, *Asian Bacchae, followers of Dionysus*

TEIRESIAS, *a blind seer*

CADMUS, *former king of Thebes*

PENTHEUS, *his grandson and present king*

A GUARD

A HERDSMAN

A MESSENGER

AGAVE, *daughter of Cadmus and mother of Pentheus*

SCENE

Before the king's palace in Thebes. Across from the gates, in the downstage area, is the tomb of Semele (DIONYSUS' mother), half-ruined and thickly covered with vine. Every now and then, a strand of smoke rises up out of the stones. Access to the city can be gained on all sides. Upstage left is the way to Mount Cithaeron.

There is a crash of thunder, followed by an eerie stillness, accentuated by the rustling of leaves. Out of it grows a distant drone of women's voices, and DIONYSUS appears.

He carries a thyrsus (a stick twined with ivy), and his scant dress, draped with animal skin, suggests the Orient. His flowing blond hair, cascading around his shoulders, and his lithe, smooth-skinned limbs complement the feline, almost feminine grace of his movements.

Dionysus
I, Dionysus, son of Zeus, am back in Thebes.   1
I was born here, of Semele, daughter of Cadmus,
blasted from her womb by a bolt of blazing thunder.
Why am I here? A god in the shape of a man,
walking by the banks of Ismenus, the waters of Dirce?
Look out there! That house in ruins,
still smoking, smoldering still with unquenchable flame,
is my mother's monument,
her thunder-dug grave,
undying evidence of spiteful Hera's rage.   10
Let's give some praise to Cadmus,

---

*Translation by Michael Cacoyannis.

817

who turned it into consecrated ground, a living temple
that I shrouded with clustering vine.
I left behind the gold-abounding lands
of Lydia and of Phrygia,
Persia's sun-beaten plains and Bactria's giant walls,
crossing the winter-scorched earth of the Medes
and the length of happy Arabia, in short,
all Asia down to its shimmering seashores
where Greeks and barbarians freely mingle   20
in teeming, shapely-towered cities,
and here I am. In Greece.
This is the first of its cities I visit.
I danced my way throughout the East,
spreading my rituals far and wide—a God
made manifest to men.
Of all Greek cities, Thebes is the one I chose
to rouse into a new awareness,
dressing Greek bodies in fawnskins,
planting the thyrsus in Greek hands,   30
my ivied spear.
My mother's sisters—
were there ever more unsisterly sisters—
gossiped that this Dionysus was no child of Zeus,
that Semele having slept with some man
proceeded—on Cadmus' cunning advice—
to attribute her sinful conception to God.
No wonder Zeus struck her dead, they would prattle,
taking a lover and brazenly lying!
Well! These sisters, all three,   40
I've stung into a frenzy and steered them
from their homes into the mountains,
where I left them raving. Complete of course
with full orgiastic trappings. What is more,
all the women of Thebes, but all,
I've sent stampeding out of doors. They're up there now,
milling with Cadmus' daughters under the fresh-smelling pines
or high upon the rocks. This town must learn,
even against its will, how much it costs
to scorn God's mysteries and to be purged.   50
So shall I vindicate my virgin mother
and reveal myself to mortals as a God,
the son of God.
Now hear this.
King Cadmus has conferred the powers of his throne
with all attending honors on his grandson, Pentheus.
This God-fighting upstart snubs me; banishes my name
from public sacrifice and private prayer.

He'll soon find out, and every Theban with him,
whose birthright is divine and whose is not.   60
Once that score is settled, I'll move on
to manifest myself in other lands. But should this town,
in blind anger, take up arms to drive my Bacchae from the hills,
I'll give them war,
leading my women's army to the charge.
To this end,
I have disguised myself as a mortal,
adopting the ways and features of a man.
[*The* CHORUS OF ASIAN BACCHAE *appears during the following lines, coming from
the same direction as* DIONYSUS. *They wear fawnskins and garlands of ivy leaves and
flowers twined around their necks. Apart from the thyrsus, several carry skin drums of
various shapes, which they beat as the action—or their emotion—requires*]
You! Women of Tmolus, Lydia's towering mountain,
my band of initiates, you,   70
whom I unplucked from your primitive lands
to be my road companions and my friends,
raise up your native Phrygian drums
that pulse to rhythms that are mother earth's and mine.
Surround the royal home of Pentheus with your beat
and turn the city out to see. Meanwhile,
I'll make my way to those Cithaeron slopes
that seethe with Theban Bacchae
and join their dance.
[DIONYSUS *goes off toward Mount Cithaeron to a rising crescendo of drumbeats*]

Chorus
Out of the heart of Asia   80
down from the sacred heights of Tmolus
have I come. For the God—
Bromius, Bacchus, Dionysus—
fatigue is sweet to the limbs,
and effortless effort the trek
when you are shouting with joy.
Who is there in the street? Who?
Who is lurking in the house? Stand still,
stand back and hold your breath,
while I chant a prayer immemorial,   90
in praise of Dionysus.
Oh, happy the man who, blessed by his knowledge of God,
discovers purity.
Who opens his heart to togetherness.
Who joins in mountain-dancing
and sacred cleansing rituals. He,
who sanctifies the orgies of Cybele,
the mother of fertility,

waving the thyrsus high,
crowning his head with ivy,   100
in honor of Dionysus.
Go, Bacchae, go, go, go! Bring
God's godly son—our Bromius—
down from the Phrygian hills
out into the spacious streets of Greece—
the home of Dionysus.
Him,
whom his mother carried
to premature and painful birth
when in a crash of thunder   110
she was death-struck by a fiery bolt.
But quicker than death,
Zeus swept him up and plunged him
into a makeshift womb—
secure from Hera's eyes—
in the thick of his thigh,
stitched with stitches of gold.
As time ripened into fate
he delivered the bull-horned God
and crowned him with a crown of serpents.   120
Thus was created the custom
for thyrsus-carrying maenads
to twine snakes in their hair.

Oh, Thebes, Semele's nurse,
crest your walls with ivy.
Burst into greenness, burst
into a blaze of bryony,
take up the bacchanalian beat
with branches of oak and of fir,
cover your flesh with fawnskin   130
fringed with silver-white fleece
and lifting the fennel,
touch God
in a fit of sanctified frenzy.
Then all at once, the whole land will dance!
Bacchus will lead the dancing throngs to the mountain,
the mountain,
which is home to that mob of women,
who rebelled against shuttle and loom
answering the urge   140
of Dionysus.

Oh holy heights of Crete
cradling the caves of the Curetes

where Zeus was born.
There, the triple-crested Corybantes
traced in vibrant skin
the circle of my joy.
They married its percussive strength
to the wailing sweetness of flutes,
then put it into Rhea's hands   150
to draw the earth-beat out
and make it throb in Bacchic song.
In time, the frenzied Satyrs
from the Mother-Goddess stole the drum
and struck up dances for the feasts,
held every second year,
to honor and give joy to Dionysus.

How sweet to the body, when
breaking loose from the mountain revels
you collapse to the ground in a fawnskin   160
after hunting the goat.
How sweet the kill—
the fresh-smelling blood—
the sacramental relishing
of raw flesh . . .

Oh Asia, great mother,
my distant mountain home!
How the mind races back
to those peaks that clang in glory,
of Bromius, evoë . . .   170
Your ground flows with milk,
flows with wine, flows with nectar from the bees.
Like smoke from a Syrian incense,
the fragrant God arises with his torch of pine.
He runs, he dances in a whirl of flame,
he rouses the faithful
crazing their limbs with his roar,
while he races the wind,
his soft hair streaming behind.
And his call resounds like thunder: 180
"Go, my bacchae, go!
Let Tmolus with its golden streams
reverberate with songs of Dionysus,
and the vibrant crash of drums.
Sing out in joy
with loud Phrygian cries,
while the holy sweet-throated flute
climbs the holy scale and the scaling maenads climb

up the mountain,
the mountain."   190

It is then, that a girl like me
knows happiness. When she is free,
like a filly playfully prancing
around its mother,
in fields without fences.

[*The* CHORUS *withdraws silently to one side as* TEIRESIAS *enters, ivy-crowned and with
a fawnskin over his shoulders. His festive dress seems oddly out of step with his old age
and ascetic bearing. Being blind, he carries a staff, tipped with ivy leaves*]

Teiresias
Who is at the gates? Go call Cadmus out,
Cadmus, son of Agenor who sailed from distant Sidon
to build the fortress walls of Thebes.
Just say Teiresias wants him. He already knows
why I am here. We made a pact, he and I   200
—old me with him who is older still—
to take up the thyrsus, put on our fawnskins
and top them with garlands of twirling ivy.

[CADMUS *comes out of the palace, forestalling the* GUARD *who is about to call him. Like*
TEIRESIAS, *he is very old and looks equally incongruous in his Dionysiac garb*]

Cadmus
Dear friend! I knew you were here by the sound of your voice,
the voice of wisdom that makes a wise man welcome.
I come to you ready, dressed to please God,
as indeed I should, for is not Dionysus
my own daughter's son? Now that mankind has seen his light
we must do our very best to exalt him. So!
Where should we dance? Where do we fling a leg   210
and toss our grizzly heads? It is for you
to guide me, Teiresias, though you be as ancient as I.
Initiation is your job. I'll never tire night or day,
of thumping the ground with my thyrsus. Oh, what bliss
to forget how very old one is!

Teiresias
You speak the way I feel. Young again
and just as tempted to try a little dance.

Cadmus
You don't think that a carriage—for the mountains—
would be more sensible?

Teiresias
Indeed, no.   220
That would diminish our respect for the God.

Cadmus
Then let me, being older, be your nursemaid, old man.

Teiresias
We'll let the God lead us. No need to exert ourselves.

Cadmus
Are we the only men in Thebes to dance to Bacchus?

Teiresias
The only ones with healthy minds. The rest are sick.

Cadmus
We are wasting time. Here, take my hand.

Teiresias
And you take mine. There, get a good grip.

Cadmus
After all, who am I, a mortal, to put down the Gods?

Teiresias
Only fools play speculative games with the Gods.
But we, we cling to what we learned from our fathers,   230
beliefs that are as old as time and as immune
to the onslaught of words, no matter how clever the theory,
how complex the argument, the human mind can invent.
No doubt people will say it's a disgrace—
an old man like me, dancing, with ivy in my hair.
Well, let them! Who ever heard of God
segregating the young from the old,
saying these should dance and these should not?
He expects to be honored by one and all,
not by degrees or in sections.   240

Cadmus
Teiresias, you cannot see the light
so let my words enlighten you.
I see Pentheus, the son of Echion, to whom
I've handed over all powers of state,
rushing toward the palace.
How wild he looks! There's something in the wind.
Let's hear.
[PENTHEUS *bursts onto the stage, accompanied by his military guard. He is about the same age as Dionysus, whom he resembles in looks but little else. Austerely dressed, he is as angular in his masculinity as he is strident when, as now, he is in a rage. He does not notice* CADMUS *and* TEIRESIAS, *who have crept out of his way]*

Pentheus
What an unholy mess!

No sooner does one venture on a journey,
than rumor plagues the town and things get out of hand.   250
Our women, I am told, have left their homes,
in a religious trance—what travesty!—
and scamper up and down the wooded mountains, dancing
in honor of this newfangled God, Dionysus,
whoever he may be.
In the middle of each female group
of revelers, I hear,
stands a jar of wine, brimming! and that taking turns,
they steal away, one here, one there, to shady nooks,
where they satisfy the lechery of men,   260
pretending to be priestesses,
performing their religious duties. Ha!
That performance reeks more of Aphrodite than of Bacchus.
The ones I have already caught are being guarded, manacled
and safely locked behind bars. The others, still at large,
I shall thrash out of the mountains, the lot,
including my own mother, Agave, and her sisters
Ino and Autonoe, I'll clap them into irons, I swear,
I'll put a stop to this orgiastic filth!
The other news   270
is that some stranger has arrived in town,
a sorcerer from Lydia, a conjurer of sorts,
with golden scented hair tumbling down to his shoulders,
a skin that glows like wine, and eyes
that promise Aphrodite's secret charms.
He spends his nights and days with girls, I hear,
enticing them with his Bacchic witchcraft.
Just let me catch him hanging round these streets,
and his thyrsus-tapping, hair-tossing days are over.
His body will be looking for his head.   280
He is the one who spreads the tale
that Dionysus is a God,
hatched from the thigh of Zeus,
in which he had been sewn. As if we didn't know
the truth about Dionysus and his liar of a mother,
both of them burned to a cinder by a bolt of flame
hurled by Zeus, her so-called bedmate.
Foul-mouthed foreigner! His tongue will earn him
the foulest punishment my power can pronounce.
Death by hanging! Let him be warned, whoever he may be.   290
[*He turns to go and sees* TEIRESIAS *first, then* CADMUS]
Ye Gods! What new marvel have we here? Teiresias,
the prophet, all dolled up in spotted skins!
And my mother's father—how grotesque—
playing bacchant with his wand and all!

I am ashamed, sir! How can a man so old
be so devoid of sense!
Take off that ivy, will you?
And drop that thyrsus. Now! Do you hear?
This is all *your* doing, Teiresias! Using him,
to launch this new God to the masses.   300
Convenient, isn't it? Give religion a boost
and prophets grow fat, raking in the profits
from reading the stars and fire-magic.
You can thank your white hairs for being here and not in prison,
chained with those raving females; just the place for frauds
who encourage their obnoxious rituals. Take my word,
when women are allowed to feast on wine, there is no telling
to what lengths their filthy minds will go!

Chorus
The blasphemy of the man! Who are you
to think you can insult the Gods? Or Cadmus,   310
who sowed the seed from which you sprang?
Are you so bent on shaming your father's house?

Teiresias
When a sensible man
has a good cause to defend, to be eloquent
is no great feat. Your tongue is so nimble
one might think you had some sense, but your words
contain none at all. The powerful man
who matches insolence with glibness is worse than a fool.
He is a public danger!
This new God whom you dismiss,   320
no words of mine can attain
the greatness of his coming power in Greece. Young man,
two are the forces most precious to mankind.
The first is Demeter, the Goddess.
She is the Earth—or any name you wish to call her—
and she sustains humanity with solid food.
Next came the son of the virgin, Dionysus,
bringing the counterpart to bread, wine
and the blessings of life's flowing juices.
His blood, the blood of the grape,   330
lightens the burden of our mortal misery.
When, after their daily toils, men drink their fill,
sleep comes to them, bringing release from all their troubles.
There is no other cure for sorrow. Though himself a God,
it is his blood we pour out
to offer thanks to the Gods. And through him,
we are blessed.
You mock the legend

of his being stitched inside the thigh of Zeus!
Let me teach you how legends are born.   340
When Zeus snatched the infant God out of the flames
and lifted him to Olympus, Hera, his wife,
schemed to have him thrown out of heaven. But Zeus,
with typical God's wit, devised his own counterplot.
He tore some pieces off the sky that envelopes the earth,
and presented them to nagging Hera
as the salvaged limbs of the child,
while he rushed the real Dionysus to safety.
Men, however, through retelling a story,
often wander from the truth. In time,   350
out of a mere play of words, grew this myth,
that the child had been salvaged *in* the limbs of Zeus.
This God is also a prophet. Possession by his ecstasy,
his sacred frenzy, opens the soul's prophetic eyes.
Those whom his spirit takes over completely
often with frantic tongues foretell the future.
His power even stretches to the realm of war.
You can see an army, positioned and ready for battle,
drop their spears and run for their lives
crazed out of their wits, by the grace of Dionysus.   360
A day will come when you shall see him
straddling the rocks of Delphi amid a blaze of torches,
leaping from peak to peak, swinging and hurling high
his thyrsus, the emblem of his glory
acclaimed throughout Greece. So Pentheus,
listen to me. Do not mistake the rule of force
for true power. Men are not shaped by force.
Nor should you boast of wisdom, when everyone but you
can see how sick your thoughts are. Instead,
welcome this God to Thebes. Exalt him with wine,   370
garland your head and join the Bacchic revels.
It's not for Dionysus to force women to be modest.
As in all things, moderation depends on our nature.
Remember this! No amount of Bacchic revels
can corrupt an honest woman.
Also, remember your own deep pleasure
when the crowds swarm outside your gates
and shout glory to your name.
Why should not *he*
be glad to have his name exalted?   380
I say he is.
So I—and Cadmus, whom you ridicule—
will wear our ivy crowns and will dance.
Old as we are, I promise you we'll dance.
And nothing you can ever say will make me

turn against the Gods. For you are sick,
possessed by madness so perverse, no drug can cure,
no madness can undo.

Chorus
Your words, old man,
most wisely balance 390
respect for the Gods.
Without shaming Apollo
you honor our Bromius, as a great God.
[CADMUS *approaches* PENTHEUS, *carefully trying to humor him*]

Cadmus
My boy, Teiresias has advised you well.
Stay close to us! Don't step outside the rules.
Just now you were up in the air, not thinking,
but thinking that you were. For even if you are right
and this God is not a God, why say it?
Why not call him one?
You have everything to gain from such a lie 400
that makes Semele, your aunt, the mother of a God.
Think what an honor for the whole family!
Remember Actaeon, my Actaeon, what a miserable end he came to—
my own grandson, torn limb from limb, in this very same valley
by the meat-devouring hounds that he himself had reared,
for the price of one boast: that he
was a better hunter than Artemis.
Don't risk the same fate. Here,
let me put this ivy on your head.
Join us in paying homage to Dionysus! 410
[PENTHEUS *swings around, knocking the thyrsus out of* CADMUS' *hand. The old man
staggers and falls to the ground*]

Pentheus
Keep your hands off me! Go! Run to your Bacchic revels.
I want none of your senile folly
rubbing off on me! As for him,
your tutor in idiocy, I'll deal with him.
Run, someone, straight to this man's lair,
his rock of prophecy. Dig it up with crowbars,
topple it, tear the stones from their sockets,
smash it into dust.
Throw his holy emblems to the winds, the drunken winds.
That will sting him to the quick. The rest of you, 420
scour the city, find this effeminate stranger
who afflicts our women with this new disease
and who befouls our beds. And when you catch him,
drag him here in chains.

He'll taste the people's justice when he's stoned to death,
regretting every bitter moment of his fun in Thebes.
[The GUARDS run off in several directions]

Teiresias
Poor fool! You don't know what you are saying.
You were out of your mind before. Now you are stark mad.
Come, Cadmus. The two of us will go and pray
both for this man—undeserving monster though he is—   430
and for Thebes, that the God might spare us all
from some new calamity. Take up your thyrsus
and follow me. Try to support me and I'll support you.
It would be a shocking sight, two old men
sharing one fall! But never mind. Anything
so long as Dionysus, son of Zeus, is served.
Oh Cadmus, Pentheus is another name for grief.
Watch over your house, for grief is stalking in his steps.
This is not prophecy but blatant fact.
You can tell a dangerous fool by his own words.   440
[TEIRESIAS and CADMUS exit as PENTHEUS strides into the palace]

Chorus
Holiness, power all transcending
soaring higher than the Gods
yet floating down on golden wings
to touch the earth, do you hear this man?
Do you hear the blasphemy
of Pentheus the unholy, hurled at Semele's son,
my Bromius, whom the garlanded Gods
when they feast on his bounty and his beauty
rate first among the first?

He is life's liberating force.   450
He is release of limbs and communion through dance.
He is laughter and music in flutes.
He is repose from all cares—he is sleep!
When his blood bursts from the grape
and flows across tables laid in his honor
to fuse with our blood,
he gently, gradually, wraps us in shadows
of ivy-cool sleep.

The unbridled tongue,
the arrogant frenzy of fools,   460
lead headlong to disaster.
But the tranquil life
of the wisely content
is anchored in rock and protects

the home from the storm.
The Gods may be far.
Yet, out of the hazy heavens,
they observe the ways of men.
Knowledge is not wisdom.
A knowing mind that ignores its own limits   470
has a very short span. And the man
who aims too high
never reaps what lies within his grasp.
Such is the folly—
and I know none worse—
of perversely ambitious, fanatical men.
Oh, to be in Cyprus,
the island-home of Aphrodite,
where the spirits of love
thrill the blood of men with magic breezes.   480
Or in that mythical land of the many-mouthed river
whose floods make deserts bloom.
Or where the muses play, Pieria,
whose peerless beauty
lovingly hugs the slopes of Olympus.
Oh, Bromius, my Bromius take me there!
Pave the way with romp and with prayer,
to the land of the Graces,
the land of Desire!
Where freedom is law   490
and women can revel with Bacchus.

The divine son of Zeus rejoices in festivity.
Of all his loves, the first is Peace,
the great benefactress
who cherishes the lives of young men.
He gives to the poor as he gives to the rich
the sorrow-killing drug of wine.
He hates only those who spurn
the daylight joys and the night's delights
that make life rich. How prudent   500
to keep one's heart and mind
away from those who think they know all.
Give me the simple wisdom and faith
of ordinary people. And I will make it mine.
[PENTHEUS *steps out of the palace, as several guards enter, leading* DIONYSUS. *His hands are shackled*]

Guard
Pentheus, here we are. All that you asked is done.
We hunted down the prey you sent us out to catch.

An easy job, I have to own. You see,
the animal was tame, sir. Made no attempt to run,
just stood there, very friendly, holding out his hands.
He didn't flinch or lose that flush   510
of wine-glow in his cheeks, but always smiling urged us
to tie him up and turn him in. He even stepped right up—
to save me from the trouble. That made me feel ashamed
and I mumbled: "Look, stranger, this is not my doing.
I'm just a soldier carrying out the orders of the king."
But there is more. Those raving women
that you'd clapped in chains
and locked up in your prison—
well, sir, they're gone,
they're on the loose, prancing their way into the glens,   520
laughing and calling Bacchus, their chosen God.
The chains around their feet just fell apart,
the prison doors unbarred themselves,
untouched by human hand. If you ask me,
this stranger who has come to Thebes,
is capable of many miracles.
I had my say.
The rest is up to you.

Pentheus
Untie his hands.
Now I have him in my net, no amount of agile tricks   530
can help him slip away.
[The GUARDS *unshackle* DIONYSUS' *hands and step aside, clearing the stage for the confrontation]*
So! You cut a handsome figure, I'll give you that!
Quite tempting—
I mean to women—the object, I don't doubt,
of your presence here in Thebes.
Your curls are soft!
A bit too long for wrestling, but very pretty
the way they hug your cheeks, so lovingly.
And what fair skin you have, so well looked-after!
But then, you don't expose it to the sun, do you?   540
You like the darker places,
where you can hunt desire with your beauty.
Now then! To start with, where are you from?

Dionysus
That's easy to answer, though nothing to boast of.
You must have heard of Mount Tmolus,
famous for its flowers.

Pentheus
So I have. It rings the city of Sardis.

Dionysus
I come from there. Lydia is my country.

Pentheus
Where did you learn these orgiastic rituals
that you bring to Greece?   550

Dionysus
Dionysus initiated me.
He is the son of Zeus.

Pentheus
Which Zeus? A native of those parts,
who coins new Gods?

Dionysus
No. The same Zeus who married Semele
in these parts of yours.

Pentheus
Did he possess you in your sleep
or by appearing to your eyes?

Dionysus
Face to face. He shared his mysteries with me.

Pentheus
What lies behind these mysteries, according to you?   560

Dionysus
That only the initiated may know.

Pentheus
And those who *are* initiated,
what are the benefits they gain?

Dionysus
You may not hear. Though you would gain by knowing.

Pentheus
A crafty answer, baited to sting my curiosity.

Dionysus
Wrong. Our mysteries abhor the probing ears of impious men.

Pentheus
This God you saw, or that you say you saw, what is he like?

Dionysus
Like the likeness of his choice. Not mine.

Pentheus
Another devious answer and devoid of sense.

Dionysus
What makes no sense is talking sense to a fool.   570

Pentheus
Is this the first place to which you've brought your God?

Dionysus
Throughout the Orient, people celebrate his dance.

Pentheus
I believe it. Next to the Greeks,
they're all barbarians.

Dionysus
In this, they're more civilized.
The standards differ.

Pentheus
Do you perform your mysteries
during the day or by night?

Dionysus
Mostly by night.
The dark is more conducive to worship.   580

Pentheus
You mean to lechery and bringing out the filth in women.

Dionysus
Those who look for filth, can find it at the height of noon.

Pentheus
You're going to pay for that rash, perverted mouth of yours.

Dionysus
And you for being a crass and ignorant blasphemer.

Pentheus
Oho! Our Bacchus-fiend is getting bold!
Crossing swords with words, not bad!

Dionysus
Do tell me how you'll punish me.
What torture have you in mind?

Pentheus
First, I'll chop your dainty curls off. At the roots!

Dionysus
My hair is holy. I grow it long for God.   590
[*Unable to carry out his threat,* PENTHEUS *takes another tack, trying to reestablish his authority*]

Pentheus
Next, you'll hand that thyrsus over. Now!

Dionysus
Come and take it yourself.
I hold it in the name of Dionysus.
[DIONYSUS *holds out his thyrsus, but* PENTHEUS *cannot move. In his impotence, he flings empty threats at him*]

Pentheus
Last—I'll have you bodily removed.
I'll throw you in my dungeons.

Dionysus
The God himself will set me free. I only have to ask him.

Pentheus
If you can get those raving bacchants to invoke him with you,
perhaps he will materialize!

Dionysus
He's here now. He sees what is being done to me.

Pentheus
Where *is* he? To me he's quite invisible.   600

Dionysus
Where I am. Your lack of faith has blurred your vision.

Pentheus
[*to the* GUARDS, *beside himself*]
Seize him! He's mocking me and he is mocking Thebes.

Dionysus
Let fools be warned. Place no chains on me.

Pentheus
And I say chain him. I am the only power here.

Dionysus
You do not know what your life is
or what you do, or who you are.

Pentheus
I am Pentheus, son of Echion. And Agave.

Dionysus
To boast of that name is to court your own doom.

Pentheus
Away with him!
Lock him up inside the stables, within my easy reach.   610

Let him wallow in the murky darkness that he loves
and dance his head off!
As for these women,
your fellow travelers and your accomplices in evil,
I'll either have them sold as slaves
or put their hands to different work. At my looms!
That will stop them thumping those infernal drums.
[DIONYSUS holds out his hands, encouraging the GUARDS to manacle them]

Dionysus
I shall go. But nothing fateful, that is not my fate,
can come to me.
As for you, Dionysus himself, whose Godship you deny,   620
will call you to account for your outrageous conduct.
When you lay hands on me, it is *him* you put in prison.
[The GUARDS lead DIONYSUS away. PENTHEUS exits]

Chorus
O Dirce, nymph of the sacred stream
sprung from the mighty river, Achelöus.
Once in your crystalline pools
you cradled the infant God,
snatched by Zeus, his father,
from the mouth of the living flame.
And the father cried: "Come, Dithyrambus,
born to be reborn from this male womb of mine!   630
I name you Bacchus. And Thebes
will someday know you by that name."
Why then, merciful Dirce,
when I come to you with garlands
and group-binding love, do you turn away?
Why do you spurn me? Hound me?
I swear by the clustered grape,
you will learn to care for him,
who is Bromius, great in the East.

What fury, what venomous fury   640
rages in Pentheus,
the earthborn and earthbound,
spawned by the sperm of the snake!
No man,
but a monster caged up in a man,
leaping through eyes of blood
to strike at the kill,
a vicious dwarf with giant dreams
pitting his strength against the Gods.
Soon, too soon, I fear   650
he will bind me with chains,

me, who am bound to Bacchus with freedom.
He has plunged my comrade,
my leader in the dance,
in the black depths of his dungeon.
Oh Dionysus, son of God,
do you see our sufferings?
Do you see your faithful
in helpless agony before the oppressor?   660
Oh lord, come down from Olympus.
Shake your golden thyrsus
and stifle the murderer's insolent fury.
Where are you, God?
Leading your band of revelers
through the wilds of Nysa,
haven of free-roaming beasts?
On the towering crags of Corycia?
Or in the secret glens of Olympus,
where Orpheus once, making music with his lyre,
gathered the trees around him,   670
gathered the spellbound beasts?

Oh happy, happy Pieria!
Bacchus honors you.
He will come to you with dances,
crossing the swirling torrents of Axios,
waving the whirling maenads on
across the mighty banks of Lydias,
bountiful father of rivers,
into that land of gushing waters,
blessed with the grace of its horses   680
and the fertile beauty of its pastures.
[As the CHORUS falls silent, a voice is heard—that of DIONYSUS—calling as if from the
guts of the earth. Agitated, the CHORUS scatters around the stage]

Dionysus
Io! Hear me! Oh, my bacchae!
Do you hear my cry? Io, my bacchae! Io!

Chorus
Who calls? Where does it come from, this cry,
calling in the voice of Dionysus?

Dionysus
Io! Io! Again I cry to you—
I, the son of Semele and of Zeus.

Chorus
Io, Io, lord! Our lord!
Come to us, come to your loving companions,

your group of worshipers.   690
Oh, Bromius, Bromius!

Dionysus
Earthquake almighty,
shake the floor of the world!
*[The stage grows dark. A low rumble is heard, building in intensity, until everything
seems to be reeling. The* CHORUS *sways and stumbles, crazed with fear]*

Chorus
Ah, look!
The palace of Pentheus is trembling!
It's reeling! It will collapse!
Dionysus is within the walls! Kneel to him!
The stones of the pillars are cracking!
They're crashing to the ground!
Bromius is here! Blasting the roof with his laughter!   700

Dionysus
Let the blazing bolt of lightning strike!
Burn down the palace of Pentheus! Burn it down!
*[A flash of lightning is followed by a crash of thunder, and flames leap up from Semele's
tomb]*

Chorus
Ah! Ah!
Over there, do you see?
Look how the fire leaps
out of Semele's holy tomb!
How the lurking flame
left there once by the bolt of Zeus,
springs to life!
Down, trembling maenads. Fling your bodies to the ground.   710
He rises from the ruins
of the once-mighty house,
that he himself has laid to dust.
Here he comes, the son of God.
[The women fling themselves to the ground, covering their heads. As the lights build up,
DIONYSUS *comes out of the palace and threads his way among them, helping them rise]*

Dionysus
Women of Asia, my barbarians!
Why are you cowering, trembling, on the ground?
I know! It seems you saw, as I did,
how Bacchus shook the palace of Pentheus.
But come! Rise to your feet.
Shed the fear from your limbs.   720

Chorus
Light of lights, oh leader of our holy dance!

What joy to see your face!
Without you, I was lost.

Dionysus
Have you so little faith as to despair
the moment I was led to Pentheus' murky prison?

Chorus
What else could I do?
Who would be there to protect me
if some misfortune came to you? But tell us,
how did you escape that godless man?

Dionysus
It was easy.   730
I freed myself without undue exertion!

Chorus
But were your hands not shackled?

Dionysus
Ah! There I had him, made him look an utter fool.
All the while that he was thinking he was binding *me*,
me he didn't even touch! He fed on pure illusion.
You see, in the stable where he held me,
in strictest isolation, as he thought,
he came upon a bull and straightaway
tried to bind it by the hooves and knees.
He was panting with rage, sending showers of sweat   740
flying off his body, digging teeth into his lips,
while I sat quietly by and watched. Just then,
out of nowhere, Bacchus came and shook the palace,
setting his mother's tomb ablaze with flames.
Seeing this and thinking that the palace was on fire,
Pentheus went rushing around in circles,
shouting to his slaves to carry water from the river.
Every hand was put to the toil—for nothing!
Then, afraid I had escaped, he stopped his labors,
drew his sinister sword and charged toward the palace.   750
In that very instant, Dionysus—
I'm presuming it was he, I can but guess—
planted in his path a ghost,
uncannily resembling me.
Pentheus lunged at it, slashing the luminous air
and thinking with relish that he was killing me.
But that's not all the God had in store for him!
To demolish his pride even further,
he brought the palace crashing down onto the stables.
burying them beneath a heap of rubble, a sight to make   760

my imprisonment bitter to him.
Sheer exhaustion has now made him drop his sword.
He is prostrate—as any man should be,
who dares to wage a war with God.
As for me, I calmly walked out of the palace,
to join you here,
without another thought for Pentheus.
But wait! I think I hear his footsteps, stamping through the court.
His lordship threatens to emerge. I wonder what he'll say after this!
Let him stir up a storm. He shall not ruffle me.   770
A wise man knows restraint. His strength is his detachment.
[PENTHEUS *enters furiously*]

Pentheus
It's an outrage! He's got away! From *me!*
That stranger,
that man I'd clapped in chains.
[*He spots* DIONYSUS *among the* CHORUS]
Ha! There he is!
What is the meaning of all this?
How did you escape?
How dare you show your face outside my doors?

Dionysus
Get hold of yourself! Tread lightly or you'll trip.

Pentheus
How did you get here? How did you escape?   780

Dionysus
Did I not tell you—or did you not hear—
that somebody would set me free?

Pentheus
Who? Can you only talk in empty riddles?

Dionysus
He who makes the clustering vine
grow for mankind.

Pentheus
You mean he who drives our women from their homes!

Dionysus
For that splendid insult, I'm sure Dionysus thanks you.

Pentheus
Seal off the city.
Go around the towers and bolt all gates!

Dionysus
Whatever for?   790
Can't Gods jump higher than your city's walls?

Pentheus
You're clever—very clever—
except where it counts.

Dionysus
It's where it counts the most that I am clever.
However, listen first to this man,
who comes from the mountains.
He brings you news!
We shall wait here. No, we shall not run away, I promise!
[A HERDSMAN *enters from the direction of Mount Cithaeron. He is panting with
fatigue and excitement*]

Herdsman
Pentheus, ruler of Thebes, my king,
I come straight from Cithaeron,   800
leaving behind its craggy slopes, where dazzling snowdrifts
never melt!

Pentheus
That you've come, we know. Now get on with your message.

Herdsman
I saw them. The Bacchae. Those raving women
who, stung by holy frenzy, went darting off into the wilds
in a flurry of bare feet.
I couldn't wait to tell you, King,
you and everyone in Thebes, the weird,
the awesome things they do, miraculous beyond belief.
But, first, I want to know. Can I speak freely, frankly,   810
of their goings on, or must I trim my tongue?
Truth is, I'm a little scared of your lordship.
You're so impatient, so fierce of temper—
just like a king, only more.

Pentheus
Speak on. No matter what you tell me,
it's not you that I shall blame. Besides,
to penalize a man for telling you the truth,
is wrong. But the more harrowing your tale about the Bacchae,
the more crushing the punishment that I shall inflict
upon that man who put our women up   820
to these vicious new tricks.

Herdsman
The sun's first rays had just begun

to spill their warmth upon the earth,
and I was steering my cattle up the slopes
to the pastures near the ridge, when suddenly
I see three bands of women—resting from their dance.
Autonoe at the head of one,
Ino of another,
and Agave, your mother, of the third—all fast asleep,   830
wherever exhaustion had dropped them;
some with heads lying back on pillowy branches,
others stretched out on beds of matted oak leaves,
but modestly, serenely, sir, not the way you think.
They were not drunk with wine,
or seduced by the music of flutes,
so they'd be in raptures,
or chasing wild erotic pleasures in the woods.
But then, your mother, alerted by the lowing
of our horned bulls, sprang up,
and with a ringing cry urged the Bacchae   840
to rouse themselves from sleep. And they,
shedding the bloom of sleep from their eyes, nimbly rose—
a sight miraculously orderly and graceful—
women young and old, and girls as yet unmarried.
First, they let their hair fall down their shoulders
and those whose fawnskins had come loose
fastened them up, while others girdled theirs
with snakes that licked their cheeks. Some,
mothers with newborn babies left at home,
cradled young gazelles or wild wolf cubs in their arms   850
and fed them at their full-blown breasts
that brimmed with milk.
Then they wreathed their heads with shoots
of ivy, oak and flowering bryony.
One of them lifted a thyrsus, struck a rock
and water gushed from it as cool as mountain snow.
Another drove a stick into the ground
and at the bidding of the God,
wine came bubbling up.
Those who wanted milk   860
just scratched the soil lightly with their fingers
and white streams flowed, while from their ivy-crested wands
sweet honey dripped like sparkling dew.
Oh, King,
if you had been there and had seen,
you would have offered grateful prayers to the God
you now denounce.
Well, we cowherds and shepherds of those parts
got together and discussed these marvels,

these awesome things we had witnessed. 870
And one of our crowd, one who's always sneaking up to town,
very smooth with words, held forth to us and said:
"You people living in these holy glens,
what do you say we hunt Agave out,
drag her away from her orgies and do a service to the king, her son?"
He talked good sense, we thought, so we hid ourselves
low among the thickets, waiting in ambush.
At a given hour, all the Bacchae
shook the thyrsus for the revels to start
and their voices joined into a single cry: 880
"Iacchus, son of Zeus, oh Bromius, evoë."
And the whole mountain reeled,
possessed by their ecstatic dance,
and the beasts too and the trees,
suddenly everything but everything
was on the move. Then, quite by chance,
Agave came whirling past me, and I,
leaping out from my cover in the bushes,
tried to seize her. But she called out, yelling:
"Come, my fleet-footed hounds! 890
We're being hunted by these men! Take up your thyrsus
and follow, follow me!" At this, we fled
and barely escaped being torn to pieces
by these God-struck maenads.
But our cattle—
our herds grazing on the grassy slopes—oh!
They fell upon them with their naked hands.
You could see a woman sink her nails into a cow,
with its udders full, and lift it, bellowing, high above her head.
Others dragged young heifers, ripping them apart. 900
Everywhere you looked,
ribs and cloven hooves
were flying through the air.
And from the pine branches
dangled lumps of flesh that dripped with blood. Majestic bulls,
one minute aiming their horns with all their furious pride,
the next were stumbling to the ground,
overwhelmed by the swarming hands of girls,
their bones stripped clean of all their flesh,
faster than you could blink your royal eyes. 910
Then, taking off with sudden speed, like birds,
they swooped down the hillside to the flatlands—
fattened with crops by the river Asopos—
and like a rampaging army they burst into the villages
that nestle in Cithaeron's foothills.
They ransacked everything in sight.

They snatched young children out of homes,
carried them on their shoulders along with other plunder
and everything stayed put, without being tied. Nothing,
not even bronze or iron, fell to the somber earth.   920
Flames flickered in their hair and did not burn them.
The villagers, enraged, of course, by all this havoc,
took arms against the Bacchae. Then,
what a spectacle, my king, how eerie!
Their pointed spears drew no blood,
while the women, just hurling the thyrsus,
opened wounds, the women, sir, turned men to flight!
That could not have been without some godly power.
They went back then
to the haunts from which they started,   930
those fountains which their God had sprung for them.
They washed their bodies clean of blood
and from their cheeks, the serpents licked away the stains.
Oh, my king, this God, whoever he may be,
is powerful in many things. It was he,
so they say, who gave to us, poor mortals,
the gift of wine, that numbs all sorrows.
If wine should ever cease to be,
then so will love.
No pleasures left for men.   940

Chorus

It frightens me to speak
my free thoughts
freely in a tyrant's presence.
But let the truth be told:
Among the Gods, Dionysus is second to none.

Pentheus

So, it has come!
This Bacchic violence, this hysteria,
spreading like a raging fire, is already upon us.
We are disgraced in the eyes of all Greece.
This is no time for apathy. You!   950
Go to the Electran gate, run!
Call every able-bodied man to arms!
Mobilize the cavalry in full!
Everyone who can use a sling or spring a bow,
I want them all. We march against the Bacchae.
It will be a black day indeed
when men sit back and endure such conduct from their women.
[The GUARD *runs off. The* HERDSMAN *creeps out without being noticed.* DIONYSUS
turns to PENTHEUS *and speaks to him soberly, reasoning with him, as if casting
a spell]*

Dionysus
Pentheus, nothing I can say will move you, *that* I know.
Yet even so!
In spite even of the grievous wrong you've done me,   960
I shall warn you again. Do not take arms against a God.
Let things be. Dionysus will not let you
drive his Bacchae from their sacred mountain haunts.

Pentheus
I need no lectures from you.
You've escaped from prison once—relish that!
Or do you want me to send you right back?

Dionysus
If I were you,
I would offer him a sacrifice. Not angry threats,
which, you being mortal, he a god,
is just like kicking barefoot at a rock.   970

Pentheus
Sacrifice? Exactly what I plan to offer him.
Women's blood—most suitably supplied by his own victims.
I'll drench the glens of Cithaeron with it!

Dionysus
Unless you're routed. Which you will be.
The lot of you. Just think of the disgrace!
Your shields of bronze being beaten back by sticks of ivy!

Pentheus
This stranger's like a nightmare that you can't shake off.
Whether you ignore him or kick him, he will have his say.

Dionysus
Friend, it still is possible to put things right.

Pentheus
How? By making myself a slave of my slaves?   980

Dionysus
I shall bring those women back to Thebes
without the help of weapons.

Pentheus
Ha! This is another of your artful tricks.

Dionysus
A trick? Is using my power to save you a trick?

Pentheus
No. It's a conspiracy with them—those Bacchae—
so that you can revel on forever.

Dionysus
True. Conspiracy if you like—but with a God.
*[*PENTHEUS, *who has been steadily losing ground, wavers. Suddenly, breaking out of the spell, he springs away, yelling]*

Pentheus
My arms! Go fetch my arms.
And you stop talking.

Dionysus
Ah!*   990
How would you like to *see* them
all cooped up together in the hills,
having their orgies?

Pentheus
Would I? I'd pay a fortune in gold for that.

Dionysus
Why, what gives you such a passionate desire?

Pentheus
Mind you, I would be very sorry
to see them drunk. . . .

Dionysus
But for all your sorrow
you will be delighted to see them, will you not?

Pentheus
Oh, yes, very. I could crouch beneath the pines, silently.   1000

Dionysus
However well you hide, they'll find you out.

Pentheus
That makes sense. I'll go openly! Of course!

Dionysus
Well, shall we go? You'll undertake the journey?

Pentheus
The sooner the better. I'll blame you for delaying me.

Dionysus
Wait! First you must dress yourself in something soft and feminine.

Pentheus
What! I, a man, look like a woman?

---

*This marks the turning point of the scene. Dionysus becomes wily and insinuating, drawing Pentheus deeper and deeper into his nets by bringing out his baser instincts.

Dionysus
If they see you as a man, they'll kill you.

Pentheus
You're talking sense again. Shrewd as an old wizard, aren't you?

Dionysus
Dionysus tells me what to say.

Pentheus
Sensible as your suggestion is, how can I make it work?   1010

Dionysus
I will come inside and dress you myself.

Pentheus
Dress me? In what—a woman's dress?
Oh no, I'd be ashamed.

Dionysus
I see! You're no longer keen to watch the maenads!

Pentheus
What exactly do I have to wear?

Dionysus
On your head, long flowing hair.

Pentheus
And then? What style of outfit do you have in mind?

Dionysus
Robes down to your feet and veils in your hair.

Pentheus
And to go with that? What else?

Dionysus
A dappled fawnskin and a thyrsus in your hand.   1020

Pentheus
No, never!

Dionysus
Then fight with the Bacchae.
And be ready for a bloodbath.

Pentheus
You're right.
It's good tactics to spy on them first.

Dionysus
Wiser and safer
than to invite violence by using it.

Pentheus
But how shall I pass through the city
without being seen?

Dionysus
We shall take lonely and deserted streets. I'll be your guide.   1030

Pentheus
Anything, so long as I'm not jeered at by any of those Bacchae.
I need to think it over. I'll go in . . . and decide.

Dionysus
As you please.
I am prepared for all eventualities.

Pentheus
I leave you. I shall re-emerge,
either to lead my army to the mountains
or to fall in with your plans.
[PENTHEUS *goes into the palace*]

Dionysus
Women, there goes a man walking straight into the net.
He shall visit the Bacchae
and there find punishment and death.   1040
Dionysus, to your work. I know you are near.
Be revenged on this man.
But, first, unhinge his mind,
make it floar into madness.
Sane, he never will accept to wear a woman's dress.
But once his wits have broken loose, he will.
I want the whole of Thebes to laugh
as I parade him through the streets,
laugh at this womanly man, this terrifying king,
whose arrogant threats still thunder in our ears.   1050
I shall go to him. Time to deck him out
in the clothes he shall take with him to Hades,
slaughtered by his own mother's hands.
So shall Pentheus come to know Dionysus, son of Zeus,
a God sprung from nature, like nature most cruel,
and yet, most gentle to mankind.
[DIONYSUS *follows* PENTHEUS *into the palace*]

Chorus
When, oh when,
in an all-night trance
shall I dance again,
bare feet flashing, head rushing   1060
through the coolness of leaves,
like a fawn that frolics

in the green delights of the forest,
free from the deadly snares of the hunt.
Oh, but till then,
the terror of leaping
clear of the intricate nets
and the pouncing claws of hounds
unleashed by the hunter's frenzied command,
fleeing like a shuddering breeze   1070
over the marshlands, over the river,
to the sheltering arms of the forest
to exult as the thick-sprouting trees
close their shadows around it
in dark pools of solitude
empty of men.
What is wisdom? Which
of all the God-given gifts
is more beneficial to man
than the power to hold   1080
an enemy powerless at bay?
That which is good is welcome forever.

Slowly, but implacably,
divine power moves
to strike at the arrogant man
who brazenly worships
his own image as God
and not the Gods themselves.
But they are there.
Above us, in us, around us   1090
the Gods lie subtly in ambush.
At a point in time they pounce
on the impious man.
No mortal act, no human thought
shall trespass beyond the age-old truths,
fortressed by tradition and custom.
Faith costs little.
To believe in some essence supreme
is to believe in life;
to draw strength from whatever   1100
is rooted in time
and in Nature's inscrutable logic.

What is wisdom? Which,
of all the God-given gifts
is more beneficial to man
than the power to hold
an enemy powerless at bay?
That which is good is welcome forever.

Happy the man who escapes
from the raging seas into port. 1110
Happy the man who withstands
life's assaults.
Somehow, in some way, some man surpasses some other
in position and fortune.
For the millions of men there are millions of hopes.
For some, these ripen into happiness,
for others into nothing.
Count lucky the man who is happy on this one day.
*[*DIONYSUS *emerges from the palace. He turns and calls to* PENTHEUS*]*

Dionysus
You, lusting to see what you are unfit to see,
thinking unthinkable thoughts, 1120
you, yes you, Pentheus, come out.
Reveal yourself as a woman!
Let's see this maenad in her Bacchic dress,
who goes to spy on her mother and her friends.
*[*PENTHEUS *comes slowly out of the palace. He wears a woman's dress and a veil over
his long golden curls, and he carries a thyrsus. He walks as if in a trance, trying to keep
his balance]*
Well! You look exactly
like one of Cadmus' daughters.

Pentheus
Strange! I seem to see two suns
and—two Thebes, yes,
two cities, two, each with seven gates. And you—
walking there before me—are you a bull? 1130
I could wager that you are one,
with those horns
that have sprouted from your head!
Were you one before? An animal? I mean a bull,
decidedly a bull!

Dionysus
The God is with us. Though angry before,
now he's been placated and walks beside us graciously.
Now you see what you ought to see.

Pentheus *[posing narcissistically]*
How do I look? Like Ino,
or do I carry myself more like my mother, Agave? 1140

Dionysus
Looking at you, I could swear I was seeing one of them.
Oh dear! One of your curls is out of place!
It should be tucked in as I arranged it.

Pentheus
It must have shaken loose indoors
when I was tossing my head, getting into a Bacchic mood.

Dionysus
Let me, whose job it is to serve your grace,
put it back in place! And hold your head still.

Pentheus
Come along then, fix it. I'm all yours now.

Dionysus
Your girdle too has slipped. And your skirt,
how unevenly it drapes around your ankles!   1150

Pentheus
Yes, now I see it. At least on the right.
On the left, it hangs well to the heel.

Dionysus
You may think me your best friend yet
when, much to your surprise, you see how docile the Bacchae are.

Pentheus
Do I hold the thyrsus in the right hand or the left to be like them exactly?

Dionysus
In the right.
And swing it up as you swing your right foot forward.
[He watches with wry amusement as PENTHEUS *executes his instructions]*
I do applaud the change in your mind.

Pentheus *[incongruously showing off his masculinity]*
Do you think I could lift the whole of Cithaeron,
Bacchae and all, upon my shoulders?   1160

Dionysus
If you wished, you could. Before, your mind was unsound.
Now it works the way it should.

Pentheus
Shall we take up crowbars?
Or shall I put my shoulder to the cliffs and wrench them loose,
while my hands tear down the peaks?

Dionysus
It wouldn't do to wreck the playgrounds of the nymphs,
the groves where Pan sits piping!

Pentheus
You are right. It's demeaning to conquer
women by force. I shall hide among the pines.

Dionysus
You will hide where you must hide and you'll be hidden,   1170
as well as any spy should be, when peeping on his fellow maenads.

Pentheus
I can see them now—crouched among the bushes
like mating birds, trapped in each other's loving arms.

Dionysus
Now we both know what you long to go and watch.
You may even catch them—if they don't catch you first.

Pentheus
Lead me through the very heart of Thebes.
Let them all see that I alone among them,
am *man* enough to dare.

Dionysus
You and you alone bear the burden for the city.
The struggle that awaits you is great.   1180
Your destiny is unique.
Come. I shall take you safely there.
Someone else will bring you back.

Pentheus
You mean my mother!

Dionysus
In triumph! For everyone to see.

Pentheus
It is for that I go.

Dionysus
You will be carried home—

Pentheus
You thrill me!

Dionysus
—carried in your mother's arms.

Pentheus
Now you're spoiling me!   1190

Dionysus
The way you *should* be spoiled. . . .

Pentheus
No less than I deserve.
[PENTHEUS *exits*]

Dionysus
Go, terrifying man, go your terrifying way
to the terror you'll be privileged to know,
the glory that will hoist you to the skies.
Stretch out your arms, Agave,
and you, her sisters, daughters of Cadmus.
I bring him! This man so young,
I bring him to his ultimate struggle.
The victory is mine. The victor Dionysus.   1200
The event will tell the rest.
[DIONYSUS *exits*]

Chorus
Run, swift hounds of madness, run,
run to the mountain,
find the faithful possessed,
the daughters of Cadmus,
goad them, lash them, turn them loose
on the woman-posing, woman-hating maniac
perversely spying in skirts.
His mother will spot him first,
through a crack in the rocks,   1210
through a break in the trees.
She'll cry to the maenads:
"What creature is this, prowling on the hills,
prying on the Bacchae,
these hills, our hills, the hills of the holy revels?
Who bore him? A woman?
No woman's blood in such as him.
A gorgon's seed, whelped from a she-wolf."

Arrive,
come Justice, arise,   1220
shining with the flash of your sword! And drive,
drive it clean through the throat
of the godless, lawless, ruthless son of Echion,
the earthborn, the earthbound.

Justice is balance.
His mind, unbalanced,
reels with sick, iniquitous passion,
profaning the mysteries of God,
lusting to violate Nature herself,
the Holy Mother.   1230
On he goes, up he goes,
his fury outracing his madness
as he plunges towards the unassailable goal,
the matching of visible force with invincible strength.

He will die, as he must. It is the Law.
The invisible line drawn by the Gods
that no man can overstep.
Call it humility, acceptance, or just faith.
To know that our days are but as dust,
to be content with that and love each living particle,   1240
is our only strength. But strength enough
to make our peace with grief.
Let others crowd their minds with scholarly wisdom.
Them I do not envy. I rejoice in keeping
my mind open to pursue the simple, attainable things
that are also the greatest.
Within that pursuit
lies the only known measure for happiness—
purity through loving by day and by night;
joyful acceptance of the godliness in me   1250
which reconciles me humbly with the powers beyond.

Come Justice! Arise! Arrive,
shining with the flash of your sword. And drive,
drive it clean through the throat
of the godless, lawless, ruthless son of Echion,
the earthborn, the earthbound.

Come, God—
Bromius, Bacchus, Dionysus—
burst into life, burst
into being, be a mighty bull,   1260
a hundred-headed snake,
a fire-breathing lion.
Burst into smiling life, oh Bacchus!
Smile at the hunter of the Bacchae,
smile and cast your noose.
And smiling, always smiling, watch
the maddened herd of maenads
burst upon him, bring him down,
trample him to death.
[A MESSENGER arrives running from the direction of Mount Cithaeron]

Messenger
Oh, House, once happy throughout Greece!   1270
Oh, envied race sown by Cadmus
in this Theban earth! I weep for you—
poor servant though I am!

Chorus
What is it? Is there news from the Bacchae?

Messenger
Pentheus is dead. The son of Echion is dead.

Chorus
Oh, Bromius, God of Joy! Yours is the glory!

Messenger
What did you say? Have you no shame, woman?
You rejoice at my master's misfortune?

Chorus
I'm not one of you.
To you Greeks, I'm a barbarian from the East.   1280
I speak my own language of worship.
I'm free from the fear of your chains!

Messenger
If you think the state of Thebes is short of men—

Chorus
Dionysus, not Thebes, rules over me.
Dionysus is my state.

Messenger
Well, I suppose one should excuse you.
But when disaster strikes
to jubilate after the fact is not decent.

Chorus
Tell me all. Speak. What kind of death did he die,
the oppressor, the master of oppression?   1290

Messenger
After leaving the city,
we made our way through the farmlands
to the river Asopus, and, crossing it,
we struck into the foothills of Cithaeron—
Pentheus and myself, for I was escorting my master,
and that stranger who was acting as our guide.
Finally, we reached a wooded glen,
and now we paused, our voices hushed,
our footsteps muffled by the grass,
as we glided through the trees—to see and not be seen.   1300
And there, looking down into a gorge,
sheer between two cliffs and full of streams,
we saw them, the maenads, quietly sitting
in the thick-knit shadows of the pines,
their hands aflutter with their happy tasks.
Some were dressing up their thyrsus

replacing old ivy with fresh green shoots.
Others, playful like colts, whose mouths
had just been freed from bridles, sang out in turn,
tossing their Bacchic tunes from throat to throat.   1310
Pentheus—unhappy man—
somehow could not see all those women.
"Stranger," he said, "from where we stand
I cannot quite detect those so-called maenads.
But if I climbed the tallest pine tree on the ridge
I'd have a proper view of their obscene activities."
Then I saw the stranger work a living miracle.
Gripping the highest branch of a sky-piercing pine
he firmly bent it down, down,
down to the dark earth, till it arched like a bow,   1320
as perfectly curved as a rim of wood,
flexed to hug the circle of a wheel.
So did the stranger arch that tree to the ground—
a feat no mortal hand could do.
Then, setting Pentheus astride the topmost branch,
he slowly let the sturdy trunk spring up again,
letting it glide smoothly through his grip,
so as not to throw him off.
Sheer into the sheer sky it went,
with my master riding on the top,   1330
easier for the maenads now to see than he could them.
But barely had he risen into view
when the stranger was nowhere to be seen.
And a voice clanged through the mountain air—
that of Dionysus, I suppose—calling out:
"Women! I deliver unto you
the man who mocks at you and me
and at our holy mysteries. Now punish him!"
And as he spoke, a dazzling shaft of light
flashed between heaven and earth, binding them together.   1340
The very air stood still. Throughout the glens, the trees
stifled the voice of their leaves
and in the hush, no beast was heard.
The Bacchae, who had heard the voice but not the words,
sprang up, their eyes and ears alert.
Then came the voice again. And now they knew,
Cadmus' daughters knew, the clear command of Bacchus.
Bursting forth, like a flock of racing doves,
Agave and her sisters and all the Bacchae with them
up the cliffside, through the torrents,   1350
over the boulders they leapt,
their limbs charged by the rage of their God.
And when they saw my master perched upon the pine,

first they scampered up a wall of rock,
across from where he soared, and pelted him with stones
and branches, stripped and hurled like spears.
Like hail they flung their sticks of thyrsus
at their pitiful target.
But still their aim fell short of the ill-fated wretch,
suspended on his dizzy perch,   1360
beyond their furious reach, yet trapped without escape.
At last, like a bolt of forest lightning,
they struck an oak tree clear of branches,
and using them as levers,
tried to pry the pine tree from its roots.
But even then, their efforts failed. Agave then cried out:
"Maenads come, surround the trunk
and grip it with your fists.
Shake down this climbing animal
or he'll reveal the secrets of our holy dance."   1370
A swarm of hands now swept upon the pine
and tore it from the earth. Then, plunging from the heights,
reeling toward the ground,
down, down, came Pentheus, with one continuous yell,
aware of his impending doom.
His mother,
as priestess of the ritual killing,
was first to fall upon him.
He stripped his head, tore everything away,
hoping that Agave, wretched woman,   1380
would know him and not kill him.
He touched her cheeks and cried:
"No Mother, no, it is I,
your child, your Pentheus, born to you in Echion's house!
Have pity on me, Mother, I have wronged
but do not kill your son for my offense, not me, your son!"
She was foaming at the mouth.
Her eyes bulged, rolling wildly.
There was no corner of her mind
not possessed by Bacchus.   1390
She was insane, oblivious to her son!
Seizing his left arm just above the wrist
and pushing with her foot against his chest
she wrenched his arm clean out of the shoulder.
It was not her strength that did it
but the God's power racing in her blood.
Ino, her sister, was working on the other side,
tearing off his flesh. And now Autonoe
pounced upon him, followed by the whole rabid pack.
The mountains boomed with shrill confusion—   1400

Pentheus wailing while there was still a gasp left in him,
the women howling in their triumph.
One carried off an arm,
another a foot with the boot still on it.
They laid his ribs bare—clawed them clean.
His blood still warm on their hands,
they tossed the flesh of Pentheus back and forth
like children playing games.
Nothing is left of him. His body
lies scattered—some of it on the jagged rocks,   1410
some buried in the forest thickets—
by no means easy to recover.
Except for his poor head. His mother has it,
proudly in her grip. She raises it high
on her thyrsus point—that head
she thinks is of some forest beast—
and carries it through the glades of Cithaeron,
leaving her sisters dancing with those raving women.
She is on her way here, inside the city,
exulting in her fearful and pathetic quarry.   1420
She cries out to Bacchus, calling him
"fellow-hunter," "my ally in the kill,"
"the victor of our chase"! Oh, what a victory!
What a triumph of tears! But I am going.
I want no more part of this unnatural horror.
Just let me get away, far away,
before Agave comes home.
I am but a simple man, yet to me
reverence and humility before the Gods
is best for all men. It is also the only wisdom.   1430
If only men would use it. So I think.
[*The* MESSENGER *exits, leaving the* CHORUS *in a state of fear and exultation*]

Chorus
Dance for Bacchus,
dance.
Let voices boom
in song
for the doom
of Pentheus, seed of the dragon.
Pentheus,
dragged to his death
by the folds of his female dress,   1440
pulled *down* into darkness
by the gentle thyrsus
he held so *high.*
Pentheus, the profane,

marched by a bull to his slaughter.
Oh Thebes! Oh Theban Bacchae!
What a victory you have won!
What a ringing triumph
to be drowned in wailing and tears.
Yet—salute one must   1450
the horror and the glory
of the final reckoning,
that embrace of blood
between a mother and her child
that she herself has killed.
But look! I see Agave, Pentheus' mother,
running wild-eyed toward the palace.
Prepare yourselves
for the roaring voice of the God of Joy.

[AGAVE *enters, holding the head of* PENTHEUS. *Her dress is torn and there is blood on
her hands and arms. She comes to a sudden stop as she sees the* CHORUS, *clinging to her
trophy with jealous pride*]

Agave
Women of Asia, Bacchae—   1460

Chorus
Me? What do you want of *me?*

Agave
From the mountain, I have brought it.
All the way, a tender branch
fresh-cut, with curly shoots. A beautiful catch.

Chorus
We see. And we accept you.
We shall cry out together.

Agave
Without a trap, I trapped it.
A lion—a savage whelp of a lion.
Look! Look at it!

Chorus
In what wilderness, how?   1470

Agave
Cithaeron . . .

Chorus
Cithaeron?

Agave
Killed him. Most totally.

Chorus
But who, whose hands?

Agave
Mine first! Mine is the prize for striking first!
You know what the other women are singing?
Agave, the best, Agave, most blest.

Chorus
Who else? whose hands?

Agave
Oh, Cadmus' . . .

Chorus
Cadmus! 1480

Agave
Cadmus' daughters. My sisters,
yes, but only after me, after *me,*
did *they* lay hands on the quarry.
Oh, what a fortunate hunting.

Chorus
The God knows when to smile.

Agave
Come feast with me. Share in my success.

Chorus
Share—unhappy woman?

Agave
The best is young! See how the down
blooms upon its cheek like newborn silk,
under the rich, soft mane. 1490

Chorus
The hair does make it look indeed
like a beast of the woods.

Agave
Bacchus,
skilled hunter that he is,
most skillfully unleashed his maenads
and led them to the kill.

Chorus
God is the king of hunters.

Agave
Do you praise me?

Chorus
We do—praise you.

Agave
So will Cadmus soon.   1500
So will all his people.

Chorus
And Pentheus?
Will he also praise his mother?

Agave
He *will* praise her
when he sees the lion she has caught.
It is not glorious?

Chorus
Prodigious.

Agave
Prodigiously conquered.

Chorus
You rejoice?

Agave
More! I exult!   1510
My conquest is great, plain to see!
And great the acclaim it deserves.

Chorus
Show then, poor woman, show to everyone in Thebes
this priceless trophy you have carried proudly home.
[AGAVE *parades the stage, proudly exhibiting the head of* PENTHEUS]

Agave
You, people of this high-towered city,
subjects of this mighty country, look!
Here is my trophy! *Here* is the quarry
we, your women, hunted down, yes *we*—
and not with nets or hooks or pointed spears—
but with our own bare arms, our hands, our delicate fingers.   1520
Now what are they worth, your manly boasts?
Where *is* the pride in power that relies
on hideous tools of war? *We* didn't need them.
With our hands we captured this beast of prey
and ripped it limb from limb.
But where is my father?
He is old, but he should come.
And Pentheus, my son,
where is he? Fetch him, someone. Tell him

his mother wants him. With a ladder. 1530
He shall set it up against the front
of his palace. Firmly—for he mustn't slip—
and nail high upon the highest wall,
so all the town can see
his mother's triumph in the hunt,
this lion's head, my trophy, yes *mine!*
[CADMUS *enters, followed by attendants carrying a makeshift stretcher with the covered remains of* PENTHEUS. *They remain upstage while* CADMUS *speaks]*

Cadmus
Come men, follow me.
Bear your pitiful burden
of that which was Pentheus, my Pentheus,
to his home. Follow me with— 1540
oh, those broken limbs that I painfully assembled
after a long and dismal search
up in the glens of Cithaeron, where they lay
scattered far and wide among the forest crags,
in tiny fragments, hard to find.
I had already left the mountain revels
and was entering the city with Teiresias,
when news was brought to me
of my daughters' atrocious deed.
I hurried back to the hills, to return, this time, 1550
with this boy, dismembered by the maenads.
There on the wooded slopes I saw Autonoe,
my poor Actaeon's mother, and with her Ino,
both still possessed with frenzy. But Agave, I was told,
was seen running, raving, on her way here.
Oh! Too true, alas, I see her now.
A sight to make eyes bleed!

Agave
Father!
Be proud! As proud as any mortal man can be.
For you have sired the bravest daughters ever 1560
in the world. I mean all three of us,
but me above the rest. From now on,
no more weaving at the loom, no little chores for me.
I'm meant for greater things—for hunting
savage beasts with my bare hands.
Oh Father, you see what I carry in my arms?
It is the prize I have won—yours,
to hang upon your walls.
Receive it, Father, in your hands. Rejoice in my conquest,
and summon all your friends to join our royal feast. 1570

Let them see how fortunate you are. How blest
by the splendor of my deed.

Cadmus
Oh misery, oh grief beyond all measure.
I cannot look on this, this—murder—
yes, murder, done by those pitiful hands you're so proud of!
And you would offer such a victim to the Gods,
expecting Thebes and me to sit in at your feast?
How just—yet how unfair—the price the God
had made us pay. Dionysus, lord of joy,
born of our blood, has cruelly laid us low!   1580

Agave
How disagreeable old men can be!
Why does he look so mournful?
I wish my son would emulate his mother!
Go hunting in the wilds with the young men of Thebes
and outshine them all!
But all he knows, that boy, is how to fight the Gods.
He should be scolded, Father! Yes!
And you're the one to do it. Well?
Is no one going to fetch him,
to see me in my happiness?   1590

Cadmus
Oh daughter, daughter!
If ever you come out of this and know what you have done,
you'll suffer pain insufferable. And if your mind
remains forever drugged against reality,
your happiness, being all delusion, is but the greatest misery.

Agave
What is there that is wrong?
Why all this talk of misery?
[*Making a decision,* CADMUS *approaches* AGAVE *and talks to her with low intensity,*
trying to pull her out of her trance]

Cadmus
Listen to me! Do as I say.
First, look up at the sky.

Agave
I'm looking. What am I supposed to see?   1600

Cadmus
Is it the same as always?
Or does it seem changed to your eyes?

Agave
It is brighter than before—more luminous.

Cadmus
And inside you?
Is there still that lightness? Like floating?

Agave
I do not grasp your meaning.
Yet—I feel different somehow. More—awake.
As if—something has shifted in my head.

Cadmus
Do my words reach you now?
Can you answer clearly?   1610

Agave
Yes, but I forget.
What were we talking of, Father?

Cadmus
When you reached womanhood,
whose house did you marry into?

Agave
You gave me to a man of our Theban dragon-race.
His name was Echion.

Cadmus
In your husband's house—you bore a son.
Who was he?

Agave
Pentheus. Echion's son and mine.

Cadmus
And whose face is that   1620
you're holding in your hand?

Agave
A lion's—so the hunting women say. . . .

Cadmus
Now look straight at it.
There's little effort in that.

Agave [*turning her head away*]
Ah! What is this! What am I holding?

Cadmus [*grasping her head, forcing her to look*]
Look at it! Go on looking
till you know what it is!

Agave
I see—oh, Gods, no, not this grief,
not this agony . . .

Cadmus
Does it seem like a lion now?   1630

Agave
No. It is Pentheus—his head—
in my hands.

Cadmus
We wept for him
long before you knew.

Agave
Who killed him?
How did he come into my hands?

Cadmus
Oh, merciless truth—you always come too soon.

Agave
Tell me! Now! My heart is leaping out
to the horror I must hear.

Cadmus
It was *you!* You and your sisters!   1640
You killed him!

Agave
Where? Where did he die?
Here at home? Or where?

Cadmus
In those same glens where Actaeon
was torn to pieces by his hounds.

Agave
Cithaeron? Why?
What evil fate drove him there?

Cadmus
He went to mock the God
and you, his Bacchic revelers!

Agave
But we? How did we get there?   1650

Cadmus
You were driven mad.
The whole town was possessed.

Agave
Now I see it all.
Dionysus! He destroyed us.

Cadmus
You denied his deity,
reviled his name in public.
[A pause. The violence of their despair ebbs into a quiet but piercing grief]

Agave
Father, where is the body
of my beloved son?

Cadmus
Here! I have brought it home,
broken, painfully retrieved.   1660

Agave
Broken? But are his limbs together,
decently composed?

Cadmus
What human hands could do,
ours did. Not much.

Agave
Oh, if only mine could undo what they have done.

Cadmus
Too late. When guilty people are struck mad,
their madness knows no guilt.

Agave
My guilt—my madness, yes!
But what did Pentheus have to do with that?

Cadmus
He was like you, contemptuous of the God.   1670
And in a single devastating blow, the God
has brought us down, your sisters, you, this boy—
ruining my house and me. I had no son,
no male heir of my blood but him,
sprung from your unhappy womb! And now he's gone—
abominably, shamefully cut down—
he who was the pillar of my house.
Oh, my child, my king, my grandson,
our guiding light you were,
the keeper of our future.   1680
This city held you in its awe. When you were near,
no man would dare to slight this gray old head,

for fear of you. And now I, Cadmus the great,
who sowed the Theban race and reaped a glorious harvest,
must go away, dishonored, an outcast from my home.
Oh, dearest one—to me as dear in death,
as when you were in life—
never again will you touch my face
and call me Grandfather and hug me in your arms and say:
"Has anybody done you wrong? Has anyone upset you,   1690
made you sad? Just tell me who
and, Grandfather, I'll punish him myself."
And now you're gone, as miserably dead
as I'm alive, your mother broken,
none of us left but torn by grief.
If there be any man who challenges or scorns
the unseen powers,
let him look on this boy's death and accept
that which is God.

Chorus
I grieve for you, Cadmus.   1700
Though your grandson's punishment is just.
For you it is too cruel.*

Agave [in a strange, almost impersonal voice]
Father,
you see this woman
standing where I do.
She is your daughter.
Yet nothing is there left of what she was.
In one quick stroke, her hands,
blind and driven by the Gods,
have split her life in two.   1710
Whatever was before
has crumbled, vanished,
behind a wall of blood.
For her—for me—
there's only now. An endless now,
stretching like a dark and empty desert
without past or future.
My son is dead. His mother killed him.
I am his mother. Those few words contain
horror, shame, anguish so immense   1720
that no living creature should be able to endure.
Yet I live. How or why, I do not know.

---

*From this point until the appearance of Dionysus in his divine dimension, there is a break in the manuscript. This missing text has been reconstructed by the translator, based on Latin translations.

And no longer do I ask to understand. For, if I do,
I might sin again and be denied the one last favor
that would be any mother's right to ask.

Cadmus
What is that, my daughter?

Agave
To prepare my son for his journey to the dead.
He cannot go like this! I know my hands are cursed,
polluted with blood of my blood,
yet whose but mine can make whole again   1730
that body that they proudly reared to manhood?

Cadmus
Oh, daughter! The holy laws forbid the ones who kill
to care for their victims.

Agave
My victim? Yes! But, Gods, I DID NOT KNOW!
If my son deserved to die and I deserved to kill him,
you've had your way! A little charity is all I ask!
To be allowed to wash him clean of blood with tears
and sing a dirge for every broken limb!
Oh, Father, spare me a little of the pity
that the Gods must feel for you.   1740
Just let me put my son to sleep—
and let the Gods do what they want with me.
Punish me with death or life, I do not care!
[CADMUS signals to the attendants, who approach slowly with PENTHEUS' *remains]*

Chorus
Bring forth your sorrowful burden.
Do what you can, my daughter.
But do not linger more than it is seemly.
And steel your heart against a sight
hard for any mortal eyes to bear,
but most of all a mother's.
[The attendants stop near AGAVE. *During the following lines, she sets* PENTHEUS' *head next to his mangled limbs, caressing them as she laments on her knees]*

Agave
Put him down.   1750
Oh, my child! My son!
Your mother's here
to heal your wounds and give you back your beauty,
that she herself reduced to . . . this! Oh no!
Proud head
that not so long ago these hateful eyes reviled

and now drench with tears. Rest where you belong. Remember
how once you nestled in my arms?
Oh dearest face—tender cheek, so young—
sweet mouth that suckled at my breast,   1760
now forever closed. If you could speak,
what would you say to wrench your mother's heart,
that I have not already said a thousand times!
Oh my prince!
These noble limbs that soon I should have dressed
for some young girl, your bride,
how lifeless now they lie—
unnaturally, mercilessly mangled—
Oh I cannot! Help me!
No, on—I must be strong. Go someone, bring a shroud   1770
fit for the burial of this king, my son.
My eyes shall not betray him with weakness.
*[*CADMUS *takes off his cloak and approaches* AGAVE*]*

Cadmus
Here, my daughter,
take this old man's cloak. And come away.

Agave
Yes, father. A little while and I am done.
[Ceremoniously holding the cloak over PENTHEUS' *remains]*
I wash your wounds.
With this princely shroud I cover your head.
I bind your limbs with love,
flesh of my flesh,
in life as in death,   1780
forever.
*[*AGAVE *covers the remains with the cloak. In the hush, the* CHORUS *sounds drained and disoriented]*

Chorus
O Dionysus,
we feel you near,
stirring like molten lava
under the ravaged earth,
flowing from the wounds of your trees
in tears of sap,
screaming with the rage
of your hunted beasts.

How terrible your vengeance against those   1790
who harness your forces
to their laws of unnatural order.
A free and open mind

is safe against the excesses
lurking in the secret juices of your plants.
But those who try to strangle you
in the roots of their own nature,
who oppress and are oppressed,
through you, achieve their own destruction.

[DIONYSUS *appears, suspended in space above the palace, as the bull-horned God*]

Dionysus
Hear me all! I speak to you now as Dionysus,   1800
a God revealed to mortal eyes.
I came back to this land of my virgin birth,
to suffer the indignities that only human folly can invent.
I was mocked at, chained, thrown in prison. Men like Pentheus
who abuse their power in defiance of the Gods
shall ever rediscover the inexorable terror of divine justice.
Now you, his kin, were made to kill the tyrant that you gloried in.
You are unclean. And you shall go your separate ways,
leaving Thebes forever, to rid it from the curse of your pollution.
Had you been willing to be wise when you had all,   1810
today, instead of losing all, you would be thriving allies
of the son of Zeus, your friend.

Cadmus
Spare us, Dionysus. We have sinned.

Dionysus
Too late to know me now. You did not when you should.

Agave
We were wrong and we confess.
But you are merciless!

Dionysus
I am a God.
And when insulted, Gods do not forgive.

Agave
The Gods should be above the passions of mere men.

Dionysus *[in a distant, tired voice]*
So it was ordained from the beginning   1820
by the almighty father, Zeus.

Agave
It is decided, old man. Give up.
The cruelty of the Gods demands our banishment.

Dionysus
Then go. Why delay the inevitable.

[AGAVE *and* CADMUS *begin to cross the stage, moving in opposite directions*]

Cadmus
Oh child, what a terrible fate has overtaken us,
you, your sisters, and your wretched father.
A derelict old man, I'm doomed to live,
despised, in foreign lands. For sufferings like mine
there is no respite ever. Even when I sail
down the silent river to the world of the dead   1830
I shall find no rest.

Agave
I shall live, Father. Alone, deprived of you.
[As AGAVE and CADMUS *pass each other, she turns and embraces him*]

Cadmus
Poor child,
why do you fold your arms around me,
like a swan sheltering its useless, old father?

Agave
Where am I to go? Cast out, unwanted,
whom can I turn to?

Cadmus
I do not know, my daughter,
Your father cannot help you.

Agave
Farewell, my home. Farewell, my city.   1840
I leave you for exile. My once bridal bed
I leave you for misery.
Father, I weep for you.

Cadmus
Strange! I still feel pity
for you and your sisters.

Agave
Brutal! Brutally ruthless the fate
Dionysus hurled at your house.

Dionysus *[fading away]*
Yes. And ruthlessly brutal the way
you dishonored his name in Thebes.

Agave
Farewell, my father.   1850

Cadmus
Poor child, farewell.
Oh words—how futile you can be.

Agave
Take me, someone, to my sisters,
my pitiful sisters, that I must lead to exile.
I want to go far,
out of sight of cursed Cithaeron
and Cithaeron out of my sight.
To a place no thyrsus threatens—or haunts
even in memory. Let those who wish,
be Bacchae after me.   1860

Chorus
The Gods take many forms.
They manifest themselves in unpredictable ways.
What we most expect
does not happen.
And for the least expected
God finds a way.
That is what happened here today.

. . . .

Questions for Discussion and Review

1. Medea has been variously described as a strong and independent woman, a woman mad with passion, and a witch. Using specific examples from the *Medea,* discuss which image ultimately is conveyed by the play.

2. Medea is granted refuge by King Aegeus of Athens in return for a potion that will restore his fertility. The child Aegeus fathers will turn out to be the Athenian hero Theseus. How does this relationship affect our view of Medea?

3. Compare Medea and Clytemnestra as heroines. What strengths do they have in common? How do they feel about being confined to the conventional role of women? Although they both murder members of their own families, what do their different fates reveal about moral responsibility in the two plays?

4. Compare Euripides' portrayal of Jason with the myths that present Jason as the leader of the Argonauts. Which typically heroic characteristics reappear in Euripides' Jason, and which do not?

5. Why does Pentheus regard Bacchic ecstasy as a threat to civilization? Is he right in any of his objections to surrendering the rational self to the power of emotional abandonment? In presenting his version of the myth, would Euripides urge unconditional acceptance of Dionysian frenzy? Should humans retain rational control at all times? Should one both acknowledge *and* resist instinctual passion?

6. Some critics suggest that Dionysus is ethically unacceptable because he is a cruel and vengeful god. Do you think that Euripides' tragedy provokes moral criticisms of Dionysus's character and vengeful behavior? Is Dionysus presented as a force of nature that transcends standards of human judgment? How does he represent

unconscious forces in both external nature and the human psyche? Explain your answer.

7. What do we learn from witnessing a dramatization of Dionysus's return to his home city and his punishment of close relatives who reject him? Is a prophet invariably denied honor in his hometown? (Compare the myth of the god's return with the account of Jesus' rejection by his family and former neighbors in Mark 6 and Luke 4.)

PART FOUR

The World of
Roman Myth

CHAPTER

1 8

The Roman Vision: Greek Myths and Roman Realities

KEY TOPICS/THEMES

The Romans borrowed freely from neighboring cultures, including the Etruscans and the Greeks. They especially admired Greek myth, adding it to their own myths, such as the one about the founding of Rome. They changed the Greek names and adapted the stories in four major ways: shifting their emphasis to reflect Roman views on what was important, attaching the stories to historical events and individuals, orienting them toward their overriding concern with the state of Rome, and reinterpreting them to reflect Roman values and ideas.

The Connection Between Greek and Roman Myths

Like much of Roman culture, Roman myth is eclectic, including both indigenous material and that borrowed from many neighboring peoples, especially from the Etruscans, who had dominated the region before the Romans rebelled and founded their own republic (509 B.C.), and, of course, from the Greeks. From the Etruscans, the Romans appropriated the names of several of their gods (such as Jupiter, Juno, and Minerva, whom the Romans identified with the Greek gods Zeus, Hera, and Athene), animal symbols (such as the she-wolf; Figure 18-1), and many rituals and superstitions. The Etruscans had already begun the process of urbanization, engaging in projects such as public buildings and drainage systems that the Romans would continue and expand. The Romans were also influenced by Etruscan governance and lifestyles. For example, although they would eventually reject monarchy, the Romans retained the Senate as an assembly of the heads of aristocratic families. And upper-class Etruscan women, who were better educated and less restricted than their Greek counterparts, and who were even permitted to dine on couches with

FIGURE 18-1   The She-Wolf of Rome. To this late sixth- or early fifth-century Etruscan bronze, the Roman sculptor added the twins Romulus and Remus, legendary founders of Rome. (The twins here are Renaissance reconstructions of the Roman originals, which were destroyed.) The Romans not only seized the sculpture and brought it to Rome but added to it representations of the myth of the founding of their state, making it, figuratively as well as literally, their own. This sculpture thus provides a visual image of the eclectic nature of Roman culture. *(Conservatori Museum, Rome)*

their husbands while entertaining guests (a practice Greek commentators found scandalous), also set the model for Roman women who, by the late Republic, were permitted the same freedoms.

Both the Etruscans and the Romans were influenced by the Greeks, who had established colonies in Sicily and southern Italy as early as the eighth century B.C. The Greeks exchanged with their neighbors not only goods and services but also elements of their culture and, of course, their alphabet, which both the Etruscans and the Romans adapted to the needs of their respective languages. The Romans were thus influenced by the Greeks both directly, interacting with the Greeks themselves, and indirectly, through the Etruscans, long before they conquered Greece in 146 B.C.

The Romans particularly admired the Greeks, borrowing their myths and incorporating many other aspects of Greek culture into their own. "I found Rome a city of brick," the first Roman emperor, **Augustus,** is said to have boasted, "but I left it a city of marble." Augustus's statement reflects the Roman perception of both the high cultural status and the beauty of Greek public architecture, with its elegant marble temples, as contrasted with the solid, practical brick of Roman buildings. Despite his boast, however, Augustus did not order that Rome be demolished and reconstructed in solid marble; nor could the large buildings required for a city the size of Rome have been safely constructed on the post-and-lintel system preferred by the Greeks. Rather, to make Rome resemble a Greek city while still addressing practical needs, Roman architects continued to design brick buildings supported

FIGURE 18-2   The Pantheon. A feat of engineering unprecedented in its time (c. A.D. 120), the Pantheon, a temple to all the Roman gods, enclosed a huge interior space spanned by an enormous dome. The central structure, however, was not permitted to stand on its own merits: rather, the architect added a "Greek" facade—a portico (porch) that creates the illusion of a classical Greek temple, complete with pillars that support only the roof of the porch itself.

by sturdy Roman arches, which they overlaid with marble tiles and decorated with marble "columns" (which supported nothing), sculpted onto the exterior walls, often adding a mock Greek portico (porch) at the entrance (Figure 18-2).

Beneath the facade of Augustus's "city of marble," of course, Rome was still Rome. His metaphor, however, might equally serve to describe the relationship between Greek and Roman myth. Although justifiably proud of their own skills in organization, engineering, and government, the Romans saw themselves as inferior to the Greeks in terms of literary and artistic achievements. They had adopted Greek literature (educating their children, for example, on Homer's works) and Greek myth, keeping the stories intact to maintain the veneer of Greek culture but changing the names and adapting the concepts to fit their core ideas and values. They also created links between the Greek myths they borrowed and existing Roman myths. In fact, it is largely through the works of Roman writers such as Virgil and Ovid (see Chapters 19 and 20) that the cumulative body of classical mythology—reinterpreted in characteristically Roman ways—was, in turn, transmitted to later periods of Western culture (see Chapter 21). But, of course, they didn't simply imitate the Greeks' mythology. Rather, they reinterpreted the myths in characteristically Roman ways, whether adapting them or using them to contrast and highlight their unique and specifically Roman vision.

A Roman Myth: Romulus and Remus

The most important Roman myth was probably the story of **Romulus** and **Remus** and the founding of Rome. According to this myth, **Rhea Silvia** [REE-a SIL-vih-a] (or, in some variants, **Ilia**) was assigned to the office of Vestal Virgin by her wicked uncle Amulius, who had usurped the throne of her father, Numitor. Because the Vestal Virgins, who guarded the Eternal Flame sacred to the Vesta (the goddess of the hearth, equivalent to the Greek goddess Hestia), were required to remain celibate until age forty, Amulius hoped to prevent his niece from producing heirs, who would contest his claim to the throne. However, seduced by the god **Mars,** she bore twin sons, Romulus and Remus. Determined to exterminate the line, Amulius left the infants to die in a basket on the river Tiber. Washed up safely on shore, the twins were nursed by a she-wolf (originally an Etruscan symbol) and fed bits of food by a bird until they were found and raised by a shepherd. Growing to manhood, they discovered their real identities and, aided by loyal shepherds, restored their grandfather Numitor to the throne of his city, **Alba Longa.**

The brothers, however, wanted a city of their own and argued over which one of them to name the city after. To settle the quarrel, they agreed to a contest: the winner would be the first one to see a sign from the gods—a flock of vultures. Remus first saw six, but Romulus, immediately afterward, saw twelve, which he claimed was a more powerful sign, albeit a later one. Supported by their respective followers, they fought, and Remus was killed. Or perhaps, as one variant suggests, Romulus killed him for defiantly jumping over a wall Romulus had built around the perimeter of his new city, marked out with a plow. Remus thus becomes a "foundation sacrifice," his death consecrating the walls of the city and ensuring their effectiveness as a barrier protecting the city from invasion. The city thus founded was named *Rome*—conceived according to a policy of aggressive expansion enforced by violence and as part of a divine plan.

The Rape of the Sabine Women

The new city prospered, but the shepherds-turned-warriors and the other men (often fugitives or escaped slaves) who joined them lacked potential mates—people in the surrounding towns being understandably unwilling to marry their daughters to such aggressive intruders. (Or perhaps the Romans wanted to form a link with their neighbors, the **Sabines** [SAY-binz], in order to annex their territory and secure it permanently.) Romulus invited the residents of neighboring communities, including the Sabines, to a festival. When the guests were assembled, the Romans forcibly abducted and raped the daughters of the Sabines and, refusing to return their captives, married them. Although the abduction ended in formal marriage, it is significant that Roman society was established via the subjugation of women and survived on a foundation of gender oppression.

For several years, the Sabines warred against the Romans, until the Romans' wives themselves interfered to assure their families that they were happy to be Roman wives. According to the Greek writer Plutarch (A.D. 46–120), who notes approvingly that the abduction made possible the forging of political alliances that made Rome strong enough to survive and prosper, the myth also gave rise to the custom (still often practiced in our own time) of the groom carrying the bride over the threshold of her new home; because the original Roman brides were kidnap victims, they did not voluntarily enter their abductors' homes, and so had to be carried in. The Roman and Sabine territories were then combined under a single (ultimately Roman) government. Romulus ruled, with support from commoners and soldiers, for thirty-eight years until, during a storm, he suddenly vanished in a dark cloud. Some suspected that resentful patrician senators had killed and dismembered him, but he was officially said, by the senators who witnessed the incident, to have been taken up to the heavens to be henceforth worshiped as the warrior god Quirinus.

The Feast of the Lupercalia

The origins of the Romulus and Remus myth are lost in history, but modern scholars have suggested several possible interpretations. The twins may be related, for example, to the **Lares** [LAR-eez], guardians of the spirit of the home who also became guardians of the state. The story of Romulus and Remus is also closely connected with the Feast of the Lupercalia, in honor of the god Faunus, or Pan (both associated with shepherds), a ritual the twins are credited with founding. They are said to have run completely around their village, prior to the discovery of their true identities, either naked or dressed only in loincloths made from the hides of sacrificial goats (suggesting an even more ancient initiation rite), thus chartering the official Roman ritual. Each year on February 15, two young aristocrats chosen for the honor, the Luperci, sacrificed two goats in a cave named for the she-wolf (*lupa*) said to have suckled the twins. The youths were pricked by the sacrificial knife, and the blood was then washed off with wool soaked in milk. After engaging in games and feasting on the cooked meat, the Luperci cut strips from the goat hides and ran around the base of the Palatine (one of the seven hills of Rome), whipping anyone they could with the thongs.

After a plague of miscarriages and stillbirths in Rome in 296 B.C., the ritual acquired a new function—ensuring women's fertility. According to Ovid, who places his story during the time of Romulus, widespread infertility became a problem among the Sabine women, who were told by Juno, in her role as Lucina, moon goddess and goddess of childbirth, that in order to conceive they must be impregnated by a sacred goat. Ovid attributes the explanation of Juno's will to an Etruscan augur. Thus, women who wanted to conceive presented themselves at the Lupercalia to be whipped by the goat thongs, thereby resolving the fertility problem. From that point on, the Feast of the Lupercalia included the flagellation of women who offered themselves up.

Another possible connection with the myth is found in the Saturnalia, a festival in honor of Saturn, a god associated with sowing and agriculture. In the myth, the women watched as the men performed the ritual. After their marriage, however, they participated, now as Roman matrons, in a female version, the ritual of the "Matronalia," during which men gave presents to women in honor of Juno, goddess of childbirth. This festival, the first "Mother's Day," like its counterpart in modern

America, paid token homage to women who, for the rest of the year, were subservient to men.

Whatever the Romans may have borrowed or adapted from Greek myth, the indigenous myth of Romulus and Remus and the foundation of a city that would be both secure in its walls and prosperous in its fertility—of its fields, flocks, and women—remained so compelling that the emperor Octavian considered choosing the name "Romulus" for himself before settling on "Augustus." In this way, he avoided any reminder of the centuries-old division between brothers that might recall the civil war from which Rome had just emerged in 30 B.C.

Characteristics of Roman Myth

The Focus on the City and Its History

The myth of Romulus and Remus and the founding of Rome reveals quintessentially Roman elements. First, it is focused on the city and its process of expansion from a mere plot of ground to an empire in progress, beginning with the Sabine territories, while nostalgically attesting to its roots among simple shepherds. Second, although the story begins with strong mythic components (Mars and the she-wolf), it swiftly turns to the actual history of Roman expansion into the rest of Italy.

The Patriarchal Perspective

Third, the myth's perspective is intensely patriarchal, entirely appropriate to a society in which the *pater familias,* the male head of the extended family, had literally the power of life and death over family members. Determined to father children, the original inhabitants of Rome as depicted in the foundation myth have no qualms about raping the Sabine women, thereby reenacting the original rape of Rhea Silvia by Mars. Greek myths, of course, are also highly patriarchal. But we can usually perceive in them some vestige of ambivalence, some trace of the feminine powers in the symbols whose meanings lurk beneath the surface. That the rape of the Sabine women is approved by the gods and, more revealingly, by the women themselves demonstrates both the total subservience of women in this myth and the myth's complete obliteration of the female perspective.

There are, of course, many instances of rape in Greek myths as well. And in the Roman poet Ovid's *Metamorphoses* (see Chapter 20), as in the Greek myths on which they are based, rapes are not portrayed approvingly. Nevertheless, it is instructive to contrast the myth of the Sabine women with a familiar depiction of rape in Greek myth. The abduction of Helen—along with Paris's violation of the guest–host relationship and the laws of marriage that preceded it—is treated as a violation of principles sacred to the gods, and the war that follows leads to the destruction, not the expansion, of Troy. Even more revealing is the contrast with the Greek myth of the centaurs' attempted rape of the Lapith women at the wedding of the Lapith princess. Whereas the centaurs are reviled and driven off by the Greeks for their savage, irrational behavior, the Romans are rewarded with wives, land, and divine approval for the same actions.

The Demythologizing Tendency

Finally, we can see in the Romulus and Remus story the strong resistance to its more fantastic components by contrasting the story of this city founded in violence with the Greek myth of the founding of Thebes. In the Greek myth, Cadmus sows dragon's teeth, which magically grow into a race of armed men. The armed men of Rome, however, arrive in a more pedestrian fashion—as disgruntled farmers and shepherds, runaway slaves, and fugitives from justice. And to propagate their race, they require the services not of dragons but of women. Plutarch, whose *Lives* compared figures from Greek and Roman myth and history, would surely have felt compelled, in his role as biographer and historian, to offer an alternative (and more realistic) explanation of the "divine conception" of the twins; nevertheless, his tome serves to illustrate the demythologizing impulse frequently at work in Roman myths. According to Plutarch, the story of the rape of Rhea Silvia by the war god was probably planted as a cover-up to a more likely scenario—a rape by her uncle Amulius. Plutarch's demythologizing tendency is likewise illustrated in his version of the myth of Theseus and the Minotaur: **Pasiphae,** he asserted, was in love not with a bull (*taurus,* in Greek) but with a captain of the king's guard named Taurus, who lost an athletic contest to Theseus. Similarly, he stated that Theseus went not to the Underworld but to a land governed by a king who happened to be named Pluto, who had a wife named Persephone and a dog named Cerberus. Heracles, according to Plutarch, rescued Theseus from the dog! In a similar vein, the poet Horace, in one of his odes (Book 3, Number 16), described Zeus as coming to Perseus's mother, **Danae,** safely locked in her tower, in a shower of gold, but equated the gold with bribery—which can always break down barriers.

Although such "rationalistic" explanations of mythic materials were not unknown in the work of earlier writers about Greek myth, they are for the Romans consistent with a widespread sense of pride in their own pragmatic nature. The Romans wanted their myths, but without having to relinquish their sense of themselves as practical men of the world.

The Links Between Greek and Roman Mythology

The myth of the founding of Rome, however, would not have been as satisfying had the Romans not been able to forge, in both senses of the word, a link between it and Greek mythology. In fact, the "Greek connection" was so intriguing to the Romans that there are several mythic versions of the ancestral link between the two populations. According to Hesiod, for example, Odysseus fathered two sons by Circe, whom Hesiod portrays as an Etruscan goddess. One of those sons, Latinos, may have been an eponymous ruler of the Etruscans. The Romulus and Remus story, however, was the "official" version of the linkage. Thus, not only is Romulus a son of Mars (the Roman name for the Greek god Ares), but his mother is descended from **Ascanius** [as-KAY-nih-uhs], son of **Aeneas** [ee-NEE-as], the only Trojan hero to escape the destruction of Troy. The "missing" descendants of Troy are thereby accounted for—they are Romans! And although the Trojans were not exactly Greek, they were, in effect, honorary Greeks by virtue of being featured in Homer's *Iliad.* Moreover, because Aeneas is the son of the goddess Aphrodite (whom the Romans renamed **Venus**), he is in any case half-Greek. Like Augustus's "marble city," these links between Greek and Roman myths satisfied the Romans' desire to be Greek without having to give up being Roman.

Roman Transformations of Greek Myths

The Romans went beyond merely creating a Greek connection to their own myths. They actually adopted the entire body of Greek mythology, identifying the Greek gods with their own indigenous deities, an appealing correspondence given that both often share the same Near Eastern sources or, further back, Indo-European roots. Both Zeus and Jupiter, for example, are derived from the ancient Indo-European Dyaus-Pitar (god the father). Thus, the Greek gods would not have seemed at all "foreign" to the Romans, who eagerly incorporated the Greek narratives as, in effect, additional information about their own deities. But they did not borrow mindlessly or in passive imitation. Rather, they changed as they borrowed, transforming Greek myth in four characteristic ways: they refocused the myths, redefining the characters of the gods and shifting the emphasis to those they considered especially important; they historicized the myths, attaching them to real events and individuals in Roman history; they politicized the myths, making them serve the needs of the Roman state; and they reinterpreted the myths to reflect Roman ideas and values.

The Refocusing of Myth: Greek Versus Roman Gods

The Greek pantheon is dominated by the figures of Zeus and Hera, along with Athene—the wisdom of Zeus—and Apollo, who likewise comes to embody enlightenment and the wisdom of self-knowledge and self-control. For the Romans, however, abstractions like wisdom and the pursuit of self-awareness were, though certainly important, clearly less pressing concerns than were practical problems like managing the grain supply to feed an enormous and growing population. Thus, in the Roman pantheon, although the main figures are still **Jupiter** (Figure 18-3) and **Juno** (Figure 18-4) (Roman equivalents of Zeus and Hera), Apollo and **Minerva** (the Roman counterpart of Athene) occupy a less central position. Further, **Ceres** [SEE-reez] (from whose name we derive the word *cereal* and who is the Roman version of Demeter, goddess of grain) becomes correspondingly more important. Similarly, Hestia, the Greek goddess of the hearth (the cooking fire), was mentioned only infrequently in Greek myths. Hestia's Roman counterpart, the native Roman goddess **Vesta**, however, was worshiped not only in every Roman home but in a public temple served by the Vestal Virgins, where a sacred fire that they kept always burning became the central symbol of Eternal Rome.

A similar shift of emphasis is evident in the changing attitude toward the war god. Although they admired their warrior-heroes, sometimes even making gods of them, the Greeks exalted Athene as goddess of the defensive war that saved the city but were somewhat ambivalent about Ares, the god of offensive war, whom they sometimes portrayed as two-faced and violent and not very bright. Clearly, for a nation with imperial ambitions, such a portrayal would not do. In fact, the Romans, although seeing themselves as bringers of peace, proudly traced their ancestry to

FIGURE 18-3   Jupiter. The Roman version of the Greek god Zeus, Jupiter adds a political dimension to the gods' domain. Bearing the Roman eagle at the end of his scepter, Jupiter is presented in this sculpture as a divine emblem of imperial power and a guarantor of its eternal dominion. *(Vatican Museums, Rome)*

the war god Mars (Figure 18-5). Possibly originating as an agricultural deity, Mars was portrayed as an implacable god whose purpose was to inspire the Roman legions to victory.

The Historicizing of Myth

In addition to shifting the focus of the myths and redefining the gods accordingly, the Romans, intensely proud of their own history, insisted on historicizing the myths. Greek myths, too, are often loosely based on historical events. The Troy saga, for instance, undoubtedly has some basis in a war or series of wars between the Greeks and Trojans, whose city was strategically located at the entrance to the Dardanelles; and the myth of Theseus and the Minotaur may reflect in a general way the shift of power from Crete to the mainland and the end of the colonial status of the Greek city-states. But the Romans were more precise and insistent about the historicizing process, tying the myths whenever possible to real names, dates, places, and events. Plutarch, for example, treated Romulus and Remus as historical, not mythical, figures.

Unlike the relatively timeless world of Greek myths, Roman myths are often precisely located in time and space and explained as realistically as possible.

FIGURE 18-4   Juno, Queen of Heaven
(also known as *Hera Barberini*). In this fifth-
century-B.C. sculpture, Juno (the Roman
equivalent of the Greek goddess Hera) is portrayed as a figure of royal bearing, reflecting
the dignity of her position as the most powerful Roman goddess. Like Jupiter, she is associated with the stability of the Roman state.
(Vatican Museums, Rome)

Whereas Heracles may have explored the unknown regions of the mythical North
and West, Romulus is much more interested in expanding Roman territory into
adjacent Italian lands. Descended from the gods and Homeric heroes on the mythical side, Romulus is also linked to history as the ancestor of Julius Caesar and his
great-nephew, the emperor Augustus. Virgil explained the link: Ascanius, Aeneas's
son, was nicknamed *Ilus,* and by the simple addition of another vowel picked up
over time, he became *Iulus;* thus, he was deemed the progenitor of the family of
Julii—as the family had indeed claimed since the third century B.C.—and hence of
Julius Caesar. The family tree of flesh-and-blood contemporary Romans, rooted in
the soil of mythology, sprouts real fruit. To the down-to-earth Roman sensibility,
these historical links justified the myths, even as the myths chartered real political claims. Indeed, by the fourth century B.C., several important Roman families
traced their lineage to the Trojans.

Trajan's column (Figure 18-6) is a visual illustration of the Roman fascination
with the points of intersection of myth and history. The bas-reliefs winding around
this column in scroll-like fashion tell the story of the Roman defeat of the Dacians (in what is now, as a result of that conquest, called Romania) under the emperor Trajan. In a scene at the base describing the beginning of the campaign, the
river god of the Danube supports the bridge over which the Roman legions pass.

FIGURE 18-5   Mars. Whereas the Greeks were somewhat ambivalent about their war god, Ares, the Romans proudly claimed their war god, Mars, as their ancestor. Depicted in this bronze statue as a Roman soldier, Mars personifies the military strength on which Rome relied. *(Capitolino Museum, Rome)*

FIGURE 18-6   Detail from Trajan's Column. In a typical Roman combination of myth and actual history, the 128-foot-high marble column of Trajan (located in the Forum of Trajan, Rome, A.D. 106–113) depicts, in spiral bands over 4 feet high, the emperor Trajan's two campaigns against the Dacians. In this detail near the base, the river god of the Danube supports the bridge—and hence the Roman enterprise—as columns of armored imperial troops cross the Danube River. Portraits of Emperor Trajan occur frequently in the unfolding story told in the bas-reliefs. The figure of Jupiter also appears, supporting the Roman cause. The narrative culminates in the Romans' victory, attended by the winged goddess Victory herself.

Amid realistic scenes of contemporary events of that war, in which the emperor figures prominently, Jupiter and the goddess Victory also appear. Such works, like the myths, reflect the Roman belief that art, to be useful, should instruct as well as delight. The more grounded in reality the myths were, the more they could perform their didactic function, illuminating both historical and contemporary events. The historicizing impulse sometimes even involved literalizing mythic material. For example, Greek myths traditionally include stories of Amazons, a tribe of female warriors, although there is no evidence that such women ever actually existed. In Rome, however, there is evidence in the form of inscriptions, bas-reliefs, and burial artifacts, that female gladiators performed in the arenas.

The Politicizing of Myth

A famous Roman statue features an Apollo-like portrait of the emperor Augustus with a small **Cupid**—an agent of the goddess Venus—at his feet (Figure 18-7). If history justified the myths, the myths, in turn, were used to justify political reali-

FIGURE 18-7 Augustus of Prima Porta. In this marble statue (c. 20 B.C.), the emperor Augustus is portrayed as a Roman soldier directing his troops. The portrait is recognizably Augustus himself, but idealized and slightly larger than life (6′8″), and is reminiscent of Greek sculptures of the god Apollo. The facial expression, however, is unlike those calm, detached Greek images. In characteristic Roman fashion, Augustus's expression is serious, and he is clearly intent on the business at hand. He is accompanied by a small Cupid at his feet, the real and the mythic thus intersecting. The relative proportions and positions of the two figures suggest that the real world in which Augustus actually ruled predominates, while the subordinate mythic material provides a support system: the gods are on the side of Rome. (*Vatican Museums, Rome*)

ties: in this case, the imperial regime is granted a divine connection while private emotions (here, love) are subordinated to duty to the state.

In Roman religious practices, as in their myths, the same connection between private worship and public rites prevailed. For example, Romans in their homes typically worshiped three kinds of gods: the Lares, spirits (possibly ancestral) who guarded the family; the **Penates** [pe-NAY-teez], spirits of the pantry, who also protected the house and especially its food supply; and the Vesta, goddess of the blazing hearth, where the meals were cooked. These domestic gods had their public counterparts in the state gods Jupiter, Juno, and Ceres, who performed the same protective functions for the nation as the domestic gods did for the home. Thus, even in the rituals of daily life, the Romans ended up paying service to the gods of state and hence to the state itself. This link to political life was strengthened when deceased emperors were deified and their spirits were said to have joined the other guardians of Rome.

One scholar, T. P. Wiseman, speculates that the Romulus and Remus myth itself is a product of Roman politics. In the original version of the myth, he argues, there was a single eponymous founder, Romulus; the figure of Remus was not added until the late third century B.C., only to be killed off, in the myth, in reflection of the class division in ancient Rome. Remus, he says, represented the plebians (common people), who twice seceded from Rome and refused to serve in the military, while Romulus represented the patricians (aristocracy). The actual political rift was resolved through a series of legal reforms that granted the plebians a somewhat greater share of political power. The myth of Remus's death, Wiseman claims, is perhaps a symbolic blood sacrifice to consecrate the foundation of the state. In fact, he suggests, human sacrifice to ensure the security of the city's foundation walls may actually have been performed.

For the Romans, in myths as in other aspects of their lives, all roads led to Rome. It is true, of course, that Greek myths were often used to express political ideas. Aeschylus's *Eumenides,* for example, underwrites the Athenian court system; the *Iliad* surely comments on political values; and the spirit of Theseus was said to protect Athens. Nevertheless, the gods of the Greeks were not typically nationalistic in their political aims. Although individual Greek localities had their resident deities (indeed, every stream or grove seems to have had its local nymph or god), the major gods, the Olympians, were not gods of specific places—of, say, Argos or Mycenae or Troy. Rather, they were *the* gods—of Trojans and of Greeks. Roman gods, in contrast, were emphatically Roman. And although conquest spread their worship to many lands, the gods themselves remained identified as gods of Rome, as gods who had a vested interest in Roman destiny. Thus, even Ovid, recounting myths of adventure and love in the *Metamorphoses,* set the tales within the framework of Roman ambitions. Roman destiny, further, was divinely predetermined: the establishment and maintenance of Eternal Rome and the incorporation of all the earth within its borders. This obsession with Rome was so pervasive that even writers who were skeptical of the "official" view of the state, its destiny, or its gods felt compelled to discuss it or at least to include it in their works. Rome was not a topic a Roman could simply ignore.

The Myths Reinterpreted

The use of myths to support these political aims required a major reinterpretation of the material inherited from the Greeks. Thus, the dynamic, open-ended, ambiguous, and often contradictory universe of Greek myth gave way to a universe that was teleological—that is, directed in linear fashion toward a single, inevitable goal: the subjection of all the world to the rule of Roman gods and Roman law. Consequently, all acts that furthered that goal were deemed good; all that hindered it were necessarily evil. In Roman myth as in Roman culture, *pietas*—duty to parents, gods, and state—and patriotism were inseparably linked.

The Romans had witnessed, both historically and currently, what happens when governments are unprepared for external threats or vulnerable to the outbreak of civil wars. If they were to be truly bringers of peace (an aim that, to their credit, they more or less accomplished during the long period of the **Pax Romana**), they would need to be able to count on the commitment to duty and loyalty of the citizens of their empire. Patriotism was thus neither an abstraction nor a sentimental concept—it was a survival tool. Service in the military and the discipline that made the Roman legions so successful likewise depended on the self-sacrifice and loyalty of Roman citizens. To worship and obey the gods of Rome, then, became an act of patriotism; conversely, defiance of the gods constituted both impiety and treason. (Historically, this attitude was reflected in the otherwise tolerant Romans' antagonism toward groups like the Christians and Jews, who would accept Roman governors but refuse to worship their gods.) Further, events that seemed to have human causes were, when seen from the gods' perspective (the big picture), revealed to be part of a divine plan. For the Greeks, the fall of Troy was more the consequence of choices made by a Paris, a Priam, or a Hector; for the Romans, Troy fell so that Rome could arise, and Aeneas had to go into exile so that the Romans could claim Trojan as well as Latin ancestry. In such a universe, there can ultimately be no tragedy—only history incompletely understood.

The Roman Hero

The ego-driven hero of Greek myth typically set his ambiguous, divided nature against a confusing and contradictory world and succeeded by acquiring self-knowledge while maintaining his integrity. Such a hero, however, was far too concerned with his own needs and goals and far too prone, in his reckless pursuit of immortality, to commit antisocial acts to constitute a proper role model for Romans. Along with the powers of Mars and the territorial ambitions of Romulus, the Romans wanted their heroes to exemplify the ideal Roman soldier and citizen, adamant and unswerving in championing the Roman way. For a state in which, unlike the Greek polis, we can see the beginnings of the modern nation-state, in which citizenship transcends tribal and regional loyalties, such dedication is mandatory. It is not surprising, then, that the Latin epics were self-consciously didactic and that they were intentionally employed in the education of young Romans to inculcate proper models of appropriate masculine identity in the context of the state and its citizens' national responsibilities.

Three qualities nostalgically associated with the early republic are essential for the Roman hero: *gravitas,* or seriousness of purpose and devotion to duty (especially duty to the state); *pietas,* or duty to one's parents, the state, and the gods of Rome; and *frugalitas,* or the idealizing of the simple life, free from the distractions of vanity and self-indulgence, qualities associated in Roman myth and epics with women. The proper Roman hero subordinates his own needs to those of the state he serves, accepts whatever burdens and sacrifices patriotic duty imposes on him, and does not ask to be rewarded. It is enough that Rome be immortal—sharing in the immortality of the state, he finds all the fulfillment he needs.

Nor should the properly masculine Roman hero indulge in the emotional excesses of his Greek counterparts—duty requires that he avoid giving way to passionate excesses of grief, anger, or rage. Certainly, the Romans admired the Greek heroes of myth and even perpetuated the cult of Hercules (the Latin name for

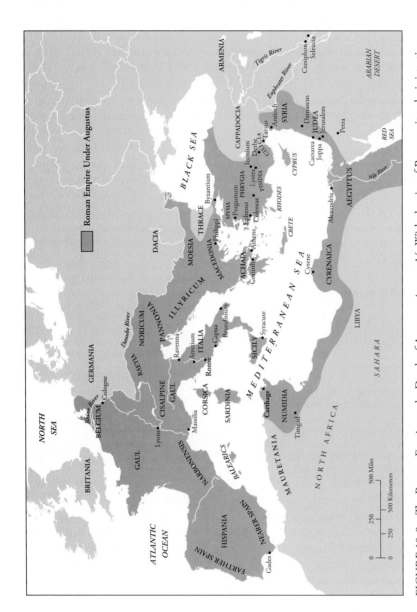

FIGURE 18-8   The Roman Empire at the Death of Augustus in A.D. 14. With the city of Rome as its administrative capitol, the empire governed most of the Mediterranean basin. Its subjects included people representing a wide variety of language groups and cultures.

Heracles), maintaining an altar to him (the Ara Maxima, or Greatest Altar) and claiming, as both Virgil and the Roman historian Livy attest, that Hercules passed through Rome while bringing the cattle of Geryon back from the Underworld. But for a Hercules or an Achilles to behave in Augustan Rome as these heroes sometimes did in Greek myth would have been considered outrageous. Further, the Roman hero does not invest such emotional energy in his own life that the prospect of his death becomes the one overwhelming fact determining his choices. Rather, he must recognize that his individual life occupies one brief instant in a long span of history. To become obsessed with his personal needs or private sufferings would perpetuate the illusion of egocentrism: in fact, neither his triumphs nor his tragedies matter, except insofar as they contribute to the ultimate goal—the triumph of Eternal Rome.

Such heroes will, of course, be rewarded—but not in this life. For true patriots, Elysium awaits, in the Underworld, where worthy souls can sing, curry their horses, polish their chariots, and, of course (this being a Roman version of paradise), partake in the inevitable feast.

. . . .

Questions for Discussion and Review

1. The Romans, who were great admirers of Greek culture, borrowed Greek myths but altered them to reflect their own values and ideas. Describe at least two ways in which the Romans transformed Greek myths.

2. Contrast the rape of the Sabine women with the Greek myth in which the centaurs attempt to rape the Lapith women. What do these two myths suggest about the female perspective in the Roman and Greek cultures, respectively? How do Greek and Roman myths differ in their response to rape?

3. In what ways does Romulus reflect a specifically Roman concept of the hero? Consider his ancestry, his attitude toward the city and its role, and his self-image.

4. Explain how the Roman hero differs from his Greek counterpart. What qualities of a Hercules or an Achilles would a Roman admire? What aspects of their behavior might a Roman hero disapprove of?

Virgil's Roman Epic: The *Aeneid*

KEY TOPICS/THEMES

Virgil's Aeneid, *the great Roman "sequel" to the Homeric epics, describes the wanderings of Aeneas, the only Trojan hero to escape from the destruction of Troy, along with his father, his son, and a band of retainers. After a series of adventures, including a year spent in Carthage as the consort of Queen Dido, he makes his way, commanded by Jupiter, to Italy. After a prolonged war there, he marries a Latin princess and becomes the progenitor of the Romans. Although paying tribute to both the* Odyssey *and the* Iliad, *Virgil transforms Greek myths and heroes and presents a uniquely Roman epic with a uniquely Roman hero.*

Virgil

Publius Vergilius Maro, known as Virgil (70–19 B.C.), was raised in Mantua on his father's successful farm. Sent to Rome to complete his education, he witnessed in dismay the civil wars that began in 48 B.C., marking Rome's painful transition from republic to empire (Figure 19-1). His own family farm was confiscated during that chaotic time. Determined that such disorder should not recur, Virgil supported the empire, seeing the emperor Augustus, its most visible symbol, as a restorer of peace and civil order.

A careful poet, Virgil wrote slowly and revised extensively. His work includes two groups of pastoral poems (the *Eclogues* and the *Georgics*) that nostalgically idealize the peaceful simplicity of the rural life of farmers and shepherds. These works, highly appealing to the residents of a city characterized by the noise, crowds, traffic, and other tensions of urban life as we still know them, made Virgil the most popular poet of his time.

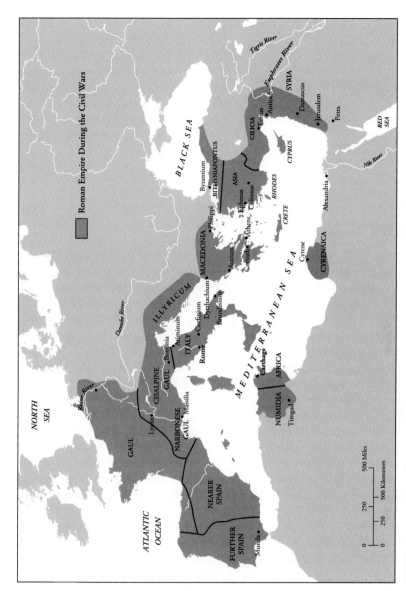

FIGURE 19-1 Map of Rome During the Civil Wars. Rome by this time had already expanded its empire to include areas not only in Europe but also in Asia, North Africa, and the Middle East.

Emperor Augustus himself encouraged and funded Virgil's work on his epic poem, the *Aeneid* [ee-NEE-id], to which he devoted the last eleven years of his life. Not yet finished with his revisions, Virgil ordered the manuscript to be burned at his death, but Augustus prevented its destruction—and no wonder! Apart from his personal admiration for the poem, what better public relations device could an emperor imagine than to have the nation's most honored poet describe the empire and its current ruler as divinely inspired? Whatever interpretations later readers might have, it is clear that the emperor and his court found this work a most flattering tribute to both emperor and empire.

The *Aeneid:* Significant Themes and Characters

The Greek Connection

The characteristic Augustan desire to infuse a Roman work with an aura of classical Greece is manifested in the *Aeneid* in several ways. Determined to be the Roman Homer, Virgil wrote in an elegant style, calculated to elevate the Latin tongue from the prosaic language of everyday affairs to a self-consciously poetic vehicle with a cultural status equal to that of Greek—a foreign language that educated Romans would have learned as part of their formal schooling.

In addition to asserting the genealogical link that makes Augustus into a descendant of the mythical Trojan **Aeneas** (see Chapter 18), Virgil frequently reminds his readers of the similarities between his epic and Homer's. Not only does he adopt all the standard features of the Homeric epic, beginning with the invocation of the Muse, he also draws explicit parallels between his work and Homer's. The first six books of the *Aeneid* are carefully modeled on the *Odyssey.* The wanderings of a hero trying to get home, the search for a bride, the devotion of Aeneas to his son, the following of Odysseus's route from Troy (so that Aeneas lands, for example, at the Cyclops's cave just as Odysseus did), the danger of temptation by a woman who would keep him from his journey if she could—all point to the similarities between the two works.

In Book 7, with a second invocation, Virgil shifts gears and, to describe his battle scenes, models the rest of the work on the *Iliad.* The parallels include the councils of the gods, their rivalries and interventions, the relationship between the hero and his divine mother, the gathering of the troops (including one army led by a woman), and the death of the hero's best friend at the hands of his rival.

The Historicizing of Myth   Despite the Greek veneer, however, the *Aeneid* is a thoroughly Roman poem. Like his contemporaries, Virgil was concerned with the historicizing of myth, linking the characters of the story with individual events and persons in Roman history. At several crucial points in the narrative, the poet has reliable characters (the god Jupiter; the hero's father, Anchises) recount the "history" of Rome, giving dates even to mythological events: Aeneas will rule **Latium** [LAY-shee-uhm] for three years, and his son will rule for thirty years and build a new city at Alba Longa, which will be the capital for three hundred years until Romulus builds Rome itself. The narration recounts the conquest of Greece—delayed ven-

The World of Roman History

753 B.C.	Traditional date of Rome's founding by Romulus and Remus
510	Expulsion of Tarquin; traditional date of the establishment of the Roman Republic
264–241	First Punic War; Roman army enters Sicily
218–201	Second Punic War; Hannibal invades Italy and is defeated by Scipio Africanus at Battle of Zama (202)
149–146	Third Punic War; Carthage destroyed (146)
60	First Triumvirate formed by Pompey, Crassus, and Julius Caesar
47–44	Dictatorship of Caesar; assassinated in 44
43	Second Triumvirate formed by Antony, Octavian, and Lepidus; defeats opposition at Battle of Philippi (42)
41–32	Marc Antony rules eastern empire
31	Octavian defeats Antony at Battle of Actium
27 B.C.–A.D. 14	Reign of Augustus (Octavian)
c. 4 B.C.–A.D. 33	Life of Jesus of Nazareth; First Gospel (c. A.D. 70)
313	Constantine issues the Edict of Milan, making Christianity the empire's favored religion

geance for the destruction of Troy—and the expansion of Rome, and culminates in the reigns of Julius and his grandnephew Augustus Caesar, who will renew a Golden Age in Latium. Similarly, Aeneas's shield, forged for him by **Vulcan** (the Latin name for Hephaestus) as Achilles' was, depicts contemporary Roman events, including the Battle of Actium (31 B.C.) between Marc Antony and Octavian (who shortly thereafter became Emperor Augustus).

Another example of the linkage of myth and history occurs in the curse that **Dido** [DYE-doh] calls down on Aeneas when he abandons her. She calls for an "avenger" from **Carthage** who will make endless war on Rome, thus predicting both the series of **Punic Wars** that Rome fought with Carthage and the invasion of Rome during the second of those wars (218–201 B.C.) by the Carthaginian general **Hannibal,** who wreaked devastation from which the nation never fully recovered. (For a more complete chronology of the world of Roman history, see the accompanying box.) Most educated Romans, who were quite familiar with the dates of their own history, would probably have been aware that the Carthaginian portion of Virgil's tale involved, in fact, a bit of "revisionist" history. Not only did Troy's "fall" occur too long before the founding of Carthage for any such figures as Aeneas and Dido to have met, but also, earlier tradition portrayed Dido as both a good leader and a highly moral person, one who would never have engaged in a publicly flaunted extramarital affair. The anachronisms are compounded when Aeneas, arriving at Carthage, finds scenes of the destruction of Troy already carved on the temple of Juno. But the link between myth and actual events—Hannibal's invasion of Italy and the eventual Roman destruction of Carthage—was apparently too appealing an opportunity to pass up. That Augustus began reconstructing Carthage as a Roman colony, and that the Phoenician goddess Tannit was, in Romanized Carthage, identified as Juno-Tannit, may also have played a part.

The Role of the City   The first role of the city, as described by Aeneas himself when he visits Carthage, is to create the conditions under which civilized life can flourish: to establish just laws and good government (the prerequisites for civic order and justice); to erect buildings and monuments; to encourage the arts, theater, trade, and commerce; and to enclose them all within walls that serve to mark off the city's legal boundaries and to protect its inhabitants. The Romans' concern with boundaries and barriers such as borders, ramparts, and walls, which was reflected in the earlier myth that describes Romulus marking off his territory with a plow, is evident throughout the *Aeneid*. Jupiter, for example, promises Venus that the walls of Rome will surely rise. When Aeneas first enters Carthage, he comments enviously on the happiness of those "whose walls already rise." In fact, almost every mention of a city in the epic includes a reference to its walls, so that the walls come to stand for the entire city and the way of life and the people it contains.

Although we don't get to see Rome itself in the *Aeneid*, we do get to watch Carthage under construction, a model for Aeneas to admire, until Dido (queen of Carthage), caught up in her love affair with Aeneas, forgets her responsibilities; her neglect of duty is thus a warning to the would-be Roman. In this process, the appointed leader is in charge. If he or she neglects the task, the city will suffer: Carthage, as every Roman knew, was ultimately destroyed by Rome (146 B.C.). Troy, defending the self-indulgent Paris, was also destroyed.

But it is not enough to create peace and order within one city's borders and walls if there are enemies outside. Thus, the second role of the city is to spread its civilization, to "curb haughty nations by justice," to "teach the ways of peace to those they conquer"—even if it must fight endless wars to do so. Like many well-intentioned modern nations, the peace-loving Romans apparently fought wars, which they hated, in order to create the conditions that would end the necessity for war. Although in recent years we have come to consider such acts and intentions as imperialist aggression, in their own time the Romans' vision of one world united under Roman auspices was not necessarily considered undesirable.

Many lands actually welcomed the Romans who, along with their governors and their gods, brought the blessings of security, advanced technology (as they constructed water and sanitation systems and built roads that still function today), an improved economy (as goods and services were traded), education (as young people from the colonies came to Roman universities to study), and opportunities both for Roman citizenship and for advancement in the vast Roman bureaucracy. Further, whenever possible, the Romans respected the cultures they absorbed, usually allowing the colonial peoples to maintain their own language, culture, and religion.

The Roman Hero

In the *Iliad*—the story of Troy—we met the hero Achilles in the opening lines of the poem; in the *Odyssey,* although we didn't actually meet Odysseus until Book 5, we heard of him (and of the poet's judgment of him) in the proem (the introductory section) that opens the work. Not so in the Roman epic: the subject of the *Aeneid*—its real hero—is not a man but a city and the nation that shares its name. In the opening line, the poet announces his subject: "arms" and "a man." Clearly, the "arms"—warfare—come first, whereas the "man" remains anonymous for the first 130 lines of the poem.

The focus on the city skews the portrayal of the human contenders in one very specific and exclusively Roman direction. In the *Iliad,* Hector and Achilles faced each other as equals, respecting each other's worth and honor. But in the *Aeneid,* though **Turnus** is portrayed with considerable sympathy and though he and Aeneas are equally skilled and courageous, they are seen from the Roman perspective. That is, Aeneas is a patriot, but Turnus, who does what Aeneas does but on the wrong side, is repeatedly described as "mad" and "fanatical"—an enemy to Rome and, as he explicitly states, to Jupiter. He is thus a foil to Aeneas in war, as Dido was in love. In the *Iliad,* Zeus respected and sympathized with both sides. In the *Aeneid,* there is no question about which is the good side: Turnus fights for personal glory, whereas Aeneas fights for gods and country—for Rome. An exchange such as that between Hector and Ajax in the *Iliad*—Trojan and Greek fighting to a draw, proving their prowess, and exchanging gifts—is not possible here. War is no longer a game fought for the glory of the players; war is now grim—and avoidable. If only Rome's opponents would do the sensible thing and yield peacefully to the inevitable, the "iron gates of war" would close forever. Until then, the kind of peace found in the Roman image of **Arcadia** as a peaceable kingdom of gardens and shepherds will remain a dream of the Golden Age long past (associated by the Romans with the "good old days" of the early republic) or of the life in Elysium to come. The persistence in Roman culture of nostalgia for the imagined simplicity of the past and the fondness of well-to-do Romans for country villas for pastoral weekend retreats are expressed in these mythic images, perhaps representing an undercurrent of suspicion that the price paid for civilization—even (or perhaps especially) one as glorious as Rome's—was too high.

In return for their troubles, the Greek heroes received some kind of reward: Achilles got his glory, and Odysseus his family and home. Meanwhile, the hero of the *Aeneid* will not even get to see the promised land for which he risks his life and sacrifices everything—his comfort, his home, his wife, his lover, his friends (including Palinarus, the helmsman, and the Arcadian prince **Pallas** himself), along with his freedom and his fortune. What kind of hero would sacrifice so much to gain so little?

Aeneas: An Exemplary Roman

Aeneas is presented from the beginning of the epic as a man "remarkable for goodness," who is nevertheless forced by the gods to bear the burden of being the founder of Rome. Achilles, offered two fates, chose to fight (and die) at Troy; Odysseus, despite many tempting alternatives, chose to go home to Ithaca, whatever the risks. Aeneas, however, has no such choices. From the beginning, he is the victim of divine politics. So that Rome may come into being, Troy falls, and he is ordered by his mother, the goddess Venus, to flee to "Italy," a region he's never seen or even heard of. When he falls in love with Dido, he stays with her until **Mercury** orders him to leave: "You must set sail" is the message Mercury brings from Jupiter. For the Roman hero, unlike his Greek counterpart, his only choice is in the way he accepts his destiny.

Why, the poet asks, would the gods impose such suffering on such a good man? Can the gods be malevolent? The answer, not stated explicitly until Aeneas's visit to the Underworld in Book 6, is already implied in the opening dozen lines of the poem: it is for the good of Rome. Conscious of his responsibility to the gods, to his son, and to the future of Rome (if you won't do it for yourself, his mother and Jupiter both ask him, would you deny your son the walls of Rome?), Aeneas accepts his burdens—despite his sorrow at the losses he has experienced—not only with the tranquility that the Roman philosophers urged but with the kind of zeal, once he is committed, that characterized the Greek heroes' pursuit of their own more personal goals. This contrast in the Greek and Roman heroes' sense of their own identities is revealed even in the epithets attached to their names. For the Greek heroes, the epithets described personal skills or qualities—"wily Odysseus," "swift-footed Achilles." For Aeneas, however, the epithets describe moral commitments and responsibilities—"pious Aeneas," "father Aeneas"—qualities so utterly given in his character that he can use them to describe himself: "I am pious Aeneas," he says, introducing himself to Dido. As such, one of his burdens is quite literal: he is responsible for carrying the household gods of Troy—the Lares, the Penates, and the Vesta—to Rome, where they eventually will be established as the gods of Rome, and where, in the temple of the Vesta (the hearth fire of the state), the Eternal Flame of Rome will be kept burning.

Aeneas's Discipline   Another difference between Aeneas and the Greek heroes is his self-control. Achilles was naturally excessive; and Odysseus was typically impulsive, giving in to curiosity or egotism until he acquired self-control and a sense of responsibility the hard way, through painful experience. Aeneas, however, seems to come already equipped with the Roman virtues of responsibility and self-discipline. The visits of the two heroes, Aeneas and Odysseus, to the land of the Cyclopes are instructive. There, in the place where Odysseus's impulsive egotism got him into trouble with Poseidon, Aeneas exhibits both self-control and compassion: he takes aboard an enemy sailor, Achaemenides, supposedly "left behind" by the irresponsible Odysseus (an incident that appears nowhere in Homer but that clearly illustrates the virtues that Virgil attributed to his more proper Roman hero). In another ironic comment on Homer's Odysseus, Aeneas insists that the Trojans do not land at Carthage to raid the city—"to loot the household gods of Libya, or to drive down stolen booty toward the beaches."

The difference between Greek and Roman heroes is most blatantly revealed in a pair of parallel incidents in Book 10, in which Virgil contrasts the behavior of the Greek-style hero Turnus (explicitly compared to "a new Achilles") with that of the Roman hero Aeneas. Turnus, an experienced general, comes on the young prince

Pallas, in his first battle, on the battlefield. He not only kills the young man but strips him of his gold belt and wears it to boast of his victory. For Turnus, the glory is in the body count, and the belt is his trophy. In a similar incident, Aeneas comes on a young Latin soldier, **Lausus,** who is taking incredible risks to defend his father, a notorious tyrant. So struck is Aeneas by the young man's pious devotion to the idea of fatherhood that, remembering his own father, Aeneas treats Lausus respectfully, offering him the opportunity to avoid the encounter. When Lausus insists on fighting and is killed, Aeneas makes a point of refusing to strip the armor, instead returning the corpse with honor to the youth's companions.

Aeneas's Rage   Despite his courtesy and stated preference for treaties rather than battles, Aeneas is not passive. Not only does he fight like a demon when necessary, but when aroused, "his wrath is terrible." Unlike Achilles', though, Aeneas's anger is not fueled by slights to his ego. It is only when he experiences a deep sense of moral outrage that he allows his anger to express itself in the service of a higher goal: when he comes on Helen in the ruins of Troy; when Turnus kills Pallas and strips his armor; when the Latins violate treaty after treaty; and, of course, after their last battle, when Aeneas sees Pallas's belt on Turnus's shoulder. But he does learn, in the course of his experience, to control the occasions when he allows that anger to be translated into action. When he meets Helen, his mother, Venus, must temper his instinctive desire to kill her on the spot, just as Athene tempered Achilles' urge to kill Agamemnon during their quarrel. Venus instructs her son in the gods' perspective; by the time of Aeneas's encounter with Turnus, no god needs to intervene—Aeneas has adopted the gods' perspective as his own.

Women in the *Aeneid*

Like the heroes, the women, both divine and human, in the *Aeneid* are divided into those who are on the Roman side and those who are Rome's enemies. On the pro-Roman side are Aeneas's wife, **Creusa** [kree-OO-sa], and his mother, Venus.

Creusa   In an image that emphasizes the epic's patriarchal focus, Aeneas escapes from Troy carrying his father (the burden of the past) on his back and leading his son (his duty toward the future) by the hand (Figure 19-2). His wife, Creusa, left to follow along, lags behind and is killed by Greek soldiers. When Aeneas realizes that she is missing, he goes back to find her but discovers only her shade (or ghost). In a scene reminiscent of Odysseus's attempt to embrace the shade of his mother in Hades, he tries three times to embrace her, only to find nothing there but air—an apt image of her insubstantial value when compared with the larger enterprise of founding Rome.

The behavior of Creusa's shade nevertheless represents a model of Roman devotion to duty. Characterizing Aeneas's weeping as "fanatic sorrow," she instructs him to accept the gods' arrangement of their destinies, to seek a new kingdom and a new bride, and to stop fretting and get on with his mission. That is the last we hear of her, or of mourning—a revealing contrast to the extended funeral games (exactly like those Achilles held in honor of Patroclus) that Aeneas holds for his dead father. Women in Roman myth clearly are expendable.

FIGURE 19-2   Aeneas and Anchises. Shown in this Attic vase painting
(c. 510 B.C.) carrying his father, Anchises, on his back and leading his son,
Ascanius, by the hand, Aeneas is an apt emblem of the duty of a Roman
hero—or a Roman citizen: to carry on the ancient traditions, to sustain the
Roman state, and to lead it to an even greater future. But that great responsibility is clearly a heavy burden: Aeneas, his head with its great helmet bowed,
droops under the weight. *(Martin von Wagner Museum, Wurzburg)*

Marriage and the Family   Marriage, for the Romans, is a sacred institution. But
marriages are made for political or economic reasons—love is not essential. Thus,
Aeneas will wed the Latin princess **Lavinia** in order to cement the bond between
Latins and Trojans, despite her overt hostility and his lack of any personal relationship with her, thus recapitulating the original Romans' capture of and subsequent
marriage to the Sabine women. And Dido, whom he loves, he does not marry—an
omission he reminds her of ("I have never entered into such agreements," he says)
when she, thinking of him as her husband, begs him to stay. The political function
of marriage reflects the actual state of affairs in Augustan Rome. Beginning during
the disruptions of the civil wars, the number of divorces and extramarital liaisons
increased, as women gradually gained more social and economic independence. To
underwrite social stability and reassert male control, Augustus made the marriage
laws more rigid, requiring widowers to remarry and to select women of their own
class, and making it illegal for men to ignore their wives' adultery (a ruling that
would backfire when his own family members were later implicated).

In this patriarchal world, fatherhood is essential. Motherhood, however, is subsumed in the larger affairs of state. Lavinia's mother, **Amata**, for example, explaining her disapproval of King **Latinus**'s plan to break their daughter's engagement to Turnus and marry her instead to Aeneas, is simply dismissed.

Two Mothers: Thetis and Venus   It is also instructive to contrast the maternal relationship, outwardly similar, of Thetis and Achilles to that of Venus and Aeneas. The two mothers have similar functions, carrying messages between Zeus/Jupiter and their respective sons or appealing to Hephaestus/Vulcan for new shields when their sons are about to go into battle. But their goals for their respective offspring differ radically. Thetis wanted to protect Achilles from harm; of his two fates, she'd clearly prefer the safer choice—long life, even without glory. Not so Venus: committed to her own political agenda, as well as to her son's political responsibilities as future father of his country, she wants him to found Rome even if it means struggle, sacrifice, and sorrow for him personally. Thus, she participates in the plot with Juno to cause him to fall in love with Dido in order to protect his ships—and his mission—knowing that he will have to leave and will suffer emotionally as a result. Venus, of course, is all-too-familiar with the consequences of abandoning self-control and yielding to the "madness" of desire. According to the Homeric *Hymn to Aphrodite,* Aphrodite (Venus) herself is driven by such "madness" to make love to the mortal Anchises, the result being the birth of none other than Aeneas.

Juno and Juturna   On the anti-Roman side are Juno (always described, until she yields to Jupiter, as "savage Juno") and the goddess **Juturna** (the "fanatic" sister of Turnus). Between them, these two goddesses encourage Dido's neglect of Carthage, the fury of Amata (queen of Latium), Turnus's rage, the Latins' repeated breaking of treaties, and acts of violence such as the burning of Aeneas's ships. They even interfere in trying to deprive Aeneas of victory by preventing him from finding Turnus on the battlefield, often plucking him up, chariot and all, and depositing him, much to his consternation, on the other side of the river.

Even more revealing of the "savage" goddess's chthonic powers (she is characterized throughout the epic as violent and irrational), Juno calls up the powers of **Allecto,** one of the Furies, from her home in the Underworld. Associated by Virgil with the poison of the Gorgon, she sends a snake into the breast of Amata and implants a firebrand in the heart of Turnus, driving both mad, so that Amata is compelled to Bacchic frenzies and Turnus to equally frenzied violence in war.

Thus, whether they are loved or hated, men are victims of the terrible goddesses. Juno may not have the power to change Jupiter's plan for Rome, but she can delay its implementation, just as Poseidon delayed Odysseus from reaching home. But the difference is revealing. Poseidon's interference was caused by Odysseus's own pride, his vain boasting that revealed his identity to the Cyclops, and its duration (a finite sentence that Zeus insisted must not exceed the crime) coincided with Odysseus's moral development. Juno's delaying the founding of Rome and her persecution of Aeneas are not in proportion to Aeneas's behavior or moral condition. As many scholars have noted, even Turnus, whom Juno ostensibly protects, is destroyed in the process, and Aeneas, despite Venus's assistance, never gets to see the promised city of Rome—nor will anyone for several centuries. Meanwhile, the firebrand of war will keep burning. According to some readers, Juno thus has, in effect, the last word, despite "yielding" to Jupiter. In fact, immediately after Juno and Jupiter settle affairs between themselves, Jupiter himself sends a Fury to paralyze Turnus, setting him up for Aeneas to slay.

Dido   Between these pro- and anti-Roman extremes is the figure of Dido. Like Aeneas, caught up in an affair beyond her control, she is portrayed sympathetically —the victim, in turn, of the gods and of Aeneas, who loves her and then, ordered by the gods, rather unceremoniously abandons her. Aeneas is not gifted, like Odysseus, with "honeyed words" to let her down gently. Virgil grants Dido a long lament in which she expresses her grief and sorrow. But the contrast to the *Odyssey* is revealing. Portraying Aeneas as sitting at Dido's table and telling his story in flashbacks, Virgil connects Dido with two women in Homer's epic. One is Nausicaa, in whose father's hall Odysseus tells his own tale. But unlike Alcinuous, who offers Odysseus half his kingdom and his daughter, Nausicaa, if he wants to stay, and free passage home if he wants to leave, Dido's offer to share her kingdom with Aeneas has a catch—he must stay. And unlike Nausicaa, Dido is overwhelmed by her visitor's departure. By attempting, in effect, to imprison her lover, Dido reflects not Nausicaa but Calypso, who keeps Odysseus as her prisoner and sex slave, until Hermes brings the message from Zeus that she must release him.

Virgil's contemporaries would surely have seen a parallel between Dido and, in their own recent history, Cleopatra, the Egyptian queen who loved the Roman general (and Julius Caesar's associate) Marc Antony. She bore him three children during his prolonged stay in Egypt, and when Antony was defeated by Octavian (later known as Augustus) at the Battle of Actium, Egypt was subordinated to Rome, and Antony's career was in ruins. Cleopatra and Antony both committed suicide. Like Cleopatra, with whom she is implicitly compared in the later description of Aeneas's shield, Dido has abandoned her city and compromised her reputation, all for love—and now she has lost that. In anger and despair, she curses Aeneas, calls for an avenger, and commits suicide. In her rage, she, too, embodies the spirit of the Furies, calling up unending warfare. Pitying her in her agony, as she dies an unmerited death brought on by her emotional frenzy, Juno sends **Iris** to free her spirit from her body, ending her misery.

On a personal level, Virgil clearly sympathizes with Dido in her predicament, just as he does with Turnus; neither understands what has gone wrong. Dido has devoted herself to love as Turnus has to honor, and both die bewildered, watching a world they thought they understood crumble about them. In Dido's death (as in Turnus's, which Virgil likewise presents sympathetically), we see the poet burying with honor a set of values long admired by, but no longer appropriate for, contemporary Romans.

Wrapped up in the pursuit of purely personal satisfactions, Dido has abandoned her responsibility and neglected her city-in-progress. Many modern readers find Aeneas cold, and even inhuman, in his response to Dido. However, she has allowed her emotions to get the better of her self-control. A good Roman would have mourned briefly and then gotten back to work, as Aeneas did on losing Creusa. Indeed, Creusa herself sets the model, insisting that he get on with his mission.

It is not Dido's plight itself but her response to the burdens and sorrows of her life that is characterized as understandable but ultimately un-Roman—a foil to

Aeneas's proper response. Virgil is sorry for Dido (witness Aeneas's appeal to her shade in the Underworld, which she rejects). But although the worthy Roman sheds "tears for passing things"—for Creusa, for Troy, for Dido, for Pallas, for all the personal betrayals, losses, and sorrows that life entails—and even memorializes them in stone, or in verse, he must not allow sorrow to prevent him from carrying out his duty to Rome or from seeing the historical perspective, from which his personal fate is relatively insignificant.

In addition to being un-Roman in her response, Dido is also a woman, and like Cleopatra, she becomes an emblem of what happens, both to the individual and to the state, when women are allowed to rule. Depicted as changeable as well as overemotional, Dido first aids Aeneas and then curses him, just as she initially refuses to consider remarriage and then wants to marry Aeneas. The only steadfast female in the epic is Creusa, and she is conveniently dead! Even Camilla, the Volscian female warrior (equivalent to the Amazon Penthesilia, whom Achilles fought and killed), is portrayed as distracted by trivia: she chases after a splendidly arrayed Trojan warrior because she covets his costume, all purple and gold. "Blind to all else," as the poet describes her, she neither sees nor hears the fatal blow coming. It is clear that females, especially those with armies at their command, must be defeated to ensure social and political order in Rome, just as Roman females must be kept in their proper (and properly subordinate) place—again recapitulating the politically useful myth about the Sabine women, who not only accepted their subordinate condition but also stopped their fathers and brothers from attacking Rome.

The Gods and Human Fate

In one of the most revealing scenes in the epic, Venus tears away the "cloud" from Aeneas's eyes so that he can see the destruction of Troy from the gods' viewpoint. In a superficially similar scene in the *Iliad,* Athene removed the cloud from the eyes of Diomedes so that he could distinguish the gods from the humans on the battlefield. The differences, however, are striking: whereas in the Greek epic the gods and humans were caught up in the same battle, in the Roman version human action is ultimately an illusion—at best, the humans are agents in a divine plan they cannot see or comprehend. They may think that Greeks fight with Trojans, but it is actually gods doing battle with gods, Venus reveals. Thus, there is no point in Aeneas's killing Helen—she isn't the real cause of the Trojan War. If Troy falls, it falls so that Rome can eventually arise. The most significant things Aeneas can reclaim from the ruins of Troy, apart from his son (who will be the ancestor of the Romans), are the Vesta (the statue of the hearth goddess) and the Eternal Flame (the divine spirit of Rome), which Aeneas is to keep burning until it can be enshrined anew in the Eternal City itself.

At every level in the *Aeneid,* human destiny is revealed to be a function of divine politics. Even love, that most intimate of emotions, is not exempt: Venus and Juno, each for her own political aims, cause Dido and Aeneas to fall in love—Venus to protect Aeneas's Roman mission by ensuring that Dido won't attack him or burn his ships, Juno to transfer Rome's destiny as Eternal City to Carthage. The goddesses, acting on a script they have prewritten, further cause the two to consummate their love in a carefully prepared setting—a cave in which they take shelter from a storm arranged by Juno. That intrusion of the political into the personal was not confined to myths: under Augustus, the interference of the state in the personal lives of individuals was such that Augustus oversaw the passing of laws to regulate (and even require) marriage (and remarriage, after divorce or widowhood), with heavy financial penalties for those who failed to comply.

Unlike the *Iliad,* in which "fates" were always plural, or the *Odyssey,* in which one's destiny was determined by one's moral status, in the *Aeneid,* humans find themselves acting out roles in a scenario the gods have devised. Their only choices lie in how to respond to the burdens the gods dole out. Jupiter assures Venus from the very first that her "children's fate is firm," that Rome will indeed be established, prosper, and endure.

The Underworld

In the Underworld, Aeneas is guided by the **Cumaean Sibyl** [koo-MEE-an SIB-il], the priestess who is the oracle at the shrine of Apollo at Cumae (the location of an early Greek colony in Italy) where Aeneas first reaches the Italian coast. He is also instructed by the shade of his father, Anchises, from whom he finally learns his ultimate destiny and the meaning of his suffering. It is then that the key question—Why is a good man compelled by the gods to suffer?—is at last answered.

Borrowing from Homer's description of Odysseus's journey to the Underworld, with additional details extrapolated from Plato's description in his dialogue *Phaedo,* Virgil elaborates on an Underworld divided into nine circles, each administering eternal justice to a different category of human souls. The upper circles include the innocent (such as infants and martyrs) and the suicides, and there is a separate circle for the "Fields of Mourning," those who were "consumed with bitter love." It is here that Aeneas meets the shade of Dido, still unreconciled to her fate, who turns from him as the eternally unforgiving Ajax did from Odysseus.

The road through the Underworld then divides. The highway to the left leads to **Tartarus,** where various kinds of wickedness are punished; the road to the right leads toward **Elysium,** where the souls of the blessed spend eternity. (Wherever the Romans went, they seem to have built highways, complete with road signs!)

It is here that the shade of **Anchises,** like Tiresias in the *Odyssey,* points his son toward the path that will lead him to his goal. As both moral guide to the upper world and tour guide to the lower, he explains to Aeneas how the good are eventually rewarded—not in their lives on earth, where sorrow and loss may prevail even for the deserving, but in eternity. In a modification of the doctrine of reincarnation of souls borrowed from Plato, Anchises tells Aeneas that, for most souls, awareness of the "Universal Mind" within them is dulled by the body and that the resulting blindness clings even after death. Consequently, most souls, washed clean of memory by the river **Lethe** [LEE-thee], are recycled every millennium until they can manage to purify themselves sufficiently. A few—pure priests, proud patriots, and pious poets (Virgil himself undoubtedly one of them)—escape the endless cycle of reincarnations and enter Elysium, where they spend eternity, Roman style, listening to music, feasting, currying their horses, and polishing their chariots and weapons.

This, in the long run, is the eternal reward for service—for those who accept the burdens and losses and who serve Rome faithfully. From this perspective, to get overly upset about the pains (or overly committed to the pleasures) of life in the present world is to take the short view. In the big picture, everyone gets exactly what he or she deserves.

Anchises also gets the opportunity here to explain the future of Rome, from the founding to the reign of Augustus, who will renew the Golden Age and extend his empire to the ends of the earth, making war redundant. Rome's unique contribution to the renewal of the Golden Age will be its mastery of the art of government and its ability—through conquest if necessary—to bring and teach peace to all the world. Having seen Elysium, Aeneas is understandably reluctant to leave. Nevertheless, with the vision of Rome before him, he accepts the burden of his mission with a new sense of commitment. We never again hear him complaining that his life is not his own. From this point on, he never hesitates. To achieve that grand vision, no suffering, no sacrifice is too great.

An Ironic View Some contemporary scholars interpret this vision of "Rome triumphant" as ironic. One might ask whether Augustus would have continued to provide government funds to the poet or would have rescued the poem from the flames to which Virgil consigned it in his will if he had seen it as condemning himself and his plans or even as presenting them ambivalently. (It is perhaps for just such a suspicion that he may have later forced the poet Ovid into exile.)

Personal political views apart, there is some evidence to support the ironic view. On leaving Elysium, Aeneas is led through the Gate of Ivory, traditionally the source of false dreams (as opposed to the Gates of Horn, which led to true or prophetic dreams). Is Virgil a prophet of Rome's grandeur or of its doom, prefigured here in the gloom of the Underworld? In a complex work such as this, to be sure, many readings are possible. But could Augustus have missed such a broad hint? The image of the two gates through which all dreams pass is hardly an esoteric reference whose meaning might have eluded a mere politician; it was, after all, a commonplace metaphor. It even occurred in the *Iliad,* which every Roman schoolboy no doubt read. And although an ironic reading is conceivable, the fact that readers and scholars for almost two millennia thereafter did not note the possibility suggests that, whatever inherent meaning we might now find in the material, the poet and his contemporaries did not detect in the image of the Gate of Ivory an implicit rejection of the Augustan vision. Further, even if Anchises' vision is deceptive, Jupiter himself has already made the same statement at the beginning of the epic, reciting the future history of Rome to Venus. And he will repeat it to Juno at the end.

Surely, Virgil never implies that founding or preserving Rome will be quick or easy, or without pain or loss—on the contrary. In fact, Anchises alludes to but denies his son a prevision of the death of Pallas, perhaps fearing that such foreknowledge would keep Aeneas from persevering. But the difficulties entailed do not deny the value of the vision itself. Rome, after all, did come about, and, the hated civil wars over, Virgil and his fellow poets (his friend Horace, for instance, who also wrote poems celebrating Augustus) seemed to share in the sense of relief and the renewed hope for the future. Further, if Eternal Rome, was, in fact, a dream, it may have been a dream worth holding onto.

Finally, we might recall here the Roman preference for demythologizing their mythic material and presenting it more realistically. In the real world, even in a culture given to superstition, people simply don't go to the Underworld. Nevertheless, to share in the tradition of epic heroes before him, Aeneas, presented by Virgil as a historical, and not simply mythological, figure, must go there as well. Presenting the obligatory voyage of the hero to the Underworld as an illusion, a false dream, allows the poet to have it both ways—to present his vision and to explain away its more difficult-to-swallow components. And yet, it would not be altogether inconsistent with this vision of hope for Virgil to have used the Underworld episode as a subtle reminder that around the edges of every dream lurks the possibility of nightmare.

The Last Battle

As in the *Iliad,* the climax of the *Aeneid* is the long-delayed combat between the two opposing warriors, and once again the contrast between the *Iliad* and the *Aeneid* is revealing. In Homer's work, the tension between the possible outcomes was stressed—even if the audience knew how it would end, the participants (including the gods) did not. Until the last moment, Apollo had hopes for Hector. And when Zeus held up his scales, he did not know in advance which side would sink down. In the *Aeneid,* Jupiter possesses a similar pair of scales, one of many Homeric trappings that Virgil borrows. But it is ultimately a meaningless gesture. Not only does Jupiter himself weight the scales, adding two "different fates," but the gods know in advance the outcome of the battle, as does the shade of Anchises in the Underworld. Before Aeneas and Turnus even meet on the battlefield, Juno yields and asks instead for a union of the two peoples: the Latins will be allowed to keep their name and language, and will become one larger, eclectic culture, Latin and Trojan (Greek) merged; and Juno will be worshiped alongside Jupiter as queen of the Roman gods. Only then does the no-longer-climactic battle take place.

When Aeneas finally encounters Turnus, he defeats the Latin general fairly rapidly, taking advantage of the paralysis of terror wrought by the Fury sent by Jupiter. Indeed, Juturna, Turnus's goddess-sister and charioteer, sees that Fury and leaves her brother, recognizing Jupiter's impending destruction of Turnus, before the battle with Aeneas actually occurs. Turnus is reduced to begging on his knees for mercy, not for his corpse to be respected, as Hector had, but for his life. Achilles, in the parallel Homeric encounter, enraged at Hector for killing Patroclus and wearing his helmet, would not listen to any such pleas. Aeneas, in contrast, is moved to be compassionate and is about to grant Turnus's request when he sees the belt of Pallas that the Latin had boastfully confiscated and worn to display his prowess, as heroes in the *Iliad* regularly did.

Two Views of Aeneas   Some readers argue that this scene, too, is presented ironically, showing an Aeneas corrupted by war and by his role as the agent of an exploitative, imperialist government. Beginning as a model Roman hero, he becomes just like the Greeks—another Achilles, who coldheartedly murders a man begging for mercy. Aeneas's last act, they argue, reveals how service to such a government institution gradually undermines the humanity of those who serve it. Others see the "two Aeneases" as representing the gap between public figure and private individual that political leaders must experience, requiring a public display of confidence and suppression of private doubts. (One writer asserts that the contradictions in Aeneas's character are the result of Virgil's having changed his mind in the middle of writing but not having finished the necessary revisions.)

Such interpretations may help rescue the work for contemporary readers whose sensibilities are offended by a poet who both supports the establishment and portrays at least some circumstances in which violence is acceptable. But those interpretations must be argued despite Virgil's repeated presentation of Turnus's fanatic behavior. It is true, of course, that Turnus is a victim, trapped by the gods, as were Aeneas and Dido. But sympathy is not the same as approval. And neither Dido nor Turnus is merely a victim. Turnus is also a cruel, fanatical, ego-driven, and treacherous man.

Another View of Aeneas   One might alternatively argue that Aeneas starts out as a Greek-style hero—witness his Achilles-like rage at Helen, which Venus must interrupt by seizing his hand (just as Athene in the *Iliad* prevented Achilles from stabbing Agamemnon), and his Odysseus-like lingering on the couch of Dido. But already he is more compassionate (he rescues Achaemenides) and more civilized (he doesn't "raid" Carthage). And instructed (and occasionally scolded) by Venus and Jupiter, he learns to become a complete Roman hero, his outbursts of rage now coming only when the state is at risk or the gods are offended or denied. In fact, one scholar, Thomas Van Nortwick, argues that Turnus is Aeneas's "second self" and that, in killing Turnus, Aeneas is "killing" the old-style, heroic self that he has outgrown. It is significant that no god intervenes when, following the death of Pallas, Aeneas is uncharacteristically savage in battle. There is, pointedly, no parallel here to the equivalent scene in the *Iliad* when the river god Scamander attacked Achilles, who had been venting his rage and heaping corpses into the river. The very same gods who condemned both Achilles' and Turnus's behavior apparently approve of Aeneas's.

Further, beneath the momentary surface resemblances between Achilles and Aeneas, important differences emerge. First, whereas Patroclus was an experienced fighter (albeit no Achilles) who killed twenty-seven men in his last moments, Pallas is a youth in his first battle, an unfair match to begin with, as Virgil earlier made clear. Thus, for Turnus to brag about the kill and to wear Pallas's belt is not only a reversion to the older heroic model but also an unwarranted boast—Pallas is a relatively easy mark. Second, Jupiter himself takes pains to comment on the inappropriateness of Turnus's wearing the belt and warns that punishment will inevitably follow.

Moreover, unlike Achilles, who vowed to eat Hector's body raw, Aeneas is tempted to show mercy—an exact inversion of the earlier scene in which he is tempted to kill Helen—only to have the moral outrage of that senseless and shameful killing propel him to act *against* instinct and do what the gods have already acknowledged must be done. Only then, in an outburst of what the later Roman poet Juvenal (c. A.D. 60–128) called *saeva indignatio* (righteous indignation), does the otherwise restrained Aeneas allow himself to vent his rage in violence and kill Turnus. That his rage helps him overcome his initial reluctance, that he kills in anger and precisely *not* with the cool detachment of a state assassin, and that he feels compelled even in the act of killing Turnus to shout that it is Pallas who kills him makes his final act, one might argue, more rather than less human. Like the shades of the suitors in the *Odyssey,* Turnus's shade flees to Hades, unrepentant and angry still. If there was once a gap between the private man, tormented by personal feelings forever thwarted by the gods, and the public man, destined to bear the burden of Rome's future, that gap closes at last at this moment.

The *Aeneid*: An Overview

Virgil, then, presents us with a complex work featuring a character who, for better or worse, grows and changes, and a multiple and often ambivalent perspective on the events portrayed. The world of the *Aeneid* is one in which individuals, burdened by the need to serve and driven and even deceived by gods with political agendas of their own, are bound to suffer "loss on bitter loss." The question becomes, Is the goal worth the sacrifice? Even if the answer turns out to be no, what choice is there? Not only do the gods do what they must do, regardless of the consequences to individuals, but the humans, to be moral (not merely government) agents, must do what they believe is right, and not merely what is comfortable. Finally, what is the alternative? Rome in general and Virgil in particular had already witnessed the alternative, and nothing in the gloom of the Underworld could match the horrors of the real-life wars, both foreign and civil, that produced not human freedom but only terror and chaos. Of course Virgil was ambivalent about war—what compassionate human being isn't?

There is certainly a conflict between humanism and war, and there may well be a conflict between humanism and government. But to argue (as Freud did) that war is the price we pay for civilization and then to argue (as Freud did not) that the price is too high is to condemn humans to live in a psychological netherworld where the terrible forces of unrestrained libido are in control. However imperfect a ruler Augustus might be, the alternative to a world ruled by Augustus, Virgil seems to imply, is a world ruled by Allecto.

AENEID*

Virgil

BOOK 1

I sing of arms and of a man: his fate   1
had made him fugitive; he was the first
to journey from the coasts of Troy as far
as Italy and the Lavinian shores.
Across the lands and waters he was battered
beneath the violence of High Ones, for
the savage Juno's unforgetting anger;
and many sufferings were his in war—
until he brought a city into being
and carried in his gods to Latium;   10
from this have come the Latin race, the lords
of Alba, and the ramparts of high Rome.

Tell me the reason, Muse: what was the wound
to her divinity, so hurting her
that she, the queen of gods, compelled a man
remarkable for goodness to endure
so many crises, meet so many trials?
Can such resentment hold the minds of gods?

There was an ancient city they called Carthage—
a colony of refugees from Tyre—   20
a city facing Italy, but far
away from Tiber's mouth: extremely rich
and, when it came to waging war, most fierce.
This land was Juno's favorite—it is said—
more dear than her own Samos; here she kept
her chariot and armor; even then
the goddess had this hope and tender plan:
for Carthage to become the capital
of nations, if the Fates would just consent.
But she had heard that, from the blood of Troy,   30
a race had come that some day would destroy
the citadels of Tyre; from it, a people
would spring, wide-ruling kings, men proud in battle
and destined to annihilate her Libya.
The Fates had so decreed. And Saturn's daughter—
in fear of this, remembering the old war

---

*Translation by Allen Mandelbaum.

909

that she had long since carried on at Troy
for her beloved Argos (and, indeed,
the causes of her bitterness, her sharp
and savage hurt, had not yet left her spirit;   40
for deep within her mind lie stored the judgment
of Paris and the wrong done to her scorned
beauty, the breed she hated, and the honors
that had been given ravished Ganymede)—
was angered even more; for this, she kept
far off from Latium the Trojan remnant
left by the Greeks and pitiless Achilles.
For long years they were cast across all waters,
fate-driven, wandering from sea to sea.
It was so hard to found the race of Rome.   50

. . . .

[Juno persuades Aeolus, the wind god, to send a hurricane to damage Aeneas's ships. Several are lost, but to prevent total destruction, Neptune calms the seas. Aeneas lands the remainder on Libya's coast:]

And now Aeneas' weary crewmen hurry
to find the nearest land along their way.
They turn toward Libya's coast. There is a cove
within a long, retiring bay; and there
an island's jutting arms have formed a harbor
where every breaker off the high sea shatters
and parts into the shoreline's winding shelters.
Along this side and that there towers, vast,
a line of cliffs, each ending in like crags;
beneath the ledges tranquil water lies   60
silent and wide; the backdrop—glistening
forests and, beetling from above, a black
grove, thick with bristling shadows. Underneath
the facing brow: a cave with hanging rocks,
sweet waters, seats of living stone, the home
of nymphs. And here no cable holds tired ships,
no anchor grips them fast with curving bit.

Aeneas shelters here with seven ships—
all he can muster, all the storm has left.
The Trojans, longing so to touch the land,   70
now disembark to gain the wished-for sands.

. . . .

[Aeneas sees that his followers are fed and then addresses them:]

"O comrades—surely we're not ignorant
of earlier disasters, we who have suffered
things heavier than this—our god will give

an end to this as well. You have neared the rage
of Scylla and her caves' resounding rocks;
and you have known the Cyclops' crags; call back
your courage, send away your grieving fear.
Perhaps one day you will remember even
these our adversities with pleasure. Through   80
so many crises and calamities
we make for Latium, where fates have promised
a peaceful settlement. It is decreed
that there the realm of Troy will rise again.
Hold out, and save yourself for kinder days."

These are his words; though sick with heavy cares,
he counterfeits hope in his face; his pain
is held within, hidden. His men make ready
the game that is to be their feast; they flay
the deer hide off the ribs; the flesh lies naked.   90
Some slice off quivering strips and pierce them with
sharp spits, while on the beach the others set
caldrons of brass and tend the flame. With food
their strength comes back again. Along the grass
they stretch and fill their bellies full of fat
venison meat and well-aged wine. That done—
their hunger banished by their feasting and
the tables cleared—their talk is long, uncertain
between their hope and fear, as they ask after
their lost companions, wondering if their comrades   100
are still alive or if they have undergone
the final change and can no longer hear
when called upon. Especially the pious
Aeneas moans within himself the loss
now of the vigorous Orontes, now
of Amycus, the cruel end of Lycus,
the doom of brave Cloanthus, of brave Gyas.

Their food and talk were done when Jupiter,
while gazing from the peaks of upper air
across the waters winged with canvas and   110
low-lying lands and shores and widespread peoples,
stood high upon the pinnacle of heaven
until he set his sight on Libya's kingdom.
And as he ponders this, the saddened Venus,
her bright eyes dimmed and tearful, speaks to him:

"O you who, with eternal rule, command
and govern the events of gods and men,
and terrify them with your thunderbolt,
what great offense has my Aeneas given,

what is his crime, what have the Trojans done   120
that, having undergone so many deaths,
the circle of all lands is shut against them—
and just because of Italy? Surely
you have sworn that out of them, in time to come,
with turning years, the Romans will be born
and, from the resurrected blood of Teucer,
rise up as rulers over sea and land?
What motive, Father, made you change? That promise
was solace for Troy's fall and its sad ruin;
I weighed this fate against the adverse fates.   130
But now their former fortune still pursues
the Trojans driven by so many evils.
Great king, is there no end to this ordeal?
Antenor could escape the Argive army,
then make his way through the Illyrian bays,
the inner lands of the Liburnians,
and safely cross the source of the Timavus,
where, with a mighty mountain's roar, it rushes
through nine mouths, till its flood bursts, overwhelming
the fields beneath with its resounding waters.   140
Yet here he planted Padua, a town
and home for Teucrians, and gave his nation
a name and then hung up the arms of Troy;
and now, serene, he tastes tranquillity.
But we, your very children, we whom you
had promised heaven's heights, have lost our ships—
unspeakable! Just for the rage of one
we are betrayed, kept far from Italy.
Is this the way you give us back our scepter?"

But then he smiled upon her—Jupiter,   150
father of men and gods—just as he calms
the heavens and the storms. He lightly kissed
his daughter's lips; these were his words to Venus:
"My Cytherea, that's enough of fear;
your children's fate is firm; you'll surely see
the walls I promised you, Lavinium's city;
and you shall carry your great-hearted son,
Aeneas, high as heaven's stars. My will
is still the same; I have not changed. Your son
(I now speak out—I know this anxiousness   160
is gnawing at you; I unroll the secret
scroll of the Fates, awake its distant pages)
shall wage tremendous war in Italy
and crush ferocious nations and establish

a way of life and walls for his own people—
until the time of his third summer as
the king of Latium, until he has passed
three winters since he overcame the Latins.
But then the boy Ascanius, who now
is carrying Iülus as his surname (while   170
the state of Ilium held fast, he still
was known as Ilus), with his rule shall fill
the wheeling months of thirty mighty years.
He shall remove his kingdom from Lavinium
and, powerful, build Alba Longa's walls.
For full three hundred years, the capital
and rule of Hector's race shall be at Alba,
until a royal priestess, Ilia,
with child by Mars, has brought to birth twin sons.
And then, rejoicing in the tawny hide   180
of his nursemaid, the she-wolf, Romulus
shall take the rulership and build the walls
of Mars' own city. Romulus shall call
that people 'Romans,' after his own name.
I set no limits to their fortunes and
no time; I give them empire without end.
Then even bitter Juno shall be changed;
for she, who now harasses lands and heavens
with terror, then shall hold the Romans dear
together with me, cherishing the masters   190
of all things, and the race that wears the toga.
This is what I decree. An age shall come
along the way of gliding lustra when
the house born of Assaracus shall hold
both Phthia and illustrious Mycenae
and rule defeated Argos. Then a Trojan
Caesar shall rise out of that splendid line.
His empire's boundary shall be the Ocean;
the only border to his fame, the stars.
His name shall be derived from great Iülus,   200
and shall be Julius. In time to come,
no longer troubled, you shall welcome him
to heaven, weighted with the Orient's wealth;
he, too, shall be invoked with prayers. With battle
forgotten, savage generations shall
grow generous. And aged Faith and Vesta,
together with the brothers, Romulus
and Remus, shall make laws. The gruesome gates
of war, with tightly welded iron plates,
shall be shut fast. Within, unholy Rage   210

shall sit on his ferocious weapons, bound
behind his back by a hundred knots of brass;
he shall groan horribly with bloody lips."

The words of Jupiter are done. He sends
the son of Maia down from heaven that
the newfound lands and fortresses of Carthage
be opened wide in welcome to the Trojans;
that Dido, ignorant of destiny,
not drive away Aeneas from her boundaries.
He flies across the great air; using wings   220
as oars, he quickly lands on Libyan shores.
He does as he was told. And the Phoenicians
now set aside their savagery before
the will of god; and Dido, above all,
receives into her spirit kindliness,
a gracious mind to greet the Teucrians.

But, nightlong, many cares have held the pious
Aeneas. And as soon as gracious daylight
is given to him, this is his decision:
to go out and explore this foreign country,   230
to learn what shores the wind has brought him to,
who lives upon this land—it is untilled—
are they wild beasts or men—and then to tell
his comrades what he has found. He hides his fleet
inside the narrows of the wooded cove,
beneath a hollow rock shut in by trees,
with bristling shades around. And he himself,
only Achates at his side, moves on;
he brandishes two shafts tipped with broad iron.

But in the middle of the wood, along   240
the way, his mother showed herself to him.
The face and dress she wore were like a maiden's,
her weapons like a girl's from Sparta or
those carried by Harpalyce of Thrace
when she tires out her horses, speeding faster
even than rapid Hebrus as she races.
For, as a huntress would, across her shoulder,
Venus had slung her bow in readiness;
her hair was free, disheveled by the wind;
her knees were bare; her tunic's flowing folds   250
were gathered in a knot. And she speaks first:
"Young men there! Can you tell me if by chance
you have seen one of my sisters pass—she wore
a quiver and a spotted lynx's hide—

while she was wandering here or, with her shouts,
chasing a foaming boar along its course?"

So Venus. Answering, her son began:
"I have not seen or heard your sister, maiden—
or by what name am I to call you, for
your voice is not like any human voice.   260
O goddess, you must be Apollo's sister
or else are to be numbered with the nymphs!
Whoever you may be, do help us, ease
our trials; do tell us underneath what skies,
upon what coasts of earth we have been cast;
we wander, ignorant of men and places,
and driven by the wind and the vast waves.
Before your altars many victims will
fall at our hands, as offerings to you."

Then Venus: "I can hardly claim such honor.   270
The girls of Tyre are used to wearing quivers
and bind their calves with scarlet hunting boots.
You see a Punic country, men of Tyre,
the city of Agenor; but at the border
the Libyans lie—a tribe that swears by war.
Our ruler here is Dido, she who left
her city when she had to flee her brother.
The tale of wrong is intricate and long,
but I shall trace its chief events in order.

"Her husband was Sychaeus: wealthiest   280
landowner in Phoenicia. For her father
had given her, a virgin, to Sychaeus
and joined them with the omens of first marriage.
Unhappy Dido loved him with much passion.
Pygmalion, her brother, held the kingdom
of Tyre; beyond all men he was a monster
in crime. Between Sychaeus and her brother
dividing fury came. Pygmalion—
unholy, blind with lust for gold—in secret
now catches Dido's husband off his guard   290
and cuts him down by sword before the altars,
heedless of his own sister's love. For long
he kept this hidden and, insidious,
invented many stories to mock Dido—
she is sick and longing—with an empty hope.
But in her sleep, to Dido came the very
image of her unburied husband; he
lifted his pallid face—amazingly—

and laid bare to his wife the cruel altars,
his breast impaled upon the blade, revealing   300
to her the hidden horror of the house.
He urges her to speed her flight, to leave
her homeland; and to help her journey, he
discloses ancient treasure in the earth,
a hoard of gold and silver known to none.
And Dido, moved by this, prepared her flight
and her companions. Now there come together
both those who felt fierce hatred for the tyrant
and those who felt harsh fear. They seize the ships
that happen to be ready, loading them   310
with gold. The wealth of covetous Pygmalion
is carried overseas. A woman leads.
They landed at the place where now you see
the citadel and high walls of new Carthage
rising; and then they bought the land called Byrsa,
'The Hide,' after the name of that transaction
(they got what they were able to enclose
inside a bull's skin). But who, then, are you?
From what coasts have you come? Where are you going?"
To these her questions he replied with sighs;   320
he drew his words from deep within his breast:

"O goddess, if I tracked my story back
until its first beginning, were there time
to hear the annals of our trials, then
the evening would have shut Olympus' gates
and gathered in the day before I ended.
But we were sailing out from ancient Troy—
if Troy means anything to you—across
strange seas when, as it willed, a tempest drove us
upon the coasts of Libya. I am pious   330
Aeneas, and I carry in my ships
my household gods together with me, rescued
from Argive enemies; my fame is known
beyond the sky. I seek out Italy,
my country, my ancestors born of Jove.
When I set out upon the Phrygian sea,
I had twice-ten ships, and my goddess-mother
showed me the way; I followed my firm fates.
Now I am left with scarcely seven galleys,
ships shattered by the waves and the east wind;   340
and I myself, a needy stranger, roam
across the wilderness of Libya; I
am driven out of Europe, out of Asia."

But Venus had enough of his complaints,
and so she interrupted his lament:

"Whoever you may be, I hardly think
the heaven-dwellers hold a grudge against you:
the breath of life is yours, and you are near
a Tyrian city. Only make your way
until you reach the palace of the queen.   350
For I can tell you truthfully: your comrades
are given back to you, your fleet is saved
and driven toward sure waters by the winds
that shifted to the north—unless my parents
have taught me augury to no good end.
Look there, where you can make out twice-six swans
that gladly file along, whom once the bird
of Jupiter had scattered, swooping down
from upper air into the open sky.
And now, in long array, they either seem   360
to settle down or else to hover, waiting
and watching those that have already landed;
and just as they, returning, play with rustling
wings, as they wheel about the sky in crews,
and give themselves to song—not otherwise
your ships and youths are either in the harbor
or near its mouth with swelling sails. Only
move on and follow where this pathway leads."

These were the words of Venus. When she turned,
her neck was glittering with a rose brightness;   370
her hair anointed with ambrosia,
her head gave all a fragrance of the gods;
her gown was long and to the ground; even
her walk was sign enough she was a goddess.
And when Aeneas recognized his mother,
he followed her with these words as she fled:
"Why do you mock your son—so often and
so cruelly—with these lying apparitions?
Why can't I ever join you, hand to hand,
to hear, to answer you with honest words?"   380

So he reproaches her, then takes the road
to Carthage. But as goddess, Venus cloaks
Aeneas and Achates in dark mist;
she wraps them in a cape of cloud so thick
that none can see or touch them or delay
their way or ask why they had come. And she
herself glides through the skies to Paphos, gladly

revisiting her home, her temple and
her hundred altars fragrant with fresh garlands
and warm with their Sabaean frankincense.   390

Meanwhile Aeneas and the true Achates
press forward on their path. They climb a hill
that overhangs the city, looking down
upon the facing towers. Aeneas marvels
at the enormous buildings, once mere huts,
and at the gates and tumult and paved streets.
The eager men of Tyre work steadily:
some build the city walls or citadel—
they roll up stones by hand; and some select
the place for a new dwelling, marking out   400
its limits with a furrow; some make laws,
establish judges and a sacred senate;
some excavate a harbor; others lay
the deep foundations for a theater,
hewing tremendous pillars from the rocks,
high decorations for the stage to come.
Just as the bees in early summer, busy
beneath the sunlight through the flowered meadows,
when some lead on their full-grown young and others
press out the flowing honey, pack the cells   410
with sweet nectar, or gather in the burdens
of those returning; some, in columns, drive
the drones, a lazy herd, out of the hives;
the work is fervent, and the fragrant honey
is sweet with thyme. "How fortunate are those
whose walls already rise!" Aeneas cries
while gazing at the rooftops of the city.
Then, sheltered by a mist, astoundingly,
he enters in among the crowd, mingling
together with the Tyrians. No one sees him.   420

Just at the center of the city stood
a thickly shaded wood; this was the place
where, when they landed, the Phoenicians first—
hurled there by whirlwind and by wave—dug up
an omen that Queen Juno had pointed out:
the head of a fierce stallion. This had meant
the nation's easy wealth and fame in war
throughout the ages. Here Sidonian Dido
was building a stupendous shrine for Juno,
enriched with gifts and with the goddess' statue,   430
where flights of steps led up to brazen thresholds;
the architraves were set on posts of brass;
the grating hinges of the doors were brass.

Within this grove, the sights—so strange to him—
have, for the first time, stilled Aeneas' fear;
here he first dared to hope he had found shelter,
to trust more surely in his shattered fortunes.
For while he waited for the queen, he studied
everything in that huge sanctuary,
marveling at a city rich enough   440
for such a temple, at the handiwork
of rival artists, at their skillful tasks.
He sees the wars of Troy set out in order:
the battles famous now through all the world,
the sons of Atreus and of Priam, and
Achilles, savage enemy to both.
He halted. As he wept, he cried: "Achates,
where on this earth is there a land, a place
that does not know our sorrows? Look! There is Priam!
Here, too, the honorable finds its due   450
and there are tears for passing things; here, too,
things mortal touch the mind. Forget your fears;
this fame will bring you some deliverance."
He speaks. With many tears and sighs he feeds
his soul on what is nothing but a picture.

He watched the warriors circling Pergamus:
here routed Greeks were chased by Trojan fighters
and here the Phrygian troops pursued by plumed
Achilles in his chariot. Nearby,
sobbing, he recognized the snow-white canvas   460
tents of King Rhesus—with his men betrayed,
while still in their first sleep, and then laid waste,
with many dead, by bloody Diomedes,
who carried off their fiery war horses
before they had a chance to taste the pastures
of Troy, or drink the waters of the Xanthus.

Elsewhere Young Troilus, the unhappy boy—
he is matched unequally against Achilles—
runs off, his weapons lost. He is fallen flat;
his horses drag him on as he still clings   470
fast to his empty chariot, clasping
the reins. His neck, his hair trail on the ground,
and his inverted spear inscribes the dust.
Meanwhile the Trojan women near the temple
of Pallas, the unkindly; hair disheveled,
sad, beating at their breasts, as suppliants,
they bear the robe of offering. The goddess
averts her face, her eyes fast to the ground.

Three times Achilles had dragged Hector round
the walls of Troy, selling his lifeless body   480
for gold. And then, indeed, Aeneas groans
within the great pit of his chest, deeply;
for he can see the spoils, the chariot,
the very body of his friend, and Priam
pleading for Hector with defenseless hands.
He also recognized himself in combat
with the Achaean chiefs, then saw the Eastern
battalions and the weapons of black Memnon.
Penthesilea in her fury leads
the ranks of crescent-shielded Amazons.   490
She flashes through her thousands; underneath
her naked breast, a golden girdle; soldier-
virgin and queen, daring to war with men.

But while the Dardan watched these scenes in wonder,
while he was fastened in a stare, astonished,
the lovely-bodied Dido neared the temple,
a crowding company of youths around her.
And just as, on the banks of the Eurotas
or through the heights of Cynthus, when Diana
incites her dancers, and her followers,   500
a thousand mountain-nymphs, press in behind her,
she wears a quiver slung across her shoulder;
and as she makes her way, she towers over
all other goddesses; gladness excites
Latona's silent breast: even so, Dido;
so, in her joy, she moved among the throng
as she urged on the work of her coming kingdom.

And then below the temple's central dome—
facing the doorway of the goddess, guarded
by arms—she took her place on a high throne.   510
Dido was dealing judgments to her people
and giving laws, apportioning the work
of each with fairness or by drawing lots;
when suddenly Aeneas sees, as they
press forward through the mighty multitude,
Sergestus, Antheus, and the brave Cloanthus,
and other Trojans whom the black whirlwind
had scattered on the waters, driven far
to other coasts. Aeneas is astounded;
both joy and fear have overcome Achates.   520
They burned to join right hands with their companions,
but this strange happening confuses them.
They stay in hiding, screened by folds of fog,

and wait to see what fortune found their friends,
on what beach they have left the fleet, and why
they come; for these were men who had been chosen
from all the ships to ask for grace, who now
made for the temple door with loud outcries.

When they had entered and received their leave
to speak in Dido's presence, then the eldest,   530
Ilioneus, calmly began: "O Queen,
whom Jupiter has granted this: to bring
to being a new city, curbing haughty
nations by justice—we, unhappy Trojans,
men carried by the winds across all seas,
beg you to keep the terror of fire from
our fleet, to spare a pious race, to look
on us with kindliness. We do not come
to devastate your homes and with the sword
to loot the household gods of Libya or   540
to drive down stolen booty toward the beaches.
That violence is not within our minds;
such arrogance is not for the defeated.
There is a place the Greeks have named Hesperia,
an ancient land with strong arms and fat soil.
Its colonists were the Oenotrians.
Now rumor runs that their descendants call
that nation 'Italy,' after their leader.
Our prows were pointed there when suddenly,
rising upon the surge, stormy Orion   550
drove us against blind shoals; and insolent
south winds then scattered us, undone by brine,
across the crushing sea, the pathless rocks.
A few of us have drifted to your shores.
What kind of men are these? Or is your country
so barbarous that it permits this custom?
We are denied the shelter of the beach;
they goad us into war; they will not let us
set foot upon the border of their land.
If you despise the human race and mortal   560
weapons, then still consider that the gods
remember right and wrong. We had a king,
Aeneas, none more just, no one more pious,
no man his better in the arts of war.
If fate has saved this man, if he still feeds
upon the upper air, if he is not
laid low to rest among the cruel Shades,
then we are not afraid and you will not
repent if you compete with him in kindness.

Within Sicilian territory, too,   570
are fields and cities and the famed Acestes,
born of the blood of Troy. Let us haul up
our fleet, smashed by the winds, along your beaches
and fit out timber from your forests, trim
our oars; and if we find our king and comrades
and are allowed to turn toward Italy
and Latium, then let us sail out gladly.
But if our shelter there has been denied us,
and you, the finest father of the Trojans,
were swallowed by the sea of Libya, and   580
no hope is left us now for Iülus, then
at least let us seek out again the straits
of Sicily, the land from which we sailed.
There houses wait for us, and King Acestes."
So spoke Ilioneus. The other sons
of Dardanus approved his words with shouts.

Then Dido softly, briefly answers him:
"O Teucrians, enough of fear, cast out
your cares. My kingdom is new; hard circumstances
have forced me to such measures for our safety,   590
to post guards far and wide along our boundaries.
But who is ignorant of Aeneas' men?
Who has not heard of Troy, its acts and heroes,
the flames of that tremendous war? We Tyrians
do not have minds so dull, and we are not
beyond the circuit of the sun's yoked horses.
Whatever you may choose—Hesperia and
the fields of Saturn, or the land of Eryx
and King Acestes—I shall send you safe
with escort, I shall help you with my wealth.   600
And should you want to settle in this kingdom
on equal terms with me, then all the city
I am building now is yours. Draw up your ships.
I shall allow no difference between
the Tyrian and the Trojan. Would your king,
Aeneas, too, were present, driven here
by that same south wind. I, in fact, shall send
my trusted riders out along the shores,
to comb the farthest coasts of Libya and
to see if, cast out of the waters, he   610
is wandering through the forests or the cities."

The words of Dido stir the brave Achates
and father Aeneas; long since, both of them
had burned to break free from their cloud. Achates
speaks first to his companion: "Goddess-born,

what counsel rises in your spirit now?
You see that everything is safe, our ships
and sailors saved. And only one is missing,
whom we ourselves saw sink among the waves.
All else is as your mother said it would be."   620

Yet he was hardly done when suddenly
the cloud that circled them is torn; it clears
away to open air. And there Aeneas
stood, glittering in that bright light, his face
and shoulders like a god's. Indeed, his mother
had breathed upon her son becoming hair,
the glow of a young man, and in his eyes,
glad handsomeness: such grace as art can add
to ivory, or such as Parian marble
or silver shows when set in yellow gold.   630
But then, surprising all, he tells the queen:
"The man you seek is here. I stand before you,
Trojan Aeneas, torn from Libyan waves.
O you who were alone in taking pity
on the unutterable trials of Troy,
who welcome us as allies to your city
and home—a remnant left by Greeks, harassed
by all disasters known on land and sea,
in need of everything—we cannot, Dido,
repay you, then, with gratitude enough   640
to match your merits, neither we nor any
Dardans scattered over this great world.
May gods confer on you your due rewards,
if deities regard the good, if justice
and mind aware of right count anywhere.
What happy centuries gave birth to you?
What splendid parents brought you into being?
While rivers run into the sea and shadows
still sweep the mountain slopes and stars still pasture
upon the sky, your name and praise and honor   650
shall last, whatever be the lands that call me."
This said, he gives his right hand to his friend
Ilioneus; his left he gives Serestus;
then turns to brave Cloanthus and brave Gyas.

First at the very sight of him, and then
at all he had endured, Sidonian Dido
was startled. And she told the Trojan this:
"You, goddess-born, what fortune hunts you down
through such tremendous trials? What violence
has forced you onto these ferocious shores?   660
Are you that same Aeneas, son of Dardan

Anchises, whom the gracious Venus bore
beside the banks of Phrygian Simois?
Indeed, I still remember banished Teucer,
a Greek who came to Sidon from his native
kingdom, when with the help of Belus he
was seeking out new realms (my father Belus
was plundering then, as victor, wealthy Cyprus).
And even then I learned of Troy's disaster,
and of your name and of the kings of Greece.   670
And though he was the Trojans' enemy,
Teucer would often praise the Teucrians
and boast that he was born of their old race.
Thus, young men, you are welcome to our halls.
My destiny, like yours, has willed that I,
a veteran of hardships, halt at last
in this country. Not ignorant of trials,
I now can learn to help the miserable."

So Dido speaks. At once she leads Aeneas
into the royal palace and announces   680
her offerings in the temples of the gods.
But meanwhile she does not neglect his comrades.
She sends down to the beaches twenty bullocks,
a hundred fat lambs with their ewes, and Bacchus'
glad gift of wine. Within the palace gleam
the furnishings of royal luxury;
the feast is readied in the atrium.
And there are draperies of noble purple
woven with art; and plates of massive silver
upon the tables; and, engraved in gold,   690
the sturdy deeds of Dido's ancestors,
a long, long line of happenings and heroes
traced from the first beginnings of her race.

Aeneas (for his father's love could not
permit his mind to rest) now quickly sends
Achates to the Trojan ships, to carry
these tidings to Ascanius, to lead
Aeneas' son up to the walls of Carthage:
all his paternal love and care are for
Ascanius. He also tells Achates   700
to bring back gifts snatched from the wreck of Troy:
a tunic stiff with images of gold,
and then a veil whose fringes were of saffron
acanthus—these once worn by Argive Helen,
who had borne them off to Troy and her unlawful
wedding when she had fled Mycenae—splendid
gifts of her mother Leda; and besides,

the scepter that had once been carried by
Ilione, eldest of Priam's daughters,
a necklace set with pearls, and then a crown   710
that had twin circles set with jewels and gold.
And hurrying to do all he was told,
Achates made his way down to the boats.

But in her breast the Cytherean ponders
new stratagems, new guile: that Cupid, changed
in form and feature, come instead of sweet
Ascanius and, with his gifts, inflame
the queen to madness and insinuate
a fire in Dido's very bones. For Venus
is much afraid of that deceptive house   720
and of the Tyrians with their double tongues.
The thought of savage Juno burns; by night
her care returns. Her words are for winged Love:

"Son, you are my only strength, my only power;
son, you who scorn the shafts of the great Father's
Typhoean thunderbolts, I flee to you
for refuge; suppliant, I call upon
the force within your godhead. For you know
how, through the hatred of resentful Juno,
across the sea and every shore your brother   730
Aeneas has been hunted down; and often
you have sorrowed with my sorrow. Now Phoenician
Dido has hold of him; with sweet words she
would make him stay. The hospitality
of Juno—and where it may lead—makes me
afraid; at such a turn I know she'll not
be idle. So, before she has a chance,
I plan to catch the queen by craftiness,
to girdle Dido with a flame, so that
no god can turn her back; I'll hold her fast   740
with great love for Aeneas. Hear me now;
I need your help to carry out this plot.
Ascanius, my dearest care, is ready
to go along to the Sidonian city,
called by his loving father, carrying
gifts saved from Troy in flames and from the sea.
But I shall lull the royal boy to sleep
on high Cythera or Idalium
and hide him in my holy house, so that
he cannot know—or interrupt—our trap.   750
And you will need—for one night and no more—
to counterfeit his features; as a boy,
to wear that boy's familiar face, and so

when Dido, joyful, draws you close during
the feasting and the flowing wine, when she
embraces you, and kisses tenderly,
your breath can fill her with a hidden flame,
your poison penetrate, deceivingly."

Love does what his dear mother asks. He sheds
his wings and gladly tries the walk of Iülus.   760
But Venus pours upon Ascanius
a gentle rest. She takes him to her breast
caressingly; and as a goddess can,
she carries him to her Idalium
where, in high groves, mild marjoram enfolds him
in flowers and the breath of its sweet shade.
Now Cupid's on his way, as he was told.
Gladly—Achates is his guide—he brings
the Tyrians royal gifts. As he arrives,
he finds the banqueting begun, the queen   770
already settled on her couch of gold
beneath resplendent awnings, at the center.
Father Aeneas and the Trojan warriors
now gather; they recline on purple covers.
The servants pour out water for their hands
and promptly offer bread from baskets and
bring towels smooth in texture for the guests.
Inside are fifty handmaids at their stations—
their care to stock the storerooms and to honor
the household gods with fire—and a hundred   780
more women, and as many male attendants
of equal age with them, to load the tables
with food and place the cups. The Tyrians, too,
have gathered, crowding through the happy halls—
all these invited to brocaded couches.
They marvel at Aeneas' gifts, at Iülus—
the god's bright face and his fictitious words—
and at the cloak, the veil adorned with saffron
acanthus borders. And above all, luckless
Dido—doomed to face catastrophe—   790
can't sate her soul, inflamed by what she sees;
the boy, the gifts excite her equally.
And he pretends to satisfy a father's
great love by hanging on Aeneas' neck
in an embrace. Then he seeks out the queen.
Her eyes cling fast to him, and all her heart;
at times she fondles him upon her lap—
for Dido does not know how great a god
is taking hold of her poor self. But Cupid,
remembering his mother, Venus, slowly   800

begins to mist the memory of Sychaeus
and with a living love tries to surprise
her longings gone to sleep, her unused heart.
And at the first pause in the feast the tables
are cleared away. They fetch enormous bowls
and crown the wine with wreaths. The uproar grows;
it swells through all the palace; voices roll
across the ample halls; the lamps are kindled—
they hang from ceilings rich with golden panels—
and flaming torches overcome the night.   810
And then the queen called for a golden cup,
massive with jewels, that Belus once had used,
Belus and all the Tyrian line; she filled
that golden cup with wine. The hall fell still.
"O Jupiter, for they say you are author
of laws for host and guest, do grant that this
may be a day of happiness for those
who come from Tyre and Troy, and may our sons
remember it. May Bacchus, gladness-giver,
and gracious Juno, too, be present here;   820
and favor, Tyrians, this feast with honor."
Her words were done. She offered her libation,
pouring her wine upon the boards; and then
she was the first to take the cup, but only
touching her lips to it. She passed it next
to Bitias and spurred him to be quick.
He drained the foaming cup with eagerness
and drenched himself in that gold flood; in turn
the other chieftains drank. Long-haired Iopas,
whom mighty Atlas once had taught, lifts up   830
his golden lyre, sounding through the hall.
He sings the wandering moon; the labors of
the sun; the origins of men and beasts,
of water and of fire; and of Arcturus,
the stormy Hyades, and the twin Bears;
and why the winter suns so rush to plunge
in Ocean: what holds back the lingering nights.
The Tyrians applaud again, again.
The Trojans follow. So the luckless Dido
drew out the night with varied talk. She drank   840
long love and asked Aeneas many questions:
of Priam; Hector; how Aurora's son
was armed; and now, how strong were Diomedes'
horses; now, how tremendous was Achilles.

"No, come, my guest," she calls, "and tell us all
things from the first beginning: Grecian guile,
your people's trials, and then your journeyings.

For now the seventh summer carries you,
a wanderer, across the lands and waters."

BOOK 2

[Aeneas tells his story to Dido:]

A sudden silence fell on all of them;   1
their eyes were turned, intent on him. And father
Aeneas, from his high couch, then began:

"O Queen—too terrible for tongues the pain
you ask me to renew, the tale of how
the Danaans could destroy the wealth of Troy,
that kingdom of lament: for I myself
saw these things; I took large part in them.
What Myrmidon or what Dolopian,
what soldier even of the harsh Ulysses,   10
could keep from tears in telling such a story?
But now the damp night hurries from the sky
into the sea; the falling stars persuade
to sleep. But if you long so much to learn
our suffering, to hear in brief the final
calamity of Troy—although my mind,
remembering, recoils in grief, and trembles,
I shall try.

          "The captains of the Danaans,
now weak with war and beaten back by fate,
and with so many gliding years gone by,   20
are able to construct, through the divine
art of Minerva, a mountainous horse.
They weave its ribs with sawed-off beams of fir,
pretending that it is an offering
for safe return. At least, that is their story.
Then in the dark sides of the horse they hide
men chosen from the sturdiest among them;
they stuff their soldiers in its belly, deep
in that vast cavern: Greeks armed to the teeth.

. . . .

[Aeneas describes the Trojan Horse and the treachery of Sinon, who lied to the Trojans in order to persuade them to accept the gift, deceiving them by false tears. As Troy is falling, the shade of Hector appears to Aeneas, giving him responsibility to carry the Vesta and other holy objects from Troy to Rome. Watching in horror as the youngest son of Priam is murdered before his father's eyes, Aeneas is reminded of his own family. He discovers that all of his troops are gone:]

"Before me rose Creüsa, left alone,   30
my plundered home, the fate of small Iülus.

I look behind and scan the troops around me;
all of my men, worn out, have quit the battle,
have cast their bodies down along the ground
or fallen helplessly into the flames.

"And now that I am left alone, I see
the daughter of Tyndareos clinging
to Vesta's thresholds, crouching silently
within a secret corner of the shrine;
bright conflagrations give me light as I   40
wander and let my eyes read everything.
For she, in terror of the Trojans—set
against her for the fall of Pergamus—
and of the Danaans' vengeance and the anger
of her abandoned husband; she, the common
Fury of Troy and of her homeland, she
had hid herself; she crouched, a hated thing,
beside the altars. In my mind a fire
is burning; anger spurs me to avenge
my falling land, to exact the debt of crime.   50
'Is she to have it so: to leave unharmed,
see Sparta and her home Mycenae, go—
a victor queen in triumph—to look on
her house and husband, parents, children, trailing
a train of Trojan girls and Phrygian slaves?
Shall Troy have been destroyed by fire, Priam
been beaten by the blade, the Dardan shore
so often soaked with blood, to this end? No.
For though there is no memorable name
in punishing a woman and no gain   60
of honor in such victory, yet I
shall have my praise for blotting out a thing
of evil, for my punishing of one
who merits penalties; and it will be
a joy to fill my soul with vengeful fire,
to satisfy the ashes of my people.'

"And carried off by my mad mind, I was
still blurting out these words when, with such brightness
as I had never seen, my gracious mother
stood there before me; and across the night   70
she gleamed with pure light, unmistaken goddess,
as lovely and as tall as she appears
whenever she is seen by heaven's beings.
And while she caught and held my right hand fast,
she spoke these words to me with her rose lips:
'My son, what bitterness has kindled this
fanatic anger? Why this madness? What

of all your care for me—where has it gone?
Should you not first seek out your father, worn
with years, Anchises, where you left him; see   80
if your own wife, Creüsa, and the boy
Ascanius are still alive? The Argive
lines ring them all about; and if my care
had not prevented such an end, by now
flames would have swept them off, the hostile sword
have drunk their blood. And those to blame are not
the hated face of the Laconian woman,
the daughter of Tyndareos, or Paris:
it is the gods' relentlessness, the gods',
that overturns these riches, tumbles Troy   90
from its high pinnacle. Look now—for I
shall tear away each cloud that cloaks your eyes
and clogs your human seeing, darkening
all things with its damp fog: you must not fear
the orders of your mother; do not doubt,
but carry out what she commands. For here,
where you see huge blocks ripped apart and stones
torn free from stones and smoke that joins with dust
in surges, Neptune shakes the walls, his giant
trident is tearing Troy from its foundations;   100
and here the first to hold the Scaean gates
is fiercest Juno; girt with iron, she
calls furiously to the fleet for more
Greek troops. Now turn and look: Tritonian Pallas
is planted there; upon the tallest towers
she glares with her storm cloud and her grim Gorgon.
And he who furnishes the Greeks with force
that favors and with spirit is the Father
himself, for he himself goads on the gods
against the Dardan weapons. Son, be quick   110
to flee, have done with fighting. I shall never
desert your side until I set you safe
upon your father's threshold.' So she spoke,
then hid herself within the night's thick shadows.
Ferocious forms appear—the fearful powers
of gods that are the enemies of Troy.

"At this, indeed, I saw all Ilium
sink down into the fires; Neptune's Troy
is overturned: even as when the woodsmen
along a mountaintop are rivals in   120
their striving to bring down an ancient ash,
hacked at with many blows of iron and ax;
it always threatens falling, nodding with

its trembling leaves and tossing crest until,
slowly, slowly, the wounds have won; it gives
one last great groan, then wrenches from the ridges
and crashes into ruin. I go down
and, guided by a god, move on among
the foes and fires; weapons turn aside,
the flames retire where I make my way.   130

"But now, when I had reached my father's threshold,
Anchises' ancient house, our home—and I
longed so to carry him to the high mountains
and sought him first—he will not let his life
be drawn out after Troy has fallen, he
will not endure exile: 'You whose lifeblood
is fresh, whose force is still intact and tough,
you hurry your escape; if heaven's lords
had wanted longer life for me, they would
have saved my home. It is enough—and more—   140
that I have lived beyond one fall and sack
of Troy. Call out your farewell to my body
as it is now, thus laid out, thus; and then
be gone. I shall find death by my own hand;
the enemy will pity me and seek
my spoils. The loss of burial is easy.
For hated by the gods and useless, I
have lingered out my years too long already,
since that time when the father of the High Ones
and king of men let fly his thunderbolt   150
against me with the winds, touched me with lightning.'

"These were the words he used. He did not move.
We stood in tears—my wife, Creüsa, and
Ascanius and all the household—begging
my father not to bring down everything
along with him and make our fate more heavy.
He will not have it. What he wants is set;
he will not leave his place. Again I take
to arms and, miserable, long for death.
What other stratagem or chance is left?   160
And then I ask: 'My father, had you thought
I could go off and leave you here? Could such
unholiness fall from a father's lips?
For if it please the High Ones that no thing
be left of this great city, if your purpose
must still persist, if you want so to add
yourself and yours to Ilium's destruction—
why then, the door to death is open: Pyrrhus—

who massacres the son before his father's
eyes, and then kills the father at the altars—   170
still hot from Priam's blood, will soon be here.
And was it, then, for this, my gracious mother,
that you have saved me from the blade, the fire—
that I might see the enemy within
the heart of home, my son Ascanius,
my father, and Creüsa at their side,
all butchered in each other's blood? My men,
bring arms; the last light calls upon the beaten.
Let be, and let me at the Greeks again,
to make my way back to new battles. Never   180
shall we all die this day without revenge.'

"At that I girded on my sword again
and fixed it firm, passing my left hand through
my shield strap as I hurried from the house.
But suddenly Creüsa held me fast
beside the threshold; clinging to my feet,
she lifted young Iülus to his father:
'If you go off to die, then take us, too,
to face all things with you; but if your past
still lets you put your hope in arms, which now   190
you have put on, then first protect this house.
To whom is young Iülus left, to whom
your father and myself, once called your wife?'

"So did Creüsa cry; her wailing filled
my father's house. But even then there comes
a sudden omen—wonderful to tell:
between the hands, before the faces of
his grieving parents, over Iülus' head
there leaps a lithe flametip that seems to shed
a radiance; the tongue of fire flickers,   200
harmless, and plays about his soft hair, grazes
his temples. Shuddering in our alarm,
we rush to shake the flames out of his hair
and quench the holy fire with water. But
Anchises raised his glad eyes to the stars
and lifted heavenward his voice and hands:
'O Jupiter, all-able one, if you
are moved by any prayers, look on us.
I only ask you this: if by our goodness
we merit it, then, Father, grant to us   210
your help and let your sign confirm these omens.'

"No sooner had the old man spoken so
than sudden thunder crashed upon the left,

and through the shadows ran a shooting star,
its trail a torch of flooding light. It glides
above the highest housetops as we watch,
until the brightness that has marked its course
is buried in the woods of Ida: far
and wide the long wake of that furrow shines,
and sulphur smokes upon the land. At last,   220
won over by this sign, my father rises,
to greet the gods, to adore the sacred star:
'Now my delay is done; I follow; where
you lead, I am. Gods of my homeland, save
my household, save my grandson. Yours, this omen;
and Troy is in your keeping. Yes, I yield.
My son, I go with you as your companion.'

"These were his words. But now the fire roars
across the walls; the tide of flame flows nearer.
'Come then, dear father, mount upon my neck;   230
I'll bear you on my shoulders. That is not
too much for me. Whatever waits for us,
we both shall share one danger, one salvation.
Let young Iülus come with me, and let
my wife Creüsa follow at a distance.
And servants, listen well to what I say:
along the way, just past the city walls,
in an abandoned spot there is a mound,
an ancient shrine of Ceres; and nearby
an ancient cypress stands, one that our fathers'   240
devotion kept alive for many years.
From different directions, we shall meet
at this one point. My father, you will carry
the holy vessels and our homeland's gods.
Filthy with war, just come from slaughter, I
must never touch these sacred things until
I bathe myself within a running stream.'

"This said, I spread a tawny lion skin
across my bent neck, over my broad shoulders,
and then take up Anchises; small Iülus   250
now clutches my right hand; his steps uneven,
he is following his father; and my wife
moves on behind. We journey through dark places;
and I, who just before could not be stirred
by any weapons cast at me or by
the crowds of Greeks in charging columns, now
am terrified by all the breezes, startled
by every sound, in fear for son and father.

"And now, as I approached the gates and thought
I had found the way of my escape, the sudden   260
and frequent tramp of feet was at my ears;
and peering through the shades, Anchises cries:
'My son, take flight; my son, they are upon us.
I see their gleaming shields, the flashing bronze.'
At this alarm I panicked: some unfriendly
god's power ripped away my tangled mind.
For while I take a trackless path, deserting
the customary roads, fate tears from me
my wife Creüsa in my misery.
I cannot say if she had halted or   270
had wandered off the road or slumped down, weary.
My eyes have never had her back again.
I did not look behind for her, astray,
or think of her before we reached the mound
and ancient, sacred shrine of Ceres; here
at last, when all were gathered, she alone
was missing—gone from husband, son, companions.

"What men, what gods did I in madness not
accuse? Did I see anything more cruel
within the fallen city? I commit   280
Ascanius, Anchises, and the gods
of Troy to my companions, hiding them
inside a winding valley. I myself
again seek out the city, girding on
my gleaming arms. I want to meet all risks
again, return through all of Troy, again
give back my life to danger. First I seek
the city walls, the gateway's shadowed thresholds
through which I had come before. And I retrace
my footsteps; through the night I make them out.   290
My spirit is held by horror everywhere;
even the very silence terrifies.
Then I move homeward—if by chance, by chance,
she may have made her way there. But the Danaans
had flooded in and held the house. At once
the hungry conflagration rolls before
the wind, high as the highest rooftop; flames
are towering overhead, the boiling tide
is raging to the heavens. I go on;
again I see the house of Priam and   300
the fortress. Down the empty porticoes,
in Juno's sanctuary, I can see
both Phoenix and the fierce Ulysses, chosen
as guardians, at watch over the booty.

And here, from every quarter, heaped together,
are Trojan treasures torn from burning altars—
the tables of the gods, and plundered garments,
and bowls of solid gold; and Trojan boys
and trembling women stand in a long line.

"And more, I even dared to cast my cries   310
across the shadows; in my sorrow, I—
again, again, in vain—called for Creüsa;
my shouting filled the streets. But as I rushed
and raged among the houses endlessly,
before my eyes there stood the effigy
and grieving shade of my Creüsa, image
far larger than the real. I was dismayed;
my hair stood stiff, my voice held fast within
my jaws. She spoke; her words undid my cares:

"'O my sweet husband, is there any use   320
in giving way to such fanatic sorrow?
For this could never come to pass without
the gods' decree; and you are not to carry
Creüsa as your comrade, since the king
of high Olympus does not grant you that.
Along your way lie long exile, vast plains
of sea that you must plow; but you will reach
Hesperia, where Lydian Tiber flows,
a tranquil stream, through farmers' fruitful fields.
There days of gladness lie in wait for you: 330
a kingdom and a royal bride. Enough
of tears for loved Creüsa. I am not
to see the haughty homes of Myrmidons
or of Dolopians, or be a slave
to Grecian matrons—I, a Dardan woman
and wife of Venus' son. It is the gods'
great Mother who keeps me upon these shores.
And now farewell, and love the son we share.'

"When she was done with words—I weeping and
wanting to say so many things—she left   340
and vanished in transparent air. Three times
I tried to throw my arms around her neck;
three times the Shade I grasped in vain escaped
my hands—like fleet winds, most like a winged dream.

"And so at last, when night has passed, I go
again to my companions. Here I find,
to my surprise, new comrades come together,
vast numbers, men and women, joined for exile,

a crowd of sorrow. Come from every side,
with courage and with riches, they are ready   350
for any lands across the seas where I
may lead them. Now the star of morning rose
above high Ida's ridges, guiding the day.
The Danaans held the gates' blockaded thresholds.
There was no hope of help. Then I gave way
and, lifting up my father, made for the mountains."

BOOK 3

[Aeneas tells Dido of the divine command to seek out Italy. He describes his wanderings, including his encounters with the Harpies, filthy birds that foul everything they
touch. Helenus, a priest, tells him of the sign by which he will recognize the future
site of Rome when he arrives there—a white sow with thirty suckling pigs under a
holly branch. Arriving at the Cyclops's cave, Aeneas comes on a sailor, Achaemenides,
apparently left behind by Odysseus. Although Achaemenides is a Greek, and therefore an enemy of Troy, Aeneas rescues him. At last, Aeneas and his men arrive at
Libya. Meanwhile, Anchises, Aeneas's father, dies. With this last grief, Aeneas, now
"father Aeneas," ends his tale.]

BOOK 4

Too late. The queen is caught between love's pain   1
and press. She feeds the wound within her veins;
she is eaten by a secret flame. Aeneas'
high name, all he has done, again, again
come like a flood. His face, his words hold fast
her breast. Care strips her limbs of calm and rest.

A new dawn lights the earth with Phoebus' lamp
and banishes damp shadows from the sky
when restless Dido turns to her heart's sharer:
"Anna, my sister, what dreams make me shudder?   10
Who is this stranger guest come to our house?
How confident he looks, how strong his chest
and arms! I think—and I have cause—that he
is born of gods. For in the face of fear
the mean must fall. What fates have driven him!
What trying wars he lived to tell! Were it not
my sure, immovable decision not
to marry anyone since my first love
turned traitor, when he cheated me by death,
were I not weary of the couch and torch,   20
I might perhaps give way to this one fault.
For I must tell you, Anna, since the time
Sychaeus, my poor husband, died and my
own brother splashed our household gods with blood,
Aeneas is the only man to move

my feelings, to overturn my shifting heart.
I know too well the signs of the old flame.
But I should call upon the earth to gape
and close above me, or on the almighty
Father to take his thunderbolt, to hurl   30
me down into the shades, the pallid shadows
and deepest night of Erebus, before
I'd violate you, Shame, or break your laws!
For he who first had joined me to himself
has carried off my love, and may he keep it
and be its guardian within the grave."
She spoke. Her breast became a well of tears.

And Anna answers: "Sister, you more dear
to me than light itself, are you to lose
all of your youth in dreary loneliness,   40
and never know sweet children or the soft
rewards of Venus? Do you think that ashes
or buried Shades will care about such matters?
Until Aeneas came, there was no suitor
who moved your sad heart—not in Libya nor,
before, in Tyre: you always scorned Iarbas
and all the other chiefs that Africa,
a region rich in triumphs, had to offer.
How can you struggle now against a love
that is so acceptable? Have you forgotten   50
the land you settled, those who hem you in?
On one side lie the towns of the Gaetulians,
a race invincible, and the unbridled
Numidians and then the barbarous Syrtis.
And on the other lies a barren country,
stripped by the drought and by Barcaean raiders,
raging both far and near. And I need not
remind you of the wars that boil in Tyre
and of your brother's menaces and plots.
For I am sure it was the work of gods   60
and Juno that has held the Trojan galleys
fast to their course and brought them here to Carthage.
If you marry Aeneas, what a city
and what a kingdom, sister, you will see!
With Trojan arms beside us, so much greatness
must lie in wait for Punic glory! Only
pray to the gods for their good will, and having
presented them with proper sacrifices,
be lavish with your Trojan guests and weave
excuses for delay while frenzied winter   70
storms out across the sea and shatters ships,

while wet Orion blows his tempest squalls
beneath a sky that is intractable."

These words of Anna fed the fire in Dido.
Hope burned away her doubt, destroyed her shame.
First they moved on from shrine to shrine, imploring
the favor of the gods at every altar.
They slaughter chosen sheep, as is the custom,
and offer them to Ceres the lawgiver,
to Phoebus, Father Bacchus, and—above all—   80
to Juno, guardian of marriage. Lovely
Dido holds the cup in her right hand;
she pours the offering herself, midway
between a milk-white heifer's horns. She studies
slit breasts of beasts and reads their throbbing guts.
But oh the ignorance of augurs! How
can vows and altars help one wild with love?
Meanwhile the supple flame devours her marrow;
within her breast the silent wound lives on.
Unhappy Dido burns. Across the city   90
she wanders in her frenzy—even as
a heedless hind hit by an arrow when
a shepherd drives for game with darts among
the Cretan woods and, unawares, from far
leaves winging steel inside her flesh; she roams
the forests and the wooded slopes of Dicte,
the shaft of death still clinging to her side.
So Dido leads Aeneas around the ramparts,
displays the wealth of Sidon and the city
ready to hand; she starts to speak, then falters   100
and stops in midspeech. Now day glides away.
Again, insane, she seeks out that same banquet,
again she prays to hear the trials of Troy,
again she hangs upon the teller's lips.

But now the guests are gone. The darkened moon,
in turn, conceals its light, the setting stars
invite to sleep; inside the vacant hall
she grieves alone and falls upon the couch
that he has left. Absent, she sees, she hears
the absent one or draws Ascanius,   110
his son and counterfeit, into her arms,
as if his shape might cheat her untellable love.

Her towers rise no more; the young of Carthage
no longer exercise at arms or build
their harbors or sure battlements for war;
the works are idle, broken off; the massive,

menacing rampart walls, even the crane,
defier of the sky, now lie neglected.

As soon as Jove's dear wife sees that her Dido
is in the grip of such a scourge and that   120
no honor can withstand this madness, then
the daughter of Saturn faces Venus: "How
remarkable indeed: what splendid spoils
you carry off, you and your boy; how grand
and memorable is the glory if
one woman is beaten by the guile of two
gods. I have not been blind. I know you fear
our fortresses, you have been suspicious of
the houses of high Carthage. But what end
will come of all this hate? Let us be done   130
with wrangling. Let us make, instead of war,
an everlasting peace and plighted wedding.
You have what you were bent upon: she burns
with love; the frenzy now is in her bones.
Then let us rule this people—you and I—
with equal auspices; let Dido serve
a Phrygian husband, let her give her Tyrians
and her pledged dowry into your right hand."

But Venus read behind the words of Juno
the motive she had hid: to shunt the kingdom   140
of Italy to Libyan shores. And so
she answered Juno: "Who is mad enough
to shun the terms you offer? Who would prefer
to strive with you in war? If only fortune
favor the course you urge. For I am ruled
by fates and am unsure if Jupiter
would have the Trojans and the men of Tyre
become one city, if he likes the mingling
of peoples and the writing of such treaties.
But you are his wife and it is right for you   150
to try his mind, to entreat him. Go. I'll follow."

Queen Juno answered her: "That task is mine.
But listen now while in few words I try
to tell you how I mean to bring about
this urgent matter. When tomorrow's Titan
first shows his rays of light, reveals the world,
Aeneas and unhappy Dido plan
to hunt together in the forest. Then
while horsemen hurry to surround the glades
with nets, I shall pour down a black raincloud,   160
in which I have mixed hail, to awaken all

the heavens with my thundering. Their comrades
will scatter under cover of thick night.
Both Dido and the Trojan chief will reach
their shelter in the same cave. I shall be there.
And if I can rely on your goodwill,
I shall unite the two in certain marriage
and seal her as Aeneas' very own;
and this shall be their wedding." Cytherea
said nothing to oppose the plan; she granted   170
what Juno wanted, smiling at its cunning.
Meanwhile Aurora rose; she left the Ocean.
And when her brightness fills the air, select
young men move from the gates with wide-meshed nets
and narrow snares and broad-blade hunting spears,
and then Massylian horsemen hurry out
with strong, keen-scented hounds. But while the chieftains
of Carthage wait at Dido's threshold, she
still lingers in her room. Her splendid stallion,
in gold and purple, prances, proudly champing   180
his foaming bit. At last the queen appears
among the mighty crowd; upon her shoulders
she wears a robe of Sidon with embroidered
borders. Her quiver is of gold, her hair
has knots and ties of gold, a golden clasp
holds fast her purple cloak. Her Trojan comrades
and glad Ascanius advance behind her.
Aeneas, who is handsome past all others,
himself approaches now to join her, linking
his hunting band to hers. Just as Apollo,   190
when in the winter he abandoned Lycia
and Xanthus' streams to visit his maternal
Delos, where he renews the dances—Cretans,
Dryopians, and painted Agathyrsi,
mingling around the altars, shout—advances
upon the mountain ridges of high Cynthus
and binds his flowing hair with gentle leaves
and braids its strands with intertwining gold;
his arrows clatter on his shoulder: no
less graceful is Aeneas as he goes;   200
an equal beauty fills his splendid face.
And when they reach the hills and pathless thickets,
the wild she-goats, dislodged from stony summits,
run down the ridges; from another slope
stags fling themselves across the open fields;
they mass their dusty bands in flight, forsaking
the hillsides. But the boy Ascanius
rides happy in the valleys on his fiery

stallion as he passes on his course
now stags, now goats; among the lazy herds   210
his prayer is for a foaming boar or that
a golden lion come down from the mountain.

Meanwhile confusion takes the sky, tremendous
turmoil, and on its heels, rain mixed with hail.
The scattered train of Tyre, the youth of Troy,
and Venus' Dardan grandson in alarm
seek different shelters through the fields; the torrents
roar down the mountains. Dido and the Trojan
chieftain have reached the same cave. Primal Earth
and Juno, queen of marriages, together   220
now give the signal: lightning fires flash,
the upper air is witness to their mating,
and from the highest hilltops shout the nymphs.
That day was her first day of death and ruin.
For neither how things seem nor how they are deemed
moves Dido now, and she no longer thinks
of furtive love. For Dido calls it marriage,
and with this name she covers up her fault.

Then, swiftest of all evils, Rumor runs
straightway through Libya's mighty cities—Rumor,   230
whose life is speed, whose going gives her force.
Timid and small at first, she soon lifts up
her body in the air. She stalks the ground;
her head is hidden in the clouds. Provoked
to anger at the gods, her mother Earth
gave birth to her, last come—they say—as sister
to Coeus and Enceladus; fast-footed
and lithe of wing, she is a terrifying
enormous monster with as many feathers
as she has sleepless eyes beneath each feather   240
(amazingly), as many sounding tongues
and mouths, and raises up as many ears.
Between the earth and skies she flies by night,
screeching across the darkness, and she never
closes her eyes in gentle sleep. By day
she sits as sentinel on some steep roof
or on high towers, frightening vast cities;
for she holds fast to falsehood and distortion
as often as to messages of truth.
Now she was glad. She filled the ears of all   250
with many tales. She sang of what was done
and what was fiction, chanting that Aeneas,
one born of Trojan blood, had come, that lovely

Dido has deigned to join herself to him,
that now, in lust, forgetful of their kingdom,
they take long pleasure, fondling through the winter,
the slaves of squalid craving. Such reports
the filthy goddess scatters everywhere
upon the lips of men. At once she turns
her course to King Iarbas; and his spirit   260
is hot, his anger rages at her words.
Iarbas was the son of Hammon by
a ravished nymph of Garamantia.
In his broad realm he had built a hundred temples,
a hundred handsome shrines for Jupiter.
There he had consecrated sleepless fire,
the everlasting watchman of the gods;
the soil was rich with blood of slaughtered herds,
and varied garlands flowered on the thresholds.
Insane, incited by that bitter rumor,   270
he prayed long—so they say—to Jupiter;
he stood before the altars in the presence
of gods, a suppliant with upraised hands:
"All-able Jove, to whom the Moorish nation,
feasting upon their figured couches, pour
Lenaean sacrifices, do you see
these things? Or, Father, are we only trembling
for nothing when you cast your twisting thunder?
Those fires in the clouds that terrify
our souls—are they but blind and aimless lightning   280
that only stirs our empty mutterings?
A woman, wandering within our borders,
paid for the right to build a tiny city.
We gave her shore to till and terms of tenure.
She has refused to marry me, she has taken
Aeneas as a lord into her lands.
And now this second Paris, with his crew
of half-men, with his chin and greasy hair
bound up beneath a bonnet of Maeonia,
enjoys his prey; while we bring offerings   290
to what we have believed to be your temples,
still cherishing your empty reputation."

And as he prayed and clutched the altar stone,
all-able Jupiter heard him and turned
his eyes upon the royal walls, upon
the lovers who had forgotten their good name.
He speaks to Mercury, commanding him:
"Be on your way, my son, call up the Zephyrs,
glide on your wings, speak to the Dardan chieftain

who lingers now at Tyrian Carthage, paying   300
not one jot of attention to the cities
the Fates have given him. Mercury, carry
across the speeding winds the words I urge:
his lovely mother did not promise such
a son to us; she did not save him twice
from Grecian arms for this—but to be master
of Italy, a land that teems with empire
and seethes with war; to father a race from Teucer's
high blood, to place all earth beneath his laws.
But if the brightness of such deeds is not   310
enough to kindle him, if he cannot
attempt the task for his own fame, does he—
a father—grudge Ascanius the walls
of Rome? What is he pondering, what hope
can hold him here among his enemies,
not caring for his own Ausonian sons
or for Lavinian fields. He must set sail.
And this is all; my message lies in this."

His words were ended. Mercury made ready
to follow his great father's orders. First   320
he laces on his golden sandals: winged
to bear him, swift as whirlwinds, high across
the land and water. Then he takes his wand;
with this he calls pale spirits up from Orcus
and down to dreary Tartarus sends others;
he uses this to give sleep and recall it,
and to unseal the eyes of those who have died.
His trust in this, he spurs the winds and skims
the troubled clouds. And now in flight, he sights
the summit and high sides of hardy Atlas   330
who props up heaven with his crest—Atlas,
whose head is crowned with pines and battered by
the wind and rain and always girdled by
black clouds; his shoulders' cloak is falling snow;
above the old man's chin the rivers rush;
his bristling beard is stiff with ice. Here first
Cyllene's god poised on his even wings
and halted; then he hurled himself headlong
and seaward with his body, like a bird
that, over shores and reefs where fishes throng,   340
swoops low along the surface of the waters.
Not unlike this, Cyllene's god between
the earth and heaven as he flies, cleaving
the sandy shore of Libya from the winds
that sweep from Atlas, father of his mother.

As soon as his winged feet have touched the outskirts,
he sees Aeneas founding fortresses
and fashioning new houses. And his sword
was starred with tawny jasper, and the cloak
that draped his shoulders blazed with Tyrian purple—   350
a gift that wealthy Dido wove for him;
she had run golden thread along the web.
And Mercury attacks at once. "Are you
now laying the foundation of high Carthage,
as servant to a woman, building her
a splendid city here? Are you forgetful
of what is your own kingdom, your own fate?
The very god of gods, whose power sways
both earth and heaven, sends me down to you
from bright Olympus. He himself has asked me   360
to carry these commands through the swift air:
what are you pondering or hoping for
while squandering your ease in Libyan lands?
For if the brightest of such deeds is not
enough to kindle you—if you cannot
attempt the task for your own fame—remember
Ascanius growing up, the hopes you hold
for Iülus, your own heir, to whom are owed
the realm of Italy and land of Rome."
So did Cyllene's god speak out. He left   370
the sight of mortals even as he spoke
and vanished into the transparent air.

This vision stunned Aeneas, struck him dumb;
his terror held his hair erect; his voice
held fast within his jaws. He burns to flee
from Carthage; he would quit these pleasant lands,
astonished by such warnings, the command
of gods. What can he do? With what words dare
he face the frenzied queen? What openings
can he employ? His wits are split, they shift   380
here, there; they race to different places, turning
to everything. But as he hesitated,
this seemed the better plan: he calls Sergestus
and Mnestheus and the strong Serestus, and
he asks them to equip the fleet in silence,
to muster their companions on the shore,
to ready all their arms, but to conceal
the reasons for this change; while he himself—
with gracious Dido still aware of nothing
and never dreaming such a love could ever   390
be broken—would try out approaches, seek

the tenderest, most tactful time for speech,
whatever dexterous way might suit his case.
And all are glad. They race to carry out
the orders of Aeneas, his commands.

But Dido—for who can deceive a lover?—
had caught his craftiness; she quickly sensed
what was to come; however safe they seemed,
she feared all things. That same unholy Rumor
brought her these hectic tidings: that the boats   400
were being armed, made fit for voyaging.
Her mind is helpless; raging frantically,
inflamed, she raves throughout the city—just
as a Bacchante when, each second year,
she is startled by the shaking of the sacred
emblems, the orgies urge her on, the cry
"o Bacchus" calls to her by night; Cithaeron
incites her with its clamor. And at last
Dido attacks Aeneas with these words:

"Deceiver, did you even hope to hide   410
so harsh a crime, to leave this land of mine
without a word? Can nothing hold you back—
neither your love, the hand you pledged, nor even
the cruel death that lies in wait for Dido?
Beneath the winter sky are you preparing
a fleet to rush away across the deep
among the north winds, you who have no feeling?
What! Even if you were not seeking out
strange fields and unknown dwellings, even if
your ancient Troy were still erect, would you   420
return to Troy across such stormy seas?
Do you flee me? By tears, by your right hand—
this sorry self is left with nothing else—
by wedding, by the marriage we began,
if I did anything deserving of you
or anything of mine was sweet to you,
take pity on a fallen house, put off
your plan, I pray—if there is still place for prayers.
Because of you the tribes of Libya, all
the Nomad princes hate me, even my   430
own Tyrians are hostile; and for you
my honor is gone and that good name that once
was mine, my only claim to reach the stars.
My guest, to whom do you consign this dying
woman? I must say 'guest': this name is all
I have of one whom once I called my husband.

Then why do I live on? Until Pygmalion,
my brother, batters down my walls, until
Iarbas the Gaetulian takes me prisoner?
Had I at least before you left conceived   440
a son in me; if there were but a tiny
Aeneas playing by me in the hall,
whose face, in spite of everything, might yet
remind me of you, then indeed I should
not seem so totally abandoned, beaten."
Her words were ended. But Aeneas, warned
by Jove, held still his eyes; he struggled, pressed
care back within his breast. With halting words
he answers her at last: "I never shall
deny what you deserve, the kindnesses   450
that you could tell; I never shall regret
remembering Elissa for as long
as I remember my own self, as long
as breath is king over these limbs. I'll speak
brief words that fit the case. I never hoped
to hide—do not imagine that—my flight;
I am not furtive. I have never held
the wedding torches as a husband; I
have never entered into such agreements.
If fate had granted me to guide my life   460
by my own auspices and to unravel
my troubles with unhampered will, then I
should cherish first the town of Troy, the sweet
remains of my own people and the tall
rooftops of Priam would remain, my hand
would plant again a second Pergamus
for my defeated men. But now Grynean
Apollo's oracle would have me seize
great Italy, the Lycian prophecies
tell me of Italy: there is my love,   470
there is my homeland. If the fortresses
of Carthage and the vision of a city
in Libya can hold you, who are Phoenician,
why, then, begrudge the Trojans' settling on
Ausonian soil? There is no harm: it is
right that we, too, seek out a foreign kingdom.
For often as the night conceals the earth
with dew and shadows, often as the stars
ascend, afire, my father's anxious image
approaches me in dreams. Anchises warns   480
and terrifies. I see the wrong I have done
to one so dear, my boy Ascanius,
whom I am cheating of Hesperia,

the fields assigned by fate. And now the gods'
own messenger, sent down by Jove himself—
I call as witness both our lives—has brought
his orders through the swift air. My own eyes
have seen the god as he was entering
our walls—in broad daylight. My ears have drunk
his words. No longer set yourself and me   490
afire. Stop your quarrel. It is not
my own free will that leads to Italy."

But all the while Aeneas spoke, she stared
askance at him, her glance ran this way, that.
She scans his body with her silent eyes.
Then Dido thus, inflamed, denounces him:

"No goddess was your mother, false Aeneas,
and Dardanus no author of your race;
the bristling Caucasus was father to you
on his harsh crags; Hyrcanian tigresses   500
gave you their teats. And why must I dissemble?
Why hold myself in check? For greater wrongs?
For did Aeneas groan when I was weeping?
Did he once turn his eyes, or, overcome,
shed tears or pity me, who was his loved one?
What shall I cry out first? And what shall follow?
No longer now does mighty Juno or
our Father, son of Saturn, watch this earth
with righteous eyes. Nowhere is certain trust.
He was an outcast on the shore, in want.   510
I took him in and madly let him share
my kingdom; his lost fleet and his companions
I saved from death. Oh I am whirled along
in fire by the Furies! First the augur
Apollo, then the Lycian oracles,
and now, sent down by Jove himself, the gods'
own herald, carrying his horrid orders.
This seems indeed to be a work for High Ones,
a care that can disturb their calm. I do not
refute your words. I do not keep you back.   520
Go then, before the winds, to Italy.
Seek out your kingdom overseas; indeed,
if there be pious powers still, I hope
that you will drink your torments to the lees
among sea rocks and, drowning, often cry
the name of Dido. Then, though absent, I
shall hunt you down with blackened firebrands;
and when chill death divides my soul and body,

a Shade, I shall be present everywhere.
Depraved, you then will pay your penalties.   530
And I shall hear of it, and that report
will come to me below, among the Shadows."

Her speech is broken off; heartsick, she shuns
the light of day, deserts his eyes; she turns
away, leaves him in fear and hesitation,
Aeneas longing still to say so much.
As Dido faints, her servants lift her up;
they carry her into her marble chamber;
they lay her body down upon the couch.

But though he longs to soften, soothe her sorrow   540
and turn aside her troubles with sweet words,
though groaning long and shaken in his mind
because of his great love, nevertheless
pious Aeneas carries out the gods'
instructions. Now he turns back to his fleet.

. . . .

[Dido utters a long lament over her fate. Furious at Aeneas, she appeals to Juno, Hecate, and the Furies to punish Aeneas with suffering and calls for an avenger:]

"These things I plead; these final words I pour
out of my blood. Then, Tyrians, hunt down
with hatred all his sons and race to come;
send this as offering unto my ashes.
Do not let love or treaty tie our peoples.   550
May an avenger rise up from my bones,
one who will track with firebrand and sword
the Dardan settlers, now and in the future,
at any time that ways present themselves.
I call your shores to war against their shores,
your waves against their waves, arms with their arms.
Let them and their sons' sons learn what is war."

This said, she ran her mind to every side,
for she was seeking ways with which to slice—
as quickly as she can—the hated light;   560
and then, with these brief words, she turned to Barce,
Sychaeus' nurse—for Dido's own was now
black ashes in Phoenicia, her old homeland:
"Dear nurse, call here to me my sister Anna;
and tell her to be quick to bathe her body
with river water; see that she brings cattle
and all that is appointed for atonement.
So must my sister come; while you yourself
bind up your temples with a pious fillet.

I mean to offer unto Stygian Jove   570
the sacrifices that, as is ordained,
I have made ready and begun, to put
an end to my disquiet and commit
to flames the pyre of the Trojan chieftain."
So Dido spoke. And Barce hurried off;
she moved with an old woman's eagerness.

But Dido, desperate, beside herself
with awful undertakings, eyes bloodshot
and rolling, and her quivering cheeks flecked
with stains and pale with coming death, now bursts   580
across the inner courtyards of her palace.
She mounts in madness that high pyre, unsheathes
the Dardan sword, a gift not sought for such
an end. And when she saw the Trojan's clothes
and her familiar bed, she checked her thought
and tears a little, lay upon the couch
and spoke her final words: "O relics, dear
while fate and god allowed, receive my spirit
and free me from these cares; for I have lived
and journeyed through the course assigned by fortune.   590
And now my Shade will pass, illustrious,
beneath the earth; I have built a handsome city,
have seen my walls rise up, avenged a husband,
won satisfaction from a hostile brother:
o fortunate, too fortunate—if only
the ships of Troy had never touched our coasts."
She spoke and pressed her face into the couch.
"I shall die unavenged, but I shall die,"
she says, "Thus, thus, I gladly go below
to shadows. May the savage Dardan drink   600
with his own eyes this fire from the deep
and take with him the omen of my death."

Then Dido's words were done, and her companions
can see her fallen on the sword; the blade
is foaming with her blood, her hands are bloodstained.
Now clamor rises to the high rooftop.
Now rumor riots through the startled city.
The lamentations, keening, shrieks of women
sound through the houses; heavens echo mighty
wailings, even as if an enemy   610
were entering the gates, with all of Carthage
or ancient Tyre in ruins, and angry fires
rolling across the homes of men and gods.

. . . .

BOOK 5

[Having escaped from Carthage, Aeneas holds funeral games to commemorate the death of his father, Anchises. Neptune casts the helmsman Palinarus into the sea as a sacrifice to Juno's anger.]

BOOK 6

[Guided by the Cumaean Sibyl, Aeneas enters the Underworld, where he uses the Golden Bough to compel Charon to ferry him across the River Styx:]

. . . .

The journey they began can now continue.   1
They near the riverbank. Even the boatman,
while floating on the Styx, had seen them coming
across the silent grove and toward the shore.
He does not wait for greeting but attacks,
insulting with these words: "Enough! Stop there!
Whoever you may be who make your way,
so armed, down to our waters, tell me now
why you have come. This is the land of shadows,
of Sleep and drowsy Night; no living bodies   10
can take their passage in the ship of Styx.
Indeed, I was not glad to have Alcides
or Theseus or Pirithoüs cross the lake,
although the three of them were sons of gods
and undefeated in their wars. Alcides
tried to drag off in chains the guardian
of Tartarus; he tore him, trembling, from
the king's own throne. The others tried to carry
the queen away from Pluto's wedding chamber."

Apollo's priestess answered briefly: "We   20
bring no such trickery; no need to be
disturbed; our weapons bear no violence;
for us, the mighty watchman can bark on
forever in his cavern, frightening
the bloodless shades; Proserpina can keep
the threshold of her uncle faithfully.
Trojan Aeneas, famed for piety
and arms, descends to meet his father, down
into the deepest shades of Erebus.
And if the image of such piety   30
is not enough to move you, then"—and here
she shows the branch concealed beneath her robe—
"you may yet recognize this bough." At this
the swollen heart of Charon stills its anger.
He says no more. He wonders at the sacred
gift of the destined wand, so long unseen,

and turns his blue-black keel toward shore. He clears
the other spirits from the gangways and
long benches and, meanwhile, admits the massive
Aeneas to the boat, the vessel's seams   40
groaning beneath the weight as they let in
marsh water through the chinks. At last he sets
the priestess and the soldier safe across
the stream in ugly slime and blue-gray sedge.

These regions echo with the triple-throated
bark of the giant Cerberus, who crouches,
enormous, in a cavern facing them.
The Sibyl, seeing that his neck is bristling
with snakes, throws him a honeyed cake of wheat
with drugs that bring on sleep. His triple mouths   50
yawn wide with rapid hunger as he clutches
the cake she cast. His giant back falls slack
along the ground; his bulk takes all the cave.
And when the beast is buried under sleep,
Aeneas gains the entrance swiftly, leaves
the riverbank from which no one returns.

Here voices and loud lamentations echo:
the souls of infants weeping at the very
first threshold—torn away by the black day,
deprived of their sweet life, ripped from the breast,   60
plunged into bitter death. And next to them
are those condemned to die upon false charges.
These places have not been assigned, indeed,
without a lot, without a judge; for here
Minos is magistrate. He shakes the urn
and calls on the assembly of the silent,
to learn the lives of men and their misdeeds.
The land that lies beyond belongs to those
who, although innocent, took death by their
own hands; hating the light, they threw away   70
their lives. But now they long for the upper air,
and even to bear want and trials there.
But fate refuses them: the melancholy
marshland, its ugly waters, hem them in,
the prisoners of Styx and its nine circles.

Nearby, spread out on every side, there lie
the Fields of Mourning: this, their given name.
And here, concealed by secret paths, are those
whom bitter love consumed with brutal waste;
a myrtle grove encloses them; their pains   80
remain with them in death. Aeneas sees

Phaedra and Procris and sad Eriphyle,
who pointed to the wounds inflicted by
her savage son; he sees Pasiphaë
and then Evadne; and Laodamia
and Caeneus, once a youth and now a woman,
changed back again by fate to her first shape.

Among them, wandering in that great forest,
and with her wound still fresh: Phoenician Dido.
And when the Trojan hero recognized her   90
dim shape among the shadows (just as one
who either sees or thinks he sees among
the cloud banks, when the month is young, the moon
rising), he wept and said with tender love:
"Unhappy Dido, then the word I had
was true? That you were dead? That you pursued
your final moment with the sword? Did I
bring only death to you? Queen, I swear by
the stars, the gods above, and any trust
that may be in this underneath, I was   100
unwilling when I had to leave your shores.
But those same orders of the gods that now
urge on my journey through the shadows, through
abandoned, thorny lands and deepest night,
drove me by their decrees. And I could not
believe that with my going I should bring
so great a grief as this. But stay your steps.
Do not retreat from me. Whom do you flee?
This is the last time fate will let us speak."
These were the words Aeneas, weeping, used,   110
trying to soothe the burning, fierce-eyed Shade.
She turned away, eyes to the ground, her face
no more moved by his speech than if she stood
as stubborn flint or some Marpessan crag.
At last she tore herself away; she fled—
and still his enemy—into the forest
of shadows, where Sychaeus, once her husband,
answers her sorrows, gives her love for love.
Nevertheless, Aeneas, stunned by her
unkindly fate, still follows at a distance   120
with tears and pity for her as she goes.

He struggles on his given way again.
Now they have reached the borderlands of this
first region, the secluded home of those
renowned in war. Here he encounters Tydeus,
Parthenopaeus, famous soldier, and
the pale shade of Adrastus; here are men

mourned in the upper world, the Dardan captains
fallen in battle. And for all of these,
on seeing them in long array, he grieves: 130
for Glaucus, Medon, and Thersilochus,
the three sons of Antenor; Polyboetes,
who was a priest of Ceres; and Idaeus,
still clinging to his chariot, his weapons.
The spirits crowd Aeneas right and left,
and it is not enough to see him once;
they want to linger, to keep step with him,
to learn the reasons for his visit there.
But when the Grecian chieftains and the hosts
of Agamemnon see the hero and   140
his weapons glittering across the shadows,
they tremble with an overwhelming terror;
some turn their backs in flight, as when they once
sought out their ships; some raise a thin war cry;
the voice they now have mocks their straining throats.

And here Aeneas saw the son of Priam,
Deiphobus, all of his body mangled,
his face torn savagely, his face and both
his hands, his ears lopped off his ravaged temples,
his nostrils slashed by a disgraceful wound.   150
How hard it was to recognize the trembling
Shade as he tried to hide his horrid torments.
Aeneas does not wait to hear his greeting
but with familiar accents speaks to him:
"Deiphobus, great warrior, and born
of Teucer's brilliant blood, who made you pay
such brutal penalties? Who was allowed
to do such violence to you? For Rumor
had told me that on that last night, worn out
by your vast slaughter of the Greeks, you sank   160
upon a heap of tangled butchery.
Then I myself raised up an empty tomb
along Rhoeteum's shore; three times I called
loudly upon your Shade. Your name and weapons
now mark the place. I could not find you, friend,
or bury you, before I left, within
your native land." The son of Priam answered:

"My friend, you left no thing undone; you paid
Deiphobus and his dead Shade their due.
But I was cast into these evils by   170
my own fate and the deadly treachery
of the Laconian woman; it was she
who left me these memorials. You know

and must remember all too well how we
spent that last night among deceiving pleasures.
For when across high Pergamus the fatal
horse leaped and, in its pregnant belly, carried
armed infantry, she mimed a choral dance
and, shrieking in a Bacchic orgy, paced
the Phrygian women; it was she herself   180
who held a giant firebrand and, from
the citadel, called in the Danaans.
I lay, sleep-heavy, worn with cares, within
our luckless bridal chamber, taken by
a sweet, deep rest much like the peace of death.
And meanwhile my incomparable wife
has stripped the house of every weapon, even
removing from beneath my head my trusted
sword; and she throws the doorway open, calls
her Menelaeus to my palace, hoping   190
her lover surely will be grateful for
this mighty favor, and her infamy
for old misdeeds will be forgotten. Why
delay? They burst into my room. The son
of Aeolus joins them as a companion,
encourager of outrage. Gods, requite
the Greeks for this if with my pious lips
I ask for satisfaction. But, in turn,
come tell me what misfortunes bring you here
alive? Have you been driven here by sea   200
wanderings or by warnings of the gods?
What fate so wearies you that you would visit
these sad and sunless dwellings, restless lands?"

But as they talked together, through the sky
Aurora with her Chariot of rose
had passed her midpoint; and they might have spent
all this allotted time with words had not
the Sibyl, his companion, warned him thus:
"The night is near, Aeneas, and we waste
our time with tears. For here the road divides   210
in two directions: on the right it runs
beneath the ramparts of great Dis, this is
our highway to Elysium; the wicked
are punished on the left—that path leads down
to godless Tartarus." Deiphobus:
"Do not be angry, mighty priestess, I
now leave to fill the count, return to darkness.
Go on, our glory, go; know better fates."
He said no more; his steps turned at these words.

Aeneas suddenly looks back; beneath   220
a rock upon his left he sees a broad
fortress encircled by a triple wall
and girdled by a rapid flood of flames
that rage: Tartarean Phlegethon whirling
resounding rocks. A giant gateway stands
in front, with solid adamantine pillars—
no force of man, not even heaven's sons,
enough to level these in war; a tower
of iron rises in the air; there sits
Tisiphone, who wears a bloody mantle.   230
She guards the entrance, sleepless night and day.
Both groans and savage scourgings echo there,
and then the clang of iron and dragging chains.

Aeneas stopped in terror, and the din
held him. "What kind of crimes are these? Virgin,
o speak! What penalties are paid here? What
loud lamentations fill the air?" The priestess
began: "Great captain of the Teucrians,
no innocent can cross these cursed thresholds;
but when the goddess Hecate made me   240
the guardian of Avernus' groves, then she
revealed the penalties the gods decreed
and guided me through all the halls of hell.
The king of these harsh realms is Rhadamanthus
the Gnosian: he hears men's crimes and then
chastises and compels confession for
those guilts that anyone, rejoicing, hid—
but uselessly—within the world above,
delaying his atonement till too late,
beyond the time of death. Tisiphone   250
at once is the avenger, armed with whips;
she leaps upon the guilty, lashing them;
in her left hand she grips her gruesome vipers
and calls her savage company of sisters.
And now at last the sacred doors are opened,
their hinges grating horribly. You see
what kind of sentry stands before the entrance,
what shape is at the threshold? Fiercer still,
the monstrous Hydra lives inside; her fifty
black mouths are gaping. Tartarus itself   260
then plunges downward, stretching twice as far
as is the view to heaven, high Olympus.
And here the ancient family of Earth,
the sons of Titan who had been cast down
by thunderbolts, writhe in the deepest gulf.

Here, too, I saw the giant bodies of
the twin sons of Aloeus, those who tried
to rip high heaven with their hands, to harry
Jove from his realms above. I saw Salmoneus:
how brutal were the penalties he paid 270
for counterfeiting Jove's own fires and
the thunders of Olympus. For he drove
four horses, brandishing a torch; he rode
triumphant through the tribes of Greece and through
the city in the heart of Elis, asking
for his own self the honor due to gods:
a madman who would mime the tempests and
inimitable thunder with the clang
of bronze and with the tramp of horn-foot horses.
But through the thick cloud banks all-able Jove 280
let fly his shaft—it was no firebrand
or smoky glare of torches: an enormous
blast of the whirlwind drove Salmoneus headlong.
And I saw Tityos, the foster child
of Earth, mother of all, his body stretched
on nine whole acres; and a crooked-beaked
huge vulture feeds upon his deathless liver
and guts that only grow the fruits of grief.
The vulture has his home deep in the breast
of Tityos, and there he tears his banquets 290
and gives no rest even to new-grown flesh.
And must I tell you of Ixion and
Pirithoüs, the Lapithae? Of those
who always stand beneath a hanging black
flint rock that is about to slip, to fall,
forever threatening? And there are those
who sit before high banquet couches, gleaming
upon supports of gold; before their eyes
a feast is spread in royal luxury,
but near at hand reclines the fiercest Fury: 300
they cannot touch the tables lest she leap
with lifted torch and thundering outcries.
And here are those who in their lives had hated
their brothers or had struck their father or
deceived a client or (the thickest swarm)
had brooded all alone on new-won treasure
and set no share apart for kin and friends;
those slain for their adultery; those who followed
rebellious arms or broke their pledge to masters—
imprisoned, all await their punishment. 310
And do not ask of me what penalty,
what shape or fate has overwhelmed their souls.

For some are made to roll a giant boulder,
and some are stretched along the spokes of wheels.
Sad Theseus has to sit and sit forever;
and miserable Phlegyas warns them all—
his roaring voice bears witness through the darkness:
'Be warned, learn justice, do not scorn the gods!'
Here is one who sold his fatherland for gold
and set a tyrant over it; he made   320
and unmade laws for gain. This one assailed
the chamber of his daughter and compelled
forbidden mating. All dared horrid evil
and reached what they had dared. A hundred tongues,
a hundred mouths, an iron voice were not
enough for me to gather all the forms
of crime or tell the names of all the torments."
So did the aged priestess of Apollo
speak, and she adds, "But come now, on your way,
complete the task you chose, Let us be quick.   330
I see the walls the Cyclops forged, the gates
with arching fronts, where we were told to place
our gifts." She has spoken. Side by side they move
along the shaded path; and hurrying
across the space between, they near the doors.
Aeneas gains the entrance, and he sprinkles
his body with fresh water, then he sets
the bough across the threshold facing them.

Their tasks were now completed; they had done
all that the goddess had required of them.   340
They came upon the lands of gladness, glades
of gentleness, the Groves of Blessedness—
a gracious place. The air is generous;
the plains wear dazzling light; they have their very
own sun and their own stars. Some exercise
their limbs along the green gymnasiums
or grapple on the golden sand, compete
in sport, and some keep time with moving feet
to dance and chant. There, too, the Thracian priest,
the long-robed Orpheus, plays, accompanying   350
with seven tones; and now his fingers strike
the strings, and now his quill of ivory.
The ancient race of Teucer, too, is here,
most handsome sons, great-hearted heroes born
in better years: Assaracus and Ilus
and Dardanus, who founded Pergamus.
From far Aeneas wonders at their phantom
armor and chariots; their spears are planted,

fixed in the ground; their horses graze and range
freely across the plain. The very same   360
delight that once was theirs in life—in arms
and chariots and care to pasture their
sleek steeds—has followed to this underearth.

And here to right and left he can see others:
some feasting on the lawns; and some chanting
glad choral paeans in a fragrant laurel
grove. Starting here, Eridanus in flood
flows through a forest to the world above.
Here was the company of those who suffered
wounds, fighting for their homeland; and of those   370
who, while they lived their lives, served as pure priests;
and then the pious poets, those whose songs
were worthy of Apollo; those who had
made life more civilized with newfound arts;
and those whose merits won the memory
of men: all these were crowned with snow-white garlands.
And as they streamed around her there, the Sibyl
addressed them, and Musaeus before all—
he stood, his shoulders towering above
a thronging crowd whose eyes looked up to him: 380
"O happy souls and you the best of poets,
tell us what land, what place it is that holds
Anchises. It is for his sake we have come
across the mighty streams of Erebus."

The hero answered briefly: "None of us
has one fixed home: we live in shady groves
and settle on soft riverbanks and meadows
where fresh streams flow. But if the will within
your heart is bent on this, then climb the hill
and I shall show to you an easy path."   390
He spoke, and led the way, and from the ridge
he pointed out bright fields. Then they descend.

But in the deep of a green valley, father
Anchises, lost in thought, was studying
the souls of all his sons to come—though now
imprisoned, destined for the upper light.
And as it happened, he was telling over
the multitude of all his dear descendants,
his heroes' fates and fortunes, works and ways.
And when he saw Aeneas cross the meadow,   400
he stretched out both hands eagerly, the tears
ran down his cheeks, these words fell from his lips:

"And have you come at last, and has the pious
love that your father waited for defeated
the difficulty of the journey? Son,
can I look at your face, hear and return
familiar accents? So indeed I thought,
imagining this time to come, counting
the moments, and my longing did not cheat me.
What lands and what wide waters have you journeyed   410
to make this meeting possible? My son,
what dangers battered you? I feared the kingdom
of Libya might do so much harm to you."

Then he: "My father, it was your sad image,
so often come, that urged me to these thresholds.
My ships are moored on the Tyrrhenian.
O father, let me hold your right hand fast,
do not withdraw from my embrace." His face
was wet with weeping as he spoke. Three times
he tried to throw his arms around Anchises'   420
neck; and three times the Shade escaped from that
vain clasp—like light winds, or most like swift dreams.

Meanwhile, Aeneas in a secret valley
can see a sheltered grove and sounding forests
and thickets and the stream of Lethe flowing
past tranquil dwellings. Countless tribes and peoples
were hovering there: as in the meadows, when
the summer is serene, the bees will settle
upon the many-colored flowers and crowd
the dazzling lilies—all the plain is murmuring.   430
The sudden sight has startled him. Aeneas,
not knowing, asks for reasons, wondering
about the rivers flowing in the distance,
the heroes swarming toward the riverbanks.
Anchises answers him: "These are the spirits
to whom fate owes a second body, and
they drink the waters of the river Lethe,
the care-less drafts of long forgetfulness.
How much, indeed, I longed to tell you of them,
to show them to you face to face, to number   440
all of my seed and race, that you rejoice
the more with me at finding Italy."

"But, Father, can it be that any souls
would ever leave their dwelling here to go
beneath the sky of earth, and once again

take on their sluggish bodies? Are they madmen?
Why this wild longing for the light of earth?"
"Son, you will have the answer; I shall not
keep you in doubt," Anchises starts and then
reveals to him each single thing in order.   490

"First, know, a soul within sustains the heaven
and earth, the plains of water, and the gleaming
globe of the moon, the Titan sun, the stars;
and mind, that pours through every member, mingles
with that great body. Born of these: the race
of men and cattle, flying things, and all
the monsters that the sea has bred beneath
its glassy surface. Fiery energy
is in these seeds, their source is heavenly;
but they are dulled by harmful bodies, blunted   460
by their own earthly limbs, their mortal members.
Because of these, they fear and long, and sorrow
and joy, they do not see the light of heaven;
they are dungeoned in their darkness and blind prison.
And when the final day of life deserts them,
then, even then, not every ill, not all
the plagues of body quit them utterly;
and this must be, for taints so long congealed
cling fast and deep in extraordinary
ways. Therefore they are schooled by punishment   470
and pay with torments for their old misdeeds:
some there are purified by air, suspended
and stretched before the empty winds; for some
the stain of guilt is washed away beneath
a mighty whirlpool or consumed by fire.
First each of us must suffer his own Shade;
then we are sent through wide Elysium—
a few of us will gain the Fields of Gladness—
until the finished cycle of the ages,
with lapse of days, annuls the ancient stain   480
and leaves the power of ether pure in us,
the fire of spirit simple and unsoiled.
But all the rest, when they have passed time's circle
for a millennium, are summoned by
the god to Lethe in a great assembly
that, free of memory, they may return
beneath the curve of the upper world, that they
may once again begin to wish for bodies."
Anchises ended, drew the Sibyl and
his son into the crowd, the murmuring throng,   490
then gained a vantage from which he could scan

all of the long array that moved toward them,
to learn their faces as they came along:

"Listen to me: my tongue will now reveal
the fame that is to come from Dardan sons
and what Italian children wait for you—
bright souls that are about to take your name;
in them I shall unfold your fates. The youth
you see there, leaning on his headless spear,
by lot is nearest to the light; and he   500
will be the first to reach the upper air
and mingle with Italian blood; an Alban,
his name is Silvius, your last-born son.
For late in your old age Lavinia,
your wife, will bear him for you in the forest;
and he will be a king and father kings;
through him our race will rule in Alba Longa.
Next Procas stands, pride of the Trojan race;
then Capys, Numitor, and he who will
restore your name as Silvius Aeneas,   510
remarkable for piety and arms
if he can ever gain his Alban kingdom.
What young men you see here, what powers they
display, and how they bear the civic oak
that shades their brows! For you they will construct
Nomentum, Gabii, Fidena's city,
and with the ramparts of Collatia,
Pometia and Castrum Inui,
and Bola, Cora, they will crown the hills.
These will be names that now are nameless lands.   520

"More: Romulus, a son of Mars. He will
join Numitor, his grandfather, on earth
when Ilia, his mother, gives him birth
out of the bloodline of Assaracus.
You see the double plumes upon his crest:
his parent Mars already marks him out
with his own emblem for the upper world.
My son, it is beneath his auspices
that famous Rome will make her boundaries
as broad as earth itself, will make her spirit   530
the equal of Olympus, and enclose
her seven hills within a single wall,
rejoicing in her race of men: just as
the Berecynthian mother, tower-crowned,
when, through the Phrygian cities, she rides on
her chariot, glad her sons are gods, embraces

a hundred sons of sons, and every one
a heaven-dweller with his home on high.

"Now turn your two eyes here, to look upon
your Romans, your own people. Here is Caesar   540
and all the line of Iülus that will come
beneath the mighty curve of heaven. This,
this is the man you heard so often promised—
Augustus Caesar, son of a god, who will
renew a golden age in Latium,
in fields where Saturn once was king, and stretch
his rule beyond the Garamantes and
the Indians—a land beyond the paths
of year and sun, beyond the constellations,
where on his shoulders heaven-holding Atlas   550
revolves the axis set with blazing stars.

.   .   .   .

[The shade of Anchises, telling Aeneas of the wars he must wage, warns him not to
let war be "native to his mind" and advises the future Caesar to show tolerance.
Aeneas leaves the Underworld through the Gate of Ivory, traditionally the gate of
false dreams.]

BOOK 7

[Aeneas and his ships land in Italy. Virgil begins this, his "greater theme," with a second invocation, this time to deal with "arms." Lavinia, daughter of King Latinus, is
wooed by many, including Turnus, the Ausonian prince, who is favored by Lavinia's
mother. But King Latinus is told by an oracle to marry Lavinia not to a Latin but to
a stranger who will raise their name above the stars. Juno renews her threat: Aeneas
will be another Paris, to destroy yet another Troy. She persuades Allecto, the spirit of
violence and war from the Underworld, to arouse Lavinia's mother and also Turnus,
who, thus enraged, calls for war. The series of alliances and a catalogue of the huge
armies and their leaders are described.]

BOOK 8

[The river god Tibernius shows Aeneas the sign of the white sow and the thirty suckling pigs and assures him of his fate. He tells Aeneas to seek alliance with Evander,
king of Arcadia and father of Prince Pallas, who freely offers to join Aeneas. Arcadia
will be the future site of Rome. Venus, Aeneas's mother, persuades Vulcan to aid the
Trojans. The god forges a shield for Aeneas decorated with scenes depicting the history of Rome-to-be, including Augustus Caesar, shown leading the Italian Senate and
the people, the household gods, and the great gods to battle.]

.   .   .   .

But Pallas casts his spear with massive force   1
and tears his bright sword from its hollow scabbard.
The spearhead flies and strikes just where the armor
of Turnus rises to the shoulders, tugs

its way straight through the shield edge, and at last
it even grazes his tremendous body.
Then Turnus, poising long his lance of oak,
one tipped with pointed steel, aims it at Pallas
and cries: "Now see if my shaft pierces more."
So Turnus spoke. The lance head shudders through   10
the very center of the shield, across
so many plates of iron, plates of bronze,
so many layers of bulls' hides, driving through
the corselet and enormous chest of Pallas.
Hopeless, he plucks the warm tip from the wound;
his blood and life flow out by one same path.
He falls upon his wound; his armor clangs
above him; as he dies, his bloody mouth
strikes on the hostile ground. Then Turnus stands
above him, crying: "O Arcadians,   20
remember, take my words back to Evander:
just as he has deserved, I send him Pallas!
Whatever comfort lies in burial
I freely give. His welcome to Aeneas
will not have cost your King Evander little."
This said, his left foot pressed upon the body,
and he ripped off the ponderous belt of Pallas,
on which a scene of horror was engraved:
a band of fifty bridegrooms, foully slaughtered
one wedding night, and bloodied marriage chambers.   30
This had been carved in lavish gold by Clonus,
the son of Eurytus; now Turnus revels
and glories in his taking of the plunder.
O mind of man that does not know the end
or future fates, nor how to keep the measure
when we are fat with pride at things that prosper!
A time will come to Turnus when he will long
to purchase at great price an untouched Pallas,
when he will hate this trophy and this day.

BOOK 9

[The battle begins. Turnus tries to set the Trojan ships on fire, but they are rescued by
Jupiter at the command of Cybele (his mother) herself. On the field, Turnus exhibits
"rage and insane desire for slaughter," in contrast to the restraint of Aeneas.]

BOOK 10

[Jupiter requests of the gods in council a league of peace, but Venus and Juno cannot agree. Then Jupiter insists that the gods not intervene in humans' battles. On the
field, Turnus kills Pallas, stripping him of the gold belt. The narrator himself steps
in here to comment on Turnus's overweaning pride and the fact that he will come to

regret this act. Pallas's death arouses Aeneas's fury, and he plunges into battle "with
hating heart," kicking the bodies of his victims. He searches for Turnus, but Juno
tricks Turnus into fleeing the battle, at which Turnus is dismayed. The "pointless
anger" and countless deaths are enumerated. Despite his anger, Aeneas sympathizes
with the youth Lausus, who piously sacrifices himself to save his father, although
his father is the greatest tyrant in Italy. Reminded of his own father, Aeneas offers
to let Lausus go, but Lausus insists on fighting. Aeneas kills him but, in contrast to
Turnus's treatment of Pallas, does not strip him of his armor.]

. . . .

For there the Lord of Fire had wrought the story 1
of Italy, the Romans' victories,
since he was not unskilled in prophecy
or one who cannot tell the times to come.
There he had set the generations of
Ascanius, and all their wars, in order.
There, too, he made a mother-wolf, reclining
in Mars' green cavern; and at play beside her,
twin boys were hanging at her dugs; fearless,
they sucked their mother. She, at this, bent back 10
her tapered neck to lick them each in turn
and shape their bodies with her tongue. Not far
from this he set the Romans and the Sabine
women they carried off—against all law—
while in the crowded theater the great
Circensian games were under way; and sudden
war then broke out again between the Romans
and aged Tatius, king of austere Cures.
Next, Romulus and Tatius, these same kings,
their quarrels set to rest, stood at Jove's altar; 20
both, armed and cup in hand and having offered
a sow as sacrifice, swore league and friendship.
Not far from this, two chariots that rushed
in different directions tore apart
Mettus (but then you should have kept your word,
o man of Alba!); Tullus hauled the guts
of that conniving man into the forest;
the briers dripped with splattered blood. There, too,
Porsenna, asking Rome to readmit
the banished Tarquin, hemmed the city in 30
with strangling siege; Aeneas' sons rushed on
the sword for freedom's sake. You might have seen
Porsenna as one wild and menacing,
since Cocles dared tear down the Tiber's bridge,
and Cloelia broke her chains and swam the river.

Carved in the upper part was Manlius,
the guardian of the Tarpeian rock,

who stood before the temple gates, defender
of the high Capitol; the new-carved palace
was shaggy with the straw of Romulus.   40
And here a silver goose fluttered across
the gilded colonnades, signaling that
the Gauls were at the threshold. Through the brush
the Gauls crept toward the tower, under cover
of darkness and dense night. Their hair is golden;
and golden, too, their clothes, set-off by gleaming,
striped cloaks; their milk-white necks are bound in gold;
each brandishes two Alpine javelins
and, with an oblong shield, defends his body.
Here in relief were carved the nude Luperci   50
and dancing Salian priests, with woolen caps
and shields that fell from heaven; through the city
chaste matrons in their cushioned carriages
led sacred rites. Away from these scenes Vulcan
added the house of Tartarus, the high
doorways of Dis, the penalties of crime;
and Catiline, you hanging from a cliff
that threatens, trembling at the Furies' faces;
and, set apart, the pious who receive
their laws from Cato. Bordering these scenes,   60
he carved a golden image of the sea,
yet there were blue-gray waters and white foam
where dolphins bright with silver cut aross
the tide and swept the waves with circling tails.

Across the center of the shield were shown
the ships of brass, the strife of Actium:
you might have seen all of Leucata's bay
teeming with war's array, waves glittering
with gold. On his high stern Augustus Caesar
is leading the Italians to battle,   70
together with the senate and the people,
the household gods and Great Gods; his bright brows
pour out a twin flame, and upon his head
his father's Julian star is glittering.
Elsewhere Agrippa towers on the stern;
with kindly winds and gods he leads his squadron;
around his temples, glowing bright, he wears
the naval crown, magnificent device,
with its ships' beaks. And facing them, just come
from conquering the peoples of the dawn,   80
from the red shores of the Erythraean Sea—
together with barbaric riches, varied
arms—is Antonius. He brings with him
Egypt and every power of the East

and farthest Bactria; and—shamefully—
behind him follows his Egyptian wife.
The squadrons close headlong; and all the waters
foam, turn by drawn-back oars and by the prows
with triple prongs. They seek the open seas;
you could believe the Cyclades, uprooted,   90
now swam upon the waters or steep mountains
had clashed with mountains as the crewmen thrust
in their great galleys at the towering sterns.
Torches of hemp and flying darts of steel
are flung by hand, and Neptune's fields are red
with strange bloodshed. Among all this the queen
calls to her squadrons with their native sistrum;
she has not yet looked back at the twin serpents
that swim behind her. Every kind of monster
god—and the barking god, Anubis, too—   100
stands ready to cast shafts against Minerva
and Venus and at Neptune. In the middle
of all the struggle, Mars, engraved in steel,
rages beside fierce Furies from the sky;
and Discord, joyous, strides in her rent robe;
Bellona follows with a bloodstained whip.
But Actian Apollo, overhead,
had seen these things; he stretched his bow; and all
of Egypt and of India, and all
the Arabs and Sabaeans, turned their backs   110
and fled before this terror. The queen herself
was seen to woo the winds, to spread her sails,
and now, yes now, let fall the slackened ropes.
The Lord of Fire had fashioned her within
the slaughter, driven on by wave and west wind,
pale with approaching death; but facing this,
he set the Nile, his giant body mourning,
opening wide his folds and all his robes,
inviting the defeated to his blue-gray
breast and his sheltering streams. But entering   120
the walls of Rome in triple triumph, Caesar
was dedicating his immortal gift
to the Italian gods: three hundred shrines
throughout the city. And the streets reechoed
with gladness, games, applause; in all the temples
were bands of matrons, and in all were altars;
and there, before these altars, slaughtered steers
were scattered on the ground. Caesar himself
is seated at bright Phoebus' snow-white porch,
and he reviews the spoils of nations and   130
he fastens them upon the proud doorposts.
The conquered nations march in long procession,

as varied in their armor and their dress
as in their languages. Here Mulciber
had modeled Nomad tribes and Africans,
loose-robed; the Carians; the Leleges;
Geloni armed with arrows. And he showed
Euphrates, moving now with humbler waves;
the most remote of men, the Morini;
the Rhine with double horns; the untamed Dahae; 140
and, river that resents its bridge, the Araxes.

Aeneas marvels at his mother's gift,
the scenes on Vulcan's shield; and he is glad
for all these images, though he does not
know what they mean. Upon his shoulder he
lifts up the fame and fate of his sons' sons.

BOOK 11

[As the bodies pile up, the Latins ask for a truce to bury the dead. Aeneas insists that
he has no quarrel with the Latin people but fights only because the king violated their
initial alliance. Turnus, meanwhile, "delirious with courage," objects to the truce.
The fighting resumes, but the Latins gradually lose ground in battle.]

BOOK 12

[The battles continue, with both heroes fighting valiantly. King Latinus offers to surrender in order to save Turnus, but "fanatic" Turnus asks only to "barter death for
glory." Aeneas and Turnus agree to face each other in single combat. Aeneas vows,
if victorious, to build his own city and to name it after Lavinia and not subject Italians to his rule. But Juno incites Juturna (Turnus's sister, a river goddess) to break
the treaty and renew general war. She tricks the Latins by showing them a false omen
of victory. Aeneas, trying to keep his men from responding to the Latin charge, is
wounded by an arrow shot by an unknown hand. In the fray that ensues, Aeneas seeks
out Turnus, refusing to fight the others. But Juturna has removed Turnus's chariot
from the battle:]

. . . .

Aeneas' anger seethes; 1
excited by the treachery of Turnus,
whose chariot and horses have been carried
far off, and having often pleaded with
Jove and the altars of the shattered treaty,
at last Aeneas charges into battle;
and terrible, with Mars behind him, he
awakens brutal, indiscriminate
slaughter, he lets his violence run free.
What god can now unfold for me in song 10
all of the bitterness and butchery
and deaths of chieftains—driven now by Turnus,
now by the Trojan hero, each in turn

throughout that field? O Jupiter, was it
your will that nations destined to eternal
peace should have clashed in such tremendous turmoil?

. . . .

**[Only now does Aeneas feel compelled to attack the city. Meanwhile, Turnus realizes
that his sister has tricked him and that, in her attempt to save him, she has caused the
destruction of both himself and Latium. Turnus is furious and humiliated:]**

Confused by all these shifting images
of ruin, Turnus stood astounded, staring
and silent. In his deepest heart there surge
tremendous shame and madness mixed with sorrow   20
and love whipped on by frenzy and a courage
aware of its own worth. As soon as shadows
were scattered and his mind saw light again,
in turmoil then, he turned his burning eyes
upon the walls and, from his chariot, looked
back to that splendid city. There a whirlwind
of flames was rolling on, storey by storey,
skyward, and gripping fast a tower—one
that he himself had built, of tight-packed timbers;
beneath it wheels were set; above it, tall   30
drawbridges. "Sister, fate has won; do not
delay me; let us follow where both god
and cruel fortune call; I am set to face
Aeneas, set to suffer death in all
its bitterness; sister, no longer will
you see me in disgrace. I beg you, let
me rage this madness out before I die."
So Turnus; then he left his chariot, leaped
down to the field; charging through enemies,
through shafts, he quits his grieving sister; swift,   40
he crashes through the center of the ranks.
Just as a rock when, from a mountaintop,
it hurtles headlong, having been torn up
by wind or washed away by a wheeling storm
or loosened by the long lapse of the years;
the mass, enormous, with a mighty thrust
drives down the slope and bounds upon the earth,
rolls woods and herds and men along its course:
so Turnus rushes through the scattered bands
up to the city walls, there where the ground   50
is soaked in shed blood and the air is shrill
with shafts. He signals with his hand, then shouts
aloud: "Rutulians, stop now; and you,
Italians, stay your steel; whatever chance
is here belongs to me; it is more just
for me alone to pay this covenant,

decide this war by sword." And then they all
drew back and left the center free for combat.

But when he hears the name of Turnus, father
Aeneas leaves the ramparts and tall towers;   60
he casts aside delay, breaks off the siege;
and now, exultant, joyous, and tremendous,
he pounds upon his shield—as huge as Athos,
as Eryx, or as father Apenninus
himself when, roaring, with his trembling oaks
he lifts his snow-topped summit skyward, glad.
Now all—Rutulians, Trojans, and Italians—
turned eagerly to look: both those who manned
high battlements and those below, who ran
a battering ram against the walls; they slung   70
their weapons off their shoulders. King Latinus
himself is wonderstruck to see such giant
men—born within such distant, different lands—
now come together for this trial by steel.
And they, as soon as space was cleared for them
along the open plain, first fling their spears
from far, then swiftly rush to fight; they dash
the brass of clanging shields together. Earth
groans, and their frequent sword blows double; chance
and courage mingle into one. Just as,   80
on giant Sila or on tall Taburnus,
when two bulls charge together into battle
with butting brows, the herdsmen fall back; all
the flock is mute with fear; the heifers wonder
who is to rule the forest, whom the herds
must follow; and the bulls with massive force
trade wounds; they gore with struggling horns; they bathe
their necks and shoulders in a stream of blood;
their groans and bellows echo through the grove:
so did the Daunian hero and the Trojan   90
Aeneas clash their shields; their violence
fills all the air. There Jupiter himself
holds up two scales in equal balance, then
he adds two different fates, one on each hand:
whom this trial dooms, what weight sinks down to death.
Now Turnus, thinking he is safe, springs out:
he rises up to his full height; with sword
upraised, he strikes. The Trojans and the anxious
Italians shout: the tension takes both ranks.
But, treacherous, that blade breaks off, deserts   100
fanatic Turnus at his blow's midstroke
had flight not helped him then. As soon as he
sees that strange hilt in his defenseless hand,

he runs away, swifter than the east wind.
They say that in his first wild dash to battle,
when mounting on his chariot, he had left
his father's sword behind and, rushing, snatched
the weapon of his charioteer, Metiscus;
so long as routed Trojans turned their backs,
that sword had served him well, but when it met   110
the armor that the God of Fire had forged,
the mortal blade, like brittle ice, had splintered;
the fragments glitter on the yellow sand.
So Turnus madly flees across the field;
now here, then there, he wheels in wayward circles.
The Trojans in a dense ring press against him;
to one side lies the vast Laurentian marsh,
and on the other, high walls hem him in.

And though the arrow wound within his knees
stays and delays him, nonetheless Aeneas   120
runs after Turnus. Keen, he presses on
against his trembling enemy, foot to foot:
even as, when a hunting dog has found
a stag hemmed in beside a stream or hedged
by fear before the netting's crimson feathers,
he chases, barking, pressing near; the stag,
in terror of the snare and of the river's
high banks, wheels back and forth a thousand ways;
and yet the lively Umbrian hound hangs close
to him with gaping mouth; at every instant   130
he grasps, he grinds his jaws but, baffled, bites
on nothing. Then indeed the shouting rises;
the shores and lakes resound; confusion takes
the skies. But Turnus, even as he flies
away, rebukes all his Rutulian ranks;
he calls on each by name, he shouts for his
familiar blade. And for his part, Aeneas
now menaces with death and instant ruin
the head of anyone who dares draw near;
he threatens to tear down the city and   140
he terrifies the shuddering Italians;
though wounded, he keeps on. Five times they circle
the field and, just as many times, weave back,
this way and that. They seek no trifling prize:
what they strive for is Turnus' blood and life.

Just here, by chance, had stood a bitter-leaved
wild olive tree, sacred to Faunus; sailors
had long since venerated it; when saved
from waves, they fastened here their offerings

to the Laurentians' god; here they would hang   150
their votive garments. Heedless of this custom,
the Teucrians had carried off the sacred
tree trunk to clear the field, to lay it bare
for battle. Here the shaft Aeneas first
had cast at Turnus stood; its impetus
had carried it and held it fast in that
tenacious root. The Dardan bent, wanting
to wrench his shaft free, then with spear, to catch
the warrior whom he could not overtake
on foot. And Turnus, wild with terror, cries: 160
"I pray you, Faunus, pity me; and you,
most gracious Earth, hold fast that steel if I
have ever kept your rites—those that Aeneas'
men have profaned by war." He spoke, invoked
the help of gods with prayers that were not useless;
for though Aeneas struggled long and lingered
above the gripping root, no force of his
could loose the spearhead from that tough wood's bite.
While, fierce, he wrenches, tugs, the Daunian
goddess, Juturna, once again takes on   170
the form of Turnus' charioteer, Metiscus;
she runs and gives his blade back to her brother.
But Venus, furious that this was granted
the daring nymph, drew near; and then she tore
Aeneas' spearhead free from that deep root.
Both men are high in heart; they face each other,
their arms and courage fresh again—one trusts
his sword; the other, tall and fierce, his shaft—
Aeneas, Turnus, breathless for Mars' contest.

Meanwhile Olympus' king calls out to Juno   180
as from a golden cloud she scans the battle:
"Wife, how can this day end? What is there left
for you to do? You know, and say you know,
that, as a deity, Aeneas is owed
to heaven, that the fates will carry him
high as the stars. What is your plan? What is
the hope that keeps you lingering in these
chill clouds? And was it seemly for a god
to be profaned by a human wound? Or for
a sword that had been lost to be restored   190
to Turnus (without you, Juturna could
do nothing)? Was it right to give fresh force
to those who are defeated? Stop at last;
give way to what I now ask: do not let
so great a sorrow gnaw at you in silence;
do not let your sweet lips so often press

your bitter cares on me. This is the end.
You have harassed the Trojans over land
and wave, have kindled brutal war, outraged
Latinus' home, and mingled grief and marriage: 200
you cannot pass beyond this point." So, Jove;
the goddess, Saturn's daughter, yielding, answered:

"Great Jupiter, it was indeed for this—
my knowing what you wish—that I have left
both Turnus and the earth, unwillingly.
Were it not so, you would not see me now
alone upon my airy throne, enduring
everything; but girt with flames, I should
be standing on the battlefield itself,
to drag the Trojans toward the war they hate.   210
I do confess that I urged on Juturna
to help her luckless brother; I approved
her daring greater things to save his life;
yet not to aim an arrow, not to stretch
her bow. I swear this by the pitiless
high fountainhead of Styx, the only pledge
that fills the upper gods with dread. And now
I yield; detesting wars, I give them up.
And only this—which fates do not forbid—
I beg of you, for Latium, for your   220
own father's greatness, for the race of Saturn:
when with their happy wedding rites they reach
a peace—so be it—when they both unite
in laws and treaties, do not let the native-
born Latins lose their ancient name, become
Trojans, or be called Teucrians; do not
make such men change their language or their dress.
Let Latium still be, let Alban kings
still rule for ages; let the sons of Rome
be powerful in their Italian courage.   230
Troy now is fallen; let her name fall, too."

And Jupiter smiled at her then; the maker
of men and things said: "Surely you are sister
to Jove, a second child of Saturn, for
deep in your breast there surge such tides of anger.
But come, give up this useless madness: I
now grant your wish and willingly, vanquished,
submit. For the Ausonians will keep
their homeland's words and ways; their name will stay;
the body of the Teucrians will merge   240
with Latins, and their name will fall away.
But I shall add their rituals and customs

to the Ausonians', and make them all—
and with one language—Latins. You will see
a race arise from this that, mingled with
the blood of the Ausonians, will be
past men, even past gods, in piety;
no other nation will pay you such honor."
Juno agreed to this; with gladness she
then changed her mind. She quit the skies, her cloud.   250

. . . .

[Jupiter sends a Fury to terrify Turnus. Juturna recognizes Jupiter's intentions, and,
sorrowing for the impending loss of her brother, she plunges into the river's depths to
spend her immortal life in grief. At last, the combat between Aeneas and Turnus takes
place:]

And now Aeneas charges straight at Turnus.
He brandishes a shaft huge as a tree,
and from his savage breast he shouts: "Now what
delay is there? Why, Turnus, do you still
draw back from battle? It is not for us
to race against each other, but to meet
with cruel weapons, hand to hand. Go, change
yourself into all shapes; by courage and
by craft collect whatever help you can;
take wing, if you so would, toward the steep stars   260
or hide yourself within the hollow earth."
But Turnus shakes his head: "Your burning words,
ferocious Trojan, do not frighten me;
it is the gods alone who terrify me,
and Jupiter, my enemy." He says
no more, but as he looks about he sees
a giant stone, an ancient giant stone
that lay at hand, by chance, upon the plain,
set there as boundary mark between the fields
to keep the farmers free from border quarrels.   270
And twice-six chosen men with bodies such
as earth produces now could scarcely lift
that stone upon their shoulders. But the hero,
anxious and running headlong, snatched the boulder;
reaching full height, he hurled it at the Trojan.
But Turnus does not know if it is he
himself who runs or goes or lifts or throws
that massive rock; his knees are weak; his blood
congeals with cold. The stone itself whirls through
the empty void but does not cross all of   280
the space between; it does not strike a blow.
Just as in dreams of night, when languid rest
has closed our eyes, we seem in vain to wish

to press on down a path, but as we strain,
we falter, weak; our tongues can say nothing,
the body loses its familiar force,
no voice, no word, can follow: so whatever
courage he calls upon to find a way,
the cursed goddess keeps success from Turnus.
Then shifting feelings overtake his heart;   290
he looks in longing at the Latin ranks
and at the city, and he hesitates,
afraid; he trembles at the coming spear.
He does not know how he can save himself,
what power he has to charge his enemy;
he cannot see his chariot anywhere;
he cannot see the charioteer, his sister.

In Turnus' wavering Aeneas sees
his fortune; he holds high the fatal shaft;
he hurls it far with all his body's force.   300
No boulder ever catapulted from
siege engine sounded so, no thunderbolt
had ever burst with such a roar. The spear
flies on like a black whirlwind, carrying
its dread destruction, ripping through the border
of Turnus' corselet and the outer rim
of Turnus' seven-plated shield; hissing,
it penetrates his thigh. The giant Turnus,
struck, falls to earth; his knees bend under him.
All the Rutulians leap up with a groan,   310
and all the mountain slopes around reecho;
tall forests, far and near, return that voice.
Then humble, suppliant, he lifts his eyes
and, stretching out his hand, entreating, cries:
"I have indeed deserved this; I do not
appeal against it; use your chance. But if
there is a thought of a dear parent's grief
that now can touch you, then I beg you, pity
old Daunus—in Anchises you had such
a father—send me back or, if you wish,   320
send back my lifeless body to my kin.
For you have won, and the Ausonians
have seen me, beaten, stretch my hands; Lavinia
is yours; then do not press your hatred further."

Aeneas stood, ferocious in his armor;
his eyes were restless and he stayed his hand;
and as he hesitated, Turnus' words
began to move him more and more—until

high on the Latin's shoulder he made out
the luckless belt of Pallas, of the boy   330
whom Turnus had defeated, wounded, stretched
upon the battlefield, from whom he took
this fatal sign to wear upon his back,
this girdle glittering with familiar studs.
And when his eyes drank in this plunder, this
memorial of brutal grief, Aeneas,
aflame with rage—his wrath was terrible—
cried: "How can you who wear the spoils of my
dear comrade now escape me? It is Pallas
who strikes, who sacrifices you, who takes   340
this payment from your shameless blood." Relentless,
he sinks his sword into the chest of Turnus.
His limbs fell slack with chill; and with a moan
his life, resentful, fled to Shades below.

. . . .

Questions for Discussion and Review

1. In what specific ways is the *Aeneid* like the *Iliad* and the *Odyssey?* What themes, plot structures, and even specific episodes in the *Aeneid* resemble those of the Homeric epics? Why does Virgil want to remind us of the similarities between his work and Homer's?

2. In what ways is Aeneas similar to his Homeric counterparts Achilles and Odysseus? In what ways is he different?

3. Why does Aeneas fall in love with Dido? Later, why does he leave her? What part do the gods play in both of those events?

4. What heroic qualities does Aeneas share with Turnus? In what ways are they different in their attitudes toward war, their methods of fighting, and their moral values?

5. Compare the relationship between Thetis and her son Achilles in the *Iliad* with that between Venus and Aeneas in the *Aeneid*. How does each divine mother help her son? What goal does each goddess have in mind?

6. Why does Aeneas go to the Underworld? What does he learn there? How does his new perspective affect his behavior afterward?

7. Compare the role of Jupiter in the *Aeneid* with that of Zeus in the *Iliad*. How do their powers differ? What goals does each envision? What does each god do to fulfill his plan? How successful is he in bringing it about?

8. Describe some of the ways in which myth and real history intersect in the *Aeneid*. What historical events and figures appear in the poem? How are they related to the mythic events and themes?

9. In their final battle, Aeneas rejects Turnus's plea for mercy and kills him. How should we evaluate this act? Defend your position with specific references to the poem.

2O

The Retelling of Greek Myths: Ovid's *Metamorphoses*

KEY TOPICS/THEMES

Ovid retells Greek myths in a continuous narrative that focuses on the theme of change. Sometimes comic, sometimes bitter in tone, his tales portray the world of myth (and, some would say, the world of Augustan Rome) as a place where everything—love, the gods, and time itself— changes and thus betrays people's hopes and expectations. The only way to cope with such constant flux is to be transformed into something immobile (like the laurel tree in "Apollo and Daphne" in Book 1) or inanimate (like the human statues in "The Story of Perseus" in Book 5). The tales are framed by a vision of Rome and end with "The Deification of Caesar" (Book 15) and the poet's hope that Rome will endure forever—so that he can have a perpetual audience for his poems!

Ovid

In the case of the poet Ovid (43 B.C.–A.D. 17), the connection between myth and politics turned all too literal. Something in Ovid's elegant and witty writings (which included such works as the *Art of Love* and the collection of tales called *Metamorphoses*—a retelling of many Greek myths) apparently offended Augustus, who in A.D. 8 banished Ovid from Rome, forcing him to spend his last decade in exile in a town on the shores of the Black Sea. Perhaps Augustus thought that Ovid's worldly, sometimes comic, and sometimes cynical depictions of the lecherous pursuits of gods and humans too obviously undermined the "official" image of a sober Roman citizenry and its politically correct deities. More likely, Ovid's love poems put the sexual exploits of Augustus's immediate family, especially his daughter Julia, in the public spotlight. Further, unlike the "official" interpretation of the story of the Sabine women favored by Augustus (who identified himself with Romulus) to support his increased restrictions on both marriage and women's freedoms, Ovid's version stresses the savagery of the original act. The implication is that Rome's very stability not only is rooted in violence but depends for its continuity on a sustaining of that violence—clearly not a view that would have been regarded with approval by Augustan officialdom.

The *Metamorphoses:* Significant Themes and Characters

The Story of Creation

Ovid's theme in *Metamorphoses* is "bodies changed." One of the most remarkable aspects of the poem is that, instead of an anthology of separate myths, Ovid offers a series of narrative links that allow one tale to flow into another in a continuous stream, thus reflecting his theme of transformations in the structure of the poem itself.

Like Hesiod, he begins with the story of creation—the changes in the body of the cosmos itself. Ovid's universe, like Hesiod's, is in a state of perpetual flux—only more so. He describes a world in which time dissolves all—even the earth itself—to water, to air, to fire, and back to earth again, just as individuals in the myths change from human to animal and other forms, and just as Troy is transformed into Rome. The changes in Ovid's universe, however, move largely in one direction: from chaos to order, from motion to stasis. In Hesiod's description of creation, primal chaos is depicted with a certain exuberance, as Hesiod celebrates, in his catalogues and genealogies, the proliferation of life. For Ovid, in contrast, chaos is an intolerable condition in which the very atoms of the universe war with one another. It is not until god, or nature, separates the warring components of the universe—decreeing a proper place for each in the eternal order, subdividing all creation and, as might be expected from Roman gods, marking out boundaries—that Ovid can celebrate the emergence of the stars. The bureaucratically organized universe thus produced is divided into zones just as Rome was divided into wards. The boundaries between social classes, even among the gods, are as essential to the proper order as are the borders between zones and territories. Even the dwellings of the gods on Olympus are segregated into neighborhoods, with the lesser gods inhabiting a poorer section.

The Comic Tone

As some scholars have noted, in such references to contemporary Roman society, Ovid is poking fun at Augustus (who, along with other important Romans, lived on the Palatine Hill), equating him with Jupiter and perhaps satirizing the folly and pretentiousness of the Augustan court. Hoping to add dignity to Roman life and, presumably, to enhance his own reputation, Augustus had attempted to revive not only neglected Roman religious rites but even the worship of the Greek god Apollo. He also sought to impose moral restraints on a society whose elite patrician class was used to a lifestyle characterized by various kinds of self-indulgence. In 18 B.C., for example, Augustus made adultery a crime; however, he was subsequently embarrassed by the blatantly licentious behavior of his daughter Julia and, constrained by his own laws, had to banish her from Rome. His granddaughter was banished for the same reason. As several modern readers have pointed out, there is an element of bathos (a sudden dropping off in tone) as Ovid moves from a description of Mount Olympus to a reference to the Palatine Hill. Indeed, throughout much of the *Metamorphoses,* there is an undercurrent of downsizing of the myths, bringing them to the level of ordinary experience, and an element of parody, mocking the foibles of the gods, the follies and hypocrisies of Augustan society, and perhaps even Augustus himself.

Echo and Narcissus

In the story of Echo and Narcissus, Ovid describes the twin follies of **Echo,** a woman whose discourse was so dependent on others' that she was unable either to begin or to end a conversation on her own initiative, and **Narcissus,** an unusually beautiful young man who was so self-absorbed that he was incapable of relating to any other being, male or female, human or divine.

Ovid tells how Echo serves Jove (Jupiter) by chattering to distract Juno while Jove makes love to nameless nymphs. She thus incurs Juno's anger. The goddess punishes Echo by rendering her capable only of repeating the last statement she has heard, exaggerating the reflective characteristics already present in Echo's speech.

Echo falls in love with Narcissus, an odd pairing of complementary foibles: the woman who cannot express what is inside herself paired with the man who cannot respond to anything outside himself. But the slightly comical overtones of that initial ironic juxtaposition soon give way to a far bleaker perspective. Narcissus, of course, rejects Echo, as he rejects all the women and young men who pursue him, his lack of capacity for love an insult to the powers of Aphrodite and Eros. Persistent but endlessly frustrated in her hopeless pursuit of Narcissus, Echo is gradually reduced to the condition of a disembodied voice.

Meanwhile, one of the young men Narcissus has rejected prays that Narcissus himself will come to feel tormented by the pains of unrequited love he has caused in so many others. Carrying to its most extreme form the self-infatuation of Narcissus, the goddess of vengeance, Nemesis, causes Narcissus to fall in love with his own reflection on the surface of a pond, as if Eros, denied an external object, turns inward, with deadly results. Like Echo, Narcissus is disembodied, dissolving into the watery image of himself visible on the pond's surface, until nothing is left of him but the flower that still bears his name (see Color plate 16).

The Golden Age

As is often the case in satire, beneath the witty, comic surface lurks a more serious indictment, as Ovid moves beyond folly to vice, from the ludicrous to the vicious, resulting in a dual vision between whose perspectives the poet can range at will.

Like Hesiod, Ovid tells the myth of the Ages of Man (Book 1). But Ovid gives equal attention to those aspects of Roman life for which the Golden Age had no need: judges, laws, and punishments; ships, soldiers, and weapons; and aggression and anxiety. In contrast, he somewhat ambivalently, and occasionally even bitterly, presents the Iron Age of contemporary Rome, characterized by greed, war, violence, and those very important Roman figures—surveyors—who marked off the boundaries of private property. Caught between the terrifying prospect of anarchy and the almost equally frightening "threat" of law, the Romans—even a poet who had experienced firsthand just how fearful the law can be—dreaded disorder more. The role of government, then, in this fallen world of the Iron Age, is to use the force of law and, if necessary, of arms to impose order on an anarchic world. The subtle tension exhibited in Virgil's *Aeneid* between the fear of chaos and the fear of law—the fleeting suspicion that perhaps the price paid for the benefits of Roman civilization might have been too high—becomes even more explicit in Ovid's works and is reflected in the characteristic Roman nostalgia for the Golden Age, or the early republic.

The Nightmare World

In Ovid's poem, however, the nostalgic impulse is short-lived. In a more sinister vein, many of Ovid's tales move beyond follies to vices, portraying a nightmarish world characterized by lust, rape, betrayal, and revenge. Several scholars, having made the link between Jupiter and Augustus in the earlier sections of the poem, now see these more appalling stories as commentaries on the cruelty of those in power—of the Augustan state and the emperor himself. It is difficult to say, in those cases in which the poet himself omits any obvious hints of the comic, whether he intended such a comment. It is clear, however, in this world in which gods turn on humans, that cruelty and violence are so pervasive that the only escape possible is through transformation into less-than-human or even inanimate states beyond the reach of pain. If Aeneas can be said, as some of Virgil's modern readers claim, to have been emotionally dehumanized by his experience, Ovid's mythic characters are literally so. Men and women, driven by uncontrollable inner urges or relentlessly pursued by individuals—or gods—who are thus driven, are saved only by being changed into trees, rocks, or even constellations.

Perseus

In "The Story of Perseus" (Books 4–5), we can see most blatantly this compulsion toward immobility. Whereas, for example, Odysseus was content to fight a hundred suitors one at a time, **Perseus,** in Ovid's retelling, finds that method too exhausting and inefficient. Instead, he merely whips out the Gorgon's head and instantly transforms all of Andromeda's former suitors to stone. Although that mass transformation is, of course, part of the ancient Greek Perseus myth, Ovid goes on to describe, in stark detail, the suitors' tears frozen on their faces for eternity. And Perseus, in a marvelous comic touch, offers the marble "statue" of her former fiancé to **Andromeda,** to set up in her new home. But the image also conveys the more serious theme of the desperate striving for permanence. In these men-turned-statues, we can see, in its most literal form, the Roman petrification of Greek myth. And, of course, Perseus and Andromeda are themselves eventually honored by becoming constellations.

Apollo and Daphne

Traditional Roman heroes like Romulus and Aeneas are, in Ovid's version, transformed into gods. But not even the gods themselves are exempt from the inevitable pitfalls and failures of sensual love. The gods' desires, like those of humans, remain unfulfilled, as the objects of their desire turn into beasts, trees, or flowers before their outstretched hands. Apollo, for instance, may be the god of archery, but he is himself subject to the darts of Cupid (Book 1). "Burning" with futile love for **Daphne,** who rejects both men and marriage (see Chapter 7), he pursues her until she is turned by her father, a river god, into a laurel tree, an etiological tale explaining not only why the laurel leaves thereafter remain sacred to Apollo, but also why Roman heroes wear laurel crowns, and why the laurel appears over the entrance to Augustus's hall. But being thus honored proves small consolation to the god, who, instead of achieving erotic bliss, finds himself rather foolishly embracing the trunk of a tree (Figure 20-1). Because of Augustus's particular interest in reviving the worship of Apollo along with other elements of Greek culture, some scholars see in this tale an attempt to mock Augustus's plans by portraying the god whom he admires as ridiculous. But for Daphne, who, to escape a "fate worse than death," must be dehumanized, the consequences are anything but comical.

Orpheus and Eurydice

Unlike Echo and Narcissus, who are incapable of love, **Orpheus** and **Eurydice** [oo-RIH-dih-see] fail to fulfill their love because of forces beyond their, or anyone's, control. At the very moment of their marriage, Eurydice is bitten by a serpent, associated with the chthonic figure of Medusa, "rough with snakes." The "poison of the serpent," death itself, takes Eurydice, and she dies. Her distraught husband/lover, the musician Orpheus, does what the warrior-heroes used to do: he descends to the Underworld. But whereas those heroes typically made such quests to escape domesticity, Orpheus, inverting the heroic mode, makes the journey to retrieve his wife— to restore domesticity. Indeed, more like Demeter seeking reunion with Persephone than like a Heracles or a Theseus seeking his own immortality, Orpheus even offers to die himself if Eurydice cannot be released from the Underworld. Thus, he refuses the warrior's defiant stance: he does not come, he insists, to bind the "triple-throated" hound Cerberus. Trusting that, because love is "famous" in the upper world, it will be similarly honored in the lower, Orpheus appeals to Hades and Persephone, in light of their love for each other, to release Eurydice.

Attempting to pursue love beyond the grave, Orpheus brings together the forces of Eros (Love) and Thanatos (Death). But Orpheus is not in love with death; rather, his descent to the Underworld is a variant of the mythic tradition that embraces such couples as Venus and Adonis, the Egyptian lovers Isis and Osiris, or the Babylonian lovers Ishtar and Tammuz. In those stories, it is usually the goddess who

FIGURE 20-1   Apollo and Daphne. In this marble statue (1622–1625),
the Italian sculptor Gianlorenzo Bernini depicts the erotic pursuit of
Daphne by the god Apollo. Responding to his daughter's plea to be rescued
from the impending rape, Daphne's father, a river god, turns her into a
laurel tree. Bernini's sculpture captures the moment of transformation of
Daphne into the laurel tree: just as Apollo's hand arrests her flight, her forward motion is thrust upward. Her hair, still flowing as she twists to avoid
him, sprouts leaves, and the bark begins enclosing her legs and trunk, protecting her as it immobilizes her. *(Galleria Borghese, Rome)*

reaches beyond death to bring her consort back from the Underworld to some form
of rebirth.

All people, Orpheus argues, belong to the Underworld eventually: he simply
wants Eurydice's death to happen later, "in the ripeness of years." What has betrayed these lovers is change, time itself. For a brief interval, as Orpheus charms the
inhabitants of the Underworld with his music, time does seem to stop: the Furies
themselves weep, and the punishments of sinners in Tartarus cease. Orpheus's request to stop time, or to reverse it—to undo death—is granted, on one condition:

he must not look back as he leads Eurydice up again to the world of light. But it is impossible for Orpheus not to look back. Indeed, he already has done so: the descent into the Underworld, an attempt to reverse time, itself constitutes a looking back. And whereas the traditional warrior-hero achieves a form of rebirth as a result of his trip to the Underworld, no such thing occurs during the hero's life in this tale.

Unlike many of the later versions of the story of Orpheus and Eurydice, in which Orpheus turns back because he distrusts either the gods or Eurydice herself, Ovid's Orpheus explicitly turns back "in love." Nor does Eurydice reproach her husband for doing so. Nevertheless, "in a moment," the poet tells us, Eurydice is gone. Even mutual and seemingly perfect love is not eternal. The ultimate dissolution of the self in death is the final metamorphosis: death is the ultimate betrayal.

Having lost Eurydice, Orpheus rejects the love of women and turns to young men instead. As he wanders the hills playing his lyre, Orpheus appears to have acquired a function akin to a fertility god: trees appear in his wake, reminding us of Orpheus's similarities to Demeter and Dionysus. Thus, Orpheus incorporates qualities of both Apollo, god of music, and Dionysus, the "twice-born" agricultural god.

In the story that follows Orpheus's in Ovid's poem, Apollo also pursues a youth, **Cyparissus**, who, in turn, loves a pet deer; but moving from one kind of love object to another, regardless of gender or species, does not mitigate the ineluctable powers of time and change. Lamenting the loss of his beloved deer, Cyparissus is turned into a cypress tree, associated with mourning. The juxtaposition in the poem—of the trees into which Apollo's lovers are transformed and the trees that spring up on the hills where Orpheus wanders—suggests that the hills are littered with the transformed remnants of Orpheus's male lovers as well.

The Death of Orpheus

Delaying the story of the death of Orpheus and returning to it later, immediately after the story of Venus and Adonis, Ovid implies a link between the two Underworld experiences. According to the tradition that Ovid describes, Orpheus is killed and mutilated by maenads, women who followed Orpheus as they did Dionysus. Angered by his rejection of women, they silence his lyre—his Apollonian voice—which is rendered, for the first time, useless. The women then perform a sparagmos ritual in which Orpheus, like Dionysus, is torn limb from limb; he is also compared to Actaeon, the "doomed stag" destroyed by the women whom Ovid compares to Actaeon's hounds.

Orpheus's head (along with his lyre) is flung into a river, from which it is rescued by Apollo himself, who "freezes" it, performing the only form of metamorphosis still possible: he turns it, gaping jaws and all, to stone. Ovid's description of that transformation to a condition of stillness, beyond the reach of change, is reminiscent of his treatment of the story of Perseus, whose rivals were similarly petrified.

Throughout Ovid's version of the Orpheus myth, some sort of rivalry is suggested between Apollo, who communicates in mediated form through the voice of another (the Oracle at Delphi, the lyre), and Dionysus (Bacchus), whose unmediated epiphanies the maenads have experienced but which Orpheus has denied them. In Ovid's tale, however, the two gods—dual aspects of Orpheus himself—are reconciled. Bacchus, mourning Orpheus's death, punishes the women who rejected

Orpheus and turns them, like Daphne, into trees. Orpheus himself, meanwhile, rejoins Eurydice in the Underworld where he can, the poet assures us, look back without loss: in this world, Ovid seems to imply, betrayal is a universal condition—only sorrow lasts. But in the same sort of consolation that Virgil held out for the Roman hero Aeneas, only in the afterlife, at last, can pious poets sing their songs forever.

The Apotheosis of Caesar

Despite (or rather, as a result of) all the changes he describes, the spirit of Rome, in Ovid's work, emerges triumphant, and the *Metamorphoses* ends with "The Deification of Caesar" (Book 15) and his transformation from mortal to celestial body to preside henceforth over the divine destiny of Rome. This section of the work, tracing Roman history from the fall of Troy to Ovid's own time, is fairly serious in tone, its occasional comic touches muted. For all the problems of the Augustan Age, Ovid did not confuse the present actors with the script or reject its larger vision.

In one last, subtle irony, Ovid implies in the "Epilogue" (Book 15) that his own fame will be carried above the stars—that is, above Caesar's! Nevertheless, Ovid is aware of how dependent even the most critical poet is on the stability of the society in which his poems can be transmitted. Like Shakespeare's magician Prospero in *The Tempest,* Ovid has woven an "insubstantial pageant" of shapes that shift before our eyes. And however much he might criticize Roman government, it is only when Rome is at last stabilized that the poet can be confident that the work which summons those airy shapes into our presence will endure beyond the reach of time. Only then, when the history of Rome becomes its own glorious monument, can the omnipresent threat of perpetual change—the fear that, should Roman vigilance ever slip, the world would revert to the chaos from which it came—at last cease.

Fortunately for modern readers, although Rome fell, Ovid, despite his fears, endured to become not only one of our best sources of information about Greek myth but also one of the key influences on Western culture (see Chapter 21).

Excerpts from the
METAMORPHOSES*
Ovid

BOOK 1

My intention is to tell of bodies changed   1
To different forms; the gods, who made the changes,
Will help me—or I hope so—with a poem
That runs from the world's beginning to our own days.

The Creation

Before the ocean was, or earth, or heaven,
Nature was all alike, a shapelessness,
Chaos, so-called, all rude and lumpy matter,
Nothing but bulk, inert, in whose confusion
Discordant atoms warred: there was no sun
To light the universe; there was no moon   10
With slender silver crescents filling slowly;
No earth hung balanced in surrounding air;
No sea reached far along the fringe of shore.
Land, to be sure, there was, and air, and ocean,
But land on which no man could stand, and water
No man could swim in, air no man could breathe,
Air without light, substance forever changing,
Forever at war: within a single body
Heat fought with cold, wet fought with dry, the hard
Fought with the soft, things having weight contended   20
With weightless things.
                 Till God, or kindlier Nature,
Settled all argument, and separated
Heaven from earth, water from land, our air
From the high stratosphere, a liberation
So things evolved, and out of blind confusion
Found each its place, bound in eternal order,
The force of fire, that weightless element,
Leaped up and claimed the highest place in heaven;
Below it, air; and under them the earth
Sank with its grosser portions; and the water,   30
Lowest of all, held up, held in, the land.

---

*Translation by Rolfe Humphries.

Whatever god it was, who out of chaos
Brought order to the universe, and gave it
Division, subdivision, he molded earth,
In the beginning, into a great globe,
Even on every side, and bade the waters
To spread and rise, under the rushing winds,
Surrounding earth; he added ponds and marshes,
He banked the river-channels, and the waters
Feed earth or run to sea, and that great flood   40
Washes on shores, not banks. He made the plains
Spread wide, the valleys settle, and the forest
Be dressed in leaves; he made the rocky mountains
Rise to full height, and as the vault of Heaven
Has two zones, left and right, and one between them
Hotter than these, the Lord of all Creation
Marked on the earth the same design and pattern.
The torrid zone too hot for men to live in,
The north and south too cold, but in the middle
Varying climate, temperature and season.   50
Above all things the air, lighter than earth,
Lighter than water, heavier than fire,
Towers and spreads; there mist and cloud assemble,
And fearful thunder and lightning and cold winds,
But these, by the Creator's order, held
No general dominion; even as it is,
These brothers brawl and quarrel; though each one
Has his own quarter, still, they come near tearing
The universe apart. Eurus is monarch
Of the lands of dawn, the realms of Araby,   60
The Persian ridges under the rays of morning.
Zephyrus holds the west that glows at sunset,
Boreas, who makes men shiver, holds the north,
Warm Auster governs in the misty southland,
And over them all presides the weightless ether,
Pure without taint of earth.
                            These boundaries given,
Behold, the stars, long hidden under darkness,
Broke through and shone, all over the spangled heaven,
Their home forever, and the gods lived there,
And shining fish were given the waves for dwelling   70
And beasts the earth, and birds the moving air.

But something else was needed, a finer being,
More capable of mind, a sage, a ruler,
So Man was born, it may be, in God's image,
Or Earth, perhaps, so newly separated
From the old fire of Heaven, still retained

Some seed of the celestial force which fashioned
Gods out of living clay and running water.
All other animals look downward; Man,
Alone, erect, can raise his face toward Heaven.   80

The Four Ages

The Golden Age was first, a time that cherished
Of its own will, justice and right; no law.
No punishment, was called for; fearfulness
Was quite unknown, and the bronze tablets held
No legal threatening; no suppliant throng
Studied a judge's face; there were no judges,
There did not need to be. Trees had not yet
Been cut and hollowed, to visit other shores.
Men were content at home, and had no towns
With moats and walls around them; and no trumpets   90
Blared out alarums; things like swords and helmets
Had not been heard of. No one needed soldiers.
People were unaggressive, and unanxious;
The years went by in peace. And Earth, untroubled,
Unharried by hoe or plowshare, brought forth all
That men had need for, and those men were happy,
Gathering berries from the mountain-sides,
Cherries, or blackcaps, and the edible acorns.
Spring was forever, with a west wind blowing
Softly across the flowers no man had planted,   100
And Earth, unplowed, brought forth rich grain; the field,
Unfallowed, whitened with wheat, and there were rivers
Of milk, and rivers of honey, and golden nectar
Dripped from the dark-green oak-trees.
                              After Saturn
Was driven to the shadowy land of death,
And the world was under Jove, the Age of Silver
Came in, lower than gold, better than bronze.
Jove made the springtime shorter, added winter,
Summer, and autumn, the seasons as we know them.
That was the first time when the burnt air glowed   110
White-hot, or icicles hung down in winter.
And men built houses for themselves; the caverns,
The woodland thickets, and the bark-bound shelters
No longer served; and the seeds of grain were planted
In the long furrows, and the oxen struggled
Groaning and laboring under the heavy yoke.

Then came the Age of Bronze, and dispositions
Took on aggressive instincts, quick to arm,
Yet not entirely evil. And last of all

The Iron Age succeeded, whose base vein   120
Let loose all evil: modesty and truth
And righteousness fled earth, and in their place
Came trickery and slyness, plotting, swindling,
Violence and the damned desire of having.
Men spread their sails to winds unknown to sailors,
The pines came down their mountain-sides, to revel
And leap in the deep waters, and the ground,
Free, once, to everyone, like air and sunshine,
Was stepped off by surveyors. The rich earth,
Good giver of all the bounty of the harvest,   130
Was asked for more; they dug into her vitals,
Pried out the wealth a kinder lord had hidden
In Stygian shadow, all that precious metal,
The root of evil. They found the guilt of iron,
And gold, more guilty still. And War came forth
That uses both to fight with; bloody hands
Brandished the clashing weapons. Men lived on plunder.
Guest was not safe from host, nor brother from brother,
A man would kill his wife, a wife her husband,
Stepmothers, dire and dreadful, stirred their brews   140
With poisonous aconite, and sons would hustle
Fathers to death, and Piety lay vanquished,
And the maiden Justice, last of all immortals,
Fled from the bloody earth.
                               Heaven was no safer.
Giants attacked the very throne of Heaven,
Piled Pelion on Ossa, mountain on mountain
Up to the very stars. Jove struck them down
With thunderbolts, and the bulk of those huge bodies
Lay on the earth, and bled, and Mother Earth,
Made pregnant by that blood, brought forth new bodies,   150
And gave them, to recall her older offspring,
The forms of men. And this new stock was also
Contemptuous of gods, and murder-hungry
And violent. You would know they were sons of blood.

Jove's Intervention

And Jove was witness from his lofty throne
Of all this evil, and groaned as he remembered
The wicked revels of Lycaon's table,
The latest guilt, a story still unknown
To the high gods. In awful indignation
He summoned them to council. No one dawdled.   160
Easily seen when the night skies are clear,
The Milky Way shines white. Along this road
The gods move toward the palace of the Thunderer,

His royal halls, and, right and left, the dwellings
Of other gods are open, and guests come thronging.
The lesser gods live in a meaner section,
An area not reserved, as this one is,
For the illustrious Great Wheels of Heaven.
(Their Palatine Hill, if I might call it so.)

They took their places in the marble chamber   170
Where high above them all their king was seated,
Holding his ivory scepter, shaking out
Thrice, and again, his awful locks, the sign
That made the earth and stars and ocean tremble,
And then he spoke, in outrage: "I was troubled
Less for the sovereignty of all the world
In that old time when the snake-footed giants
Laid each his hundred hands on captive Heaven.
Monstrous they were, and hostile, but their warfare
Sprung from one source, one body. Now, wherever   180
The sea-gods roar around the earth, a race
Must be destroyed, the race of men. I swear it!
I swear by all the Stygian rivers gliding
Under the world, I have tried all other measures.
The knife must cut the cancer out, infection
Averted while it can be, from our numbers.
Those demigods, those rustic presences,
Nymphs, fauns, and satyrs, wood and mountain dwellers,
We have not yet honored with a place in Heaven,
But they should have some decent place to dwell in,   190
In peace and safety. Safety? Do you reckon
They will be safe, when I, who wield the thunder,
Who rule you all as subjects, am subjected
To the plottings of the barbarous Lycaon?"

They burned, they trembled. Who was this Lycaon,
Guilty of such rank infamy? They shuddered
In horror, with a fear of sudden ruin,
As the whole world did later, when assassins
Struck Julius Caesar down, and Prince Augustus
Found satisfaction in the great devotion   200
That cried for vengeance, even as Jove took pleasure,
Then, in the gods' response. By word and gesture
He calmed them down, awed them again to silence,
And spoke once more:

The Story of Lycaon

                    "He has indeed been punished.
On that score have no worry. But what he did,
And how he paid, are things that I must tell you.

I had heard the age was desperately wicked,
I had heard, or so I hoped, a lie, a falsehood,
So I came down, as man, from high Olympus,
Wandered about the world. It would take too long   210
To tell you how widespread was all that evil.
All I had heard was grievous understatement!
I had crossed Maenala, a country bristling
With dens of animals, and crossed Cyllene,
And cold Lycaeus' pine woods. Then I came
At evening, with the shadows growing longer,
To an Arcadian palace, where the tyrant
Was anything but royal in his welcome.
I gave a sign that a god had come, and people
Began to worship, and Lycaon mocked them,   220
Laughed at their prayers, and said: 'Watch me find out
Whether this fellow is a god or mortal,
I can't tell quickly, and no doubt about it.'
He planned, that night, to kill me while I slumbered;
That was his way to test the truth. Moreover,
And not content with that, he took a hostage,
One sent by the Molossians, cut his throat,
Boiled pieces of his flesh, still warm with life,
Broiled others, and set them before me on the table.
That was enough. I struck, and the bolt of lightning   230
Blasted the household of that guilty monarch.
He fled in terror, reached the silent fields,
And howled, and tried to speak. No use at all!
Foam dripped from his mouth; bloodthirsty still, he turned
Against the sheep, delighting still in slaughter,
And his arms were legs, and his robes were shaggy hair,
Yet he is still Lycaon, the same grayness,
The same fierce face, the same red eyes, a picture
Of bestial savagery. One house has fallen,
But more than one deserves to. Fury reigns   240
Over all the fields of Earth. They are sworn to evil,
Believe it. Let them pay for it, and quickly!
So stands my purpose."
                    Part of them approved
With words and added fuel to his anger,
And part approved with silence, and yet all
Were grieving at the loss of humankind,
Were asking what the world would be, bereft
Of mortals: who would bring their altars incense?
Would earth be given the beasts, to spoil and ravage?
Jove told them not to worry; he would give them   250
Another race, unlike the first, created
Out of a miracle; he would see to it.

He was about to hurl his thunderbolts
At the whole world, but halted, fearing Heaven
Would burn from fire so vast, and pole to pole
Break out in flame and smoke, and he remembered
The fates had said that some day land and ocean,
The vault of Heaven, the whole world's mighty fortress,
Besieged by fire, would perish. He put aside
The bolts made in Cyclopean workshops; better,   260
He thought, to drown the world by flooding water.

The Flood

So, in the cave of Aeolus, he prisoned
The North-wind, and the West-wind, and such others
As ever banish cloud, and he turned loose
The South-wind, and the South-wind came out streaming
With dripping wings, and pitch-black darkness veiling
His terrible countenance. His beard is heavy
With rain-cloud, and his hoary locks a torrent,
Mists are his chaplet, and his wings and garments
Run with the rain. His broad hands squeeze together   270
Low-hanging clouds, and crash and rumble follow
Before the cloudburst, and the rainbow, Iris,
Draws water from the teeming earth, and feeds it
Into the clouds again. The crops are ruined,
The farmers' prayers all wasted, all the labor
Of a long year, comes to nothing.
                              And Jove's anger,
Unbounded by his own domain, was given
Help by his dark-blue brother. Neptune called
His rivers all, and told them, very briefly,
To loose their violence, open their houses,   280
Pour over embankments, let the river horses
Run wild as ever they would. And they obeyed him.
His trident struck the shuddering earth; it opened
Way for the rush of waters. The leaping rivers
Flood over the great plains. Not only orchards
Are swept away, not only grain and cattle,
Not only men and houses, but altars, temples,
And shrines with holy fires. If any building
Stands firm, the waves keep rising over its roof-top,
Its towers are under water, and land and ocean   290
Are all alike, and everything is ocean,
An ocean with no shore-line.
                              Some poor fellow
Seizes a hill-top; another, in a dinghy,
Rows where he used to plough, and one goes sailing
Over his fields of grain or over the chimney

Of what was once his cottage. Someone catches
Fish in the top of an elm-tree, or an anchor
Drags in green meadow-land, or the curved keel brushes
Grape-arbors under water. Ugly sea-cows
Float where the slender she-goats used to nibble   300
The tender grass, and the Nereids come swimming
With curious wonder, looking, under water,
At houses, cities, parks, and groves. The dolphins
Invade the woods and brush against the oak-trees;
The wolf swims with the lamb; lion and tiger
Are borne along together; the wild boar
Finds all his strength is useless, and the deer
Cannot outspeed that torrent; wandering birds
Look long, in vain, for landing-place, and tumble,
Exhausted, into the sea. The deep's great license   310
Has buried all the hills, and new waves thunder
Against the mountain-tops. The flood has taken
All things, or nearly all, and those whom water,
By chance, has spared, starvation slowly conquers.

Deucalion and Pyrrha

Phocis, a fertile land, while there was land,
Marked for Oetean from Boeotian fields.
It was ocean now, a plain of sudden waters.
There Mount Parnassus lifts its twin peaks skyward,
High, steep, cloud-piercing. And Deucalion came there
Rowing his wife. There was no other land,   320
The sea had drowned it all. And here they worshipped
First the Corycian nymphs and native powers,
Then Themis, oracle and fate-revealer.
There was no better man than this Deucalion,
No one more fond of right; there was no woman
More scrupulously reverent than Pyrrha.
So, when Jove saw the world was one great ocean,
Only one woman left of all those thousands,
And only one man left of all those thousands,
Both innocent and worshipful, he parted   330
The clouds, turned loose the North-wind, swept them off,
Showed earth to heaven again, and sky to land,
And the sea's anger dwindled, and King Neptune
Put down his trident, calmed the waves, and Triton,
Summoned from far down under, with his shoulders
Barnacle-strewn, loomed up above the waters,
The blue-green sea-god, whose resounding horn
Is heard from shore to shore. Wet-bearded, Triton
Set lip to that great shell, as Neptune ordered,
Sounding retreat, and all the lands and waters   340

Heard and obeyed. The sea has shores; the rivers,
Still running high, have channels; the floods dwindle,
Hill-tops are seen again; the trees, long buried,
Rise with their leaves still muddy. The world returns.

Deucalion saw that world, all desolation,
All emptiness, all silence, and his tears
Rose as he spoke to Pyrrha: "O my wife,
The only woman, now, on all this earth
My consort and my cousin and my partner
In these immediate dangers, look! Of all the lands   350
To East or West, we two, we two alone,
Are all the population. Ocean holds
Everything else; our foothold, our assurance,
Are small as they can be, the clouds still frightful.
Poor woman—well, we are not all alone—
Suppose you had been, how would you bear your fear?
Who would console your grief? My wife, believe me,
Had the sea taken you, I would have followed.
If only I had the power, I would restore
The nations as my father did, bring clay   360
To life with breathing. As it is, we two
Are all the human race, so Heaven has willed it,
Samples of men, mere specimens."
                                        They wept,
And prayed together, and having wept and prayed,
Resolved to make petition to the goddess
To seek her aid through oracles. Together
They went to the river-water, the stream Cephisus,
Still far from clear, but flowing down its channel,
And they took river-water, sprinkled foreheads,
Sprinkled their garments, and they turned their steps   370
To the temple of the goddess, where the altars
Stood with the fires gone dead, and ugly moss
Stained pediment and column. At the stairs
They both fell prone, kissed the chill stone in prayer:
"If the gods' anger ever listens
To righteous prayers, O Themis, we implore you,
Tell us by what device our wreck and ruin
May be repaired. Bring aid, most gentle goddess,
To sunken circumstance."
                                And Themis heard them,
And gave this oracle: "Go from the temple,   380
Cover your heads, loosen your robes, and throw
Your mother's bones behind you!" Dumb, they stood
In blank amazement, a long silence, broken
By Pyrrha finally: she would not do it!

With trembling lips she prays whatever pardon
Her disobedience might merit, but this outrage
She dare not risk, insult her mother's spirit
By throwing her bones around. In utter darkness
They voice the cryptic saying over and over,
What can it mean? They wonder. At last Deucalion   390
Finds the way out: "I might be wrong, but surely
The holy oracles would never counsel
A guilty act. The earth is our great mother,
And I suppose those bones the goddess mentions
Are the stones of earth; the order means to throw them,
The stones, behind us."

                She was still uncertain,
And he by no means sure, and both distrustful
Of that command from Heaven; but what damage,
What harm, would there be in trying? They descended,
Covered their heads, loosened their garments, threw   410
The stones behind them as the goddess ordered.
The stones—who would believe it, had we not
The unimpeachable witness of Tradition?—
Began to lose their hardness, to soften, slowly,
To take on form, to grow in size, a little,
Become less rough, to look like human beings,
Or anyway as much like human beings
As statues do, when the sculptor is only starting,
Images half blocked out. The earthy portion,
Damp with some moisture, turned to flesh, the solid   410
Was bone, the veins were as they always had been.
The stones the man had thrown turned into men,
The stones the woman threw turned into women,
Such being the will of God. Hence we derive
The hardness that we have, and our endurance
Gives proof of what we have come from.

                    Other forms
Of life came into being, generated
Out of the earth: the sun burnt off the dampness,
Heat made the slimy marshes swell; as seed
Swells in a mother's womb to shape and substance,   420
So new forms came to life. When the Nile river
Floods and recedes and the mud is warmed by sunshine,
Men, turning over the earth, find living things,
And some not living, but nearly so, imperfect,
On the verge of life, and often the same substance
Is part alive, part only clay. When moisture
Unites with heat, life is conceived; all things
Come from this union. Fire may fight with water,
But heat and moisture generate all things,

Their discord being productive. So when earth, 430
After that flood, still muddy, took the heat,
Felt the warm fire of sunlight, she conceived,
Brought forth, after their fashion, all the creatures,
Some old, some strange and monstrous.

                  One, for instance,
She bore unwanted, a gigantic serpent,
Python by name, whom the new people dreaded,
A huge bulk on the mountain-side. Apollo,
God of the glittering bow, took a long time
To bring him down, with arrow after arrow
He had never used before except in hunting 440
Deer and the skipping goats. Out of the quiver
Sped arrows by the thousand, till the monster,
Dying, poured poisonous blood on those black wounds.
In memory of this, the sacred games,
Called Pythian, were established, and Apollo
Ordained for all young winners in the races,
On foot or chariot, for victorious fighters,
The crown of oak. That was before the laurel,
That was before Apollo wreathed his forehead
With garlands from that tree, or any other. 450

Apollo and Daphne

Now the first girl Apollo loved was Daphne,
Whose father was the river-god Peneus,
And this was no blind chance, but Cupid's malice.
Apollo, with pride and glory still upon him
Over the Python slain, saw Cupid bending
His tight-strung little bow. "O silly youngster,"
He said, "What are you doing with such weapons?
Those are for grown-ups! The bow is for my shoulders;
I never fail in wounding beast or mortal,
And not so long ago I slew the Python 460
With countless darts; his bloated body covered
Acre on endless acre, and I slew him!
The torch, my boy, is enough for you to play with,
To get the love-fires burning. Do not meddle
With honors that are mine!" And Cupid answered:
"Your bow shoots everything, Apollo—maybe—
But mine will fix you! You are far above
All creatures living, and by just that distance
Your glory less than mine." He shook his wings,
Soared high, came down to the shadows of Parnassus, 470
Drew from his quiver different kinds of arrows,
One causing love, golden and sharp and gleaming,
The other blunt, and tipped with lead, and serving

To drive all love away, and this blunt arrow
He used on Daphne, but he fired the other,
The sharp and golden shaft, piercing Apollo
Through bones, through marrow, and at once he loved
And she at once fled from the name of lover,
Rejoicing in the woodland hiding places
And spoils of beasts which she had taken captive,   480
A rival of Diana, virgin goddess.
She had many suitors, but she scorned them all;
Wanting no part of any man, she travelled
The pathless groves, and had no care whatever
For husband, love, or marriage. Her father often
Said, "Daughter, give me a son-in-law!" and "Daughter,
Give me some grandsons!" But the marriage torches
Were something hateful, criminal, to Daphne,
So she would blush, and put her arms around him,
And coax him: "Let me be a virgin always;   490
Diana's father said she might. Dear father!
Dear father—please!" He yielded, but her beauty
Kept arguing against her prayer. Apollo
Loves at first sight; he wants to marry Daphne,
He hopes for what he wants—all wishful thinking!—
Is fooled by his own oracles. As stubble
Burns when the grain is harvested, as hedges
Catch fire from torches that a passer-by
Has brought too near, or left behind in the morning,
So the god burned, with all his heart, and burning   500
Nourished that futile love of his by hoping.
He sees the long hair hanging down her neck
Uncared for, says, "But what if it were combed?"
He gazes at her eyes—they shine like stars!
He gazes at her lips, and knows that gazing
Is not enough. He marvels at her fingers,
Her hands, her wrists, her arms, bare to the shoulder,
And what he does not see he thinks is better.
But still she flees him, swifter than the wind,
And when he calls she does not even listen: 510
"Don't run away, dear nymph! Daughter of Peneus,
Don't run away! I am no enemy,
Only your follower: don't run away!
The lamb flees from the wolf, the deer the lion,
The dove, on trembling wing, flees from the eagle.
All creatures flee their foes. But I, who follow,
Am not a foe at all. Love makes me follow,
Unhappy fellow that I am, and fearful
You may fall down, perhaps, or have the briars
Make scratches on those lovely legs, unworthy   520

To be hurt so, and I would be the reason.
The ground is rough here. Run a little slower,
And I will run, I promise, a little slower.
Or wait a minute: be a little curious
Just who it is you charm. I am no shepherd,
No mountain-dweller, I am not a ploughboy,
Uncouth and stinking of cattle. You foolish girl,
You don't know who it is you run away from,
That must be why you run. I am lord of Delphi
And Tenedos and Claros and Patara.   530
Jove is my father. I am the revealer
Of present, past and future; through my power
The lyre and song make harmony; my arrow
Is sure in aim—there is only one arrow surer,
The one that wounds my heart. The power of healing
Is my discovery; I am called the Healer
Through all the world: all herbs are subject to me.
Alas for me, love is incurable
With any herb; the arts which cure the others
Do me, their lord, no good!"

                              He would have said   540
Much more than this, but Daphne, frightened, left him
With many words unsaid, and she was lovely
Even in flight, her limbs bare in the wind,
Her garments fluttering, and her soft hair streaming,
More beautiful than ever. But Apollo,
Too young a god to waste his time in coaxing,
Came following fast. When a hound starts a rabbit
In an open field, one runs for game, one safety,
He has her, or thinks he has, and she is doubtful
Whether she's caught or not, so close the margin,   550
So ran the god and girl, one swift in hope,
The other in terror, but he ran more swiftly,
Borne on the wings of love, gave her no rest,
Shadowed her shoulder, breathed on her streaming hair.
Her strength was gone, worn out by the long effort
Of the long flight; she was deathly pale, and seeing
The river of her father, cried "O help me,
If there is any power in the rivers,
Change and destroy the body which has given
Too much delight!" And hardly had she finished,   560
When her limbs grew numb and heavy, her soft breasts
Were closed with delicate bark, her hair was leaves,
Her arms were branches, and her speedy feet
Rooted and held, and her head became a tree top,
Everything gone except her grace, her shining.
Apollo loved her still. He placed his hand

Where he had hoped and felt the heart still beating
Under the bark; and he embraced the branches
As if they still were limbs, and kissed the wood,
And the wood shrank from his kisses, and the god   570
Exclaimed: "Since you can never be my bride,
My tree at least you shall be! Let the laurel
Adorn, henceforth, my hair, my lyre, my quiver:
Let Roman victors, in the long procession,
Wear laurel wreaths for triumph and ovation.
Beside Augustus' portals let the laurel
Guard and watch over the oak, and as my head
Is always youthful, let the laurel always
Be green and shining!" He said no more. The laurel,
Stirring, seemed to consent, to be saying *Yes*.   580

There is a grove in Thessaly, surrounded
By woodlands with steep slopes; men call it Tempe.
Through this the Peneus River's foamy waters
Rise below Pindus mountain. The cascades
Drive a fine smoky mist along the tree tops,
Frail clouds, or so it seems, and the roar of the water
Carries beyond the neighborhood. Here dwells
The mighty god himself, his holy of holies
Is under a hanging rock; it is here he gives
Laws to the nymphs, laws to the very water.   590
And here came first the streams of his own country
Not knowing what to offer, consolation
Or something like rejoicing: crowned with poplars
Sperchios came, and restless Enipeus,
Old Apidanus, Aeas, and Amphrysos
The easy-going. And all the other rivers
That take their weary waters into oceans
All over the world, came there, and only one
Was absent, Inachus, hiding in his cavern,
Salting his stream with tears, oh, most unhappy,   600
Mourning a daughter lost. Her name was Io,
Who might, for all he knew, be dead or living,
But since he cannot find her anywhere
He thinks she must be nowhere, and his sorrow
Fears for the worst.

BOOK 3 Echo and Narcissus

           And so Tiresias,   1
Famous through all Aonian towns and cities,
Gave irreproachable answers to all comers
Who sought his guidance. One of the first who tested
The truths he told was a naiad of the river,

Liriope, whom the river-god, Cephisus
Embraced and ravished in his watery dwelling.
In time she bore a child, most beautiful
Even as child, gave him the name Narcissus,
And asked Tiresias if the boy would ever   10
Live to a ripe old age. Tiresias answered:
"Yes, if he never knows himself." How silly
Those words seemed, for how long! But as it happened,
Time proved them true—the way he died, the strangeness
Of his infatuation.
                        Now Narcissus
Was sixteen years of age, and could be taken
Either for boy or man; and boys and girls
Both sought his love, but in that slender stripling
Was pride so fierce no boy, no girl, could touch him.
He was out hunting one day, driving deer   20
Into the nets, when a nymph named Echo saw him,
A nymph whose way of talking was peculiar
In that she could not start a conversation
Nor fail to answer other people talking.
Up to this time Echo still had a body,
She was not merely voice. She liked to chatter,
But had no power of speech except the power
To answer in the words she last had heard.
Juno had done this: when she went out looking
For Jove on top of some nymph among the mountains,   30
Echo would stall the goddess off by talking
Until the nymphs had fled. Sooner or later
Juno discovered this and said to Echo:
"The tongue that made a fool of me will shortly
Have shorter use, the voice be brief hereafter."
Those were not idle words; now Echo always
Says the last thing she hears, and nothing further.
She saw Narcissus roaming through the country,
Saw him, and burned, and followed him in secret,
Burning the more she followed, as when sulphur   40
Smeared on the rim of torches, catches fire
When other fire comes near it. Oh, how often
She wanted to come near with coaxing speeches,
Make soft entreaties to him! But her nature
Sternly forbids; the one thing not forbidden
Is to make answers. She is more than ready
For words she can give back. By chance Narcissus
Lost track of his companions, started calling
"Is anybody here?" and "Here!" said Echo.
He looked around in wonderment, called louder   50
"Come to me!" "Come to me!" came back the answer.

He looked behind him, and saw no one coming;
"Why do you run from me?" and heard his question
Repeated in the woods. "Let us get together!"
There was nothing Echo would ever say more gladly,
"Let us get together!" And, to help her words,
Out of the woods she came, with arms all ready
To fling around his neck. But he retreated:
"Keep your hands off," he cried, "and do not touch me!
I would die before I give you a chance at me."   60
"I give you a chance at me," and that was all
She ever said thereafter, spurned and hiding,
Ashamed, in the leafy forests, in lonely caverns.
But still her love clings to her and increases
And grows on suffering; she cannot sleep,
She frets and pines, becomes all gaunt and haggard,
Her body dries and shrivels till voice only
And bones remain, and then she is voice only
For the bones are turned to stone. She hides in woods
And no one sees her now along the mountains,   70
But all may hear her, for her voice is living.

She was not the only one on whom Narcissus
Had visited frustration; there were others,
Naiads or Oreads, and young men also
Till finally one rejected youth, in prayer,
Raised up his hands to Heaven: "May Narcissus
Love one day, so, himself, and not win over
The creature whom he loves!" Nemesis heard him,
Goddess of Vengeance, and judged the plea was righteous.
There was a pool, silver with shining water,   80
To which no shepherds came, no goats, no cattle,
Whose glass no bird, no beast, no falling leaf
Had ever troubled. Grass grew all around it,
Green from the nearby water, and with shadow
No sun burned hotly down on. Here Narcissus,
Worn from the heat of hunting, came to rest
Finding the place delightful, and the spring
Refreshing for the thirsty. As he tried
To quench his thirst, inside him, deep within him,
Another thirst was growing, for he saw   90
An image in the pool, and fell in love
With that unbodied hope, and found a substance
In what was only shadow. He looks in wonder,
Charmed by himself, spell-bound, and no more moving
Than any marble statue. Lying prone
He sees his eyes, twin stars, and locks as comely
As those of Bacchus or the god Apollo,

Smooth cheeks, and ivory neck, and the bright beauty
Of countenance, and a flush of color rising
In the fair whiteness. Everything attracts him   100
That makes him so attractive. Foolish boy,
He wants himself; the loved becomes the lover,
The seeker sought, the kindler burns. How often
He tries to kiss the image in the water,
Dips in his arms to embrace the boy he sees there,
And finds the boy, himself, elusive always,
Not knowing what he sees, but burning for it,
The same delusion mocking his eyes and teasing.
Why try to catch an always fleeing image,
Poor credulous youngster? What you seek is nowhere,   110
And if you turn away, you will take with you
The boy you love. The vision is only shadow,
Only reflection, lacking any substance.
It comes with you, it stays with you, it goes
Away with you, if you can go away.
No thought of food, no thought of rest, can make him
Forsake the place. Stretched on the grass, in shadow,
He watches, all unsatisfied, that image
Vain and illusive, and he almost drowns
In his own watching eyes. He rises, just a little,   120
Enough to lift his arms in supplication
To the trees around him, crying to the forest:
"What love, whose love, has ever been more cruel?
You woods should know: you have given many lovers
Places to meet and hide in; has there ever,
Through the long centuries, been anyone
Who has pined away as I do? He is charming,
I see him, but the charm and sight escape me.
I love him and I cannot seem to find him!
To make it worse, no sea, no road, no mountain,   130
No city-wall, no gate, no barrier, parts us
But a thin film of water. He is eager
For me to hold him. When my lips go down
To kiss the pool, his rise, he reaches toward me.
You would think that I could touch him—almost nothing
Keeps us apart. Come out, whoever you are!
Why do you tease me so? Where do you go
When I am reaching for you? I am surely
Neither so old or ugly as to scare you,
And nymphs have been in love with me. You promise,   140
I think, some hope with a look of more than friendship.
You reach out arms when I do, and your smile
Follows my smiling; I have seen your tears
When I was tearful; you nod and beckon when I do;

Your lips, it seems, answer when I am talking
Though what you say I cannot hear. I know
The truth at last. He is myself! I feel it,
I know my image now. I burn with love
Of my own self; I start the fire I suffer.
What shall I do? Shall I give or take the asking?   150
What shall I ask for? What I want is with me,
My riches make me poor. If I could only
Escape from my own body! If I could only—
How curious a prayer from any lover—
Be parted from my love! And now my sorrow
Is taking all my strength away; I know
I have not long to live, I shall die early,
And death is not so terrible, since it takes
My trouble from me; I am sorry only
The boy I love must die: we die together."   160
He turned again to the image in the water,
Seeing it blur through tears, and the vision fading,
And as he saw it vanish, he called after:
"Where are you going? Stay: do not desert me,
I love you so. I cannot touch you; let me
Keep looking at you always, and in looking
Nourish my wretched passion!" In his grief
He tore his garment from the upper margin,
Beat his bare breast with hands as pale as marble,
And the breast took on a glow, a rosy color,   170
As apples are white and red, sometimes, or grapes
Can be both green and purple. The water clears,
He sees it all once more, and cannot bear it.
As yellow wax dissolves with warmth around it,
As the white frost is gone in morning sunshine,
Narcissus, in the hidden fire of passion,
Wanes slowly, with the ruddy color going,
The strength and hardihood and comeliness,
Fading away, and even the very body
Echo had loved. She was sorry for him now,   180
Though angry still, remembering; you could hear her
Answer "Alas!" in pity, when Narcissus
Cried out "Alas!" You could hear her own hands beating
Her breast when he beat his. "Farewell, dear boy,
Beloved in vain!" were his last words, and Echo
Called the same words to him. His weary head
Sank to the greensward, and death closed the eyes
That once had marveled at their owner's beauty.
And even in Hell, he found a pool to gaze in,
Watching his image in the Stygian water.   190
While in the world above, his naiad sisters

Mourned him, and dryads wept for him, and Echo
Mourned as they did, and wept with them, preparing
The funeral pile, the bier, the brandished torches,
But when they sought his body, they found nothing,
Only a flower with a yellow center
Surrounded with white petals.

BOOK 4   Perseus

[Cadmus and Harmonia, rulers of Thebes who had refused to worship Bacchus, were changed into serpents.]

They had one comfort in their changed condition: 1
India, conquered, worshipped Bacchus; Greece
Thronged to his temples. King Acrisius only,
Of the same stock, still kept him out of Argos,
Took arms against the god, would not admit him
The son of Jove. Nor would he grant that Perseus
Was also son of Jove, the child begotten
On Danae in the golden rain. But truth
Is powerful: Acrisius learned repentance
For his attack on the god, and his denial   10
Of his own grandson. Bacchus was in Heaven,
But Perseus, bringing back the wondrous trophy
Of the snake-haired monster, through the thin air was cleaving
His way on whirring wings. As he flew over
The Libyan sands, drops from the Gorgon's head
Fell bloody on the ground, and earth received them
Turning them into vipers. For this reason
Libya, today, is full of deadly serpents.

From there he drove through space, the warring winds
Bearing him every way, as a squall is driven.   20
From his great height he looked on lands outspread
Far, far below; he flew the whole world over,
Saw the cold Bears, three times, and saw the Crab
With curving claws, three times, whirled often eastward,
Whirled often to the west. As the day ended,
Fearful of night, he came down for a landing
On the West's edge, the realm of Atlas, seeking
A little rest, till the Morning-star should waken
The fires of dawn, and Dawn lead out the chariot
Of the new day. Atlas, Iapetus' offspring,   30
Loomed over all men in his great bulk of body.
He ruled this land and the sea whose waters take
The Sun's tired horses and the weary wheels
At the long day's end. He had a thousand herds,
No neighbors, and he had a tree, all shining

With gold, whose golden leaves hid golden branches,
Whose golden branches hung with golden apples.
Perseus greeted Atlas: "If the glory
Of lofty birth has any meaning for you,
I am the son of Jove; if you prefer   40
To wonder at great deeds, you will find that mine
Are very wonderful. I ask for rest,
For friendly shelter." But Atlas, doubtful,
Thought of an ancient oracle of Themis:
Atlas, the time will come when your tree loses
Its gold, and the marauder is Jove's son.
Fearful of this, Atlas had walled his orchard,
Given its keeping to a monstrous dragon,
And kept all strangers off. He answered Perseus:
"Get out of here, you liar! Neither Jove   50
Nor glory gets you entrance here." He added
A lusty shove, though Perseus resisted,
Argued, and tried appeasement. But at last,
Inferior in strength (for who could equal
The strength of Atlas?), he told the giant:
"Well, anyway, since you will give me nothing,
I have something here for you!" He turned his back,
Held up, with his left hand behind his body,
Medusa's terrible head, and big, as he was,
Atlas was all at once a mountain: beard   60
And hair were forests, and his arms and shoulders
Were mountain-ridges; what had been his head
Was the peak of the mountain, and his bones were boulders.
But still he grew, for so the gods had willed it,
And his great bulk upheld the starry Heaven.

And Aeolus by now had closed the winds
In their eternal prison; the bright star
That wakes men to their toil, had risen brightly
In the clear morning air, and Perseus fastened
His winged sandals to his feet, took up   70
The scimitar, and soared aloft. Below him
Lay many lands, and finally he saw
The Ethiopians, King Cepheus' people.
There the god Ammon, not without injustice,
Ordered a daughter, who had not deserved it,
To pay the penalty for her mother's talking,
And Perseus saw her there, Andromeda,
Bound by the arms to the rough rocks; her hair,
Stirred in a gentle breeze, and her warm tears flowing
Proved her not marble, as he thought, but woman.   80
She was beautiful, so much so that he almost

Forgot to move his wings. He came down to her
Saying: "My dear, the chains that ought to bind you
Are love-knots rather than shackles. May I ask you
Your name, your country, the reason for this bondage?"
At first she made no answer, too much the virgin
To speak to any man; she would have hidden
Her modest features with her hands, but could not
Since they were bound. Her eyes were free, and filling
With rising tears. And Perseus urged her, gently,   90
Not to seem too unwilling, but to tell him
What wrong she had done, if any; so, at last,
She gave her name, her country, adding further
How her mother had bragged too much about her beauty.
She had not told it all, when the sea roared
And over the sea a monster loomed and towered
Above the wave. She cried aloud. Her parents
Were near at hand, both grieving, but the mother
More justly so, and they brought no help with them,
Only the kind of tears and vain embraces   100
Proper on such occasions. This struck Perseus
As pretty futile. "There is time, and plenty,
For weeping, later," he told them, "but the moment
For help is very short. If I were here as suitor,
I, Perseus, son of Jove and Danae,
Conqueror of the snaky-headed Gorgon,
The daring flier through the winds of Heaven,
You would accept me, I think, before all others.
But to such great endowments I am trying
To add, with the gods' blessing, a greater service.   110
If I save her by my valor, do I have her?"
What could they say but Yes? They promised also
A kingdom as her dowry.
                    As a galley
Bears down, with all the sturdy sweating rowers
Driving it hard, so came the monster, thrusting
The water on both sides in a long billow.
A slinger from the cliff could almost hit him
When Perseus rose cloudward, and his shadow
Fell on the surface, and the monster, seeing
That shadow, raged against it. As an eagle   120
Sees, in open field, a serpent sunning
Its mottled back, comes swooping down upon it,
Grasps it behind its head, to miss the poison
Sent through the deadly fangs, and buries talons
In scaly neck, so Perseus came plunging
In his steep dive down air, attacked the monster
That roared as the right shoulder took the sword-blade

Up to the hilt. The wound hurt deep, the sea-beast
Reared, lashed, and dived, and thrashed, as a wild-boar does
When the hounds bay around him. Perseus rose   130
When the fangs struck, he poised, he sought for openings
Along the barnacled back, along the sides,
At tapering fishy tail; the monster's vomit
Was blood and salty water. The winged sandals
Grew heavy from that spew, and Perseus dared not
Depend upon them further. He found a rock
Projecting out of the sea when the waves were still,
Hidden in storm. There he hung on, from there
He struck, again, again, and the sword went deep
Into the vitals, and the shores re-echoed   140
To Heaven with applause. Father and mother,
Rejoicing, hail their son-in-law, the savior
Of all the house. The chains are loosened
From the girl's arms, and she comes slowly forward,
The cause, and the reward, of all that labor.
Water is brought so that the victor may
Wash his hands clean of blood; before he washes,
Lest the hard sand injure the Gorgon's head,
He makes it soft with leaves, and over them
Strews sea-weed for a cover, and puts down   150
Medusa's head. And the twigs, all fresh and pliant,
Absorb another force, harden and stiffen
In branch and leaves. The sea-nymphs test the wonder
With other boughs, and the same wonder happens
To their delight, and they use the twigs as seedlings,
Strewing them over the water, and even now
Such is the nature of coral, that it hardens,
Exposed to air, a vine below the surface.

Now Perseus built three altars to three gods,
The left for Mercury, the right for Pallas,   160
The central one for Jove, and sacrificed
Heifer and bull and yearling steer. He wanted
No dowry save Andromeda in payment
Of his reward. And Love and Hymen shook
The marriage-torches, fires fed fat on incense,
Glowing and fragrant, and the garlands hung
Down from the timbers, and the lyre and flute
And song made music, proof of happy spirits.
Great doors swung open, and the golden halls
Were set for splendid banqueting, and courtiers   170
Came thronging to the tables.
                              So they feasted
And took their fill of wine, and all were happy,

And Perseus asked them questions about the region,
People and customs and the native spirit.
They told him, and they asked in turn: "Now tell us,
Heroic Perseus, how you slew the Gorgon."
He told them how there lay, beneath cold Atlas,
A place protected by the bulk of the mountain
Where dwelt twin sisters, daughters, both, of Phorcys.
They had one eye between them, and they shared it,   180
Passing it from one sister to the other,
And he contrived to steal it, being so handed,
And slipped away, going by trackless country,
Rough woods and jagged rocks, to the Gorgons' home.
On all sides, through the fields, along the highways,
He saw the forms of men and beasts, made stone
By one look at Medusa's face. He also
Had seen that face, but only in reflection
From the bronze shield his left hand bore; he struck
While snakes and Gorgon both lay sunk in slumber,   190
Severed the head, and from that mother's bleeding
Were born the swift-winged Pegasus and his brother.

And he went on to tell them of his journeys,
His perils over land and sea, the stars
He had brushed on flying pinions. And they wanted
Still more, and someone asked him why Medusa,
Alone of all the sisters, was snaky-haired.
Their guest replied: "That, too, is a tale worth telling.
She was very lovely once, the hope of many
An envious suitor, and of all her beauties   200
Her hair most beautiful—at least I heard so
From one who claimed he had seen her. One day Neptune
Found her and raped her, in Minerva's temple,
And the goddess turned away, and hid her eyes
Behind her shield, and, punishing the outrage
As it deserved, she changed her hair to serpents,
And even now, to frighten evil-doers,
She carries on her breastplate metal vipers
To serve as awful warning of her vengeance."

[As the story continues in Book 5, Phineus, Andromeda's previous fiancé, accuses Perseus of stealing his promised bride and attacks the hero. A huge fight breaks out, and Perseus, seriously outnumbered, raises the Gorgon's head, turning his enemies to stone. He petrifies Phineus as he pleads for mercy, promising the statue to Andromeda.]

BOOK 10   Orpheus and Eurydice

So Hymen left there, clad in saffron robe,   1
Through the great reach of air, and took his way
To the Ciconian country, where the voice

Of Orpheus called him, all in vain. He came there,
True, but brought with him no auspicious words,
No joyful faces, lucky omens. The torch
Sputtered and filled the eyes with smoke; when swung,
It would not blaze: bad as the omens were,
The end was worse, for as the bride went walking
Across the lawn, attended by her naiads,   10
A serpent bit her ankle, and she was gone.
Orpheus mourned her to the upper world,
And then, lest he should leave the shades untried,
Dared to descend to Styx, passing the portal
Men call Taenarian. Through the phantom dwellers,
The buried ghosts, he passed, came to the king
Of that sad realm, and to Persephone,
His consort, and he swept the strings, and chanted:
"Gods of the world below the world, to whom
All of us mortals come, if I may speak   20
Without deceit, the simple truth is this:
I came here, not to see dark Tartarus,
Nor yet to bind the triple-throated monster
Medusa's offspring, rough with snakes. I came
For my wife's sake, whose growing years were taken
By a snake's venom. I wanted to be able
To bear this; I have tried to. Love has conquered.
This god is famous in the world above,
But here, I do not know. I think he may be
Or is it all a lie, that ancient story   30
Of an old ravishment, and how he brought
The two of you together? By these places
All full of fear, by this immense confusion,
By this vast kingdom's silences, I beg you,
Weave over Eurydice's life, run through too soon.
To you we all, people and things, belong,
Sooner or later, to this single dwelling
All of us come, to our last home; you hold
Longest dominion over humankind.
She will come back again, to be your subject,   40
After the ripeness of her years; I am asking
A loan and not a gift. If fate denies us
This privilege for my wife, one thing is certain:
I do not want to go back either; triumph
In the death of two."
                    And with his words, the music
Made the pale phantoms weep: Ixion's wheel
Was still, Tityos' vultures left the liver,
Tantalus tried no more to reach for the water,
And Belus' daughters rested from their urns,

And Sisyphus climbed on his rock to listen.   50
That was the first time ever in all the world
The Furies wept. Neither the king nor consort
Had harshness to refuse him, and they called her,
Eurydice. She was there, limping a little
From her late wound, with the new shades of Hell.
And Orpheus received her, but one term
Was set: he must not, till he passed Avernus,
Turn back his gaze, or the gift would be in vain.

They climbed the upward path, through absolute silence,
Up the steep murk, clouded in pitchy darkness,   60
They were near the margin, near the upper land,
When he, afraid that she might falter, eager to see her,
Looked back in love, and she was gone, in a moment.
Was it he, or she, reaching out arms and trying
To hold or to be held, and clasping nothing
But empty air? Dying the second time,
She had no reproach to bring against her husband,
What was there to complain of? One thing, only:
He loved her. He could hardly hear her calling
Farewell! when she was gone.
                        The double death   70
Stunned Orpheus, like the man who turned to stone
At sight of Cerberus, or the couple of rock,
Olenos and Lethaea, hearts so joined
One shared the other's guilt, and Ida's mountain,
Where rivers run, still holds them, both together.
In vain the prayers of Orpheus and his longing
To cross the river once more; the boatman Charon
Drove him away. For seven days he sat there
Beside the bank, in filthy garments, and tasting
No food whatever. Trouble, grief, and tears   80
Were all his sustenance. At last, complaining
The gods of Hell were cruel, he wandered on
To Rhodope and Haemus, swept by the north winds,
Where, for three years, he lived without a woman
Either because marriage had meant misfortune
Or he had made a promise. But many women
Wanted this poet for their own, and many
Grieved over their rejection. His love was given
To young boys only, and he told the Thracians
That was the better way: *enjoy that springtime,*   90
Take those first flowers!
                        There was a hill, and on it
A wide-extending plain, all green, but lacking
The darker green of shade, and when the singer

Came there and ran his fingers over the strings,
The shade came there to listen. The oak-tree came,
And many poplars, and the gentle lindens,
The beech, the virgin laurel, and the hazel
Easily broken, the ash men use for spears,
The shining silver-fir, the ilex bending
Under its acorns, the friendly sycamore,   100
The changing-colored maple, and the willows
That love the river-waters, and the lotus
Favoring pools, and the green boxwood came,
Slim tamarisks, and myrtle, and viburnum
With dark-blue berries, and the pliant ivy,
The tendrilled grape, the elms, all dressed with vines,
The rowan-trees, the pitch-pines, and the arbute
With the red fruit, the palm, the victor's triumph,
The bare-trunked pine with spreading leafy crest,
Dear to the mother of the gods since Attis   110
Put off his human form, took on that likeness,
And the cone-shaped cypress joined them, now a tree,
But once a boy, loved by the god Apollo
Master of lyre and bow-string, both together.

BOOK 11   The Death of Orpheus

So with his singing Orpheus drew the trees,   1
The beasts, the stones, to follow, when, behold!
The mad Ciconian women, fleeces flung
Across their maddened breasts, caught sight of him
From a near hill-top, as he joined his song
To the lyre's music. One of them, her tresses
Streaming in the light air, cried out: "Look there!
There is our despiser!" and she flung a spear
Straight at the singing mouth, but the leafy wand
Made only a mark and did no harm. Another   10
Let fly a stone, which, even as it flew,
Was conquered by the sweet harmonious music,
Fell at his feet, as if to ask for pardon.
But still the warfare raged, there was no limit,
Mad fury reigned, and even so, all weapons
Would have been softened by the singer's music,
But there was other orchestration: flutes
Shrilling, and trumpets braying loud, and drums,
Beating of breasts, and howling, so the lyre
Was overcome, and then at last the stones   20
Reddened with blood, the blood of the singer, heard
No more through all that outcry. All the birds
Innumerable, fled, and the charmed snakes,

The train of beasts, Orpheus' glory, followed.
The Maenads stole the show. Their bloody hands
Were turned against the poet; they came thronging
Like birds who see an owl, wandering in daylight;
They bayed him down, as in the early morning,
Hounds circle the doomed stag beside the game-pits.
They rushed him, threw the wands, wreathed with green leaves,   30
Not meant for such a purpose; some threw clods,
Some branches torn from the tree, and some threw stones,
And they found fitter weapons for their madness.
Not far away there was a team of oxen
Plowing the field, and near them farmers, digging
Reluctant earth, and sweating over their labor,
Who fled before the onrush of this army
Leaving behind them hoe and rake and mattock
And these the women grabbed, and slew the oxen
Who lowered horns at them in brief defiance   40
And were torn limb from limb, and then the women
Rushed back to murder Orpheus, who stretched out
His hands in supplication, and whose voice,
For the first time, moved no one. They struck him down,
And through those lips to which the rocks had listened,
To which the hearts of savage beasts responded,
His spirit found its way to winds and air.

The birds wept for him, and the throng of beasts,
The flinty rocks, the trees which came so often
To hear his song, all mourned. The trees, it seemed,   50
Shook down their leaves, as if they might be women
Tearing their hair, and rivers, with their tears,
Were swollen, and their naiads and their dryads
Mourned in black robes. The poet's limbs lay scattered
Where they were flung in cruelty or madness,
But Hebrus River took the head and lyre
And as they floated down the gentle current
The lyre made mournful sounds, and the tongue murmured
In mournful harmony, and the banks echoed
The strains of mourning. On the sea, beyond   60
Their native stream, they came at last to Lesbos
And grounded near the city of Methymna.
And here a serpent struck at the head, still dripping
With sea-spray, but Apollo came and stopped it,
Freezing the open jaws to stone, still gaping.
And Orpheus' ghost fled under the earth, and knew
The places he had known before, and, haunting
The fields of the blessed, found Eurydice
And took her in his arms, and now together

And side by side they wander, or Orpheus follows 70
Or goes ahead, and may, with perfect safety,
Look back for his Eurydice.
                                    But Bacchus
Demanded punishment for so much evil.
Mourning his singer's loss, he bound those women,
All those who saw the murder, in a forest,
Twisted their feet to roots, and thrust them deep
Into unyielding earth. As a bird struggles
Caught in a fowler's snare, and flaps and flutters
And draws its bonds the tighter by its struggling,
Even so the Thracian women, gripped by the soil, 80
Fastened in desperate terror, writhed and struggled,
But the roots held. They looked to see their fingers,
Their toes, their nails, and saw the bark come creeping
Up the smooth legs; they tried to smite their thighs
With grieving hands, and struck on oak; their breasts
Were oak, and oak their shoulders, and their arms
You well might call long branches and be truthful.

BOOK 15   The Deification of Caesar

[After summarizing the early history of Rome, Ovid ends on the story of Asclepius
(Aesculapius), god of medicine, who arrives in Rome in the form of a serpent to cure a
deadly plague.]

                                    The old god 1
Came to our shrines from foreign lands, but Caesar
Is god in his own city. First in war,
And first in peace, victorious, triumphant,
Planner and governor, quick-risen to glory,
The newest star in Heaven, and more than this,
And above all, immortal through his son.
No work, in all of Caesar's great achievement,
Surpassed this greatness, to have been the father
Of our own Emperor. To have tamed the Britons, 10
Surrounded by the fortress of their ocean,
To have led a proud victorious armada
Up seven-mouthed Nile, to have added to the empire
Rebel Numidia, Libya, and Pontus
Arrogant with the name of Mithridates,
To have had many triumphs, and deserved
Many more triumphs: this was truly greatness,
Greatness surpassed only by being father
Of one yet greater, one who rules the world
As proof that the immortal gods have given 20
Rich blessing to the human race, so much so
We cannot think him mortal, our Augustus,

Therefore our Julius must be made a god
To justify his son.
                    And golden Venus
Saw this, and saw, as well, the murder plotted
Against her priest, the assassins in their armor,
And she grew pale with fear. "Behold," she cried
To all the gods in turn, "Behold, what treason
Threatens me with its heavy weight, what ambush
Is set to take Iulus' last descendant!   30
Must this go on forever? Once again
The spear of Diomedes strikes to wound me,
The walls of Troy fall over me in ruins,
Once more I see my son, long-wandering,
Storm-tossed, go down to the shades, and rise again
To war with Turnus, or to speak more truly,
With Juno. It is very foolish of me
To dwell on those old sufferings, for my fear,
My present fear, has driven them from my mind.
Look: Do you see them whetting their evil daggers?   40
Avert this crime, before the fires of Vesta
Drown in their high-priest's blood!"
                                    The anxious goddess
Cried these complaints through Heaven, and no one listened.
The gods were moved, and though they could not shatter
The iron mandates of the ancient sisters,
They still gave certain portents of the evil
To come upon the world. In the dark storm-clouds
Arms clashed and trumpets blared, most terrible,
And horns heard in the sky warned men of crime,
And the sun's visage shone with lurid light   50
On anxious lands. Firebrands were seen to flash
Among the stars, the clouds dripped blood, rust-color
Blighted the azure Morning-Star, and the Moon
Rode in a blood-red car. The Stygian owl
Wailed in a thousand places; ivory statues
Dripped tears in a thousand places, and wailing traveled
The holy groves, and threats were heard. No victim
Paid expiation, and the liver warned
Of desperate strife to come, the lobe found cloven
Among the entrails. In the market place,   60
Around the homes of men and the gods' temples
Dogs howled by night, and the shadows of the silent
Went roaming, and great earthquakes shook the city.
No warning of the gods could check the plotting
Of men, avert the doom of fate. Drawn swords
Were borne into a temple; nowhere else
In the whole city was suitable for murder
Save where the senate met.

Then Venus beat

Her breast with both her hands, and tried to hide him,
Her Caesar, in a cloud, as she had rescued   70
Paris from Menelaus, as Aeneas
Fled Diomedes' sword. And Jove spoke to her:
"My daughter, do you think your power alone
Can move the fates no power can ever conquer?
Enter the home of the Three Sisters: there
You will see the records, on bronze and solid iron,
Wrought with tremendous effort, and no crashing
Of sky, no wrath of lightning, no destruction
Shall make them crumble. They are safe, forever.
There you will find engraved on adamant   80
The destinies of the race, unchangeable.
I have read them, and remembered; I will tell you
So you may know the future. He has finished
The time allotted him, this son you grieve for;
His debt to earth is paid. But he will enter
The Heaven as a god, and have his temples
On earth as well: this you will see fulfilled,
Will bring about, you and his son together.
He shall inherit both the name of Caesar
And the great burden, and we both shall help him   90
Avenge his father's murder. Under him
Mutina's conquered walls will sue for mercy,
Pharsalia know his power, and Philippi
Run red with blood again, and one more Pompey
Go down to death in the Sicilian waters.
A Roman general's Egyptian woman,
Foolish to trust that liaison, will perish
For all her threats that our own Capitol
Would serve Canopus. Need I bring to mind
Barbarian lands that border either ocean?   100
Whatever lands men live on, the world over,
Shall all be his to rule, and the seas also.
And when peace comes to all the world, his mind
Will turn to law and order, civil justice,
And men will learn from his sublime example,
And he, still looking forward toward the future,
The coming generations, will give order
That his good wife's young son should take his name,
His duty when he lays the burden down,
Though he will live as long as ancient Nestor   110
Before he comes to heaven to greet his kinsmen.
Now, in the meantime, from the murdered body
Raise up the spirit, set the soul of Julius
As a new star in Heaven, to watch over
Our market place, our Capitol."

He ended,
And Venus, all unseen, came to the temple,
Raised from the body of Caesar the fleeting spirit,
Not to be lost in air, but borne aloft
To the bright stars of Heaven. As she bore it,
She felt it burn, released it from her bosom,   120
And saw it rise, beyond the moon, a comet
Rising, not falling, leaving the long fire
Behind its wake, and gleaming as a star.
And now he sees his son's good acts, confessing
They are greater than his own, for once rejoicing
In being conquered. But the son refuses
To have his glories set above his father's;
Fame will not heed him, for she heeds no mortal,
Exalts him, much against his will, resists him
In this one instance only. So must Atreus   130
Defer to Agamemnon; so does Theseus
Surpass Aegeus, and Achilles Peleus,
And—(one more instance where the father's glory
Yields to the son's)—Saturn is less than Jove.
Jove rules the lofty citadels of Heaven,
The kingdoms of the triple world, but Earth
Acknowledges Augustus. Each is father
As each is lord. O gods, Aeneas' comrades,
To whom the fire and sword gave way, I pray you,
And you, O native gods of Italy,   140
Quirinus, father of Rome, and Mars, the father
Of Rome's unconquered sire, and Vesta, honored
With Caesar's household gods, and Apollo, tended
With reverence as Vesta is, and Jove,
Whose temple crowns Tarpeia's rock, O gods,
However many, whom the poet's longing
May properly invoke, far be the day,
Later than our own era, when Augustus
Shall leave the world he rules, ascend to Heaven,
And there, beyond our presence, hear our prayers!   150

The Epilogue

Now I have done my work. It will endure,
I trust, beyond Jove's anger, fire and sword,
Beyond Time's hunger. The day will come, I know,
So let it come, that day which has no power
Save over my body, to end my span of life
Whatever it may be. Still, part of me,
The better part, immortal, will be borne
Above the stars; my name will be remembered
Wherever Roman power rules conquered lands,

I shall be read, and through all centuries,   160
If prophecies of bards are ever truthful,
I shall be living, always.

. . . .

Questions for Discussion and Review

1. What are the "Ages of Man" according to Ovid? Compare Ovid's description of the Ages of Man with that of the Greek poet Hesiod (see Chapter 4). What characteristically Roman views and ideas does Ovid incorporate in his version of the myth?

2. How does Ovid characterize his own time? What does he value about Roman life? What does he fear? What does he criticize?

3. What does Apollo want from Daphne? Why does she refuse him? What does Apollo's attempted rape suggest about the relationship between humans and gods?

4. How would you describe Perseus's character as portrayed by Ovid? How does he differ from the hero of the Greek Perseus myths (see Chapter 10)? How does Perseus's attitude toward Andromeda in Ovid's poem differ from that in the Greek myth?

5. Both Ovid and Virgil raise the issue of "Eternal Rome" in their poems. Compare and contrast their views. Does each poet value the concept that his nation is destined to last forever or subject that idea to an ironic critique? How does each see Caesar's role? Defend your views with specific references to each work.

6. How does the story of Orpheus and Eurydice compare or contrast with descents into the Underworld, such as those of Heracles, Persephone, or Adonis?

PART FIVE

The Western World's
Transformations of Myth

CHAPTER

21

The Persistence of Myth

KEY TOPICS/THEMES

Despite a period of relative decline between the time of the fall of Rome and the late Middle Ages, classical mythology has endured throughout the history of Western culture—through translations and revivals, through adaptations and reinterpretations, through the borrowing of themes and images, and through the use of key figures and symbols. During some periods of history, certain mythic figures (such as Icarus during the Renaissance or Prometheus during the Romantic period) even became symbols of the central ideas or concerns of the age.

The Decline and Revival of Classical Mythology

Perhaps the most remarkable attribute of classical mythology is its persistence. Long after ceasing to have even the remotest connections to belief systems, these myths continued to resonate, reflecting continuing human concerns and providing an enduring cultural resource transcending the boundaries of politics, language, religion, and time itself.

Classical mythology has not, of course, retained a constant level of popular appeal. In fact, its survival has hardly been a foregone conclusion. During the era following the collapse of the Roman Empire in the West, the rise and spread of Christianity and a long period of economic and political disorder in Europe contributed to the general disappearance of literacy, as well as to a radical change in perspective. Among the effects was a loss of knowledge of or interest in classical learning of all kinds. Although it never entirely disappeared, classical mythology was considered particularly inappropriate for a Christian audience, primarily because of its "pagan" deities. Further, the new guide for human behavior—the imitation of Christ, with its focus on humility and otherworldliness—theoretically negated the mythic hero as an appropriate role model (though that concept, too, survived by being

1019

transposed into an acceptably Christian context in such heroes as Roland and the ostensibly Christian Beowulf).

As literacy gradually became more widespread again in the late Middle Ages, it was through the works of writers like Virgil and Ovid that growing numbers of readers rediscovered classical mythology and reclaimed large portions of the mythological landscape, despite its pagan character. The example of Virgil, in fact, eased the process of assimilating the mythic material into the Christian worldview. In the fourth of a series of poems called the *Eclogues,* Virgil had referred to a child who would come to redeem Rome. Claiming this allusion as Virgil's "prediction" of the Coming of Christ allowed medieval Christian readers to justify their attention to a pagan poet. In his three-part poem the *Commedia* (later known as the *Divine Comedy*), the Italian poet Dante expanded the trip to the Underworld from Book 6 of Virgil's *Aeneid* into the subject of the entire first book (the *Inferno*) of his poem, transforming Aeneas's voyage into a spiritual journey of the soul. He also made Virgil himself into a literary character, portraying the Roman poet as his guide through both Hell and Purgatory. Dante placed the pagan **Ulysses** [oo-LIS-seez] (Odysseus) in Hell for daring to sail beyond the world's limits to Mount Purgatory, and borrowed many mythological details of Virgil's Underworld, from the River Styx to figures such as **Charon, Cerberus,** and **Minos.** Virgil's *Aeneid* remained, into the eighteenth century and beyond, the staple of European education, providing an introduction to the larger body of classical mythology that artists, composers, and writers would draw on for centuries to come.

Meanwhile, the Courtly Love tradition, beginning in the twelfth century, sparked a revived interest in Ovid's *Art of Love.* This tradition was first expressed in the poetry of the French troubadours and explained in a treatise (*The Art of Courtly Love*) by Andreas Capellanus, chaplain at the court of Eleanor of Aquitaine. The concept of Courtly Love defined passionate love as a powerful, ennobling force. Because such love was usually adulterous, it was considered sinful by the Church. The poets thus turned to secular sources, such as Ovid, for their inspiration. Ovid's metaphor of service to Eros—or Cupid, the god of love whose darts and arrows inflame lovers—pervades love poems from Dante's own sonnets, *La Vita Nuova (The New Life),* to Petrarch's cycle of sonnets *To Laura.* Petrarch's contemporary, the English poet Chaucer, included a translation of one of Petrarch's sonnets in *Troilus and Criseyde* (c. 1385), a narrative poem describing the tragic love story of Hector's brother and his lover. These, in turn, became the model for innumerable secular love poems from the early Renaissance to the present day, providing another vehicle by which the heritage of Greek and Roman mythology could be transmitted to the modern world.

The Later Uses of Classical Mythology

The popular uses of images from classical mythology in the modern world include fields as diverse as psychology, sociology, television, and advertising, to name a few. Indeed, so common are these images that we are often scarcely aware of the mythic components of advertisements, such as the logos of tire companies (Atlas, the Titan who held the sky on his shoulders), or of floral delivery services (Hermes with his winged sandals), or the "cupids" whose hearts and arrows adorn Valentine's Day cards. There are mythological references even in apparently abstract phrases like "the culture of narcissism" (a description of an era when people seem obsessed with gratification of their personal needs), which alludes to the myth of **Narcissus,** the young man who fell in love with his own image.

Methods of Transmission

Even if we focused solely on literature and the arts, a complete list of works that incorporate elements of classical mythology would require hundreds of pages. But despite this scope and diversity, mythic material is most frequently transmitted in four basic ways: (1) rendering ancient plays or poems accessible to modern readers by translating them into modern languages or by reviving them in contemporary performances; (2) updating (by reinterpreting or adapting) ancient stories, plays, or poems to make them relevant to contemporary audiences; (3) taking advantage of an audience's familiarity with mythic materials by incorporating their themes and images to create a double vision, ancient and modern, either to reinforce or to contrast the two visions in thematic counterpoint; or (4) using a specific mythic figure as an emblem or symbol of an idea that an artist, writer, composer, or director wishes to expound or explore.

Translations and Revivals

In ancient Greece itself, of course, as in Rome (as long as educated Romans learned Greek), translations weren't necessary. But by the Middle Ages, the vernacular European languages had replaced Latin as the language of everyday speech, though Latin was retained as a religious and literary language; meanwhile, the study of Greek dwindled. When interest in classical writers was revived in the Renaissance, the study of Greek once again became popular with humanist scholars, who set about searching for Greek and Roman manuscripts. Even prior to the fall of Constantinople to the Turks in 1453, many Greek scholars had migrated to Italy, often bringing their prized ancient manuscripts with them and thus fueling the ongoing classical revival. As learning and the taste for classical works spread beyond the elite circles of humanist scholars, translations became necessary. One influential Renaissance translator was the English poet and playwright George Chapman, who was the first to translate Homer's work into English (1616). Later, Alexander Pope did his own translation, rendering the *Iliad* in rhymed couplets, reflecting the eighteenth-century perception of a harmonious and meticulously organized universe in which common sense reigned:

> The King of men, on public counsels bent,
> Convened the princes in his ample tent;
> Each seized a portion of the kingly feast,
> But stayed his hand when thirst and hunger ceased.
> Then Nestor spoke, for wisdom long approved,
> And, slowly rising, thus the council moved:
> "Monarch of nations! whose superior sway

Assembled states and lords of earth obey,
The laws and sceptres to thy hand are given,
And millions own the care of thee and heaven.

. . . .

Thee, prince! it fits alike to speak and hear,
Pronounce with judgment, with regard give ear,
To see no wholesome motion be withstood,
And ratify the best for public good. (9.121–135)

Each era since has produced its own crop of translations, reflective of current tastes. As scholars learned more about the ancient world and its languages, both the accuracy and the readability of the texts improved, and many fine modern translations became widely available.

Adaptations, Revisions, and "Updatings"

The practice of writing "revisionist" versions of extant works began as early as the era of the classical playwrights themselves: Aeschylus, Sophocles, and Euripides wrote plays dramatizing their versions of the same myths as did their fellow playwrights and competitors. Each of the three, for instance, had his own version of the story of the revenge of Orestes and Electra. And although the basic plot outlines remained unchanged, their interpretations and judgments of the action differed radically. For example, Aeschylus's Oresteian trilogy praises the Athenian jury system as superior to a system of justice administered either by individual humans or by gods who have agendas of their own. In contrast, Euripides' *Electra* comments on the ability of important, well-connected people like Orestes and Electra to get off lightly even after committing the most appalling crimes while peasants and villagers, who are portrayed as comparatively noble and generous, go unrewarded. Ovid, too, rewrote Greek myths in terms that reflected the sensibilities of his Roman audience, as did the Roman playwright Seneca. Slightly later, the African writer Apuleius inserted his own version of the tale of Cupid and Psyche in his Latin work *The Golden Ass*.

The Revival of Drama   When, after a prolonged interruption during the Dark and Middle Ages, classical drama was revived in the Renaissance, playwrights began revising dramas to fit their own conceptions. Some of the earliest plays, such as *Hercules Furens* (1561), were composed and performed in London at the Inns of Court by university students who showed great fondness for the plays of Seneca, as did William Shakespeare (*Titus Andronicus*, 1594). Later examples include the grand Baroque moral tragedies of the seventeenth-century French playwright Jean Racine (*Phaedre*, 1677, and *Andromache*, 1677, for example) and the twentieth-century rewrites of the American playwright Eugene O'Neill (for example, his trilogy *Mourning Becomes Electra*, 1931, a version of Aeschylus's *Oresteia*). And the French existentialist dramatists Andre Gide (*Oedipus*, 1931), Jean Giraudoux (*Electra*, 1937), Jean-Paul Sartre (*The Flies*, 1943, also a version of the Orestes myth), and Jean Anouilh collectively formed a kind of mini-industry of mythological dramas.

Anouilh, for example, wrote a version of *Antigone* (1944) that would have been especially meaningful to a French audience during World War II. In Sophocles' version, the heroine's determination to bury her brother's body in defiance of the law decreed by her uncle Creon is portrayed as a courageous upholding of the gods' moral law in the face of the decrees of a tyrant. In Anouilh's hands, her defiant self-sacrifice is reframed as an example of an existential act of commitment—of asserting one's freedom to define oneself morally in a universe whose absurdity is underlined by the author's portrayal of Creon and his henchmen as members of the Vichy government (French collaborators with the Nazis who were at that time occupying France). More recently, Luis Alfaro's *Electricidad* (2007) relocates the revenge killings of the *Oresteia* to the cholo gang culture of East Los Angeles.

Musical and Literary Adaptations   Nor are the adaptations confined to plays. In fact, the invention of opera itself may be traced to a desire to revive Greek drama in its "original" form. The Florentine Camarata, a group of Italian humanists devoted to literature and the arts, believed that the Greeks and Romans sang rather than spoke their tragedies in stage performance. They were determined to revive the ancient practice, which they believed to be a perfect marriage of poetry and music. To fulfill that aim, Ottavio Rinuccini, a court poet of the Medici family, wrote *Daphne* (c. 1594), a text based on Greek myth set to music, which is generally taken to be the first opera in European history. Its music has been lost, and thus Rinuccini's second such work, *Eurydice* (1600), also based on a Greek myth, is considered the first complete opera.

It is the Baroque composer Claudio Monteverdi, however, who is credited with creating modern opera as we know it, unifying all the vocal, instrumental, and dramatic elements. When he wrote his first opera (*Orpheus*, 1607), he, too, turned to Greek myth and, like Rinuccini, chose to retell the story of **Orpheus** and **Eurydice**. Many opera composers since—from Henry Purcell (*Dido and Aeneas*, 1689), to Richard Strauss (*Electra*, 1909), to Igor Stravinsky (*Oedipus Rex*, 1927)—have continued to use adaptations of works based on classical myths as the sources of their libretti.

Further continuing the tradition of adaptation of mythology were poets such as William Shakespeare ("Venus and Adonis," 1593) and novelists such as John Barth (whose *Chimera*, 1972, tells the stories of three heroes, including Perseus and Bellerophon) and James Joyce (whose novel *Ulysses*, 1914, updates the *Odyssey*, setting it in early twentieth-century Dublin). More recently, the Caribbean poet Derek Walcott dramatized the Homeric epic in *The Odyssey: A Stage Version* (1992). The *Odyssey*, in fact, has had continuing appeal as the basis for revisions of myths, including some with a feminist perspective. Charles Frazier's novel *Cold Mountain* (1998), which sets the story of Odysseus and Penelope in the Blue Ridge Mountains during the Civil War, gives more attention to Ada (the Penelope character) than do traditional reworkings of the myth, while Indian American novelist Bharati Mukherjee's *Jasmine* (1989), set in India, New York, and Iowa, portrays the heroine herself as the Odysseus character. Canadian novelist Margaret Atwood focuses the tale altogether on Penelope and her handmaids in *The Penelopiad* (2006).

Nor is this process confined to music and literature: the Coen brothers' film *O Brother, Where Art Thou?* (2000) sets the *Odyssey* in early twentieth-century America, depicting the adventures of Ulysses, a con artist and prison escapee trying to get home to prevent the remarriage of his divorced wife, Penny, to a rival. In a different (but similarly comic) vein, Eric Showalter's *Age of Bronze, Volume I: A Thousand Ships* tells the story of Troy in an archaeologically correct, impeccably illustrated comic book. And, as modern readers might expect, there are even cyber-text variants. For example, in Charles Mee's Internet version of the third play of Aeschylus's *Oresteia,* called *Orestes 2.0,* the writer invites Web browsers to adapt his work at will, a challenge accepted by Ann Tracy, whose adaptation, *Orestes 2.5,* was performed in Sacramento (2002).

The Use of Mythic Themes and Images

Rather than adapt entire myths, plays, or epics, many artists, writers, and compos-ers have based their work more loosely on mythic themes or have employed mythic images. These include brief allusions in a single line of poetry or prose, inspirations of the spirit of a musical composition, and concrete embodiments of a feeling or idea or point of view in a novel, poem, painting, film, or even photograph or dance (Figure 21-1).

Thus, to cite a mere handful of examples, the Renaissance painter Sandro Bot-ticelli depicted the birth of Venus (see Color Plate 1), revealing the grace, beauty, and harmonious nature of Love. Half a century later, in the Mannerist style, Jean Cousin the Elder placed Eve, the "first Pandora" (see Color Plate 2), in the tradi-tional pose of the reclining Venus, depicting her with one hand on her jar and the

FIGURE 21-1   Philip Trager, *The Abduction,* 1996. This striking photo of a performance of *Persephone,* choreographed by Ralph Lemon, was commissioned by the Jacob's Pillow Dance Festival, Dance Anthology Project, as part of a collaborative effort by photographer, choreographer, and dancers. The photo shows Persephone being pursued by Hades. *(Photo © Philip Trager, 1996)*

FIGURE 21-2   Claude Lorrain, *Coast View of Delos with Aeneas,* 1672. In this pastoral scene, which anticipates the neoclassical style, the landscape has become the real subject, a peaceful, bucolic scene tastefully adorned with structures in imitation of Greek architecture to lend a "classical" flavor. The human figures who occupied most of the space in paintings from the Renaissance through the middle of the seventeenth century have been reduced to the point that they are absorbed into the landscape and are almost incidental—a fitting reflection of an age that saw itself as made up of "pygmies" whose achievements could never surpass those of the "giants," such as Homer and Virgil, of ancient Greece and Rome. *(National Gallery, London)*

other resting on a skull, suggesting a more ambivalent response. The painter Claude Lorrain recreated a scene from the *Aeneid* (Figure 21-2)—a vision of a "Golden Age" that reflected the order, balance, and symmetry of neoclassical ideals. Many of Lorrain's paintings depicted similar scenes, and portrayals of the Golden Age remained popular throughout the period.

The Victorian poet Alfred, Lord Tennyson ("Ulysses," 1842) picked up where Homer left off, imagining the frustrations of an aged and enervated Odysseus longing for the thrill of one last voyage. More recently, Constantine Cavafy's poem "Ithaca" (1911) imagines the adventurous journey we all embark on to our own private Ithaca, relishing the voyage itself rather than the destination:

> Ithaca gave you the marvelous journey.
> Without her you wouldn't have set out.
> She hasn't anything else to give.

Similarly, in the early twentieth century, the poet William Butler Yeats ("Leda and the Swan," 1923) used the myth of the conception of Helen of Troy to consider

FIGURE 21-3   Salvador Dali, *Leda Atomica*, 1948. In this surrealist painting, Leda (actually a portrait of the artist's wife, Gala) sits on a "throne" floating in space, as the swan floats beside her. In the original myth, the swan is Zeus in disguise, who would make love to Leda, thereby conceiving Helen and setting in motion the destruction of Troy; here, the swan looks like nothing more than a domestic fowl. The juxtaposition, as in a dream, of the literal and the symbolic, of the real and the imaginary, of solid objects suspended in unreal space, renders in visual terms the nature of mythology itself. *(Collection of the artist)*

the irony of seemingly transient moments causing enormously destructive consequences. The modern surrealist painter Salvador Dali rendered the same myth in a much more cerebral and nonthreatening fashion (Figure 21-3).

W. H. Auden ("The Shield of Achilles," 1952) rewrote Homer's description of the two sides of Achilles' shield, with its contrasting scenes of peace and war, to comment on the illusions of heroism and the stupidity of power enforced by violence. A similar use of mythic images can be found in the work of Pablo Picasso, who did a series of etchings illustrating Ovid's *Metamorphoses*. The images he employed in the *Minotauromachy* (Figure 21-4) reappeared two years later in *Guernica* (Figure 21-5), a stark black-and-white painting depicting the horrors of the Spanish Civil War. Salvador Dali used the Ovidian tale of Narcissus to explore the unconscious images generated by a personality undergoing transformation in *The Metamorphosis of Narcissus* (see Color Plate 16).

Extended Uses of Mythic Themes   Examples of more extended uses of mythic themes and images include such diverse works as John Updike's novel *The Centaur* (1962), in which the divided creature of myth is identified with the conflicting impulses and desires of a Pennsylvania high school student, and James Joyce's *Portrait of the Artist as a Young Man* (1916), whose hero, a young poet, is compared with Daedalus, King Minos's "artificer" who designed both the labyrinth at Knossos (the institution of the Catholic Church in Joyce's version) and the waxen wings (now equated with the powers of poetry) with which to escape its confines. Bernard Malamud's novel *The Natural* (1952)—like the film based on it (1984, directed by Barry Levinson)—has a baseball player hero who undergoes experiences similar to those of both Achilles and Odysseus and who even has a bat hand-carved from a

FIGURE 21-4   Pablo Picasso, *Minotauromachy,* 1935. Picasso, who at the time of this painting had recently done a series of etchings illustrating Ovid's *Metamorphoses,* often turned to classical themes. The figure of the Minotaur reappears frequently in his paintings and etchings. In this etching, "The Battle of the Minotaur," the half-human beast creates terror and chaos. Amid the carnage, he points a sword toward a little girl holding a candle and a bouquet of flowers—a peace offering? Has she, like Ariadne, let Theseus (the man on the ladder?) into the labyrinth, naively trusting that he would destroy the monster within with no consequences? This Minotaur has taken the sword of the female matador sent to kill him; her body lies dead across the back of the horse, whose guts pour out on the ground. While the man hurries to escape up the ladder, the two women in the window regard the doves on the windowsill. Are they indifferent, thinking themselves safe up there, or merely unaware of the threat of war? *(Museum of Modern Art, New York)*

hickory tree (reminiscent of Achilles' "Pelian ash"), with Zeus's own symbol, the lightning bolt, emblazoned on it. Philip Roth's novel *The Human Stain* (2001) also employs traditional mythic themes, in this case the Oedipus story. In Roth's tale, the "stain" on Oedipus's identity results not from inherited curses, but from the burden of his mixed-race parentage, which he denies, leaving home in an attempt to escape his heritage, and ironically seeking freedom and self-determination by marrying the mother he would have wanted. In yet another invocation of the Oedipus story, Haruki Murakami's novel *Kafka on the Shore* (2002) centers the tale on the riddles of identity plaguing a runaway fifteen-year-old Japanese boy.

In these and countless other works based on mythic themes or images, the mythic material provides a way of understanding in greater depth the individual experiences depicted. These authors take advantage of the continuing relevance of the myths to the immutability of the human condition while using the same myths to comment, sometimes ironically, on the experiences they describe.

FIGURE 21-5   Pablo Picasso, *Guernica,* 1937. In this enormous painting (11′6″ × 25′8″), Picasso uses many of the images from the *Minotauromachy* (see Figure 21-4)—the disjointed bodies, the screaming horse, the girl holding the lamp, and even the bull—to depict the horrors of the saturation-bombing of the town of Guernica by insurgents during the Spanish Civil War. In this painting, however, no one, not even the bull, escapes the carnage, and the flowers lie trampled near the now-broken blade. The artist's exclusion of color and combining of cubist and expressionist techniques—the avoidance of three-dimensional forms, the suggestion of "collage" in the newsprintlike sections of the horse's body, the distortion of eyes that reveal inner and outer perspectives simultaneously—allow him to depict raw, unmediated emotions. Instead of the conventional view through the frame of a "window" that gives viewers a glimpse of events happening to others, this painting is a nightmare that traps viewers inside the horror, re-creating the experience of the original victims: the only rational response to this painting is a scream. *(Prado, Madrid)*

Myth as Emblem

Some writers, in the sciences and social sciences as well as the arts, have seized on a specific mythic figure to function as an emblem or symbol of a specific idea. Thus, the psychoanalyst Sigmund Freud used the figure of Oedipus to embody the unconscious, infantile erotic drives to which, he argued, all humans are subject (*The Interpretation of Dreams,* 1900). And Albert Camus, an existentialist writer, chose **Sisyphus** (who was condemned to push an enormous boulder repeatedly up a mountain, only to have it roll down the other side) as a concrete embodiment of the choices individuals make to define themselves in an absurd world in that moment when they decide, each time, to push the stone up the mountain once more (*The Myth of Sisyphus,* 1942). Similarly, contemporary ecologists have singled out the figure of Gaea, the ancient earth goddess, to signify the essential interrelationship of all components of earth's biosphere. And feminist psychologists employ the same goddess—both viewed in her own right and divided into separate functions in such goddesses as Hera, Athene, Artemis, and Aphrodite—as emblems of various components of the female psyche (Jean Shinoda Bolen, *Goddesses in Everywoman,* 1984).

More recently, John Gray (*Men Are from Mars, Women Are from Venus,* 1992) uses the mythic lovers in his title as emblems of the problems of communication between the genders in modern relationships. John Shay (*Achilles in Vietnam: Com-*

bat Trauma and the Undoing of Character, 1994), a psychiatrist treating Vietnam War veterans suffering from post-traumatic stress disorders, uses Homer's Achilles to illuminate the afflictions of modern combat veterans while tapping the modern soldiers' experiences to clarify what also happens to Achilles: the sense of betrayal, the withdrawal from one's society, and the "berserk state" that is the climax of extreme combat trauma, apparently, whether in ancient battles or in those of our own era. Shay also relates the trials of Odysseus's homecoming to the difficulties modern soldiers experience on returning from combat (*Odysseus in America: Combat Trauma and the Trials of Homecoming,* 2002).

A very different approach to the psychological applications of myth occurs in Jeanette Winterson's *Weight* (2005). In a narrative told from the first-person perspective, she uses the myth of Atlas and Heracles to explore the poles of the quest for identity—fate and freedom, endurance and strength—personified by these two figures, and addresses the need to make appropriate choices regarding both one's individual journey and the burdens the world imposes.

Mythology even proves useful in fields as seemingly remote as botany. Throughout *The Botany of Desire: A Plant's-Eye View of the World* (2002), Michael Pollan contrasts the cultural impetus behind the cultivation of the apple, for which he uses Dionysus as an emblem, versus that of the tulip, embodying, he claims, the spirit of Apollo. Pollan describes John Chapman, known in American legend as "Johnny Appleseed," as "the American Dionysus," a figure of freedom inhabiting the slippery boundaries between male and female, human and divine, animal and human, while the tulip embodies Apollonian clarity, order, logic, and individuality.

Myth and Cultural History

Precisely because they have lasted so long, myths, in whatever form they have been transmitted, can be extremely useful tools for students of cultural history. For example, because so many myths continue to be adapted and reinterpreted, historians can study the various revisions as barometers of cultural change. Thus, the story of the musician Orpheus and his ill-fated descent into the Underworld to rescue his beloved Eurydice can be variously portrayed as a grand but tragic passion, or as a descent into the depths of the human psyche or into the abyss of existential despair, or even as a comment on the destructive effect of patriarchal male–female relationships. H. D. (Hilda Doolittle) takes this latter approach, lamenting in her poem "Eurydice" the "arrogance" and self-sufficiency of Orpheus, who can neither leave Eurydice at peace in the Underworld nor allow her to emerge on her own terms (1917, 1925).

Indeed, the story of Orpheus and Eurydice has been interpreted in these and many other ways in such works as the operas of Monteverdi (*Orpheus,* 1607), Christoph Willibald Gluck (*Orpheus and Eurydice,* 1762), and Franz Joseph Haydn (*Orpheus and Eurydice,* 1791) and a play by Anouilh (*Eurydice,* 1941), among many others. The story has likewise been retold in film, such as *Orpheus* (1949, directed by Jean Cocteau) and *The Fugitive Kind* (1960, directed by Sidney Lumet), itself a version of Tennessee Williams's play *Orpheus Descending* (1957). In the Brazilian film *Black Orpheus* (1958, directed by Marcel Camus), the Underworld is the

Brazilian Carnival, during which, with normal constraints and inhibitions lifted, the demonic forces of violence and unreason are unleashed. More recently, in *The Hip-Hop Waltz of Eurydice* by Iranian-born playwright Reza Abdoh (an example of performance art staged at the Los Angeles Theatre Center in 1991), the Underworld is portrayed as one segment of the contemporary gay/lesbian subculture, complete with punk costumes and gender reversal (Orpheus is played by a woman, Eurydice by a man)—a nightmare vision of a world living under the threat of AIDS, in which Hades is a fascist police captain and Orpheus goes to hell on a motorcycle. In Salman Rushdie's novel *The Ground Beneath Her Feet* (1999), Orpheus and Eurydice become rock superstars. And in Czeslaw Milosz's poem "Orpheus and Eurydice" (2006) the poet Orpheus descends from the glass-paneled entrance of Hades to Persephone's palace on a series of elevators, passing through corridors guarded by electronic dogs.

In the fine arts, similar series of transformations can be traced. For example, in a pair of seventeenth-century paintings done only eighteen years apart, two artists—Peter Paul Rubens and Nicolas Poussin—depicted the same event, the rape of the Sabine women (Figures 21-6 and 21-7). In these two versions of the same theme, one can almost see the shift from Baroque to neoclassical sensibility occur. Ruben's foreshortened, intensely violent painting, with its naked, contorted bodies and writhing motion, places the viewer menacingly close, almost within the scene itself. In Poussin's painting, in contrast, the women are more decorously clothed, and virtually the entire action is confined within the triangle whose apex is pointed to by the hand of the woman to the left of center and the sword of the man to the right of center. Poussin moves the point of view discreetly back, presenting a more detached, more controlled, even heroic spectacle, all taking place under the watchful eye of the Roman soldier on the pedestal.

Not only can paintings reinterpret myths, but those paintings themselves can be used as sources for further commentary. Consider the way in which Jean-Auguste-Dominique Ingres's painting the *Apotheosis of Homer* (Figure 21-8) is dismantled and commented on ironically in Dali's painting of the same name (Figure 21-9).

Versions of Venus   The many interpretations of Venus in painting and sculpture through the ages (Figures 21-10 through 21-19) provide an extended illustration of changes in taste, style, and vision that reveal as much about their own eras as about the goddess herself. For instance, the calm depiction of divine beauty in the *Venus de Milo* (see Figure 21-10) of the second century B.C. differs from the more human but still idealized beauty of Botticelli's Renaissance painting *Venus and Mars* (see Color Plate 11). In stark contrast, the mannerist interpretations of Titian reveal the goddess in more blatantly sensuous fashion while showing her from more than one perspective. His reclining *Venus of Urbino* (see Figure 21-11) watches the viewer watching her, while his *Venus with the Mirror* (see Figure 21-12) multiplies perspectives still further by having the viewers watch Venus while she watches us in a mirror. Finally, Salvador Dali's surrealist sculpture, *Venus de Milo of the Drawers* (see Figure 21-19), parodies the original, reminding us through his hollow plaster figure that "Venus" is an abstract concept into which we must insert, like socks in a drawer, whatever meaning we choose.

FIGURE 21-6   Peter Paul Rubens, *Rape of the Daughters of Leucippus,* c. 1618. In the contrast between this painting by Rubens and the nearly contemporary one by Nicolas Poussin (see Figure 21-7) interpreting the same myth of the founding of the Roman people, the transformation from Baroque to neoclassical sensibility is evident. In Rubens's intensely Baroque work, the human figures are in the foreground and occupy most of the large canvas (7′3″ × 6′10″). The figures are approximately life-size, and the foreshortening of perspective puts the viewer right into the scene, intensifying the dramatic effects and getting the viewer personally involved. The writhing bodies of the victims and the twisted configurations of horses and men form intersecting spirals that create a vortex of movement in the center of the painting. But while the viewer instinctively sympathizes with the victims, the latter are nevertheless portrayed in such sensuous fashion that the painting augments the same erotic appeal the rapists are responding to. Forced in this way to assume the perspectives of both victim and rapist, the viewer is implicated in the very act he or she must deplore. *(Alte Pinakothek, Munich)*

FIGURE 21-7   Nicolas Poussin, *Rape of the Sabine Women,* 1636–1637. In contrast to Rubens's painting (see Figure 21-6), there are no ambiguities in Poussin's version of the same event, which clearly moves toward the neoclassical mode. Though there are far more figures in this almost equally large painting (5′1″ × 6′10″), they are less threatening to the viewer. Smaller in scale relative to the size of the canvas and further diminished by the backdrop of buildings and sky, they are also organized into a clear, controlling pattern —a classical equilateral triangle with its apex in the light behind the upraised hand of the woman in the center. The Roman attackers are portrayed as heroic in appearance, in contrast to Rubens's twisted bodies juxtaposed against the horses, whose animal natures the rapists seem to be emulating. The event has also been moved from the countryside to an urban setting so that the stable forms of classical buildings and columns (looking, indeed, as if the Romans had already built their city there) help enclose and contain the violence. The women here are clothed so that a sense of decorum is maintained even in the midst of the abduction. Finally, the figure of Romulus, mythical founder of Rome, on the podium of the temple (and thus presumably acting with the approval of the gods), appears to be directing the action, emphasizing the sense that everything is under control. *(Metropolitan Museum of Art, New York)*

Myth as Cultural Icon

Sometimes a whole generation latches onto a particular mythic figure, who then becomes a kind of cultural icon to which everyone seems to pay tribute. Notable examples of such occurrences include Icarus in the Renaissance and Prometheus in the Romantic period.

FIGURE 21-8   Jean-Auguste-Dominique Ingres, *Apotheosis of Homer,* 1827. In Ingres's tribute to the Greek poet, shown in this painting receiving from the winged figure of Victory the laurel crown as Prince of Poets and being welcomed into the company of the divine, we see, in effect, the "apotheosis" of neoclassical painting at its most extreme—an idealized and essentially static world realistically portrayed with great precision. The triangle made of actual portraits of artists and writers through the ages and forming an apex at the crown is visually repeated in the two figures personifying the *Iliad* (left) and the *Odyssey* (right) seated on the steps beneath their "father." A third triangle is formed by the entablature of the temple behind. This painting also literally enshrines the neoclassical belief that writers and artists, however "great" they may be in their own time, can at best imitate and pay tribute to, but can never hope to equal or surpass, the "giants" of the past. *(Louvre, Paris)*

FIGURE 21-9   Salvador Dali, *Apotheosis of Homer,* 1945. In this surrealist version, Dali literally deconstructs Ingres's painting (see Figure 21-8) and with it the illusions of an "eternal" art whose rules and value are unchanging. Dali reduces "Homer" to a broken bit of statuary, a relic, while the solid temple of the Muse itself melts. An ethereal horse (Pegasus?) tries to throw off riders who are attempting to hitch a ride to the stars by desperately clinging to its back, symbolic of the ancient myth. On the right, a skeletal wooden figure mourns over an empty sarcophagus, which suggests not resurrection but desecration of the dead: the corpse lies outside, untended, on the cart. *(Private collection)*

FIGURE 21-10   Aphrodite of Melos *(Venus de Milo),* c. 200–
150 B.C. A Hellenistic version of the classical goddess of love,
Aphrodite is depicted in this statue as elegant, beautiful, and
dignified. *(Louvre, Paris)*

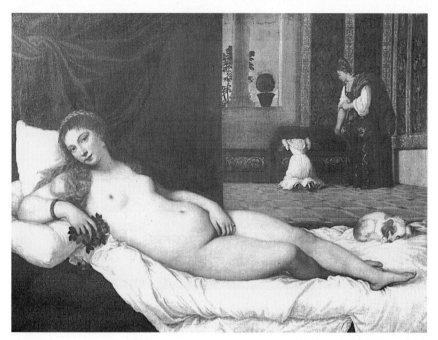

FIGURE 21-11   Titian, *Venus of Urbino,* 1538. The traditional "reclining Venus" in this painting is unbalanced, in characteristic mannerist fashion, by the extended perspective behind the two figures in the background and the perspective lines on the floor tile that draw the eye toward them. The dog on the bed also distracts our view from the goddess. Her knowing expression and the position of her hand accent the self-conscious sensuality of the portrait. By looking directly at the viewer, the goddess arouses the viewer's equally self-conscious response. *(Uffizi Gallery, Florence)*

FIGURE 21-12   Titian, *Venus with the Mirror,* 1555. Perspectives multiply dizzyingly in this theatrically lit painting, as we watch this luxuriously sensual Venus who gazes in the mirror. But the face in the mirror reveals that, while we watch her, she is watching not herself but us! Who is the voyeur, and who is the object? Breaking the one-way mirror that usually allows us to see into a painting while not being seen ourselves, Titian shatters the barrier that normally separates the "real" world of the viewer from the "unreal" world of "art" and makes the viewer conscious of having been caught intruding on Venus's privacy. *(National Gallery of Art, Mellon Collection, Washington, D.C.)*

FIGURE 21-13   Nicolas Poussin, *Mars and Venus,* c. 1628. In contrast to Botticelli's version of the scene (see Color Plate 11), Poussin's painting moves the figures farther back and creates further detachment by adding members to the "audience." The landscape becomes correspondingly more significant. *(Augustus Hemenway Fund and Arthur William Wheelwright Fund. Courtesy, Museum of Fine Arts, Boston)*

FIGURE 21-14   François Boucher, *The Toilet of Venus,* 1740. In this delicate painting, a slender, pretty, rather young-looking Venus is attended by cherubic Cupids in a lush, highly ornate setting. In typical rococo style, this symmetry of the classical style is overlaid with a profusion of decorative embellishments so that Venus herself takes on the air of another elegant ornament. *(Metropolitan Museum of Art, New York)*

FIGURE 21-15   Antonio Canova, *Pauline Bonaparte as Venus,* 1808. In this extremely flattering, life-size marble sculpture, Canova pays tribute to Napoleon's desire to revive the Roman Empire by portraying his sister, Pauline Borghese (née Bonaparte), in the traditional reclining Venus posture. *(Galleria Borghese, Rome)*

FIGURE 21-16   Edouard Manet, *Olympia,* 1863. Manet's *Olympia,* portrayed as Venus reclining, was a famous Parisian prostitute, shown here boldly staring back at the viewer as her maid brings flowers from an admirer. The painting scandalized Manet's contemporaries, which delighted the artist and his friends. The selection of scenes from ordinary and often urban life, as opposed to the "traditional" subjects of academic art, was typical of the Impressionists, who found their inspiration in Manet's work. *(Musée de l'Impressionisme, Paris)*

FIGURE 21-17   Arestide Maillol, *Torso of Venus,*
1925. Maillol's tribute to classical form, unlike its
original predecessors, never had a head or limbs.
The bronze sculpture focuses on the traditional "at
ease" posture of the torso, with one hip raised and
one knee bent, as an interesting, quasi-abstract
solid shape, calling our attention to its weight,
volume, and contours, rather than to its represen-
tational elements. *(Gallerie Dina Vierny, Paris)*

FIGURE 21-18   Jules Pascin,
Back View of Venus, 1924–
1925. Like Maillol's sculpture
(see Figure 21-17), Pascin's
painting, with its reversed
view, heavy black contours,
and almost obliterated head,
focuses our attention on line
and shape rather than realistic
representation. *(Musée d'Art
Moderne de la Ville de Paris)*

FIGURE 21-19   Salvador Dali, *Venus de Milo of the Drawers,* 1936. Dali's sculpture deconstructs the *Venus de Milo* (see Figure 21-10), just as his *Apotheosis of Homer* (see Figure 21-9) does with Ingres's painting of the same subject (see Figure 21-8). This plaster statue reminds us that sculpture is an artifice—an occupier of volume, a container of space, to be filled (and interpreted) as we choose. One ironic (and typically Daliesque) note: The "brain" drawer is missing. *(Private collection)*

The Renaissance

During the Renaissance (a word first used by the Italian poet Petrarch to describe the rebirth of the cultural achievements of Greece and Rome), the writings of Homer, as well as those of Ovid, Plutarch, and Seneca, joined those of Virgil and many others already popularized in the late medieval period as mythology shared in the general classical revival. The earlier rejection of pagan ideas yielded to the desire of the Christian humanists to unify their religious beliefs with their secular aesthetic and intellectual interests. Thus, "service to the god of love," Eros, is a phrase Renaissance writers often used without the slightest awareness of implicit blasphemy. Alternatively, the poet may have confessed awareness of the contradiction but played on the pun, referring to both Christ and Cupid as "god of love," as did John Donne in "Love's Deity": "I long to talk with some old lover's ghost / Who died before the god of love was born" (lines 1–2). When forced to choose, Renaissance poets may have even opted for Cupid: for example, in Sir Philip Sidney's sonnet from the series *Astrophel and Stella,* the poet deals with the conflict between Ovidian images and Christian beliefs, between the compelling impulses of the heart toward erotic love and the theoretical journey of the soul toward heaven. Maintaining that precarious balance so typical of the paradoxical stance that Renaissance scholars termed "Christian humanism," Sidney manages to have it both ways. Thus, he confesses that, although Cupid's darts may be dismissed as mere poetic artifice, the erotic drive overwhelms any purely theoretical intention as surely as if there were a god called Cupid who took unerring aim at human hearts.

FIGURE 21-20   Michelangelo, *David,* 1501–1504. A celebration of the beauty of the human body and the potential of the human being, this marble figure of David, of heroic proportions (18′), is portrayed with the same godlike body and air of repose that classical sculptors used in representing the god Apollo. *(Galleria dell'Accademia, Florence)*

During the Renaissance, biblical figures such as David (in Michelangelo's sculpture; Figure 21-20) and Adam and Eve (in his painting on the Sistine Chapel ceiling) are portrayed as Greek gods, whereas mythological characters (as in Lucas Cranach the Elder's *Judgment of Paris;* Figure 21-21) are depicted in Renaissance costumes and settings. Throughout Europe, artists began to go out of their way to invoke the Muses and re-create the Graces of an earlier age. Mythological themes abounded in the paintings, inspired the music, adorned the architecture, and filled the pages of the poems, plays, and stories, providing everything from brief allusions to complete plots. Further, a renewed enthusiasm for the heroic model of experience is evident in Benvenuto Cellini's sculpture *Perseus and Medusa* (Figure 21-22).

Icarus

Amid the cornucopia of mythological subjects, one figure seems to express best the fears and aspirations of the time—**Icarus,** the boy who flew too high. For the Greeks, the myth of Icarus was a lesson in the necessity of the golden mean of moderation and self-control. The Renaissance Icarus, however, came to be admired for having the audacity to break through the limits of convention and ordinary experience—a tragic figure whose fall into the sea is the price he pays for a glimpse of a higher vision, for a moment of transcendence at the peak of a brief but glorious trajectory.

Dramatized in figures like the conqueror Tamburlaine (in the play by that name by the Elizabethan playwright Christopher Marlowe, c. 1588) or the seeker of forbidden knowledge Doctor Faustus (Marlowe, c. 1588), Icarus embodied the

FIGURE 21-21   Lucas Cranach the Elder, *Judgment of Paris,* 1530. In Cranach's painting, Paris is a Renaissance soldier, who looks up at the Cupid aiming arrows from the tree while the three goddesses—Athene at the right, wearing the helmet, Hera at the left, and Aphrodite in the center—calmly, almost indifferently, await the inevitable. The fact that the men are wearing Renaissance battle gear not only updates (and thus universalizes) the myth but also underlines the inevitability of the consequences—the Trojan War for which Paris is already prepared. *(Staatliche Kunsthalle, Karlsruhe)*

paradoxical condition of the Renaissance hero—a modern, secular figure in a still-medieval, as well as Christian, universe. Although doomed to fail, he must literally hit his head against the ceiling of ordained limits—in its most extreme form, the limit is the threat of damnation itself—in order to fulfill the ambition that defines his humanity. Faustus, for example, sells his soul to the devil (or the devil's servant Mephistophilis) in return for forbidden knowledge, recapitulating the humanistic defiance earlier captured in the myths of Prometheus, Pandora, and Eve.

Perceived as a threat to orthodoxy, Icarus must certainly fall:

> His waxen wings did mount above his reach
> And melting heavens conspired his overthrow. (Marlowe, Prologue)

But his "aspiring mind" and his quest for "knowledge infinite" (as Marlowe described it in *Tamburlaine,* Part 1) made him one of the most compelling images of the age.

The Fall of Icarus   If images such as Icarus can become cultural symbols, they can also be used to signal changing cultural values. Thus, Pieter Breughel the Elder, in his painting *The Fall of Icarus* (see Color Plate 12), moves the figure of Icarus from center stage to an insignificant—and almost indistinguishable—spot in a corner of the painting: only the legs, jutting out of the sea, reveal the drowning boy, while the rest of the world, indifferent, goes about its business. In this painting, Breughel signals a shift in values (which occurred somewhat earlier on the Continent than in more remote places like England). Instead of the obsessively human-centered world of the Renaissance, we here assume the asymmetrical Baroque perspective of a world

FIGURE 21-22   Benvenuto Cellini, *Perseus and Medusa,* 1545–1554. Cellini's rather menacing bronze sculpture puts the figure of the hero on an ornate pedestal, as he grips his sword and stands in triumph on the body of Medusa, holding her severed head aloft. *(Loggia dei Lanzi, Florence)*

adrift in an infinite universe in which individuals have no intrinsic significance and the nobility essential for heroic tragedy is impossible or irrelevant.

The Romantic Age: Prometheus

In the Romantic period, it is Prometheus who seems to have leaped out of the annals of mythology into the consciousness of an entire generation. Identified with the creative energy, the heroic rebellion against oppressive authority, and the sense of being reborn into a new age unleashed by the French Revolution, Prometheus captured the imagination of artists, composers, poets, and novelists alike in works as diverse as Lord Byron's poem "Prometheus" (1801) and Percy Bysshe Shelley's *Prometheus Unbound* (1818), a lyric drama offered in answer to Aeschylus's *Prometheus Bound.*

In the preface to his play, Shelley speaks for his contemporaries as he explains,

I was averse from a catastrophe so feeble as that of reconciling the Champion with the Oppressor of mankind [the presumed ending of Aeschylus's trilogy]. The moral interest of the fable, which is so powerfully sustained by the sufferings and endurance of Prometheus, would be annihilated if we could conceive him as unsaying his high language and quailing before his . . . perfidious adversary [Zeus].

Shelley goes on to compare Prometheus to Satan (as depicted in John Milton's Christian epic *Paradise Lost,* 1674), who also defied divine authority. But Shelley finds Prometheus preferable because,

in addition to courage, and majesty, and firm and patient opposition to omnipotent force, he is susceptible of being described as exempt from the taints of ambition, envy, revenge, and a desire for personal aggrandisement. . . .

Prometheus, Shelley concludes, is the "type of the highest perfection of moral and intellectual nature, impelled by the purest and truest motives to the best and noblest ends." In the last speech of the play, Demagorgon celebrates the Titan's triumph over tyranny:

This is the day, which down the void abysm
At the Earth-born's spell yawns for Heaven's despotism,
    And Conquest is dragged captive through the deep:
Love, from its awful throne of patient power
In the wise heart, from the last giddy hour
    Of dread endurance, from the slippery, steep,
And narrow verge of crag-like agony, springs
And folds over the world its healing wings.

. . . .

To suffer woes which Hope thinks infinite;
To forgive wrongs darker than death or night;
    To defy Power, which seems omnipotent;
To live, and bear; to hope till Hope creates
From its own wreck the thing it contemplates;
    Neither to change, nor falter, not repent;

This, like thy glory, Titan, is to be
Good, great and joyous, beautiful and free;
This alone is Life, Joy, Empire, and Victory. (4.554–578)

Prometheus and Napoleon The myth created an aura around historical events and powerful personalities as well. Napoleon, who rather enjoyed having himself portrayed as a Greek god (Figure 21-23), was imaginatively linked with Prometheus until he "betrayed" the Revolution by declaring himself emperor. Beethoven's Third Symphony (the *Eroica,* 1804), which incorporates musical material from his earlier composition *The Creatures of Prometheus,* was originally dedicated to Napoleon, but Beethoven angrily removed the dedication in response to that betrayal. Napoleon thus revealed exactly those traits that Shelley had identified with Satan. The exhilarating spirit of freedom, released from all restraints, can also be a source of terror.

Prometheus and Satan The convergence of the redemptive and the demonic in Shelley's juxtaposition of Prometheus and Satan was not coincidental. The image of Satan-as-hero prompted a revival of interest in the poetry of Milton, whose *Paradise*

FIGURE 21-23 Antonio Canova, *Napoleon,* 1802–1810. In this larger-than-life marble sculpture (11′8″), Canova rather unrealistically portrays Napoleon as having the beauty of a Greek god (compare with Figure 7-1) combined with the power of Jupiter, whose imperial staff he bears. (The fig leaf over the genitals is a concession to the sensibility of the time.) Canova, who was, in fact, not an enthusiast for the Napoleonic regime, was more or less forced to do this sculpture, an offer from the emperor that he couldn't refuse. *(Wellington Museum, London)*

Lost, itself based on classical models, had portrayed the Archenemy in terms that the Romantics found intensely appealing: the poet William Blake even asserted that Milton was "of the Devil's party without knowing it." In a similar juxtaposition, Percy Bysshe Shelley's wife, Mary Wollstonecraft Shelley, titled her novel *Frankenstein, or the Modern Prometheus* (1818). Her protagonist, defying conventional moral limits in order to release the human spirit from "lifeless clay" into a more sublime state, comments on his intention to "explore unknown powers" and to reveal the secrets of creation:

> Life and death appeared to me ideal bounds, which I should first break through, and pour a torrent of light into our dark world. A new species would bless me as its creator and source. . . .

What this "god" creates, however, turns out to be monstrous.

During the Renaissance, such pursuit of forbidden knowledge was identified with Faustus, who was, in turn, compared with Icarus, the daring boy. Then, after a long hiatus during the seventeenth and eighteenth centuries, when acts of individual transcendence were not sought after or admired, Faustus himself was revived in the Romantic period, as in the German poet Johann Wolfgang von Goethe's version (*Faust,* Part 1, 1801). Goethe's poetic drama, in turn, inspired a series of lithographs illustrating scenes from Goethe's novel by the French artist Eugene Delacroix (1828), as well as operas by Charles-François Gounod (*Faust,* 1859) and Hector Berlioz (*The Damnation of Faust,* 1846). However, this Romantic Faust is compared not with Icarus but with the rebel Prometheus.

The Future of Myth

There are seemingly few areas of modern experience impervious to the uses of our mythological heritage. While we have focused, for the most part, on serious endeavors in the arts and sciences, other enterprises, from politics to humor, also take advantage of myth's capacity to enhance our understanding, as illustrated in this political cartoon (2004) from the "Non Sequitur" series by Wiley Miller:

FIGURE 21-24   (Non Sequitur © *2004 Wiley Miller. Distributed by Universal Press Syndicate. Reprinted with permission. All right reserved.*)

In all the varied forms in which classical myths have been passed on to us through the millennia, they have retained their power to compel our attention and to reveal to us, in myriad ways, their complex capacity for conveying meaning. They will undoubtedly continue to move us for a long time to come, expressing both the continuity of the human spirit and its infinite variety in as yet unimagined ways.

Excerpts from the
INFERNO*
Dante

BOOK 1 (CANTO 26, CIRCLE 8, BOLGIA 8)†

[Guided by the shade of Virgil, the poet visits the section of Hell where Ulysses and other Greek heroes are confined.]

. . . .

I stood on the bridge, and leaned out from the edge;　　　　　　　1
　　so far, that but for a jut of rock I held to
　　I should have been sent hurtling from the ledge

without being pushed. And seeing me so intent,
　　my Guide said: "There are souls within those flames;
　　each sinner swathes himself in his own torment."

"Master," I said, "your words make me more sure,
　　but I had seen already that it was so
　　and meant to ask what spirit must endure

the pains of that great flame which splits away　　　　　　　　10
　　in two great horns, as if it rose from the pyre
　　where Eteocles and Polynices lay?"

He answered me: "Forever round this path
　　Ulysses and Diomede move in such dress,
　　united in pain as once they were in wrath;

there they lament the ambush of the Horse
　　which was the door through which the noble seed
　　of the Romans issued from its holy source;

there they mourn that for Achilles slain
　　sweet Deidamia weeps even in death;　　　　　　　　　　20
　　there they recall the Palladium in their pain."

"Master," I cried, "I pray you and repray
　　till my prayer becomes a thousand—if these souls
　　can still speak from the fire, oh let me stay

---

*Translation by John Ciardi.

†Circle 8 spreads out over several cantos. The separate subdivisions are called *bolgias*, or "ditches in the Underworld, in which different categories of sinners are contained."

until the flame draws near! Do not deny me:
  You see how fervently I long for it!"
  And he to me: "Since what you ask is worthy,

it shall be. But be still and let me speak;
  for I know your mind already, and they perhaps
  might scorn your manner of speaking, since they were Greek."   30

And when the flame had come where time and place
  seemed fitting to my Guide, I heard him say
  these words to it: "O you two souls who pace

together in one flame!—if my days above
  won favor in your eyes, if I have earned
  however much or little of your love

in writing my High Verses, do not pass by,
  but let one of you be pleased to tell where he,
  having disappeared from the known world, went to die."

As if it fought the wind, the greater prong   40
  of the ancient flame began to quiver and hum;
  then moving its tip as if it were the tongue

that spoke, gave out a voice above the roar.
  "When I left Circe," it said, "who more than a year
  detained me near Gaëta long before

Aeneas came and gave the place that name,
  not fondness for my son, nor reverence
  for my aged father, nor Penelope's claim

to the joys of love, could drive out of my mind
  the lust to experience the far-flung world   50
  and the failings and felicities of mankind.

I put out on the high and open sea,
  with a single ship and only those few souls
  who stayed true when the rest deserted me.

As far as Morocco and as far as Spain
  I saw both shores; and I saw Sardinia
  and the other islands of the open main.

I and my men were stiff and slow with age
  when we sailed at last into the narrow pass
  where, warning all men back from further voyage,   60

Hercules' Pillars rose upon our sight.
  Already I had left Ceuta on the left;
  Seville now sank behind me on the right.

'Shipmates,' I said, 'who through a hundred thousand
    perils have reached the West, do not deny
    to the brief remaining watch our senses stand

experience of the world beyond the sun.
    Greeks! You were not born to live like brutes,
    but to press on toward manhood and recognition!'

With this brief exhortation I made my crew   70
    so eager for the voyage I could hardly
    have held them back from it when I was through;

and turning our stern toward morning, our bow toward night,
    we bore southwest out of the world of man;
    we made wings of our oars for our fool's flight.

That night we raised the other pole ahead
    with all its stars, and ours had so declined
    it did not rise out of its ocean bed.

Five times since we had dipped our bending oars
    beyond the world, the light beneath the moon   80
    had waxed and waned, when dead upon our course

we sighted, dark in space, a peak* so tall
    I doubted any man had seen the like.
    Our cheers were hardly sounded, when a squall

broke hard upon our bow from the new land:
    three times it sucked the ship and the sea about
    as it pleased Another to order and command.

At the fourth, the poop rose and the bow went down
till the sea closed over us and the light was gone."

---

*Mount Purgatory.

SONNET 5 from *Astrophel and Stella*

Sir Philip Sidney

It is most true that eyes are formed to serve   1
   The inward light, and that the heavenly part
   Ought to be king, from whose rules who do swerve,
   Rebels to nature, strive for their own smart.
It is most true what we call Cupid's dart
   An image is which for ourselves we carve,
   And, fools, adore in temple of our heart
   Till that good god make church and churchman starve.
True, that true beauty virtue is indeed,
   Whereof this beauty can be but a shade,   10
   Which elements with mortal mixture breed.
True, that on earth we are but pilgrims made,
   And should in soul up to our country move;
   True, and yet true that I must Stella love.

PROMETHEUS*

George Gordon, Lord Byron

1

Titan! to whose immortal eyes   1
   The sufferings of mortality,
   Seen in their sad reality,
Were not as things that gods despise;
What was thy pity's recompense?
A silent suffering, and intense;
The rock, the vulture, and the chain,
All that the proud can feel of pain,
The agony they do not show,
The suffocating sense of woe,   10
Which speaks but in its loneliness,
And then is jealous lest the sky
Should have a listener, nor will sigh
   Until its voice is echoless.

2

Titan! to thee the strife was given
   Between the suffering and the will,
   Which torture where they cannot kill;
And the inexorable Heaven,
And the deaf tyranny of Fate,
The ruling principle of Hate,   20
Which for its pleasure doth create
The things it may annihilate,
Refused thee even the boon to die:
The wretched gift Eternity
Was thine—and thou hast borne it well.
All that the Thunderer wrung from thee
Was but the menace which flung back
On him the torments of thy rack;
The fate thou didst so well foresee,
But would not to appease him tell;   30
And in thy Silence was his Sentence,
And in his Soul a vain repentance,
And evil dread so ill dissembled,
That in his hand the lightnings trembled.

---

*Diodati, July 1816.

3

Thy Godlike crime was to be kind,
 To render with thy precepts less
 The sum of human wretchedness,
And strengthen Man with his own mind;
And baffled as thou wert from high,
Still in thy patient energy, 40
In the endurance, and repulse
 Of thine impenetrable Spirit,
Which Earth and Heaven could not convulse,
 A mighty lesson we inherit:
Thou art a symbol and a sign
 To Mortals of their fate and force;
Like thee, Man is in part divine,
 A troubled stream from a pure source;
And Man in portions can foresee
His own funereal destiny; 50
His wretchedness, and his resistance,
And his sad unallied existence:
To which his Spirit may oppose
Itself—and equal to all woes,
 And a firm will, and a deep sense,
 Which even in torture can descry
  Its own concenter'd recompense,
 Triumphant where it dares defy,
 And making Death a Victory.

ULYSSES*

Alfred, Lord Tennyson

It little profits that an idle king,   1
By this still hearth, among these barren crags,
Match'd with an aged wife, I mete and dole
Unequal laws unto a savage race,
That hoard, and sleep, and feed, and know not me.
I cannot rest from travel; I will drink
Life to the lees. All times I have enjoy'd
Greatly, have suffer'd greatly, both with those
That loved me, and alone; on shore, and when
Thro' scudding drifts the rainy Hyades   10
Vext the dim sea. I am become a name;
For always roaming with a hungry heart
Much have I seen and known,—cities of men
And manners, climates, councils, governments,
Myself not least, but honor'd of them all,—
And drunk delight of battle with my peers,
Far on the ringing plains of windy Troy.
I am a part of all that I have met;
Yet all experience is an arch wherethro'
Gleams that untravell'd world whose margin fades   20
For ever and for ever when I move.
How dull it is to pause, to make an end,
To rust unburnish'd, not to shine in use!
As tho' to breathe were life! Life piled on life
Were all too little, and of one to me
Little remains; but every hour is saved
From that eternal silence, something more,
A bringer of new things; and vile it were
For some three suns to store and hoard myself,
And this gray spirit yearning in desire   30
To follow knowledge like a sinking star,
Beyond the utmost bound of human thought.
    This is my son, mine own Telemachus,
To whom I leave the sceptre and the isle,—
Well-loved of me, discerning to fulfil
This labor, by slow prudence to make mild
A rugged people, and thro' soft degrees
Subdue them to the useful and the good.
Most blameless is he, centred in the sphere

---

*First printed in 1842, and unaltered.

Of common duties, decent not to fail   40
In offices of tenderness, and pay
Meet adoration to my household gods,
When I am gone. He works his work, I mine.
   There lies the port; the vessel puffs her sail;
There gloom the dark, broad seas. My mariners,
Souls that have toil'd, and wrought, and thought with me,—
That ever with a frolic welcome took
The thunder and the sunshine, and opposed
Free hearts, free foreheads,—you and I are old;
Old age hath yet his honor and his toil.   50
Death closes all; but something ere the end,
Some work of noble note, may yet be done,
Not unbecoming men that strove with Gods.
The lights begin to twinkle from the rocks;
The long day wanes; the slow moon climbs; the deep
Moans round with many voices. Come, my friends.
'Tis not too late to seek a newer world.
Push off, and sitting well in order smite
The sounding furrows; for my purpose holds
To sail beyond the sunset, and the baths   60
Of all the western stars, until I die.
It may be that the gulfs will wash us down;
It may be we shall touch the Happy Isles,
And see the great Achilles, whom we knew.
Tho' much is taken, much abides; and tho'
We are not now that strength which in old days
Moved earth and heaven, that which we are, we are,—
One equal temper of heroic hearts,
Made weak by time and fate, but strong in will
To strive, to seek, to find, and not to yield.   70

LEDA AND THE SWAN

William Butler Yeats

A sudden blow: the great wings beating still   1
Above the staggering girl, her thighs caressed
By the dark webs, her nape caught in his bill,
He holds her helpless breast upon his breast.

How can those terrified vague fingers push
The feathered glory from her loosening thighs?
And how can body, laid in that white rush,
But feel the strange heart beating where it lies?

A shudder in the loins engenders there
The broken wall, the burning roof and tower   10
And Agamemnon dead.
                        Being so caught up,
So mastered by the brute blood of the air,
Did she put on his knowledge with his power
Before the indifferent beak could let her drop?

THE SHIELD OF ACHILLES

W. H. Auden

        She looked over his shoulder   1
            For vines and olive trees,
        Marble well-governed cities
            And ships upon untamed seas,
        But there on the shining metal
            His hands had put instead
        An artificial wilderness
            And a sky like lead.

A plain without a feature, bare and brown,
    No blade of grass, no sign of neighborhood,   10
Nothing to eat and nowhere to sit down,
    Yet, congregated on its blankness, stood
    An unintelligible multitude,
A million eyes, a million boots in line,
Without expression, waiting for a sign.

Out of the air a voice without a face
    Proved by statistics that some cause was just
In tones as dry and level as the place:
    No one was cheered and nothing was discussed:
    Column by column in a cloud of dust   20
They marched away enduring a belief
Whose logic brought them, somewhere else, to grief.

        She looked over her shoulder
            For ritual pieties,
        White flower-garlanded heifers,
            Libation and sacrifice,
        But there on the shining metal
            Where the altar should have been,
        She saw by his flickering forge-light
            Quite another scene.   30

Barbed wire enclosed an arbitrary spot
    Where bored officials lounged (one cracked a joke)
And sentries sweated for the day was hot:
    A crowd of ordinary decent folk
    Watched from without and neither moved nor spoke
As three pale figures were led forth and bound
To three posts driven upright in the ground.

The mass and majesty of this world, all
    That carries weight and always weighs the same
Lay in the hands of others; they were small   40
    And could not hope for help and no help came:
    What their foes liked to do was done, their shame
Was all the worst could wish; they lost their pride
And died as men before their bodies died.

      She looked over his shoulder
        For athletes at their games,
      Men and women in a dance
        Moving their sweet limbs
      Quick, quick, to music,
        But there on the shining shield   50
      His hands had set no dancing-floor
        But a weed-choked field.

A ragged urchin, aimless and alone,
    Loitered about that vacancy; a bird
Flew up to safety from his well-aimed stone:
    That girls are raped, that two boys knife a third,
    Were axioms to him, who'd never heard
Of any world where promises were kept,
Or one could weep because another wept.

      The thin-lipped armorer,   60
        Hephaestos, hobbled away,
      Thetis of the shining breasts
        Cried out in dismay
      At what the god had wrought
        To please her son, the strong
      Iron-hearted man-slaying Achilles
        Who would not live long.

MUSÉE DES BEAUX ARTS

W. H. Auden

About suffering they were never wrong, 1
The Old Masters: how well they understood
Its human position; how it takes place
While someone else is eating or opening a window or just walking dully along;
How, when the aged are reverently, passionately waiting
For the miraculous birth, there always must be
Children who did not specially want it to happen, skating
On a pond at the edge of the wood:
They never forgot
That even the dreadful martyrdom must run its course 10
Anyhow in a corner, some untidy spot
Where the dogs go on with their doggy life and the torturer's horse
Scratches its innocent behind on a tree.

In Breughel's *Icarus,* for instance: how everything turns away
Quite leisurely from the disaster; the ploughman may
Have heard the splash, the forsaken cry,
But for him it was not an important failure; the sun shone
As it had to on the white legs disappearing into the green
Water; and the expensive delicate ship that must have seen
Something amazing, a boy falling out of the sky, 20
Had somewhere to get to and sailed calmly on.

THE POMEGRANATE

Eavan Boland

The only legend I have ever loved is   1
The story of a daughter lost in hell.
And found and rescued there.
Love and blackmail are the gist of it.
Ceres and Persephone the names.
And the best thing about the legend is
I can enter it anywhere. And have.
As a child in exile in
A city of fogs and strange consonants,
I read it first and at first I was   10
An exiled child in the crackling dusk of
The underworld, the stars blighted. Later
I walked out in a summer twilight
Searching for my daughter at bedtime.
When she came running I was ready
To make any bargain to keep her.
I carried her back past whitebeams.
And wasps and honey-scented buddleias.
But I was Ceres then and I knew
Winter was in store for every leaf   20
On every tree on that road.
Was inescapable for each one we passed.
And for me.
It is winter
And the stars are hidden.
I climb the stairs and stand where I can see
My child asleep beside her teen magazines,
Her can of Coke, her plate of uncut fruit.
The pomegranate! How did I forget it?
She could have come home and been safe   30
And ended the story and all
Our heartbroken searching but she reached
Out a hand and plucked a pomegranate.
She put out her hand and pulled down
The French sound for apple and
The noise of stone and the proof
That even in the place of death,
At the heart of legend, in the midst
Of rocks full of unshed tears
Ready to be diamonds by the time   40
The story was told, a child can be

Hungry. I could warn her. There is still a chance.
The rain is cold. The road is flint-coloured.
The suburb has cars and cable television.
The veiled stars are above ground.
It is another world. But what else
Can a mother give her daughter but such
Beautiful rifts in time?
If I defer the grief I will diminish the gift.
The legend must be hers as well as mine.   50
She will enter it. As I have.
She will wake up. She will hold
The papery, flushed skin in her hand.
And to her lips. I will say nothing.

CASSANDRA, IRAQ

C. K. Williams

1.

She's magnificent, as we imagine women must be
who foresee and foretell and are right and disdained.

This is the difference between we who are like her
in having been right and disdained, and we as we are.

Because we, in our foreseeings, our having been right,
are repulsive to ourselves, fat and immobile, like toads.

Not toads in the garden, who after all are what they are,
but toads in the tale of death in the desert of sludge.

2.

In this tale of lies, of treachery, of superfluous dead,
were there ever so many who were right and disdained?

With no notion of what to do next? If we were true seers,
as prescient as she, as frenzied, we'd know what to do next.

We'd twitter, as she did, like birds; we'd warble, we'd trill.
But what would it be really, to *twitter,* to *warble,* to *trill?*

Is it *ee-ee-ee,* like having a child? Is it *uh-uh-uh,* like a wound?
Or is it inside, like a blow, silent to everyone but yourself?

3.

Yes, inside, I remember, *oh-oh-oh:* it's where grief
is just about to be spoken, but all at once can't be: *oh.*

When you no longer can "think" of what things like lies,
like superfluous dead, so many, might mean: *oh.*

Cassandra will be abducted at the end of her tale, and die.
Even she can't predict how. Stabbed? Shot? Blown to bits?

Her abductor dies, too, though, in a gush of gore, in a net.
That we know; she foresaw that—in a gush of gore, in a net.

. . . .

Questions for Discussion and Review

1. How does Dante portray Ulysses's motives and goals? How is his portrayal in the *Inferno* different from Homer's portrayal in the *Odyssey?* Where does Dante's Ulysses sail to on his last voyage? Why is he punished for it? How does Dante's version of Ulysses's last voyage differ from Tennyson's?

2. (a) Explain Yeats's interpretation of the tragedy of Troy in his poem "Leda and the Swan." (b) Contrast Yeats's poem with Dali's painting *Leda Atomica* (see Figure 21-3). Explain Leda's role in bringing about the war in the painting and in the poem, and compare it with Zeus's role. Why is Zeus not named in the poem or pictured in the painting?

3. Compare W. H. Auden's "The Shield of Achilles" with Homer's description of the shield in the *Iliad*. How do the differences reflect ancient versus modern beliefs or values? How does each portray war?

4. Compare Salvador Dali's *Venus de Milo of the Drawers* (see Figure 21-19), with the original *Venus de Milo* (see Figure 21-10). What does Dali's version suggest about the goddess of love? Why did the modern artist depict the figure with drawers? What does the sculpture suggest those drawers might contain?

5. (a) How does the Breughel painting *The Fall of Icarus* (Color Plate 12) comment on the Renaissance interpretation of Icarus as a tragic hero? (b) How does W. H. Auden's sonnet "Musée des Beaux Arts" comment on Breughel's painting? Is Auden's view more like the Renaissance view or more like Breughel's?

6. In a detailed analysis of Rubens's *Rape of the Daughters of Leucippus* and Poussin's *Rape of the Sabine Women* (see Figures 21-6 and 21-7), explain how the two paintings present different interpretations of this event from Roman mythology. How do the choices of a close-up view versus greater distance, of few versus many figures, and of a rural versus an urban setting affect the interpretation portrayed in each painting?

7. Choose two illustrations from the section "Versions of Venus" (see Figures 21-10 through 21-19), and compare and contrast the two artists' views of the goddess. If possible, relate the differences to the times in which each artist lived.

8. Compare the figure of Prometheus in Byron's poem with that of Aeschylus's *Prometheus Bound*. What political and moral values are associated with each figure?

9. Discuss the metaphor of Cupid, the "god of love," in Sidney's sonnet from *Astrophel and Stella*. What attitude toward Cupid is present? How does the poet's use of Cupid reflect his attitude toward the woman he loves? Explain how the image of Cupid is related to the poet's own religious beliefs.

(The following questions require outside sources.)

10. Read either Sophocles' or Euripides' version of *Electra,* and compare it to Aeschylus's Oresteian trilogy. How do the playwrights' interpretations of the major characters and of the roles of the gods differ? What purpose do the minor characters each author introduces serve in reinforcing the particular play's perspective?

11. Read Jean Anouilh's play *Antigone,* and compare it to Sophocles' version. How does each playwright portray the protagonist (Antigone) and the antagonist (Creon)?

How do their personal and political motives differ? How does each play reflect contemporary problems or concerns in the world of the author?

12. Choose one chapter from Joyce's novel *Ulysses* or one scene from Derek Walcott's *The Odyssey: A Stage Version,* and compare it with the corresponding book in Homer's *Odyssey*. What do they have in common? What did the modern author do to make the Homeric poem relevant to the twentieth-century reader?

13. Watch the film *The Natural* (1984, directed by Barry Levinson). In what specific ways are the film and its hero like the *Iliad*? In what specific ways do they resemble the *Odyssey*? How is the modern sports hero similar to or different from the ancient epic hero in his inner nature, his relationship with his peers, and the problems he encounters?

14. Read Cavafy's poem "Ithaca," and compare his portrayal of Odysseus's journey with that of either Tennyson or Homer. What remains constant in the two versions? What changes?

Works Cited

Cavafy, Constantine. *The Complete Poems of Cavafy.* Trans. Rae Dalven. New York: Harcourt Brace Jovanovich, 1976.

Marlowe, Christopher. *The Tragic History of Doctor Faustus.* New York: Appleton, 1950.

Pope, Alexander. *The Best of Pope.* Ed. George Sherburn. 1929. New York: Ronald, 1940.

Shelley, Mary Wollstonecraft. *Frankenstein, or the Modern Prometheus.* New York: New American Library, 1965.

Shelley, Percy Bysshe. *Poetical Works.* Ed. Thomas Hutchinson and G. M. Matthews. Oxford: Oxford UP, 1970.

A Selected List of Primary Works That Reinterpret Classical Myths

Fiction

Atwood, Margaret. *The Penelopiad* (2006).

Barth, John. *Chimera* (1972).

Frazier, Charles. *Cold Mountain* (1998).

Joyce, James. *Portrait of the Artist as a Young Man* (1916).

———. *Ulysses* (1922).

Malamud, Bernard. *The Natural* (1952).

Mukherjee, Bharati. *Jasmine* (1989).

Murakami, Haruki. *Kafka on the Shore* (2002).

Roth, Philip. *The Human Stain* (2001).

Rushdie, Salman. *The Ground Beneath Her Feet* (1999).

Shelley, Mary Wollstonecraft. *Frankenstein, or the Modern Prometheus* (1818).

Updike, John. *The Centaur* (1962).

Winterson, Jeanette. *Weight* (2006).

Poetry

Auden, W. H. "Musée des Beaux Arts" (1938).

———. "The Shield of Achilles" (1952).

Boland, Eavan. "The Pomegranate" (1994).

Byron, George Gordon, Lord. "Prometheus" (1816).

Cavafy, Constantine. "Ithaca" (1911).

Dante. *Divine Comedy* (1314–1321).

H. D. (Hilda Doolittle). "Eurydice" (1917, 1925).

Jarrell, Randall. "The Birth of Venus" (1952).

———. "Orestes at Tauris" (1948).

———. "The Sphinx's Riddle to Oedipus" (1960).

Lawrence, D. H. "The Argonauts" (1933).

Lowell, Robert. "Falling Asleep over the *Aeneid*" (1950).

Milosz, Czeslaw. "Orpheus and Eurydice" (2006).

Plath, Sylvia. "Two Sisters of Persephone" (1951).

Rukeyser, Muriel. "Myth" (1973).

Shakespeare, William. "Venus and Adonis" (1593).

Tennyson, Alfred, Lord. "Ulysses" (1842).

Williams, C. K. "Cassandra, Iraq" (2006).

Yeats, William Butler. "Colonus' Praise" (1928).

———. "Leda and the Swan" (1923).

Drama

Abdoh, Reza. *The Hip-Hop Waltz of Eurydice* (1991).

Alfaro, Luis. *Electricidad* (2007).

Anouilh, Jean. *Antigone* (1944).

———. *Eurydice* (1941).

———. *Medea* (1946).

Cocteau, Jean. *La Machine Infernale* (1934).

———. *Orpheus* (1927).

Eliot, T. S. *Family Reunion* (1935).

Gide, André. *Oedipus* (1931).

———. *Theseus* (1946).

Giraudoux, Jean. *Amphitryon 38* (1938).

———. *Electra* (1937).

O'Neill, Eugene. *Desire Under the Elms* (1924).

———. *Mourning Becomes Electra* (1931).

Racine, Jean. *Andromache* (1667).

———. *Iphigenia at Aulis* (1674).

———. *Phaedre* (1677).

Sartre, Jean-Paul. *The Flies* (1943).

Shelley, Percy Bysshe. *Prometheus Unbound* (1811).

Walcott, Derek. *The Odyssey: A Stage Version* (1992).

Williams, Tennessee. *Orpheus Descending* (1957).

Painting

Botticelli, Sandro. *Birth of Venus* (1480).

———. *Venus and Mars* (1485).

Boucher, François. *The Toilet of Venus* (1740).

Breughel, Pieter, the Elder. *The Fall of Icarus* (1555–1556).

Bronzino, Agnolo. *Allegory of Venus* (1550).

Cousin, Jean, the Elder. *Eva Prima Pandora* (1538).

Cranach, Lucas, the Elder. *Judgment of Paris* (1530).

———. *Venus* (1532).

Dali, Salvador. *Apotheosis of Homer* (1945).

———. *Leda Atomica.* (1948).

———. *The Metamorphosis of Narcissus* (1936–1937).

Delacroix, Eugene. *Dante and Vergil in Hell* (1822).

El Greco. *Laocoon* (1610).

Ingres, Jean-Auguste-Dominique. *Apotheosis of Homer* (1827).

———. *Oedipus and the Sphinx* (1808).

Lorrain, Claude. *Coast View of Delos with Aeneas* (1672).

Pascin, Jules. *Back View of Venus* (1924–1925).

Picasso, Pablo. *Minotauromachia* (1935).

———. *Ovid's Metamorphoses* [etchings] (1931).

Poussin, Nicolas. *Mars and Venus* (1630).

———. *Rape of the Sabine Women* (1636–1637).

Rubens, Peter Paul. *Rape of the Daughters of Leucippus* (1618).

———. *The Toilet of Venus* (1613).

Tintoretto. *The Marriage of Bacchus and Ariadne* (c. 1577–1588).

Titian. *Bacchus and Ariadne* (1520).

———. *Venus and Adonis* (1562).

———. *Venus of Urbino* (1538).

———. *Venus with the Mirror* (1555).

Sculpture

Bernini, Gianlorenzo. *Apollo and Daphne* (1622–1625).

Canova, Antonio. *Napoleon* (1802–1810).

———. *Pauline Bonaparte as Venus* (1808).

Cellini, Benvenuto. *Perseus and Medusa* (1545–1554).

Dali, Salvador. *Venus de Milo of the Drawers* (1936).

Girardon, François. *Apollo Attended by the Nymphs* (c. 1666–1672).

Maillol, Arestide. *Torso of Venus* (1925).

Pollaiuolo, Antonio. *Hercules Strangling Antaeus* (c. 1475).

Music

Barber, Patricia. *Metamorphoses* (2006).

Beethoven, Ludwig von. *The Creatures of Prometheus* (1801).

Berlioz, Hector. *The Trojans* (1856–1858).

Britten, Benjamin. *Phaedra* (1975).

Faure, Gabriel. *Penelope* (1913).

Gabrieli, Giovanni. *Oedipus Tyrannus* (1585).

Gluck, Christoph Willibald. *Echo and Narcissus* (1779).

———. *Iphigenia Among the Taurians* (1779).

———. *Iphigenia at Aulis* (1774).

———. *Orpheus and Eurydice* (1762).

Handel, George Frideric. *Hercules* (1745).

———. *Semele* (1743).

Haydn, Franz Joseph. *Orpheus and Eurydice* (1791).

Monteverdi, Claudio. *Orpheus* (1607).

———. *The Return of Ulysses* (1637).

Offenbach, Jacques. *Orpheus in the Underworld* (1858).

Parry, Sir Charles Hasting Hubert. *Prometheus Unbound* (1880).

Purcell, Henry. *Dido and Aeneas* (1689).

Rinuccini, Ottavio. *Eurydice* (1600).

Strauss, Richard. *Ariadne on Naxos* (1916).

———. *Electra* (1909).

Stravinsky, Igor. *Oedipus Rex* (1927).

———. *Persephone* (1934).

Walton, William. *Troilus and Cressida* (1954).

Film

Black Orpheus. Directed by Marcel Camus (1958).

Clash of the Titans. Directed by Desmond Davis (1981).

The Fugitive Kind. Directed by Sidney Lumet (1960).

The Natural. Directed by Barry Levinson (1984).

O Brother, Where Art Thou? Directed by Joel and Ethan Coen (2000).

Orpheus. Directed by Jean Cocteau (1949).

Medea. Directed by Pier Pasolini (1970).

Troy. Directed by Wolfgang Petersen (2004).

Dance

Barber, Samuel. *Cave of the Heart (Medea's Meditation and Dance of Vengeance)* (for Martha Graham, 1946).

Noverre, Jean Georges. *Medea and Jason* (1763).

Stravinsky, Igor. *Apollo* (choreographed by George Balanchine, 1928).

Mixed Media (Photography, Dance, Poetry, Drama, Internet)

Mee, Charles. *Orestes 2.0* (2001).

Tracy, Ann. *Orestes 2.5* (2002).

Trager, Philip, and Ralph Lemon. *Persephone* (1996).

Glossary

Achaeans   Homer's most common term for the Greeks who besieged Troy; he also called them *Argives* or *Danaans*.

Achates   In Virgil's *Aeneid,* the faithful friend and companion of Aeneas.

Acheron [AK-e-rahn]   One of the main rivers of Hades's realm.

Achilles [a-KIL-leez]   Son of the sea nymph Thetis and the mortal Peleus; in Homer's *Iliad,* the most formidable Greek warrior at Troy.

Acropolis   In Athens, the steep fortified hill atop which stand the Parthenon and other temples dedicated to Athene.

Actaeon [ak-TEE-ahn]   The son of Aristaeus and Autonoe, daughter of Cadmus. When he offended Artemis, either by boasting of his superior hunting abilities or by observing her bathing, the goddess changed him into a stag, and he was torn apart by his hounds.

Adam   According to the Book of Genesis, the first human being, whom Yahweh eventually divided into male and female; his name means "humankind."

Admetus   The king of Pherae in Thessaly whom Apollo served as shepherd in penance for having slain the Python at Delphi. According to a variant of the myth, Zeus forced Apollo to serve Admetus after the god had killed the Cyclops, who had created the thunderbolt Zeus used in slaying Apollo's son Asclepius.

Adonis   The youth whom Aphrodite (Venus) loved and who was slain by a wild boar. He resembles certain aspects of Dionysus in that he is a male fertility figure symbolizing the natural cycle of vegetative growth, death, and regeneration.

Aegeus [EE-jee-uhs]   King of Athens and father of the hero Theseus, he gave refuge to Medea after she escaped from Corinth. When he thought Theseus had been killed by the Minotaur, he committed suicide by leaping into the sea named after him.

aegis [EE-jis]   The breastplate of Zeus—a protective garment decorated with a Gorgon's head and surrounded by a fringe of snakes—commonly worn by Athene in her role as goddess of victory.

Aegisthus [ee-JIS-thuhs]   Son of Thyestes and his daughter Pelopia, he became Clytemnestra's lover and was slain by Orestes.

Aeneas [ee-NEE-as]   Son of Aphrodite (Venus) and Anchises, a mortal Trojan prince, and the hero of Virgil's *Aeneid.* After Troy's fall, he journeyed to Italy, where he founded a dynasty that eventually produced Romulus and Remus, the legendary founders of Rome.

Aeolus   Greek god of the winds.

Aesculapius   Latin name for Asclepius.

Agamemnon   Son of Atreus and brother of Menelaus, he was commander in chief of the Greek expedition against Troy. Murdered by his wife Clytemnestra, he was avenged by his children Orestes and Electra.

Agave [a-GAY-vee]   Daughter of Harmonia and King Cadmus (founder of Thebes), she was the sister of Semele, Ino, and Autonoe and the mother of Pentheus.

agon   In Greek drama, the term denoting the contest, struggle, or conflict between the principal characters.

Ajax   A leading Greek warrior in the Trojan War who went mad after losing a contest to Odysseus for Achilles' armor. His name is also spelled *Aias.*

Alba Longa   In the *Aeneid,* an Italian city founded by Aeneas's son Ascanius.

Alcestis   Title character of Euripides' tragedy about a wife who volunteered to die in place of her husband, Admetus.

Alcinous [al-SIN-oh-uhs]   King of the Phaeacians, husband of Arete, and father of Nausicaa, he received Odysseus hospitably on his island of Scheria (traditionally identified as Corfu).

Alcmene   The wife of Amphitryon and mother of Heracles, she was said to be the last of the mortal women seduced by Zeus.

Alexandros   Another name for Paris, the Trojan prince who abducted Helen.

Allecto   One of the Furies called up from the Underworld in the *Aeneid*.

allegory   A literary narrative in which persons, places, and events are given a symbolic meaning.

Amata   Queen of Latium and mother of Lavinia, whom Aeneas married.

Amazons   A tribe of formidable female warriors who lived apart from men.

ambrosia   Food of the Olympian gods.

amor [ah-MOHR]   In Roman myth, a personification of love.

Amphitryon   Son of Alceus (son of Perseus), he married Alcmene and became the father of Iphicles, Heracles' half-brother.

anagnorisis   In tragedy, the recognition scene in which a character discovers a previously unknown fact or relationship.

Anchises   Trojan prince, father of the hero Aeneas by Aphrodite.

Andromache [an-DROM-a-kee]   Wife of Hector, Troy's leading defender, and mother of Astyanax.

Andromeda   A maiden chained to a rock as prey for a sea monster. She was rescued by Perseus, who then turned her uncle Phineus to stone by showing him the head of Medusa.

anima   Jungian term for the feminine principle residing in the male psyche.

animus   Jungian term for the masculine principle residing in the female psyche.

Antenor   A wise Trojan counselor, he advocated Helen's return to the Greeks.

anthropomorphism   The practice of attributing human characteristics to something not human; particularly, ascribing human form to a deity.

Anticleia [an-tih-KLEE-a]   Daughter of Autolycus, wife of Laertes, and mother of Odysseus, she died mourning for her son during his long absence from Ithaca. Her ghost appeared to Odysseus in the Underworld.

Antigone [an-TIG-oh-nee]   Daughter of Oedipus and Jocasta, she was her blinded father's guide in Sophocles' *Oedipus at Colonus* and the heroine of *Antigone*.

Aphrodite [af-roh-DYE-tee] (Venus)   Goddess of love and beauty; in Hesiod, she was born from the castration of Uranus; in Homer, she was the daughter of Zeus and Dione.

Apollo   Son of Zeus and Leto, he is also called *Phoebus*, the radiant god of light, music, prophecy, and the arts. His most famous shrine was at Delphi, where his priestess, the Pythia, proclaimed the divine will. His son, Asclepius, the first physician, was patron of the healing arts.

Arcadia   A mountainous region in the south of Greece, sacred to Pan, Hermes, and Apollo, and associated with shepherds.

Archaic period   The period of Greek history, roughly 800–480 B.C., characterized by the rise of the polis and other distinctively Greek institutions, including the creation of the Homeric epics.

archetype   The primal form or original pattern from which all other things of a like nature are descended. In myth, the term refers to characters, ideas, or actions that represent the supreme and/or essential examples of a universal type, components of the "collective unconscious."

Areopagus   The "hill of Ares (Mars)," a spur of the Athenian Acropolis, where Athene established a court for homicides; the site of Orestes' trial in the *Eumenides*.

Ares [AR-eez] (Mars)   Son of Zeus and Hera, he is the personification of male aggression and the fighting spirit, an unpopular god in Greece but highly respected in Rome, where he was identified with Mars, an Italian god of agriculture and war.

Arete [a-REE-tee]   Wife of Alcinous, king of the Phaeacians, she was noted for her wisdom and hospitality.

Argives   Homeric term for the Greeks who fought at Troy; virtually interchangeable with *Achaeans* or *Danaans*.

Argonauts Fifty Greek heroes who sailed with Jason aboard the *Argo* to obtain the Golden Fleece.

Argos The region ruled by Agamemnon, whose capital was Mycenae.

Argus (1) The hundred-eyed monster whom Hera appointed to spy on Zeus; when Hermes killed him, Hera placed his eyes in the peacock's tail. (2) The faithful dog of Odysseus who died immediately after recognizing that his master had returned to Ithaca.

Ariadne [ar-ih-AD-nee] Daughter of Minos and Pasiphae, king and queen of Knossos on Crete, and sister of Phaedra. After helping Theseus to kill the Minotaur and fleeing Crete with him, she was abandoned by Theseus on the island of Naxos, where Dionysus married her and made her immortal.

Aristotle Greek philosopher (384–322 B.C.), a disciple of Plato, and tutor of Alexander of Macedonia. A scientist and logician, he also wrote the *Poetics,* a work of literary criticism.

Artemis [AR-te-mis] (Diana) Daughter of Zeus and Leto and twin sister of Apollo, she is virgin goddess of wildlife and the hunt. Although her arrows can inflict the pains of childbirth, she champions women's societies, such as that formed by the Amazons.

Ascanius [as-KAY-nih-uhs] Son of Aeneas by the Trojan princess Creusa. He is also called *Iulus.*

Asclepius [as-KLEE-pee-uhs] (Aesculapius) Son of Apollo and Coronis, the Greek founder and patron of medicine. When his skills brought the dead back to life, Zeus killed him with a thunderbolt.

Atalanta A virgin huntress who competed with the heroes in their athletic contests and heroic adventures, including the expedition of the Argonauts and the Calydonian Boar Hunt. She refused to marry unless a suitor could defeat her in a footrace at which losers would be killed. Either Hippomenes or Milanion distracted her by scattering three of Aphrodite's golden apples and won the race.

Ate Minor goddess personifying moral blindness.

Athene [uh-THEE-nuh] (Minerva) Virgin daughter of Zeus born from her father's brain, she was goddess of wisdom, women's handicrafts, and victory in war.

Athens Dominant Greek city-state during the fifth century B.C., center of the intellectual and artistic developments that created the historical Golden Age.

Atlantis According to Plato's *Timaeus* and *Critias,* a legendary civilization that sank beneath the sea, perhaps a Minoan city on the volcanic island of Thera (Santorini) that was obliterated by an eruption in 1628 B.C.

Atlas Titan brother of Prometheus whom Zeus ordered to hold up the broad vault of the sky.

Atreides Homeric term meaning "son of Atreus," referring to Agamemnon or Menelaus. (The plural is *Atreidae.*)

Atreus [AY-tre-uhs] A son of Pelops and king of Mycenae, he was the father of Agamemnon and Menelaus.

Atropos One of the three Fates, she blindly cut the thread of life spun and measured by her sisters Clotho and Lachesis.

Attica Province in east-central Greece ruled by Athens.

Attis Young male consort of the Phrygian goddess Cybele, who drove him mad so that he castrated himself.

Augustus First Roman emperor (30 B.C.–A.D. 14), and indirect sponsor of Virgil's *Aeneid.*

Aulis Seaport at which Greek troops assembled before sailing to Troy; site of Iphigenia's sacrifice.

Aurora [ah-ROR-uh] The Roman goddess of dawn, a counterpart of the Greek Eos, daughter of Hyperion and Theia.

autochthon One supposedly sprung from the ground he or she inhabits, a person derived from earth.

Autolycus [ah-TUHL-ih-kuhs] A son of Hermes infamous for his trickery, he was the father of Anticleia, mother of Odysseus.

bacchae Female worshipers of Dionysus (Bacchus).

bacchants Ecstatic worshipers of Dionysus (Bacchus).

Bacchus [BAH-kuhs] Another name for Dionysus.

Baucis The aged wife of Philemon, rewarded for her hospitality.

Bellerophon [bel-LER-oh-fahn] Son of Glaucus (son of Sisyphus) who killed the Chimaera and defeated the Amazons; he tried to ride to heaven on the winged horse Pegasus. He is also called *Bellerophontes.*

Boeotia A fertile province bordering Attica in central Greece, the principal city of which was Thebes.

Boreas Personification of the North Wind.

Brauronia A Greek festival featuring an initiation rite for young girls, who ran races as bears in honor of Artemis.

Briseis Daughter of Brises (ally of the Trojans) and the captive of Achilles whom Agamemnon confiscated, provoking the wrath that ignited the *Iliad*'s action.

Bromius Another name for Dionysus.

Bronze (Age of) See **Five Ages.**

Cadmus Founder and king of Thebes, husband of Harmonia, and father of Agave, Autonoe, Ino, and Semele. As a young man, he slew a dragon and (by Athene's direction) planted its teeth, from which warriors sprang up. These fought among themselves until only five remained alive; the surviving five built Thebes and were the ancestors of the Theban aristocracy.

caduceus A wand entwined by two serpents and topped by a pair of wings, emblematic of Hermes as Zeus's personal messenger and herald; it is also associated with Asclepius, god of healing.

Caesar, Julius Roman general, statesman, and dictator (100–44 B.C.); after conquering Gaul (France), Caesar led his armies across the Rubicon into Italy, where his presumed ambition to make himself king triggered his assassination.

Calchas Prophet who accompanied the Achaeans to Troy.

Calliope Muse of epic poetry invoked by Homer and Hesiod.

Callisto A virgin follower of Artemis, raped by Zeus and turned into a bear. In one version of her myth, she was nearly shot by her son Arcas but was rescued by Zeus, who transformed her into the Great Bear constellation.

Calypso Minor goddess embodying female sexuality who held Odysseus captive for seven years on the island of Ogygia.

Carthage Powerful colony of Tyre on the north coast of Africa, directly south of Rome. The chief threat to Roman imperialism, it was destroyed by Scipio Africanus in 146 B.C.

Cassandra Daughter of Priam and Hecuba, she was Apollo's virgin prophet; part of Agamemnon's booty from Troy, she was brought to Argos, where Clytemnestra murdered her.

Castor and **Pollux** (Polydeuces) Twin brothers celebrated for their devotion to each other, they were born from the same union of Zeus and Leda that produced Helen and Clytemnestra.

catharsis Aristotle's term for the emotional effect of tragedy, the purging or cleansing of the emotions of pity and fear.

centaur A creature half-man, half-horse; symbol of humanity's divided nature.

Cerberus [SER-ber-uhs] The three-headed watchdog of Hades.

Ceres [SEE-reez] Roman equivalent of Demeter, goddess of grain and earth's fertility.

Chaos In Hesiod, a yawning chasm, one of four primal entities from which the universe evolved. In Ovid, it was the primal disorder or dark confusion of matter that was later shaped into an ordered system (cosmos).

Charon [KA-rohn] Ancient boatman of the Underworld who ferried souls across the River Styx, the symbolic boundary between life and death.

charter myths Traditional tales that serve to justify or validate some custom or practice, such as Hesiod's story about Prometheus's tricking Zeus into accepting an inferior sacrifice.

Charybdis [ka-RIB-dis] Female monster who, with Scylla, guarded the Straits of Messina between Italy and Sicily; a whirlpool that sucked ships underwater.

Chimaera A fire-breathing monster with a lion's head, goat's body, and dragon's tail, traditionally an inhabitant of Hades' realm.

Chiron [KYE-rahn] A wise old centaur who tutored several famous heroes, including Jason and Achilles.

chorus The band of dancers and singers that performs in a Greek play, sometimes participating in the action but more commonly commenting on and interpreting the principal characters' actions.

Chryseis In the *Iliad,* daughter of Chryses (priest of Apollo) whom Agamemnon was forced to return to her father after the god inflicted a plague on the Greek army.

Chrysothemis Daughter of Agamemnon and Clytemnestra, a sister of Electra and Orestes.

chthonic [THOH-nik] Term relating to earth or the infernal regions, commonly associated with goddesses of fertility and/or death and regeneration.

Circe [SIR-see] In the *Odyssey,* the enchantress who turned the hero's men into swine; she instructed Odysseus on the way to Hades' kingdom and warned him of Scylla and Charybdis. According to some myths, Odysseus fathered a son, Telegonus, by her.

City (or Great) Dionysia An annual festival in Athens honoring Dionysus during which tragedies, comedies, and other dramatic and musical performances were staged.

Classical period The period of Greek history, roughly 480–323 B.C., characterized by phenomenal creativity in art, architecture, drama, history, philosophy, and science.

Clio The Muse of history.

Clotho One of the three fates. (See **Atropos.**)

Clytemnestra [klye-tem-NES-tra] The leading female character in the *Oresteia,* she was the daughter of Tyndareus (or Zeus) and Leda, sister of Helen, wife of Agamemnon, mistress of Aegisthus, and mother of Iphigenia, Electra, Chrysothemis, and Orestes. After murdering Agamemnon, she was slain by Orestes.

Cocytus [koh-SYE-tuhs] One of the four main rivers of the Underworld, it is the River of Lamentation (Wailing).

Colchis Home of Medea, on the remote shores of the Black Sea.

Colonus Suburb of Athens, birthplace of Sophocles, and site of Oedipus's death.

cosmogony A theory about the origin or birth of the universe (cosmos).

cosmology A theory or belief describing the natural order or structure of the universe.

cosmos Greek term for the harmonious structure of the universe.

Creon [KREE-on] (1) Greek word for ruler. (2) In Sophocles' Theban plays, Jocasta's brother. (3) In Euripides' *Medea,* king of Corinth.

Creusa [kree-OO-sa] (1) In the *Aeneid,* daughter of Priam, first wife of Aeneas, and mother of Ascanius (Iulus); she was killed in the fall of Troy. (2) In the *Medea,* the daughter of Corinth's king, Jason's intended bride.

Croesus King of Lydia (560–546 B.C.), famous for his great wealth. His kingdom was captured by Cyrus, founder of the Persian Empire.

Cronus [KROH-nuhs] Titan son of Gaea (Gaia) and Uranus, he deposed his father and ruled the cosmos until overthrown by his youngest son, Zeus. The Romans later identified him with Saturn.

Cumaean Sibyl [koo-MEE-an SIB-il] Italian counterpart of the Delphic Oracle, her shrine was located at Cumae, the oldest Greek colony in the Bay of Naples region. In the *Aeneid,* she acted as Aeneas's guide through the Underworld.

cuneiform [kue-NEE-uh-form] The wedge-shaped script invented by the ancient Sumerians about 3200 B.C. and later adopted by the Akkadians and other Mesopotamian peoples; the earliest form of writing.

Cupid   The Latin name for Eros, god of love.

Cybele [SIB-e-lee]   Asiatic mother goddess whom the Greeks identified with Rhea. Many of her priests were eunuchs, supposedly imitating the self-castration of Cybele's lover Attis.

Cyclopes   (1) The three sons of Gaea and Uranus: Brontes (Thunder), Steropes (Lightning), and Arges (Thunderbolt). Zeus released them from Tartarus, where Cronus had confined them, and enlisted their help in overthrowing the Titans. (2) In the *Odyssey*, a race of savage, one-eyed giants who lived in caves on Sicily. (The singular is *cyclops*.) (See **Polyphemus.**)

Cynthia   Epithet of Artemis, particularly when identified with the moon.

Cyparissus   A son of Telephus who, for his unusually good looks, was beloved by several gods, including Zephyrus and Apollo. When Cyparissus accidentally killed the stag that was his favorite companion, he asked heaven to let him grieve forever. As a result, he was changed into a cypress, the tree of mourning.

Cypris   Epithet for Aphrodite, who was supposed to have emerged from the sea on the shores of Cyprus.

Daedalus [DEE-duh-luhs]   Master architect who designed the labyrinth at Knossos for King Minos. When Minos tried to keep him and his son Icarus prisoner on Crete, Daedalus fashioned wings for their escape. (See **Icarus.**)

Danaans   Another term for *Achaeans*.

Danae [DA-na-ee]   Mother of the hero Perseus, who was sired by Zeus in a shower of gold. Cast into the sea in a chest with her son, Danae was unexpectedly rescued. (See **Perseus.**)

Daphne   A nymph beloved of Apollo, she was changed into a laurel tree, the leaves of which were thereafter sacred to the god.

Dardanus   Legendary founder of Troy, he and his descendants were persecuted by Hera because Zeus had been the lover of his mother, Electra, a daughter of the Titan Atlas whom Zeus changed into a star, one of the Pleiades; when Troy fell, Electra left the constellation and became a comet.

Dark Ages (Greek)   The obscure period of Greek history following the collapse of Mycenaean civilization about 1100 B.C. It ended with the Greek renaissance in Ionia during the eighth century B.C.

Deianeira [dee-ya-NYE-ra]   Second wife of Heracles.

Deiphobus   Son of Priam and Hecuba, he was the prince of Troy who married Helen after Paris's death.

Delos   Aegean island sacred to Apollo and Artemis, and the site of their birth.

Delphi [DEL-phee]   Ancient shrine of prophecy on the slopes of Mount Parnassus, site of Apollo's Oracle. Formerly a sanctuary of Themis and other chthonic goddesses, it was earlier called Pytho.

Delphic Oracle   The priestess (Pythia) who acted as Apollo's mouthpiece or prophet at Delphi, the most sacred prophetic institution in Greece.

Demeter [de-MEE-ter] (Ceres)   Daughter of Cronus and Rhea, she was the Olympian goddess of agricultural fertility. Her myth is closely related to that of her daughter Persephone. (See **Persephone.**)

Demodocus [de-MAH-dah-kuhs]   In the *Odyssey*, the Phaeacian bard or minstrel who sang of the Trojan War at King Alcinous's court.

Demophon   (1) Son of Celeus and Metanira and the younger brother of Triptolemus. When searching for Persephone, Demeter became Demophon's nursemaid and tried to make him immortal by holding him in the fire, until the process was interrupted by the child's mother. (2) The son of Theseus and Phaedra (or Ariadne) who fought in the Trojan War.

Deucalion   The son of Prometheus, who is warned by his father of Zeus's plan to drown the human race in a global flood. Prometheus instructs Deucalion to build a boat for himself and his wife Pyrrha. After the deluge, Deucalion and Pyrrha have a son, Hellen, eponymous ancestor of the Greeks. Ovid tells the story in his *Metamorphoses.*

deus ex machina The "god from the machine," a mechanical device used in Greek theater production to lift an actor impersonating a god onto the stage. The term refers to the practice of introducing a divine being to resolve problems that human characters cannot untangle.

Diana The Latin name for Artemis, goddess of the hunt and commonly identified with the moon.

Dido [DYE-doh] Queen and founder of Carthage, she befriended the shipwrecked Aeneas and was later deserted by him at Jupiter's command.

Diomede(s) [dye-oh-MEE-deez] Youngest and one of the most effective Greek fighters in the Trojan War, he even battled against Ares and Aphrodite.

Dione According to some traditions, Titan mother of Aphrodite.

Dionysus [dye-oh-NYE-suhs] Son of Zeus and Semele and god of the vine that produces wine, he was a male fertility figure who represented a great variety of natural forces, including the vegetative cycle of life, growth, death, and rebirth, and the conflicting power of human passions. He is also called *Bacchus, Bromius,* and *Liber.*

Dionysus Zagreus [dye-oh-NYE-suhs ZAG-re-uhs] In the Orphic version of the Dionysus myth, a son of Zeus and Persephone swallowed by Zeus and reborn as the son of Zeus and Semele.

dioscuri Term meaning "youths of god (Zeus)," refers to Castor and Pollux (Polydeuces, Greek form of Latinized name), twin sons of Zeus and Leda.

Dirae Roman name for the Furies.

Dis Latin name for Hades or Pluto, god of the Underworld.

dithyramb [DITH-ih-ram] Ecstatic dance or choral song performed in honor of Dionysus, out of which tragedy is said to have evolved.

divination Ancient practice of trying to foretell the future from such phenomena as the flight of birds or the condition of internal organs in sacrificial animals.

Dorians A Greek people, distinctive linguistically and culturally from other Greeks, who controlled Argos and Sparta following the Mycenaean collapse.

dragon A monstrous serpent or other reptile, commonly with wings, that typically represented chaotic or evil forces.

Echo Wood nymph cursed by Hera, she wasted away to a mere voice for the unrequited love of Narcissus.

Eden In biblical tradition, a primordial garden from which the first human couple was banished; it represents one version of humanity's lost Golden Age, a theme also found in Hesiod.

ego Latin first-person pronoun, the "I" that Freud's translators use to designate the center of individual consciousness.

Eileithyia(e) [ye-lye-THYE-ya] Daughter of Hera, a minor goddess of childbirth.

Electra Daughter of Agamemnon and Clytemnestra and sister of Orestes, she conspired with her brother to avenge their murdered father.

Eleusinian [el-oo-SIN-ee-uhn] **Mysteries** A cult at the town of Eleusis involving the worship of Demeter, Persephone, and Triptolemus. Initiates were sworn to secrecy.

Elpenor In the *Odyssey,* one of the hero's crew who dies after falling from the roof of Circe's palace; at Hades' portal, his ghost appears to Odysseus asking for proper burial.

Elysium [e-LIZ-ih-uhm], or **Elysian fields** A posthumous realm of earthly delights reserved for those especially favored by the gods.

Endymion A handsome shepherd boy with whom the moon goddess Selene fell in love; he sleeps eternally.

Enuma Elish Ancient Babylonian creation epic celebrating Marduk's victory over an older generation of gods, a Near Eastern counterpart to Hesiod's *Theogony.*

Eos [EE-ohs] A personification of the dawn, she was the sister of Selene and Helios and later identified by the Romans with Aurora.

ephebe A class of Greek youths, approximately eighteen to twenty years old, who underwent systematic educational and physical training to serve the polis as hoplites.

epic A long narrative poem, in exalted and sometimes deliberately archaic style, that recounts the adventures, in war or travel, of a national hero whose qualities represent the essential values of his society. The Homeric epic typically employs a number of standard poetic devices, such as invoking the Muse, posing an "epic question," and announcing an "epic theme," such as the wrath of Achilles.

Epic of Gilgamesh An ancient Mesopotamian narrative celebrating the heroic exploits of a legendary king of Uruk famous for slaying monsters and journeying to a mythical paradise, where his ancestor Utnapishtim told him of a prehistoric deluge.

epilogue In a Greek play, whatever is spoken after the chorus's final exit.

Epimetheus [ep-ih-MEE-thee-uhs] A brother of Prometheus who, on man's behalf, accepted the Olympian gods' gift of Pandora; his name means "afterthought."

epiphany The appearance or manifestation of a divine being; a revelatory perception of almost supernatural intensity.

episode In Greek drama, the scene occurring between two choral odes; an act.

epode In Greek drama, the part of a choral song that follows the strophe and antistrophe; it is sung while the chorus stands still.

Erebus Personification of primal darkness, the offspring of Chaos, it came to represent the intense gloom of Hades.

Erechtheus [e-REK-thee-uhs] Legendary early king or founder of Athens, to whom a temple on the Acropolis was dedicated.

Erinyes [e-RIN-ih-eez] Greek term for the Furies.

Eris Personification of strife or discord. The term can also mean the spirit of competition for excellence.

Eros [AIR-ohs] (Cupid) God of love and sexual desire, he was represented as an unbegotten primal force (Hesiod) or as the son of Ares and Aphrodite (Homer).

Eteocles [e-TEE-oh-kleez] Son of Oedipus and Jocasta, he was killed in a duel with his brother Polyneices.

etiology A branch of knowledge dealing with causes, it refers to the proposition that all myths represent attempts to explain the origins of natural, social, or psychological phenomena.

Eumenides [oo-MEN-ih-deez] Greek name for the Kindly Ones, formerly the Furies.

Europa A princess of Tyre whom Zeus, in the form of a bull, kidnapped and took to Crete, where she became the mother of Minos and Rhadamanthus.

Eurydice [oo-RIH-dih-see] Wife of Orpheus, whom he tried to retrieve from Hades.

Eurynomos [oo-RIH-noh-mohs] An Underworld demon who devoured the flesh of dead bodies, leaving only the bones.

exodos In Greek drama, the final speech sung by the chorus as it leaves the stage.

Fate The mysterious power of destiny that shapes human lives and history. (See **Moirae**.)

Fauna Roman woodland goddess.

Faunus Minor Roman woodland deity who presided over crops, herds, and fields and who had the ability to foresee the future. He is commonly identified with Pan.

Five Ages (Hesiod) The five stages of (mythic) human history, which Hesiod divides symbolically into ages of gold, silver, bronze, heroes, and iron (the present age); with the exception of the heroic age, each successive stage represents a marked decline in human society.

Flora Roman goddess of fertility, associated with spring and flowers.

folklore Traditional customs, tales, and beliefs of a people.

folktales Anonymous stories that originate and circulate orally among a people.

Fortuna   Roman goddess, the "first-born daughter" of Jupiter, a personification of fate. She was associated with Fors, a divinity of chance, in the phrase *Fors Fortuna*. She is also identified with Tyche, the Greek goddess of chance and luck.

Furies (Dirae)   Born from Uranus's blood, they were goddesses of blood vengeance; in Aeschylus, they were daughters of Night. They are also called the *Erinyes*.

Gaea [JEE-uh] (Gaia)   The Greeks' original Earth Mother, a primal divine power coeval with Chaos. After producing Uranus (Sky), she mated with him to produce the Titans.

Ganymede   Trojan shepherd boy with whom Zeus fell in love and, in the shape of an eagle, carried off to heaven, where he became cupbearer to the gods.

Gemini   The divine twins, Castor and Pollux, whom Zeus changed into a starry constellation, giving a part of the zodiac its name.

genius   In Roman religion, the indwelling procreative spirit of a man or place that imparts distinction or power.

Geryon   A three-headed giant whom Heracles killed.

Gilgamesh   Legendary ruler of Uruk, a city-state in ancient Sumer; the hero of the world's oldest narrative poem.

Glaucus   In the *Iliad,* a grandson of Bellerophon, co-leader of the Lycian allies of the Trojans who foolishly exchanged his gold armor for the bronze armor of Diomede(s).

Golden Age   (1) The mythic period of primal innocence described in Hesiod's poems. (2) The historical period of Athenian political and cultural supremacy (c. 480–404 B.C.) that produced enduring models of excellence in art, literature, drama, architecture, and philosophy. See also **Five Ages.**

Golden Fleece   The wool of a golden ram given to the king of Colchis and, with Medea's help, stolen by Jason.

Gorgons   Three hideous sisters with snakes for hair and with hypnotic eyes. Medusa, the only mortal Gorgon, had a gaze so terrifying that she could turn men to stone. With Athene's help, Perseus beheaded her.

Graces, the   Three goddesses personifying beauty and charm, inspirers of artistic creation.

Graiae [GRYE-eye]   Three ancient women who had been born old, they had only one eye and one tooth among them, which they shared in rotation. They were named Enyo, Pephredo, and Dino and lived in the far West, where the sun never shone. Sisters of the Gorgons, they were tricked by Perseus into revealing the three objects he needed to kill Medusa.

Great Goddess, the   Ancient parthenogenetic goddess (worshiped in Old Europe and many other cultures) whose functions included overseeing the cycle of life, death, and regeneration. Originally a creator deity, she eventually acquired association with agriculture and was worshiped as an earth goddess. Gaea is the oldest form of the Great Goddess specific to Greek myth.

Hades [HAY-deez] (Dis)   (1) Son of Cronus and Rhea and brother of Zeus, he was given dominion over the Underworld; he is also called *Pluto*. (2) The subterranean realm of the dead, which is named after its gloomy ruler.

Haemon   Son of Creon, and fiancé to Antigone, he committed suicide when his father condemned his bride-to-be to death.

hamartia   In Greek tragedy, a term derived from the verb "missing the mark," to fall short in judgment, understanding, or action; the term Aristotle used to denote a serious error in judgment of the tragic hero.

Hannibal   General of the Carthaginians who led the invasion of Italy in the Second Punic War.

Harmonia   Daughter of Ares and Aphrodite and wife of Cadmus, founder and king of Thebes.

Harpies   Three vicious winged female demons believed to kidnap human victims.

Hebe [HEE-bee] (Juventas)   Daughter of Zeus and Hera and a personification of youth, she was cupbearer of the Olympian gods until displaced by Ganymede. After Heracles' deification, he married Hebe, symbol of the gods' eternal youthfulness.

Hecate [HEK-uh-tee]   In Hesiod, a great and gracious goddess; in later myth, a creature of darkness and the Underworld, patron of magic and witchcraft.

hecatomb   In Greek ritual, originally the sacrifice of a hundred oxen; over time, the term came to mean the sacrifice of any large number of animals.

Hecatoncheires   Zeus's allies in the Titanomachy. (See **Hundred-handed.**)

Hector   Son of Priam and Hecuba and chief defender of Troy against the invading Achaeans, he was abandoned by his patron Apollo and slain by Achilles. An account of his funeral rites closes the *Iliad*.

Hecuba [HEK-oo-ba]   Wife of Priam and queen of Troy, she was the mother of Hector, Paris, Cassandra, and many other noble children, nearly all of whom were killed as a result of the Trojan War.

Helen   Daughter of Zeus and Leda; sister of Clytemnestra, Castor, and Pollux; and wife of Menelaus. Tyndareus, her legal father, made each of her innumerable suitors swear to uphold her marriage to whichever husband she selected, an oath that bound many Greek heroes after Paris took her to Troy.

Helios [HEE-lee-ohs]   Son of Hyperion, he was god of the sun.

Hellas [HEL-luhs]   The ancient Greeks' name for their country.

Hellenes [HEL-lee-neez]   Name the Greeks used in classical times to denote the Greek people, who were reputedly descended from a mythical ancestor, Hellen.

Hellenistic period   The period of Greek history following Alexander's death in 323 B.C., and characterized by a creative synthesis of native Greek (Hellenic) and eastern cultures.

Hephaestus [he-FES-tuhs] (Vulcan)   Son of Hera (Hesiod) or of Hera and Zeus (Homer), he was god of fire and the forge, the master of metalcraft who built the Olympians' palace and fashioned armor for Achilles. He was married to Aphrodite, who preferred Ares as her lover.

Hera [HEE-ra] (Juno)   Daughter of Cronus and Rhea and sister and wife of Zeus, she was goddess of marriage and domesticity. Her matriarchal spirit ill fit the patriarchal rule of Zeus.

Heracles [HER-a-kleez] (Hercules)   Son of Zeus and the mortal Alcmene (who was married to Amphitryon), he was the strongest and the most long-suffering of all Greek heroes; best known for the Twelve Labors imposed on him by King Eurystheus, he was eventually rewarded with immortality on Olympus.

Hermaphroditus   Son of Hermes and Aphrodite, he was physically united with the nymph Salmacis, acquiring the characteristics of both sexes.

Hermes [HER-meez] (Mercury)   Son of Zeus and Maia, he was primarily his father's messenger and an embodiment of extreme mobility. The guide of dead souls, he was also patron of travelers, merchants, highwaymen, gamblers, and thieves.

Hermione   Daughter of Helen and Menelaus, she was first married to Neoptolemus (son of Achilles) and then to Orestes, son of Agamemnon.

Heroes (Age of)   See **Five Ages.**

Hesiod   Greek poet of the late eighth century B.C., author of the *Theogony* and *Works and Days*.

Hesperides [hes-PER-ih-deez]   Known as *Nymphs of the Setting Sun* or *Daughters of the Evening,* they lived in the far West and guarded a tree bearing golden apples.

Hestia [HES-tee-uh] (Vesta)   Eldest daughter of Cronus and Rhea and virgin sister of Zeus, she guarded the Olympian hearth.

hieros gamos [HYE-rohs GAHM-ohs]   A sacred marriage in which male and female entities, human or divine, are united in a way that ensures or promotes peace and fecundity.

Hippolytus [hip-PAHL-ih-tuhs]   Son of Theseus and Antiope, queen of the Amazons, he was falsely accused of sexual assault by his stepmother, Phaedra, and, when his deceived father cursed him, killed by a monster from the sea.

Homer   Name that the ancient Greeks attributed to the (otherwise unknown) poet of the *Iliad* and the *Odyssey*, the father of epic poetry.

Horae   The three daughters of Zeus and Themis who personified justice (Dike), order (Eunomia), and peace (Eirene). Guardians of natural law, they regulated the seasons and the smooth functioning of the cosmos.

hubris [HYOO-bris]   The kind of excessive pride that blinds the tragic hero to his own limitations, offends the gods, and initiates his doom.

humanism   A conviction that individual human beings occupy a central place in society and the cosmos, a belief in the inherent worth and dignity of all humanity.

Hundred-handed   Three giant sons of Gaea and Uranus who fought on Zeus's side when he battled the Titans. Their names were Cottus, Briareus, and Gyges.

Hyacinthus   A youth whom both Apollo and Zephyrus loved; when Apollo and Hyacinthus were throwing the discus, the jealous Zephyrus interfered, striking the boy with the discus and killing him, after which he was changed into the flower bearing his name.

Hydra   A seven-headed monster that ravaged Argos and was slain by Heracles.

Hylas   The boy whom Heracles loved, lost ashore while looking for water during the voyage of the Argonauts.

Hymen   Son of Apollo and one of the Muses, he was the god of marriage.

Hyperion [hye-PEER-ee-uhn]   Titan son of Uranus and Gaea, and father of Helios, Selene, and Eos; a personification of the sun.

Hypnos   A personification of sleep, he was the twin brother of Thanatos (Death).

Icarus [IK-uh-ruhs]   Son of Daedalus who flew from Crete on artificial wings his father had constructed. Ignoring Daedalus's warning, he flew too close to the sun, whose rays melted the wax holding the wings together, causing him to fall to his death.

ichor [IH-kohr]   The colorless liquid that flowed instead of blood in the veins of the Greek gods.

icon   Greek term for "image." In classical Greek art, typically a painted or carved representation of a divine being, human, or animal.

id   English translation of the Freudian term for the unconscious welter of amoral appetites and instincts residing in every human psyche.

Ida, Mount   (1) The mountain in Crete on which Zeus was born and hidden from Cronus. (2) A mountain near Troy.

Ilia   Daughter of the Roman king Numitor, a Vestal Virgin who became by Mars the mother of Romulus and Remus. She is also called *Rhea Silvia*.

Ilion (Ilium)   The name of Priam's city, Troy.

image   The mental picture and/or physical sensation evoked by a verbal description, such as Homer's graphic depiction of Odysseus's attempt to embrace the shade of his dead mother, Anticleia (*Odyssey*, Book 11).

individualism   A belief that each human being has a unique value that grants one the right to personal freedom and the opportunity to fulfill one's full human potential.

Indo-European   Linguistic term designating an unrecorded prehistoric language spoken in Europe and western Asia, from which an interrelated group of languages, including Greek, Latin, French, and English, are descended.

Ino   Daughter of Cadmus and Harmonia who nursed the infant Dionysus after Semele's death. When Hera drove her mad, she threw herself into the sea and was transformed into Leucothea, the white goddess of sea foam, a friend to sailors.

invocation of the Muse   A literary convention in which a poet formally asks Calliope, Muse of epic poetry, to inspire his composition.

Io   A young priestess of Hera in Argos whom Zeus raped and whom Hera vindictively changed into a heifer and drove mad with a gadfly.

Ion   Son of Apollo and Creusa who, according to some traditions, was the ancestor of the Ionian Greeks.

Iphigenia [if-ih-je-NYE-a]   Daughter of Agamemnon and Clytemnestra whom her father sacrificed at Aulis to prevent the Greeks' expedition against Troy from being disbanded.

Iris   A personification of the rainbow and Hera's special messenger, she was married to Zephyrus, the West Wind.

Iron (Age of)   See **Five Ages.**

irony   A literary term based on the Greek word *eironeia,* meaning a "pretense" or "simulation in speech." Dramatic irony occurs when a character acts inappropriately because he or she is ignorant of facts of which the audience is aware, as when Oedipus rashly condemned the man guilty of Laius's murder.

Iulus   Another name for Ascanius, son of Aeneas and Creusa.

Ithaca   Island kingdom of Odysseus, the rulership of which was bestowed on him by his parents, Laertes and Anticleia.

ithyphallic   A term denoting figures displaying an erect penis, such as satyrs.

Ixion   After Zeus had mercifully pardoned him for murder, Ixion treacherously tried to seduce Hera, for which Zeus bound him on an eternally revolving wheel in Tartarus.

Janus   Roman god of doorways, beginnings, and endings, he is pictured having two faces looking in two different directions. The month of January is named after him.

Jason   Greek adventurer who led fifty Argonauts on a quest across the Black Sea for the Golden Fleece. After marrying Medea, who had helped him steal the fleece from her father, Jason divorced her. Her reaction is dramatized in Euripides' *Medea.*

Jocasta [joh-KAS-ta]   Widow of Laius, mother and wife of Oedipus, sister of Creon, and mother of Ismene, Antigone, Eteocles, and Polyneices.

Jove   Abbreviated Roman name for Zeus, king of the gods.

judgment of Paris   The decision that Paris, a Trojan prince, made in selecting Aphrodite as the most beautiful goddess, thereby earning the wrath of Hera and Athene and ensuring the destruction of Troy.

Julius Caesar   See **Caesar, Julius.**

Juno   Roman name for Hera, queen of the gods.

Jupiter   The Roman equivalent of Zeus, king of the Olympian gods.

Juturna   Italian goddess of fountains; in the *Aeneid,* she was the devoted sister of Turnus.

Juventas   Latin equivalent of Hebe, Greek personification of divine youthfulness.

Keres   Hideous winged demons who, like the Fates (Moirae), were daughters of Night. Associated with personifications of death and doom, they may represent the destinies assigned persons at birth.

Kore [KOHR-ee]   A Greek term meaning "maid," commonly applied to Persephone, daughter of Demeter.

Labyrinth   The maze that Daedalus built for King Minos to house the Minotaur.

Lacedemonia   Region in southeast Greece, the political center of which was Sparta.

Lachesis   One of the three Fates. (See **Atropos.**)

Laertes [lay-ER-teez]   Son of Arcesius and Chalcomedusa, he married Anticleia, by whom he fathered Odysseus.

Laius [LAY-uhs]   Father of Oedipus and first husband of Jocasta, he brought a curse on his family by eloping with Chrysippus, the son of his host, Pelops.

Lamia   A reptilian female who stole unwary children.

Laocoon [lay-AHK-oh-ahn]   Trojan priest who warned against taking the Wooden Horse into Troy and who was crushed by giant sea serpents.

Lares [LAR-eez]   In Roman religion, the deified spirits of family ancestors.

Latinus   King of Latium and father of Lavinia, whom Aeneas married.

Latium [LAY-shee-uhm]   Region on the Tiber River in western Italy where the Latins lived. Rome was founded near its northern border.

Lausus A young soldier killed by Aeneas in battle but honored for bravely defending his father.

Lavinia Daughter of King Latinus and Queen Amata, she became Aeneas's second wife.

Leda Wife of Tyndareus (king of Sparta) by whom Zeus fathered Helen, Clytemnestra, Castor, and Pollux (Polydeuces).

legend A story transmitted from the distant past, especially one based at least in part on some historical event.

Lemnos Volcanic island in the Aegean Sea on which Philoctetes was abandoned by the Achaeans.

Lenaea Athenian drama festival held annually in January at which comedies were performed.

Lethe [LEE-thee] In Hades, the River of Forgetfulness.

Leto [LEE-toh] Titan goddess by whom Zeus fathered Artemis and Apollo.

libido In Freudian psychoanalysis, the psychic energy associated with instinctual biological drives, especially sexual desire.

lot In the Greek concept of Fate, the peculiar mixture of good and evil that each person is assigned in life.

Lupercalia An ancient Roman festival featuring a ritual in which women who wanted to conceive were flagellated by two young men, the Luperci, who ran around the foot of the Palatine Hill, wielding goat-hide thongs.

lyre A small, hand-held stringed musical instrument used to accompany songs or recitations of poetry.

maenads [MEE-nadz] Female worshipers of Dionysus, commonly called *Bacchae* or *Bacchants,* who dressed in fawn skins and carried a thyrsus while performing ecstatic dances.

Manes In Roman religion, the spirits of the dead, thought to be hostile to the living and euphemistically called the *Kindly Ones.*

Marduk Chief god of the Babylonian pantheon, the son of Ea (god of wisdom), and creator-hero of the *Enuma Elish.*

Mars Roman god of agriculture and war identified with the Greek Ares.

Medea [me-DEE-a] Sorceress daughter of Aeetes (king of Colchis) and wife of Jason, whom she enabled to obtain the Golden Fleece. When he abandoned her for a Greek wife, she killed their children.

Medusa The only mortal Gorgon, whose terrifying gaze turned men to stone. With Athene's help, Perseus beheaded her.

Megara [ME-ga-ra] The first wife of Heracles.

Melpomone Muse of tragedy, commonly represented in a tragic mask.

Menelaus [men-e-LAY-uhs] Son of Atreus, younger brother of Agamemnon, husband of Helen, and king of Sparta.

Mercury Roman name for Hermes, messenger of the Olympian gods.

metaphor A figure of speech in which one object is used to describe the quality of another; an implied comparison of one thing to another, inferring that the first has a hitherto unrecognized likeness to the second (for example, Achilles is a *lion*—meaning that he has the courage, strength, and savagery of the king of beasts).

Metis [MEE-tis] Personification of wise advice; Zeus's first wife, whom he swallowed to produce Athene.

Midas A legendary king of Phrygia who got his wish that everything he touched would turn to gold.

mimesis Aristotle's term for imitation, the mother of all art.

Minerva Italian goddess of crafts and trade guilds, later identified with Athene as martial defender of the state. With Jupiter and Juno, she was a member of the chief Roman triad of divinities.

Minoan [mih-NOH-an] Term describing the earliest European civilization (c. 2500–

1400 B.C.), which was centered on Crete and other Aegean islands and was characterized by elaborate palace complexes, such as that of King Minos at Knossos.

Minos [MYE-nohs]   Name of a king—or line of kings—who ruled at Knossos on Crete. The son of Zeus and Europa, Minos married Pasiphae, whose unnatural union with a bull produced the Minotaur.

Minotaur [MIN-oh-tahr]   A monster half-human, half-bull, produced from Pasiphae's union with the sacred bull of Poseidon, it was confined in the Labyrinth at Knossos and slain by Theseus.

Mnemosyne [nee-MAHS-ih-nee]   Personification of memory, daughter of Uranus and Gaea, and, by Zeus, the mother of the Muses.

Moirae   The three Fates, pictured as ancient women who spun, wove, and cut off the individual threads signifying human lives. Named Atropos, Clotho, and Lachesis, they were the daughters of Zeus and Themis.

monotheism   The belief in one God.

Morpheus   Son of Hypnos (Sleep), and the god of dreams.

Museaus   A legendary pre-Homeric poet said to have been either the teacher or pupil of Orpheus.

Muses, the   The nine daughters of Zeus and Mnemosyne, patrons of literature and the fine arts.

Mycenae [mye-SEE-nee]   Ancient Greek city, capital of Agamemnon, after which the Mycenaean civilization is named.

Mycenaean [mye-see-NEE-uhn]   Term describing the first mainland Greek civilization (c. 1600–1100 B.C.); deeply influenced by the older Minoan culture, Mycenaean society produced the large majority of Greek myths, including the Trojan War saga.

Myrmidons   Achilles' faithful troops who accompanied him to Troy.

mysteries   Secret cults typically involving chthonic or fertility deities, such as Demeter and Persephone or Dionysus and Orpheus, that promised their initiates the gods' protection and a joyous afterlife.

myth   From the Greek word *mythos,* a story typically involving gods and/or heroes whose adventures represent significant aspects of human experience.

mythology   (1) The systematic study of myth. (2) A set or collection of myths, such as classical mythology.

naiads   Nymphs who dwelled in rivers, springs, or lakes.

Narcissus   A beautiful youth beloved by Echo but who, refusing to love anyone else, fell in love with his own image.

narratology   The critical study of structure in narratives.

nature myth   A theory of myth that sees all myths as disguised representations of natural phenomena, such as the cycle of the seasons or the alternation of sun and storm.

Nausicaa [nah-SIK-ay-a]   Daughter of King Alcinous and Queen Arete who found the shipwrecked Odysseus and befriended him at the Phaeacian court.

necessity   The power of Fate or Destiny that determined how all things must be, it was generally conceived of as a force superior to both gods and human beings.

nectar   The drink of the Olympian gods that sustained their eternal youthfulness.

nemesis   (1) In Homer, the power of retributive justice, the punishment that overtook wrongdoers. (2) In Aristotle, the term describing the fall of the tragic hero.

Neoptolemus   Son of Achilles and Deidamia, known as *Pyrrhus* (yellow haired). When Troy fell, he murdered Priam and took Andromache captive but later married Hermione and was killed by Orestes.

Neptune   Roman name for Poseidon, god of the sea and earthquakes.

Nereus   In Homer, the old man of the sea, father of the nereids, or sea nymphs, the most famous of which was Thetis, mother of Achilles.

Nestor   Aged king of Pylos, famous for his sagacity, who advised the Greek expedition to Troy.

Nessus A centaur whom Heracles killed for attempting to rape Deianeira (Heracles' wife). Nessus gave Deianeira his garment steeped in the poison of the Hydra, a gift that later caused Heracles' painful death.

Nike Personification of victory, to whom a temple was dedicated on the Athenian Acropolis.

Niobe Daughter of Tantalus, sister of Pelops, and wife of Amphion, king of Thebes, she foolishly boasted that, because she had twelve (or fourteen) children, she was the superior of Leto, who had only two. Leto's twins, Artemis and Apollo, shot all but two of her children. Eternally weeping, Niobe was changed into stone.

numen In Roman religion, the force or spirit inhabiting each earthly place or object—a cave, tree, or spring—as well as each person. Certain places or objects were felt to be numinous, or filled with the sense or presence of divinity.

nymphs Female spirits that dwelled in natural formations, such as rivers, forests, mountains, or fields. Although long-lived, they were not necessarily immortal.

Ocean (Oceanus) (1) In primitive Greek geography, a gigantic river that encircled the earth. (2) A Titan son of Gaea and Uranus, he was the father of all rivers.

ode From the Greek word *oide,* meaning "song." (1) The lyrics that the chorus sings in Greek drama. (2) A stately, dignified song performed in honor of gods, legendary heroes, or prizewinning athletes, such as the odes of Pindar (c. 522–443 B.C.).

Odysseus [oh-DIS-ee-uhs] (Ulysses) Son of Laertes and Anticleia, husband of Penelope, father of Telemachus, king of Ithaca, and favorite of Athene, he was celebrated for his prudence, ingenuity, and resourcefulness among the Greek forces at Troy, the fall of which he engineered. Hero of the *Odyssey,* he demonstrated an endurance and adaptability that determined his successful return to Ithaca.

Oedipus [E-dih-puhs] Son of Laius and Jocasta; father (by Jocasta) of Ismene, Antigone, Eteocles, and Polyneices; and king of Thebes; his myth demonstrates human inability to circumvent the gods' will.

Ogygia [oh-JIJ-ih-a] Island home of the nymph Calypso, location unknown.

Olympia Religious center on the Peloponnesian Peninsula where, every four years (beginning in 776 B.C.), the most famous Greek athletic contests were held.

Olympus, Mount (1) A high mountain along the northern border between Thessaly and Greece proper, near the valley of Tempe, sacred to Apollo. (2) The mythical dwelling place of the Olympian gods, located somewhere in the sky.

oracle (1) The word or utterance of a god, usually a command or prophecy about the future. (2) The person inspired to deliver a divine proclamation, such as the Delphic Oracle.

orchestra In a Greek theater, the circular arena, lower than the main stage, where the chorus danced and sang.

Orestes [ah-RES-teez] Son of Agamemnon and Clytemnestra, brother of Iphigenia and Electra, and husband of Hermione (daughter of Helen).

Orion A giant hunter who was transformed into a major constellation.

Orpheus [OR-fee-uhs] The archetypal poet and singer who descended into Hades to rescue his wife, Eurydice, he later suffered sparagmos, after which his lyre, symbol of divine harmony, was transformed into a constellation.

Orphism A particularly obscure mystery cult in which devotees were initiated into the secrets of moral transfiguration and future immortality.

Osiris Egyptian guide and judge of the dead, brother and husband of Isis, and (posthumously) father of Horus. He underwent sparagmos, resurrection, and deification, which suggested to the Greeks that he was an African manifestation of Dionysus.

paean (1) A song of thanksgiving or triumph; a hymn of praise. (2) A choral ode invoking the healing power of Apollo. (3) In later times, a song chanted to Ares before marching to war.

Palladium   A small wooden statue of Pallas Athene, the possession of which the Trojans believed would protect their city. After Odysseus stole it, Troy fell.

Pallas   (1) A title of Athene, meaning unknown. (2) A Titan who, by Styx, fathered Nike (Victory). (3) In the *Aeneid,* a son of Evander whom Turnus kills.

Pan   A son of Hermes and a daughter of Dryops (leader of an ancient pre-Greek people), he was the quintessential nature deity, usually pictured as a goat from the waist down, with a human torso, a goat's horns, and pointed ears. Patron of goatherds and flocks, he roamed the wilderness playing the panpipes and pursuing nymphs.

Panathenaea [pan-ath-e-NEE-a]   Athens' major annual festival honoring its patron, Athene. It included athletic, poetry, and musical contests and culminated in a great procession to the Acropolis.

Pandarus   A Trojan commander who broke the armistice with the Greeks, treacherously wounding Menelaus. He was then killed by Diomede(s).

Pandora   In Hesiod, the first woman, created by Hephaestus from clay and adorned by Athene with every attraction. She was designed by Zeus to weaken humankind.

Pantheon   (1) Term meaning "all the gods." (2) A circular temple built by Hadrian in Rome.

parados   The ode sung by a Greek chorus during its first appearance on stage.

paradox   A statement or condition in which two or more apparently contradictory elements are in some sense true or valid. An oxymoron such as Hesiod's description of Pandora as a "lovely evil" is one type of paradox.

Paris   Trojan prince, son of Priam and Hecuba and younger brother of Hector, he selected Aphrodite as the most beautiful goddess, abducted Helen as his prize, and thereby sealed Troy's doom. He is also called *Alexandros.*

Parnassus, Mount   A rugged mountain on whose slopes Delphi is located; a landform sacred to Apollo and the Muses.

parody   An imitation of a literary work that deliberately distorts or exaggerates its style or content, thereby opening it to ridicule.

parthenogenesis   The phenomenon by which a female was able to reproduce without being fertilized by a male.

Parthenon   The Doric temple to *Athene Parthenos* (Athene the Virgin) that was built atop the Athenian Acropolis in the fifth century B.C.

Pasiphae [pah-SIF-a-ee]   Daughter of Helios, sister of Circe, wife of King Minos of Crete, and mother of Ariadne, Phaedra, and (by a bull) the Minotaur.

pathos   That part of a Greek tragedy that depicts the suffering and/or death of the hero.

patriarch   A father, founder, or venerable leader of a family, clan, or group.

patriarchy   A social-political system in which male leadership and values dominate.

Patroclus [pa-TROH-kluhs]   Son of Menoetius (one of Helen's former suitors) and beloved friend of Achilles, whom he accompanied to Troy. His death galvanized Achilles to return to the war.

Pax Romana   The "Roman Peace," the political stability that Roman imperial efficiency imposed on the Mediterranean world from the reign of Augustus (30 B.C.–A.D. 14) until the death of Marcus Aurelius in A.D. 180.

Pegasus   A winged horse that sprang from the blood of Medusa after Perseus beheaded her.

Peleus   The mortal to whom the gods married Thetis after Zeus learned that if he had a son by Thetis the boy would be stronger than his father. After Achilles' birth—when Peleus showed the first sign of aging—Thetis deserted him.

Pelias [PEE-lih-uhs]   A son of Poseidon and Tyro who usurped the kingdom of his brother Aeson, father of Jason.

Peloponnesian War   A disastrous war (431–404 B.C.) between the rival states of Athens and Sparta and their respective allies, ending with Sparta's victory.

Peloponnesus   The southern peninsula of Greece, where Argos, Mycenae, Sparta, and Pylos were located.

Pelops [PEE-lahps]   Son of Tantalus (king of Phrygia), he was served by his father to the gods at a banquet. After Demeter—absorbed in her grief for Persephone—took a bite from his shoulder, the gods restored it with an ivory replacement. The Peloponnesian Peninsula is named after him; his sons included Atreus and Thyestes.

Penates [pe-NAY-teez]   Roman deities of hearth and home, their images were kept in each Roman house and in a temple of the state.

Penelope   Daughter of Icarius of Sparta and Periboea, a naiad, and wife of Odysseus and mother of Telemachus, she was a model of the loyal and prudent wife.

Pentheus [PEN-thee-uhs]   Son of Agave and Echion (one of the men born when Cadmus sowed the dragon's teeth), he was the young king of Thebes who opposed the introduction of Dionysus's cult into his realm, for which the god destroyed him.

Pericles [PER-ik-leez]   Leader of the Athenian democracy (c. 460–429 B.C.) and sponsor of the rebuilding of the Acropolis, whose temples included the Parthenon.

peripeteia [per-ih-pe-TEE-uh]   In tragedy, the sudden reversal or unexpected change of the hero's fortunes, as when the conquering hero Agamemnon was brought down by his wife.

Persephone [per-SEF-oh-nee]   Daughter of Zeus and his sister Demeter, she personified the grain harvest. When Hades took her to the Underworld, her mother (symbolizing the fertility of the soil) fell into such extreme grief that the gods ordered Persephone's return to the daylight world for most of the year. She is also called *Proserpina* and *Kore (Core)*, the Maiden.

Perseus   Son of Zeus and Danae, he beheaded Medusa, wed Andromeda, and (in some myths) founded Mycenae.

Persian Wars   A series of three Persian invasions into Greece that continued the westward expansion of Persia begun by Cyrus the Great, conqueror of Babylon (539 B.C.). The Greeks repelled the Persians and their allies at Marathon (490 B.C.), but not until after the sea battles at Salamis (480) and Mycale (479) did the Persians permanently retreat into Asia. Herodotus (c. 450 B.C.) left a detailed account of these events.

personification   A literary device by which an abstract quality is given human or divine form, as when Homer made Panic (the sudden fear that seizes a crowd) and Rout (the impulse to flee the battlefield) actual personages. Eros personifies human sexual desire as Eos signifies the dawn.

Phaedra [FE-drah]   Daughter of King Minos and Pasiphae, wife of Theseus (king of Athens), and stepmother of Theseus's son Hippolytus, with whom she fell in love and later denounced to his father after he rejected her advances.

Phaethon [FEE-e-thahn]   Son of Helios (or Apollo) and Clymene who convinced his father to let him drive the chariot of the sun across heaven, with catastrophic results.

Philemon and **Baucis**   In Ovid, an aged couple who hospitably received Zeus and Hermes (Jupiter and Mercury) when they posed as poor travelers.

Philoctetes   Greek hero to whom Heracles bequeathed a magic bow and arrow that never failed to hit its target. In Sophocles' *Philoctetes,* Odysseus visited Lemnos, where Philoctetes had been abandoned because he suffered from a stinking wound that did not heal. Using the trusting young Neoptolemus as his foil, Odysseus plotted to steal the bow after a prophet announced that Troy could not be taken without it.

Phlegethon   The fiery river of the Underworld that, in a huge waterfall, joined the Cocytus to form the Acheron.

Phoebus   An epithet of Apollo, meaning the "shining one." (See **Apollo.**)

Phoenix   (1) Mythological Egyptian bird that lived for five hundred years and then consumed itself in flames; from its ashes a new bird arose. (2) In the *Iliad,* Achilles' old teacher who tried to persuade the hero to rejoin his comrades at Troy.

Phrynichus   An early tragedian, the first to produce plays about contemporary history, such as the *Capture of Miletus.*

pietas   The supreme Roman virtue of duty toward the family, state, and gods, expressed in action rather than thought.

Pillars of Heracles The massive rock formations guarding the narrow passage of Gibraltar linking the Mediterranean Sea and the Atlantic Ocean.

Pirithous [pye-RITH-oh-uhs] King of the Lapiths who accompanied his friend Theseus into the Underworld to abduct Persephone, for which sacrilege he was condemned to being bound forever in an iron chair.

Pisistratus The Athenian tyrant during whose administration (560–527 B.C.) were instituted the public recitations of Homer at the Panathenaea and the tragic competitions at the City Dionysia.

Plato Athenian philosopher (427–347 B.C.) who taught that the material world is only a flawed reflection of a perfect spiritual realm, from which the human soul descends to earth to be born in a mortal body and to which it returns for judgment after death.

Pleiades A constellation of seven stars, supposedly the daughters of Atlas who were pursued by Orion and changed into heavenly bodies.

plot The structure or arrangement of incidents in a play or other literary work so that they form a coherent design, typically involving elements of conflict, crisis, and resolution.

Plutarch A Greek biographer who wrote "parallel" lives of famous Romans and Greeks.

Pluto [PLOO-toh] The "wealth giver," an epithet of Hades, whose subterranean realm contained precious minerals and other treasures. (See **Hades.**)

Plutus [PLOO-tuhs] A son of Demeter and Iasion and the personification of wealth.

polis Greek term for the city-state, such as Athens or Sparta.

pollution A state of ritual or moral impurity incurred by the committing of a crime such as homicide. Until a polluted person had expiated his guilt, he was driven from his homeland as unclean and likely to bring on the gods' wrath.

Polyneices [pol-ih-NYE-seez] Son of Oedipus and Jocasta, he was killed in a battle for the throne of Thebes by his brother Eteocles.

Polyphemus A Cyclops, a one-eyed cannibalistic giant whom Odysseus blinded and who retaliated with a curse enforced by his father, Poseidon.

polytheism The belief in a multiplicity of gods.

Poseidon [poh-SYE-duhn] (Neptune) Son of Cronus and Rhea, brother of Zeus, and husband of Amphitrite (a nereid); god of the sea and earthquakes, he used his three-pronged trident to raise storms and swamp ships.

Priam King of Troy, husband of Hecuba, and father of Hector, Paris, Cassandra, and (by various concubines) fifty sons.

Procrustes A brigand (said to be a son of Poseidon) who kidnapped and murdered travelers on the road between Athens and Eleusis. He laid his victims on an iron bed: if they were too short he stretched them out to fit the bed frame; if too tall, he cut off their extremities. Theseus beheaded him.

prologue In Greek drama, whatever is spoken before the entrance of the chorus.

Prometheus [proh-MEE-thee-uhs] A Titan cousin of Zeus and son of Iapetus and Clymene, he was punished by Zeus for befriending humanity. Prometheus's theft of fire signified his enlightenment of primitive men, rescuing them from the mental darkness of ignorance and savagery. After suffering for millennia the repeated tearing out of his liver by Zeus's fierce eagle, Prometheus was eventually reconciled to his enemy and ascended to Olympus, where he was honored as the divine fire-bearer.

Proserpina The Latin name of Persephone, daughter of Demeter and Zeus.

protagonist In Greek drama, the "first actor," the major character.

Proteus A son of Poseidon or Ocean (Oceanus), he had to tell the future of anyone who held him down. He tried to elude capture by changing his form into that of an animal, plant, or element, such as fire, water, or wind.

Psyche (1) The Greek word for "soul," it refers to the mental, emotional, and psychological makeup of a human being. (2) Perhaps the last major myth created in classical antiquity: the story of a beautiful young woman named Psyche who, after many hardships and ordeals, at last married Love (Eros or Cupid) and ascended to join the gods on Olympus, a tale representing the human soul as being destined to achieve divine immortality. The myth is contained in the Roman writer Apuleius's novel the *Golden Ass.*

psychology   A science that investigates the human mind and behavior.

Punic Wars   A series of three wars between Rome and Carthage that ended with the latter's total destruction (146 B.C.), foreshadowed in the *Aeneid* by Dido's fatal affair with Aeneas.

Pylades [PYE-la-deez]   Loyal friend of Orestes who accompanied him to Mycenae.

Pylos   Kingdom of old Nestor, which Telemachus visited while searching for his father.

Pyrrha   Wife of Deucalion, with whom she survives the global deluge. See **Deucalion.**

Pyrrhus   A name of Neoptolemus, son of Achilles.

Pythagoras   Greek philosopher and mathematician (sixth century B.C.) who taught the transmigration of souls, a belief that the immortal soul undergoes a series of incarnations in different bodies, including those of animals and plants.

Pythia [PITH-ee-uh]   Title of Apollo's virgin priestess at Delphi, a name commemorating the god's victory over Python.

Pytho [PYE-thoh]   An ancient name of Delphi, where Apollo dispensed his oracles.

Python [PYE-thuhn]   The serpent that guarded the ancient Delphic shrine of Themis and that Apollo killed with his arrow.

Quirinus   A Roman warrior god identified with Romulus after the latter's death.

recognition   From the Greek *anagnorisis,* in Greek drama it refers to the scene in which a character becomes aware of some previously unknown but highly significant fact, such as Electra's recognition of her long-lost brother Orestes or Oedipus's fatal discovery of his true identity.

Remus   Son of Mars and a Vestal Virgin, he was the twin brother of Romulus.

reversal   In Greek tragedy, the point at which the hero's fortunes suddenly change (usually for the worse), or an action that produces the opposite of what was expected.

Rhadamanthus   Son of Zeus and Europa who, with his brother Minos, became a judge of the dead and ruler of Elysium.

Rhapsode, Rhapsodist   Originally a poet who recited his own works; later, a professional singer of Homeric poems, such as those who performed at the Panathenaea.

Rhea [REE-a]   Titan wife of Cronus and mother of Zeus, Poseidon, Hades, Hera, and Hestia, she was sometimes identified with the Asiatic goddess Cybele.

Rhea Silvia [REE-a SIL-vih-a]   In some myths, the Vestal Virgin mother of Romulus and Remus. She is also known as *Ilia.*

ritual   The established form for a ceremony, a formalized set of words, gestures, or actions assiduously repeated in customary order, especially the prescribed order of a religious rite. According to some mythographers, all myths are related to ritual observances.

Romulus   Son of Mars and Rhea Silvia (a Vestal Virgin) and founder of Rome (traditionally 753 B.C.), he killed his twin brother Remus for criticizing the inadequacy of the walls he had built around Rome.

Sabines [SAY-binz]   In Roman tradition, inhabitants of central Italy at the time of Romulus, whose women the Romans abducted.

saga   A series or extensive collection of traditional tales about a person, place, or events, such as those concerning Thebes or the Trojan War.

Saturn   An Italian god whom the Romans identified with Cronus.

Saturnalia   An annual Roman festival held December 17–19 in honor of Saturn, the rebirth of the sun after the winter solstice, and the sowing of crops—a forerunner of Christmas.

satyr [SAY-ter]   Generally human in appearance, but with a horse's tail and ears, the satyr was characterized by lust and cowardice, a symbol of the amoral and animalistic aspects of human nature.

satyr play The ribald farce that followed the presentation of a tragic trilogy at the City Dionysia, it reaffirmed the comic and sexual aspects of human life.

Scylla [SIL-la] In the *Odyssey*, a female monster who, with Charybdis, guarded the Straits of Messina between Italy and Sicily. A whirlpool, Charybdis sucked ships down to their doom, while multiarmed Scylla seized and ate any who came within her reach.

Selene [se-LEE-nee] A Titan daughter of Hyperion (or Helios), she personified the moon.

Semele [SEM-uh-lee] Daughter of Cadmus and Harmonia, sister of Agave, and mother (by Zeus) of Dionysus, she was consumed in Zeus's lightning when she demanded to see him in his true form. Dionysus later rescued her from Hades and escorted her to heaven.

serpent A reptile that can represent evil, such as Typhoeus or the dragon of chaos; alternatively, it can also signify the beneficent or healing powers of nature, such as the snakes associated with Apollo's son Asclepius. The ancient Goddess of Crete was also depicted with serpents, as were classical representations of Athene.

shadow A term used in Jungian psychology to denote the unconscious part of the personality consisting of emotions or qualities that were repressed as the psyche developed. Although the shadow contains many negative or potentially destructive drives that can motivate antisocial or self-defeating behavior—greed, shame, lust, envy, hatred, selfishness—it also harbors abilities and talents that were never cultivated because they were not encouraged and is thus a source of positive psychic energy.

Shame In Hesiod, a personification of the social attitude that (correctly) makes wrongdoers ashamed of their bad behavior; its absence leads to social injustice and moral anarchy.

Sheol The biblical Underworld, counterpart of Hades.

Sibyl Title of Apollo's virgin prophetess at Cumae who guided Aeneas through the subterranean kingdom of Hades.

Silen [sih-LEEN] Human–animal hybrid usually portrayed as an old man whose bestial appearance and antic behavior belie an inner wisdom.

Silenus [sye-LEE-nuhs] A mythic creature of wild nature, half-man, half-animal in form, typically depicted with a horse's ears and tail. Despite his partly bestial appearance and association with Bacchic revels, Silenus was known for his great wisdom and tutored the young Dionysus. Similarly hybrid figures, the silens (sileni) were depicted on Greek vases as drunken old men with equine features.

Silver (Age of) See **Five Ages.**

simile An explicit comparison between two unlike objects, using *as* or *like.* In an "epic simile," the poet typically creates an extended comparison that likens two objects or classes of objects at such length that the subject is temporarily forgotten, as when Homer compares soldiers slain in battle to falling autumn leaves.

Sinon In the *Aeneid*, a Greek spy who persuaded the Trojans to take the Wooden Horse into their city.

Sirens Female creatures, half-bird, half-woman, whose songs lured passing sailors to shipwreck and death.

Sisyphus [SIS-ih-fuhs] Founder of Corinth who, for his greed and deceit, was condemned in Tartarus forever to roll a huge stone uphill, from whence it always rolled down again.

skene In Greek drama, the small building at the back of the stage that the actors used as a dressing room; the source of the word *scenery.*

Socrates Athenian philosopher (c. 469–399 B.C.) and friend and teacher of Plato, he was condemned to death for questioning assumptions deemed essential to maintain civic order and security.

sparagmos [spuh-RAHG-mohs] The ritual tearing asunder of a young male sacrificial victim, a dismemberment associated with Osiris, Dionysus, Pentheus, and Orpheus, as well as numerous Near Eastern dying and rising gods, such as Attis, Tammuz, and Adonis.

Sparta (1) In Mycenaean times, the luxurious capital of Helen and Menelaus. (2) In classical times, the austere city-state that was run like a totalitarian military camp.

Sphinx Enigmatic creature with the head of a woman, body of a lion, and wings of an eagle, infamous for killing anyone who tried but failed to solve its riddles.

strophe In Greek drama, the choral ode sung while the chorus moved from one side of the orchestra to the other; the antistrophe was the part sung while the chorus rotated in the reverse direction.

structuralism A method of critical analysis postulating that the human mind has an innate tendency to impose patterns or structured systems on experience, such as the tendency to perceive the world as a duality of opposites. The function of myth is to mediate or reconcile these polarities.

Styx (1) The oldest child of Oceanus and Tethys, she aided Zeus in his battle with the Titans, for which Zeus honored her by making vows sworn in Styx's name irrevocable even for gods. (2) River in the Underworld marking the boundary between life and death.

superego A Freudian term denoting a major component of the psyche that reflects parental and societal restraints imposed on the individual.

symbol In literary criticism, anything—person, place, or object—that stands for something else, typically suggesting a higher or more abstract meaning than the literal entity itself. The fire that Prometheus stole from heaven symbolized all the civilized arts and skills associated with light and dominion over nature.

syncretism The practice of combining two or more originally distinct ideas or religious traditions to create a new composite religion or set of beliefs.

Tantalus Son of Zeus and father of Pelops, whose flesh he served to the Olympians, an act for which he was condemned to eternal torment in Tartarus.

Tarquin Name of two Etruscan kings of ancient Rome.

Tartarus [TAHR-tahr-uhs] The dark abyss beneath Hades' realm where Zeus chained the fallen Titans and where the wicked suffered torment.

Telemachus [tee-LEM-a-kuhs] Son of Penelope and Odysseus who helped his father destroy his mother's hundred suitors.

Teucer Son of Telamon, the most skilled Greek archer in the war against Troy.

Thanatos [THAN-a-tohs] The personification of Death, he was the twin brother of Hypnos (Sleep).

Thebes Leading city of Boeotia, founded by Cadmus and home of Oedipus and his family.

Themis [THEE-mis] A Titan goddess, daughter of Gaea and Uranus, who personified justice and law; in some myths, she was the mother of Prometheus. Even after Apollo's cult was established there, she had a prophetic shrine at Delphi.

theriomorphism The practice of depicting divine beings in animal form.

Thersites In the *Iliad,* a mean-spirited common soldier whom Odysseus beat for daring to argue with his superiors.

Theseus [THEE-see-uhs] Son of Aegeus and legendary king of Athens, he won fame by slaying the Minotaur at Minos's palace on Crete. He fathered Hippolytus by the Amazon Antiope and later married Phaedra, daughter of Minos.

Thesmophoria [thes-moh-FOHR-ee-uh] A festival honoring Demeter in which only women (excluding virgins) participated.

Thespis Although some scholars doubt his historicity, he was probably an Athenian playwright (c. 534 B.C.), known as the father of drama for having created the first role for an actor.

Thetis A sea nymph married to Peleus, by whom she had Achilles.

Thyestes Brother of Atreus and father of Aegisthus.

Tiresias [tih-REE-sih-as] Blind Theban prophet who had temporarily been changed into a woman, giving him the experience to settle a quarrel between Hera and Zeus over which sex has the greater capacity for sexual pleasure. Hera blinded him for his candid answer, while Zeus gave him long life and insight.

Titans Race of giant gods whom Gaea and Uranus begot and whom Zeus overthrew and imprisoned in Tartarus.

tragedy   In Greek literature, a serious play containing a pathos, or scene of suffering, that was performed at the City Dionysia.

trilogy   In Greek tragedy, a series of three plays dealing with a common subject or theme, of which the *Oresteia* is the only surviving example.

Triptolemus [trip-TOHL-e-muhs]   The young man whom Demeter chose to travel the world teaching the skills of agriculture, in some accounts identified with the child whom Demeter tried to make immortal. He was associated with Demeter and Persephone in the Eleusinian Mysteries.

Trojan Horse   The hollow wooden horse that concealed Odysseus and other Achaeans and that was left as a parting gift when the Greeks pretended to leave Troy. It was so large that the Trojans had to tear down part of their protective walls to take it into their city.

Trojan War   The ten-year siege of Troy led by Agamemnon to retrieve Helen, who had eloped with Paris, a Trojan prince.

Troy (Ilium)   The city of Priam and Hecuba that the Greeks, under Agamemnon, destroyed (c. 1200 B.C.). Guarding the trade routes between the Mediterranean and the Black Sea, it was located near modern Hissarlik, Turkey.

Turnus   In the *Aeneid,* the Italian king of the Rutulians and suitor of Lavinia. After killing Pallas, he was slain by Aeneas.

Tyndareus   King of Sparta and reputed father of Helen (whom most traditions say is the daughter of Zeus).

Typhoeus [tye-FEE-uhs]   A monstrous giant, in appearance half-human and half-reptile, with one hundred dragon heads; the child of Gaea and Tartarus, a manifestation of the dragon of chaos that Zeus had to defeat before assuming control of the cosmos.

Typhon   A reptilian child of Hera, an incarnation of storm winds.

tyrant   The ruler of a Greek city-state who had neither inherited nor been elected to his position, although he could be appointed to assume governmental control, as was the Athenian Solon. Commonly used to denote a usurper who seized control through a military coup d'etat, the term was eventually applied to a political despot.

Ulysses [oo-LIS-seez]   The Latin name for Odysseus, king of Ithaca.

Uranus [OOR-a-nuhs]   The original sky god and son-husband of Gaea, he was castrated and deposed by his "crafty" son Cronus.

Venus   Italian goddess of gardens and flowers identified with Aphrodite.

Vesta [VES-tuh]   Roman name for Hestia, goddess of the hearth. In Rome, the Vestal Virgins were charged with the sacred duty of keeping alight the Eternal Flame signifying the Roman state.

Vulcan   Roman name for Hephaestus, god of fire and the forge.

Xanthus   Achilles' horse, which prophesied his master's death.

Yahweh   Personal name of Israel's God, commonly misrendered in English as "the Lord."

Zephyrus   Personification of the West Wind.

Zeus (Jove, Jupiter)   The youngest son of Cronus and Rhea, king of the Olympian gods, a personification of atmospheric phenomena—particularly storms and lightning—and the cosmic guarantor of justice, oath keeping, civic order, and kingship. As head of the Greek pantheon, he was the ultimate court of appeal for both humans and gods. All other Olympians were either his siblings or children, including his sister-wife Hera.

ziggurat [ZIG-oo-rat]   An ancient Mesopotamian temple tower built of successively recessed levels topped by a shrine to the god it commemorated.

Selected Bibliography

Chapter 1 Introduction to Greek Myth

Apollodorus (of Athens). *The Library of Greek Mythology.* Rev. ed. Trans. Robin Hard. (Oxford World Classics). New York: Oxford UP, 1999.

Boardman, John, Jasper Griffin, and Oswyn Murray, eds. *Greece and the Hellenistic World.* Oxford: Oxford UP, 1988.

Bruno, Vincent J., ed. *The Parthenon.* New York: Norton, 1974.

Burkert, Walter. *Greek Religion.* Trans. John Raffan. 1985. Reprint, Cambridge: Harvard UP, 2006.

———. *Homo Necans: The Anthropology of Ancient Greek Sacrificial Ritual and Myth.* Trans. Peter Bing. Berkeley: U of California P, 1983.

———. *Structure and History in Greek Mythology and Ritual.* Berkeley: U of California P, 1979.

Buxton, Richard. *The Complete World of Greek Mythology.* London: Thames & Hudson, 2004.

———. *Imaginary Greece: The Contexts of Mythology.* 1994. Reprint, Cambridge: Cambridge UP, 2002.

Calasso, Roberto. *The Marriage of Cadmus and Harmony.* Trans. Tim Parks. New York: Knopf, 1993.

Carpenter, T. H. *Art and Myth in Ancient Greece.* London: Thames, 1991.

Detienne, Marcel. *The Creation of Mythology.* Trans. Margaret Cook. Chicago: U of Chicago P, 1986.

Dundes, Alan, ed. *Sacred Narrative: Readings in the Theory of Myth.* Berkeley: U of California P, 1984.

Edmunds, Lowell, ed. *Approaches to Greek Myth.* 1990. Reprint, Baltimore: Johns Hopkins UP, 2007.

Gantz, Timothy. *Early Greek Myth.* Baltimore: Johns Hopkins UP, 1993.

Graf, Fritz. *Greek Mythology: An Introduction.* Trans. Thomas Marier. 1993. Reprint, Baltimore: Johns Hopkins UP, 1996.

Grimal, Pierre. *The Dictionary of Classical Mythology.* Trans. A. R. Maxwell-Hyslop. Oxford: Blackwell, 1986.

Guthrie, W. K. C. *The Greeks and Their Gods.* Boston: Beacon, 1955.

Hornblower, Simon, and Antony Spawforth, eds. *The Oxford Classical Dictionary.* 3rd ed., rev. New York: Oxford UP, 2003.

———. *The Oxford Companion to Classical Civilization.* New York: Oxford UP, 1998.

Howatson, M. C., ed. *The Oxford Companion to Classical Literature.* 2nd ed. New York: Oxford UP, 1989. (Paperback, 2006)

Hyginus. *Astronomica.* Ed. Paul Chatelain and P. Legendre. Paris: Libraire Honore Champion, 1909.

———. *Fabulae.* Ed. H. J. Rose. Leyden: Sythoff, 1933.

Nilsson, Martin P. *The Mycenaean Origin of Greek Mythology.* New York: Norton, n.d.

Pausanias. *Guide to Greece.* Trans. Peter Levi. New York: Penguin, 1971. Vol. 1 of *Central Greece.*

Plutarch. *The Rise and Fall of Athens: Nine Greek Lives by Plutarch.* Trans. Ian Scott-Kilvert. Baltimore: Penguin, 1960.

Price, Simon. *Religions of the Ancient Greeks.* 1999. Reprint, New York: Cambridge UP, 2004.

Shapiro, H. A. *Myth into Art: Poet and Painter in Classical Greece.* New York: Routledge, 1994.

Chapter 2   Ways of Interpreting Myth

Bal, Mieke. *Narratology: Introduction to the Theory of Narrative.* 2nd ed. Toronto: U of Toronto P, 1997.

Birenbaum, Harvey. *Myth and Mind.* UP of America, 1988.

Burkert, Walter. *Homo Necans: The Anthropology of Ancient Greek Sacrificial Ritual and Myth.* Trans. Peter Bing. Berkeley: U of California P, 1983.

———. *Structure and History in Greek Mythology.* Berkeley: U of California P, 1979.

Campbell, Joseph. *The Hero with a Thousand Faces.* 2nd ed. Princeton: Princeton UP, 1968.

———. *The Masks of God: Occidental Mythology.* New York: Penguin, 1964.

Detienne, Marcel. *The Writing of Orpheus: Greek Myth in Cultural Context.* Trans. Janet Lloyd. Baltimore: Johns Hopkins UP, 2003.

Doherty, Lillian. *Gender and the Interpretation of Classical Myth.* London: Duckworth, 2001.

Doniger, Wendy. *The Implied Spider: Politics and Theology in Myth.* New York: Columbia UP, 1998.

Dowden, Ken. *The Uses of Greek Mythology.* London: Routledge, 1992.

Eisner, Robert. *The Road to Daulis: Psychoanalysis, Psychology, and Classical Mythology.* Syracuse: Syracuse UP, 1987.

Evans, Richard I. *Dialogue with C. G. Jung.* 2nd ed. New York: Praeger, 1981.

Ferguson, John. *Among the Gods: An Archaeological Exploration of Greek Religion.* New York: Routledge, 1990.

Frazer, Sir James G. *The New Golden Bough.* Ed. T. H. Gaster. New York: Criterion, 1959.

Freud, Sigmund. *The Interpretation of Dreams.* 1900. New York: Basic, 1955.

———. *Totem and Taboo.* 1913. New York: Norton, 1962.

Graf, Fritz. *Greek Mythology: An Introduction.* Trans. Thomas Marier. Baltimore: Johns Hopkins UP, 1993.

Grant, Michael. *The Myths of the Greeks and the Romans.* New York: Mentor, 1964.

Harrison, Jane E. *Mythology.* New York: Harcourt, 1963.

———. *Themis.* Cleveland: Meridian, 1962.

Hawley, Richard, and Barbara Levick, eds. *Women in Antiquity: New Assessments.* New York: Routledge, 1995.

Jung, Carl G. *Man and His Symbols.* New York: Dell, 1964.

———. *Modern Man in Search of a Soul.* Trans. W. S. Dell and Cary Banes. New York: Harcourt, n.d.

———. *Psychology of the Unconscious.* New York: Dodd, 1957.

Kirk, G. S. *The Nature of Greek Myths.* New York: Penguin, 1974.

Lefkowitz, Mary R. *Women in Greek Myth.* Baltimore: Johns Hopkins UP, 1986.

Lévi-Strauss, Claude. *The Raw and the Cooked.* Trans. D. Weightman. New York: Harper, 1969.

———. *The Savage Mind.* Chicago: U of Chicago P, 1966.

Lincoln, Bruce. *Theorizing Myth: Narrative, Ideology, and Scholarship.* Chicago: U of Chicago P, 1999.

Malinowski, Bronislaw. *Crime and Custom in Savage Society.* Patterson: Littlefield, 1959.

———. *The Sexual Life of Savages.* New York: Harcourt, 1929.

Manhart, Klaus. "Likely Story: Myths Persist in Modern Culture Because of the Brain's Biological Need to Impose Order on the World." *Scientific American Mind,* 16.4 (2005): 58–63.

Mullahy, Patrick. *Oedipus, Myth and Complex: A Review of Psychoanalytic Theory.* New York: Hermitage, 1948.

Murray, Gilbert. *Five Stages of Greek Religion.* Garden City: Doubleday, 1992.

Nagy, Gregory. *Greek Mythology and Poetry.* Ithaca: Cornell UP, 1999.

Neumann, Erich. *The Origins and History of Consciousness.* Princeton: Princeton UP, 1970.

Puhvel, Jaan. *Comparative Mythology.* Baltimore: Johns Hopkins UP, 1987.

Rabinowitz, Nancy Sorkin, and Amy Richlin, eds. *Feminist Theory and the Classics.* New York: Routledge, 1993.

Ramachandran, V. S., and Sandra Blakeslee. *Phantoms in the Brain: Probing the Mysteries of the Human Mind.* New York: Morrow, 1998.

Schneiderman, Leo. *The Psychology of Myth, Folklore, and Religion.* Chicago: Nelson-Hall, 1981.

Segal, Robert A., ed. *Literary Criticism and Myth.* 6 vols. New York: Garland, 1996.

Slater, Philip E. *The Glory of Hera: Greek Mythology and the Greek Family.* Princeton: Princeton UP, 1968.

Vernant, Jean-Pierre. *Myth and Society in Ancient Greece.* New York: Zone, 1990.

Vernant, Jean-Pierre, and Pierre Vidal-Naquet. *Myth and Tragedy in Ancient Greece.* New York: Zone, 1990.

Winkler, John J. *Constraints of Desire: The Anthropology of Sex and Gender in Ancient Greece.* New York: Routledge, 1990.

Wollheim, Richard. *Sigmund Freud.* Rev. ed. Glasgow: Cambridge UP, 1989.

Zeitlin, Froma I. *Playing the Other: Gender and Society in Classical Greek Literature.* Chicago: U of Chicago P, 1996.

Chapter 3   In the Beginning: Hesiod's Creation Story

Athanassakis, Apostolos N., ed. and trans. *Hesiod: Theogony, Works and Days, Shield.* 2nd ed. Baltimore: Johns Hopkins UP, 2004.

Brown, Norman O., ed. and trans. *Theogony.* New York: Prentice-Hall, 1953.

Burkert, Walter. *The Orientalizing Revolution: Near Eastern Influence on Greek Culture in the Early Archaic Age.* (Reprint edition). Cambridge: Harvard UP, 1998.

Burn, A. R. *The World of Hesiod: A Study of the Greek Middle Ages c. 900-700 BC.* New York: Blom, 1936.

Caldwell, Richard S., ed. and trans. *Hesiod's Theogony.* Cambridge: Focus Classical Library, 1987.

Clay, Jenny Strauss. *Hesiod's Cosmos.* Cambridge: Cambridge UP, 2003.

Dalley, Stephanie. *Myths from Mesopotamia: Creation, the Flood Gilgamesh, and Others.* New York: Oxford UP, 1989.

Frankel, H. *Early Greek Poetry and Philosophy.* Trans. Moses Hadas and James Willis. Oxford: Irvington, 1975.

Friedrich, Paul. *The Meaning of Aphrodite.* Chicago: U of Chicago P, 1978.

Greene, Mott T. *Natural Knowledge in Preclassical Antiquity.* Baltimore: Johns Hopkins UP, 1992.

Griffin, Jasper. "Greek Myth and Hesiod." In John Boardman, Jasper Griffin, and Oswyn Murray, eds. *The Oxford History of the Classical World.* New York: Oxford UP, 1986.

Hine, Daryl, ed. and trans. *Works of Hesiod and the Homeric Hymns.* Chicago: U of Chicago P, 2005.

Jaeger, Werner. *Paideia: The Ideals of Greek Culture.* Vol. 1. New York: Oxford UP, 1945.

———. *The Theology of the Early Greek Philosophers.* Oxford: n.p., 1936.

Lombardo, Stanley, ed. and trans. *Hesiod: Works and Days and Theogony.* Cambridge: Hackett, 1993.

Most, Glenn W., ed. and trans. *Hesiod.* (Loeb Classical Library). Cambridge, MA: Harvard UP, 2006.

Penglase, Charles. *Greek Myths and Mesopotamia: Parallels and Influence in the Homeric Hymns and Hesiod.* New York: Routledge, 1994.

Pucci, P. *Hesiod and the Language of Poetry.* Baltimore: n.p., 1977.

Walcot, P. *Envy and the Greeks.* Warminster: n.p., 1978.

———. *Hesiod and the Near East.* Cardiff: U of Wales P, 1964.

West, M. L. *The East Face of Helicon: West Asiatic Elements in Greek Poetry and Myth.* Rev. ed. New York: Oxford UP, 1999.

———, ed. and trans. *Theogony and Works and Days.* New York: Oxford UP, 1988.

Chapter 4 Alienation of the Human and Divine: Prometheus, Fire, and Pandora

Dundes, Alan, ed. *The Flood Myth.* Berkeley: U of California P, 1988.

Gottschalk, Richard. *Homer and Hesiod, Myth and Philosophy.* Lanham, MD: UP of America, 2000.

Griffith, Mark. *Aeschylus: Prometheus Bound.* New York: Cambridge UP, 1983.

Herington, C. J. *Aeschylus.* New Haven: Yale UP, 1986.

Hogan, James C. *A Commentary on the Complete Greek Tragedies: Aeschylus.* Chicago: U of Chicago P, 1985.

Kerényi, Carl. *Prometheus: Archetypal Images of Human Existence.* Trans. Ralph Manheim. Princeton: Princeton UP, 1991.

Panofsky, Dora, and Erwin Panofsky. *Pandora's Box: The Changing Aspects of a Mythical Symbol.* 3rd ed. Princeton: Princeton UP, 1991.

Solomon, Friedrich. *Hesiod and Aeschylus.* 1949. n.p.: Johnson Reprint, 1967.

Thomson, George. *Aeschylus and Athens.* London: Lawrence, 1941.

West, M. L., ed. and trans. *Theogony and Works and Days.* New York: Oxford UP, 1988.

Winnington-Ingram, R. P. *Studies in Aeschylus.* New York: Cambridge UP, 1983.

Chapter 5 The Divine Woman in Greek Mythology

Baring, Anne, and Jules Cashford. *The Myth of the Goddess: Evolution of an Image.* London: Penguin, 1993.

Berger, Pamela. *The Goddess Obscured: Transformations of the Grain Protectress from Goddess to Saint.* Boston: Beacon, 1985.

Eliade, Mircea. *Patterns in Comparative Religion.* Trans. Rosemary Sheed. 1949. Cleveland: World, 1958.

Foley, Helene. *The Homeric "Hymn to Demeter."* Princeton: Princeton UP, 1994.

Gadon, Elinor W. *The Once and Future Goddess: A Symbol for Our Times.* San Francisco: Harper, 1989.

Gilligan, Carol. *In a Different Voice: Psychological Theory and Women's Development.* Cambridge: Harvard UP, 1982.

Gimbutas, Marija. *The Language of the Goddess.* New York: Harper, 1989.

Goodison, Lucy, and Christine Morris, eds. *Ancient Goddesses: The Myths and Evidence.* Madison: U of Wisconsin P, 1999.

Kerényi, C. *Eleusis: Archetypal Image of Mother and Daughter.* 1967. New York: Schocken, 1977.

MacGillivray, J. Alexander. "Labyrinths and Bull-Leapers." *Archaeology* (Nov./Dec. 2000): 53–55.

McLean, Adam. *The Triple Goddess: An Exploration of the Archetypal Feminine.* Grand Rapids: Phanes, 1989.

Meyer, Marvin W., ed. *The Ancient Mysteries: A Sourcebook. Sacred Texts of the Mystery Religions of the Ancient Mediterranean World.* San Francisco: Harper, 1987.

Mylonas, George E. *Eleusis and the Eleusinian Mysteries.* Princeton UP, 1961.

Neumann, Erich. *The Great Mother: An Analysis of the Archetype.* Trans. Ralph Manheim. 1963. Princeton: Princeton UP, 1991.

Slater, Philip E. *The Glory of Hera: Greek Mythology and the Greek Family.* 1968. Princeton: Princeton UP, 1992.

Chapter 6 The Olympian Family of Zeus: Sharing Rule of the Universe

Athanassakis, Apostolos N., ed. and trans. *The Homeric Hymns.* 2nd ed. Baltimore: Johns Hopkins UP, 2004.

Clay, Jennie Strauss. *The Politics of Olympus: Form and Meaning in the Major Homeric Hymns.* Princeton: Princeton UP, 1989.

Dowden, Ken. *Zeus.* (Gods and Heroes of the Ancient World). New York: Routledge, 2006.

Gantz, Timothy. *Early Greek Myth.* Baltimore: Johns Hopkins UP, 1993.

Grimal, Pierre. *The Dictionary of Classical Mythology.* Trans. A. R. Maxwell-Hyslop. Oxford: Basil Blackwell, 1986.

Guthrie, W. K. C. *The Greeks and Their Gods.* Boston: Beacon, 1969.

Hornblower, Simon, and Antony Spawforth, eds. *The Oxford Classical Dictionary.* 3rd ed. New York: Oxford UP, 1996.

Hyginus. *Astronomica.* Ed. Paul Chatelain and P. Legendre. Paris: Librairie Honore Champion, 1909.

———. *Fabulae.* Ed. H. J. Rose. Leyden, Sythoff, 1933.

Kerényi, Carl. *The Gods of the Greeks.* London: Thames & Hudson, 1980.

Lefkowitz, Mary. *Greek Gods, Human Lives: What We Can Learn from Myths.* New Haven: Yale UP, 2003.

Mikalson, Jon D. *Ancient Greek Religion.* Malden, MA: Blackwell, 2004.

Moses, Brian. *An Encyclopedia of Greek and Roman Gods and Heroes.* (Pelican Big Books). Boston: Longman, 1998.

O'Brien, Joan V. *The Transformation of Hera: A Study of Ritual, Hero, and the Goddess in the Iliad.* Lanham: Rowman and Littlefield, 1993.

Otto, Walter. *The Homeric Gods: The Spiritual Significance of Greek Religion.* Trans. Moses Hadas. New York: Norton, 1979.

Sargent, Thelma. *The Homeric Hymns: A Verse Translation.* New York: Norton, 1973.

Segal, Robert. *Myth: A Very Short Introduction.* New York: Oxford UP, 2004.

Sergent, Bernard. *Homosexuality in Greek Myth.* Boston: Beacon, 1986.

Chapter 7   In Touch with the Gods: Apollo's Oracle at Delphi

Boer, Charles, trans. *The Homeric Hymns.* Rev. ed. South Kingstown, RI: Moyer Bell, 2006.

Bowden, Hugh. *Classical Athens and the Delphic Oracle: Divination and Democracy.* New York: Cambridge UP, 2005.

Broad, William J. *The Oracle: Lost Secrets and Hidden Messages of Ancient Delphi.* New York: Penguin, 2006.

De Boer, Jelle Z., and John Hale. "Was She Really Stoned? The Oracle of Delphi." *Archaeology Odyssey,* 5(6) (Nov./Dec. 2002).

De Boer, J. Z., J. R. Hale, and J. Clanton. "New Evidence of the Geological Origins of the Ancient Delphic Oracle." *Geology,* 29 (2001).

Downing, Christine. *Myths and Mysteries of Same-Sex Love.* New York: Continuum, 1989.

Eisner, Robert. *The Road to Daulis: Psychoanalysis, Psychology, and Classical Mythology.* Syracuse: Syracuse UP, 1987.

Fontrose, Joseph. *Python: A Study of Delphic Myth and Its Origins.* Berkeley: U of California P, 1959.

———. *The Delphic Oracle: Its Responses and Operations.* Berkeley: U of California P, 1978.

Parker, R. *Miasma: Pollution and Purification in Early Greek Religion.* Oxford UP, 1983.

Petrokos, Basil. *Delphi.* Athens: "Esperos" [English] Edition, 1971.

Picciardi, L. "Active Faulting at Delphi, Greece: Seismotactonic Remarks and a Hypothesis for the Geologic Environment of a Myth." *Geology,* 28 (2001).

Chapter 8   Dionysus: Rooted in Earth and Ecstasy

Alderink, Larry J. *Creation and Salvation in Ancient Orphism.* American Classical Studies 8. Chico: Scholars, 1981.

Athanassakis, Apostolos N., trans. *The Orphic Hymns: Text, Translation and Notes.* Atlanta: Society of Biblical Literature, 1988.

Boer, Charles, trans. *The Homeric Hymns.* Rev. ed. South Kingstown, RI: Moyer Bell, 2006.

Burkert, Walter. *Ancient Mystery Cults.* Cambridge: Harvard UP, 1987.

Cantarella, Eva. *Bisexuality in the Ancient World.* Trans. Cormac Ó Cuilleanáin. New Haven: Yale UP, 1992.

Carpenter, Thomas. *Dionysian Imagery in Fifth Century Athens.* New York: Oxford UP, 1997.

Dodds, E. R. *The Greeks and the Irrational.* Berkeley: U of California P, 1951.

Guthrie, W. K. C. *Orpheus and Greek Religion: A Study of the Orphic Movement.* Princeton: Princeton UP, 1993.

Kerényi, C. *Dionysos: Archetypal Image of Indestructible Life.* Trans. Ralph Manheim. Princeton: Princeton UP, 1996.

Martin, Luther H. *Hellenistic Religions: An Introduction.* Oxford: Oxford UP, 1987.

Nilsson, Martin P. *The Dionysiac Mysteries of the Hellenistic and Roman Age.* Lund: Gleerup, 1957.

Otto, Walter F. *Dionysus: Myth and Cult.* Trans. Robert B. Palmer. Bloomington: Indiana UP, 1995.

Vernant, Jean-Pierre, and Pierre Vidal-Naquet. *Myth and Tragedy in Ancient Greece.* Trans. Janet Lloyd. New York: Zone, 1988.

West, M. L. *The Orphic Poems.* Oxford: Clarendon, 1983.

Wili, Walter. "The Orphic Mysteries and the Greek Spirit." *The Mysteries: Papers from the Eranos Yearbooks.* Vol. 2. Ed. Joseph Campbell. Trans. Ralph Manheim and R. F. C. Hull. New York: Pantheon, 1955.

Chapter 9   Land of No Return: The Gloomy Kingdom of Hades

Apollodorus (of Athens). *The Library of Greek Mythology.* Rev. ed. Trans. Robin Hard (Oxford World Classics). New York: Oxford UP, 1999.

Bremmer, Jan. *The Early Greek Concept of the Soul.* Princeton: Princeton UP, 1983.

Burkert, Walter. *Greek Religion.* Trans. John Raffan. (Reprint edition). Cambridge: Harvard UP, 2006.

Calasso, Roberto. *The Marriage of Cadmus and Harmony.* Trans. Tim Parks. New York: Knopf, 1993.

Dietrich, B. C. *Death, Fate and the Gods: The Development of a Religious Idea in Greek Popular Belief and in Homer.* London: Athlone, 1965, 1967.

Eliot, Alexander. *The Universal Myths: Heroes, Gods, Tricksters and Others.* New York: New American Library, 1990.

Garland, Robert. *The Greek Way of Death.* Ithaca: Cornell UP, 1985.

Homer. *Odyssey of Homer.* "Book 11." Trans. Stanley Lombardo. Indianapolis, IN: Hackett, 2000.

Jackson, Danny P., trans. *The Epic of Gilgamesh.* Introduction by Robert D. Biggs. Bolchazy-Carducci, 1992.

Jacobsen, Thorkild. *The Treasures of Darkness: A History of Mesopotamian Religion.* New Haven: Yale UP, 1976.

McCall, Henrietta. *Mesopotamian Myths.* Austin: U of Texas P, British Museum, 1990.

Plato. "Phaedo." *The Last Days of Socrates.* Rev. ed. Trans. Hugh Tredennick. New York: Penguin, 1969.

———. *The Republic of Plato.* Trans. F. M. Cornford. Oxford: Oxford UP, 1941.

———. *The Symposium.* Trans. W. Hamilton. New York: Penguin, 1951.

Sandars, N. K., trans. *Poems of Heaven and Hell from Ancient Mesopotamia.* Baltimore: Penguin, 1971.

Segal, Charles. *Orpheus: The Myth of a Poet.* Baltimore: Johns Hopkins UP, 1989.

Vermeule, Emily. *Aspects of Death in Early Greek Art and Poetry.* Berkeley: U of California P, 1979.

West, Martin L. *The Orphic Poems.* New York: Oxford UP, 1983.

Chapter 10 Heroes of Myth: Man Divided Against Himself

Calasso, Roberto. *The Marriage of Cadmus and Harmony.* Trans. Tim Parks. New York: Knopf, 1993.

Campbell, Joseph. *The Hero with a Thousand Faces.* 1949. Cleveland: World, 1970.

Dumezil, Georges. *The Stakes of the Warrior.* Trans. David Weeks. 1968. Berkeley: U of California P, 1983.

Galinsky, G. Karl. *The Herakles Theme: The Adaptations of the Hero in Literature from Homer to the Twentieth Century.* Oxford: Blackwell, 1972.

Kirk, G. S. *The Nature of Greek Myths.* London: Penguin, 1974.

Rank, Otto. *The Myth of the Birth of the Hero.* New York: Brunner, 1952.

Segal, Robert A. Introduction. *In Quest of the Hero.* Ed. Robert A. Segal. Princeton: Princeton UP, 1990.

Slater, Philip. *The Glory of Hera: Greek Mythology and the Greek Family.* Princeton: Princeton UP, 1968.

Walker, Henry J. *Theseus and Athens.* New York: Oxford UP, 1995.

Chapter 11 Heroines of Myth: Women in Many Roles

Doherty, Lillian. *Gender and the Interpretation of Classical Myth.* London: Duckworth, 2001.

Fantham, Elaine, Helene Peet Foley, Natalie Boymel Kampen, et al. *Women in the Classical World: Image and Text.* New York: Oxford UP, 1995.

Lefkowitz, Mary F., and Maureen Fant. *Women in Greece and Rome.* Toronto: Samuel Stevens, 1977.

———. *Women's Life in Greece and Rome: A Source Book in Translation.* Baltimore: Johns Hopkins UP, 1987.

Lincoln, Bruce. *Emerging from the Chrysalis: Studies in Rituals of Women's Initiation.* Oxford: Oxford, UP, 1991.

Lyons, Deborah. *Gender and Immortality: Heroines in Ancient Greek Myth and Cult.* Princeton: Princeton UP, 1997.

Neumann, Erich. *Amor and Psyche: The Psychic Development of the Feminine.* New York: Princeton UP, 1990.

Shorter, Bani. *An Image Darkly Forming: Women and Initiation.* London: Routledge, 1987.

Zeitlin, Froma I. *Playing the Other: Gender and Society in Classical Greek Literature.* Chicago: U of Chicago P, 1996.

Chapter 12 Heroes at War: The Troy Saga

Beye, Charles Rowan. *Ancient Greek Literature and Society.* New York: Anchor, 1975.

Clarke, Howard W. *The Art of the Odyssey.* Englewood Cliffs: Prentice-Hall, 1967.

Finley, M. I. *The World of Odysseus.* 1959. Cleveland: World, 1963.

Fleischman, John. "Homer's Bones." *Discover,* July 2002: 58–65.

Griffin, Jasper. *Homer.* New York: Hill, 1980.

Hogan, James C. *A Guide to the Iliad: Based on the Translation by Robert Fitzgerald.* New York: Doubleday, 1979.

Kirk, G. S. *Homer and the Epic.* Cambridge: Cambridge UP, 1965.

Luce, J. V. *Homer and the Heroic Age.* San Francisco: Harper, 1975.

Nagy, Gregory. *The Best of the Achaeans: Concepts of the Hero in Archaic Greek Poetry.* Baltimore: Johns Hopkins UP, 1998.

O'Brien, Joan. *The Transformation of Hera: A Study of Ritual, Hero, and the Goddess in the Iliad.* Lanham: Rowman and Littlefield, 1993.

Redfield, James M. *Nature and Culture in the Iliad: The Tragedy of Hector.* Chicago: U of Chicago P, 1975.

Schein, Seth L. *The Mortal Hero: An Introduction to Homer's Iliad.* Berkeley: U of California P, 1984.

Shay, Jonathan. *Achilles in Vietnam: Combat Trauma and the Undoing of Character.* New York: Simon, 1995.

Stanford, W. B. *The Ulysses Theme.* Ann Arbor: U of Michigan P, 1963.

Van Nortwick, Thomas. *Somewhere I Have Never Travelled: The Second Self and the Hero's Journey in Ancient Epic.* New York: Oxford UP, 1992.

Whitman, Cedric. *Homer and the Heroic Tradition.* New York: Norton, 1958.

Chapter 13   A Different Kind of Hero: The Quest of Odysseus

Ahl, Frederick. *The Odyssey Re-formed.* Ithaca: Cornell UP, 1996.

Bittlestone, Robert, James Diggle, and John Underhill. *Odysseus Unbound: The Search for Homer's Ithaca.* New York: Cambridge UP, 2005.

Bloom, Harold, ed. *Homer's Odyssey.* New York: Chelsea, 1988.

Clay, Jenny Strauss. *The Wrath of Athena.* Princeton: Princeton UP, 1983.

Cook, Erwin F. *The Odyssey in Athens: Myths of Cultural Origins.* Ithaca: Cornell UP, 1995.

Fenik, Bernard. *Studies in the Odyssey.* Hermes, 30. Wiesbaden: Steiner, 1974.

Finley, John H., Jr. *Homer's Odyssey.* Cambridge: Harvard UP, 1978.

Lombardo, Stanley, trans. *Homer: Odyssey.* Cambridge: Hackett, 2000.

Louden, Bruce. *The Odyssey: Structure, Narration, and Meaning.* Baltimore: Johns Hopkins UP, 2002.

Page, Denys. *Folktales in Homer's Odyssey.* Cambridge: Harvard UP, 1973.

Schein, Seth L. *Reading the Odyssey: Selected Interpretive Essays.* Princeton: Princeton UP, 1996.

Segal, Charles. *Singers, Heroes, and Gods in the Odyssey.* Ithaca, NY: Cornell UP, 2001.

Shay, Jonathan. *Odysseus in America: Combat Trauma and the Trials of Homecoming.* New York: Scribner, 2002.

Thalmann, William G. *The Odyssey: An Epic of Return.* New York: Twayne, 1992.

Toohey, Peter. *Reading Epic: An Introduction to the Ancient Narratives.* New York: Routledge, 1993.

Chapter 14   The Theater of Dionysus: Myth and the Tragic Vision

Baldry, H. C. *The Greek Tragic Theatre.* New York: Norton, 1971.

Carpenter, Thomas H., and Christopher A. Farone, eds. *Masks of Dionysus.* Ithaca: Cornell UP, 1993.

Easterling, P. E., ed. *The Cambridge Companion to Greek Tragedy.* Cambridge: Cambridge UP, 1997.

Gregory, Justina, ed. *A Companion to Greek Tragedy.* Malden, MA: Blackwell, 2005.

Hall, Edith, ed. *Dionysus Since 69: Greek Tragedy at the Dawn of the Third Millennium.* Rev. ed. New York: Oxford UP, 2005.

Humphreys, S. C. *The Family, Women and Death.* Boston: Routledge, 1993.

Jones, John. *On Aristotle and Greek Tragedy.* New York: Oxford UP, 1962.

Kitto, H. D. F. *Greek Tragedy.* 3rd ed. New York: Routledge, 2002.

Mikalson, Jon D. *Honor Thy Gods: Popular Religion in Greek Tragedy.* Chapel Hill: U of North Carolina P, 1991.

Pickard-Cambridge, Arthur W. *Dithyramb, Tragedy, and Comedy.* 2nd ed. Ed. T. B. L. Webster. Oxford: Clarendon, 1962.

Porter, James. *The Invention of Dionysus: An Essay on the Birth of Tragedy.* Palo Alto, CA: Stanford UP, 2000.

Sewall, Richard B. *The Vision of Tragedy.* New Haven: Yale UP, 1965.

Storey, Ian C., and Arlene Allen. *A Guide to Ancient Greek Drama.* (Blackwell Guides to Classical Literature). Malden, MA: Blackwell, 2005.

Vernant, Jean-Pierre, and Pierre Vidal-Naquet. *Myth and Tragedy in Ancient Greece.* Trans. Janet Lloyd. New York: Zone, 1988.

Walton, J. M. *The Greek Sense of Theatre: Tragedy Reviewed.* London: n.p., 1984.

Webster, T. B. L. *The Greek Chorus.* London: Methuen, 1970.

———. *Greek Theatre Production.* London: Methuen, 1956.

Winkler, John J., and Froma I. Zeitlin, eds. *Nothing to Do with Dionysus? Athenian Drama and Its Social Context.* Princeton: Princeton UP, 1990.

Zeitlin, Froma I. *Playing the Other: Gender and Society in Classical Greek Literature.* Chicago: U of Chicago P, 1996.

Chapter 15   The House of Atreus: Aeschylus's *Oresteia*

Aeschylus. *Seven Plays.* Trans. Edward Marshead. El Paso: El Paso Norte Press, 2006.

Bloom, Harold, ed. *Aeschylus: Comprehensive Research and Study Guide.* New York: Chelsea House, 2001.

Goldhill, Simon. *Aeschylus: The Oresteia.* New York: Cambridge UP, 1992.

———. *Reading Greek Tragedy.* London: Cambridge UP, 1986.

Grene, David, and Richmond Lattimore, eds. *The Complete Greek Tragedies: Aeschylus.* Chicago: U of Chicago P, 1992.

Heringon, C. J. *Aeschylus.* New Haven: Yale UP, 1986.

Hogan, James C. *A Commentary on the Complete Greek Tragedies: Aeschylus.* Chicago: U of Chicago P, 1985.

Kott, Jan. *The Eating of the Gods: An Interpretation of Greek Tragedy.* New York: Vintage, 1970.

Podlecki, A. *The Political Background of Aeschylean Tragedy.* Michigan: U of Michigan P, 1966.

Rosenmeyer, Thomas G. *The Art of Aeschylus.* Berkeley: U of California P, 1982.

Simon, Bennett. *The Tragic Drama and the Family: Psychoanalytic Studies from Aeschylus to Beckett.* New Haven: Yale UP, 1988.

Thomson, George. *Aeschylus and Athens.* London: Lawrence and Wishart, 1987.

———. *Aeschylus: The Oresteia.* 5th ed. New York: Dell, 1965.

Tyrrell, William B., and Frieda S. Brown. *Athenian Myths and Institutions.* New York: Oxford UP, 1991.

Zak, William F. *The Polis and the Divine Order: The Oresteia, Sophocles, and the Defense of Democracy.* Lewisburg: Bucknell UP, 1995.

Chapter 16   The Tragic House of Laius: Sophocles' Oedipus Cycle

Bloom, Harold, ed. *Sophocles: Modern Critical Views.* New York: Chelsea, 1990.

Fergusson, Francis. *The Idea of a Theater.* 1949. Garden City: Doubleday, 1953.

Grene, David. *Reality and the Heroic Pattern: Last Plays of Ibsen, Shakespeare and Sophocles.* Chicago: U of Chicago P, 1967.

Knox, Bernard M. W. *The Heroic Temper: Studies in Sophoclean Tragedy.* Berkeley: U of California P, 1964.

———. *Oedipus at Thebes: Sophocles' Tragic Hero and His Time.* New Haven: Yale UP, 1998.

Pucci, Pietro. *Oedipus and the Fabrication of the Father: Oedipus Tyrannus in Modern Criticism and Philosophy.* Baltimore: Johns Hopkins UP, 1992.

Van Nortwick, Thomas. *Oedipus: The Meaning of a Masculine Life.* Norman: U of Oklahoma P, 1998.

Vellacott, Philip. *Sophocles and Oedipus: A Study of Oedipus Tyrannus with a New Translation.* Ann Arbor: U of Michigan P, 1971.

Vernant, Jean-Pierre, and Pierre Vidal-Naquet. *Myth and Tragedy in Ancient Greece.* Trans. Janet Lloyd. New York: Zone, 1990.

Whitman, Cedric H. *Sophocles: A Study of Heroic Humanism.* Cambridge: Harvard UP, 1956.

Chapter 17   A Different Perspective on Tragedy: Euripides' *Medea* and the *Bacchae*

Clauss, James J., and Sarah Iles Johnston, eds. *Medea: Essays on Medea in Myth, Literature, Philosophy and Art*. Princeton: Princeton UP, 1997.

Conacher, D. J. *Euripidean Drama: Myth, Theme and Structure*. Toronto: U of Toronto P, 1967.

Dodds, E. R. *Euripides' Bacchae*. Oxford: Clarendon, 1960.

Greenwood, Leonard Hugh Graham. *Aspects of Euripidean Tragedy*. 1953. New York: Russell, 1972.

Grene, David, and Richmond Lattimore, eds. *The Complete Greek Tragedies, Volume 3: Euripides*. Chicago: U of Chicago Press, 1992.

Lucas, D. W. *The Greek Tragic Poets*. 2nd ed. New York: Norton, 1959.

Meagher, Robert. *Mortal Vision: The Wisdom of Euripides*. New York: St. Martin's, 1989.

Mills, Sophie. *Euripides: Bacchae*. (Duckworth Companions to Greek and Roman Tragedy). London: Gerald Duckworth, 2006.

Oranje, H. *Euripides' Bacchae: The Play and Its Audience*. Leiden: Brill, 1984.

Powell, Anton. *Euripides, Women, and Sexuality*. London: Routledge, 1990.

Pucci, Pietro. *The Violence of Pity in Euripides' Medea*. Ithaca: Cornell UP, 1980.

Segal, Charles. *Dionysiac Poetics and Euripides' "Bacchae."* 2nd ed. Princeton: Princeton UP, 1997.

Welsford, Enid. *The Fool*. New York: Doubleday, 1961.

Winkler, John J., and Froma I. Zeitlin, eds. *Nothing to do with Dionysus? Athenian Drama in its Social Context*. Princeton: Princeton UP, 1990.

Winnington-Ingram, R. P. *Euripides and Dionysus: An Interpretation of the Bacchae*. Cambridge: Cambridge UP, 1948.

Chapter 18   The Roman Vision: Greek Myths and Roman Realities

Barr, Robert. "British Dig Finds Evidence of a Woman Gladiator." *Sacramento Bee,* 13 Sept. 2000: A11.

Cairns, Francis. *Virgil's Augustan Epic*. Cambridge: Cambridge UP, 1989.

Christ, Karl. *The Romans: An Introduction to Their History and Civilisation*. Trans. Christopher Holme. Berkeley: U of California P, 1984.

Fantham, Elaine, Helene Peet Foley, Natalie Boymel Kampsen, et. al. *Women in the Classical World: Image and Text*. New York: Oxford UP, 1994.

Feeney, Denis. *Literature and Religion at Rome: Cultures, Contexts and Beliefs*. Cambridge: Cambridge UP, 1999.

Grant, Michael. *History of Rome*. New York: Scribner, 1978.

Hexter, Ralph, and Daniel Selden, eds. *Innovations of Antiquity*. New York: Routledge, 1992.

Lefkowitz, Mary F., and Maureen Fant. *Women in Greece and Rome*. Toronto: Samuel Stevens, 1977.

Ogilvie, R. M. *Roman Literature and Society*. London: Penguin, 1980.

Wiseman, T. P. *Remus: A Roman Myth*. Cambridge: Cambridge UP, 1995.

Woodman, Tony, and David West, eds. *Poetry and Politics in the Age of Augustus*. Cambridge: Cambridge UP, 1984.

Chapter 19   Virgil's Roman Epic: The *Aeneid*

Bloom, Harold, ed. *Virgil: Modern Critical Views*. New York: Chelsea, 1986.

Hexter, Ralph, and Daniel Selden, eds. *Innovations of Antiquity*. New York: Routledge, 1992.

Johnson, W. R. *Darkness Visible: A Study of Vergil's Aeneid*. Berkeley: U of California P, 1976.

Keith, A. M. *Engendering Rome: Women in Latin Epic*. Cambridge: Cambridge UP, 2000.

O' Hara, James J. *Death and the Optimistic Prophecy in Vergil's Aeneid.* Princeton: Princeton UP, 1990.

Poschl, Viktor. *The Art of Virgil: Image and Symbol in the Aeneid.* Trans. Gerda Seligson. Ann Arbor: U of Michigan P, 1962.

Van Nortwick, Thomas. *Somewhere I Have Never Travelled: The Second Self and the Hero's Journey in Ancient Epic.* New York: Oxford UP, 1992.

Williams, R. D. *Virgil.* Greece and Rome: New Surveys in the Classics 1. Oxford: Clarendon, 1967.

Wiltshire, Susan Ford. *Public and Private in Vergil's "Aeneid."* Amherst: U of Massachusetts P, 1989.

Chapter 20   The Retelling of Greek Myths: Ovid's *Metamorphoses*

Barnard, Mary E. *The Myth of Apollo and Daphne from Ovid to Quevedo: Love, Agon and the Grotesque.* Durham: Duke UP, 1987.

Brooks, Otis. *Ovid as an Epic Poet.* 2nd ed. Cambridge: Cambridge UP, 1970.

Forbes Irving, P. M. C. *Metamorphoses in Greek Myths.* Oxford: Clarendon, 1990.

Hexter, Ralph, and Daniel Selden, eds. *Innovations of Antiquity.* New York: Routledge, 1992.

Wall, Kathleen. *The Callisto Myth from Ovid to Atwood: Initiation and Rape in Literature.* Kingston: McGill-Queen's UP, 1988.

Warner, Maria. *Fantastic Metamorphoses, Other Worlds: Ways of Telling the Self.* Oxford: Oxford UP, 2002.

Wilkinson, L. P. *Ovid Surveyed: An Abridgement for the General Reader of "Ovid Recalled."* Cambridge: Cambridge UP, 1962.

Chapter 21   The Persistence of Myth

Brombert, Victor, ed. *The Hero in Literature.* New York: Fawcett, 1969.

Bush, Douglas. *Mythology and the Renaissance Tradition in English Poetry.* 1932. New York: Norton, 1963.

———. *Mythology and the Romantic Tradition in English Poetry.* 1937. New York: Norton, 1963.

Reid, Jane Davidson, with Chris Rohmann. *The Oxford Guide to Classical Mythology in the Arts, 1300-1990s.* 2 vols. Oxford: Oxford UP, 1993.

Stanford, W. B. *The Ulysses Theme: A Study in the Adaptability of a Traditional Hero.* 2nd ed. Ann Arbor: U of Michigan P, 1968.

Credits

a division of Random House, Inc.; **984** From Ovid, *Metamorphoses*, translated by Rolfe Humphries. Copyright, 1955, Indiana University Press. Reprinted by permission of Indiana University Press; **1047** From *The Divine Comedy* by Dante Alighieri, translated by John Ciardi. Copyright 1954, 1957, 1959, 1960, 1961, 1965, 1967, 1970 by the Ciardi Family Publishing Trust. Used by permission of W. W. Norton & Company, Inc.; **1055** William Butler Yeats, "Leda and the Swan." Reprinted with the permission of Scribner, an imprint of Simon & Schuster Adult Publishing Group, and A P Watt Ltd on behalf of Michael B Yeats, from *The Collected Works of W. B. Yeats, Volume I: The Poems*, Revised and edited by Richard J. Finneran. Copyright © 1928 by The Macmillan Company; copyright renewed © 1956 by Georgie Yeats. All rights reserved; **1056** "The Shield of Achilles," copyright 1952 by W. H. Auden, from *Collected Poems* by W. H. Auden. Used by permission of Random House, Inc.; **1058** "Musée des Beaux Arts," copyright 1940 and renewed 1968 by W. H. Auden, from *Collected Poems* by W. H. Auden. Used by permission of Random House, Inc.; **1059** "The Pomegranate," from *In a Time of Violence* by Eavan Boland. Copyright © 1994 by Eavan Boland. Used by permission of W. W. Norton & Company, Inc. and Carcanet Press Limited; **1061** C. K. Williams, "Cassandra, Iraq," *The New Yorker*, April 3, 2006. Reprinted by permission of the author.

PHOTOS **Page 1** Archaeological Receipts Fund (TAP),Greece; **4** AKG London; **5** *top* Acropolis Museum, Athens/Archaeological Receipts Fund (TAP), Greece; **5** *bottom* Museo Arqueológico Nacional Serrano; **6** Museo Archeologico Nazionale, Taranto; **7** Bettmann/Corbis; **17** The British Museum, London; **18** *top* The British Museum, London; **18** *bottom* Archaeological Receipts Fund (TAP), Greece; **19** *top* The British Museum, London; **19** *bottom* The British Museum, London; **27** PhotoEdit; **28** Archaeological Receipts Fund (TAP), Greece; **29** Archaeological Receipts Fund (TAP), Greece; **30** Nimatallah/Art Resource; **31** © 1996 Rene Burri/Magnum Photos; **40** The Vatican Museum; **49** Alinari/Art Resource; **50** Alinari/Art Resource; **59** Alinari/Art Resource; **62** *top* Archaeological Receipts Fund (TAP), Greece; **62** *bottom* Archaeological Receipts Fund (TAP), Greece; **69** The British Museum, London; **71** Alinari/Art Resource; **77** Alinari/Art Resource; **78** The British Museum, London; **79** Erich Lessing/AKG London; **80** Archaeological Institute of the Dodecanese; **81** Museo del Prado, Madrid; **83** The British Museum, London; **84** Museo Archeologico Regionale, Palermo; **85** Staatliche Antikensammlungen und Glyptothek; **107** RMN/ADAGP/Art Resource; **111** The British Museum, London; **113** Ashmolean Museum; **120** Alinari/Art Resource; **121** Alinari/Art Resource; **123** Alinari/Art Resource; **125** Alinari/Art Resource; **127** Scala/Art Resource; **146** American Museum of Natural History; **148** Alinari/Art Resource; **150** Alinari/Art Resource; **151** Archaeological Receipts Fund (TAP), Greece; **152** Alinari/Art Resource; **153** The British Museum, London; **156** Archaeological Receipts Fund (TAP), Greece; **158** Archaeological Receipts Fund (TAP), Greece; **159** The British Museum, London; **162** The British Museum, London; **164** Hirmer Fotoarchiv, Munich; **183** Hirmer Fotoarchiv, Munich; **188** Archaeological Receipts Fund (TAP), Greece; **190** Alinari/Art Resource; **194** Alinari/Art Resource; **195** RMN/ADAGP/Art Resource; **197** Archaeological Receipts Fund (TAP), Greece; **198** Alinari/Art Resource; **199** Archaeological Receipts Fund (TAP), Greece; **201** *top* Archaeological Receipts Fund (TAP), Greece; **201** *bottom* Archaeological Receipts Fund (TAP), Greece; **202** RMN/ADAGP/Art Resource; **203** Courtesy of the Museum of Fine Arts, Boston; **204** *top* The British Museum, London; **204** *bottom* RMN/ADAGP/Art Resource; **206** Foto Marburg/Art Resource; **207** Archaeological Receipts Fund (TAP), Greece; **210** The Art Archive/The Picture Desk; **213** Courtesy of the Vatican Museums; **214** Alinari/Art Resource; **215** RMN/ADAGP/Art Resource; **217** The J.Paul Getty Museum; **238** Courtesy of the Vatican Museums; **240** Metropolitan Museum of Art; **241** *top* The Allard Pierson Museum; **241** *bottom* Archaeological Receipts Fund (TAP), Greece; **245** *left* Archaeological Receipts Fund (TAP), Greece; **245** *right* Archaeological Receipts Fund (TAP), Greece; **246** Courtesy of the Vatican Museums; **248** Staatliche Museen Zu Berlin; **250** Erich Lessing/Art Resource; **252** Archaeological Receipts Fund (TAP), Greece; **267** Alinari/Art Resource; **269** Ecole Francaise d'Athenes; **270** Staatliche Antikensammlungen und Glyptothek; **271** The Bridgeman Art Library; **272** Museo Archeologico Nazionale, Ferrara; **274** Alinari/Art Resource; **275** Hirmer Fotoarchiv, Munich; **277** *top* Hirmer Fotoarchiv, Munich; **277** *bottom* Hirmer Fotoarchiv, Munich; **278** *top* Courtesy of the Museum of Fine Arts, Boston; **278** *bottom* Alinari/Art Resource; **279** Alinari/Art Resource; **281** *top* Scala/Art Resource; **281** *bottom left* Scala/Art Resource; **281** *bottom right* Scala/Art Resource; **282** Giraudon/Art Resource; **296** The British Museum, London; **298** Archaeological Receipts Fund (TAP), Greece; **299** Metropolitan Museum of Art; **300** *left* Staatliche Antikensammlungen und

Glyptothek; **300** *right* Staatliche Antikensammlungen und Glyptothek; **301** Alinari/Art Resource; **302** The British Museum, London; **303** RMN/ADAGP/Art Resource; **305** Erich Lessing/Art Resource, NY; **306** RMN/ADAGP/Art Resource; **309** The Granger Collection; **318** Staatliche Museen Zu Berlin; **321** Museo Archeologico Regionale, Palermo; **325** Réunion des Musées Nationaux/Art Resource; **326** University of Pennsylvania Museum; **327** Staatliche Antikensammlungen und Glyptothek; **328** Bettmann/Corbis; **329** The British Museum, London; **330** Archaeological Receipts Fund (TAP), Greece; **331** Staatliche Antikensammlungen und Glyptothek; **334** The British Museum, London; **335** The British Museum, London; **339** Photo: H.Lewandowski/RMN/ADAGP/Art Resource; **340** Metropolitan Museum of Art; **346** The Israel Museum, Jerusalem; **347** Courtesy of the Museum of Fine Arts, Boston; **348** The British Museum, London; **351** Photo: H. Lewandowski/RMN/ADAGP/Art Resource; **354** Nimatallah/Art Resource; **356** Staatliche Antikensammlungen und Glyptothek; **361** Staatliche Antikensammlungen und Glyptothek; **368** The Vatican Museum; **377** *top* Photo: H. Lewandowski. Louvre, Paris, France. Réunion des Musées Nationaux/Art Resource; **377** *bottom* The British Museum, London; **378** Kunsthistorisches Museum, Vienna; **381** Metropolitan Museum of Art; **463** *top* Staatliche Museen Zu Berlin; **463** *bottom* Staatliche Museen Zu Berlin; **466** Il Museo Archeologico Nazionale di Sperlonga; **467** Alinari/Art Resource; **468** Hirmer Fotoarchiv, Munich; **469** Courtesy of Museum of Fine Arts, Boston; **470** Scala/Art Resource; **471** Archaeological Receipts Fund (TAP), Greece; **472** Courtesy of Museum of Fine Arts, Boston; **475** The British Museum, London; **478** The British Museum, London; **480** Scala/Art Resource; **481** Hirmer Fotoarchiv, Munich; **541** Courtesy of the Museum of Fine Arts, Boston; **546** Photo: Claire Niggli/Antikenmuseum Basel und Sammlung Ludwig; **548** Ancient Art & Architecture Collection; **550** Metropolitan Museum of Art; **551** Staatliche Museen Zu Berlin; **554** Staatliche Museen Zu Berlin; **561** The British Museum, London; **563** Scala/Art Resource; **565** Courtesy of the Museum of Fine Arts, Boston; **566** Courtesy of the Museum of Fine Arts, Boston; **567** Museo Archeologico Nazionale, Ferrara; **568** Courtesy of the Museum of Fine Arts, Boston; **569** Kunsthistorisches Museum, Vienna; **570** National Archeological Museum, Naples; **571** Archaeological Receipts Fund (TAP), Greece; **572** Alinari/Art Resource; **643** RMN/ADAGP/Art Resource; **644** Photo: H. Lewandowski/RMN/ADAGP/Art Resource; **652** Cabinet des Modailles/Bibliotheque Nationale de France; **654** Courtesy of the Vatican Museums; **758** Alinari/Art Resource; **760** Erich Lessing/Art Resource; **763** The Cleveland Museum of Art; **766** Scala/Art Resource; **767** The British Museum, London; **769** RMN/ADAGP/Art Resource; **770** Courtesy of the Vatican Museums; **771** National Archeological Museum, Naples; **772** Courtesy of the Museum of Fine Arts, Boston; **773** Courtesy of the Museum of Fine Arts, Boston; **873** Courtesy of the Vatican Museums; **876** Alinari/Art Resource; **877** Alinari/Art Resource; **883** Courtesy of the Vatican Museums; **884** Courtesy of the Vatican Museums; **885** Alinari/Art Resource; **886** Alinari/Art Resource; **887** Courtesy of the Vatican Museums; **900** Photo: K.Oehrlein/Martin von Wagner Museum, Universitat Wurzburg; **981** Galleria Borghese, Rome; **1017** National Gallery of Art, Washington, D.C.; **1024** Philip Trager/Wesleyan University Press; **1025** National Gallery, London; **1026** Descharnes & Descharnes Sarl, Paris. © 2000 Foundation ARS Gala-Salvador Dali VEGAP, Madrid/ARS, New York; **1027** Digital Image © The Museum of Modern Art/Licensed by SCALA/Art Resource, NY; **1028** Giraudon/Art Resource; **1031** Erich Lessing/Art Resource, NY; **1032** Metropolitan Museum of Art; **1033** *top* RMN/ADAGP/Art Resource; **1033** *bottom* Descharnes & Descharnes Sarl, Paris. © 2000 Foundation ARS Gala-Salvador Dali VEGAP, Madrid/ARS, New York; **1034** RMN/ADAGP/Art Resource; **1035** *top* Foto Marburg/Art Resource; **1035** *bottom* National Gallery of Art, Washington, D.C.; **1036** *top* Courtesy of Museum of Fine Arts, Boston; **1036** *bottom* Metropolitan Museum of Art; **1037** *top* Galleria Borghese, Rome; **1037** *bottom* Photo: Gerard Blot. RMN/ADAGP/Art Resource; **1038** *top* Réunion des Musées Nationaux/Art Resource, NY; **1038** *bottom* Musee d'Art Moderne de la Ville de Paris. © P.M.V.P./Ladet for the photo #1983 MAM0371; **1039** Descharnes & Descharnes Sarl, Paris. © 2000 Foundation ARS Gala-Salvador Dali VEGAP, Madrid/ARS, New York; **1040** Scala/Art Resource; **1041** Staatliche Kunsthalle, Karlsruhe; **1042** Alinari/Art Resource; **1044** Victoria and Albert Museum.

COLOR PLATES **CP-1** Sandro Botticelli, "Birth of Venus", c. 1480. Uffizi Gallery, Florence. Scala/Art Resource; **CP-2** Jean Cousin the Elder, "Eva Prima Pandora", 1538. Louvre, Paris. RMN/ADAGP/Art Resource; **CP-3** Jacopo Tintoretto, "The Origin of the Milky Way". National Gallery, London. National Gallery, London; **CP-4** Thomas Hart Benton, "Persephone", 1938. The Nelson-Atkins Mu-

Index

Page references in **_bold italics_** refer to primary works. Page references in _italics_ refer to boxed material. Page references in **bold** refer to illustrations.